ESSENTIAL MATHEMATICS FOR

ECONOMIC
ANALYSIS

ESSENTIAL MATHEMATICS FOR

ECONOMIC ANALYSIS

FOURTH EDITION

Knut Sydsæter and Peter Hammond

with Arne Strøm

This Licensed Edition is published by Dorling Kindersley (India) Pvt. Ltd, Copyright © 2014 by arrangement with Pearson Education Ltd, United Kingdom.

ISBN 978-93-325-1739-4

First Impression

This edition is manufactured in India and is authorized for sale only in India, Bangladesh, Bhutan, Pakistan, Nepal, Sri Lanka and the Maldives. Circulation of this edition outside of these territories is UNAUTHORIZED.

Published by Dorling Kindersley (India) Pvt. Ltd., licensees of Pearson Education in South Asia.

Head Office: 7th Floor, knowledge Boulevard, A-8(A) Sector-62, Noida (U.P) 201309, India
Registered Office: 11 Community Centre, Panchsheel Park, New Delhi 110 017, India.

Printed in India by HT Media Ltd.

To the memory of my parents Elsie (1916–2007) and Fred (1916–2008), my first teachers of Mathematics, basic Economics, and many more important things.

— Peter

CONTENTS

PREFACE

I came to the position that mathematical analysis is not one of many ways of doing economic theory: It is the only way. Economic theory is mathematical analysis. Everything else is just pictures and talk.
—R. E. Lucas, Jr. (2001)

Purpose

The subject matter that modern economics students are expected to master makes significant mathematical demands. This is true even of the less technical "applied" literature that students will be expected to read for courses in fields such as public finance, industrial organization, and labour economics, amongst several others. Indeed, the most relevant literature typically presumes familiarity with several important mathematical tools, especially calculus for functions of one and several variables, as well as a basic understanding of multivariable optimization problems with or without constraints. Linear algebra is also used to some extent in economic theory, and a great deal more in econometrics.

The purpose of *Essential Mathematics for Economic Analysis*, therefore, is to help economics students acquire enough mathematical skill to access the literature that is most relevant to their undergraduate study. This should include what some students will need to conduct successfully an undergraduate research project or honours thesis.

As the title suggests, this is a book on *mathematics*, whose material is arranged to allow progressive learning of mathematical topics. That said, we do frequently emphasize economic applications. These not only help motivate particular mathematical topics; we also want to help prospective economists acquire mutually reinforcing intuition in both mathematics and economics. Indeed, as the list of examples on the inside front cover suggests, a considerable number of economic concepts and ideas receive some attention.

We emphasize, however, that this is not a book about economics or even about mathematical economics. Students should learn economic theory systematically from other courses, which use other textbooks. We will have succeeded if they can concentrate on the economics in these courses, having already thoroughly mastered the relevant mathematical tools this book presents.

Special Features and Accompanying Material

All sections of the book, except one, conclude with problems, often quite numerous. There are also many review problems at the end of each chapter. Answers to almost all problems are provided at the end of the book, sometimes with several steps of the solution laid out.

There are two main sources of supplementary material. The first, for both students and their instructors, is via MyMathLab Global. Students who have arranged access to this web site for our book will be able to generate a practically unlimited number of additional problems which test how well some of the key ideas presented in the text have been understood. More explanation of this system is offered after this preface. The same web page also has a "student resources" tab with access to a *Student's Manual* with more extensive answers (or, in the case of a few of the most theoretical or difficult problems in the book, the only answers) to problems marked with the symbol (SM).

The second source, for instructors who adopt the book for their course, is an *Instructor's Manual* that may be downloaded from the publisher's Instructor Resource Centre.

In addition, for courses with special needs, there is a brief online appendix on trigonometric functions and complex numbers. This is also available via MyMathLab Global.

Prerequisites

Experience suggests that it is quite difficult to start a book like this at a level that is really too elementary.[1] These days, in many parts of the world, students who enter college or university and specialize in economics have an enormous range of mathematical backgrounds and aptitudes. These range from, at the low end, a rather shaky command of elementary algebra, up to real facility in the calculus of functions of one variable. Furthermore, for many economics students, it may be some years since their last formal mathematics course. Accordingly, as mathematics becomes increasingly essential for specialist studies in economics, we feel obliged to provide as much quite elementary material as is reasonably possible. Our aim here is to give those with weaker mathematical backgrounds the chance to get started, and even to acquire a little confidence with some easy problems they can really solve on their own.

To help instructors judge how much of the elementary material students really know before starting a course, the *Instructor's Manual* provides some diagnostic test material. Although each instructor will obviously want to adjust the starting point and pace of a course to match the students' abilities, it is perhaps even more important that each individual student appreciates his or her own strengths and weaknesses, and receives some help and guidance in overcoming any of the latter. This makes it quite likely that weaker students will benefit significantly from the opportunity to work through the early more elementary chapters, even if they may not be part of the course itself.

As for our economic discussions, students should find it easier to understand them if they already have a certain very rudimentary background in economics. Nevertheless, the text has often been used to teach mathematics for economics to students who are studying elementary economics at the same time. Nor do we see any reason why this material cannot

---

[1] In a recent test for 120 first-year students intending to take an elementary economics course, there were 35 different answers to the problem of expanding $(a + 2b)^2$.

be mastered by students interested in economics before they have begun studying the subject in a formal university course.

Topics Covered

After the introductory material in Chapters 1 to 3, a fairly leisurely treatment of single-variable differential calculus is contained in Chapters 4 to 8. This is followed by integration in Chapter 9, and by the application to interest rates and present values in Chapter 10. This may be as far as some elementary courses will go. Students who already have a thorough grounding in single variable calculus, however, may only need to go fairly quickly over some special topics in these chapters such as elasticity and conditions for global optimization that are often not thoroughly covered in standard calculus courses.

We have already suggested the importance for budding economists of multivariable calculus (Chapters 11 and 12), of optimization theory with and without constraints (Chapters 13 and 14), and of the algebra of matrices and determinants (Chapters 15 and 16). These six chapters in some sense represent the heart of the book, on which students with a thorough grounding in single variable calculus can probably afford to concentrate. In addition, several instructors who have used previous editions report that they like to teach the elementary theory of linear programming, which is therefore covered in Chapter 17.

The ordering of the chapters is fairly logical, with each chapter building on material in previous chapters. The main exception concerns Chapters 15 and 16 on linear algebra, as well as Chapter 17 on linear programming, most of which could be fitted in almost anywhere after Chapter 3. Indeed, some instructors may reasonably prefer to cover some concepts of linear algebra before moving on to multivariable calculus, or to cover linear programming before multivariable optimization with inequality constraints.

Satisfying Diverse Requirements

The less ambitious student can concentrate on learning the key concepts and techniques of each chapter. Often, these appear boxed and/or in colour, in order to emphasize their importance. Problems are essential to the learning process, and the easier ones should definitely be attempted. These basics should provide enough mathematical background for the student to be able to understand much of the economic theory that is embodied in applied work at the advanced undergraduate level.

Students who are more ambitious, or who are led on by more demanding teachers, can try the more difficult problems. They can also study the material in smaller print. The latter is intended to encourage students to ask why a result is true, or why a problem should be tackled in a particular way. If more readers gain at least a little additional mathematical insight from working through these parts of our book, so much the better.

The most able students, especially those intending to undertake postgraduate study in economics or some related subject, will benefit from a fuller explanation of some topics than we have been able to provide here. On a few occasions, therefore, we take the liberty of referring to our more advanced companion volume, *Further Mathematics for Economic Analysis* (usually abbreviated to FMEA). This is written jointly with our respective colleagues Atle Seierstad and Arne Strøm in Oslo and, in a new forthcoming edition, with Andrés Carvajal at Warwick. In particular, FMEA offers a proper treatment of topics like second-order conditions for optimization, and the concavity or convexity of functions of more than two variables—topics that we think go rather beyond what is really "essential" for all economics students.

Changes in the Fourth Edition

We have been gratified by the number of students and their instructors from many parts of the world who appear to have found the first three editions useful.[2] We have accordingly been encouraged to revise the text thoroughly once again. There are numerous minor changes and improvements, including the following in particular:

(1) The main new feature is MyMathLab Global, explained on the page after this preface, as well as on the back cover.

(2) New problems have been added for each chapter.

(3) Some of the figures have been improved.

Acknowledgements

Over the years we have received help from so many colleagues, lecturers at other institutions, and students, that it is impractical to mention them all.

Still, for some time now Arne Strøm, also at the Department of Economics of the University of Oslo, has been an indispensable member of our production team. His mastery of the intricacies of the TEX typesetting system and his exceptional ability to spot errors and inaccuracies have been of enormous help. As long overdue recognition of his contribution, we have added his name on the front cover of this edition.

Apart from our very helpful editors, with Kate Brewin at Pearson Education in charge, we should particularly like to thank Arve Michaelsen at Matematisk Sats in Norway for major assistance with the macros used to typeset the book, and for the figures.

Very special thanks also go to professor Fred Böker at the University of Göttingen, who is not only responsible for translating previous editions into German, but has also shown exceptional diligence in paying close attention to the mathematical details of what he was translating. We appreciate the resulting large number of valuable suggestions for improvements and corrections that he continues to provide.

To these and all the many unnamed persons and institutions who have helped us make this text possible, including some whose anonymous comments on earlier editions were forwarded to us by the publisher, we would like to express our deep appreciation and gratitude. We hope that all those who have assisted us may find the resulting product of benefit to their students. This, we can surely agree, is all that really matters in the end.

Knut Sydsæter and Peter Hammond

Oslo and Warwick, March 2012

---

[2] Different English versions of this book have been translated into Albanian, German, Hungarian, Italian, Portuguese, Spanish, and Turkish.

PUBLISHER'S ACKNOWLEDGEMENTS

We are grateful to the following for permission to reproduce copyright material:

Text
Epigraph from the Preface from R.E. Lucas, Jr. (2001); Epigraph Chapter 9 by I.N. Stewart; Epigraph Chapter 15 by J.H. Drèze; Epigraph Chapter 16 by The Estate of Max Rosenlicht.

In some instances we have been unable to trace the owners of copyright material, and we would appreciate any information that would enable us to do so.

1

INTRODUCTORY TOPICS I:
ALGEBRA

Is it right I ask;
is it even prudence;
to bore thyself and bore the students?
—Mephistopheles to Faust *(From Goethe's Faust.)*

This introductory chapter basically deals with elementary algebra, but we also briefly consider a few other topics that you might find that you need to review. Indeed, tests reveal that even students with a good background in mathematics often benefit from a brief review of what they learned in the past. These students should browse through the material and do some of the less simple problems. Students with a weaker background in mathematics, or who have been away from mathematics for a long time, should read the text carefully and then do most of the problems. Finally, those students who have considerable difficulties with this chapter should turn to a more elementary book on algebra.

1.1 The Real Numbers

We start by reviewing some important facts and concepts concerning numbers. The basic numbers are

$$1, \ 2, \ 3, \ 4, \ \ldots \qquad \textbf{(natural numbers)}$$

also called positive integers. Of these 2, 4, 6, 8, . . . are the **even numbers**, whereas 1, 3, 5, 7, . . . are the **odd numbers**. Though familiar, such numbers are in reality rather abstract and advanced concepts. Civilization crossed a significant threshold when it grasped the idea that a flock of four sheep and a collection of four stones have something in common, namely "fourness". This idea came to be represented by symbols such as the primitive :: (still used on dominoes or playing cards), the Roman numeral IV, and eventually the modern 4. This key notion is grasped and then continually refined as young children develop their mathematical skills.

The positive integers, together with 0 and the negative integers $-1, -2, -3, -4, \ldots$, make up the integers, which are

$$0, \ \pm 1, \ \pm 2, \ \pm 3, \ \pm 4, \ \ldots \qquad \textbf{(integers)}$$

They can be represented on a **number line** like the one shown in Fig. 1 (where the arrow gives the direction in which the numbers increase).

Figure 1 The number line

The **rational numbers** are those like $3/5$ that can be written in the form a/b, where a and b are both integers. An integer n is also a rational number, because $n = n/1$. Other examples of rational numbers are

$$\frac{1}{2}, \quad \frac{11}{70}, \quad \frac{125}{7}, \quad -\frac{10}{11}, \quad 0 = \frac{0}{1}, \quad -19, \quad -1.26 = -\frac{126}{100}$$

The rational numbers can also be represented on the number line. Imagine that we first mark $1/2$ and all the multiples of $1/2$. Then we mark $1/3$ and all the multiples of $1/3$, and so forth. You can be excused for thinking that "finally" there will be no more places left for putting more points on the line. But in fact this is quite wrong. The ancient Greeks already understood that "holes" would remain in the number line even after all the rational numbers had been marked off. For instance, there are no integers p and q such that $\sqrt{2} = p/q$. Hence, $\sqrt{2}$ is not a rational number. (Euclid proved this fact in around the year 300 BC.)

The rational numbers are therefore insufficient for measuring all possible lengths, let alone areas and volumes. This deficiency can be remedied by extending the concept of numbers to allow for the so-called irrational numbers. This extension can be carried out rather naturally by using decimal notation for numbers, as explained below.

The way most people write numbers today is called the **decimal system**, or the **base 10 system**. It is a positional system with 10 as the base number. Every natural number can be written using only the symbols, $0, 1, 2, \ldots, 9$, which are called **digits**. You may recall that a digit is either a finger or a thumb, and that most humans have 10 digits. The positional system defines each combination of digits as a sum of powers of 10. For example,

$$1984 = 1 \cdot 10^3 + 9 \cdot 10^2 + 8 \cdot 10^1 + 4 \cdot 10^0$$

Each natural number can be uniquely expressed in this manner. With the use of the signs $+$ and $-$, all integers, positive or negative, can be written in the same way. Decimal points also enable us to express rational numbers other than natural numbers. For example,

$$3.1415 = 3 + 1/10^1 + 4/10^2 + 1/10^3 + 5/10^4$$

Rational numbers that can be written exactly using only a finite number of decimal places are called **finite decimal fractions**.

Each finite decimal fraction is a rational number, but not every rational number can be written as a finite decimal fraction. We also need to allow for **infinite decimal fractions** such as

$$100/3 = 33.333\ldots$$

where the three dots indicate that the digit 3 is repeated indefinitely.

If the decimal fraction is a rational number, then it will always be **recurring** or **periodic**—that is, after a certain place in the decimal expansion, it either stops or continues to repeat a finite sequence of digits. For example, $11/70 = 0.1\,\underbrace{571428}\,\underbrace{571428}\,5\ldots$ with the sequence of six digits 571428 repeated infinitely often.

The definition of a real number follows from the previous discussion. We define a **real number** as an arbitrary infinite decimal fraction. Hence, a real number is of the form $x = \pm m.\alpha_1\alpha_2\alpha_3\ldots$, where m is a nonnegative integer, and α_n $(n = 1, 2\ldots)$ is an infinite series of digits, each in the range 0 to 9. We have already identified the periodic decimal fractions with the rational numbers. In addition, there are infinitely many new numbers given by the nonperiodic decimal fractions. These are called **irrational numbers.** Examples include $\sqrt{2}$, $-\sqrt{5}$, π, $2^{\sqrt{2}}$, and $0.12112111211112\ldots$.

We mentioned earlier that each rational number can be represented by a point on the number line. But not all points on the number line represent rational numbers. It is as if the irrational numbers "close up" the remaining holes on the number line after all the rational numbers have been positioned. Hence, an unbroken and endless straight line with an origin and a positive unit of length is a satisfactory model for the real numbers. We frequently state that there is a *one-to-one correspondence* between the real numbers and the points on a number line. Often, too, one speaks of the "real line" rather than the "number line".

The set of rational numbers as well as the set of irrational numbers are said to be "dense" on the number line. This means that between any two different real numbers, irrespective of how close they are to each other, we can always find both a rational and an irrational number—in fact, we can always find infinitely many of each.

When applied to the real numbers, the four basic arithmetic operations always result in a real number. The only exception is that we cannot divide by 0.[1]

$$\frac{p}{0} \text{ is not defined for any real number } p$$

This is very important and should not be confused with $0/a = 0$, for all $a \neq 0$. Notice especially that $0/0$ is not defined as any real number. For example, if a car requires 60 litres of fuel to go 600 kilometres, then its fuel consumption is $60/600 = 10$ litres per 100 kilometres. However, if told that a car uses 0 litres of fuel to go 0 kilometres, we know nothing about its fuel consumption; $0/0$ is completely undefined.

---

[1] "Black holes are where God divided by zero." (Steven Wright)

1. Which of the following statements are true?

(a) 1984 is a natural number.

(b) -5 is to the right of -3 on the number line.

(c) -13 is a natural number.

(d) There is no natural number that is not rational.

(e) 3.1415 is not rational.

(f) The sum of two irrational numbers is irrational.

(g) $-3/4$ is rational.

(h) All rational numbers are real.

2. Explain why the infinite decimal expansion $1.01001000100001000001\ldots$ is not a rational number.

1.2 Integer Powers

You should recall that we often write 3^4 instead of the product $3 \cdot 3 \cdot 3 \cdot 3$, that $\frac{1}{2} \cdot \frac{1}{2} \cdot \frac{1}{2} \cdot \frac{1}{2} \cdot \frac{1}{2}$ can be written as $\left(\frac{1}{2}\right)^5$, and that $(-10)^3 = (-10)(-10)(-10) = -1000$. If a is any number and n is any natural number, then a^n is defined by

$$a^n = \underbrace{a \cdot a \cdot \ldots \cdot a}_{n \text{ factors}}$$

The expression a^n is called the **nth power** of a; here a is the **base**, and n is the **exponent**. We have, for example, $a^2 = a \cdot a$, $x^4 = x \cdot x \cdot x \cdot x$, and

$$\left(\frac{p}{q}\right)^5 = \frac{p}{q} \cdot \frac{p}{q} \cdot \frac{p}{q} \cdot \frac{p}{q} \cdot \frac{p}{q}$$

where $a = p/q$, and $n = 5$. By convention, $a^1 = a$, a "product" with only one factor.

We usually drop the multiplication sign if this is unlikely to create misunderstanding. For example, we write abc instead of $a \cdot b \cdot c$, but it is safest to keep the multiplication sign in $1.05^3 = 1.05 \cdot 1.05 \cdot 1.05$.

We define further

$$a^0 = 1 \quad \text{for } a \neq 0$$

Thus, $5^0 = 1$, $(-16.2)^0 = 1$, and $(x \cdot y)^0 = 1$ (if $x \cdot y \neq 0$). But if $a = 0$, we do not assign a numerical value to a^0; the expression 0^0 is *undefined*.

We also need to define powers with negative exponents. What do we mean by 3^{-2}? It turns out that the sensible definition is to set 3^{-2} equal to $1/3^2 = 1/9$. In general,

$$a^{-n} = \frac{1}{a^n}$$

whenever n is a natural number and $a \neq 0$. In particular, $a^{-1} = 1/a$. In this way we have defined a^x for all integers x.

Calculators usually have a power key, denoted by $\boxed{y^x}$ or $\boxed{a^x}$, which can be used to compute powers. Make sure you know how to use it by computing 2^3 (which is 8), 3^2 (which is 9), and 25^{-3} (which is 0.000064).

Properties of Powers

There are some rules for powers that you really must not only know by heart, but understand why they are true. The two most important are:

$$\text{(i) } a^r \cdot a^s = a^{r+s} \qquad \text{(ii) } (a^r)^s = a^{rs}$$

Note carefully what these rules say. According to rule (i), powers with the same base are multiplied by *adding* the exponents. For example,

$$a^3 \cdot a^5 = \underbrace{a \cdot a \cdot a}_{3 \text{ factors}} \cdot \underbrace{a \cdot a \cdot a \cdot a \cdot a}_{5 \text{ factors}} = \underbrace{a \cdot a \cdot a \cdot a \cdot a \cdot a \cdot a \cdot a}_{3+5=8 \text{ factors}} = a^{3+5} = a^8$$

Here is an example of rule (ii):

$$(a^2)^4 = \underbrace{a \cdot a}_{2 \text{ factors}} \cdot \underbrace{a \cdot a}_{2 \text{ factors}} \cdot \underbrace{a \cdot a}_{2 \text{ factors}} \cdot \underbrace{a \cdot a}_{2 \text{ factors}} = \underbrace{a \cdot a \cdot a \cdot a \cdot a \cdot a \cdot a \cdot a}_{2 \cdot 4 = 8 \text{ factors}} = a^{2 \cdot 4} = a^8$$

Division of two powers with the same base goes like this:

$$a^r \div a^s = \frac{a^r}{a^s} = a^r \frac{1}{a^s} = a^r \cdot a^{-s} = a^{r-s}$$

Thus we divide two powers with the same base by *subtracting* the exponent in the denominator from that in the numerator. For example, $a^3 \div a^5 = a^{3-5} = a^{-2}$.

Finally, note that

$$(ab)^r = \underbrace{ab \cdot ab \cdot \ldots \cdot ab}_{r \text{ factors}} = \underbrace{a \cdot a \cdot \ldots \cdot a}_{r \text{ factors}} \cdot \underbrace{b \cdot b \cdot \ldots \cdot b}_{r \text{ factors}} = a^r b^r$$

and

$$\left(\frac{a}{b}\right)^r = \underbrace{\frac{a}{b} \cdot \frac{a}{b} \cdot \ldots \cdot \frac{a}{b}}_{r \text{ factors}} = \frac{\overbrace{a \cdot a \cdot \ldots \cdot a}^{r \text{ factors}}}{\underbrace{b \cdot b \cdot \ldots \cdot b}_{r \text{ factors}}} = \frac{a^r}{b^r} = a^r b^{-r}$$

These rules can be extended to cases where there are several factors. For instance,

$$(abcde)^r = a^r b^r c^r d^r e^r$$

We saw that $(ab)^r = a^r b^r$. What about $(a+b)^r$? One of the most common errors committed in elementary algebra is to equate this to $a^r + b^r$. For example, $(2+3)^3 = 5^3 = 125$, but $2^3 + 3^3 = 8 + 27 = 35$. Thus,

$$(a+b)^r \neq a^r + b^r \qquad \text{(in general)}$$

EXAMPLE 1   Simplify[2]   (a) $x^p x^{2p}$ (b) $t^s \div t^{s-1}$ (c) $a^2 b^3 a^{-1} b^5$ (d) $\dfrac{t^p t^{q-1}}{t^r t^{s-1}}$.

Solution:

(a) $x^p x^{2p} = x^{p+2p} = x^{3p}$

(b) $t^s \div t^{s-1} = t^{s-(s-1)} = t^{s-s+1} = t^1 = t$

(c) $a^2 \upsilon^3 a^{-1} b^5 = a^2 a^{-1} b^3 b^5 = a^{2-1} b^{3+5} = a^1 b^8 = ab^8$

(d) $\dfrac{t^p \cdot t^{q-1}}{t^r \cdot t^{s-1}} = \dfrac{t^{p+q-1}}{t^{r+s-1}} = t^{p+q-1-(r+s-1)} = t^{p+q-1-r-s+1} = t^{p+q-r-s}$

EXAMPLE 2   If $x^{-2} y^3 = 5$, compute $x^{-4} y^6$, $x^6 y^{-9}$, and $x^2 y^{-3} + 2x^{-10} y^{15}$.

Solution: In computing $x^{-4} y^6$, how can we make use of the assumption that $x^{-2} y^3 = 5$? A moment's reflection might lead you to see that $(x^{-2} y^3)^2 = x^{-4} y^6$, and hence $x^{-4} y^6 = 5^2 = 25$. Similarly,

$$x^6 y^{-9} = (x^{-2} y^3)^{-3} = 5^{-3} = 1/125$$

$$x^2 y^{-3} + 2x^{-10} y^{15} = (x^{-2} y^3)^{-1} + 2(x^{-2} y^3)^5 = 5^{-1} + 2 \cdot 5^5 = 6250.2$$

NOTE 1   An important motivation for introducing the definitions $a^0 = 1$ and $a^{-n} = 1/a^n$ is that we want the rules for powers to be valid for negative and zero exponents as well as for positive ones. For example, we want $a^r \cdot a^s = a^{r+s}$ to be valid when $r = 5$ and $s = 0$. This requires that $a^5 \cdot a^0 = a^{5+0} = a^5$, so we must choose $a^0 = 1$. If $a^n \cdot a^m = a^{n+m}$ is to be valid when $m = -n$, we must have $a^n \cdot a^{-n} = a^{n+(-n)} = a^0 = 1$. Because $a^n \cdot (1/a^n) = 1$, we *must* define a^{-n} to be $1/a^n$.

NOTE 2   It is easy to make mistakes when dealing with powers. The following examples highlight some common sources of confusion.

(a) There is an important difference between $(-10)^2 = (-10)(-10) = 100$, and $-10^2 = -(10 \cdot 10) = -100$. The square of minus 10 is not equal to minus the square of 10.

(b) Note that $(2x)^{-1} = 1/(2x)$. Here the product $2x$ is raised to the power of -1. On the other hand, in the expression $2x^{-1}$ only x is raised to the power -1, so $2x^{-1} = 2 \cdot (1/x) = 2/x$.

(c) The volume of a ball with radius r is $\frac{4}{3}\pi r^3$. What will the volume be if the radius is doubled? The new volume is $\frac{4}{3}\pi (2r)^3 = \frac{4}{3}\pi (2r)(2r)(2r) = \frac{4}{3}\pi 8r^3 = 8\left(\frac{4}{3}\pi r^3\right)$, so the volume is 8 times the initial one. (If we made the mistake of "simplifying" $(2r)^3$ to $2r^3$, the result would imply only a doubling of the volume; this should be contrary to common sense.)

Compound Interest

Powers are used in practically every branch of applied mathematics, including economics. To illustrate their use, recall how they are needed to calculate compound interest.

---

[2] Here and throughout the book we strongly suggest that when you attempt to solve a problem, you cover the solution and then gradually reveal the proposed answer to see if you are right.

Suppose you deposit $1000 in a bank account paying 8% interest at the end of each year.[3] After one year you will have earned $1000 \cdot 0.08 = \$80$ in interest, so the amount in your bank account will be $1080. This can be rewritten as

$$1000 + \frac{1000 \cdot 8}{100} = 1000 \left(1 + \frac{8}{100}\right) = 1000 \cdot 1.08$$

Suppose this new amount of $1000 \cdot 1.08$ is left in the bank for another year at an interest rate of 8%. After a second year, the extra interest will be $1000 \cdot 1.08 \cdot 0.08$. So the total amount will have grown to

$$1000 \cdot 1.08 + (1000 \cdot 1.08) \cdot 0.08 = 1000 \cdot 1.08(1 + 0.08) = 1000 \cdot (1.08)^2$$

Each year the amount will increase by the factor 1.08, and we see that at the end of t years it will have grown to $1000 \cdot (1.08)^t$.

If the original amount is $\$K$ and the interest rate is $p\%$ per year, by the end of the first year, the amount will be $K + K \cdot p/100 = K(1 + p/100)$ dollars. The growth factor per year is thus $1 + p/100$. In general, after t (whole) years, the original investment of $\$K$ will have grown to an amount

$$K \left(1 + \frac{p}{100}\right)^t$$

when the interest rate is $p\%$ per year (and interest is added to the capital every year—that is, there is compound interest).

This example illustrates a general principle:

A quantity K which increases by p% per year will have increased after t years to

$$K \left(1 + \frac{p}{100}\right)^t$$

Here $1 + \dfrac{p}{100}$ *is called the* **growth factor** *for a growth of p%.*

If you see an expression like $(1.08)^t$ you should immediately be able to recognize it as the amount to which $1 has grown after t years when the interest rate is 8% per year. How should you interpret $(1.08)^0$? You deposit $1 at 8% per year, and leave the amount for 0 years. Then you still have only $1, because there has been no time to accumulate any interest, so that $(1.08)^0$ *must* equal 1.

NOTE 3 $1000 \cdot (1.08)^5$ is the amount you will have in your account after 5 years if you invest $1000 at 8% interest per year. Using a calculator, you find that you will have approximately $1469.33. A rather common mistake is to put $1000 \cdot (1.08)^5 = (1000 \cdot 1.08)^5 = (1080)^5$. This is 10^{12} (or a trillion) times the right answer.

---

[3] Remember that 1% means one in a hundred, or 0.01. So 23%, for example, is $23 \cdot 0.01 = 0.23$. To calculate 23% of 4000, we write $4000 \cdot \frac{23}{100} = 920$ or $4000 \cdot 0.23 = 920$.

EXAMPLE 3   A new car has been bought for $15 000 and is assumed to decrease in value (depreciate) by 15% per year over a six-year period. What is its value after 6 years?

Solution: After one year its value is down to

$$15\,000 - \frac{15\,000 \cdot 15}{100} = 15\,000\left(1 - \frac{15}{100}\right) = 15\,000 \cdot 0.85 = 12\,750$$

After two years its value is $15\,000 \cdot (0.85)^2 = 10\,837.50$, and so on. After six years we realize that its value must be $15\,000 \cdot (0.85)^6 \approx 5\,657$.

This example illustrates a general principle:

A quantity K which decreases by p% per year, will after t years have decreased to

$$K\left(1 - \frac{p}{100}\right)^t$$

Here $1 - \dfrac{p}{100}$ *is called the* **growth factor** *for a decline of p%.*

Do We Really Need Negative Exponents?

How much money should you have deposited in a bank 5 years ago in order to have $1000 today, given that the interest rate has been 8% per year over this period? If we call this amount x, the requirement is that $x \cdot (1.08)^5$ must equal $1000, or that $x \cdot (1.08)^5 = 1000$. Dividing by 1.08^5 on both sides yields

$$x = \frac{1000}{(1.08)^5} = 1000 \cdot (1.08)^{-5}$$

(which is approximately $681). Thus, $\$(1.08)^{-5}$ is what you should have deposited 5 years ago in order to have $1 today, given the constant interest rate of 8%.

In general, $\$P(1 + p/100)^{-t}$ *is what you should have deposited t years ago in order to have* $P *today, if the interest rate has been p% every year.*

1. Compute: (a) 10^3 (b) $(-0.3)^2$ (c) 4^{-2} (d) $(0.1)^{-1}$

2. Write as powers of 2:   (a) 4   (b) 1   (c) 64   (d) 1/16

3. Write as powers:

(a) $15 \cdot 15 \cdot 15$ (b) $\left(-\frac{1}{3}\right)\left(-\frac{1}{3}\right)\left(-\frac{1}{3}\right)$ (c) $\frac{1}{10}$ (d) 0.0000001

(e) $t\,t\,t\,t\,t\,t$ (f) $(a-b)(a-b)(a-b)$ (g) $a\,a\,b\,b\,b\,b$ (h) $(-a)(-a)(-a)$

In Problems 4–6 expand and simplify.

4. (a) $2^5 \cdot 2^5$ (b) $3^8 \cdot 3^{-2} \cdot 3^{-3}$ (c) $(2x)^3$ (d) $(-3xy^2)^3$

5. (a) $\dfrac{p^{24}p^3}{p^4 p}$ (b) $\dfrac{a^4 b^{-3}}{(a^2 b^{-3})^2}$ (c) $\dfrac{3^4(3^2)^6}{(-3)^{15}3^7}$ (d) $\dfrac{p^\gamma (pq)^\sigma}{p^{2\gamma + \sigma}q^{\sigma - 2}}$

6. (a) $2^0 \cdot 2^1 \cdot 2^2 \cdot 2^3$ (b) $\left(\dfrac{4}{3}\right)^3$ (c) $\dfrac{4^2 \cdot 6^2}{3^3 \cdot 2^3}$

     (d) $x^5 x^4$ (e) $y^5 y^4 y^3$ (f) $(2xy)^3$

     (g) $\dfrac{10^2 \cdot 10^{-4} \cdot 10^3}{10^0 \cdot 10^{-2} \cdot 10^5}$ (h) $\dfrac{(k^2)^3 k^4}{(k^3)^2}$ (i) $\dfrac{(x+1)^3(x+1)^{-2}}{(x+1)^2(x+1)^{-3}}$

7. The surface area of a sphere with radius r is $4\pi r^2$.

     (a) By what factor will the surface area increase if the radius is tripled?

     (b) If the radius increases by 16%, by how many % will the surface area increase?

8. Which of the following equalities are true and which are false? Justify your answers. (Note: a and b are positive, m and n are integers.)

     (a) $a^0 = 0$ (b) $(a+b)^{-n} = 1/(a+b)^n$ (c) $a^m \cdot a^m = a^{2m}$

     (d) $a^m \cdot b^m = (ab)^{2m}$ (e) $(a+b)^m = a^m + b^m$ (f) $a^n \cdot b^m = (ab)^{n+m}$

9. Complete the following:

     (a) $xy = 3$ implies $x^3 y^3 = \ldots$ (b) $ab = -2$ implies $(ab)^4 = \ldots$

     (c) $a^2 = 4$ implies $(a^8)^0 = \ldots$ (d) n integer implies $(-1)^{2n} = \ldots$

10. Compute the following: (a) 13% of 150   (b) 6% of 2400   (c) 5.5% of 200

11. A box containing 5 balls costs \$8.50. If the balls are bought individually, they cost \$2.00 each. How much cheaper is it, in percentage terms, to buy the box as opposed to buying 5 individual balls?

12. Give economic interpretations to each of the following expressions and then use a calculator to find the approximate values:

     (a) $50 \cdot (1.11)^8$ (b) $10\,000 \cdot (1.12)^{20}$ (c) $5000 \cdot (1.07)^{-10}$

13. (a) \$12\,000 is deposited in an account earning 4% interest per year. What is the amount after 15 years?

     (b) If the interest rate is 6% each year, how much money should you have deposited in a bank 5 years ago to have \$50\,000 today?

14. A quantity increases by 25% each year for 3 years. How much is the combined percentage growth p over the three year period?

15. (a) A firm's profit increased from 1990 to 1991 by 20%, but it decreased by 17% from 1991 to 1992. Which of the years 1990 and 1992 had the higher profit?

     (b) What percentage decrease in profits from 1991 to 1992 would imply that profits were equal in 1990 and 1992?

1.3 Rules of Algebra

You are certainly already familiar with the most common rules of algebra. We have already used some in this chapter. Nevertheless, it may be useful to recall those that are most important. If a, b, and c are arbitrary numbers, then:

(a) $a + b = b + a$

(b) $(a + b) + c = a + (b + c)$

(c) $a + 0 = a$

(d) $a + (-a) = 0$

(e) $ab = ba$

(f) $(ab)c = a(bc)$

(g) $1 \cdot a = a$

(h) $aa^{-1} = 1$ for $a \neq 0$

(i) $(-a)b = a(-b) = -ab$

(j) $(-a)(-b) = ab$

(k) $a(b + c) = ab + ac$

(l) $(a + b)c = ac + bc$

These rules are used in the following examples:

$5 + x^2 = x^2 + 5$

$x\frac{1}{3} = \frac{1}{3}x$

$(-3)5 = 3(-5) = -(3 \cdot 5) = -15$

$3x(y + 2z) = 3xy + 6xz$

$(a + 2b) + 3b = a + (2b + 3b) = a + 5b$

$(xy)y^{-1} = x(yy^{-1}) = x$

$(-6)(-20) = 120$

$(t^2 + 2t)4t^3 = t^2 4t^3 + 2t4t^3 = 4t^5 + 8t^4$

The algebraic rules can be combined in several ways to give:

$$a(b - c) = a[b + (-c)] = ab + a(-c) = ab - ac$$
$$x(a + b - c + d) = xa + xb - xc + xd$$
$$(a + b)(c + d) = ac + ad + bc + bd$$

Figure 1 provides a geometric argument for the last of these algebraic rules for the case in which the numbers a, b, c, and d are all positive. The area $(a + b)(c + d)$ of the large rectangle is the sum of the areas of the four small rectangles.

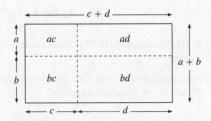

Figure 1

Recall the following three "quadratic identities", which are so important that you should definitely memorize them.

$$(a + b)^2 = a^2 + 2ab + b^2$$
$$(a - b)^2 = a^2 - 2ab + b^2$$
$$(a + b)(a - b) = a^2 - b^2$$

The last of these is called the *difference-of-squares formula*. The proofs are very easy. For example, $(a+b)^2$ means $(a+b)(a+b)$, which equals $aa + ab + ba + bb = a^2 + 2ab + b^2$.

EXAMPLE 1   Expand: (a) $(3x + 2y)^2$ (b) $(1 - 2z)^2$ (c) $(4p + 5q)(4p - 5q)$.

Solution:

(a) $(3x + 2y)^2 = (3x)^2 + 2(3x)(2y) + (2y)^2 = 9x^2 + 12xy + 4y^2$

(b) $(1 - 2z)^2 = 1 - 2 \cdot 1 \cdot 2 \cdot z + (2z)^2 = 1 - 4z + 4z^2$

(c) $(4p + 5q)(4p - 5q) = (4p)^2 - (5q)^2 = 16p^2 - 25q^2$

We often encounter parentheses with a minus sign in front. Because $(-1)x = -x$,

$$-(a + b - c + d) = -a - b + c - d$$

In words: *When removing a pair of parentheses with a minus in front, change the signs of* **all** *the terms within the parentheses—do not leave any out.*

We saw how to multiply two factors, $(a+b)$ and $(c+d)$. How do we compute such products when there are several factors? Here is an example:

$$(a + b)(c + d)(e + f) = \big[(a + b)(c + d)\big](e + f) = \big(ac + ad + bc + bd\big)(e + f)$$

$$= (ac + ad + bc + bd)e + (ac + ad + bc + bd)f$$

$$= ace + ade + bce + bde + acf + adf + bcf + bdf$$

Alternatively, write $(a + b)(c + d)(e + f) = (a + b)\big[(c + d)(e + f)\big]$, then expand and show that you get the same answer.

EXAMPLE 2   Expand $(r + 1)^3$.

Solution:

$$(r + 1)^3 = \big[(r + 1)(r + 1)\big](r + 1) = (r^2 + 2r + 1)(r + 1) = r^3 + 3r^2 + 3r + 1$$

Illustration: A ball with radius r metres has a volume of $\frac{4}{3}\pi r^3$ cubic metres. By how much does the volume expand if the radius increases by 1 metre? The solution is

$$\tfrac{4}{3}\pi(r + 1)^3 - \tfrac{4}{3}\pi r^3 = \tfrac{4}{3}\pi(r^3 + 3r^2 + 3r + 1) - \tfrac{4}{3}\pi r^3 = \tfrac{4}{3}\pi(3r^2 + 3r + 1)$$

Algebraic Expressions

Expressions involving letters such as $3xy - 5x^2y^3 + 2xy + 6y^3x^2 - 3x + 5yx + 8$ are called *algebraic expressions*. We call $3xy$, $-5x^2y^3$, $2xy$, $6y^3x^2$, $-3x$, $5yx$, and 8 the *terms* in the expression that is formed by adding all the terms together. The numbers 3, -5, 2, 6, -3, and 5 are the *numerical coefficients* of the first six terms. Two terms where only the numerical coefficients are different, such as $-5x^2y^3$ and $6y^3x^2$, are called *terms of the same type*. In order to simplify expressions, we collect terms of the same type. Then within each term, we put numerical coefficients first and place the letters in alphabetical order. Thus,

$$3xy - 5x^2y^3 + 2xy + 6y^3x^2 - 3x + 5yx + 8 = x^2y^3 + 10xy - 3x + 8$$

EXAMPLE 3   Expand and simplify: $(2pq - 3p^2)(p + 2q) - (q^2 - 2pq)(2p - q)$.

Solution:

$$(2pq - 3p^2)(p + 2q) - (q^2 - 2pq)(2p - q)$$
$$= 2pqp + 2pq2q - 3p^3 - 6p^2q - (q^2 2p - q^3 - 4pqp + 2pq^2)$$
$$= 2p^2q + 4pq^2 - 3p^3 - 6p^2q - 2pq^2 + q^3 + 4p^2q - 2pq^2$$
$$= -3p^3 + q^3$$

Factoring

When we write $49 = 7 \cdot 7$ and $672 = 2 \cdot 2 \cdot 2 \cdot 2 \cdot 2 \cdot 3 \cdot 7$, we have *factored* these numbers. Algebraic expressions can often be factored in a similar way. For example, $6x^2y = 2 \cdot 3 \cdot x \cdot x \cdot y$ and $5x^2y^3 - 15xy^2 = 5 \cdot x \cdot y \cdot y(xy - 3)$.

EXAMPLE 4   Factor each of the following:

(a) $5x^2 + 15x$ (b) $-18b^2 + 9ab$ (c) $K(1+r) + K(1+r)r$ (d) $\delta L^{-3} + (1-\delta)L^{-2}$

Solution:

(a) $5x^2 + 15x = 5x(x + 3)$

(b) $-18b^2 + 9ab = 9ab - 18b^2 = 3 \cdot 3b(a - 2b)$

(c) $K(1+r) + K(1+r)r = K(1+r)(1+r) = K(1+r)^2$

(d) $\delta L^{-3} + (1-\delta)L^{-2} = L^{-3}[\delta + (1-\delta)L]$

The "quadratic identities" can often be used in reverse for factoring. They sometimes enable us to factor expressions that otherwise appear to have no factors.

EXAMPLE 5   Factor each of the following:

(a) $16a^2 - 1$ (b) $x^2y^2 - 25z^2$ (c) $4u^2 + 8u + 4$ (d) $x^2 - x + \frac{1}{4}$

Solution:

(a) $16a^2 - 1 = (4a + 1)(4a - 1)$

(b) $x^2y^2 - 25z^2 = (xy + 5z)(xy - 5z)$

(c) $4u^2 + 8u + 4 = 4(u^2 + 2u + 1) = 4(u + 1)^2$

(d) $x^2 - x + \frac{1}{4} = (x - \frac{1}{2})^2$

NOTE 1 To factor an expression means to express it as a *product* of simpler factors. Note that $9x^2 - 25y^2 = 3 \cdot 3 \cdot x \cdot x - 5 \cdot 5 \cdot y \cdot y$ does *not* factor $9x^2 - 25y^2$. A correct factoring is $9x^2 - 25y^2 = (3x - 5y)(3x + 5y)$.

Sometimes one has to show a measure of inventiveness to find a factoring:

$$4x^2 - y^2 + 6x^2 + 3xy = (4x^2 - y^2) + 3x(2x + y)$$
$$= (2x + y)(2x - y) + 3x(2x + y)$$
$$= (2x + y)(2x - y + 3x)$$
$$= (2x + y)(5x - y)$$

Although it might be difficult, or impossible, to find a factoring, it is very easy to verify that an algebraic expression has been factored correctly by simply multiplying the factors. For example, we check that

$$x^2 - (a + b)x + ab = (x - a)(x - b)$$

by expanding $(x - a)(x - b)$.

Most algebraic expressions *cannot* be factored. For example, there is no way to write $x^2 + 10x + 50$ as a product of simpler factors.[4]

PROBLEMS FOR SECTION 1.3

In Problems 1–5, expand and simplify.

1. (a) $-3 + (-4) - (-8)$ (b) $(-3)(2 - 4)$ (c) $(-3)(-12)(-\frac{1}{2})$

(d) $-3[4 - (-2)]$ (e) $-3(-x - 4)$ (f) $(5x - 3y)9$

(g) $2x\left(\dfrac{3}{2x}\right)$ (h) $0 \cdot (1 - x)$ (i) $-7x\dfrac{2}{14x}$

2. (a) $5a^2 - 3b - (-a^2 - b) - 3(a^2 + b)$ (b) $-x(2x - y) + y(1 - x) + 3(x + y)$

(c) $12t^2 - 3t + 16 - 2(6t^2 - 2t + 8)$ (d) $r^3 - 3r^2s + s^3 - (-s^3 - r^3 + 3r^2s)$

3. (a) $-3(n^2 - 2n + 3)$ (b) $x^2(1 + x^3)$ (c) $(4n - 3)(n - 2)$

(d) $6a^2b(5ab - 3ab^2)$ (e) $(a^2b - ab^2)(a + b)$ (f) $(x - y)(x - 2y)(x - 3y)$

4. (a) $(ax + b)(cx + d)$ (b) $(2 - t^2)(2 + t^2)$ (c) $(u - v)^2(u + v)^2$

(SM) **5.** (a) $(2t - 1)(t^2 - 2t + 1)$ (b) $(a + 1)^2 + (a - 1)^2 - 2(a + 1)(a - 1)$

(c) $(x + y + z)^2$ (d) $(x + y + z)^2 - (x - y - z)^2$

---

[4] If we introduce complex numbers, however, then $x^2 + 10x + 50$ *can* be factored.

6. Expand each of the following:

(a) $(x + 2y)^2$ (b) $\left(\dfrac{1}{x} - x\right)^2$ (c) $(3u - 5v)^2$ (d) $(2z - 5w)(2z + 5w)$

7. (a) $201^2 - 199^2 =$ (b) If $u^2 - 4u + 4 = 1$, then $u =$ (c) $\dfrac{(a+1)^2 - (a-1)^2}{(b+1)^2 - (b-1)^2} =$

8. Compute $1000^2/(252^2 - 248^2)$ without using a calculator.

9. Verify the following cubic identities, which are occasionally useful:

(a) $(a + b)^3 = a^3 + 3a^2b + 3ab^2 + b^3$ (b) $(a - b)^3 = a^3 - 3a^2b + 3ab^2 - b^3$

(c) $a^3 - b^3 = (a - b)(a^2 + ab + b^2)$ (d) $a^3 + b^3 = (a + b)(a^2 - ab + b^2)$

In Problems 10 to 15, factor the given expressions.

10. (a) $21x^2y^3$ (b) $3x - 9y + 27z$ (c) $a^3 - a^2b$ (d) $8x^2y^2 - 16xy$

11. (a) $28a^2b^3$ (b) $4x + 8y - 24z$ (c) $2x^2 - 6xy$ (d) $4a^2b^3 + 6a^3b^2$

(e) $7x^2 - 49xy$ (f) $5xy^2 - 45x^3y^2$ (g) $16 - b^2$ (h) $3x^2 - 12$

12. (a) $x^2 - 4x + 4$ (b) $4t^2s - 8ts^2$ (c) $16a^2 + 16ab + 4b^2$ (d) $5x^3 - 10xy^2$

(SM) **13.** (a) $a^2 + 4ab + 4b^2$ (b) $K^2L - L^2K$ (c) $K^{-4} - LK^{-5}$

(d) $9z^2 - 16w^2$ (e) $-\frac{1}{5}x^2 + 2xy - 5y^2$ (f) $a^4 - b^4$

14. (a) $5x + 5y + ax + ay$ (b) $u^2 - v^2 + 3v + 3u$ (c) $P^3 + Q^3 + Q^2P + P^2Q$

15. (a) $K^3 - K^2L$ (b) $KL^3 + KL$ (c) $L^2 - K^2$

(d) $K^2 - 2KL + L^2$ (e) $K^3L - 4K^2L^2 + 4KL^3$ (f) $K^{-3} - K^{-6}$

1.4 Fractions

Recall that

$$a \div b = \frac{a}{b} \quad \begin{matrix} \leftarrow \text{numerator} \\ \leftarrow \text{denominator} \end{matrix}$$

For example, $5 \div 8 = \frac{5}{8}$. For typographical reasons we often write $5/8$ instead of $\frac{5}{8}$. Of course, $5 \div 8 = 0.625$. In this case, we have written the fraction as a decimal number. The fraction $5/8$ is called a *proper fraction* because 5 is less than 8. The fraction $19/8$ is an *improper fraction* because the numerator is larger than (or equal to) the denominator. An improper fraction can be written as a *mixed number*:

$$\frac{19}{8} = 2 + \frac{3}{8} = 2\frac{3}{8}$$

Here $2\frac{3}{8}$ means 2 *plus* $3/8$. On the other hand, $2 \cdot \frac{3}{8} = \frac{2 \cdot 3}{8} = \frac{3}{4}$ (by the rules reviewed in what follows). Note, however, that $2\frac{x}{8}$ means $2 \cdot \frac{x}{8}$; the notation $\frac{2x}{8}$ or $2x/8$ is obviously preferable in this case. Indeed, $\frac{19}{8}$ or $19/8$ is probably better than $2\frac{3}{8}$ because it also helps avoid ambiguity.

The most important properties of fractions are listed below, with simple numerical examples. It is absolutely essential for you to master these rules, so you should carefully check that you know each of them.

Rule:

Example:

(1) $\dfrac{a \cdot \cancel{c}}{b \cdot \cancel{c}} = \dfrac{a}{b}$ ($b \neq 0$ and $c \neq 0$)

$\dfrac{21}{15} = \dfrac{7 \cdot \cancel{3}}{5 \cdot \cancel{3}} = \dfrac{7}{5}$

(2) $\dfrac{-a}{-b} = \dfrac{(-a) \cdot (-1)}{(-b) \cdot (-1)} = \dfrac{a}{b}$

$\dfrac{-5}{-6} = \dfrac{5}{6}$

(3) $-\dfrac{a}{b} = (-1)\dfrac{a}{b} = \dfrac{(-1)a}{b} = \dfrac{-a}{b}$

$-\dfrac{13}{15} = (-1)\dfrac{13}{15} = \dfrac{(-1)13}{15} = \dfrac{-13}{15}$

(4) $\dfrac{a}{c} + \dfrac{b}{c} = \dfrac{a+b}{c}$

$\dfrac{5}{3} + \dfrac{13}{3} = \dfrac{18}{3} = 6$

(5) $\dfrac{a}{b} + \dfrac{c}{d} = \dfrac{a \cdot d + b \cdot c}{b \cdot d}$

$\dfrac{3}{5} + \dfrac{1}{6} = \dfrac{3 \cdot 6 + 5 \cdot 1}{5 \cdot 6} = \dfrac{23}{30}$

(6) $a + \dfrac{b}{c} = \dfrac{a \cdot c + b}{c}$

$5 + \dfrac{3}{5} = \dfrac{5 \cdot 5 + 3}{5} = \dfrac{28}{5}$

(7) $a \cdot \dfrac{b}{c} = \dfrac{a \cdot b}{c}$

$7 \cdot \dfrac{3}{5} = \dfrac{21}{5}$

(8) $\dfrac{a}{b} \cdot \dfrac{c}{d} = \dfrac{a \cdot c}{b \cdot d}$

$\dfrac{4}{7} \cdot \dfrac{5}{8} = \dfrac{4 \cdot 5}{7 \cdot 8} = \dfrac{\cancel{4} \cdot 5}{7 \cdot 2 \cdot \cancel{4}} = \dfrac{5}{14}$

(9) $\dfrac{a}{b} \div \dfrac{c}{d} = \dfrac{a}{b} \cdot \dfrac{d}{c} = \dfrac{a \cdot d}{b \cdot c}$

$\dfrac{3}{8} \div \dfrac{6}{14} = \dfrac{3}{8} \cdot \dfrac{14}{6} = \dfrac{\cancel{3} \cdot \cancel{2} \cdot 7}{\cancel{2} \cdot 2 \cdot 2 \cdot \cancel{3}} = \dfrac{7}{8}$

Rule (1) is very important. It is the rule used to reduce fractions by factoring the numerator and the denominator, then cancelling *common factors* (that is, dividing both the numerator and denominator by the same nonzero quantity).

EXAMPLE 1   Simplify: (a) $\dfrac{5x^2yz^3}{25xy^2z}$ (b) $\dfrac{x^2 + xy}{x^2 - y^2}$ (c) $\dfrac{4 - 4a + a^2}{a^2 - 4}$

Solution:

(a) $\dfrac{5x^2yz^3}{25xy^2z} = \dfrac{\cancel{5} \cdot \cancel{x} \cdot x \cdot \cancel{y} \cdot \cancel{z} \cdot z \cdot z}{\cancel{5} \cdot 5 \cdot \cancel{x} \cdot \cancel{x} \cdot y \cdot \cancel{z}} = \dfrac{xz^2}{5y}$ (b) $\dfrac{x^2 + xy}{x^2 - y^2} = \dfrac{x(x+y)}{(x-y)(x+y)} = \dfrac{x}{x-y}$

(c) $\dfrac{4 - 4a + a^2}{a^2 - 4} = \dfrac{(a-2)(a-2)}{(a-2)(a+2)} = \dfrac{a-2}{a+2}$

When we use rule (1) in reverse, we are *expanding* the fraction. For example, $5/8 = 5 \cdot 125/8 \cdot 125 = 625/1000 = 0.625$.

When we simplify fractions, only *common* factors can be removed. A frequently occurring error is illustrated in the following example.

$$\textbf{Wrong!} \quad \rightarrow \quad \frac{2\cancel{x} + 3y}{\cancel{x}y} = \frac{2 + 3\cancel{x}}{\cancel{x}} = \frac{2 + 3}{1} = 5$$

In fact, the numerator and the denominator in the fraction $(2x + 3y)/xy$ do not have any common factors. But a correct simplification is this: $(2x + 3y)/xy = 2/y + 3/x$.

Another error is shown in the next example.

$$\textbf{Wrong!} \quad \rightarrow \quad \frac{x}{x^2 + 2x} = \frac{x}{x^2} + \frac{x}{2x} = \frac{1}{x} + \frac{1}{2}$$

A correct way of simplifying the fraction is to cancel the common factor x, which yields the fraction $1/(x + 2)$.

Rules (4)–(6) are those used to add fractions. Note that (5) follows from (1) and (4):

$$\frac{a}{b} + \frac{c}{d} = \frac{a \cdot d}{b \cdot d} + \frac{c \cdot b}{d \cdot b} = \frac{a \cdot d + b \cdot c}{b \cdot d}$$

and we see easily that, for example,

$$\frac{a}{b} - \frac{c}{d} + \frac{e}{f} = \frac{adf}{bdf} - \frac{cbf}{bdf} + \frac{ebd}{bdf} = \frac{adf - cbf + ebd}{bdf} \qquad (*)$$

If the numbers b, d, and f have common factors, the computation carried out in $(*)$ involves unnecessarily large numbers. We can simplify the process by first finding the least common denominator (LCD) of the fractions. To do so, factor each denominator completely; the LCD is the product of all the distinct factors that appear in any denominator, each raised to the highest power to which it gets raised in any denominator. The use of the LCD is demonstrated in the following example.

EXAMPLE 2   Simplify the following:

(a) $\dfrac{1}{2} - \dfrac{1}{3} + \dfrac{1}{6}$ (b) $\dfrac{2 + a}{a^2 b} + \dfrac{1 - b}{ab^2} - \dfrac{2b}{a^2 b^2}$ (c) $\dfrac{x - y}{x + y} - \dfrac{x}{x - y} + \dfrac{3xy}{x^2 - y^2}$

Solution:

(a) The LCD is 6 and so $\dfrac{1}{2} - \dfrac{1}{3} + \dfrac{1}{6} = \dfrac{1 \cdot 3}{2 \cdot 3} - \dfrac{1 \cdot 2}{2 \cdot 3} + \dfrac{1}{2 \cdot 3} = \dfrac{3 - 2 + 1}{6} = \dfrac{2}{6} = \dfrac{1}{3}$

(b) The LCD is $a^2 b^2$ and so

$$\frac{2 + a}{a^2 b} + \frac{1 - b}{ab^2} - \frac{2b}{a^2 b^2} = \frac{(2 + a)b}{a^2 b^2} + \frac{(1 - b)a}{a^2 b^2} - \frac{2b}{a^2 b^2}$$

$$= \frac{2b + ab + a - ba - 2b}{a^2 b^2} = \frac{a}{a^2 b^2} = \frac{1}{ab^2}$$

(c) The LCD is $(x + y)(x - y)$ and so

$$\frac{x - y}{x + y} - \frac{x}{x - y} + \frac{3xy}{x^2 - y^2} = \frac{(x - y)(x - y)}{(x - y)(x + y)} - \frac{(x + y)x}{(x + y)(x - y)} + \frac{3xy}{(x - y)(x + y)}$$

$$= \frac{x^2 - 2xy + y^2 - x^2 - xy + 3xy}{(x - y)(x + y)} = \frac{y^2}{x^2 - y^2}$$

An Important Note

What do we mean by $1 - \frac{5-3}{2}$? It means that from the number 1, we subtract the number $\frac{5-3}{2} = \frac{2}{2} = 1$. Therefore, $1 - \frac{5-3}{2} = 0$. Alternatively,

$$1 - \frac{5 - 3}{2} = \frac{2}{2} - \frac{(5 - 3)}{2} = \frac{2 - (5 - 3)}{2} = \frac{2 - 5 + 3}{2} = \frac{0}{2} = 0$$

In the same way,

$$\frac{2 + b}{ab^2} - \frac{a - 2}{a^2 b}$$

means that we subtract $(a - 2)/a^2 b$ from $(2 + b)/ab^2$:

$$\frac{2 + b}{ab^2} - \frac{a - 2}{a^2 b} = \frac{(2 + b)a}{a^2 b^2} - \frac{(a - 2)b}{a^2 b^2} = \frac{(2 + b)a - (a - 2)b}{a^2 b^2} = \frac{2(a + b)}{a^2 b^2}$$

It is a good idea first to enclose in parentheses the numerators of the fractions, as in the next example.

EXAMPLE 3   Simplify the expression $\dfrac{x - 1}{x + 1} - \dfrac{1 - x}{x - 1} - \dfrac{-1 + 4x}{2(x + 1)}$.

Solution:

$$\frac{x - 1}{x + 1} - \frac{1 - x}{x - 1} - \frac{-1 + 4x}{2(x + 1)} = \frac{(x - 1)}{x + 1} - \frac{(1 - x)}{x - 1} - \frac{(-1 + 4x)}{2(x + 1)}$$

$$= \frac{2(x - 1)^2 - 2(1 - x)(x + 1) - (-1 + 4x)(x - 1)}{2(x + 1)(x - 1)}$$

$$= \frac{2(x^2 - 2x + 1) - 2(1 - x^2) - (4x^2 - 5x + 1)}{2(x + 1)(x - 1)}$$

$$= \frac{x - 1}{2(x + 1)(x - 1)} = \frac{1}{2(x + 1)}$$

We prove (9) by writing $(a/b) \div (c/d)$ as a ratio of fractions:[5]

$$\frac{a}{b} \div \frac{c}{d} = \frac{\frac{a}{b}}{\frac{c}{d}} = \frac{b \cdot d \cdot \frac{a}{b}}{b \cdot d \cdot \frac{c}{d}} = \frac{\cancel{b} \cdot d \cdot a}{\cancel{b} \cdot \frac{b \cdot \cancel{d} \cdot c}{\cancel{d}}} = \frac{d \cdot a}{b \cdot c} = \frac{a \cdot d}{b \cdot c} = \frac{a}{b} \cdot \frac{d}{c}$$

---

[5] Illustration (one easily becomes thirsty reading this stuff): You buy half a litre of a soft drink. Each sip is one fiftieth of a litre. How many sips? Answer: $(1/2) \div (1/50) = 25$.

When we deal with fractions of fractions, we should be sure to emphasize which is the fraction line of the dominant fraction. For example,

$$\frac{\dfrac{a}{b}}{c} \quad \text{means} \quad a \div \frac{b}{c} = \frac{ac}{b} \qquad \text{whereas} \qquad \frac{\dfrac{a}{b}}{c} \quad \text{means} \quad \frac{a}{b} \div c = \frac{a}{bc} \qquad (*)$$

Of course, it is safer to write $\dfrac{a}{b/c}$ or $a/(b/c)$ in the first case, and $\dfrac{a/b}{c}$ or $(a/b)/c$ in the second case. As a numerical example of $(*)$,

$$\frac{1}{\dfrac{3}{5}} = \frac{5}{3} \qquad \text{whereas} \qquad \frac{\dfrac{1}{3}}{5} = \frac{1}{15}$$

PROBLEMS FOR SECTION 1.4

In Problems 1 and 2, simplify the various expressions.

1. (a) $\dfrac{3}{7} + \dfrac{4}{7} - \dfrac{5}{7}$ (b) $\dfrac{3}{4} + \dfrac{4}{3} - 1$ (c) $\dfrac{3}{12} - \dfrac{1}{24}$ (d) $\dfrac{1}{5} - \dfrac{2}{25} - \dfrac{3}{75}$

     (e) $3\dfrac{3}{5} - 1\dfrac{4}{5}$ (f) $\dfrac{3}{5} \cdot \dfrac{5}{6}$ (g) $\left(\dfrac{3}{5} \div \dfrac{2}{15}\right) \cdot \dfrac{1}{9}$ (h) $\dfrac{\frac{2}{3} + \frac{1}{4}}{\frac{3}{4} + \frac{3}{2}}$

2. (a) $\dfrac{x}{10} - \dfrac{3x}{10} + \dfrac{17x}{10}$ (b) $\dfrac{9a}{10} - \dfrac{a}{2} + \dfrac{a}{5}$ (c) $\dfrac{b+2}{10} - \dfrac{3b}{15} + \dfrac{b}{10}$

     (d) $\dfrac{x+2}{3} + \dfrac{1-3x}{4}$ (e) $\dfrac{3}{2b} - \dfrac{5}{3b}$ (f) $\dfrac{3a-2}{3a} - \dfrac{2b-1}{2b} + \dfrac{4b+3a}{6ab}$

3. Cancel common factors:

     (a) $\dfrac{325}{625}$ (b) $\dfrac{8a^2b^3c}{64abc^3}$ (c) $\dfrac{2a^2 - 2b^2}{3a + 3b}$ (d) $\dfrac{P^3 - PQ^2}{(P+Q)^2}$

4. If $x = 3/7$ and $y = 1/14$, find the simplest forms of these fractions:

     (a) $x + y$ (b) $\dfrac{x}{y}$ (c) $\dfrac{x-y}{x+y}$ (d) $\dfrac{13(2x - 3y)}{2x + 1}$

(SM) **5.** Simplify:

     (a) $\dfrac{1}{x-2} - \dfrac{1}{x+2}$ (b) $\dfrac{6x + 25}{4x + 2} - \dfrac{6x^2 + x - 2}{4x^2 - 1}$ (c) $\dfrac{18b^2}{a^2 - 9b^2} - \dfrac{a}{a + 3b} + 2$

     (d) $\dfrac{1}{8ab} - \dfrac{1}{8b(a+2)}$ (e) $\dfrac{2t - t^2}{t+2} \cdot \left(\dfrac{5t}{t-2} - \dfrac{2t}{t-2}\right)$ (f) $2 - \dfrac{a\left(1 - \frac{1}{2a}\right)}{0.25}$

6. Simplify the following:

(a) $\dfrac{2}{x} + \dfrac{1}{x+1} - 3$

(b) $\dfrac{t}{2t+1} - \dfrac{t}{2t-1}$

(c) $\dfrac{3x}{x+2} - \dfrac{4x}{2-x} - \dfrac{2x-1}{x^2-4}$

(d) $\dfrac{\dfrac{1}{x} + \dfrac{1}{y}}{\dfrac{1}{xy}}$

(e) $\dfrac{\dfrac{1}{x^2} - \dfrac{1}{y^2}}{\dfrac{1}{x^2} + \dfrac{1}{y^2}}$

(f) $\dfrac{\dfrac{a}{x} - \dfrac{a}{y}}{\dfrac{a}{x} + \dfrac{a}{y}}$

7. Verify that $x^2 + 2xy - 3y^2 = (x + 3y)(x - y)$, and then simplify the expression

$$\frac{x-y}{x^2+2xy-3y^2} - \frac{2}{x-y} - \frac{7}{x+3y}$$

8. Simplify:

(a) $\left(\dfrac{1}{4} - \dfrac{1}{5}\right)^{-2}$

(b) $n - \dfrac{n}{1 - \dfrac{1}{n}}$

(c) $\dfrac{1}{1 + x^{p-q}} + \dfrac{1}{1 + x^{q-p}}$

(d) $\dfrac{\dfrac{1}{x-1} + \dfrac{1}{x^2-1}}{x - \dfrac{2}{x+1}}$

(e) $\dfrac{\dfrac{1}{(x+h)^2} - \dfrac{1}{x^2}}{h}$

(f) $\dfrac{\dfrac{10x^2}{x^2-1}}{\dfrac{5x}{x+1}}$

1.5 Fractional Powers

In textbooks and research articles on economics we constantly see powers with fractional exponents such as $K^{1/4}L^{3/4}$ and $Ar^{2.08}p^{-1.5}$. How do we define a^x when x is a rational number? Of course, we would like the usual rules for powers still to apply.

You probably know the meaning of a^x if $x = 1/2$. In fact, if $a \geq 0$ and $x = 1/2$, then we define $a^x = a^{1/2}$ as equal to $\sqrt{a}$, the **square root** of a. Thus, $a^{1/2} = \sqrt{a}$ is defined as the nonnegative number that when multiplied by itself gives a. This definition makes sense because $a^{1/2} \cdot a^{1/2} = a^{1/2+1/2} = a^1 = a$. Note that a real number multiplied by itself must always be ≥ 0, whether that number is positive, negative, or zero. Hence,

$$a^{1/2} = \sqrt{a} \qquad \text{(valid if } a \geq 0)$$

For example, $\sqrt{16} = 16^{1/2} = 4$ because $4^2 = 16$ and $\sqrt{\dfrac{1}{25}} = \dfrac{1}{5}$ because $\dfrac{1}{5} \cdot \dfrac{1}{5} = \dfrac{1}{25}$. If a and b are nonnegative numbers (with $b \neq 0$ in (ii)), then

$$\text{(i)} \quad \sqrt{ab} = \sqrt{a}\sqrt{b} \qquad \text{(ii)} \quad \sqrt{\dfrac{a}{b}} = \dfrac{\sqrt{a}}{\sqrt{b}}$$

which can also be written $(ab)^{1/2} = a^{1/2}b^{1/2}$ and $(a/b)^{1/2} = a^{1/2}/b^{1/2}$. For example, $\sqrt{16 \cdot 25} = \sqrt{16} \cdot \sqrt{25} = 4 \cdot 5 = 20$, and $\sqrt{9/4} = \sqrt{9}/\sqrt{4} = 3/2$.

Note that formulas (i) and (ii) are not valid if a or b or both are negative. For example, $\sqrt{(-1)(-1)} = \sqrt{1} = 1$, whereas $\sqrt{-1} \cdot \sqrt{-1}$ is not defined (unless one uses complex numbers).

NOTE 1 Recall that, in general, $(a+b)^r \neq a^r + b^r$. For $r = 1/2$, this implies that we have

$$\sqrt{a+b} \neq \sqrt{a} + \sqrt{b} \qquad \text{(in general)}$$

The following observation illustrates just how frequently this fact is overlooked. During an examination in a basic course in mathematics for economists, 22% of 190 students simplified $\sqrt{1/16 + 1/25}$ incorrectly and claimed that it was equal to $1/4 + 1/5 = 9/20$. (The correct answer is $\sqrt{41/400} = \sqrt{41}/20$.) In a test for another group of 138 students, 40% made the same mistake.

NOTE 2 $(-2)^2 = 4$ and $2^2 = 4$. Thus both $x = -2$ and $x = 2$ are solutions of the equation $x^2 = 4$. Therefore we have $x^2 = 4$ if and only if $x = \pm\sqrt{4} = \pm 2$. Note, however, that the symbol $\sqrt{4}$ means *only* 2, not -2.

By using a calculator, we find that $\sqrt{2} \div \sqrt{3} \approx 0.816$. Without a calculator, the division $\sqrt{2} \div \sqrt{3} \approx 1.414 \div 1.732$ would be tedious. But if we expand the fraction by rationalizing the denominator—that is, if we multiply both numerator and denominator by the same term in order to remove expressions with roots in the denominator, it becomes easier:

$$\frac{\sqrt{2}}{\sqrt{3}} = \frac{\sqrt{2} \cdot \sqrt{3}}{\sqrt{3} \cdot \sqrt{3}} = \frac{\sqrt{2 \cdot 3}}{3} = \frac{\sqrt{6}}{3} \approx \frac{2.448}{3} = 0.816$$

Sometimes the difference-of-squares formula of Section 1.3 can be used to eliminate square roots from the denominator of a fraction:

$$\frac{1}{\sqrt{5} + \sqrt{3}} = \frac{\sqrt{5} - \sqrt{3}}{(\sqrt{5} + \sqrt{3})(\sqrt{5} - \sqrt{3})} = \frac{\sqrt{5} - \sqrt{3}}{5 - 3} = \frac{1}{2}(\sqrt{5} - \sqrt{3})$$

Nth Roots

What do we mean by $a^{1/n}$, where n is a natural number, and a is positive? For example, what does $5^{1/3}$ mean? If the rule $(a^r)^s = a^{rs}$ is still to apply in this case, we must have $(5^{1/3})^3 = 5^1 = 5$. This implies that $5^{1/3}$ must be a solution of the equation $x^3 = 5$. This equation can be shown to have a unique positive solution, denoted by $\sqrt[3]{5}$, the *cube root* of 5. Therefore, we must define $5^{1/3}$ as $\sqrt[3]{5}$.

In general, $(a^{1/n})^n = a^1 = a$. Thus, $a^{1/n}$ is a solution of the equation $x^n = a$. This equation can be shown to have a unique positive solution denoted by $\sqrt[n]{a}$, the **nth root** of a:

$$a^{1/n} = \sqrt[n]{a}$$

In words: *if a is positive and n is a natural number, then $a^{1/n}$ is the unique positive number that, raised to the nth power, gives a—that is, $(a^{1/n})^n = a$.*

EXAMPLE 1   Compute (a) $\sqrt[3]{27}$ (b) $(1/32)^{1/5}$ (c) $(0.0001)^{0.25} = (0.0001)^{1/4}$.

Solution:

(a) $\sqrt[3]{27} = 3$, because $3^3 = 27$.   (b) $(1/32)^{1/5} = 1/2$ because $(1/2)^5 = 1/32$.

(c) $(0.0001)^{1/4} = 0.1$ because $(0.1)^4 = 0.0001$.

EXAMPLE 2   An amount \$5000 in an account has increased to \$10 000 in 15 years. What (constant) yearly interest rate p has been used?

Solution: After 15 years the amount of \$5000 has grown to $5000\,(1 + p/100)^{15}$, so we have the equation

$$5000\left(1 + \frac{p}{100}\right)^{15} = 10\,000 \quad \text{or} \quad \left(1 + \frac{p}{100}\right)^{15} = 2$$

In general, $(a^t)^{1/t} = a^1 = a$ for $t \neq 0$. Raising each side to the power of 1/15 yields

$$1 + \frac{p}{100} = 2^{1/15} \quad \text{or} \quad p = 100(2^{1/15} - 1)$$

With a calculator we find $p \approx 4.73$.

We proceed to define $a^{p/q}$ whenever p is an integer, q is a natural number, and $a > 0$. Consider first $5^{2/3}$. We have already defined $5^{1/3}$. For rule $(a^r)^s = a^{rs}$ to apply, we must have $5^{2/3} = (5^{1/3})^2$. So we must define $5^{2/3}$ as $\left(\sqrt[3]{5}\right)^2$. In general, for $a > 0$, we define

$$a^{p/q} = \left(a^{1/q}\right)^p = \left(\sqrt[q]{a}\right)^p \qquad \text{(p an integer, q a natural number)}$$

From the properties of exponents,

$$a^{p/q} = \left(a^{1/q}\right)^p = \left(a^p\right)^{1/q} = \sqrt[q]{a^p}$$

Thus, to compute $a^{p/q}$, we could either first take the qth root of a and raise the result to p, or first raise a to the power p and then take the qth root of the result. We obtain the same answer either way. For example,

$$4^{7/2} = (4^7)^{1/2} = 16384^{1/2} = 128 = 2^7 = (4^{1/2})^7$$

EXAMPLE 3   Compute: (a) $16^{3/2}$ (b) $16^{-1.25}$ (c) $(1/27)^{-2/3}$

Solution:

(a) $16^{3/2} = (16^{1/2})^3 = 4^3 = 64$

(b) $16^{-1.25} = 16^{-5/4} = \dfrac{1}{16^{5/4}} = \dfrac{1}{\left(\sqrt[4]{16}\right)^5} = \dfrac{1}{2^5} = \dfrac{1}{32}$

(c) $(1/27)^{-2/3} = 27^{2/3} = \left(\sqrt[3]{27}\right)^2 = 3^2 = 9$

EXAMPLE 4   Simplify the following expressions so that the answers contain only positive exponents:

(a) $\dfrac{a^{3/8}}{a^{1/8}}$

(b) $(x^{1/2}x^{3/2}x^{-2/3})^{3/4}$

(c) $\left(\dfrac{10p^{-1}q^{2/3}}{80p^2q^{-7/3}}\right)^{-2/3}$

Solution:

(a) $\dfrac{a^{3/8}}{a^{1/8}} = a^{3/8-1/8} = a^{2/8} = a^{1/4} = \sqrt[4]{a}$

(b) $(x^{1/2}x^{3/2}x^{-2/3})^{3/4} = (x^{1/2+3/2-2/3})^{3/4} = (x^{4/3})^{3/4} = x$

(c) $\left(\dfrac{10p^{-1}q^{2/3}}{80p^2q^{-7/3}}\right)^{-2/3} = (8^{-1}p^{-1-2}q^{2/3-(-7/3)})^{-2/3} = 8^{2/3}p^2q^{-2} = 4\dfrac{p^2}{q^2}$

NOTE 3   Tests reveal that many students, while they are able to handle quadratic identities, nevertheless make mistakes when dealing with more complicated powers. Here are examples taken from recent tests:

(i) $(1+r)^{20}$ is *not* equal to $1^{20} + r^{20}$.

(ii) If $u = 9 + x^{1/2}$, it does *not* follow that $u^2 = 81 + x$; instead $u^2 = 81 + 18x^{1/2} + x$.

(iii) $(e^x - e^{-x})^p$ is *not* equal to $e^{xp} - e^{-xp}$ (unless $p = 1$).

NOTE 4   If q is an odd number and p is an integer, $a^{p/q}$ can be defined even when $a < 0$. For example, $(-8)^{1/3} = \sqrt[3]{-8} = -2$, because $(-2)^3 = -8$. However, in defining $a^{p/q}$ when $a < 0$, q must be odd. If not, we could get contradictions such as "$-2 = (-8)^{1/3} = (-8)^{2/6} = \sqrt[6]{(-8)^2} = \sqrt[6]{64} = 2$".

When computing $a^{p/q}$ it is often easier to first find $\sqrt[q]{a}$ and then raise the result to the pth power. For example, $(-64)^{5/3} = (\sqrt[3]{-64})^5 = (-4)^5 = -1024$.

PROBLEMS FOR SECTION 1.5

1. Compute:

   (a) $\sqrt{9}$

   (b) $\sqrt{1600}$

   (c) $(100)^{1/2}$

   (d) $\sqrt{9+16}$

   (e) $(36)^{-1/2}$

   (f) $(0.49)^{1/2}$

   (g) $\sqrt{0.01}$

   (h) $\sqrt{\dfrac{1}{25}}$

2. Decide whether each "?" should be replaced by $=$ or $\neq$. Justify your answer. (Assume that a and b are positive.)

   (a) $\sqrt{25 \cdot 16}$? $\sqrt{25} \cdot \sqrt{16}$

   (b) $\sqrt{25 + 16}$? $\sqrt{25} + \sqrt{16}$

   (c) $(a+b)^{1/2}$? $a^{1/2} + b^{1/2}$

   (d) $(a+b)^{-1/2}$? $(\sqrt{a+b})^{-1}$

3. Solve for x:

   (a) $\sqrt{x} = 9$

   (b) $\sqrt{x} \cdot \sqrt{4} = 4$

   (c) $\sqrt{x+2} = 25$

   (d) $\sqrt{3} \cdot \sqrt{5} = \sqrt{x}$

   (e) $2^{2-x} = 8$

   (f) $2^x - 2^{x-1} = 4$

4. Rationalize the denominator and simplify:

(a) $\dfrac{6}{\sqrt{7}}$

(b) $\dfrac{\sqrt{32}}{\sqrt{2}}$

(c) $\dfrac{\sqrt{3}}{4\sqrt{2}}$

(d) $\dfrac{\sqrt{54}-\sqrt{24}}{\sqrt{6}}$

(e) $\dfrac{2}{\sqrt{3}\sqrt{8}}$

(f) $\dfrac{4}{\sqrt{2y}}$

(g) $\dfrac{x}{\sqrt{2x}}$

(h) $\dfrac{x(\sqrt{x}+1)}{\sqrt{x}}$

(SM) **5.** Simplify the following expressions by making the denominators rational:

(a) $\dfrac{1}{\sqrt{7}+\sqrt{5}}$

(b) $\dfrac{\sqrt{5}-\sqrt{3}}{\sqrt{5}+\sqrt{3}}$

(c) $\dfrac{x}{\sqrt{3}-2}$

(d) $\dfrac{x\sqrt{y}-y\sqrt{x}}{x\sqrt{y}+y\sqrt{x}}$

(e) $\dfrac{h}{\sqrt{x+h}-\sqrt{x}}$

(f) $\dfrac{1-\sqrt{x+1}}{1+\sqrt{x+1}}$

6. Compute without using a calculator:

(a) $\sqrt[3]{125}$

(b) $(243)^{1/5}$

(c) $(-8)^{1/3}$

(d) $\sqrt[3]{0.008}$

7. Using a calculator, find approximations to:

(a) $\sqrt[3]{55}$

(b) $(160)^{1/4}$

(c) $(2.71828)^{1/5}$

(d) $(1+0.0001)^{10000}$

8. The population of a nation increased from 40 million to 60 million in 12 years. What is the yearly percentage rate of growth p?

9. Compute the following without using a calculator:

(a) $81^{1/2}$

(b) $64^{-1/3}$

(c) $16^{-2.25}$

(d) $\left(\dfrac{1}{3^{-2}}\right)^{-2}$

10. Simplify: (a) $\left(27x^{3p}y^{6q}z^{12r}\right)^{1/3}$

(b) $\dfrac{(x+15)^{4/3}}{(x+15)^{5/6}}$

(c) $\dfrac{8\sqrt[3]{x^2}\,\sqrt[4]{y}\,\sqrt{1/z}}{-2\sqrt[3]{x}\sqrt{y^5}\sqrt{z}}$

11. Simplify the following expressions so that each contains only a single exponent.

(a) $\left(((a^{1/2})^{2/3})^{3/4}\right)^{4/5}$

(b) $a^{1/2}a^{2/3}a^{3/4}a^{4/5}$

(c) $\left(((3a)^{-1})^{-2}(2a^{-2})^{-1}\right)/a^{-3}$

(d) $\dfrac{\sqrt[3]{a}\,a^{1/12}\,\sqrt[4]{a^3}}{a^{5/12}\sqrt{a}}$

(SM) **12.** Which of the following equations are valid for all x and y?

(a) $(2^x)^2 = 2^{x^2}$

(b) $3^{x-3y} = \dfrac{3^x}{3^{3y}}$

(c) $3^{-1/x} = \dfrac{1}{3^{1/x}}$ $(x\neq 0)$

(d) $5^{1/x} = \dfrac{1}{5^x}$ $(x\neq 0)$

(e) $a^{x+y} = a^x + a^y$

(f) $2^{\sqrt{x}}\cdot 2^{\sqrt{y}} = 2^{\sqrt{xy}}$ $(x$ and y positive)

13. If a firm uses x units of input in process A, it produces $32x^{3/2}$ units of output. In the alternative process B, the same input produces $4x^3$ units of output. For what levels of input does process A produce more than process B?

1.6 Inequalities

The real numbers consist of the positive numbers, 0, and the negative numbers. If a is a positive number, we write $a > 0$ (or $0 < a$), and we say that a is greater than zero. A fundamental property of the positive numbers is:

$$a > 0 \text{ and } b > 0 \quad \text{imply} \quad a + b > 0 \text{ and } a \cdot b > 0 \qquad (1)$$

If the number c is negative, we write $c < 0$ (or $0 > c$).

In general, we say that *the number a is greater than the number b*, and we write $a > b$ (or $b < a$), if $a - b$ is positive:

$$a > b \quad \text{means that} \quad a - b > 0$$

Thus, $4.11 > 3.12$ because $4.11 - 3.12 = 0.99 > 0$, and $-3 > -5$ because $-3 - (-5) = 2 > 0$. On the number line (see Fig. 1) $a > b$ means that a lies to the right of b.

When $a > b$, we often say that a *is strictly greater than* b in order to emphasize that $a = b$ is ruled out. If $a > b$ or $a = b$, then we write $a \geq b$ (or $b \leq a$) and say that a is *greater than or equal to b*.

$$a \geq b \quad \text{means that} \quad a - b \geq 0$$

For example, $4 \geq 4$ and $4 \geq 2$. Note in particular that it *is* correct to write $4 \geq 2$, because $4 - 2$ *is* positive or 0.

We call $>$ and $<$ *strict* inequalities, whereas $\geq$ and $\leq$ are *weak* inequalities. The difference is often very important in economic analysis.

One can prove a number of important properties of $>$ and $\geq$. For example,

$$\text{If } a > b, \quad \text{then} \quad a + c > b + c \text{ for all } c \qquad (2)$$

The argument is simple: For all numbers a, b, and c, $(a+c)-(b+c) = a+c-b-c = a-b$. Hence, if $a - b > 0$, then $a + c - (b + c) > 0$, and the conclusion follows. On the number line, this implication is self-evident (here c is chosen to be negative):

Figure 1

At the risk of being trivial, here is an interpretation of this rule. If one day the temperature in New York is higher than that in London, and the temperature at both places then increases (or decreases) by the same number of degrees, then the ensuing New York temperature is still higher than that in London.

To deal with more complicated inequalities involves using the following properties:

$$\text{If } a > b \text{ and } b > c, \quad \text{then } a > c \qquad (3)$$

$$\text{If } a > b \text{ and } c > 0, \quad \text{then } ac > bc \qquad (4)$$

$$\text{If } a > b \text{ and } c < 0, \quad \text{then } ac < bc \qquad (5)$$

$$\text{If } a > b \text{ and } c > d, \quad \text{then } a + c > b + d \qquad (6)$$

All four properties remain valid when each $>$ is replaced by $\geq$, and each $<$ by $\leq$. The properties all follow easily from (1). For example, (5) is proved as follows. Suppose $a > b$ and $c < 0$. Then $a - b > 0$ and $-c > 0$, so according to (1), $(a - b)(-c) > 0$. Hence $-ac + bc > 0$, implying that $ac < bc$.

According to (4) and (5):

(a) If the two sides of an inequality are multiplied by a positive number, the direction of the inequality is preserved.

(b) If the two sides of an inequality are multiplied by a negative number, the direction of the inequality is reversed.

It is important that you understand these rules, and realize that they correspond to everyday experience. For instance, (4) can be interpreted this way: given two rectangles with the same base, the one with the larger height has the larger area.

EXAMPLE 1   Find what values of x satisfy $3x - 5 > x - 3$.

Solution: Adding 5 to both sides of the inequality yields $3x - 5 + 5 > x - 3 + 5$, or $3x > x + 2$. Adding $(-x)$ to both sides yields $3x - x > x - x + 2$, so $2x > 2$, and after dividing by the positive number 2, we get $x > 1$. The argument can obviously be reversed, so the solution is $x > 1$.

Sign Diagrams

EXAMPLE 2   Check whether the inequality $(x - 1)(3 - x) > 0$ is satisfied for $x = -3$, $x = 2$, and $x = 5$. Then find all the values x that satisfy the same inequality.

Solution: For $x = -3$, we have $(x - 1)(3 - x) = (-4) \cdot 6 = -24 < 0$; for $x = 2$, we have $(x - 1)(3 - x) = 1 \cdot 1 = 1 > 0$; and for $x = 5$, we have $(x - 1)(3 - x) = 4 \cdot (-2) = -8 < 0$. Hence, the inequality is satisfied for $x = 2$, but not for $x = -3$ or $x = 5$.

To find the entire solution set, we use a *sign diagram*. The sign variation for each factor in the product is determined. For example, the factor $x - 1$ is negative when $x < 1$, is 0 when $x = 1$, and is positive when $x > 1$. This sign variation is represented in the diagram.

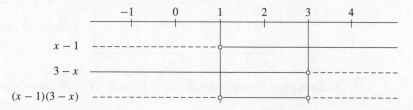

The upper dashed line to the left of the vertical line $x = 1$ indicates that $x - 1 < 0$ if $x < 1$; the small circle indicates that $x - 1 = 0$ when $x = 1$; and the solid line to the right of $x = 1$ indicates that $x - 1 > 0$ if $x > 1$. In a similar way, we represent the sign variation for $3 - x$.

The sign variation of the product is obtained as follows. If $x < 1$, then $x - 1$ is negative and $3 - x$ is positive, so the product is negative. If $1 < x < 3$, both factors are positive, so the product is positive. If $x > 3$, then $x - 1$ is positive and $3 - x$ is negative, so the product is negative. Conclusion: The solution set consists of those x that are greater than 1, but less than 3. So

$$(x - 1)(3 - x) > 0 \quad \text{if and only if} \quad 1 < x < 3$$

EXAMPLE 3 Find all values of p that satisfy $\dfrac{2p - 3}{p - 1} > 3 - p$.

Solution: It is tempting to begin by multiplying each side of the inequality by $p - 1$. However, then we must distinguish between the two cases, $p - 1 > 0$ and $p - 1 < 0$, because if we multiply through by $p - 1$ when $p - 1 < 0$, we have to reverse the inequality sign. There is an alternative method, which makes it unnecessary to distinguish between two different cases. We begin by adding $p - 3$ to both sides. This yields

$$\frac{2p - 3}{p - 1} + p - 3 > 0$$

Making $p - 1$ the common denominator gives

$$\frac{2p - 3 + (p - 3)(p - 1)}{p - 1} > 0 \quad \text{or} \quad \frac{p(p - 2)}{p - 1} > 0$$

because $2p - 3 + (p - 3)(p - 1) = 2p - 3 + p^2 - 4p + 3 = p^2 - 2p = p(p - 2)$. To find the solution set of this inequality, we again use a sign diagram. On the basis of the sign variations for p, $p - 2$, and $p - 1$, the sign variation for $p(p - 2)/(p - 1)$ is determined. For example, if $0 < p < 1$, then p is positive and $(p - 2)$ is negative, so $p(p - 2)$ is negative. But $p - 1$ is also negative on this interval, so $p(p - 2)/(p - 1)$ is positive. Arguing this way for all the relevant intervals leads to the following sign diagram. (The original inequality has no meaning when $p = 1$. This is symbolized by a diagonal cross in the sign diagram.)

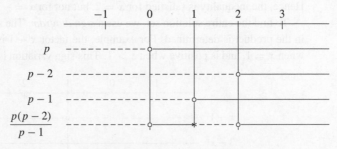

So the original inequality is satisfied if and only if $0 < p < 1$ or $p > 2$.

WARNING 1 The most common error committed in solving inequalities is precisely that indicated in Example 3: If we multiply by $p - 1$, the inequality is preserved *only* if $p - 1$ is positive—that is, if $p > 1$.

WARNING 2   It is vital that you really understand the method of sign diagrams. A common error is illustrated by the following example. Find the solution set for

$$\frac{(x-2)+3(x+1)}{x+3} \leq 0$$

"Solution": We construct the sign diagram:

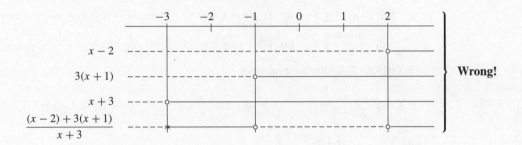

According to this diagram, the inequality should be satisfied for $x < -3$ and for $-1 \leq x \leq 2$. However, for $x = -4 \ (< -3)$, the fraction reduces to 15, which is positive. What went wrong? Suppose $x < -3$. Then $x - 2 < 0$ and $3(x+1) < 0$ and, therefore, the numerator $(x-2)+3(x+1)$ is negative. Because the denominator $x+3$ is also negative for $x < -3$, the fraction is positive. The sign variation for the fraction in the diagram is, therefore, completely wrong. The product of two negative numbers is positive, but their sum is negative, and not positive as the wrong sign diagram suggests. We obtain a correct solution to the given problem by first collecting terms in the numerator so that the inequality becomes $(4x+1)/(x+3) \leq 0$. A sign diagram for this inequality reveals the correct answer, which is $-3 < x \leq -1/4$.

Double Inequalities

Two inequalities that are valid simultaneously are often written as a *double inequality*. If, for example, $a \leq z$ and moreover $z < b$, it is natural to write $a \leq z < b$. (On the other hand, if $a \leq z$ and $z > b$, but we do not know which is the larger of a and b, then we cannot write $a \leq b < z$ or $b \leq a \leq z$, and we do *not* write $a \leq z > b$.)

EXAMPLE 4   One day, the lowest temperature in Buenos Aires was 50°F, and the highest was 77°F. What is the corresponding temperature variation in degrees Celsius? (If F denotes degrees Fahrenheit and C denotes degrees Celsius, then $F = \frac{9}{5}C + 32$.)

Solution: We have $50 \leq \frac{9}{5}C + 32 \leq 77$. Subtracting 32 from each term yields $50 - 32 \leq \frac{9}{5}C \leq 77 - 32$, or $18 \leq \frac{9}{5}C \leq 45$. Dividing these inequalities by 9/5 (or multiplying by 5/9) yields $10 \leq C \leq 25$. The temperature thus varied between 10°C and 25°C.

PROBLEMS FOR SECTION 1.6

1. Decide which of the following inequalities are true:

   (a) $-6.15 > -7.16$ (b) $6 \geq 6$ (c) $(-5)^2 \leq 0$ (d) $-\frac{1}{2}\pi < -\frac{1}{3}\pi$

   (e) $\dfrac{4}{5} > \dfrac{6}{7}$ (f) $2^3 < 3^2$ (g) $2^{-3} < 3^{-2}$ (h) $\dfrac{1}{2} - \dfrac{2}{3} < \dfrac{1}{4} - \dfrac{1}{3}$

2. Find what values of x satisfy:

   (a) $-x - 3 \leq 5$ (b) $3x + 5 < x - 13$ (c) $3x - (x - 1) \geq x - (1 - x)$

   (d) $\dfrac{2x - 4}{3} \leq 7$ (e) $\frac{1}{3}(1 - x) \geq 2(x - 3)$ (f) $\dfrac{t}{24} - (t + 1) + \dfrac{3t}{8} < \dfrac{5}{12}(t + 1)$

In Problems 3–6, solve the inequalities.

3. (a) $\dfrac{x + 2}{x - 1} < 0$ (b) $\dfrac{2x + 1}{x - 3} > 1$ (c) $5a^2 \leq 125$

SM 4. (a) $2 < \dfrac{3x + 1}{2x + 4}$ (b) $\dfrac{120}{n} + 1.1 \leq 1.85$ (c) $g^2 - 2g \leq 0$

   (d) $\dfrac{1}{p - 2} + \dfrac{3}{p^2 - 4p + 4} \geq 0$ (e) $\dfrac{-n - 2}{n + 4} > 2$ (f) $x^4 < x^2$

SM 5. (a) $(x - 1)(x + 4) > 0$ (b) $(x - 1)^2(x + 4) > 0$ (c) $(x - 1)^3(x - 2) \leq 0$

   (d) $(5x - 1)^{10}(x - 1) < 0$ (e) $(5x - 1)^{11}(x - 1) < 0$ (f) $\dfrac{3x - 1}{x} > x + 3$

   (g) $\dfrac{x - 3}{x + 3} < 2x - 1$ (h) $x^2 - 4x + 4 > 0$ (i) $x^3 + 2x^2 + x \leq 0$

6. (a) $1 \leq \frac{1}{3}(2x - 1) + \frac{8}{3}(1 - x) < 16$ (b) $-5 < \dfrac{1}{x} < 0$ (c) $\dfrac{(1/x) - 1}{(1/x) + 1} \geq 1$

7. Decide whether the following inequalities are valid for all x and y:

   (a) $x + 1 > x$ (b) $x^2 > x$ (c) $x + x > x$ (d) $x^2 + y^2 \geq 2xy$

8. (a) The temperature for storing potatoes should be between 4°C and 6°C. What are the corresponding temperatures in degrees Fahrenheit? (See Example 4.)

   (b) The freshness of a bottle of milk is guaranteed for 7 days if it is kept at a temperature between 36°F and 40°F. Find the corresponding temperature variation in degrees Celsius.

HARDER PROBLEM

9. If a and b are two positive numbers, the numbers m_A, m_G, and m_H defined by

$$m_A = \frac{1}{2}(a + b), \qquad m_G = \sqrt{ab}, \qquad \text{and} \qquad \frac{1}{m_H} = \frac{1}{2}\left(\frac{1}{a} + \frac{1}{b}\right)$$

are called the **arithmetic**, **geometric**, and **harmonic means** of a and b. Prove that

$$m_A \geq m_G \geq m_H$$

with strict inequalities unless $a = b$. (*Hint:* You should first test these inequalities by choosing some specific numbers, using a calculator if you wish. To show that $m_A \geq m_G$, start with the obvious inequality $(\sqrt{a} - \sqrt{b})^2 \geq 0$, and then expand. To show that $m_G \geq m_H$, start by showing that $\sqrt{xy} \leq \frac{1}{2}(x + y)$. Then let $x = 1/a$, $y = 1/b$.)

1.7   Intervals and Absolute Values

Let a and b be any two numbers on the real line. Then we call the set of all numbers that lie between a and b an **interval**. In many situations, it is important to distinguish between the intervals that include their endpoints and the intervals that do not. When $a < b$, there are four different intervals that all have a and b as endpoints, as shown in Table 1.

Table 1

Notation	Name	The interval consists of all x satisfying:
(a, b)	The **open** interval from a to b.	$a < x < b$
$[a, b]$	The **closed** interval from a to b.	$a \leq x \leq b$
$(a, b]$	A **half-open** interval from a to b.	$a < x \leq b$
$[a, b)$	A **half-open** interval from a to b.	$a \leq x < b$

Note that an open interval includes neither of its endpoints, but a closed interval includes both of its endpoints. A half-open interval contains one of its endpoints, but not both. All four intervals, however, have the same length, $b - a$.

We usually illustrate intervals on the number line as in Fig. 1, with included endpoints represented by dots, and excluded endpoints at the tips of arrows.

Figure 1 $A = [-4, -2]$, $B = [0, 1)$, and $C = (2, 5)$

The intervals mentioned so far are all *bounded intervals*. We also use the word "interval" to signify certain unbounded sets of numbers. For example, we have

$$[a, \infty) = \text{all numbers } x \text{ with } x \geq a$$

$$(-\infty, b) = \text{all numbers } x \text{ with } x < b$$

with "∞" as the common symbol for infinity. The symbol ∞ is not a number at all, and therefore the usual rules of arithmetic do not apply to it. In the notation $[a, \infty)$, the symbol ∞ is only intended to indicate that we are considering the collection of *all* numbers larger than or equal to a, without any upper bound on the size of the number. Similarly, $(-\infty, b)$ has no lower bound. From the preceding, it should be apparent what we mean by (a, ∞) and $(-\infty, b]$. The collection of all real numbers is also denoted by the symbol $(-\infty, \infty)$.

Absolute Value

Let a be a real number and imagine its position on the real line. The distance between a and 0 is called the *absolute value* of a. If a is positive or 0, then the absolute value is the number a itself; if a is negative, then because distance must be positive, the absolute value is equal to the positive number $-a$.

The **absolute value** of a is denoted by $|a|$, and

$$|a| = \begin{cases} a & \text{if } a \geq 0 \\ -a & \text{if } a < 0 \end{cases} \tag{1}$$

For example, $|13| = 13, |-5| = -(-5) = 5, |-1/2| = 1/2$, and $|0| = 0$. Note in particular that $|-a| = |a|$.

NOTE 1   It is a common fallacy to assume that a must denote a positive number, even if this is not explicitly stated. Similarly, on seeing $-a$, many students are led to believe that this expression is always negative. Observe, however, that the number $-a$ is positive when a itself is negative. For example, if $a = -5$, then $-a = -(-5) = 5$. Nevertheless, it is often a useful convention in economics to define variables so that, as far as possible, their values are positive rather than negative.

EXAMPLE 1

(a) Compute $|x - 2|$ for $x = -3, x = 0$, and $x = 4$.

(b) Rewrite $|x - 2|$ using the definition of absolute value.

Solution:

(a) For $x = -3, |x - 2| = |-3 - 2| = |-5| = 5$. For $x = 0, |x - 2| = |0 - 2| = |-2| = 2$. For $x = 4, |x - 2| = |4 - 2| = |2| = 2$.

(b) According to the definition (1), $|x - 2| = x - 2$ if $x - 2 \geq 0$, that is, $x \geq 2$. However, $|x - 2| = -(x - 2) = 2 - x$ if $x - 2 < 0$, that is, $x < 2$. Hence,

$$|x - 2| = \begin{cases} x - 2, & \text{if } x \geq 2 \\ 2 - x, & \text{if } x < 2 \end{cases}$$

Let x_1 and x_2 be two arbitrary numbers. The *distance* between x_1 and x_2 on the number line is $x_1 - x_2$ if $x_1 \geq x_2$, and $-(x_1 - x_2)$ if $x_1 < x_2$. Therefore, we have

$$|x_1 - x_2| = |x_2 - x_1| = \textbf{distance} \text{ between } x_1 \text{ and } x_2 \text{ on the number line} \tag{2}$$

In Fig. 2 we have indicated geometrically that the distance between 7 and 2 is 5, whereas the distance between -3 and -5 is equal to 2, because $|-3-(-5)| = |-3+5| = |2| = 2$.

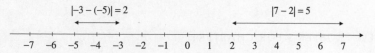

Figure 2   The distances between 7 and 2 and between -3 and -5.

Suppose $|x| = 5$. What values can x have? There are only two possibilities: either $x = 5$ or $x = -5$, because no other numbers have absolute values equal to 5. Generally, if a is greater than or equal to 0, then $|x| = a$ means that $x = a$ or $x = -a$. Because $|x| \geq 0$ for all x, the equation $|x| = a$ has no solution when $a < 0$.

If a is a positive number and $|x| < a$, then the distance from x to 0 is less than a. Furthermore, when a is nonnegative, and $|x| \leq a$, the distance from x to 0 is less than or equal to a. In symbols:

$$|x| < a \text{ means that } -a < x < a \qquad (3)$$

$$|x| \leq a \text{ means that } -a \leq x \leq a \qquad (4)$$

EXAMPLE 2   Find all the x such that

$$|3x - 2| \leq 5$$

Check first to see if this inequality holds for $x = -3$, $x = 0$, $x = 7/3$, and $x = 10$.

Solution: For $x = -3$, $|3x - 2| = |-9 - 2| = 11$; for $x = 0$, $|3x - 2| = |-2| = 2$; for $x = 7/3$, $|3x - 2| = |7 - 2| = 5$; and for $x = 10$, $|3x - 2| = |30 - 2| = 28$. Hence, the given inequality is satisfied for $x = 0$ and $x = 7/3$, but not for $x = -3$ and $x = 10$.

From (4) the inequality $|3x - 2| \leq 5$ means that $-5 \leq 3x - 2 \leq 5$. Adding 2 to all three expressions gives

$$-5 + 2 \leq 3x - 2 + 2 \leq 5 + 2$$

or $-3 \leq 3x \leq 7$. Dividing by 3 gives $-1 \leq x \leq 7/3$.

PROBLEMS FOR SECTION 1.7

1. Calculate $|2x - 3|$ for $x = 0$, $1/2$, and $7/2$.

2. (a) Calculate $|5 - 3x|$ for $x = -1$, 2, and 4.

   (b) Solve the equation $|5 - 3x| = 0$.

   (c) Rewrite $|5 - 3x|$ by using the definition of absolute value.

3. Determine x such that

   (a) $|3 - 2x| = 5$ (b) $|x| \leq 2$ (c) $|x - 2| \leq 1$

   (d) $|3 - 8x| \leq 5$ (e) $|x| > \sqrt{2}$ (f) $|x^2 - 2| \leq 1$

4. A 5-metre iron bar is to be produced. The bar may not deviate by more than 1 mm from its stated length. Write a specification for the bar's length x in metres: (a) by using a double inequality; (b) with the aid of an absolute-value sign.

REVIEW PROBLEMS FOR CHAPTER 1

1. (a) What is three times the difference between 50 and x?

   (b) What is the quotient between x and the sum of y and 100?

   (c) If the price of an item is a including 20% VAT (value added tax), what is the price before VAT?

   (d) A person buys x_1, x_2, and x_3 units of three goods whose prices per unit are respectively p_1, p_2, and p_3. What is the total expenditure?

   (e) A rental car costs F dollars per day in fixed charges and b dollars per kilometre. How much must a customer pay to drive x kilometres in 1 day?

   (f) A company has fixed costs of F dollars per year and variable costs of c dollars per unit produced. Find an expression for the total cost per unit (total average cost) incurred by the company if it produces x units in one year.

   (g) A person has an annual salary of $\$L$ and then receives a raise of $p\%$ followed by a further increase of $q\%$. What is the person's new yearly salary?

2. Express as single real numbers in decimal notation:

   (a) 5^3
   (b) 10^{-3}
   (c) $\dfrac{1}{3^{-3}}$
   (d) $\dfrac{-1}{10^{-3}}$

   (e) $3^{-2}3^3$
   (f) $(3^{-2})^{-3}$
   (g) $-\left(\dfrac{5}{3}\right)^0$
   (h) $\left(-\dfrac{1}{2}\right)^{-3}$

3. Which of the following expressions are defined, and what are their values?

   (a) $(0+2)^0$
   (b) 0^{-2}
   (c) $\dfrac{(10)^0}{(0+1)^0}$
   (d) $\dfrac{(0+1)^0}{(0+2)^0}$

4. Simplify:

   (a) $(2^3 2^{-5})^3$
   (b) $\left(\dfrac{2}{3}\right)^{-1} - \left(\dfrac{4}{3}\right)^{-1}$
   (c) $(3^{-2} - 5^{-1})^{-1}$
   (d) $(1.12)^{-3}(1.12)^3$

(SM) 5. Simplify:

   (a) $(2x)^4$
   (b) $(2^{-1} - 4^{-1})^{-1}$
   (c) $\dfrac{24x^3 y^2 z^3}{4x^2 y z^2}$

   (d) $\left[-(-ab^3)^{-3}(a^6 b^6)^2\right]^3$
   (e) $\dfrac{a^5 \cdot a^3 \cdot a^{-2}}{a^{-3} \cdot a^6}$
   (f) $\left[\left(\dfrac{x}{2}\right)^3 \cdot \dfrac{8}{x^{-2}}\right]^{-3}$

6. Compute: (a) 12% of 300   (b) 5% of 2000   (c) 6.5% of 1500

7. Give economic interpretations to each of the following expressions and then use a calculator to find the approximate values:

   (a) $100 \cdot (1.01)^8$ (b) $50\,000 \cdot (1.15)^{10}$ (c) $6000 \cdot (1.03)^{-8}$

8. (a) \$100 000 is deposited into an account earning 8% interest per year. What is the amount after 10 years?

   (b) If the interest rate is 8% each year, how much money should you have deposited in a bank 6 years ago to have \$25 000 today?

(SM) 9. Expand and simplify:

   (a) $a(a-1)$ (b) $(x-3)(x+7)$ (c) $-\sqrt{3}\left(\sqrt{3}-\sqrt{6}\right)$ (d) $\left(1-\sqrt{2}\right)^2$

   (e) $(x-1)^3$ (f) $(1-b^2)(1+b^2)$ (g) $(1+x+x^2+x^3)(1-x)$ (h) $(1+x)^4$

10. Complete the following:

    (a) $x^{-1}y^{-1}=3$ implies $x^3y^3=\cdots$ (b) $x^7=2$ implies $(x^{-3})^6(x^2)^2=\cdots$

    (c) $\left(\dfrac{xy}{z}\right)^{-2}=3$ implies $\left(\dfrac{z}{xy}\right)^6=\cdots$ (d) $a^{-1}b^{-1}c^{-1}=1/4$ implies $(abc)^4=\cdots$

11. Factor the expressions

    (a) $25x-5$ (b) $3x^2-x^3y$ (c) $50-x^2$ (d) $a^3-4a^2b+4ab^2$

(SM) 12. Factor the expressions

    (a) $5(x+2y)+a(x+2y)$ (b) $(a+b)c-d(a+b)$ (c) $ax+ay+2x+2y$

    (d) $2x^2-5yz+10xz-xy$ (e) p^2-q^2+p-q (f) $u^3+v^3-u^2v-v^2u$

13. Compute the following without using a calculator:

    (a) $16^{1/4}$ (b) $243^{-1/5}$ (c) $5^{1/7} \cdot 5^{6/7}$ (d) $(4^8)^{-3/16}$

    (e) $64^{1/3}+\sqrt[3]{125}$ (f) $(-8/27)^{2/3}$ (g) $(-1/8)^{-2/3}+(1/27)^{-2/3}$ (h) $\dfrac{1000^{-2/3}}{\sqrt[3]{5^{-3}}}$

14. Solve the following equations for x:

    (a) $2^{2x}=8$ (b) $3^{3x+1}=1/81$ (c) $10^{x^2-2x+2}=100$

15. Find the unknown x in each of the following equations:

    (a) $25^5 \cdot 25^x=25^3$ (b) $3^x-3^{x-2}=24$ (c) $3^x \cdot 3^{x-1}=81$

    (d) $3^5+3^5+3^5=3^x$ (e) $4^{-6}+4^{-6}+4^{-6}+4^{-6}=4^x$ (f) $\dfrac{2^{26}-2^{23}}{2^{26}+2^{23}}=\dfrac{x}{9}$

(SM) 16. Simplify: (a) $\dfrac{s}{2s-1}-\dfrac{s}{2s+1}$ (b) $\dfrac{x}{3-x}-\dfrac{1-x}{x+3}-\dfrac{24}{x^2-9}$ (c) $\dfrac{\dfrac{1}{x^2y}-\dfrac{1}{xy^2}}{\dfrac{1}{x^2}-\dfrac{1}{y^2}}$

(SM) **17.** Reduce the following fractions:

(a) $\dfrac{25a^3b^2}{125ab}$ (b) $\dfrac{x^2 - y^2}{x + y}$ (c) $\dfrac{4a^2 - 12ab + 9b^2}{4a^2 - 9b^2}$ (d) $\dfrac{4x - x^3}{4 - 4x + x^2}$

18. Solve the following inequalities:

(a) $2(x - 4) < 5$ (b) $\dfrac{1}{3}(y - 3) + 4 \geq 2$ (c) $8 - 0.2x \leq \dfrac{4 - 0.1x}{0.5}$

(d) $\dfrac{x - 1}{-3} > \dfrac{-3x + 8}{-5}$ (e) $|5 - 3x| \leq 8$ (f) $|x^2 - 4| \leq 2$

19. Using a mobile phone costs \$30 per month, and an additional \$0.16 per minute of use.

(a) What is the cost for one month if the phone is used for a total of x minutes?

(b) What are the smallest and largest numbers of *hours* you can use the phone in a month if the monthly telephone bill is to be between \$102 and \$126?

20. If a rope could be wrapped around the Earth's surface at the equator, it would be approximately circular and about 40 million metres long. Suppose we wanted to extend the rope to make it 1 metre above the equator at every point. How many more metres of rope would be needed? (The circumference of a circle with radius r is $2\pi r$.)

21. (a) Prove that $a + \dfrac{a \cdot p}{100} - \dfrac{\left(a + \dfrac{a \cdot p}{100}\right) \cdot p}{100} = a\left[1 - \left(\dfrac{p}{100}\right)^2\right]$.

(b) An item initially costs \$2000 and then its price is increased by 5%. Afterwards the price is lowered by 5%. What is the final price?

(c) An item initially costs a dollars and then its price is increased by p%. Afterwards the (new) price is lowered by p%. What is the final price of the item? (After considering this problem, look at the expression in part (a).)

(d) What is the result if one first *lowers* a price by p% and then *increases* it by p%?

22. (a) If $a > b$, is it necessarily true that $a^2 > b^2$?

(b) Show that if $a + b > 0$, then $a > b$ implies $a^2 > b^2$.

23. (a) If $a > b$, use numerical examples to check whether $1/a > 1/b$, or $1/a < 1/b$.

(b) Prove that if $a > b$ and $ab > 0$, then $1/b > 1/a$.

24. Prove that (i) $|ab| = |a| \cdot |b|$ and (ii) $|a + b| \leq |a| + |b|$, for all real numbers a and b. (The inequality in (ii) is called the **triangle inequality**.)

(SM) **25.** Consider an equilateral triangle, and let P be an arbitrary point within the triangle. Let h_1, h_2, and h_3 be the shortest distances from P to each of the three sides. Show that the sum $h_1 + h_2 + h_3$ is independent of where point P is placed in the triangle. (*Hint:* Compute the area of the triangle as the sum of three triangles.)

2

INTRODUCTORY TOPICS II:

EQUATIONS

...and mathematics is nourished by dreamers
—as it nourishes them.
—D'Arcy W. Thompson (1940)

S cience uses mathematical models, which often include one or more equations whose solution determines the magnitudes of some variables we would like to understand better. Economics is no exception. Accordingly, this chapter considers some types of equation that appear frequently in economic models.

Many students are used to dealing with algebraic expressions and equations involving only *one* variable (usually x). Often, however, they have difficulties at first in dealing with expressions involving several variables with a wide variety of names, and denoted by different letters. For economists, however, it is very important to be able to handle such algebraic expressions and equations with ease.

2.1 How to Solve Simple Equations

Consider the following simple examples,

$$\text{(a) } 3x + 10 = x + 4 \qquad \text{(b) } \frac{z}{z-5} + \frac{1}{3} = \frac{-5}{5-z} \qquad \text{(c) } Y = C + I$$

Equation (a) contains the *variable* x, whereas (b) has the variable z, and equation (c) has the three variables Y, C, and I.

To *solve* an equation means to find all values of the variables for which the equation is satisfied. For equation (a) this is easy. In order to isolate the unknown x on one side of the equation, we add $-x$ to both sides. This gives $2x + 10 = 4$. Adding -10 to both sides of this equation yields $2x = 4 - 10 = -6$. Dividing by 2 we get the solution $x = -3$.

If any value of a variable makes an expression in an equation undefined, that value is not allowed. Thus, the choice $z = 5$ is not allowed in (b) because it makes the expressions $z/(z-5)$ and $-5/(5-z)$ undefined, because they are $5/0$ and $-5/0$, respectively. As we shall show in Example 3 below, equation (b) has no solutions.

Equation (c) has many solutions, one of which is $Y = 1000$, $C = 700$, and $I = 300$.

For problem (a) the solution procedure was probably well known. The method we used is summed up in the following frame, noting that two equations which have exactly the same solutions are called *equivalent*.

To get equivalent equations, do the following on both sides of the equality sign:

(A) add (or subtract) the same number,

(B) multiply (or divide) by the same number $\neq 0$.

When faced with more complicated equations involving parentheses and fractions, we usually begin by multiplying out the parentheses, and then we multiply both sides of the equation by the lowest common denominator for all the fractions. Here is an example.

EXAMPLE 1   Solve the equation $6p - \frac{1}{2}(2p - 3) = 3(1 - p) - \frac{7}{6}(p + 2)$.

Solution: First multiply out all the parentheses: $6p - p + \frac{3}{2} = 3 - 3p - \frac{7}{6}p - \frac{7}{3}$. Second, multiply both sides by 6 to clear all the fractions: $36p - 6p + 9 = 18 - 18p - 7p - 14$. Third, gather terms: $55p = -5$. Thus $p = -5/55 = -1/11$.

The next two examples show that sometimes a surprising degree of care is needed to find the right solutions.

EXAMPLE 2   Solve the equation $\dfrac{x + 2}{x - 2} - \dfrac{8}{x^2 - 2x} = \dfrac{2}{x}$.

Solution: Since $x^2 - 2x = x(x - 2)$, the common denominator is $x(x - 2)$. We see that $x = 2$ and $x = 0$ both make the equation absurd, because then at least one of the denominators becomes 0. Provided $x \neq 0$ and $x \neq 2$, we can multiply both sides of the equation by the common denominator $x(x - 2)$ to obtain

$$\frac{x + 2}{x - 2} \cdot x(x - 2) - \frac{8}{x(x - 2)} \cdot x(x - 2) = \frac{2}{x} \cdot x(x - 2)$$

Cancelling common factors reduces this to $(x + 2)x - 8 = 2(x - 2)$ or $x^2 + 2x - 8 = 2x - 4$ and so $x^2 = 4$. Equations of the form $x^2 = a$, where $a > 0$, have two solutions $x = \sqrt{a}$ and $x = -\sqrt{a}$. In our case, $x^2 = 4$ has solutions $x = 2$ and $x = -2$. But $x = 2$ makes the original equation absurd, so *only $x = -2$ is a solution.*

EXAMPLE 3   Solve the equation $\dfrac{z}{z - 5} + \dfrac{1}{3} = \dfrac{-5}{5 - z}$.

Solution: We see that z cannot be 5. Remembering this restriction, multiply both sides by $3(z - 5)$. This gives

$$3z + z - 5 = 15$$

which has the unique solution $z = 5$. Because we had to assume $z \neq 5$, we must conclude that no solution exists for the original equation.

Often, solving a problem in economic analysis requires formulating an appropriate algebraic equation.

EXAMPLE 4   A firm manufactures a commodity that costs $20 per unit to produce. In addition, the firm has fixed costs of $2000. Each unit is sold for $75. How many units must be sold if the firm is to meet a profit target of $14 500?

Solution: If the number of units produced and sold is denoted by Q, then the revenue of the firm is $75Q$ and the total cost of production is $20Q + 2000$. Because profit is the difference between total revenue and total cost, it can be written as $75Q - (20Q + 2000)$. Because the profit target is 14 500, the equation

$$75Q - (20Q + 2000) = 14\,500$$

must be satisfied. It is easy to find the solution $Q = 16\,500/55 = 300$ units.

PROBLEMS FOR SECTION 2.1

In Problems 1–3, solve each of the equations.

1. (a) $5x - 10 = 15$ (b) $2x - (5 + x) = 16 - (3x + 9)$

(c) $-5(3x - 2) = 16(1 - x)$ (d) $4x + 2(x - 4) - 3 = 2(3x - 5) - 1$

(e) $\frac{2}{3}x = -8$ (f) $(8x - 7)5 - 3(6x - 4) + 5x^2 = x(5x - 1)$

(g) $x^2 + 10x + 25 = 0$ (h) $(3x - 1)^2 + (4x + 1)^2 = (5x - 1)(5x + 1) + 1$

2. (a) $3x + 2 = 11$ (b) $-3x = 21$ (c) $3x = \frac{1}{4}x - 7$

(d) $\dfrac{x - 3}{4} + 2 = 3x$ (e) $\dfrac{1}{2x + 1} = \dfrac{1}{x + 2}$ (f) $\sqrt{2x + 14} = 16$

SM 3. (a) $\dfrac{x - 3}{x + 3} = \dfrac{x - 4}{x + 4}$ (b) $\dfrac{3}{x - 3} - \dfrac{2}{x + 3} = \dfrac{9}{x^2 - 9}$ (c) $\dfrac{6x}{5} - \dfrac{5}{x} = \dfrac{2x - 3}{3} + \dfrac{8x}{15}$

4. Solve the following problems by first formulating an equation in each case:

(a) The sum of twice a number and 5 is equal to the difference between the number and 3. Find the number.

(b) The sum of three successive natural numbers is 10 more than twice the smallest of them. Find the numbers.

(c) Jane receives double pay for every hour she works over and above 38 hours per week. Last week, she worked 48 hours and earned a total of $812. What is Jane's regular hourly wage?

(d) James has invested $15 000 at an annual interest rate of 10%. How much additional money should he invest at the interest rate of 12% if he wants the total interest earned by the end of the year to equal $2100?

(e) When Mr. Barnes passed away, 2/3 of his estate was left to his wife, 1/4 was shared by his children, and the remainder, $100 000, was donated to a charity. How big was Mr. Barnes's estate?

(SM) **5.** Solve the following equations:

(a) $\dfrac{3y-1}{4} - \dfrac{1-y}{3} + 2 = 3y$ (b) $\dfrac{4}{x} + \dfrac{3}{x+2} = \dfrac{2x+2}{x^2+2x} + \dfrac{7}{2x+4}$

(c) $\dfrac{2 - \dfrac{z}{1-z}}{1+z} = \dfrac{6}{2z+1}$ (d) $\dfrac{1}{2}\left(\dfrac{p}{2} - \dfrac{3}{4}\right) - \dfrac{1}{4}\left(1 - \dfrac{p}{3}\right) - \dfrac{1}{3}(1-p) = -\dfrac{1}{3}$

6. A person has y euros to spend on three kinds of fruit, namely apples, bananas, and cherries. She decides to spend $\frac{1}{3}y$ euros on each kind. The prices in euros per kilo are 3 for apples, 2 for bananas, and 6 for cherries. What is the total weight of fruit she buys, and how much does she pay per kilo of fruit? (This is an example of "dollar cost" averaging. See Problem 11.5.3.)

2.2 Equations with Parameters

Economists often use mathematical models to describe the relationship between different economic phenomena. These models enable them to explain the interdependence of different economic variables. In macroeconomic models, which are designed to explain the broad outlines of a country's economy, examples of such variables include the gross domestic product (GDP), total consumption, and total investment.

Simple relationships between two variables can often be described by a linear equation. Examples of such linear equations in two variables x and y are

(a) $y = 10x$ (b) $y = 3x + 4$ (c) $y = -\dfrac{8}{3}x - \dfrac{7}{2}$

These equations have a common structure which makes it possible to write down a general equation covering all the special cases:

$$y = ax + b \tag{1}$$

where a and b are real numbers. For example, letting $a = 3$ and $b = 4$ yields equation (b).

The general equation (1) describes a whole class of linear equations where x and y are the variables. The letters a and b are called **parameters**, and they take on different values. Linear equations are studied in more detail in Section 4.4.

We often need to solve equations with "strange" letters denoting the variables. In addition, there might be several parameters involved. Here are two typical examples:

EXAMPLE 1   Consider the basic macroeconomic model

(i) $Y = C + \bar{I}$ (ii) $C = a + bY$ $\qquad\qquad$ (∗)

where Y is the gross domestic product (GDP), C is consumption, and $\bar{I}$ is total investment, which is treated as fixed.[1] Here a and b are positive parameters of the model, with $b < 1$.

---

[1] In economics, we often use a bar over a symbol to indicate that it is fixed. An alternative notation is to use the superscript 0, e.g. $Y = C + I^0$, or the subscript 0, e.g. $Y = C + I_0$.

Equation (i) says that GDP, by definition, is the sum of consumption and total investment. Equation (ii) says that consumption is a linear function of GDP.

Special cases of the model are obtained by choosing particular numerical values for the parameters, such as $\bar{I} = 100$, $a = 500$, $b = 0.8$, or $\bar{I} = 150$, $a = 600$, $b = 0.9$. Thus

$$
\text{(iii)} \quad
\begin{aligned}
Y &= C + 100 \\
C &= 500 + 0.8Y
\end{aligned}
\qquad
\text{(iv)} \quad
\begin{aligned}
Y &= C + 150 \\
C &= 600 + 0.9Y
\end{aligned}
$$

Solve model ($*$) for Y in terms of $\bar{I}$ and the parameters.

Solution: Substituting $C = a + bY$ into (i) gives

$$
Y = a + bY + \bar{I}
$$

Now rearrange this equation so that all the terms containing Y are on the left-hand side. This can be done by adding $-bY$ to both sides, thus cancelling the bY term on the right-hand side to give

$$
Y - bY = a + \bar{I}
$$

Notice that the left-hand side is equal to $(1 - b)Y$, so $(1 - b)Y = a + \bar{I}$. Dividing both sides by $1 - b$, so that the coefficient of Y becomes 1, then gives the answer, which is

$$
Y = \frac{a}{1 - b} + \frac{1}{1 - b}\bar{I} \tag{$**$}
$$

This solution is a formula expressing the **endogenous** variable Y in terms of the **exogenous** variable $\bar{I}$ and the parameters a and b. The formula can be applied to particular values of the constants, such as $\bar{I} = 100$, $a = 500$, $b = 0.8$, to give the right answer in every case. Note the power of this approach: The model is solved only once, and then numerical answers are found simply by substituting appropriate numerical values for the parameters of the model.

Economists usually call the two equations in ($*$) the **structural form** of the model, whereas ($**$) is one part of the **reduced form** that expresses endogenous variables as functions of exogenous variables. (The other part of the reduced form is the equation $C = (a + b\bar{I})/(1 - b)$ that determines the second endogenous variable C.)

EXAMPLE 2   Suppose the total demand for money in the economy is given by the formula

$$
M = \alpha Y + \beta(r - \gamma)^{-\delta}
$$

where M is the quantity of money in circulation, Y is national income, r is the interest rate, while α, β, γ, and δ are positive parameters.

(a) Solve the equation for r.

(b) For the USA during the period 1929–1952, the parameters have been estimated as $\alpha = 0.14$, $\beta = 76.03$, $\gamma = 2$, and $\delta = 0.84$. Show that r is then given by

$$
r = 2 + \left(\frac{76.03}{M - 0.14Y} \right)^{25/21}
$$

Solution:

(a) It follows easily from the given equation that $(r - \gamma)^{-\delta} = (M - \alpha Y)/\beta$. Then raising each side to the power $-1/\delta$ yields

$$r - \gamma = \left(\frac{M - \alpha Y}{\beta}\right)^{-1/\delta}, \quad \text{or} \quad r = \gamma + \left(\frac{\beta}{M - \alpha Y}\right)^{1/\delta} \qquad (*)$$

where we used the fact that $(a/b)^{-p} = (b/a)^p$.

(b) In this case $1/\delta = 1/0.84 = 100/84 = 25/21$, and the required formula follows immediately from $(*)$.

PROBLEMS FOR SECTION 2.2

1. Find the value of Y in the models (iii) and (iv) in Example 1. Verify that formula $(**)$ gives the same result.

(SM) 2. Solve the following equations for x:

(a) $\dfrac{1}{ax} + \dfrac{1}{bx} = 2$

(b) $\dfrac{ax + b}{cx + d} = A$

(c) $\dfrac{1}{2}px^{-1/2} - w = 0$

(d) $\sqrt{1 + x} + \dfrac{ax}{\sqrt{1 + x}} = 0$

(e) $a^2x^2 - b^2 = 0$

(f) $(3 + a^2)^x = 1$

3. Solve each equation for the variable suggested:

(a) $q = 0.15p + 0.14$ for p (supply of rice in India)

(b) $S = \alpha + \beta P$ for P (supply function)

(c) $A = \frac{1}{2}gh$ for g (the area of a triangle)

(d) $V = \frac{4}{3}\pi r^3$ for r (the volume of a ball)

(e) $AK^\alpha L^\beta = Y_0$ for L (production function)

(SM) 4. Solve the following equations for the indicated variables:

(a) $\alpha x - a = \beta x - b$ for x

(b) $\sqrt{pq} - 3q = 5$ for p

(c) $Y = 94 + 0.2(Y - (20 + 0.5Y))$ for Y

(d) $K^{1/2}\left(\dfrac{1}{2}\dfrac{r}{w}K\right)^{1/4} = Q$ for K

(e) $\dfrac{\frac{1}{2}K^{-1/2}L^{1/4}}{\frac{1}{4}L^{-3/4}K^{1/2}} = \dfrac{r}{w}$ for L

(f) $\dfrac{1}{2}pK^{-1/4}\left(\dfrac{1}{2}\dfrac{r}{w}\right)^{1/4} = r$ for K

(SM) 5. Solve for the indicated variable:

(a) $\dfrac{1}{s} + \dfrac{1}{T} = \dfrac{1}{t}$ for s

(b) $\sqrt{KLM} - \alpha L = B$ for M

(c) $\dfrac{x - 2y + xz}{x - z} = 4y$ for z

(d) $V = C\left(1 - \dfrac{T}{N}\right)$ for T

2.3 Quadratic Equations

This section reviews the method for solving quadratic (also called second-degree) equations. The general quadratic equation has the form

$$ax^2 + bx + c = 0 \qquad (a \neq 0) \tag{1}$$

where a, b, and c are given constants, and x is the unknown. If we divide each term by a, we get the equivalent equation $x^2 + (b/a)x + c/a = 0$. If $p = b/a$ and $q = c/a$, the equation is

$$x^2 + px + q = 0 \tag{2}$$

Two special cases are easy to handle. If $q = 0$ (there is no constant term), the equation reduces to $x^2 + px = 0$. This is equivalent to $x(x + p) = 0$. Since the product of two numbers can be 0 only if at least one of the numbers is 0, we conclude that $x = 0$ or $x = -p$. Using the symbol $\iff$ to denote "if and only if", we have

$$x^2 + px = 0 \iff x = 0 \quad \text{or} \quad x = -p$$

This means that the equation $x^2 + px = 0$ has the solutions $x = 0$ and $x = -p$, but no others. (See Section 3.4.)

If $p = 0$ (there is no term involving x), the equation (2) reduces to $x^2 + q = 0$. Then $x^2 = -q$, and there are two possibilities. If $q > 0$, then the equation has no solutions. In the alternative case when $q \leq 0$, one has

$$x^2 + q = 0 \iff x = \pm\sqrt{-q} \qquad (q \leq 0)$$

EXAMPLE 1   Solve the equations:

(a) $5x^2 - 8x = 0$ (b) $x^2 - 4 = 0$ (c) $x^2 + 3 = 0$

Solution:

(a) Dividing each term by 5 yields $x^2 - (8/5)x = x(x - 8/5) = 0$, so $x = 0$ or $x = 8/5$.

(b) The equation yields $x^2 = 4$, and hence, $x = \pm\sqrt{4} = \pm 2$, which means that x is either 2 or -2. (Alternatively: $x^2 - 4 = (x + 2)(x - 2) = 0$, so $x = 2$ or $x = -2$.)

(c) Because x^2 is ≥ 0, the left-hand side of the equation $x^2 + 3 = 0$ is always strictly positive and the equation has no solution.

Harder Cases

If equation (2) has both coefficients different from 0, solving it becomes harder. Consider, for example, $x^2 - (4/3)x - 1/4 = 0$. We could, of course, try to find the values of x that satisfy the equation by trial and error. However, it is not easy that way to find the only two solutions, which are $x = 3/2$ and $x = -1/6$.

NOTE 1 Here are two attempts to solve the equation that fail:

(a) A first attempt rearranges $x^2 - (4/3)x - 1/4 = 0$ to give $x^2 - (4/3)x = 1/4$, and $x(x - 4/3) = 1/4$. Thus, the product of x and $x - 4/3$ must be 1/4. But there are infinitely many pairs of numbers whose product is 1/4, so this is of very little help in finding x.

(b) A second attempt is to divide each term by x to get $x - 4/3 = 1/4x$. Because the equation involves terms in both x and $1/x$, as well as a constant term, we have made no progress whatsoever.

Evidently, we need a completely new idea in order to find the solution of equation (2). If you are only interested in formulas that always give you the solutions to (1) or (2) (provided they have solutions), proceed directly to the boxed formulas shown later. If you are interested in understanding why those formulas work, read on.

EXAMPLE 2   Solve the equation $x^2 + 8x - 9 = 0$.

Solution: It is natural to begin by moving 9 to the right-hand side:

$$x^2 + 8x = 9 \qquad (*)$$

However, because x occurs in two terms, it is not obvious how to proceed. A method called *completing the square*, one of the oldest tricks in mathematics, turns out to work. In the present case this method involves adding 16 to each side of the equation to get

$$x^2 + 8x + 16 = 9 + 16 \qquad (**)$$

The point of adding 16 is that the left-hand side is then a complete square: $x^2 + 8x + 16 = (x + 4)^2$. Thus, equation $(**)$ takes the form

$$(x + 4)^2 = 25 \qquad (***)$$

The equation $z^2 = 25$ has two solutions, $z = \pm\sqrt{25} = \pm 5$. Thus, $(***)$ implies that either $x + 4 = 5$ or $x + 4 = -5$. The required solutions are, therefore, $x = 1$ and $x = -9$.

Alternatively, equation $(***)$ can be written as $(x + 4)^2 - 5^2 = 0$. Using the difference-of-squares formula yields $(x + 4 - 5)(x + 4 + 5) = 0$, which reduces to $(x - 1)(x + 9) = 0$, so we have the following *factorization*

$$x^2 + 8x - 9 = (x - 1)(x + 9)$$

Note that $(x - 1)(x + 9)$ is 0 precisely when $x = 1$ or $x = -9$.

The General Case

We now apply the method of completing the squares to the quadratic equation (2). This equation obviously has the same solutions as

$$x^2 + px = -q$$

One half of the coefficient of x is $p/2$. Adding the square of this number to each side of the equation yields

$$x^2 + px + (p/2)^2 = (p/2)^2 - q$$

The left-hand side has now been made a complete square (of $x + p/2$), so

$$(x + p/2)^2 = p^2/4 - q \qquad (*)$$

Note that if $p^2/4 - q < 0$, then the right-hand side is negative. Because $(x + p/2)^2$ is nonnegative for all choices of x, we conclude that if $p^2/4 - q < 0$, then neither of the equations $(*)$ and (2) has any solution. On the other hand, if $p^2/4 - q > 0$, then $(*)$ yields two possibilities:

$$x + p/2 = \sqrt{p^2/4 - q} \qquad \text{and} \qquad x + p/2 = -\sqrt{p^2/4 - q}$$

Then the values of x are easily found. These formulas are correct even if $p^2/4 - q = 0$, though then they give just the one solution $x = -p/2$ twice over. In conclusion:

$$x^2 + px + q = 0 \qquad \text{if and only if} \qquad x = -\frac{p}{2} \pm \sqrt{\frac{p^2}{4} - q} \qquad \left(\frac{p^2}{4} \geq q \right) \qquad (3)$$

Faced with an equation of the type (1), we can always find its solutions by first dividing the equation by a and then using (3). Sometimes it is convenient to have the formula for the solution of (1) in terms of the coefficients a, b, and c. Dividing equation (1) by a, we get $x^2 + px + q = 0$ with $p = b/a$ and $q = c/a$. Substituting these values in (3) gives the solutions $x = -b/2a \pm \sqrt{b^2/4a^2 - c/a}$. To summarize:

QUADRATIC FORMULA

If $b^2 - 4ac \geq 0$ and $a \neq 0$, then

$$ax^2 + bx + c = 0 \qquad \text{if and only if} \qquad x = \frac{-b \pm \sqrt{b^2 - 4ac}}{2a} \qquad (4)$$

It is probably a good idea to spend a few minutes of your life memorizing this formula (or formula (3)) thoroughly. Once you have done so, you can immediately write down the solutions of any quadratic equation. Only if $b^2 - 4ac \geq 0$ are the solutions real numbers. If we use the formula when $b^2 - 4ac < 0$, the square root of a negative number appears and no real solution exists. The solutions are often called the **roots** of the equation.

EXAMPLE 3   Use the quadratic formula to find the solutions (or roots) of $2x^2 - 2x - 40 = 0$.

Solution: Write the equation as $2x^2 + (-2)x + (-40) = 0$. Because $a = 2$, $b = -2$, and $c = -40$, the quadratic formula (4) yields

$$x = \frac{-(-2) \pm \sqrt{(-2)^2 - 4 \cdot 2 \cdot (-40)}}{2 \cdot 2} = \frac{2 \pm \sqrt{4 + 320}}{4} = \frac{2 \pm 18}{4} = \frac{1}{2} \pm \frac{9}{2}$$

The solutions are, therefore, $x = \frac{1}{2} + \frac{9}{2} = 5$ and $x = \frac{1}{2} - \frac{9}{2} = -4$.

If we use formula (3) instead, we divide each term by 2 and get $x^2 - x - 20 = 0$, so

$$x = 1/2 \pm \sqrt{1/4 + 20} = 1/2 \pm \sqrt{81/4} = 1/2 \pm 9/2$$

which gives the same solutions as before.

Suppose $p^2/4 - q \geq 0$ and let x_1 and x_2 be the solutions of (2). By using the same difference-of-squares formula as we did to obtain the factorization in Example 2, one can rewrite equation (2) as $(x - x_1)(x - x_2) = 0$. Furthermore, it follows that

---

If x_1 and x_2 are the solutions of $ax^2 + bx + c = 0$ given by (4), then

$$ax^2 + bx + c = a(x - x_1)(x - x_2)$$

(5)

This is a very important result, because it shows how to factor a general quadratic function. If $b^2 - 4ac < 0$, there is no factorization of $ax^2 + bx + c$. If $b^2 - 4ac = 0$, then $x_1 = x_2$ and $ax^2 + bx + c = a(x - x_1)^2 = a(x - x_2)^2$.

EXAMPLE 4   Factor (if possible) the following quadratic polynomials:

(a) $\frac{1}{3}x^2 + \frac{2}{3}x - \frac{14}{3}$ (b) $-2x^2 + 40x - 600$

Solution:

(a) $\frac{1}{3}x^2 + \frac{2}{3}x - \frac{14}{3} = 0$ has the same solutions as $x^2 + 2x - 14 = 0$. By formula (3), its solutions are $x = -1 \pm \sqrt{1 + 14} = -1 \pm \sqrt{15}$, and these are the solutions of the given equation also. Then from (5),

$$\tfrac{1}{3}x^2 + \tfrac{2}{3}x - \tfrac{14}{3} = \tfrac{1}{3}\big(x - (-1 + \sqrt{15})\big)\big(x - (-1 - \sqrt{15})\big) = \tfrac{1}{3}(x + 1 - \sqrt{15})(x + 1 + \sqrt{15})$$

(b) For $-2x^2 + 40x - 600 = 0$, $a = -2$, $b = 40$, and $c = -600$, so $b^2 - 4ac = 1600 - 4800 = -3200$. Therefore, no factoring exists in this case.

NOTE 2   The quadratic formula is very useful, since it gives the solutions to any quadratic equation. But you should not be a "quadratic formula fanatic" and use it always. If $b = 0$ or $c = 0$, we explained at the beginning of this section how the equation can be solved very easily. During a recent exam, one extreme "quadratic formula fanatic", when faced with solving the equation $(x - 4)^2 = 0$, expanded the parentheses to obtain $x^2 - 8x + 16 = 0$, and then used the quadratic formula eventually to get the (correct) answer, $x = 4$. What would you have done?

Consider again equation (2) with solutions x_1 and x_2 given by (3). Expanding the right-hand side of the identity $x^2 + px + q = (x - x_1)(x - x_2)$ corresponding to (5) yields $x^2 + px + q = x^2 - (x_1 + x_2)x + x_1 x_2$. Equating like powers of x gives $x_1 + x_2 = -p$ and $x_1 x_2 = q$. (The same formulas are obtained by adding and multiplying the two solutions found in (3).) Thus:

If x_1 and x_2 are the roots of $x^2 + px + q = 0$, then

$$x_1 + x_2 = -p \quad \text{and} \quad x_1 x_2 = q$$

$\qquad(6)$

In words, the sum of the roots is minus the coefficient of the first-order term and the product is the constant term.

PROBLEMS FOR SECTION 2.3

1. Solve the following quadratic equations (if they have solutions):

  (a) $15x - x^2 = 0$ (b) $p^2 - 16 = 0$ (c) $(q - 3)(q + 4) = 0$

  (d) $2x^2 + 9 = 0$ (e) $x(x + 1) = 2x(x - 1)$ (f) $x^2 - 4x + 4 = 0$

2. Solve the following quadratic equations by using the method of completing the square, and factor (if possible) the left-hand side:

  (a) $x^2 - 5x + 6 = 0$ (b) $y^2 - y - 12 = 0$ (c) $2x^2 + 60x + 800 = 0$

  (d) $-\frac{1}{4}x^2 + \frac{1}{2}x + \frac{1}{2} = 0$ (e) $m(m - 5) - 3 = 0$ (f) $0.1p^2 + p - 2.4 = 0$

Solve the equations in 3–4 by using the quadratic formula:

3. (a) $r^2 + 11r - 26 = 0$ (b) $3p^2 + 45p = 48$ (c) $20\,000 = 300K - K^2$

  (d) $r^2 + (\sqrt{3} - \sqrt{2})r = \sqrt{6}$ (e) $0.3x^2 - 0.09x = 0.12$ (f) $\dfrac{1}{24} = p^2 - \dfrac{1}{12}p$

4. (a) $x^2 - 3x + 2 = 0$ (b) $5t^2 - t = 3$ (c) $6x = 4x^2 - 1$

  (d) $9x^2 + 42x + 44 = 0$ (e) $30\,000 = x(x + 200)$ (f) $3x^2 = 5x - 1$

(SM) 5. (a) Find the lengths of the sides of a rectangle whose perimeter is 40 cm and whose area is 75 cm^2.

  (b) Find two successive natural numbers whose sum of squares is 13.

  (c) In a right-angled triangle, the hypotenuse is 34 cm. One of the short sides is 14 cm longer than the other. Find the lengths of the two short sides.

  (d) A motorist drove 80 km. In order to save 16 minutes, he had to drive 10 km/h faster than usual. What was his usual driving speed?

6. Solve the following equations:

  (a) $x^3 - 4x = 0$ (b) $x^4 - 5x^2 + 4 = 0$ (c) $z^{-2} - 2z^{-1} - 15 = 0$

2.4 Linear Equations in Two Unknowns

This section reviews some methods for solving two linear equations with two unknowns.

EXAMPLE 1   Find the values of x and y that satisfy both of the equations

$$2x + 3y = 18$$
$$3x - 4y = -7$$

(∗)

We need to find the values of x and y that satisfy *both* equations.

METHOD 1   First, solve one of the equations for one of the variables in terms of the other; then substitute the result into the other equation. This leaves only one equation in one unknown, which is easily solved.

To apply this method to system (∗), we can solve the first equation for y in terms of x. In fact, $2x + 3y = 18$ implies that $3y = 18 - 2x$ and, hence, $y = 6 - \frac{2}{3}x$. Substituting this expression for y into the second equation in (∗) gives

$$3x - 4\left(6 - \tfrac{2}{3}x\right) = -7$$
$$3x - 24 + \tfrac{8}{3}x = -7$$
$$9x - 72 + 8x = -21$$
$$17x = 51$$

Hence, $x = 3$. Then we find y by using $y = 6 - \frac{2}{3}x$ once again to obtain $y = 6 - \frac{2}{3} \cdot 3 = 4$. The solution of (∗) is therefore $x = 3$ and $y = 4$.

Such a solution should always be checked by direct substitution. Indeed, substituting $x = 3$ and $y = 4$ in (∗) gives $2 \cdot 3 + 3 \cdot 4 = 18$ and $3 \cdot 3 - 4 \cdot 4 = -7$.

METHOD 2   This method is based on eliminating one of the variables by adding or subtracting a multiple of one equation from the other. For system (∗), suppose we want to eliminate y. Suppose we multiply the first equation in (∗) by 4 and the second by 3. Then the coefficients of y in both equations will be the same except for the sign. If we then add the transformed equations, the term in y disappears and we obtain

$$
\begin{aligned}
8x + 12y &= 72 \\
9x - 12y &= -21 \\
\hline
17x \phantom{{}+12y} &= 51
\end{aligned}
$$

Hence, $x = 3$. To find the value for y, substitute 3 for x in either of the original equations and solve for y. This gives $y = 4$, which agrees with the earlier result.

We end this section by using Method 2 to solve a general linear system with two equations and two unknowns:

$$ax + by = c$$
$$dx + ey = f$$

(1)

Here $a, b, c, d, e,$ and f are arbitrary given numbers, whereas x and y are the unknowns. If we let $a = 2$, $b = 3$, $c = 18$, $d = 3$, $e = -4$, and $f = -7$, then this reduces to system (∗). Using Method 2, we multiply the first equation by e and the second by $-b$ to obtain

$$
\begin{array}{r}
aex + bey = ce \\
-bdx - bey = -bf \\
\hline
(ae - bd)x \qquad\quad = ce - bf
\end{array}
$$

which gives the value for x. We can substitute back in (1) to find y, and the result is

$$x = \frac{ce - bf}{ae - bd}, \qquad\qquad y = \frac{af - cd}{ae - bd} \qquad (2)$$

We have found expressions for both x and y.

These formulas break down if the denominator $ae - bd$ in both fractions is equal to 0. This case requires special attention.

PROBLEMS FOR SECTION 2.4

Solve the systems of equations in 1–3:

1. (a) $\begin{aligned} x - y &= 5 \\ x + y &= 11 \end{aligned}$ (b) $\begin{aligned} 4x - 3y &= 1 \\ 2x + 9y &= 4 \end{aligned}$ (c) $\begin{aligned} 3x + 4y &= 2.1 \\ 5x - 6y &= 7.3 \end{aligned}$

2. (a) $\begin{aligned} 5x + 2y &= 3 \\ 2x + 3y &= -1 \end{aligned}$ (b) $\begin{aligned} x - 3y &= -25 \\ 4x + 5y &= 19 \end{aligned}$ (c) $\begin{aligned} 2x + 3y &= 3 \\ 6x + 6y &= -1 \end{aligned}$

3. (a) $\begin{aligned} 2K + L &= 11.35 \\ K + 4L &= 25.8 \end{aligned}$ (b) $\begin{aligned} 23p + 45q &= 181 \\ 10p + 15q &= 65 \end{aligned}$ (c) $\begin{aligned} 0.01r + 0.21s &= 0.042 \\ -0.25r + 0.55s &= -0.47 \end{aligned}$

(SM) **4.** (a) Find two numbers whose sum is 52 and whose difference is 26.

(b) Five tables and 20 chairs cost $1800, whereas 2 tables and 3 chairs cost $420. What is the price of each table and each chair?

(c) A firm produces a good in two qualities, A and B. For the coming year, the estimated output of A is 50% higher than that of B. The profit per unit sold is $300 for A and $200 for B. If the profit target is $13 000 over the next year, how much of each of the two qualities must be produced?

(d) At the beginning of the year a person had a total of $10 000 in two accounts. The interest rates were 5% and 7.2% per year, respectively. If the person has made no transfers during the year, and has earned a total of $676 interest, what was the initial balance in each of the two accounts?

2.5 Nonlinear Equations

This chapter has already considered some types of equation frequently occurring in economic models. In this section we consider some additional types that are often encountered later in the book, particularly in connection with optimization problems.

Recall that a product of two or more factors is 0 if and only if at least one of the factors is 0. This fact is used again and again. Consider the following examples.

EXAMPLE 1   Solve each of the following three separate equations:

(a) $x^3\sqrt{x+2} = 0$ (b) $x(y+3)(z^2+1)\sqrt{w-3} = 0$ (c) $x^2 - 3x^3 = 0$

Solution:

(a) If $x^3\sqrt{x+2} = 0$, then either $x^3 = 0$ or $\sqrt{x+2} = 0$. The equation $x^3 = 0$ has only the solution $x = 0$, while $\sqrt{x+2} = 0$ gives $x = -2$. The solutions of the equation are therefore $x = 0$ and $x = -2$.

(b) There are four factors in the product. One of the factors, $z^2 + 1$, is never 0. Hence, the solutions are: $x = 0$ or $y = -3$ or $w = 3$.

(c) Start by factoring: $x^2 - 3x^3 = x^2(1 - 3x)$. The product $x^2(1 - 3x)$ is 0 if and only if $x^2 = 0$ or $1 - 3x = 0$. Hence, the solutions are $x = 0$ and $x = 1/3$.

NOTE 1   When trying to solve an equation, an easy way to make a serious mistake is to cancel a factor which might be zero. It is important to check that the factor being cancelled really is not zero. For instance, suppose one cancels the common factor x^2 in the equation $x^2 = 3x^3$. The result is $1 = 3x$, implying that $x = 1/3$. The solution $x = 0$ has been lost.

In general,

$$ab = ac \quad \text{is equivalent to} \quad a = 0 \quad \text{or} \quad b = c \tag{1}$$

because the equation $ab = ac$ is equivalent to $ab - ac = 0$, or $a(b - c) = 0$. This product is 0 when $a = 0$ or $b = c$.

If $ab = ac$ and $a \neq 0$, we conclude from (1) that $b = c$.

EXAMPLE 2   What conclusions about the variables can we draw if

(a) $x(x + a) = x(2x + b)$ (b) $\lambda y = \lambda z^2$ (c) $xy^2(1 - y) - 2\lambda(y - 1) = 0$

Solution:

(a) $x = 0$ or $x + a = 2x + b$. The last equation gives $x = a - b$. The solutions are therefore $x = 0$ and $x = a - b$.

(b) $\lambda = 0$ or $y = z^2$. (It is easy to "forget" the possibility that $\lambda = 0$.)

(c) The equation is equivalent to

$$xy^2(1 - y) + 2\lambda(1 - y) = 0, \quad \text{that is} \quad (1 - y)(xy^2 + 2\lambda) = 0$$

We conclude from the last equation that $1 - y = 0$ or $xy^2 + 2\lambda = 0$, that is $y = 1$ or $\lambda = -\frac{1}{2}xy^2$.

Consider finally some equations involving fractions. Recall that the fraction a/b is not defined if $b = 0$. If $b \neq 0$, however, then $a/b = 0$ is equivalent to $a = 0$.

EXAMPLE 3   Solve the following equations:

(a) $\dfrac{1 - K^2}{\sqrt{1 + K^2}} = 0$ (b) $\dfrac{45 + 6r - 3r^2}{(r^4 + 2)^{3/2}} = 0$ (c) $\dfrac{x^2 - 5x}{\sqrt{x^2 - 25}} = 0$

Solution:

(a) The denominator is never 0, so the fraction is 0 when $1 - K^2 = 0$, that is when $K = \pm 1$.

(b) Again the denominator is never 0. The fraction is 0 when $45 + 6r - 3r^2 = 0$, that is $3r^2 - 6r - 45 = 0$. Solving this quadratic equation, we find that $r = -3$ or $r = 5$.

(c) The numerator is equal to $x(x - 5)$, which is 0 if $x = 0$ or $x = 5$. At $x = 0$ the denominator is $\sqrt{-25}$, which is not defined, and at $x = 5$ the denominator is 0. We conclude that the equation has no solutions.

PROBLEMS FOR SECTION 2.5

Solve the equations in Problems 1–2:

1. (a) $x(x + 3) = 0$ (b) $x^3(1 + x^2)(1 - 2x) = 0$ (c) $x(x - 3) = x - 3$

   (d) $\sqrt{2x + 5} = 0$ (e) $\dfrac{x^2 + 1}{x(x + 1)} = 0$ (f) $\dfrac{x(x + 1)}{x^2 + 1} = 0$

(SM) 2. (a) $\dfrac{5 + x^2}{(x - 1)(x + 2)} = 0$ (b) $1 + \dfrac{2x}{x^2 + 1} = 0$

   (c) $\dfrac{(x + 1)^{1/3} - \frac{1}{3}x(x + 1)^{-2/3}}{(x + 1)^{2/3}} = 0$ (d) $\dfrac{x}{x - 1} + 2x = 0$

(SM) 3. Examine what conclusions can be drawn about the variables if:

   (a) $z^2(z - a) = z^3(a + b)$, $a \neq 0$ (b) $(1 + \lambda)\mu x = (1 + \lambda)y\mu$

   (c) $\dfrac{\lambda}{1 + \mu} = \dfrac{-\lambda}{1 - \mu^2}$ (d) $ab - 2b - \lambda b(2 - a) = 0$

REVIEW PROBLEMS FOR CHAPTER 2

In Problems 1–2, solve each of the equations.

1. (a) $3x - 20 = 16$ (b) $-5x + 8 + 2x = -(4 - x)$ (c) $-6(x - 5) = 6(2 - 3x)$

   (d) $\dfrac{4 - 2x}{3} = -5 - x$ (e) $\dfrac{5}{2x - 1} = \dfrac{1}{2 - x}$ (f) $\sqrt{x - 3} = 6$

(SM) **2.** (a) $\dfrac{x-3}{x-4} = \dfrac{x+3}{x+4}$ (b) $\dfrac{3(x+3)}{x-3} - 2 = 9\dfrac{x}{x^2-9} + \dfrac{27}{(x+3)(x-3)}$

(c) $\dfrac{2x}{3} = \dfrac{2x-3}{3} + \dfrac{5}{x}$ (d) $\dfrac{x-5}{x+5} - 1 = \dfrac{1}{x} - \dfrac{11x+20}{x^2-5x}$

3. Solve the following equations for the variables specified:

(a) $x = \frac{2}{3}(y-3) + y$ for y (b) $ax - b = cx + d$ for x

(c) $AK\sqrt{L} = Y_0$ for L (d) $px + qy = m$ for y

(e) $\dfrac{\dfrac{1}{1+r} - a}{\dfrac{1}{1+r} + b} = c$ for r (f) $Px(Px + Q)^{-1/3} + (Px + Q)^{2/3} = 0$ for x

4. Consider the macro model

$$\text{(i)} \ Y = C + \bar{I} + G, \qquad \text{(ii)} \ C = b(Y - T), \qquad \text{(iii)} \ T = tY$$

where the parameters b and t lie in the interval $(0, 1)$, Y is the gross domestic product (GDP), C is consumption, $\bar{I}$ is total investment, T denotes taxes, and G is government expenditure.

(a) Express Y and C in terms of $\bar{I}$, G, and the parameters.

(b) What happens to Y and C as t increases?

(SM) **5.** Solve the following equations for the variables indicated:

(a) $3K^{-1/2}L^{1/3} = 1/5$ for K (b) $(1 + r/100)^t = 2$ for r

(c) $p - abx_0^{b-1} = 0$ for x_0 (d) $\left[(1-\lambda)a^{-\rho} + \lambda b^{-\rho}\right]^{-1/\rho} = c$ for b

6. Solve the following quadratic equations:

(a) $z^2 = 8z$ (b) $x^2 + 2x - 35 = 0$ (c) $p^2 + 5p - 14 = 0$

(d) $12p^2 - 7p + 1 = 0$ (e) $y^2 - 15 = 8y$ (f) $42 = x^2 + x$

7. Solve the following equations:

(a) $(x^2 - 4)\sqrt{5-x} = 0$ (b) $(x^4 + 1)(4 + x) = 0$ (c) $(1-\lambda)x = (1-\lambda)y$

8. Johnson invested $1500, part of it at 15% interest and the remainder at 20%. His total yearly income from the two investments was $275. How much did he invest at each rate?

9. If $5^{3x} = 25^{y+2}$ and $x - 2y = 8$, then what is $x - y$?

HARDER PROBLEM

10. Solve the following systems of equations:

(a) $\begin{array}{l} \dfrac{2}{x} + \dfrac{3}{y} = 4 \\[2mm] \dfrac{3}{x} - \dfrac{2}{y} = 19 \end{array}$ (b) $\begin{array}{l} 3\sqrt{x} + 2\sqrt{y} = 2 \\[2mm] 2\sqrt{x} - 3\sqrt{y} = \dfrac{1}{4} \end{array}$ (c) $\begin{array}{l} x^2 + y^2 = 13 \\[2mm] 4x^2 - 3y^2 = 24 \end{array}$

3
INTRODUCTORY TOPICS III:
MISCELLANEOUS

Everything should be made as simple as possible, but not simpler.
—Albert Einstein

This chapter starts with sums and summation notation. Most economic students will need these for their statistics and econometrics courses in particular.

Arguments in mathematics require tight logical reasoning; arguments in economic analysis are no exception to this rule. We therefore present some basic concepts from logic. A brief section on mathematical proofs might be useful for more ambitious students.

A short introduction to set theory comes next. The chapter winds up with a discussion of mathematical induction. Very occasionally, this is used directly in economic arguments. More often, it is needed to understand mathematical results which economists often use.

3.1 Summation Notation

Economists often make use of census data. Suppose a country is divided into six regions. Let N_i denote the population in region i. Then the total population is given by

$$N_1 + N_2 + N_3 + N_4 + N_5 + N_6$$

It is convenient to have an abbreviated notation for such lengthy sums. The capital Greek letter sigma Σ is conventionally used as a **summation symbol**, and the sum is written as

$$\sum_{i=1}^{6} N_i$$

This reads "the sum from $i = 1$ to $i = 6$ of N_i". If there are n regions, then

$$N_1 + N_2 + \cdots + N_n \qquad (*)$$

is one possible notation for the total population. Here the dots $\cdots$ indicate that the obvious previous pattern continues, but comes to an end just before the last term N_n.

In summation or sigma notation, we use the summation symbol Σ and write

$$\sum_{i=1}^{n} N_i$$

This tells us to form the sum of all the terms that result when we substitute successive integers for i, starting with $i = 1$ and ending with $i = n$. The symbol i is called the **index of summation**. It is a "dummy variable" that can be replaced by any other letter (which has not already been used for something else). Thus, both $\sum_{j=1}^{n} N_j$ and $\sum_{k=1}^{n} N_k$ represent the same sum as (∗).

The upper and lower limits of summation can both vary. For example,

$$\sum_{i=30}^{35} N_i = N_{30} + N_{31} + N_{32} + N_{33} + N_{34} + N_{35}$$

is the total population in the six regions numbered from 30 to 35.

More generally, suppose p and q are integers with $q \geq p$. Then

$$\sum_{i=p}^{q} a_i = a_p + a_{p+1} + \cdots + a_q$$

denotes the sum that results when we substitute successive integers for i, starting with $i = p$ and ending with $i = q$. If the upper and lower limits of summation are the same, then the "sum" reduces to one term. And if the upper limit is less than the lower limit, then there are no terms at all, so the usual convention is that the "sum" reduces to zero.

EXAMPLE 1   Compute: (a) $\displaystyle\sum_{i=1}^{5} i^2$ (b) $\displaystyle\sum_{k=3}^{6}(5k - 3)$ (c) $\displaystyle\sum_{j=0}^{2} \frac{(-1)^j}{(j + 1)(j + 3)}$.

Solution:

(a) $\displaystyle\sum_{i=1}^{5} i^2 = 1^2 + 2^2 + 3^2 + 4^2 + 5^2 = 1 + 4 + 9 + 16 + 25 = 55$

(b) $\displaystyle\sum_{k=3}^{6}(5k - 3) = (5 \cdot 3 - 3) + (5 \cdot 4 - 3) + (5 \cdot 5 - 3) + (5 \cdot 6 - 3) = 78$

(c) $\displaystyle\sum_{j=0}^{2} \frac{(-1)^j}{(j + 1)(j + 3)} = \frac{1}{1 \cdot 3} + \frac{-1}{2 \cdot 4} + \frac{1}{3 \cdot 5} = \frac{40 - 15 + 8}{120} = \frac{33}{120} = \frac{11}{40}$

Sums and the summation notation occur frequently in economics. Often, there are several variables or parameters in addition to the summation index. It is important to be able to interpret such sums. In each case, the summation symbol tells you that there is a sum of terms. The sum results from substituting successive integers for the summation index, starting with the lower limit and ending with the upper limit.

EXAMPLE 2   Expand   (a) $\displaystyle\sum_{i=1}^{n} p_t^{(i)} q^{(i)}$ (b) $\displaystyle\sum_{j=-3}^{i} x^{5-j} y^j$ (c) $\displaystyle\sum_{i=1}^{N} (x_{ij} - \bar{x}_j)^2$

Solution:

(a) $\displaystyle\sum_{i=1}^{n} p_t^{(i)} q^{(i)} = p_t^{(1)} q^{(1)} + p_t^{(2)} q^{(2)} + \cdots + p_t^{(n)} q^{(n)}$

(b) $\displaystyle\sum_{j=-3}^{1} x^{5-j} y^j = x^{5-(-3)} y^{-3} + x^{5-(-2)} y^{-2} + x^{5-(-1)} y^{-1} + x^{5-0} y^0 + x^{5-1} y^1$

$$= x^8 y^{-3} + x^7 y^{-2} + x^6 y^{-1} + x^5 + x^4 y$$

(c) $\displaystyle\sum_{i=1}^{N} (x_{ij} - \bar{x}_j)^2 = (x_{1j} - \bar{x}_j)^2 + (x_{2j} - \bar{x}_j)^2 + \cdots + (x_{Nj} - \bar{x}_j)^2$

Note that t is *not* an index of summation in (a), and j is *not* an index of summation in (c).

EXAMPLE 3   Write the following sums using summation notation:

(a) $1 + 3 + 3^2 + 3^3 + \cdots + 3^{81}$ (b) $a_i^6 + a_i^5 b_j + a_i^4 b_j^2 + a_i^3 b_j^3 + a_i^2 b_j^4 + a_i b_j^5 + b_j^6$

Solution:

(a) This is easy if we note that $1 = 3^0$ and $3 = 3^1$, so that the sum can be written as $3^0 + 3^1 + 3^2 + 3^3 + \cdots + 3^{81}$. The general term is 3^i, and we have

$$1 + 3 + 3^2 + 3^3 + \cdots + 3^{81} = \sum_{i=0}^{81} 3^i$$

(b) This is more difficult. Note, however, that the indices i and j never change. Also, the exponent for a_i decreases step by step from 6 to 0, whereas that for b_j increases from 0 to 6. The general term has the form $a_i^{6-k} b_j^k$, where k varies from 0 to 6. Thus,

$$a_i^6 + a_i^5 b_j + a_i^4 b_j^2 + a_i^3 b_j^3 + a_i^2 b_j^4 + a_i b_j^5 + b_j^6 = \sum_{k=0}^{6} a_i^{6-k} b_j^k$$

EXAMPLE 4   **(Price Indices)**   In order to summarize the overall effect of price changes for several different goods within a country, a number of alternative *price indices* have been suggested. Consider a "basket" of n commodities. For $i = 1, \ldots, n$, define

$$q^{(i)} = \text{number of units of good } i \text{ in the basket}$$

$$p_0^{(i)} = \text{price per unit of good } i \text{ in year } 0$$

$$p_t^{(i)} = \text{price per unit of good } i \text{ in year } t$$

Then

$$\sum_{i=1}^{n} p_0^{(i)} q^{(i)} = p_0^{(1)} q^{(1)} + p_0^{(2)} q^{(2)} + \cdots + p_0^{(n)} q^{(n)}$$

is the cost of the basket in year 0, whereas

$$\sum_{i=1}^{n} p_t^{(i)} q^{(i)} = p_t^{(1)} q^{(1)} + p_t^{(2)} q^{(2)} + \cdots + p_t^{(n)} q^{(n)}$$

is the cost of the basket in year t. A price index for year t, with year 0 as the base year, is defined as

$$\frac{\displaystyle\sum_{i=1}^{n} p_t^{(i)} q^{(i)}}{\displaystyle\sum_{i=1}^{n} p_0^{(i)} q^{(i)}} \cdot 100 \qquad \textbf{(price index)} \tag{1}$$

If the cost of the basket is 1032 in year 0 and the cost of the same basket in year t is 1548, then the price index is $(1548/1032) \cdot 100 = 150$.

In the case where the quantities $q^{(i)}$ are levels of consumption in the base year 0, this is called the **Laspeyres price index**. But if the quantities $q^{(i)}$ are levels of consumption in the year t, this is called the **Paasche price index**.

PROBLEMS FOR SECTION 3.1

1. Evaluate the following sums:

   (a) $\displaystyle\sum_{i=1}^{10} i$

   (b) $\displaystyle\sum_{k=2}^{6} (5 \cdot 3^{k-2} - k)$

   (c) $\displaystyle\sum_{m=0}^{5} (2m + 1)$

   (d) $\displaystyle\sum_{l=0}^{2} 2^{2^l}$

   (e) $\displaystyle\sum_{i=1}^{10} 2$

   (f) $\displaystyle\sum_{j=1}^{4} \frac{j+1}{j}$

2. Expand the following sums:

   (a) $\displaystyle\sum_{k=-2}^{2} 2\sqrt{k+2}$

   (b) $\displaystyle\sum_{i=0}^{3} (x + 2i)^2$

   (c) $\displaystyle\sum_{k=1}^{n} a_{ki} b^{k+1}$

   (d) $\displaystyle\sum_{j=0}^{m} f(x_j)\, \Delta x_j$

SM 3. Express these sums in summation notation:

   (a) $4 + 8 + 12 + 16 + \cdots + 4n$

   (b) $1^3 + 2^3 + 3^3 + 4^3 + \cdots + n^3$

   (c) $1 - \dfrac{1}{3} + \dfrac{1}{5} - \dfrac{1}{7} + \cdots + (-1)^n \dfrac{1}{2n+1}$

   (d) $a_{i1} b_{1j} + a_{i2} b_{2j} + \cdots + a_{in} b_{nj}$

   (e) $3x + 9x^2 + 27x^3 + 81x^4 + 243x^5$

   (f) $a_i^3 b_{i+3} + a_i^4 b_{i+4} + \cdots + a_i^p b_{i+p}$

   (g) $a_i^3 b_{i+3} + a_{i+1}^4 b_{i+4} + \cdots + a_{i+p}^{p+3} b_{i+p+3}$

   (h) $81\,297 + 81\,495 + 81\,693 + 81\,891$

4. Compute the price index (1) if $n = 3$, $p_0^{(1)} = 1$, $p_0^{(2)} = 2$, $p_0^{(3)} = 3$, $p_t^{(1)} = 2$, $p_t^{(2)} = 3$, $p_t^{(3)} = 4$, $q^{(1)} = 3$, $q^{(2)} = 5$, and $q^{(3)} = 7$.

5. Insert the appropriate limits of summation in the sums on the right-hand side.

   (a) $\displaystyle\sum_{k=1}^{10} (k-2)t^k = \sum_{m=} mt^{m+2}$

   (b) $\displaystyle\sum_{n=0}^{N} 2^{n+5} = \sum_{j=} 32 \cdot 2^{j-1}$

6. Officially there is a long-run goal of free labour mobility throughout the European Economic Area, to which 30 nations currently belong. For the year 2011, let c_{ij} denote the number of workers who moved their main place of work from nation i to nation j, $i \neq j$. If, say, $i = 25$ and $j = 10$, then we write $c_{25,10}$ for c_{ij}. If $i = j$ we let $c_{ij} = 0$. Explain the meaning of the sums: (a) $\sum_{j=1}^{30} c_{ij}$, (b) $\sum_{i=1}^{30} c_{ij}$.

(SM) 7. Decide which of the following equalities are generally valid. (Note in particular the correct answer to (b).)

(a) $\displaystyle\sum_{k=1}^{n} ck^2 = c \sum_{k=1}^{n} k^2$ (b) $\displaystyle\left(\sum_{i=1}^{n} a_i\right)^2 = \sum_{i=1}^{n} a_i^2$ (c) $\displaystyle\sum_{j=1}^{n} b_j + \sum_{j=n+1}^{N} b_j = \sum_{j=1}^{N} b_j$

(d) $\displaystyle\sum_{k=3}^{7} 5^{k-2} = \sum_{k=0}^{4} 5^{k+1}$ (e) $\displaystyle\sum_{i=0}^{n-1} a_{i,j}^2 = \sum_{k=1}^{n} a_{k-1,j}^2$ (f) $\displaystyle\sum_{k=1}^{n} \frac{a_k}{k} = \frac{1}{k} \sum_{k=1}^{n} a_k$

3.2 Rules for Sums. Newton's Binomial Formula

The following properties of the sigma notation are helpful when manipulating sums:

$$\sum_{i=1}^{n} (a_i + b_i) = \sum_{i=1}^{n} a_i + \sum_{i=1}^{n} b_i \qquad \textbf{(additivity property)} \qquad (1)$$

$$\sum_{i=1}^{n} ca_i = c \sum_{i=1}^{n} a_i \qquad \textbf{(homogeneity property)} \qquad (2)$$

The proofs are straightforward. For example, (2) is proved by noting that

$$\sum_{i=1}^{n} ca_i = ca_1 + ca_2 + \cdots + ca_n = c(a_1 + a_2 + \cdots + a_n) = c \sum_{i=1}^{n} a_i$$

The homogeneity property (2) states that a constant factor can be moved outside the summation sign. In particular, if $a_i = 1$ for all i, then

$$\sum_{i=1}^{n} c = nc \qquad (3)$$

which just states that a constant c summed n times is equal to n times c.

The summation rules can be applied in combination to give formulas like

$$\sum_{i=1}^{n} (a_i + b_i - 2c_i + d) = \sum_{i=1}^{n} a_i + \sum_{i=1}^{n} b_i - 2 \sum_{i=1}^{n} c_i + nd$$

EXAMPLE 1   Evaluate the sum

$$\sum_{m=2}^{n} \frac{1}{(m-1)m} = \frac{1}{1 \cdot 2} + \frac{1}{2 \cdot 3} + \cdots + \frac{1}{(n-1)n}$$

by using the identity $\dfrac{1}{(m-1)m} = \dfrac{1}{m-1} - \dfrac{1}{m}$.

Solution:

$$\sum_{m=2}^{n} \frac{1}{m(m-1)} = \sum_{m=2}^{n} \left(\frac{1}{m-1} - \frac{1}{m} \right) = \sum_{m=2}^{n} \frac{1}{m-1} - \sum_{m=2}^{n} \frac{1}{m}$$

$$= \left(\frac{1}{1} + \frac{1}{2} + \frac{1}{3} + \cdots + \frac{1}{n-1} \right) - \left(\frac{1}{2} + \frac{1}{3} + \cdots + \frac{1}{n-1} + \frac{1}{n} \right) = 1 - \frac{1}{n}$$

To derive the last equality, note that most of the terms cancel pairwise. The only exceptions are the first term within the first parentheses and the last term within the last parentheses. This powerful trick is commonly used to calculate some special sums of this kind. See Problem 3.

EXAMPLE 2   The **arithmetic mean** (or **mean**) μ_x of T numbers $x_1, x_2, \ldots, x_T$ is their average, defined as the sum of all the numbers divided by T, the number of terms. That is, $\mu_x = \frac{1}{T} \sum_{i=1}^{T} x_i$. Prove that $\sum_{i=1}^{T} (x_i - \mu_x) = 0$ and $\sum_{i=1}^{T} (x_i - \mu_x)^2 = \sum_{i=1}^{T} x_i^2 - T\mu_x^2$.

Solution: The difference $x_i - \mu_x$ is the deviation between x_i and the mean. We prove first that the sum of these deviations is 0, using the foregoing definition of μ_x:

$$\sum_{i=1}^{T} (x_i - \mu_x) = \sum_{i=1}^{T} x_i - \sum_{i=1}^{T} \mu_x = \sum_{i=1}^{T} x_i - T\mu_x = T\mu_x - T\mu_x = 0$$

Furthermore, the sum of the squares of the deviations is

$$\sum_{i=1}^{T} (x_i - \mu_x)^2 = \sum_{i=1}^{T} (x_i^2 - 2\mu_x x_i + \mu_x^2) = \sum_{i=1}^{T} x_i^2 - 2\mu_x \sum_{i=1}^{T} x_i + \sum_{i=1}^{T} \mu_x^2$$

$$= \sum_{i=1}^{T} x_i^2 - 2\mu_x T\mu_x + T\mu_x^2 = \sum_{i=1}^{T} x_i^2 - T\mu_x^2$$

Dividing by T, we see that the mean square deviation or **variance** $(1/T) \sum_{i=1}^{T} (x_i - \mu_x)^2$ must equal the mean square, $(1/T) \sum_{i=1}^{T} x_i^2$, minus the square of the mean, μ_x^2.

Useful Formulas

A (very) demanding teacher once asked his students to sum $81\,297 + 81\,495 + 81\,693 + \cdots + 100\,899$. There are 100 terms and the difference between successive terms is constant and equal to 198. Gauss, later one of the world's leading mathematicians, was in the class, and (at age 9) is reputed to have given the right answer in only a few minutes. Problem 5 asks you to match Gauss, but we will provide some help first.

Applied to the easier problem of finding the sum $x = 1 + 2 + \cdots + n$, Gauss's argument was probably as follows: First, write the sum x in two ways

$$x = 1 + 2 + \cdots + (n-1) + n$$
$$x = n + (n-1) + \cdots + 2 + 1$$

Summing vertically term by term gives

$$2x = (1+n) + [2 + (n-1)] + \cdots + [(n-1) + 2] + (n+1)$$
$$= (1+n) + (1+n) + \cdots + (1+n) + (1+n) = n(1+n)$$

Thus, solving for x gives the result:

$$\sum_{i=1}^{n} i = 1 + 2 + \cdots + n = \tfrac{1}{2}n(n+1) \qquad (4)$$

The following two summation formulas are occasionally useful in economics. Check to see if they are true for $n = 1, 2$, and 3. For proofs, see Problem 3.7.2.

$$\sum_{i=1}^{n} i^2 = 1^2 + 2^2 + 3^2 + \cdots + n^2 = \tfrac{1}{6}n(n+1)(2n+1) \qquad (5)$$

$$\sum_{i=1}^{n} i^3 = 1^3 + 2^3 + 3^3 + \cdots + n^3 = \left(\tfrac{1}{2}n(n+1)\right)^2 = \left(\sum_{i=1}^{n} i\right)^2 \qquad (6)$$

Newton's Binomial Formula

We all know that $(a+b)^1 = a + b$ and $(a+b)^2 = a^2 + 2ab + b^2$. Using the latter equality and writing $(a+b)^3 = (a+b)(a+b)^2$ and $(a+b)^4 = (a+b)(a+b)^3$, we find that

$$(a+b)^1 = a + b$$
$$(a+b)^2 = a^2 + 2ab + b^2$$
$$(a+b)^3 = a^3 + 3a^2b + 3ab^2 + b^3$$
$$(a+b)^4 = a^4 + 4a^3b + 6a^2b^2 + 4ab^3 + b^4$$

The corresponding formula for $(a+b)^m$, where m is any natural number, can be expressed as follows:

NEWTON'S BINOMIAL FORMULA

$$(a+b)^m = a^m + \binom{m}{1}a^{m-1}b + \cdots + \binom{m}{m-1}ab^{m-1} + \binom{m}{m}b^m \qquad (7)$$

This formula involves the **binomial coefficients** $\binom{m}{k}$ which are defined, for $m = 1, 2, \ldots$ and for $k = 0, 1, 2, \ldots, m$, by

$$\binom{m}{k} = \frac{m(m-1)\cdots(m-k+1)}{k!}, \qquad \binom{m}{0} = 1$$

where $k!$, read as "k factorial", is standard notation for the product $1 \cdot 2 \cdot 3 \cdots (k-1) \cdot k$ of the first k numbers, with the convention that $0! = 1$.

In general, $\binom{m}{1} = m$ and $\binom{m}{m} = 1$. When $m = 5$, for example, we have

$$\binom{5}{2} = \frac{5 \cdot 4}{1 \cdot 2} = 10, \qquad \binom{5}{3} = \frac{5 \cdot 4 \cdot 3}{1 \cdot 2 \cdot 3} = 10, \qquad \binom{5}{4} = \frac{5 \cdot 4 \cdot 3 \cdot 2}{1 \cdot 2 \cdot 3 \cdot 4} = 5$$

Then (7) gives $(a+b)^5 = a^5 + 5a^4b + 10a^3b^2 + 10a^2b^3 + 5ab^4 + b^5$.

The coefficients occurring in the expansions for successive powers of $(a + b)$ form the following pattern, called **Pascal's triangle** (though it was actually known in China by about the year 1100, long before Blaise Pascal was born):

$$
\begin{array}{ccccccccccccccccc}
 & & & & & & & & 1 \\
 & & & & & & & 1 & & 1 \\
 & & & & & & 1 & & 2 & & 1 \\
 & & & & & 1 & & 3 & & 3 & & 1 \\
 & & & & 1 & & 4 & & 6 & & 4 & & 1 \\
 & & & 1 & & 5 & & 10 & & 10 & & 5 & & 1 \\
 & & 1 & & 6 & & 15 & & 20 & & 15 & & 6 & & 1 \\
 & 1 & & 7 & & 21 & & 35 & & 35 & & 21 & & 7 & & 1 \\
1 & & 8 & & 28 & & 56 & & 70 & & 56 & & 28 & & 8 & & 1 \\
\end{array}
$$

$$1 \quad 9 \quad 36 \quad 84 \quad 126 \quad 126 \quad 84 \quad 36 \quad 9 \quad 1$$

This table can be continued indefinitely. The numbers in this triangle are indeed the binomial coefficients. For instance, the numbers in row 6 (when the first row is numbered 0) are

$$\binom{6}{0} \quad \binom{6}{1} \quad \binom{6}{2} \quad \binom{6}{3} \quad \binom{6}{4} \quad \binom{6}{5} \quad \binom{6}{6}$$

Note first that the numbers are symmetric about the middle line. This symmetry can be expressed as

$$\binom{m}{k} = \binom{m}{m-k} \tag{8}$$

For example, $\binom{6}{2} = 15 = \binom{6}{4}$. Second, apart from the 1 at both ends of each row, each number is the sum of the two adjacent numbers in the row above. For instance, 56 in the eighth row is equal to the sum of 21 and 35 in the seventh row. In symbols,

$$\binom{m+1}{k+1} = \binom{m}{k} + \binom{m}{k+1} \tag{9}$$

In Problem 4 you are asked to prove these two properties.

PROBLEMS FOR SECTION 3.2

1. Use the results in (4) and (5) to find $\sum_{k=1}^{n}(k^2 + 3k + 2)$.

2. Use Newton's binomial formula to find $(a + b)^6$.

3. (a) Prove that $\sum_{k=1}^{8}(a_{k+1} - a_k) = a_9 - a_1$, and, generally, that $\sum_{k=1}^{n}(a_{k+1} - a_k) = a_{n+1} - a_1$.

   (b) Use the result in (a) to compute the following:

   (i) $\displaystyle\sum_{k=1}^{50}\left(\frac{1}{k} - \frac{1}{k+1}\right)$ (ii) $\displaystyle\sum_{k=1}^{12}\left(3^{k+1} - 3^k\right)$ (iii) $\displaystyle\sum_{k=1}^{n}\left(ar^{k+1} - ar^k\right)$

4. (a) Prove that $\dbinom{5}{3} = \dfrac{5!}{2!\,3!}$, and in general that

$$\binom{m}{k} = \frac{m!}{(m-k)!\,k!} \tag{10}$$

   (b) Verify by direct computation that $\dbinom{8}{3} = \dbinom{8}{8-3}$ and $\dbinom{8+1}{3+1} = \dbinom{8}{3} + \dbinom{8}{3+1}$.

   (c) Use (10) to verify (8) and (9).

5. Prove the summation formula for an **arithmetic series**,

$$\sum_{i=0}^{n-1}(a + id) = na + \frac{n(n-1)d}{2}$$

Apply the result to find the sum Gauss is supposed to have calculated at age 9.

3.3 Double Sums

Often one has to combine several summation signs. Consider, for example, the following rectangular array of numbers:

$$\begin{array}{cccc}
a_{11} & a_{12} & \cdots & a_{1n} \\
a_{21} & a_{22} & \cdots & a_{2n} \\
\vdots & \vdots & & \vdots \\
a_{m1} & a_{m2} & \cdots & a_{mn}
\end{array} \tag{1}$$

The array can be regarded as a *spreadsheet*. A typical number in the array is of the form a_{ij}, where $1 \le i \le m$ and $1 \le j \le n$. (For example, a_{ij} may indicate the total revenue of a firm from its sales in region i in month j.) There are $n \cdot m$ numbers in all. Let us find the sum of all the numbers in the array by first summing all the numbers in each of the m rows, then adding all these row sums. The m different row sums can be written in the form $\sum_{j=1}^{n} a_{1j}, \sum_{j=1}^{n} a_{2j}, \ldots, \sum_{j=1}^{n} a_{mj}$. (In our example, these row sums are the total revenues in each region summed over all the n months.) The sum of these m sums is equal to $\sum_{j=1}^{n} a_{1j} + \sum_{j=1}^{n} a_{2j} + \cdots + \sum_{j=1}^{n} a_{mj}$, which can be written as $\sum_{i=1}^{m} \left(\sum_{j=1}^{n} a_{ij} \right)$. If instead we add the numbers in each of the n columns first and then add these sums, we get

$$\sum_{i=1}^{m} a_{i1} + \sum_{i=1}^{m} a_{i2} + \cdots + \sum_{i=1}^{m} a_{in} = \sum_{j=1}^{n} \left(\sum_{i=1}^{m} a_{ij} \right)$$

(How do you interpret this sum in our economic example?) In both these cases, we have calculated the sum of all the numbers in the array. For this reason, we must have

$$\sum_{i=1}^{m} \sum_{j=1}^{n} a_{ij} = \sum_{j=1}^{n} \sum_{i=1}^{m} a_{ij}$$

where, following usual practice, we have deleted the parentheses. This formula says that *in a (finite) double sum, the order of summation is immaterial*. It is important to note that the summation limits for i and j are independent of each other.

EXAMPLE 1   Compute $\sum_{i=1}^{3} \sum_{j=1}^{4} (i + 2j)$.

Solution:

$$\sum_{i=1}^{3} \sum_{j=1}^{4} (i + 2j) = \sum_{i=1}^{3} \left[(i + 2) + (i + 4) + (i + 6) + (i + 8) \right]$$

$$= \sum_{i=1}^{3} (4i + 20) = 24 + 28 + 32 = 84$$

You should check that the result is the same by summing over i first instead.

PROBLEMS FOR SECTION 3.3

(SM) 1. Expand and compute the following double sums:

(a) $\sum_{i=1}^{3} \sum_{j=1}^{4} i \cdot 3^j$ (b) $\sum_{s=0}^{2} \sum_{r=2}^{4} \left(\frac{rs}{r+s} \right)^2$ (c) $\sum_{i=1}^{m} \sum_{j=1}^{n} (i + j^2)$ (d) $\sum_{i=1}^{m} \sum_{j=1}^{2} i^j$

2. Consider a group of individuals each having a certain number of units of m different goods. Let a_{ij} denote the number of units of good i owned by person j ($i = 1, \ldots, m$; $j = 1, \ldots, n$). Explain in words the meaning of the following sums:

(a) $\sum_{j=1}^{n} a_{ij}$ (b) $\sum_{i=1}^{m} a_{ij}$ (c) $\sum_{j=1}^{n} \sum_{i=1}^{m} a_{ij}$

3. Prove that the sum of all the numbers in the triangular table

$$
\begin{array}{ccccc}
a_{11} & & & & \\
a_{21} & a_{22} & & & \\
a_{31} & a_{32} & a_{33} & & \\
\vdots & \vdots & \vdots & \ddots & \\
a_{m1} & a_{m2} & a_{m3} & \cdots & a_{mm}
\end{array}
$$

can be written as $\displaystyle\sum_{i=1}^{m}\left(\sum_{j=1}^{i} a_{ij}\right)$ and also as $\displaystyle\sum_{j=1}^{m}\left(\sum_{i=j}^{m} a_{ij}\right)$.

HARDER PROBLEM

(SM) **4.** Consider the $m \cdot n$ numbers a_{ij} in the rectangular array (1). Denote the arithmetic mean of them all by $\bar{a}$, and the mean of all the numbers in the jth column by $\bar{a}_j$, so that

$$
\bar{a} = \frac{1}{mn}\sum_{r=1}^{m}\sum_{s=1}^{n} a_{rs}, \qquad \bar{a}_j = \frac{1}{m}\sum_{r=1}^{m} a_{rj}
$$

Prove that $\bar{a}$ is the mean of the column sums $\bar{a}_j$ $(j = 1, \ldots, n)$ and that

$$
\sum_{r=1}^{m}\sum_{s=1}^{m}(a_{rj} - \bar{a})(a_{sj} - \bar{a}) = m^2(\bar{a}_j - \bar{a})^2 \tag{$*$}
$$

3.4 A Few Aspects of Logic

We have emphasized the role of mathematical models in the empirical sciences, especially in economics. The more complicated the phenomena to be described, the more important it is to be exact. Errors in models applied to practical situations can have catastrophic consequences. For example, in the early stages of the US space programme, a rocket costing millions of dollars to develop had to be destroyed only seconds after launch because a semicolon was missing in the computer program controlling its guidance system. A more recent example is the Mars lander which burned up early in the year 2000 because of a confusion between metric and US units of measurement.

Although the consequences may be less dramatic, errors in mathematical reasoning also occur easily. Here is a typical example of how a student (or even a professor) might use faulty logic and thus end up with an incorrect answer to a problem.

EXAMPLE 1   Find a possible solution for the equation

$$
x + 2 = \sqrt{4 - x}
$$

"Solution": Squaring each side of the equation gives $(x + 2)^2 = (\sqrt{4 - x})^2$, and thus $x^2 + 4x + 4 = 4 - x$. Rearranging this last equation gives $x^2 + 5x = 0$. Cancelling x results in $x + 5 = 0$, and therefore $x = -5$.

According to this reasoning, the answer should be $x = -5$. Let us check this. For $x = -5$, we have $x + 2 = -3$. Yet $\sqrt{4 - x} = \sqrt{9} = 3$, so this answer is incorrect. In Example 4 we explain how the error arose. (Note the wisdom of checking your answer whenever you think you have solved an equation.)

This example highlights the dangers of routine calculation without adequate thought. It may be easier to avoid similar mistakes after studying the structure of logical reasoning.

Propositions

Assertions that are either true or false are called statements, or **propositions.** Most of the propositions in this book are mathematical ones, but other kinds may arise in daily life. "All individuals who breathe are alive" is an example of a true proposition, whereas the assertion "all individuals who breathe are healthy" is a false proposition. Note that if the words used to express such an assertion lack precise meaning, it will often be difficult to tell whether it is true or false. For example, the assertion "67 is a large number" is neither true nor false without a precise definition of "large number".

Implications

In order to keep track of each step in a chain of logical reasoning, it often helps to use implication arrows.

Suppose P and Q are two propositions such that whenever P is true, then Q is necessarily true. In this case, we usually write

$$P \implies Q \qquad\qquad (*)$$

This is read as "P implies Q", or "if P, then Q", or "Q is a consequence of P". Other ways of expressing the same implication include "Q if P", "P only if Q", and "Q is an implication of P". The symbol $\implies$ is an **implication arrow,** and it points in the direction of the logical implication. Here are some examples of correct implications.

EXAMPLE 2   (a) $x > 2 \implies x^2 > 4$

(b) $xy = 0 \implies x = 0$ or $y = 0$

(c) x is a square $\implies x$ is a rectangle

(d) x is a healthy person $\implies x$ breathes without difficulty

Notice that the word "or" in mathematics means the "inclusive or", signifying that "P or Q" includes the case when P and Q are both true.

In certain cases where the implication $(*)$ is valid, it may also be possible to draw a logical conclusion in the other direction:

$$Q \implies P$$

In such cases, we can write both implications together in a single **logical equivalence**:

$$P \iff Q$$

We then say that "P is equivalent to Q". Because we have both "P if Q" and "P only if Q", we also say that "P if and only if Q", which is often written "P iff Q" for short. The symbol $\iff$ is an **equivalence arrow.**

In Example 2, we see that the implication arrow in (b) could be replaced with the equivalence arrow, because it is also true that $x = 0$ or $y = 0$ implies $xy = 0$. Note, however, that no other implication in Example 2 can be replaced by the equivalence arrow. For even if x^2 is larger than 4, it is not necessarily true that x is larger than 2 (for instance, x might be -3); also, a rectangle is not necessarily a square; and, finally, just because person x breathes without difficulty does not mean that x is healthy.

Necessary and Sufficient Conditions

There are other commonly used ways of expressing that proposition P implies proposition Q, or that P is equivalent to Q. Thus, if proposition P implies proposition Q, we state that P is a "sufficient condition" for Q. After all, for Q to be true, it is sufficient that P is true. Accordingly, we know that if P is satisfied, then it is certain that Q is also satisfied. In this case, we say that Q is a "necessary condition" for P, for Q must necessarily be true if P is true. Hence,

P is a **sufficient condition** for Q means: $P \implies Q$

Q is a **necessary condition** for P means: $P \implies Q$

If we formulate the implication in Example 2 (c) in this way, it would read:

A sufficient condition for x to be a rectangle is that x be a square.

or

A necessary condition for x to be a square is that x be a rectangle.

The corresponding way to express $P \iff Q$ verbally is simply: *P is a necessary and sufficient condition for Q*.

It is evident from this that it is very important to distinguish between the propositions "P is a necessary condition for Q" (meaning $Q \implies P$) and "P is a sufficient condition for Q" (meaning $P \implies Q$). To emphasize the point, consider two propositions:

Breathing is a necessary condition for a person to be healthy.

Breathing is a sufficient condition for a person to be healthy.

The first proposition is clearly true. But the second is false, because sick people are still breathing.

In the following pages, we shall repeatedly refer to necessary and sufficient conditions. Understanding them and the difference between them is a necessary condition for understanding much of economic analysis. It is not a sufficient condition, alas!

Solving Equations

Implication and equivalence arrows are very useful in helping to avoid mistakes in solving equations. Consider first the following example.

EXAMPLE 3   Find all x such that $(2x - 1)^2 - 3x^2 = 2\left(\frac{1}{2} - 4x\right)$.

Solution: By expanding $(2x - 1)^2$ and also multiplying out the right-hand side, we obtain a new equation that obviously has the same solutions as the original one:

$$(2x - 1)^2 - 3x^2 = 2\left(\tfrac{1}{2} - 4x\right) \iff 4x^2 - 4x + 1 - 3x^2 = 1 - 8x$$

Adding $8x - 1$ to each side of the second equation and then gathering terms gives an equivalent equation:

$$4x^2 - 4x + 1 - 3x^2 = 1 - 8x \iff x^2 + 4x = 0$$

Now $x^2 + 4x = x(x + 4)$, and the latter expression is 0 if and only if $x = 0$ or $x = -4$. That is,

$$x^2 + 4x = 0 \iff x(x + 4) = 0 \iff x = 0 \quad \text{or} \quad x = -4$$

Putting everything together, we have derived a chain of equivalence arrows showing that the given equation is fulfilled for the two values $x = 0$ and $x = -4$, and for no other values of x.

EXAMPLE 4   Find all x such that $x + 2 = \sqrt{4 - x}$. (Recall Example 1.)

Solution: Squaring both sides of the given equation yields

$$\left(x + 2\right)^2 = \left(\sqrt{4 - x}\right)^2$$

Consequently, $x^2 + 4x + 4 = 4 - x$, that is, $x^2 + 5x = 0$. From the latter equation it follows that

$$x(x + 5) = 0 \quad \text{which yields} \quad x = 0 \text{ or } x = -5$$

Thus, a necessary condition for x to solve $x + 2 = \sqrt{4 - x}$ is that $x = 0$ or $x = -5$. Inserting these two possible values of x into the original equation shows that only $x = 0$ satisfies the equation. The unique solution to the equation is, therefore, $x = 0$.

In finding the solution to Example 1, why was it necessary to test whether the values we found were actually solutions, whereas this step was unnecessary in Example 3? To answer this, we must analyse the logical structure of our solution to Example 1. Using implication arrows marked by letters, we can express the solution as follows:

$$x + 2 = \sqrt{4 - x} \overset{(a)}{\implies} (x + 2)^2 = 4 - x \overset{(b)}{\implies} x^2 + 4x + 4 = 4 - x$$

$$\overset{(c)}{\implies} x^2 + 5x = 0 \overset{(d)}{\implies} x(x + 5) = 0 \overset{(e)}{\implies} x = 0 \text{ or } x = -5$$

Implication (a) is true (because $a = b \implies a^2 = b^2$ and $\left(\sqrt{a}\right)^2 = a$). *It is important to note, however, that the implication cannot be replaced by an equivalence.* If $a^2 = b^2$, then either $a = b$ or $a = -b$; it need not be true that $a = b$. Implications (b), (c), (d), and (e) are also all true; moreover, all could have been written as equivalences, though this is not necessary in order to find the solution. Therefore, a chain of implications has been obtained that leads from the equation $x + 2 = \sqrt{4 - x}$ to the proposition "$x = 0$ or $x = -5$". Because the implication (a) cannot be reversed, there is no corresponding chain of implications going in the opposite direction. We have verified that if the number x satisfies $x + 2 = \sqrt{4 - x}$, then x must be either 0 or -5; no other value can satisfy the given equation. However, we have not yet shown that either 0 or -5 really satisfies the equation. Only after we try inserting 0 and -5 into the equation do we see that $x = 0$ is the only solution. *Note that in this case, the test we have suggested not only serves to check our calculations, but is also a logical necessity.*

Looking back at the wrong "solution" to Example 1, we now realize that the false argument involved two errors. Firstly, the implication $x^2 + 5x = 0 \Rightarrow x + 5 = 0$ is wrong, because $x = 0$ is also a solution of $x^2 + 5x = 0$. Secondly, it is logically necessary to check if 0 or -5 really satisfies the equation.

The method used in solving Example 4 is the most common. It involves setting up a chain of implications that starts from the given equation and ends with all the possible solutions. By testing each of these trial solutions in turn, we find which of them really do satisfy the equation. Even if the chain of implications is also a chain of equivalences, such a test is always a useful check of both logic and calculations.

PROBLEMS FOR SECTION 3.4

1. There are many other ways to express implications and equivalences, apart from those already mentioned. Use appropriate implication or equivalence arrows to represent the following propositions:

   (a) The equation $2x - 4 = 2$ is fulfilled only when $x = 3$.

   (b) If $x = 3$, then $2x - 4 = 2$.

   (c) The equation $x^2 - 2x + 1 = 0$ is satisfied if $x = 1$.

   (d) If $x^2 > 4$, then $|x| > 2$, and conversely.

2. Solve the equation $\dfrac{(x + 1)^2}{x(x - 1)} + \dfrac{(x - 1)^2}{x(x + 1)} - 2\dfrac{3x + 1}{x^2 - 1} = 0.$

3. Consider the following six implications and decide in each case: (i) if the implication is true; and (ii) if the converse implication is true. (x, y, and z are real numbers.)

   (a) $x = 2$ and $y = 5 \implies x + y = 7$ (b) $(x - 1)(x - 2)(x - 3) = 0 \implies x = 1$

   (c) $x^2 + y^2 = 0 \implies x = 0$ or $y = 0$ (d) $x = 0$ and $y = 0 \implies x^2 + y^2 = 0$

   (e) $xy = xz \implies y = z$ (f) $x > y^2 \implies x > 0$

4. Consider the proposition $2x + 5 \geq 13$.

(a) Is the condition $x \geq 0$ necessary, or sufficient, or both necessary and sufficient for the inequality to be satisfied?

(b) Answer the same question when $x \geq 0$ is replaced by $x \geq 50$.

(c) Answer the same question when $x \geq 0$ is replaced by $x \geq 4$.

5. Solve the following equations:

(a) $x + 2 = \sqrt{4x + 13}$ (b) $|x + 2| = \sqrt{4 - x}$ (c) $x^2 - 2|x| - 3 = 0$

SM **6.** Solve the following equations:

(a) $\sqrt{x - 4} = \sqrt{x + 5} - 9$ (b) $\sqrt{x - 4} = 9 - \sqrt{x + 5}$

SM **7.** Fill in the blank rectangles with "iff" (if and only if) when this results in a true statement, or alternatively with "if" or "only if".

(a) $x = \sqrt{4}$ ⬜ $x = 2$ (b) $x(x + 3) < 0$ ⬜ $x > -3$

(c) $x^2 < 9$ ⬜ $x < 3$ (d) $x(x^2 + 1) = 0$ ⬜ $x = 0$

(e) $x^2 > 0$ ⬜ $x > 0$ (f) $x^4 + y^4 = 0$ ⬜ $x = 0$ or $y = 0$

8. Consider the following attempt to solve the equation $x + \sqrt{x + 4} = 2$:

"From the given equation, it follows that $\sqrt{x + 4} = 2 - x$. Squaring both sides gives $x + 4 = 4 - 4x + x^2$. After rearranging the terms, it is seen that this equation implies $x^2 - 5x = 0$. Cancelling x, we obtain $x - 5 = 0$ and this equation is satisfied when $x = 5$."

(a) Mark with arrows the implications or equivalences expressed in the text. Which ones are correct?

(b) Solve the equation correctly.

HARDER PROBLEM

SM **9.** If P is a statement, the *negation* of P is denoted by $\neg P$. If P is true, then $\neg P$ is false, and vice versa. For example, the negation of the statement $2x + 3y \leq 8$ is $2x + 3y > 8$. For each of the following 6 propositions, state the negation as simply as possible.

(a) $x \geq 0$ and $y \geq 0$.

(b) All x satisfy $x \geq a$.

(c) Neither x nor y is less than 5.

(d) For each $\varepsilon > 0$, there exists a $\delta > 0$ such that B is satisfied.

(e) No one can help liking cats.

(f) Everyone loves somebody some of the time.

3.5 Mathematical Proofs

In every branch of mathematics, the most important results are called **theorems.** Construct-ing logically valid proofs for these results often can be very complicated. For example, the "four-colour theorem" states that any map in the plane needs at most four colours in order that all adjacent regions can be given different colours. Proving this involved checking hundreds of thousands of different cases, a task that was impossible without a sophisticated computer program.

In this book, we often omit formal proofs of theorems. Instead, the emphasis is on providing a good intuitive grasp of what the theorems tell us. However, although proofs do not form a major part of this book, it is still useful to understand something about the different types of proof that are used in mathematics.

Every mathematical theorem can be formulated as an implication

$$P \implies Q \qquad (*)$$

where P represents a proposition or a series of propositions called *premises* ("what we know"), and Q represents a proposition or a series of propositions that are called the *con-clusions* ("what we want to know").

Usually, it is most natural to prove a result of the type $(*)$ by starting with the premises P and successively working forward to the conclusions Q; we call this a **direct proof**. Sometimes, however, it is more convenient to prove the implication $P \implies Q$ by an **indirect proof**. In this case, we begin by supposing that Q is not true, and on that basis demonstrate that P cannot be true either. This is completely legitimate, because we have the following equivalence:

$$P \implies Q \quad \text{is equivalent to} \quad not\ Q \implies not\ P$$

It is helpful to consider how this rule of logic applies to a concrete example:

If it is raining, the grass is getting wet.

asserts precisely the same thing as

If the grass is not getting wet, then it is not raining.

EXAMPLE 1   Use the two methods of proof to prove that $-x^2 + 5x - 4 > 0 \implies x > 0$.

Solution:

(a) *Direct proof:* Suppose $-x^2 + 5x - 4 > 0$. Adding $x^2 + 4$ to each side of the inequality gives $5x > x^2 + 4$. Because $x^2 + 4 \geq 4$, for all x, we have $5x > 4$, and so $x > 4/5$. In particular, $x > 0$.

(b) *Indirect proof:* Suppose $x \leq 0$. Then $5x \leq 0$ and so $-x^2 + 5x - 4$, as a sum of three nonpositive terms, is ≤ 0.

Deductive vs. Inductive Reasoning

The two methods of proof just outlined are both examples of *deductive reasoning* — that is, reasoning based on consistent rules of logic. In contrast, many branches of science use *inductive reasoning*. This process draws general conclusions based only on a few (or even many) observations. For example, the statement that "the price level has increased every year for the last n years; therefore, it will surely increase next year too", demonstrates inductive reasoning. This inductive approach is nevertheless of fundamental importance in the experimental and empirical sciences, despite the fact that conclusions based upon it never can be absolutely certain. Indeed, in economics, such examples of inductive reasoning (or the implied predictions) often turn out to be false, with hindsight.

In mathematics, inductive reasoning is not recognized as a form of proof. Suppose, for instance, that students in a geometry course are asked to show that the sum of the angles of a triangle is always 180 degrees. If they painstakingly measure as accurately as possible 1000 different triangles, demonstrating that in each case the sum of the angles is 180, it would still not serve as a proof for the assertion. It would represent a very good indication that the proposition is true, but it is not a mathematical proof. Similarly, in business economics, the fact that a particular company's profits have risen for each of the past 20 years is no guarantee that they will rise once again this year.

PROBLEMS FOR SECTION 3.5

1. Which of the following statements are equivalent to the (dubious) statement: "If inflation increases, then unemployment decreases"?

   (a) For unemployment to decrease, inflation must increase.

   (b) A sufficient condition for unemployment to decrease is that inflation increases.

   (c) Unemployment can only decrease if inflation increases.

   (d) If unemployment does not decrease, then inflation does not increase.

   (e) A necessary condition for inflation to increase is that unemployment decreases.

2. Analyse the following epitaph: (a) using logic; (b) from a poetic viewpoint.

   > Those who knew him, loved him.
   > Those who loved him not, knew him not.

3. Show by an indirect proof: If x and y are integers and xy is an odd number, then x and y are both odd.

3.6 Essentials of Set Theory

In daily life, we constantly group together objects of the same kind. For instance, we refer to the faculty of a university to signify all the members of the academic staff. A garden refers to all the plants that are growing in it. We talk about all Scottish firms with more than 300 employees, all taxpayers in Germany who earned between 50 000 and 100 000 euros in 2004. In all these cases, we have a collection of objects viewed as a whole. In mathematics, such a collection is called a **set**, and its objects are called its **elements**, or its **members**.

How is a set specified? The simplest method is to list its members, in any order, between the two braces { and }. An example is the set $S = \{a, b, c\}$ whose members are the first three letters in the English alphabet. Or it might be a set consisting of three members represented by the letters a, b, and c. For example, if $a = 0$, $b = 1$, and $c = 2$, then $S = \{0, 1, 2\}$. Also, S denotes the set of roots of the cubic equation $(x - a)(x - b)(x - c) = 0$ in the unknown x, where a, b, and c are any three real numbers.

Two sets A and B are considered **equal** if each element of A is an element of B and each element of B is an element of A. In this case, we write $A = B$. This means that the two sets consist of exactly the same elements. Consequently, $\{1, 2, 3\} = \{3, 2, 1\}$, because the order in which the elements are listed has no significance; and $\{1, 1, 2, 3\} = \{1, 2, 3\}$, because a set is not changed if some elements are listed more than once.

Alternatively, suppose that you are to eat a meal at a restaurant that offers a choice of several main dishes. Four choices might be feasible—fish, pasta, omelette, and chicken. Then the *feasible set* F has these four members, and is fully specified as

$$F = \{\text{fish, pasta, omelette, chicken}\}$$

Notice that the order in which the dishes are listed does not matter. The feasible set remains the same even if the order of the items on the menu is changed.

Specifying a Property

Not every set can be defined by listing all its members, however. For one thing, some sets are infinite—that is, they contain infinitely many members.

Actually, such infinite sets are rather common in economics. Take, for instance, the *budget set* that arises in consumer theory. Suppose there are two goods with quantities (for example, weights of two kinds of fruit) denoted by real numbers x and y. Suppose one unit of these goods can be bought at prices p and q, respectively. A consumption bundle (x, y) is a pair of quantities of the two goods. Its value at prices p and q is $px + qy$. Suppose that a consumer has an amount m to spend on the two goods. Then the *budget constraint* is $px + qy \leq m$ (assuming that the consumer is free to underspend). If one also accepts that the quantity consumed of each good must be nonnegative, then the *budget set*, which will be denoted by B, consists of those consumption bundles (x, y) satisfying the three inequalities $px + qy \leq m$, $x \geq 0$, and $y \geq 0$. (The set B is shown in Fig. 4.4.12.) Standard notation for such a set is

$$B = \{(x, y) : px + qy \leq m, \ x \geq 0, \ y \geq 0\} \tag{1}$$

The braces { } are still used to denote "the set consisting of". However, instead of listing all the members, which is impossible for the infinite set of points in the triangular budget set B, the specification of the set B is given in two parts. To the left of the colon, (x, y) is used to denote the typical member of B, here a consumption bundle that is specified by listing the respective quantities of the two goods. To the right of the colon, the three properties that these typical members must satisfy are all listed, and the set thereby specified. This is an example of the general specification:

$$S = \{\text{typical member : defining properties}\}$$

Note that it is not just infinite sets that can be specified by properties—finite sets can also be specified in this way. Indeed, even some finite sets almost *have* to be specified in this way, such as the set of all the more than 7 billion human beings currently alive.

Set Membership

As we stated earlier, sets contain members or elements. There is some convenient standard notation that denotes the relation between a set and its members. First,

$$x \in S$$

indicates that x *is an element of* S. Note the special symbol $\in$ (which is a variant of the Greek letter ε, or "epsilon").

To express the fact that x is *not* a member of S, we write $x \notin S$. For example, $d \notin \{a, b, c\}$ says that d is not an element of the set $\{a, b, c\}$.

For additional illustrations of set membership notation, let us return to the main dish example. Confronted with the choice from the set $F = \{\text{fish, pasta, omelette, chicken}\}$, let s denote your actual selection. Then, of course, $s \in F$. This is what we mean by "feasible set"—it is possible only to choose some member of that set but nothing outside it.

Let A and B be any two sets. Then A is a **subset** of B if it is true that every member of A is also a member of B. Then we write $A \subseteq B$. In particular, $A \subseteq A$. From the definitions we see that $A = B$ if and only if $A \subseteq B$ and $B \subseteq A$.

Set Operations

Sets can be combined in many different ways. Especially important are three operations: union, intersection, and the difference of sets, as shown in Table 1.

Table 1

Notation	Name	The set consists of:
$A \cup B$	A **union** B	The elements that belong to at least one of the sets A and B
$A \cap B$	A **intersection** B	The elements that belong to both A and B
$A \setminus B$	A **minus** B	The elements that belong to A, but not to B

Thus,

$$A \cup B = \{x : x \in A \text{ or } x \in B\}$$
$$A \cap B = \{x : x \in A \text{ and } x \in B\}$$
$$A \setminus B = \{x : x \in A \text{ and } x \notin B\}$$

EXAMPLE 1   Let $A = \{1, 2, 3, 4, 5\}$ and $B = \{3, 6\}$. Find $A \cup B, A \cap B, A \setminus B$, and $B \setminus A$.

Solution: $A \cup B = \{1, 2, 3, 4, 5, 6\}, A \cap B = \{3\}, A \setminus B = \{1, 2, 4, 5\}, B \setminus A = \{6\}$.

An economic example can be obtained by considering workers in Europe in 2001. Let A be the set of all those workers who had an income of at least 15 000 and let B be the set of all who had a net worth of at least 150 000. Then $A \cup B$ would be those workers who earned at least 15 000 or who had a net worth of at least 150 000, whereas $A \cap B$ are those workers who earned at least 15 000 and who also had a net worth of at least 150 000. Finally, $A \setminus B$ would be those who earned at least 15 000 but who had less than 150 000 in net worth.

If two sets A and B have no elements in common, they are said to be **disjoint**. The symbol "Ø" denotes the set that has no elements. It is called the **empty set**. Thus, the sets A and B are disjoint if and only if $A \cap B = \emptyset$.

A collection of sets is often referred to as a **family** of sets. When considering a certain family of sets, it is often natural to think of each set in the family as a subset of one particular fixed set Ω, hereafter called the **universal set.** In the previous example, the set of all European workers in 2001 would be an obvious choice for a universal set.

If A is a subset of the universal set Ω, then according to the definition of difference, $\Omega \setminus A$ is the set of elements of Ω that are not in A. This set is called the **complement** of A in Ω and is sometimes denoted by $\complement A$, so that $\complement A = \Omega \setminus A$. Other ways of denoting the complement of A include A^c and $\tilde{A}$.

When using the notation $\complement A$ or some equivalent, it is important to be clear about which universal set Ω is used to construct the complement.

EXAMPLE 2   Let the universal set Ω be the set of all students at a particular university. Moreover, let F denote the set of female students, M the set of all mathematics students, C the set of students in the university choir, B the set of all biology students, and T the set of all students who play tennis. Describe the members of the following sets: $\Omega \setminus M$, $M \cup C$, $F \cap T$, $M \setminus (B \cap T)$, and $(M \setminus B) \cup (M \setminus T)$.

Solution: $\Omega \setminus M$ consists of those students who are not studying mathematics, $M \cup C$ of those students who study mathematics and/or are in the choir. The set $F \cap T$ consists of those female students who play tennis. The set $M \setminus (B \cap T)$ has those mathematics students who do not both study biology and play tennis. Lastly, the set $(M \setminus B) \cup (M \setminus T)$ has those students who either are mathematics students not studying biology or mathematics students who do not play tennis. Do you see that the last two sets are equal? (For arbitrary sets M, B, and T, it is true that $(M \setminus B) \cup (M \setminus T) = M \setminus (B \cap T)$. It will be easier to verify this equality after you have read the following discussion of Venn diagrams.)

Venn Diagrams

When considering the relationships between several sets, it is instructive and extremely helpful to represent each set by a region in a plane. The region is drawn so that all the elements belonging to a certain set are contained within some closed region of the plane. Diagrams constructed in this manner are called **Venn diagrams.** The definitions discussed in the previous section can be illustrated as in Fig. 1, with shading where appropriate.

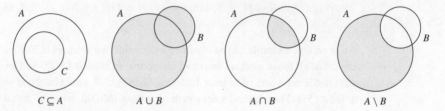

$C \subseteq A$ $A \cup B$ $A \cap B$ $A \setminus B$

Figure 1 Venn diagrams

By using the definitions directly, or by illustrating sets with Venn diagrams, one can derive formulas that are universally valid regardless of which sets are being considered. For example, the formula $A \cap B = B \cap A$ follows immediately from the definition of the intersection between two sets. It is somewhat more difficult to verify directly from the definitions that the following relationship is valid for all sets A, B, and C:

$$A \cap (B \cup C) = (A \cap B) \cup (A \cap C) \tag{$*$}$$

With the use of a Venn diagram, however, we easily see that the sets on the right- and left-hand sides of the equality sign both represent the shaded set in Fig. 2. The equality in $(*)$ is therefore valid.

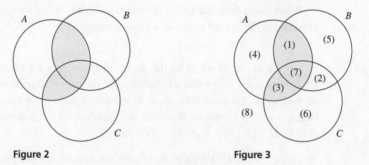

Figure 2   **Figure 3**

It is important for this kind of argument that the three sets A, B, and C in a Venn diagram be drawn to allow for all possible relations between an element and each of the three sets. In other words, as in Fig. 3, the following eight different sets all should be nonempty:

(1) $(A \cap B) \setminus C$ (2) $(B \cap C) \setminus A$ (3) $(C \cap A) \setminus B$ (4) $A \setminus (B \cup C)$

(5) $B \setminus (C \cup A)$ (6) $C \setminus (A \cup B)$ (7) $A \cap B \cap C$ (8) $\complement(A \cup B \cup C)$

Notice, however, that this way of representing sets in the plane becomes unmanageable if four or more sets are involved, because then there would have to be at least $16 (= 2^4)$ regions in any such Venn diagram.

From the definition of intersection and union (or by the use of Venn diagrams), it easily follows that $A \cup (B \cup C) = (A \cup B) \cup C$ and that $A \cap (B \cap C) = (A \cap B) \cap C$. Consequently, it does not matter where the parentheses are placed. In such cases, the parentheses can be dropped and the expressions written as $A \cup B \cup C$ and $A \cap B \cap C$. Note, however, that the parentheses cannot generally be moved in the expression $A \cap (B \cup C)$, because this set is not always equal to $(A \cap B) \cup C$. Prove this fact by considering the case where $A = \{1, 2, 3\}$, $B = \{2, 3\}$, and $C = \{4, 5\}$, or by using a Venn diagram.

Cantor

Georg Cantor, the founder of set theory, is regarded as one of history's great mathematicians. This is not because of his contributions to the development of the useful, but relatively trivial, aspects of set theory outlined above. Rather, Cantor is remembered for his profound study of infinite sets. Below we try to give just a hint of his theory's implications.

A collection of individuals are gathering in a room that has a certain number of chairs. How can we find out if there are exactly as many individuals as chairs? One method would be to count the chairs and count the individuals, and then see if they total the same number. Alternatively, we could ask all the individuals to sit down. If they all have a seat to themselves and there are no chairs unoccupied, then there are exactly as many individuals as chairs. In that case each chair corresponds to an individual and each individual corresponds to a chair.

Generally we say that two sets of elements have the same **cardinality**, if there is a one-to-one correspondence between the sets. This definition is also valid for sets with an infinite number of elements. Cantor demonstrated a surprising consequence of this definition—that the set of natural numbers, $\mathbb{N}$, and the set of rational numbers, $\mathbb{Q}$, have the same cardinality (even though $\mathbb{N}$ is a proper subset of $\mathbb{Q}$!). On the other hand, the set of real numbers, $\mathbb{R}$, and the set $\mathbb{N}$ do not have the same cardinality. Also, $\mathbb{R}$ has the same cardinality as the set of all irrational numbers. Cantor struggled for three years to prove an even more surprising result—that there are as many points in a square as there are points on one of the edges of the square, in the sense that the two sets have the same cardinality. In a letter to Dedekind dated 1877, Cantor wrote of this result: "Je le vois, mais je ne le crois pas." (*"I see it, but I do not believe it."*)

PROBLEMS FOR SECTION 3.6

1. Let $A = \{2, 3, 4\}$, $B = \{2, 5, 6\}$, $C = \{5, 6, 2\}$, and $D = \{6\}$.

   (a) Determine which of the following statements are true: $4 \in C$; $5 \in C$; $A \subseteq B$; $D \subseteq C$; $B = C$; and $A = B$.

   (b) Find $A \cap B$; $A \cup B$; $A \setminus B$; $B \setminus A$; $(A \cup B) \setminus (A \cap B)$; $A \cup B \cup C \cup D$; $A \cap B \cap C$; and $A \cap B \cap C \cap D$.

2. Let F, M, C, B, and T be the sets in Example 2. Describe the following sets: $F \cap B \cap C$, $M \cap F$, and $((M \cap B) \setminus C) \setminus T$.

3. A survey revealed that 50 people liked coffee and 40 liked tea. Both these figures include 35 who liked both coffee and tea. Finally, 10 did not like either coffee or tea. How many people in all responded to the survey?

4. With reference to Example 2, write the following statements in set terminology:

   (a) All biology students are mathematics students.

   (b) There are female biology students in the university choir.

   (c) No tennis player studies biology.

   (d) Those female students who neither play tennis nor belong to the university choir all study biology.

5. Make a complete list of all the different subsets of the set $\{a, b, c\}$. How many are there if the empty set and the set itself are included? Do the same for the set $\{a, b, c, d\}$.

6. Determine which of the following formulas are true. If any formula is false, find a counter-example to demonstrate this, using a Venn diagram if you find it helpful.

   (a) $A \setminus B = B \setminus A$ (b) $A \subseteq B \iff A \cup B = B$

   (c) $A \subseteq B \iff A \cap B = A$ (d) $A \cap B = A \cap C \implies B = C$

   (e) $A \cup B = A \cup C \implies B = C$ (f) $A \setminus (B \setminus C) = (A \setminus B) \setminus C$

7. If A is a set with a finite number of elements, let $n(A)$ denote the number of elements in A. If A and B are arbitrary finite sets, prove the following:

   (a) $n(A \cup B) = n(A) + n(B) - n(A \cap B)$

   (b) $n(A \setminus B) = n(A) - n(A \cap B)$

8. (a) One thousand people took part in a survey to reveal which newspaper, A, B, or C, they had read on a certain day. The responses showed that 420 had read A, 316 had read B, and 160 had read C. These figures include 116 who had read both A and B, 100 who had read A and C, and 30 who had read B and C. Finally, all these figures include 16 who had read all three papers.

   (i) How many had read A, but not B?

   (ii) How many had read C, but neither A nor B?

   (iii) How many had read neither A, B, nor C?

   (b) Denote the complete set of all 1000 persons in the survey by Ω (the universal set). Applying the notation in Problem 7, we have $n(A) = 420$ and $n(A \cap B \cap C) = 16$, for example. Describe the numbers given in (i), (ii), and (iii) of part (a) using the same notation. Why is $n(\Omega \setminus (A \cup B \cup C)) = n(\Omega) - n(A \cup B \cup C)$?

3.7 Mathematical Induction

Proof by induction is an important technique for verifying formulas involving natural numbers. For instance, consider the sum of the first n odd numbers. We observe that

$$1 = 1 \ = 1^2$$
$$1 + 3 = 4 \ = 2^2$$
$$1 + 3 + 5 = 9 \ = 3^2$$
$$1 + 3 + 5 + 7 = 16 = 4^2$$
$$1 + 3 + 5 + 7 + 9 = 25 = 5^2$$

This suggests a general pattern, with the sum of the first n odd numbers equal to n^2:

$$1 + 3 + 5 + \cdots + (2n - 1) = n^2 \qquad (*)$$

To prove that this is generally valid, we can proceed as follows. Suppose that the formula in $(*)$ is correct for a certain natural number $n = k$, so that

$$1 + 3 + 5 + \cdots + (2k - 1) = k^2$$

By adding the next odd number $2k + 1$ to each side, we get

$$1 + 3 + 5 + \cdots + (2k - 1) + (2k + 1) = k^2 + (2k + 1)$$

But the right-hand side is the square of $k + 1$, so we have formula $(*)$ with $n = k + 1$. Hence, we have proved that if the sum of the first k odd numbers is k^2, then the sum of the first $k + 1$ odd numbers equals $(k + 1)^2$. This implication, together with the fact that $(*)$ really is valid for $n = 1$, implies that $(*)$ is generally valid. For we have just shown that if $(*)$ is true for $n = 1$, then it is true for $n = 2$; that if it is true for $n = 2$, then it is true for $n = 3$; ...; that if it is true for $n = k$, then it is true for $n = k + 1$; and so on.

A proof of this type is called a *proof by (mathematical) induction*. It requires showing first that the formula is indeed valid for $n = 1$, and second that, *if* the formula is valid for $n = k$, then it is also valid for $n = k + 1$. It follows by induction that the formula is valid for all natural numbers n.

EXAMPLE 1   Prove by induction that, for all positive integers n,

$$3 + 3^2 + 3^3 + 3^4 + \cdots + 3^n = \tfrac{1}{2}(3^{n+1} - 3) \qquad (**)$$

Solution: For $n = 1$, both sides are 3. Suppose $(**)$ is true for $n = k$. Then

$$3 + 3^2 + 3^3 + 3^4 + \cdots + 3^k + 3^{k+1} = \tfrac{1}{2}(3^{k+1} - 3) + 3^{k+1} = \tfrac{1}{2}(3^{k+2} - 3)$$

which is $(**)$ for $n = k + 1$. Thus, by induction, $(**)$ is true for all n.

On the basis of these examples, the general structure of an induction proof can be explained as follows: We want to prove that a mathematical formula $A(n)$ which depends on n is valid for all natural numbers n. In the two previous examples, the respective statements $A(n)$ were

$$A(n) : 1 + 3 + 5 + \cdots + (2n - 1) = n^2$$
$$A(n) : 3 + 3^2 + 3^3 + 3^4 + \cdots + 3^n = \tfrac{1}{2}(3^{n+1} - 3)$$

The steps required in each proof are as follows: First, verify that $A(1)$ is valid, which means that the formula is correct for $n = 1$. Then prove that for each natural number k, if $A(k)$ is true, it follows that $A(k + 1)$ must be true. Here $A(k)$ is called *the induction hypothesis*, and the step from $A(k)$ to $A(k + 1)$ is called *the induction step* in the proof. When $A(1)$ holds and the induction step is proved for an arbitrary natural number k, then, by induction, statement $A(n)$ is true for all n. The general principle can now be formulated:

THE PRINCIPLE OF MATHEMATICAL INDUCTION

Suppose that $A(n)$ is a statement for all natural numbers n and that

(a) $A(1)$ is true

(b) for each natural number k, if the induction hypothesis $A(k)$ is true, then
    $A(k + 1)$ is true

Then $A(n)$ is true for all natural numbers n.

(1)

The principle of induction seems intuitively evident. If the truth of $A(k)$ for each k implies the truth of $A(k + 1)$, then because $A(1)$ is true, $A(2)$ must be true, which, in turn, means that $A(3)$ is true, and so on. (An analogy: Consider a ladder with an infinite number of steps. Suppose you can climb the first step and suppose, moreover, that after each step, you can always climb the next. Then you are able to climb up to any step.)

The principle of mathematical induction can easily be generalized to the case in which we have a statement $A(n)$ for each integer greater than or equal to an arbitrary integer n_0. Suppose we can prove that $A(n_0)$ is valid and moreover that, for each $k \geq n_0$, if $A(k)$ is true, then $A(k + 1)$ is true. If follows that $A(n)$ is true for all $n \geq n_0$.

PROBLEMS FOR SECTION 3.7

1. Prove statement (3.2.4) by induction:

$$1 + 2 + 3 + \cdots + n = \tfrac{1}{2}n(n + 1) \qquad (*)$$

2. Prove formulas (3.2.5) and (3.2.6) by induction.

(SM) **3.** Prove the following by induction:

$$\frac{1}{1 \cdot 2} + \frac{1}{2 \cdot 3} + \frac{1}{3 \cdot 4} + \cdots + \frac{1}{n(n + 1)} = \frac{n}{n + 1} \qquad (*)$$

(SM) **4.** $1^3 + 2^3 + 3^3 = 36$ is divisible by 9. Prove by induction that the sum $n^3 + (n+1)^3 + (n+2)^3$ of three consecutive cubes is always divisible by 9.

5. Let $A(n)$ be the statement: "Any collection of n professors in one room all have the same income". Consider the following "induction argument": $A(1)$ is obviously true. Suppose $A(k)$ is true for some natural number k. We will then prove that $A(k+1)$ is true. So take any collection of $k + 1$ professors in one room and send one of them outside. The remaining k professors all have the same income by the induction hypothesis. Bring the professor back inside and send another outside instead. Again the remaining professors will have the same income. But then all the $k + 1$ professors will have the same income. By induction, this proves that all n professors have the same income. What is wrong with this argument?

REVIEW PROBLEMS FOR CHAPTER 3

1. Evaluate the following sums:

(a) $\displaystyle\sum_{i=1}^{4} \frac{1}{i(i+2)}$

(b) $\displaystyle\sum_{j=5}^{9}(2j - 8)^2$

(c) $\displaystyle\sum_{k=1}^{5} \frac{k-1}{k+1}$

2. Evaluate the following sums:

(a) $\displaystyle\sum_{n=2}^{5}(n-1)^2(n+2)$

(b) $\displaystyle\sum_{k=1}^{5}\left(\frac{1}{k} - \frac{1}{k+1}\right)$

(c) $\displaystyle\sum_{i=-2}^{3}(i+3)^i$

(d) $\displaystyle\sum_{i=0}^{4}\binom{4}{i}$

3. Express these sums in summation notation:

(a) $3 + 5 + 7 + \cdots + 199 + 201$

(b) $\dfrac{2}{1} + \dfrac{3}{2} + \dfrac{4}{3} + \cdots + \dfrac{97}{96}$

4. Express these sums in summation notation:

(a) $4 \cdot 6 + 5 \cdot 7 + 6 \cdot 8 + \cdots + 38 \cdot 40$

(b) $\dfrac{1}{x} + \dfrac{1}{x^2} + \cdots + \dfrac{1}{x^n}$

(c) $1 + \dfrac{x^2}{3} + \dfrac{x^4}{5} + \dfrac{x^6}{7} + \cdots + \dfrac{x^{32}}{33}$

(d) $1 - \dfrac{1}{2} + \dfrac{1}{3} - \dfrac{1}{4} + \cdots - \dfrac{1}{80} + \dfrac{1}{81}$

5. Which of these equalities are always right and which of them are sometimes wrong?

(a) $\displaystyle\sum_{i=1}^{n} a_i = \sum_{j=3}^{n+2} a_{j-2}$

(b) $\displaystyle\sum_{i=1}^{n}(a_i + b_i)^2 = \sum_{i=1}^{n} a_i^2 + \sum_{i=1}^{n} b_i^2$

(c) $\displaystyle\sum_{k=0}^{n} 5a_{k+1,j} = 5\sum_{k=1}^{n+1} a_{k,j}$

(d) $\displaystyle\sum_{i=1}^{3}\left(\frac{a_i}{b_i}\right) = \frac{\displaystyle\sum_{i=1}^{3} a_i}{\displaystyle\sum_{i=1}^{3} b_i}$

(SM) **6.** Consider the following implications and decide in each case: (i) if the implication is true; (ii) if the converse implication is true. (x and y are real numbers.)

(a) $x = 5$ and $y = -3 \implies x + y = 2$

(b) $x^2 = 16 \implies x = 4$

(c) $(x - 3)^2(y + 2) > 0 \implies y > -2$

(d) $x^3 = 8 \implies x = 2$

7. Let $A = \{1, 3, 4\}$, $B = \{1, 4, 6\}$, $C = \{2, 4, 3\}$, and $D = \{1, 5\}$. Find $A \cap B$; $A \cup B$; $A \setminus B$; $B \setminus A$; $(A \cup B) \setminus (A \cap B)$; $A \cup B \cup C \cup D$; $A \cap B \cap C$; and $A \cap B \cap C \cap D$.

8. Let the universal set be $\Omega = \{1, 2, 3, 4, \ldots, 11\}$ and define $A = \{1, 4, 6\}$ and $B = \{2, 11\}$. Find $A \cap B$; $A \cup B$; $\Omega \setminus B$; $\complement A = \Omega \setminus A$.

(SM) 9. A liberal arts college has 1000 students. The numbers studying various languages are: English (E) 780; French (F) 220; and Spanish (S) 52. These figures include 110 who study English and French, 32 who study English and Spanish, 15 who study French and Spanish. Finally, all these figures include 10 students taking all three languages.

  (a) How many study English and French, but not Spanish?

  (b) How many study English, but not French?

  (c) How many study no languages?

(SM) 10. Find the sums:

  (a) $R = 3 + 5 + 7 + \cdots + 197 + 199 + 201$

  (b) $S = 1001 + 2002 + 3003 + \cdots + 8008 + 9009 + 10010$

HARDER PROBLEM

(SM) 11. (a) Prove that $(1 + x)^2 \geq 1 + 2x$ for all x.

  (b) Prove that $(1 + x)^3 \geq 1 + 3x$ for all $x \geq -3$.

  (c) Prove by induction that for all natural numbers n and all $x \geq -1$,

$$(1 + x)^n \geq 1 + nx \qquad \textbf{(Bernoulli's inequality)}$$

4

FUNCTIONS OF ONE VARIABLE

—mathematics is not so much a subject
as a way of studying any subject,
not so much a science as a way of life.
—G. Temple (1981)

Functions are important in practically every area of pure and applied mathematics, including mathematics applied to economics. The language of economic analysis is full of terms like demand and supply functions, cost functions, production functions, consumption functions, etc. In this chapter we present a discussion of functions of one real variable, illustrated by some very important economic examples.

4.1 Introduction

One variable is a function of another if the first variable *depends* upon the second. For instance, the area of a circle is a function of its radius. If the radius r is given, then the area A is determined. In fact $A = \pi r^2$, where π is the numerical constant $3.14159\ldots$.

One does not need a mathematical formula to convey the idea that one variable is a function of another: A table can also show the relationship. For instance, Table 1 shows the development of annual total personal consumption expenditure, measured in current euros, without allowing for inflation, in the European Union for the period 2003–2009.

Table 1 Personal consumption expenditure in the EU, 2003–2009 (in billions of euros)

Year	2003	2004	2005	2006	2007	2008	2009
Personal consumption	5 912.0	6 181.8	6 461.7	6 773.1	7 099.8	7 184.3	6 886.0

This table defines consumption expenditure as a function of the calendar year.

In ordinary conversation we sometimes use the word "function" in a similar way. For example, we might say that the infant mortality rate of a country is a function of the quality of its health care, or that a country's national product is a function of the level of investment.

The dependence between two real variables can also be illustrated by means of a graph. In Fig. 1 we have drawn a curve that allegedly played an important role some years ago in the discussion of "supply side economics". It shows the presumed relationship between a country's income tax rate and its total income tax revenue. Obviously, if the tax rate is 0%, then tax revenue is 0. However, if the tax rate is 100%, then tax revenue will also be (about) 0, since nobody is willing to work if their entire income is going to be confiscated. This curve, which has generated considerable controversy, is supposed to have been drawn on the back of a restaurant napkin by an American economist, Arthur Laffer, who then later popularized its message with the public. (Actually, many economists previously had the same idea.)

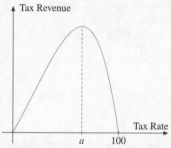

Figure 1 The "Laffer curve", which relates tax revenue to tax rates

In some instances a graph is preferable to a formula. A case in point is an electrocardiogram (ECG) showing the heartbeat pattern of a patient. Here the doctor studies the pattern of repetitions directly from the graphs; the patient might die before the doctor could understand a formula approximating the ECG picture.

All of the relationships discussed above have one characteristic in common: A definite rule relates each value of one variable to a definite value of another variable. In the ECG example the function is the rule showing electrical activity as a function of time.

In all of our examples it is implicitly assumed that the variables are subject to certain constraints. For instance, in Table 1 only the years between 1998 and 2004 are relevant.

4.2 Basic Definitions

The examples in the preceding section lead to the following general definition, with D a set of real numbers:

> A (real-valued) **function** of a real variable x with **domain** D is a rule that assigns a unique real number to each real number x in D. As x varies over the whole domain, the set of all possible resulting values $f(x)$ is called the **range** of f.

The word "rule" is used in a very broad sense. *Every* rule with the properties described is called a function, whether that rule is given by a formula, described in words, defined by a table, illustrated by a curve, or expressed by any other means.

Functions are given letter names, such as f, g, F, or φ. If f is a function and x is a number in its domain D, then $f(x)$ denotes the number that the function f assigns to x. The symbol $f(x)$ is pronounced "f of x", or often just "f x". It is important to note the difference between f, which is a symbol for the function (the rule), and $f(x)$, which denotes the value of f at x.

If f is a function, we sometimes let y denote the value of f at x, so

$$y = f(x)$$

Then we call x the **independent variable**, or the **argument** of f, whereas y is called the **dependent variable**, because the value y (in general) depends on the value of x. The domain of the function f is then the set of all possible values of the independent variable, whereas the range is the set of corresponding values of the dependent variable. In economics, x is often called the *exogenous* variable, which is supposed to be fixed *outside* the economic model, whereas for each given x the equation $y = f(x)$ serves to determine the *endogenous* variable y *inside* the economic model.

A function is often defined by a formula such as $y = 8x^2 + 3x + 2$. The function is then the rule $x \mapsto 8x^2 + 3x + 2$ that assigns the number $8x^2 + 3x + 2$ to each value of x.

Functional Notation

To become familiar with the relevant notation, it helps to look at some examples of functions that are defined by formulas.

EXAMPLE 1   A function is defined for all numbers by the following rule:

Assign to any number its third power

This function will assign $0^3 = 0$ to 0, $3^3 = 27$ to 3, $(-2)^3 = (-2)(-2)(-2) = -8$ to -2, and $(1/4)^3 = 1/64$ to 1/4. In general, it assigns the number x^3 to the number x. If we denote this third power function by f, then

$$f(x) = x^3$$

So $f(0) = 0^3 = 0$, $f(3) = 3^3 = 27$, $f(-2) = (-2)^3 = -8$, $f(1/4) = (1/4)^3 = 1/64$.

Substituting a for x in the formula for f gives $f(a) = a^3$, whereas

$$f(a+1) = (a+1)^3 = (a+1)(a+1)(a+1) = a^3 + 3a^2 + 3a + 1$$

NOTE 1   A common error is to presume that $f(a) = a^3$ implies $f(a+1) = a^3 + 1$. The error can be illustrated by considering a simple interpretation of f. If a is the edge of a cube measured in metres, then $f(a) = a^3$ is the volume of the cube measured in cubic metres (or m^3). Suppose that each edge of the cube expands by 1 m. Then the volume of the new cube is $f(a+1) = (a+1)^3$ m^3. The number $a^3 + 1$ can be interpreted as the number obtained when the volume of a cube with edge a is increased by 1 m^3. In fact, $f(a+1) = (a+1)^3$ is quite a bit more than $a^3 + 1$, as illustrated in Figs. 1 and 2.

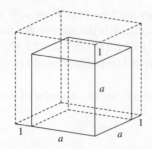

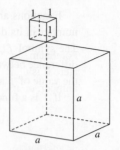

Figure 1 Volume $f(a+1) = (a+1)^3$ **Figure 2** Volume $a^3 + 1$

EXAMPLE 2   The total dollar cost of producing x units of a product is given by

$$C(x) = 100x\sqrt{x} + 500$$

for each nonnegative integer x. Find the cost of producing 16 units. Suppose the firm produces a units; find the *increase* in the cost from producing one additional unit.

Solution: The cost of producing 16 units is found by substituting 16 for x in the formula for $C(x)$:

$$C(16) = 100 \cdot 16\sqrt{16} + 500 = 100 \cdot 16 \cdot 4 + 500 = 6900$$

The cost of producing a units is $C(a) = 100a\sqrt{a} + 500$, and the cost of producing $a + 1$ units is $C(a + 1)$. Thus the increase in cost is

$$C(a + 1) - C(a) = 100(a + 1)\sqrt{a + 1} + 500 - 100a\sqrt{a} - 500$$

$$= 100\big[(a + 1)\sqrt{a + 1} - a\sqrt{a}\,\big]$$

In economic theory, we often study functions that depend on a number of parameters, as well as the independent variable. An obvious generalization of Example 2 follows.

EXAMPLE 3   Suppose that the cost of producing x units of a commodity is

$$C(x) = Ax\sqrt{x} + B \qquad \text{(A and B are constants)}$$

Find the cost of producing 0, 10, and $x + h$ units.

Solution: The cost of producing 0 units is $C(0) = A \cdot 0 \cdot \sqrt{0} + B = 0 + B = B$. (Parameter B simply represents fixed costs. These are the costs that must be paid whether or not anything is actually produced, such as a taxi driver's annual licence fee.) Similarly, $C(10) = A10\sqrt{10} + B$. Finally, substituting $x + h$ for x in the given formula gives

$$C(x + h) = A(x + h)\sqrt{x + h} + B$$

So far we have used x to denote the independent variable, but we could just as well have used almost any other symbol. For example, all of the following formulas define exactly the same function (and hence we can set $f = g = \varphi$):

$$1 \mapsto 1^4 = 1, \qquad k \mapsto k^4, \quad \text{and} \quad 1/y \mapsto (1/y)^4$$

or alternatively

$$f(x) = x^4, \qquad g(t) = t^4, \qquad \varphi(\xi) = \xi^4$$

For that matter, we could also express this function as $x \mapsto x^4$, or alternatively as $f(\cdot) = (\cdot)^4$. Here it is understood that the dot between the parentheses can be replaced by an arbitrary number, or an arbitrary letter, or even another function (like $1/y$). Thus,

$$1 \mapsto 1^4 = 1, \qquad k \mapsto k^4, \qquad \text{and} \qquad 1/y \mapsto (1/y)^4$$

or alternatively

$$f(1) = 1^4 = 1, \qquad f(k) = k^4, \qquad \text{and} \qquad f(1/y) = (1/y)^4$$

Domain and Range

The definition of a function is not really complete unless its domain is either obvious or specified explicitly. The natural domain of the function f defined by $f(x) = x^3$ is the set of all real numbers. In Example 2, where $C(x) = 100x\sqrt{x} + 500$ denotes the cost of producing x units of a product, the domain was specified as the set of nonnegative integers. Actually, a more natural domain is the set of numbers $0, 1, 2, \ldots, x_0$, where x_0 is the maximum number of items the firm can produce. For a producer like an iron mine, however, where output x is a continuous variable, the natural domain is the closed interval $[0, x_0]$.

We shall adopt the convention that *if a function is defined using an algebraic formula, the domain consists of all values of the independent variable for which the formula gives a unique value (unless another domain is explicitly mentioned).*

EXAMPLE 4   Find the domains of   (a) $f(x) = \dfrac{1}{x+3}$ and   (b) $g(x) = \sqrt{2x+4}$.

Solution:
(a) For $x = -3$, the formula reduces to the meaningless expression "$1/0$". For all other values of x, the formula makes $f(x)$ a well-defined number. Thus, the domain consists of all numbers $x \neq -3$.
(b) The expression $\sqrt{2x+4}$ is uniquely defined for all x such that $2x + 4$ is nonnegative. Solving the inequality $2x + 4 \geq 0$ for x gives $x \geq -2$. The domain of g is therefore the interval $[-2, \infty)$.

Let f be a function with domain D. The set of all values $f(x)$ that the function assumes is called the *range* of f. Often, we denote the domain of f by D_f, and the range by R_f. These concepts are illustrated in Fig. 3, using the idea of the graph of a function. (Graphs are discussed in the next section.)

Alternatively, we can think of any function f as an engine operating so that if x in the domain is an input, the output is $f(x)$. (See Fig. 4.) The range of f is then all the numbers we get as output using all numbers in the domain as inputs. If we try to use as an input a number not in the domain, the engine does not work, and there is no output.

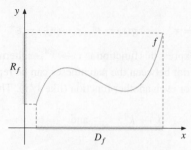

Figure 3 The domain and range of f

Figure 4 Function engine

EXAMPLE 5   Show that the number 4 belongs to the range of the function defined by $g(x) = \sqrt{2x + 4}$. Find the entire range of g. (The result of Example 4 shows that g has domain $[-2, \infty)$.)

Solution: To show that 4 is in the range of g, we must find a number x such that $g(x) = 4$. That is, we must solve the equation $\sqrt{2x + 4} = 4$ for x. By squaring both sides of the equation, we get $2x + 4 = 4^2 = 16$, that is, $x = 6$. Because $g(6) = 4$, the number 4 does belong to the range R_g.

In order to determine the whole range of g, we must answer the question: As x runs through the whole of the interval $[-2, \infty)$, what are all the possible values of $\sqrt{2x + 4}$? For $x = -2$, one has $\sqrt{2x + 4} = 0$, and $\sqrt{2x + 4}$ can never be negative. We claim that whatever number $y_0 \geq 0$ is chosen, there exists a number x_0 such that $\sqrt{2x_0 + 4} = y_0$. Indeed, squaring each side of this last equation gives $2x_0 + 4 = y_0^2$. Hence, $2x_0 = y_0^2 - 4$, which implies that $x_0 = \frac{1}{2}(y_0^2 - 4)$. Because $y_0^2 \geq 0$, we have $x_0 = \frac{1}{2}(y_0^2 - 4) \geq \frac{1}{2}(-4) = -2$. Hence, for every number $y_0 \geq 0$, we have found a number $x_0 \geq -2$ such that $g(x_0) = y_0$. The range of g is, therefore, $[0, \infty)$.

Even if a function is completely specified by a formula, including a specific domain, it is not always easy to find the range of the function. For example, without using the methods of differential calculus, it is hard to find R_f exactly when $f(x) = 3x^3 - 2x^2 - 12x - 3$ and $D_f = [-2, 3]$.

A function f is called **increasing** if $x_1 < x_2$ implies $f(x_1) \leq f(x_2)$, and **strictly increasing** if $x_1 < x_2$ implies $f(x_1) < f(x_2)$. *Decreasing* and *strictly decreasing* functions are defined in the obvious way. (See Section 6.3.) The function g in Example 5 is strictly increasing in $[-2, \infty)$.

Calculators (including calculator programs on personal computers or smart phones) often have many special functions built into them. For example, most of them have the $\boxed{\sqrt{\ }}$ key, which when given a number x, returns the square root of the number, $\sqrt{x}$. If we enter a nonnegative number such as 25, and press the square root key, then the number 5 appears. If we enter -3, then "Error", or "Not a number" is shown, which is the way the calculator tells us that $\sqrt{-3}$ is not defined (within the real number system).

PROBLEMS FOR SECTION 4.2

SM 1. (a) Let $f(x) = x^2 + 1$. Compute $f(0)$, $f(-1)$, $f(1/2)$, and $f(\sqrt{2})$.

(b) For what values of x is it true that

(i) $f(x) = f(-x)$?   (ii) $f(x+1) = f(x) + f(1)$?   (iii) $f(2x) = 2f(x)$?

2. Suppose $F(x) = 10$, for all x. Find $F(0)$, $F(-3)$, and $F(a+h) - F(a)$.

3. Let $f(t) = a^2 - (t-a)^2$, where a is a constant.

(a) Compute $f(0)$, $f(a)$, $f(-a)$, and $f(2a)$.   (b) Compute $3f(a) + f(-2a)$.

4. (a) For $f(x) = \dfrac{x}{1+x^2}$, compute $f(-1/10)$, $f(0)$, $f(1/\sqrt{2})$, $f(\sqrt{\pi})$, and $f(2)$.

(b) Show that $f(-x) = -f(x)$ for all x, and that $f(1/x) = f(x)$ for $x \neq 0$.

5. Let $F(t) = \sqrt{t^2 - 2t + 4}$. Compute $F(0)$, $F(-3)$, and $F(t+1)$.

6. The cost of producing x units of a commodity is given by $C(x) = 1000 + 300x + x^2$.

(a) Compute $C(0)$, $C(100)$, and $C(101) - C(100)$.

(b) Compute $C(x+1) - C(x)$, and explain in words the meaning of the difference.

7. (a) H. Schultz has estimated the demand for cotton in the US for the period 1915–1919 to be $D(P) = 6.4 - 0.3P$ (with appropriate units for the price P and the quantity $D(P)$). Find the demand in each case if the price is 8, 10, and 10.22.

(b) If the demand is 3.13, what is the price?

8. (a) If $f(x) = 100x^2$, show that for all t, $f(tx) = t^2 f(x)$.

(b) If $P(x) = x^{1/2}$, show that for all $t \geq 0$, $P(tx) = t^{1/2} P(x)$.

9. (a) The cost of removing $p\%$ of the impurities in a lake is given by $b(p) = \dfrac{10p}{105 - p}$. Find $b(0)$, $b(50)$, and $b(100)$.

(b) What does $b(50+h) - b(50)$ mean (where $h \geq 0$)?

10. Only for very special "additive" functions is it true that $f(a+b) = f(a) + f(b)$ for all a and b. Determine whether $f(2+1) = f(2) + f(1)$ for the following:

(a) $f(x) = 2x^2$ (b) $f(x) = -3x$ (c) $f(x) = \sqrt{x}$

11. (a) If $f(x) = Ax$, show that $f(a+b) = f(a) + f(b)$ for all a and b.

(b) If $f(x) = 10^x$, show that $f(a+b) = f(a) \cdot f(b)$ for all natural numbers a and b.

12. A student claims that $(x+1)^2 = x^2 + 1$. Can you use a geometric argument to show that this is wrong?

(SM) 13. Find the domains of the functions defined by the following formulas:

(a) $y = \sqrt{5 - x}$ (b) $y = \dfrac{2x - 1}{x^2 - x}$ (c) $y = \sqrt{\dfrac{x - 1}{(x - 2)(x + 3)}}$

14. (a) Find the domain of the function f defined by the formula $f(x) = \dfrac{3x + 6}{x - 2}$.

   (b) Show that the number 5 is in the range of f by finding a number x such that $(3x + 6)/(x - 2) = 5$.

   (c) Show that the number 3 is not in the range of f.

15. Find the domain and the range of $g(x) = 1 - \sqrt{x + 2}$.

4.3 Graphs of Functions

Recall that a **rectangular** (or a **Cartesian**) coordinate system is obtained by first drawing two perpendicular lines, called coordinate axes. The two axes are respectively the x-*axis* (or the *horizontal axis*) and the y-*axis* (or the *vertical axis*). The intersection point O is called the *origin*. We measure the real numbers along each of these lines, as shown in Fig. 1. The unit distance on the x-axis is not necessarily the same as on the y-axis, although this is the case in Fig. 1.

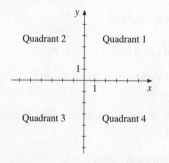

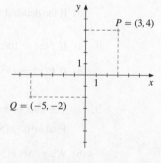

Figure 1 A coordinate system   **Figure 2** Points $(3, 4)$ and $(-5, -2)$

The rectangular coordinate system in Fig. 1 is also called the xy-**plane**. The coordinate axes separate the plane into four quadrants, which traditionally are numbered as in Fig. 1. Any point P in the plane can be represented by a unique pair (a, b) of real numbers. These can be found by drawing dashed lines, like those in Figure 2, which are perpendicular to the two axes. The point represented by (a, b) lies at the intersection of the vertical straight line $x = a$ with the horizontal straight line $y = b$.

Conversely, any pair of real numbers represents a unique point in the plane. For example, in Fig. 2, if the ordered pair $(3, 4)$ is given, the corresponding point P lies at the intersection of $x = 3$ with $y = 4$. Thus, P lies 3 units to the right of the y-axis and 4 units above the x-axis. We call $(3, 4)$ the **coordinates** of P. Similarly, Q lies 5 units to the left of the y-axis and 2 units below the x-axis, so the coordinates of Q are $(-5, -2)$.

Note that we call (a, b) an **ordered pair**, because the order of the two numbers in the pair is important. For instance, $(3, 4)$ and $(4, 3)$ represent two different points.

As you surely know, each function of one variable can be represented by a graph in such a rectangular coordinate system. Such a representation helps us visualize the function. This is because the shape of the graph reflects the properties of the function.

The **graph** of a function f is simply the set of all points $(x, f(x))$, where x belongs to the domain of f.

EXAMPLE 1   Consider the function $f(x) = x^2 - 4x + 3$. The values of $f(x)$ for some special choices of x are given in the following table.

Table 1 Values of $f(x) = x^2 - 4x + 3$

x	0	1	2	3	4
$f(x) = x^2 - 4x + 3$	3	0	−1	0	3

Plot the points $(0, 3)$, $(1, 0)$, $(2, -1)$, $(3, 0)$, and $(4, 3)$ obtained from the table in an xy-plane, and draw a smooth curve through these points.

Solution: This is done in Fig. 3. The graph is called a parabola. (See Section 4.6.)

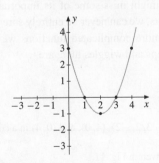

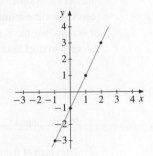

Figure 3 The graph of $f(x) = x^2 - 4x + 3$

Figure 4 The graph of $g(x) = 2x - 1$

EXAMPLE 2   Find some of the points on the graph of $g(x) = 2x - 1$, and sketch it.

Solution: One has $g(-1) = 2 \cdot (-1) - 1 = -3$, $g(0) = 2 \cdot 0 - 1 = -1$, and $g(1) = 2 \cdot 1 - 1 = 1$. Moreover, $g(2) = 3$. There are infinitely many points on the graph, so we cannot write them all down. In Fig. 4 the four points $(-1, -3)$, $(0, -1)$, $(1, 1)$, and $(2, 3)$ are marked off, and they seem to lie on a straight line. That line is the graph.

Some Important Graphs

Some special functions occur so often in applications that you should learn to recognize their graphs. You should in each case make a table of function values to confirm the form of these graphs.

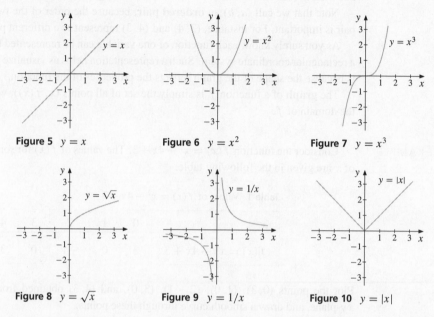

Figure 5 $y = x$

Figure 6 $y = x^2$

Figure 7 $y = x^3$

Figure 8 $y = \sqrt{x}$

Figure 9 $y = 1/x$

Figure 10 $y = |x|$

NOTE 1 When we try to plot the graph of a function, we must try to include a sufficient number of points, otherwise we might miss some of its important features. Actually, by merely plotting a finite set of points, we can never be entirely sure that there are no wiggles or bumps we have missed. For more complicated functions we have to use differential calculus to decide how many bumps and wiggles there are.

PROBLEMS FOR SECTION 4.3

1. Plot the points $(2, 3)$, $(-3, 2)$, $(-3/2, -2)$, $(4, 0)$, and $(0, 4)$ in a coordinate system.

2. The graph of the function f is given in Fig. 11.
   (a) Find $f(-5)$, $f(-3)$, $f(-2)$, $f(0)$, $f(3)$, and $f(4)$ by examining the graph.
   (b) Determine the domain and the range of f.

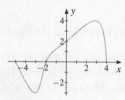

Figure 11

In problems 3–6 fill in the tables and draw the graphs of the functions.

3.

x	0	1	2	3	4
$g(x) = -2x + 5$					

4.

x	−2	−1	0	1	2	3	4
$h(x) = x^2 - 2x - 3$							

5.

x	−2	−1	0	1	2
$F(x) = 3^x$					

6.

x	−2	−1	0	1	2	3
$G(x) = 1 - 2^{-x}$						

4.4 Linear Functions

Linear functions occur very often in economics. They are defined as follows.

$$y = ax + b \qquad (a \text{ and } b \text{ are constants})$$

The graph of the equation is a straight line. If we let f denote the function that assigns y to x, then $f(x) = ax + b$, and f is called a **linear** function.

Take an arbitrary value of x. Then

$$f(x + 1) - f(x) = a(x + 1) + b - ax - b = a$$

This shows that a measures the change in the value of the function when x increases by 1 unit. For this reason, the number a is the **slope** of the line (or the function).

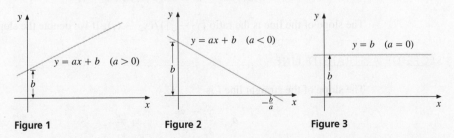

Figure 1   Figure 2   Figure 3

If the slope a is positive, the line slants upward to the right, and the larger the value of a, the steeper is the line. On the other hand, if a is negative, then the line slants downward to the right, and the absolute value of a measures the steepness of the line. For example, when $a = -3$, the steepness is 3. In the special case when $a = 0$, the steepness is zero, because the line is horizontal. Algebraically, we have $y = ax + b = b$ for all x. The three different cases are illustrated in Figs. 1 to 3. If $x = 0$, then $y = ax + b = b$, and b is called the **y-intercept** (or often just the intercept).

EXAMPLE 1   Find and interpret the slopes of the following straight lines.

(a) $C = 55.73x + 182\,100\,000$ Estimated cost function for the US Steel Corp. (1917–1938). (C is the total cost in dollars per year, and x is the production of steel in tons per year).

(b) $q = -0.15p + 0.14$ Estimated annual demand function for rice in India for the period 1949–1964. (p is price in Indian rupees, and q is consumption per person.)

Solution:

(a) The slope is 55.73, which means that if production increases by 1 ton, then the cost *increases* by $55.73.

(b) The slope is -0.15, which tells us that if the price increases by one Indian rupee, then the quantity demanded *decreases* by 0.15 units.

How do we compute the slope of a straight line in the plane? Here is an easy way. Pick two different points on the line $P = (x_1, y_1)$ and $Q = (x_2, y_2)$, as shown in Fig. 4.

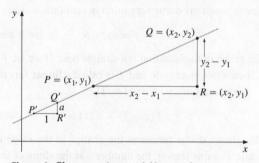

Figure 4   Slope $a = (y_2 - y_1)/(x_2 - x_1)$.

The slope of the line is the ratio $(y_2 - y_1)/(x_2 - x_1)$. If we denote the slope by a, then:

SLOPE OF A STRAIGHT LINE

The **slope** of the straight line l is

$$a = \frac{y_2 - y_1}{x_2 - x_1}, \qquad x_1 \neq x_2$$

where (x_1, y_1) and (x_2, y_2) are any two distinct points on l.

Multiplying both the numerator and the denominator of $(y_2 - y_1)/(x_2 - x_1)$ by -1, we obtain $(y_1 - y_2)/(x_1 - x_2)$. This shows that it does not make any difference which point is P and which is Q. Moreover, the properties of similar triangles imply that the ratios $Q'R'/P'R'$ and QR/PR in Fig. 4 must be equal. For this reason, the number $a = (y_2 - y_1)/(x_2 - x_1)$ is equal to the change in the value of y when x increases by 1 unit.

EXAMPLE 2   Determine the slopes of the three straight lines l, m, and n.

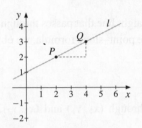

Figure 5 The line l

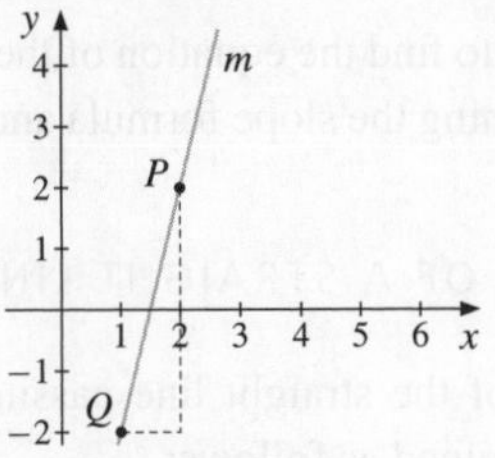

Figure 6 The line m

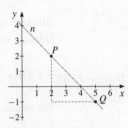

Figure 7 The line n

Solution: The lines l, m, and n all pass through $P = (2, 2)$. In Fig. 5 the point Q is $(4, 3)$, whereas in Fig. 6 it is $(1, -2)$, and in Fig. 7 it is $(5, -1)$. Therefore, the respective slopes of the lines l, m, and n are

$$a_l = \frac{3 - 2}{4 - 2} = \frac{1}{2}, \qquad a_m = \frac{-2 - 2}{1 - 2} = 4, \qquad a_n = \frac{-1 - 2}{5 - 2} = -1$$

The Point–Slope and Point–Point Formulas

Let us find the equation of a straight line l passing through the point $P = (x_1, y_1)$ with slope a. If (x, y) is any other point on the line, the slope a is given by the formula:

$$\frac{y - y_1}{x - x_1} = a$$

Multiplying each side by $x - x_1$, we obtain $y - y_1 = a(x - x_1)$. Hence,

POINT—SLOPE FORMULA OF A STRAIGHT LINE

The equation of the straight line passing through (x_1, y_1) with slope a is

$$y - y_1 = a(x - x_1)$$

Note that when using this formula, x_1 and y_1 are fixed numbers giving the coordinates of the fixed point. On the other hand, x and y are variables denoting the coordinates of an arbitrary point on the line.

EXAMPLE 3   Find the equation of the line through $(-2, 3)$ with slope -4. Then find the y-intercept and the point at which this line intersects the x-axis (the x-intercept).

Solution: The point–slope formula with $(x_1, y_1) = (-2, 3)$ and $a = -4$ gives

$$y - 3 = (-4)(x - (-2)) \quad \text{or} \quad y - 3 = -4(x + 2) \quad \text{or} \quad 4x + y = -5$$

The y-intercept has $x = 0$, so $y = -5$. The line intersects the x-axis at the point where $y = 0$, that is, where $4x = -5$, so $x = -5/4$. The point of intersection with the x-axis is therefore $(-5/4, 0)$. (Draw a graph.)

Often we need to find the equation of the straight line that passes through two given distinct points. Combining the slope formula and the point–slope formula, we obtain the following:

POINT—POINT FORMULA OF A STRAIGHT LINE

The equation of the straight line passing through (x_1, y_1) and (x_2, y_2), where $x_1 \neq x_2$, is obtained as follows:

1. Compute the slope of the line, $a = \dfrac{y_2 - y_1}{x_2 - x_1}$

2. Substitute the expression for a into the point–slope formula: $y - y_1 = a(x - x_1)$. The result is

$$y - y_1 = \frac{y_2 - y_1}{x_2 - x_1}(x - x_1)$$

EXAMPLE 4   Find the equation of the line passing through $(-1, 3)$ and $(5, -2)$.

Solution: Let $(x_1, y_1) = (-1, 3)$ and $(x_2, y_2) = (5, -2)$. Then the point–point formula gives

$$y - 3 = \frac{-2 - 3}{5 - (-1)}\big[x - (-1)\big] \quad \text{or} \quad y - 3 = -\frac{5}{6}(x + 1) \quad \text{or} \quad 5x + 6y = 13$$

Graphical Solutions of Linear Equations

Section 2.4 dealt with algebraic methods for solving a system of two linear equations in two unknowns. The equations are linear, so their graphs are straight lines. The coordinates of any point on a line satisfy the equation of that line. Thus, the coordinates of any point of intersection of these two lines will satisfy both equations. This means that any point where these lines intersect will satisfy the equation system.

EXAMPLE 5   Solve each of the following three pairs of equations graphically:

(a) $\begin{aligned} x + y &= 5 \\ x - y &= -1 \end{aligned}$ (b) $\begin{aligned} 3x + y &= -7 \\ x - 4y &= 2 \end{aligned}$ (c) $\begin{aligned} 3x + 4y &= 2 \\ 6x + 8y &= 24 \end{aligned}$

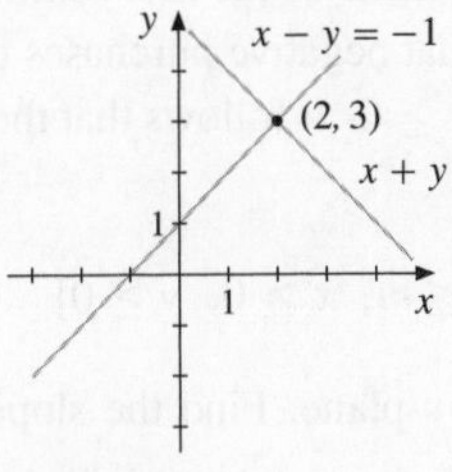

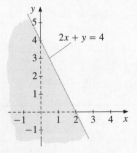

Figure 8 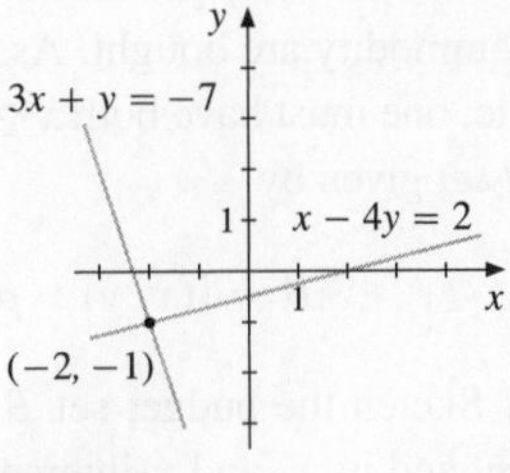   Figure 9 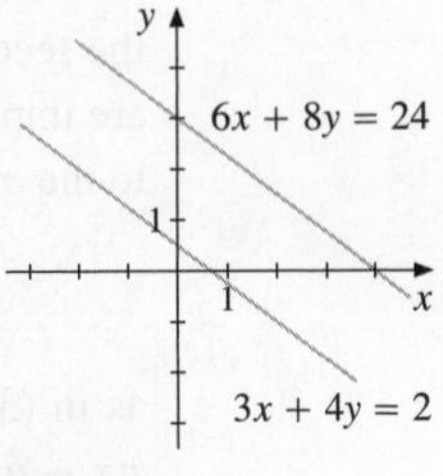   Figure 10

(a) Figure 8 shows the graphs of the straight lines $x + y = 5$ and $x - y = -1$. There is only one point of intersection, which is $(2, 3)$. The solution of the system is, therefore, $x = 2$, $y = 3$.

(b) Figure 9 shows the graphs of the straight lines $3x + y = -7$ and $x - 4y = 2$. There is only one point of intersection, which is $(-2, -1)$. The solution of the system is, therefore, $x = -2$, $y = -1$.

(c) Figure 10 shows the graphs of the straight lines $3x + 4y = 2$ and $6x + 8y = 24$. These lines are parallel and have no point of intersection. The system has no solutions.

Linear Inequalities

This section concludes by discussing how to represent linear inequalities geometrically. We present two examples.

EXAMPLE 6   Sketch in the xy-plane the set of all pairs of numbers (x, y) that satisfy the inequality $2x + y \leq 4$. (Using set notation, this set is $\{(x, y) : 2x + y \leq 4\}$.)

Solution: The inequality can be written as $y \leq -2x + 4$. The set of points (x, y) that satisfy the equation $y = -2x + 4$ is a straight line. Therefore, the set of points (x, y) that satisfy the inequality $y \leq -2x + 4$ must have y-values below those of points on the line $y = -2x + 4$. So it must consist of all points that lie on or below this line. See Fig. 11.

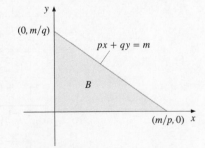

Figure 11 $\{(x, y) : 2x + y \leq 4\}$

Figure 12 Budget set: $px + qy \leq m$, $x \geq 0$, and $y \geq 0$

EXAMPLE 7   A person has \$$m$ to spend on the purchase of two commodities. The prices of the two commodities are \$$p$ and \$$q$ per unit. Suppose x units of the first commodity and y units of the second commodity are bought. Assuming that negative purchases of either commodity are impossible, one must have both $x \geq 0$ and $y \geq 0$. It follows that the person is restricted to the *budget set* given by

$$B = \{(x, y) : \; px + qy \leq m, \; x \geq 0, \; y \geq 0\}$$

as in (3.6.1). Sketch the budget set B in the xy-plane. Find the slope of the budget line $px + qy = m$, and its x- and y-intercepts.

Solution: The set of points (x, y) that satisfy $x \geq 0$ and $y \geq 0$ is the first (nonnegative) quadrant. If we impose the additional requirement that $px + qy \leq m$, we obtain the triangular domain B shown in Fig. 12.

If $px + qy = m$, then $qy = -px + m$ and so $y = (-p/q)x + m/q$. This shows that the slope is $-p/q$. The budget line intersects the x-axis when $y = 0$. Then $px = m$, so $x = m/p$. The budget line intersects the y-axis when $x = 0$. Then $qy = m$, so $y = m/q$. So the two points of intersection are $(m/p, 0)$ and $(0, m/q)$, as shown in Fig. 12.

PROBLEMS FOR SECTION 4.4

1. Find the slopes of the lines passing through the following pairs of points:

    (a) $(2, 3)$ and $(5, 8)$ (b) $(-1, -3)$ and $(2, -5)$ (c) $\left(\frac{1}{2}, \frac{3}{2}\right)$ and $\left(\frac{1}{3}, -\frac{1}{5}\right)$

2. Draw graphs for the following straight lines:

    (a) $3x + 4y = 12$ (b) $\dfrac{x}{10} - \dfrac{y}{5} = 1$ (c) $x = 3$

3. Suppose demand D for a good is a linear function of its price per unit, P. When price is \$10, demand is 200 units, and when price is \$15, demand is 150 units. Find the demand function.

4. Find the slopes of the five lines L_1 to L_5 shown in the figure, and give equations describing them.

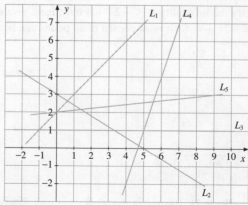

Figure 13

5. Decide which of the following relationships are linear:

(a) $5y + 2x = 2$ (b) $P = 10(1 - 0.3t)$ (c) $C = (0.5x + 2)(x - 3)$

(d) $p_1 x_1 + p_2 x_2 = R$ (p_1, p_2, and R constants)

6. A printing company quotes the price of $1400 for producing 100 copies of a report, and $3000 for 500 copies. Assuming a linear relation, what would be the price of printing 300 copies?

7. Determine the equations for the following straight lines:

(a) L_1 passes through $(1, 3)$ and has a slope of 2.

(b) L_2 passes through $(-2, 2)$ and $(3, 3)$.

(c) L_3 passes through the origin and has a slope of $-1/2$.

(d) L_4 passes through $(a, 0)$ and $(0, b)$ (suppose $a \neq 0$).

8. Sketch in the xy-plane the set of all pairs of numbers (x, y) that satisfy the following inequalities:

(a) $2x + 4y \geq 5$ (b) $x - 3y + 2 \leq 0$ (c) $100x + 200y \leq 300$

9. Solve the following three systems of equations graphically:

(a) $\begin{aligned} x - y &= 5 \\ x + y &= 1 \end{aligned}$ (b) $\begin{aligned} x + y &= 2 \\ x - 2y &= 2 \\ x - y &= 2 \end{aligned}$ (c) $\begin{aligned} 3x + 4y &= 1 \\ 6x + 8y &= 6 \end{aligned}$

(SM) **10.** Sketch in the xy-plane the set of all pairs of numbers (x, y) that satisfy all the following three inequalities:

$$3x + 4y \leq 12, \qquad x - y \leq 1, \qquad \text{and} \qquad 3x + y \geq 3$$

4.5 Linear Models

Linear relations occur frequently in mathematical models. The relationship between the Celsius and Fahrenheit temperature scales, $F = \frac{9}{5}C + 32$ (see Example 1.6.4), is an example of an exact (by definition) linear relation between two variables. Most of the linear models in economics are approximations to more complicated models. Two typical relations are those shown in Example 4.4.1. Statistical methods have been devised to construct linear functions that approximate the actual data as closely as possible. Let us consider a very naive attempt to construct a linear model based on some population data.

EXAMPLE 1   A United Nations report estimated that the European population was 641 million in 1960, and 705 million in 1970. Use these estimates to construct a linear function of t that approximates the population in Europe (in millions), where t is the number of years from 1960 ($t = 0$ is 1960, $t = 1$ is 1961, and so on). Then use the function to estimate the population in 1975, 2000, and 1930.

Solution: If P denotes the population in millions, we construct an equation of the form $P = at + b$. We know that the graph must pass through the points $(t_1, P_1) = (0, 641)$ and $(t_2, P_2) = (10, 705)$. So we use the point–point formula, replacing x and y with t and P, respectively. This gives

$$P - 641 = \frac{705 - 641}{10 - 0}(t - 0) = \frac{64}{10}t \quad \text{or} \quad P = 6.4\,t + 641 \qquad (*)$$

In Table 1, we have compared our estimates with UN forecasts. Note that because $t = 0$ corresponds to 1960, $t = -30$ will correspond to 1930.

Note that the slope of line $(*)$ is 6.4. This means that if the European population had developed according to $(*)$, then the annual increase in the population would have been constant and equal to 6.4 million.

Table 1 Population estimates for Europe

Year	1930	1975	2000
t	−30	15	40
UN estimates	573	728	854
Formula $(*)$ gives	449	737	897

Actually, Europe's population grew unusually fast during the 1960s. Of course, it grew unusually slowly when millions died during the war years 1939–1945. We see that formula $(*)$ does not give very good results compared to the UN estimates. For a better way to model population growth see Example 4.9.1.

EXAMPLE 2   (**The Consumption Function**)   In Keynesian macroeconomic theory, total consumption expenditure on goods and services, C, is assumed to be a function of national income Y, with

$$C = f(Y)$$

In many models, following Keynes's associate R. F. Kahn, the consumption function is assumed to be linear, so that

$$C = a + bY$$

The slope b is called the **marginal propensity to consume**. If C and Y are measured in billions of dollars, the number b tells us by how many billions of dollars consumption increases if national income increases by 1 billion dollars. Following Kahn's insight, the number b is usually thought to lie between 0 and 1.

In a study of the US economy for the period 1929–1941, T. Haavelmo estimated the consumption function: $C = 95.05 + 0.712\,Y$. Here, the marginal propensity to consume is equal to 0.712.

EXAMPLE 3   (**Supply and Demand**)   Over a fixed period of time such as a week, the quantity of a specific good that consumers demand (that is, are willing to buy) will depend on the price of that good. Usually, as the price increases the demand will decrease.[1] Also, the number of units that the producers are willing to supply to the market during a certain period depends on the price they are able to obtain. Usually, the supply will increase as the price increases. So typical demand and supply curves are as indicated in Fig. 1.

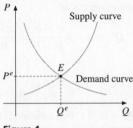

Figure 1   **Figure 2**

The point E in Fig. 1, at which demand is equal to supply, represents an **equilibrium**. The price P^e at which this occurs is the **equilibrium price** and the corresponding quantity Q^e is the **equilibrium quantity**. The equilibrium price is thus the price at which consumers will buy the same amount of the good as the producers wish to sell at that price.

As a very simple example, consider the following linear demand and supply functions:

$$\text{(i)} \ D = 100 - P \qquad\qquad \text{(ii)} \ S = 10 + 2P$$

or in inverse form, $P = 100 - D$ and $P = \frac{1}{2}S - 5$, as in Fig. 2. The quantity demanded D equals the quantity supplied S provided $100 - P = 10 + 2P$, that is, $3P = 90$. So the equilibrium price is $P^e = 30$, with equilibrium quantity $Q^e = 70$.

NOTE 1   A peculiarity of Fig. 1 is that, although quantity is usually regarded as a function of price, here we measure price on the vertical axis and quantity on the horizontal axis. This has been standard practice in elementary price theory since the fundamental ideas of the French economist Antoine-Augustin Cournot and several other European contemporaries became popularized by the English economist Alfred Marshall in the late 19th century.

EXAMPLE 4   (**Linear Supply and Demand Functions**)   Consider the following general linear demand and supply schedules:

$$\text{(i)} \ D = a - bP \qquad\qquad \text{(ii)} \ S = \alpha + \beta P$$

---

[1] For certain luxury goods like perfume, which are often given as presents, demand might increase as the price increases. For absolutely essential goods, like insulin for diabetics, demand might be almost independent of the price. Occasionally dietary staples could also be "Giffen goods" for which demand rises as price rises. The explanation offered is that these foodstuffs are so essential to a very poor household's survival that a rise in price lowers real income substantially, and so makes alternative sources of nourishment even less affordable.

Here a and b are positive parameters of the demand function D, while α and β are positive parameters of the supply function.

Such linear supply and demand functions play an important role in economics. It is often the case that the market for a particular commodity, such as copper, can be represented approximately by suitably estimated linear demand and supply functions.

The equilibrium price P^e occurs where demand equals supply. Hence $D = S$ at $P = P^e$ implying that $a - bP^e = \alpha + \beta P^e$, or $a - \alpha = (\beta + b)P^e$. The corresponding equilibrium quantity is $Q^e = a - bP^e$. So equilibrium occurs at

$$P^e = \frac{a - \alpha}{\beta + b}, \qquad Q^e = a - b\frac{a - \alpha}{\beta + b} = \frac{a\beta + \alpha b}{\beta + b}$$

PROBLEMS FOR SECTION 4.5

1. The consumption function $C = 4141 + 0.78\,Y$ was estimated for the UK during the period 1949–1975. What is the marginal propensity to consume?

2. Find the equilibrium price for each of the two linear models of supply and demand:

   (a) $D = 75 - 3P$, $\quad S = 20 + 2P$ $\qquad$ (b) $D = 100 - 0.5P$, $\quad S = 10 + 0.5P$

3. The total cost C of producing x units of some commodity is a linear function of x. Records show that on one occasion, 100 units were made at a total cost of \$200, and on another occasion, 150 units were made at a total cost of \$275. Express the linear equation for total cost C in terms of the number of units x produced.

4. The expenditure of a household on consumer goods, C, is related to the household's income, y, in the following way: When the household's income is \$1000, the expenditure on consumer goods is \$900, and whenever income increases by \$100, the expenditure on consumer goods increases by \$80. Express the expenditure on consumer goods as a function of income, assuming a linear relationship.

5. For most assets such as cars, stereo equipment, and furniture, the value decreases, or *depreciates*, each year. If the value of an asset is assumed to decrease by a fixed percentage of the original value each year, it is referred to as *straight line depreciation*.

   (a) Suppose the value of a car which initially costs \$20 000 depreciates by 10% of its original value each year. Find a formula for its value $P(t)$ after t years.

   (b) If a \$500 washing machine is completely depreciated after 10 years (straight line depreciation), find a formula for its value $W(t)$ after t years.

6. (a) According to the 20th report of the International Commission on Whaling, the number N of fin whales in the Antarctic for the period 1958–1963 was estimated to be

   $$N = -17\,400\,t + 151\,000, \qquad 0 \le t \le 5$$

   where $t = 0$ corresponds to January 1958, $t = 1$ corresponds to January 1959, and so on. According to this equation, how many fin whales would be left in April 1960?

   (b) If the decrease continued at the same rate, when would there be no fin whales left? (Actually, the 1993 estimate was approximately 21 000.)

4.6 Quadratic Functions

Economists often find that linear functions are too simple for modelling economic phenom-ena with acceptable accuracy. Indeed, many economic models involve functions that either decrease down to some minimum value and then increase, or else increase up to some max-imum value and then decrease. Some simple functions with this property are the general **quadratic** functions

$$f(x) = ax^2 + bx + c \qquad (a, b, \text{ and } c \text{ are constants, } a \neq 0) \qquad (1)$$

(If $a = 0$, the function is linear; hence, the restriction $a \neq 0$.) In general, the graph of $f(x) = ax^2 + bx + c$ is called a **parabola**. The shape of this parabola roughly resembles $\cap$ when $a < 0$ and $\cup$ when $a > 0$. Three typical cases are illustrated in Fig. 1. The graphs are symmetric about the **axis of symmetry**, which is the vertical dashed line in each of the three cases.

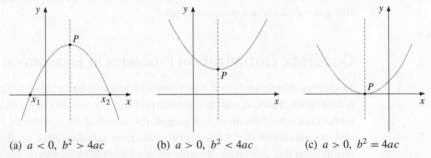

(a) $a < 0, \ b^2 > 4ac$ (b) $a > 0, \ b^2 < 4ac$ (c) $a > 0, \ b^2 = 4ac$

Figure 1 The graph of the parabola $y = ax^2 + bx + c$ for different values of a, b, and c

In order to investigate the function $f(x) = ax^2 + bx + c$ in more detail, we should find the answers to the following questions:

A. For which values of x (if any) is $ax^2 + bx + c = 0$?

B. What are the coordinates of the maximum/minimum point P, also called the **vertex** of the parabola?

The answer to question A was given by the quadratic formula (2.3.4) and the subsequent discussion of that formula. The easiest way to handle question B is to use derivatives, which is the topic of Chapter 6. (See Problem 6.2.6.) However, let us briefly consider how the "method of completing the squares" from Section 2.3 can be used to answer question B.

In fact, this method yields

$$f(x) = ax^2 + bx + c = a\left(x + \frac{b}{2a}\right)^2 - \frac{b^2 - 4ac}{4a} \qquad (2)$$

as is easily verified by expanding the right-hand side and gathering terms.

Now, when x varies, only the value of $a(x + b/2a)^2$ changes. This term is equal to 0 only when $x = -b/2a$, and if $a > 0$, it is never less than 0. This means that when $a > 0$, then the function $f(x)$ attains its minimum when $x = -b/2a$, and the value of $f(x)$ is then equal to $f(-b/2a) = -(b^2 - 4ac)/4a = c - b^2/4a$. If $a < 0$ on the other hand, then $a(x + b/2a)^2 \leq 0$ for all x, and the squared term is equal to 0 only when $x = -b/2a$. Hence, $f(x)$ attains its maximum when $x = -b/2a$ in this second case.

To summarize, we have shown the following:

$$\text{If } a > 0, \text{ then } f(x) = ax^2 + bx + c \text{ has its } \textbf{minimum} \text{ at } x = -b/2a \qquad (3)$$

$$\text{If } a < 0, \text{ then } f(x) = ax^2 + bx + c \text{ has its } \textbf{maximum} \text{ at } x = -b/2a \qquad (4)$$

The axis of symmetry for a parabola is the vertical line through its vertex, which is the point P in all three cases of Fig. 1.[2] Indeed, formula (2) implies that, for any number u, one has

$$f\left(-\frac{b}{2a} + u\right) = au^2 - \frac{b^2 - 4ac}{4a} = f\left(-\frac{b}{2a} - u\right)$$

It follows that the quadratic function $f(x) = ax^2 + bx + c$ is symmetric about the vertical line $x = -b/2a$ which passes through P.

Quadratic Optimization Problems in Economics

Much of economic analysis is concerned with optimization problems. Economics, after all, is the science of choice, and optimization problems are the form in which economists usually model choice mathematically. A general discussion of such problems must be postponed until we have developed the necessary tools from calculus. Here we show how the simple results from this section on maximizing quadratic functions can be used to illustrate some basic economic ideas.

EXAMPLE 1   The price P per unit obtained by a firm in producing and selling Q units is $P = 102 - 2Q$, and the cost of producing and selling Q units is $C = 2Q + \frac{1}{2}Q^2$. Then the profit is[3]

$$\pi(Q) = PQ - C = (102 - 2Q)Q - (2Q + \tfrac{1}{2}Q^2) = 100Q - \tfrac{5}{2}Q^2$$

Find the value of Q which maximizes profits, and the corresponding maximal profit.

Solution: Using formula (4) we find that profit is maximized at

$$Q = Q^* = -\frac{100}{2(-\frac{5}{2})} = 20 \qquad \text{with} \qquad \pi^* = \pi(Q^*) = -\frac{100^2}{4(-\frac{5}{2})} = 1000$$

This example is a special case of the monopoly problem studied in the next example.

---

[2] The function f is symmetric about $x = x_0$ if $f(x_0 + t) = f(x_0 - t)$ for all x. See Section 5.2.

[3] In mathematics π is used to denote the constant ratio $3.1415\ldots$ between the circumference of a circle and its diameter. In economics, this constant is not used very often. Also, p and P usually denote a price, so π has come to denote profit.

EXAMPLE 2   (**A Monopoly Problem**)   Consider a firm that is the only seller of the commodity it produces, possibly a patented medicine, and so enjoys a monopoly. The total costs of the monopolist are assumed to be given by the quadratic function

$$C = \alpha Q + \beta Q^2, \qquad Q \geq 0$$

of its output level Q, where α and β are positive constants. For each Q, the price P at which it can sell its output is assumed to be determined from the linear "inverse" demand function

$$P = a - bQ, \qquad Q \geq 0$$

where a and b are constants with $a > 0$ and $b \geq 0$. So for any nonnegative Q, the total revenue R is given by the quadratic function $R = PQ = (a - bQ)Q$, and profit by the quadratic function

$$\pi(Q) = R - C = (a - bQ)Q - \alpha Q - \beta Q^2 = (a - \alpha)Q - (b + \beta)Q^2$$

Assuming that the monopolist's objective is to maximize the profit function $\pi = \pi(Q)$, find the optimal output level Q^M and the corresponding optimal profit π^M.

Solution: By using (4), we see that there is a maximum of π at

$$Q^M = \frac{a - \alpha}{2(b + \beta)} \qquad \text{with} \qquad \pi^M = \frac{(a - \alpha)^2}{4(b + \beta)} \tag{$*$}$$

This is valid if $a > \alpha$; if $a \leq \alpha$, the firm will not produce, but will have $Q^M = 0$ and $\pi^M = 0$. The two cases are illustrated in Figs. 2 and 3. In Fig. 3, the part of the parabola to the left of $Q = 0$ is dashed, because it is not really relevant given the natural requirement that $Q \geq 0$. The price and cost associated with Q^M in $(*)$ can be found by routine algebra.

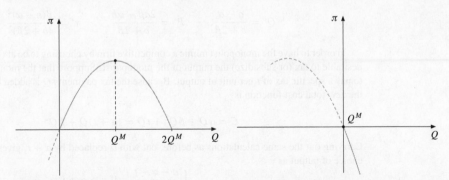

Figure 2 The profit function, $a > \alpha$ **Figure 3** The profit function, $a \leq \alpha$

If we put $b = 0$ in the price function $P = a - bQ$, then $P = a$ for all Q. In this case, the firm's choice of quantity does not influence the price at all and so the firm is said to be *perfectly competitive.* By replacing a by P in our previous expressions, we see that profit is maximized for a perfectly competitive firm at

$$Q^* = \frac{P - \alpha}{2\beta} \qquad \text{with} \qquad \pi^* = \frac{(P - \alpha)^2}{4\beta} \qquad (**)$$

provided that $P > \alpha$. If $P \le \alpha$, then $Q^* = 0$ and $\pi^* = 0$.

Solving the first equation in $(**)$ for P yields $P = \alpha + 2\beta Q^*$. Thus, the equation

$$P = \alpha + 2\beta Q \qquad (***)$$

represents the *supply curve* of this perfectly competitive firm for $P > \alpha$. For $P \le \alpha$, the profit-maximizing output Q^* is 0. The supply curve relating the price on the market to the firm's choice of output quantity is shown in Fig. 4; it includes all the points of the line segment between the origin and $(0, \alpha)$, where the price is too low for the firm to earn any profit by producing a positive output.

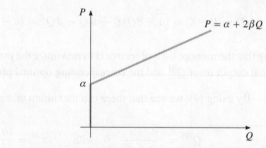

Figure 4 The supply curve of a perfectly competitive firm

Let us return to the monopoly firm (which has no supply curve). If it could somehow be made to act like a competitive firm, taking price as given, it would be on the supply curve $(***)$. Given the demand curve $P = a - bQ$, equilibrium between supply and demand occurs when $(***)$ is also satisfied, and so $P = a - bQ = \alpha + 2\beta Q$. Solving the second equation for Q, and then substituting for P and π in turn, we see that the respective equilibrium levels of output, price, and profit would be

$$Q^e = \frac{a - \alpha}{b + 2\beta}, \qquad P^e = \frac{2a\beta + \alpha b}{b + 2\beta}, \qquad \pi^e = \frac{\beta(a - \alpha)^2}{(b + 2\beta)^2}$$

In order to have the monopolist mimic a competitive firm by choosing to be at (Q^e, P^e), it may be desirable to tax (or subsidize) the output of the monopolist. Suppose that the monopolist is required to pay a specific tax of t per unit of output. Because the tax payment tQ is added to the firm's costs, the new total cost function is

$$C = \alpha Q + \beta Q^2 + tQ = (\alpha + t)Q + \beta Q^2$$

Carrying out the same calculations as before, but with α replaced by $\alpha + t$, gives the monopolist's choice of output as

$$Q_t^M = \begin{cases} \dfrac{a - \alpha - t}{2(b + \beta)}, & \text{if } a \ge \alpha + t \\[2mm] 0, & \text{otherwise} \end{cases}$$

So $Q_t^M = Q^e$ when $(a - \alpha - t)/2(b + \beta) = (a - \alpha)/(b + 2\beta)$. Solving this equation for t yields $t = -(a - \alpha)b/(b + 2\beta)$. Note that t is actually negative, indicating the desirability of *subsidizing* the output of the monopolist in order to encourage additional production. (Of course, subsidizing monopolists is usually felt to be unjust, and many additional complications need to be considered carefully before formulating a desirable policy for dealing with monopolists. Still the previous analysis suggests that if it is desirable to lower a monopolist's price or its profit, this is much better done directly than by taxing its output.)

PROBLEMS FOR SECTION 4.6

1. (a) Let $f(x) = x^2 - 4x$. Complete the following table and use it to sketch the graph of f:

x	-1	0	1	2	3	4	5
$f(x)$							

(b) Using (3), determine the minimum point of f.

(c) Solve the equation $f(x) = 0$.

2. (a) Let $f(x) = -\frac{1}{2}x^2 - x + \frac{3}{2}$. Complete the following table and sketch the graph of f:

x	-4	-3	-2	-1	0	1	2
$f(x)$							

(b) Using (4), determine the maximum point of f.

(c) Solve the equation $-\frac{1}{2}x^2 - x + \frac{3}{2} = 0$ for x.

(d) Show that $f(x) = -\frac{1}{2}(x - 1)(x + 3)$, and use this to study how the sign of $f(x)$ varies with x. Compare the result with the graph.

3. Determine the maximum/minimum points by using (3) or (4):

(a) $x^2 + 4x$　　　　　(b) $x^2 + 6x + 18$　　　　　(c) $-3x^2 + 30x - 30$

(d) $9x^2 - 6x - 44$　　　(e) $-x^2 - 200x + 30\,000$　　(f) $x^2 + 100x - 20\,000$

4. Find all the zeros of each quadratic function in Problem 3, and write each function in the form $a(x - x_1)(x - x_2)$ (if possible).

5. Find solutions to the following equations, where p and q are parameters.

(a) $x^2 - 3px + 2p^2 = 0$　　(b) $x^2 - (p + q)x + pq = 0$　　(c) $2x^2 + (4q - p)x = 2pq$

6. A model by A. Sandmo in the theory of efficient loan markets involves the function

$$U(x) = 72 - (4 + x)^2 - (4 - rx)^2$$

where r is a constant. Find the value of x for which $U(x)$ attains its largest value.

7. (a) A farmer has 1000 metres of fence wire with which to make a rectangular enclosure, as illustrated in the figure below. Find the areas of the three rectangles whose bases are 100, 250, and 350 metres.

(b) Let the base have length $250 + x$. Then the height is $250 - x$ (see Fig. 5). What choice of x gives the maximum area?[4]

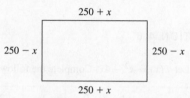

$$250 + x$$

$$250 - x \qquad\qquad 250 - x$$

$$250 + x$$

Figure 5

8. (a) If a cocoa shipping firm sells Q tons of cocoa in the UK, the price received is given by $P_E = \alpha_1 - \frac{1}{3}Q$. On the other hand, if it buys Q tons from its only source in Ghana, the price it has to pay is given by $P_G = \alpha_2 + \frac{1}{6}Q$. In addition, it costs γ per ton to ship cocoa from its supplier in Ghana to its customers in the UK (its only market). The numbers α_1, α_2, and γ are all positive. Express the cocoa shipper's profit as a function of Q, the number of tons shipped.

(b) Assuming that $\alpha_1 - \alpha_2 - \gamma > 0$, find the profit-maximizing shipment of cocoa. What happens if $\alpha_1 - \alpha_2 - \gamma \leq 0$?

(c) Suppose the government of Ghana imposes an export tax on cocoa of t per ton. Find the new expression for the shipper's profits and the new quantity shipped.

(d) Calculate the Ghanaian government's export tax revenue T as a function of t, and compare the graph of this function with the Laffer curve presented in Section 4.1.

(e) Advise the Ghanaian government on how to obtain as much tax revenue as possible.

HARDER PROBLEM

(SM) **9.** Let $a_1, a_2, \ldots, a_n$ and $b_1, b_2, \ldots, b_n$ be arbitrary real numbers. We claim that the following inequality (called the **Cauchy–Schwarz inequality**) is always valid:

$$(a_1b_1 + a_2b_2 + \cdots + a_nb_n)^2 \leq (a_1^2 + a_2^2 + \cdots + a_n^2)(b_1^2 + b_2^2 + \cdots + b_n^2) \qquad (5)$$

(a) Check the inequality for $a_1 = -3$, $a_2 = 2$, $b_1 = 5$, and $b_2 = -2$. (Then $n = 2$.)

(b) Prove (5) by means of the following trick: first, define f for all x by

$$f(x) = (a_1x + b_1)^2 + \cdots + (a_nx + b_n)^2$$

It should be obvious that $f(x) \geq 0$ for all x. Write $f(x)$ as $Ax^2 + Bx + C$, where the expressions for A, B, and C are related to the terms in (5). Because $Ax^2 + Bx + C \geq 0$ for all x, we must have $B^2 - 4AC \leq 0$. Why? The conclusion follows.

---

[4] It is reported that certain surveyors in antiquity wrote contracts with farmers to sell them rectangular pieces of land in which only the perimeter was specified. As a result, the lots were long narrow rectangles.

4.7 Polynomials

After considering linear and quadratic functions, the logical next step is to examine **cubic functions** of the form

$$f(x) = ax^3 + bx^2 + cx + d \qquad (a, b, c, \text{ and } d \text{ are constants; } a \neq 0) \qquad (1)$$

It is relatively easy to examine the behaviour of linear and quadratic functions. Cubic functions are considerably more complicated, because the shape of their graphs changes drastically as the coefficients a, b, c, and d vary. Two examples are given in Figs. 1 and 2.

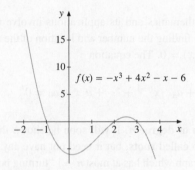

Figure 1 A cubic function   **Figure 2** A cubic cost function

Cubic functions do occasionally appear in economic models. Let us look at an example.

EXAMPLE 1   Consider a firm producing a single commodity. The total cost of producing Q units of the commodity is $C(Q)$. Cost functions often have the following properties: First, $C(0)$ is positive, because an initial fixed expenditure is involved. When production increases, costs also increase. In the beginning, costs increase rapidly, but the rate of increase slows down as production equipment is used for a higher proportion of each working week. However, at high levels of production, costs again increase at a fast rate, because of technical bottlenecks and overtime payments to workers, for example. It can be shown that the cubic cost function $C(Q) = aQ^3 + bQ^2 + cQ + d$ exhibits this type of behaviour provided that $a > 0, b < 0$, $c > 0, d > 0$, and $3ac > b^2$. Such a function is sketched in Fig. 2.

Cubic cost functions whose coefficients have a different sign pattern have also been studied. For instance, a study of a particular electric power generating plant revealed that over a certain period, the cost of fuel y as a function of output Q was given by $y = -Q^3 + 214.2Q^2 - 7900Q + 320700$. (This cost function cannot be valid for all Q, however, because it suggests that fuel costs would be negative for large enough Q.)

The detailed study of cubic functions is made easier by applying the differential calculus, as will be seen later.

General Polynomials

Linear, quadratic, and cubic functions are all examples of **polynomials**. The function P defined for all x by

$$P(x) = a_n x^n + a_{n-1} x^{n-1} + \cdots + a_1 x + a_0 \qquad (a\text{'s are constants}; a_n \neq 0) \qquad (2)$$

is called the **general polynomial of degree** n with **coefficients** $a_n, a_{n-1}, \ldots, a_0$. When $n = 4$, we obtain $P(x) = a_4 x^4 + a_3 x^3 + a_2 x^2 + a_1 x + a_0$, which is the general quartic function, or polynomial of degree 4. Neither $5 + \dfrac{1}{x^2}$ nor $\dfrac{1}{x^3 - x + 2}$ are polynomials, however.

Numerous problems in mathematics and its applications involve polynomials. Often, one is particularly interested in finding the number and location of the **zeros** of $P(x)$—that is, the values of x such that $P(x) = 0$. The equation

$$a_n x^n + a_{n-1} x^{n-1} + \cdots + a_1 x + a_0 = 0 \qquad (3)$$

is called the **general equation of degree** n. It will soon be shown that this equation has *at most* n (real) solutions, also called **roots**, but it need not have any. The corresponding nth-degree polynomial has a graph which has at most $n - 1$ "turning points", but there may be fewer such points. For example, the 100th-degree equation $x^{100} + 1 = 0$ has no solutions because $x^{100} + 1$ is always greater than or equal to 1, and its graph has only one turning point.

According to the **fundamental theorem of algebra**, every polynomial of the form (2) can be written as a product of polynomials of degree 1 or 2.

Factoring Polynomials

Let $P(x)$ and $Q(x)$ be two polynomials for which the degree of $P(x)$ is greater than or equal to the degree of $Q(x)$. Then there always exist unique polynomials $q(x)$ and $r(x)$ such that

$$P(x) = q(x)Q(x) + r(x) \qquad (4)$$

where the degree of $r(x)$ is less than the degree of $Q(x)$. This fact is called the **remainder theorem**. When x is such that $Q(x) \neq 0$, then (4) can be written in the form

$$\frac{P(x)}{Q(x)} = q(x) + \frac{r(x)}{Q(x)}$$

where $r(x)$ is the remainder. If $r(x) = 0$, we say that $Q(x)$ *is a factor of* $P(x)$, or that $P(x)$ *is divisible by* $Q(x)$. Then $P(x) = q(x)Q(x)$ or $P(x)/Q(x) = q(x)$.

An important special case is when $Q(x) = x - a$. Then $Q(x)$ is of degree 1, so the remainder $r(x)$ must have degree 0, and is therefore a constant. In this special case, for all x,

$$P(x) = q(x)(x - a) + r$$

For $x = a$ in particular, we get $P(a) = r$. *Hence, $x - a$ divides $P(x)$ if and only if $P(a) = 0$.* This important observation can be formulated as follows:

> The polynomial $P(x)$ has the factor $x - a \iff P(a) = 0$ (5)

EXAMPLE 2 Prove that $x - 5$ is a factor of the polynomial $P(x) = x^3 - 3x^2 - 50$.

Solution: $P(5) = 125 - 75 - 50 = 0$, so according to (5), $x - 5$ divides $P(x)$. (In fact, $P(x) = (x - 5)(x^2 + 2x + 10)$.)

NOTE 1 It follows from (5) that an nth-degree polynomial $P(x)$ can have *at most n* different zeros. The reason is that each zero gives rise to a different factor of the form $x - a$. Then, as an nth-degree polynomial, $P(x)$ can have at most n such factors. The result in (5) is often used when we try to factor polynomials.

NOTE 2 **(Integer Solutions)** Each integer m which satisfies the cubic equation

$$-x^3 + 4x^2 - x - 6 = 0 \qquad (*)$$

must satisfy the equation $m(-m^2 + 4m - 1) = 6$. Since $-m^2 + 4m - 1$ is also an integer, m must be a factor of the constant term 6. Thus ± 1, ± 2, ± 3, and ± 6 are the only possible integer solutions. Direct substitution into the left-hand side (LHS) of equation $(*)$ reveals that of these eight possibilities, -1, 2, and 3 are roots of the equation. A third-degree equation has at most three roots, so we have found them all. In fact,

$$-x^3 + 4x^2 - x - 6 = -(x + 1)(x - 2)(x - 3)$$

In general:

> Suppose that $a_n, a_{n-1}, \ldots, a_1, a_0$ are all integers. Then all possible integer roots of the equation
>
> $$a_n x^n + a_{n-1} x^{n-1} + \cdots + a_1 x + a_0 = 0$$ (6)
>
> must be factors of the constant term a_0.

EXAMPLE 3 Find all possible integer roots of the equation $\frac{1}{2}x^3 - x^2 + \frac{1}{2}x - 1 = 0$.

Solution: We multiply both sides of the equation by 2 to obtain an equation whose coefficients are all integers:

$$x^3 - 2x^2 + x - 2 = 0$$

Now, all integer solutions of the equation must be factors of 2. So only ± 1 and ± 2 can be integer solutions. A check shows that $x = 2$ is the only integer solution. In fact, because $x^3 - 2x^2 + x - 2 = (x - 2)(x^2 + 1)$, there is only one real root.

EXAMPLE 4   Find possible quadratic and cubic functions which have the graphs in Figs. 3 and 4 respectively.

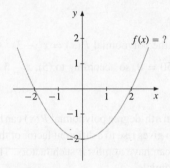

Figure 3

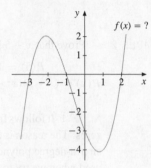

Figure 4

Solution: Figure 3: Since the graph intersects the x-axis at the two points $x = -2$ and $x = 2$, we try the quadratic function $f(x) = a(x-2)(x+2)$. Then $f(0) = -4a$. According to the graph, $f(0) = -2$, so $a = 1/2$, and hence

$$f(x) = \tfrac{1}{2}(x - 2)(x + 2) = \tfrac{1}{2}x^2 - 2$$

Figure 4: Because the equation $f(x) = 0$ has roots $x = -3, -1, 2$, we try the cubic function $f(x) = b(x + 3)(x + 1)(x - 2)$. Then $f(0) = -6b$. According to the graph, $f(0) = -3$. So $b = 1/2$, and hence

$$f(x) = \tfrac{1}{2}(x + 3)(x + 1)(x - 2)$$

Polynomial Division

One can divide polynomials in much the same way as one uses long division to divide numbers. To remind ourselves how long division works, consider a simple numerical example:

$$2735 \div 5 \ = 500 + 40 + 7$$
$$\underline{2500}$$
$$235$$
$$\underline{200}$$
$$35$$
$$\underline{35}$$
$$0 \quad \text{remainder}$$

Hence, $2735 \div 5 = 547$. Note that the horizontal lines instruct you to subtract the numbers above the lines. (You might be more accustomed to a different way of arranging the numbers, but the idea is the same.)

Consider next

$$(-x^3 + 4x^2 - x - 6) \div (x - 2)$$

We write the following:

$$
\begin{array}{l}
(-x^3 + 4x^2 - \ x - 6) \div (x - 2) = -x^2 \qquad\qquad\quad + 2x \qquad + 3 \\
\underline{-x^3 + 2x^2} \qquad\qquad\qquad\qquad \longleftarrow \boxed{-x^2(x-2)} \\
\quad 2x^2 - \ x \\
\quad \underline{2x^2 - 4x} \qquad\qquad\qquad\quad \longleftarrow \boxed{2x(x-2)} \longleftarrow \\
\qquad\quad 3x - 6 \\
\qquad\quad \underline{3x - 6} \qquad\qquad \longleftarrow \boxed{3(x-2)} \longleftarrow \\
\qquad\qquad\quad 0 \qquad \text{remainder}
\end{array}
$$

(You can omit the boxes, but they should help you to see what is going on.) We conclude that $(-x^3 + 4x^2 - x - 6) \div (x - 2) = -x^2 + 2x + 3$. However, it is easy to see that $-x^2 + 2x + 3 = -(x + 1)(x - 3)$. So

$$-x^3 + 4x^2 - x - 6 = -(x + 1)(x - 3)(x - 2)$$

EXAMPLE 5   Prove that the polynomial $P(x) = -2x^3 + 2x^2 + 10x + 6$ has a zero at $x = 3$, and factor the polynomial.

Solution: Inserting $x = 3$ yields $P(3) = 0$, so $x = 3$ is a zero. According to (5), the polynomial $P(x)$ has $x - 3$ as a factor. Performing the division $(-2x^3 + 2x^2 + 10x + 6) \div (x - 3)$, we find that the result is $-2(x^2 + 2x + 1) = -2(x + 1)^2$, and so $P(x) = -2(x - 3)(x + 1)^2$.

Polynomial Division with a Remainder

The division $2734 \div 5$ gives 546 and leaves the remainder 4. So $2734/5 = 546 + 4/5$. We consider a similar form of division for polynomials.

EXAMPLE 6   Perform the division: $(x^4 + 3x^2 - 4) \div (x^2 + 2x)$.

Solution:
$$
\begin{array}{l}
(x^4 \qquad\quad + 3x^2 \qquad\quad - 4) \div (x^2 + 2x) = x^2 - 2x + 7 \\
\underline{x^4 + 2x^3} \\
\quad -2x^3 + 3x^2 \qquad\quad - 4 \\
\quad \underline{-2x^3 - 4x^2} \\
\qquad\qquad 7x^2 \qquad\quad - 4 \\
\qquad\qquad \underline{7x^2 + 14x} \\
\qquad\qquad\qquad -14x - 4 \qquad \text{remainder}
\end{array}
$$

(The polynomial $x^4 + 3x^2 - 4$ has no terms in x^3 and x, so we inserted some extra space between the powers of x to make room for the terms in x^3 and x that arise in the course of the calculations.) We conclude that $x^4 + 3x^2 - 4 = (x^2 - 2x + 7)(x^2 + 2x) + (-14x - 4)$. Hence,

$$\frac{x^4 + 3x^2 - 4}{x^2 + 2x} = x^2 - 2x + 7 - \frac{14x + 4}{x^2 + 2x}$$

Rational Functions

A **rational function** is a function $R(x) = P(x)/Q(x)$ that can be expressed as the ratio of two polynomials $P(x)$ and $Q(x)$. This function is defined for all x where $Q(x) \neq 0$. The rational function $R(x)$ is called **proper** if the degree of $P(x)$ is less than the degree of $Q(x)$. When the degree of $P(x)$ is greater than or equal to that of $Q(x)$, then $R(x)$ is called an **improper** rational function. By using polynomial division, any improper rational function can be written as a polynomial plus a proper rational function, as in Example 6.

EXAMPLE 7   One of the simplest types of rational function is

$$R(x) = \frac{ax + b}{cx + d} \qquad (c \neq 0)$$

(If $c = 0$, $R(x)$ is a linear function.) The graph of R is a *hyperbola*. (See Fig. 5.1.7 for a typical example where $R(x) = (3x - 5)/(x - 2)$. See also the end of Section 5.5.) A very simple case is

$$R(x) = \frac{a}{x} \qquad (a > 0)$$

Figure 5 shows the graph of this function in the first quadrant. Note that the shaded area A is always equal to a, independent of which point P we choose on the curve, since the area is $A = x_0(a/x_0) = a$.

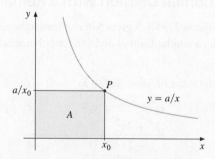

Figure 5 The area A is independent of P

Studying the behaviour of more complicated rational functions becomes easier once we have developed the proper tools from calculus. (See e.g. Problem 7.9.7.)

PROBLEMS FOR SECTION 4.7

(SM) **1.** Find all integer roots of the following equations:

   (a) $x^4 - x^3 - 7x^2 + x + 6 = 0$ (b) $2x^3 + 11x^2 - 7x - 6 = 0$

   (c) $x^4 + x^3 + 2x^2 + x + 1 = 0$ (d) $\frac{1}{4}x^3 - \frac{1}{4}x^2 - x + 1 = 0$

2. Find all integer roots of the following equations:

   (a) $x^2 + x - 2 = 0$ (b) $x^3 - x^2 - 25x + 25 = 0$ (c) $x^5 - 4x^3 - 3 = 0$

(SM) **3.** Perform the following divisions:

   (a) $(2x^3 + 2x - 1) \div (x - 1)$ (b) $(x^4 + x^3 + x^2 + x) \div (x^2 + x)$

   (c) $(x^5 - 3x^4 + 1) \div (x^2 + x + 1)$ (d) $(3x^8 + x^2 + 1) \div (x^3 - 2x + 1)$

(SM) **4.** Find possible formulas for each of the three polynomials with graphs shown in Fig. 6.

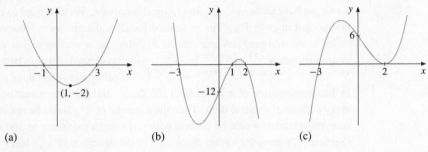

(a)   (b)   (c)

Figure 6

5. Perform the following divisions:

   (a) $(x^2 - x - 20) \div (x - 5)$ (b) $(x^3 - 1) \div (x - 1)$ (c) $(-3x^3 + 48x) \div (x - 4)$

6. Show that the division $(x^4 + 3x^2 + 5) \div (x - c)$ leaves a remainder for all values of c.

7. Prove that $R(x) = \dfrac{ax + b}{cx + d} = \dfrac{a}{c} + \dfrac{bc - ad}{c(cx + d)}$ $(c \neq 0)$.

(SM) **8.** The following function has been used in demand theory:

$$E = \alpha \frac{x^2 - \gamma x}{x + \beta} \qquad (\alpha, \beta, \text{ and } \gamma \text{ are constants})$$

Perform the division $(x^2 - \gamma x) \div (x + \beta)$, and use the result to express E as a sum of a linear function and a proper fraction.

4.8 Power Functions

Consider the general **power function** f defined by the formula

$$f(x) = Ax^r \qquad (x > 0, \ r \text{ and } A \text{ are any constants}) \tag{1}$$

We saw in Section 1.5 how the number x^r can be defined for all rational numbers r (that is, for all fractional exponents). When we consider the power function, we assume that $x > 0$. This is because for many values of r, such as $r = 1/2$, the symbol x^r is not defined for negative values of x. And we exclude $x = 0$ because 0^r is undefined if $r \leq 0$.

Here are three examples of why powers with rational exponents are needed:

A. The formula $S \approx 4.84V^{2/3}$ gives the approximate surface area S of a ball as a function of its volume V. (See Problem 6.)

B. The flow of blood (in litres per second) through the heart of an individual is approximately proportional to $x^{0.7}$, where x is the body weight.

C. The formula $Y = 2.262K^{0.203}L^{0.763}(1.02)^t$ appears in a study of the growth of national product, and shows how powers with fractional exponents can arise in economics. (Here Y is the net national product, K is capital stock, L is labour, and t is time.)

So far we have defined x^r for any rational number r. We also need to consider x^r when r is irrational in order for x^r to be defined for all real numbers r. How do we define, say, 5 raised to the irrational power π, that is 5^π? Because π is close to 3.1, we should define 5^π as approximately $5^{3.1} = 5^{31/10} = \sqrt[10]{5^{31}}$, which *is* defined. An even better approximation is $5^\pi \approx 5^{3.14} = 5^{314/100} = 5^{157/50} = \sqrt[50]{5^{157}}$. We can continue by taking more decimal places in the representation of $\pi = 3.14159\,26535, \ldots$, and our approximation will be better with every additional decimal digit. Then the meaning of 5^π should be reasonably clear. In any case, most readers would be content with just using a calculator to find that $5^\pi \approx 156.993$. (Section 7.11 provides further discussion of the definition of x^r when r is irrational.)

Graphs of Power Functions

We return to the power function $f(x) = x^r$, which is now defined for all real numbers r provided that $x > 0$. We always have $f(1) = 1^r = 1$, so the graph of the function passes through the point $(1, 1)$ in the xy-plane. The shape of the graph depends crucially on the value of r, as Figs. 1–3 indicate.

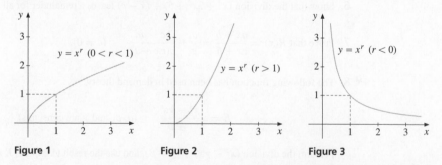

Figure 1   Figure 2   Figure 3

If $0 < r < 1$, the graph is like that in Fig. 1, which resembles the graph of $f(x) = x^{0.5}$ shown in Fig. 4.3.8. For $r > 1$ the graph is like that shown in Fig. 2. (For $r = 2$, the graph is the half of the parabola $y = x^2$ shown in Fig. 4.3.6.) Finally, for $r < 0$, the graph is shown in Fig. 3. (For $r = -1$, the graph is half of the hyperbola $y = 1/x$ shown in Fig. 4.3.9.)

Figure 4 illustrates how the graph of $y = x^r$ changes with changing positive values of the exponent.

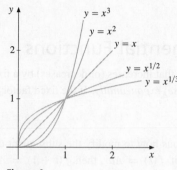

Figure 4

PROBLEMS FOR SECTION 4.8

1. Sketch the graphs of $y = x^{-3}$, $y = x^{-1}$, $y = x^{-1/2}$, and $y = x^{-1/3}$, defined for $x > 0$.

2. Use a calculator to find approximate values for (a) $\sqrt{2}^{\sqrt{2}}$ (b) π^π

3. Solve the following equations for x: (a) $2^{2x} = 8$ (b) $3^{3x+1} = 1/81$ (c) $10^{x^2-2x+2} = 100$

SM 4. Match each of the graphs A–F with one of the functions (a)–(f) in the following table. (In (f) try to find a suitable function which has the remaining graph.)

(a) $y = \frac{1}{2}x^2 - x - \frac{3}{2}$ has graph ____   (b) $y = 2\sqrt{2-x}$ has graph ____

(c) $y = -\frac{1}{2}x^2 + x + \frac{3}{2}$ has graph ____   (d) $y = \left(\frac{1}{2}\right)^x - 2$ has graph ____

(e) $y = 2\sqrt{x-2}$ has graph ____   (f) $y =$ ____ has graph ____

A

B

C

D

E

F

5. Find t when (a) $3^{5t}9^t = 27$ (b) $9^t = (27)^{1/5}/3$

6. The formulas for the surface area S and the volume V of a ball with radius r are $S = 4\pi r^2$ and $V = (4/3)\pi r^3$. Express S as a power function of V.

4.9 Exponential Functions

A quantity that increases (or decreases) by a fixed factor per unit of time is said to *increase* (or *decrease*) *exponentially*. If the fixed factor is a, this leads to the exponential function

$$f(t) = Aa^t \qquad (a \text{ and } A \text{ are positive constants}) \tag{1}$$

(It is obvious how to modify the subsequent discussion for the case when A is negative.) Note that if $f(t) = Aa^t$, then $f(t+1) = Aa^{t+1} = Aa^t \cdot a^1 = af(t)$, so the value of f at time $t + 1$ is a times the value of f at time t. If $a > 1$, then f is increasing; if $0 < a < 1$, then f is decreasing. (See Figs. 1 and 2.) Because $f(0) = Aa^0 = A$, we can write $f(t) = f(0)a^t$.

Exponential functions appear in many important economic, social, and physical models. For instance, economic growth, population growth, continuously accumulated interest, radioactive decay, and decreasing illiteracy have all been described by exponential functions. In addition, the exponential function is one of the most important functions in statistics.

NOTE 1   Observe the fundamental difference between the two functions

$$f(x) = a^x \qquad \text{and} \qquad g(x) = x^a$$

The second of these two is one of the *power functions* discussed in Section 4.8. For the exponential function a^x, it is the exponent x that varies, while the base a is constant. For the power function x^a, on the other hand, the exponent a is constant, while the base x varies.

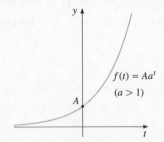

Figure 1 Graph of $f(t) = Aa^t$ $(a > 1)$

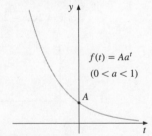

Figure 2 Graph of $f(t) = Aa^t$ $(0 < a < 1)$

EXAMPLE 1   **(Population Growth)**   Consider a growing population like that of Europe during the 20th century. In Example 4.5.1, we constructed a linear function $P = 6.4\,t + 641$, where P denotes the population in millions, $t = 0$ corresponds to the year 1960 when the population was 641 million, and $t = 10$ corresponds to the year 1970 when the population estimate was 705 million. According to this formula, the annual increase in population would be constant and equal to 6.4 million. This is a very unreasonable assumption. After all, the linear function implies that, for $t \leq -101$ (i.e., for years before 1860), the population of Europe was negative!

In fact, according to UN estimates, the European population was expected to grow by approximately 0.72% annually during the period 1960 to 2000. With a population of 641 million in 1960, the population in 1961 would then be $641 \cdot 1.0072$ (see Section 1.2), which is approximately 645 million. Next year, in 1962, it would have grown to $641 \cdot 1.0072^2$, which is approximately 650 million. If growth were to continue at 0.72% annually, the population figure would grow by the factor 1.0072 each year. Then, t years after 1960, the population would be given by

$$P(t) = 641 \cdot 1.0072^t$$

Thus, $P(t)$ is an exponential function of the form (1). For the year 2000, corresponding to $t = 40$, the formula yields the estimate $P(40) \approx 854$ million. (The actual figure turned out to be about 728 million, which shows the limitations of naive projections.)

Many countries, particularly in Africa, have recently had far faster population growth than Europe. For instance, during the 1970s and 1980s, the growth rate of Zimbabwe's population was close to 3.5% annually. If we let $t = 0$ correspond to the census year 1969 when the population was 5.1 million, the population t years after 1969 is $P(t) = 5.1 \cdot 1.035^t$. If we calculate $P(20)$, $P(40)$, and $P(60)$ using this formula, we get roughly 10, 20, and 40. Thus, the population of Zimbabwe roughly doubles after 20 years; during the next 20 years, it doubles again, and so on. We say that the *doubling time* of the population is approximately 20 years. Of course, this kind of extrapolation is quite dubious, because exponential growth of population cannot go on forever. (If the growth rate were to continue at 3.5% annually, there was no emigration, and the Zimbabwean territory did not expand, then by year 2296 each Zimbabwean would have only 1 square metre of land on average. See Problem 6.)

If $a > 1$ (and $A > 0$), the exponential function $f(t) = Aa^t$ is increasing. Its **doubling time** is the time it takes for it to double. Its value at $t = 0$ is A, so the doubling time t^* is given by the equation $f(t^*) = Aa^{t^*} = 2A$, or after cancelling A, by $a^{t^*} = 2$. Thus the doubling time of the exponential function $f(t) = Aa^t$ is the power to which a must be raised in order to get 2.[5] (In Problem 7 you will be asked to show that the doubling time is independent of which year you take as the base.)

EXAMPLE 2   Use your calculator to find the doubling time of

(a) a population (like that of Zimbabwe) increasing at 3.5% annually (thus confirming the earlier calculations)

(b) the population of Kenya in the 1980s (which then had the world's highest annual growth rate of population, 4.2%).

Solution:

(a) The doubling time t^* is given by the equation $1.035^{t^*} = 2$. Using a calculator shows that $1.035^{15} \approx 1.68$, whereas $1.035^{25} \approx 2.36$. Thus, t^* must lie between 15 and 25. Because $1.035^{20} \approx 1.99$, t^* is close to 20. In fact, $t^* \approx 20.15$.

---

[5] By using natural logarithms (see Example 4.10.2) we find that $t^* = \ln 2 / \ln a$.

(b) The doubling time t^* is given by the equation $1.042^{t^*} = 2$. Using a calculator, we find that $t^* \approx 16.85$. Thus, with a growth rate of 4.2%, Kenya's population would double in less than 17 years.

EXAMPLE 3   (**Compound Interest**)   A savings account of $\$K$ that increases by $p\%$ interest each year will have increased after t years to $K(1 + p/100)^t$ (see Section 1.2). According to this formula with $K = 1$, a deposit of \$1 earning interest at 8% per year ($p = 8$) will have increased after t years to $(1 + 8/100)^t = 1.08^t$.

Table 1 How \$1 of savings increases with time at 8% annual interest

t	1	2	5	10	20	30	50	100	200
$(1.08)^t$	1.08	1.17	1.47	2.16	4.66	10.06	46.90	2199.76	4 838 949.60

After 30 years, \$1 of savings has increased to more than \$10, and after 200 years, it has grown to more than \$4.8 million! Observe that the expression 1.08^t defines an exponential function of the type (1) with $a = 1.08$. Even if a is only slightly larger than 1, $f(t)$ will increase very quickly when t is large.

EXAMPLE 4   (**Continuous Depreciation**)   Each year the value of most assets such as cars, stereo equipment, or furniture decreases, or *depreciates*. If the value of an asset is assumed to decrease by a fixed percentage each year, then the depreciation is called *continuous*. (Straight line depreciation was discussed in Problem 4.5.5.)

Assume that a car, which at time $t = 0$ has the value P_0, depreciates at the rate of 20% each year over a 5 year period. What is its value $A(t)$ at time t, for $t = 1, 2, 3, 4, 5$?

Solution: After 1 year its value is $P_0 - (20P_0/100) = P_0(1 - 20/100) = P_0(0.8)^1$. Thereafter it depreciates each subsequent year by the factor 0.8. Thus, after t years, its value is $A(t) = P_0(0.8)^t$. In particular, $A(5) = P_0(0.8)^5 \approx 0.32P_0$, so after 5 years its value has decreased to about 32% of its original value.

The most important properties of the exponential function are summed up by the following:

THE GENERAL EXPONENTIAL FUNCTION

The **general exponential function** with base $a > 0$ is

$$f(x) = Aa^x$$

where a is the factor by which $f(x)$ changes when x increases by 1.

If $a = 1 + p/100$, where $p > 0$ and $A > 0$, then $f(x)$ will increase by $p\%$ for each unit increase in x.

If $a = 1 - p/100$, where $0 < p < 100$ and $A > 0$, then $f(x)$ will decrease by $p\%$ for each unit increase in x.

The Natural Exponential Function

Each base a of $f(x) = Aa^x$ gives a different exponential function. In mathematics, one particular value of a gives an exponential function that is far more important than all others. One might guess that $a = 2$ or $a = 10$ would be this special base. Certainly, powers to the base of 2 are important in computing, and powers to the base 10 occur in our usual decimal number system. Nevertheless, once we have studied some calculus, it will turn out that the most important base for an exponential function is an irrational number a little larger than 2.7. In fact, it is so distinguished that it is denoted by the single letter e, probably because it is the first letter of the word "exponential". Its value to 15 decimals is[6]

$$e = 2.718281828459045\ldots$$

Many formulas in calculus become much simpler when e is used as the base for exponential functions. Given this base e, the corresponding exponential function

$$f(x) = e^x \tag{2}$$

is called the **natural exponential function**. Later (in Example 7.6.2) we shall give an explicit way of approximating e^x to an arbitrary degree of accuracy. Of course, all the usual rules for powers apply also to the natural exponential function. In particular,

(a) $e^s e^t = e^{s+t}$ (b) $\dfrac{e^s}{e^t} = e^{s-t}$ (c) $(e^s)^t = e^{st}$

The graphs of $f(x) = e^x$ and $f(x) = e^{-x}$ are given in Fig. 3.

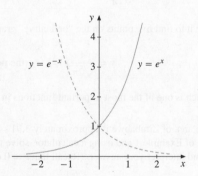

Figure 3 The graphs of $y = e^x$ and $y = e^{-x}$

Powers with e as their base, even e^1, are difficult to compute by hand. A pocket calculator with an $\boxed{e^x}$ function key can do this immediately, however. For instance, one finds that $e^{1.0} \approx 2.7183$, $e^{0.5} \approx 1.6487$, and $e^{-\pi} \approx 0.0432$.

NOTE 2   Sometimes the notation $\exp(u)$, or even $\exp u$, is used in place of e^u. If u is a complicated expression like $x^3 + x\sqrt{x - 1/x} + 5$, it is easier to read and write $\exp(x^3 + x\sqrt{x - 1/x} + 5)$ instead of $e^{x^3 + x\sqrt{x - 1/x} + 5}$.

---

[6] Though the number e had appeared over 100 years earlier, the Swiss mathematician Euler was the first to denote it by the letter e. He subsequently proved that it was irrational and calculated it to 23 decimal places.

1. If the population of Europe grew at the rate of 0.72% annually, what would be the doubling time?

2. The population of Botswana was estimated to be 1.22 million in 1989, and to be growing at the rate of 3.4% annually. If $t = 0$ denotes 1989, find a formula for the population $P(t)$ at date t. What is the doubling time?

3. A savings account with an initial deposit of \$100 earns 12% interest per year. What is the amount of savings after t years? Make a table similar to Table 1. (Stop at 50 years.)

4. Fill in the following table and sketch the graphs of $y = 2^x$ and $y = 2^{-x}$.

x	-3	-2	-1	0	1	2	3
2^x							
2^{-x}							

5. Use your calculator to fill in the following table:

x	-2	-1	0	1	2
$y = \dfrac{1}{\sqrt{2\pi}} e^{-\frac{1}{2}x^2}$					

Use it to find five points on the "bell curve" graph of

$$y = \frac{1}{\sqrt{2\pi}} e^{-\frac{1}{2}x^2} \quad \text{(the \textbf{normal density function})}$$

which is one of the most important functions in statistics.

6. The area of Zimbabwe is approximately $3.91 \cdot 10^{11}$ square metres. Referring to the text at the end of Example 1 and using a calculator, solve the equation $5.1 \cdot 10^6 \cdot 1.035^t = 3.91 \cdot 10^{11}$ for t, and interpret your answer. (Recall that $t = 0$ corresponds to 1969.)

7. With $f(t) = Aa^t$, if $f(t + t^*) = 2f(t)$, prove that $a^{t^*} = 2$. (This shows that the doubling time t^* of the general exponential function is independent of the initial time t.)

8. Which of the following equations do *not* define exponential functions of x?

   (a) $y = 3^x$ (b) $y = x^{\sqrt{2}}$ (c) $y = (\sqrt{2})^x$ (d) $y = x^x$ (e) $y = (2.7)^x$ (f) $y = 1/2^x$

9. Suppose that all prices rise at the same proportional rate in a country whose inflation rate is 19% per year. For an item that currently costs P_0, use the implied formula $P(t) = P_0(1.19)^t$ for the price after t years in order to predict the prices of:

   (a) A 20 kg bag of corn, presently costing \$16, after 5 years.

   (b) A \$4.40 can of coffee after 10 years.   (c) A \$250 000 house after 4 years.

10. Find possible exponential functions for the graphs in Fig. 4.

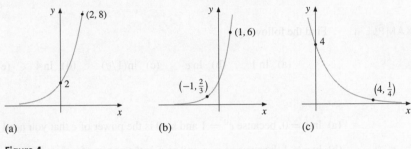

Figure 4

4.10 Logarithmic Functions

The doubling time of an exponential function $f(t) = Aa^t$ was defined as the time it takes for $f(t)$ to become twice as large. In order to find the doubling time t^*, we must solve the equation $a^{t^*} = 2$ for t^*. In economics, we often need to solve similar problems:

A. At the present rate of inflation, how long will it take the price level to triple?

B. If the world's population grows at 2% per year, how long does it take to double its size?

C. If $1000 is invested in a savings account bearing interest at the annual rate of 8%, how long does it take for the account to reach $10 000?

All these questions involve solving equations of the form $a^x = b$ for x. For instance, problem C reduces to the problem of finding which x solves the equation $1000(1.08)^x = 10\,000$.

We begin with equations in which the base of the exponential is e, which was, as you recall, the irrational number $2.718\ldots$. Here are some examples:

$$\text{(i)} \quad e^x = 4 \qquad \text{(ii)} \quad 5e^{-3x} = 16 \qquad \text{(iii)} \quad A\alpha e^{-\alpha x} = k$$

In all these equations, the unknown x occurs as an exponent. We therefore introduce the following useful definition. If $e^u = a$, we call u the **natural logarithm** of a, and we write $u = \ln a$. Hence, we have the following definition of the symbol $\ln a$:

$$e^{\ln a} = a \qquad (a \text{ is any positive number}) \tag{1}$$

Thus, $\ln a$ is the power of e you need to get a. In particular, if $e^x = 4$, then x must be $\ln 4$.

Because e^u is a strictly increasing function of u, it follows that $\ln a$ *is* uniquely determined by the definition (1). You should memorize this definition. It is the foundation for everything in this section, and for a good part of what comes later. The following example illustrates how to use this definition.

EXAMPLE 1   Find the following:

$$\text{(a) } \ln 1 \quad \text{(b) } \ln e \quad \text{(c) } \ln(1/e) \quad \text{(d) } \ln 4 \quad \text{(e) } \ln(-6)$$

Solution:

(a) $\ln 1 = 0$, because $e^0 = 1$ and so 0 is the power of e that you need to get 1.

(b) $\ln e = 1$, because $e^1 = e$ and so 1 is the power of e that you need to get e.

(c) $\ln(1/e) = \ln e^{-1} = -1$, because -1 is the power of e that you need to get $1/e$.

(d) $\ln 4$ is the power of e you need to get 4. Because $e^1 \approx 2.7$ and $e^2 = e^1 \cdot e^1 \approx 7.3$, the number $\ln 4$ must lie between 1 and 2. By using the $\boxed{e^x}$ key on a calculator, you should be able to find a good approximation to $\ln 4$ by trial and error. However, it is easier to press 4 and the $\boxed{\ln x}$ key. Then you find that $\ln 4 \approx 1.386$. Thus, $e^{1.386} \approx 4$.

(e) $\ln(-6)$ would be the power of e you need to get -6. Because e^x is positive for all x, it is obvious that $\ln(-6)$ must be undefined. (The same is true for $\ln x$ whenever $x \le 0$.) ∎

The following box collects some useful rules for natural logarithms.

RULES FOR THE NATURAL LOGARITHMIC FUNCTION LN:

(a) $\ln(xy) = \ln x + \ln y$ (x and y positive)

(The logarithm of a *product* is the *sum* of the logarithms of the factors.)

(b) $\ln \dfrac{x}{y} = \ln x - \ln y$ (x and y positive)

(The logarithm of a *quotient* is the *difference* between the logarithms of its numerator and denominator.)   (2)

(c) $\ln x^p = p \ln x$ (x positive)

(The logarithm of a *power* is the exponent multiplied by the logarithm of the base.)

(d) $\ln 1 = 0, \quad \ln e = 1, \quad x = e^{\ln x}, \ (x > 0) \quad \text{and} \quad \ln e^x = x$

To show (a), observe first that the definition of $\ln(xy)$ implies that $e^{\ln(xy)} = xy$. Furthermore, $x = e^{\ln x}$ and $y = e^{\ln y}$, so

$$e^{\ln(xy)} = xy = e^{\ln x} e^{\ln y} = e^{\ln x + \ln y} \tag{$*$}$$

where the last step uses the rule $e^s e^t = e^{s+t}$. In general, $e^u = e^v$ implies $u = v$, so we conclude from ($*$) that $\ln(xy) = \ln x + \ln y$.

The proofs of (b) and (c) are based on the rules $e^s/e^t = e^{s-t}$ and $(e^s)^t = e^{st}$, respectively, and are left to the reader. Finally, (d) displays some important properties for convenient reference.

It *is* tempting to replace $\ln(x + y)$ by $\ln x + \ln y$, but this is quite wrong. In fact, $\ln x + \ln y$ is equal to $\ln(xy)$, not to $\ln(x + y)$.

There are no simple formulas for $\ln(x + y)$ and $\ln(x - y)$.

Here are some examples that apply the previous rules.

EXAMPLE 2   Recall that the doubling time t^* of an exponential function $f(t) = Aa^t$ is given by the formula $a^{t^*} = 2$. Solve this equation for t^*.

Solution: Taking the natural logarithm of both sides of the equation yields $\ln a^{t^*} = \ln 2$. Using rule (c) we get $t^* \ln a = \ln 2$, and so $t^* = \ln 2 / \ln a$. ∎

EXAMPLE 3   Express (a) $\ln 4$, (b) $\ln \sqrt[3]{2^5}$, and (c) $\ln(1/16)$ in terms of $\ln 2$.

Solution:

(a) $\ln 4 = \ln(2 \cdot 2) = \ln 2 + \ln 2 = 2 \ln 2$. (Or: $\ln 4 = \ln 2^2 = 2 \ln 2$.)

(b) We have $\sqrt[3]{2^5} = 2^{5/3}$. Therefore, $\ln \sqrt[3]{2^5} = \ln 2^{5/3} = (5/3) \ln 2$.

(c) $\ln(1/16) = \ln 1 - \ln 16 = 0 - \ln 2^4 = -4 \ln 2$. (Or: $\ln(1/16) = \ln 2^{-4} = -4 \ln 2$.) ∎

EXAMPLE 4   Solve the following equations for x:

(a) $5e^{-3x} = 16$ (b) $A\alpha e^{-\alpha x} = k$ (c) $(1.08)^x = 10$ (d) $e^x + 4e^{-x} = 4$

Solution:

(a) Take $\ln$ of each side of the equation to obtain $\ln(5e^{-3x}) = \ln 16$. The product rule gives $\ln(5e^{-3x}) = \ln 5 + \ln e^{-3x}$. Here $\ln e^{-3x} = -3x$, by rule (d). Hence, $\ln 5 - 3x = \ln 16$, which gives

$$x = \frac{1}{3}(\ln 5 - \ln 16) = \frac{1}{3} \ln \frac{5}{16}$$

(b) We argue as in (a) and obtain $\ln(A\alpha e^{-\alpha x}) = \ln k$, or $\ln(A\alpha) + \ln e^{-\alpha x} = \ln k$, so $\ln(A\alpha) - \alpha x = \ln k$. Finally, therefore,

$$x = \frac{1}{\alpha}[\ln(A\alpha) - \ln k] = \frac{1}{\alpha} \ln \frac{A\alpha}{k}$$

(c) Again we take the ln of each side of the equation and obtain $x \ln 1.08 = \ln 10$. So the solution is $x = \ln 10/\ln 1.08$, which is ≈ 29.9. Thus, it takes just short of 30 years for $1 to increase to $10 when the interest rate is 8%. (See Table 1 in Example 4.9.3.)

(d) It is very tempting to begin with $\ln(e^x + 4e^{-x}) = \ln 4$, but this leads nowhere, because $\ln(e^x + 4e^{-x})$ cannot be further evaluated. Instead, we argue like this: Putting $u = e^x$ gives $e^{-x} = 1/e^x = 1/u$, so the equation is $u + 4/u = 4$, or $u^2 + 4 = 4u$. Solving this quadratic equation for u yields $u = 2$ as the only solution. Hence, $e^x = 2$, and so $x = \ln 2$.

The Function g(x) = ln x

For each positive number x, the number $\ln x$ is defined by $e^{\ln x} = x$. In other words, $u = \ln x$ is the solution of the equation $e^u = x$. This definition is illustrated in Fig. 1. We call the resulting function

$$g(x) = \ln x \qquad (x > 0) \tag{3}$$

the **natural logarithm** of x. Think of x as a point moving upwards on the vertical axis from the origin. As x increases from values less than 1 to values greater than 1, so $g(x)$ increases from negative to positive values. Because e^u tends to 0 as u becomes large negative, so $g(x)$ becomes large negative as x tends to 0. Repeating the definition of $\ln x$, then inserting $y = \ln x$ and taking the ln of each side, yields

(i) $e^{\ln x} = x$ for all $x > 0$ (ii) $\ln e^y = y$ for all y

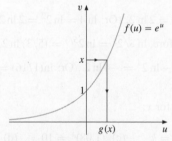 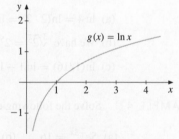

Figure 1 Illustration of the definition of $g(x) = \ln x$

Figure 2 The graph of the logarithmic function $g(x) = \ln x$

In Fig. 2 we have drawn the graph of $g(x) = \ln x$. The shape of this graph ought to be remembered. It can be obtained by reflecting the graph of Fig. 1 about the line $v = u$ so that the u- and v-axes are interchanged, and become the y- and x-axes of Fig. 2, respectively. According to Example 1, we have $g(1/e) = -1$, $g(1) = 0$, and $g(e) = 1$. Observe that this corresponds well with the graph.

Logarithms with Bases other than e

Recall that we defined $\ln x$ as the exponent to which we must raise the base e in order to obtain x. From time to time, it is useful to have logarithms based on numbers other than e. For many years, until the use of mechanical and then electronic calculators became widespread, tables of logarithms to the base 10 were frequently used to simplify complicated calculations involving multiplication, division, square roots, and so on.

Suppose that a is a fixed positive number (usually chosen > 1). If $a^u = x$, then we call u the **logarithm of x to base a** and write $u = \log_a x$. The symbol $\log_a x$ is then defined for every positive number x by the following:

$$a^{\log_a x} = x \tag{4}$$

For instance, $\log_2 32 = 5$, because $2^5 = 32$, whereas $\log_{10}(1/100) = -2$, because $10^{-2} = 1/100$. Note that $\ln x$ is $\log_e x$.

By taking the $\ln$ on each side of (4), we obtain $\log_a x \cdot \ln a = \ln x$, so that

$$\log_a x = \frac{1}{\ln a} \ln x \tag{5}$$

This reveals that the logarithm of x in the system with base a is proportional to $\ln x$, with a proportionality factor $1/\ln a$. It follows immediately that $\log_a$ obeys the same rules as $\ln$:

(a) $\log_a(xy) = \log_a x + \log_a y$,   (b) $\log_a(x/y) = \log_a x - \log_a y$

(c) $\log_a x^p = p \log_a x$,   (d) $\log_a 1 = 0$ and $\log_a a = 1$ (6)

For example, (a) follows from the corresponding rule for $\ln$:

$$\log_a(xy) = \frac{1}{\ln a} \ln(xy) = \frac{1}{\ln a}(\ln x + \ln y) = \frac{1}{\ln a} \ln x + \frac{1}{\ln a} \ln y = \log_a x + \log_a y$$

PROBLEMS FOR SECTION 4.10

1. Express as multiples of $\ln 3$:   (a) $\ln 9$ (b) $\ln \sqrt{3}$ (c) $\ln \sqrt[5]{3^2}$ (d) $\ln \dfrac{1}{81}$

2. Solve the following equations for x:

(a) $3^x = 8$ (b) $\ln x = 3$ (c) $\ln(x^2 - 4x + 5) = 0$

(d) $\ln[x(x - 2)] = 0$ (e) $\dfrac{x \ln(x + 3)}{x^2 + 1} = 0$ (f) $\ln(\sqrt{x} - 5) = 0$

(SM) **3.** Solve the following equations for x:

(a) $3^x 4^{x+2} = 8$ (b) $3 \ln x + 2 \ln x^2 = 6$ (c) $4^x - 4^{x-1} = 3^{x+1} - 3^x$

(d) $\log_2 x = 2$ (e) $\log_x e^2 = 2$ (f) $\log_3 x = -3$

(SM) **4.** (a) Let $f(t) = Ae^{rt}$ and $g(t) = Be^{st}$, with $A > 0$, $B > 0$, and $r \neq s$. Solve the equation $f(t) = g(t)$ for t.

(b) In 1990 the GNP (gross national product) of China was estimated to be $1.2 \cdot 10^{12}$ US dollars, and the rate of growth was estimated to be $r = 0.09$. By comparison, the GNP for the USA was reported as \$5.6 \cdot 10^{12}$, with an estimated rate of growth of $s = 0.02$. If the GNP of each country continued to grow exponentially at the rates $r = 0.09$ and $s = 0.02$, respectively, when would the GNP of the two nations be the same?

5. Which of the following formulas are always true and which are sometimes false (all variables are positive)?

(a) $(\ln A)^4 = 4 \ln A$ (b) $\ln B = 2 \ln \sqrt{B}$ (c) $\ln A^{10} - \ln A^4 = 3 \ln A^2$

6. Which of the following formulas are always true and which are sometimes false (all variables are positive)?

(a) $\ln \dfrac{A+B}{C} = \ln A + \ln B - \ln C$

(b) $\ln \dfrac{A+B}{C} = \ln(A+B) - \ln C$

(c) $\ln \dfrac{A}{B} + \ln \dfrac{B}{A} = 0$

(d) $p \ln(\ln A) = \ln(\ln A^p)$

(e) $p \ln(\ln A) = \ln(\ln A)^p$

(f) $\dfrac{\ln A}{\ln B + \ln C} = \ln A(BC)^{-1}$

7. Simplify the following expressions:

(a) $\exp\big[\ln(x)\big] - \ln\big[\exp(x)\big]$

(b) $\ln\big[x^4 \exp(-x)\big]$

(c) $\exp\big[\ln(x^2) - 2\ln y\big]$

REVIEW PROBLEMS FOR CHAPTER 4

1. (a) Let $f(x) = 3 - 27x^3$. Compute $f(0)$, $f(-1)$, $f(1/3)$, and $f(\sqrt[3]{2})$.

(b) Show that $f(x) + f(-x) = 6$ for all x.

2. (a) Let $F(x) = 1 + \dfrac{4x}{x^2 + 4}$. Compute $F(0)$, $F(-2)$, $F(2)$, and $F(3)$.

(b) What happens to $F(x)$ when x becomes large positive or negative?

(c) Give a rough sketch of the graph of F.

3. Figure A combines the graphs of a quadratic function f and a linear function g. Use the graphs to find those x where: (i) $f(x) \le g(x)$ (ii) $f(x) \le 0$ (iii) $g(x) \ge 0$.

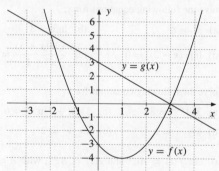

Figure A

4. Find the domains of:

(a) $f(x) = \sqrt{x^2 - 1}$

(b) $g(x) = \dfrac{1}{\sqrt{x-4}}$

(c) $h(x) = \sqrt{(x-3)(5-x)}$

5. (a) The cost of producing x units of a commodity is given by $C(x) = 100 + 40x + 2x^2$. Find $C(0)$, $C(100)$, and $C(101) - C(100)$.

(b) Find $C(x+1) - C(x)$, and explain in words the meaning of the difference.

6. Find the slopes of the straight lines   (a) $y = -4x + 8$ (b) $3x + 4y = 12$ (c) $\dfrac{x}{a} + \dfrac{y}{b} = 1$

7. Find equations for the following straight lines:

   (a) L_1 passes through $(-2, 3)$ and has a slope of -3.

   (b) L_2 passes through $(-3, 5)$ and $(2, 7)$.

   (c) L_3 passes through (a, b) and $(2a, 3b)$ (suppose $a \neq 0$).

8. If $f(x) = ax + b$, $f(2) = 3$, and $f(-1) = -3$, then $f(-3) = ?$

9. Fill in the following table, then make a rough sketch of the graph of $y = x^2 e^x$.

x	-5	-4	-3	-2	-1	0	1
$y = x^2 e^x$							

10. Find the equation for the parabola $y = ax^2 + bx + c$ that passes through the three points $(1, -3)$, $(0, -6)$, and $(3, 15)$. (*Hint:* Determine a, b, and c.)

11. (a) If a firm sells Q tons of a product, the price P received per ton is $P = 1000 - \frac{1}{3}Q$. The price it has to pay per ton is $P = 800 + \frac{1}{5}Q$. In addition, it has transportation costs of 100 per ton. Express the firm's profit π as a function of Q, the number of tons sold, and find the profit-maximizing quantity.

    (b) Suppose the government imposes a tax on the firm's product of 10 per ton. Find the new expression for the firm's profits $\hat{\pi}$ and the new profit-maximizing quantity.

12. In Example 4.6.1, suppose a tax of t per unit produced is imposed. If $t < 100$, what production level now maximizes profits?

13. (a) A firm produces a commodity and receives \$100 for each unit sold. The cost of producing and selling x units is $20x + 0.25x^2$ dollars. Find the production level that maximizes profits.

    (b) A tax of \$10 per unit is imposed. What is now the optimal production level?

    (c) Answer the question in (b) if the sales price per unit is p, the total cost of producing and selling x units is $\alpha x + \beta x^2$, and the tax per unit is t.

SM 14. Write the following polynomials as products of linear factors:

    (a) $p(x) = x^3 + x^2 - 12x$ (b) $q(x) = 2x^3 + 3x^2 - 18x + 8$

15. Which of the following divisions leave no remainder? (a and b are constants; n is a natural number.)

    (a) $(x^3 - x - 1)/(x - 1)$ (b) $(2x^3 - x - 1)/(x - 1)$

    (c) $(x^3 - ax^2 + bx - ab)/(x - a)$ (d) $(x^{2n} - 1)/(x + 1)$

16. Find the values of k that make the polynomial $q(x)$ divide the polynomial $p(x)$:

    (a) $p(x) = x^2 - kx + 4$; $q(x) = x - 2$ (b) $p(x) = k^2 x^2 - kx - 6$; $q(x) = x + 2$

    (c) $p(x) = x^3 - 4x^2 + x + k$; $q(x) = x + 2$ (d) $p(x) = k^2 x^4 - 3kx^2 - 4$; $q(x) = x - 1$

(SM) **17.** The cubic function $p(x) = \frac{1}{4}x^3 - x^2 - \frac{11}{4}x + \frac{15}{2}$ has three real zeros. Verify that $x = 2$ is one of them, and find the other two.

18. In 1964 a five-year plan was introduced in Tanzania. One objective was to double the real per capita income over the next 15 years. What is the average annual rate of growth of real income per capita required to achieve this objective?

(SM) **19.** Figure B shows the graphs of two functions f and g. Check which of the constants a, b, c, p, q, and r are > 0, $= 0$, or < 0.

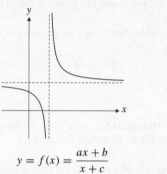
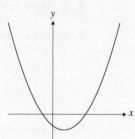

$$y = f(x) = \frac{ax + b}{x + c} \qquad\qquad y = g(x) = px^2 + qx + r$$

Figure B

20. (a) Determine the relationship between the Celsius (C) and Fahrenheit (F) temperature scales when you know that (i) the relation is linear; (ii) water freezes at $0°C$ and $32°F$; and (iii) water boils at $100°C$ and $212°F$.

(b) Which temperature is represented by the same number in both scales?

21. Solve for t: (a) $x = e^{at+b}$ (b) $e^{-at} = 1/2$ (c) $\dfrac{1}{\sqrt{2\pi}}e^{-\frac{1}{2}t^2} = \dfrac{1}{8}$

(SM) **22.** Prove the following equalities (with appropriate restrictions on the variables):

(a) $\ln x - 2 = \ln(x/e^2)$
(b) $\ln x - \ln y + \ln z = \ln \dfrac{xz}{y}$

(c) $3 + 2\ln x = \ln(e^3 x^2)$
(d) $\dfrac{1}{2}\ln x - \dfrac{3}{2}\ln\dfrac{1}{x} - \ln(x+1) = \ln\dfrac{x^2}{x+1}$

5

PROPERTIES
OF FUNCTIONS

*The paradox is now fully established that the
utmost abstractions are the true weapons with
which to control our thought of concrete facts.*
—A.N. Whitehead

This chapter begins by examining more closely functions of one variable and their graphs. In particular, we shall consider how changes in a function relate to shifts in its graph, and how to construct new functions from old ones. Next we discuss when a function has an inverse, and explain how an inverse function reverses the effect of the original function, and vice versa.

Any equation in two variables can be represented by a curve (or a set of points) in the *xy*-plane. Some examples illustrate this. The chapter ends with a discussion of the general concept of a function, which is one of the most fundamental in mathematics, of great importance also in economics.

5.1 Shifting Graphs

Bringing a significant new oil field into production will affect the supply curve for oil, with consequences for its equilibrium price. Adopting an improved technology in the production of a commodity will imply an upward shift in its production function. This section studies in general how the graph of a function $f(x)$ relates to the graphs of the functions

$$f(x) + c, \quad f(x + c), \quad cf(x), \quad \text{and} \quad f(-x)$$

Here c is a positive or negative constant. Before formulating any general rules, consider the following example.

EXAMPLE 1   We know the graph of $y = \sqrt{x}$, which is one of those drawn in Fig. 1. Sketch the graphs of $y = \sqrt{x} + 2$, $y = \sqrt{x} - 2$, $y = \sqrt{x + 2}$, $y = \sqrt{x - 2}$, $y = 2\sqrt{x}$, $y = -\sqrt{x}$, and $y = \sqrt{-x}$.

Solution: The graphs of $y = \sqrt{x} + 2$ and $y = \sqrt{x} - 2$, shown in Fig. 1, are obviously obtained by moving the graph of $y = \sqrt{x}$ upwards or downwards by two units, respectively.

The function $y = \sqrt{x + 2}$ is defined for $x + 2 \geq 0$, that is, for $x \geq -2$. Its graph, which is shown in Fig. 2, is obtained by moving the graph of $y = \sqrt{x}$ two units to the left. In the same way the graph of $y = \sqrt{x - 2}$ is obtained by moving the graph of $y = \sqrt{x}$ two units to the right, as shown in Fig. 2.

The graph of $y = 2\sqrt{x}$ is obtained by stretching the graph of f vertically upwards by a factor of two, as shown in Fig. 3. The graph of $y = -\sqrt{x}$ is obtained by reflecting the graph of $y = \sqrt{x}$ about the x-axis, as shown in Fig. 4.

Finally, the function $y = \sqrt{-x}$, is defined for $-x \geq 0$, that is, for $x \leq 0$, and its graph is shown in Fig. 5. It is obtained by reflecting the graph of $y = \sqrt{x}$ about the y-axis.

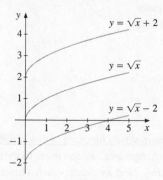

Figure 1 $y = \sqrt{x} \pm 2$

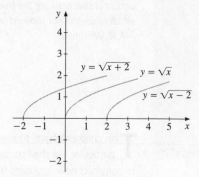

Figure 2 $y = \sqrt{x \pm 2}$

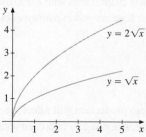

Figure 3 $y = \sqrt{x}$ and $y = 2\sqrt{x}$

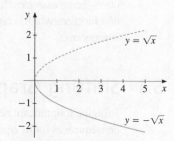

Figure 4 $y = \pm\sqrt{x}$

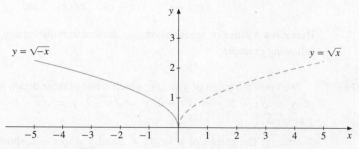

Figure 5 $y = \sqrt{\pm x}$

General rules for shifting the graph of $y = f(x)$:

(i) If $y = f(x)$ is replaced by $y = f(x) + c$, the graph is moved upwards by c units if $c > 0$ (downwards if $c < 0$).

(ii) If $y = f(x)$ is replaced by $y = f(x + c)$, the graph is moved c units to the left if $c > 0$ (to the right if $c < 0$).

(iii) If $y = f(x)$ is replaced by $y = cf(x)$, the graph is stretched vertically if $c > 0$ (stretched vertically and reflected about the x-axis if $c < 0$).

(iv) If $y = f(x)$ is replaced by $y = f(-x)$, the graph is reflected about the y-axis.

(1)

NOTE 1 If the independent variable is y and $x = g(y)$, then in the recipe one should interchange the words "upwards" with "to the right", and "downwards" with "to the left".

Combining these rules with Figures 4.3.5–4.3.10, a large number of useful graphs can be sketched with ease, as the following example illustrates.

EXAMPLE 2   Sketch the graphs of   (i) $y = 2 - (x + 2)^2$ (ii) $y = \dfrac{1}{x - 2} + 3$

Solution:

(i) First $y = x^2$ is reflected about the x-axis to obtain the graph of $y = -x^2$. This graph is then moved 2 units to the left, which results in the graph of $y = -(x + 2)^2$. Finally, this new graph is raised by 2 units, and we obtain the graph shown in Fig. 6.

(ii) The graph of $y = 1/(x - 2)$ is obtained by moving the graph of $y = 1/x$ in Fig. 4.3.9 2 units to the right. By moving the new graph 3 units up, we get the graph in Fig. 7.

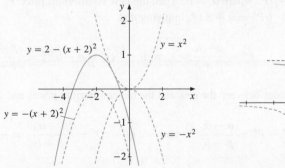

Figure 6 $y = 2 - (x + 2)^2$ **Figure 7** $y = 1/(x - 2) + 3$

EXAMPLE 3   In Example 4.5.3 we studied the simple demand and supply functions

$$D = 100 - P, \qquad S = 10 + 2P \qquad (*)$$

which gave the equilibrium price $P^e = 30$ with corresponding quantity $Q^e = 70$. Suppose that there is a shift to the right in the supply curve, so that the new supply at price P is $\tilde{S} = 16 + 2P$. Then the new equilibrium price $\tilde{P}^e$ is determined by the equation $100 - \tilde{P}^e = 16 + 2\tilde{P}^e$, which gives $\tilde{P}^e = 28$, with corresponding quantity $\tilde{Q}^e = 100 - 28 = 72$. Hence the new equilibrium price is lower than the old one, while the quantity is higher. The outward shift in the supply curve from S to $\tilde{S}$ implies that the equilibrium point moves down to the right along the unchanged demand curve. This is shown in Fig. 8.

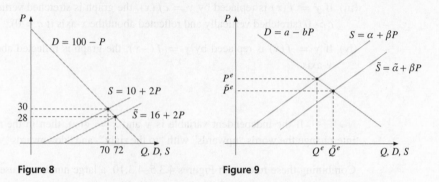

Figure 8   **Figure 9**

In Example 4.5.4 we studied the general linear demand and supply functions

$$D = a - bP, \qquad S = \alpha + \beta P$$

The equilibrium price P^e and corresponding equilibrium quantity Q^e were given by

$$P^e = \frac{a - \alpha}{\beta + b}, \qquad Q^e = \frac{a\beta + \alpha b}{\beta + b}$$

Suppose that there is a shift in the supply curve so that the new supply at each price P is $\tilde{S} = \tilde{\alpha} + \beta P$, where $\tilde{\alpha} > \alpha$. Then the new equilibrium price $\tilde{P}^e$ is determined by the equation $a - b\tilde{P}^e = \tilde{\alpha} + \beta \tilde{P}^e$, implying that

$$\tilde{P}^e = \frac{a - \tilde{\alpha}}{\beta + b}, \qquad \text{with} \qquad \tilde{Q}^e = a - b\tilde{P}^e = \frac{a\beta + \tilde{\alpha} b}{\beta + b}$$

The differences between the new and the old equilibrium prices and quantities are

$$\tilde{P}^e - P^e = \frac{\alpha - \tilde{\alpha}}{\beta + b} \qquad \text{and} \qquad \tilde{Q}^e - Q^e = \frac{(\tilde{\alpha} - \alpha)b}{\beta + b} = -b(\tilde{P}^e - P^e)$$

We see that $\tilde{P}^e$ is less than P^e (because $\tilde{\alpha} > \alpha$), while $\tilde{Q}^e$ is larger than Q^e. This is shown in Fig. 9. The rightward shift in the supply curve from S to $\tilde{S}$ implies that the equilibrium point moves down and to the right along the unchanged demand curve. Upward shifts in the supply curve resulting from, for example, taxation or increased cost, can be analysed in the same way. So can shifts in the demand curve.

EXAMPLE 4   Suppose a person earning y (dollars) in a given year pays $f(y)$ (dollars) in income tax. The government decides to reduce taxes. One proposal is to allow every individual to deduct d dollars from their taxable income before the tax is calculated. An alternative proposal involves calculating income tax on the full amount of taxable income, and then allowing each person a "tax credit" that deducts c dollars from the total tax due. Illustrate graphically the two proposals for a "normal" tax function f, and mark off the income y^* where the two proposals yield the same tax revenue.

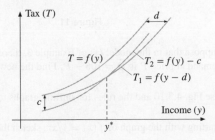

Figure 10 The graphs of $T_1 = f(y-d)$ and $T_2 = f(y)-c$

Solution: Figure 10 illustrates the situation for a "progressive" tax schedule in which the average tax rate, $T/y = f(y)/y$, is an increasing function of y. First draw the graph of the original tax function, $T = f(y)$. If taxable income is y and the deduction is d, then $y - d$ is the reduced taxable income, and so the tax liability is $f(y-d)$. By shifting the graph of the original tax function d units to the right, we obtain the graph of $T_1 = f(y-d)$.

The graph of $T_2 = f(y) - c$ is obtained by lowering the graph of $T = f(y)$ by c units. The income y^* which gives the same tax under the two different schemes is given by the equation

$$f(y^* - d) = f(y^*) - c$$

Note that $T_1 > T_2$ when $y < y^*$, but that $T_1 < T_2$ when $y > y^*$. Thus, the tax credit is worth more to those with low incomes; the deduction is worth more to those with high incomes (as one might expect).

PROBLEMS FOR SECTION 5.1

1. Use Fig. 4.3.6 and rules for shifting graphs to sketch the graphs of

  (a) $y = x^2 + 1$ (b) $y = (x+3)^2$ (c) $y = 3 - (x+1)^2$

2. If $y = f(x)$ has the graph suggested in Fig. 11, sketch the graphs of

  (a) $y = f(x-2)$ (b) $y = f(x) - 2$ (c) $y = f(-x)$

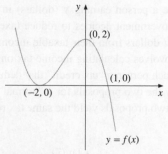

Figure 11

3. Suppose that in the model (∗) of Example 3, there is a positive shift in demand so that the new demand at price P is $\tilde{D} = 106 - P$. Find the new equilibrium point and illustrate.

4. Use Fig. 4.3.10 and the rules for shifting graphs to sketch the graph of $y = 2 - |x + 2|$.

5. Starting with the graph of $f(x) = 1/x^2$, sketch the graph of $g(x) = 2 - (x + 2)^{-2}$.

6. Suppose in Example 4 that $f(y) = Ay + By^2$ where A and B are positive parameters. Find y^* in this case.

5.2   New Functions from Old

Figure 1 gives a graphical representation of the number of male and female students registered at a certain university in the period 1986 to 1997.

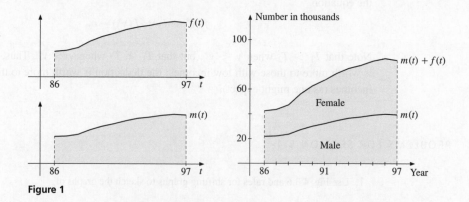

Figure 1

Let $f(t)$ and $m(t)$ denote the number of female and male students in year t, while $n(t)$ denotes the total number of students. Of course,

$$n(t) = f(t) + m(t)$$

The graph of the total number $n(t)$ is obtained by piling the graph of $f(t)$ on top of the graph of $m(t)$. Suppose in general that f and g are functions which both are defined in a set A of real numbers. The function F defined by the formula $F(x) = f(x) + g(x)$ is called the **sum** of f and g, and we write $F = f + g$. The function G defined by $G(x) = f(x) - g(x)$ is called the **difference** between f and g, and we write $G = f - g$.

Sums and differences of functions are often seen in economic models. Consider the following typical examples.

EXAMPLE 1   The cost of producing Q units of a commodity is $C(Q)$. The cost per unit of output, $A(Q) = C(Q)/Q$, is called the average cost.

$$A(Q) = C(Q)/Q \qquad \text{(average cost)}$$

If, in particular, $C(Q) = aQ^3 + bQ^2 + cQ + d$ is a cubic cost function of the type shown in Fig. 4.7.2, the average cost is

$$A(Q) = aQ^2 + bQ + c + d/Q, \qquad Q > 0$$

Thus $A(Q)$ is a sum of a quadratic function $y = aQ^2 + bQ + c$ and the hyperbola $y = d/Q$. Figure 2 shows how the graph of the average cost function $A(Q)$ is obtained by piling the graph of the hyperbola $y = d/Q$ onto the graph of the parabola $y = aQ^2 + bQ + c$.

Note that for small values of Q the graph of $A(Q)$ is close to the graph of $y = d/Q$, while for large values of Q, the graph is close to the parabola (since d/Q is small when Q is large).

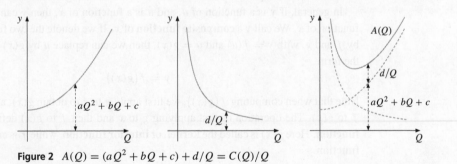

Figure 2 $A(Q) = (aQ^2 + bQ + c) + d/Q = C(Q)/Q$

Let $R(Q)$ denote the **revenues** obtained by producing (and selling) Q units. Then the **profit** $\pi(Q)$ is given by

$$\pi(Q) = R(Q) - C(Q)$$

An example showing how to construct the graph of the profit function $\pi(Q)$ is given in Fig. 3. In this case the firm gets a fixed price p per unit, so that the graph of $R(Q)$ is a straight line through the origin. The graph of $-C(Q)$ must be added to that of $R(Q)$. The production level which maximizes profit is Q^*.

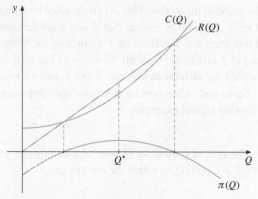

Figure 3 $\pi(Q) = R(Q) - C(Q)$

Products and Quotients

If f and g are defined in a set A, the function F defined by $F(x) = f(x) \cdot g(x)$ is called the **product** of f and g, and we put $F = f \cdot g$ (or fg). The function F defined where $g(x) \neq 0$ by $F(x) = f(x)/g(x)$ is called the **quotient** of f and g, and we write $F = f/g$. We have already seen examples of these operations. It is difficult to give useful general rules about the behaviour of the graphs of fg and f/g given the graphs of f and g.

Composite Functions

Suppose the demand for a commodity is a function x of its price p. Suppose that price p is not constant, but depends on time t. Then it is natural to regard x as a function of t.

In general, if y is a function of u, and u is a function of x, then y can be regarded as a function of x. We call y a **composite function** of x. If we denote the two functions involved by f and g, with $y = f(u)$ and $u = g(x)$, then we can replace u by $g(x)$ and so write y in the form

$$y = f\big(g(x)\big)$$

Note that when computing $f\big(g(x)\big)$, we first apply g to x to obtain $g(x)$, and then we apply f to $g(x)$. The operation of first applying g to x and then f to $g(x)$ defines a **composite function**. Here $g(x)$ is called the **kernel**, or **interior function**, while f is called the **exterior function**.

NOTE 1 The function that maps x to $f\big(g(x)\big)$ is often denoted by $f \circ g$. This is read as "f of g" or "f after g", and is called the **composition** of f with g. Correspondingly, $g \circ f$ denotes the function that maps x to $g\big(f(x)\big)$. Thus, we have

$$(f \circ g)(x) = f\big(g(x)\big) \qquad \text{and} \qquad (g \circ f)(x) = g\big(f(x)\big)$$

Usually, $f \circ g$ and $g \circ f$ are quite different functions. For instance, if $g(x) = 2 - x^2$ and $f(u) = u^3$, then $(f \circ g)(x) = (2 - x^2)^3$, whereas $(g \circ f)(x) = 2 - (x^3)^2 = 2 - x^6$; the two resulting polynomials are not the same.

It is easy to confuse $f \circ g$ with $f \cdot g$, especially typographically. But these two functions are defined in entirely different ways. When we evaluate $f \circ g$ at x, we first compute $g(x)$ and then evaluate f at $g(x)$. On the other hand, the product $f \cdot g$ of f and g is the function whose value at a particular number x is simply the product of $f(x)$ and $g(x)$, so $(f \cdot g)(x) = f(x) \cdot g(x)$.

Many calculators have several built-in functions. When we enter a number x_0 and press the key for the function f, we obtain $f(x_0)$. When we compute a composite function given f and g, and try to obtain the value of $f\big(g(x)\big)$, we proceed in a similar manner: enter the number x_0, then press the g key to get $g(x_0)$, and again press the f key to get $f(g(x_0))$. Suppose the machine has the functions $\boxed{1/x}$ and $\boxed{\sqrt{x}}$. If we enter the number 9, then press $\boxed{1/x}$ followed by $\boxed{\sqrt{x}}$, we get $1/3 = 0.33\ldots$ The computation we have performed can be illustrated as follows:

$$
\boxed{1/x} \qquad\qquad \boxed{\sqrt{x}}
$$
$$
9 \quad \longrightarrow \quad 1/9 \quad \longrightarrow \quad 1/3.
$$

Using function notation, $f(x) = \sqrt{x}$ and $g(x) = 1/x$, so $f(g(x)) = f(1/x) = \sqrt{1/x} = 1/\sqrt{x}$. In particular, $f(g(9)) = 1/\sqrt{9} = 1/3$.

EXAMPLE 2   Write the following as composite functions:

(a) $y = (x^3 + x^2)^{50}$ (b) $y = e^{-(x-\mu)^2}$ (μ is a constant)

Solution:

(a) You should ask yourself: What is the natural way of computing the values of this function? Given a value of x, you first compute $x^3 + x^2$, which gives the interior function, $g(x) = x^3 + x^2$. Then take the fiftieth power of the result, so the exterior function is $f(u) = u^{50}$. Hence,

$$
f(g(x)) = f(x^3 + x^2) = (x^3 + x^2)^{50}
$$

(b) We can choose the interior function as $g(x) = -(x - \mu)^2$ and the exterior function as $f(u) = e^u$. Then
$$
f(g(x)) = f(-(x - \mu)^2) = e^{-(x-\mu)^2}
$$

We could also have chosen $g(x) = (x - \mu)^2$ and $f(u) = e^{-u}$.

Symmetry

The function $f(x) = x^2$ satisfies $f(-x) = f(x)$, as indeed does any even power x^{2n} (with n an integer, positive or negative). So if $f(-x) = f(x)$ for all x in the domain of f, implying that the graph of f is **symmetric about the y-axis** as shown in Fig. 4, then f is called an **even** function.

On the other hand, any odd power x^{2n+1} (with n an integer) such as $f(x) = x^3$ satisfies $f(-x) = -f(x)$. So if $f(-x) = -f(x)$ for all x in the domain of f, implying that the graph of f is **symmetric about the origin**, as shown in Fig. 5, then f is called an **odd** function.

Finally, f is **symmetric about** a if $f(a + x) = f(a - x)$ for all x. The *graph* of f is then **symmetric about the line** $x = a$ as in Fig. 6. In Sec. 4.6 we showed that the quadratic function $f(x) = ax^2 + bx + c$ is symmetric about $x = -b/2a$. The function $y = e^{-(x-\mu)^2}$ from Example 2(b) is symmetric about $x = \mu$.

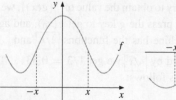

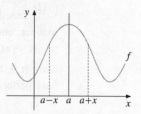

Figure 4 Even function   **Figure 5** Odd function   **Figure 6** Symmetric about $x = a$

PROBLEMS FOR SECTION 5.2

1. Show graphically how you find the graph of $y = \frac{1}{4}x^2 + 1/x$ by adding the graph of $1/x$ to the graph of $y = \frac{1}{4}x^2$. Assume $x > 0$.

2. Sketch the graphs of: (a) $y = \sqrt{x} - x$ (b) $y = e^x + e^{-x}$ (c) $y = e^{-x^2} + x$

3. If $f(x) = 3x - x^3$ and $g(x) = x^3$, compute: $(f + g)(x)$, $(f - g)(x)$, $(fg)(x)$, $(f/g)(x)$, $f(g(1))$, and $g(f(1))$.

4. Let $f(x) = 3x + 7$. Compute $f(f(x))$. Find the value x^* when $f(f(x^*)) = 100$.

5. Compute $\ln(\ln e)$ and $(\ln e)^2$. What do you notice? (This illustrates how, if we define the function f^2 by $f^2(x) = (f(x))^2$, then, in general, $f^2(x) \neq f(f(x))$.)

5.3   Inverse Functions

Suppose that the demand quantity D for a commodity depends on the price per unit P according to

$$D = \frac{30}{P^{1/3}}$$

This formula tells us directly the demand D corresponding to a given price P. If, for example, $P = 27$, then $D = 30/27^{1/3} = 10$. So D is a function of P. That is, $D = f(P)$ with $f(P) = 30/P^{1/3}$. Note that demand decreases as the price increases.

If we look at the matter from a producer's point of view, however, it may be more natural to treat output as something it can choose and consider the resulting price. The producer wants to know the *inverse* function, in which price depends on the quantity sold.

This functional relationship is obtained by solving $D = 30/P^{1/3}$ for P. First we obtain $P^{1/3} = 30/D$ and then $(P^{1/3})^3 = (30/D)^3$, so that the original equation is equivalent to

$$P = \frac{27\,000}{D^3}$$

This equation gives us directly the price P corresponding to a given output D. For example, if $D = 10$, then $P = 27\,000/10^3 = 27$. In this case, P is a function $g(D)$ of D, with $g(D) = 27\,000/D^3$.

The two variables D and P in this example are related in a way that allows each to be regarded as a function of the other. In fact, the two functions

$$f(P) = 30p^{-1/3} \qquad \text{and} \qquad g(D) = 27\,000D^{-3}$$

are *inverses* of each other. We say that f is the inverse of g, and that g is the inverse of f.

Note that the two functions f and g convey exactly the same information. For example, the fact that demand is 10 at price 27 can be expressed using either f or g:

$$f(27) = 10 \qquad \text{or} \qquad g(10) = 27$$

In Example 4.5.3 we considered an even simpler demand function $D = 100 - P$. Solving for P we get $P = 100 - D$, which was referred to as the inverse demand function.

Suppose in general that f is a function with domain $D_f = A$, meaning that to each x in A there corresponds a unique number $f(x)$. Recall that if f has domain A, then the range of f is the set $B = R_f = \{f(x) : x \in A\}$, which is also denoted by $f(A)$. The range B consists of all numbers $f(x)$ obtained by letting x vary in A. Furthermore, f is said to be **one-to-one** in A if f never has the same value at any two different points in A. In other words, for each one y in B, there is exactly one x in A such that $y = f(x)$. Equivalently, f is one-to-one in A provided that it has the property that, whenever x_1 and x_2 both lie in A and $x_1 \neq x_2$, then $f(x_1) \neq f(x_2)$. It is evident that if a function is strictly increasing in all of A, or strictly decreasing in all of A, then it is one-to-one. A particular one-to-one function f is illustrated in Fig. 1; another function g that is not one-to-one is shown in Fig. 2.

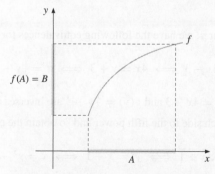

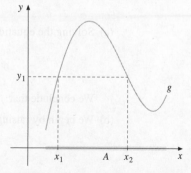

Figure 1 f is one-to-one with domain A and range B. f has an inverse

Figure 2 g is *not* one-to-one and hence has no inverse over A. Which x-value should be associated with y_1?

DEFINITION OF INVERSE FUNCTION

Let f be a function with domain A and range B. If and only if f is one-to-one, it has an **inverse function** g with domain B and range A. The function g is given by the following rule: For each y in B, the value $g(y)$ is the unique number x in A such that $f(x) = y$. Then
(1)

$$g(y) = x \iff y = f(x) \qquad (x \in A, \ y \in B)$$

A direct implication of (1) is that

$$g(f(x)) = x \ \text{ for all } x \text{ in } A \qquad \text{and} \qquad f(g(y)) = y \ \text{ for all } y \text{ in } B \tag{2}$$

The equation $g(f(x)) = x$ shows what happens if we first apply f to x and then apply g to $f(x)$: we get x back because g *undoes what f did to x*. Note that if g is the inverse of a function f, then f is also the inverse of g.

NOTE 1   If g is the inverse of f, it is standard to use the notation f^{-1} for g. This sometimes leads to confusion. If a is a number, then a^{-1} means $1/a$. But $f^{-1}(x)$ does *not* mean $1/f(x) = (f(x))^{-1}$. For example: *The functions defined by $y = 1/(x^2+2x+3)$ and $y = x^2 + 2x + 3$ are **not** inverses of each other, but reciprocals.*

In simple cases, we can use the same method as in the introductory example to find the inverse of a given function (and hence automatically verify that the inverse exists). Some more examples follow.

EXAMPLE 1   Solve the following equations for x and find the corresponding inverse functions:

(a) $y = 4x - 3$ (b) $y = \sqrt[5]{x+1}$ (c) $y = \dfrac{3x-1}{x+4}$

Solution:
(a) Solving the equation for x, we have the following equivalences for all x and all y:

$$y = 4x - 3 \iff 4x = y + 3 \iff x = \tfrac{1}{4}y + \tfrac{3}{4}$$

We conclude that $f(x) = 4x - 3$ and $g(y) = \tfrac{1}{4}y + \tfrac{3}{4}$ are inverses of each other.

(b) We begin by raising each side to the fifth power and so obtain the equivalences

$$y = \sqrt[5]{x+1} \iff y^5 = x + 1 \iff x = y^5 - 1$$

These are valid for all x and all y. Hence, we have shown that $f(x) = \sqrt[5]{x+1}$ and $g(y) = y^5 - 1$ are inverses of each other.

(c) Here we begin by multiplying both sides of the equation by $x + 4$ to obtain $y(x + 4) = 3x - 1$. From this equation, we obtain $yx + 4y = 3x - 1$ or $x(3 - y) = 4y + 1$. Hence,

$$x = \frac{4y + 1}{3 - y}$$

We conclude that $f(x) = (3x - 1)/(x + 4)$ and $g(y) = (4y + 1)/(3 - y)$ are inverses of each other. Observe that f is only defined for $x \neq -4$, and g is only defined for $y \neq 3$. So the equivalence in (1) is valid only with these restrictions.

A Geometric Characterization of Inverse Functions

In our introductory example, we saw that $f(P) = 30p^{-1/3}$ and $g(D) = 27\,000D^{-3}$ were inverse functions. Because of the concrete interpretation of the symbols P and D, it was natural to describe the functions the way we did. In other circumstances, it may be convenient to use the same variable as argument in both f and g. In Example 1(a), we saw that $f(x) = 4x - 3$ and $g(y) = \frac{1}{4}y + \frac{3}{4}$ were inverses of each other. If also we use x instead of y as the variable of the function g, we find that

$$f(x) = 4x - 3 \quad \text{and} \quad g(x) = \tfrac{1}{4}x + \tfrac{3}{4} \quad \text{are inverses of each other} \quad (*)$$

In the same way, on the basis of Example 1(b) we can say that

$$f(x) = (x + 1)^{1/5} \quad \text{and} \quad g(x) = x^5 - 1 \quad \text{are inverses of each other} \quad (**)$$

There is an interesting geometric property of the graphs of inverse functions. For the pairs of inverse functions in $(*)$ and $(**)$, the graphs of f and g are mirror images of each other with respect to the line $y = x$. This is illustrated in Figs. 3 and 4.

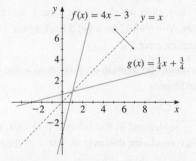

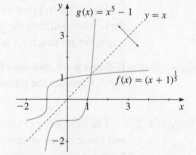

Figure 3 f and g are inverses of each other   **Figure 4** f and g are inverses of each other

Suppose in general that f and g are inverses of each other. The fact that (a, b) lies on the graph f means that $b = f(a)$. According to (1), this implies that $g(b) = a$, so that (b, a) lies on the graph of g. Because (a, b) and (b, a) lie symmetrically about the line $y = x$ (see Problem 8), we have the following conclusion:

When two functions f and g are inverses of each other, then the graphs of
$y = f(x)$ and $y = g(x)$ are symmetric about the line $y = x$. (The units on the coordinate axes must be same.) $\qquad$ (3)

NOTE 2 When the functions f and g are inverses of each other, then by definition (1), the equations $y = f(x)$ and $x = g(y)$ are equivalent. The two functions actually have exactly the same graph, though in the second case we should think of x depending on y, instead of the other way around. On the other hand, the graphs of $y = f(x)$ and $y = g(x)$ are symmetric about the line $y = x$.

For instance, Examples 4.5.3 and 5.1.3 discuss demand and supply curves. These can be thought of as the graphs of a function where quantity Q depends on price P, or equivalently of the inverse function where price P depends on quantity Q.

In all the examples examined so far, the inverse could be expressed in terms of known formulas. It turns out that even if a function has an inverse, it may be impossible to express it in terms of a function we know. *Inverse functions are actually an important source of new functions.* A typical case arises in connection with the exponential function. In Section 4.9 we showed that $y = e^x$ is strictly increasing and that it tends to 0 as x tends $-\infty$ and to ∞ as x tends to ∞. For each positive y there exists a uniquely determined x such that $e^x = y$. In Section 4.10 we called the new function the natural logarithm function, ln, and we have the equivalence $y = e^x \iff x = \ln y$. The *functions $f(x) = e^x$ and $g(y) = \ln y$ are therefore inverses of each other.* Because the ln function appears in so many connections, it is tabulated, and moreover represented by a separate key on many calculators.

If a calculator has a certain function f represented by a key, then it will usually have another which represents its inverse function f^{-1}. If, for example, it has an $\boxed{e^x}$-key, it also has an $\boxed{\ln x}$-key. Since $f^{-1}(f(x)) = x$, if we enter a number x, press the $\boxed{f}$-key and then press the $\boxed{f^{-1}}$-key, then we should get x back again. Try to enter 5, use the $\boxed{e^x}$-key and then the $\boxed{\ln x}$-key. You should then get 5 back again. (One reason why you might not get exactly 5 is a rounding error.)

If f and g are inverses of each other, the domain of f is equal to the range of g, and vice versa. Consider the following examples.

EXAMPLE 2 The function $f(x) = \sqrt{3x + 9}$, defined in the interval $[-3, \infty)$, *is* strictly increasing and hence has an inverse. Find a formula for the inverse. Use x as the free variable for both functions.

Solution: When x increases from -3 to ∞, $f(x)$ increases from 0 to ∞, so the range of f is $[0, \infty)$. Hence f has an inverse g defined on $[0, \infty)$. To find a formula for the inverse, we solve the equation $y = \sqrt{3x + 9}$ for x. Squaring gives $y^2 = 3x + 9$, which solved for x gives $x = \frac{1}{3}y^2 - 3$. Interchanging x and y in this expression to make x the free variable, we find that the inverse function of f is $y = g(x) = \frac{1}{3}x^2 - 3$, defined on $[0, \infty)$. See Fig. 5.

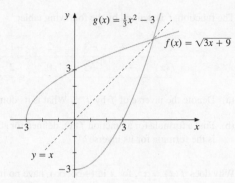

Figure 5

EXAMPLE 3   Consider the function f defined by the formula $f(x) = 4\ln(\sqrt{x+4}-2)$.

(a) For which values of x is $f(x)$ defined? Determine the range of f.

(b) Find a formula for its inverse. Use x as the free variable.

Solution:

(a) In order for $\sqrt{x+4}$ to be defined, x must be ≥ -4. But we also have to make sure that $\sqrt{x+4}-2 > 0$, otherwise the logarithm is not defined. Now, $\sqrt{x+4}-2 > 0$ means that $\sqrt{x+4} > 2$, or $x+4 > 4$, that is, $x > 0$. The domain of f is therefore $(0, \infty)$. As x varies from near 0 to ∞, $f(x)$ increases from $-\infty$ to ∞. The range of f is therefore $(-\infty, \infty)$.

(b) If $y = 4\ln(\sqrt{x+4}-2)$, then $\ln(\sqrt{x+4}-2) = y/4$, so that $\sqrt{x+4}-2 = e^{y/4}$ and then $\sqrt{x+4} = 2+e^{y/4}$. By squaring each side we obtain $x+4 = (2+e^{y/4})^2 = 4 + 4e^{y/4} + e^{y/2}$, so that $x = 4e^{y/4} + e^{y/2}$. The inverse function, with x as the free variable, is therefore $y = e^{x/2}+4e^{x/4}$. It is defined in $(-\infty, \infty)$ with range $(0, \infty)$.

PROBLEMS FOR SECTION 5.3

1. Demand D as a function of price P is given by

$$D = \frac{32}{5} - \frac{3}{10}P$$

Solve the equation for P and find the inverse function.

2. The demand D for sugar in the US in the period 1915–1929, as a function of the price P, was estimated by H. Schultz as

$$D = f(P) = \frac{157.8}{P^{0.3}} \qquad (D \text{ and } P \text{ are measured in appropriate units})$$

Solve the equation for P and so find the inverse of f.

3. Find the domains, ranges, and inverses of the functions given by the four formulas

(a) $y = -3x$ (b) $y = 1/x$ (c) $y = x^3$ (d) $y = \sqrt{\sqrt{x}-2}$

(SM) **4.** The function f is defined by the following table:

x	-4	-3	-2	-1	0	1	2
$f(x)$	-4	-2	0	2	4	6	8

(a) Denote the inverse of f by f^{-1}. What is its domain? What is the value of $f^{-1}(2)$?

(b) Find a formula for a function $f(x)$, defined for all real x, which agrees with this table. What is the formula for its inverse?

5. Why does $f(x) = x^2$, for x in $(-\infty, \infty)$, have no inverse function? Show that f restricted to $[0, \infty)$ has an inverse, and find that inverse.

6. Formalize the following statements:

(a) Halving and doubling are inverse operations.

(b) The operation of multiplying a number by 3 and then subtracting 2 is the inverse of the operation of adding 2 to the number and then dividing by 3.

(c) The operation of subtracting 32 from a number and then multiplying the result by 5/9 is the inverse of the operation of multiplying a number by 9/5 and then adding 32. "Fahrenheit to Celsius, and Celsius to Fahrenheit". (See Example 1.6.4.)

7. If f is the function that tells you how many kilograms of carrots you can buy for a specified amount of money, then what does f^{-1} tell you?

8. (a) Draw a coordinate system in the plane. Show that points $(3, 1)$ and $(1, 3)$ are symmetric about the line $y = x$, and the same for $(5, 3)$ and $(3, 5)$.

(b) Use properties of congruent triangles to prove that points (a, b) and (b, a) in the plane are symmetric about the line $y = x$. What is the point half-way between these two points?

(SM) **9.** Find inverses of the following functions (use x as the independent variable):

(a) $f(x) = (x^3 - 1)^{1/3}$ (b) $f(x) = \dfrac{x+1}{x-2}$ (c) $f(x) = (1 - x^3)^{1/5} + 2$

(SM) **10.** The functions defined by the following formulas are strictly increasing in their domains. Find the domain of each inverse function, and a formula for the corresponding inverse.

(a) $y = e^{x+4}$ (b) $y = \ln x - 4, \ x > 0$ (c) $y = \ln\left(2 + e^{x-3}\right)$

HARDER PROBLEM

11. Find the inverse of $f(x) = \frac{1}{2}(e^x - e^{-x})$. (*Hint:* You need to solve a quadratic equation in $z = e^x$.)

5.4   Graphs of Equations

The equations

$$x\sqrt{y} = 2, \qquad x^2 + y^2 = 16, \qquad \text{and} \qquad y^3 + 3x^2 y = 13$$

are three examples of equations in two variables x and y. A **solution** of such an equation is an ordered pair (a, b) such that the equation is satisfied when we replace x by a and y by b. The **solution set** of the equation is the set of all solutions. Representing all pairs in the solution set in a Cartesian coordinate system gives a set called the **graph** of the equation.

EXAMPLE 1   Find some solutions of each of the equations $x\sqrt{y} = 2$ and $x^2 + y^2 = 16$, and try to sketch their graphs.

Solution: From $x\sqrt{y} = 2$ we obtain $y = 4/x^2$. Hence it is easy to find corresponding values for x and y as given in Table 1.

Table 1   Solutions of $x\sqrt{y} = 2$

x	1	2	4	6
y	4	1	1/4	1/9

The graph is drawn in Fig. 1, along with the four points in the table.

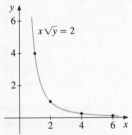

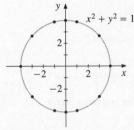

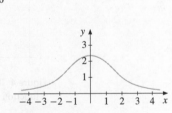

Figure 1 $x\sqrt{y} = 2$ **Figure 2** $x^2 + y^2 = 16$ **Figure 3** $y^3 + 3x^2 y = 13$

For $x^2 + y^2 = 16$, if $y = 0$, $x^2 = 16$, so $x = \pm 4$. Thus $(4, 0)$ and $(-4, 0)$ are two solutions. Table 2 combines these with some other solutions.

Table 2   Solutions of $x^2 + y^2 = 16$

x	-4	-3	-1	0	1	3	4
y	0	$\pm\sqrt{7}$	$\pm\sqrt{15}$	± 4	$\pm\sqrt{15}$	$\pm\sqrt{7}$	0

In Fig. 2 we have plotted the points given in the table, and the graph seems to be a circle. (This is confirmed in the next section.)

EXAMPLE 2   What can you say about the graph of the equation $y^3 + 3x^2y = 13$?

Solution: If $x = 0$, then $y^3 = 13$, so that $y = \sqrt[3]{13} \approx 2.35$. Hence $(0, \sqrt[3]{13})$ lies on the graph. Note that if (x_0, y_0) lies on the graph, so does $(-x_0, y_0)$, since x is raised to the second power. Hence the graph is symmetric about the y-axis. You may notice that $(2, 1)$, and hence $(-2, 1)$, are solutions. (Additional points can found by solving the equation for x, to obtain $x = \pm\sqrt{(13 - y^3)/3y}$.)

If we write the equation in the form

$$y = \frac{13}{y^2 + 3x^2} \qquad (*)$$

we see that no point (x, y) on the graph can have $y \le 0$, so that the whole graph lies above the x-axis. From $(*)$ it also follows that if x is large positive or negative, then y must be small. Figure 3 displays the graph, drawn by computer program, which accords with these findings.

Vertical-Line Test

Graphs of different functions can have innumerable different shapes. However, not all curves in the plane are graphs of functions. By definition, a function assigns to each point x in the domain only one y-value. *The graph of a function therefore has the property that a vertical line through any point on the x-axis has at most one point of intersection with the graph.* This simple *vertical-line test* is illustrated in Figs. 4 and 5.

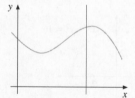

Figure 4 The graph represents a function

Figure 5 The graph does *not* represent a function

The graph of the circle $x^2 + y^2 = 16$, shown in Fig. 2, is a typical example of a graph that does *not* represent a function, since it does not pass the vertical-line test. A vertical line $x = a$ for any a with $-4 < a < 4$ intersects the circle at *two* points. Solving the equation $x^2 + y^2 = 16$ for y, we obtain $y = \pm\sqrt{16 - x^2}$. Note that the upper semicircle alone is the graph of the function $y = \sqrt{16 - x^2}$, and the lower semicircle is the graph of the function $y = -\sqrt{16 - x^2}$. Both these functions are defined on the interval $[-4, 4]$.

Choosing Units

A function of one variable is a rule assigning numbers in its range to numbers in its domain. When we describe an empirical relationship by means of a function, we must first choose the units of measurement. For instance we might measure time in years, days, or weeks.

We might measure money in dollars, yen, or euros. The choice we make will influence the visual impression conveyed by the graph of the function.

Figure 6 illustrates a standard trick which is often used to influence people's impressions of empirical relationships. In both diagrams time is measured in years and consumption in billions of dollars. They both graph the same function. But if you were trying to impress an audience with the performance of the national economy, which one would you choose?

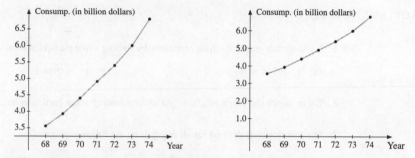

Figure 6 Graphical representations of the same function with different units of measurement

Compound Functions

Sometimes a function is defined in several pieces, by giving a separate formula for each of a number of disjoint parts of the domain. Two examples of such **compound functions** are presented next.

EXAMPLE 3   Draw the graph of the function f defined by

$$f(x) = \begin{cases} -x & \text{for } x \le 0 \\ x^2 & \text{for } 0 < x \le 1 \\ 1.5 & \text{for } x > 1 \end{cases}$$

Solution: The graph is drawn in Fig. 7. The arrow at $(1, 1.5)$ indicates that this point is not part of the graph of the function. The function has a *discontinuity* at $x = 1$. (See Section 7.8.)

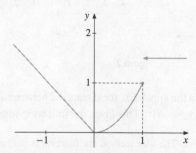

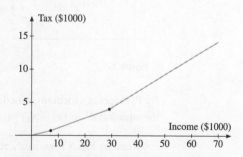

Figure 7 Graph of the function in Example 3

Figure 8 US Federal Income Tax in 2004

EXAMPLE 4   (US Federal Income Tax (2004) for Single Persons) In Fig. 8 we show a part of the graph of this income tax function.[1] The marginal rate of tax on income up to $7150 was 10%, on income between $7151 and $29050 it was 15%, then on income between $29051 and $70350 it was 25%. For income above this level there are higher marginal rates; the highest has 35% for income above $319100.

PROBLEMS FOR SECTION 5.4

(SM) **1.** Try to sketch graphs of these equations by finding some particular solutions.

(a) $x^2 + 2y^2 = 6$ 　　　　　　　　　　　　(b) $y^2 - x^2 = 1$

2. Try to sketch the graph of $\sqrt{x} + \sqrt{y} = 5$ by finding some particular solutions.

3. The function F is defined for all $R_N \geq 0$ by the following formulas:

$$F(R_N) = \begin{cases} 0 & \text{for } R_N \leq 7500 \\ 0.044(R_N - 7500) & \text{for } R_N > 7500 \end{cases}$$

Compute $F(100\,000)$, and sketch the graph of F.

5.5 Distance in the Plane. Circles

Let $P_1 = (x_1, y_1)$ and $P_2 = (x_2, y_2)$ be two points in the xy-plane as shown in Fig. 1.

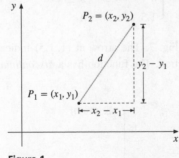

Figure 1

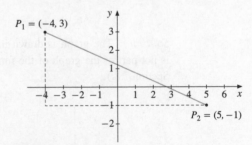

Figure 2

By Pythagoras's theorem, stated in the appendix, the distance d between P_1 and P_2 satisfies the equation $d^2 = (x_2 - x_1)^2 + (y_2 - y_1)^2$. This gives the following important formula:

---

[1] Of course, Fig. 8 is an idealization. The true income tax function is defined only for integral numbers of dollars—or, more precisely, it is a discontinuous "step function" which jumps up slightly whenever income rises by another dollar.

DISTANCE FORMULA

The distance between the points (x_1, y_1) and (x_2, y_2) is

$$d = \sqrt{(x_2 - x_1)^2 + (y_2 - y_1)^2}$$

(1)

We considered two points in the first quadrant to prove the distance formula. It turns out that the same formula is valid irrespective of where the two points P_1 and P_2 lie. Note also that since $(x_1 - x_2)^2 = (x_2 - x_1)^2$ and $(y_1 - y_2)^2 = (y_2 - y_1)^2$, it makes no difference which point is P_1 and which is P_2.

Some find formula (1) hard to grasp. In words it tells us that we can find the distance between two points in the plane as follows:

Take the difference between the x-coordinates and square what you get. Do the same with the y-coordinates. Add the results and then take the square root.

EXAMPLE 1   Find the distance d between $P_1 = (-4, 3)$ and $P_2 = (5, -1)$. (See Fig. 2.)

Solution: Using (1) with $x_1 = -4$, $y_1 = 3$ and $x_2 = 5$, $y_2 = -1$, we have

$$d = \sqrt{(5 - (-4))^2 + (-1 - 3)^2} = \sqrt{9^2 + (-4)^2} = \sqrt{81 + 16} = \sqrt{97} \approx 9.85$$

Circles

Let (a, b) be a point in the plane. *The circle with radius r and centre at (a, b) is the set of all points (x, y) whose distance from (a, b) is equal to r.* Applying the distance formula to the typical point (x, y) on the circle shown in Fig. 3 gives

$$\sqrt{(x - a)^2 + (y - b)^2} = r$$

Squaring each side yields:

EQUATION OF A CIRCLE

The equation of a circle with centre at (a, b) and radius r is

$$(x - a)^2 + (y - b)^2 = r^2$$

(2)

A graph of (2) is shown in Fig. 3. Note that if we let $a = b = 0$ and $r = 4$, then (2) reduces to $x^2 + y^2 = 16$. This is the equation of a circle with centre at $(0, 0)$ and radius 4, as shown in Fig. 5.4.2.

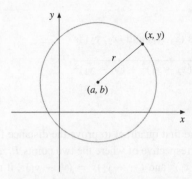

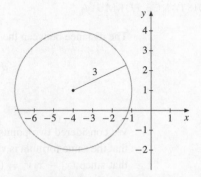

Figure 3 Circle with centre at (a, b) and radius r

Figure 4 Circle with centre at $(-4, 1)$ and radius 3

EXAMPLE 2   Find the equation of the circle with centre at $(-4, 1)$ and radius 3.

Solution: Here $a = -4$, $b = 1$, and $r = 3$. (See Fig. 4.) So according to (2), the equation for the circle is

$$(x + 4)^2 + (y - 1)^2 = 9 \qquad (*)$$

Expanding the squares to obtain $x^2 + 8x + 16 + y^2 - 2y + 1 = 9$, and then collecting terms, we have

$$x^2 + y^2 + 8x - 2y + 8 = 0 \qquad (**)$$

The equation of the circle given in $(**)$ has the disadvantage that we cannot immediately read off its centre and radius. If we are given equation $(**)$, however, we can use the method of "completing the squares" to deduce $(*)$ from $(**)$. See Problem 5.

Ellipses and Hyperbolas

A very important type of curve in physics and astronomy is the ellipse. (After all, the planets, including the Earth, move around the Sun in orbits that are approximately elliptical.) Occasionally, ellipses also appear in economics and statistics. The simplest type of ellipse has the equation

$$\frac{(x - x_0)^2}{a^2} + \frac{(y - y_0)^2}{b^2} = 1 \qquad \textbf{(ellipse)} \qquad (3)$$

This ellipse has centre at (x_0, y_0) and its graph is shown in Fig. 5. Note that when $a = b$, the ellipse degenerates into a circle.

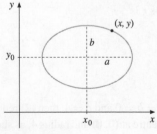

Figure 5 Ellipse

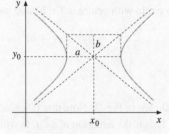

Figure 6 Hyperbola

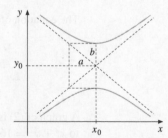

Figure 7 Hyperbola

Figures 6 and 7 show the graphs of the two **hyperbolas**

$$\frac{(x-x_0)^2}{a^2} - \frac{(y-y_0)^2}{b^2} = +1 \quad \text{and} \quad \frac{(x-x_0)^2}{a^2} - \frac{(y-y_0)^2}{b^2} = -1 \quad (4)$$

respectively. The asymptotes are the dashed lines in Figs. 6 and 7. They are the same pair in each figure. Their equations are $y - y_0 = \pm\frac{b}{a}(x - x_0)$.

We end this section by noting that the graph of the general quadratic equation

$$Ax^2 + Bxy + Cy^2 + Dx + Ey + F = 0 \quad (5)$$

where A, B, and C are not all 0, will have one of the following shapes:

- If $4AC > B^2$, either an ellipse (possibly a circle), or a single point, or empty.

- If $4AC = B^2$, either a parabola, or one line or two parallel lines, or empty.

- If $4AC < B^2$, either a hyperbola, or two intersecting lines.

PROBLEMS FOR SECTION 5.5

1. Determine the distances between the following pairs of points:

    (a) $(1, 3)$ and $(2, 4)$ (b) $(-1, 2)$ and $(-3, 3)$ (c) $(3/2, -2)$ and $(-5, 1)$

    (d) (x, y) and $(2x, y + 3)$ (e) (a, b) and $(-a, b)$ (f) $(a, 3)$ and $(2 + a, 5)$

2. The distance between $(2, 4)$ and $(5, y)$ is $\sqrt{13}$. Find y. (Explain geometrically why there must be two values of y.)

3. Find the distances between each pair of points:

    (a) $(3.998, 2.114)$ and $(1.130, -2.416)$ (b) $(\pi, 2\pi)$ and $(-\pi, 1)$

4. Find the equations of the circles with:

    (a) Centre at $(2, 3)$ and radius 4.   (b) Centre at $(2, 5)$ and one point at $(-1, 3)$.

5. To show that the graph of $x^2 + y^2 - 10x + 14y + 58 = 0$ is a circle, we can argue like this: First rearrange the equation to read $(x^2 - 10x) + (y^2 + 14y) = -58$. Completing the two squares gives: $(x^2 - 10x + 5^2) + (y^2 + 14y + 7^2) = -58 + 5^2 + 7^2 = 16$. Thus the equation becomes

$$(x - 5)^2 + (y + 7)^2 = 16$$

whose graph is a circle with centre $(5, -7)$ and radius $\sqrt{16} = 4$. Use this method to find the centre and the radius of the two circles with equations:

    (a) $x^2 + y^2 + 10x - 6y + 30 = 0$ (b) $3x^2 + 3y^2 + 18x - 24y = -39$

6. Prove that if the distance from a point (x, y) to the point $(-2, 0)$ is twice the distance from (x, y) to $(4, 0)$, then (x, y) must lie on the circle with centre $(6, 0)$ and radius 4.

7. In Example 4.7.7 we considered the function $y = (ax + b)/(cx + d)$, and we claimed that for $c \neq 0$ the graph was a hyperbola. See how this accords with the classification below (5).

HARDER PROBLEM

(SM) 8. Show that the graph of

$$x^2 + y^2 + Ax + By + C = 0 \qquad (A, B, \text{ and } C \text{ constants}) \qquad (*)$$

is a circle if $A^2 + B^2 > 4C$. Find its centre and radius. (See Problem 5.) What happens if $A^2 + B^2 \leq 4C$?

5.6 General Functions

So far we have studied functions of one variable. These are functions whose domain is a set of real numbers, and whose range is also a set of real numbers. Yet a realistic description of many economic phenomena requires considering a large number of variables simultaneously. For example, the demand for a good like butter is a function of several variables such as the price of the good, the prices of complements like bread, substitutes like olive oil or margarine, as well as consumers' incomes, their doctors' advice, and so on.

Actually, you have probably already seen many special functions of several variables. For instance, the formula $V = \pi r^2 h$ for the volume V of a cylinder with base radius r and height h involves a function of two variables. (Of course, in this case $\pi \approx 3.14159$ is a mathematical constant.) A change in one of these variables will not affect the value of the other variable. For each pair of positive numbers (r, h), there is a definite value for the volume V. To emphasize that V depends on the values of both r and h, we write

$$V(r, h) = \pi r^2 h$$

For $r = 2$ and $h = 3$, we obtain $V(2, 3) = 12\pi$, whereas $r = 3$ and $h = 2$ give $V(3, 2) = 18\pi$. Also, $r = 1$ and $h = 1/\pi$ give $V(1, 1/\pi) = 1$. Note in particular that $V(2, 3) \neq V(3, 2)$.

In some abstract economic models, it may be enough to know that there is some functional relationship between variables, without specifying the dependence more closely. For instance, suppose a market sells three commodities whose prices per unit are respectively p, q, and r. Then economists generally assume that the demand for one of the commodities by an individual with income m is given by a function $f(p, q, r, m)$ of four variables, without necessarily specifying the precise form of that function.

An extensive discussion of functions of several variables begins in Chapter 11. This section introduces an even more general type of function. In fact, general functions of the kind presented here are of fundamental importance in practically every area of pure and applied mathematics, including mathematics applied to economics. Here is the general definition:

A **function** is a rule which to each element in a set A associates one and only one element in a set B. (1)

The following indicates how very wide is the concept of a function.

EXAMPLE 1 (a) The function that assigns to each triangle in a plane the area of that triangle (measured, say, in cm^2).

(b) The function that determines the social security number, or other identification number, of each taxpayer.

(c) The function that for each point P in a horizontal plane determines the point lying 3 units above P.

(d) Let A be the set of possible actions that a person can choose in a certain situation. Suppose that every action a in A produces a certain result (say, a certain profit) $\varphi(a)$. In this way, we have defined a function φ with domain A.

If we denote the function by f, the set A is called the **domain** of f, and B is called the **target** or the **codomain**. The two sets A and B need not consist of numbers, but can be sets of arbitrary elements. The definition of a function requires three objects to be specified:

(i) A domain A

(ii) A target B

(iii) A rule that assigns a *unique* element in B to *each* element in A.

Nevertheless, in many cases, we refrain from specifying the sets A and/or B explicitly when it is obvious from the context what these sets are.

An important requirement in the definition of a function is that to each element in the domain A, there corresponds a *unique* element in the target B. While it is meaningful to talk about the function that assigns the natural mother to every child, the rule that assigns the aunt to any child does not, in general, define a function, because many children have more than one aunt. Explain why the following rule, as opposed to the one in Example 1(c), does not define a function: "to a point P in the plane assign a point that lies 3 units from P".

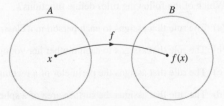

Figure 1 A function from A to B

If f is a function with domain A and target B, we often say that f is a **function from A to B**, and write $f : A \rightarrow B$. The functional relationship is often represented as in Fig. 1. Other words that are sometimes used instead of "function" include **transformation** and **map** or **mapping**.

The particular value $f(x)$ is often called the **image** of the element x by the function f. The set of elements in B that are images of at least one element in A is called the **range** of the function. Thus, the range is a subset of the target. If we denote the range of f by R_f, then $R_f = \{f(x) : x \in A\}$. This is also written as $f(A)$. The range of the function in Example 1(a) is the set of all positive numbers. Explain why the range of the function in (c) must be a whole plane.

The definition of a function requires that only *one* element in B be assigned to each element in A. However, different elements in A might be mapped to the same element in B. In Example 1(a), for instance, many different triangles have the same area. If each element of B is the image of at most one element in A, the function f is called **one-to-one**. Otherwise, if one or more elements of B are the images of more than one element in A, the function f is many-to-one. (If a relation is one-to-many, it is not even a function.)

The social security function in Example 1(b) is one-to-one, because two different taxpayers should always have different social security numbers. Can you explain why the function defined in Example 1(c) is also one-to-one, whereas the function that assigns to each child his or her mother is not?

Inverse Functions

The definition of inverse function in Sec. 5.3 can easily be extended to general functions. Suppose f is a one-to-one function from a set A to a set B, and assume that the range of f is all of B. We can then define a function g from B to A by the following obvious rule: Assign to each element v of B the one and only element $u = g(v)$ of A that f maps to v—that is, the u satisfying $v = f(u)$. Because f is one-to-one, there can be only one u in A such that $v = f(u)$, so g is a function, its domain is B and its target and range are both equal to A. The function g is called the **inverse function** of f. For instance, the inverse of the social security function mentioned in Example 1(b) is the function that, to each social security number in its range, assigns the person carrying that number.

PROBLEMS FOR SECTION 5.6

(SM) 1. Which of the following rules define functions?

(a) The rule that assigns to each person in a classroom his or her height.

(b) The rule that assigns to each mother her youngest child alive today.

(c) The rule that assigns the perimeter of a rectangle to its area.

(d) The rule that assigns the surface area of a spherical ball to its volume.

(e) The rule that assigns the pair of numbers $(x + 3, y)$ to the pair of numbers (x, y).

2. Determine which of the functions defined in Problem 1 are one-to-one, and which then have an inverse. Determine each inverse when it exists.

REVIEW PROBLEMS FOR CHAPTER 5

1. Use Fig. 4.3.10 and the rules for shifting graphs to sketch the graphs of
   (a) $y = |x| + 1$
   (b) $y = |x + 3|$
   (c) $y = 3 - |x + 1|$

2. If $f(x) = x^3 - 2$ and $g(x) = (1 - x)x^2$, compute: $(f + g)(x)$, $(f - g)(x)$, $(fg)(x)$, $(f/g)(x)$, $f(g(1))$, and $g(f(1))$.

3. (a) Consider the demand and supply curves
   $$D = 150 - \tfrac{1}{2}P, \qquad S = 20 + 2P$$
   Find the equilibrium price P^*, and the corresponding quantity Q^*.

   (b) Suppose a tax of \$2 per unit is imposed on the producer. How will this influence the equilibrium price?

   (c) Compute the total revenue obtained by the producer before the tax is imposed (R^*) and after ($\hat{R}$).

4. Demand D as a function of price P is given by $D = \tfrac{32}{5} - \tfrac{3}{10}P$. (See Problem 4.2.7 for an economic interpretation.) Solve the equation for P and find the inverse demand function.

5. The demand D for a product as a function of the price P is given by $D = 120 - 5P$. Solve the equation for P and so find the inverse demand function.

6. Find the inverses of the functions given by the formulas:
   (a) $y = 100 - 2x$
   (b) $y = 2x^5$
   (c) $y = 5e^{3x-2}$

(SM) 7. The following functions are strictly increasing in their domains. Find the domains of their inverses and formulas for the inverses. Use x as the free variable.
   (a) $f(x) = 3 + \ln(e^x - 2), \quad x > \ln 2$
   (b) $f(x) = \dfrac{a}{e^{-\lambda x} + a}, \quad a$ and λ positive, $x \in (-\infty, \infty)$

8. Determine the distances between the following pairs of points:
   (a) $(2, 3)$ and $(5, 5)$
   (b) $(-4, 4)$ and $(-3, 8)$
   (c) $(2a, 3b)$ and $(2 - a, 3b)$

9. Find the equations of the circles with:
   (a) Centre at $(2, -3)$ and radius 5.
   (b) Centre at $(-2, 2)$ and a point at $(-10, 1)$.

10. A point P moves in the plane so that it is always equidistant from each of the points $A = (3, 2)$ and $B = (5, -4)$. Find a simple equation that the coordinates (x, y) of P must satisfy. (*Hint:* Compute the square of the distance from P to A and to B, respectively.)

11. Each person in a team is known to have red blood cells that belong to one and only one of four blood groups denoted A, B, AB, and O. Consider the function that assigns each person in the team to his or her blood group. Can this function be one-to-one if the team consists of at least five persons?

6

DIFFERENTIATION

To think of it [differential calculus] merely as a
more advanced technique is to miss its real content.
In it, mathematics becomes a dynamic mode of thought,
and that is a major mental step in the ascent of man.
—J. Bronowski (1973)

A n important topic in many scientific disciplines, including economics, is the study of how quickly quantities change over time. In order to compute the future position of a planet, to predict the growth in population of a biological species, or to estimate the future demand for a commodity, we need information about rates of change.

The concept used to describe the rate of change of a function is the derivative, which is *the* central concept in mathematical analysis. This chapter defines the derivative of a function and presents some of the important rules for calculating it.

Isaac Newton (1642–1727) and Gottfried Wilhelm Leibniz (1646–1716) discovered most of these general rules independently of each other. This initiated differential calculus, which has been the foundation for the development of modern science. It has also been of central importance to the theoretical development of modern economics.

6.1 Slopes of Curves

Even though in economics we are usually interested in the derivative as a rate of change, we begin this chapter with a geometrical motivation for the concept. When we study the graph of a function, we would like to have a precise measure of the steepness of the graph at a point.

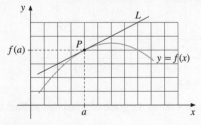

Figure 1 $f'(a) = 1/2$

We know that for the line $y = px + q$, the number p denotes its slope. If p is large and positive, then the line rises steeply from left to right; if p is large and negative, the line falls steeply. But for an arbitrary function f, what is the steepness of its graph? A natural answer is to define the steepness or **slope** of a curve *at a particular point* as the slope of the tangent to the curve at that point—that is, as the slope of the straight line which just touches the curve at that point. For the curve in Fig. 1 the steepness at point P is seen to be $1/2$, because the slope of the tangent line L is $1/2$.

In Fig. 1, the point P has coordinates $(a, f(a))$. The slope of the tangent to the graph at P is called the **derivative** of $f(x)$ at $x = a$, and we denote this number by $f'(a)$ (read as "f prime a"). In general, we have

$$f'(a) = \text{the slope of the tangent to the curve } y = f(x) \text{ at the point } (a, f(a))$$

Thus, in Fig. 1, we have $f'(a) = 1/2$.

EXAMPLE 1   Find $f'(1)$, $f'(4)$, and $f'(7)$ for the function whose graph is shown in Fig. 2.

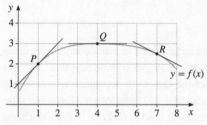

Figure 2

Solution: At $P = (1, 2)$, the tangent goes through the point $(0, 1)$, and so has slope 1. At the point $Q = (4, 3)$ the tangent is horizontal, and so has slope 0. At $R = (7, 2\frac{1}{2})$, the tangent goes through $(8, 2)$, and so has slope $-\frac{1}{2}$. Hence, $f'(1) = 1$, $f'(4) = 0$, and $f'(7) = -\frac{1}{2}$.

PROBLEMS FOR SECTION 6.1

1. Figure 3 shows the graph of a function f. Find the values of $f(3)$ and $f'(3)$.

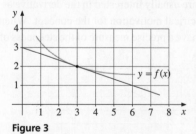

Figure 3

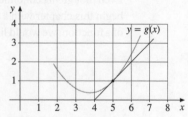

Figure 4

2. Figure 4 shows the graph of a function g. Find the values of $g(5)$ and $g'(5)$.

6.2   Tangents and Derivatives

The previous section gave a rather vague definition of the tangent to a curve at a point. All we said is that it is a straight line which just touches the curve at that point. We now give a more formal definition of the same concept.

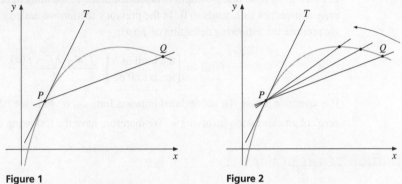

Figure 1   Figure 2

The geometrical idea behind the definition is easy to understand. Consider a point P on a curve in the xy-plane (see Fig. 1). Take another point Q on the curve. The entire straight line through P and Q is called a *secant*. If we keep P fixed, but let Q move along the curve toward P, then the secant will rotate around P, as indicated in Fig. 2. The limiting straight line PT toward which the secant tends is called the **tangent (line)** to the curve at P. Suppose that the curve in Figs. 1 and 2 is the graph of a function f. The approach illustrated in Fig. 2 allows us to find the slope of the tangent PT to the graph of f at the point P.

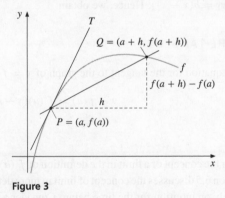

Figure 3

Figure 3 reproduces the curve, the points P and Q, and the tangent PT in Fig. 2. Point P in Fig. 3 has the coordinates $(a, f(a))$. Point Q lies close to P and is also on the graph of f. Suppose that the x-coordinate of Q is $a + h$, where h is a small number $\neq 0$. Then the x-coordinate of Q is not a (because $Q \neq P$), but a number close to a. Because Q lies on the graph of f, the y-coordinate of Q is equal to $f(a + h)$. Hence, the point Q has coordinates $(a + h, f(a + h))$. The slope m_{PQ} of the secant PQ is therefore

$$m_{PQ} = \frac{f(a + h) - f(a)}{h}$$

This fraction is often called a **Newton quotient** of f. Note that when $h = 0$, the fraction becomes 0/0 and so is undefined. But choosing $h = 0$ corresponds to letting $Q = P$. When Q moves toward P along the graph of f, the x-coordinate of Q, which is $a + h$, must tend to a, and so h tends to 0. Simultaneously, the secant PQ tends to the tangent to the graph at P. This suggests that we ought to *define* the slope of the tangent at P as the number that m_{PQ} approaches as h tends to 0. In the previous section we called this number $f'(a)$. So we propose the following definition of $f'(a)$:

$$f'(a) = \left\{ \begin{matrix} \text{the limit as } h \\ \text{tends to 0 of} \end{matrix} \right\} \frac{f(a + h) - f(a)}{h}$$

It is common to use the abbreviated notation $\lim_{h \to 0}$, or $\lim\limits_{h \to 0}$, for "the limit as h tends to zero" of an expression involving h. We therefore have the following definition:

DEFINITION OF THE DERIVATIVE

The derivative of the function f at point a, denoted by $f'(a)$, is given by the formula

$$f'(a) = \lim_{h \to 0} \frac{f(a + h) - f(a)}{h}$$

(1)

The number $f'(a)$ gives the slope of the tangent to the curve $y = f(x)$ at the point $(a, f(a))$. The equation for a straight line passing through (x_1, y_1) and having a slope b is given by $y - y_1 = b(x - x_1)$. Hence, we obtain:

DEFINITION OF THE TANGENT

The equation for the tangent to the graph of $y = f(x)$ at the point $(a, f(a))$ is

$$y - f(a) = f'(a)(x - a)$$

(2)

So far the concept of a limit in the definition of $f'(a)$ is mathematically somewhat imprecise. Section 6.5 discusses the concept of limit in more detail. Because it is relatively complicated, we rely on intuition for the time being. Consider a simple example.

EXAMPLE 1   Use (1) to compute $f'(a)$ when $f(x) = x^2$. Find in particular $f'(1/2)$ and $f'(-1)$. Give geometric interpretations, and find the equation for the tangent at the point $(1/2, 1/4)$.

Solution: For $f(x) = x^2$, we have $f(a + h) = (a + h)^2 = a^2 + 2ah + h^2$, and so $f(a + h) - f(a) = (a^2 + 2ah + h^2) - a^2 = 2ah + h^2$. Hence, for all $h \neq 0$, we obtain

$$\frac{f(a + h) - f(a)}{h} = \frac{2ah + h^2}{h} = \frac{h(2a + h)}{h} = 2a + h$$

(∗)

because we can cancel h whenever $h \neq 0$. But as h tends to 0, so $2a + h$ obviously tends to $2a$. Thus, we can write

$$f'(a) = \lim_{h \to 0} \frac{f(a + h) - f(a)}{h} = \lim_{h \to 0} (2a + h) = 2a$$

This shows that when $f(x) = x^2$, then $f'(a) = 2a$. For $a = 1/2$, we obtain $f'(1/2) = 2 \cdot 1/2 = 1$. Similarly, $f'(-1) = 2 \cdot (-1) = -2$.

Figure 4 provides a geometric interpretation of $(*)$. In Fig. 5, we have drawn the tangents to the curve $y = x^2$ corresponding to $a = 1/2$ and $a = -1$. At $a = 1/2$, we have $f(a) = (1/2)^2 = 1/4$ and $f'(1/2) = 1$. According to (2), the equation of the tangent is $y - 1/4 = 1 \cdot (x - 1/2)$ or $y = x - 1/4$. (Show that the other tangent drawn in Fig. 5 has the equation $y = -2x - 1$.) Note that the formula $f'(a) = 2a$ shows that $f'(a) < 0$ when $a < 0$, and $f'(a) > 0$ when $a > 0$. Does this agree with the graph?

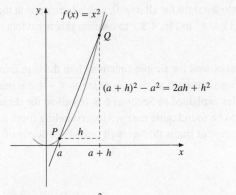

Figure 4 $f(x) = x^2$

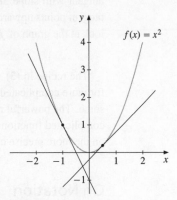

Figure 5 $f(x) = x^2$

If f is a relatively simple function, we can find $f'(a)$ by using the following recipe:

RECIPE FOR COMPUTING $f'(a)$

(A) Add h to a and compute $f(a + h)$.

(B) Compute the corresponding change in the function value: $f(a + h) - f(a)$.

(C) For $h \neq 0$, form the Newton quotient $\dfrac{f(a + h) - f(a)}{h}$.   (3)

(D) Simplify the fraction in step (C) as much as possible. Wherever possible, cancel h from the numerator and denominator.

(E) Then $f'(a)$ is the limit of $\dfrac{f(a + h) - f(a)}{h}$ as h tends to 0.

Let us apply this recipe to another example.

EXAMPLE 2   Compute $f'(a)$ when $f(x) = x^3$.

Solution: We follow the recipe in (3).

(A) $f(a+h) = (a+h)^3 = a^3 + 3a^2h + 3ah^2 + h^3$

(B) $f(a+h) - f(a) = (a^3 + 3a^2h + 3ah^2 + h^3) - a^3 = 3a^2h + 3ah^2 + h^3$

(C)–(D) $\dfrac{f(a+h) - f(a)}{h} = \dfrac{3a^2h + 3ah^2 + h^3}{h} = 3a^2 + 3ah + h^2$

(E) As h tends to 0, so $3ah + h^2$ also tends to 0; hence, the entire expression $3a^2 + 3ah + h^2$ tends to $3a^2$. Therefore, $f'(a) = 3a^2$.

We have thus shown that the graph of the function $f(x) = x^3$ at the point $x = a$ has a tangent with slope $3a^2$. Note that $f'(a) = 3a^2 > 0$ when $a \neq 0$, and $f'(0) = 0$. The tangent points upwards to the right for all $a \neq 0$, and is horizontal at the origin. You should look at the graph of $f(x) = x^3$ in Fig. 4.3.7 to confirm this behaviour.

The recipe in (3) works well for simple functions like those in Examples 1 and 2. But for more complicated functions such as $f(x) = \sqrt{3x^2 + x + 1}$ it is unnecessarily cumbersome. The powerful rules explained in Sections 6.6–6.8 allow the derivatives of even quite complicated functions to be found quite easily. Understanding these rules, however, relies on the more precise concept of limits that we will provide in Section 6.5.

On Notation

We showed in Example 1 that if $f(x) = x^2$, then for every a we have $f'(a) = 2a$. We frequently use x as the symbol for a quantity that can take any value, so we write $f'(x) = 2x$. Using this notation, our results from the two last examples are as follows:

$$f(x) = x^2 \implies f'(x) = 2x \tag{4}$$

$$f(x) = x^3 \implies f'(x) = 3x^2 \tag{5}$$

The result in (4) is a special case of the following rule, which you are asked to show in Problem 6.

$$f(x) = ax^2 + bx + c \implies f'(x) = 2ax + b \qquad (a, b, \text{ and } c \text{ are constants}) \tag{6}$$

For $a = 1$, $b = c = 0$, this reduces to (4). Here are some other special cases of (6):

$f(x) = 3x^2 + 2x + 5 \qquad\qquad \implies f'(x) = 2 \cdot 3x + 2 = 6x + 2$

$f(x) = -16 + \frac{1}{2}x - \frac{1}{16}x^2 \qquad \implies f'(x) = \frac{1}{2} - \frac{1}{8}x$

$f(x) = (x - p)^2 = x^2 - 2px + p^2 \implies f'(x) = 2x - 2p \qquad (p \text{ is a constant})$

If we use y to denote the typical value of the function $y = f(x)$, we often denote the derivative simply by y'. We can then write $y = x^3 \Longrightarrow y' = 3x^2$.

Several other forms of notation for the derivative are often used in mathematics and its applications. One of them, originally due to Leibniz, is called the **differential notation**. If $y = f(x)$, then in place of $f'(x)$, we write

$$\frac{dy}{dx} = dy/dx \qquad \text{or} \qquad \frac{df(x)}{dx} = df(x)/dx \qquad \text{or} \qquad \frac{d}{dx}f(x)$$

For instance, if $y = x^2$, then

$$\frac{dy}{dx} = 2x \qquad \text{or} \qquad \frac{d}{dx}(x^2) = 2x$$

We can think of the symbol d/dx as an instruction to differentiate what follows with respect to x. Differentiation occurs so often in mathematics that it has become standard to use **w.r.t.** as an abbreviation for "with respect to". At this point, we will only think of the symbol dy/dx as meaning $f'(x)$ and will not consider how it might relate to dy divided by dx. Later chapters discuss this notation in greater detail.

When we use letters other than f, x, and y, the notation for the derivative changes accordingly. For example:

$$P(t) = t^2 \Longrightarrow P'(t) = 2t; \quad Y = K^3 \Longrightarrow Y' = 3K^2; \quad \text{and} \quad A = r^2 \Longrightarrow dA/dr = 2r$$

PROBLEMS FOR SECTION 6.2

1. Let $f(x) = 4x^2$. Show that $f(5 + h) - f(5) = 40h + 4h^2$. Hence,

$$\frac{f(5 + h) - f(5)}{h} = 40 + 4h$$

Using this result, find $f'(5)$. Compare the answer with (6).

2. (a) Let $f(x) = 3x^2 + 2x - 1$. Show that for $h \neq 0$,

$$\frac{f(x + h) - f(x)}{h} = 6x + 2 + 3h$$

Use this result to find $f'(x)$.

(b) Find in particular $f'(0)$, $f'(-2)$, and $f'(3)$. Find also the equation of the tangent to the graph at the point $(0, -1)$.

3. (a) The demand function for a commodity with price P is given by the formula $D(P) = a - bP$. Find $dD(P)/dP$.

(b) The cost of producing x units of a commodity is given by the formula $C(x) = p + qx^2$. Find $C'(x)$, the *marginal cost* (see Section 6.4).

4. Show that

$$f(x) = \frac{1}{x} = x^{-1} \implies f'(x) = -\frac{1}{x^2} = -x^{-2}$$

(*Hint:* Show that $[f(x+h) - f(x)]/h = -1/x(x+h)$.)

(SM) 5. In each case, find the slope of the tangent to the graph of f at the specified point:

(a) $f(x) = 3x + 2$ at $(0, 2)$ (b) $f(x) = x^2 - 1$ at $(1, 0)$

(c) $f(x) = 2 + 3/x$ at $(3, 3)$ (d) $f(x) = x^3 - 2x$ at $(0, 0)$

(e) $f(x) = x + 1/x$ at $(-1, -2)$ (f) $f(x) = x^4$ at $(1, 1)$

6. (a) If $f(x) = ax^2 + bx + c$, show that $[f(x+h) - f(x)]/h = 2ax + b + ah$. Use this to show that $f'(x) = 2ax + b$.

(b) For what value of x is $f'(x) = 0$? Explain this result in the light of (4.6.3) and (4.6.4).

7. The figure shows the graph of a function f. Determine the sign of the derivative $f'(x)$ at each of the four points a, b, c, and d.

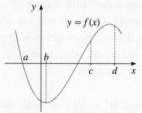

Figure 6

(SM) 8. (a) Show that $\left(\sqrt{x+h} - \sqrt{x}\right)\left(\sqrt{x+h} + \sqrt{x}\right) = h$.

(b) If $f(x) = \sqrt{x}$, show that $[f(x+h) - f(x)]/h = 1/\left(\sqrt{x+h} + \sqrt{x}\right)$.

(c) Use the result in part (b) to show that for $x > 0$,

$$f(x) = \sqrt{x} \implies f'(x) = \frac{1}{2\sqrt{x}} = \frac{1}{2}x^{-1/2}$$

9. (a) If $f(x) = ax^3 + bx^2 + cx + d$, show that

$$\frac{f(x+h) - f(x)}{h} = 3ax^2 + 2bx + c + 3axh + ah^2 + bh$$

and hence find $f'(x)$.

(b) Show that the result in part (a) generalizes Example 2 and Problem 6(a).

HARDER PROBLEM

10. Show that

$$f(x) = x^{1/3} \implies f'(x) = \tfrac{1}{3}x^{-2/3}$$

(*Hint:* Prove that $[(x+h)^{1/3} - x^{1/3}][(x+h)^{2/3} + (x+h)^{1/3}x^{1/3} + x^{2/3}] = h$. Then follow the argument used to solve Problem 8.)

6.3 Increasing and Decreasing Functions

The terms *increasing* and *decreasing* functions have been used previously to describe the behaviour of a function as we travel from *left to right* along its graph. In order to establish a definite terminology, we introduce the following definitions. We assume that f is defined in an interval I and that x_1 and x_2 are numbers from that interval.

If $f(x_2) \geq f(x_1)$ whenever $x_2 > x_1$, then f is **increasing** in I

If $f(x_2) > f(x_1)$ whenever $x_2 > x_1$, then f is **strictly increasing** in I

If $f(x_2) \leq f(x_1)$ whenever $x_2 > x_1$, then f is **decreasing** in I

If $f(x_2) < f(x_1)$ whenever $x_2 > x_1$, then f is **strictly decreasing** in I

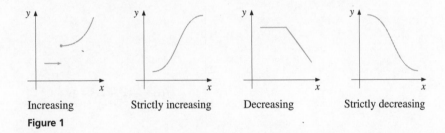

Increasing   Strictly increasing   Decreasing   Strictly decreasing

Figure 1

Figure 1 illustrates these definitions. Note that we allow an increasing (or decreasing) function to have sections where the graph is horizontal. This does not quite agree with common language. Few people would say that their salary increases when it stays constant!

To find out on which intervals a function is (strictly) increasing or (strictly) decreasing using the definitions, we have to consider the sign of $f(x_2) - f(x_1)$ whenever $x_2 > x_1$. This is usually quite difficult to do directly by checking the values of $f(x)$ at different points x. In fact, we already know a good test of whether a function is increasing or decreasing, in terms of the sign of its derivative:

$$f'(x) \geq 0 \text{ for all } x \text{ in the interval } I \iff f \text{ is increasing in } I \tag{1}$$

$$f'(x) \leq 0 \text{ for all } x \text{ in the interval } I \iff f \text{ is decreasing in } I \tag{2}$$

Using the fact that the derivative of a function is the slope of the tangent to its graph, the equivalences in (1) and (2) seem almost obvious. An observation which is equally correct is the following:

$$f'(x) = 0 \text{ for all } x \text{ in the interval } I \iff f \text{ is constant in } I \tag{3}$$

A precise proof of (1)–(3) relies on the mean-value theorem. See Note 8.4.2.

EXAMPLE 1   Use result (6) in the previous section to find the derivative of $f(x) = \frac{1}{2}x^2 - 2$. Then examine where f is increasing/decreasing.

Solution: We find that $f'(x) = x$, which is ≥ 0 for $x \geq 0$ and ≤ 0 if $x \leq 0$, and thus $f'(0) = 0$. We conclude that f is increasing in $[0, \infty)$ and decreasing in $(-\infty, 0]$. Draw the graph of f.

EXAMPLE 2   Examine where $f(x) = -\frac{1}{3}x^3 + 2x^2 - 3x + 1$ is increasing/decreasing. Use the result in Problem 9 of the previous section to find its derivative.

Solution: The formula in the problem can be used with $a = -1/3$, $b = 2$, $c = -3$, and $d = 1$. Thus $f'(x) = -x^2 + 4x - 3$. Solving the equation $f'(x) = -x^2 + 4x - 3 = 0$ yields $x = 1$ and $x = 3$, and thus $f'(x) = -(x - 1)(x - 3) = (x - 1)(3 - x)$. A sign diagram for $(x - 1)(3 - x)$ (see Example 1.6.2) reveals that $f'(x) = (x - 1)(3 - x)$ is ≥ 0 in the interval $[1, 3]$, and ≤ 0 in $(-\infty, 1]$ and in $[3, \infty)$. We conclude that $f(x)$ is increasing in $[1, 3]$, but decreasing in $(-\infty, 1]$ and in $[3, \infty)$. See Fig. 2.

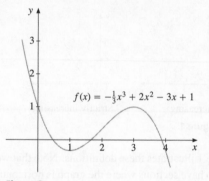

Figure 2

If $f'(x)$ is strictly positive in an interval, the function should be strictly increasing. Indeed,

$$f'(x) > 0 \text{ for all } x \text{ in the interval } I \implies f(x) \text{ is strictly increasing in } I \qquad (4)$$

$$f'(x) < 0 \text{ for all } x \text{ in the interval } I \implies f(x) \text{ is strictly decreasing in } I \qquad (5)$$

The implications in (4) and (5) give sufficient conditions for f to be strictly increasing or decreasing. They cannot be reversed to give necessary conditions. For example, if $f(x) = x^3$, then $f'(0) = 0$. Yet f is strictly increasing. (See Problem 3.)

NOTE 1 In student papers (and economics books), the following statement is often seen: "Suppose that f is strictly increasing—that is, $f'(x) > 0$." The example $f(x) = x^3$ shows that the statement is wrong. A function can be strictly increasing even though the derivative is 0 at certain points. In fact, suppose that $f'(x) \geq 0$ for all x in I and $f'(x) = 0$ at only a finite number of points in I. Then $f'(x) > 0$ in any subinterval between two adjacent zeros of $f'(x)$, and so f is strictly increasing on each such subinterval. It follows that f is strictly increasing on the whole interval.

1. By using (1) and (2) in this section, as well as (6) in the previous section, examine where $f(x) = x^2 - 4x + 3$ is increasing/decreasing. (Compare with Fig. 4.3.3.)

2. Examine where $f(x) = -x^3 + 4x^2 - x - 6$ is increasing/decreasing. (Use the result in Problem 9 in the previous section. Compare with Fig. 4.7.1.)

3. Show that $f(x) = x^3$ is strictly increasing. (*Hint:* Consider the sign of
$$x_2^3 - x_1^3 = (x_2 - x_1)(x_1^2 + x_1 x_2 + x_2^2) = (x_2 - x_1)\left[\left(x_1 + \tfrac{1}{2}x_2\right)^2 + \tfrac{3}{4}x_2^2\right].)$$

6.4 Rates of Change

The derivative of a function at a particular point was defined as the slope of the tangent to its graph at that point. Economists interpret the derivative in many important ways, starting with the rate of change of an economic variable.

Suppose that a quantity y is related to a quantity x by $y = f(x)$. If x has the value a, then the value of the function is $f(a)$. Suppose that a is changed to $a + h$. The new value of y is $f(a + h)$, and the change in the value of the function when x is changed from a to $a + h$ is $f(a + h) - f(a)$. The change in y per unit change in x has a particular name, the *average rate of change of f over the interval from a to $a + h$*. It is equal to

$$\frac{f(a + h) - f(a)}{h}$$

Note that this fraction is precisely the Newton quotient of f. Taking the limit as h tends to 0 gives the derivative of f at a, which we interpret as follows:

The **instantaneous rate of change** of f at a is $f'(a)$

This very important concept appears whenever we study quantities that change. When time is the independent variable, we often use the "dot notation" for differentiation with respect to time. For example, if $x(t) = t^2$, we write $\dot{x}(t) = 2t$.

Sometimes we are interested in studying the proportion $f'(a)/f(a)$, interpreted as follows:

The **relative rate of change** of f at a is $\dfrac{f'(a)}{f(a)}$

In economics, relative rates of change are often seen. Sometimes they are called **proportional rates of change**. They are usually quoted in percentages per unit of time—for example, percentages per year (or per annum, for those who think Latin is still a useful language). Often we will describe a variable as increasing at, say, 3% a year if there is a relative rate of change of 3/100 each year.

EXAMPLE 1   Let $N(t)$ be the number of individuals in a population (of, say, humans, animals, or plants) at time t. If t increases to $t + h$, then the change in population is equal to $N(t + h) - N(t)$ individuals. Hence,

$$\frac{N(t + h) - N(t)}{h}$$

is *the average rate of change*. Taking the limit as h tends to 0 gives $\dot{N}(t) = dN/dt$ for *the rate of change of population at time t.*

In Example 4.5.1 the formula $P = 6.4t + 641$ was used (misleadingly) as an estimate of Europe's population (in millions) at a date which comes t years after 1960. In this case, the rate of change is $dP/dt = 6.4$ million per year, the same for all t.

EXAMPLE 2   Let $K(t)$ be the capital stock in an economy at time t. The rate of change $\dot{K}(t)$ of $K(t)$ is called the **rate of investment**[1] at time t. It is usually denoted by $I(t)$, so

$$\dot{K}(t) = I(t) \tag{1}$$

EXAMPLE 3   Consider a firm producing some commodity in a given period, and let $C(x)$ denote the cost of producing x units. The derivative $C'(x)$ at x is called the **marginal cost** at x. According to the definition, it is equal to

$$C'(x) = \lim_{h \to 0} \frac{C(x + h) - C(x)}{h} \qquad \text{(\textbf{marginal cost})} \tag{2}$$

When h is small in absolute value, we obtain the approximation

$$C'(x) \approx \frac{C(x + h) - C(x)}{h} \tag{3}$$

Thus for h small, a linear approximation to $C(x + h) - C(x)$, the **incremental cost** of producing h units of extra output, is $hC'(x)$, the product of the marginal cost and the change in output. This is true even when $h < 0$, signifying a decrease in output and, provided that $C'(x) > 0$, a lower cost.

NOTE 1   Putting $h = 1$ in (3) makes marginal cost *approximately equal* to

$$C'(x) \approx C(x + 1) - C(x) \tag{4}$$

This is approximately equal to the incremental cost $C(x + 1) - C(x)$, that is, the *additional cost of producing one more unit than x.* In elementary economics books marginal cost is often defined as the difference $C(x + 1) - C(x)$ because more appropriate concepts from differential calculus cannot be used.

---

[1] Actually, it is the *net* rate of investment. Some investment is needed to replace depreciated capital; including this as well gives *gross* investment.

This book will sometimes offer economic interpretations of a derivative that, like Note 1, consider the change in a function when a variable x is increased by one whole unit; it would be more accurate to consider the change in the function per unit increase, for small increases. Here is an example.

EXAMPLE 4   Let $C(x)$ denote the cost in millions of dollars for removing $x\%$ of the pollution in a lake. Give an economic interpretation of the equality $C'(50) = 3$.

Solution: Because of the linear approximation $C(50+h) - C(50) \approx hC'(50)$, the precise interpretation of $C'(50) = 3$ is that, starting at 50%, for each 1% of pollution that is removed, the extra cost is about 3 million dollars. Less precisely, $C'(50) = 3$ means that it costs about 3 million dollars extra to remove 51% instead of 50% of the pollution.

NOTE 2   Following Example 3, economists often use the word "marginal" to indicate a derivative. To mention just two of many examples we shall encounter, the **marginal propensity to consume** is the derivative of the consumption function with respect to income; similarly, the **marginal product** (or **productivity**) of labour is the derivative of the production function with respect to labour input.

Empirical Functions

The very definition of the derivative assumes that arbitrarily small increments in the independent variable are possible. In practical problems it is impossible to implement, or even measure, arbitrarily small changes in the variable. For example, economic quantities that vary with time, such as a nation's domestic product or the number of its people who are employed, are usually measured at intervals of days, weeks, or years. Further, the cost functions of the type we discussed in Example 2 are often defined only for integer values of x. In all these cases, the variables only take discrete values. The graphs of such functions, therefore, will only consist of discrete points. For functions of this type in which time and numbers both change discretely, the concept of the derivative is not defined. To remedy this, the actual function is usually replaced by a "smooth" function that is a "good approximation" to the original function.

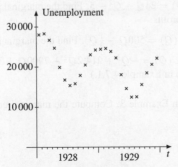

Figure 1 Unemployment in Norway (1928–1929)

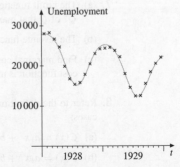

Figure 2 A smooth curve approximating the points in Fig. 1.

As an illustration, Fig. 1 graphs observations of the number of registered unemployed in Norway for each month of the years 1928–1929. This was a period in which Norway was still largely an agricultural economy, in which unemployment rose during the autumn and fell during the spring. In Fig. 2 we show the graph of a "smooth" function that approximates the points plotted in Fig. 1.

PROBLEMS FOR SECTION 6.4

1. Let $C(x) = x^2 + 3x + 100$ be the cost function of a firm. Show that the average per unit rate of change when x is changed from 100 to $100 + h$ is

$$\frac{C(100 + h) - C(100)}{h} = 203 + h \qquad (h \neq 0)$$

What is the marginal cost $C'(100)$? Use (6.2.6) to find $C'(x)$ and, in particular, $C'(100)$.

2. If the cost function of a firm is $C(x) = kx + I$, give economic interpretations of the parameters k and I.

3. If the total saving of a country is a function $S(Y)$ of the national product Y, then $S'(Y)$ is called the *marginal propensity to save* (MPS). Find the MPS for the following functions:

(a) $S(Y) = a + bY$ (b) $S(Y) = 100 + 0.1Y + 0.0002Y^2$

4. If the tax a family pays is a function of its income y given by $T(y)$, then $T'(y)$ is called the *marginal tax rate*. Characterize the following tax function by determining its marginal rate:

$$T(y) = ty \qquad (t \text{ is a constant number in } (0, 1))$$

5. Let $x(t)$ denote the number of barrels of oil left in a well at time t, where time is measured in minutes. What is the interpretation of $\dot{x}(0) = -3$?

6. The total cost of producing x units of a commodity is $C(x) = x^3 - 90x^2 + 7500x$, $x \geq 0$.

(a) Compute the marginal cost function $C'(x)$. (Use the result in Problem 6.2.9.)

(b) For which value of x is the marginal cost the least?

7. (a) The profit function is $\pi(Q) = 24Q - Q^2 - 5$. Find the marginal profit, and find the value Q^* of Q that maximizes profits.

(b) The revenue function is $R(Q) = 500Q - \frac{1}{3}Q^3$. Find the marginal revenue.

(c) Find marginal cost when $C(Q) = -Q^3 + 214.2Q^2 - 7900Q + 320\,700$. (This particular cost function is mentioned in Example 4.7.1.)

8. Refer to the definition given in Example 3. Compute the marginal cost in the following two cases:

(a) $C(x) = a_1 x^2 + b_1 x + c_1$

(b) $C(x) = a_1 x^3 + b_1$

6.5 A Dash of Limits

In Section 6.2 we defined the derivative of a function based on the concept of a limit. The same concept has many other uses in mathematics, as well as in economic analysis, so now we should take a closer look. Here we give a preliminary definition and formulate some important rules for limits. In Section 7.9, we discuss the limit concept more closely.

EXAMPLE 1   Consider the function F defined by the formula

$$F(x) = \frac{e^x - 1}{x}$$

where $e \approx 2.7$ is the base for the natural exponential function. (See Section 4.9.) Note that if $x = 0$, then $e^0 = 1$, and the fraction collapses to the absurd expression "0/0". Thus, the function F is not defined for $x = 0$, but one can still ask what happens to $F(x)$ when x is close to 0. Using a calculator (except when $x = 0$), we find the values shown in Table 1.

Table 1 Values of $F(x) = (e^x - 1)/x$ when x is close to 0

x	-1	-0.1	-0.001	-0.0001	0.0	0.0001	0.001	0.1	1
$F(x)$	0.632	0.956	0.999	1.000	*	1.000	1.001	1.052	1.718

* not defined

From the table it appears that as x gets closer and closer to 0, so the fraction $F(x)$ gets closer and closer to 1. It therefore seems reasonable to assume that $F(x)$ tends to 1 in the limit as x tends to 0. We write[2]

$$\lim_{x \to 0} \frac{e^x - 1}{x} = 1 \quad \text{or} \quad \frac{e^x - 1}{x} \to 1 \quad \text{as} \quad x \to 0$$

Figure 1 shows a portion of the graph of F. The function F is defined for all x, except at $x = 0$, and $\lim_{x \to 0} F(x) = 1$. (A small circle is used to indicate that the corresponding point $(0, 1)$ is not in the graph of F.)

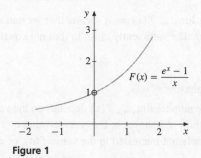

Figure 1

---

[2] Indeed, later it will be shown that the number e is defined so that this limit is 1.

Suppose, in general, that a function f is defined for all x near a, but not necessarily at $x = a$. *Then we say that $f(x)$ has the number A as its limit as x tends to a, if $f(x)$ tends to A as x tends to (but is not equal to) a.* We write

$$\lim_{x \to a} f(x) = A \quad \text{or} \quad f(x) \to A \quad \text{as} \quad x \to a$$

It is possible, however, that the value of $f(x)$ does not tend to any fixed number as x tends to a. Then we say that $\lim_{x \to a} f(x)$ *does not exist*, or that $f(x)$ *does not have a limit as x tends to a.*

EXAMPLE 2   Examine the limit $\lim_{h \to 0} \dfrac{\sqrt{h + 1} - 1}{h}$ using a calculator.

Solution: By choosing numbers h close to 0, we find the following table:

Table 2 Values of $F(h) = (\sqrt{h + 1} - 1)/h$ when h is close to 0

h	−0.5	−0.2	−0.1	−0.01	0.0	0.01	0.1	0.2	0.5
$F(h)$	0.586	0.528	0.513	0.501	*	0.499	0.488	0.477	0.449

* not defined

This suggests that $\lim_{h \to 0} \dfrac{\sqrt{h + 1} - 1}{h} = 0.5$.

The limits we claim to have found in Examples 1 and 2 are both based on a rather shaky numerical procedure. For instance, in Example 2, can we really be certain that our guess is correct? Could it be that if we chose h values even closer to 0, the fraction would tend to a limit other than 0.5, or maybe not have any limit at all? Further numerical computations will support our belief that the initial guess is correct, but we can never make a table that has *all* the values of h close to 0, so numerical computation alone can never establish with certainty what the limit is. This illustrates the need to have a rigorous procedure for finding limits, based on a precise mathematical definition of the limit concept. This definition is given in Section 7.8, but here we merely give a preliminary definition which will convey the right idea.

Writing $\lim_{x \to a} f(x) = A$ means that we can make $f(x)$ as close to A as we want for all x sufficiently close to (but not equal to) a.   (1)

We emphasize:

(a) The number $\lim_{x \to a} f(x)$ depends on the value of $f(x)$ for x-values close to a, but not on how f behaves at the precise value of $x = a$. When finding $\lim_{x \to a} f(x)$, we are simply not interested in the value $f(a)$, or even in whether f is defined at a.

(b) When we compute $\lim_{x \to a} f(x)$, we must take into consideration x-values on both sides of a.

Rules for Limits

Since limits cannot really be determined merely by numerical computations, we use simple rules instead. Their validity can be shown later once we have a precise definition of the limit concept. These rules are very straightforward and we have even used a few of them already in the previous section.

Suppose that f and g are defined as functions of x in a neighbourhood of a (but not necessarily at a). Then we have the following rules written down in a way that makes them easy to refer to later:[3]

RULES FOR LIMITS

If $\lim_{x \to a} f(x) = A$ and $\lim_{x \to a} g(x) = B$, then

(a) $\lim_{x \to a} \left(f(x) \pm g(x) \right) = A \pm B$

(b) $\lim_{x \to a} \left(f(x) \cdot g(x) \right) = A \cdot B$ (2)

(c) $\lim_{x \to a} \dfrac{f(x)}{g(x)} = \dfrac{A}{B}$ (if $B \neq 0$)

(d) $\lim_{x \to a} \left(f(x) \right)^r = A^r$ (if A^r is defined and r is any real number)

It is easy to give intuitive explanations for these rules. Suppose that $\lim_{x \to a} f(x) = A$ and that $\lim_{x \to a} g(x) = B$. Then we know that, when x is close to a, then $f(x)$ is close to A and $g(x)$ is close to B. So intuitively the sum $f(x) + g(x)$ is close to $A + B$, the difference $f(x) - g(x)$ is close to $A - B$, the product $f(x)g(x)$ is close to $A \cdot B$, and so on.

These rules can be used repeatedly to obtain new extended rules such as

$$\lim_{x \to a} [f_1(x) + f_2(x) + \cdots + f_n(x)] = \lim_{x \to a} f_1(x) + \lim_{x \to a} f_2(x) + \cdots + \lim_{x \to a} f_n(x)$$
$$\lim_{x \to a} [f_1(x) \cdot f_2(x) \cdots f_n(x)] = \lim_{x \to a} f_1(x) \cdot \lim_{x \to a} f_2(x) \cdots \lim_{x \to a} f_n(x)$$

In words: *the limit of a sum is the sum of the limits, and the limit of a product is equal to the product of the limits.*

Suppose the function $f(x)$ is equal to the same constant value c for every x. Then

$$\lim_{x \to a} c = c \qquad \text{(at every point } a\text{)}$$

It is also evident that if $f(x) = x$, then

$$\lim_{x \to a} f(x) = \lim_{x \to a} x = a \qquad \text{(at every point } a\text{)}$$

Combining these two simple limits with the general rules allows easy computation of the limits for certain combinations of functions.

---

[3] Using the identities $f(x) - g(x) = f(x) + (-1)g(x)$, and $f(x)/g(x) = f(x)(g(x))^{-1}$, it is clear that some of these rules follow from others.

EXAMPLE 3   Compute the following limits:

(a) $\lim_{x \to -2} (x^2 + 5x)$ (b) $\lim_{x \to 4} \dfrac{2x^{3/2} - \sqrt{x}}{x^2 - 15}$ (c) $\lim_{x \to a} Ax^n$

Solution: Using the rules for limits specified in (2), we get

(a) $\lim_{x \to -2} (x^2 + 5x) = \lim_{x \to -2} (x \cdot x) + \lim_{x \to -2} (5 \cdot x)$

$$= \left(\lim_{x \to -2} x \right)\left(\lim_{x \to -2} x \right) + \left(\lim_{x \to -2} 5 \right)\left(\lim_{x \to -2} x \right)$$

$$= (-2)(-2) + 5 \cdot (-2) = -6$$

(b) $\lim_{x \to 4} \dfrac{2x^{3/2} - \sqrt{x}}{x^2 - 15} = \dfrac{2 \lim_{x \to 4} x^{3/2} - \lim_{x \to 4} \sqrt{x}}{\lim_{x \to 4} x^2 - 15} = \dfrac{2 \cdot 4^{3/2} - \sqrt{4}}{4^2 - 15} = \dfrac{2 \cdot 8 - 2}{16 - 15} = 14$

(c) $\lim_{x \to a} Ax^n = \left(\lim_{x \to a} A \right)\left(\lim_{x \to a} x^n \right) = A \cdot \left(\lim_{x \to a} x \right)^n = A \cdot a^n$

It was easy to find the limits in this last example by using the rules specified in (2). Examples 1 and 2 are more difficult. They involve a fraction whose numerator and denominator both tend to 0. A simple observation can sometimes help us find such limits (provided that they exist). Because $\lim_{x \to a} f(x)$ can only depend on the values of f when x is close to, but not equal to a, we have the following:

If the functions f and g are equal for all x close to a (but not necessarily at $x = a$), then $\lim_{x \to a} f(x) = \lim_{x \to a} g(x)$ whenever either limit exists.   (3)

Here are some examples of how this rule works.

EXAMPLE 4   Compute the limit $\lim_{x \to 2} \dfrac{3x^2 + 3x - 18}{x - 2}$.

Solution: We see that both numerator and denominator tend to 0 as x tends to 2. Because the numerator $3x^2 + 3x - 18$ is equal to 0 for $x = 2$, it has $x - 2$ as a factor. In fact, $3x^2 + 3x - 18 = 3(x - 2)(x + 3)$. Hence,

$$f(x) = \frac{3x^2 + 3x - 18}{x - 2} = \frac{3(x - 2)(x + 3)}{x - 2}$$

For $x \neq 2$, we can cancel $x - 2$ from both numerator and denominator to obtain $3(x + 3)$. So the functions $f(x)$ and $g(x) = 3(x + 3)$ are equal for all $x \neq 2$. By (3), it follows that

$$\lim_{x \to 2} \frac{3x^2 + 3x - 18}{x - 2} = \lim_{x \to 2} 3(x + 3) = 3(2 + 3) = 15$$

EXAMPLE 5   Compute the following limits: (a) $\lim\limits_{h \to 0} \dfrac{\sqrt{h+1}-1}{h}$ (b) $\lim\limits_{x \to 4} \dfrac{x^2-16}{4\sqrt{x}-8}$.

Solution:

(a) The numerator and the denominator both tend to 0 as h tends to 0. Here we must use a little trick. We multiply both numerator and denominator by $\sqrt{h+1}+1$ to get

$$\frac{\sqrt{h+1}-1}{h} = \frac{\left(\sqrt{h+1}-1\right)\left(\sqrt{h+1}+1\right)}{h\left(\sqrt{h+1}+1\right)} = \frac{h+1-1}{h\left(\sqrt{h+1}+1\right)} = \frac{1}{\sqrt{h+1}+1}$$

where the common factor h has been cancelled. For all $h \neq 0$ (and $h \geq -1$), the given function is equal to $1/(\sqrt{h+1}+1)$, which tends to $1/2$ as h tends to 0. We conclude that the limit of our function is equal to $1/2$, which confirms the result in Example 2.

(b) We must try to simplify the fraction because $x = 4$ gives $0/0$. Again we can use a trick to factorize the fraction as follows:

$$\frac{x^2-16}{4\sqrt{x}-8} = \frac{(x+4)(x-4)}{4\left(\sqrt{x}-2\right)} = \frac{(x+4)\left(\sqrt{x}+2\right)\left(\sqrt{x}-2\right)}{4\left(\sqrt{x}-2\right)} \qquad (*)$$

Here we have used the factorization $x - 4 = \left(\sqrt{x}+2\right)\left(\sqrt{x}-2\right)$, which is correct for $x \geq 0$. In the last fraction of $(*)$, we can cancel $\sqrt{x} - 2$ when $\sqrt{x} - 2 \neq 0$—that is, when $x \neq 4$. Using (3) again gives

$$\lim_{x \to 4} \frac{x^2-16}{4\sqrt{x}-8} = \lim_{x \to 4} \frac{1}{4}(x+4)(\sqrt{x}+2) = \frac{1}{4}(4+4)(\sqrt{4}+2) = 8$$

PROBLEMS FOR SECTION 6.5

1. Determine the following by using the rules for limits:

(a) $\lim\limits_{x \to 0} (3 + 2x^2)$

(b) $\lim\limits_{x \to -1} \dfrac{3+2x}{x-1}$

(c) $\lim\limits_{x \to 2} (2x^2 + 5)^3$

(d) $\lim\limits_{t \to 8} \left(5t + t^2 - \frac{1}{8}t^3\right)$

(e) $\lim\limits_{y \to 0} \dfrac{(y+1)^5 - y^5}{y+1}$

(f) $\lim\limits_{z \to -2} \dfrac{1/z + 2}{z}$

2. Examine the following limits numerically by using a calculator:

(a) $\lim\limits_{h \to 0} \dfrac{2^h - 1}{h}$

(b) $\lim\limits_{h \to 0} \dfrac{3^h - 1}{h}$

(c) $\lim\limits_{\lambda \to 0} \dfrac{3^{\lambda} - 2^{\lambda}}{\lambda}$

3. Consider the following limit: $\lim\limits_{x \to 1} \dfrac{x^2 + 7x - 8}{x - 1}$.

(a) Examine the limit numerically by making a table of values of the fraction when x is close to 1.

(b) Find the limit precisely by using the method in Example 4.

4. Compute the following limits:

(a) $\lim\limits_{x \to 2} (x^2 + 3x - 5)$

(b) $\lim\limits_{y \to -3} \dfrac{1}{y + 8}$

(c) $\lim\limits_{x \to 0} \dfrac{x^3 - 2x - 1}{x^5 - x^2 - 1}$

(d) $\lim\limits_{x \to 0} \dfrac{x^3 + 3x^2 - 2x}{x}$

(e) $\lim\limits_{h \to 0} \dfrac{(x+h)^3 - x^3}{h}$

(f) $\lim\limits_{x \to 0} \dfrac{(x+h)^3 - x^3}{h}$ $(h \neq 0)$

(SM) 5. Compute the following limits:

(a) $\lim\limits_{h \to 2} \dfrac{\dfrac{1}{3} - \dfrac{2}{3h}}{h - 2}$

(b) $\lim\limits_{x \to 0} \dfrac{x^2 - 1}{x^2}$

(c) $\lim\limits_{t \to 3} \sqrt[3]{\dfrac{32t - 96}{t^2 - 2t - 3}}$

(d) $\lim\limits_{h \to 0} \dfrac{\sqrt{h + 3} - \sqrt{3}}{h}$

(e) $\lim\limits_{t \to -2} \dfrac{t^2 - 4}{t^2 + 10t + 16}$

(f) $\lim\limits_{x \to 4} \dfrac{2 - \sqrt{x}}{4 - x}$

(SM) 6. If $f(x) = x^2 + 2x$, compute the following limits:

(a) $\lim\limits_{x \to 1} \dfrac{f(x) - f(1)}{x - 1}$

(b) $\lim\limits_{x \to 2} \dfrac{f(x) - f(1)}{x - 1}$

(c) $\lim\limits_{h \to 0} \dfrac{f(2 + h) - f(2)}{h}$

(d) $\lim\limits_{x \to a} \dfrac{f(x) - f(a)}{x - a}$

(e) $\lim\limits_{h \to 0} \dfrac{f(a + h) - f(a)}{h}$

(f) $\lim\limits_{h \to 0} \dfrac{f(a + h) - f(a - h)}{h}$

HARDER PROBLEM

7. Compute the following limits. (*Hint:* For part (b), write the fraction as a function of $u = \sqrt[3]{27 + h}$.)

(a) $\lim\limits_{x \to 2} \dfrac{x^2 - 2x}{x^3 - 8}$

(b) $\lim\limits_{h \to 0} \dfrac{\sqrt[3]{27 + h} - 3}{h}$

(c) $\lim\limits_{x \to 1} \dfrac{x^n - 1}{x - 1}$ (n is a natural number)

6.6 Simple Rules for Differentiation

The derivative of a function f was defined by the formula

$$f'(x) = \lim_{h \to 0} \frac{f(x + h) - f(x)}{h} \qquad (*)$$

If this limit exists, we say that f is **differentiable** at x. The process of finding the derivative of a function is called **differentiation**. It is useful to think of this as an operation that transforms one function f into a new function f'. The function f' is then defined for the values of x where the limit in $(*)$ exists. If $y = f(x)$, we can use the symbols y' and dy/dx as alternatives to $f'(x)$.

In Section 6.2 we used formula $(*)$ to find the derivatives of some simple functions. However, it is difficult and time consuming to apply the definition directly in each separate case. We now embark on a systematic programme to find general rules which ultimately will give mechanical and efficient procedures for finding the derivative of very many differentiable functions specified by a formula, even one that is complicated. We start with some simple rules.

If f is a constant function, then its derivative is 0:

$$f(x) = A \Longrightarrow f'(x) = 0 \qquad (1)$$

The result is easy to see geometrically. The graph of $f(x) = A$ is a straight line parallel to the x-axis. The tangent to the graph is the line itself, which has slope 0 at each point (see Fig. 1). You should now use the definition of $f'(x)$ to get the same answer.

The next two rules are also very useful.

$$y = A + f(x) \implies y' = f'(x) \qquad \text{(Additive constants disappear)} \qquad (2)$$

$$y = Af(x) \implies y' = Af'(x) \qquad \text{(Multiplicative constants are preserved)} \qquad (3)$$

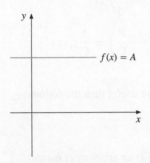

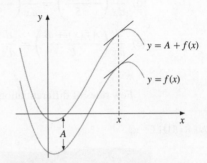

Figure 1 The derivative of a constant is 0.

Figure 2 The two graphs have parallel tangents for every x, so the functions have the same derivatives.

Rule (2) is illustrated in Fig. 2, where A is positive. The graph of $A + f(x)$ is that of $f(x)$ shifted upwards by A units in the direction of the y-axis. So the tangents to the two curves $y = f(x)$ and $y = f(x) + A$ at the same value of x must be parallel. In particular, they must have the same slope. Again you should try to use the definition of $f'(x)$ to give a formal proof of this assertion.

Let us prove rule (3) by using the definition of a derivative. If $g(x) = Af(x)$, then $g(x + h) - g(x) = Af(x + h) - Af(x) = A[f(x + h) - f(x)]$, and so

$$g'(x) = \lim_{h \to 0} \frac{g(x + h) - g(x)}{h} = A \lim_{h \to 0} \frac{f(x + h) - f(x)}{h} = Af'(x)$$

Here is an economic illustration of rule (3). Suppose $f(t)$ denotes the sales revenue at time t of firm A, and firm B's sales revenue $g(t)$ at each time is 3 times as large as that of A. Then the growth rate of B's revenues is 3 times as large as that of A. In mathematical notation: $g(t) = 3f(t) \implies g'(t) = 3f'(t)$. However, the firms' *relative* growth rates $f'(t)/f(t)$ and $g'(t)/g(t)$ will be equal.

In Leibniz's notation, the three results are as follows:

$$\frac{d}{dx} A = 0, \qquad \frac{d}{dx}[A + f(x)] = \frac{d}{dx} f(x), \qquad \frac{d}{dx}[Af(x)] = A \frac{d}{dx} f(x)$$

EXAMPLE 1   Suppose we know $f'(x)$, and that $C \neq 0$. Find the derivatives of

(a) $5 + f(x)$ (b) $f(x) - \frac{1}{2}$ (c) $4f(x)$ (d) $-\dfrac{f(x)}{5}$ (e) $\dfrac{Af(x) + B}{C}$

Solution: We obtain

(a) $\dfrac{d}{dx}(5 + f(x)) = f'(x)$

(b) $\dfrac{d}{dx}\left(f(x) - \tfrac{1}{2}\right) = \dfrac{d}{dx}\left(-\tfrac{1}{2} + f(x)\right) = f'(x)$

(c) $\dfrac{d}{dx}(4f(x)) = 4f'(x)$

(d) $\dfrac{d}{dx}\left(-\dfrac{f(x)}{5}\right) = \dfrac{d}{dx}\left(-\dfrac{1}{5}f(x)\right) = -\dfrac{1}{5}f'(x)$

(e) $\dfrac{d}{dx}\left(\dfrac{Af(x) + B}{C}\right) = \dfrac{d}{dx}\left(\dfrac{A}{C}f(x) + \dfrac{B}{C}\right) = \dfrac{A}{C}f'(x)$

Few rules of differentiation are more useful than the following:

POWER RULE

$$f(x) = x^a \implies f'(x) = ax^{a-1} \qquad (a \text{ is an arbitrary constant}) \qquad (4)$$

For $a = 2$ and $a = 3$ this rule was confirmed in Section 6.2. The method used in these two examples can be generalized to the case where a is an arbitrary natural number. Later we shall see that the rule is valid for all real numbers a.

EXAMPLE 2 Use (4) to compute the derivative of: (a) $y = x^5$ (b) $y = 3x^8$ (c) $y = \dfrac{x^{100}}{100}$.

Solution:

(a) $y = x^5 \implies y' = 5x^{5-1} = 5x^4$ (b) $y = 3x^8 \implies y' = 3 \cdot 8x^{8-1} = 24x^7$

(c) $y = \dfrac{x^{100}}{100} = \dfrac{1}{100}x^{100} \implies y' = \dfrac{1}{100}100x^{100-1} = x^{99}$

EXAMPLE 3 Use (4) to compute:

(a) $\dfrac{d}{dx}\left(x^{-0.33}\right)$ (b) $\dfrac{d}{dr}(-5r^{-3})$ (c) $\dfrac{d}{dp}(Ap^\alpha + B)$ (d) $\dfrac{d}{dx}\left(\dfrac{A}{\sqrt{x}}\right)$

Solution:

(a) $\dfrac{d}{dx}\left(x^{-0.33}\right) = -0.33x^{-0.33-1} = -0.33x^{-1.33}$

(b) $\dfrac{d}{dr}(-5r^{-3}) = (-5)(-3)r^{-3-1} = 15r^{-4}$

(c) $\dfrac{d}{dp}(Ap^\alpha + B) = A\alpha p^{\alpha-1}$

(d) $\dfrac{d}{dx}\left(\dfrac{A}{\sqrt{x}}\right) = \dfrac{d}{dx}(Ax^{-1/2}) = A\left(-\dfrac{1}{2}\right)x^{-1/2-1} = -\dfrac{A}{2}x^{-3/2} = \dfrac{-A}{2x\sqrt{x}}$

EXAMPLE 4   The so-called **Pareto income distribution** is described by the formula

$$f(r) = \frac{B}{r^\beta} = Br^{-\beta}, \qquad r > 0 \tag{5}$$

where B and β are positive constants and r is income measured in, say, dollars. Here $f(r)\Delta r$ is approximately the proportion of the population who earn between r and $r + \Delta r$ dollars. See Section 9.4. The distribution function gives a good approximation for incomes above a certain threshold level. For these, empirical estimates of β have usually been in the interval $2.4 < \beta < 2.6$. Compute $f'(r)$ and comment on its sign.

Solution: We find that $f'(r) = -\beta Br^{-\beta-1} = -\beta B/r^{\beta+1}$, so $f'(r) < 0$, and $f(r)$ is strictly decreasing.

PROBLEMS FOR SECTION 6.6

1. Compute the derivatives of the following functions of x:

   (a) $y = 5$ (b) $y = x^4$ (c) $y = 9x^{10}$ (d) $y = \pi^7$

2. Suppose we know $g'(x)$. Find expressions for the derivatives of the following:

   (a) $2g(x) + 3$ (b) $-\frac{1}{6}g(x) + 8$ (c) $\dfrac{g(x) - 5}{3}$

3. Find the derivatives of the following:

   (a) x^6 (b) $3x^{11}$ (c) x^{50} (d) $-4x^{-7}$

   (e) $\dfrac{x^{12}}{12}$ (f) $-\dfrac{2}{x^2}$ (g) $\dfrac{3}{\sqrt[3]{x}}$ (h) $-\dfrac{2}{x\sqrt{x}}$

4. Compute the following: (a) $\dfrac{d}{dr}(4\pi r^2)$ (b) $\dfrac{d}{dy}\left(Ay^{b+1}\right)$ (c) $\dfrac{d}{dA}\left(\dfrac{1}{A^2\sqrt{A}}\right)$

5. Explain why

$$f'(a) = \lim_{x \to a} \frac{f(x) - f(a)}{x - a}$$

   Use this to find $f'(a)$ when $f(x) = x^2$.

6. For each of the following functions, find a function $F(x)$ that has $f(x)$ as its derivative, that is $F'(x) = f(x)$. (Note that you are not asked to find $f'(x)$.)

   (a) $f(x) = x^2$ (b) $f(x) = 2x + 3$ (c) $f(x) = x^a$ $(a \neq -1)$

HARDER PROBLEM

7. The following limits all take the form $\lim_{h\to 0}[f(a+h) - f(a)]/h$. Use your knowledge of derivatives to find the limits.

   (a) $\lim_{h\to 0} \dfrac{(5+h)^2 - 5^2}{h}$ (b) $\lim_{s\to 0} \dfrac{(s+1)^5 - 1}{s}$ (c) $\lim_{h\to 0} \dfrac{5(x+h)^2 + 10 - 5x^2 - 10}{h}$

6.7 Sums, Products, and Quotients

If we know $f'(x)$ and $g'(x)$, then what are the derivatives of $f(x) + g(x)$, $f(x) - g(x)$, $f(x) \cdot g(x)$, and $f(x)/g(x)$? You will probably guess the first two correctly, but are less likely to be right about the last two (unless you have already learned the answers).

Sums and Differences

Suppose f and g are both defined in a set A of real numbers.

DIFFERENTIATION OF SUMS AND DIFFERENCES

If both f and g are differentiable at x, then the sum $f + g$ and the difference $f - g$ are both differentiable at x, and

$$F(x) = f(x) \pm g(x) \implies F'(x) = f'(x) \pm g'(x)$$

(1)

In Leibniz's notation:

$$\frac{d}{dx}\big(f(x) \pm g(x)\big) = \frac{d}{dx}f(x) \pm \frac{d}{dx}g(x)$$

Proof for the case $F(x) = f(x) + g(x)$: The Newton quotient of F is

$$\frac{F(x+h) - F(x)}{h} = \frac{(f(x+h) + g(x+h)) - (f(x) + g(x))}{h}$$

$$= \frac{f(x+h) - f(x)}{h} + \frac{g(x+h) - g(x)}{h}$$

When $h \to 0$, the last two fractions tend to $f'(x)$ and $g'(x)$, respectively, and thus the sum of the fractions tends to $f'(x) + g'(x)$. Hence,

$$F'(x) = \lim_{h \to 0} \frac{F(x+h) - F(x)}{h} = f'(x) + g'(x)$$

The proof of the other case is similar—only some of the signs change in an obvious way. ∎

EXAMPLE 1   Compute $\dfrac{d}{dx}\big(3x^8 + x^{100}/100\big)$.

Solution: $\frac{d}{dx}\big(3x^8 + x^{100}/100\big) = \frac{d}{dx}(3x^8) + \frac{d}{dx}\big(x^{100}/100\big) = 24x^7 + x^{99}$, where we used (1) and the results from Example 6.6.2.

EXAMPLE 2   In Example 6.4.3, $C(x)$ denoted the cost of producing x units of some commodity in a given period. If $R(x)$ is the revenue from selling those x units, then the profit function is the difference between the revenues and the costs, $\pi(x) = R(x) - C(x)$. According to (1), $\pi'(x) = R'(x) - C'(x)$. In particular, $\pi'(x) = 0$ when $R'(x) = C'(x)$. In words: *Marginal profit is 0 when marginal revenue is equal to marginal cost.*

Rule (1) can be extended to sums of an arbitrary number of terms. For example,

$$\frac{d}{dx}(f(x) - g(x) + h(x)) = f'(x) - g'(x) + h'(x)$$

which we see by writing $f(x) - g(x) + h(x)$ as $(f(x) - g(x)) + h(x)$, and then using (1).

Using the rules above makes it easy to differentiate any polynomial.

Products

Suppose $f(x) = x$ and $g(x) = x^2$, then $(f \cdot g)(x) = x^3$. Here $f'(x) = 1$, $g'(x) = 2x$, and $(f \cdot g)'(x) = 3x^2$. Hence, the derivative of $(f \cdot g)(x)$ is *not* equal to $f'(x) \cdot g'(x) = 2x$. The correct rule for differentiating a product is a little more complicated.

THE DERIVATIVE OF A PRODUCT

If both f and g are differentiable at the point x, then so is $F = f \cdot g$, and

$$F(x) = f(x) \cdot g(x) \Longrightarrow F'(x) = f'(x) \cdot g(x) + f(x) \cdot g'(x)$$

(2)

Briefly formulated: *The derivative of the product of two functions is equal to the derivative of the first times the second, plus the first times the derivative of the second.* The formula, however, is much easier to digest than these words.

In Leibniz's notation, the product rule is expressed as:

$$\frac{d}{dx}\left[f(x) \cdot g(x)\right] = \left[\frac{d}{dx}f(x)\right] \cdot g(x) + f(x) \cdot \left[\frac{d}{dx}g(x)\right]$$

Before demonstrating why (2) is valid, here are two examples:

EXAMPLE 3   Use (2) to find $h'(x)$ when $h(x) = (x^3 - x) \cdot (5x^4 + x^2)$.

Solution: We see that $h(x) = f(x) \cdot g(x)$ with $f(x) = x^3 - x$ and $g(x) = 5x^4 + x^2$. Here $f'(x) = 3x^2 - 1$ and $g'(x) = 20x^3 + 2x$. Thus,

$$h'(x) = f'(x) \cdot g(x) + f(x) \cdot g'(x) = (3x^2 - 1) \cdot (5x^4 + x^2) + (x^3 - x) \cdot (20x^3 + 2x)$$

Usually we simplify the answer by expanding to obtain just one polynomial. Simple computation gives

$$h'(x) = 35x^6 - 20x^4 - 3x^2$$

Alternatively, we can begin by expanding the expression for $h(x)$. Do so and verify that you get the same expression for $h'(x)$ as before.

EXAMPLE 4   We illustrate the product rule for differentiation in a simple economic setting. Let $D(P)$ denote the demand function for a product. By selling $D(P)$ units at price P per unit, the producer earns revenue $R(P)$ given by $R(P) = PD(P)$. Usually $D'(P)$ is negative because demand goes down when the price increases. According to the product rule for differentiation,

$$R'(P) = D(P) + PD'(P) \qquad (*)$$

For an economic interpretation, suppose P increases by one dollar. The revenue $R(P)$ changes for two reasons. First, $R(P)$ increases by $1 \cdot D(P)$, because each of the $D(P)$ units brings in one dollar more. But a one dollar increase in the price per unit causes demand to change by $D(P+1) - D(P)$ units, which is approximately $D'(P)$. The (positive) loss due to a one dollar increase in the price per unit is then $-PD'(P)$, which must be subtracted from $D(P)$ to obtain $R'(P)$, as in equation $(*)$. The resulting expression merely expresses the simple fact that $R'(P)$, the total rate of change of $R(P)$, is what you gain minus what you lose.

We have now seen how to differentiate products of two functions. What about products of more than two functions? For example, suppose that

$$y = f(x)g(x)h(x)$$

What is y'? We extend the same technique shown earlier and put $y = \big[f(x)g(x)\big]h(x)$. Then the product rule gives

$$
\begin{aligned}
y' &= [f(x)g(x)]'\, h(x) + [f(x)g(x)]\, h'(x) \\
&= \big[f'(x)g(x) + f(x)g'(x)\big] h(x) + f(x)g(x)h'(x) \\
&= f'(x)g(x)h(x) + f(x)g'(x)h(x) + f(x)g(x)h'(x)
\end{aligned}
$$

If none of the three functions is equal to 0, we can write the result in the following way:[4]

$$\frac{(fgh)'}{fgh} = \frac{f'}{f} + \frac{g'}{g} + \frac{h'}{h}$$

By analogy, it is easy to write down the corresponding result for a product of n functions. In words, the relative rate of growth of the product is the sum of the relative rates at which each factor is changing.

Proof of (2):   Suppose f and g are differentiable at x, so that the two Newton quotients

$$\frac{f(x+h) - f(x)}{h} \qquad \text{and} \qquad \frac{g(x+h) - g(x)}{h}$$

tend to the limits $f'(x)$ and $g'(x)$, respectively, as h tends to 0. We must show that the Newton quotient of F also tends to a limit, which is given by $f'(x)g(x) + f(x)g'(x)$. The Newton quotient of F is

$$\frac{F(x+h) - F(x)}{h} = \frac{f(x+h)g(x+h) - f(x)g(x)}{h} \qquad (*)$$

---

[4] If all the variables are positive, this result is easier to show using logarithmic differentiation. See Section 6.11.

To proceed further we must somehow transform the right-hand side (RHS) to involve the Newton quotients of f and g. We use a trick: The numerator of the RHS is unchanged if we both subtract and add the number $f(x)g(x + h)$. Hence, with a suitable regrouping of terms, we have

$$\frac{F(x + h) - F(x)}{h} = \frac{f(x + h)g(x + h) - f(x)g(x + h) + f(x)g(x + h) - f(x)g(x)}{h}$$

$$= \frac{f(x + h) - f(x)}{h} g(x + h) + f(x) \frac{g(x + h) - g(x)}{h}$$

As h tends to 0, the two Newton quotients tend to $f'(x)$ and $g'(x)$, respectively. Now we can write $g(x + h)$ for $h \neq 0$ as

$$g(x + h) = \left[\frac{g(x + h) - g(x)}{h} \right] h + g(x)$$

By the product rule for limits and the definition of $g'(x)$, this tends to $g'(x) \cdot 0 + g(x) = g(x)$ as h tends to 0. It follows that the Newton quotient of F tends to $f'(x)g(x) + f(x)g'(x)$ as h tends to 0.   ∎

Quotients

Suppose $F(x) = f(x)/g(x)$, where f and g are differentiable in x with $g(x) \neq 0$. Bearing in mind the complications in the formula for the derivative of a product, one should be somewhat reluctant to make a quick guess as to the correct formula for $F'(x)$.

In fact, it is quite easy to find the formula for $F'(x)$ if we *assume* that $F(x)$ *is* differentiable. From $F(x) = f(x)/g(x)$ it follows that $f(x) = F(x)g(x)$. Thus, the product rule gives $f'(x) = F'(x) \cdot g(x) + F(x) \cdot g'(x)$. Solving for $F'(x)$ yields $F'(x) \cdot g(x) = f'(x) - F(x) \cdot g'(x)$, and so

$$F'(x) = \frac{f'(x) - F(x)g'(x)}{g(x)} = \frac{f'(x) - [f(x)/g(x)]\, g'(x)}{g(x)}$$

Multiplying both numerator and denominator of the last fraction by $g(x)$ gives the following important formula.

THE DERIVATIVE OF A QUOTIENT

If f and g are differentiable at x and $g(x) \neq 0$, then $F = f/g$ is differentiable at x, and

$$F(x) = \frac{f(x)}{g(x)} \implies F'(x) = \frac{f'(x) \cdot g(x) - f(x) \cdot g'(x)}{\left(g(x) \right)^2} \tag{3}$$

In words: *The derivative of a quotient is equal to the derivative of the numerator times the denominator minus the numerator times the derivative of the denominator, this difference then being divided by the square of the denominator.* In simpler notation, we have

$$\left(\frac{f}{g} \right)' = \frac{f'g - fg'}{g^2}$$

NOTE 1   In the product rule formula, the two functions appear symmetrically, so that it is easy to remember. In the formula for the derivative of a quotient, the expressions in the numerator must be in the right order. Here is how you check that you have the order right. Write down the formula you believe is correct. Put $g \equiv 1$. Then $g' \equiv 0$, and your formula ought to reduce to f'. If you get $-f'$, then your signs are wrong.

EXAMPLE 5   Compute $F'(x)$ and $F'(4)$ when $F(x) = \dfrac{3x-5}{x-2}$.

Solution: We apply (3) with $f(x) = 3x-5$, $g(x) = x-2$. Then $f'(x) = 3$ and $g'(x) = 1$. So we obtain, for $x \neq 2$:

$$F'(x) = \frac{3 \cdot (x-2) - (3x-5) \cdot 1}{(x-2)^2} = \frac{3x - 6 - 3x + 5}{(x-2)^2} = \frac{-1}{(x-2)^2}$$

To find $F'(4)$, we put $x = 4$ in the formula for $F'(x)$ to get $F'(4) = -1/(4-2)^2 = -1/4$. Note that $F'(x) < 0$ for all $x \neq 2$. Hence F is strictly decreasing both for $x < 2$ and for $x > 2$. Note that $(3x-5)/(x-2) = 3 + 1/(x-2)$. The graph is shown in Fig. 5.1.7.

EXAMPLE 6   Let $C(x)$ be the total cost of producing x units of a commodity. Then $C(x)/x$ is the *average cost* of producing x units. Find an expression for $\frac{d}{dx}\left[C(x)/x\right]$.

Solution:

$$\frac{d}{dx}\left(\frac{C(x)}{x}\right) = \frac{C'(x)x - C(x)}{x^2} = \frac{1}{x}\left(C'(x) - \frac{C(x)}{x}\right) \tag{4}$$

Note that the marginal cost $C'(x)$ exceeds the average cost $C(x)/x$ if and only if average cost increases as output increases. (In a similar way, if a basketball team recruits a new player, the average height of the team increases if and only if the new player's height exceeds the old average height.)

The formula for the derivative of a quotient becomes more symmetric if we consider relative rates of change. By using (3), simple computation shows that

$$F(x) = \frac{f(x)}{g(x)} \quad \Longrightarrow \quad \frac{F'(x)}{F(x)} = \frac{f'(x)}{f(x)} - \frac{g'(x)}{g(x)} \tag{5}$$

The relative rate of change of a quotient is equal to the relative rate of change of the numerator minus the relative rate of change of the denominator.

Let $W(t)$ be the nominal wage rate and $P(t)$ the price index at time t. Then $w(t) = W(t)/P(t)$ is called the **real wage rate**. According to (5),

$$\frac{\dot{w}(t)}{w(t)} = \frac{\dot{W}(t)}{W(t)} - \frac{\dot{P}(t)}{P(t)}$$

The relative rate of change of the real wage rate is equal to the difference between the relative rates of change of the nominal wage rate and the price index. Thus, if nominal wages increase at the rate of 5% per year but prices rise by 6% per year, then real wages fall by 1%. Also, if inflation leads to wages and prices increasing at the same relative rate, then the real wage rate is constant.

PROBLEMS FOR SECTION 6.7

In Problems 1–4, differentiate the functions defined by the various formulas.

1. (a) $x + 1$ (b) $x + x^2$ (c) $3x^5 + 2x^4 + 5$

     (d) $8x^4 + 2\sqrt{x}$ (e) $\frac{1}{2}x - \frac{3}{2}x^2 + 5x^3$ (f) $1 - 3x^7$

2. (a) $\frac{3}{5}x^2 - 2x^7 + \frac{1}{8} - \sqrt{x}$ (b) $(2x^2 - 1)(x^4 - 1)$ (c) $\left(x^5 + \frac{1}{x}\right)(x^5 + 1)$

SM 3. (a) $\dfrac{1}{x^6}$ (b) $x^{-1}(x^2 + 1)\sqrt{x}$ (c) $\dfrac{1}{\sqrt{x^3}}$ (d) $\dfrac{x + 1}{x - 1}$

     (e) $\dfrac{x + 1}{x^5}$ (f) $\dfrac{3x - 5}{2x + 8}$ (g) $3x^{-11}$ (h) $\dfrac{3x - 1}{x^2 + x + 1}$

4. (a) $\dfrac{\sqrt{x} - 2}{\sqrt{x} + 1}$ (b) $\dfrac{x^2 - 1}{x^2 + 1}$ (c) $\dfrac{x^2 + x + 1}{x^2 - x + 1}$

5. Let $x = f(L)$ be the output when L units of labour are used as input. Assume that $f(0) = 0$, $f'(L) > 0$, and $f''(L) < 0$ for $L > 0$. Average productivity is $g(L) = f(L)/L$.

  (a) Let $L^* > 0$. Indicate on a figure the values of $f'(L^*)$ and $g(L^*)$. Which is the larger?

  (b) How does the average productivity change when labour input increases?

SM 6. For each of the following functions, determine the intervals where it is increasing.

  (a) $y = 3x^2 - 12x + 13$ (b) $y = \frac{1}{4}(x^4 - 6x^2)$ (c) $y = \dfrac{2x}{x^2 + 2}$ (d) $y = \dfrac{x^2 - x^3}{2(x + 1)}$

SM 7. Find the equations for the tangents to the graphs of the following functions at the specified points:

  (a) $y = 3 - x - x^2$ at $x = 1$ (b) $y = \dfrac{x^2 - 1}{x^2 + 1}$ at $x = 1$

  (c) $y = \left(\dfrac{1}{x^2} + 1\right)(x^2 - 1)$ at $x = 2$ (d) $y = \dfrac{x^4 + 1}{(x^2 + 1)(x + 3)}$ at $x = 0$

8. Consider the extraction of oil from a well. Let $x(t)$ be the rate of extraction in barrels per day and $p(t)$ the price in dollars per barrel at time t. Then $R(t) = p(t)x(t)$ is the revenue in dollars per day. Find an expression for $\dot{R}(t)$, and give it an economic interpretation in the case when $p(t)$ and $x(t)$ are both increasing. (*Hint:* $R(t)$ increases for two reasons ...)

SM 9. Differentiate the following functions w.r.t. t:

  (a) $\dfrac{at + b}{ct + d}$ (b) $t^n \left(a\sqrt{t} + b\right)$ (c) $\dfrac{1}{at^2 + bt + c}$

10. If $f(x) = \sqrt{x}$, then $f(x) \cdot f(x) = x$. Use the product rule to find a formula for $f'(x)$. Compare this with the result in Problem 6.2.8.

11. Prove the power rule

$$y = x^a \implies y' = ax^{a-1}$$

for $a = -n$, where n is a natural number, by using the relation $f(x) = x^{-n} = 1/x^n$ and the quotient rule (3).

6.8 Chain Rule

Suppose that y is a function of u, and that u is a function of x. Then y is a composite function of x. Suppose that x changes. This gives rise to a two-stage "chain reaction": first, u reacts directly to the change in x; second, y reacts to this change in u. If we know the rates of change du/dx and dy/du, then what is the rate of change dy/dx? It turns out that the relationship between these rates of change is simply:

$$\frac{dy}{dx} = \frac{dy}{du} \cdot \frac{du}{dx} \qquad \text{(Chain Rule)} \qquad (1)$$

A slightly more detailed formulation says that *if y is a differentiable function of u, and u is a differentiable function of x, then y is a differentiable function of x*, and (1) holds.

An important special case is when $y = u^a$. Then $dy/du = au^{a-1}$, and the chain rule yields the **generalized power rule**:

$$y = u^a \implies y' = au^{a-1}u' \qquad (u = g(x)) \qquad (2)$$

It is easy to remember the chain rule when using Leibniz's notation. The left-hand side of (1) is exactly what results if we "cancel" the du on the right-hand side. Of course, because dy/du and du/dx are not fractions (but merely symbols for derivatives) and du is not a number, cancelling is not defined.[5]

The chain rule is very powerful. Facility in applying it comes from a lot of practice.

EXAMPLE 1 (a) Find dy/dx when $y = u^5$ and $u = 1 - x^3$.

(b) Find dy/dx when $y = \dfrac{10}{(x^2 + 4x + 5)^7}$.

Solution:

(a) Here we can use (1) directly. Since $dy/du = 5u^4$ and $du/dx = -3x^2$, we have

$$\frac{dy}{dx} = \frac{dy}{du} \cdot \frac{du}{dx} = 5u^4(-3x^2) = -15x^2u^4 = -15x^2(1 - x^3)^4$$

(b) If we write $u = x^2 + 4x + 5$, then $y = 10u^{-7}$. By the generalized power rule, one has

$$\frac{dy}{dx} = 10(-7)u^{-8}u' = -70u^{-8}(2x + 4) = \frac{-140(x + 2)}{(x^2 + 4x + 5)^8}$$

---

[5] It has been suggested that proving (1) by cancelling du is not much better than proving that $64/16 = 4$ by cancelling the two sixes: $\cancel{6}4/1\cancel{6} = 4$.

NOTE 1   After a little training, the intermediate steps become unnecessary. For example, to differentiate the composite function

$$y = (\underbrace{1 - x^3}_{u})^5$$

suggested by Example 1(a), we can *think* of y as $y = u^5$, where $u = 1 - x^3$. We can then differentiate both u^5 and $1 - x^3$ in our heads, and immediately write down $y' = 5(1 - x^3)^4(-3x^2)$.

NOTE 2   If you differentiate $y = x^5/5$ using the quotient rule, you obtain the right answer, but commit a small "mathematical crime". This is because it is much easier to write y as $y = (1/5)x^5$ to get $y' = (1/5)5x^4 = x^4$. In the same way, it is unnecessarily cumbersome to apply the quotient rule to the function given in Example 1(b). The generalized power rule is much more effective.

EXAMPLE 2   Differentiate the functions

(a) $y = (x^3 + x^2)^{50}$ (b) $y = \left(\dfrac{x - 1}{x + 3}\right)^{1/3}$ (c) $y = \sqrt{x^2 + 1}$

Solution:

(a) $y = (x^3 + x^2)^{50} = u^{50}$ where $u = x^3 + x^2$, so $u' = 3x^2 + 2x$. Then (2) gives

$$y' = 50u^{50-1} \cdot u' = 50(x^3 + x^2)^{49}(3x^2 + 2x)$$

(b) Again we use (2): $y = \left(\dfrac{x - 1}{x + 3}\right)^{1/3} = u^{1/3}$ where $u = \dfrac{x - 1}{x + 3}$. The quotient rule gives

$$u' = \frac{1 \cdot (x + 3) - (x - 1) \cdot 1}{(x + 3)^2} = \frac{4}{(x + 3)^2}$$

and hence

$$y' = \frac{1}{3}u^{(1/3)-1} \cdot u' = \frac{1}{3}\left(\frac{x - 1}{x + 3}\right)^{-2/3} \cdot \frac{4}{(x + 3)^2}$$

(c) Note first that $y = \sqrt{x^2 + 1} = (x^2 + 1)^{1/2}$, so $y = u^{1/2}$ where $u = x^2 + 1$. Hence,

$$y' = \frac{1}{2}u^{(1/2)-1} \cdot u' = \frac{1}{2}(x^2 + 1)^{-1/2} \cdot 2x = \frac{x}{\sqrt{x^2 + 1}}$$

The formulation of the chain rule might appear abstract and difficult. However, when we interpret the derivatives involved in (1) as rates of change, the chain rule becomes rather intuitive, as the next example from economics will indicate.

EXAMPLE 3   The demand x for a commodity depends on price p. Suppose that price p is not constant, but depends on time t. Then x is a composite function of t, and according to the chain rule,

$$\frac{dx}{dt} = \frac{dx}{dp} \cdot \frac{dp}{dt} \qquad\qquad (*)$$

Suppose, for instance, that the demand for butter decreases by 5000 pounds if the price goes up by $1 per pound. So $dx/dp \approx -5000$. Suppose further that the price per pound increases by $0.05 per month, so $dp/dt \approx 0.05$. What is the decrease in demand in pounds per month?

Solution: Because the price per pound increases by $0.05 per month, and the demand decreases by 5000 pounds for every dollar increase in the price, the demand *decreases* by approximately $5000 \cdot 0.05 = 250$ pounds per month. This means that $dx/dt \approx -250$ (measured in pounds per month). Note how this argument confirms that $(*)$ holds approximately, at least.

The next example uses the chain rule several times.

EXAMPLE 4   Find $x'(t)$ when $x(t) = 5(1 + \sqrt{t^3 + 1})^{25}$.

Solution: The initial step is easy. Let $x(t) = 5u^{25}$, where $u = 1 + \sqrt{t^3 + 1}$, to obtain

$$x'(t) = 5 \cdot 25u^{24}\,\frac{du}{dt} = 125u^{24}\,\frac{du}{dt} \qquad (*)$$

The new feature in this example is that we cannot write down du/dt at once. Finding du/dt requires using the chain rule a second time. Let $u = 1 + \sqrt{v} = 1 + v^{1/2}$, where $v = t^3 + 1$. Then

$$\frac{du}{dt} = \tfrac{1}{2}v^{(1/2)-1} \cdot \frac{dv}{dt} = \tfrac{1}{2}v^{-1/2} \cdot 3t^2 = \tfrac{1}{2}(t^3 + 1)^{-1/2} \cdot 3t^2 \qquad (**)$$

From $(*)$ and $(**)$, we get

$$x'(t) = 125\left(1 + \sqrt{t^3 + 1}\right)^{24} \cdot \tfrac{1}{2}(t^3 + 1)^{-1/2} \cdot 3t^2$$

Suppose, as in the last example, that x is a function of u, u is a function of v, and v is in turn a function of t. Then x is a composite function of t, and the chain rule can be used twice to obtain

$$\frac{dx}{dt} = \frac{dx}{du} \cdot \frac{du}{dv} \cdot \frac{dv}{dt}$$

This is precisely the formula used in the last example. Again the notation is suggestive because the left-hand side is exactly what results if we "cancel" both du and dv on the right-hand side.

An Alternative Formulation of the Chain Rule

Although Leibniz's notation makes it very easy to remember the chain rule, it suffers from the defect of not specifying where each derivative is evaluated. We remedy this by introducing names for the functions involved. So let $y = f(u)$ and $u = g(x)$. Then y can be written as

$$y = f(g(x))$$

Here y is a *composite function* of x, as considered in Section 5.2, with $g(x)$ as the *kernel*, and f as the *exterior function*.

THE CHAIN RULE

If g is differentiable at x_0 and f is differentiable at $u_0 = g(x_0)$, then $F(x) = f(g(x))$ is differentiable at x_0, and

$$F'(x_0) = f'(u_0)g'(x_0) = f'(g(x_0))g'(x_0)$$

(3)

In words: *to differentiate a composite function, first differentiate the exterior function w.r.t. the kernel, then multiply by the derivative of the kernel.*

EXAMPLE 5   Find the derivative of $F(x) = f(g(x))$ at $x_0 = -3$ if $f(u) = u^3$ and $g(x) = 2 - x^2$.

Solution: In this case, $f'(u) = 3u^2$ and $g'(x) = -2x$. So according to (3), $F'(-3) = f'(g(-3))g'(-3)$. Now $g(-3) = 2 - (-3)^2 = 2 - 9 = -7$; $g'(-3) = 6$; and $f'(g(-3)) = f'(-7) = 3(-7)^2 = 3 \cdot 49 = 147$. So $F'(-3) = f'(g(-3))g'(-3) = 147 \cdot 6 = 882$. ∎

Proof of (3):   In simplified notation, with $y = F(x) = f(u)$ and $u = g(x)$, as above, it is tempting to argue as follows: Since $u = g(x)$ is continuous, $\Delta u = g(x) - g(x_0) \to 0$ as $x \to x_0$, and so

$$F'(x_0) = \lim_{\Delta x \to 0} \frac{\Delta y}{\Delta x} = \lim_{\Delta x \to 0} \left(\frac{\Delta y}{\Delta u} \cdot \frac{\Delta u}{\Delta x} \right) = \lim_{\Delta u \to 0} \frac{\Delta y}{\Delta u} \cdot \lim_{\Delta x \to 0} \frac{\Delta u}{\Delta x} = \frac{dy}{du} \cdot \frac{du}{dx} = f'(u_0)g'(x_0)$$

There is a catch, however, because Δu may be equal to 0 for values of x arbitrarily close to x_0, and then $\Delta y / \Delta u$ will be undefined. To avoid division by zero, define functions φ and γ as follows:

$$\varphi(u) = \begin{cases} \dfrac{f(u) - f(u_0)}{u - u_0} & \text{if } u \neq u_0 \\ f'(u_0) & \text{if } u = u_0 \end{cases}, \qquad \gamma(x) = \begin{cases} \dfrac{g(x) - g(x_0)}{x - x_0} & \text{if } x \neq x_0 \\ g'(x_0) & \text{if } x = x_0 \end{cases}$$

Then $\lim_{u \to u_0} \varphi(u) = \varphi(u_0)$ and $\lim_{x \to x_0} \gamma(x) = \gamma(x_0)$. Moreover,

$$f(u) - f(u_0) = \varphi(u)(u - u_0) \qquad \text{and} \qquad g(x) - g(x_0) = \gamma(x)(x - x_0)$$

for all u in an interval around u_0 and all x in an interval around x_0. It follows that, for h close to 0,

$$F(x_0 + h) - F(x_0) = f(g(x_0 + h)) - f(g(x_0))$$
$$= \varphi(g(x_0 + h)) \cdot (g(x_0 + h) - g(x_0)) = \varphi(g(x_0 + h)) \cdot \gamma(x_0 + h) \cdot h$$

and so

$$F'(x_0) = \lim_{h \to 0} \frac{F(x_0 + h) - F(x_0)}{h} = \varphi(g(x_0))\gamma(x_0) = f'(g(x_0))g'(x_0)$$ ∎

PROBLEMS FOR SECTION 6.8

1. Use the chain rule (1) to find dy/dx for the following:

    (a) $y = 5u^4$ where $u = 1 + x^2$ (b) $y = u - u^6$ where $u = 1 + 1/x$

2. Compute the following:

    (a) dY/dt when $Y = -3(V + 1)^5$ and $V = \frac{1}{3}t^3$.

    (b) dK/dt when $K = AL^a$ and $L = bt + c$ (A, a, b, and c are positive constants).

(SM) **3.** Find the derivatives of the following functions, where a, p, q, and b are constants:

(a) $y = \dfrac{1}{(x^2 + x + 1)^5}$

(b) $y = \sqrt{x + \sqrt{x + \sqrt{x}}}$

(c) $y = x^a (px + q)^b$

4. If Y is a function of K, and K is a function of t, find the formula for the derivative of Y with respect to t at $t = t_0$.

5. If $Y = F(K)$ and $K = h(t)$, find the formula for dY/dt.

6. Compute dx/dp for the demand function $x = b - \sqrt{ap - c}$, where a, b, and c are positive constants, while x is the number of units demanded, and p is the price per unit, with $p > c/a$.

7. Find a formula for $h'(x)$ when   (i) $h(x) = f(x^2)$ (ii) $h(x) = f(x^n g(x))$.

8. Let $s(t)$ be the distance in kilometres a car goes in t hours. Let $B(s)$ be the number of litres of fuel the car uses to go s kilometres. Provide an interpretation of the function $b(t) = B(s(t))$, and find a formula for $b'(t)$. $b'(t) = B'(s) \cdot s'(t)$

9. Suppose that $C = 20q - 4q \left(25 - \tfrac{1}{2}x\right)^{1/2}$, where q is a constant and $x < 50$. Find dC/dx.

10. Differentiate each of the following in two different ways:

(a) $y = (x^4)^5 = x^{20}$

(b) $y = (1 - x)^3 = 1 - 3x + 3x^2 - x^3$

11. (a) Suppose you invest 1000 euros at $p\%$ interest per year. Then after 10 years you will have $K = g(p)$ euros. Give economic interpretations to: (i) $g(5) \approx 1629$ (ii) $g'(5) \approx 155$.

(b) To check the numbers in (a), find a formula for $g(p)$, and then compute $g(5)$ and $g'(5)$.

12. If f is differentiable at x, find expressions for the derivatives of the following functions:

(a) $x + f(x)$

(b) $\left[f(x)\right]^2 - x$

(c) $\left[f(x)\right]^4$

(d) $x^2 f(x) + \left[f(x)\right]^3$

(e) $x f(x)$

(f) $\sqrt{f(x)}$

(g) $\dfrac{x^2}{f(x)}$

(h) $\dfrac{\left[f(x)\right]^2}{x^3}$

6.9 Higher-Order Derivatives

The derivative f' of a function f is often called the **first derivative** of f. If f' is also differentiable, then we can differentiate f' in turn. The result $(f')'$ is called the **second derivative**, written more concisely as f''. We use $f''(x)$ to denote the second derivative of f evaluated at the particular point x.

EXAMPLE 1   Find $f'(x)$ and $f''(x)$ when $f(x) = 2x^5 - 3x^3 + 2x$.

Solution: The rules for differentiating polynomials imply that $f'(x) = 10x^4 - 9x^2 + 2$. Then we differentiate each side of this equality to get $f''(x) = 40x^3 - 18x$.

The different forms of notation for the second derivative are analogous to those for the first derivative. For example, we write $y'' = f''(x)$ in order to denote the second derivative of $y = f(x)$. The Leibniz notation for the second derivative is also used. In the notation dy/dx or $df(x)/dx$ for the first derivative, we interpreted the symbol d/dx as an operator indicating that what follows is to be differentiated with respect to x. The second derivative is obtained by using the operator d/dx twice: $f''(x) = (d/dx)(d/dx)f(x)$. We usually think of this as $f''(x) = (d/dx)^2 f(x)$, and so write it as follows:

$$f''(x) = \frac{d^2 f(x)}{dx^2} = d^2 f(x)/dx^2 \quad \text{or} \quad y'' = \frac{d^2 y}{dx^2} = d^2 y/dx^2$$

Pay special attention to where the superscripts 2 are placed.

Of course, the notation for the second derivative must change if the variables have other names.

EXAMPLE 2   (a) Find Y'' when $Y = AK^a$ is a function of K ($K > 0$), with A and a as constants.

(b) Find $d^2 L/dt^2$ when $L = \dfrac{t}{t+1}$, and $t \geq 0$.

Solution:

(a) Differentiating $Y = AK^a$ with respect to K gives $Y' = AaK^{a-1}$. A second differentiation with respect to K yields $Y'' = Aa(a-1)K^{a-2}$.

(b) First, we use the quotient rule to find that

$$\frac{dL}{dt} = \frac{d}{dt}\left(\frac{t}{t+1}\right) = \frac{1 \cdot (t+1) - t \cdot 1}{(t+1)^2} = (t+1)^{-2}$$

Then,

$$\frac{d^2 L}{dt^2} = -2(t+1)^{-3} = \frac{-2}{(t+1)^3}$$

Convex and Concave Functions

Recall from Section 6.3 how the sign of the first derivative determines whether a function is increasing or decreasing on an interval I. If $f'(x) \geq 0$ ($f'(x) \leq 0$) on I, then f is increasing (decreasing) on I, and conversely. The second derivative $f''(x)$ is the derivative of $f'(x)$. Hence:

$$f''(x) \geq 0 \text{ on } I \iff f' \text{ is increasing on } I \tag{1}$$

$$f''(x) \leq 0 \text{ on } I \iff f' \text{ is decreasing on } I \tag{2}$$

The equivalence in (1) is illustrated in Fig. 1. The slope of the tangent, $f'(x)$, is increasing as x increases. On the other hand, the slope of the tangent to the graph in Fig. 2 is decreasing as x increases. (To help visualize this, imagine sliding a ruler along the curve and keeping it aligned with the tangent to the curve at each point. As the ruler moves along the curve from left to right, the tangent rotates counterclockwise in Fig. 1, clockwise in Fig. 2.)

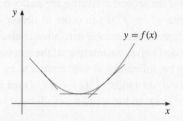

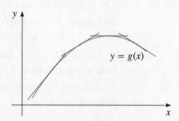

Figure 1 The slope of the tangent increases as x increases. $f'(x)$ is increasing.

Figure 2 The slope of the tangent decreases as x increases. $g'(x)$ is decreasing.

Suppose that f is continuous in the interval I and twice differentiable in the interior of I. Then we can introduce the following definitions:

$$f \text{ is } \mathbf{convex} \text{ on } I \iff f''(x) \geq 0 \text{ for all } x \text{ in } I$$

$$f \text{ is } \mathbf{concave} \text{ on } I \iff f''(x) \leq 0 \text{ for all } x \text{ in } I$$

(3)

These properties are illustrated in Fig. 3, which should be studied carefully. Whether a function is concave or convex is crucial to many results in economic analysis, especially the many that involve maximization or minimization problems. We note that often I is the whole real line, in which case the interval is not mentioned explicitly.

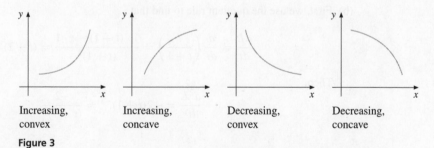

Increasing, convex

Increasing, concave

Decreasing, convex

Decreasing, concave

Figure 3

EXAMPLE 3

Check the convexity/concavity of the following functions:

$$\text{(a) } f(x) = x^2 - 2x + 2 \qquad \text{and} \qquad \text{(b) } f(x) = ax^2 + bx + c$$

Solution:

(a) Here $f'(x) = 2x - 2$ so $f''(x) = 2$. Because $f''(x) > 0$ for all x, f is convex.

(b) Here $f'(x) = 2ax + b$, so $f''(x) = 2a$. If $a = 0$, then f is linear. In this case, the function f meets both the definitions in (3), so it is both concave and convex. If $a > 0$, then $f''(x) > 0$, so f is convex. If $a < 0$, then $f''(x) < 0$, so f is concave. The last two cases are illustrated by the graphs in Fig. 4.6.1.

We consider two typical examples of convex and concave functions.

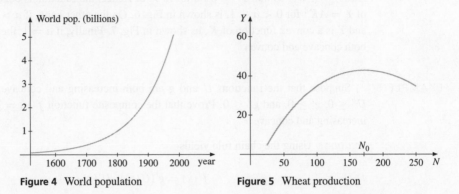

Figure 4 World population   **Figure 5** Wheat production

Figure 4 shows a rough graph of the function P, for dates between 1500 and 2000, where

$$P(t) = \text{world population (in billions) in year } t$$

It appears from the figure that not only is $P(t)$ increasing, but the rate of increase increases. (Each year the *increase* becomes larger.) So, for the last five centuries, $P(t)$ has been convex.

The graph in Fig. 5 shows the crop of wheat $Y(N)$ when N pounds of fertilizer per acre are used. The curve is based on fertilizer experiments in Iowa during 1952. The function has a maximum at $N = N_0 \approx 172$. Increasing the amount of fertilizer beyond N_0 will cause wheat production to decline. Moreover, $Y(N)$ is concave. If $N < N_0$, increasing N by one unit will *increase* $Y(N)$ by less, the larger is N. On the other hand, if $N > N_0$, increasing N by one unit will *decrease* $Y(N)$ by more, the larger is N.

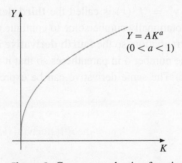
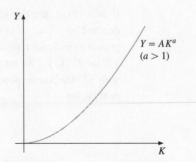

Figure 6 Concave production function   **Figure 7** Convex production function

EXAMPLE 4

Examine the concavity/convexity of the production function

$$Y = AK^a \qquad (A > 0,\ a > 0)$$

defined for all $K \geq 0$.

Solution: From Example 2(a), $Y'' = Aa(a - 1)K^{a-2}$. If $a \in (0, 1)$, then the coefficient $Aa(a - 1) < 0$, so that $Y'' < 0$ for all $K > 0$. Hence, the function is concave. The graph of $Y = AK^a$ for $0 < a < 1$, is shown in Fig. 6. On the other hand, if $a > 1$, then $Y'' > 0$ and Y is a convex function of K, as shown in Fig. 7. Finally, if $a = 1$, then Y is linear, so both concave and convex.

EXAMPLE 5   Suppose that the functions U and g are both increasing and concave, with $U' \geq 0$, $U'' \leq 0$, $g' \geq 0$, and $g'' \leq 0$. Prove that the composite function $f(x) = g(U(x))$ is also increasing and concave.

Solution: Using the chain rule yields

$$f'(x) = g'(U(x)) \cdot U'(x) \tag{$*$}$$

Because g' and U' are both ≥ 0, so $f'(x) \geq 0$. Hence, f is increasing. (*An increasing transformation of an increasing function is increasing.*)

In order to compute $f''(x)$, we must differentiate the product of the two functions $g'(U(x))$ and $U'(x)$. According to the chain rule, the derivative of $g'(U(x))$ is equal to $g''(U(x)) \cdot U'(x)$. Hence,

$$f''(x) = g''(U(x)) \cdot (U'(x))^2 + g'(U(x)) \cdot U''(x) \tag{$**$}$$

Because $g'' \leq 0$, $g' \geq 0$, and $U'' \leq 0$, it follows that $f''(x) \leq 0$. (*An increasing concave transformation of a concave function is concave.*)

Nth-Order Derivatives

If $y = f(x)$, the derivative of $y'' = f''(x)$ is called the **third derivative**, customarily denoted by $y''' = f'''(x)$. It is notationally cumbersome to continue using more and more primes to indicate repeated differentiation, so the **fourth derivative** is usually denoted by $y^{(4)} = f^{(4)}(x)$. (We must put the number 4 in parentheses so that it will not get confused with y^4, the fourth power of y.) The same derivative can be expressed as d^4y/dx^4. In general, let

$$y^{(n)} = f^{(n)}(x) \quad \text{or} \quad \frac{d^n y}{dx^n} \qquad \text{denote the } n\text{th derivative of } f \text{ at } x$$

The number n is called the **order** of the derivative. For example, $f^{(6)}(x_0)$ denotes the sixth derivative of f calculated at x_0, found by differentiating six times.

EXAMPLE 6   Compute all the derivatives up to and including order 4 of

$$f(x) = 3x^{-1} + 6x^3 - x^2 \qquad (x \neq 0)$$

Solution: Repeated differentiation gives

$$f'(x) = -3x^{-2} + 18x^2 - 2x, \qquad f''(x) = 6x^{-3} + 36x - 2,$$
$$f'''(x) = -18x^{-4} + 36 \qquad f^{(4)}(x) = 72x^{-5}$$

PROBLEMS FOR SECTION 6.9

1. Compute the second derivatives of:

   (a) $y = x^5 - 3x^4 + 2$ (b) $y = \sqrt{x}$ (c) $y = (1 + x^2)^{10}$

2. Find d^2y/dx^2 when $y = \sqrt{1 + x^2} = (1 + x^2)^{1/2}$.

3. Compute:

   (a) y'' for $y = 3x^3 + 2x - 1$ (b) Y''' for $Y = 1 - 2x^2 + 6x^3$

   (c) d^3z/dt^3 for $z = 120t - (1/3)t^3$ (d) $f^{(4)}(1)$ for $f(z) = 100z^{-4}$

4. Find $g''(2)$ when $g(t) = \dfrac{t^2}{t-1}$.

5. Find formulas for y'' and y''' when $y = f(x)g(x)$.

6. Find d^2L/dt^2 when $L = 1/\sqrt{2t - 1}$.

7. If $u(y)$ denotes an individual's utility of having income (or consumption) y, then

$$R = -yu''(y)/u'(y)$$

   is the coefficient of **relative risk aversion**. ($R_A = R/y$ is the degree of **absolute risk aversion**.) Compute R for the following utility functions (where A_1, A_2, and ρ are positive constants with $\rho \neq 1$, and we assume that $y > 0$):

   (a) $u(y) = \sqrt{y}$ (b) $u(y) = A_1 - A_2y^{-2}$ (c) $u(y) = A_1 + A_2y^{1-\rho}/(1 - \rho)$

8. Let $U(x) = \sqrt{x}$ and $g(u) = u^3$. Then $f(x) = g(U(x)) = x^{3/2}$, which is not a concave function. Why does this not contradict the conclusion in Example 5?

9. The US defence secretary claimed in 1985 that Congress had reduced the defence budget. Representative Gray pointed out that the budget had not been reduced; Congress had only reduced the rate of increase. If P denotes the size of the defence budget, translate the statements into statements about the signs of P' and P''.

10. Sentence in a newspaper: "The rate of increase of bank loans is increasing at an increasing rate". If $L(t)$ denotes total bank loans at time t, represent the sentence by a mathematical statement about the sign of an appropriate derivative of L.

6.10 Exponential Functions

Exponential functions were introduced in Section 4.9. They were shown to be well suited in describing certain economic phenomena such as growth and compound interest. In particular we introduced the *natural* exponential function, $f(x) = e^x$, where $e \approx 2.7$. (Recall the alternative notation, $f(x) = \exp(x)$.)

Now we explain why this particular exponential function deserves to be called "natural". Consider the Newton quotient of $f(x) = e^x$, which is

$$\frac{f(x+h) - f(x)}{h} = \frac{e^{x+h} - e^x}{h} \qquad (*)$$

If this fraction tends to a limit as h tends to 0, then $f(x) = e^x$ is differentiable and $f'(x)$ is precisely equal to this limit.

To simplify the right-hand side of $(*)$, we make use of the rule $e^{x+h} = e^x \cdot e^h$ to write $e^{x+h} - e^x$ as $e^x(e^h - 1)$. So $(*)$ can be rewritten as

$$\frac{f(x+h) - f(x)}{h} = e^x \cdot \frac{e^h - 1}{h}$$

We now evaluate the limit of the right-hand side as $h \to 0$. Note that e^x is a constant when we vary only h. As for $(e^h - 1)/h$, in Example 6.5.1 we argued that this fraction tends to 1 as h tends to 0. (Although in that example the variable was x and not h.) It follows that

$$f(x) = e^x \quad \implies \quad f'(x) = e^x \qquad (1)$$

Thus the **natural exponential function** $f(x) = e^x$ *has the remarkable property that its derivative is equal to the function itself.* This is the main reason why the function appears so often in mathematics and applications.

Another implication of (1) is that $f''(x) = e^x$. Because $e^x > 0$ for all x, both $f'(x)$ and $f''(x)$ are positive. Hence, both f and f' are strictly increasing. This confirms the increasing convex shape indicated in Fig. 4.9.3.

Combining (1) with the other rules of differentiation, we can differentiate many expressions involving the exponential function e^x.

EXAMPLE 1   Find the first and second derivatives of   (a) $y = x^3 + e^x$ (b) $y = x^5 e^x$ (c) $y = e^x/x$

Solution: (a) We find that $y' = 3x^2 + e^x$ and $y'' = 6x + e^x$.

(b) We have to use the product rule: $y' = 5x^4 e^x + x^5 e^x = x^4 e^x (5 + x)$. To compute y'', we differentiate $y' = 5x^4 e^x + x^5 e^x$ once more to obtain

$$y'' = 20x^3 e^x + 5x^4 e^x + 5x^4 e^x + x^5 e^x = x^3 e^x (x^2 + 10x + 20)$$

(c) The quotient rule yields

$$y = \frac{e^x}{x} \implies y' = \frac{e^x x - e^x \cdot 1}{x^2} = \frac{e^x(x-1)}{x^2}$$

Differentiating $y' = \dfrac{e^x x - e^x}{x^2}$ once more w.r.t. x gives

$$y'' = \frac{(e^x x + e^x - e^x)x^2 - (e^x x - e^x)2x}{(x^2)^2} = \frac{e^x(x^2 - 2x + 2)}{x^3}$$

Combining (1) with the chain rule allows some rather complicated functions to be differentiated. First, note that $y = e^{g(x)} = e^u \implies y' = e^u \cdot u' = e^{g(x)} \cdot g'(x)$, so that

$$y = e^{g(x)} \implies y' = e^{g(x)} g'(x) \tag{2}$$

EXAMPLE 2   Differentiate:

(a) $y = e^{-x}$ (b) $y = x^p e^{ax}$ (p and a are constants)   (c) $y = \sqrt{e^{2x} + x}$

Solution:

(a) Direct use of (2) gives $y = e^{-x} \implies y' = e^{-x} \cdot (-1) = -e^{-x}$. This derivative is always negative, so the function is strictly decreasing. Furthermore, $y'' = e^{-x} > 0$, so the function is convex. This agrees with the graph shown in Fig. 4.9.3.

(b) The derivative of e^{ax} is ae^{ax}. Hence, using the product rule,

$$y' = px^{p-1}e^{ax} + x^p a e^{ax} = x^{p-1}e^{ax}(p + ax)$$

(c) Let $y = \sqrt{e^{2x} + x} = \sqrt{u}$, with $u = e^{2x} + x$. Then $u' = 2e^{2x} + 1$, where we used the chain rule. Using the chain rule again, we obtain

$$y = \sqrt{e^{2x} + x} = \sqrt{v} \implies y' = \frac{1}{2\sqrt{v}} \cdot v' = \frac{2e^{2x} + 1}{2\sqrt{e^{2x} + x}}$$

EXAMPLE 3   Find the intervals where the following functions are increasing:

(a) $y = \dfrac{e^x}{x}$ (b) $y = x^4 e^{-2x}$ (c) $y = xe^{-\sqrt{x}}$

Solution:

(a) According to Example 1(c), $y' = \dfrac{e^x(x-1)}{x^2}$, so $y' \geq 0$ when $x \geq 1$. Thus y is increasing in $[1, \infty)$.

(b) According to Example 2(b), with $p = 4$ and $a = -2$, we have $y' = x^3 e^{-2x}(4 - 2x)$. A sign diagram reveals that y is increasing in $[0, 2]$.

(c) The function is only defined for $x \geq 0$. Using the chain rule, for $x > 0$ the derivative of $e^{-\sqrt{x}}$ is $-e^{-\sqrt{x}}/2\sqrt{x}$, so by the product rule, the derivative of $y = xe^{-\sqrt{x}}$ is

$$y' = 1 \cdot e^{-\sqrt{x}} - \frac{xe^{-\sqrt{x}}}{2\sqrt{x}} = e^{-\sqrt{x}}\left(1 - \frac{1}{2}\sqrt{x}\right)$$

where we have used the fact that $x/\sqrt{x} = \sqrt{x}$. It follows that y is increasing when $x > 0$ and $1 - \frac{1}{2}\sqrt{x} \geq 0$. Because $y = 0$ when $x = 0$ and $y > 0$ when $x > 0$, it follows that y is increasing in $[0, 4]$.

NOTE 1 A common error when differentiating exponential functions is to believe that the derivative of e^x is "xe^{x-1}". This is due to confusing the exponential function with a power function.

SURVEY OF THE PROPERTIES OF THE NATURAL EXPONENTIAL FUNCTION

The natural exponential function

$$f(x) = \exp(x) = e^x \qquad (e = 2.71828\ldots)$$

is differentiable, strictly increasing and convex. In fact,

$$f(x) = e^x \implies f'(x) = f(x) = e^x$$

The following properties hold for all exponents s and t:

(a) $e^s e^t = e^{s+t}$ (b) $e^s / e^t = e^{s-t}$ (c) $(e^s)^t = e^{st}$

Moreover,

$$e^x \to 0 \quad \text{as} \quad x \to -\infty, \qquad e^x \to \infty \quad \text{as} \quad x \to \infty$$

Differentiating Other Exponential Functions

So far we have considered only the derivative of e^x, where $e = 2.71828\ldots$. How can we differentiate $y = a^x$, where a is any other positive number? According to definition (4.10.1), we have $a = e^{\ln a}$. So, using the general property $(e^r)^s = e^{rs}$, we have the formula

$$a^x = \left(e^{\ln a}\right)^x = e^{(\ln a)x}$$

This shows that in functions involving the expression a^x, we can just as easily work with the special exponential function e^{bx}, where b is a constant equal to $\ln a$. In particular, we can differentiate a^x by differentiating $e^{x \ln a}$. According to (2), with $g(x) = (\ln a)x$, we have

$$y = a^x \implies y' = a^x \ln a \tag{3}$$

EXAMPLE 4   Find the derivatives of (a) $f(x) = 10^{-x}$ (b) $g(x) = x2^{3x}$

Solution:

(a) $f(x) = 10^{-x} = 10^u$ where $u = -x$. Using (3) and the chain rule gives $f'(x) = -10^{-x} \ln 10$.

(b) We differentiate 2^{3x} by letting $y = 2^{3x} = 2^u$, where $u = 3x$. By the chain rule, $y' = (2^u \ln 2)u' = (2^{3x} \ln 2) \cdot 3 = 3 \cdot 2^{3x} \ln 2$, and using the product rule we obtain

$$g'(x) = 1 \cdot 2^{3x} + x \cdot 3 \cdot 2^{3x} \ln 2 = 2^{3x}(1 + 3x \ln 2)$$

PROBLEMS FOR SECTION 6.10

1. Find the first-order derivatives of:

   (a) $y = e^x + x^2$ (b) $y = 5e^x - 3x^3 + 8$ (c) $y = \dfrac{x}{e^x}$ (d) $y = \dfrac{x + x^2}{e^x + 1}$.

   (e) $y = -x - 5 - e^x$ (f) $y = x^3 e^x$ (g) $y = e^x x^{-2}$ (h) $y = (x + e^x)^2$

2. Find the first-order derivatives w.r.t. t of the following functions (a, b, c, p, and q are constants).

   (a) $x = (a + bt + ct^2)e^t$ (b) $x = \dfrac{p + qt^3}{te^t}$ (c) $x = \dfrac{(at + bt^2)^2}{e^t}$

3. Find the first and second-order derivatives of:

   (a) $y = e^{-3x}$ (b) $y = 2e^{x^3}$ (c) $y = e^{1/x}$ (d) $y = 5e^{2x^2 - 3x + 1}$

(SM) 4. Find the intervals where the following functions are increasing:

   (a) $y = x^3 + e^{2x}$ (b) $y = 5x^2 e^{-4x}$ (c) $y = x^2 e^{-x^2}$

5. Find the intervals where the following functions are increasing:

   (a) $y = x^2 / e^{2x}$ (b) $y = e^x - e^{3x}$ (c) $y = \dfrac{e^{2x}}{x + 2}$

6. Find:

   (a) $\dfrac{d}{dx}\left(e^{(e^x)}\right)$ (b) $\dfrac{d}{dt}\left(e^{t/2} + e^{-t/2}\right)$ (c) $\dfrac{d}{dt}\left(\dfrac{1}{e^t + e^{-t}}\right)$ (d) $\dfrac{d}{dz}\left(e^{z^3} - 1\right)^{1/3}$

7. Differentiate: (a) $y = 5^x$ (b) $y = x2^x$ (c) $y = x^2 2^{x^2}$ (d) $y = e^x 10^x$.

6.11 Logarithmic Functions

In Section 4.10 we introduced the natural logarithmic function, $g(x) = \ln x$. It is defined for all $x > 0$ and has the following graph (reproduced from Fig. 4.10.2):

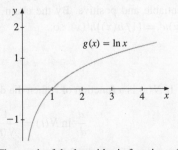

Figure 1 The graph of the logarithmic function $g(x) = \ln x$

According to Section 5.3, the function $g(x) = \ln x$ has $f(x) = e^x$ as its *inverse*. If we *assume* that $g(x) = \ln x$ has a derivative for all $x > 0$, we can easily find that derivative. To do so, we differentiate w.r.t. x the equation defining $g(x) = \ln x$, which is

$$e^{g(x)} = x \tag{$*$}$$

Using (6.10.2), we get $e^{g(x)}g'(x) = 1$. Since $e^{g(x)} = x$, this implies $xg'(x) = 1$, and thus

$$g(x) = \ln x \implies g'(x) = \frac{1}{x} \tag{1}$$

Thus, the derivative of $\ln x$ at x is simply the number $1/x$. For $x > 0$, we have $g'(x) > 0$, so that $g(x)$ is *strictly* increasing. Note moreover that $g''(x) = -1/x^2$, which is less than 0 for all $x > 0$, so that $g(x)$ is concave. This confirms the shape of the graph in Fig. 1. In fact, the growth of $\ln x$ is quite slow. For example, $\ln x$ does not attain the value 10 until $x > 22\,026$, because $\ln x = 10$ gives $x = e^{10} \approx 22\,026.5$.

EXAMPLE 1   Compute y' and y'' when: (a) $y = x^3 + \ln x$ (b) $y = x^2 \ln x$ (c) $y = \ln x / x$.

Solution:

(a) We find easily that $y' = 3x^2 + 1/x$. Furthermore, $y'' = 6x - 1/x^2$.

(b) The product rule gives

$$y' = 2x \ln x + x^2(1/x) = 2x \ln x + x$$

Differentiating the last expression w.r.t. x gives $y'' = 2 \ln x + 2x(1/x) + 1 = 2 \ln x + 3$.

(c) Here we use the quotient rule:

$$y' = \frac{(1/x)x - (\ln x) \cdot 1}{x^2} = \frac{1 - \ln x}{x^2}$$

Differentiating again yields

$$y'' = \frac{-(1/x)x^2 - (1 - \ln x)2x}{(x^2)^2} = \frac{2 \ln x - 3}{x^3}$$

Often, we need to consider composite functions involving natural logarithms. Because $\ln u$ is defined only when $u > 0$, a composite function of the form $y = \ln h(x)$ will only be defined for values of x satisfying $h(x) > 0$.

Combining the rule for differentiating $\ln x$ with the chain rule allows us to differentiate many different types of function. Suppose, for instance, that $y = \ln h(x)$, where $h(x)$ is differentiable and positive. By the chain rule, $y = \ln u$ with $u = h(x)$ implies that $y' = (1/u)u' = \left(1/h(x)\right)h'(x)$, so:

$$y = \ln h(x) \implies y' = \frac{h'(x)}{h(x)} \tag{2}$$

NOTE 1   If $N(t)$ is a function of t, then the derivative of its natural logarithm

$$\frac{d}{dt} \ln N(t) = \frac{1}{N(t)} \frac{dN(t)}{dt} = \frac{\dot{N}(t)}{N(t)}$$

is the relative rate of growth of $N(t)$.

EXAMPLE 2   Find the domains of the following functions and compute their derivatives:

$$\text{(a)} \ \ y = \ln(1 - x) \qquad \text{(b)} \ \ y = \ln(4 - x^2) \qquad \text{(c)} \ \ y = \ln\left(\frac{x-1}{x+1}\right) - \frac{1}{4}x$$

Solution:

(a) $\ln(1 - x)$ is defined if $1 - x > 0$, that is if $x < 1$. To find its derivative, we use (2) with
$h(x) = 1 - x$. Then $h'(x) = -1$, so (2) gives

$$y' = \frac{-1}{1 - x} = \frac{1}{x - 1}$$

(b) $\ln(4 - x^2)$ is defined if $4 - x^2 > 0$, that is if $(2 - x)(2 + x) > 0$. This is satisfied if
and only if $-2 < x < 2$. Formula (2) gives

$$y' = \frac{-2x}{4 - x^2} = \frac{2x}{x^2 - 4}$$

(c) We can write $y = \ln u - \frac{1}{4}x$, where $u = (x - 1)/(x + 1)$. For the function to be defined,
we require that $u > 0$. A sign diagram shows that this is satisfied if $x < -1$ or $x > 1$.
Using (2), we obtain

$$y' = \frac{u'}{u} - \frac{1}{4} \qquad \text{where} \qquad u' = \frac{1 \cdot (x + 1) - 1 \cdot (x - 1)}{(x + 1)^2} = \frac{2}{(x + 1)^2}$$

So

$$y' = \frac{2(x + 1)}{(x + 1)^2(x - 1)} - \frac{1}{4} = \frac{9 - x^2}{4(x^2 - 1)} = \frac{(3 - x)(3 + x)}{4(x - 1)(x + 1)}$$

EXAMPLE 3   Find the intervals where the following functions are increasing:

$$\text{(a)} \ \ y = x^2 \ln x \qquad \text{(b)} \ \ y = 4x - 5\ln(x^2 + 1) \qquad \text{(c)} \ \ y = 3\ln(1 + x) + x - \tfrac{1}{2}x^2$$

Solution:

(a) The function is defined for $x > 0$, and

$$y' = 2x \ln x + x^2(1/x) = x(2\ln x + 1)$$

Hence, $y' \geq 0$ when $\ln x \geq -1/2$, that is, when $x \geq e^{-1/2}$. Thus y is increasing in
$[e^{-1/2}, \infty)$.

(b) We find that

$$y' = 4 - \frac{10x}{x^2 + 1} = \frac{4(x - 2)\left(x - \tfrac{1}{2}\right)}{x^2 + 1}$$

A sign diagram reveals that y is increasing in each of the intervals $(-\infty, \tfrac{1}{2}]$ and $[2, \infty)$.

(c) The function is defined for $x > -1$, and

$$y' = \frac{3}{1 + x} + 1 - x = \frac{(2 - x)(2 + x)}{x + 1}$$

A sign diagram reveals that y is increasing in $(-1, 2]$.

SURVEY OF THE PROPERTIES OF THE NATURAL LOGARITHM

The natural logarithmic function

$$g(x) = \ln x$$

is differentiable, strictly increasing and concave in $(0, \infty)$. In fact,

$$g'(x) = 1/x, \qquad g''(x) = -1/x^2$$

By definition, $e^{\ln x} = x$ for all $x > 0$, and $\ln e^x = x$ for all x. The following properties hold for all $x > 0$, $y > 0$:

(a) $\ln(xy) = \ln x + \ln y$ (b) $\ln(x/y) = \ln x - \ln y$ (c) $\ln x^p = p \ln x$

Moreover,

$$\ln x \to -\infty \quad \text{as} \quad x \to 0 \quad \text{(from the right)}, \qquad \ln x \to \infty \quad \text{as} \quad x \to \infty$$

Logarithmic Differentiation

When differentiating an expression containing products, quotients, roots, powers, and combinations of these, it is often an advantage to use **logarithmic differentiation**. The method is illustrated by two examples:

EXAMPLE 4   Find the derivative of $y = x^x$ defined for all $x > 0$.

Solution: The power rule of differentiation, $y = x^a \implies y' = ax^{a-1}$, requires the exponent a to be a constant, while the rule $y = a^x \implies y' = a^x \ln a$ requires that the base a is constant. In the expression x^x both the exponent and the base vary with x, so neither of the two rules can be used.

Begin by taking the natural logarithm of each side, $\ln y = x \ln x$. Differentiating w.r.t. x gives $y'/y = 1 \cdot \ln x + x(1/x) = \ln x + 1$. Multiplying by $y = x^x$ gives us the result:

$$y = x^x \implies y' = x^x (\ln x + 1)$$

EXAMPLE 5   Find the derivative of $y = [A(x)]^\alpha [B(x)]^\beta [C(x)]^\gamma$, where α, β, and γ are constants and A, B, and C are positive functions.

Solution: First, take the natural logarithm of each side to obtain

$$\ln y = \alpha \ln(A(x)) + \beta \ln(B(x)) + \gamma \ln(C(x))$$

Differentiation with respect to x yields

$$\frac{y'}{y} = \alpha \frac{A'(x)}{A(x)} + \beta \frac{B'(x)}{B(x)} + \gamma \frac{C'(x)}{C(x)}$$

Multiplying by y we have

$$y' = \left[\alpha \frac{A'(x)}{A(x)} + \beta \frac{B'(x)}{B(x)} + \gamma \frac{C'(x)}{C(x)} \right] [A(x)]^\alpha [B(x)]^\beta [C(x)]^\gamma$$

In Section 4.10 we showed (see equation (5)) that the logarithm of x in the system with base a is proportional to $\ln x$, with a proportionality factor $1/\ln a$: $\log_a x = \frac{1}{\ln a} \ln x$. It follows immediately that

$$y = \log_a x \implies y' = \frac{1}{\ln a} \frac{1}{x} \tag{3}$$

Approximating the Number e

If $g(x) = \ln x$, then $g'(x) = 1/x$, and, in particular, $g'(1) = 1$. Using in turn the definition of $g'(1)$, the fact that $\ln 1 = 0$, together with the rule $\ln x^p = p \ln x$, we obtain

$$1 = g'(1) = \lim_{h \to 0} \frac{\ln(1+h) - \ln 1}{h} = \lim_{h \to 0} \frac{1}{h} \ln(1+h) = \lim_{h \to 0} \ln(1+h)^{1/h}$$

Because $\ln(1+h)^{1/h}$ tends to 1 as h tends to 0, it follows that $(1+h)^{1/h}$ itself must tend to e:

$$e = \lim_{h \to 0} (1+h)^{1/h} \tag{4}$$

The following table has been computed using a pocket calculator, and it seems to confirm that the decimal expansion we gave for e starts out correctly. (Of course, this by no means proves that the limit exists.)

Table 1 Values of $(1+h)^{1/h}$ when h gets smaller and smaller

h	1	1/2	1/10	1/1000	1/100 000	1/1 000 000
$(1+h)^{1/h}$	2	2.25	2.5937...	2.7169...	2.71825...	2.718281828...

From the table we can see that closer and closer approximations to e are obtained by choosing h smaller and smaller. (A much better way to approximate e^x, for general real x, is suggested in Example 7.6.2.)

Power Functions

In Section 6.6 we claimed that, for all real numbers a,

$$f(x) = x^a \implies f'(x) = ax^{a-1} \tag{$*$}$$

This important rule has only been established for certain special values of a, particularly the rational numbers. Because $x = e^{\ln x}$, we have $x^a = (e^{\ln x})^a = e^{a \ln x}$. Using the chain rule, we obtain

$$\frac{d}{dx}(x^a) = \frac{d}{dx}(e^{a \ln x}) = e^{a \ln x} \cdot \frac{a}{x} = x^a \frac{a}{x} = ax^{a-1}$$

This justifies using the same power rule even when a is an irrational number.

1. Compute the first- and second-order derivatives of:

(a) $y = \ln x + 3x - 2$ (b) $y = x^2 - 2\ln x$ (c) $y = x^3 \ln x$ (d) $y = \dfrac{\ln x}{x}$

2. Find the derivative of:

(a) $y = x^3 (\ln x)^2$ (b) $y = \dfrac{x^2}{\ln x}$ (c) $y = (\ln x)^{10}$ (d) $y = (\ln x + 3x)^2$

SM **3.** Find the derivative of:

(a) $\ln(\ln x)$ (b) $\ln \sqrt{1 - x^2}$ (c) $e^x \ln x$ (d) $e^{x^3} \ln x^2$

(e) $\ln(e^x + 1)$ (f) $\ln(x^2 + 3x - 1)$ (g) $2(e^x - 1)^{-1}$ (h) $e^{2x^2 - x}$

4. Determine the domains of the functions defined by:

(a) $y = \ln(x + 1)$ (b) $y = \ln\left(\dfrac{3x - 1}{1 - x}\right)$ (c) $y = \ln|x|$

SM **5.** Determine the domains of the functions defined by:

(a) $y = \ln(x^2 - 1)$ (b) $y = \ln(\ln x)$ (c) $y = \dfrac{1}{\ln(\ln x) - 1}$

SM **6.** Find the intervals where the following functions are increasing:

(a) $y = \ln(4 - x^2)$ (b) $y = x^3 \ln x$ (c) $y = \dfrac{(1 - \ln x)^2}{2x}$

7. Find the equation for the tangent to the graph of

(a) $y = \ln x$ at the points with x-coordinates   (i) 1   (ii) $\frac{1}{2}$ (iii) e

(b) $y = xe^x$ at the points with x-coordinates   (i) 0   (ii) 1   (iii) -2

8. Use logarithmic differentiation to find $f'(x)/f(x)$ when:

(a) $f(x) = \left(\dfrac{x + 1}{x - 1}\right)^{1/3}$ (b) $f(x) = x^{2x}$ (c) $f(x) = \sqrt{x - 2}\,(x^2 + 1)(x^4 + 6)$

SM **9.** Differentiate the following functions using logarithmic differentiation:

(a) $y = (2x)^x$ (b) $y = x^{\sqrt{x}}$ (c) $y = (\sqrt{x})^x$

10. Prove that if u and v are differentiable functions of x, and $u > 0$, then

$$y = u^v \;\Rightarrow\; y' = u^v\left(v' \ln u + \dfrac{vu'}{u}\right)$$

HARDER PROBLEM

(SM) **11.** If $f(x) = e^x - 1 - x$, then $f'(x) = e^x - 1 > 0$ for all $x > 0$. The function $f(x)$ is therefore strictly increasing in the interval $[0, \infty)$. Since $f(0) = 0$, it follows that $f(x) > 0$ for all $x > 0$, and so $e^x > 1 + x$ for all $x > 0$. Use the same method to prove the following inequalities:

(a) $e^x > 1 + x + x^2/2$ for $x > 0$

(b) $\frac{1}{2}x < \ln(1 + x) < x$ for $0 < x < 1$

(c) $\ln x < 2(\sqrt{x} - 1)$ for $x > 1$

REVIEW PROBLEMS FOR CHAPTER 6

1. Let $f(x) = x^2 - x + 2$. Show that $[f(x + h) - f(x)]/h = 2x - 1 + h$, and use this result to find $f'(x)$.

2. Let $f(x) = -2x^3 + x^2$. Compute $[f(x + h) - f(x)]/h$, and find $f'(x)$.

3. Compute the first- and second-order derivatives of the following functions:

(a) $y = 2x - 5$ (b) $y = \frac{1}{3}x^9$ (c) $y = 1 - \frac{1}{10}x^{10}$ (d) $y = 3x^7 + 8$

(e) $y = \frac{x - 5}{10}$ (f) $y = x^5 - x^{-5}$ (g) $y = \frac{x^4}{4} + \frac{x^3}{3} + \frac{5^2}{2}$ (h) $y = \frac{1}{x} + \frac{1}{x^3}$

4. Let $C(Q)$ denote the cost of producing Q units per month of a commodity. What is the interpretation of $C'(1000) = 25$? Suppose the price obtained per unit is fixed at 30 and that the current output per month is 1000. Is it profitable to increase production?

5. For each of the following functions, find the equation for the tangent to the graph at the specified point:

(a) $y = -3x^2$ at $x = 1$ (b) $y = \sqrt{x} - x^2$ at $x = 4$ (c) $y = \frac{x^2 - x^3}{x + 3}$ at $x = 1$

6. Let $A(x)$ denote the dollar cost of building a house with a floor area of x square metres. What is the interpretation of $A'(100) = 250$?

7. Differentiate the following functions:

(a) $f(x) = x(x^2 + 1)$ (b) $g(w) = w^{-5}$ (c) $h(y) = y(y - 1)(y + 1)$

(d) $G(t) = \frac{2t + 1}{t^2 + 3}$ (e) $\varphi(\xi) = \frac{2\xi}{\xi^2 + 2}$ (f) $F(s) = \frac{s}{s^2 + s - 2}$

8. Find the derivatives: (a) $\frac{d}{da}(a^2 t - t^2)$ (b) $\frac{d}{dt}(a^2 t - t^2)$ (c) $\frac{d}{d\varphi}\left(x\varphi^2 - \sqrt{\varphi}\right)$

9. Use the chain rule to find dy/dx for the following:

(a) $y = 10u^2$ and $u = 5 - x^2$ (b) $y = \sqrt{u}$ and $u = \frac{1}{x} - 1$

10. Compute the following:

    (a) dZ/dt when $Z = (u^2 - 1)^3$ and $u = t^3$.

    (b) dK/dt when $K = \sqrt{L}$ and $L = 1 + 1/t$.

11. If $a(t)$ and $b(t)$ are positive-valued differentiable functions of t, and if A, α, and β are constants, find expressions for $\dot{x}/x$ where:

    (a) $x = \left(a(t)\right)^2 b(t)$ (b) $x = A\left(a(t)\right)^{\alpha}\left(b(t)\right)^{\beta}$ (c) $x = A\left((a(t))^{\alpha} + (b(t))^{\beta}\right)^{\alpha+\beta}$

12. If $R = S^{\alpha}$, $S = 1 + \beta K^{\gamma}$, and $K = At^p + B$, find an expression for dR/dt.

13. Find the derivatives of the following functions, where a, b, p, and q are constants:

    (a) $h(L) = (L^a + b)^p$ (b) $C(Q) = aQ + bQ^2$ (c) $P(x) = \left(ax^{1/q} + b\right)^q$

14. Find the first-order derivatives of:

    (a) $y = -7e^x$ (b) $y = e^{-3x^2}$ (c) $y = \dfrac{x^2}{e^x}$ (d) $y = e^x \ln(x^2 + 2)$

    (e) $y = e^{5x^3}$ (f) $y = 2 - x^4 e^{-x}$ (g) $y = (e^x + x^2)^{10}$ (h) $y = \ln\left(\sqrt{x} + 1\right)$

⒮ⓜ 15. Find the intervals where the following functions are increasing:

    (a) $y = (\ln x)^2 - 4$ (b) $y = \ln(e^x + e^{-x})$ (c) $y = x - \dfrac{3}{2}\ln(x^2 + 2)$

16. (a) Suppose $\pi(Q) = QP(Q) - cQ$, where P is a differentiable function and c is a constant. Find an expression for $d\pi/dQ$.

    (b) Suppose $\pi(L) = PF(L) - wL$, where F is a differentiable function and P and w are constants. Find an expression for $d\pi/dL$.

DERIVATIVES IN USE

Although this may seem a paradox, all science is dominated by the idea of approximation.
—Bertrand Russell

Many economic models involve functions that are defined implicitly by one or more equations. In some simple but economically relevant cases, we begin this chapter by showing how to compute derivatives of such functions, including how to differentiate the inverse. It is very important for economists to master the technique of implicit differentiation.

Next we consider linear approximations and differentials, followed by a discussion of quadratic and higher-order polynomial approximations. Section 7.6 studies Taylor's formula, which makes it possible to analyse the resulting error when a function is approximated by a polynomial.

A discussion of the important economic concept of elasticity follows in Section 7.7.

The word *continuous* is common even in everyday language. We use it, in particular, to characterize changes that are gradual rather than sudden. This usage is closely related to the idea of a continuous function. In Section 7.8 we discuss this concept and explain its close relationship with the limit concept. Limits and continuity are key ideas in mathematics, and also very important in the application of mathematics to economic problems. The preliminary discussion of limits in Section 6.5 was necessarily very sketchy. In Section 7.9 we take a closer look at this concept and extend it in several directions.

Next we present the intermediate value theorem, which makes precise the idea that a continuous function has a "connected" graph. This makes it possible to prove that certain equations have solutions. A brief discussion of Newton's method for finding approximate solutions to equations is given. A short section on infinite sequences follows. Finally, Section 7.12 presents l'Hôpital's rule for indeterminate forms, which is sometimes useful for evaluating limits.

7.1 Implicit Differentiation

We know how to differentiate functions given by explicit formulas like $y = f(x)$. Now we consider how to differentiate functions defined implicitly by an equation such as $g(x, y) = c$, where c is a constant. We begin with a very simple case.

EXAMPLE 1   Consider the following equation in x and y,

$$xy = 5 \qquad (*)$$

If $x = 1$, then $y = 5$. Also, $x = 3$ gives $y = 5/3$. And $x = 5$ gives $y = 1$. In general, for each number $x \neq 0$, there is a unique number y such that the pair (x, y) satisfies the equation. We say that equation $(*)$ *defines y implicitly as a function of x*. The graph of equation $(*)$ for $x > 0$ is shown in Fig. 1.

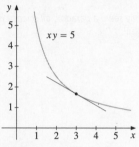

Figure 1 $xy = 5, x > 0$

Economists often need to know the slope of the tangent at an arbitrary point on such a graph, i.e. to know the derivative of y as a function of x. The answer can be found by implicit differentiation of equation $(*)$, which defines y as a function of x. If we denote this function by f, then replacing y by $f(x)$ gives

$$xf(x) = 5 \qquad \text{for all} \quad x > 0 \qquad (**)$$

Because the left and right sides of the equation are equal for all $x > 0$, the derivative of the left-hand side w.r.t. x must be equal to the derivative of the right-hand side w.r.t. x. The derivative of the constant 5 is 0. When we differentiate $xf(x)$, we must use the product rule. Therefore, by differentiating $(**)$ w.r.t. x, we obtain

$$1 \cdot f(x) + xf'(x) = 0$$

It follows that for $x > 0$,

$$f'(x) = -\frac{f(x)}{x}$$

If $x = 3$, then $f(3) = 5/3$, and thus $f'(3) = -(5/3)/3 = -5/9$, which agrees with Fig. 1.

Usually, we do not introduce a name like f for y as a function of x. Instead, we differentiate $(*)$ directly w.r.t. x, recalling that y is a differentiable function of x, and so we write $y + xy' = 0$. Solving for y' gives

$$y' = -\frac{y}{x} \qquad (***)$$

For this particular example, there is another way to find the answer. Solving equation $(*)$ for y gives $y = 5/x = 5x^{-1}$, and hence direct differentiation gives $y' = 5(-1)x^{-2} = -5/x^2$. Note that substituting $5/x$ for y in $(***)$ yields $y' = -5/x^2$ again.

EXAMPLE 2   The graph of

$$y^3 + 3x^2 y = 13 \qquad (*)$$

was studied in Example 5.4.2. It passes through the point $(2, 1)$. Find the slope of the graph at that point. (The graph is shown in Fig. 2.)

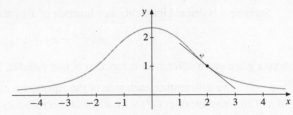

Figure 2 The graph of $y^3 + 3x^2 y = 13$

Solution: Since there is no simple way of expressing y as an explicit function of x, we use implicit differentiation. We think of replacing y with an unspecified function of x wherever y occurs. Then $y^3 + 3x^2 y$ becomes a function of x which is equal to the constant 13 for all x. So the derivative of $y^3 + 3x^2 y$ w.r.t. x must be equal to zero for all x. According to the chain rule, the derivative of y^3 w.r.t. x is equal to $3y^2 y'$. Using the product rule, the derivative of $3x^2 y$ is equal to $6xy + 3x^2 y'$. Hence, differentiating $(*)$ gives

$$3y^2 y' + 6xy + 3x^2 y' = 0 \qquad (**)$$

Solving this equation for y' yields

$$y' = \frac{-6xy}{3x^2 + 3y^2} = \frac{-2xy}{x^2 + y^2} \qquad (***)$$

For $x = 2$, $y = 1$ we find $y' = -4/5$, which agrees with Fig. 2.

Examples 1 and 2 illustrate the following general method.

THE METHOD OF IMPLICIT DIFFERENTIATION

If two variables x and y are related by an equation, to find y':

(a) Differentiate each side of the equation w.r.t. x, considering y as a function of x. (Usually, you will need the chain rule.)

(b) Solve the resulting equation for y'.

The next section shows several economic examples. A particularly important application of this method occurs in the next chapter where we consider what happens to the solution of an optimization problem when parameters change.

EXAMPLE 3   The equation $x^2 y^3 + (y + 1)e^{-x} = x + 2$ defines y as a differentiable function of x in a neighbourhood of $(x, y) = (0, 1)$. Compute y' at this point.

Solution: Implicit differentiation w.r.t. x gives

$$2xy^3 + x^2 3y^2 y' + y' e^{-x} + (y+1)(-e^{-x}) = 1$$

Inserting $x = 0$ and $y = 1$ yields $y' + 2(-1) = 1$, implying that $y' = 3$.

EXAMPLE 4   Suppose y is defined implicitly as a function of x by the equation

$$g(xy^2) = xy + 1 \qquad (*)$$

where g is a given differentiable function of one variable. Find an expression for y'.

Solution: We differentiate each side of the equation w.r.t. x, considering y as a function of x. The derivative of $g(xy^2)$ w.r.t. x is $g'(xy^2)(y^2 + x2yy')$. So differentiating $(*)$ yields $g'(xy^2)(y^2 + x2yy') = y + xy'$. Solving for y' gives us

$$y' = \frac{y(yg'(xy^2) - 1)}{x(1 - 2yg'(xy^2))}$$

The Second Derivative of Functions Defined Implicitly

The following examples suggest how to compute the second derivative of a function that is defined implicitly by an equation.

EXAMPLE 5   Compute y'' when y is given implicitly as a function of x by

$$xy = 5$$

Solution: In Example 1 we found by implicit differentiation that $y + xy' = 0$. Differentiating this equation implicitly w.r.t. x once more, while recognizing that both y and y' depend on x, we obtain

$$y' + y' + xy'' = 0$$

Inserting the expression $-y/x$ we already have for y' gives $-2y/x + xy'' = 0$. Solving for y'' finally yields

$$y'' = \frac{2y}{x^2}$$

We see that if $y > 0$, then $y'' > 0$, which accords with Fig. 1 since the graph is convex. Because $y = 5/x$, we also get $y'' = 10/x^3$.

In this simple case, we can check the answer directly. Since $y = 5x^{-1}$ and $y' = -5x^{-2}$, we have $y'' = 10x^{-3}$.

In order to find y'' we can also use formula $(***)$ in Example 1 and differentiate the fraction w.r.t. x, again taking into account that y depends on x:

$$y'' = -\frac{y'x - y}{x^2} = -\frac{(-y/x)x - y}{x^2} = \frac{2y}{x^2}$$

EXAMPLE 6   For the function defined by the equation $y^3 + 3x^2 y = 13$ in Example 2, find y'' at the point $(2, 1)$.

Solution: The easiest approach is to differentiate equation (∗∗) in Example 2 w.r.t. x. The derivative of $3y^2y'$ w.r.t. x is $(6yy')y' + 3y^2y'' = 6y(y')^2 + 3y^2y''$. The two other terms are differentiated in the same way, and we obtain

$$6y(y')^2 + 3y^2y'' + 6y + 6xy' + 6xy' + 3x^2y'' = 0$$

Inserting $x = 2$, $y = 1$, and $y' = -4/5$ (see Example 2), then solving the resulting equation, gives $y'' = 78/125$. (An alternative method is to differentiate the fraction in (∗∗∗) in Example 2 w.r.t. x.)

PROBLEMS FOR SECTION 7.1

1. Find y' by implicit differentiation if $3x^2 + 2y = 5$. Check by solving the equation for y and then differentiating.

2. For the equation $x^2y = 1$, find dy/dx and d^2y/dx^2 by implicit differentiation. Check by solving the equation for y and then differentiating.

SM 3. Find dy/dx and d^2y/dx^2 by implicit differentiation when (a) $x - y + 3xy = 2$ (b) $y^5 = x^6$

4. A curve in the uv-plane is given by $u^2 + uv - v^3 = 0$. Compute dv/du by implicit differentiation. Find the point (u, v) on the curve where $dv/du = 0$ and $u \neq 0$.

5. Suppose that y is a differentiable function of x that satisfies the equation

$$2x^2 + 6xy + y^2 = 18$$

Find y' and y'' at the point $(x, y) = (1, 2)$.

6. For each of the following equations, answer the question: If $y = f(x)$ is a differentiable function that satisfies the equation, what is y'? (a is a positive constant.)

(a) $x^2 + y^2 = a^2$ (b) $\sqrt{x} + \sqrt{y} = \sqrt{a}$ (c) $x^4 - y^4 = x^2y^3$ (d) $e^{xy} - x^2y = 1$

7. (a) Find the slope of the tangent line to the curve

$$2xy - 3y^2 = 9$$

at $(x, y) = (6, 1)$.

(b) Compute also the second derivative at this point.

SM 8. Suppose y is defined implicitly as a function of x by the following equations, where g is a given differentiable function of one variable. Find an expression for y'.

(a) $xy = g(x) + y^3$ (b) $g(x + y) = x^2 + y^2$ (c) $(xy + 1)^2 = g(x^2y)$

9. Suppose F is a differentiable function of one variable with $F(0) = 0$ and $F'(0) \neq -1$. Find an expression for y' at the point $(x, y) = (1, 0)$ if y is defined implicitly as a differentiable function of x by the equation

$$x^3F(xy) + e^{xy} = x$$

ⓈⓂ **10.** (a) The elegant curve shown in Figure 3 is known as a *lemniscate*. It is given by the equation

$$(x^2 + y^2)^2 = a^2(x^2 - y^2) \qquad (a \text{ is a positive constant})$$

Find the slope of the tangent to this curve at a point (x, y) where $y \neq 0$.

(b) Determine those points on the curve where the tangent is parallel to the x-axis.

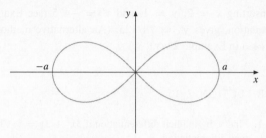

Figure 3 A lemniscate

7.2 Economic Examples

Few mathematical techniques are more important in economics than implicit differentiation. This is because so many functions in economic models are defined implicitly by an equation or a system of equations. Often the variables have other names than x and y, so one needs to practise differentiating equations with other names for the variables.

EXAMPLE 1   In a standard macroeconomic model for determining national income in a closed economy, it is assumed that

$$\text{(i) } Y = C + I \qquad \text{(ii) } C = f(Y)$$

Here (ii) is the consumption function discussed in Example 4.5.2, whereas (i) states that the national income Y is divided up between consumption C and investment I. Assume that $f'(Y)$, the *marginal propensity to consume*, exists and lies between 0 and 1.

(a) Suppose first that $C = f(Y) = 95.05 + 0.712\,Y$ (see Example 4.5.2), and use equations (i) and (ii) to find Y in terms of I.

(b) Inserting the expression for C from (ii) into (i) gives $Y = f(Y) + I$. Suppose that this equation defines Y as a differentiable function of I. Find an expression for dY/dI.

(c) Assuming that $f''(x)$ also exists, find $Y'' = d^2Y/dI^2$.

Solution:

(a) In this case, we find that $Y = 95.05 + 0.712\,Y + I$. Solving for Y yields

$$Y = (95.05 + I)/(1 - 0.712) \approx 3.47\,I + 330.03$$

In particular, $dY/dI \approx 3.47$, so if I is increased by \$1 billion, then the corresponding increase in the national income is approximately 3.47 billion dollars.

(b) Differentiating $Y = f(Y) + I$ w.r.t. I, and using the chain rule, we have

$$\frac{dY}{dI} = f'(Y)\frac{dY}{dI} + 1 \qquad \text{or} \qquad \frac{dY}{dI}\left[1 - f'(Y)\right] = 1 \qquad (*)$$

Solving for dY/dI yields

$$\frac{dY}{dI} = \frac{1}{1 - f'(Y)} \qquad (**)$$

For example, if $f'(Y) = 1/2$, then $dY/dI = 2$. If $f'(Y) = 0.712$, then $dY/dI \approx 3.47$. In general, we see that because of the assumption that $f'(Y)$ lies between 0 and 1, so $1 - f'(Y)$ also lies between 0 and 1. Hence $1/\left(1 - f'(Y)\right)$ is always greater than 1. In this model, therefore, a \$1 billion increase in investment will always lead to a more than \$1 billion increase in the national income. Also, the greater is $f'(Y)$, the marginal propensity to consume, the smaller is $1 - f'(Y)$, and so the greater is dY/dI.

(c) We differentiate the first equation in $(*)$ implicitly w.r.t. I. The derivative of $f'(Y)$ w.r.t. I is $f''(Y)(dY/dI)$. According to the product rule, the derivative of the product $f'(Y)(dY/dI)$ w.r.t. I is $f''(Y)(dY/dI)(dY/dI) + f'(Y)(d^2Y/dI^2)$. Hence,

$$\frac{d^2Y}{dI^2} = f''(Y)\left(\frac{dY}{dI}\right)^2 + f'(Y)\frac{d^2Y}{dI^2}$$

Since $dY/dI = 1/(1 - f'(Y))$, easy algebra yields

$$\frac{d^2Y}{dI^2} = \frac{f''(Y)}{\left[1 - f'(Y)\right]^3}$$

EXAMPLE 2   In the linear supply and demand model of Example 4.5.4, suppose that a tax of t per unit is imposed on consumers' purchases, thus raising the price they face from P to $P + t$. Then

$$D = a - b(P + t), \qquad S = \alpha + \beta P \qquad (*)$$

Here a, b, α, and β are positive constants. The equilibrium price is determined by equating supply and demand, so that

$$a - b(P + t) = \alpha + \beta P \qquad (**)$$

(a) Equation $(**)$ implicitly defines the price P as a function of the unit tax t. Compute dP/dt by implicit differentiation. What is its sign? What is the sign of $\frac{d}{dt}(P + t)$? Check the result by first solving equation $(**)$ for P and then finding dP/dt explicitly.

(b) Compute tax revenue T as a function of t. For what value of t does the quadratic function T reach its maximum?

(c) Generalize the foregoing model by assuming that $D = f(P + t)$ and $S = g(P)$, where f and g are differentiable functions with $f' < 0$ and $g' > 0$. The equilibrium condition

$$f(P + t) = g(P)$$

defines P implicitly as a differentiable function of t. Find an expression for dP/dt by implicit differentiation. Illustrate geometrically.

Solution:

(a) Differentiating (∗∗) w.r.t. t yields $-b(dP/dt+1) = \beta\, dP/dt$. Solving for dP/dt gives

$$\frac{dP}{dt} = \frac{-b}{b+\beta}$$

We see that dP/dt is negative. Because P is the price received by the producer, this price will go down if the tax rate t increases. But $P+t$ is the price paid by the consumer. Because

$$\frac{d}{dt}(P+t) = \frac{dP}{dt} + 1 = \frac{-b}{b+\beta} + 1 = \frac{-b+b+\beta}{b+\beta} = \frac{\beta}{b+\beta}$$

we see that $0 < d(P+t)/dt < 1$. Thus, the consumer price increases, but by less than the increase in the tax.

If we solve (∗∗) for P, we obtain

$$P = \frac{a - \alpha - bt}{b+\beta} = \frac{a-\alpha}{b+\beta} - \frac{b}{b+\beta}t$$

This equation shows that the equilibrium producer price is a linear function of the tax per unit, with slope $-b/(b+\beta)$.

(b) The total tax revenue is $T = St = (\alpha + \beta P)t$, where P is the equilibrium price. Thus,

$$T = \left[\alpha + \beta \left(\frac{a-\alpha}{b+\beta} - \frac{b}{b+\beta}t \right) \right]t = \frac{-b\beta}{b+\beta}t^2 + \frac{a\beta + \alpha b}{b+\beta}t$$

This quadratic function has its maximum at $t = (\alpha b + \beta a)/2b\beta$.

(c) Differentiating the equation $f(P+t) = g(P)$ w.r.t. t yields

$$f'(P+t)\left(\frac{dP}{dt} + 1 \right) = g'(P) \frac{dP}{dt} \tag{∗}$$

Solving for dP/dt gives

$$\frac{dP}{dt} = \frac{f'(P+t)}{g'(P) - f'(P+t)}$$

Because $f' < 0$ and $g' > 0$, we see that dP/dt is negative in this case as well. Moreover,

$$\frac{d}{dt}(P+t) = \frac{dP}{dt} + 1 = \frac{f'(P+t)}{g'(P) - f'(P+t)} + 1 = \frac{g'(P)}{g'(P) - f'(P+t)}$$

which implies that $0 < d(P+t)/dt < 1$.

Figure 1 has a graph which illustrates this answer. As usual in economics, we have quantity on the horizontal axis, and price on the vertical axis. The demand function with the tax is $D = f(P+t)$. Its graph is obtained by shifting the graph of $D = f(P)$ — or equivalently, the graph of the inverse demand curve $P = f^{-1}(Q)$ — down t units, so it becomes $P = f^{-1}(Q) - t$, or $Q = f(P+t)$. The figure confirms that, when t increases, the new equilibrium E' corresponds to a decreased price P. Nevertheless, $P + t$ increases because the decrease in P is smaller than the increase in t.

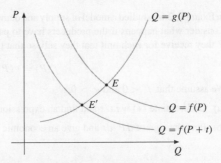

Figure 1 Shift in the demand curve

1. According to Herman Wold, the demand Q for butter in Stockholm during the period 1925–1937 was related to the price P by the equation $Q \cdot P^{1/2} = 38$. Find dQ/dP by implicit differentiation. Check the answer by using a different method to compute the derivative.

2. (a) Consider a profit-maximizing firm producing a single commodity. If the firm gets a fixed price P per unit sold, its profit from selling Q units is $\pi(Q) = PQ - C(Q)$, where $C(Q)$ is the cost function. Assume that $C'(Q) > 0$ and $C''(Q) > 0$. In Example 8.5.1, it will be shown that $Q = Q^* > 0$ maximizes profits provided

$$P = C'(Q^*) \qquad\qquad (*)$$

Thus, at the optimum, marginal cost must equal the price per unit. By implicit differentiation of $(*)$ w.r.t. P, find an expression for dQ^*/dP.

   (b) Comment on the sign of dQ^*/dP.

3. Consider the equation

$$AP^{-\alpha}r^{-\beta} = S$$

where A, α, β, and S are positive constants. Take natural logarithms of both sides and find dP/dr by implicit differentiation. Determine its sign. (Economic interpretation: There is a constant supply S of a commodity whose demand is a decreasing function of its price P and the interest rate r. Problem: How does the equilibrium price react to an increase in the interest rate?)

4. (a) A standard macroeconomic model for income determination in an open economy is

$$\text{(i)} \ \ Y = C + I + \bar{X} - M \qquad \text{(ii)} \ \ C = f(Y) \qquad \text{(iii)} \ \ M = g(Y)$$

where $0 < f'(Y) < 1$. Here $\bar{X}$ is an exogenous constant that denotes exports, whereas M denotes the volume of imports. The function g in (iii) is called an *import function*. By inserting (ii) and (iii) into (i), we obtain an equation that defines Y as a function of exogenous investment I. Find an expression for dY/dI by implicit differentiation. What is the likely sign of $g'(Y)$? Discuss the sign of dY/dI.

   (b) Find an expression for d^2Y/dI^2.

5. Find an expression for d^2P/dt^2 in Example 2(c) by differentiating $(*)$ w.r.t. t.

6. In Example 2 we studied a model of supply and demand where a tax is imposed on the consumers. Consider what happens if the producers have to pay a fraction t ($0 < t < 1$) of the sales price P they receive for each unit that they sell, so that the equilibrium condition is

$$f(P) = g(P - tP) \qquad (*)$$

We assume that $f' < 0$ and $g' > 0$.

(a) Differentiate (*) w.r.t. t and find an expression for dP/dt.

(b) Find the sign of dP/dt and give an economic interpretation.

7.3 Differentiating the Inverse

Section 5.3 dealt with inverse functions. As explained there, if f is a one-to-one function defined on an interval I, it has an inverse function g defined on the range $f(I)$ of f. What is the relationship between the derivatives of f and g?

EXAMPLE 1   Provided that $a \neq 0$, the two linear functions $f(x) = ax + b$ and $g(x) = (x - b)/a$ are inverses of each other. (Verify this.) The graphs are straight lines which are symmetric about the line $y = x$. The slopes are respectively a and $1/a$. Look back at Fig. 5.3.3 and notice that this result is confirmed, since the slope of f is 4 and the slope of g is 1/4.

In general, if f and g are inverses of each other, then

$$g\big(f(x)\big) = x \qquad \text{for all } x \text{ in } I \qquad (1)$$

By implicit differentiation, *provided that* both f and g are differentiable, we can easily find the relationship between the derivatives of f and g. Indeed, differentiating (1) w.r.t. x gives $g'\big(f(x)\big)f'(x) = 1$, so that if $f'(x) \neq 0$, then

$$g'\big(f(x)\big) = \frac{1}{f'(x)} \qquad (2)$$

It follows from (2) that f' and g' have the same sign. If f is strictly increasing (decreasing), then g is strictly increasing (decreasing), and vice versa.

The most important facts about inverse functions are summed up in this theorem:

THEOREM 7.3.1 (INVERSE FUNCTIONS)

If f is differentiable and strictly increasing (or strictly decreasing) in an interval I, then f has an inverse function g, which is strictly increasing (strictly decreasing) in the interval $f(I)$. If x_0 is an interior point of I and $f'(x_0) \neq 0$, then g is differentiable at $y_0 = f(x_0)$ and

$$g'(y_0) = \frac{1}{f'(x_0)} \qquad (y_0 = f(x_0)) \qquad (3)$$

NOTE 1 Formula (3) is used as follows to find the derivative of g at a point y_0. First find, if possible, the point x_0 in I at which $f(x_0) = y_0$. Thereafter, compute $f'(x)$, and then find $f'(x_0)$. If $f'(x_0) \neq 0$, then g has a derivative at y_0 given by $g'(y_0) = 1/f'(x_0)$.

The geometric interpretation of formula (3) is shown in Fig. 1, where f and g are inverses of each other. Let the slope of the tangent at P be $a = f'(x_0)$. At the point Q, the x-coordinate is $f(x_0)$, and the slope of the tangent at that point is $g'(f(x_0))$. This number is equal to $1/a$. (In the figure, $a \approx 1/3$, and $1/a \approx 3$.)

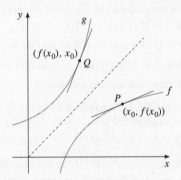

Figure 1 If the slope at P is a, then the slope at Q is $1/a$.

EXAMPLE 2   Suppose the function f is defined for all x by the following formula

$$f(x) = x^5 + 3x^3 + 6x - 3$$

Show that f has an inverse function g. Use formula (3) to find $g'(7)$. (Note that $f(1) = 7$.)

Solution: Differentiating $f(x)$ yields $f'(x) = 5x^4 + 9x^2 + 6$. Clearly, $f'(x) > 0$ for all x, so f is strictly increasing and consequently it is one-to-one. It therefore has an inverse function g. To find $g'(7)$, we use formula (3) with $x_0 = 1$ and $y_0 = 7$. Since $f'(1) = 20$, we obtain $g'(7) = 1/f'(1) = 1/20$. Note that we have found $g'(7)$ exactly even though it is impossible to find any algebraic formula for the inverse function g.

EXAMPLE 3   Suppose that f and g are twice differentiable functions which are inverses of each other. By differentiating (2) w.r.t. x, find an expression for $g''(f(x))$ where $f'(x) \neq 0$. Do f'' and g'' have the same, or opposite signs?

Solution: Differentiating (2) w.r.t. x yields $g''(f(x))f'(x) = (-1)(f'(x))^{-2}f''(x)$. It follows that if $f'(x) \neq 0$, then

$$g''(f(x)) = -\frac{f''(x)}{(f'(x))^3} \tag{4}$$

If $f' > 0$, then $f''(x)$ and $g''(f(x))$ have opposite signs, but they have the same sign if $f' < 0$. (In particular, if f is increasing and concave, the inverse g is increasing and convex as in Fig. 1.)

NOTE 2 It is common to present the formula in (3) in the deceptively simple way:

$$\frac{dx}{dy} = \frac{1}{dy/dx} \qquad (5)$$

as if dx and dy can be manipulated like ordinary numbers. Formula (4) shows that similar use of the differential notation for second derivatives fails drastically. The "formula $d^2x/dy^2 = 1/(dy^2/d^2x)$", for instance, makes no sense at all.

EXAMPLE 4   Suppose that, instead of the linear demand function of Example 4.5.4, one has the **log-linear** function $\ln Q = a - b \ln P$.

(a) Express Q as a function of P, and show that $dQ/dP = -bQ/P$.

(b) Express P as a function of Q, and find dP/dQ.

(c) Check that your answer satisfies (5).

Solution: (a) Taking exponentials gives $Q = e^{a-b\ln P} = e^a (e^{\ln P})^{-b} = e^a P^{-b}$, so $dQ/dP = -be^a P^{-b-1} = -bQ/P$. (b) Solving $Q = e^a P^{-b}$ for P gives $P = e^{a/b} Q^{-1/b}$, so $dP/dQ = (-1/b)e^{a/b} Q^{-1-1/b}$. (c) $dP/dQ = (-1/b)P/Q = 1/(dQ/dP)$.

Comments: (i) $P = e^{a/b} Q^{-1/b}$ is the inverse demand function, which is also log-linear. (ii) El $Q_P = -b$ is the (constant) price elasticity of demand. (iii) El $P_Q = -1/b$ is the (constant) elasticity of inverse demand.

PROBLEMS FOR SECTION 7.3

1. The function defined for all x by $f(x) = e^{2x-2}$ has an inverse g. Use formula (3) to find $g'(1)$. Check your result by finding a formula for g.

2. (a) The function f is defined for $|x| \le 2$ by the formula $f(x) = \frac{1}{3}x^3\sqrt{4 - x^2}$. Find the intervals where f increases, and the intervals where f decreases, then sketch its graph.

   (b) Explain why f has an inverse g on $[0, \sqrt{3}]$, and find $g'(\frac{1}{3}\sqrt{3})$. (*Hint:* $f(1) = \frac{1}{3}\sqrt{3}$.)

3. (a) Let f be defined by

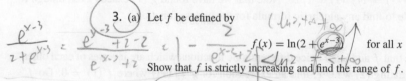

   $$f(x) = \ln(2 + e^{x-3}) \qquad \text{for all } x$$

   Show that f is strictly increasing and find the range of f.

   (b) Find an expression for the inverse function g of f. Where is g defined?

   (c) Verify that $f'(3) = 1/g'(f(3))$.

4. According to Problem 5.3.2, the demand for sugar in the USA in the period 1915–1929, as a function of the price P, was given by $D = 157.8/P^{0.3}$. Find dP/dD by using (5).

⑤Ⓜ 5. Use (5) to find dx/dy when:

   (a) $y = e^{-x-5}$ (b) $y = \ln(e^{-x} + 3)$ (c) $xy^3 - x^3 y = 2x$

7.4 Linear Approximations

Much of modern economic analysis relies on numerical calculations, nearly always only approximate. Often, therefore, rather than work with a complicated function, we approximate it by one that is much simpler. Since linear functions are especially simple, it seems natural to try using a "linear approximation" first.

Consider a function $f(x)$ that is differentiable at $x = a$. Suppose we approximate the graph of f by its tangent line at $(a, f(a))$, as shown in Fig. 1. This tangent line is the graph of the function $y = p(x) = f(a) + f'(a)(x - a)$ (see 6.2.2). Algebraically, therefore:

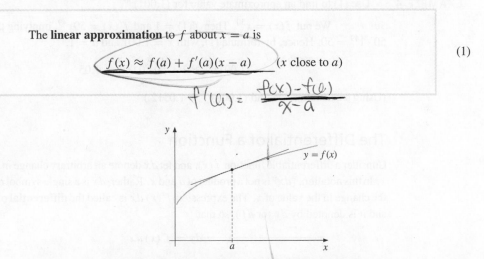

The **linear approximation** to f about $x = a$ is

$$f(x) \approx f(a) + f'(a)(x - a) \qquad (x \text{ close to } a)$$

(1)

$$f'(a) = \frac{f(x) - f(a)}{x - a}$$

Figure 1 Approximation of a function by its tangent

Note that both $f(x)$ and its linear approximation $p(x)$ have the same value and the same derivative at $x = a$.[1]

EXAMPLE 1   Find the linear approximation to $f(x) = \sqrt[3]{x}$ about $x = 1$.

Solution: We have $f(x) = \sqrt[3]{x} = x^{1/3}$, so $f(1) = 1$, and $f'(x) = \frac{1}{3}x^{-2/3}$, so $f'(1) = \frac{1}{3}$. Inserting these values into formula (1) when $a = 1$ yields

$$\sqrt[3]{x} \approx f(1) + f'(1)(x - 1) = 1 + \tfrac{1}{3}(x - 1) \qquad (x \text{ close to } 1)$$

For example, $\sqrt[3]{1.03} \approx 1 + \frac{1}{3}(1.03 - 1) = 1.01$. The correct value to 4 decimals is 1.0099.

EXAMPLE 2   Use (1) to show that $\ln(1 + x) \approx x$ for x close to 0.

Solution: With $f(x) = \ln(1 + x)$, we get $f(0) = 0$ and $f'(x) = 1/(1 + x)$, so $f'(0) = 1$. Then (1) yields $\ln(1 + x) \approx x$.

---

[1] One can prove that if f is differentiable, then $f(x) - f(a) = f'(a)(x - a) + \varepsilon(x - a)$ where $\varepsilon \to 0$ as $x \to a$. (If $x - a$ is very small, then ε is very small, and $\varepsilon(x - a)$ is "very very small".)

EXAMPLE 3   **(Rule of 70)** If an amount K earns yearly interest $p\%$, the doubling time is $t^* = \ln 2 / \ln(1 + p/100)$. (See Example 4.10.2.) If we use the approximations $\ln 2 \approx 0.7$ and $\ln(1 + x) \approx x$, then

$$t^* = \frac{\ln 2}{\ln(1 + p/100)} \approx \frac{0.7}{p/100} = \frac{70}{p}$$

This yields the "rule of 70" according to which, if the interest rate is $p\%$, then the doubling time is approximately 70 divided by p. For instance, if $p = 3.5$, then t^* is 20, which is close to the exact value $t^* = \ln 2 / \ln 1.035 \approx 20.1$.

EXAMPLE 4   Use (1) to find an approximate value for $(1.001)^{50}$.

Solution: We put $f(x) = x^{50}$. Then $f(1) = 1$ and $f'(x) = 50x^{49}$, implying that $f'(1) = 50 \cdot 1^{49} = 50$. Hence, by formula (1), with $x = 1.001$ and $a = 1$,

$$(1.001)^{50} \approx 1 + 50 \cdot 0.001 = 1.05$$

(Using a calculator, we find $(1.001)^{50} \approx 1.0512$.)

The Differential of a Function

Consider a differentiable function $f(x)$, and let dx denote an arbitrary change in the variable x. In this notation, "dx" is not a product of d and x. Rather, dx is a single symbol representing the change in the value of x. The expression $f'(x)\,dx$ is called the **differential** of $y = f(x)$, and it is denoted by dy (or df), so that

$$dy = f'(x)\,dx \tag{2}$$

Note that dy is proportional to dx, with $f'(x)$ as the factor of proportionality.

Now, if x changes by dx, then the corresponding change in $y = f(x)$ is

$$\Delta y = f(x + dx) - f(x) \tag{3}$$

In the approximation (1), suppose we replace x by $x + dx$ and a by x. The result is $f(x + dx) \approx f(x) + f'(x)\,dx$. Using the definitions of dy and Δy in (2) and (3) above, we get $\Delta y \approx dy = f'(x)\,dx$.

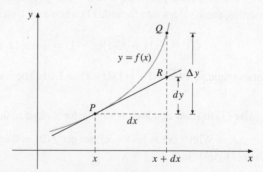

Figure 2 A geometric representation of the differential dy and $\Delta y = f(x + dx) - f(x)$

The differential dy is not the actual increment in y as x is changed to $x+dx$, but rather the change in y that would occur if y continued to change at the fixed rate $f'(x)$ as x changes to $x + dx$. Fig. 2 illustrates the difference between Δy and dy. Consider, first, the movement from P to Q along the curve $y = f(x)$: as x changes by dx, the actual change in the vertical height of the point is Δy. Suppose instead that we are only allowed to move along the tangent to the graph at P. Thus, as we move from P to R along the tangent, the change in height that corresponds to dx is dy. As in Fig. 2, the approximation $\Delta y \approx dy$ is usually better if dx is smaller in absolute value. This is because the length $|RQ| = |\Delta y - dy|$ of the line segment RQ, representing the difference between Δy and dy, tends to 0 as dx tends to 0. In fact, $|RQ|$ becomes small so fast that the ratio $|RQ|/dx$ tends to 0 as $dx \to 0$.

Rules for Differentials

The notation $(d/dx)(\cdot)$ calls for the expression in parentheses to be differentiated with respect to x. For example, $(d/dx)(x^3) = 3x^2$. In the same way, we let $d(\cdot)$ denote the differential of whatever is inside the parentheses.

EXAMPLE 5   Compute the following differentials:

(a) $d\left(Ax^a + B\right)$ (A, B, and a are constants)

(b) $d\left(f(K)\right)$ (f is a differentiable function of K)

Solution:

(a) Putting $f(x) = Ax^a + B$, we get $f'(x) = Aax^{a-1}$, so $d\left(Ax^a + B\right) = Aax^{a-1}\,dx$.

(b) $d\,(f(K)) = f'(K)\,dK$.

All the usual rules for differentiation can be expressed in terms of differentials. If f and g are two differentiable functions of x, then the following rules hold.

RULES FOR DIFFERENTIALS

$$(f \cdot g)' = f'g + g'f$$

$$d(af + bg) = a\,df + b\,dg \qquad \text{(a and b are constants)}$$

$$d(fg) = g\,df + f\,dg \qquad \frac{d}{dx}(fg) = \frac{d}{dx}f \cdot g + \frac{d}{dx}g \cdot f \qquad (4)$$

$$d\left(\frac{f}{g}\right) = \frac{g\,df - f\,dg}{g^2} \qquad (g \neq 0) \qquad d(fg) = dfg + dgf$$

Here is a proof of the second of these formulas (the others are proved in the same way):

$$d(fg) = (fg)'\,dx = (f'g + fg')\,dx = gf'\,dx + fg'\,dx = g\,df + f\,dg \qquad \blacksquare$$

Suppose that $y = f(x)$ and that $x = g(t)$ is a function of t. Then $y = h(t) = f\left(g(t)\right)$ is a function of t. The differential of $y = h(t)$ is $dy = h'(t)\,dt$. According to the chain rule, $h'(t) = f'(g(t))\,g'(t)$, so that $dy = f'\left(g(t)\right)g'(t)\,dt$. Because $x = g(t)$, the differential of x is equal to $dx = g'(t)\,dt$, and therefore, $dy = f'(x)\,dx$.

This shows that *if* $y = f(x)$, *then the differential of y is equal to* $dy = f'(x)\,dx$, *whether x depends on another variable or not.*

Economists often use differentials in their models. A typical example follows.

EXAMPLE 6   Consider again the model in Example 7.2.1:

$$\text{(i) } Y = C + I \qquad \text{(ii) } C = f(Y)$$

Find the differential dY expressed in terms of dI. If employment $N = g(Y)$ is also a function of Y, find the differential dN expressed in terms of dI.

Solution: Taking differentials in (i) and (ii), we obtain

$$\text{(iii) } dY = dC + dI \qquad \text{(iv) } dC = f'(Y)\,dY$$

Substituting dC from (iv) into (iii) and solving for dY yields

$$dY = \frac{1}{1 - f'(Y)}\,dI$$

which is the same formula found previously. From $N = g(Y)$, we get $dN = g'(Y)\,dY$, so

$$dN = \frac{g'(Y)}{1 - f'(Y)}\,dI$$

Economists usually claim that $g'(Y) > 0$ (employment increases as national income increases) and $f'(Y)$, the marginal propensity to consume, is between 0 and 1. From the formula for dN, these claims imply that if investment increases, then employment increases. ∎

PROBLEMS FOR SECTION 7.4

1. Prove that

$$\sqrt{1 + x} \approx 1 + \tfrac{1}{2}x$$

   for x close to 0, and illustrate this approximation by drawing the graphs of $y = 1 + \tfrac{1}{2}x$ and $y = \sqrt{1 + x}$ in the same coordinate system.

2. Use (1) to find the linear approximation to $f(x) = (5x + 3)^{-2}$ about $x = 0$.

(SM) 3. Find the linear approximations to the following functions about $x = 0$:

   (a) $f(x) = (1 + x)^{-1}$ (b) $f(x) = (1 + x)^5$ (c) $f(x) = (1 - x)^{1/4}$

4. Find the linear approximation to $F(K) = AK^\alpha$ about $K = 1$.

5. Find the following differentials (where p, q, and r are constants):

   (a) $d(10x^3)$ (b) $d(5x^3 - 5x^2 + 5x + 5)$ (c) $d(1/x^3)$ (d) $d(\ln x)$

   (e) $d(x^p + x^q)$ (f) $d(x^p x^q)$ (g) $d(px + q)^r$ (h) $d(e^{px} + e^{qx})$

6. (a) Prove that $(1 + x)^m \approx 1 + mx$ for x close to 0. Use this to find approximations to the following numbers:

   (b) (i) $\sqrt[3]{1.1} = \left(1 + \frac{1}{10}\right)^{1/3}$ (ii) $\sqrt[5]{33} = 2\left(1 + \frac{1}{32}\right)^{1/5}$ (iii) $\sqrt[3]{9} = \sqrt[3]{8 + 1}$ (iv) $(0.98)^{25}$

7. Compute $\Delta y = f(x + dx) - f(x)$ and the differential $dy = f'(x)\, dx$ for the following:

   (a) $f(x) = x^2 + 2x - 3$ when $x = 2$ and: (i) $dx = 1/10$;   (ii) $dx = 1/100$

   (b) $f(x) = 1/x$ when $x = 3$ and: (i) $dx = -1/10$;   (ii) $dx = -1/100$

   (c) $f(x) = \sqrt{x}$ when $x = 4$ and: (i) $dx = 1/20$;   (ii) $dx = 1/100$

(SM) 8. (a) The equation
$$3xe^{xy^2} - 2y = 3x^2 + y^2$$
defines y as a differentiable function of x about the point $(x, y) = (1, 0)$. Find the slope of the graph at this point by implicit differentiation.

   (b) What is the linear approximation to y about $x = 1$?

9. (a) A circle with radius r has area $A(r) = \pi r^2$. Then $A'(r) = 2\pi r$, the circumference of the circle. Explain geometrically the approximation $A(r + dr) - A(r) \approx 2\pi r\, dr$.

   (b) Explain geometrically the approximation $V(r + dr) - V(r) \approx 4\pi r^2\, dr$, where $V(r) = \frac{4}{3}\pi r^3$ is the volume and $V'(r) = 4\pi r^2$ is the surface area of a sphere with radius r.

10. If an amount K is charged to a credit card on which interest is $p\%$ per year, then unless some payments are made beforehand, after t years the balance will have grown to $K_t = K(1 + p/100)^t$ (even without any penalty charges). Using the approximation $\ln(1 + p/100) \approx p/100$ (derived in Example 2), prove that $\ln K_t \approx \ln K + pt/100$. Find the percentage interest rate p at which the balance doubles after t years.

11. Find the linear approximation to the following function about the point $\mu = 0$:
$$g(\mu) = A(1 + \mu)^{a/(1+b)} - 1 \qquad (A, a, \text{ and } b \text{ are positive constants})$$

7.5 Polynomial Approximations

The previous section discussed approximations of functions of one variable by linear functions. In particular, Example 7.4.1 established the approximation

$$\sqrt[3]{x} \approx 1 + \tfrac{1}{3}(x - 1) \qquad (x \text{ close to 1})$$

In this case, at $x = 1$, the functions $y = \sqrt[3]{x}$ and $y = 1 + \frac{1}{3}(x - 1)$ both have the same value 1, and the same derivative $1/3$.

Approximation by linear functions may well be insufficiently accurate. So it is natural to try quadratic approximations, or approximations by polynomials of a higher order.

Quadratic Approximations

We begin by showing how a twice differentiable function $y = f(x)$ can be approximated near $x = a$ by a quadratic polynomial

$$f(x) \approx p(x) = A + B(x - a) + C(x - a)^2$$

With a fixed, there are three coefficients A, B, and C to determine. We use three conditions to do so. Specifically, at $x = a$, we arrange that $f(x)$ and $p(x) = A + B(x-a) + C(x-a)^2$ should have: (i) the same value; (ii) the same derivative; and (iii) the same second derivative. In symbols, we require $f(a) = p(a)$, $f'(a) = p'(a)$, and $f''(a) = p''(a)$. Now $p'(x) = B + 2C(x - a)$ and $p''(x) = 2C$, so, after inserting $x = a$ into our expressions for $p(x)$, $p'(x)$, and $p''(x)$, it follows that $A = p(a)$, $B = p'(a)$, and $C = \frac{1}{2}p''(a)$. This justifies the following:

The **quadratic approximation** to $f(x)$ about $x = a$ is

$$f(x) \approx f(a) + f'(a)(x - a) + \tfrac{1}{2}f''(a)(x - a)^2 \qquad (x \text{ close to } a)$$

(1)

Note that, compared with (7.4.1), we have simply added one extra term. For $a = 0$, in particular, we obtain the following:

$$f(x) \approx f(0) + f'(0)x + \tfrac{1}{2}f''(0)x^2 \qquad (x \text{ close to } 0) \tag{2}$$

EXAMPLE 1   Find the quadratic approximation to $f(x) = \sqrt[3]{x}$ about $x = 1$.

Solution: Here $f'(x) = \frac{1}{3}x^{-2/3}$ and $f''(x) = \frac{1}{3}\left(-\frac{2}{3}\right)x^{-5/3}$. It follows that $f'(1) = \frac{1}{3}$ and $f''(1) = -\frac{2}{9}$. Because $f(1) = 1$, using (1) yields

$$\sqrt[3]{x} \approx 1 + \tfrac{1}{3}(x - 1) - \tfrac{1}{9}(x - 1)^2 \qquad (x \text{ close to } 1)$$

For example, $\sqrt[3]{1.03} \approx 1 + \frac{1}{3} \cdot 0.03 - \frac{1}{9}(0.03)^2 = 1 + 0.01 - 0.0001 = 1.0099$. This is correct to 4 decimals, and so it is better than the linear approximation derived in Example 7.4.1. ∎

EXAMPLE 2   Find the quadratic approximation to $y = y(x)$ about $x = 0$ when y is defined implicitly as a function of x near $(x, y) = (0, 1)$ by $xy^3 + 1 = y$.

Solution: Implicit differentiation w.r.t. x yields

$$y^3 + 3xy^2 y' = y' \tag{*}$$

Substituting $x = 0$ and $y = 1$ into (*) gives $y' = 1$. Differentiating (*) w.r.t. x now yields

$$3y^2 y' + (3y^2 + 6xyy')y' + 3xy^2 y'' = y''$$

Substituting $x = 0$, $y = 1$, and $y' = 1$, we obtain $y'' = 6$. Hence, according to (2),

$$y(x) \approx y(0) + y'(0)x + \tfrac{1}{2}y''(0)x^2 = 1 + x + 3x^2$$

Higher-Order Approximations

So far, we have considered linear and quadratic approximations. For functions with third- and higher-order derivatives, we can find even better approximations near one point by using polynomials of a higher degree. Suppose we want to approximate a function $f(x)$ over an interval centred at $x = a$ with an nth-degree polynomial of the form

$$p(x) = A_0 + A_1(x - a) + A_2(x - a)^2 + A_3(x - a)^3 + \cdots + A_n(x - a)^n \qquad (3)$$

Because $p(x)$ has $n + 1$ coefficients, we can impose the following $n + 1$ conditions on this polynomial:

$$f(a) = p(a), \ f'(a) = p'(a), \ \ldots, \ f^{(n)}(a) = p^{(n)}(a)$$

These conditions require that $p(x)$ and its first n derivatives agree with the value of $f(x)$ and its first n derivatives at $x = a$. Let us see what these conditions become when $n = 3$. In this case,

$$p(x) = A_0 + A_1(x - a) + A_2(x - a)^2 + A_3(x - a)^3$$

and we find that

$$p'(x) = A_1 + 2A_2(x - a) + 3A_3(x - a)^2$$
$$p''(x) = 2A_2 + 2 \cdot 3A_3(x - a)$$
$$p'''(x) = 2 \cdot 3A_3$$

Thus, when $x = a$, we have $p(a) = A_0$, $p'(a) = 1! \, A_1$, $p''(a) = 2! \, A_2$, $p'''(a) = 3! \, A_3$. This implies the following approximation:

$$f(x) \approx f(a) + \frac{1}{1!}f'(a)(x - a) + \frac{1}{2!}f''(a)(x - a)^2 + \frac{1}{3!}f'''(a)(x - a)^3$$

Thus, we have added an extra term to the quadratic approximation (1).

The general case follows the same pattern, and we obtain the following approximation to $f(x)$ by an nth-degree polynomial:

Approximation to $f(x)$ about $x = a$:

$$f(x) \approx f(a) + \frac{f'(a)}{1!}(x - a) + \frac{f''(a)}{2!}(x - a)^2 + \cdots + \frac{f^{(n)}(a)}{n!}(x - a)^n \qquad (4)$$

The polynomial on the right-hand side of (4) is called the nth-order **Taylor polynomial** (or Taylor approximation) for f about $x = a$.

The function f and its nth-order Taylor polynomial have such a high degree of contact at $x = a$ that it is reasonable to expect the approximation in (4) to be good over some (possibly small) interval centred about $x = a$. The next section analyses the error that results from using such polynomial approximations. In the case when f is itself a polynomial whose degree does not exceed n, the formula becomes exact, without any approximation error at any point.

EXAMPLE 3   Find the third-order Taylor approximation of $f(x) = \sqrt{1+x}$ about $x = 0$.

Solution: We write $f(x) = \sqrt{1+x} = (1+x)^{1/2}$. Then

$$f'(x) = \tfrac{1}{2}(1+x)^{-1/2}$$
$$f''(x) = \tfrac{1}{2}\left(-\tfrac{1}{2}\right)(1+x)^{-3/2}$$
$$f'''(x) = \tfrac{1}{2}\left(-\tfrac{1}{2}\right)\left(-\tfrac{3}{2}\right)(1+x)^{-5/2}$$

Putting $x = 0$ gives $f(0) = 1$, $f'(0) = 1/2$, $f''(0) = (1/2)(-1/2) = -1/4$, and finally $f'''(0) = (1/2)(-1/2)(-3/2) = 3/8$. Hence, by (4) for the case $n = 3$, we have

$$f(x) \approx 1 + \frac{1}{1!}\frac{1}{2}x + \frac{1}{2!}\left(-\frac{1}{4}\right)x^2 + \frac{1}{3!}\frac{3}{8}x^3 = 1 + \frac{1}{2}x - \frac{1}{8}x^2 + \frac{1}{16}x^3$$

EXAMPLE 4   Apply the approximation (4) to $f(x) = e^x$ about $x = 0$.

Solution: This case is particularly simple, because all derivatives of f are equal to e^x, and thus $f^{(k)}(0) = 1$ for all $k = 1, 2, \ldots, n$. Hence (4) yields

$$e^x \approx 1 + \frac{x}{1!} + \frac{x^2}{2!} + \cdots + \frac{x^n}{n!} \tag{5}$$

which is an important result.

PROBLEMS FOR SECTION 7.5

1. Find quadratic approximations to each of the following functions about the specified point:

   (a) $f(x) = (1+x)^5$, $x = 0$

   (b) $F(K) = AK^\alpha$, $K = 1$

   (c) $f(\varepsilon) = \left(1 + \tfrac{3}{2}\varepsilon + \tfrac{1}{2}\varepsilon^2\right)^{1/2}$, $\varepsilon = 0$

   (d) $H(x) = (1-x)^{-1}$, $x = 0$

(SM) 2. Find the fifth-order Taylor polynomial of $f(x) = \ln(1+x)$ about $x = 0$.

(SM) 3. Find the Taylor polynomial of order 2 about $x = 0$ for $f(x) = 5\big(\ln(1+x) - \sqrt{1+x}\,\big)$.

4. A study of attitudes to risk is based on the following approximation to a consumer's utility function. Explain how to derive this approximation.

$$U(y + M - s) \approx U(y) + U'(y)(M - s) + \tfrac{1}{2}U''(y)(M - s)^2$$

5. Find the quadratic approximation for y about $(x, y) = (0, 1)$ when y is defined implicitly as a function of x by the equation $1 + x^3 y + x = y^{1/2}$.

6. Let the function $x(t)$ be given by the conditions $x(0) = 1$ and

$$\dot{x}(t) = tx(t) + 2\big[x(t)\big]^2$$

Determine the second-order Taylor polynomial for $x(t)$ about $t = 0$.

7. Establish the approximation $\quad e^{\sigma\sqrt{t/n}} \approx 1 + \sigma\sqrt{t/n} + \sigma^2 t/2n$.

8. Establish the approximation $\quad \left(1 + \dfrac{p}{100}\right)^n \approx 1 + n\dfrac{p}{100} + \dfrac{n(n-1)}{2}\left(\dfrac{p}{100}\right)^2$.

9. The function h is defined for all $x > 0$ by

$$h(x) = \frac{x^p - x^q}{x^p + x^q} \qquad (p > q > 0)$$

Find the first-order Taylor polynomial about $x = 1$ for $h(x)$.

7.6 Taylor's Formula

The previous section presented polynomial approximations. In particular, the **nth-order Taylor polynomial** approximation of $f(x)$ about $x = 0$ is

$$f(x) \approx f(0) + \frac{1}{1!}f'(0)x + \frac{1}{2!}f''(0)x^2 + \cdots + \frac{1}{n!}f^{(n)}(0)x^n \qquad (*)$$

Any approximation like $(*)$ is of limited use unless something is known about the error it implies. Taylor's formula remedies this deficiency. This formula is often used by economists, and is regarded as one of the main results in mathematical analysis.

Consider the approximation in $(*)$. Except at $x = 0$, function $f(x)$ and the Taylor polynomial on the RHS of $(*)$ are usually different. The difference between the two will depend on x as well as on n, and is called the *remainder* after n terms. We denote it by $R_{n+1}(x)$. Hence, by definition,

$$f(x) = f(0) + \frac{1}{1!}f'(0)x + \cdots + \frac{1}{n!}f^{(n)}(0)x^n + R_{n+1}(x) \qquad (1)$$

The following theorem gives an important explicit formula for the remainder.[2] (The proof will be given in Note 8.4.3.)

---

[2] The English mathematician Brook Taylor had already found polynomial approximations of the general form $(*)$ in 1715. Lagrange proved (2) approximately 50 years later.

LAGRANGE'S FORM OF THE REMAINDER

Suppose f is $n+1$ times differentiable in an interval including 0 and x. Then the remainder $R_{n+1}(x)$ given in (1) can be written as

$$R_{n+1}(x) = \frac{1}{(n+1)!} f^{(n+1)}(c) x^{n+1} \tag{2}$$

for some number c between 0 and x.

Using this formula for $R_{n+1}(x)$ in (1), we obtain

TAYLOR'S FORMULA

$$f(x) = f(0) + \frac{1}{1!} f'(0)x + \cdots + \frac{1}{n!} f^{(n)}(0)x^n + \frac{1}{(n+1)!} f^{(n+1)}(c) x^{n+1} \tag{3}$$

Note that the remainder resembles the preceding terms in the sum. The only difference is that in the formula for the remainder, $f^{(n+1)}$ is evaluated at a point c, where c is some unspecified number between 0 and x, whereas in all the previous terms, the derivatives are evaluated at 0. The number c is not fixed because it depends, in general, on x as well as on n.

If we put $n = 1$ in formula (3), we obtain

$$f(x) = f(0) + f'(0)x + \tfrac{1}{2} f''(c)x^2 \qquad \text{for some } c \text{ between 0 and } x \tag{4}$$

This formula tells us that $\tfrac{1}{2} f''(c)x^2$ is the error that results if we replace $f(x)$ with its linear approximation about $x = 0$.

How do we use the remainder formula? It suggests an upper limit for the error that results if we replace f with its nth Taylor polynomial. Suppose, for instance, that for all x in an interval I, the absolute value of $f^{(n+1)}(x)$ is at most M. Then we can conclude that in this interval

$$|R_{n+1}(x)| \leq \frac{M}{(n+1)!} |x|^{n+1} \tag{5}$$

Note that if n is a large number and if x is close to 0, then $|R_{n+1}(x)|$ is small for two reasons: first, if n is large, the number $(n+1)!$ in the denominator in (5) is large; second, if $|x|$ is less than 1, then $|x|^{n+1}$ is also small when n is large.

EXAMPLE 1   Use formula (4) to approximate the function

$$f(x) = \sqrt{25 + x} = (25 + x)^{1/2}$$

Then use it to estimate both $\sqrt{25.01}$ and the absolute value of the remainder.

Solution: To apply formula (4), we differentiate to obtain

$$f'(x) = \frac{1}{2}(25+x)^{-1/2}, \qquad f''(x) = \frac{1}{2}\left(-\frac{1}{2}\right)(25+x)^{-3/2}$$

It follows that $f(0) = 5$, whereas $f'(0) = 1/10$ and $f''(c) = -(1/4)(25+c)^{-3/2}$. So by (4), for some c between 0 and x, one has

$$\sqrt{25+x} = 5 + \frac{1}{10}x + \frac{1}{2}\left(-\frac{1}{4}\right)(25+c)^{-3/2}x^2 = 5 + \frac{1}{10}x - \frac{1}{8}(25+c)^{-3/2}x^2 \quad (*)$$

In order to estimate $\sqrt{25.01}$, we write $25.01 = 25 + 0.01$ and use $(*)$. If $x = 0.01$, then c lies between 0 and 0.01, so $25 + c > 25$. Then $(25+c)^{-3/2} < (25)^{-3/2} = 1/125$, so the absolute value of the remainder is

$$|R_2(0.01)| = \left|\frac{-1}{8}(25+c)^{-3/2}\left(\frac{1}{100}\right)^2\right| \leq \frac{1}{80\,000} \cdot \frac{1}{125} = 10^{-7}$$

We conclude that $\sqrt{25.01} \approx 5 + 1/10 \cdot 1/100 = 5.001$, with an error less than 10^{-7}. ∎

EXAMPLE 2   Find Taylor's formula for $f(x) = e^x$, and estimate the error term for $n = 3$ and $x = 0.1$.

Solution: From Example 4 in the previous section, it follows that there exists a number c between 0 and x such that

$$e^x = 1 + \frac{x}{1!} + \frac{x^2}{2!} + \cdots + \frac{x^n}{n!} + \frac{x^{n+1}}{(n+1)!}e^c \tag{6}$$

One can prove that for each fixed number x the remainder term in (6) approaches 0 as n approaches infinity. Using (6) one can therefore find the value of e^x for any x to an arbitrary degree of accuracy. However, if $|x|$ is large, a large number of terms have to be used in order to obtain a good degree of accuracy, because the remainder approaches 0 very slowly as n approaches infinity.

For $n = 3$ and $x = 0.1$, we obtain for some c in the interval $(0, 0.1)$,

$$e^{0.1} = 1 + \frac{1}{10} + \frac{1}{200} + \frac{1}{6000} + \frac{(0.1)^4}{24}e^c \tag{*}$$

For $c < 0.1$, we have $e^c < e^{0.1}$. We claim that $e^{0.1} < 1.2$. To prove this note that $(1.2)^{10} \approx 6.2 > e$, so $e < (1.2)^{10}$ and thus $e^c < e^{0.1} < ((1.2)^{10})^{0.1} = 1.2$, implying that

$$\left|R_4\left(\frac{1}{10}\right)\right| = \frac{(0.1)^4}{24}e^c < \frac{1}{240\,000} 1.2 = 0.000\,005 = 5 \cdot 10^{-6}$$

The error that results from dropping the remainder from $(*)$ is therefore less than $5 \cdot 10^{-6}$. ∎

NOTE 1   Suppose we consider the Taylor formula on an interval about $x = a$ instead of $x = 0$. The first $n + 1$ terms on the right-hand side of (3) become replaced by those of (7.5.4), and the new remainder is

$$R_{n+1}(x) = \frac{1}{(n+1)!} f^{(n+1)}(c)(x - a)^{n+1} \qquad (c \text{ is between } x \text{ and } a) \qquad (7)$$

It is easy to show that (7) follows from (1) and (2) by considering the function g defined by $g(t) = f(a + t)$ when t is close to 0.

PROBLEMS FOR SECTION 7.6

1. Write Taylor's formula (3) with $n = 2$ for $f(x) = \ln(1 + x)$.

2. Use the approximation $(1 + x)^m \approx 1 + mx + \frac{1}{2}m(m - 1)x^2$ to find values of

(a) $\sqrt[3]{25}$ (b) $\sqrt[5]{33}$

(*Hint:* Note that $\sqrt[3]{25} = 3(1 - 2/27)^{1/3}$.) Check these approximations by using a calculator.

3. Show that $\sqrt[3]{9} = 2\,(1 + 1/8)^{1/3}$. Use formula (3) (with $n = 2$) to compute $\sqrt[3]{9}$ to the third decimal.

SM 4. Let $g(x) = \sqrt[3]{1 + x}$.

(a) Find the Taylor polynomial of $g(x)$ of order 2 about the origin.

(b) For $x \geq 0$ show that $|R_3(x)| \leq 5x^3/81$.

(c) Find $\sqrt[3]{1003}$ to 7 significant digits.

7.7   Why Economists Use Elasticities

Economists often study how demand for a certain commodity such as coffee reacts to price changes. We can ask by how many units such as kilograms the quantity demanded will change per dollar increase in price. In this way, we obtain a concrete number, measured in units of the commodity per unit of money. There are, however, several unsatisfactory aspects to this way of measuring the sensitivity of demand to price changes. For instance, a $1 increase in the price of a kilo of coffee may be considerable, whereas a $1 increase in the price of a car is insignificant.

This problem arises because the sensitivity of demand to price changes is being measured in the same arbitrary units as those used to measure both quantity demanded and price. The difficulties are eliminated if we use relative changes instead. We ask by what percentage the quantity demanded changes when the price increases by 1%. The number we obtain in this way will be independent of the units in which both quantities and prices are measured. This number is called the **price elasticity of demand**, measured at a given price.

In 1960, the price elasticity of butter in a certain country was estimated to be -1. This means that an increase of 1% in the price would lead to a decrease of 1% in the demand, if all the other factors that influence the demand remained constant. The price elasticity for potatoes was estimated to be -0.2. What is the interpretation? Why do you think the absolute value of this elasticity is so much less than that for butter?

Assume now that the demand for a commodity can be described by the function

$$x = D(p)$$

of the price p. When the price changes from p to $p + \Delta p$, the quantity demanded, x, also changes. The absolute change in x is $\Delta x = D(p + \Delta p) - D(p)$, and the *relative* (or proportional) change is

$$\frac{\Delta x}{x} = \frac{D(p + \Delta p) - D(p)}{D(p)}$$

The ratio between the relative change in the quantity demanded and the relative change in the price is

$$\frac{\Delta x}{x} \Big/ \frac{\Delta p}{p} = \frac{p}{x} \frac{\Delta x}{\Delta p} = \frac{p}{D(p)} \frac{D(p + \Delta p) - D(p)}{\Delta p} \qquad (*)$$

When $\Delta p = p/100$ so that p increases by 1%, then $(*)$ becomes $(\Delta x / x) \cdot 100$, which is the percentage change in the quantity demanded. We call the proportion in $(*)$ *the average elasticity of x in the interval* $[p, p + \Delta p]$. Observe that the number defined in $(*)$ depends both on the price change Δp and on the price p, but is unit-free. Thus, it makes no difference whether the quantity is measured in tons, kilograms, or pounds, or whether the price is measured in dollars, pounds, or euros.

We would like to define the elasticity of D at p so that it does not depend on the size of the increase in p. We can do this if D is a differentiable function of p. For then it is natural to define the elasticity of D w.r.t. p as the limit of the ratio in $(*)$ as Δp tends to 0. Because the Newton quotient $[D(p + \Delta p) - D(p)]/\Delta p$ tends to $D'(p)$ as Δp tends to 0, we obtain:

The elasticity of $D(p)$ with respect to p is $\dfrac{p}{D(p)} \dfrac{dD(p)}{dp}$

Usually, we get a good approximation to the elasticity by letting $\Delta p / p = 1/100 = 1\%$ and computing $p \, \Delta x / (x \, \Delta p)$.

The General Definition of Elasticity

The above definition of elasticity concerned a function determining quantity demanded as a function of price. Economists, however, also consider income elasticities of demand, when demand is regarded as a function of income. They also consider elasticities of supply, elasticities of substitution, and several other kinds of elasticity. It is therefore helpful to see how elasticity can be defined for a general differentiable function. If f is differentiable at x and $f(x) \neq 0$, we define the elasticity of f w.r.t. x as

$$\text{El}_x \, f(x) = \frac{x}{f(x)} f'(x) \qquad (\textbf{elasticity of } f \text{ w.r.t. } x) \tag{1}$$

EXAMPLE 1   Find the elasticity of $f(x) = Ax^b$ (A and b are constants, with $A \neq 0$).

Solution: In this case, $f'(x) = Abx^{b-1}$. Hence, $\text{El}_x \, Ax^b = (x/Ax^b)Abx^{b-1} = b$, so

$$f(x) = Ax^b \implies \text{El}_x \, f(x) = b \tag{2}$$

The elasticity of the power function Ax^b w.r.t. x is simply the exponent b. So this function has constant elasticity. In fact, it is the only type of function which has constant elasticity. This is shown in Problem 9.9.6.

EXAMPLE 2   Assume that the quantity demanded of a particular commodity is given by

$$D(p) = 8000p^{-1.5}$$

Compute the elasticity of $D(p)$ and find the exact percentage change in quantity demanded when the price increases by 1% from $p = 4$.

Solution: Using (2) we find that $\text{El}_p \, D(p) = -1.5$, so that an increase in the price of 1% causes quantity demanded to decrease by about 1.5%.

In this case we can compute the decrease in demand exactly. When the price is 4, the quantity demanded is $D(4) = 8000 \cdot 4^{-1.5} = 1000$. If the price $p = 4$ is increased by 1%, the new price will be $4 + 4/100 = 4.04$, so that the *change* in demand is

$$D(4.04) - D(4) = 8000 \cdot 4.04^{-1.5} - 1000 = -14.81$$

The percentage change in demand from $D(4)$ is $-(14.81/1000) \cdot 100 = -1.481\%$.

EXAMPLE 3   Let $D(P)$ denote the demand function for a product. By selling $D(P)$ units at price P, the producer earns revenue $R(P)$ given by $R(P) = PD(P)$. The elasticity of $R(P)$ w.r.t. P is

$$\text{El}_P \, R(P) = \frac{P}{PD(P)} \frac{d}{dP}[PD(P)] = \frac{1}{D(P)}[D(P) + PD'(P)] = 1 + \text{El}_P \, D(P)$$

Observe that if $\text{El}_P \, D(P) = -1$, then $\text{El}_P \, R(P) = 0$. Thus, when the price elasticity of the demand at a point is equal to -1, a small price change will have (almost) no influence on the revenue. More generally, the marginal revenue dR/dP generated by a price change is positive if the price elasticity of demand is greater than -1, and negative if the elasticity is less than -1.

NOTE 1

- If $|\text{El}_x\, f(x)| > 1$, then f is elastic at x.
- If $|\text{El}_x\, f(x)| = 1$, then f is unit elastic at x.
- If $|\text{El}_x\, f(x)| < 1$, then f is inelastic at x.
- If $|\text{El}_x\, f(x)| = 0$, then f is perfectly inelastic at x.
- If $|\text{El}_x\, f(x)| = \infty$, then f is perfectly elastic at x.

NOTE 2 If $y = f(x)$ has an inverse function $x = g(y)$, then Theorem 7.3.1 implies that

$$\text{El}_y(g(y)) = \frac{y}{g(y)} g'(y) = \frac{f(x)}{x} \frac{1}{f'(x)} = \frac{1}{\text{El}_x\, f(x)} \tag{3}$$

A formula that corresponds to (7.3.5) is

$$\text{El}_y\, x = \frac{1}{\text{El}_x\, y} \tag{4}$$

There are some rules for elasticities of sums, products, quotients, and composite functions that are occasionally useful. You might like to derive these rules by solving Problem 9.

Elasticities as Logarithmic Derivatives

Suppose that two variables x and y are related by the equation

$$y = Ax^b \qquad (x, y, \text{ and } A \text{ are positive}) \tag{5}$$

as in Example 1. Taking the natural logarithm of each side of (5) while applying the rules for logarithms, we find that (5) is equivalent to the equation

$$\ln y = \ln A + b \ln x \tag{6}$$

From (6), we see that $\ln y$ is a linear function of $\ln x$, and so we say that (6) is a **log-linear** relation between x and y. The transformation from (5) to (6) is often seen in economic models, sometimes using logarithms to a base other than e.

For the function defined by (5), we know from Example 1 that $\text{El}_x\, y = b$. So from (6) we see that $\text{El}_x\, y$ is equal to the (double) logarithmic derivative $d \ln y / d \ln x$, which is the constant slope of this log-linear relationship.

This example illustrates the general rule that elasticities are equal to such logarithmic derivatives. In fact, whenever x and y are both positive variables, with y a differentiable function of x, a proof based on repeatedly applying the chain rule shows that

$$\text{El}_x\, y = \frac{x}{y} \frac{dy}{dx} = \frac{d \ln y}{d \ln x} \tag{7}$$

1. Find the elasticities of the functions given by the following formulas:

   (a) $3x^{-3}$ (b) $-100x^{100}$ (c) $\sqrt{x}$ (d) $A/x\sqrt{x}$ (A constant)

2. A study in transport economics uses the relation $T = 0.4K^{1.06}$, where K is expenditure on building roads, and T is a measure of traffic volume. Find the elasticity of T w.r.t. K. In this model, if expenditure increases by 1%, by what percentage (approximately) does traffic volume increase?

3. (a) A study of Norway's State Railways revealed that, for rides up to 60 km, the price elasticity of the volume of passenger demand was approximately -0.4. According to this study, what is the consequence of a 10% increase in fares?

   (b) The corresponding elasticity for journeys over 300 km was calculated to be approximately -0.9. Can you think of a reason why this elasticity is larger in absolute value than the previous one ?

4. Use definition (1) to find $\text{El}_x y$ for the following (a and p are constants):

   (a) $y = e^{ax}$ (b) $y = \ln x$ (c) $y = x^p e^{ax}$ (d) $y = x^p \ln x$

5. Prove that $\text{El}_x (f(x))^p = p\,\text{El}_x f(x)$ (p is a constant).

6. The demand D for apples in the US as a function of income r for the period 1927 to 1941 was estimated as $D = Ar^{1.23}$, where A is a constant. Find and interpret the elasticity of D w.r.t. r. (This elasticity is called the income elasticity of demand, or the *Engel elasticity*.)

7. Voorhees and colleagues studied the transportation systems in 37 American cities and estimated the average travel time to work, m (in minutes), as a function of the number of inhabitants, N. They found that $m = e^{-0.02}N^{0.19}$. Write the relation in log-linear form. What is the value of m when $N = 480\,000$?

8. Show that

$$\text{El}_x\big(Af(x)\big) = \text{El}_x\, f(x) \qquad \text{(multiplicative constants vanish)}$$

$$\text{El}_x\big(A + f(x)\big) = \frac{f(x)\,\text{El}_x\, f(x)}{A + f(x)} \qquad \text{(additive constants remain)}$$

HARDER PROBLEMS

SM 9. Prove that if f and g are positive-valued differentiable functions of x and A is a constant, then the following rules hold (where we write, for instance, $\text{El}_x f$ instead of $\text{El}_x f(x)$).

   (a) $\text{El}_x A = 0$ (b) $\text{El}_x(fg) = \text{El}_x f + \text{El}_x g$

   (c) $\text{El}_x\left(\dfrac{f}{g}\right) = \text{El}_x f - \text{El}_x g$ (d) $\text{El}_x(f + g) = \dfrac{f\,\text{El}_x f + g\,\text{El}_x g}{f + g}$

   (e) $\text{El}_x(f - g) = \dfrac{f\,\text{El}_x f - g\,\text{El}_x g}{f - g}$ (f) $\text{El}_x\, f\big(g(x)\big) = \text{El}_u\, f(u)\text{El}_x u$ $(u = g(x))$

10. Use the rules of Problem 9 to evaluate the following:

(a) $\text{El}_x(-10x^{-5})$ (b) $\text{El}_x(x + x^2)$ (c) $\text{El}_x(x^3 + 1)^{10}$

(d) $\text{El}_x(\text{El}_x 5x^2)$ (e) $\text{El}_x(1 + x^2)$ (f) $\text{El}_x\left(\dfrac{x-1}{x^5+1}\right)$

7.8 Continuity

Roughly speaking, a function $y = f(x)$ is continuous if small changes in the independent variable x lead to small changes in the function value y. Geometrically, *a function is continuous on an interval if its graph is connected—that is, it has no breaks*. An example is indicated in Fig. 1.

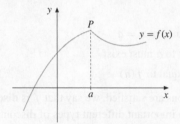

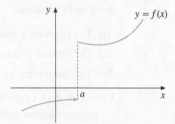

Figure 1 A continuous function   **Figure 2** A discontinuous function

It is often said that a function is continuous if its graph can be drawn without lifting one's pencil off the paper. On the other hand, if the graph makes one or more jumps, we say that f is *discontinuous*. Thus, the function whose graph is shown in Fig. 2 is discontinuous at $x = a$, but continuous at all other points of its domain. The graph indicates that $f(x) < 0$ for all $x < a$, but $f(x) > 0$ for all $x \geq a$, so there is a jump at $x = a$.

Why are we interested in distinguishing between continuous and discontinuous functions? One important reason is that we must usually work with numerical approximations. For instance, if a function f is given by some formula and we wish to compute $f(\sqrt{2})$, we usually take it for granted that we can compute $f(1.4142)$ and obtain a good approximation to $f(\sqrt{2})$. In fact, this implicitly assumes that f is continuous. Then, because 1.4142 is close to $\sqrt{2}$, the value $f(1.4142)$ must be close to $f(\sqrt{2})$.

In applications of mathematics to natural sciences and economics, a function will often represent how some phenomenon changes over time. Continuity of the function will then reflect continuity of the phenomenon, in the sense of gradual rather than sudden changes. For example, a person's body temperature is a function of time which changes from one value to another only after passing through all the intermediate values.

On the other hand, the market price of Brent crude oil is actually a discontinuous function of time when examined closely enough. One reason is that the price (measured in dollars or some other currency) must always be a rational number. A second, more interesting, reason for occasional large jumps in the price is the sudden arrival of news or a rumour that significantly affects either the demand or supply function—for example, a sudden change in the relevant tax policy of a major oil-exporting country.

The concept of continuity just discussed must obviously be made more precise before we can use it in mathematical arguments. We need a definition of continuity not based solely on geometric intuition.

Continuity in Terms of Limits

As discussed above, a function $y = f(x)$ is continuous at $x = a$ if small changes in x lead to small changes in $f(x)$. Stated differently, if x is close to a, then $f(x)$ must be close to $f(a)$. This motivates the following definition:

$$f \text{ is \textbf{continuous} at } x = a \text{ if } \lim_{x \to a} f(x) = f(a) \tag{1}$$

Hence, we see that in order for f to be continuous at $x = a$, the following three conditions must all be fulfilled:

 (i) The function f must be defined at $x = a$

 (ii) The limit of $f(x)$ as x tends to a must exist

 (iii) This limit must be exactly equal to $f(a)$

Unless all three of these conditions are satisfied, we say that f is **discontinuous** at a.

Figure 3 below indicates two important different types of discontinuity that can occur. At $x = a$, the function is discontinuous because $f(x)$ clearly has no limit as x tends to a. Hence, condition (ii) is not satisfied. This is an "irremovable" discontinuity. On the other hand, the limit of $f(x)$ as x tends to b exists and is equal to A. Because $A \neq f(b)$, however, condition (iii) is not satisfied, so f is discontinuous at b. This is a "removable" discontinuity that would disappear if the function were redefined at $x = b$ to make $f(b)$ equal to A.

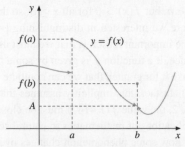

Figure 3 f has two points of discontinuity. $x = a$ is an irremovable and $x = b$ is a removable discontinuity point for f

Properties of Continuous Functions

Mathematicians have discovered many important results that are true only for continuous functions. It is therefore important to be able to determine whether or not a given function is continuous. The rules for limits given in Section 6.5 make it is easy to establish continuity of many types of function.

First, note that $\lim_{x \to a} c = c$ and $\lim_{x \to a} x = a$ at each point a. Hence, the two functions

$$f(x) = c \quad \text{and} \quad f(x) = x \quad \text{are continuous everywhere} \tag{2}$$

This is as it should be, because the graphs of these functions are straight lines.

Next, definition (1) and the limit rules in (6.5.2) immediately imply parts (a)–(c) of the following:

RESULTS ON CONTINUOUS FUNCTIONS

If f and g are continuous at a, then

(a) $f + g$ and $f - g$ are continuous at a

(b) fg and f/g (if $g(a) \neq 0$) are continuous at a

(c) $[f(x)]^r$ is continuous at a if $[f(a)]^r$ is defined   (r any real number)

(d) If f is continuous and has an inverse on the interval I, then its inverse f^{-1} is continuous on $f(I)$.

$$(3)$$

For instance, to prove the first part of (b), if both f and g are continuous at a, then $f(x) \to f(a)$ and $g(x) \to g(a)$ as $x \to a$. But then, according to rules for limits, $f(x)g(x) \to f(a)g(a)$ as $x \to a$, which means precisely that fg is continuous at $x = a$. The result in part (d) is a little trickier to prove, but it is easy to believe because the graphs of f and its inverse f^{-1} are symmetric about the line $y = x$.

By combining (2) and (3), it follows that functions like $h(x) = x + 8$ and $k(x) = 3x^3 + x + 8$ are continuous. In general, because a polynomial is a sum of continuous functions, it is continuous everywhere. Moreover, a rational function

$$R(x) = P(x)/Q(x) \qquad (P(x) \text{ and } Q(x) \text{ are polynomials})$$

is continuous at all x where $Q(x) \neq 0$.

Consider a composite function $f(g(x))$ where f and g are assumed to be continuous. If x is close to a, then continuity of g at a implies that $g(x)$ is close to $g(a)$. In turn, $f(g(x))$ becomes close to $f(g(a))$ because f is continuous at $g(a)$, and thus $f(g(x))$ is continuous at a. In short, *composites of continuous functions are continuous:* If g is continuous at $x = a$, and f is continuous at $g(a)$, then $f\big(g(x)\big)$ is continuous at $x = a$. In general:

Any function that can be constructed from continuous functions by combining one or more operations of addition, subtraction, multiplication, division (except by zero), and composition, is continuous at all points where it is defined.

$$(4)$$

By using the results just discussed, a mere glance at the formula defining a function will usually suffice to determine the points at which it is continuous.

EXAMPLE 1   Determine at which values of x the functions f and g are continuous:

(a) $f(x) = \dfrac{x^4 + 3x^2 - 1}{(x-1)(x+2)}$ (b) $g(x) = (x^2 + 2)\left(x^3 + \dfrac{1}{x}\right)^4 + \dfrac{1}{\sqrt{x+1}}$

Solution:

(a) This is a rational function that is continuous at all x, except where the denominator $(x-1)(x+2)$ vanishes. Hence, f is continuous at all x different from 1 and -2.

(b) This function is defined when $x \neq 0$ and $x + 1 > 0$. Hence, g is continuous in the domain $(-1, 0) \cup (0, \infty)$.

Knowing where a function is continuous simplifies the computation of many limits. If f is continuous at $x = a$, then the limit of $f(x)$ as x tends to a is found simply by evaluating $f(a)$. For instance, since the function $f(x) = x^2 + 5x$ we studied in Example 6.5.3(a) is a continuous function of x,

$$\lim_{x \to -2} (x^2 + 5x) = f(-2) = (-2)^2 + 5(-2) = 4 - 10 = -6$$

Of course, simply finding $f(-2)$ like this is much easier than using the rules for limits.

Compound functions, such as Examples 5.4.3 and 5.4.4, are defined "piecewise" by different formulas which apply to disjoint intervals. Such functions are frequently discontinuous at the junction points. As another example, the amount of postage you pay for a letter is a discontinuous function of the weight. (As long as we use preprinted stamps, it would be extremely inconvenient to have the "postage function" be even approximately continuous.) On the other hand, given any tax schedule that looks like the one in Example 5.4.4, the tax you pay as a function of your net income is (essentially) a continuous function (although many people seem to believe that it is not).

PROBLEMS FOR SECTION 7.8

1. Which of the following functions are likely to be continuous functions of time?

   (a) The price in the Zurich gold market of an ounce of gold.

   (b) The height of a growing child.

   (c) The height of an aeroplane above sea level.

   (d) The distance travelled by a car.

2. Let f and g be defined for all x by

$$f(x) = \begin{cases} x^2 - 1, & \text{for } x \leq 0 \\ -x^2, & \text{for } x > 0 \end{cases} \quad \text{and} \quad g(x) = \begin{cases} 3x - 2, & \text{for } x \leq 2 \\ -x + 6, & \text{for } x > 2 \end{cases}$$

Draw a graph of each function. Is f continuous at $x = 0$? Is g continuous at $x = 2$?

(SM) **3.** Determine the values of x at which each of the functions defined by the following formulas is continuous:

(a) $x^5 + 4x$

(b) $\dfrac{x}{1-x}$

(c) $\dfrac{1}{\sqrt{2-x}}$

(d) $\dfrac{x}{x^2+1}$

(e) $\dfrac{x^8 - 3x^2 + 1}{x^2 + 2x - 2}$

(f) $\dfrac{1}{\sqrt{x}} + \dfrac{x^7}{(x+2)^{3/2}}$

4. Draw the graph of y as a function of x if y depends on x as indicated in Fig. 4—that is, y is the height of the aeroplane above the point on the ground vertically below. Is y a continuous function of x?

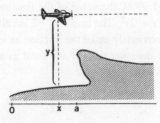

Figure 4

5. For what value of a is the following function continuous for all x?

$$f(x) = \begin{cases} ax - 1, & \text{for } x \leq 1 \\ 3x^2 + 1, & \text{for } x > 1 \end{cases}$$

6. Sketch the graph of a function f that is one-to-one on an interval, but neither strictly increasing nor strictly decreasing. (*Hint:* f cannot be continuous.)

7.9 More on Limits

Section 6.5 gave a preliminary discussion of limits. We now supplement this with some additional concepts and results, still keeping the discussion at an intuitive level. The reason for this gradual approach is that it is important and quite easy to acquire a working knowledge of limits. Experience suggests, however, that the precise definition is rather difficult to understand, as are proofs based on this definition.

Suppose f is defined for all x close to a, but not necessarily at a. According to Section 6.5, as x tends to a, the function $f(x)$ has A as its limit provided that the number $f(x)$ can be made as close to A as one pleases by making x sufficiently close to (but not equal to) a. Then we say that the limit exists. Now consider a case in which the limit does not exist.

EXAMPLE 1   Examine $\displaystyle\lim_{x \to -2} \dfrac{1}{(x+2)^2}$ using a pocket calculator.

Solution: Choosing x-values close to -2, we obtain the values in Table 1.

Table 1   Values of $1/(x + 2)^2$ when x is close to -2

x	-1.8	-1.9	-1.99	-1.999	-2.0	-2.001	-2.01	-2.1	-2.2
$\dfrac{1}{(x+2)^2}$	25	100	10000	1000000	*	1000000	10000	100	25

*not defined

As x gets closer and closer to -2, we see that the value of the fraction becomes larger and larger. By extending the values in the table, we see, for example, that for $x = -2.0001$ and $x = -1.9999$, the value of the fraction is 100 million. Figure 1 shows the graph of $f(x) = 1/(x + 2)^2$. The line $x = -2$ is called a **vertical asymptote** for the graph of f.

We can obviously make the fraction as large as we like by choosing x sufficiently close to -2, so it does not tend to any limit as x tends to -2. Instead, we say that it tends to infinity, and write

$$\frac{1}{(x + 2)^2} \to \infty \qquad \text{as} \qquad x \to -2$$

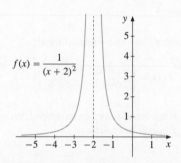

$$f(x) = \frac{1}{(x + 2)^2}$$

Figure 1 $f(x) \to \infty$ as $x \to -2$

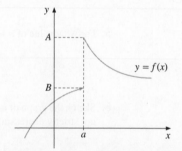

$$y = f(x)$$

Figure 2 $\displaystyle\lim_{x \to a} f(x)$ does not exist

(Note that ∞ is NOT a number, so ∞ is not a limit.)

One-Sided Limits

The function whose graph is shown in Fig. 2 also fails to have a limit as x tends to a. However, it seems from the figure that if x tends to a with values less than a, then $f(x)$ tends to the number B. We say, therefore, that the *limit of $f(x)$ as x tends to a from below is B*, and we write

$$\lim_{x \to a^-} f(x) = B \quad \text{or} \quad f(x) \to B \text{ as } x \to a^-$$

Analogously, also referring to Fig. 2, we say that the *limit of $f(x)$ as x tends to a from above is A*, and we write

$$\lim_{x \to a^+} f(x) = A \quad \text{or} \quad f(x) \to A \text{ as } x \to a^+$$

We call these *one-sided limits*, the first *from below* and the second *from above*. They can also be called the *left limit* and *right limit*, respectively.

A necessary and sufficient condition for the (ordinary) limit to exist is that the two one-sided limits of f at a exist and are equal:

$$\lim_{x \to a} f(x) = A \quad \Longleftrightarrow \quad \left[\lim_{x \to a^-} f(x) = A \text{ and } \lim_{x \to a^+} f(x) = A \right] \qquad (1)$$

It should now also be clear what is meant by

$$f(x) \to \pm\infty \text{ as } x \to a^- \quad \text{and} \quad f(x) \to \pm\infty \text{ as } x \to a^+$$

EXAMPLE 2   Figure 3 shows the graph of a function f defined on $[0, 9]$. Use the figure to check that the following limits seem correct:

$$\lim_{x \to 2} f(x) = 3, \quad \lim_{x \to 4^-} f(x) = 1/2, \quad \lim_{x \to 4^+} f(x) = 3, \quad \text{“} \lim_{x \to 6} f(x) = -\infty \text{”}$$

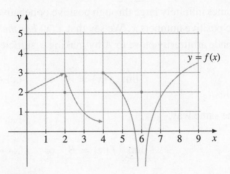

Figure 3

EXAMPLE 3   Explain the following limits:

$$\frac{1}{\sqrt{2 - x}} \to \infty \text{ as } x \to 2^-, \qquad \frac{-1}{\sqrt{x - 2}} \to -\infty \text{ as } x \to 2^+$$

Solution: If x is slightly smaller than 2, then $2 - x$ is small and positive. Hence, $\sqrt{2 - x}$ is close to 0, and $1/\sqrt{2 - x}$ is a large positive number. For example, $1/\sqrt{2 - 1.9999} = 1/\sqrt{0.0001} = 100$. As x tends to 2^-, so $1/\sqrt{2 - x}$ tends to ∞.

The other limit is similar, because if x is slightly larger than 2, then $\sqrt{x - 2}$ is positive and close to 0, and $-1/\sqrt{x - 2}$ is a large negative number.

One-Sided Continuity

The introduction of one-sided limits allows us to define one-sided continuity. Suppose f is defined on the half-open interval $(c, a]$. If $f(x)$ tends to $f(a)$ as x tends to a^-, we say that f is *left continuous* at a. Similarly, if f is defined on $[a, d)$, we say that f is *right continuous* at a if $f(x)$ tends to $f(a)$ as x tends to a^+. Because of (1), we see that a function f is continuous at a if and only if f is both left and right continuous at a.

EXAMPLE 4   Figure 3 shows that f is right continuous at $x = 4$ since $\lim_{x \to 4^+} f(x)$ exists and is equal to $f(4) = 3$. At $x = 2$, $\lim_{x \to 2^-} f(x) = \lim_{x \to 2^+} f(x) = 3$, but $f(2) = 2$, so f is neither right nor left continuous at $x = 2$.

If a function f is defined on a closed bounded interval $[a, b]$, we usually say that f is continuous in $[a, b]$ if it is continuous at each point of the open interval (a, b), and is in addition right continuous at a and left continuous at b. It should be obvious how to define continuity on half-open intervals. The continuity of a function at all points of an interval (including one-sided continuity at the end points) is often a minimum requirement we impose when speaking about "well-behaved" functions.

Limits at Infinity

We can also use the language of limits to describe the behaviour of a function as its argument becomes infinitely large through positive or negative values. Let f be defined for arbitrarily large positive numbers x. We say that $f(x)$ *has the limit A as x tends to infinity* if $f(x)$ can be made arbitrarily close to A by making x sufficiently large. We write

$$\lim_{x \to \infty} f(x) = A \quad \text{or} \quad f(x) \to A \text{ as } x \to \infty$$

In the same way,

$$\lim_{x \to -\infty} f(x) = B \quad \text{or} \quad f(x) \to B \text{ as } x \to -\infty$$

indicates that $f(x)$ can be made arbitrarily close to B by making x a sufficiently large negative number. The two limits are illustrated in Fig. 4. The horizontal line $y = A$ is a (horizontal) **asymptote** for the graph of f as x tends to ∞, whereas $y = B$ is a (horizontal) asymptote for the graph as x tends to $-\infty$.

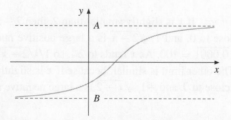

Figure 4 $y = A$ and $y = B$ are horizontal asymptotes

EXAMPLE 5   Examine the following functions as $x \to \infty$ and as $x \to -\infty$:

(a) $f(x) = \dfrac{3x^2 + x - 1}{x^2 + 1}$
(b) $g(x) = \dfrac{1 - x^5}{x^4 + x + 1}$

Solution:

(a) A rough argument is as follows: If x is a large negative or a large positive number, then the term $3x^2$ "dominates" in the numerator, whereas x^2 dominates in the denominator. Thus, if $|x|$ is a large number, $f(x)$ behaves like the fraction $3x^2/x^2 = 3$. We conclude that $f(x)$ tends to 3 as $|x|$ tends to ∞.

More formally, away from $x = 0$ we can divide each term in the numerator and the denominator by the highest power of x, which is x^2, to obtain

$$f(x) = \frac{3x^2 + x - 1}{x^2 + 1} = \frac{3 + (1/x) - (1/x^2)}{1 + (1/x^2)}$$

If x is large in absolute value, then both $1/x$ and $1/x^2$ are close to 0. Thus, $f(x)$ is arbitrarily close to 3 if $|x|$ is sufficiently large, and $f(x) \to 3$ both as $x \to -\infty$ and $x \to \infty$.

(b) A first rough argument is that if $|x|$ is a large number, then $g(x)$ behaves like the fraction $-x^5/x^4 = -x$. Therefore, $g(x) \to -\infty$ as $x \to \infty$, whereas $g(x) \to \infty$ as $x \to -\infty$. More formally,

$$g(x) = \frac{1 - x^5}{x^4 + x + 1} = \frac{(1/x^4) - x}{1 + (1/x^3) + 1/x^4}$$

You should now finish the argument yourself along the lines given in part (a).

Warnings

We have extended the original definition of a limit in several different directions. For these extended limit concepts, the previous rules for finite limits set out in Section 6.5 still apply. For example, all those rules remain valid if we consider left-hand limits or right-hand limits. Also, if we replace $x \to a$ by $x \to \infty$ or $x \to -\infty$, then again the corresponding limit properties hold. Provided at least one of the two limits A and B is nonzero, the four rules in (6.5.2) remain valid if at most one of A and B is infinite.

When $f(x)$ and $g(x)$ both tend to ∞ as x tends to a, however, much more care is needed. Because $f(x)$ and $g(x)$ can each be made arbitrarily large if x is sufficiently close to a, both $f(x) + g(x)$ and $f(x)g(x)$ can also be made arbitrarily large. But, in general, we cannot say what are the limits of $f(x) - g(x)$ and $f(x)/g(x)$. The limits of these expressions will depend on how "fast" $f(x)$ and $g(x)$, respectively, tend to ∞ as x tends to a. Briefly formulated:

$$f(x) \to \infty \quad \text{and} \quad g(x) \to \infty \quad \text{as} \quad x \to a \implies \begin{cases} f(x) + g(x) \to \infty & \text{as } x \to a \\ f(x)g(x) \to \infty & \text{as } x \to a \\ f(x) - g(x) \to ? & \text{as } x \to a \\ f(x)/g(x) \to ? & \text{as } x \to a \end{cases}$$

The two question marks mean that we cannot determine the limits of $f(x) - g(x)$ and $f(x)/g(x)$ without more information about f and g. We do not even know if these limits exist or not. The following example illustrates some of the possibilities.

EXAMPLE 6   Let $f(x) = 1/x^2$ and $g(x) = 1/x^4$. As $x \to 0$, so $f(x) \to \infty$ and $g(x) \to \infty$. Examine the limits as $x \to 0$ of the following expressions:

$$f(x) - g(x), \qquad g(x) - f(x), \qquad \frac{f(x)}{g(x)}, \qquad \frac{g(x)}{f(x)}$$

Solution: $f(x) - g(x) = (x^2 - 1)/x^4$. As $x \to 0$, the numerator tends to -1 and the denominator to 0. The fraction therefore tends to $-\infty$. For the other three limits we have:

$$g(x) - f(x) = \frac{1 - x^2}{x^4} \to \infty, \qquad \frac{f(x)}{g(x)} = x^2 \to 0, \qquad \frac{g(x)}{f(x)} = \frac{1}{x^2} \to \infty$$

These examples serve to illustrate that infinite limits require extreme care. Let us consider some other tricky examples. Suppose we study the product $f(x)g(x)$ of two functions, where $g(x)$ tends to 0 as x tends to a. Will the product $f(x)g(x)$ also tend to 0 as x tends to a? Not necessarily. If $f(x)$ tends to a limit A, then we know that $f(x)g(x)$ tends to $A \cdot 0 = 0$. On the other hand, if $f(x)$ tends to $\pm\infty$, then it is easy to construct examples in which the product $f(x)g(x)$ does not tend to 0 at all. (You should try to construct some examples of your own before turning to Problem 3.)

Continuity and Differentiability

Consider the function f graphed in Fig. 5.

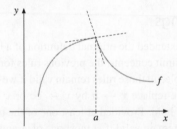

Figure 5 f is continuous, but not differentiable at $x = a$

At point $(a, f(a))$ the graph does not have a (unique) tangent. Thus f has no derivative at $x = a$, but f is continuous at $x = a$. So a function can be continuous at a point without being differentiable at that point. (For a standard example, see the graph of $f(x) = |x|$ shown in Fig. 4.3.10 which is continuous everywhere, but not differentiable at $x = 0$.)

On the other hand, it is easy to see that differentiability implies continuity:

If f is differentiable at $x = a$, then f is continuous at $x = a$ (2)

Proof: The function f is continuous at $x = a$ provided $f(a + h) - f(a)$ tends to 0 as $h \to 0$. Now, for $h \neq 0$,

$$f(a + h) - f(a) = \frac{f(a + h) - f(a)}{h} \cdot h \qquad (*)$$

If f is differentiable at $x = a$, the Newton quotient $[f(a + h) - f(a)]/h$ tends to the number $f'(a)$ as $h \to 0$. So the right-hand side of $(*)$ tends to $f'(a) \cdot 0 = 0$ as $h \to 0$. Thus, f is continuous at $x = a$. ∎

Suppose that f is some function whose Newton quotient $[f(a+h) - f(a)]/h$ tends to a limit as h tends to 0 through positive values. Then the limit is called the *right derivative* of f at a. The *left derivative* of f at a is defined similarly, and we use the notation

$$f'(a^+) = \lim_{h \to 0^+} \frac{f(a+h) - f(a)}{h}, \qquad f'(a^-) = \lim_{h \to 0^-} \frac{f(a+h) - f(a)}{h} \qquad (3)$$

if the one-sided limits exist. If f is continuous at a and has left and right derivatives satisfying $f'(a^+) \neq f'(a^-)$, then the graph of f is said to have a **kink** at $(a, f(a))$.

EXAMPLE 7   (US Federal income tax (2004) for single persons) This income tax function was discussed in Example 5.4.4. Figure 5.4.8 gives the graph of the tax function. If $t(x)$ denotes the tax paid at income x, its graph has corners at $x = 7150$, at $x = 29\,050$, and at $x = 70\,350$. We see, for instance, that $t'(29\,050^-) = 0.15$ because the tax is 15 cents on the last dollar earned before reaching 29 050. Also, $t'(29\,050^+) = 0.25$ because the tax is 25 cents on the first dollar earned above 29 050. Because $t'(29\,050^-) \neq t'(29\,050^+)$, the tax function t is not differentiable at $x = 29\,050$. Check that $t'(70\,350^+) = 0.28$.

A Rigorous Definition of Limits

Our preliminary definition of the limit concept in Section 6.5 was as follows:

> $\lim_{x \to a} f(x) = A$ means that we can make $f(x)$ as close to A as we want, for all x sufficiently close to (but not equal to) a.

The closeness, or, more generally, the distance, between two numbers can be measured by the absolute value of the difference between them. Using absolute values, the definition can be reformulated in this way:

> $\lim_{x \to a} f(x) = A$ means that *we can make* $|f(x) - A|$ *as small as we want for all* $x \neq a$ *with* $|x - a|$ *sufficiently small.*

Towards the end of the 19th century some of the world's best mathematicians at the time gradually realized that this definition can be made precise in the following way:

> We say that $f(x)$ has limit (or tends to) A as x tends to a, and write $\lim_{x \to a} f(x) = A$, if for each number $\varepsilon > 0$ there exists a number $\delta > 0$ such that $|f(x) - A| < \varepsilon$ for every x with $0 < |x - a| < \delta$.   (4)

This is the definition on which all mathematically rigorous work on limits is based. It is illustrated in Fig. 6. The definition implies that the graph of f must remain within the rectangular box $PQRS$, for all $x \neq a$ in $(a - \delta, a + \delta)$.

It should be regarded as a part of your general mathematical education *to have seen* this ε-δ definition of the limit concept. However, in this book we rely only on an intuitive understanding of limits.

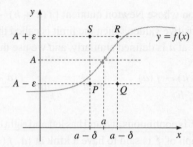

Figure 6 Illustration of definition (4)

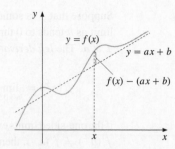

Figure 7 $y = ax + b$ is an asymptote as $x \to \infty$ for the graph of f

PROBLEMS FOR SECTION 7.9

(SM) 1. Evaluate the following limits:

(a) $\lim\limits_{x \to 0^+} (x^2 + 3x - 4)$

(b) $\lim\limits_{x \to 0^-} \dfrac{x + |x|}{x}$

(c) $\lim\limits_{x \to 0^+} \dfrac{x + |x|}{x}$

(d) $\lim\limits_{x \to 0^+} \dfrac{-1}{\sqrt{x}}$

(e) $\lim\limits_{x \to 3^+} \dfrac{x}{x - 3}$

(f) $\lim\limits_{x \to 3^-} \dfrac{x}{x - 3}$

2. Evaluate: (a) $\lim\limits_{x \to \infty} \dfrac{x - 3}{x^2 + 1}$ (b) $\lim\limits_{x \to -\infty} \sqrt{\dfrac{2 + 3x}{x - 1}}$ (c) $\lim\limits_{x \to \infty} \dfrac{(ax - b)^2}{(a - x)(b - x)}$

3. Let $f_1(x) = x$, $f_2(x) = x$, $f_3(x) = x^2$, and $f_4(x) = 1/x$. Determine $\lim\limits_{x \to \infty} f_i(x)$ for $i = 1, 2,$
3, 4, and discuss whether the rules for limits in Section 6.5 apply to the limits as $x \to \infty$.

(a) $f_1(x) + f_2(x)$

(b) $f_1(x) - f_2(x)$

(c) $f_1(x) - f_3(x)$

(d) $f_1(x)/f_2(x)$

(e) $f_1(x)/f_3(x)$

(f) $f_1(x) f_2(x)$

(g) $f_1(x) f_4(x)$

(h) $f_3(x) f_4(x)$

(SM) 4. The nonvertical line $y = ax + b$ is said to be an **asymptote** as $x \to \infty$ (or $x \to -\infty$) to the
curve $y = f(x)$ if

$$f(x) - (ax + b) \to 0 \quad \text{as} \quad x \to \infty \;(\text{or } x \to -\infty)$$

This condition means that the vertical distance between the point $(x, f(x))$ on the curve and the
point $(x, ax + b)$ on the line tends to 0 as $x \to \pm\infty$. (See Fig. 7.)
   Suppose $f(x) = P(x)/Q(x)$ is a rational function where the degree of the polynomial
$P(x)$ is *one greater* than that of the polynomial $Q(x)$. In this case $f(x)$ will have an asymptote
that can be found by performing the polynomial division $P(x) \div Q(x)$ to obtain a polynomial
of degree 1, plus a remainder term that tends to 0 as $x \to \pm\infty$. (See Section 4.7.) Use this
method to find asymptotes for the graph of each of the following functions of x:

(a) $\dfrac{x^2}{x + 1}$

(b) $\dfrac{2x^3 - 3x^2 + 3x - 6}{x^2 + 1}$

(c) $\dfrac{3x^2 + 2x}{x - 1}$

(d) $\dfrac{5x^4 - 3x^2 + 1}{x^3 - 1}$

5. Consider the cost function defined for $x \geq 0$ by

$$C(x) = A\frac{x(x+b)}{x+c} + d$$

Here A, b, c, and d are positive constants. Find the asymptotes.

6. Graph the function f defined by $f(x) = 0$ for $x \leq 0$, and $f(x) = x$ for $x > 0$. Compute $f'(0^+)$ and $f'(0^-)$.

(SM) **7.** Consider the function f defined by the formula

$$f(x) = \frac{3x}{-x^2 + 4x - 1}$$

Compute $f'(x)$ and use a sign diagram to determine where the function increases. (The function is not defined for $x = 2 \pm \sqrt{3}$.)

7.10 Intermediate Value Theorem. Newton's Method

An important reason for introducing the concept of a continuous function was to make precise the idea of a function whose graph is connected—that is, it lacks any breaks. The following result, which can be proved by using the ε-δ definition of limit, expresses this property in mathematical language.

THEOREM 7.10.1 (THE INTERMEDIATE VALUE THEOREM)

Let f be a function continuous in the closed interval $[a, b]$.

(i) If $f(a)$ and $f(b)$ have different signs, then there is at least one c in (a, b) such that $f(c) = 0$.

(ii) If $f(a) \neq f(b)$, then for every *intermediate value* y in the open interval between $f(a)$ and $f(b)$ there is at least one c in (a, b) such that $f(c) = y$.

The conclusion in part (ii) follows from applying part (i) to the function $g(x) = f(x) - y$. You should draw a figure to help convince yourself that a function for which there is no such c must have at least one discontinuity.

Theorem 7.10.1 is important in assuring the existence of solutions to some equations that cannot be solved explicitly.

EXAMPLE 1   Prove that the following equation has at least one solution c between 0 and 1:

$$x^6 + 3x^2 - 2x - 1 = 0$$

Solution: The polynomial

$$f(x) = x^6 + 3x^2 - 2x - 1$$

is continuous for all x—in particular for x in $[0, 1]$. Moreover, $f(0) = -1$ and $f(1) = 1$. According to Theorem 7.10.1, there exists at least one number c in $(0, 1)$ such that $f(c) = 0$.

Sometimes we need to prove that certain equations have unique solutions. Consider the following example.

EXAMPLE 2   Prove that the equation

$$2x - 5e^{-x}(1 + x^2) = 0$$

has a unique solution, which lies in the interval $(0, 2)$.

Solution: Define $g(x) = 2x - 5e^{-x}(1 + x^2)$. Then $g(0) = -5$ and $g(2) = 4 - 25/e^2$. In fact $g(2) > 0$ because $e > 5/2$. According to the intermediate value theorem, therefore, the continuous function g must have at least one zero in $(0, 2)$. Moreover, note that

$$g'(x) = 2 + 5e^{-x}(1 + x^2) - 10xe^{-x} = 2 + 5e^{-x}(1 - 2x + x^2) = 2 + 5e^{-x}(x - 1)^2$$

But then $g'(x) > 0$ for all x, so g is strictly increasing. It follows that g can have only one zero.

Newton's Method

The intermediate value theorem can often be used to show that an equation $f(x) = 0$ has a solution in a given interval, but it gives no additional information about the location of the zero. In this subsection we shall explain a method which usually leads to a good approximate solution in an efficient way. The method was first suggested by Newton and it has an easy geometric explanation.

Consider the graph of the function $y = f(x)$ shown in Fig. 1. It has a zero at $x = a$, but this zero is not known. To find it, start with an initial estimate, x_0, of a. (It is an advantage to start with x_0 not too far from a, if possible.) In order to improve the estimate, construct the tangent line to the graph at the point $(x_0, f(x_0))$, and find the point x_1 at which the tangent crosses the x-axis, as shown in Fig. 1.

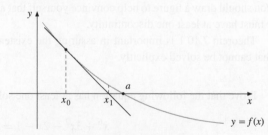

Figure 1 Illustration of Newton's method

Usually x_1 is a significantly better estimate of a than x_0. After having found x_1, repeat the procedure by constructing the tangent line to the curve at the point $(x_1, f(x_1))$. Denote by x_2 the point where this new tangent line crosses the x-axis. Repeating this procedure, we obtain a sequence of points which usually converges very quickly to a.

It is easy to find formulas for x_1, x_2, ... The slope of the tangent at x_0 is $f'(x_0)$. According to the point–slope formula, the equation for the tangent line through the point $(x_0, f(x_0))$ with slope $f'(x_0)$ is given by

$$y - f(x_0) = f'(x_0)(x - x_0)$$

At the point where this tangent line crosses the x-axis, we have $y = 0$ and $x = x_1$. Hence $-f(x_0) = f'(x_0)(x_1 - x_0)$. Solving this equation for x_1, we get

$$x_1 = x_0 - \frac{f(x_0)}{f'(x_0)}$$

Similarly, given x_1, the formula for x_2 is

$$x_2 = x_1 - \frac{f(x_1)}{f'(x_1)}$$

In general, one has the following formula for the $(n + 1)$th approximation x_{n+1}, expressed in terms of the nth approximation x_n:

NEWTON'S METHOD

As long as $f'(x_n) \neq 0$, Newton's method generates the sequence of points given by the formula

$$x_{n+1} = x_n - \frac{f(x_n)}{f'(x_n)}, \qquad n = 0, 1, \ldots \tag{1}$$

Usually, the sequence $\{x_n\}$ converges quickly to a zero of f.

EXAMPLE 3   Find an approximate value for the zero of

$$f(x) = x^6 + 3x^2 - 2x - 1$$

in the interval $[0, 1]$, using Newton's method once (see Example 1).

Solution: Choose $x_0 = 1$. Then $f(x_0) = f(1) = 1$. Because $f'(x) = 6x^5 + 6x - 2$, we have $f'(1) = 10$. Hence, equation (1) for $n = 0$ yields

$$x_1 = 1 - \frac{f(1)}{f'(1)} = 1 - \frac{1}{10} = \frac{9}{10} = 0.9$$

EXAMPLE 4   Use Newton's method twice to find an approximate value for $\sqrt[15]{2}$.

Solution: We need an equation of the form $f(x) = 0$ which has $x = \sqrt[15]{2} = 2^{1/15}$ as a root. The equation $x^{15} = 2$ has this root, so we let $f(x) = x^{15} - 2$. Choose $x_0 = 1$. Then $f(x_0) = f(1) = -1$, and because $f'(x) = 15x^{14}$, we have $f'(1) = 15$. Thus, for $n = 0$, (1) gives

$$x_1 = 1 - \frac{f(1)}{f'(1)} = 1 - \frac{-1}{15} = \frac{16}{15} \approx 1.0667$$

Moreover,

$$x_2 = x_1 - \frac{f(x_1)}{f'(x_1)} = \frac{16}{15} - \frac{f(16/15)}{f'(16/15)} = \frac{16}{15} - \frac{(16/15)^{15} - 2}{15(16/15)^{14}} \approx 1.04729412$$

This is actually correct to 8 decimal places.[3]

NOTE 1   In most cases Newton's method is very efficient, but it can happen that the sequence $\{x_n\}$ defined in (1) does not converge. Figure 2 shows an example where x_1 is a much worse approximation to a than x_0 was. Of course, the formula (1) breaks down if $f'(x_n) = 0$. Usually, Newton's method fails only if the absolute value of $f'(x_n)$ becomes too small, for some n.

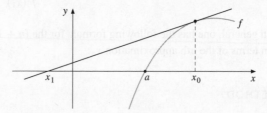

Figure 2

How Fast Does Newton's Method Converge (If it Does)?

THEOREM 7.10.2 (CONVERGENCE OF NEWTON'S METHOD)

Suppose in (1) that f is twice differentiable with $f(x^*) = 0$ and $f'(x^*) \neq 0$. Suppose too there exist both $K > 0$ and $\delta > 0$ with $K\delta < 1$ such that

$$\frac{|f(x)f''(x)|}{f'(x)^2} \leq K|x - x^*|$$

for all x in the open interval $I = (x^* - \delta, x^* + \delta)$. Then, provided that the sequence $\{x_n\}$ in (1) starts at an x_0 in I, it will converge to x^*, with an error $\|x_n - x^*\|$ that satisfies $|x_n - x^*| \leq (\delta K)^{2^n}/K$.

---

[3] A frequently used rule of thumb says that, to obtain an approximation that is correct to n decimal places, use Newton's method until it gives the same n decimal places twice in a row.

1. Show that each of the following equations has at least one root in the given interval.

   (a) $x^7 - 5x^5 + x^3 - 1 = 0$ in $(-1, 1)$ (b) $x^3 + 3x - 8 = 0$ in $(1, 3)$

   (c) $\sqrt{x^2 + 1} = 3x$ in $(0, 1)$ (d) $e^{x-1} = 2x$ in $(0, 1)$

2. Explain why anybody taller than 1 metre was once exactly 1 metre tall.

3. Find a better approximation to $\sqrt[3]{17} \approx 2.5$ by using Newton's method once.

SM 4. The equation $x^4 + 3x^3 - 3x^2 - 8x + 3 = 0$ has an integer root. Find it. The three additional roots are close to -1.9, 0.4, and 1.5. Find better approximations by using Newton's method once for each root that is not an integer.

5. The equation $(2x)^x = 15$ has a solution which is approximately an integer. Find a better approximation by using Newton's method once.

6. In Fig. 1, $f(x_0) > 0$ and $f'(x_0) < 0$. Moreover, x_1 is to the right of x_0. Verify that this agrees with the formula (1) for $n = 0$. Check the other combinations of signs for $f(x_0)$ and $f'(x_0)$ to see both geometrically and analytically on which side of x_0 the point x_1 lies.

7.11 Infinite Sequences

We often encounter functions like those in Newton's method which associate a number $s(n)$ to each natural number n. Such a function is called an **infinite sequence**, or just a sequence. Its terms $s(1)$, $s(2)$, $s(3)$,..., $s(n)$,... are usually denoted by using subscripts: s_1, s_2, s_3, ..., s_n, ... We use the notation $\{s_n\}_{n=1}^{\infty}$, or simply $\{s_n\}$, for an arbitrary infinite sequence. For example, if $s(n) = 1/n$, $n = 1, 2, 3, \ldots$, then the terms of the sequence are

$$1, \frac{1}{2}, \frac{1}{3}, \frac{1}{4}, \ldots, \frac{1}{n}, \ldots$$

If we choose n large enough, the terms of this sequence can be made as small as we like. We say that the sequence *converges* to 0. In general, we introduce the following definition:

    *A sequence $\{s_n\}$ is said to **converge** to a number s if s_n can be made arbitrarily close to s by choosing n sufficiently large.* We write

$$\lim_{n \to \infty} s_n = s \quad \text{or} \quad s_n \to s \text{ as } n \to \infty$$

This definition is just a special case of the previous definition that $f(x) \to A$ as $x \to \infty$. All the ordinary limit rules in Section 6.5 apply to limits of sequences.

    A sequence that does not converge to any real number is said to **diverge**. Explain why the two sequences

$$\{2^n\}_{n=0}^{\infty} \quad \text{and} \quad \{(-1)^n\}_{n=1}^{\infty}$$

both diverge. Occasionally, as in the first of these sequences, the starting index is not 1, but another integer, here 0.

EXAMPLE 1   For $n \geq 3$ let A_n be the area of a regular n-gon (i.e. a polygon with n equal sides and n equal angles) inscribed in a circle with radius 1. For $n = 3$, A_3 is the area of a triangle; for $n = 4$, A_4 is the area of a square; for $n = 5$, A_5 is the area of a pentagon; and so on (see Fig. 1).

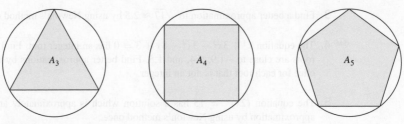

Figure 1

The area A_n increases with n, but is always less than π, the area of a circle with radius 1. It seems intuitively evident that we can make the difference between A_n and π as small as we wish provided that n becomes sufficiently large, so that

$$A_n \to \pi \quad \text{as} \quad n \to \infty$$

In this example, A_1 and A_2 have no meaning, so the sequence starts with A_3.

EXAMPLE 2   In Section 6.11 we argued that $\lim_{h \to 0} (1 + h)^{1/h}$ is $e = 2.718\ldots$. If we let $h = 1/n$, where the natural number $n \to \infty$ as $h \to 0$, we obtain the following important limit:

$$e = \lim_{n \to \infty} (1 + 1/n)^n \tag{1}$$

Irrational Numbers as Limits of Sequences

The sequence $\{A_n\}$ in Example 1 converges to the irrational number $\pi = 3.14159265\ldots$. Another sequence that converges to π starts this way: $s_1 = 3.1$, $s_2 = 3.14$, $s_3 = 3.141$, $s_4 = 3.1415$, etc. Each new number is obtained by including an additional digit in the decimal expansion for π. For this sequence, $s_n \to \pi$ as $n \to \infty$.

Consider an arbitrary irrational number r. Just as for π, the decimal expansion of r will define one particular sequence r_n of rational numbers that converges to r.

Section 1.5 defined the power a^x when x is rational, and Section 4.8 suggested how to define a^x when x is irrational, by considering the special case of 5^π.

Let r be an arbitrary irrational number. Then there exists a sequence r_n of rational numbers such that $r_n \to r$ as $n \to \infty$. The power a^{r_n} is well-defined for all n. Since r_n converges to r, it is reasonable to define a^r as the limit of a^{r_n} as n approaches infinity:

$$a^r = \lim_{n \to \infty} a^{r_n} \tag{$*$}$$

Actually, there are infinitely many sequences $\{r_n\}$ of rational numbers that converge to any given irrational number r. Nevertheless, one can show that the limit in $(*)$ exists and is independent of which sequence we choose.

1. Let $\alpha_n = \dfrac{3-n}{2n-1}$ and $\beta_n = \dfrac{n^2 + 2n - 1}{3n^2 - 2}$, $n = 1, 2, \ldots$. Find the following limits:

   (a) $\lim\limits_{n\to\infty} \alpha_n$ (b) $\lim\limits_{n\to\infty} \beta_n$ (c) $\lim\limits_{n\to\infty} (3\alpha_n + 4\beta_n)$

   (d) $\lim\limits_{n\to\infty} \alpha_n \beta_n$ (e) $\lim\limits_{n\to\infty} \alpha_n/\beta_n$ (f) $\lim\limits_{n\to\infty} \sqrt{\beta_n - \alpha_n}$

2. Examine the convergence of the sequences whose general terms are as follows:

   (a) $s_n = 5 - \dfrac{2}{n}$ (b) $s_n = \dfrac{n^2 - 1}{n}$ (c) $s_n = \dfrac{3n}{\sqrt{2n^2 - 1}}$

3. Prove that $e^x = \lim\limits_{n\to\infty} (1 + x/n)^n$ for $x > 0$. (The same limit is valid also for $x < 0$.)

7.12 L'Hôpital's Rule

We often need to examine the limit as x tends to a of a quotient in which both numerator and denominator tend to 0. Then we write

$$\lim_{x \to a} \frac{f(x)}{g(x)} = \frac{\text{``0''}}{0}$$

We call such a limit an **indeterminate form of type 0/0**. Here a may be replaced by a^+, a^-, ∞, or $-\infty$. The words "indeterminate form" indicate that the limit (or one-sided limit) cannot be found without further examination.

We start with the simple case of an indeterminate form $f(x)/g(x)$ where f and g are differentiable and $f(a) = g(a) = 0$. When $x \neq a$ and $g(x) \neq g(a)$, then some routine algebra allow us to express

$$\frac{f(x)}{g(x)} = \frac{[f(x) - f(a)]/(x - a)}{[g(x) - g(a)]/(x - a)}$$

as the ratio of two Newton quotients. Letting $x \to a$, we see that provided $g'(a) \neq 0$, the fraction on the right-hand side tends to $f'(a)/g'(a)$. This gives the following result:

L'HÔPITAL'S RULE (SIMPLE VERSION)

If $f(a) = g(a) = 0$ and $g'(a) \neq 0$, then

$$\lim_{x \to a} \frac{f(x)}{g(x)} = \frac{f'(a)}{g'(a)} \tag{1}$$

According to (1), we can find the limit of an indeterminate form of type "0/0" by differentiating the numerator and the denominator separately.

EXAMPLE 1   Use (1) to confirm the limit found in Example 6.5.1—namely,

$$\lim_{x \to 0} \frac{f(x)}{g(x)} = \lim_{x \to 0} \frac{e^x - 1}{x} = 1$$

Solution: In this case $f(0) = e^0 - 1 = 0$ and $g(0) = 0$. Moreover, $f'(x) = e^x$ and $g'(x) = 1$. Thus from (1)

$$\lim_{x \to 0} \frac{e^x - 1}{x} = \frac{f'(0)}{g'(0)} = \frac{1}{1} = 1$$

EXAMPLE 2   Compute $\lim_{\lambda \to 0} \dfrac{x^\lambda - y^\lambda}{\lambda}$ $(x > 0, \ y > 0)$.

Solution: In this limit x and y are kept fixed. Define $f(\lambda) = x^\lambda - y^\lambda$ and $g(\lambda) = \lambda$. Then, $f(0) = g(0) = 0$. Using the rule $(a^x)' = a^x \ln a$, we obtain $f'(\lambda) = x^\lambda \ln x - y^\lambda \ln y$, so that $f'(0) = \ln x - \ln y$. Moreover, $g'(\lambda) = 1$, so $g'(0) = 1$. Using l'Hôpital's rule,

$$\lim_{\lambda \to 0} \frac{x^\lambda - y^\lambda}{\lambda} = \ln x - \ln y = \ln \frac{x}{y}$$

In particular, if $y = 1$, then

$$\lim_{\lambda \to 0} \frac{x^\lambda - 1}{\lambda} = \ln x \tag{2}$$

which is a useful result.

Suppose we have a "0/0" form as in (1), but that $f'(a)/g'(a)$ is also of the type "0/0". Because $g'(a) = 0$, the argument for (1) breaks down. What do we do then? The answer is to differentiate once more both numerator and denominator separately. If we still obtain an expression of the type "0/0", we go on differentiating numerator and denominator repeatedly until the limit is determined (if possible). Here is an example from statistics.

EXAMPLE 3   Find $\lim_{x \to 0} \dfrac{e^{xt} - 1 - xt}{x^2}$.

Solution: The numerator and denominator are both 0 at $x = 0$. Applying l'Hôpital's rule twice, we have

$$\lim_{x \to 0} \frac{e^{xt} - 1 - xt}{x^2} = \frac{\text{``0''}}{0} = \lim_{x \to 0} \frac{te^{xt} - t}{2x} = \frac{\text{``0''}}{0} = \lim_{x \to 0} \frac{t^2 e^{xt}}{2} = \frac{1}{2}t^2$$

NOTE 1 Here are some important warnings concerning the most common errors in applying l'Hôpital's rule:

1. Check that you really do have an indeterminate form; otherwise, the method usually gives an erroneous result (see Problem 4).

2. Do not differentiate f/g as a fraction, but compute f'/g' instead.

The method explained here and used to solve Example 3 is built on the following theorem. Note that the requirements on f and g are weaker than might have appeared from the examples presented so far. For instance, f and g need not even be differentiable at $x = a$. Thus the theorem actually gives a more general version of l'Hôpital's rule.

THEOREM 7.12.1 (L'HÔPITAL'S RULE FOR ''0/0'' FORMS)

Suppose that f and g are differentiable in an interval (α, β) that contains a, except possibly at a, and suppose that $f(x)$ and $g(x)$ both tend to 0 as x tends to a. If $g'(x) \neq 0$ for all $x \neq a$ in (α, β), and if $\lim_{x \to a} f'(x)/g'(x) = L$, then

$$\lim_{x \to a} \frac{f(x)}{g(x)} = \lim_{x \to a} \frac{f'(x)}{g'(x)} = L$$

This is true whether L is finite, ∞, or $-\infty$.

Extensions of L'Hôpital's Rule

L'Hôpital's rule can be extended to some other cases. For instance, a can be an endpoint of the interval (α, β). Thus, $x \to a$ can be replaced by $x \to a^+$ or $x \to a^-$. Also it is easy to see that a may be replaced by ∞ or $-\infty$ (see Problem 6). The rule also applies to other indeterminate forms such as "$\pm\infty/\pm\infty$", although the proof is more complicated (see Problem 7). Here is an example:

$$\lim_{x \to \infty} \frac{\ln x}{x} = \frac{\text{``}\infty\text{''}}{\infty} = \lim_{x \to \infty} \frac{1/x}{1} = 0 \tag{3}$$

Indeed, a variety of other indeterminate forms can sometimes be transformed into expressions of the type we have already mentioned by means of algebraic manipulations or substitutions.

EXAMPLE 4   Find $L = \lim_{x \to \infty} \left(\sqrt[5]{x^5 - x^4} - x \right)$.

Solution: We reduce this "$\infty - \infty$" case to a "0/0" case by some algebraic manipulation. Note first that for $x \neq 0$,

$$\sqrt[5]{x^5 - x^4} - x = \left[x^5(1 - 1/x)\right]^{1/5} - x = x(1 - 1/x)^{1/5} - x$$

Thus,

$$\lim_{x \to \infty} (\sqrt[5]{x^5 - x^4} - x) = \lim_{x \to \infty} \frac{(1 - 1/x)^{1/5} - 1}{1/x} = \frac{\text{"0"}}{0}$$

Using l'Hôpital's rule, we have

$$L = \lim_{x \to \infty} \frac{(1/5)\,(1 - 1/x)^{-4/5}\,(1/x^2)}{-1/x^2} = \lim_{x \to \infty} \left[-\frac{1}{5}\left(1 - \frac{1}{x}\right)^{-4/5}\right] = -\frac{1}{5}$$

EXAMPLE 5   Consider the CES ("constant elasticity of substitution") function

$$F(K, L) = A\left(aK^{-\varrho} + (1 - a)L^{-\varrho}\right)^{-1/\varrho} \qquad (*)$$

where $A > 0$, $K > 0$, $L > 0$, $a \in (0, 1)$, and $\varrho \neq 0$. (Functions of two variables are studied systematically in Chapter 11.) Keeping A, K, L, and a fixed, apply l'Hôpital's rule to $z = \ln[F(K, L)/A]$ as $\varrho \to 0$ in order to show that $F(K, L)$ converges to the Cobb–Douglas function $AK^a L^{1-a}$.

Solution: We get

$$z = \ln\left(aK^{-\varrho} + (1 - a)L^{-\varrho}\right)^{-1/\varrho} = -\ln\left(aK^{-\varrho} + (1 - a)L^{-\varrho}\right)/\varrho \to \text{"0/0"} \quad \text{as } \varrho \to 0$$

Because $(d/d\varrho)K^{-\varrho} = -K^{-\varrho} \ln K$ and $(d/d\varrho)L^{-\varrho} = -L^{-\varrho} \ln L$, applying l'Hôpital's rule gives

$$\lim_{\varrho \to 0} z = \lim_{\varrho \to 0} \left(\frac{aK^{-\varrho} \ln K + (1 - a)L^{-\varrho} \ln L}{aK^{-\varrho} + (1 - a)L^{-\varrho}}\right)\Big/ 1$$

$$= a \ln K + (1 - a) \ln L = \ln K^a L^{1-a}$$

Hence $e^z \to K^a L^{1-a}$, and the conclusion follows.

An Important Limit

If a is an arbitrary number greater than 1, then $a^x \to \infty$ as $x \to \infty$. For example, $(1.0001)^x \to \infty$ as $x \to \infty$. Furthermore, if p is an arbitrary positive number, then $x^p \to \infty$ as $x \to \infty$. If we compare $(1.0001)^x$ and x^{1000}, it is clear that the former increases quite slowly at first, whereas the latter increases very quickly. Nevertheless, $(1.0001)^x$ eventually "overwhelms" x^{1000}. In general,

$$\lim_{x \to \infty} \frac{x^p}{a^x} = 0 \qquad (a > 1, \, p \text{ is a fixed positive number}) \qquad (4)$$

For example x^2/e^x and $x^{10}/(1.1)^x$ will both tend to 0 as x tends to ∞. This result is actually quite remarkable. It can be expressed briefly by saying that, for an arbitrary base $a > 1$, *the exponential function a^x increases faster than any power x^p of x. Even more succinctly:* "Exponentials overwhelm powers." (If $p \leq 0$, the limit is obviously 0.)

To prove (4), we consider the logarithm of the left-hand side, which is

$$\ln \frac{x^p}{a^x} = p \ln x - x \ln a = x \left(p \frac{\ln x}{x} - \ln a \right) \tag{$*$}$$

Now, as $x \to \infty$, we have $\ln x/x \to 0$ because of (3). So the term in parentheses in $(*)$ converges to $-\ln a$, which is negative because $a > 1$. It follows that $\ln(x^p/a^x) \to -\infty$, and so $x^p/a^x = \exp[\ln(x^p/a^x)] \to 0$ because $e^z \to 0$ as $z \to -\infty$.

PROBLEMS FOR SECTION 7.12

1. Use l'Hôpital's rule to find:

(a) $\displaystyle\lim_{x \to 3} \frac{3x^2 - 27}{x - 3}$ (b) $\displaystyle\lim_{x \to 0} \frac{e^x - 1 - x - \frac{1}{2}x^2}{3x^3}$ (c) $\displaystyle\lim_{x \to 0} \frac{e^{-3x} - e^{-2x} + x}{x^2}$

2. Find the limits: (a) $\displaystyle\lim_{x \to a} \frac{x^2 - a^2}{x - a}$ (b) $\displaystyle\lim_{x \to 0} \frac{2\sqrt{1 + x} - 2 - x}{2\sqrt{1 + x + x^2} - 2 - x}$

(SM) **3.** Use l'Hôpital's rule to find the following limits:

(a) $\displaystyle\lim_{x \to 1} \frac{x - 1}{x^2 - 1}$ (b) $\displaystyle\lim_{x \to -2} \frac{x^3 + 3x^2 - 4}{x^3 + 5x^2 + 8x + 4}$ (c) $\displaystyle\lim_{x \to 2} \frac{x^4 - 4x^3 + 6x^2 - 8x + 8}{x^3 - 3x^2 + 4}$

(d) $\displaystyle\lim_{x \to 1} \frac{\ln x - x + 1}{(x - 1)^2}$ (e) $\displaystyle\lim_{x \to 1} \frac{1}{x - 1} \ln \left(\frac{7x + 1}{4x + 4} \right)$ (f) $\displaystyle\lim_{x \to 1} \frac{x^x - x}{1 - x + \ln x}$

4. Find the following limits:

(a) $\displaystyle\lim_{x \to \infty} \frac{\ln x}{\sqrt{x}}$ (b) $\displaystyle\lim_{x \to 0^+} x \ln x$ (c) $\displaystyle\lim_{x \to 0^+} (xe^{1/x} - x)$

5. Find the error in the following:

$$\lim_{x \to 1} \frac{x^2 + 3x - 4}{2x^2 - 2x} = \lim_{x \to 1} \frac{2x + 3}{4x - 2} = \lim_{x \to 1} \frac{2}{4} = \frac{1}{2}$$

What is the correct value of the first limit?

6. With $\beta > 0$ and $\gamma > 0$, find $\displaystyle\lim_{v \to 0^+} \frac{1 - (1 + v^\beta)^{-\gamma}}{v}$.   (Consider first the case $\beta = 1$.)

HARDER PROBLEMS

7. Suppose that f and g are both differentiable for all large x and that $f(x)$ and $g(x)$ both tend to 0 as $x \to \infty$. If in addition, $\lim_{x \to \infty} g'(x) \neq 0$, show that

$$\lim_{x \to \infty} \frac{f(x)}{g(x)} = \frac{\text{"0"}}{0} = \lim_{x \to \infty} \frac{f'(x)}{g'(x)}$$

by introducing $x = 1/t$ in the first fraction and then using l'Hôpital's rule as $t \to 0^+$.

(SM) **8.** Suppose that $\lim_{x \to a} f(x)/g(x) = \text{``}\pm\infty/\pm\infty\text{''} = L \neq 0$. By applying l'Hôpital's rule to the equivalent limit, $\lim_{x \to a} [1/g(x)]/[1/f(x)] = \text{``}0/0\text{''}$, show that $L = \lim_{x \to a} [f'(x)/g'(x)]$ provided this limit exists. (Ignore cases where $f'(x)$ or $g'(x)$ tends to 0 as x tends to a.)

REVIEW PROBLEMS FOR CHAPTER 7

1. For each of the following equations, find dy/dx and d^2y/dx^2 by implicit differentiation:

  (a) $5x + y = 10$ (b) $xy^3 = 125$ (c) $e^{2y} = x^3$

  Check by solving each equation for y as a function of x, then differentiating.

2. Compute y' when y is defined implicitly by the equation $y^5 - xy^2 = 24$. Is y' ever 0?

3. The graph of the equation $x^3 + y^3 = 3xy$ passes through the point $(3/2, 3/2)$. Find the slope of the tangent line to the curve at this point. (This equation has a nice graph which is called *Descartes's folium*. See the figure in the answer to this problem.)

4. (a) Find the slope of the tangent to the curve $x^2 y + 3y^3 = 7$ at $(x, y) = (2, 1)$.

  (b) Prove that $y'' = -210/13^3$ at $(2, 1)$.

5. If $K^{1/3} L^{1/3} = 24$, compute dL/dK by implicit differentiation.

6. The equation

$$\ln y + y = 1 - 2 \ln x - 0.2(\ln x)^2$$

  defines y as a function of x for $x > 0$, $y > 0$. Compute y' and show that $y' = 0$ for $x = e^{-5}$.

7. Consider the following macroeconomic model

  (i) $Y = C + I$ (ii) $C = f(Y - T)$ (iii) $T = \alpha + \beta Y$

  where Y is national income, C is consumption, T denotes taxes, and α and β are constants. Assume that $f' \in (0, 1)$ and $\beta \in (0, 1)$.

  (a) From equations (i)–(iii) derive the equation $Y = f((1 - \beta)Y - \alpha) + I$.

  (b) Differentiate the equation in (a) implicitly w.r.t. I and find an expression for dY/dI.

  (c) Examine the sign of dY/dI.

8. (a) Find y' when y is given implicitly by the equation

$$x^2 - xy + 2y^2 = 7$$

  (b) Find the points where the graph has horizontal tangent and the points where it has vertical tangent. Do your results accord with Fig. A which shows the graph of the equation?

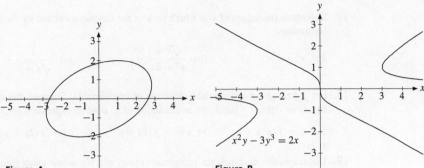

Figure A   **Figure B**

9. (a) The graph of the equation $x^2y - 3y^3 = 2x$ passes through the point $(x, y) = (-1, 1)$. Find the slope of the graph at this point.

   (b) Find the points at which the curve has vertical tangent. Show that no point on the curve has a horizontal tangent. (You may want to check that your answers are consistent with the graph of the equation given in Fig. B.)

SM 10. (a) Determine the domain and the range of the function f defined by the formula

$$f(x) = \frac{1}{2} \ln \frac{1+x}{1-x}$$

   (b) Prove that f has an inverse g, and find a formula for the inverse. Note that $f(\frac{1}{2}) = \frac{1}{2} \ln 3$. Find $g'(\frac{1}{2} \ln 3)$ in two different ways.

11. (a) Let $f(x)$ be defined for all $x > 0$ by

$$f(x) = (\ln x)^3 - 2(\ln x)^2 + \ln x$$

   Compute $f(e^2)$ and find the zeros of $f(x)$.

   (b) Prove that $f(x)$ defined on $[e, \infty)$ has an inverse function h and determine $h'(2)$.

SM 12. Find the quadratic approximations to the following functions about $x = 0$:

   (a) $f(x) = \ln(2x + 4)$ (b) $g(x) = (1 + x)^{-1/2}$ (c) $h(x) = xe^{2x}$

13. Find the differentials:

   (a) $d(\sqrt{1 + x^2})$ (b) $d(4\pi r^2)$ (c) $d(100K^4 + 200)$ (d) $d(\ln(1 - x^3))$

14. Compute the differential of $f(x) = \sqrt{1 + x^3}$. What is the approximate change in $f(x)$ when x changes from $x = 2$ to $x = 2 + dx$, where $dx = 0.2$?

SM 15. Use formula (7.6.6) with $n = 5$ to find an approximate value of $\sqrt{e}$. Show that the answer is correct to three decimal places. (*Hint:* For $0 < c < 1/2$, $e^c < e^{1/2} < 2$.)

16. Find the quadratic approximation to $y = y(x)$ about $(x, y) = (0, 1)$ when y is defined implicitly as a function of x by the equation $y + \ln y = 1 + x$.

17. Determine the values of x at which each of the functions defined by the following formulas is continuous:

    (a) $e^x + e^{1/x}$

    (b) $\dfrac{\sqrt{x} + 1/x}{x^2 + 2x + 2}$

    (c) $\dfrac{1}{\sqrt{x+2}} + \dfrac{1}{\sqrt{2-x}}$

18. Let f be a given differentiable function of one variable. Suppose that each of the following equations defines y implicitly as a function of x. Find an expression for y' in each case.

    (a) $x = f(y^2)$

    (b) $xy^2 = f(x) - y^3$

    (c) $f(2x + y) = x + y^2$

19. The respective demands for margarine (marg) and for meals away from home (mah) in the UK during the period 1920–1937, as functions of personal income r, were estimated to be $D_{marg} = Ar^{-0.165}$ and $D_{mah} = Br^{2.39}$, for suitable constants A and B. Find and interpret the (Engel) elasticities of D_{marg} and D_{mah} w.r.t. r.

20. Find the elasticities of the functions given by the following formulas:

    (a) $50x^5$

    (b) $\sqrt[3]{x}$

    (c) $x^3 + x^5$

    (d) $\dfrac{x-1}{x+1}$

21. The equation $x^3 - x - 5 = 0$ has a root close to 2. Find an approximation by using Newton's method once, with $x_0 = 2$.

22. Prove that $f(x) = e^{\sqrt{x}} - 3$ has a unique zero in the interval $[1, 4]$. Find an approximate value for this zero by using Newton's method once, with $x_0 = 1$.

SM 23. Evaluate the limits:

    (a) $\lim\limits_{x \to 3^-} (x^2 - 3x + 2)$

    (b) $\lim\limits_{x \to -2^+} \dfrac{x^2 - 3x + 14}{x + 2}$

    (c) $\lim\limits_{x \to -1} \dfrac{3 - \sqrt{x + 17}}{x + 1}$

    (d) $\lim\limits_{x \to 0} \dfrac{(2 - x)e^x - x - 2}{x^3}$

    (e) $\lim\limits_{x \to 3} \left(\dfrac{1}{x - 3} - \dfrac{5}{x^2 - x - 6} \right)$

    (f) $\lim\limits_{x \to 4} \dfrac{x - 4}{2x^2 - 32}$

    (g) $\lim\limits_{x \to 2} \dfrac{x^2 - 3x + 2}{x - 2}$

    (h) $\lim\limits_{x \to -1} \dfrac{4 - \sqrt{x + 17}}{2x + 2}$

    (i) $\lim\limits_{x \to \infty} \dfrac{(\ln x)^2}{3x^2}$

SM 24. Examine the following limit for different values of the constants a, b, c, and d, assuming that b and d are positive:

$$\lim\limits_{x \to 0} \dfrac{\sqrt{ax + b} - \sqrt{cx + d}}{x}$$

25. Evaluate $\lim\limits_{x \to 0} \dfrac{a^x - b^x}{e^{ax} - e^{bx}}$ $(a \neq b, a$ and b positive$)$

26. The equation $x^{21} - 11x + 10 = 0$ has a root at $x = 1$, and another root in the interval $(0, 1)$. Starting from $x_0 = 0.9$, use Newton's method as many times as necessary to find the latter root to 3 decimal places.

8

SINGLE-VARIABLE OPTIMIZATION

If you want literal realism,
look at the world around you;
if you want understanding,
look at theories.
—R. Dorfman (1964)

Finding the best way to do a specific task involves what is called an **optimization problem**. Examples abound in almost all areas of human activity. A manager seeks those combinations of inputs (such as capital and labour) that maximize profit or minimize cost. A doctor might want to know when is the best time of day to inject a drug, so as to avoid the concentration in the bloodstream becoming dangerously high. A farmer might want to know what amount of fertilizer per square yard will maximize profits. An oil company may wish to find the optimal rate of extraction from one of its wells.

Studying an optimization problem of this sort systematically requires a mathematical model. Constructing one is usually not easy, and only in simple cases will the model lead to the problem of maximizing or minimizing a function of a single variable—the main topic of this chapter.

In general, no mathematical methods are more important in economics than those designed to solve optimization problems. Though economic optimization problems usually involve several variables, the examples of quadratic optimization in Section 4.6 indicate how useful economic insights can be gained even from simple one-variable optimization.

8.1 Introduction

Those points in the domain of a function where it reaches its largest and its smallest values are usually referred to as maximum and minimum points. If we do not need to bother about the distinction between maxima and minima, we call them **extreme points**. Thus, if $f(x)$ has domain D, then

$$c \in D \text{ is a } \textbf{maximum point} \text{ for } f \iff f(x) \leq f(c) \text{ for all } x \in D \qquad (1)$$

$$d \in D \text{ is a } \textbf{minimum point} \text{ for } f \iff f(x) \geq f(d) \text{ for all } x \in D \qquad (2)$$

In (1), we call $f(c)$ the **maximum value**, and in (2), we call $f(d)$ the **minimum value**. If the value of f at c is strictly larger than at any other point in D, then c is a **strict maximum point**. Similarly, d is a **strict minimum point** if $f(x) > f(d)$ for all $x \in D$, $x \neq d$. As collective names, we use the terms **optimal points** and **values**, or **extreme points** and **values**.

If f is any function with domain D, then the function $-f$ is defined in D by $(-f)(x) = -f(x)$. Note that $f(x) \leq f(c)$ for all x in D if and only if $-f(x) \geq -f(c)$ for all x in D. Thus, c maximizes f in D if and only if c minimizes $-f$ in D. This simple observation, which is illustrated in Fig. 1, can be used to convert maximization problems to minimization problems and vice versa.

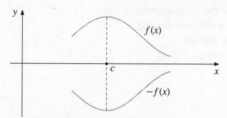

Figure 1 The point c is a maximum point for $f(x)$ and a minimum point for $-f(x)$

Sometimes we can find the maximum and minimum points of a function simply by studying the formula that defines it.

EXAMPLE 1   Find possible maximum and minimum points for:

(a) $f(x) = 3 - (x - 2)^2$ (b) $g(x) = \sqrt{x - 5} - 100, \quad x \geq 5$

Solution:

(a) Because $(x - 2)^2 \geq 0$ for all x, it follows that $f(x) \leq 3$ for all x. But $f(x) = 3$ when $(x - 2)^2 = 0$ at $x = 2$. Therefore, $x = 2$ is a maximum point for f. Because $f(x) \to -\infty$ as $x \to \infty$, the function f has no minimum.

(b) Since $\sqrt{x - 5} \geq 0$ for all $x \geq 5$, it follows that $f(x) \geq -100$ for all $x \geq 5$. Since $f(5) = -100$, we conclude that $x = 5$ is a minimum point. Since $f(x) \to \infty$ as $x \to \infty$, the function f has no maximum.

Rarely can we find extreme points as simply as in the example. The main task of this chapter is to explain how to locate possible extreme points in more complicated cases. An essential observation is a result which you have already observed: If f is a differentiable function that has a maximum or minimum at an interior point c of its domain, then the tangent line to its graph must be horizontal (parallel to the x-axis) at that point. Hence, $f'(c) = 0$. Points c at which $f'(c) = 0$ are called **stationary** (or **critical**) **points** for f. Precisely formulated, one has the following theorem:

THEOREM 8.1.1 NECESSARY FIRST-ORDER CONDITION

Suppose that a function f is differentiable in an interval I and that c is an interior point of I. For $x = c$ to be a maximum or minimum point for f in I, a necessary condition is that it is a stationary point for f—i.e. that $x = c$ satisfies the equation

$$f'(x) = 0 \qquad \textbf{(first-order condition)}$$

Proof: Suppose that f has a maximum at c (the proof in the case when c is a minimum point is similar). If the absolute value of h is sufficiently small, then $c + h \in I$ because c is an interior point of I. Because c is a maximum point, $f(c + h) - f(c) \leq 0$. If h is sufficiently small and positive, the Newton quotient $[f(c + h) - f(c)]/h \leq 0$. The limit of this quotient as $h \to 0^+$ is therefore ≤ 0 as well. But because $f'(c)$ exists, this limit is equal to $f'(c)$, so $f'(c) \leq 0$. For negative values of h, on the other hand, we get $[f(c + h) - f(c)]/h \geq 0$. The limit of this expression as $h \to 0^-$ is therefore ≥ 0. So $f'(c) \geq 0$. We have now proved that $f'(c) \leq 0$ and $f'(c) \geq 0$, so $f'(c) = 0$. ∎

Before starting to explore systematically other properties of maxima and minima, we provide some geometric examples. They will indicate for us the role played by the stationary points of a function in the theory of optimization.

Figure 2 shows the graph of a function f defined in an interval $[a, b]$ having two stationary points, c and d. At c, there is a maximum; at d, there is a minimum.

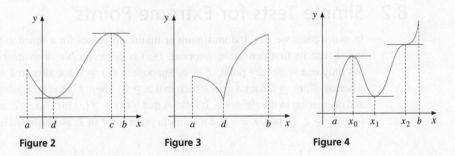

Figure 2   **Figure 3**   **Figure 4**

In Fig. 3, the function has no stationary points. There is a maximum at the end point b and a minimum at d. At d, the function is not differentiable. At b, the derivative (the left-hand derivative) is not 0.

Theorem 8.1.1 implies that $f'(x) = 0$ is a *necessary* condition for a differentiable function f to have a maximum or minimum at an interior point x in its domain. The condition is far from sufficient. This is indicated in Fig. 4 where f has three stationary points, x_0, x_1, and x_2. At the end point a there is a minimum, whereas f does not have any maximum value because it approaches ∞ as x tends to b. At the stationary point x_0 the function f has a "local maximum", in the sense that its value at that point is higher than at all neighbouring points. Similarly, at x_1 it has a local "minimum", whereas at x_2 there is a stationary point that is neither a local maximum nor a local minimum. In fact, x_2 is a special case of an *inflection point*.

In many economic problems the only possible maximum and minimum points will occur where the function is indeed stationary, as shown in Fig. 2. Nevertheless, Figs. 3 and 4 illustrate situations that *can* occur, also in economic problems.

Actually, all three figures represent important possibilities that can occur in single-variable optimization problems. Because the theory is so important in economics, we must not simply rely on vague geometric insights. Instead, we must develop a firmer analytical foundation by formulating precise mathematical results.

PROBLEMS FOR SECTION 8.1

1. Use non-calculus arguments similar to those in Example 1 in order to find the maximum or minimum points for the following functions:

   (a) $f(x) = \dfrac{8}{3x^2 + 4}$ (b) $g(x) = 5(x + 2)^4 - 3$ (c) $h(x) = \dfrac{1}{1 + x^4}$, $x \in [-1, 1]$

2. Use non-calculus arguments similar to those in Example 1 in order to find the maximum or minimum points for the following functions:

   (a) $F(x) = \dfrac{-2}{2 + x^2}$ (b) $G(x) = 2 - \sqrt{1 - x}$ (c) $H(x) = 100 - e^{-x^2}$

8.2 Simple Tests for Extreme Points

In many cases we can find maximum or minimum values for a function just by studying the sign of its first derivative. Suppose $f(x)$ is differentiable in an interval I and that it has only one stationary point, $x = c$. Suppose $f'(x) \geq 0$ for all x in I such that $x \leq c$, whereas $f'(x) \leq 0$ for all x in I such that $x \geq c$. Then $f(x)$ is increasing to the left of c and decreasing to the right of c. It follows that $f(x) \leq f(c)$ for all $x \leq c$, and $f(c) \geq f(x)$ for all $x \geq c$. Hence, $x = c$ is a maximum point for f in I, as illustrated in Fig. 1.

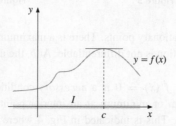

Figure 1 $x = c$ is a maximum point

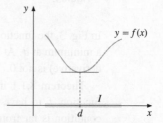

Figure 2 $x = d$ is a minimum point

With obvious modifications, a similar result holds for minimum points, as illustrated in Fig. 2. Briefly stated:[1]

---

[1] Many books in mathematics for economists instruct students always to check so-called second-order conditions, even when this first-derivative test is much easier to use.

THEOREM 8.2.1 (FIRST-DERIVATIVE TEST FOR MAXIMUM/MINIMUM)

If $f'(x) \geq 0$ for $x \leq c$ and $f'(x) \leq 0$ for $x \geq c$, then $x = c$ is a maximum point for f.

If $f'(x) \leq 0$ for $x \leq c$ and $f'(x) \geq 0$ for $x \geq c$, then $x = c$ is a minimum point for f.

EXAMPLE 1   Measured in milligrams per litre, the concentration of a drug in the bloodstream t hours after injection is given by the formula

$$c(t) = \frac{t}{t^2 + 4}, \qquad t \geq 0$$

Find the time of maximum concentration.

Solution: Differentiating with respect to t yields

$$c'(t) = \frac{1 \cdot (t^2 + 4) - t \cdot 2t}{(t^2 + 4)^2} = \frac{4 - t^2}{(t^2 + 4)^2} = \frac{(2 + t)(2 - t)}{(t^2 + 4)^2}$$

For $t \geq 0$, the term $2 - t$ alone determines the algebraic sign of the fraction, because the other terms are positive. In fact, if $t \leq 2$, then $c'(t) \geq 0$, whereas if $t \geq 2$, then $c'(t) \leq 0$. We conclude that $t = 2$ maximizes $c(t)$. Thus, the concentration of the drug is highest 2 hours after injection. Because $c(2) = 0.25$, the maximum concentration is 0.25 milligrams.

EXAMPLE 2   Consider the function f defined for all x by

$$f(x) = e^{2x} - 5e^x + 4 = (e^x - 1)(e^x - 4)$$

(a) Find the zeros of $f(x)$ and compute $f'(x)$.

(b) Find the intervals where f increases and decreases, and determine possible extreme points and values.

(c) Examine $\lim_{x \to -\infty} f(x)$. Sketch the graph of f.

Solution:

(a) $f(x) = (e^x - 1)(e^x - 4) = 0$ when $e^x = 1$ and when $e^x = 4$. Hence $f(x) = 0$ for $x = 0$ and for $x = \ln 4$. By differentiating the first expression for $f(x)$, we obtain $f'(x) = 2e^{2x} - 5e^x$.

(b) $f'(x) = 2e^{2x} - 5e^x = e^x(2e^x - 5)$. Thus $f'(x) = 0$ for $e^x = 5/2 = 2.5$, that is, $x = \ln 2.5$. Furthermore, $f'(x) \leq 0$ for $x \leq \ln 2.5$, and $f'(x) \geq 0$ for $x \geq \ln 2.5$. So $f(x)$ is decreasing in the interval $(-\infty, \ln 2.5]$ and increasing in $[\ln 2.5, \infty)$. Hence $f(x)$ has a minimum at $x = \ln 2.5$, and $f(\ln 2.5) = (2.5 - 1)(2.5 - 4) = -2.25$. Since $f(x) \to \infty$ as $x \to \infty$, $f(x)$ has no maximum.

(c) When $x \to -\infty$, then e^x tends to 0, and $f(x)$ tends to 4. The graph is drawn in Fig. 3. ($y = 4$ is an asymptote as $x \to -\infty$.)

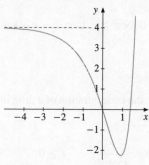

Figure 3 $f(x) = e^{2x} - 5e^x + 4$

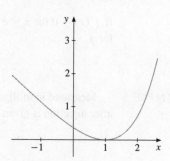

Figure 4 $f(x) = e^{x-1} - x$

Extreme Points for Concave and Convex Functions

Recall the definitions of concave and convex functions in Section 6.9. Suppose that f is concave, with $f''(x) \le 0$ for all x in an interval I. Then $f'(x)$ is decreasing in I. If $f'(c) = 0$ at an interior point c of I, then $f'(x)$ must be ≥ 0 to the left of c, while $f'(x) \le 0$ to the right of c. This implies that the function itself is increasing to the left of c and decreasing to the right of c. We conclude that $x = c$ is a maximum point for f in I. We obviously get a corresponding result for a minimum of a convex function.

THEOREM 8.2.2 (MAXIMUM/MINIMUM FOR CONCAVE/CONVEX FUNCTIONS)

Suppose f is a concave (convex) function in an interval I. If c is a stationary point for f in the interior of I, then c is a maximum (minimum) point for f in I.

EXAMPLE 3   Consider the function f defined for all x by $f(x) = e^{x-1} - x$. Show that f is convex and find its minimum point. Sketch the graph.

Solution: $f'(x) = e^{x-1} - 1$ and $f''(x) = e^{x-1} > 0$, so f is convex. Note that $f'(x) = e^{x-1} - 1 = 0$ for $x = 1$. From Theorem 8.2.2 it follows that $x = 1$ minimizes f. See Fig. 4 for the graph.

PROBLEMS FOR SECTION 8.2

1. Let y denote the weekly average quantity of pork produced in Chicago during 1948 (in millions of pounds) and let x be the total weekly work effort (in thousands of hours). Nichols estimated the relation

$$y = -2.05 + 1.06x - 0.04x^2$$

Determine the value of x that maximizes y by studying the sign variation of y'.

SM **2.** Find the derivative of the function h defined for all x by the formula $h(x) = \dfrac{8x}{3x^2 + 4}$.
Note that $h(x) \to 0$ as $x \to \pm\infty$. Use the sign variation of $h'(x)$ to find the extreme points of $h(x)$.

3. The height of a flowering plant after t months is given by

$$h(t) = \sqrt{t} - \tfrac{1}{2}t, \qquad t \in [0, 3]$$

At what time is the plant at its tallest?

4. Show that

$$f(x) = \frac{2x^2}{x^4 + 1} \;\Rightarrow\; f'(x) = \frac{4x(1 + x^2)(1 + x)(1 - x)}{(x^4 + 1)^2}$$

and find the maximum value of f on $[0, \infty)$.

5. Find possible extreme points for $g(x) = x^3 \ln x$, $x \in (0, \infty)$.

6. Find possible extreme points for $f(x) = e^{3x} - 6e^x$, $x \in (-\infty, \infty)$.

7. Find the maximum of $y = x^2 e^{-x}$ on $[0, 4]$.

SM **8.** Use Theorem 8.2.2 to find the values of x that maximize/minimize the functions given by the following formulas:

(a) $y = e^x + e^{-2x}$ (b) $y = 9 - (x - a)^2 - 2(x - b)^2$ (c) $y = \ln x - 5x, \;\; x > 0$

9. Consider n numbers $a_1, a_2, \ldots, a_n$. Find the number $\bar{x}$ which gives the best approximation to these numbers, in the sense of minimizing

$$d(x) = (x - a_1)^2 + (x - a_2)^2 + \cdots + (x - a_n)^2$$

HARDER PROBLEM

SM **10.** After the North Sea flood catastrophe in 1953, the Dutch government initiated a project to determine the optimal height of the dykes. One of the models involved finding the value of x minimizing

$$f(x) = I_0 + kx + Ae^{-\alpha x} \qquad (x \geq 0)$$

Here x denotes the extra height in metres that should be added to the dykes, $I_0 + kx$ is the construction cost, and $Ae^{-\alpha x}$ is an estimate of the expected loss caused by flooding. The parameters I_0, k, A, and α are all positive constants.

(a) Suppose that $A\alpha > k$ and find $x_0 > 0$ that minimizes $f(x)$.

(b) The constant A is defined as $A = p_0 V(1 + 100/\delta)$, where p_0 is the probability that the dykes will be flooded if they are not rebuilt, V is an estimate of the cost of flood damage, and δ is an interest rate. Show that $x_0 = \dfrac{1}{\alpha} \ln \left[\dfrac{\alpha p_0 V}{k} \left(1 + \dfrac{100}{\delta} \right) \right]$. Examine what happens to x_0 when one of the variables p_0, V, δ, or k increases. Comment on the reasonableness of the results.[2]

---

[2] The problem is discussed in D. van Dantzig, "Economic Decision Problems for Flood Prevention". *Econometrica*, 24 (1956): 276–287.

8.3 Economic Examples

This section presents some interesting examples of economic optimization problems.

EXAMPLE 1   Suppose $Y(N)$ bushels of wheat are harvested per acre of land when N pounds of fertilizer per acre are used. If P is the dollar price per bushel of wheat and q is the dollar price per pound of fertilizer, then profits in dollars per acre are

$$\pi(N) = PY(N) - qN, \qquad N \geq 0$$

Suppose there exists N^* such that $\pi'(N) \geq 0$ for $N \leq N^*$, whereas $\pi'(N) \leq 0$ for $N \geq N^*$. Then N^* maximizes profits, and $\pi'(N^*) = 0$. That is, $PY'(N^*) - q = 0$, so

$$PY'(N^*) = q \qquad\qquad (*)$$

Let us give an economic interpretation of this condition. Suppose N^* units of fertilizer are used and we contemplate increasing N^* by one unit. What do we gain? If N^* increases by one unit, then $Y(N^*+1) - Y(N^*)$ more bushels are produced. Now $Y(N^*+1) - Y(N^*) \approx Y'(N^*)$. For each of these bushels, we get P dollars, so

by increasing N^* by one unit, we gain $\approx PY'(N^*)$ dollars

On the other hand,

by increasing N^* by one unit, we lose q dollars

because this is the cost of one unit of fertilizer. Hence, we can interpret $(*)$ as follows: In order to maximize profits, you should increase the amount of fertilizer to the level N^* at which an additional pound of fertilizer equates the changes in your gains and losses from the extra pound.

(a) In an (unrealistic) example $Y(N) = \sqrt{N}$, $P = 10$, and $q = 0.5$. Find the amount of fertilizer which maximizes profits in this case.

(b) An agricultural study in Iowa estimated the yield function $Y(N)$ for the year 1952 as

$$Y(N) = -13.62 + 0.984N - 0.05N^{1.5}$$

If the price of wheat is \$1.40 per bushel and the price of fertilizer is \$0.18 per pound, find the amount of fertilizer that maximizes profits.

Solution:

(a) The profit function is

$$\pi(N) = PY(N) - qN = 10N^{1/2} - 0.5N, \qquad N \geq 0$$

Then $\pi'(N) = 10(1/2)N^{-1/2} - 0.5 = 5N^{-1/2} - 0.5$. We see that $\pi'(N^*) = 0$ when $(N^*)^{-1/2} = 0.1$, hence $N^* = 100$. Moreover, it follows that $\pi'(N) \geq 0$ when $N \leq 100$ and $\pi'(N) \leq 0$ when $N \geq 100$. We conclude that $N^* = 100$ maximizes profits. See Fig. 1.

(b) In this case

$$\pi(N) = 1.4(-13.62 + 0.984N - 0.05N^{1.5}) - 0.18N$$
$$= -19.068 + 1.1976N - 0.07N^{1.5}$$

so that

$$\pi'(N) = 1.1976 - 0.07 \cdot 1.5N^{0.5} = 1.1976 - 0.105\sqrt{N}$$

Hence $\pi'(N^*) = 0$ when $0.105\sqrt{N^*} = 1.1976$. This implies that

$$\sqrt{N^*} = 1.1976/0.105 \approx 11.4 \quad \text{or} \quad N^* \approx (11.4)^2 \approx 130$$

By studying the expression for $\pi'(N)$, we see that $\pi'(N)$ is positive to the left of N^* and negative to the right of N^*. Hence, $N^* \approx 130$ maximizes profits. The graph of $\pi(N)$ is shown in Fig. 2.

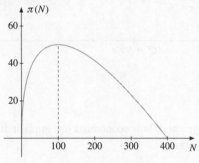

Figure 1 $\pi(N) = 10N^{1/2} - 0.5N$ **Figure 2** Profit function in Example 1(b)

EXAMPLE 2   (a) The total cost of producing Q units of a commodity is

$$C(Q) = 2Q^2 + 10Q + 32, \qquad Q > 0$$

Find the value of Q which minimizes $A(Q) = C(Q)/Q = 2Q + 10 + 32/Q$, the average cost.

(b) The total cost of producing Q units of a commodity is

$$C(Q) = aQ^2 + bQ + c, \qquad Q > 0$$

where a, b, and c are positive constants. Show that the average cost function

$$A(Q) = C(Q)/Q = aQ + b + c/Q$$

has a minimum at $Q^* = \sqrt{c/a}$. In the same coordinate system, draw the graphs of the average cost, the marginal cost, and the straight line $P = aQ + b$.

Solution:

(a) We find that $A'(Q) = 2 - 32/Q^2$ and $A''(Q) = 64/Q^3$. Since $A''(Q) > 0$ for all $Q > 0$, A is convex, and since $A'(Q) = 0$ for $Q = 4$, this is a minimum point.

(b) We find that $A'(Q) = a - c/Q^2$ and $A''(Q) = 2c/Q^3$. Since $A''(Q) > 0$ for all $Q > 0$, A is convex, and since $A'(Q) = 0$ for $Q^* = \sqrt{c/a}$, this is a minimum point. The graphs are drawn in Fig. 3. (We see that at the minimum point Q^*, marginal cost is equal to average cost. This is no coincidence because it is true in general that $A'(Q) = 0$ if and only if $C'(Q) = A(Q)$. (See Example 6.7.6.) The minimum average cost is $A(Q^*) = a\sqrt{c/a} + b + c/\sqrt{c/a} = \sqrt{ac} + b + \sqrt{ac} = 2\sqrt{ac} + b$.)

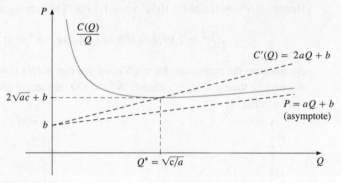

Figure 3

The following example is typical of how economists use implicit differentiation in connection with optimization problems.

EXAMPLE 3   A monopolist is faced with the demand function $P(Q)$ denoting the price when output is Q. The monopolist has a constant average cost k per unit produced.

(a) Find the profit function $\pi(Q)$, and prove that the first-order condition for maximal profit at $Q^* > 0$ is

$$P(Q^*) + Q^* P'(Q^*) = k \qquad (*)$$

(b) By implicitly differentiating $(*)$, find how the monopolist's choice of optimal production is affected by changes in k.

(c) How does the optimal profit react to a change in k?

Solution: (a) The profit function is $\pi(Q) = QP(Q) - kQ$, and $\pi'(Q) = P(Q) + QP'(Q) - k$. In order for $Q^* > 0$ to maximize $\pi(Q)$, one must have $\pi'(Q^*) = 0$, i.e. $P(Q^*) + Q^* P'(Q^*) = k$.

(b) Assuming that equation $(*)$ defines Q^* as a differentiable function of k, we obtain

$$P'(Q^*)\frac{dQ^*}{dk} + \frac{dQ^*}{dk}P'(Q^*) + Q^* P''(Q^*)\frac{dQ^*}{dk} = 1$$

Solving for dQ^*/dk gives

$$\frac{dQ^*}{dk} = \frac{1}{Q^* P''(Q^*) + 2P'(Q^*)}$$

(c) Because $\pi(Q^*) = Q^* P(Q^*) - kQ^*$, differentiating w.r.t. k gives

$$\frac{d\pi(Q^*)}{dk} = \frac{dQ^*}{dk}P(Q^*) + Q^*P'(Q^*)\frac{dQ^*}{dk} - Q^* - k\frac{dQ^*}{dk}$$

But the three terms containing dQ^*/dk all cancel because of the first-order condition (∗). So $d\pi^*/dk = -Q^*$. Thus, if the cost increases by one unit, the optimal profit will decrease by (approximately) Q^*, the optimal output level.

PROBLEMS FOR SECTION 8.3

1. (a) A firm produces $Q = 2\sqrt{L}$ units of a commodity when L units of labour are employed. If the price obtained per unit is 160 euros, and the price per unit of labour is 40 euros, what value of L maximizes profits $\pi(L)$?

   (b) A firm produces $Q = f(L)$ units of a commodity when L units of labour are employed. Assume that $f'(L) > 0$ and $f''(L) < 0$. If the price obtained per unit is 1 and price per unit of labour is w, what is the first-order condition for maximizing profits at $L = L^*$?

   (c) By implicitly differentiating the first-order condition in (b) w.r.t. w, find how L^* changes when w changes.

SM 2. (a) Suppose in Example 3 that $P(Q) = a - Q$, and assume that $0 < k < a$. Find the profit-maximizing output Q^* and the associated monopoly profit $\pi(Q^*)$.

   (b) How does the monopoly profit react to changes in k? Find $d\pi(Q^*)/dk$.

   (c) The government argues that the monopoly produces too little. It wants to induce the monopolist to produce $\hat{Q} = a - k$ units by granting a subsidy s per unit output. Calculate the subsidy s required to reach the target.

3. A square tin plate whose edges are 18 cm long is to be made into an open square box of depth x cm by cutting out equally sized squares of width x in each corner and then folding over the edges. Draw a figure, and show that the volume of the box is

$$V(x) = x(18 - 2x)^2 = 4x^3 - 72x^2 + 324x, \qquad x \in [0, 9]$$

Also find the maximum point of V in $[0, 9]$.

4. In an economic model, the proportion of families whose income is no more than x, and who have a home computer, is given by

$$p(x) = a + k(1 - e^{-cx}) \qquad (a, k, \text{ and } c \text{ are positive constants})$$

Determine $p'(x)$ and $p''(x)$. Does $p(x)$ have a maximum? Sketch the graph of p.

5. The tax T a person pays on gross income W is given by $T = a(bW + c)^p + kW$, where a, b, c, and k are positive constants, and $p > 1$. Then the average tax rate is

$$\overline{T}(W) = \frac{T}{W} = a\frac{(bW + c)^p}{W} + k$$

Find the value of W that minimizes the average tax rate.

8.4   The Extreme Value Theorem

The main theorems used so far in this chapter to locate extreme points require the function to be steadily increasing on one side of the point and steadily decreasing on the other side. Many functions with a derivative whose sign varies in a more complicated way may still have a maximum or minimum. This section shows how to locate possible extreme points for an important class of such functions.

Examples such as those illustrated in Figs. 2–4 of Section 8.1 show how not all functions have extreme points. The following theorem gives important sufficient conditions for their existence.

THEOREM 8.4.1   (EXTREME VALUE THEOREM)

Suppose that f is a continuous function over a closed and bounded interval $[a, b]$. Then there exist a point d in $[a, b]$ where f has a minimum, and a point c in $[a, b]$ where f has a maximum, so that

$$f(d) \leq f(x) \leq f(c) \qquad \text{for all } x \text{ in } [a, b]$$

NOTE 1   One of the most common misunderstandings of the extreme value theorem is illustrated by the following statement from a student's exam paper: "The function is continuous, but since it is not defined on a closed, bounded interval, the extreme value theorem shows that there is no maximum." The misunderstanding here is that, although the conditions of the theorem are sufficient, they certainly are not *necessary* for the existence of an extreme point. In Problem 9, you are asked to study a function defined in an interval that is neither closed nor bounded, and moreover the function is not even continuous. Even so, it has both a maximum and a minimum.

The proof of the extreme value theorem is surprisingly difficult. Yet the result is not hard to believe. Imagine, for example, a cyclist going for a ride along some mountain roads. Since roads avoid going over cliffs, the height of the road above sea level is a continuous function of the distance travelled, as illustrated in Fig. 1. As that figure also shows, the trip must take the cyclist over some highest point P, as well as through a lowest point Q. (These points could also be at the start or finish of the ride.)

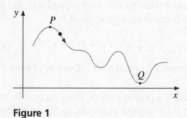

Figure 1

Searching for Maxima/Minima

Suppose we know that a function f has a maximum and/or a minimum in some bounded interval I. The optimum must occur either at an interior point of I, or else at one of the end points. If it occurs at an interior point (inside the interval I) and if f is differentiable, then the derivative f' is zero at that point. In addition, there is the possibility that the optimum occurs at a point where f is not differentiable. Hence, every extreme point must belong to one of the following three different sets:

(a) Interior points in I where $f'(x) = 0$

(b) End points of I (if included in I)

(c) Interior points in I where f' does not exist

Points satisfying any one of these three conditions will be called *candidate extreme points*. Whether they are actual extreme points depends on a careful comparison of function values, as explained below.

A typical example showing that a minimum can occur at a point of type (c) is shown in Fig. 8.1.3. However, most functions that economists study are differentiable everywhere. The following recipe, therefore, covers most problems of interest.

Problem: Find the maximum and minimum values of a differentiable function f defined on a closed, bounded interval $[a, b]$.

Solution:

(I) Find all stationary points of f in (a, b)—that is, find all points x in (a, b) that satisfy the equation $f'(x) = 0$. (1)

(II) Evaluate f at the end points a and b of the interval and also at all stationary points.

(III) The largest function value found in (II) is the maximum value, and the smallest function value is the minimum value of f in $[a, b]$.

A differentiable function is continuous, so the extreme value theorem assures us that maximum and minimum points do exist. Following the procedure just given, we can, in principle, find these extreme points.

EXAMPLE 1   Find the maximum and minimum values for

$$f(x) = 3x^2 - 6x + 5, \qquad x \in [0, 3]$$

Solution: The function is differentiable everywhere, and $f'(x) = 6x - 6 = 6(x - 1)$. Hence $x = 1$ is the only stationary point. The candidate extreme points are the end points 0 and 3, as well as $x = 1$. We calculate the value of f at these three points. The results are $f(0) = 5$, $f(3) = 14$, and $f(1) = 2$. We conclude that the maximum value is 14, obtained at $x = 3$, and the minimum value is 2 at $x = 1$.

EXAMPLE 2   Find the maximum and minimum values of

$$f(x) = \tfrac{1}{4}x^4 - \tfrac{5}{6}x^3 + \tfrac{1}{2}x^2 - 1, \qquad x \in [-1, 3]$$

Solution: The function is differentiable everywhere, and

$$f'(x) = x^3 - \tfrac{5}{2}x^2 + x = x\left(x^2 - \tfrac{5}{2}x + 1\right)$$

Solving the quadratic equation $x^2 - \tfrac{5}{2}x + 1 = 0$, we get the roots $x = 1/2$ and $x = 2$. Thus $f'(x) = 0$ for $x = 0, 1/2$, and 2. These three points, together with the two end points -1 and 3 of the interval $[-1, 3]$, constitute the five candidate extreme points. We find that $f(-1) = 7/12$, $f(0) = -1$, $f(1/2) = -185/192$, $f(2) = -5/3$, and $f(3) = 5/4$. Thus the maximum value of f is $5/4$ at $x = 3$. The minimum value is $-5/3$ at $x = 2$.

Note that it is unnecessary to study the sign variation of $f'(x)$ or to use other tests such as second-order conditions in order to verify that we have found the maximum and minimum values.

In the two previous examples we had no trouble in finding the solutions to the equation $f'(x) = 0$. However, in some cases, finding all the solutions to $f'(x) = 0$ might constitute a formidable or even insuperable problem. For instance,

$$f(x) = x^{26} - 32x^{23} - 11x^5 - 2x^3 - x + 28, \qquad x \in [-1, 5]$$

is a continuous function, so it does have a maximum and a minimum in $[-1, 5]$. Yet it is impossible to find any exact solution to the equation $f'(x) = 0$.

Difficulties of this kind are often encountered in practical optimization problems. In fact, only in very special cases can the equation $f'(x) = 0$ be solved exactly. Fortunately, there are standard numerical methods for use on a computer that in most cases will find points arbitrarily close to the actual solutions of such equations—see, for example, Newton's method discussed in Section 7.10.

The Mean Value Theorem

This optional section deals with the mean value theorem, which is a principal tool for the precise demonstration of results in calculus.

Consider a function f defined on an interval $[a, b]$, and suppose that the graph of f is connected and lacks corners, as illustrated in Fig. 2. Because the graph of f joins A to B by a connected curve having a tangent at each point, it is geometrically plausible that for at least one value of x between a and b, the tangent to the graph at x should be parallel to the line AB. In Fig. 2, x^* appears to be such a value of x. The line AB has slope $[f(b) - f(a)]/(b - a)$. So the condition for the tangent line at $(x^*, f(x^*))$ to be parallel to the line AB is that $f'(x^*) = [f(b) - f(a)]/(b - a)$. In fact, x^* can be chosen so that the vertical distance between the graph of f and AB is as large as possible. The proof that follows is based on this fact.

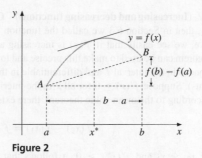

Figure 2

THEOREM 8.4.2 (THE MEAN VALUE THEOREM)

If f is continuous in the closed bounded interval $[a, b]$, and differentiable in the open interval (a, b), then there exists at least one interior point x^* in (a, b) such that

$$f'(x^*) = \frac{f(b) - f(a)}{b - a}$$

(2)

Proof: According to the point–point formula, the straight line through A and B in Fig. 2 has the equation

$$y - f(a) = \frac{f(b) - f(a)}{b - a}(x - a)$$

The function

$$g(x) = f(x) - f(a) - \frac{f(b) - f(a)}{b - a}(x - a)$$

therefore measures the vertical distance between the graph of f and the line AB. Note that

$$g'(x) = f'(x) - \frac{f(b) - f(a)}{b - a}$$

(∗)

Obviously, $g(a) = g(b) = 0$. The function $g(x)$ inherits from f the properties of being continuous in $[a, b]$ and differentiable in (a, b). By the extreme value theorem, $g(x)$ has a maximum and a minimum over $[a, b]$. Because $g(a) = g(b)$, at least one of these extreme points x^* must lie in (a, b). Theorem 8.1.1 tells us that $g'(x^*) = 0$, and the conclusion follows from (∗). ∎

EXAMPLE 3   Test the mean value theorem on $f(x) = x^3 - x$ in $[0, 2]$.

Solution: We find that $[f(2) - f(0)]/(2 - 0) = 3$ and $f'(x) = 3x^2 - 1$. The equation $f'(x) = 3$ has two solutions, $x = \pm 2\sqrt{3}/3$. Because the positive root $x^* = 2\sqrt{3}/3 \in (0, 2)$, we have

$$f'(x^*) = \frac{f(2) - f(0)}{2 - 0}$$

Thus, the mean value theorem is confirmed in this case.

NOTE 2 (**Increasing and decreasing functions**)   Over any interval I, if $f(x_2) \geq f(x_1)$ whenever $x_2 > x_1$, then in Section 6.3 we called the function f *increasing* in I. Using the definition of the derivative, we see easily that if $f(x)$ is increasing and differentiable, then $f'(x) \geq 0$. The mean value theorem can be used to make this precise and to prove the converse. Let f be a function which is continuous in the interval I and differentiable in the interior of I (that is, at points other than the end points). Suppose $f'(x) \geq 0$ for all x in the interior of I. Let $x_2 > x_1$ be two arbitrary numbers in I. According to the mean value theorem, there exists a number x^* in (x_1, x_2) such that

$$f(x_2) - f(x_1) = f'(x^*)(x_2 - x_1) \tag{$*$}$$

Because $x_2 > x_1$ and $f'(x^*) \geq 0$, it follows that $f(x_2) \geq f(x_1)$, so $f(x)$ is increasing. This proves (6.3.1). The equivalence in (6.3.2) can be proved by considering the condition for $-f$ to be increasing. Finally, (6.3.3) involves both f and $-f$ being increasing. Alternatively it follows easily by using equation $(*)$.

NOTE 3 (**Proof of Lagrange's remainder formula (7.6.2)**)   We start by proving that the formula is correct for $n = 1$. This means that we want to prove formula (7.6.4). For $x \neq 0$, define the function $S(x)$ implicitly by the equation

$$f(x) = f(0) + f'(0)x + \tfrac{1}{2}S(x)x^2 \tag{$*$}$$

If we can prove that there exists a number c between 0 and x such that $S(x) = f''(c)$, then (7.6.4) is established. Keep x fixed and define the function g for all t between 0 and x by

$$g(t) = f(x) - [f(t) + f'(t)(x - t) + \tfrac{1}{2}S(x)(x - t)^2] \tag{$**$}$$

Then $(*)$ and $(**)$ imply that $g(0) \doteq f(x) - [f(0) + f'(0)x + \tfrac{1}{2}S(x)x^2] = 0$ and that $g(x) = f(x) - [f(x) + 0 + 0] = 0$. So, by the mean value theorem, there exists a number c strictly between 0 and x such that $g'(c) = 0$. Differentiating $(**)$ with respect to t, with x fixed, we get

$$g'(t) = -f'(t) + f'(t) - f''(t)(x - t) + S(x)(x - t)$$

Thus, $g'(c) = -f''(c)(x - c) + S(x)(x - c)$. Because $g'(c) = 0$ and $c \neq x$, it follows that $S(x) = f''(c)$. Hence, we have proved (7.6.4).

The proof for the case when $n > 1$ is based on the same idea, generalizing $(*)$ and $(**)$ in the obvious way.   ∎

PROBLEMS FOR SECTION 8.4

1. Find the maximum and minimum and draw the graph of

$$f(x) = 4x^2 - 40x + 80, \qquad x \in [0, 8]$$

(SM) 2. Find the maximum and minimum of each function over the indicated interval:

(a) $f(x) = -2x - 1, \qquad [0, 3]$ (b) $f(x) = x^3 - 3x + 8, \qquad [-1, 2]$

(c) $f(x) = \dfrac{x^2 + 1}{x}, \qquad [\tfrac{1}{2}, 2]$ (d) $f(x) = x^5 - 5x^3, \qquad [-1, \sqrt{5}]$

(e) $f(x) = x^3 - 4500x^2 + 6 \cdot 10^6 x, \qquad [0, 3000]$

3. Suppose the function g is defined for all $x \in [-1, 2]$ by $g(x) = \frac{1}{5}(e^{x^2} + e^{2-x^2})$. Calculate $g'(x)$ and find the extreme points of g.

4. A sports club plans to charter a plane, and charge its members 10% commission on the price they pay to buy seats. That price is arranged by the charter company. The standard fare for each passenger is $800. For each additional person above 60, all travellers (including the first 60) get a discount of $10. The plane can take at most 80 passengers.

(a) How much commission is earned when there are 61, 70, 80, and $60 + x$ passengers?

(b) Find the number of passengers that maximizes the total commission earned by the sports club.

5. Let the function f be defined for $x \in [1, e^3]$ by

$$f(x) = (\ln x)^3 - 2(\ln x)^2 + \ln x$$

(a) Compute $f(e^{1/3})$, $f(e^2)$, and $f(e^3)$. Find the zeros of $f(x)$.

(b) Find the extreme points of f.

(c) Show that f defined over $[e, e^3]$ has an inverse function g and determine $g'(2)$.

HARDER PROBLEMS

(SM) **6.** For the following functions determine all numbers x^* in the specified intervals such that $f'(x^*) = [f(b) - f(a)]/(b - a)$:

(a) $f(x) = x^2$ in $[1, 2]$ (b) $f(x) = \sqrt{1 - x^2}$ in $[0, 1]$

(c) $f(x) = 2/x$ in $[2, 6]$ (d) $f(x) = \sqrt{9 + x^2}$ in $[0, 4]$

7. You are supposed to sail from point A in a lake to point B. What does the mean value theorem have to say about your trip?

8. Is the function f defined for all $x \in [-1, 1]$ by

$$f(x) = \begin{cases} x & \text{for } x \in (-1, 1) \\ 0 & \text{for } x = -1 \text{ and for } x = 1 \end{cases}$$

continuous? Does f attain a maximum or minimum?

9. Let f be defined for all x in $(0, \infty)$ by

$$f(x) = \begin{cases} x + 1 & \text{for } x \in (0, 1] \\ 1 & \text{for } x \in (1, \infty) \end{cases}$$

Prove that f attains maximum and minimum values. Verify that nevertheless *none* of the conditions in the extreme value theorem is satisfied.

8.5 Further Economic Examples

EXAMPLE 1   A firm that produces a single commodity wants to maximize its profits. The total revenue generated in a certain period by producing and selling Q units is $R(Q)$ dollars, whereas $C(Q)$ denotes the associated total dollar cost. The profit obtained as a result of producing and selling Q units is then

$$\pi(Q) = R(Q) - C(Q) \qquad (*)$$

We assume that because of technical limitations, there is a maximum quantity $\bar{Q}$ that can be produced by the firm in a given period. We assume too that R and C are differentiable functions of Q in the interval $[0, \bar{Q}]$. The profit function π is then differentiable, so continuous. Consequently π does have a maximum value. In special cases, that maximum might occur at $Q = 0$ or at $Q = \bar{Q}$. If not, it has an "interior maximum" where the production level Q^* satisfies $\pi'(Q^*) = 0$, and so

$$R'(Q^*) = C'(Q^*) \qquad (**)$$

Hence, *production should be adjusted to a point where the marginal revenue is equal to the marginal cost.*

Let us assume that the firm gets a fixed price P per unit sold. Then $R(Q) = PQ$, and $(**)$ takes the form

$$P = C'(Q^*) \qquad (***)$$

Thus, in the case when the firm has no control over the price, *production should be adjusted to a level at which the marginal cost is equal to the price per unit of the commodity* (assuming an interior maximum).

It is quite possible that the firm has functions $R(Q)$ and $C(Q)$ for which equation $(**)$ has several solutions. If so, the maximum profit occurs at that point Q^* among the solutions of $(**)$ which gives the highest value of $\pi(Q^*)$.

Equation $(**)$ has an economic interpretation rather like that for the corresponding optimality condition in Example 8.3.1. Indeed, suppose we contemplate increasing production from the level Q^* by one unit. We would increase revenue by the amount $R(Q^* + 1) - R(Q^*) \approx R'(Q^*)$. We would increase cost by the amount $C(Q^* + 1) - C(Q^*) \approx C'(Q^*)$. Equation $(**)$ equates $R'(Q^*)$ and $C'(Q^*)$, so that the approximate extra revenue earned by selling an extra unit is offset by the approximate extra cost of producing that unit.

EXAMPLE 2   Suppose that the firm in the preceding example obtains a fixed price $P = 121$ per unit, and that the cost function is

$$C(Q) = 0.02Q^3 - 3Q^2 + 175Q + 500$$

The firm can produce at most $\bar{Q} = 110$ units.

(a) Make a table of the values of the functions $R(Q) = 121Q$, $C(Q)$, and $\pi(Q) = R(Q) - C(Q)$ for $Q = 0, 10, 30, 50, 70, 90,$ and 110. Draw the graphs of $R(Q)$ and $C(Q)$ in the same coordinate system.

(b) Answer the following questions (approximately) by using the graphs in (a):

(i) How many units must be produced in order for the firm to make a profit?

(ii) How many units must be produced for the profit to be 2000 dollars?

(iii) Which production level maximizes profits?

(c) Answer the question in (b)(iii) by computation.

(d) What is the smallest price per unit the firm must charge in order not to lose money, if capacity is fully utilized (that is if it produces 110 units)?

Solution:

(a) We form the following table:

Table 1

Q	0	10	30	50	70	90	110
$R(Q) = 121Q$	0	1210	3630	6050	8470	10890	13310
$C(Q)$	500	1970	3590	4250	4910	6530	10070
$\pi(Q) = R(Q) - C(Q)$	−500	−760	40	1800	3560	4360	3240

The graphs of $R(Q)$ and $C(Q)$ are shown in Fig. 1.

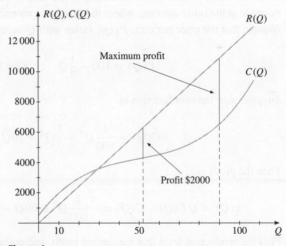

Figure 1

(b) (i) The firm earns a profit if $\pi(Q) > 0$, that is when $R(Q) > C(Q)$. On the figure we see that $R(Q) > C(Q)$ when Q is larger than (approximately) 30.

(ii) We must find where the "gap" between $R(Q)$ and $C(Q)$ is 2000. This occurs when $Q \approx 52$.

(iii) The profit is the largest when the gap between $R(Q)$ and $C(Q)$ is the largest. This seems to occur when $Q \approx 90$.

(c) When the formula for $C'(Q)$ is inserted into equation (∗∗∗) of the preceding example, because $P = 121$, the result is

$$121 = 0.06Q^2 - 6Q + 175$$

Solving this quadratic equation yields $Q = 10$ and $Q = 90$. We know that $\pi(Q)$ must have a maximum point in $[0, 110]$, and there are four candidates: $Q = 0, 10, 90,$ and 110. Using Table 1, we see that

$$\pi(0) = -500, \quad \pi(10) = -760, \quad \pi(90) = 4360, \quad \pi(110) = 3240$$

The firm therefore attains maximum profit by producing 90 units.

(d) If the price per unit is P, the profit from producing 110 units is

$$\pi(110) = P \cdot 110 - C(110) = 110P - 10\,070$$

The smallest price P which ensures that the firm does not lose money when producing 110 units, satisfies $\pi(110) = 0$, that is $110P = 10\,070$ with solution $P \approx 91.55$. This is the average cost of producing 110 units. The price must be at least 91.55 dollars if revenue is going to be enough to cover the cost of producing at full capacity.

EXAMPLE 3   In the model of the previous example, the firm took the price as given. Consider an example at the other extreme, where the firm has a monopoly in the sale of the commodity. Assume that the price per unit, $P(Q)$, varies with Q according to the formula

$$P(Q) = 100 - \frac{1}{3}Q, \qquad Q \in [0, 300]$$

Suppose now the cost function is

$$C(Q) = \frac{1}{600}Q^3 - \frac{1}{3}Q^2 + 50Q + \frac{1000}{3}$$

Then the profit is

$$\pi(Q) = QP(Q) - C(Q) = -\frac{1}{600}Q^3 + 50Q - \frac{1000}{3}, \qquad Q \in [0, 300]$$

Find the production level that maximizes profit, and compute the maximum profit.

Solution: The derivative of $\pi(Q)$ is $\pi'(Q) = -\frac{1}{200}Q^2 + 50$. Hence

$$\pi'(Q) = 0 \quad \text{for} \quad Q^2 = 10\,000, \quad \text{that is} \quad Q = 100$$

(The other possibility, $Q = -100$, is not permissible.) The values of $\pi(Q)$ at the end points of $[0, 300]$ are $\pi(0) = -1000/3$ and $\pi(300) = -91\,000/3$. Since $\pi(100) = 3000$, we conclude that $Q = 100$ maximizes profit, and the maximum profit is 3000.

EXAMPLE 4   ("**Either a Borrower or a Lender Be**")[3] A student has current income y_1 and expects future income y_2. She plans current consumption c_1 and future consumption c_2 in order to maximize the utility function

$$U = \ln c_1 + \frac{1}{1+\delta} \ln c_2, \qquad c_1, c_2 > 0$$

where δ is her discount rate. If she borrows now, so that $c_1 > y_1$, then future consumption, after repaying the loan amount $c_1 - y_1$ with interest charged at rate r, will be

$$c_2 = y_2 - (1+r)(c_1 - y_1)$$

Alternatively, if she saves now, so that $c_1 < y_1$, then future consumption will be

$$c_2 = y_2 + (1+r)(y_1 - c_1)$$

after receiving interest at rate r on her savings. Find the optimal borrowing or saving plan.

Solution: Whether the student borrows or saves, second period consumption is

$$c_2 = y_2 - (1+r)(c_1 - y_1)$$

in either case. So the student will want to maximize

$$U = \ln c_1 + \frac{1}{1+\delta} \ln[y_2 - (1+r)(c_1 - y_1)] \qquad (*)$$

We can obviously restrict attention to the interval $0 < c_1 < y_1 + (1+r)^{-1} y_2$, where both c_1 and c_2 are positive. Differentiating $(*)$ w.r.t. the choice variable c_1 gives

$$\frac{dU}{dc_1} = \frac{1}{c_1} - \frac{1+r}{1+\delta} \cdot \frac{1}{y_2 - (1+r)(c_1 - y_1)}$$

Rewriting the fractions so that they have a common denominator yields

$$\frac{dU}{dc_1} = \frac{(1+\delta)[y_2 - (1+r)(c_1 - y_1)] - (1+r)c_1}{c_1(1+\delta)[y_2 - (1+r)(c_1 - y_1)]}$$

Rearranging the numerator and equating the derivative to 0, we have

$$\frac{dU}{dc_1} = \frac{(1+\delta)[(1+r)y_1 + y_2] - (2+\delta)(1+r)c_1}{c_1(1+\delta)[y_2 - (1+r)(c_1 - y_1)]} = 0 \qquad (**)$$

The unique solution of this equation is

$$c_1^* = \frac{(1+\delta)[(1+r)y_1 + y_2]}{(2+\delta)(1+r)} = y_1 + \frac{(1+\delta)y_2 - (1+r)y_1}{(2+\delta)(1+r)}$$

From $(**)$, we see that for $c_1 < c_1^*$ one has $dU/dc_1 > 0$, whereas for $c_1 > c_1^*$ one has $dU/dc_1 < 0$. We conclude that c_1^* indeed maximizes U. Moreover, the student lends if and only if $(1+\delta)y_2 < (1+r)y_1$. In the more likely case when $(1+\delta)y_2 > (1+r)y_1$ because future income is considerably higher than present income, she will borrow. Only if by some chance $(1+\delta)y_2$ is exactly equal to $(1+r)y_1$ will she be neither a borrower nor a lender. However, this discussion has neglected the difference between borrowing and lending rates of interest that one always observes in reality.

---

[3] According to Shakespeare, Polonius's advice to Hamlet was: "Neither a borrower nor a lender be".

PROBLEMS FOR SECTION 8.5

1. With reference to Example 1, suppose that

$$R(Q) = 10Q - \frac{Q^2}{1000}, \quad C(Q) = 5000 + 2Q, \quad Q \in [0, 10\,000]$$

Find the value of Q that maximizes profits.

2. (a) With reference to Example 1, let

$$R(Q) = 80Q \quad \text{and} \quad C(Q) = Q^2 + 10Q + 900$$

The firm can at most produce 50 units. Draw the graphs of R and C in the same coordinate system.

   (b) Answer the following questions both graphically and by computation:
   (i) How many units must be produced for the firm to make a profit?
   (ii) How many units must be produced for the firm to maximize profits?

3. A pharmaceutical firm produces penicillin. The sales price per unit is 200, while the cost of producing x units is given by

$$C(x) = 500\,000 + 80x + 0.003x^2$$

The firm can produce at most 30 000 units. What value of x maximizes profits?

(SM) 4. Consider Example 1 and find the production level that maximizes profits when

   (i) $R(Q) = 1840Q, \quad C(Q) = 2Q^2 + 40Q + 5000$
   (ii) $R(Q) = 2240Q, \quad C(Q) = 2Q^2 + 40Q + 5000$
   (iii) $R(Q) = 1840Q, \quad C(Q) = 2Q^2 + 1940Q + 5000$

5. The price a firm obtains for a commodity varies with demand Q according to the formula $P(Q) = 18 - 0.006Q$. Total cost is $C(Q) = 0.004Q^2 + 4Q + 4500$.

   (a) Find the firm's profit $\pi(Q)$ and the value of Q that maximizes profit.

   (b) Find a formula for the elasticity of $P(Q)$ w.r.t. Q, and find the particular value Q^* of Q at which the elasticity is equal to -1.

   (c) Show that the marginal revenue is 0 at Q^*.

6. With reference to Example 1, let

$$R(Q) = PQ \quad \text{and} \quad C(Q) = aQ^b + c$$

where P, a, b, and c are positive constants, and $b > 1$. Find the value of Q that maximizes the profit

$$\pi(Q) = PQ - (aQ^b + c)$$

Make use of Theorem 8.2.2.

8.6   Local Extreme Points

So far this chapter has discussed what are often referred to as *global* optimization problems. The reason for this terminology is that we have been seeking the largest or smallest values of a function when we compare the function values "globally"—that is, at *all* points in the domain without exception. In applied optimization problems, especially those arising in economics, it is usually these **global** (or **absolute**) maxima and minima that are of interest. However, sometimes one is interested in the local maxima and minima of a function. In this case, we compare the function value at the point in question only with alternative function values at nearby points.

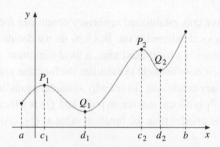

Figure 1 c_1, c_2, and b are local maximum points; a, d_1, and d_2 are local minimum points

Consider Fig. 1 and think of the graph as representing the profile of a landscape. Then the mountain tops P_1 and P_2 represent local maxima, whereas the valley bottoms Q_1 and Q_2 represent local minima. The precise definitions are as follows:

The function f has a **local (or relative) maximum (minimum)** at c, if there exists an interval (α, β) about c such that $f(x) \leq (\geq) f(c)$ for all x in (α, β) which are in the domain of f.   (1)

NOTE 1   These definitions imply that point a in Fig. 1 is a local minimum point, while b is a local (and global) maximum point. Some authors restrict the definition of local maximum/minimum points only to *interior* points of the domain of the function. According to this definition, a global maximum point that is not an interior point of the domain is not a local maximum point. It seems desirable that a global maximum/minimum point should always be a local maximum/minimum point as well, so we stick to definition (1).

Function values corresponding to local maximum (minimum) points are called **local maximum (minimum) values**. As collective names we use **local extreme points** and **local extreme values**.

In searching for (global) maximum and minimum points, Theorem 8.1.1 was very useful. Actually, the same result is valid for local extreme points: *At a local extreme point in the interior of the domain of a differentiable function, the derivative must be zero.* This is clear if we recall that the proof of Theorem 8.1.1 needed to consider the behaviour of the function in only a small interval about the optimal point. Consequently, in order to find possible local maxima and minima for a function f defined in an interval I, we can again search among the following types of point:

(i) Interior points in I where $f'(x) = 0$

(ii) End points of I (if included in I)

(iii) Interior points in I where f' does not exist

We have thus established *necessary* conditions for a function f defined in an interval I to have a local extreme point. But how do we decide whether a point satisfying the necessary conditions is a local maximum, a local minimum, or neither? In contrast to global extreme points, it does not help to calculate the function value at the different points satisfying these necessary conditions. To see why, consider again the function whose graph is given in Fig. 1. Point P_1 is a local maximum point and Q_2 is a local minimum point, but the function value at P_1 is *smaller* than the function value at Q_2. (Point Q_2 is higher than P_1.)

The First-Derivative Test

There are two main ways of determining whether a given stationary point is a local maximum, a local minimum, or neither. One of them is based on studying the sign of the first derivative about the stationary point, and is an easy modification of Theorem 8.2.1.

THEOREM 8.6.1   (FIRST-DERIVATIVE TEST FOR LOCAL EXTREME POINTS)

Suppose c is a stationary point for $y = f(x)$.

(a) If $f'(x) \geq 0$ throughout some interval (a, c) to the left of c and $f'(x) \leq 0$ throughout some interval (c, b) to the right of c, then $x = c$ is a local maximum point for f.

(b) If $f'(x) \leq 0$ throughout some interval (a, c) to the left of c and $f'(x) \geq 0$ throughout some interval (c, b) to the right of c, then $x = c$ is a local minimum point for f.

(c) If $f'(x) > 0$ both throughout some interval (a, c) to the left of c and throughout some interval (c, b) to the right of c, then $x = c$ is not a local extreme point for f. The same conclusion holds if $f'(x) < 0$ on both sides of c.

Only case (c) is not already covered by Theorem 8.2.1. In fact, if $f'(x) > 0$ in (a, c) and also in (c, b), then $f(x)$ is strictly increasing in $(a, c]$ as well as in $[c, b)$. Then $x = c$ cannot be a local extreme point.

EXAMPLE 1   Classify the stationary points of $f(x) = \frac{1}{9}x^3 - \frac{1}{6}x^2 - \frac{2}{3}x + 1$.

Solution: We get $f'(x) = \frac{1}{3}(x+1)(x-2)$, so $x = -1$ and $x = 2$ are the stationary points. The sign diagram for $f'(x)$ is:

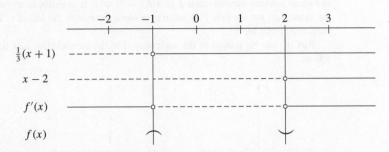

We conclude from this sign diagram that $x = -1$ is a local maximum point whereas $x = 2$ is a local minimum point.

EXAMPLE 2   Classify the stationary points of $f(x) = x^2 e^x$.

Solution: Differentiating, we get $f'(x) = 2xe^x + x^2 e^x = xe^x(2+x)$. Then $f'(x) = 0$ for $x = 0$ and for $x = -2$. A sign diagram shows that f has a local maximum point at $x = -2$ and a local (and global) minimum point at $x = 0$. (The graph of f is given in Fig. A4.R.9 in the answer section.)

The Second-Derivative Test

For most problems of practical interest in which an explicit function is specified, the first-derivative test on its own will determine whether a stationary point is a local maximum, a local minimum, or neither. Note that the theorem requires knowing the sign of $f'(x)$ at points both to the left and to the right of the given stationary point. The next test requires knowing the first two derivatives of the function, but only at the stationary point itself.

THEOREM 8.6.2 (SECOND-DERIVATIVE TEST)

Let f be a twice differentiable function in an interval I, and let c be an interior point of I. Then:

(a) $f'(c) = 0$ and $f''(c) < 0 \implies x = c$ is a strict local maximum point.

(b) $f'(c) = 0$ and $f''(c) > 0 \implies x = c$ is a strict local minimum point.

(c) $f'(c) = 0$ and $f''(c) = 0 \implies$?

Proof: To prove part (a), assume $f'(c) = 0$ and $f''(c) < 0$. By definition of $f''(c)$ as the derivative of $f'(x)$ at c,

$$f''(c) = \lim_{h \to 0} \frac{f'(c + h) - f'(c)}{h} = \lim_{h \to 0} \frac{f'(c + h)}{h}$$

Because $f''(c) < 0$, it follows that $f'(c + h)/h < 0$ if $|h|$ is sufficiently small. In particular, if h is a small positive number, then $f'(c + h) < 0$, so f' is negative in an interval to the right of c. In the same way, we see that f' is positive in some interval to the left of c. But then c is a strict local maximum point for f.

Part (b) can be proved in the same way. For the inconclusive part (c), see the comments that follow. ∎

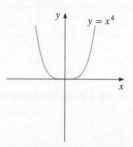

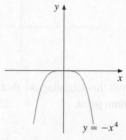

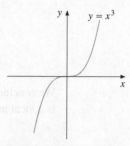

Figure 2 $f'(0) = f''(0) = 0$, and 0 is a minimum point

Figure 3 $f'(0) = f''(0) = 0$, and 0 is a maximum point

Figure 4 $f'(0) = f''(0) = 0$, and 0 is an inflection point

The theorem leaves unsettled case (c) where $f'(c) = f''(c) = 0$. Then "anything" can happen. Each of three functions $f(x) = x^4$, $f(x) = -x^4$, and $f(x) = x^3$ satisfies $f'(0) = f''(0) = 0$. At $x = 0$, they have, as shown in Figs. 2 to 4 respectively, a minimum, a maximum, and what in Section 8.7 will be called a point of inflection. Usually (as here), the first-derivative test can be used to classify stationary points at which $f'(c) = f''(c) = 0$.

EXAMPLE 3   Classify the stationary points of

$$f(x) = \tfrac{1}{9}x^3 - \tfrac{1}{6}x^2 - \tfrac{2}{3}x + 1$$

by using the second-derivative test.

Solution: We saw in Example 1 that $f'(x) = \tfrac{1}{3}x^2 - \tfrac{1}{3}x - \tfrac{2}{3} = \tfrac{1}{3}(x + 1)(x - 2)$, with two stationary points $x = -1$ and $x = 2$. Furthermore, $f''(x) = \tfrac{2}{3}x - \tfrac{1}{3}$, so that $f''(-1) = -1$ and $f''(2) = 1$. From Theorem 8.6.2 it follows that $x = -1$ is a local maximum point and $x = 2$ is a local minimum point. This confirms the results in Example 1.

EXAMPLE 4   Classify the stationary points of $f(x) = x^2 e^x$ by using the second-derivative test.

Solution: From Example 2, $f'(x) = 2xe^x + x^2 e^x$, with $x = 0$ and $x = -2$ as the two stationary points. The second derivative of f is

$$f''(x) = 2e^x + 2xe^x + 2xe^x + x^2 e^x = e^x(2 + 4x + x^2)$$

We find that $f''(0) = 2 > 0$ and $f''(-2) = -2e^{-2} < 0$. From Theorem 8.6.2 it follows that $x = 0$ is a local minimum point and $x = -2$ is a local maximum point. This confirms the results in Example 2.

Theorem 8.6.2 can be used to obtain a useful necessary condition for local extrema. Suppose that f is twice differentiable in the interval I and that c is an interior point of I where there is a local maximum. Then $f'(c) = 0$. Moreover, $f''(c) > 0$ is impossible, because by Theorem 8.6.2(b) this inequality would imply that c is a strict local minimum. Hence, $f''(c)$ has to be ≤ 0. In the same way, we see that $f''(c) \geq 0$ is a necessary condition for local minimum. Briefly formulated:

$$c \text{ is a local maximum for } f \implies f''(c) \leq 0 \tag{2}$$

$$c \text{ is a local minimum for } f \implies f''(c) \geq 0 \tag{3}$$

Many results in economic analysis rely on postulating an appropriate sign for the second derivative rather than suitable variations in the sign of the first derivative.

EXAMPLE 5   Suppose that the firm in Example 8.5.1 faces a sales tax of t dollars per unit. The firm's profit from producing and selling Q units is then

$$\pi(Q) = R(Q) - C(Q) - tQ$$

In order to maximize profits at some quantity Q^* satisfying $0 < Q^* < \bar{Q}$, one must have $\pi'(Q^*) = 0$. Hence,

$$R'(Q^*) - C'(Q^*) - t = 0 \tag{$*$}$$

Suppose $R''(Q^*) < 0$ and $C''(Q^*) > 0$. Equation $(*)$ implicitly defines Q^* as a differentiable function of t. Find an expression for dQ^*/dt and discuss its sign. Also compute the derivative w.r.t. t of the optimal value $\pi(Q^*)$ of the profit function, and show that $d\pi(Q^*)/dt = -Q^*$.

Solution: Differentiating $(*)$ with respect to t yields

$$R''(Q^*)\frac{dQ^*}{dt} - C''(Q^*)\frac{dQ^*}{dt} - 1 = 0$$

Solving for dQ^*/dt gives

$$\frac{dQ^*}{dt} = \frac{1}{R''(Q^*) - C''(Q^*)} \tag{$**$}$$

The sign assumptions on R'' and C'' imply that $dQ^*/dt < 0$. Thus, the optimal number of units produced will decline if the tax rate t increases.

The optimal value of the profit function is $\pi(Q^*) = R(Q^*) - C(Q^*) - tQ^*$. Taking into account the dependence of Q^* on t, we get

$$\frac{d\pi(Q^*)}{dt} = R'(Q^*)\frac{dQ^*}{dt} - C'(Q^*)\frac{dQ^*}{dt} - Q^* - t\frac{dQ^*}{dt}$$

$$= \left[R'(Q^*) - C'(Q^*) - t \right]\frac{dQ^*}{dt} - Q^* = -Q^*$$

Note how the square bracket disappears from this last expression because of the first-order condition $(*)$. This is an instance of the "envelope theorem", which will be discussed in Section 14.7. For each 1 cent increase in the sales tax, profit decreases by approximately Q^* cents, where Q^* is the number of units produced at the optimum.

PROBLEMS FOR SECTION 8.6

1. Consider the function f defined for all x by $f(x) = x^3 - 12x$. Find the stationary points of f and classify them by using both the first- and second-derivative tests.

(SM) **2.** Determine possible local extreme points and values for the following functions:

(a) $f(x) = -2x - 1$ (b) $f(x) = x^3 - 3x + 8$ (c) $f(x) = x + \dfrac{1}{x}$

(d) $f(x) = x^5 - 5x^3$ (e) $f(x) = \frac{1}{2}x^2 - 3x + 5$ (f) $f(x) = x^3 + 3x^2 - 2$

(SM) **3.** A function f is given by the formula

$$f(x) = \left(1 + \frac{2}{x}\right)\sqrt{x + 6}$$

(a) Find the domain of f and the intervals where $f(x)$ is positive.

(b) Find possible local extreme points.

(c) Examine $f(x)$ as $x \to 0^-$, $x \to 0^+$, and $x \to \infty$. Also determine the limit of $f'(x)$ as $x \to \infty$. Does f have a maximum or a minimum in the domain?

4. Figure 5 graphs the *derivative* of a function f. Which of the points a, b, c, d, and e are local maximum points for f, local minimum points for f, or neither?

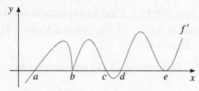

Figure 5

5. What requirements must be imposed on the constants a, b, and c in order that

$$f(x) = x^3 + ax^2 + bx + c$$

(a) will have a local minimum at $x = 0$?

(b) will have stationary points at $x = 1$ and $x = 3$?

6. Find the local extreme points of   (a) $f(x) = x^3 e^x$ (b) $g(x) = x^2 2^x$.

HARDER PROBLEM

(SM) **7.** Find the local extreme points of

$$f(x) = x^3 + ax + b$$

Use the answer to show that the equation $f(x) = 0$ has three different real roots if and only if $4a^3 + 27b^2 < 0$.

8.7 Inflection Points

Recall that in Section 6.9 we defined a twice differentiable function $f(x)$ to be concave (convex) in an interval I if $f''(x) \leq 0 \, (\geq)$ for all x in I. Points at which a function changes from being convex to being concave, or *vice versa*, are called **inflection points**. For twice differentiable functions they can be defined this way:

INFLECTION POINTS

The point c is called an **inflection point** for the function f if there exists an interval (a, b) about c such that:

(a) $f''(x) \geq 0$ in (a, c) and $f''(x) \leq 0$ in (c, b), \hfill (1)

or

(b) $f''(x) \leq 0$ in (a, c) and $f''(x) \geq 0$ in (c, b).

Briefly, $x = c$ is an inflection point if $f''(x)$ *changes sign* at $x = c$. Then we also refer to the point $(c, f(c))$ as an inflection point on the graph. Figure 1 gives an example.

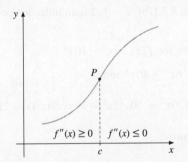

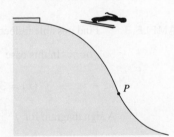

Figure 1 Point P is an inflection point on the graph $(x = c$ is an inflection point for the function)

Figure 2 The point P, where the slope is steepest, is an inflection point

Figure 2 shows the profile of a ski jump. Point P, where the slope is steepest, is an inflection point.

When looking for possible inflection points of a function, we usually use part (b) in the following theorem:

THEOREM 8.7.1 (TEST FOR INFLECTION POINTS)

Let f be a function with a continuous second derivative in an interval I, and let c be an interior point of I.

(a) If c is an inflection point for f, then $f''(c) = 0$.

(b) If $f''(c) = 0$ and f'' changes sign at c, then c is an inflection point for f.

Proof:

(a) Because $f''(x) \leq 0$ on one side of c and $f''(x) \geq 0$ on the other, and because f'' is continuous, it must be true that $f''(c) = 0$.

(b) If f'' changes sign at c, then c is an inflection point for f, according to (1).   ∎

This theorem implies that $f''(c) = 0$ is a *necessary* condition for c to be an inflection point. It is not a sufficient condition, however, because $f''(c) = 0$ does not imply that f'' changes sign at $x = c$. A typical case is given in the next example.

EXAMPLE 1   Show that $f(x) = x^4$ does not have an inflection point at $x = 0$, even though $f''(0) = 0$.

Solution: Here $f'(x) = 4x^3$ and $f''(x) = 12x^2$, so that $f''(0) = 0$. But $f''(x) > 0$ for all $x \neq 0$, and so f'' does not change sign at $x = 0$. Hence, $x = 0$ is not an inflection point. (In fact, it is a global minimum, of course, as shown in Fig. 8.6.2.)

EXAMPLE 2   Find possible inflection points for $f(x) = \frac{1}{9}x^3 - \frac{1}{6}x^2 - \frac{2}{3}x + 1$.

Solution: From Example 3 in the previous section we find that $f''(x) = \frac{2}{3}x - \frac{1}{3} = \frac{2}{3}\left(x - \frac{1}{2}\right)$. Hence, $f''(x) \leq 0$ for $x \leq 1/2$, whereas $f''(1/2) = 0$ and $f''(x) \geq 0$ for $x > 1/2$. According to Theorem 8.7.1(b), $x = 1/2$ is an inflection point for f.

EXAMPLE 3   Find possible inflection points for $f(x) = x^6 - 10x^4$.

Solution: In this case $f'(x) = 6x^5 - 40x^3$ and

$$f''(x) = 30x^4 - 120x^2 = 30x^2(x^2 - 4) = 30x^2(x - 2)(x + 2)$$

A sign diagram for f'' is as follows:

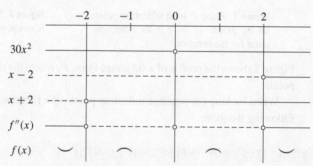

From the sign diagram we see that f'' changes sign at $x = -2$ and at $x = 2$, so these are inflection points. Since f'' does not change sign at $x = 0$, it is not an inflection point, even though $f''(0) = 0$.

Economic models often involve functions having inflection points. The cost function in Fig. 4.7.2 is a typical example. Here is another.

EXAMPLE 4   A firm produces a commodity using only one input. Let $x = f(v)$, $v \geq 0$, be the maximum output obtainable when v units of the input are used. Then f is called a **production function**. It is often assumed that the function is "S-shaped". That is, the marginal product $f'(v)$ is increasing up to a certain production level v_0, and then decreasing. Such a production function is indicated in Fig. 3. If f is twice differentiable, then $f''(v)$ is ≥ 0 in $[0, v_0]$ and ≤ 0 in $[v_0, \infty)$. Hence, f is first convex and then concave, with v_0 as an inflection point. Note that at v_0 a unit increase in input gives the maximum increase in output.

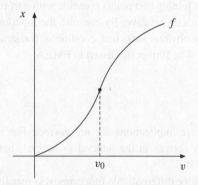

Figure 3 f is an S-shaped production function; v_0 is an inflection point

More General Definitions of Concave and Convex Functions

So far the convexity and concavity properties of functions have been defined by looking at the sign of the second derivative. An alternative geometric characterization of convexity and concavity suggests a more general definition that is valid even for functions that are not differentiable.

A function f is called **concave (convex)** if the line segment joining any two points on the graph is below (above) the graph, or on the graph.

(2)

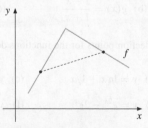

Figure 4 f is concave

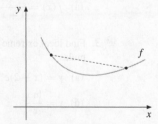

Figure 5 f is convex

These definitions are illustrated in Figs. 4 and 5. Because the graph has a "corner" in Fig. 4, this function is not even differentiable, let alone twice differentiable. For twice differentiable functions, however, one can prove that (2) is equivalent to the definitions in (6.9.3).

In order to use definition (2) to examine the convexity/concavity of a given function, we need an algebraic formulation. This will be discussed in FMEA.

Strictly Concave and Strictly Convex Functions

A function f is called **strictly concave (convex)** if the line segment joining any two points on the graph is strictly below (above) the graph (except at the end points of the segment). For instance, the function whose graph is shown in Fig. 4 has two linear pieces, on which line segments joining two points coincide with part of the graph. Thus this function is concave, but not strictly concave. By contrast, the function graphed in Fig. 5 is strictly convex.

Fairly obvious sufficient conditions for strict concavity/convexity are the following, which will be further discussed in FMEA:

$$f''(x) < 0 \text{ for all } x \in (a, b) \implies f(x) \text{ is strictly concave in } (a, b)$$
$$f''(x) > 0 \text{ for all } x \in (a, b) \implies f(x) \text{ is strictly convex in } (a, b)$$

$$(3)$$

The reverse implications are not correct. For instance, one can prove that $f(x) = x^4$ is strictly convex in the interval $(-\infty, \infty)$, but $f''(x)$ is not > 0 everywhere, because $f''(0) = 0$.

For twice differentiable functions, it is usually much easier to check concavity/convexity by considering the sign of the second derivative than by using the definitions in (2). However, in theoretical arguments, the definitions in (2) are often very useful, especially because they generalize easily to functions of several variables. (See FMEA.)

PROBLEMS FOR SECTION 8.7

1. Let f be defined for all x by $f(x) = x^3 + \frac{3}{2}x^2 - 6x + 10$.

   (a) Find the stationary points of f and determine the intervals where f increases.

   (b) Find the inflection point for f.

2. Decide where the following functions are convex and determine possible inflection points:

   (a) $f(x) = \dfrac{x}{1 + x^2}$

   (b) $g(x) = \dfrac{1 - x}{1 + x}$

   (c) $h(x) = xe^x$

SM 3. Find local extreme points and inflection points for the functions defined by the following formulas:

   (a) $y = (x + 2)e^{-x}$

   (b) $y = \ln x + 1/x$

   (c) $y = x^3 e^{-x}$

   (d) $y = \dfrac{\ln x}{x^2}$

   (e) $y = e^{2x} - 2e^x$

   (f) $y = (x^2 + 2x)e^{-x}$

4. (a) A competitive firm receives a price p for each unit of its output, and pays a price w for each unit of its only variable input. It also incurs set-up costs of F. Its output from using x units of variable input is $f(x) = \sqrt{x}$. Determine the firm's revenue, cost, and profit functions.

   (b) Write the first-order condition for profit maximization, and give it an economic interpretation. Check whether profit really is maximized at a point satisfying the first-order condition.

5. Find the extreme points and inflection points of the function f whose graph is given in Fig. 6.

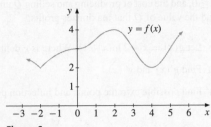

Figure 6

6. Find numbers a and b such that the graph of $f(x) = ax^3 + bx^2$ passes through $(-1, 1)$ and has an inflection point at $x = 1/2$.

7. Find the intervals where the following cubic cost function, defined for $x \geq 0$, is convex and where it is concave. Find also the unique inflection point.

$$C(x) = ax^3 + bx^2 + cx + d, \qquad a > 0, \quad b < 0, \quad c > 0, \quad d > 0$$

8. Use the same coordinate system to draw the graphs of two concave functions f and g, both defined for all x. Let the function h be defined by

$$h(x) = \min\{f(x), g(x)\}$$

(For each given x, the number $h(x)$ is the smaller of $f(x)$ and $g(x)$.) Draw the graph of h and explain why it is also concave.

REVIEW PROBLEMS FOR CHAPTER 8

1. (a) Let $f(x) = \dfrac{x^2}{x^2 + 2}$. Compute $f'(x)$ and determine where $f(x)$ is increasing/decreasing.

   (b) Find possible inflection points.

   (c) Determine the limit of $f(x)$ as $x \to \pm\infty$, and sketch the graph of $f(x)$.

2. A firm's production function is $Q(L) = 12L^2 - \frac{1}{20}L^3$, where L denotes the number of workers, with $L \in [0, 200]$.

   (a) What size of the work force (L^*) maximizes output $Q(L)$? What size of the work force (L^{**}) maximizes output per worker, $Q(L)/L$?

   (b) Note that $Q'(L^{**}) = Q(L^{**})/L^{**}$. Is this a coincidence?

3. A farmer has 1000 metres of fence wire with which to make a rectangular enclosure, as in Problem 4.6.7. This time, however, one side of the enclosure will be a straight river bank, along which no fencing is needed. What should be the dimensions of the enclosure in order to maximize area?

4. By producing and selling Q units of some commodity a firm earns total revenue $R(Q) = -0.0016Q^2 + 44Q$ and incurs cost $C(Q) = 0.0004Q^2 + 8Q + 64\,000$.

   (a) What production level Q^* maximizes profits?

   (b) The elasticity $\mathrm{El}_Q C(Q) \approx 0.12$ for $Q = 1000$. Interpret this result.

5. The price P per unit obtained by a firm in producing and selling Q units is $P = a - bQ^2$, $Q \geq 0$, and the cost of producing and selling Q units is $C = \alpha - \beta Q$. All constants are positive. Find the value of Q that maximizes profits.

6. (a) Let $g(x) = x - 2\ln(x + 1)$. Where is g defined?

   (b) Find $g'(x)$ and $g''(x)$.

   (c) Find possible extreme points and inflection points. Sketch the graph.

7. Let $f(x) = \ln(x + 1) - x + \dfrac{x^2}{2} - \dfrac{x^3}{6}$.

   (a) Find the domain D_f and prove that $f'(x) = \dfrac{x^2 - x^3}{2(x + 1)}$ for $x \in D_f$.

   (b) Find possible extreme points and inflection points.

   (c) Check $f(x)$ as $x \to (-1)^+$, and sketch the graph on the interval $(-1, 2]$.

⑤Ⓜ 8. Consider the function h defined for all x by $h(x) = \dfrac{e^x}{2 + e^{2x}}$.

   (a) Where is h increasing/decreasing? Find possible maximum and minimum points for h.

   (b) Why does h defined on $(-\infty, 0]$ have an inverse? Find an expression for the inverse function.

9. Let $f(x) = \left(e^{2x} + 4e^{-x}\right)^2$.

   (a) Find $f'(x)$ and $f''(x)$.

   (b) Determine where f is increasing/decreasing, and show that f is convex.

   (c) Find possible global extreme points for f.

HARDER PROBLEMS

⑤Ⓜ 10. (a) Consider the function

$$f(x) = \frac{x}{\sqrt[3]{x^2 - a}} \quad (a > 0)$$

   Find the domain D_f of f and the intervals where $f(x)$ is positive. Show that the graph of f is symmetric about the origin.

   (b) Where is f increasing and where is it decreasing? Find possible local extreme points.

   (c) Find possible inflection points for f.

⑤Ⓜ 11. Classify the stationary points of $f(x) = \dfrac{6x^3}{x^4 + x^2 + 2}$ by using the first-derivative test. Sketch the graph of f.

9

INTEGRATION

The main topic of the preceding three chapters was differentiation, which can be directly applied to many interesting economic problems. Economists, however, especially when doing statistics, often face the mathematical problem of finding a function from information about its derivative. This process of reconstructing a function from its derivative can be regarded as the "inverse" of differentiation. Mathematicians call this *integration*.

There are simple formulas that have been known since ancient times for calculating the area of any triangle, and so of any polygon that, by definition, is entirely bounded by straight lines. Over 4000 years ago, however, the Babylonians were concerned with accurately measuring the area of plane surfaces, like circles, that are not bounded by straight lines. Solving this kind of area problem is intimately related to integration, as will be explained in Section 9.2.

Apart from providing an introduction to integration, this chapter will also discuss some important applications of integrals that economists are expected to know. A brief introduction to some simple differential equations concludes the chapter.

9.1 Indefinite Integrals

Suppose we do not know the function F, but we have been told that its derivative is equal to x^2, so that $F'(x) = x^2$. What is F? Since the derivative of x^3 is $3x^2$, we see that $\frac{1}{3}x^3$ has x^2 as its derivative. But so does $\frac{1}{3}x^3 + C$ where C is an arbitrary constant, since additive constants disappear with differentiation.

In fact, let $G(x)$ denote an arbitrary function having x^2 as its derivative. Then the derivative of $G(x) - \frac{1}{3}x^3$ is equal to 0 for all x. But a function that has derivative equal to 0 for all x must be constant. (See (6.3.3).)

This shows that

$$F'(x) = x^2 \iff F(x) = \tfrac{1}{3}x^3 + C$$

with C as an arbitrary constant.

EXAMPLE 1   Assume that the marginal cost function of a firm is

$$C'(x) = 2x^2 + 2x + 5$$

and that the fixed costs are 100. Find the cost function $C(x)$.

Solution: Considering separately each of the three terms in the expression for $C'(x)$, we realize that the cost function must have the form $C(x) = \frac{2}{3}x^3 + x^2 + 5x + c$, because if we differentiate this function we obtain precisely $2x^2 + 2x + 5$. But the fixed costs are 100, which means that $C(0) = 100$. Inserting $x = 0$ into the proposed formula for $C(x)$ yields $c = 100$. Hence, the required cost function must be

$$C(x) = \frac{2}{3}x^3 + x^2 + 5x + 100$$

Suppose $f(x)$ and $F(x)$ are two functions of x having the property that $f(x) = F'(x)$ for all x in some interval I. We pass from F to f by taking the derivative, so the reverse process of passing from f to F could appropriately be called taking the **antiderivative**. But following usual mathematical practice, we call F an **indefinite integral** of f over the interval I, and denote it by $\int f(x)\,dx$. Two functions having the same derivative throughout an interval must differ by a constant, so:

DEFINITION OF THE INDEFINITE INTEGRAL

$$\int f(x)\,dx = F(x) + C \quad \text{when} \quad F'(x) = f(x) \quad (C \text{ is an arbitrary constant}) \qquad (1)$$

For instance, the solution to Example 1 implies that

$$\int (2x^2 + 2x + 5)\,dx = \frac{2}{3}x^3 + x^2 + 5x + C$$

The symbol $\int$ is the **integral sign**, and the function $f(x)$ appearing in (1) is the **integrand**. Then we write dx to indicate that x is the **variable of integration**. Finally, C is a **constant of integration**. We read (1) this way: The indefinite integral of $f(x)$ w.r.t. x is $F(x)$ plus a constant. We call it an *indefinite* integral because $F(x) + C$ is not to be regarded as one definite function, but as a whole class of functions, all having the same derivative f.

Differentiating each side of (1) shows directly that

$$\frac{d}{dx} \int f(x)\,dx = f(x) \qquad (2)$$

i.e., that the derivative of an indefinite integral equals the integrand. Also, (1) can obviously be rewritten as

$$\int F'(x)\,dx = F(x) + C \qquad (3)$$

Thus, *integration and differentiation cancel each other out.*

Some Important Integrals

There are some important integration formulas which follow immediately from the corresponding rules for differentiation.

Let a be a fixed number $\neq -1$. Because the derivative of $x^{a+1}/(a+1)$ is x^a, one has

$$\int x^a \, dx = \frac{1}{a+1} x^{a+1} + C \qquad (a \neq -1) \tag{4}$$

This very important result states that the indefinite integral of any power of x (except x^{-1}) is obtained by increasing the exponent of x by 1, then dividing by the new exponent, and finally adding a constant of integration. Here are three prominent examples.

EXAMPLE 2

(a) $\displaystyle \int x \, dx = \int x^1 \, dx = \frac{1}{1+1} x^{1+1} + C = \frac{1}{2} x^2 + C$

(b) $\displaystyle \int \frac{1}{x^3} \, dx = \int x^{-3} \, dx = \frac{1}{-3+1} x^{-3+1} + C = -\frac{1}{2x^2} + C$

(c) $\displaystyle \int \sqrt{x} \, dx = \int x^{1/2} \, dx = \frac{1}{\frac{1}{2}+1} x^{\frac{1}{2}+1} + C = \frac{2}{3} x^{3/2} + C$

When $a = -1$, the formula in (4) is not valid, because the right-hand side involves division by zero and so becomes meaningless. The integrand is then $1/x$, and the problem is thus to find a function having $1/x$ as its derivative. Now $\ln x$ has this property, but it is only defined for $x > 0$. Note, however, that $\ln(-x)$ is defined for $x < 0$, and according to the chain rule, its derivative is $[1/(-x)](-1) = 1/x$. Recall too that $|x| = x$ when $x \geq 0$ and $|x| = -x$ when $x < 0$. Thus, whether $x > 0$ or $x < 0$, we have

$$\int \frac{1}{x} \, dx = \ln |x| + C \tag{5}$$

Consider next the exponential function. The derivative of e^x is e^x. Thus $\int e^x \, dx = e^x + C$. More generally,

$$\int e^{ax} \, dx = \frac{1}{a} e^{ax} + C \qquad (a \neq 0) \tag{6}$$

because the derivative of $(1/a)e^{ax}$ is e^{ax}. For $a > 0$ we can write $a^x = e^{(\ln a)x}$. As a special case of (6), when $\ln a \neq 0$ because $a \neq 1$, we obtain

$$\int a^x \, dx = \frac{1}{\ln a} a^x + C \qquad (a > 0 \text{ and } a \neq 1) \tag{7}$$

The above were examples of how knowing the derivative of a function given by a formula automatically gives us a corresponding indefinite integral. Indeed, suppose it were possible to construct a complete table with every formula that we knew how to differentiate in the first column, and the corresponding derivative in the second column. For example, corresponding to the entry $y = x^2 e^x$ in the first column, there would be $y' = 2xe^x + x^2 e^x$ in the second column. Because integration is the reverse of differentiation, we infer the corresponding integration result that $\int (2xe^x + x^2 e^x)\, dx = x^2 e^x + C$ for a constant C.

Even after this superhuman effort, you would look in vain for e^{-x^2} in the second column of this table. The reason is that there is no "elementary" function that has e^{-x^2} as its derivative. (See Section 9.3.) Indeed, the integral of e^{-x^2} is a new special "error function" that plays a prominent role in statistics because of its relationship to the "normal distribution"—see Problem 4.9.5.

Using the proper rules systematically allows us to *differentiate* very complicated functions. On the other hand, finding the indefinite integral of even quite simple functions can be very difficult, or even impossible. Where it is possible, mathematicians have developed a number of *integration methods* to help in the task. Some of these methods will be explained in the rest of this chapter.

It is usually quite easy, however, to check whether a proposed indefinite integral is correct. We simply differentiate the proposed function to see if its derivative really is equal to the integrand.

EXAMPLE 3   Verify that for $x > 0$, $\displaystyle\int \ln x \, dx = x \ln x - x + C$.

Solution: We put $F(x) = x \ln x - x + C$. Then $F'(x) = 1 \cdot \ln x + x \cdot (1/x) - 1 = \ln x + 1 - 1 = \ln x$, which shows that the integral formula is correct.

Some General Rules

The two differentiation rules $(aF(x))' = aF'(x)$ and $(F(x) + G(x))' = F'(x) + G'(x)$ immediately imply the following integration rules

$$\int af(x)\, dx = a \int f(x)\, dx \qquad (a \text{ is a constant}) \tag{8}$$

$$\int [f(x) + g(x)]\, dx = \int f(x)\, dx + \int g(x)\, dx \tag{9}$$

The first of these rules says that a constant factor can be moved outside the integral, while the other shows that the integral of a sum is the sum of the integrals.

Repeated use of these properties yields the general rule:

$$\int [a_1 f_1(x) + \cdots + a_n f_n(x)]\, dx = a_1 \int f_1(x)\, dx + \cdots + a_n \int f_n(x)\, dx \tag{10}$$

EXAMPLE 4   Use rule (10) to evaluate   (a) $\displaystyle\int (3x^4 + 5x^2 + 2)\, dx$ (b) $\displaystyle\int \left(\frac{3}{x} - 8e^{-4x}\right) dx$

Solution:

(a)
$$\int (3x^4 + 5x^2 + 2)\,dx = 3\int x^4\,dx + 5\int x^2\,dx + 2\int 1\,dx$$
$$= 3\left(\tfrac{1}{5}x^5 + C_1\right) + 5\left(\tfrac{1}{3}x^3 + C_2\right) + 2(x + C_3)$$
$$= \tfrac{3}{5}x^5 + \tfrac{5}{3}x^3 + 2x + 3C_1 + 5C_2 + 2C_3$$
$$= \tfrac{3}{5}x^5 + \tfrac{5}{3}x^3 + 2x + C$$

Because C_1, C_2, and C_3 are arbitrary constants, $3C_1 + 5C_2 + 2C_3$ is also an arbitrary constant. So in the last line we have replaced it by just one constant C. In future examples of this kind, we will usually drop the two middle lines of the displayed equations.

(b) $\displaystyle \int \left(\frac{3}{x} - 8e^{-4x}\right) dx = 3\int \frac{1}{x}\,dx + (-8)\int e^{-4x}\,dx = 3\ln|x| + 2e^{-4x} + C$

So far, we have always used x as the variable of integration. In applications, the variables often have other labels, but this makes no difference to the rules of integration.

EXAMPLE 5   Evaluate: (a) $\displaystyle \int \frac{B}{r^{2.5}}\,dr$ (b) $\displaystyle \int (a + bq + cq^2)\,dq$ (c) $\displaystyle \int (1+t)^5\,dt$

Solution:

(a) Writing $B/r^{2.5}$ as $Br^{-2.5}$, formula (4) can be used with r replacing x, and so

$$\int \frac{B}{r^{2.5}}\,dr = B\int r^{-2.5}\,dr = B\frac{1}{-2.5+1}r^{-2.5+1} + C = -\frac{B}{1.5r^{1.5}} + C$$

(b) $\displaystyle \int (a + bq + cq^2)\,dq = aq + \tfrac{1}{2}bq^2 + \tfrac{1}{3}cq^3 + C$

(c) $\displaystyle \int (1+t)^5\,dt = \tfrac{1}{6}(1+t)^6 + C$

PROBLEMS FOR SECTION 9.1

1. Find the following integrals by using (4):

(a) $\displaystyle \int x^{13}\,dx$ (b) $\displaystyle \int x\sqrt{x}\,dx$ (c) $\displaystyle \int \frac{1}{\sqrt{x}}\,dx$ (d) $\displaystyle \int \sqrt{x\sqrt{x\sqrt{x}}}\,dx$

2. Find the following integrals:

(a) $\displaystyle \int e^{-x}\,dx$ (b) $\displaystyle \int e^{\frac{1}{4}x}\,dx$ (c) $\displaystyle \int 3e^{-2x}\,dx$ (d) $\displaystyle \int 2^x\,dx$

3. In the manufacture of a product, the marginal cost of producing x units is $C'(x)$ and fixed costs are $C(0)$. Find the total cost function $C(x)$ when:

(a) $C'(x) = 3x + 4$, $C(0) = 40$ (b) $C'(x) = ax + b$, $C(0) = C_0$

SM **4.** Find the following integrals:

(a) $\int (t^3 + 2t - 3)\,dt$ (b) $\int (x-1)^2\,dx$ (c) $\int (x-1)(x+2)\,dx$

(d) $\int (x+2)^3\,dx$ (e) $\int \left(e^{3x} - e^{2x} + e^x\right)dx$ (f) $\int \dfrac{x^3 - 3x + 4}{x}\,dx$

SM **5.** Find the following integrals: (a) $\int \dfrac{(y-2)^2}{\sqrt{y}}\,dy$ (b) $\int \dfrac{x^3}{x+1}\,dx$ (c) $\int x(1+x^2)^{15}\,dx$

(*Hint:* In part (a), first expand $(y-2)^2$, and then divide each term by $\sqrt{y}$. In part (b), do polynomial division as in Section 4.7. In part (c), what is the derivative of $(1+x^2)^{16}$?)

6. Show that

(a) $\int x^2 \ln x\,dx = \frac{1}{3}x^3 \ln x - \frac{1}{9}x^3 + C$

(b) $\int \sqrt{x^2+1}\,dx = \frac{1}{2}x\sqrt{x^2+1} + \frac{1}{2}\ln\left(x + \sqrt{x^2+1}\right) + C$

7. Suppose that $f(0) = 2$ and that the *derivative* of f has the graph given in Fig. 1. Sketch the graph of $f(x)$, and find an explicit function $f(x)$ which has this graph. (Suggest first a formula for $f'(x)$.)

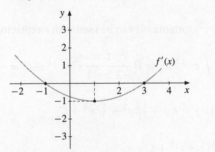

Figure 1 For Problem 7   **Figure 2** For Problem 8

8. Suppose that $f(0) = 0$ and that the *derivative* of f has the graph given in Fig. 2. Sketch the graph of $f(x)$ and find an explicit function $f(x)$ which has this graph.

9. Prove that $\int 2x \ln(x^2 + a^2)\,dx = (x^2 + a^2)\ln(x^2 + a^2) - x^2 + C.$

10. (a) Show that $\int (ax+b)^p\,dx = \dfrac{1}{a(p+1)}(ax+b)^{p+1} + C$ $(a \neq 0,\ p \neq -1)$

(b) Evaluate   (i) $\int (2x+1)^4\,dx$ (ii) $\int \sqrt{x+2}\,dx$ (iii) $\int \dfrac{1}{\sqrt{4-x}}\,dx.$

11. Find $F(x)$ if   (a) $F'(x) = \frac{1}{2}e^x - 2x$ and $F(0) = \frac{1}{2}$;   (b) $F(0) = x(1-x^2)$ and $F(1) = \frac{5}{12}$.

12. Find the general form of a function f whose second derivative, $f''(x)$, is x^2. If we require in addition that $f(0) = 1$ and $f'(0) = -1$, what is $f(x)$?

SM **13.** Suppose that $f''(x) = x^{-2} + x^3 + 2$ for $x > 0$, and $f(1) = 0$, $f'(1) = 1/4$. Find $f(x)$.

9.2 Area and Definite Integrals

This section will show how the concept of the integral can be used to calculate the area of many plane regions. This problem has been important in economics for over 4000 years. Like all major rivers, the Tigris and Euphrates in Mesopotamia (now part of Iraq) and the Nile in Egypt would occasionally change course as a result of severe floods. Some farmers would gain new land from the river, while others would lose land. Since taxes were often assessed on land area, it became necessary to re-calculate the area of a parcel of land whose boundary might be an irregularly shaped river bank.

Rather later, but still around 360 B.C., the Greek mathematician Eudoxos developed a general *method of exhaustion* for determining the areas of irregularly shaped plane regions. The idea was to exhaust the area by inscribing within it an expanding sequence of polygonal regions, whose area can be calculated exactly by summing the areas of a finite collection of triangles. Provided this sequence does indeed "exhaust" the area by including every point in the limit, we can define the *area* of the region as the limit of the increasing sequence of areas of the inscribed polygonal regions.

Eudoxos and Archimedes, amongst others, used the method of exhaustion in order to determine quite accurate approximations to the areas of a number of specific plane regions, especially for a circular disk. (See Example 7.11.1 for an illustration of how this might work.) The method, however, turned out to work only in some special cases, largely because of the algebraic problems encountered. Nearly 1900 years passed after Eudoxos before an exact method could be devised, combining what we now call integration with the new differential calculus due to Newton and Leibniz. Besides allowing areas to be measured with complete accuracy, their ideas have many other applications. Demonstrating the precise logical relationship between differentiation and integration is one of the main achievements of mathematical analysis. It has even been argued that this discovery is the single most important in all of science.

The problem to be considered and solved in this section is illustrated in Fig. 1: *How do we compute the area A under the graph of a continuous and nonnegative function f over the interval [a, b]?*

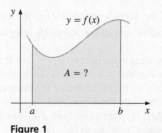

Figure 1

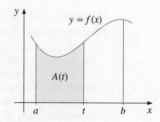

Figure 2

Let t be an arbitrary point in $[a, b]$, and let $A(t)$ denote the area under the curve $y = f(x)$ over the interval $[a, t]$, as shown in Fig. 2. Clearly, $A(a) = 0$, because there is no area from a to a. On the other hand, the area in Fig. 1 is $A = A(b)$. It is obvious from Fig. 2 that, because f is always positive, $A(t)$ increases as t increases. Suppose we increase t by a positive amount Δt. Then $A(t + \Delta t)$ is the area under the curve $y = f(x)$ over the interval $[a, t + \Delta t]$. Hence, $A(t + \Delta t) - A(t)$ is the area ΔA under the curve over the interval $[t, t + \Delta t]$, as shown in Fig. 3.

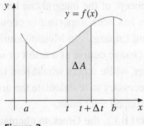

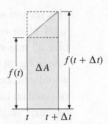

Figure 3   Figure 4

In Fig. 4, the area ΔA has been magnified. It cannot be larger than the area of the rectangle with base Δt and height $f(t + \Delta t)$, nor smaller than the area of the rectangle with base Δt and height $f(t)$. Hence, for all $\Delta t > 0$, one has

$$f(t)\, \Delta t \le A(t + \Delta t) - A(t) \le f(t + \Delta t)\, \Delta t \tag{*}$$

Because $\Delta t > 0$, this implies

$$f(t) \le \frac{A(t + \Delta t) - A(t)}{\Delta t} \le f(t + \Delta t) \tag{**}$$

Let us consider what happens to (**) as $\Delta t \to 0$. The interval $[t, t + \Delta t]$ shrinks to the single point t, and by continuity of f, the value $f(t + \Delta t)$ approaches $f(t)$. The Newton quotient $[A(t + \Delta t) - A(t)]/\Delta t$ is squeezed between $f(t)$ and a quantity $f(t + \Delta t)$ that tends to $f(t)$. This quotient must therefore tend to $f(t)$ in the limit as $\Delta t \to 0$.

So we arrive at the remarkable conclusion that the function $A(t)$, which measures the area under the graph of f over the interval $[a, t]$, is differentiable, with derivative given by

$$A'(t) = f(t) \quad \text{for all } t \text{ in } (a, b) \tag{***}$$

This proves that *the derivative of the area function $A(t)$ is the curve's "height" function $f(t)$, and the area function is therefore one of the indefinite integrals of $f(t)$.*[1]

---

[1] The function f in the figures is increasing in the interval $[t, t + \Delta t]$. It is easy to see that the same conclusion is obtained whenever the function f is continuous on the closed interval $[t, t + \Delta t]$. On the left-hand side of (*), just replace $f(t)$ by $f(c)$, where c is a minimum point of the continuous function f in the interval; and on the right-hand side, replace $f(t + \Delta t)$ by $f(d)$, where d is a maximum point of f in $[t, t + \Delta t]$. By continuity, both $f(c)$ and $f(d)$ must tend to $f(t)$ as $\Delta t \to 0$. So (***) holds also for general continuous functions f.

Let us now use x as the free variable, and suppose that $F(x)$ is an arbitrary indefinite integral of $f(x)$. Then $A(x) = F(x) + C$ for some constant C. Recall that $A(a) = 0$. Hence, $0 = A(a) = F(a) + C$, so $C = -F(a)$. Therefore,

$$A(x) = F(x) - F(a) \quad \text{where} \quad F(x) = \int f(x)\,dx \qquad (1)$$

Suppose $G(x)$ is another function with $G'(x) = f(x)$. Then $G(x) = F(x) + C$ for some constant C, and so $G(x) - G(a) = F(x) + C - (F(a) + C) = F(x) - F(a)$. This argument tells us that the area we compute using (1) is independent of which indefinite integral of f we choose.

EXAMPLE 1   Calculate the area under the parabola $f(x) = x^2$ over the interval $[0, 1]$.

Solution: The area in question is the shaded region in Fig. 5. The area is equal to $A = F(1) - F(0)$ where $F(x)$ is an indefinite integral of x^2. Now, $\int x^2\,dx = \frac{1}{3}x^3 + C$, so we choose $F(x) = \frac{1}{3}x^3$. Thus the required area is

$$A = F(1) - F(0) = \frac{1}{3} \cdot 1^3 - \frac{1}{3} \cdot 0^3 = \frac{1}{3}$$

Figure 5 suggests that this answer is reasonable, because the shaded region appears to have roughly 1/3 the area of a square whose side is of length 1.

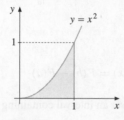

Figure 5

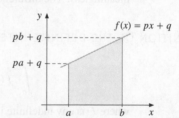

Figure 6

The argument leading to (1) is based on rather intuitive considerations. Formally, mathematicians choose to *define* the area under the graph of a continuous and nonnegative function f over the interval $[a, b]$ as the number $F(b) - F(a)$, where $F'(x) = f(x)$. The concept of area that emerges agrees with the usual concept for regions bounded by straight lines. The next example verifies this in a special case.

EXAMPLE 2   Find the area A under the straight line $f(x) = px + q$ over the interval $[a, b]$, where a, b, p, and q are all positive, with $b > a$.

Solution: The area is shown shaded in Fig. 6. It is equal to $F(b) - F(a)$ where $F(x)$ is an indefinite integral of $px + q$. Now, $\int (px + q)\,dx = \frac{1}{2}px^2 + qx + C$. The obvious choice of an indefinite integral is $F(x) = \frac{1}{2}px^2 + qx$, and so

$$A = F(b) - F(a) = \left(\tfrac{1}{2}pb^2 + qb\right) - \left(\tfrac{1}{2}pa^2 + qa\right) = \tfrac{1}{2}p(b^2 - a^2) + q(b - a)$$

As Fig. 6 shows, the area A is the sum of a rectangle whose area is $(b - a)(pa + q)$, and a triangle whose area is $\frac{1}{2}p(b - a)^2$, which you should check gives the same answer.

The Definite Integral

Let f be a continuous function defined in the interval $[a, b]$. Suppose that the function F is continuous in $[a, b]$ and has a derivative with $F'(x) = f(x)$ for every x in (a, b). Then the difference $F(b) - F(a)$ is called the **definite integral** of f over $[a, b]$. We observed above that this difference does not depend on which of the indefinite integrals of f we choose as F. The definite integral of f over $[a, b]$ is therefore a *number* that depends only on the function f and the numbers a and b. We denote this number by

$$\int_a^b f(x)\,dx \tag{2}$$

This notation makes explicit the function $f(x)$ we integrate and the interval of integration $[a, b]$. The numbers a and b are called, respectively, the **lower** and **upper limit of integration**. The variable x is a *dummy variable* in the sense that it could be replaced by any other variable that does not occur elsewhere in the expression. For instance,

$$\int_a^b f(x)\,dx = \int_a^b f(y)\,dy = \int_a^b f(\xi)\,d\xi$$

are all equal (to $F(b) - F(a)$). But do not write anything like $\int_a^y f(y)\,dy$, with the same variable as both the upper limit and the dummy variable of integration, because that is meaningless. The difference $F(b) - F(a)$ is denoted by $\left. \vphantom{\int} \right|_a^b F(x)$, or by $\left[F(x)\right]_a^b$. Thus:

DEFINITION OF THE DEFINITE INTEGRAL

$$\int_a^b f(x)\,dx = \left. \vphantom{\int} \right|_a^b F(x) = F(b) - F(a) \tag{3}$$

where F is any indefinite integral of f over an interval containing both a and b.

EXAMPLE 3   Evaluate   (a) $\displaystyle\int_2^5 e^{2x}\,dx$ (b) $\displaystyle\int_{-2}^2 (x - x^3 - x^5)\,dx$

Solution:

(a) Because $\displaystyle\int e^{2x}\,dx = \tfrac{1}{2}e^{2x} + C$, $\displaystyle\int_2^5 e^{2x}\,dx = \left. \vphantom{\int} \right|_2^5 \tfrac{1}{2}e^{2x} = \tfrac{1}{2}e^{10} - \tfrac{1}{2}e^4 = \tfrac{1}{2}e^4(e^6 - 1)$.

(b) $\displaystyle\int_{-2}^2 (x - x^3 - x^5)\,dx = \left. \vphantom{\int} \right|_{-2}^2 (\tfrac{1}{2}x^2 - \tfrac{1}{4}x^4 - \tfrac{1}{6}x^6) = (2 - 4 - \tfrac{64}{6}) - (2 - 4 - \tfrac{64}{6}) = 0$.

After reading the next subsection and realizing that the graph of $f(x) = x - x^3 - x^5$ is symmetric about the origin, you should understand better why the answer must be 0.

Definition (3) does not necessarily require $a < b$. However, if $a > b$ and $f(x)$ is positive throughout the interval $[b, a]$, then $\int_a^b f(x)\,dx$ is a negative number.

Note that we have defined the definite integral without necessarily giving it a geometric interpretation as the area under a curve. In fact, depending on the context, it can have different interpretations. For instance, if $f(r)$ is an income distribution function, then $\int_a^b f(r)\,dr$ is the proportion of people with income between a and b. (See Section 9.4.)

Although the notation for definite and indefinite integrals is similar, the two integrals are entirely different. In fact, $\int_a^b f(x)\,dx$ denotes a single number, whereas $\int f(x)\,dx$ represents any one of the infinite set of functions all having $f(x)$ as their derivative.

Area when f(x) Is Negative

If $f(x) \geq 0$ over $[a, b]$, then

$$\int_a^b f(x)\,dx \quad \text{is the area below the graph of } f \text{ over } [a, b] \tag{4}$$

If f is defined in $[a, b]$ and $f(x) \leq 0$ for all x in $[a, b]$, then the graph of f, the x-axis, and the lines $x = a$ and $x = b$ still enclose an area. This area is $-\int_a^b f(x)\,dx$, with a minus sign before the integral because the area of a region must be positive (or zero), whereas the definite integral is negative.

EXAMPLE 4   Figure 7 shows the graph of $f(x) = e^{x/3} - 3$. Evaluate the shaded area A between the x-axis and this graph over the interval $[0, 3\ln 3]$. (Note that $f(3\ln 3) = 0$.)

Solution: Because $f(x) \leq 0$ in the interval $[0, 3\ln 3]$, we obtain

$$A = -\int_0^{3\ln 3} \left(e^{x/3} - 3\right) dx = -\Big|_0^{3\ln 3} (3e^{x/3} - 3x)$$

$$= -(3e^{\ln 3} - 3 \cdot 3\ln 3) + 3e^0 = -9 + 9\ln 3 + 3 = 9\ln 3 - 6 \approx 3.89$$

Is the answer reasonable? Yes, because the shaded set in Fig. 7 seems to have an area somewhat less than that of the triangle enclosed by the points $(0, 0)$, $(0, -2)$, and $(4, 0)$, whose area is 4, and a little more than the area of the inscribed triangle with vertices $(0, 0)$, $(0, -2)$, and $(3\ln 3, 0)$, whose area is $3\ln 3 \approx 3.30$.

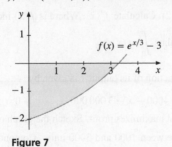

Figure 7   **Figure 8**

Suppose the function f is defined and continuous in $[a, b]$, and that it is positive in some subintervals, negative in others, as shown in Fig. 8. Let c_1, c_2, c_3 denote three roots of the equation $f(x) = 0$—that is, three points where the graph crosses the x-axis. The definite integral $\int_a^b f(x)\,dx$ is the sum of the two shaded areas above the x-axis, minus the sum of the two shaded areas below the x-axis. The total area bounded by the graph of f, the x-axis, and the lines $x = a$ and $x = b$, on the other hand, is calculated by computing the positive areas in each subinterval $[a, c_1]$, $[c_1, c_2]$, $[c_2, c_3]$, and $[c_3, b]$ in turn according to the previous definitions, and then adding these areas. Specifically, the shaded area is

$$-\int_a^{c_1} f(x)\,dx + \int_{c_1}^{c_2} f(x)\,dx - \int_{c_2}^{c_3} f(x)\,dx + \int_{c_3}^{b} f(x)\,dx$$

In fact, this illustrates a general result: the area between the graph of a function f and the x-axis is given by the definite integral $\int_a^b |f(x)|\,dx$ of the absolute value of the integrand $f(x)$, which equals the area under the graph of the nonnegative-valued function $|f(x)|$.

PROBLEMS FOR SECTION 9.2

1. Compute the areas under the graphs of (a) $f(x) = x^3$ and (b) $f(x) = x^{10}$ over $[0, 1]$.

2. Compute the area bounded by the graph of the function over the indicated interval. In (c), sketch the graph and indicate by shading the area in question.

   (a) $f(x) = 3x^2$ in $[0, 2]$ (b) $f(x) = x^6$ in $[0, 1]$

   (c) $f(x) = e^x$ in $[-1, 1]$ (d) $f(x) = 1/x^2$ in $[1, 10]$

3. Compute the area A bounded by the graph of $f(x) = 1/x^3$, the x-axis, and the two lines $x = -2$ and $x = -1$. Make a drawing. (*Hint:* $f(x) < 0$ in $[-2, -1]$.)

4. Compute the area A bounded by the graph of $f(x) = \frac{1}{2}(e^x + e^{-x})$, the x-axis, and the lines $x = -1$ and $x = 1$.

SM 5. Evaluate the following integrals:

   (a) $\displaystyle\int_0^1 x\,dx$ (b) $\displaystyle\int_1^2 (2x + x^2)\,dx$ (c) $\displaystyle\int_{-2}^3 \left(\tfrac{1}{2}x^2 - \tfrac{1}{3}x^3\right) dx$

   (d) $\displaystyle\int_0^2 (t^3 - t^4)\,dt$ (e) $\displaystyle\int_1^2 \left(2t^5 - \frac{1}{t^2}\right) dt$ (f) $\displaystyle\int_2^3 \left(\frac{1}{t-1} + t\right) dt$

SM 6. (a) Let $f(x) = x(x - 1)(x - 2)$. Calculate $f'(x)$. Where is $f(x)$ increasing?

   (b) Sketch the graph and calculate $\displaystyle\int_0^1 f(x)\,dx$.

7. (a) The profit of a firm as a function of its output x is given by

   $$f(x) = 4000 - x - 3\,000\,000/x, \quad x > 0$$

   Find the level of output that maximizes profit. Sketch the graph of f.

   (b) The actual output varies between 1000 and 3000 units. Compute the average profit $I = \dfrac{1}{2000}\displaystyle\int_{1000}^{3000} f(x)\,dx$.

8. Evaluate the integrals

   (a) $\displaystyle\int_1^3 \frac{3x}{10}\,dx$ (b) $\displaystyle\int_{-3}^{-1} \xi^2\,d\xi$ (c) $\displaystyle\int_0^1 \alpha e^{\beta\tau}\,d\tau$ ($\beta \neq 0$)   (d) $\displaystyle\int_{-2}^{-1} \frac{1}{y}\,dy$

9.3 Properties of Definite Integrals

From the definition of the definite integral, a number of properties can be derived. If f is a continuous function in an interval that contains a, b, and c, then

$$\int_a^b f(x)\,dx = -\int_b^a f(x)\,dx \tag{1}$$

$$\int_a^a f(x)\,dx = 0 \tag{2}$$

$$\int_a^b \alpha f(x)\,dx = \alpha \int_a^b f(x)\,dx \quad (\alpha \text{ an arbitrary number}) \tag{3}$$

$$\int_a^b f(x)\,dx = \int_a^c f(x)\,dx + \int_c^b f(x)\,dx \tag{4}$$

All these rules follow easily from definition (3) in the previous section. For example, (4) can be proved as follows: Let F be continuous in $[a, b]$, and suppose that $F'(x) = f(x)$ for all x in an interval big enough to include a, b, and c. Then

$$\int_a^c f(x)\,dx + \int_c^b f(x)\,dx = \big[F(c) - F(a)\big] + \big[F(b) - F(c)\big]$$

$$= F(b) - F(a) = \int_a^b f(x)\,dx$$

When the definite integral is interpreted as an area, (4) is the additivity property of areas, as illustrated in Fig. 1. Of course, (4) easily generalizes to the case in which we partition the interval $[a, b]$ into an arbitrary finite number of subintervals.

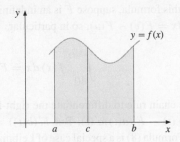

Figure 1 $\int_a^b f(x)\,dx = \int_a^c f(x)\,dx + \int_c^b f(x)\,dx$

Equations (3) and (4) are counterparts for definite integrals of, respectively, the constant multiple property (9.1.8) and the summation property (9.1.9) for indefinite integrals. In fact, if f and g are continuous in $[a, b]$, and if α and β are real numbers, then it is easy to prove that

$$\int_a^b \big[\alpha f(x) + \beta g(x)\big]\,dx = \alpha \int_a^b f(x)\,dx + \beta \int_a^b g(x)\,dx \tag{5}$$

This rule can obviously be extended to more than two functions.

Differentiation w.r.t. the Limits of Integration

Suppose that $F'(x) = f(x)$ for all x in an open interval (a, b). Suppose too that $a < t < b$. It follows that $\int_a^t f(x)\,dx = \big|_a^t F(x) = F(t) - F(a)$, so

$$\frac{d}{dt} \int_a^t f(x)\,dx = F'(t) = f(t) \tag{6}$$

In words: *The derivative of the definite integral w.r.t. the upper limit of integration is equal to the integrand evaluated at that limit.*

Correspondingly, $\int_t^b f(x)\,dx = \big|_t^b F(x) = F(b) - F(t)$, so that

$$\frac{d}{dt} \int_t^b f(x)\,dx = -F'(t) = -f(t) \tag{7}$$

In words: *The derivative of the definite integral w.r.t. the lower limit of integration is equal to minus the integrand evaluated at that limit.*

NOTE 1   Suppose that $f(x) \geq 0$ and $t < b$. We can interpret $\int_t^b f(x)\,dx$ as the area below the graph of f over the interval $[t, b]$. Then the interval shrinks as t increases, and the area will decrease. So the fact that the derivative in (7) is negative is not surprising.

The results in (6) and (7) can be generalized. In fact, if $a(t)$ and $b(t)$ are differentiable and $f(x)$ is continuous, then

$$\frac{d}{dt} \int_{a(t)}^{b(t)} f(x)\,dx = f(b(t))\,b'(t) - f(a(t))\,a'(t) \tag{8}$$

To prove this formula, suppose F is an indefinite integral of f, so that $F'(x) = f(x)$. Then $\int_u^v f(x)\,dx = F(v) - F(u)$, so in particular,

$$\int_{a(t)}^{b(t)} f(x)\,dx = F(b(t)) - F(a(t))$$

Using the chain rule to differentiate the right-hand side of this equation w.r.t. t, we obtain $F'(b(t))b'(t) - F'(a(t))a'(t)$. But $F'(b(t)) = f(b(t))$ and $F'(a(t)) = f(a(t))$, so (8) results. (Formula (8) is a special case of Leibniz's formula discussed in FMEA, Section 4.2.)

Continuous Functions are Integrable

Suppose $f(x)$ is a continuous function in $[a, b]$. Then we defined $\int_a^b f(x)\,dx$ as the number $F(b) - F(a)$, provided that $F(x)$ is some function whose derivative is $f(x)$. In some cases, we are able to find an explicit expression for $F(x)$. For instance, we can evaluate $\int_0^1 x^5\,dx$ as $1/6$ because $(1/6)x^6$ has x^5 as its derivative. On the other hand, it is impossible to find an explicit standard function of x whose derivative is the positive valued function $f(x) = (1/\sqrt{2\pi})e^{-x^2/2}$ (the standard normal density function in statistics). Yet $f(x)$ really is continuous on any interval $[a, b]$ of the real line, so the area under the graph of f over this interval definitely exists and is equal to $\int_a^b f(x)dx$. (See the graph of f in the answer to problem 4.9.5.)

In fact, one can prove that any continuous function has an antiderivative. Here are some integrals that really are impossible to "solve", except by introducing special new functions:

$$\int e^{x^2}\,dx, \quad \int e^{-x^2}\,dx, \quad \int \frac{e^x}{x}\,dx, \quad \int \frac{1}{\ln x}\,dx, \quad \int \frac{1}{\sqrt{x^4+1}}\,dx \qquad (9)$$

The Riemann Integral

The kind of integral discussed so far, which is based on the antiderivative, is called the *Newton–Leibniz* (N–L) *integral*. Several other kinds of integral are considered by mathematicians. For continuous functions, they all give the same result as the N–L integral. We briefly sketch the so-called *Riemann integral*. The idea behind the definition is closely related to the exhaustion method that was described in Section 9.2.

Let f be a *bounded* function in the interval $[a, b]$, and let n be a natural number. Subdivide $[a, b]$ into n parts by choosing points $a = x_0 < x_1 < x_2 < \cdots < x_{n-1} < x_n = b$. Put $\Delta x_i = x_{i+1} - x_i$, $i = 0, 1, \ldots, n-1$, and choose an arbitrary number ξ_i in each interval $[x_i, x_{i+1}]$ (draw a figure). The sum

$$f(\xi_0)\Delta x_0 + f(\xi_1)\Delta x_1 + \cdots + f(\xi_{n-1})\Delta x_{n-1}$$

is called a *Riemann sum* associated with the function f. This sum will depend on f as well as on the subdivision and on the choice of the different ξ_i. Suppose that, when n approaches infinity and simultaneously the largest of the numbers $\Delta x_0, \Delta x_1, \ldots, \Delta x_{n-1}$ approaches 0, the limit of the sum exists. Then f is called *Riemann integrable* (R integrable) in the interval $[a, b]$, and we put

$$\int_a^b f(x)\,dx = \lim \sum_{i=0}^{n-1} f(\xi_i)\,\Delta x_i$$

Textbooks on mathematical analysis show that the value of the integral is independent of how the ξ_i are chosen. They also show that every continuous function is R integrable, and that the R integral in this case satisfies (9.2.3). The N–L integral and the R integral thus coincide for continuous functions. But the R integral is defined for some (discontinuous) functions whose N–L integral does not exist.

PROBLEMS FOR SECTION 9.3

1. Evaluate the following integrals:

(a) $\displaystyle\int_0^5 (x + x^2)\,dx$ (b) $\displaystyle\int_{-2}^2 (e^x - e^{-x})\,dx$ (c) $\displaystyle\int_2^{10} \frac{dx}{x-1}$ (d) $\displaystyle\int_0^1 2xe^{x^2}\,dx$

(e) $\displaystyle\int_{-4}^4 (x-1)^3\,dx$ (f) $\displaystyle\int_1^2 (x^5 + x^{-5})\,dx$ (g) $\displaystyle\int_0^4 \tfrac{1}{2}\sqrt{x}\,dx$ (h) $\displaystyle\int_1^2 \frac{1+x^3}{x^2}\,dx$

2. If $\displaystyle\int_a^b f(x)\,dx = 8$ and $\displaystyle\int_a^c f(x)\,dx = 4$, what is $\displaystyle\int_c^b f(x)\,dx$?

3. If $\displaystyle\int_0^1 (f(x) - 2g(x))\,dx = 6$ and $\displaystyle\int_0^1 (2f(x) + 2g(x))\,dx = 9$, find $I = \displaystyle\int_0^1 (f(x) - g(x))\,dx$.

(SM) 4. (a) Evaluate the integral $\int_0^1 x^p(x^q + x^r)\,dx$, where p, q, and r are positive constants.

(b) Find the function $f(x)$ if $f'(x) = ax^2 + bx$, and

(i) $f'(1) = 6$ (ii) $f''(1) = 18$ (iii) $\int_0^2 f(x)\,dx = 18$

(SM) 5. Evaluate the following integrals (in (d) all constants are positive):

(a) $\int_0^3 (\frac{1}{3}e^{3t-2} + (t+2)^{-1})\,dt$

(b) $\int_0^1 (x^2 + 2)^2\,dx$

(c) $\int_0^1 \dfrac{x^2 + x + \sqrt{x+1}}{x+1}\,dx$

(d) $\int_1^b \left(A\dfrac{x+b}{x+c} + \dfrac{d}{x} \right)\,dx$

6. (a) Put $F(x) = \int_0^x (t^2+2)\,dt$ and $G(x) = \int_0^{x^2} (t^2+2)\,dt$. Find $F'(x)$ and $G'(x)$.

(b) Define $H(t) = \int_0^{t^2} K(\tau)e^{-\rho\tau}\,d\tau$, where $K(\tau)$ is a given continuous function and ρ is a constant. Find $H'(t)$.

7. Find:

(a) $\dfrac{d}{dt}\int_0^t x^2\,dx$ (b) $\dfrac{d}{dt}\int_t^3 e^{-x^2}\,dx$ (c) $\dfrac{d}{dt}\int_{-t}^t \dfrac{dx}{\sqrt{x^4+1}}$ (d) $\dfrac{d}{d\lambda}\int_{-\lambda}^2 (f(t) - g(t))\,dt$

8. Find the area between the two parabolas defined by the equations $y+1 = (x-1)^2$ and $3x = y^2$. (The points of intersection have integer coordinates.)

HARDER PROBLEMS

(SM) 9. A theory of investment has used a function W defined for all $T > 0$ by

$$W(T) = \frac{K}{T}\int_0^T e^{-\varrho t}\,dt \qquad (K \text{ and } \varrho \text{ are positive constants})$$

Evaluate the integral, then prove that $W(T)$ takes values in the interval $(0, K)$ and is strictly decreasing. (*Hint:* Problem 6.11.11.)

(SM) 10. Consider the function f defined for $x > 0$ by the formula $f(x) = 4\ln(\sqrt{x+4} - 2)$.

(a) Show that f has an inverse function g, and find a formula for g.

(b) Draw the graphs of f and g in the same coordinate system.

(c) Give a geometric interpretation of $A = \int_5^{10} 4\ln(\sqrt{x+4} - 2)\,dx$, and explain why

$$A = 10 \cdot a - \int_0^a (e^{x/2} + 4e^{x/4})\,dx, \qquad \text{where} \quad a = f(10)$$

Use this equality to express A in terms of a.

9.4 Economic Applications

We motivated the definite integral as a tool for computing the area under a curve. However, the integral has many other important interpretations. In statistics, many important probability distributions are expressed as integrals of continuous probability density functions. This section presents some examples showing the importance of integrals in economics.

Extraction from an Oil Well

Assume that at time $t = 0$ an oil producer starts extracting oil from a well that contains K barrels at that time. Let us define

$$x(t) = \text{number of barrels of oil that is left at time } t$$

In particular, $x(0) = K$. Assuming it is impractical to put oil back into the well, $x(t)$ is a decreasing function of t. The amount of oil that is extracted in a time interval $[t, t + \Delta t]$ (where $\Delta t > 0$) is $x(t) - x(t + \Delta t)$. Extraction per unit of time is, therefore,

$$\frac{x(t) - x(t + \Delta t)}{\Delta t} = -\frac{x(t + \Delta t) - x(t)}{\Delta t} \tag{*}$$

If we assume that $x(t)$ is differentiable, then as $\Delta t \to 0$ the fraction $(*)$ tends to $-\dot{x}(t)$. Letting $u(t)$ denote the **rate of extraction** at time t, we have

$$\dot{x}(t) = -u(t) \qquad \text{with} \qquad x(0) = K \tag{1}$$

The solution to equation (1) is

$$x(t) = K - \int_0^t u(\tau)\, d\tau \tag{2}$$

Indeed, we check (2) as follows. First, setting $t = 0$ gives $x(0) = K$. Moreover, differentiating (2) w.r.t. t according to rule (9.3.6) yields $\dot{x}(t) = -u(t)$.

The result (2) may be interpreted as follows: The amount of oil left at time t is equal to the initial amount K, minus the total amount that has been extracted during the time span $[0, t]$, namely $\int_0^t u(\tau)\, d\tau$.

If the rate of extraction is constant, with $u(t) = \bar{u}$, then (2) yields

$$x(t) = K - \int_0^t \bar{u}\, d\tau = K - \Big|_0^t \bar{u}\tau = K - \bar{u}t$$

In particular, the well will be empty when $x(t) = 0$, or when $K - \bar{u}t = 0$, that is when $t = K/\bar{u}$. (Of course, this particular answer could have been found more directly, without recourse to integration.)

The example illustrates two concepts that it is important to distinguish in many economic arguments. The quantity $x(t)$ is a *stock*, measured in barrels. On the other hand, $u(t)$ is a *flow*, measured in barrels *per unit of time*.

Income Distribution

In many countries, data collected by income tax authorities can be used to reveal some properties of the income distribution within a given year, as well as how the distribution changes from year to year.

Suppose we measure annual income in dollars and let $F(r)$ denote the proportion of individuals that receive no more than r dollars in a particular year. Thus, if there are n individuals in the population, $nF(r)$ is the number of individuals with income no greater than r. If r_0 is the lowest and r_1 is the highest (registered) income in the group, we are interested in the function F defined on the interval $[r_0, r_1]$. By definition, F is not continuous and therefore also not differentiable in $[r_0, r_1]$, because r has to be a multiple of \$0.01 and $F(r)$ has to be a multiple of $1/n$. However, if the population consists of a large number of individuals, then it is usually possible to find a "smooth" function that gives a good approximation to the true income distribution. Assume, therefore, that F is a function with a continuous derivative denoted by f, so that $f(r) = F'(r)$ for all r in (r_0, r_1). According to the definition of the derivative, we have

$$f(r) \, \Delta r \approx F(r + \Delta r) - F(r)$$

for all small Δr. Thus, $f(r) \, \Delta r$ is approximately equal to the proportion of individuals who have incomes between r and $r + \Delta r$. The function f is called an **income density function**, and F is the associated **cumulative distribution function**.[2]

Suppose that f is a continuous income distribution for a certain population with incomes in the interval $[r_0, r_1]$. If $r_0 \leq a \leq b \leq r_1$, then the previous discussion and the definition of the definite integral imply that $\int_a^b f(r) \, dr$ is the proportion of individuals with incomes in $[a, b]$. Thus,

$$n \int_a^b f(r) \, dr = \text{the \textbf{number of individuals} with incomes in } [a, b] \qquad (3)$$

We will now find an expression for the combined income of those who earn between a and b dollars. Let $M(r)$ denote the total income of those who earn no more than r dollars during the year, and consider the income interval $[r, r + \Delta r]$. There are approximately $nf(r) \, \Delta r$ individuals with incomes in this interval. Each of them has an income approximately equal to r, so that the total income of these individuals, $M(r + \Delta r) - M(r)$, is approximately equal to $nrf(r) \, \Delta r$. So we have

$$\frac{M(r + \Delta r) - M(r)}{\Delta r} \approx nrf(r)$$

The approximation improves (in general) as Δr decreases. By taking the limit as $\Delta r \to 0$, we obtain $M'(r) = nrf(r)$. Integrating over the interval from a to b gives $M(b) - M(a) = n \int_a^b rf(r) \, dr$. Hence,

$$n \int_a^b rf(r) \, dr = \text{\textbf{total income} of individuals with income in } [a, b] \qquad (4)$$

---

[2] Readers who know some elementary statistics will see the analogy with probability density functions and with cumulative (probability) distribution functions.

The argument that leads to (4) can be made more exact: $M(r + \Delta r) - M(r)$ is the total income of those who have income in the interval $[r, r + \Delta r]$, when $\Delta r > 0$. In this income interval, there are $n[F(r + \Delta r) - F(r)]$ individuals each of whom earns at least r and at most $r + \Delta r$. Thus,

$$nr\big[F(r + \Delta r) - F(r)\big] \leq M(r + \Delta r) - M(r) \leq n(r + \Delta r)\big[F(r + \Delta r) - F(r)\big] \qquad (*)$$

If $\Delta r > 0$, division by Δr yields

$$nr \frac{F(r + \Delta r) - F(r)}{\Delta r} \leq \frac{M(r + \Delta r) - M(r)}{\Delta r} \leq n(r + \Delta r) \frac{F(r + \Delta r) - F(r)}{\Delta r} \qquad (**)$$

(If $\Delta r < 0$, then the inequalities in $(*)$ are left unchanged, whereas those in $(**)$ are reversed.) Letting $\Delta r \to 0$ gives $nr F'(r) \leq M'(r) \leq nr F'(r)$, so that $M'(r) = nr F'(r) = nr f(r)$. ∎

The ratio between the total income and the number of individuals belonging to a certain income interval $[a, b]$ is called the mean income for the individuals in this income interval. Therefore,

$$\left. \begin{array}{r} \textbf{Mean income} \text{ of individuals with} \\ \text{incomes in the interval } [a, b] \end{array} \right\} : \quad m = \frac{\displaystyle\int_a^b r f(r)\, dr}{\displaystyle\int_a^b f(r)\, dr} \qquad (5)$$

A function that approximates actual income distributions quite well, particularly for large incomes, is the **Pareto distribution**. In this case, the proportion of individuals who earn at most r dollars is given by

$$f(r) = \frac{B}{r^\beta} \qquad (6)$$

Here B and β are positive constants. Empirical estimates of β are usually in the range $2.4 < \beta < 2.6$. For values of r close to 0, the formula is of no use. In fact, the integral $\int_0^a f(r)\, dr$ diverges to ∞, as will be seen using the arguments of Section 9.7.

EXAMPLE 1   Consider a population of n individuals in which the income density function for those with incomes between a and b is given by $f(r) = B/r^{2.5}$. Here $b > a > 0$, and B is positive. Determine the mean income of this group.

Solution: According to (3), the total number of individuals in this group is

$$N = n \int_a^b B r^{-2.5}\, dr = nB \Big|_a^b \big(-\tfrac{2}{3} r^{-1.5}\big) = \tfrac{2}{3} nB \big(a^{-1.5} - b^{-1.5}\big)$$

According to (4), the total income of these individuals is

$$M = n \int_a^b r B r^{-2.5}\, dr = nB \int_a^b r^{-1.5}\, dr = -2nB \Big|_a^b r^{-0.5} = 2nB \big(a^{-0.5} - b^{-0.5}\big)$$

So the mean income of the group is

$$m = \frac{M}{N} = 3 \frac{a^{-0.5} - b^{-0.5}}{a^{-1.5} - b^{-1.5}}$$

Suppose that b is very large. Then $b^{-0.5}$ and $b^{-1.5}$ are both close to 0, and so $m \approx 3a$. The mean income of those who earn at least a is therefore approximately $3a$.

The Influence of Income Distribution on Demand

Obviously each consumer's demand for a particular commodity depends on its price p. In addition, economists soon learn that it depends on the consumer's income r as well. Here, we consider the total demand quantity for a group of consumers whose individual demands are given by the same continuous function $D(p, r)$ of the single price p, as well as of individual income r whose distribution is given by a continuous density function $f(r)$ on the interval $[a, b]$.

Given a particular price p, let $T(r)$ denote the total demand for the commodity by all individuals whose income does not exceed r. Consider the income interval $[r, r + \Delta r]$. There are approximately $nf(r)\,\Delta r$ individuals with incomes in this interval. Because each of them demands approximately $D(p, r)$ units of the commodity, the total demand of these individuals will be approximately $nD(p, r)f(r)\,\Delta r$. However, the actual total demand of individuals with incomes in the interval $[r, r + \Delta r]$ is $T(r + \Delta r) - T(r)$, by definition. So we must have $T(r + \Delta r) - T(r) \approx nD(p, r)f(r)\,\Delta r$, and thus

$$\frac{T(r + \Delta r) - T(r)}{\Delta r} \approx nD(p, r)f(r)$$

The approximation improves (in general) as Δr decreases. Taking the limit as $\Delta r \to 0$, we obtain $T'(r) = nD(p, r)f(r)$. By definition of the definite integral, $T(b) - T(a) = n\int_a^b D(p, r)f(r)\,dr$. But $T(b) - T(a)$ is the desired measure of total demand for the commodity by all the individuals in the group. In fact, this total demand will depend on the price p. So we denote it by $x(p)$, and thus we have

$$x(p) = \int_a^b nD(p, r)f(r)\,dr \qquad \textbf{(total demand)} \qquad (7)$$

EXAMPLE 2   Let the income distribution function be that of Example 1, and let $D(p, r) = Ap^{-1.5}r^{2.08}$. Compute the total demand.

Solution: Using (7) gives

$$x(p) = \int_a^b nAp^{-1.5}r^{2.08}Br^{-2.5}\,dr = nABp^{-1.5}\int_a^b r^{-0.42}\,dr$$

Hence,

$$x(p) = nABp^{-1.5}\left.\frac{1}{0.58}r^{0.58}\right|_a^b = \frac{nAB}{0.58}p^{-1.5}(b^{0.58} - a^{0.58})$$

Consumer and Producer Surplus

Economists are interested in studying how much consumers and producers as a whole benefit (or lose) when market conditions change. A common (but theoretically questionable) measure of these benefits used by many applied economists is the total amount of consumer and producer surplus defined below.[3] At the equilibrium point E in Fig. 1, demand is equal to supply. The corresponding equilibrium price P^* is the one which induces consumers to purchase (demand) precisely the same aggregate amount that producers are willing to offer

---

[3] See, for example, H. Varian: *Intermediate Microeconomics: A Modern Approach*, 8th ed., Norton, 2009 for a closer treatment.

(supply) at that price, as in Example 4.5.3. According to the demand curve in Fig. 1, there are consumers who are willing to pay more than P^* per unit. In fact, even if the price is almost as high as P_1, some consumers still wish to buy some units at that price. The total amount "saved" by all such consumers is called the **consumer surplus**.

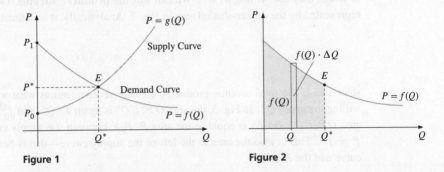

Figure 1   **Figure 2**

Consider the small rectangle indicated in Fig. 2. It has base ΔQ and height $f(Q)$, so its area is $f(Q) \cdot \Delta Q$. It is approximately the maximum additional amount that consumers as a whole are willing to pay for an extra ΔQ units at price $f(Q)$, after they have already bought Q units. For those willing to buy the commodity at price P^* or higher, the total amount they are willing to pay is the total area below the demand curve over the interval $[0, Q^*]$, that is $\int_0^{Q^*} f(Q)\,dQ$. This area is shaded in Fig. 2. If all consumers together buy Q^* units of the commodity, the total cost is $P^* Q^*$. This represents the area of the rectangle with base Q^* and height P^*. It can therefore be expressed as the integral $\int_0^{Q^*} P^*\,dQ$. The consumer surplus is defined as the integral

$$\text{CS} = \int_0^{Q^*} [f(Q) - P^*]\,dQ \tag{8}$$

which equals the total amount consumers are willing to pay for Q^*, minus what they actually pay. In Fig. 3, $\int_0^{Q^*} f(Q)\,dQ$ is the area $O P_1 E Q^*$, whereas $O P^* E Q^*$ is $P^* Q^*$. So CS is equal to the area $P^* P_1 E$ between the demand curve and the horizontal line $P = P^*$. This is also the area to the left of the demand curve—that is between the demand curve and the P-axis. So the consumer surplus CS is the lighter-shaded area in Fig. 3.

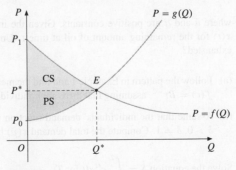

Figure 3

Most producers also derive positive benefit or "surplus" from selling at the equilibrium price P^* because they would be willing to supply the commodity for less than P^*. In Fig. 3, even if the price is almost as low as P_0, some producers are still willing to supply the commodity. Consider the total surplus of all the producers who receive more than the price at which they are willing to sell. We call this the **producer surplus**. Geometrically it is represented by the darker-shaded area in Fig. 3. Analytically, it is defined by

$$PS = \int_0^{Q^*} [P^* - g(Q)]\,dQ \tag{9}$$

since this is the total revenue producers actually receive, minus what would make them willing to supply Q^*. In Fig. 3, the area OP^*EQ^* is again P^*Q^*, and $\int_0^{Q^*} g(Q)\,dQ$ is the area OP_0EQ^*. So PS is equal to the area P^*P_0E between the supply curve and the line $P = P^*$. This is also the area to the left of the supply curve—that is between the supply curve and the P-axis.

EXAMPLE 3   Suppose that the demand curve is $P = f(Q) = 50 - 0.1Q$ and the supply curve is $P = g(Q) = 0.2Q + 20$. Find the equilibrium price and compute the consumer and producer surplus.

Solution: The equilibrium quantity is determined by the equation $50 - 0.1Q^* = 0.2Q^* + 20$, which gives $Q^* = 100$. Then $P^* = 0.2Q^* + 20 = 40$. Hence,

$$CS = \int_0^{100} [50 - 0.1Q - 40]\,dQ = \int_0^{100} [10 - 0.1Q]\,dQ = \Big|_0^{100} (10Q - 0.05Q^2) = 500$$

$$PS = \int_0^{100} [40 - (0.2Q + 20)]\,dQ = \int_0^{100} [20 - 0.2Q]\,dQ = \Big|_0^{100} (20Q - 0.1Q^2) = 1000$$

PROBLEMS FOR SECTION 9.4

1. Assume that the rate of extraction $u(t)$ from an oil well decreases exponentially over time, with

$$u(t) = \bar{u}e^{-at}$$

where $\bar{u}$ and a are positive constants. Given the initial stock $x(0) = K$, find an expression $x(t)$ for the remaining amount of oil at time t. Under what condition will the well never be exhausted?

(SM) 2. (a) Follow the pattern in Example 1 and find the mean income m over the interval $[b, 2b]$ when $f(r) = Br^{-2}$, assuming that there are n individuals in the population.

(b) Assume that the individuals' demand function is $D(p, r) = Ap^\gamma r^\delta$ with $A > 0\ \gamma < 0$, $\delta > 0, \delta \neq 1$. Compute the total demand $x(p)$ by using formula (7).

3. Solve the equation $S = \int_0^T e^{rt}\,dt$ for T.

4. Let $K(t)$ denote the capital stock of an economy at time t. Then **net investment** at time t, denoted by $I(t)$, is given by the rate of increase $\dot{K}(t)$ of $K(t)$.

(a) If $I(t) = 3t^2 + 2t + 5$ $(t \geq 0)$, what is the total increase in the capital stock during the interval from $t = 0$ to $t = 5$?

(b) If $K(t_0) = K_0$, find an expression for the total increase in the capital stock from time $t = t_0$ to $t = T$ when the investment function $I(t)$ is as in part (a).

5. An oil company is planning to extract oil from one of its fields, starting today at $t = 0$, where t is time measured in years. It has a choice between two extraction profiles f and g giving the rates of flow of oil, measured in barrels per year. Both extraction profiles last for 10 years, with $f(t) = 10t^2 - t^3$ and $g(t) = t^3 - 20t^2 + 100t$ for t in $[0, 10]$.

(a) Sketch the two profiles in the same coordinate system.

(b) Show that $\int_0^t g(\tau)\, d\tau \geq \int_0^t f(\tau)\, d\tau$ for all t in $[0, 10]$.

(c) The company sells its oil at a price per unit given by $p(t) = 1 + 1/(t + 1)$. Total revenues from the two profiles are then given by $\int_0^{10} p(t) f(t)\, dt$ and $\int_0^{10} p(t) g(t)\, dt$ respectively. Compute these integrals. Which of the two extraction profiles earns the higher revenue?

6. Suppose that the demand and supply curves are $P = f(Q) = 200 - 0.2Q$ and $P = g(Q) = 20 + 0.1Q$, respectively. Find the equilibrium price and quantity, and compute the consumer and producer surplus.

7. Suppose the demand and supply curves are $P = f(Q) = \dfrac{6000}{Q + 50}$, $P = g(Q) = Q + 10$. Find the equilibrium price and quantity, and compute the consumer and producer surplus.

9.5 Integration by Parts

Mathematicians, statisticians and economists often need to evaluate integrals like $\int x^3 e^{2x}\, dx$, whose integrand is a product of two functions. We know that $\frac{1}{4}x^4$ has x^3 as its derivative and that $\frac{1}{2}e^{2x}$ has e^{2x} as its derivative, but $(\frac{1}{4}x^4)(\frac{1}{2}e^{2x})$ certainly does not have $x^3 e^{2x}$ as its derivative. In general, because the derivative of a product is *not* the product of the derivatives, the integral of a product is not the product of the integrals.

The correct rule for differentiating a product allows us to derive an important and useful rule for integrating products. The product rule for differentiation states that

$$\big(f(x)g(x)\big)' = f'(x)g(x) + f(x)g'(x) \qquad (*)$$

Now take the indefinite integral of each side in $(*)$, and then use the rule for integrating a sum. The result is

$$f(x)g(x) = \int f'(x)g(x)\, dx + \int f(x)g'(x)\, dx$$

where the constants of integration have been left implicit in the indefinite integrals on the right-hand side of this equation. Rearranging this last equation yields the following formula:

FORMULA FOR INTEGRATION BY PARTS

$$\int f(x)g'(x)\,dx = f(x)g(x) - \int f'(x)g(x)\,dx \qquad (1)$$

At first sight, this formula does not look at all helpful. Yet the examples that follow show how this impression is quite wrong, once one has learned to use the formula properly.

Indeed, suppose we are asked to integrate a function $H(x)$ that can be written in the form $f(x)g'(x)$. By using (1), the problem can be transformed into that of integrating $f'(x)g(x)$. Usually, a function $H(x)$ can be written as $f(x)g'(x)$ in several different ways. The point is, therefore, to choose f and g so that it is easier to find $\int f'(x)g(x)\,dx$ than it is to find $\int f(x)g'(x)\,dx$.

EXAMPLE 1   Use integration by parts to evaluate $\int xe^x\,dx$.

Solution: In order to use (1), we must write the integrand in the form $f(x)g'(x)$. Let $f(x) = x$ and $g'(x) = e^x$, implying that $g(x) = e^x$. Then $f(x)g'(x) = xe^x$, and so

$$\underset{\substack{\uparrow \quad\quad \uparrow \\ f(x)\ g'(x)}}{\int x\ \cdot\ e^x\ dx} = \underset{\substack{\uparrow \quad \uparrow \\ f(x)\ g(x)}}{x\ \cdot\ e^x} - \underset{\substack{\uparrow \quad \uparrow \\ f'(x)\ g(x)}}{\int 1\ \cdot\ e^x\,dx} = xe^x - \int e^x\,dx = xe^x - e^x + C$$

The derivative of $xe^x - e^x + C$ is indeed $e^x + xe^x - e^x = xe^x$, so the integration has been carried out correctly.

An appropriate choice of f and g enabled us to evaluate the integral. Let us see what happens if we interchange the roles of f and g, and try $f(x) = e^x$ and $g'(x) = x$ instead. Then $g(x) = \frac{1}{2}x^2$. Again $f(x)g'(x) = e^x x = xe^x$, and by (1):

$$\underset{\substack{\uparrow \quad\quad \uparrow \\ f(x)\ g'(x)}}{\int e^x\ \cdot\ x\ dx} = \underset{\substack{\uparrow \quad\quad \uparrow \\ f(x)\ g(x)}}{e^x\ \cdot\ \tfrac{1}{2}x^2} - \underset{\substack{\uparrow \quad\quad \uparrow \\ f'(x)\ g(x)}}{\int e^x\ \cdot\ \tfrac{1}{2}x^2\,dx}$$

In this case, the integral on the right-hand side is more complicated than the original one. Thus, this second choice of f and g does not simplify the integral.

The example illustrates that we must be careful how we split the integrand. Insights into making a good choice, if there is one, come only with practice.

Sometimes integration by parts works not by producing a simpler integral, but one that is similar, as in (a) of the next example.

EXAMPLE 2   Evaluate the following: (a) $I = \int \dfrac{1}{x} \ln x\,dx$ (b) $J = \int x^3 e^{2x}\,dx$.

Solution:

(a) Choosing $f(x) = 1/x$ and $g'(x) = \ln x$ leads nowhere. Choosing $f(x) = \ln x$ and $g'(x) = 1/x$ works better:

$$I = \int \frac{1}{x} \ln x \, dx = \int \ln x \, \frac{1}{x} \, dx = \ln x \ln x - \int \frac{1}{x} \ln x \, dx$$

$$\qquad\qquad\qquad \underset{f(x)\,g'(x)}{\downarrow\ \downarrow} \qquad\qquad \underset{f(x)\,g(x)}{\downarrow\ \downarrow} \qquad \underset{f'(x)\,g(x)}{\downarrow\ \downarrow}$$

In this case, the last integral is exactly the one we started with, namely I. So it must be true that $I = (\ln x)^2 - I + C_1$ for some constant C_1. Solving for I yields $I = \frac{1}{2}(\ln x)^2 + \frac{1}{2}C_1$. Putting $C = \frac{1}{2}C_1$, we conclude that

$$\int \frac{1}{x} \ln x \, dx = \frac{1}{2}(\ln x)^2 + C$$

(b) We begin by arguing rather loosely as follows. Differentiation makes x^3 simpler by reducing the power in the derivative $3x^2$ from 3 to 2. On the other hand, e^{2x} becomes about equally simple whether we differentiate or integrate it. Therefore, we choose $f(x) = x^3$ and $g'(x) = e^{2x}$, so that integration by parts tells us to differentiate f and integrate g'. This yields $f'(x) = 3x^2$ and we can choose $g(x) = \frac{1}{2}e^{2x}$. Therefore,

$$J = \int x^3 e^{2x} \, dx = x^3(\tfrac{1}{2}e^{2x}) - \int (3x^2)(\tfrac{1}{2}e^{2x}) \, dx = \tfrac{1}{2}x^3 e^{2x} - \tfrac{3}{2} \int x^2 e^{2x} \, dx \quad \text{(i)}$$

The last integral *is* somewhat simpler than the one we started with because the power of x has been reduced. Integrating by parts once more yields

$$\int x^2 e^{2x} \, dx = x^2(\tfrac{1}{2}e^{2x}) - \int (2x)(\tfrac{1}{2}e^{2x}) \, dx = \tfrac{1}{2}x^2 e^{2x} - \int x e^{2x} \, dx \quad \text{(ii)}$$

Using integration by parts a third and final time gives

$$\int x e^{2x} \, dx = x(\tfrac{1}{2}e^{2x}) - \int \tfrac{1}{2}e^{2x} \, dx = \tfrac{1}{2}x e^{2x} - \tfrac{1}{4}e^{2x} + C \quad \text{(iii)}$$

Successively inserting the results of (iii) and (ii) into (i) yields (with $3C/2 = c$):

$$J = \tfrac{1}{2}x^3 e^{2x} - \tfrac{3}{4}x^2 e^{2x} + \tfrac{3}{4}x e^{2x} - \tfrac{3}{8}e^{2x} + c$$

It is a good idea to double-check your work by verifying that $dJ/dx = x^3 e^{2x}$.

There is a corresponding result for definite integrals. From the definition of the definite integral and the product rule for differentiation, we have

$$\int_a^b \left[f'(x)g(x) + f(x)g'(x) \right] dx = \int_a^b \frac{d}{dx}\left[f(x)g(x) \right] dx = \Big|_a^b f(x)g(x)$$

implying that

$$\int_a^b f(x)g'(x) \, dx = \Big|_a^b f(x)g(x) - \int_a^b f'(x)g(x) \, dx \quad \text{(2)}$$

EXAMPLE 3   Evaluate $\displaystyle\int_0^{10} (1 + 0.4t)e^{-0.05t}\, dt$.

Solution: Put $f(t) = 1 + 0.4t$ and $g'(t) = e^{-0.05t}$. Then we can choose $g(t) = -20e^{-0.05t}$, and (2) yields

$$\int_0^{10} (1 + 0.4t)e^{-0.05t}\, dt = \Big|_0^{10} (1 + 0.4t)(-20)e^{-0.05t} - \int_0^{10} (0.4)(-20)e^{-0.05t}\, dt$$

$$= -100e^{-0.5} + 20 + 8\int_0^{10} e^{-0.05t}\, dt$$

$$= -100e^{-0.5} + 20 - 160(e^{-0.5} - 1) \approx 22.3$$

PROBLEMS FOR SECTION 9.5

SM **1.** Use integration by parts to evaluate the following:

(a) $\displaystyle\int xe^{-x}\, dx$ (b) $\displaystyle\int 3xe^{4x}\, dx$ (c) $\displaystyle\int (1 + x^2)e^{-x}\, dx$ (d) $\displaystyle\int x \ln x\, dx$

SM **2.** Use integration by parts to evaluate the following:

(a) $\displaystyle\int_{-1}^{1} x \ln(x + 2)\, dx$ (b) $\displaystyle\int_0^2 x2^x\, dx$ (c) $\displaystyle\int_0^1 x^2 e^x\, dx$ (d) $\displaystyle\int_0^3 x\sqrt{1 + x}\, dx$

(In (d) you should graph the integrand and decide if your answer is reasonable.)

3. Use integration by parts to evaluate the following:

(a) $\displaystyle\int_1^4 \sqrt{t}\, \ln t\, dt$ (b) $\displaystyle\int_0^2 (x - 2)e^{-x/2}\, dx$ (c) $\displaystyle\int_0^3 (3 - x)3^x\, dx$

4. Of course, $f(x) = 1 \cdot f(x)$ for any function $f(x)$. Use this fact to prove that

$$\int f(x)\, dx = xf(x) - \int xf'(x)\, dx$$

Apply this formula to $f(x) = \ln x$. Compare with Example 9.1.3.

5. Show that $\displaystyle\int x^\rho \ln x\, dx = \frac{x^{\rho+1}}{\rho + 1} \ln x - \frac{x^{\rho+1}}{(\rho + 1)^2} + C, \quad (\rho \neq -1)$.

SM **6.** Evaluate the following integrals ($r \neq 0$):

(a) $\displaystyle\int_0^T bte^{-rt}\, dt$ (b) $\displaystyle\int_0^T (a + bt)e^{-rt}\, dt$ (c) $\displaystyle\int_0^T (a - bt + ct^2)e^{-rt}\, dt$

9.6 Integration by Substitution

In this section we shall see how the chain rule for differentiation leads to an important method for evaluating many complicated integrals. We start with some simple examples.

EXAMPLE 1   Evaluate   (a) $\int (x^2 + 10)^{50} 2x \, dx$ (b) $\int_0^a xe^{-cx^2} \, dx$ $(c \neq 0)$

Solution:

(a) Attempts to use integration by parts fail. Expanding $(x^2 + 10)^{50}$ to get a polynomial of 51 terms, and then integrating term by term, would work in principle, but would be extremely cumbersome. Instead, let us introduce $u = x^2 + 10$ as a new variable. Using differential notation, we see that $du = 2x \, dx$. Inserting these into the integral in (a) yields

$$\int u^{50} \, du$$

This integral is easy, $\int u^{50} \, du = \frac{1}{51} u^{51} + C$. Because $u = x^2 + 10$, it appears that

$$\int (x^2 + 10)^{50} 2x \, dx = \frac{1}{51}(x^2 + 10)^{51} + C$$

By the chain rule, the derivative of $\frac{1}{51}(x^2 + 10)^{51} + C$ is precisely $(x^2 + 10)^{50} 2x$, so the result *is* confirmed.

(b) First we consider the indefinite integral $\int xe^{-cx^2} \, dx$ and substitute $u = -cx^2$. Then $du = -2cx \, dx$, and thus $x \, dx = -du/2c$. Therefore

$$\int xe^{-cx^2} \, dx = \int \frac{-1}{2c} e^u \, du = -\frac{1}{2c} e^u + C = -\frac{1}{2c} e^{-cx^2} + C$$

The definite integral is

$$\int_0^a xe^{-cx^2} \, dx = -\frac{1}{2c} \Big|_0^a e^{-cx^2} = \frac{1}{2c}(1 - e^{-ca^2})$$

In both of these examples, the integrand could be written in the form $f(u)u'$, where $u = g(x)$. In (a), we put $f(u) = u^{50}$ with $u = g(x) = x^2 + 10$. In (b), we put $f(u) = e^u$ with $u = g(x) = -cx^2$. Then the integrand is a constant $-1/(2c)$ multiplied by $f(g(x))g'(x)$.

Let us try the same method on the more general integral

$$\int f(g(x))g'(x) \, dx$$

If we put $u = g(x)$, then $du = g'(x) \, dx$, and so the integral reduces to $\int f(u) \, du$. Suppose we could find an antiderivative function $F(u)$ such that $F'(u) = f(u)$. Then we would have $\int f(u) \, du = F(u) + C$, which implies that

$$\int f(g(x))g'(x) \, dx = F(g(x)) + C$$

Does this purely formal method always give the right result? To convince you that it does, we use the chain rule to differentiate $F(g(x)) + C$ w.r.t. x. The derivative is $F'(g(x))g'(x)$, which is precisely equal to $f(g(x))g'(x)$, thus confirming the following rule:

INTEGRATION BY SUBSTITUTION (CHANGE OF VARIABLE)

$$\int f(g(x))g'(x)\,dx = \int f(u)\,du \qquad (u = g(x)) \tag{1}$$

NOTE 1   Precise assumptions for this formula to be valid are as follows: g is continuously differentiable, and $f(u)$ is continuous at all points u belonging to the relevant range of g.

EXAMPLE 2   Evaluate $\int 8x^2(3x^3 - 1)^{16}\,dx$.

Solution: Substitute $u = 3x^3 - 1$. Then $du = 9x^2\,dx$, so that $8x^2\,dx = \frac{8}{9}\,du$. Hence

$$\int 8x^2(3x^3 - 1)^{16}\,dx = \frac{8}{9}\int u^{16}\,du = \frac{8}{9}\cdot\frac{1}{17}u^{17} + C = \frac{8}{153}(3x^3 - 1)^{17} + C$$

The definite integral in Example 1(b) can be evaluated more simply by "carrying over" the limits of integration. We substituted $u = -cx^2$. As x varies from 0 to a, so u varies from 0 to $-ca^2$. This allows us to write:

$$\int_0^a xe^{-cx^2}\,dx = \int_0^{-ca^2}\frac{-1}{2c}e^u\,du = \frac{-1}{2c}\bigg|_0^{-ca^2} e^u = \frac{1}{2c}(1 - e^{-ca^2})$$

This method of carrying over the limits of integration can be used in general. In fact,

$$\int_a^b f(g(x))g'(x)\,dx = \int_{g(a)}^{g(b)} f(u)\,du \qquad (u = g(x)) \tag{2}$$

The argument is simple: Provided that $F'(u) = f(u)$, we obtain

$$\int_a^b f(g(x))g'(x)\,dx = \bigg|_a^b F(g(x)) = F(g(b)) - F(g(a)) = \int_{g(a)}^{g(b)} f(u)\,du$$

EXAMPLE 3   Evaluate the integral $\int_1^e \frac{1 + \ln x}{x}\,dx$.

Solution: We suggest the substitution $u = 1 + \ln x$. Then $du = (1/x)\,dx$. Also, if $x = 1$ then $u = 1$, and if $x = e$ then $u = 2$. So we have

$$\int_1^e \frac{1 + \ln x}{x}\,dx = \int_1^2 u\,du = \frac{1}{2}\bigg|_1^2 u^2 = \frac{1}{2}(4 - 1) = \frac{3}{2}$$

More Complicated Cases

The examples of integration by substitution considered so far were rather simple. More challenging applications of this integration method are studied in this subsection.

EXAMPLE 4   Try to find a substitution that allows $\int \frac{x - \sqrt{x}}{x + \sqrt{x}}\,dx$ to be evaluated (assuming $x > 0$).

Solution: Because $\sqrt{x}$ occurs in both the numerator and the denominator, we try to simplify the integral by substituting $u = \sqrt{x}$. Then $x = u^2$ and $dx = 2u\,du$, so we get

$$\int \frac{x - \sqrt{x}}{x + \sqrt{x}}\,dx = \int \frac{u^2 - u}{u^2 + u}2u\,du = 2\int \frac{u^2 - u}{u + 1}\,du = 2\int \left(u - 2 + \frac{2}{u + 1}\right)du$$

$$= u^2 - 4u + 4\ln|u + 1| + C$$

where we have performed the polynomial division $(u^2 - u) \div (u + 1)$ with a remainder, as in Section 4.7, in order to derive the third equality. Replacing u by $\sqrt{x}$ in the last expression yields the answer

$$\int \frac{x - \sqrt{x}}{x + \sqrt{x}}\,dx = x - 4\sqrt{x} + 4\ln(\sqrt{x} + 1) + C$$

where we use the fact that $\sqrt{x} + 1 > 0$ for all x.

The last example shows the method that is used most frequently. We can summarize it as follows:

METHOD FOR FINDING A COMPLICATED INTEGRAL $\int G(x)\,dx$

1. Pick out a "part" of $G(x)$ and introduce this "part" as a new variable, $u = g(x)$.
2. Compute $du = g'(x)\,dx$.
3. Using the substitution $u = g(x)$, $du = g'(x)\,dx$, transform (if possible) $\int G(x)\,dx$ to an integral of the form $\int f(u)\,du$.
4. Find (if possible) $\int f(u)\,du = F(u) + C$.
5. Replace u by $g(x)$. The final answer is then
$$\int G(x)\,dx = F(g(x)) + C$$

At step 3 of this procedure, it is crucial that the substitution results in an integrand $f(u)$ that only contains u (and du), without any x's. Probably the most common error when integrating by substitution is to replace dx by du, rather than use the correct formula $du = g'(x)\,dx$.

Note that if one particular substitution does not work, one can try another. But as explained in Section 9.3, there is always the possibility that no substitution at all will work.

EXAMPLE 5   Find the following: (a) $\displaystyle\int x^3\sqrt{1 + x^2}\,dx$ (b) $\displaystyle\int_0^1 x^3\sqrt{1 + x^2}\,dx$.

Solution: (a) We follow steps 1 to 5:

1. We pick a "part" of $x^3\sqrt{1 + x^2}$ as a new variable. Let us try $u = \sqrt{1 + x^2}$.

2. When $u = \sqrt{1 + x^2}$, then $u^2 = 1 + x^2$ and so $2u\,du = 2x\,dx$, implying that $u\,du = x\,dx$. (Note that this is easier than differentiating u directly.)

3. $\int x^3\sqrt{1+x^2}\,dx = \int x^2\sqrt{1+x^2}\,x\,dx = \int (u^2-1)uu\,du = \int (u^4-u^2)\,du$

4. $\int (u^4-u^2)\,du = \frac{1}{5}u^5 - \frac{1}{3}u^3 + C$

5. $\int x^3\sqrt{1+x^2}\,dx = \frac{1}{5}\left(\sqrt{1+x^2}\right)^5 - \frac{1}{3}\left(\sqrt{1+x^2}\right)^3 + C$

(b) We combine the results in steps 3 and 4 of part (a), while noting that $u = 1$ when $x = 0$ and $u = \sqrt{2}$ when $x = 1$. The implication is is

$$\int_0^1 x^3\sqrt{1+x^2}\,dx = \Big|_1^{\sqrt{2}} \left(\frac{1}{5}u^5 - \frac{1}{3}u^3\right) = \frac{4\sqrt{2}}{5} - \frac{2\sqrt{2}}{3} - \frac{1}{5} + \frac{1}{3} = \frac{2}{15}(\sqrt{2}+1)$$

In this example the substitution $u = 1 + x^2$ also works.

Integrating Rational Functions, and Partial Fractions

In Section 4.7 we defined a rational function as the ratio $P(x)/Q(x)$ of two polynomials. Just occasionally economists need to integrate such functions. So we will merely give two examples that illustrate a procedure one can use more generally. One example has already appeared in Problem 9.1.5(b), where the integrand was the rational function $x^3/(x+1)$. As explained in Section 4.7, this can be simplified by polynomial division with a remainder to a form that can be integrated directly.

That first example was particularly simple because the denominator is a polynomial of degree 1 in x. When degree of the denominator exceeds 1, however, it is generally necessary to combine polynomial division with a *partial fraction expansion* of the remainder. Here is an example:

EXAMPLE 6   Calculate the integral $\int \dfrac{x^4 + 3x^2 - 4}{x^2 + 2x}\,dx$.

Solution: We apply polynomial division to the integrand, which yields (see Example 4.7.6)

$$\frac{x^4 + 3x^2 - 4}{x^2 + 2x} = x^2 - 2x + 7 - \frac{14x + 4}{x^2 + 2x}$$

We can easily integrate the first 3 terms of the RHS to obtain $\int (x^2 - 2x + 7)dx = \frac{1}{3}x^3 - x^2 + 7x +$ constant. The fourth term, however, has a denominator equal to the product of the two degree-one factors x and $x + 2$. To obtain an integrand we can integrate, we expand this term as

$$\frac{14x + 4}{x(x + 2)} = \frac{A}{x} + \frac{B}{x + 2}$$

— i.e., the sum of two partial fractions, where A and B are constants to be determined. Multiplying each side of the equation by the common denominator $x(x + 2)$ gives $14x + 4 = A(x + 2) + Bx$, or equivalently $(14 - A - B)x + 4 - 2A = 0$. To make this true for all $x \neq 0$ and all $x \neq -2$ (points where the fraction is undefined), we require that both the coefficient $14 - A - B$ of x and also the constant $4 - 2A$ are 0. Solving these two simultaneous equations gives $A = 2$ and $B = 12$. Finally, therefore, we can integrate the fourth remainder term of the integrand to obtain

$$\int \frac{14x + 4}{x^2 + 2x}\,dx = \int \frac{2}{x}\,dx + \int \frac{12}{x + 2}\,dx = 2\ln|x| + 12\ln|x + 2| + C$$

Hence, the overall answer is

$$\int \frac{x^4 + 3x^2 - 4}{x^2 + 2x}\,dx = \frac{1}{3}x^3 - x^2 + 7x + 2\ln|x| + 12\ln|x + 2| + C$$

This answer, of course, can be verified by differentiation.

PROBLEMS FOR SECTION 9.6

1. Find the following integrals by using (1):

(a) $\displaystyle\int (x^2+1)^8\, 2x\, dx$ (b) $\displaystyle\int (x+2)^{10}\, dx$ (c) $\displaystyle\int \frac{2x-1}{x^2-x+8}\, dx$

(SM) 2. Find the following integrals by means of an appropriate substitution:

(a) $\displaystyle\int x(2x^2+3)^5\, dx$ (b) $\displaystyle\int x^2 e^{x^3+2}\, dx$ (c) $\displaystyle\int \frac{\ln(x+2)}{2x+4}\, dx$

(d) $\displaystyle\int x\sqrt{1+x}\, dx$ (e) $\displaystyle\int \frac{x^3}{(1+x^2)^3}\, dx$ (f) $\displaystyle\int x^5\sqrt{4-x^3}\, dx$

3. Find the following integrals:

(a) $\displaystyle\int_0^1 x\sqrt{1+x^2}\, dx$ (b) $\displaystyle\int_1^e \frac{\ln y}{y}\, dy$ (c) $\displaystyle\int_1^3 \frac{1}{x^2} e^{2/x}\, dx$ (d) $\displaystyle\int_5^8 \frac{x}{x-4}\, dx$

(In (d) you should try at least two different methods.)

4. Solve the equation $\displaystyle\int_3^x \frac{2t-2}{t^2-2t}\, dt = \ln(\tfrac{2}{3}x-1)$ for values of x satisfying $x > 2$.

5. Show that $\displaystyle\int_{t_0}^{t_1} S'(x(t))\dot{x}(t)\, dt = S(x(t_1)) - S(x(t_0))$.

HARDER PROBLEMS

(SM) 6. Calculate the following integrals:

(a) $\displaystyle\int_0^1 (x^4-x^9)(x^5-1)^{12}\, dx$ (b) $\displaystyle\int \frac{\ln x}{\sqrt{x}}\, dx$ (c) $\displaystyle\int_0^4 \frac{dx}{\sqrt{1+\sqrt{x}}}$

(SM) 7. Calculate:

(a) $\displaystyle\int_1^4 \frac{e^{\sqrt{x}}}{\sqrt{x}\,(1+e^{\sqrt{x}})}\, dx$ (b) $\displaystyle\int_0^{1/3} \frac{dx}{e^x+1}$ (c) $\displaystyle\int_{8.5}^{41} \frac{dx}{\sqrt{2x-1}-\sqrt[4]{2x-1}}$

(*Hint:* For (b), substitute $t = e^{-x}$; for (c), substitute $z^4 = 2x - 1$.)

8. Find the integral $I = \displaystyle\int \frac{x^{1/2}}{1-x^{1/3}}\, dx$.

(*Hint:* How can you simultaneously eliminate both fractional exponents in $x^{1/2}$ and $x^{1/3}$ using only one substitution?)

9. Use the method of partial fractions suggested in Example 6 to write $f(x) = \dfrac{cx+d}{(x-a)(x-b)}$

as a sum of two fractions, and use the result to integrate:

(a) $\displaystyle\int \frac{x\, dx}{(x+1)(x+2)}$ (b) $\displaystyle\int \frac{(1-2x)\, dx}{x^2-2x-15}$

9.7 Infinite Intervals of Integration

In Example 9.6.1(b) we proved that

$$\int_0^a xe^{-cx^2}\,dx = \frac{1}{2c}(1 - e^{-ca^2})$$

Suppose c is a positive number and let a tend to infinity. Then the right-hand expression tends to $1/(2c)$. This makes it seem natural to write

$$\int_0^\infty xe^{-cx^2}\,dx = \frac{1}{2c}$$

In statistics and economics it is common to encounter such integrals over an infinite interval.

In general, suppose f is a function that is continuous for all $x \geq a$. Then $\int_a^b f(x)\,dx$ is defined for each $b \geq a$. If the limit of this integral as $b \to \infty$ exists (and is finite), then we say that f is **integrable over** $[a, \infty)$, and define

$$\int_a^\infty f(x)\,dx = \lim_{b \to \infty} \int_a^b f(x)\,dx \tag{1}$$

The **improper integral** $\int_a^\infty f(x)\,dx$ is then said to **converge**. If the limit does *not* exist, however, the improper integral is said to **diverge**. If $f(x) \geq 0$ in $[a, \infty)$, we interpret the integral (1) as the *area* below the graph of f over the infinite interval $[a, \infty)$.

Analogously, we define

$$\int_{-\infty}^b f(x)\,dx = \lim_{a \to -\infty} \int_a^b f(x)\,dx \tag{2}$$

when f is continuous in $(-\infty, b]$. If this limit exists, the improper integral is said to converge. Otherwise, it diverges.

EXAMPLE 1   The *exponential distribution* in statistics is defined by the density function

$$f(x) = \lambda e^{-\lambda x} \qquad (x \geq 0; \;\; \lambda \text{ is a positive constant})$$

Show that the area below the graph of f over $[0, \infty)$ is equal to 1. (See Fig. 1.)

Solution: For $b > 0$, the area below the graph of f over $[0, b]$ is equal to

$$\int_0^b \lambda e^{-\lambda x}\,dx = \Big|_0^b \big(-e^{-\lambda x}\big) = -e^{-\lambda b} + 1$$

As $b \to \infty$, so $-e^{-\lambda b} + 1$ approaches 1. Therefore,

$$\int_0^\infty \lambda e^{-\lambda x}\,dx = \lim_{b \to \infty} \int_0^b \lambda e^{-\lambda x}\,dx = \lim_{b \to \infty}\big(-e^{-\lambda b} + 1\big) = 1$$

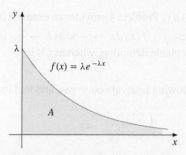

Figure 1 Area A has an unbounded base but the height decreases to 0 so rapidly that the total area is 1

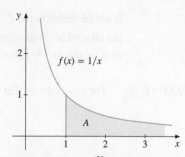

Figure 2 "$A = \int_1^\infty (1/x)\,dx = \infty$." $1/x$ does not approach 0 sufficiently fast, so the improper integral diverges

EXAMPLE 2   For $a > 1$, show that

$$\int_1^\infty \frac{1}{x^a}\,dx = \frac{1}{a-1} \tag{$*$}$$

Then study the case $a \leq 1$.

Solution: For $a \neq 1$ and $b > 1$,

$$\int_1^b \frac{1}{x^a}\,dx = \int_1^b x^{-a}\,dx = \Big|_1^b \frac{1}{1-a}x^{1-a} = \frac{1}{1-a}(b^{1-a}-1) \tag{$**$}$$

For $a > 1$, one has $b^{1-a} = 1/b^{a-1} \to 0$ as $b \to \infty$. Hence, ($*$) follows from ($**$) by letting $b \to \infty$.

For $a = 1$, the RHS of ($**$) is undefined. Nevertheless, $\int_1^b (1/x)\,dx = \ln b - \ln 1 = \ln b$, which tends to ∞ as b tends to ∞, so $\int_1^\infty (1/x)\,dx$ diverges. See Fig. 2.

For $a < 1$, the last expression in ($**$) tends to ∞ as b tends to ∞. Hence, the integral diverges in this case also.

If both limits of integration are infinite, the improper integral of a continuous function f on $(-\infty, \infty)$ is defined by

$$\int_{-\infty}^\infty f(x)\,dx = \int_{-\infty}^0 f(x)\,dx + \int_0^\infty f(x)\,dx \tag{3}$$

If *both* integrals on the right-hand side converge, the improper integral $\int_{-\infty}^\infty f(x)\,dx$ is said to *converge*; otherwise, it *diverges*. Instead of using 0 as the point of subdivision, one could use an arbitrary fixed real number c. The value assigned to the integral will always be the same, provided that the integral does converge.

It is important to note that definition (3) requires both integrals on the right-hand side to converge. Note in particular that

$$\lim_{b \to \infty} \int_{-b}^b f(x)\,dx \tag{4}$$

is *not* the definition of $\int_{-\infty}^{+\infty} f(x)\,dx$. Problem 4 provides an example in which (4) exists, yet the integral in (3) diverges because $\int_{-b}^{0} f(x)\,dx \to -\infty$ as $b \to \infty$, and $\int_{0}^{b} f(x)\,dx \to \infty$ as $b \to \infty$. So (4) is not an acceptable definition, whereas (3) is.

EXAMPLE 3   For $c > 0$, prove that the following integral converges, and find its value:

$$\int_{-\infty}^{+\infty} xe^{-cx^2}\,dx$$

Solution: In the introduction to this section we proved that $\int_{0}^{\infty} xe^{-cx^2}\,dx = 1/2c$. In the same way we see that

$$\int_{-\infty}^{0} xe^{-cx^2}\,dx = \lim_{a \to -\infty} \int_{a}^{0} xe^{-cx^2}\,dx = \lim_{a \to -\infty} \left|-\frac{1}{2c}e^{-cx^2}\right|_{a}^{0} = -\frac{1}{2c}$$

It follows that

$$\int_{-\infty}^{\infty} xe^{-cx^2}\,dx = -\frac{1}{2c} + \frac{1}{2c} = 0 \qquad (c > 0) \qquad\qquad (**)$$

In fact, the function $f(x) = xe^{-cx^2}$ satisfies $f(-x) = -f(x)$ for all x, and so its graph is symmetric about the origin. For this reason, the integral $\int_{-\infty}^{0} xe^{-cx^2}\,dx$ must also exist and be equal to $-1/2c$. (This result is very important in statistics. See Problem 12.)

Integrals of Unbounded Functions

We turn next to improper integrals where the *integrand* is not bounded. Consider first the function $f(x) = 1/\sqrt{x}$, with $x \in (0, 2]$. (See Fig. 3.)

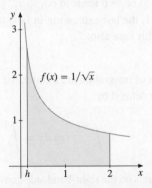

Figure 3 As $h \to 0$ the shaded area becomes unbounded, but the graph of f approaches the y-axis so quickly that the total area is finite.

Note that $f(x) \to \infty$ as $x \to 0^+$. The function f is continuous in the interval $[h, 2]$ for any fixed number h in $(0, 2)$. Therefore, the definite integral of f over the interval $[h, 2]$ exists, and in fact

$$\int_{h}^{2} \frac{1}{\sqrt{x}}\,dx = \left|2\sqrt{x}\right|_{h}^{2} = 2\sqrt{2} - 2\sqrt{h}$$

The limit of this expression as $h \to 0^+$ is $2\sqrt{2}$. Then, by definition,

$$\int_0^2 \frac{1}{\sqrt{x}}\, dx = 2\sqrt{2}$$

The improper integral is said to converge in this case, and the area below the graph of f over the interval $(0, 2]$ is $2\sqrt{2}$. The area over the interval $(h, 2]$ is shown in Fig. 3.

More generally, suppose that f is a continuous function in the interval $(a, b]$, but $f(x)$ is not defined at $x = a$. Then we can define

$$\int_a^b f(x)\, dx = \lim_{h \to 0^+} \int_{a+h}^b f(x)\, dx \tag{5}$$

if the limit exists, and the improper integral of f is said to **converge** in this case. If $f(x) \geq 0$ in $(a, b]$, we identify the integral as the *area under the graph* of f over the interval $(a, b]$.

In the same way, if f is not defined at b, we can define

$$\int_a^b f(x)\, dx = \lim_{h \to 0^+} \int_a^{b-h} f(x)\, dx \tag{6}$$

if the limit exists, in which case the improper integral of f is said to **converge**.

Suppose f is continuous in (a, b). We may not even have f defined at a or b. For instance, suppose $f(x) \to -\infty$ as $x \to a^+$ and $f(x) \to +\infty$ as $x \to b^-$. In this case, f is said to be **integrable** in (a, b), and we can define

$$\int_a^b f(x)\, dx = \int_a^c f(x)\, dx + \int_c^b f(x)\, dx \tag{7}$$

provided that both integrals on the right-hand side of (7) converge. Here c is an arbitrary fixed number in (a, b), and neither the convergence of the integral nor its value depends on the choice of c. If either of the integrals on the right-hand side of (7) does not converge, the left-hand side is not well defined.

A Comparison Test for Convergence

The following convergence test for integrals is occasionally useful because it does not require evaluation of the integral.

THEOREM 9.7.1 (A COMPARISON TEST FOR CONVERGENCE)

Suppose that f and g are continuous for all $x \geq a$ and

$$|f(x)| \leq g(x) \qquad (\text{for all } x \geq a)$$

If $\int_a^\infty g(x)\, dx$ converges, then $\int_a^\infty f(x)\, dx$ also converges, and

$$\left| \int_a^\infty f(x)\, dx \right| \leq \int_a^\infty g(x)\, dx$$

Considering the case in which $f(x) \geq 0$, Theorem 9.7.1 can be interpreted as follows: If the area below the graph of g is finite, then the area below the graph of f is finite as well, because at no point in $[a, \infty)$ does the graph of f lie above the graph of g. (Draw a figure.) This result seems quite plausible and we shall not give an analytical proof. A corresponding theorem holds for the case where the lower limit of integration is $-\infty$. Also, similar comparison tests can be proved for unbounded functions defined on bounded intervals.

EXAMPLE 4   Integrals of the form

$$\int_{t_0}^{\infty} U\big(c(t)\big) e^{-\alpha t} \, dt \qquad (*)$$

often appear in economic growth theory. Here $c(t)$ denotes consumption at time t, whereas U is an instantaneous utility function, and α is a positive discount rate. Suppose that there exist numbers M and β, with $\beta < \alpha$, such that

$$\big|U\big(c(t)\big)\big| \leq M e^{\beta t} \qquad (**)$$

for all $t \geq t_0$ and for each possible consumption level $c(t)$ at time t. Thus, the absolute value of the utility of consumption is growing at a rate less than the discount rate α. Prove that then $(*)$ converges.

Solution: From $(**)$, we have $\big|U\big(c(t)\big) e^{-\alpha t}\big| \leq M e^{-(\alpha - \beta)t}$ for all $t \geq t_0$. Moreover,

$$\int_{t_0}^{T} M e^{-(\alpha - \beta)t} \, dt = \left|_{t_0}^{T} \frac{-M}{\alpha - \beta} e^{-(\alpha - \beta)t} \right. = \frac{M}{\alpha - \beta} \left[e^{-(\alpha - \beta)t_0} - e^{-(\alpha - \beta)T} \right]$$

Because $\alpha - \beta > 0$, the last expression tends to

$$[M/(\alpha - \beta)] \, e^{-(\alpha - \beta)t_0} \qquad \text{as} \quad T \to \infty$$

From Theorem 9.7.1 it follows that $(*)$ converges.

EXAMPLE 5   The function $f(x) = e^{-x^2}$ is extremely important in statistics. When multiplied by a suitable constant (actually $1/\sqrt{\pi}$) it is the density function associated with a *Gaussian*, or *normal*, distribution. We want to show that the improper integral

$$\int_{-\infty}^{+\infty} e^{-x^2} \, dx \qquad (*)$$

converges. Recall from Section 9.1 that the indefinite integral of $f(x) = e^{-x^2}$ cannot be expressed in terms of "elementary" functions. Because $f(x) = e^{-x^2}$ is symmetric about the y-axis, one has $\int_{-\infty}^{\infty} e^{-x^2} \, dx = 2 \int_{0}^{\infty} e^{-x^2} \, dx$, so it suffices to prove that $\int_{0}^{\infty} e^{-x^2} \, dx$ converges. To show this, subdivide the interval of integration so that

$$\int_{0}^{\infty} e^{-x^2} \, dx = \int_{0}^{1} e^{-x^2} \, dx + \int_{1}^{\infty} e^{-x^2} \, dx \qquad (**)$$

Of course, $\int_{0}^{1} e^{-x^2} \, dx$ presents no problem because it is the integral of a continuous function over a bounded interval. For $x \geq 1$, one has $x^2 \geq x$ and so $0 \leq e^{-x^2} \leq e^{-x}$. Now $\int_{1}^{\infty} e^{-x} \, dx$ converges (to $1/e$), so according to Theorem 9.7.1, the integral $\int_{1}^{\infty} e^{-x^2} \, dx$ must also converge. From $(**)$, it follows that $\int_{0}^{\infty} e^{-x^2} \, dx$ converges. Thus, the integral $(*)$ does converge, but we have not found its value. In fact, more advanced techniques of integration are used in FMEA to show that

$$\int_{-\infty}^{+\infty} e^{-x^2} \, dx = \sqrt{\pi} \qquad (8)$$

PROBLEMS FOR SECTION 9.7

1. Determine the following integrals, if they converge. Indicate those that diverge.

   (a) $\displaystyle\int_1^\infty \frac{1}{x^3}\,dx$ (b) $\displaystyle\int_1^\infty \frac{1}{\sqrt{x}}\,dx$ (c) $\displaystyle\int_{-\infty}^0 e^x\,dx$ (d) $\displaystyle\int_0^a \frac{x\,dx}{\sqrt{a^2-x^2}}$ $(a > 0)$

2. Define f for all x by $f(x) = 1/(b-a)$ for $x \in [a, b]$, and $f(x) = 0$ for $x \notin [a, b]$, where $b > a$. (In statistics, f is the density function of the *uniform* (or *rectangular*) *distribution* on the interval $[a, b]$.) Find the following:

   (a) $\displaystyle\int_{-\infty}^{+\infty} f(x)\,dx$ (b) $\displaystyle\int_{-\infty}^{+\infty} xf(x)\,dx$ (c) $\displaystyle\int_{-\infty}^{+\infty} x^2 f(x)\,dx$

SM 3. In connection with Example 1, find the following:

   (a) $\displaystyle\int_0^\infty x\lambda e^{-\lambda x}\,dx$ (b) $\displaystyle\int_0^\infty (x - 1/\lambda)^2\,\lambda e^{-\lambda x}\,dx$ (c) $\displaystyle\int_0^\infty (x - 1/\lambda)^3\,\lambda e^{-\lambda x}\,dx$

   (The three numbers you obtain are called respectively the *expectation*, the *variance*, and the *third central moment* of the exponential distribution.)

4. Prove that $\displaystyle\int_{-\infty}^{+\infty} x/(1+x^2)\,dx$ diverges, but that $\displaystyle\lim_{b\to\infty}\int_{-b}^b x/(1+x^2)\,dx$ converges.

SM 5. The function f is defined for $x > 0$ by $f(x) = (\ln x)/x^3$.

   (a) Find the maximum and minimum points of f, if there are any.

   (b) Examine the convergence of $\displaystyle\int_0^1 f(x)\,dx$ and $\displaystyle\int_1^\infty f(x)\,dx$.

6. Use Theorem 9.7.1 to prove the convergence of $\displaystyle\int_1^\infty \frac{1}{1+x^2}\,dx$.

SM 7. Show that $\displaystyle\int_{-2}^3 \left(\frac{1}{\sqrt{x+2}} + \frac{1}{\sqrt{3-x}}\right) dx = 4\sqrt{5}$.

8. R. E. Hall and D. W. Jorgenson, in their article on "Tax Policy and Investment Behavior", use the integral

   $$z = \int_0^\infty e^{-rs} D(s)\,ds$$

   to represent the present discounted value, at interest rate r, of the time-dependent stream of depreciation allowances $D(s)$ $(0 \le s < \infty)$. Find z as a function of τ in the following cases:

   (a) $D(s) = 1/\tau$ for $0 \le s \le \tau$, $D(s) = 0$ for $s > \tau$. (Constant depreciation over τ years.)

   (b) $D(s) = 2(\tau - s)/\tau^2$ for $0 \le s \le \tau$, $D(s) = 0$ for $s > \tau$. (Straight-line depreciation.)

9. Suppose you evaluate $\int_{-1}^{+1}(1/x^2)\,dx$ by using the definition of the definite integral without thinking carefully. Show that you get a negative answer even though the integrand is never negative. What has gone wrong?

10. Prove that the integral $\int_0^1 \dfrac{\ln x}{\sqrt{x}} \, dx$ converges and find its value. (*Hint:* See problem 9.6.6(b).)

11. Find the integral

$$I_k = \int_1^\infty \left(\frac{k}{x} - \frac{k^2}{1+kx} \right) dx \qquad (k \text{ is a positive constant})$$

Find the limit of I_k as $k \to \infty$, if it exists.

HARDER PROBLEM

(SM) 12. In statistics, the normal, or Gaussian, density function with mean μ and variance σ^2 is defined by

$$f(x) = \frac{1}{\sigma\sqrt{2\pi}} \exp\left[-(x-\mu)^2 / 2\sigma^2 \right]$$

in the interval $(-\infty, \infty)$.[4] Prove that

(a) $\displaystyle\int_{-\infty}^{+\infty} f(x)\, dx = 1$ (b) $\displaystyle\int_{-\infty}^{+\infty} x f(x)\, dx = \mu$ (c) $\displaystyle\int_{-\infty}^{+\infty} (x - \mu)^2 f(x)\, dx = \sigma^2$

(*Hint:* Use the substitution $u = (x - \mu)/\sqrt{2}\sigma$, together with (8) and the result in Example 3.)

9.8 A Glimpse at Differential Equations

In economic growth theory, in studies of the extraction of natural resources, in many models in environmental economics, and in several other areas of economics, one encounters equations where the unknowns are functions, and where the derivatives of these functions also appear. Equations of this general type are called **differential equations**, and their study is one of the most fascinating fields of mathematics. Here we shall consider only a few simple types of such equations. We denote the independent variable by t, because most of the differential equations in economics have time as the independent variable.

We have already solved the simplest type of differential equation: Let $f(t)$ be a given function. Find all functions that have $f(t)$ as their derivative—that is, find all functions that solve $\dot{x}(t) = f(t)$ for $x(t)$. (Recall that $\dot{x}$ denotes the derivative of x w.r.t. time t.) We already know that the answer is an indefinite integral:

$$\dot{x}(t) = f(t) \iff x(t) = \int f(t)\, dt + C$$

We call $x(t) = \int f(t)\, dt + C$ the *general* solution of the equation $\dot{x}(t) = f(t)$.

Consider next some more challenging types of differential equation.

---

[4] This function, its bell-shaped graph, and a portrait of its inventor Carl Friedrich Gauss (1777–1855), appeared on the German 10-mark bank note that circulated between 1991 and 2001, in the decade before the euro was introduced.

The Law for Natural Growth

Let $x(t)$ denote an economic quantity such as the national output of China. The ratio $\dot{x}(t)/x(t)$ has previously been called the *relative rate of change* of this quantity. Several economic models postulate that the relative rate of change is approximately a constant, r. Thus,

$$\dot{x}(t) = rx(t) \qquad \text{for all } t \tag{1}$$

Which functions have a constant relative rate of change? For $r = 1$ the differential equation is $\dot{x} = x$, and we know that the derivative of $x = e^t$ is again $\dot{x} = e^t$. More generally, the function $x = Ae^t$ satisfies the equation $\dot{x} = x$ for all values of the constant A. By trial and error you will probably be able to come up with $x(t) = Ae^{rt}$ as a solution of (1). In any case, it is easy to verify: If $x = Ae^{rt}$, then $\dot{x}(t) = Are^{rt} = rx(t)$. Moreover, we can prove that no other function satisfies (1): Indeed, multiply equation (1) by the positive function e^{-rt} and collect all terms on the left-hand side. This gives

$$\dot{x}(t)e^{-rt} - rx(t)e^{-rt} = 0 \qquad \text{for all } t \tag{2}$$

Equation (2) must have precisely the same solutions as (1). But the left-hand side of this equation is the derivative of the product $x(t)e^{-rt}$. So equation (2) can be rewritten as $\frac{d}{dt}[x(t)e^{-rt}] = 0$. It follows that $x(t)e^{-rt}$ must equal a constant A. Hence, $x(t) = Ae^{rt}$. If the value of $x(t)$ at $t = 0$ is x_0, then $x_0 = Ae^0 = A$. We conclude that

$$\dot{x}(t) = rx(t), \ x(0) = x_0 \iff x(t) = x_0e^{rt} \tag{3}$$

Another way to solve (1) is to take logarithms. In fact $\frac{d}{dt}(\ln x) = \dot{x}/x = r$, so $\ln x(t) = \int r \, dt = rt + C$. This implies that $x(t) = e^{rt+C} = e^{rt}e^C = Ae^{rt}$, where $A = e^C$.

EXAMPLE 1   Let $S(t)$ denote the sales volume of a particular commodity per unit of time, evaluated at time t. In a stable market where no sales promotion is carried out, the decrease in $S(t)$ per unit of time is proportional to $S(t)$. Thus sales decelerate at the constant proportional rate $a > 0$, implying that

$$\dot{S}(t) = -aS(t)$$

(a) Find an expression for $S(t)$ when sales at time 0 are S_0.

(b) Solve the equation $S_0e^{-at} = \frac{1}{2}S_0$ for t. Interpret the answer.

Solution:

(a) This is an equation of type (1) with $x = S$ and $r = -a$. According to (3), the solution is $S(t) = S_0e^{-at}$.

(b) From $S_0e^{-at} = \frac{1}{2}S_0$, we obtain $e^{-at} = \frac{1}{2}$. Taking the natural logarithm of each side yields $-at = \ln(1/2) = -\ln 2$. Hence $t = \ln 2/a$. This is the time it takes before sales fall to half their initial level.

Equation (1) has often been called the **law for natural growth**. Whatever it may be called, this law is probably the most important differential equation that economists have to know.

Suppose that $x(t)$ denotes the number of individuals in a population at time t. The population could be, for instance, a particular colony of bacteria, or polar bears in the Arctic. We call $\dot{x}(t)/x(t)$ the *per capita growth rate* of the population. If there is neither immigration nor emigration, then the per capita rate of increase will be equal to the difference between the per capita birth and death rates. These rates will depend on many factors such as food supply, age distribution, available living space, predators, disease, and parasites, among other things.

Equation (1) specifies a simple model of population growth, the so-called **Malthus's law**. According to (3), if the per capita growth rate is constant, then the population must grow exponentially. In reality, of course, exponential growth can go on only for a limited time. Let us consider some alternative models for population growth.

Growth towards an Upper Limit

Suppose the population size $x(t)$ cannot exceed some carrying capacity K, and that the rate of change of population is proportional to its deviation from this carrying capacity:

$$\dot{x}(t) = a(K - x(t)) \tag{*}$$

With a little trick, it is easy to find all the solutions to this equation. Define a new function $u(t) = K - x(t)$, which at each time measures the deviation of the population size from the carrying capacity K. Then $\dot{u}(t) = -\dot{x}(t)$. Inserting this into (*) gives $-\dot{u}(t) = au(t)$, or $\dot{u}(t) = -au(t)$. This is an equation like (1). The solution is $u(t) = Ae^{-at}$, so that $K - x(t) = Ae^{-at}$, hence $x(t) = K - Ae^{-at}$. If $x(0) = x_0$, then $x_0 = K - A$, and so $A = K - x_0$. It follows that

$$\dot{x}(t) = a(K - x(t)), \ x(0) = x_0 \iff x(t) = K - (K - x_0)e^{-at} \tag{4}$$

In Problem 4 we shall see that the same equation describes the population in countries where the indigenous population has a fixed relative rate of growth, but where there is immigration each year. The same equation can also represent several other phenomena, some of which are discussed in the problems for this section.

EXAMPLE 2   Suppose that a population has a carrying capacity of $K = 200$ (millions) and that at time $t = 0$ there are 50 (millions). Let $x(t)$ denote the population at time t. Suppose that $a = 0.05$ and find the solution of equation (*) in this case. Sketch a graph of the solution.

Solution: Using (4) we find that

$$x(t) = 200 - (200 - 50)e^{-0.05t} = 200 - 150e^{-0.05t}$$

The graph is drawn in Fig. 1.

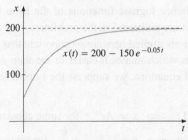

Figure 1 Growth to level 200

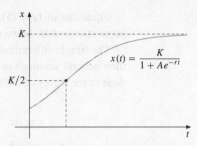

Figure 2 Logistic growth up to level K

Logistic Growth

Instead of the differential equation (∗), a more realistic assumption is that the relative rate of increase is approximately constant while the population is small, but that it converges to zero as the population approaches its carrying capacity K. A special form of this assumption is expressed by the equation

$$\dot{x}(t) = rx(t)\left(1 - \frac{x(t)}{K}\right) \tag{5}$$

Indeed, when the population $x(t)$ is small in proportion to K, so that $x(t)/K$ is small, then $\dot{x}(t) \approx rx(t)$, which implies that $x(t)$ increases (approximately) exponentially. As $x(t)$ becomes larger, however, the factor $1 - x(t)/K$ increases in significance. In general, we claim that if $x(t)$ satisfies (5) (and is not identically equal to 0), then $x(t)$ must have the form

$$x(t) = \frac{K}{1 + Ae^{-rt}} \quad \text{for some constant } A \tag{6}$$

The function x given in (6) is called a **logistic function**.

Proof of (6): We use a little trick. Suppose that $x = x(t)$ is not 0 and introduce the new variable $u = u(t) = -1 + K/x$. Then $\dot{u} = -K\dot{x}/x^2 = -Kr/x + r = -r(-1 + K/x) = -ru$. Hence $u = u(t) = Ae^{-rt}$ for some constant A. But then $-1 + K/x(t) = Ae^{-rt}$, and solving this equation for $x(t)$ yields (6). ∎

Suppose the population consists of x_0 individuals at time $t = 0$, and thus $x(0) = x_0$. Then (6) gives $x_0 = K/(1 + A)$, so that $A = (K - x_0)/x_0$. All in all, we have shown that

$$\dot{x}(t) = rx(t)\left(1 - \frac{x(t)}{K}\right), \; x(0) = x_0 \iff x(t) = \frac{K}{1 + \dfrac{K - x_0}{x_0}e^{-rt}} \tag{7}$$

If $0 < x_0 < K$, it follows from (7) that $x(t)$ is strictly increasing and that $x(t) \to K$ as $t \to \infty$ (assuming $r > 0$). We say in this case that there is *logistic growth* up to the level K. The graph of the solution is shown in Fig. 2. It has an inflection point at the height $K/2$ above the t-axis. We verify this by differentiating (5) w.r.t. t. This gives $\ddot{x} = r\dot{x}(1 - x/K) + rx(-\dot{x}/K) = r\dot{x}(1 - 2x/K) = 0$. So $\ddot{x} = 0$ when $x = K/2$, and $\ddot{x}$ changes sign at this point.

Equations of type (5), and hence logistic functions of the form (6), appear in many economic models. Some of them are discussed in the problems.

The simple differential equations studied here are so important that we present them and their general solutions in a form which makes it easier to see their structure. As is often done in the theory of differential equations, we suppress the symbol for time dependence.

$$\dot{x} = ax \quad \text{for all } t \iff x = Ae^{at} \quad \text{for some constant } A \tag{8}$$

$$\dot{x} + ax = b \quad \text{for all } t \iff x = Ae^{-at} + \frac{b}{a} \quad \text{for some constant } A \tag{9}$$

$$\dot{x} + ax = bx^2 \quad \text{for all } t \iff x = \frac{a}{b - Ae^{at}} \quad \text{for some constant } A \tag{10}$$

(In (9) we must assume that $a \neq 0$. In (10) the function $x(t) \equiv 0$ is also a solution.)

PROBLEMS FOR SECTION 9.8

1. Which of the following functions have a constant relative rate of increase, $\dot{x}/x$?

   (a) $x = 5t + 10$ (b) $x = \ln(t + 1)$ (c) $x = 5e^t$

   (d) $x = -3 \cdot 2^t$ (e) $x = e^{t^2}$ (f) $x = e^t + e^{-t}$

2. Suppose that a firm's capital stock $K(t)$ satisfies the differential equation

$$\dot{K}(t) = I - \delta K(t)$$

   where investment I is constant, and $\delta K(t)$ denotes depreciation, with δ a positive constant.

   (a) Find the solution of the equation if the capital stock at time $t = 0$ is K_0.

   (b) Let $\delta = 0.05$ and $I = 10$. Explain what happens as $t \to \infty$ when: (i) $K_0 = 150$; (ii) $K_0 = 250$.

3. Let $N(t)$ denote the number of people in a country whose homes have broadband internet. Suppose that the rate at which new people get access is proportional to the number of people who still have no access. If the population size is P, the differential equation for $N(t)$ is then

$$\dot{N}(t) = k(P - N(t))$$

   where k is a positive constant. Find the solution of this equation if $N(0) = 0$. Then find the limit of $N(t)$ as $t \to \infty$.

4. A country's annual natural rate of population growth (births minus deaths) is 2%. In addition there is a net immigration of 40 000 persons per year. Write down a differential equation for the function $N(t)$ which denotes the number of persons in the country at time t (year). Suppose that the population at time $t = 0$ is 2 000 000. Find $N(t)$.

5. Let $P(t)$ denote Europe's population in millions t years after 1960. According to UN estimates, $P(0) = 641$ and $P(10) = 705$. Suppose that $P(t)$ grows exponentially, with $P(t) = 641e^{kt}$. Compute k and then find $P(15)$ and $P(40)$ (estimates of the population in 1975 and in 2000).

6. When a colony of bacteria is subjected to strong ultraviolet light, they die as their DNA is destroyed. In a laboratory experiment it was found that the number of living bacteria decreased approximately exponentially with the length of time they were exposed to ultraviolet light. Suppose that 70.5% of the bacteria still survive after 7 seconds of exposure. What percentage will be alive after 30 seconds? How long does it take to kill 95% of the bacteria?

7. Solve the following differential equations by using one of (8)–(10):

(a) $\dot{x} = -0.5x$ (b) $\dot{K} = 0.02K$ (c) $\dot{x} = -0.5x + 5$

(d) $\dot{K} - 0.2K = 100$ (e) $\dot{x} + 0.1x = 3x^2$ (f) $\dot{K} = K(-1 + 2K)$

8. A study of British agricultural mechanization from 1950 onwards estimated that y, the number of tractors in use (measured in thousands) as a function of t (measured in years, so that $t = 0$ corresponds to 1950), was approximately given by $y(t) = 250 + x(t)$, where $x = x(t)$ satisfied the logistic differential equation

$$\dot{x} = 0.34x\,(1 - x/230)\,, \qquad x(0) = 25$$

(a) Find an expression for $y(t)$.

(b) Find the limit of $y(t)$ as $t \to \infty$, and draw the graph.

9. In a model of how influenza spreads, let $N(t)$ denote the number of persons who develop influenza t days after all members of a group of 1000 people have been in contact with a carrier of infection. Assume that

$$\dot{N}(t) = 0.39N(t)(1 - N(t)/1000)\,, \qquad N(0) = 1$$

(a) Find a formula for $N(t)$. How many develop influenza after 20 days?

(b) How many days does it take until 800 are sick?

(c) Will all 1000 people eventually get influenza?

(SM) **10.** (a) The logistic function (5) has been used for describing the stock of certain fish populations. Suppose such a population is harvested at a rate proportional to the stock, so that

$$\dot{x}(t) = rx(t)\left(1 - \frac{x(t)}{K}\right) - fx(t) \qquad (11)$$

Solve this equation, when the population at time $t = 0$ is x_0.

(b) Suppose $f > r$. Examine the limit of $x(t)$ as $t \to \infty$.

HARDER PROBLEM

11. According to *Newton's law of cooling*, the rate at which a warm object cools is proportional to the difference between the temperature of the object and the "ambient" temperature of its surroundings. If the temperature of the object at time t and the (constant) ambient temperature is C, then $\dot{T}(t) = k(C - T(t))$. Note that this is an equation of the type given in (4). At 12 noon, the police enter a room and discover a dead body. Immediately they measure its temperature, which is 35 degrees (Centigrade). At 1 pm they take the temperature again, which is now 32 degrees. The temperature in the room is constant at 20 degrees. When did the person die? (*Hint:* Let the temperature be $T(t)$, where t is measured in hours and 12 noon corresponds to $t = 0$.)

9.9 Separable and Linear Differential Equations

In this final section of the chapter we consider two general types of differential equation that are frequently encountered in economics. The discussion will be brief—for a more extensive treatment we refer to FMEA.

Separable Equations

A differential equation of the type

$$\dot{x} = f(t)g(x) \tag{1}$$

is called **separable**. The unknown function is $x = x(t)$, and its rate of change $\dot{x}$ is given as the product of a function only of t and a function only of x. A simple case is $\dot{x} = tx$, which is obviously separable, while $\dot{x} = t + x$ is not. In fact, all the differential equations studied in the previous section were separable equations of the type $\dot{x} = g(x)$, with $f(t) \equiv 1$. Equation (9.8.10), for instance, is separable, since $\dot{x} + ax = bx^2$ can be rewritten as $\dot{x} = g(x)$ where $g(x) = -ax + bx^2$.

The following general method for solving separable equations is justified in FMEA.

Method for Solving Separable Differential Equations:

A. Write equation (1) as

$$\frac{dx}{dt} = f(t)g(x) \tag{*}$$

B. Separate the variables:

$$\frac{dx}{g(x)} = f(t)\,dt$$

C. Integrate each side:

$$\int \frac{dx}{g(x)} = \int f(t)\,dt$$

D. Evaluate the two integrals (if possible) and you obtain a solution of (*) (possibly in implicit form). Solve for x, if possible.

NOTE 1 In step B we divided by $g(x)$. In fact, if $g(x)$ has a zero at $x = a$, so that $g(a) = 0$, then $x(t) \equiv a$ will be a particular solution of the equation, because the right- and left-hand sides of the equation are both 0 for all t. For instance, in the logistic equation (9.8.5), both $x(t) = 0$ and $x(t) = K$ are particular solutions.

EXAMPLE 1   Solve the differential equation

$$\frac{dx}{dt} = e^t x^2$$

and find the solution curve (often called the **integral curve**) which passes through the point $(t, x) = (0, 1)$.

Solution: We observe first that $x(t) \equiv 0$ is one (trivial) solution. To find the other solutions we follow the recipe:

Separate:
$$\frac{dx}{x^2} = e^t \, dt$$

Integrate:
$$\int \frac{dx}{x^2} = \int e^t \, dt$$

Evaluate:
$$-\frac{1}{x} = e^t + C$$

It follows that

$$x = \frac{-1}{e^t + C} \tag{$*$}$$

To find the integral curve through $(0, 1)$, we must determine the correct value of C. Because we require $x = 1$ for $t = 0$, it follows from $(*)$ that $1 = -1/(1 + C)$, so $C = -2$. Thus, the integral curve passing through $(0, 1)$ is $x = 1/(2 - e^t)$.

EXAMPLE 2   **(Economic Growth)**[5] Let $X = X(t)$ denote the national product, $K = K(t)$ the capital stock, and $L = L(t)$ the number of workers in a country at time t. Suppose that, for all $t \geq 0$,

(a) $X = \sqrt{K}\sqrt{L}$ (b) $\dot{K} = 0.4X$ (c) $L = e^{0.04t}$

Derive from these equations a single differential equation for $K = K(t)$, and find the solution of that equation when $K(0) = 10000$. (In (a) we have a Cobb–Douglas production function, (b) says that aggregate investment is proportional to output, whereas (c) implies that the labour force grows exponentially.)

Solution: From equations (a)–(c), we derive the single differential equation

$$\dot{K} = \frac{dK}{dt} = 0.4\sqrt{K}\sqrt{L} = 0.4e^{0.02t}\sqrt{K}$$

This is clearly separable. Using the recipe yields:

$$\frac{dK}{\sqrt{K}} = 0.4e^{0.02t} \, dt$$

$$\int \frac{dK}{\sqrt{K}} = \int 0.4e^{0.02t} \, dt$$

$$2\sqrt{K} = 20e^{0.02t} + C$$

If $K = 10\,000$ for $t = 0$, then $2\sqrt{10\,000} = 20 + C$, so $C = 180$. Then $\sqrt{K} = 10e^{0.02t} + 90$, and so the required solution is

$$K(t) = (10e^{0.02t} + 90)^2 = 100(e^{0.02t} + 9)^2$$

The capital–labour ratio has a somewhat bizarre limiting value in this model: $K(t)/L(t) = 100(e^{0.02t} + 9)^2/e^{0.04t} = 100[(e^{0.02t} + 9)/e^{0.02t}]^2 = 100[1 + 9e^{-0.02t}]^2 \to 100$ as $t \to \infty$.

---

[5] This is a special case of the Solow–Swan growth model. See Example 5.7.3 in FMEA.

EXAMPLE 3   Solve the separable differential equation $(\ln x)\dot{x} = e^{1-t}$.

Solution: Following the recipe yields

$$\ln x \,\frac{dx}{dt} = e^{1-t}$$

$$\ln x \, dx = e^{1-t}\, dt$$

$$\int \ln x \, dx = \int e^{1-t}\, dt$$

$$x \ln x - x = -e^{1-t} + C$$

Here we used the result in Example 9.1.3. The desired functions $x = x(t)$ are those that satisfy the last equation for all t.

NOTE 2   We usually say that we have solved a differential equation even if the unknown function (as shown in Example 3) cannot be expressed explicitly. The important point is that we have expressed the unknown function in an equation that does not include the derivative of that function.

First-Order Linear Equations

A **first-order linear differential equation** is one that can be written in the form

$$\dot{x} + a(t)x = b(t) \tag{2}$$

where $a(t)$ and $b(t)$ denote known continuous functions of t in a certain interval, and $x = x(t)$ is the unknown function. Equation (2) is called "linear" because the left-hand side is a linear function of x and $\dot{x}$.

When $a(t)$ and $b(t)$ are constants, the solution was given in (9.8.9):

$$\dot{x} + ax = b \iff x = Ce^{-at} + \frac{b}{a} \qquad (C \text{ is a constant}) \tag{3}$$

We found the solution of this equation by introducing a new variable. In fact, the equation is separable, so the recipe for separable equations will also lead us to the solution. If we let $C = 0$ we obtain the constant solution $x(t) = b/a$. We say that $x = b/a$ is an *equilibrium state*, or a *stationary state*, for the equation. Observe how this solution can be obtained from $\dot{x} + ax = b$ by letting $\dot{x} = 0$ and then solving the resulting equation for x. If the constant a is positive, then the solution $x = Ce^{-at} + b/a$ converges to b/a as $t \to \infty$. In this case, the equation is said to be **stable**, because every solution of the equation converges to an equilibrium as t approaches infinity. (Stability theory is an important issue for differential equations appearing in economics. See e.g. FMEA for an extensive discussion.)

EXAMPLE 4   Find the solution of

$$\dot{x} + 3x = -9$$

and determine whether the equation is stable.

Solution: By (3), the solution is $x = Ce^{-3t} - 3$. Here the equilibrium state is $x = -3$, and the equation is stable because $a = 3 > 0$, and $x \to -3$ as $t \to \infty$.

EXAMPLE 5

(Price Adjustment Mechanism) Let $D(P) = a - bP$ denote the demand quantity and $S(P) = \alpha + \beta P$ the supply of a certain commodity when the price is P. Here a, b, α, and β are positive constants. Assume that the price $P = P(t)$ varies with time, and that $\dot{P}$ is proportional to excess demand $D(P) - S(P)$. Thus,

$$\dot{P} = \lambda[D(P) - S(P)]$$

where λ is a positive constant. Inserting the expressions for $D(P)$ and $S(P)$ into this equation gives $\dot{P} = \lambda(a - bP - \alpha - \beta P)$. Rearranging, we then obtain

$$\dot{P} + \lambda(b + \beta)P = \lambda(a - \alpha)$$

According to (3), the solution is

$$P = Ce^{-\lambda(b+\beta)t} + \frac{a - \alpha}{b + \beta}$$

Because $\lambda(b + \beta)$ is positive, as t tends to infinity, P converges to the equilibrium price $P^e = (a - \alpha)/(b + \beta)$, for which $D(P^e) = S(P^e)$. Thus, the equation is stable.

Variable Right-Hand Side

Consider next the case where the right-hand side is not constant:

$$\dot{x} + ax = b(t) \tag{4}$$

When $b(t)$ is not constant, this equation is not separable. A clever trick helps us find the solution. We multiply each side of the equation by the positive factor e^{at}, called an **integrating factor**. This gives the equivalent equation

$$\dot{x}e^{at} + axe^{at} = b(t)e^{at} \tag{$*$}$$

This idea may not be obvious beforehand, but it works well because the left-hand side of ($*$) happens to be the exact derivative of the product xe^{at}. Thus ($*$) is equivalent to

$$\frac{d}{dt}(xe^{at}) = b(t)e^{at} \tag{$**$}$$

According to the definition of the indefinite integral, equation ($**$) holds for all t in an interval iff $xe^{at} = \int b(t)e^{at}\, dt + C$ for some constant C. Multiplying this equation by e^{-at} gives the solution for x. Briefly formulated:

$$\dot{x} + ax = b(t) \iff x = Ce^{-at} + e^{-at} \int e^{at} b(t)\, dt \tag{5}$$

EXAMPLE 6   Find the solution of

$$\dot{x} + x = t$$

and determine the solution curve passing through $(0, 0)$.

Solution: According to (5), with $a = 1$ and $b(t) = t$, the solution is given by

$$x = Ce^{-t} + e^{-t} \int te^t \, dt = Ce^{-t} + e^{-t}(te^t - e^t) = Ce^{-t} + t - 1$$

where we used integration by parts to evaluate $\int te^t \, dt$. (See Example 9.5.1.) If $x = 0$ when $t = 0$, we get $0 = C - 1$, so $C = 1$ and the required solution is $x = e^{-t} + t - 1$.   ∎

EXAMPLE 7   **(Economic Growth)** Consider the following model of economic growth in a developing country (see FMEA, Example 5.4.3 for a more general model):

(a) $X(t) = 0.2K(t)$ (b) $\dot{K}(t) = 0.1X(t) + H(t)$ (c) $N(t) = 50e^{0.03t}$

Here $X(t)$ is total domestic product per year, $K(t)$ is capital stock, $H(t)$ is the net inflow of foreign investment per year, and $N(t)$ is the size of the population, all measured at time t. In (a) we assume that the volume of production is simply proportional to the capital stock, with the factor of proportionality 0.2 being called the *average productivity of capital*. In (b) we assume that the total growth of capital per year is equal to internal savings plus net foreign investment. We assume that savings are proportional to production, with the factor of proportionality 0.1 being called the *savings rate*. Finally, (c) tells us that population increases at a constant proportional rate of growth 0.03.

Assume that $H(t) = 10e^{0.04t}$ and derive from these equations a differential equation for $K(t)$. Find its solution given that $K(0) = 200$. Find also an expression for $x(t) = X(t)/N(t)$, which is domestic product per capita.

Solution: From (a) and (b), it follows that $K(t)$ must satisfy the linear equation

$$\dot{K}(t) - 0.02K(t) = 10e^{0.04t}$$

Using (5) we obtain

$$K(t) = Ce^{0.02t} + e^{0.02t} \int e^{-0.02t} 10e^{0.04t} \, dt = Ce^{0.02t} + 10e^{0.02t} \int e^{0.02t} \, dt$$

$$= Ce^{0.02t} + (10/0.02)e^{0.04t} = Ce^{0.02t} + 500e^{0.04t}$$

For $t = 0$, $K(0) = 200 = C + 500$, so $C = -300$. Thus, the solution is

$$K(t) = 500e^{0.04t} - 300e^{0.02t} \qquad (*)$$

Per capita production is $x(t) = X(t)/N(t) = 0.2K(t)/50e^{0.03t} = 2e^{0.01t} - 1.2e^{-0.01t}$.   ∎

The solution procedure for the general linear differential equation (2) is somewhat more complicated, and we refer to FMEA.

PROBLEMS FOR SECTION 9.9

1. Solve the equation $x^4 \dot{x} = 1 - t$. Find the integral curve through $(t, x) = (1, 1)$.

SM 2. Solve the following differential equations

(a) $\dot{x} = e^{2t}/x^2$

(b) $\dot{x} = e^{-t+x}$

(c) $\dot{x} - 3x = 18$

(d) $\dot{x} = (1+t)^6/x^6$

(e) $\dot{x} - 2x = -t$

(f) $\dot{x} + 3x = te^{t^2-3t}$

3. Suppose that $y = \alpha k e^{\beta t}$ denotes production as a function of capital k, where the factor $e^{\beta t}$ is due to technical progress. Suppose that a constant fraction $s \in (0, 1)$ is saved, and that capital accumulation is equal to savings, so that we have the separable differential equation

$$\dot{k} = s\alpha k e^{\beta t}, \quad k(0) = k_0$$

The constants α, β, and k_0 are positive. Find the solution.

4. (a) Suppose $Y = Y(t)$ is national product, $C(t)$ is consumption at time t, and $\bar{I}$ is investment, which is constant. Suppose $\dot{Y} = \alpha(C + \bar{I} - Y)$ and $C = aY + b$, where a, b, and α are positive constants with $a < 1$. Derive a differential equation for Y.

(b) Find its solution when $Y(0) = Y_0$ is given. What happens to $Y(t)$ as $t \to \infty$?

SM 5. (a) In a growth model production Q is a function of capital K and labour L. Suppose that (i) $\dot{K} = \gamma Q$, (ii) $Q = K^\alpha L$, (iii) $\dot{L}/L = \beta$ with $L(0) = L_0$. Assume that $\beta \neq 0$ and $\alpha \in (0, 1)$. Derive a differential equation for K.

(b) Solve this equation when $K(0) = K_0$.

6. Find $x(t)$ when $\text{El}_t\, x(t) = a$ for all t. Assume that both t and x are positive and that a is a constant. (Recall that $\text{El}_t\, x(t)$ is the elasticity of $x(t)$ w.r.t. t.)

REVIEW PROBLEMS FOR CHAPTER 9

1. Find the following integrals:

(a) $\displaystyle\int (-16)\, dx$

(b) $\displaystyle\int 5^5\, dx$

(c) $\displaystyle\int (3 - y)\, dy$

(d) $\displaystyle\int (r - 4r^{1/4})\, dr$

(e) $\displaystyle\int x^8\, dx$

(f) $\displaystyle\int x^2 \sqrt{x}\, dx$

(g) $\displaystyle\int \frac{1}{p^5}\, dp$

(h) $\displaystyle\int (x^3 + x)\, dx$

2. Find the following integrals:

(a) $\displaystyle\int 2e^{2x}\, dx$

(b) $\displaystyle\int (x - 5e^{\frac{2}{3}x})\, dx$

(c) $\displaystyle\int (e^{-3x} + e^{3x})\, dx$

(d) $\displaystyle\int \frac{2}{x+5}\, dx$

3. Evaluate the following integrals:

(a) $\displaystyle\int_0^{12} 50\, dx$

(b) $\displaystyle\int_0^2 (x - \tfrac{1}{2}x^2)\, dx$

(c) $\displaystyle\int_{-3}^3 (u + 1)^2\, du$

(d) $\displaystyle\int_1^5 \frac{2}{z}\, dz$

(e) $\displaystyle\int_2^{12} \frac{3\, dt}{t+4}\, dt$

(f) $\displaystyle\int_0^4 v\sqrt{v^2 + 9}\, dv$

(SM) **4.** Find the following integrals:

(a) $\displaystyle\int_1^\infty \frac{5}{x^5}\,dx$ 　(b) $\displaystyle\int_0^1 x^3(1+x^4)^4\,dx$ 　(c) $\displaystyle\int_0^\infty \frac{-5t}{e^t}\,dt$ 　(d) $\displaystyle\int_1^e (\ln x)^2\,dx$

(e) $\displaystyle\int_0^2 x^2\sqrt{x^3+1}\,dx$ 　(f) $\displaystyle\int_{-\infty}^0 \frac{e^{3z}}{e^{3z}+5}\,dz$ 　(g) $\displaystyle\int_{1/2}^{e/2} x^3\ln(2x)\,dx$ 　(h) $\displaystyle\int_1^\infty \frac{e^{-\sqrt{x}}}{\sqrt{x}}\,dx$

(SM) **5.** Find the following integrals:

(a) $\displaystyle\int_0^{25} \frac{1}{9+\sqrt{x}}\,dx$ 　(b) $\displaystyle\int_2^7 t\sqrt{t+2}\,dt$ 　(c) $\displaystyle\int_0^1 57x^2\sqrt[3]{19x^3+8}\,dx$

6. Find $F'(x)$ if 　(a) $F(x)=\displaystyle\int_4^x \left(\sqrt{u}+\frac{x}{\sqrt{u}}\right)du$ 　(b) $F(x)=\displaystyle\int_{\sqrt{x}}^x \ln u\,du$

7. With $C(Y)$ as the consumption function, suppose the marginal propensity to consume is $C'(Y)=0.69$, with $C(0)=1000$. Find $C(Y)$.

8. In the manufacture of a product, the marginal cost of producing x units is $C'(x)=\alpha e^{\beta x}+\gamma$, with $\beta\neq 0$, and fixed costs are C_0. Find the total cost function $C(x)$.

9. Suppose f and g are continuous functions on $[-1,3]$ and that $\displaystyle\int_{-1}^3 (f(x)+g(x))\,dx=6$ and $\displaystyle\int_{-1}^3 (3f(x)+4g(x))\,dx=9$. Find $I=\displaystyle\int_{-1}^3 (f(x)+g(x))\,dx$.

(SM) **10.** For the following two cases, find the equilibrium price and quantity and calculate the consumer and producer surplus when the demand curve is $f(Q)$ and the supply curve is $g(Q)$:

(a) $f(Q)=100-0.05Q$ and $g(Q)=10+0.1Q$.

(b) $f(Q)=\dfrac{50}{Q+5}$ and $g(Q)=4.5+0.1Q$.

(SM) **11.** (a) Define f for $t>0$ by $f(t)=4\dfrac{(\ln t)^2}{t}$. Find $f'(t)$ and $f''(t)$.

(b) Find possible local extreme points, and sketch the graph of f.

(c) Calculate the area below the graph of f over the interval $\left[1,e^2\right]$.

12. Solve the following differential equations:

(a) $\dot{x}=-3x$ 　　(b) $\dot{x}+4x=12$ 　　(c) $\dot{x}-3x=12x^2$

(d) $5\dot{x}=-x$ 　　(e) $3\dot{x}+6x=10$ 　　(f) $\dot{x}-\frac{1}{2}x=x^2$

(SM) **13.** Solve the following differential equations:

(a) $\dot{x}=tx^2$ 　　(b) $2\dot{x}+3x=-15$ 　　(c) $\dot{x}-3x=30$

(d) $\dot{x}+5x=10t$ 　　(e) $\dot{x}+\frac{1}{2}x=e^t$ 　　(f) $\dot{x}+3x=t^2$

14. (a) Let $V(x)$ denote the number of litres of fuel left in an aircraft's fuel tank if it has flown x km. Suppose that $V(x)$ satisfies the following differential equation:

$$V'(x) = -aV(x) - b$$

(The fuel consumption per km is a constant $b > 0$. The term $-aV(x)$, with $a > 0$, is due to the weight of the fuel.) Find the solution of the equation with $V(0) = V_0$.

(b) How many km, x^*, can the plane fly if it takes off with V_0 litres in its tank?

(c) What is the minimum number of litres, V_m, needed at the outset if the plane is to fly $\hat{x}$ km?

(d) Put $b = 8$, $a = 0.001$, $V_0 = 12\,000$, and $\hat{x} = 1200$. Find x^* and V_m in this case.

15. A population of n individuals has an income density function $f(r) = (1/m)e^{-r/m}$ for r in $[0, \infty)$, where m is a positive constant. (See Section 9.4.)

(a) Show that m is the mean income.

(b) Suppose the demand function is $D(p, r) = ar - bp$. Compute the total demand $x(p)$ when the income distribution is as in (a).

HARDER PROBLEM

SM 16. A probability density function f is defined for all x by

$$f(x) = \frac{\lambda a e^{-\lambda x}}{(e^{-\lambda x} + a)^2} \qquad (a \text{ and } \lambda \text{ are positive constants})$$

(a) Show that $F(x) = \dfrac{a}{e^{-\lambda x} + a}$ is an indefinite integral of $f(x)$, and determine $\lim_{x \to \infty} F(x)$ and $\lim_{x \to -\infty} F(x)$.

(b) Show that $\displaystyle\int_{-\infty}^{x} f(t)\, dt = F(x)$, and that $F(x)$ is strictly increasing.

(c) Compute $F''(x)$ and show that F has an inflection point x_0. Compute $F(x_0)$ and sketch the graph of F.

(d) Compute $\displaystyle\int_{-\infty}^{\infty} f(x)\, dx$.

10

TOPICS IN FINANCIAL ECONOMICS

I can calculate the motions of heavenly bodies, but not the madness of people.[1]
—I. Newton (attr.)

This chapter treats some basic topics in the mathematics of finance. The main concern is how the values of investments and loans at different times are affected by interest rates.

Sections 1.2 and 4.9 have already discussed some elementary calculations involving interest rates. This chapter goes a step further and considers different interest periods. It also discusses in turn effective rates of interest, continuously compounded interest, present values of future claims, annuities, mortgages, and the internal rate of return on investment projects. The calculations involve the summation formula for geometric series, which we therefore derive.

In the last section we give a brief introduction to difference equations.

10.1 Interest Periods and Effective Rates

In advertisements that offer bank loans or savings accounts, interest is usually quoted as an *annual rate*, also called a *nominal rate*, even if the actual interest period is different. This **interest period** is the time which elapses between successive dates when interest is added to the account. For some bank accounts the interest period is one year, but recently it has become increasingly common for financial institutions to offer other interest schemes. For instance, many US bank accounts now add interest daily, some others at least monthly. If a bank offers 9% annual rate of interest with interest payments each month, then $(1/12)9\% = 0.75\%$ of the capital accrues at the end of each month. The annual rate must be divided by the number of interest periods to get the **periodic rate**—that is, the interest per period.

Suppose a principal (or capital) of S_0 yields interest at the rate $p\%$ per period (for example one year). As explained in Section 1.2, after t periods it will have increased to the amount

$$S(t) = S_0(1+r)^t \qquad \text{where} \quad r = p/100$$

Each period the principal increases by the factor $1 + r$. Note that $p\%$ means $p/100$, and we say that the **interest rate** is $p\%$ or r.

---
[1] Claimed to be Newton's reaction to the outcome of the "South Sea Bubble", a serious financial crisis in 1720, in which Newton lost money.

The formula assumes that the interest is added to the principal at the end of each period. Suppose that the annual interest rate is $p\%$, but that interest is paid biannually (i.e. twice a year) at the rate $p/2\%$. Then the principal after half a year will have increased to

$$S_0 + S_0 \frac{p/2}{100} = S_0\left(1 + \frac{r}{2}\right)$$

Each half year the principal increases by the factor $1 + r/2$. After 2 periods (= one year) it will have increased to $S_0(1 + r/2)^2$, and after t years to

$$S_0\left(1 + \frac{r}{2}\right)^{2t}$$

Note that a biannual interest payment at the rate $\frac{1}{2}r$ is better for a lender than an annual interest payment at the rate r. This follows from the fact that $(1 + r/2)^2 = 1 + r + r^2/4 > 1 + r$.

More generally, suppose that interest at the rate $p/n\%$ is added to the principal at n different times distributed more or less evenly over the year. For example, $n = 4$ if interest is added quarterly, $n = 12$ if it is added monthly, etc. Then the *principal will be multiplied by a factor* $(1 + r/n)^n$ *each year.* After t years, the principal will have increased to

$$S_0\left(1 + \frac{r}{n}\right)^{nt} \tag{1}$$

The greater is n, the faster interest accrues to the lender. (See Problem 10.2.6.)

EXAMPLE 1   A deposit of £5000 is put into an account earning interest at the annual rate of 9%, with interest paid quarterly. How much will there be in the account after 8 years?

Solution: The periodic rate r/n is $0.09/4 = 0.0225$ and the number of periods nt is $4 \cdot 8 = 32$. So formula (1) gives:

$$5000(1 + 0.0225)^{32} \approx 10\,190.52$$

EXAMPLE 2   How long will it take for the £5000 in Example 1 (with annual interest rate 9% and interest paid quarterly) to increase to £15 000?

Solution: After t quarterly payments the account will grow to $5000(1 + 0.0225)^t$. So

$$5000(1 + 0.0225)^t = 15\,000 \quad \text{or} \quad 1.0225^t = 3$$

To find t we take the natural logarithm of each side:

$$t \ln 1.0225 = \ln 3 \quad \text{(because } \ln a^p = p \ln a\text{)}$$

$$t = \frac{\ln 3}{\ln 1.0225} \approx 49.37$$

Thus it takes approximately 49.37 quarterly periods, that is approximately 12 years and four months, before the account has increased to £15 000.

Effective Rate of Interest

A consumer who needs a loan may receive different offers from several competing financial institutions. It is therefore important to know how to compare various offers. The concept of *effective interest rate* is often used in making such comparisons.

Consider a loan which implies an annual interest rate of 9% with interest at the rate $9/12 = 0.75\%$ added 12 times a year. If no interest is paid in the meantime, after one year an initial principal of S_0 will have grown to a debt of $S_0(1 + 0.09/12)^{12} \approx S_0 \cdot 1.094$. In fact, as long as no interest is paid, the debt will grow at a constant proportional rate that is (approximately) 9.4% per year. For this reason, we call 9.4% the effective yearly rate. More generally:

EFFECTIVE YEARLY RATE

When interest is added n times during the year at the rate r/n per period, then the effective yearly rate R is defined as

$$R = \left(1 + \frac{r}{n}\right)^n - 1$$

(2)

The effective yearly rate is independent of the amount S_0. For a given value of $r > 0$, it is increasing in n. (See Problem 10.2.6.)

EXAMPLE 3   What is the effective yearly rate R corresponding to an annual interest rate of 9% with interest compounded: (i) each quarter; (ii) each month?

Solution:

(i) Applying formula (2) with $r = 0.09$ and $n = 4$, the effective rate is

$$R = \left(1 + 0.09/4\right)^4 - 1 = (1 + 0.0225)^4 - 1 \approx 0.0931 \quad \text{or} \quad 9.31\%$$

(ii) In this case $r = 0.09$ and $n = 12$, so the effective rate is

$$R = \left(1 + 0.09/12\right)^{12} - 1 = (1 + 0.0075)^{12} - 1 \approx 0.0938 \quad \text{or} \quad 9.38\%$$

A typical case in which we can use the effective rate of interest to compare different financial offers is the following.

EXAMPLE 4   When investing in a savings account, which of the following offers are better: 5.9% with interest paid quarterly; or 6% with interest paid twice a year?

Solution: According to (2), the effective rates for the two offers are

$$R = \left(1 + 0.059/4\right)^4 - 1 \approx 0.0603, \qquad R = \left(1 + 0.06/2\right)^2 - 1 = 0.0609$$

The second offer is therefore better for the saver.

NOTE 1 In many countries there is an official legal definition of effective interest rate which takes into account different forms of fixed or "closing" costs incurred when initiating a loan. The **effective rate of interest** is then defined as the rate which implies that the combined present value of all the costs is equal to the size of the loan. This is the internal rate of return, as defined in Section 10.7. (Present values are discussed in Section 10.3.)

PROBLEMS FOR SECTION 10.1

1. (a) What will be the size of an account after 5 years if $8000 is invested at an annual interest rate of 5% compounded (i) monthly; (ii) daily (with 365 days in a year)?

   (b) How long does it take for the $8000 to double with monthly compounding?

2. (a) An amount $5000 earns interest at 3% per year. What will this amount have grown to after 10 years?

   (b) How long does it take for the $5000 to triple?

3. What annual percentage rate of growth is needed for a country's GDP to become 100 times as large after 100 years? ($\sqrt[100]{100} \approx 1.047$.)

4. (a) An amount of 2000 euros is invested at 7% per year. What is the balance in the account after (i) 2 years; (ii) 10 years?

   (b) How long does it take (approximately) for the balance to reach 6000 euros?

5. Calculate the effective yearly interest if the nominal rate is 17% and interest is added: (i) biannually; (ii) quarterly; (iii) monthly.

6. Which terms are preferable for a borrower: (i) an annual interest rate of 21.5%, with interest paid yearly; or (ii) an annual interest rate of 20%, with interest paid quarterly?

7. (a) A sum of $12 000 is invested at 4% annual interest. What will this amount have grown to after 15 years?

   (b) How much should you have deposited in a bank account 5 years ago in order to have $50 000 today, given that the interest rate has been 5% per year over the period?

   (c) A credit card is offered with interest on the outstanding balance charged at 2% per month. What is the effective annual rate of interest?

8. What is the nominal yearly interest rate if the effective yearly rate is 28% and interest is compounded quarterly?

10.2 Continuous Compounding

We saw in the previous section that if interest at the rate r/n is added to the principal S_0 at n different times during the year, the principal will be multiplied by a factor $(1 + r/n)^n$ each year. After t years, the principal will have increased to $S_0(1 + r/n)^{nt}$. In practice, there is a limit to how frequently interest can be added to an account. However, let us examine what happens to the expression as the annual frequency n tends to infinity. We put $r/n = 1/m$. Then $n = mr$ and so

$$S_0\left(1 + \frac{r}{n}\right)^{nt} = S_0\left(1 + \frac{1}{m}\right)^{mrt} = S_0\left[\left(1 + \frac{1}{m}\right)^m\right]^{rt} \tag{1}$$

As $n \to \infty$ (with r fixed), so $m = n/r \to \infty$, and according to Example 7.11.2, we have $(1 + 1/m)^m \to e$. Hence, the expression in (1) approaches $S_0 e^{rt}$ as n tends to infinity, implying that interest is compounded more and more frequently. In the limit, we talk about *continuous compounding* of interest:

CONTINUOUS COMPOUNDING OF INTEREST

The formula

$$S(t) = S_0 e^{rt}$$

(2)

shows how much a principal of S_0 will have increased to after t years, if the annual interest is r, and there is continuous compounding of interest.

EXAMPLE 1   Suppose the sum of £5000 is invested in an account earning interest at an annual rate of 9%. What is the balance after 8 years if interest is compounded continuously?

Solution: Using formula (2) with $r = 9/100 = 0.09$, we see that the balance is

$$5000 e^{0.09 \cdot 8} = 5000 e^{0.72} \approx 10\,272.17$$

(Compare with the result in Example 10.1.1.)

If $S(t) = S_0 e^{rt}$, then $S'(t) = S_0 r e^{rt} = r S(t)$ (according to formula (6.10.2)), and so $S'(t)/S(t) = r$. Using the terminology introduced in Section 6.4:

With continuous compounding of interest at the rate r, the principal increases at the constant relative rate r, so that $S'(t)/S(t) = r$.

From (2), we infer that $S(1) = S_0 e^r$, so that the principal increases by the factor e^r during the first year. In general, $S(t + 1) = S_0 e^{r(t+1)} = S_0 e^{rt} e^r = S(t) e^r$. Hence:

With continuous compounding of interest, the principal increases each year by a fixed factor e^r.

Comparing Different Interest Periods

Given any fixed interest rate of $p\%$ ($= 100r$) per year, continuous compounding of interest is best for the lender. (See Problem 6.) For comparatively low interest rates, however, the difference between annual and continuous compounding of interest is quite small, when the number of years of compounding is relatively small.

EXAMPLE 2   Find the amount K by which \$1 increases in the course of a year when the interest rate is 8% per year and interest is added: (a) yearly; (b) biannually; (c) continuously.

Solution: In this case $r = 8/100 = 0.08$, and we obtain

(a) $K = 1.08$ (b) $K = (1 + 0.08/2)^2 = 1.0816$ (c) $K = e^{0.08} \approx 1.08329$

If we increase either the interest rate or the number of years over which interest accumulates, then the difference between yearly and continuous compounding of interest increases.

In the previous section the effective yearly interest was defined by the formula $(1 + r/n)^n - 1$, when interest is compounded n times a year with rate r/n per period. Letting n approach infinity in this formula, we see that the expression approaches

$$e^r - 1 \tag{3}$$

This is called the **effective interest** rate with continuous compounding at the annual rate r.

PROBLEMS FOR SECTION 10.2

1. (a) How much does \$8000 grow to after 5 years if the annual interest rate is 5%, with continuous compounding?

   (b) How long does it take before the \$8000 has doubled?

2. An amount \$1000 earns interest at 5% per year. What will this amount have grown to after (a) 10 years, and (b) 50 years, when interest is compounded (i) yearly, or (ii) monthly, or (iii) continuously?

3. (a) Find the effective rate corresponding to an annual rate of 10% compounded continuously.

   (b) What is the maximum amount of compound interest that can be earned at an annual rate of 10%?

4. The value v_0 of a new car depreciates continuously at the annual rate of 10%—that is, $v(t) = v_0 e^{-\delta t}$ where $\delta = 0.1$ is the *rate of depreciation*. How many years does it take for the car to lose 90% of its original value?

5. The value of a machine depreciates continuously at the annual rate of 6%. How many years will it take for the value of the machine to halve?

HARDER PROBLEM

(SM) **6.** The argument we used to justify (2) shows in particular that $(1 + r/n)^n \to e^r$ as $n \to \infty$. For each fixed $r > 0$ we claim that $(1 + r/n)^n$ is strictly increasing in n. In particular, this implies that

$$(1 + r/n)^n < e^r \quad \text{for} \quad n = 1, 2, \ldots \tag{*}$$

This shows that continuous compounding at interest rate r is more profitable for the lender than interest payments n times a year at interest rate r/n.

To confirm these results, given any $r > 0$, define the function $g(x) = (1 + r/x)^x$ for all $x > 0$. Use logarithmic differentiation to show that

$$g'(x) = g(x)\left[\ln(1 + r/x) - \frac{r/x}{1 + r/x}\right]$$

Next, put $h(u) = \ln(1 + u) - u/(1 + u)$. Then $h(0) = 0$. Show that $h'(u) > 0$ for $u > 0$, and hence $g'(x) > 0$ for all $x > 0$. What conclusion can you draw?

10.3 Present Value

The sum of $1000 in your hand today is worth more than $1000 to be received at some future date. One important reason is that you can invest the $1000 and hope to earn some interest or other positive return.[2] If the interest rate is 11% per year, then after 1 year the original $1000 will have grown to the amount $1000(1 + 11/100) = 1110$, and after 6 years, it will have grown to $1000(1 + 11/100)^6 = 1000 \cdot (1.11)^6 \approx 1870$. This shows that, at the interest rate 11% per year, $1000 now has the same value as $1110 next year, or $1870 in 6 years time. Accordingly, if the amount $1110 is due for payment 1 year from now and the interest rate is 11% per year, then the *present value* of this amount is $1000. Because $1000 is less than $1110, we often speak of $1000 as the *present discounted value* (or PDV) of $1110 next year. The ratio $1000/$1110 = 1/(1 + 11/100) \approx 0.9009$ is called the (annual) *discount factor*, whose reciprocal 1.11 is one plus the *discount rate*, making the discount rate equal to the interest rate of 11%.

Similarly, if the interest rate is 11% per year, then the PDV of $1870 due 6 years from now is $1000. Again, the ratio $1000/$1870 \approx 0.53$ is called the *discount factor*, this time for money due in 6 years time.

Suppose that an amount K is due for payment t years after the present date. What is the *present value* when the interest rate is $p\%$ per year? Equivalently, how much must be deposited today earning $p\%$ annual interest in order to have the amount K after t years?

If interest is paid annually, an amount A will have increased to $A(1 + p/100)^t$ after t years, so that we need $A(1 + p/100)^t = K$. Thus, $A = K(1 + p/100)^{-t} = K(1 + r)^{-t}$, where $r = p/100$. Here the annual discount factor is $(1 + r)^{-1}$, and $(1 + r)^{-t}$ is the discount factor appropriate for t years.

---

[2] If prices are expected to increase, another reason for preferring $1000 today is inflation, because $1000 to be paid at some future date will buy less then than $1000 does today.

If interest is compounded continuously, then the amount A will have increased to Ae^{rt} after t years. Hence, $Ae^{rt} = K$, or $A = Ke^{-rt}$. Here e^{-rt} is the discount factor. To summarize:

PRESENT DISCOUNTED VALUE

If the interest or discount rate is $p\%$ per year and $r = p/100$, an amount K that is payable in t years has the present value (or present discounted value, or PDV):

$$K(1+r)^{-t}, \qquad \text{with annual interest payments}$$
$$Ke^{-rt}, \qquad \text{with continuous compounding of interest}$$

(1)

EXAMPLE 1   Find the present value of \$100 000 which is due for payment after 15 years if the interest rate is 6% per year, compounded (i) annually, or (ii) continuously.

Solution:

(i) According to (1), the present value is $100\,000(1 + 0.06)^{-15} \approx 41726.51$.

(ii) According to (1), the present value is $100\,000e^{-0.06 \cdot 15} = 100\,000e^{-0.9} \approx 40656.97$. As expected, the present value with continuous compounding is the smaller, because capital increases most rapidly with continuous compounding of interest.

EXAMPLE 2   (**When to Harvest a Tree?**) Consider a tree that is planted at time $t = 0$, and let $P(t)$ be its current market value at time t, where $P(t)$ is differentiable with $P(t) > 0$ for all $t \geq 0$. Assume that the interest rate is $100r\%$ per year, and assume continuous compounding of interest.

(a) At what time t^* should this tree be cut down in order to maximize its present value?

(b) The optimal cutting time t^* depends on the interest rate r. Find dt^*/dr.

Solution: (a) The present value is $f(t) = P(t)e^{-rt}$, whose derivative is

$$f'(t) = P'(t)e^{-rt} + P(t)(-r)e^{-rt} = e^{-rt}\left[P'(t) - rP(t)\right] \qquad (*)$$

A necessary condition for $t^* > 0$ to maximize $f(t)$ is that $f'(t^*) = 0$. This occurs when

$$P'(t^*) = rP(t^*) \qquad (**)$$

The tree, therefore, should be cut down at a time t^* when the relative rate of increase in the value of the tree is precisely equal to the interest rate. Of course, some conditions have to be placed on f in order for t^* to be a maximum point. It suffices to have $P'(t) \geq rP(t)$ for $t < t^*$ and $P'(t) \leq rP(t)$ for $t > t^*$.

(b) Differentiating $(**)$ w.r.t r yields $P''(t^*)\, dt^*/dr = P(t^*) + rP'(t^*)\, dt^*/dr$. Solving for dt^*/dr,

$$\frac{dt^*}{dr} = \frac{P(t^*)}{P''(t^*) - rP'(t^*)} \qquad (***)$$

NOTE 1 Differentiating (∗) w.r.t. t yields

$$f''(t) = P''(t)e^{-rt} - rP'(t)e^{-rt} - P'(t)re^{-rt} + r^2 P(t)e^{-rt}$$

Using (∗∗) we see that the second-order condition $f''(t^*) < 0$ is satisfied if and only if

$$e^{-rt}[P''(t^*) - 2rP'(t^*) + r^2 P(t^*)] = e^{-rt}[P''(t^*) - rP'(t^*)] < 0$$

in which case $dt^*/dr < 0$. Thus the optimal growing time shortens as r increases (which makes the foresters more impatient). In particular, given any $r > 0$, the optimal t^* is less than the time $\hat{t}$ that maximizes current market value $P(t)$, which is optimal only if $r = 0$.

We did not consider how the land the tree grows on may be used after harvesting—for example, by planting a new tree. This generalization is studied in Problem 10.4.8.

PROBLEMS FOR SECTION 10.3

1. Find the present value of 350 000 which is due after 10 years if the interest rate is 8% per year (i) compounded annually, or (ii) compounded continuously.

2. Find the present value of 50 000 which is due after 5 years when the interest rate is 5.75% per year, paid (i) annually, or (ii) continuously.

3. With reference to the tree-cutting problem of Example 2, consider the case where

$$f(t) = (t + 5)^2 e^{-0.05t}, \quad t \geq 0$$

   (a) Find the value of t that maximizes $f(t)$. (Study the sign variation of $f'(t)$.)

   (b) Find $\lim_{t \to \infty} f(t)$ and draw the graph of f.

10.4 Geometric Series

This section studies geometric series. These have many applications in economics and finance. Here we shall use them to calculate annuities and mortgage payments.

EXAMPLE 1   This year a firm has an annual revenue of $100 million that it expects to increase by 16% per year throughout the next decade. How large is its expected revenue in the tenth year, and what is the total revenue expected over the whole period?

Solution: The expected revenue in the second year (in millions of dollars) amounts to $100(1 + 16/100) = 100 \cdot 1.16$, and in the third year, it is $100 \cdot (1.16)^2$. In the tenth year, the expected revenue is $100 \cdot (1.16)^9$. The total revenue expected during the decade is thus

$$100 + 100 \cdot 1.16 + 100 \cdot (1.16)^2 + \cdots + 100 \cdot (1.16)^9$$

If we used a calculator to add the 10 different numbers, we would find that the sum is approximately \$2132 million.

Finding the sum in Example 1 by adding 10 different numbers on a calculator would be very tedious. When there are infinitely many terms, it is obviously impossible. There is an easier method, as we now explain.

Consider the n numbers $a, ak, ak^2, \ldots, ak^{n-1}$. Each term is obtained by multiplying its predecessor by a constant k. We wish to find the sum

$$s_n = a + ak + ak^2 + \cdots + ak^{n-2} + ak^{n-1} \tag{1}$$

of these numbers. We call this sum a (finite) **geometric series** with **quotient** k. The sum in Example 1 occurs in the case when $a = 100$, $k = 1.16$, and $n = 10$.

To find the sum s_n of the series, we use a trick. First multiply both sides of (1) by k to obtain

$$ks_n = ak + ak^2 + ak^3 + \cdots + ak^{n-1} + ak^n$$

Subtracting (1) from this equation yields

$$ks_n - s_n = ak^n - a \tag{2}$$

because all the other $n - 1$ terms cancel. This is the point of the trick. (If $k = 1$, then all terms in (1) are equal to a, and the sum is equal to $s_n = an$.) For $k \neq 1$, (2) implies that

$$s_n = a\frac{k^n - 1}{k - 1}$$

In conclusion:

SUMMATION FORMULA FOR A FINITE GEOMETRIC SERIES

$$a + ak + ak^2 + \cdots + ak^{n-1} = a\frac{k^n - 1}{k - 1} \qquad (k \neq 1) \tag{3}$$

EXAMPLE 2   For the sum in Example 1 we have $a = 100$, $k = 1.16$, and $n = 10$. Hence, (3) yields

$$100 + 100 \cdot 1.16 + \cdots + 100 \cdot (1.16)^9 = 100\frac{(1.16)^{10} - 1}{1.16 - 1}$$

Now it takes many fewer operations on the calculator than in Example 1 to show that the sum is about 2132.

Infinite Geometric Series

Consider the infinite sequence of numbers

$$1, \quad \frac{1}{2}, \quad \frac{1}{4}, \quad \frac{1}{8}, \quad \frac{1}{16}, \quad \frac{1}{32}, \quad \cdots$$

Each term in the sequence is formed by halving its predecessor, so that the nth term is $1/2^{n-1}$. The sum of the n first terms is a finite geometric series with quotient $k = 1/2$ and the first term $a = 1$. Hence, (3) gives

$$1 + \frac{1}{2} + \frac{1}{2^2} + \cdots + \frac{1}{2^{n-1}} = \frac{1 - \left(\frac{1}{2}\right)^n}{1 - \frac{1}{2}} = 2 - \frac{1}{2^{n-1}} \qquad (*)$$

We now ask what is meant by the "infinite sum"

$$1 + \frac{1}{2} + \frac{1}{2^2} + \frac{1}{2^3} + \cdots + \frac{1}{2^{n-1}} + \cdots \qquad (**)$$

Because all the terms are positive, and there are infinitely many of them, you might be inclined to think that the sum must be infinitely large. However, if we look at formula $(*)$, we see that the sum of the n first terms is equal to $2 - 1/2^{n-1}$. This number is never larger than 2, irrespective of our choice of n. As n increases, the term $1/2^{n-1}$ comes closer and closer to 0, and the sum in $(*)$ tends to 2 as limit. This makes it natural to *define* the infinite sum in $(**)$ as the number 2.

In general, we ask what meaning can be given to the "infinite sum"

$$a + ak + ak^2 + \cdots + ak^{n-1} + \cdots \qquad (4)$$

We use the same idea as in $(**)$, and consider the sum s_n of the n first terms in (4). According to (3),

$$s_n = a \frac{1 - k^n}{1 - k} \qquad (k \neq 1)$$

What happens to this expression as n tends to infinity? The answer evidently depends on k^n, because only this term depends on n. In fact, k^n tends to 0 if $-1 < k < 1$, whereas k^n does not tend to any limit if $k > 1$ or $k \leq -1$. (If you are not yet convinced that this claim is true, study the cases $k = -2$, $k = -1$, $k = -1/2$, $k = 1/2$, and $k = 2$.) It follows that if $|k| < 1$, then the sum s_n of the n first terms in (4) will tend to the limit $a/(1 - k)$ as n tends to infinity. In this case, we let the limit of (4) *define* the infinite sum, and say that the infinite series in (4) **converges**. To summarize:

SUMMATION FORMULA FOR AN INFINITE GEOMETRIC SERIES

$$a + ak + ak^2 + \cdots + ak^{n-1} + \cdots = \frac{a}{1 - k} \qquad \text{if} \quad |k| < 1 \qquad (5)$$

If we extend to infinite sums the summation notation that was introduced in Section 3.1, we can write (5) as

$$\sum_{n=1}^{\infty} ak^{n-1} = \frac{a}{1-k} \qquad \text{if} \quad |k| < 1 \tag{6}$$

If $|k| \geq 1$, we say that the infinite series (4) **diverges**. A divergent series has no (finite) sum. Divergence is obvious if $|k| > 1$. When $k = 1$, then $s_n = na$, which tends to $+\infty$ if $a > 0$ or to $-\infty$ if $a < 0$. When $k = -1$, then s_n is a when n is odd, but 0 when n is even; again there is no limit as $n \to \infty$ (if $a \neq 0$).

EXAMPLE 3   Find the sum of the infinite series

$$1 + 0.25 + (0.25)^2 + (0.25)^3 + (0.25)^4 + \cdots$$

Solution: According to formula (5) with $a = 1$ and $k = 0.25$, we have

$$1 + 0.25 + (0.25)^2 + (0.25)^3 + (0.25)^4 + \cdots = \frac{1}{1 - 0.25} = \frac{1}{0.75} = \frac{4}{3}$$

EXAMPLE 4   A rough estimate of the total oil and gas reserves under the Norwegian continental shelf at the beginning of 1999 was 13 billion ($13 \cdot 10^9$) tons (of oil equivalent). Output that year was approximately 250 million ($250 \cdot 10^6$) tons.

(a) When will the reserves be exhausted if output is kept at the same constant level?

(b) Suppose that output is reduced each year by 2% per year beginning in 1999. How long will the reserves last in this case?

Solution:

(a) The number of years for which the reserves will last is given by

$$\frac{13 \cdot 10^9}{250 \cdot 10^6} = 52$$

That is, the reserves will be exhausted around the year 2051.

(b) In 1999, output was $a = 250 \cdot 10^6$. In 2000, it would be $a - 2a/100 = a \cdot 0.98$. In 2001, it becomes $a \cdot 0.98^2$, and so on. If this continues forever, the total amount extracted will be

$$a + a \cdot 0.98 + a \cdot (0.98)^2 + \cdots + a \cdot (0.98)^{n-1} + \cdots$$

This geometric series has quotient $k = 0.98$. According to (5), the sum is

$$s = \frac{a}{1 - 0.98} = 50a$$

Since $a = 250 \cdot 10^6$, $s = 50 \cdot 250 \cdot 10^6 = 12.5 \cdot 10^9$, which is less than $13 \cdot 10^9$. The reserves will last for ever, therefore, leaving 500 million ($= 0.5 \cdot 10^9$) tons which will never be extracted.

General Series (Optional)

We briefly consider general infinite series that are not necessarily geometric,

$$a_1 + a_2 + a_3 + \cdots + a_n + \cdots \tag{7}$$

What does it mean to say that this infinite series converges? By analogy with the definition for geometric series, we form the "partial" sum s_n of the n first terms:

$$s_n = a_1 + a_2 + \cdots + a_n \tag{8}$$

In particular, $s_1 = a_1$, $s_2 = a_1 + a_2$, $s_3 = a_1 + a_2 + a_3$, and so on. As n increases, these partial sums include more and more terms of the series. Hence, if s_n tends toward a limit s as n tends to ∞, it is reasonable to consider s as the sum of *all* the terms in the series. Then we say that the infinite series is **convergent** with sum s. If s_n does not tend to a finite limit as n tends to infinity, we say that the series is **divergent**. The series then has no sum. (As with limits of functions, if $s_n \to \pm\infty$ as $n \to \infty$, this is not regarded as a limit.)

For geometric series, it was easy to determine when there is convergence because we found a simple expression for s_n. Usually, it will not be possible to find such a simple formula for the sum of the first n terms in a given series, so it can be very difficult to determine whether it converges or not. Nevertheless, there are several so-called *convergence* and *divergence criteria* that will give the answer in many cases. These criteria are seldom used directly in economics.

Let us make a general observation: If the series (7) converges, then the nth term must tend to 0 as n tends to infinity. The argument is simple: If the series is convergent, then s_n in (8) will tend to a limit s as n tends to infinity. Now $a_n = s_n - s_{n-1}$, and by the definition of convergence, s_{n-1} will also tend to s as n tends to infinity. It follows that $a_n = s_n - s_{n-1}$ must tend to $s - s = 0$ as n tends to infinity. Expressed briefly,

$$a_1 + a_2 + \cdots + a_n + \cdots \text{ converges } \implies \lim_{n\to\infty} a_n = 0 \tag{9}$$

The condition in (9) is necessary for convergence, but not sufficient. That is, a series may satisfy the condition $\lim_{n\to\infty} a_n = 0$ and yet diverge. This is shown by the following standard example:

EXAMPLE 5   The series

$$1 + \tfrac{1}{2} + \tfrac{1}{3} + \tfrac{1}{4} + \cdots + \tfrac{1}{n} + \cdots \tag{10}$$

is called the **harmonic series**. The nth term is $1/n$, which tends to 0. But the series is still divergent. To see this, we group the terms together in the following way:

$$1 + \tfrac{1}{2} + (\tfrac{1}{3} + \tfrac{1}{4}) + (\tfrac{1}{5} + \cdots + \tfrac{1}{8}) + (\tfrac{1}{9} + \cdots + \tfrac{1}{16}) + (\tfrac{1}{17} + \cdots + \tfrac{1}{32}) + \cdots \tag{$*$}$$

Between the first pair of parentheses there are two terms, one greater than $1/4$ and the other equal to $1/4$, so their sum is greater than $2/4 = 1/2$. Between the second pair of parentheses there are four terms, three greater than $1/8$ and the last equal to $1/8$, so their sum is greater than $4/8 = 1/2$. Between the third pair of parentheses there are eight terms, seven greater than $1/16$ and the last equal to $1/16$, so their sum is greater than $8/16 = 1/2$. Between the fourth pair of parentheses there are sixteen terms, fifteen greater than $1/32$ and the last equal to $1/32$, so their sum is greater than $16/32 = 1/2$. This pattern repeats itself infinitely often. Between the nth pair of parentheses there will be 2^n terms, of which $2^n - 1$ are greater than 2^{-n-1} whereas the last is equal to 2^{-n-1}, so their sum is greater than $2^n \cdot 2^{-n-1} = 1/2$. We conclude that the series in ($*$) must diverge because its sum is larger than that of an infinite number of terms all equal to $\tfrac{1}{2}$.[3]

---

[3] "The determination of $\sum 1/n$ occupied Leibniz all his life but the solution never came within his grasp." H.H. Goldstine (1977)

One can prove in general (see Problem 11) that

$$\sum_{n=1}^{\infty} \frac{1}{n^p} \text{ is convergent} \iff p > 1 \tag{11}$$

PROBLEMS FOR SECTION 10.4

1. Find the sum s_n of the finite geometric series $1 + \frac{1}{3} + \frac{1}{3^2} + \cdots + \frac{1}{3^{n-1}}$. When n approaches infinity, what is the limit of s_n? Find the sum $\sum_{n=1}^{\infty}(1/3^{n-1})$.

2. Find the sums of the following geometric series:

   (a) $\frac{1}{5} + (\frac{1}{5})^2 + (\frac{1}{5})^3 + (\frac{1}{5})^4 + \cdots$

   (b) $0.1 + (0.1)^2 + (0.1)^3 + (0.1)^4 + \cdots$

   (c) $517 + 517(1.1)^{-1} + 517(1.1)^{-2} + 517(1.1)^{-3} + \cdots$

   (d) $a + a(1+a)^{-1} + a(1+a)^{-2} + a(1+a)^{-3} + a(1+a)^{-4} + \cdots, \quad (a > 0)$

   (e) $5 + \frac{5 \cdot 3}{7} + \frac{5 \cdot 3^2}{7^2} + \cdots + \frac{5 \cdot 3^{n-1}}{7^{n-1}} + \cdots$

3. Determine whether the following series are geometric, and find the sums of those geometric series that do converge.

   (a) $8 + 1 + 1/8 + 1/64 + \cdots$ (b) $-2 + 6 - 18 + 54 - \cdots$

   (c) $2^{1/3} + 1 + 2^{-1/3} + 2^{-2/3} + \cdots$ (d) $1 - 1/2 + 1/3 - 1/4 + \cdots$

4. Examine the convergence of the following geometric series, and find their sums when they exist:

   (a) $\frac{1}{p} + \frac{1}{p^2} + \frac{1}{p^3} + \cdots$ (b) $x + \sqrt{x} + 1 + \frac{1}{\sqrt{x}} + \cdots$ (c) $\sum_{n=1}^{\infty} x^{2n}$

5. Find the sum $\sum_{k=0}^{\infty} b\left(1 + \frac{p}{100}\right)^{-k}, \quad p > 0.$

(SM) 6. Total world consumption of iron was approximately $794 \cdot 10^6$ tons in 1971. If consumption had increased by 5% each year and the resources available for mining in 1971 were $249 \cdot 10^9$ tons, how much longer would the world's iron resources have lasted?

7. The world's total consumption of natural gas was 1824 million tons oil equivalent (mtoe) in 1994. The reserves at the end of that year were estimated to be 128 300 mtoe. If consumption had increased by 2% in each of the coming years, and no new sources were ever discovered, how much longer would these reserves have lasted?

(SM) 8. (a) Consider Example 10.3.2. Assume that immediately after one tree is felled, a new tree of the same type is planted. If we assume that a new tree is planted at times t, $2t$, $3t$, etc., then the present value of all the trees will be

$$f(t) = P(t)e^{-rt} + P(t)e^{-2rt} + \cdots$$

Find the sum of this infinite geometric series.

(b) Prove that if $f(t)$ has a maximum for some $t^* > 0$, then $\dfrac{P'(t^*)}{P(t^*)} = \dfrac{r}{1 - e^{-rt^*}}$.

(c) Examine the limit of $P'(t^*)/P(t^*)$ as $r \to 0$.

9. Show that the following series diverge:

(a) $\displaystyle\sum_{n=1}^{\infty} \frac{n}{1+n}$
(b) $\displaystyle\sum_{n=1}^{\infty} (101/100)^n$
(c) $\displaystyle\sum_{n=1}^{\infty} \frac{1}{(1+1/n)^n}$

10. Examine the convergence or divergence of the following series:

(a) $\displaystyle\sum_{n=1}^{\infty} \left(\frac{100}{101}\right)^n$
(b) $\displaystyle\sum_{n=1}^{\infty} \frac{1}{\sqrt{n}}$
(c) $\displaystyle\sum_{n=1}^{\infty} \frac{1}{n^{1.00000001}}$

(d) $\displaystyle\sum_{n=1}^{\infty} \frac{1+n}{4n-3}$
(e) $\displaystyle\sum_{n=1}^{\infty} \left(-\frac{1}{2}\right)^n$
(f) $\displaystyle\sum_{n=1}^{\infty} (\sqrt{3})^{1-n}$

(SM) **11.** Use the results in Example 9.7.2 to prove (11). (*Hint:* Draw the graph of $f(x) = x^{-p}$ in $[1, \infty)$, and interpret each of the sums $\sum_{n=1}^{\infty} n^{-p}$ and $\sum_{n=2}^{\infty} n^{-p}$ geometrically as sums of an infinite number of rectangles.)

10.5 Total Present Value

Suppose that three successive annual payments are to be made, with the amount $1000 falling due after 1 year, then $1500 after 2 years, and $2000 after 3 years. How much must be deposited in an account today in order to have enough savings to cover these three payments, given that the interest rate is 11% per year? We call this amount the *present value* of the three payments.

In order to have $1000 after 1 year, we must deposit an amount x_1 today, where

$$x_1(1 + 0.11) = 1000, \qquad \text{so that} \qquad x_1 = \frac{1000}{1 + 0.11} = \frac{1000}{1.11}$$

In order to have $1500 after 2 years, we must deposit an amount x_2 today, where

$$x_2(1 + 0.11)^2 = 1500, \qquad \text{so that} \qquad x_2 = \frac{1500}{(1 + 0.11)^2} = \frac{1500}{(1.11)^2}$$

Finally, to have $2000 after 3 years, we must deposit an amount x_3 today, where

$$x_3(1 + 0.11)^3 = 2000, \qquad \text{so that} \qquad x_3 = \frac{2000}{(1 + 0.11)^3} = \frac{2000}{(1.11)^3}$$

So the total present value of the three payments, which is the total amount A that must be deposited today in order to cover all three payments, is given by

$$A = \frac{1000}{1.11} + \frac{1500}{(1.11)^2} + \frac{2000}{(1.11)^3}$$

The total is approximately $A \approx 900.90 + 1217.43 + 1462.38 = 3580.71$.

Suppose, in general, that n successive payments $a_1, \ldots, a_n$ are to be made, with a_1 being paid after 1 year, a_2 after 2 years, and so on. How much must be deposited into an account today in order to have enough savings to cover all these future payments, given that the annual interest is r? In other words, what is the *present value* of all these payments?

In order to have a_1 after 1 year, we must deposit $a_1/(1+r)$ today, to have a_2 after 2 years we must deposit $a_2/(1+r)^2$ today, and so on. The total amount P_n that must be deposited today in order to cover all n payments is therefore

$$P_n = \frac{a_1}{1+r} + \frac{a_2}{(1+r)^2} + \cdots + \frac{a_n}{(1+r)^n}. \tag{1}$$

Here P_n is the **present value** of the n instalments.

An **annuity** is a sequence of equal payments made at fixed periods of time over some time span. If $a_1 = a_2 = \cdots = a_n = a$ in (1), then (1) represents the present value of an annuity. In this case the sum in (1) is a finite geometric series with n terms. The first term is $a/(1+r)$ and the quotient is $1/(1+r)$. According to the summation formula for a geometric series, (3) in the previous section, with $k = (1+r)^{-1}$, the sum is

$$P_n = \frac{a}{(1+r)} \frac{[1-(1+r)^{-n}]}{[1-(1+r)^{-1}]} = \frac{a}{r}\left[1 - \frac{1}{(1+r)^n}\right]$$

(The second equality holds because the denominator of the middle expression reduces to r.) Hence, we have the following:

PRESENT VALUE OF AN ANNUITY

The present value of an annuity of a per payment period for n periods at the rate of interest r per period, where each payment is at the end of the period, is given by

$$P_n = \frac{a}{1+r} + \cdots + \frac{a}{(1+r)^n} = \frac{a}{r}\left[1 - \frac{1}{(1+r)^n}\right], \quad \text{where} \quad r = p/100 \tag{2}$$

This sum is illustrated below:

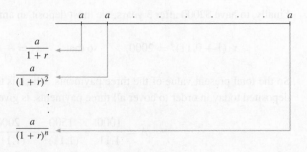

Formula (2) gives the present value of n future claims, each of a (say) dollars. If we want to find how much has accumulated in the account after n periods, immediately after the last deposit, then the **future value** F_n of the annuity is given by:

$$F_n = a + a(1+r) + a(1+r)^2 + \cdots + a(1+r)^{n-1} \tag{*}$$

This different sum is illustrated below:

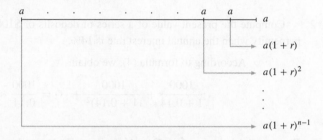

The summation formula for a geometric series yields:

$$F_n = \frac{a[1 - (1+r)^n]}{1 - (1+r)} = \frac{a}{r}[(1+r)^n - 1]$$

We can also find the (undiscounted) future value by noticing that in the special case when $a_i = a$ for all i, the terms on the right-hand side of (*) repeat those of the right-hand side of (1) when $a_1 = a_2 = \cdots = a_n = a$, but taken in the reverse order and multiplied by the interest factor $(1+r)^n$. Hence $F_n = P_n(1+r)^n = \frac{a}{r}[(1+r)^n - 1]$. So:

FUTURE VALUE OF AN ANNUITY

An amount a is deposited in an account each period for n periods, earning interest at r per period. The future (total) value of the account, immediately after the last deposit, is

$$F_n = \frac{a}{r}[(1+r)^n - 1] \tag{3}$$

EXAMPLE 1   Compute the present and the future values of a deposit of $1000 in each of the coming 8 years if the annual interest rate is 6%.

Solution: To find the present value, we apply formula (2) with $a = 1000$, $n = 8$ and $r = 6/100 = 0.06$. This gives

$$P_8 = \frac{1000}{0.06}\left(1 - \frac{1}{(1.06)^8}\right) \approx 6209.79$$

The future value is found by applying formula (3), which gives

$$F_8 = \frac{1000}{0.06}\left[(1.06)^8 - 1\right] \approx 9897.47$$

Alternatively, $F_8 = P_8(1.06)^8 \approx 6209.79(1.06)^8 \approx 9897.47$.

If $r > 0$ and we let n approach infinity in (2), then $(1 + r)^n$ approaches infinity and P_n approaches a/r. So in the limit,

$$\frac{a}{1+r} + \frac{a}{(1+r)^2} + \cdots = \frac{a}{r} \qquad (r > 0) \tag{4}$$

This corresponds to the case where an investment pays a per period in perpetuity when the interest rate is r.

EXAMPLE 2   Compute the present value of a series of deposits of \$1000 at the end of each year in perpetuity when the annual interest rate is 14%.

Solution: According to formula (4), we obtain

$$\frac{1000}{1+0.14} + \frac{1000}{(1+0.14)^2} + \cdots = \frac{1000}{0.14} \approx 7142.86$$

Present Value of a Continuous Future Income Stream

We have discussed the present value of a series of future payments made at specific discrete moments in time. It is often more natural to consider revenue as accruing continuously, like the timber yield from a large growing forest.

Suppose that income is to be received continuously from time $t = 0$ to time $t = T$ at the rate of $f(t)$ dollars per year at time t. We assume that interest is compounded continuously at rate r per year.

Let $P(t)$ denote the present discounted value (PDV) of all payments made over the time interval $[0, t]$. This means that $P(T)$ represents the amount of money you would have to deposit at time $t = 0$ in order to match what results from (continuously) depositing the income stream $f(t)$ over the time interval $[0, T]$. If Δt is any number, the present value of the income received during the interval $[t, t + \Delta t]$ is $P(t + \Delta t) - P(t)$. If Δt is a small number, the income received during this interval is approximately $f(t) \Delta t$, and the PDV of this amount is approximately $f(t)e^{-rt} \Delta t$. Thus, $P(t + \Delta t) - P(t) \approx f(t)e^{-rt} \Delta t$ and so

$$[P(t + \Delta t) - P(t)]/\Delta t \approx f(t)e^{-rt}$$

This approximation gets better the smaller is Δt, and in the limit as $\Delta t \to 0$, we have $P'(t) = f(t)e^{-rt}$. By the definition of the definite integral, $P(T) - P(0) = \int_0^T f(t)e^{-rt}\, dt$. Because $P(0) = 0$, we have the following:

PRESENT VALUE OF A CONTINUOUS INCOME STREAM

The present (discounted) value (at time 0) of a continuous income stream at the rate of $f(t)$ dollars per year over the time interval $[0, T]$, with continuously compounded interest at rate r per year, is given by

$$\text{PDV} = \int_0^T f(t)e^{-rt}\, dt$$

(5)

Equation (5) gives the value at time 0 of an income stream $f(t)$ received during the time interval $[0, T]$. The value of this amount at time T, with continuously compounded interest at rate r, is $e^{rT} \int_0^T f(t) e^{-rt}\, dt$. Because the number e^{rT} is a constant, we can rewrite the integral as $\int_0^T f(t) e^{r(T-t)}\, dt$. This is called the future discounted value (FDV) of the income stream:

FUTURE VALUE OF A CONTINUOUS INCOME STREAM

The future (discounted) value (at time T) of a continuous income stream at the rate of $f(t)$ dollars per year over the time interval $[0, T]$, with continuously compounded interest at rate r per year, is given by

$$\text{FDV} = \int_0^T f(t) e^{r(T-t)}\, dt$$

(6)

An easy modification of (5) will give us the discounted value (DV) at any time s in $[0, T]$ of an income stream $f(t)$ received during the time interval $[s, T]$. In fact, the DV at time s of income $f(t)$ received in the small time interval $[t, t + dt]$ is $f(t) e^{-r(t-s)}\, dt$. So we have the following:

DISCOUNTED VALUE OF A CONTINUOUS INCOME STREAM

The discounted value at any time s of a continuous income stream at the rate of $f(t)$ dollars per year over the time interval $[s, T]$, with continuously compounded interest at rate r per year, is given by

$$\text{DV} = \int_{t=s}^T f(t) e^{-r(t-s)}\, dt$$

(7)

EXAMPLE 3 Find the PDV and the FDV of a constant income stream of $1000 per year over the next 10 years, assuming an interest rate of $r = 8\% = 0.08$ annually, compounded continuously.

Solution:

$$\text{PDV} = \int_0^{10} 1000 e^{-0.08t}\, dt = \Big|_0^{10} 1000 \left(-\frac{e^{-0.08t}}{0.08} \right) = \frac{1000}{0.08}(1 - e^{-0.8}) \approx 6883.39$$

$$\text{FDV} = e^{0.08 \cdot 10} \text{PDV} \approx e^{0.8} \cdot 6883.39 \approx 15\,319.27$$

PROBLEMS FOR SECTION 10.5

1. What is the present value of 15 annual deposits of $3500 if the first deposit is after one year and the annual interest rate is 12%?

2. (a) An account has been dormant for many years earning interest at the constant rate of 4% per year. Now the amount is $100 000. How much was in the account 10 years ago?

   (b) At the end of each year for 4 years you deposit $10 000 into an account earning interest at a rate of 6% per year. How much is in the account at the end of the fourth year?

3. Suppose you are given the following options:

   (i) $13 000 paid after 10 years, or

   (ii) $1000 paid each year for 10 years, first payment today.

   Which of these alternatives would you choose, if the annual interest rate is 6% per year for the whole period?

4. An author is to be paid royalties for publishing a book. Two alternative offers are made:

   (a) The author can be paid $21 000 immediately,

   (b) There can be 5 equal annual payments of $4600, the first being paid at once.

   Which of these offers will be more valuable if the interest rate is 6% per annum?

5. Compute the present value of a series of deposits of $1500 at the end of each year in perpetuity when the interest rate is 8% per year.

6. A trust fund is being set up with a single payment of K. This amount is to be invested at a fixed annual interest rate of r. The fund pays out a fixed annual amount. The first payment is to be made one year after the trust fund was set up. What is the largest amount which can be paid out each year if the fund is to last for ever?

7. The present discounted value of a payment D growing at a constant rate g when the discount rate is r is given by

$$\frac{D}{1+r} + \frac{D(1+g)}{(1+r)^2} + \frac{D(1+g)^2}{(1+r)^3} + \cdots$$

where r and g are positive. What is the condition for convergence? Show that if the series converges with sum P_0, then $P_0 = D/(r-g)$.

8. Find the present and future values of a constant income stream of $500 per year over the next 15 years, assuming an interest rate of $r = 6\% = 0.06$ annually, compounded continuously.

10.6 Mortgage Repayments

When a family takes out a home mortgage at a fixed interest rate, this means that, like an annuity, equal payments are due each period—say, at the end of each month. The payments continue until the loan is paid off after, say, 20 years. Each payment goes partly to pay interest on the outstanding principal, and partly to repay principal (that is, to reduce the outstanding balance). The interest part is largest in the beginning, because interest has to be paid on the whole loan for the first period, and is smallest in the last period, because by then the outstanding balance is small. For the principal repayment, which is the difference between the fixed monthly payment and the interest, it is the other way around.

EXAMPLE 1   A person borrows $50 000 at the beginning of a year and is supposed to pay it off in 5 equal instalments at the end of each year, with interest at 15% compounding annually. Find the annual payment.

Solution: If the five repayments are each of amount a, their present value in dollars is

$$\frac{a}{1.15} + \frac{a}{(1.15)^2} + \frac{a}{(1.15)^3} + \frac{a}{(1.15)^4} + \frac{a}{(1.15)^5} = \frac{a}{0.15}\left[1 - \frac{1}{(1.15)^5}\right]$$

according to formula (10.5.2). This sum must be equal to $50 000, so

$$\frac{a}{0.15}\left[1 - \frac{1}{(1.15)^5}\right] = 50\,000 \tag{$*$}$$

This has the solution $a \approx 14\,915.78$. Alternatively, we can calculate the sum of the future values of all repayments and equate it to the future value of the original loan. This yields the equation

$$a + a(1.15) + a(1.15)^2 + a(1.15)^3 + a(1.15)^4 = 50\,000(1.15)^5$$

which is equivalent to $(*)$, and so also has the solution $a \approx 14915.78$.

To illustrate how the interest part and the principal repayment part of the yearly payment vary from year to year, we construct the following table:

Year	Payment	Interest	Principal Repayment	Outst. Balance
1	14 915.78	7 500.00	7 415.78	42 584.22
2	14 915.78	6 387.63	8 528.15	34 056.07
3	14 915.78	5 108.41	9 807.37	24 248.70
4	14 915.78	3 637.31	11 278.47	12 970.23
5	14 915.78	1 945.55	12 970.23	0

Note that the interest payment each year is 15% of the outstanding balance from the previous year. The remainder of each annual payment of $14 915.78 is the principal repayment that year, which is subtracted from the outstanding balance left over from the previous year.

Figure 1 is a chart showing each year's interest and principal repayments.

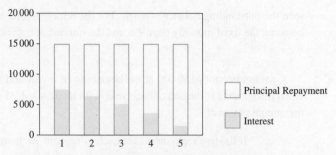

Figure 1 Interest and principal repayment in Example 1

Suppose a loan of K dollars is repaid as an annuity over n periods, at the interest rate $p\%$ per period, where the first payment a is due after one period, and the rest at equally spaced periods. According to (10.5.2), the payment a each period must satisfy

$$K = \frac{a}{r}\left[1 - \frac{1}{(1+r)^n}\right] = \frac{a}{r}[1 - (1+r)^{-n}] \tag{1}$$

Solving equation (1) for a yields

$$a = \frac{rK}{1 - (1+r)^{-n}} \tag{2}$$

where $r = p/100$. We could have used this formula in Example 1. Do so.

EXAMPLE 2   Suppose that the loan in Example 1 is being repaid by monthly payments at the end of each month with interest at the nominal rate 15% per year compounding monthly. Find the monthly payment.

Solution: The interest period is 1 month and the monthly rate is $15/12 = 1.25\%$, so that $r = 1.25/100 = 0.0125$. Also, $n = 5 \cdot 12 = 60$, so formula (2) gives:

$$a = \frac{0.0125 \cdot 50\,000}{1 - 1.0125^{-60}} \approx 1189.50 \qquad \blacksquare$$

The annuities considered so far were **ordinary** annuities where each payment is made at the *end* of the payment period. If the payment each period is made at the beginning of the period, the annuity is called an **annuity due**. This kind of annuity can be handled easily by regarding it as an ordinary annuity, except that there is an immediate initial payment.

EXAMPLE 3   A person is assuming responsibility for a \$335\,000 loan which should be repaid in 15 equal repayments of \$$a$, the first one immediately and the following after each of the coming 14 years. Find a if the annual interest rate is 14%.

Solution: The present value of the first payment is obviously a. The present value of the following 14 repayments is found by applying formula (1) with $r = 0.14$ and $n = 14$. The sum of the present values must be equal to 335\,000:

$$a + \frac{a}{0.14}\left[1 - \frac{1}{(1 + 0.14)^{14}}\right] = 335\,000$$

This reduces to $a + 6.0020715a = 335\,000$, and solving for a gives $a \approx 47\,843$. $\qquad \blacksquare$

Some lenders prefer to specify a fixed payment each period, and let the loan run for however many periods it takes to pay off the debt. This way of paying off the loan functions essentially as an annuity. The difference is that there will be a final adjustment in the last payment in order for the present value of all the payments to be equal to the borrowed amount. In this case it is convenient to use the formula obtained by solving equation (1) for n. The result is

$$\frac{rK}{a} = 1 - \frac{1}{(1+r)^n} \iff \frac{1}{(1+r)^n} = 1 - \frac{rK}{a} = \frac{a - rK}{a} \iff (1+r)^n = \frac{a}{a - rK}$$

Taking the natural logarithm of each side yields $n \ln(1+r) = \ln[a/(a - rK)]$, so:

The number of periods n needed to pay off a loan of amount K at the rate a per period, when the interest rate is r per period, is given by

$$n = \frac{\ln a - \ln(a - rK)}{\ln(1+r)}$$

(3)

EXAMPLE 4   A loan of $50 000 is to be repaid by paying $20 000, which covers both interest and the principal repayment, at the end of each of the coming years, until the loan is fully paid off. When is the loan paid off, and what is the final payment if the annual rate is 15%?

Solution: We begin by computing the number n of annual payments of $20 000 which are needed to pay off $50 000. According to (3), with $r = 0.15$, $a = 20 000$, and $K = 50 000$, we obtain:

$$n = \frac{\ln(20\,000) - \ln(20\,000 - 0.15 \cdot 50\,000)}{\ln(1 + 0.15)} \approx 3.3629$$

Thus three payments of $20 000 are needed, with an additional payment in the fourth year. Let us calculate the future value of the three payments of $20 000 three years after the loan was made. This value is:

$$20\,000 \cdot (1.15)^2 + 20\,000 \cdot 1.15 + 20\,000 = \frac{20\,000}{0.15}\left[(1.15)^3 - 1\right] \approx 69\,450$$

The future value of the $50 000 loan after the same 3 years is $50\,000 \cdot (1.15)^3 = 76\,043.75$. Thus the remaining debt after the third payment is $76\,043.75 - 69\,450 = 6593.75$. If the remaining debt and the accumulated interest are paid one year later, the amount due is $6593.75 \cdot 1.15 = 7582.81$.

Deposits within an Interest Period

Many bank accounts have an interest period of one year, or at least one month. If you deposit an amount *within* an interest period, the bank will often use simple interest, not compound interest. In this case, if you make a deposit within an interest period, then at the end of the period the amount you deposited will be multiplied by the factor $1 + rt$, where t is the remaining fraction of the interest period.

EXAMPLE 5   At the end of each quarter, beginning on March 31, 1999, a person deposits $100 in an account on which interest is paid annually at the rate 10% per year. How much is there in the account on December 31, 2001?

Solution: The deposits during 1999 are illustrated in the following figure:

31/3	30/6	30/9	31/12
100	100	100	100

These four deposits are made within the year. In order to find the balance at the end of the year (the interest period), we use simple (i.e. not compound) interest. This gives

$$100\left(1 + 0.10 \cdot \tfrac{3}{4}\right) + 100\left(1 + 0.10 \cdot \tfrac{2}{4}\right) + 100\left(1 + 0.10 \cdot \tfrac{1}{4}\right) + 100 = 415$$

Doing the same for 2000 and 2001 as well, we replace the 12 original deposits by the amount 415.00 at the end of each of the years 1999, 2000, and 2001.

31/12/1999	31/12/2000	31/12/2001
415	415	415

The balance on 31/12/2001 is $415 \cdot (1.10)^2 + 415 \cdot 1.10 + 415 = 1373.65$. So on December 31, 2001, the person has $1373.65.

1. A person borrows $80 000 at the beginning of one year, and is supposed to pay it off in 10 equal instalments at the end of each year, with interest at 7% compounding annually. Find the annual payment.

2. Suppose that the loan in Problem 1 is being repaid in equal instalments at the end of each month, with interest at the nominal rate 7% compounded monthly. Find the monthly payment.

3. (a) If you deposit $8000 in an account each year for 6 years at the rate of interest 7%, how much do you have immediately after the last deposit? How much do you have 4 years after the last deposit?

   (b) Ronald invests money in a project which triples his money in 20 years. Assuming annual compounding of interest, what is the rate of interest? What if you assume continuous compounding?

HARDER PROBLEM

4. A construction firm wants to buy a building site and has the choice between three different payment schedules:

   (a) Pay $67 000 in cash.
   (b) Pay $12 000 per year for 8 years, where the first instalment is to be paid at once.
   (c) Pay $22 000 in cash and thereafter $7000 per year for 12 years, where the first instalment is to be paid after 1 year.

   Determine which schedule is least expensive if the interest rate is 11.5% and the firm has at least $67 000 available to spend in cash. What happens if the interest rate is 12.5%?

10.7 Internal Rate of Return

Consider $n+1$ numbers $a_0, a_1, \ldots, a_n$ which represent the returns in successive years earned by an investment project. Negative numbers represent losses, positive numbers represent profits, so each a_i is actually the *net return*. Also, we think of a_i as associated with year i, whereas a_0 is associated with the present period. In most investment projects, a_0 is a big negative number, because a large expense precedes any positive returns. If we consider an interest rate of $p\%$ per year and let $r = p/100$, then the net present value of the profits accruing from the project is given by

$$A = a_0 + \frac{a_1}{1+r} + \frac{a_2}{(1+r)^2} + \cdots + \frac{a_n}{(1+r)^n}$$

Several different criteria are used to compare alternative investment projects. One is simply this: Choose the project whose profit stream has the largest present value. The interest rate to use could be an accepted rate for capital investments.

A different criterion is based on the **internal rate of return**, defined as an interest rate that makes the present value of all payments equal to 0.

As a simple example, suppose you invest an amount a which pays back b one year later. Then the rate of return is the interest rate r that makes the present value of the investment project equal to zero. That is, r must satisfy $-a + (1+r)^{-1}b = 0$, so $r = (b/a) - 1$. For example, when $a = 1000$ and $b = 1200$, the rate of return is $r = (1200/1000) - 1 = 0.2$, or 20% per year.

For a general investment project yielding returns $a_0, a_1, \ldots, a_n$, the internal rate of return is a number r such that

$$a_0 + \frac{a_1}{1+r} + \frac{a_2}{(1+r)^2} + \cdots + \frac{a_n}{(1+r)^n} = 0 \qquad (1)$$

If two investment projects both have a unique internal rate of return, then a criterion for choosing between them is to prefer the project that has the higher internal rate of return. Note that (1) is a polynomial equation of degree n in the discount factor $(1 + r)^{-1}$. In general, this equation does not have a unique positive solution r.

EXAMPLE 1   An investment project has an initial outlay of $50 000, and at the end of the next two years has returns of $30 000 and $40 000, respectively. Find the associated internal rate of return.

Solution: In this case, equation (1) takes the form

$$-50\,000 + \frac{30\,000}{1+r} + \frac{40\,000}{(1+r)^2} = 0$$

Put $s = (1+r)^{-1}$. Then the equation becomes

$$40\,000s^2 + 30\,000s - 50\,000 = 0 \qquad \text{or} \qquad 4s^2 + 3s - 5 = 0$$

This has only one positive solution, $s \approx 0.804$. Then $r = 1/s - 1 \approx 0.243$. The internal rate of return is therefore 24.3%.

NOTE 1   Suppose that $a_0 < 0$ and $a_1, \ldots, a_n$ are all > 0. Then (1) has a unique solution r^* satisfying $1 + r^* > 0$, that is, a unique internal rate of return $r^* > -1$. Also, the internal rate of return is positive if $\sum_{i=0}^{n} a_i > 0$. You are asked to prove these results in Problem 3.

PROBLEMS FOR SECTION 10.7

1. An investment project has an initial outlay of $50 000 and at the end of each of the next two years has returns of $30 000. Find the associated internal rate of return r.

2. Suppose that in (1) we have $a_0 < 0$ and $a_i = a > 0$ for $i = 1, 2, \ldots$. Find an expression for the internal rate of return in the limit as $n \to \infty$.

3. Consider an investment project with an initial loss, so that $a_0 < 0$, and thereafter no losses. Suppose also that the sum of the later profits is larger than the initial loss. Prove the two claims in Note 1. (*Hint:* Define $f(r)$ as the expression on the left side of (1). Then study the signs of $f(r)$ and $f'(r)$ on the interval $(0, \infty)$.)

4. An investment in a certain machine is expected to earn a profit of $400 000 each year. What is the maximum price that should be paid for the machine if it has a lifetime of 7 years, the interest rate is 17.5%, and the annual profit is earned at the end of each year?

HARDER PROBLEMS

(SM) 5. An investment project has an initial outlay of $100 000, and at the end of each of the next 20 years has a return of $10 000. Show that there is a unique positive internal rate of return, and find its approximate value. (*Hint:* Use $s = (1+r)^{-1}$ as a new variable. Prove that the equation you obtain for s has a unique positive solution. Verify that $s = 0.928$ is an approximate root.)

6. *A* is obliged to pay *B* $1000 yearly for 5 years, the first payment in 1 year's time. *B* sells this claim to *C* for $4340 in cash. Find an equation that determines the rate of return p that C obtains from this investment. Prove that it is a little less than 5%.

10.8 A Glimpse at Difference Equations

Many of the quantities economists study (such as income, consumption, and savings) are recorded at fixed time intervals (for example, each day, week, quarter, or year). Equations that relate such quantities at different discrete moments of time are called **difference equations**. In fact difference equations can be viewed as the discrete time counterparts of the differential equations in continuous time that were studied in Sections 9.8 and 9.9.

Let $t = 0, 1, 2, \ldots$ denote different discrete time periods or moments of time. We usually call $t = 0$ the *initial period*. If $x(t)$ is a function defined for $t = 0, 1, 2, \ldots$, we often use $x_0, x_1, x_2, \ldots$ to denote $x(0), x(1), x(2), \ldots$, and in general, we write x_t for $x(t)$.

A simple example of a first-order difference equation is

$$x_{t+1} = ax_t, \qquad t = 0, 1, \ldots \tag{1}$$

where a is a constant. This is a first-order equation because it relates the value of a function in period $t + 1$ to the value of the same function in the previous period t only.

Suppose x_0 is given. Repeatedly applying (1) gives $x_1 = ax_0, x_2 = ax_1 = a \cdot ax_0 = a^2 x_0$, $x_3 = ax_2 = a \cdot a^2 x_0 = a^3 x_0$ and so on. In general,

$$x_t = x_0 a^t, \qquad t = 0, 1, \ldots \tag{2}$$

The function $x_t = x_0 a^t$ satisfies (1) for all t, as can be verified directly. For the given value of x_0, there is clearly no other function that satisfies the equation.

EXAMPLE 1   Find the solution of the following difference equation which has $x_0 = 100$:

$$x_{t+1} = 0.2x_t, \qquad t = 0, 1, \ldots$$

From (2) we have $x_t = 100(0.2)^t$, $t = 0, 1, \ldots$.

EXAMPLE 2   Let K_t denote the balance in an account at the beginning of period t when the interest rate is r per period. (If the interest is $p\%$ per period, $r = p/100$.) Then the balance in the account at time $t + 1$ is $K_{t+1} = K_t + rK_t = (1 + r)K_t$. Hence K_t satisfies the difference equation

$$K_{t+1} = (1 + r)K_t \qquad t = 0, 1, \ldots$$

It follows immediately from (2) that

$$K_t = K_0(1 + r)^t \qquad t = 0, 1, \ldots$$

as is well known to us already from Section 1.2 and the beginning of this chapter. In general, this difference equation describes growth at the constant proportional rate r each period.

EXAMPLE 3   **(A Multiplier–Accelerator Model of Economic Growth)**   Let Y_t denote national income, I_t total investment, and S_t total saving—all in period t. Suppose that savings are proportional to national income, and that investment is proportional to the change in income from period t to $t + 1$. Then, for $t = 0, 1, 2, \ldots,$

$$\text{(i) } S_t = \alpha Y_t \qquad \text{(ii) } I_{t+1} = \beta(Y_{t+1} - Y_t) \qquad \text{(iii) } S_t = I_t$$

The last equation is the equilibrium condition that saving equals investment in each period. Here α and β are positive constants, and we assume that $\beta > \alpha > 0$. Deduce a difference equation determining the path of Y_t, given Y_0, and solve it.

Solution: From (i) and (iii), $I_t = \alpha Y_t$, and so $I_{t+1} = \alpha Y_{t+1}$. Inserting this into (ii) yields $\alpha Y_{t+1} = \beta(Y_{t+1} - Y_t)$, or $(\alpha - \beta)Y_{t+1} = -\beta Y_t$. Thus,

$$Y_{t+1} = \frac{\beta}{\beta - \alpha} Y_t = \left(1 + \frac{\alpha}{\beta - \alpha} \right) Y_t, \qquad t = 0, 1, 2, \ldots \tag{$*$}$$

Using (2) gives the solution

$$Y_t = \left(1 + \frac{\alpha}{\beta - \alpha} \right)^t Y_0, \qquad t = 0, 1, 2, \ldots$$

Linear First-Order Equations with Constant Coefficients

Consider next the first-order linear difference equation

$$x_{t+1} = ax_t + b, \qquad t = 0, 1, 2, \ldots \tag{3}$$

where a and b are constants. The equation in (1) is the special case where $b = 0$.

Starting with a given x_0, we can calculate x_t algebraically for small t. Indeed

$$x_1 = ax_0 + b$$
$$x_2 = ax_1 + b = a(ax_0 + b) + b = a^2 x_0 + (a + 1)b$$
$$x_3 = ax_2 + b = a(a^2 x_0 + (a + 1)b) + b = a^3 x_0 + (a^2 + a + 1)b$$

and so on. This makes the pattern clear. In general we have

$$x_t = a^t x_0 + (a^{t-1} + a^{t-2} + \cdots + a + 1)b$$

It is straightforward to check directly that this satisfies (3). According to the summation formula for a geometric series, $1 + a + a^2 + \cdots + a^{t-1} = (1 - a^t)/(1 - a)$, for $a \neq 1$. Thus, for $t = 0, 1, 2, \ldots,$

$$x_{t+1} = ax_t + b \quad \Longleftrightarrow \quad x_t = a^t \left(x_0 - \frac{b}{1 - a} \right) + \frac{b}{1 - a} \quad (a \neq 1) \tag{4}$$

For $a = 1$, we have $1 + a + \cdots + a^{t-1} = t$ and $x_t = x_0 + tb$ for $t = 1, 2, \ldots$.

EXAMPLE 4   Solve the difference equation $x_{t+1} = \frac{1}{3}x_t - 8$.

Solution: Using (4) we obtain the solution

$$x_t = \left(\tfrac{1}{3}\right)^t (x_0 + 12) - 12$$

Equilibrium States and Stability

Consider the solution of $x_{t+1} = ax_t + b$ given in (4). If $x_0 = b/(1-a)$, then $x_t = b/(1-a)$ for all t. The constant $x^* = b/(1-a)$ is called an **equilibrium** (or **stationary**) state for $x_{t+1} = ax_t + b$.

An alternative way of finding an equilibrium state x^* is to seek a solution of $x_{t+1} = ax_t + b$ with $x_t = x^*$ for all t. Such a solution must satisfy $x_{t+1} = x_t = x^*$ and so $x^* = ax^* + b$. Therefore, for $a \neq 1$, we get $x^* = b/(1-a)$ as before.

Suppose the constant a in (4) is less than 1 in absolute value—that is, $-1 < a < 1$. Then $a^t \to 0$ as $t \to \infty$, so (4) implies that

$$x_t \to x^* = b/(1-a) \qquad \text{as} \qquad t \to \infty$$

Hence, if $|a| < 1$, the solution converges to the equilibrium state as $t \to \infty$. The equation is then called **globally asymptotically stable**. If $|a| > 1$, then the absolute value of a^t tends to ∞ as $t \to \infty$. From (4), it follows that x_t moves farther and farther away from the equilibrium state, except when $x_0 = b/(1-a)$. Illustrations of the different possibilities are given in FMEA, Section 11.1.

EXAMPLE 5   The equation in Example 4 is stable because $a = 1/3$. The equilibrium state is -12. We see from the solution given in that example that $x_t \to -12$ as $t \to \infty$.

EXAMPLE 6   (**Mortgage Repayments**)   A particular case of the difference equation (3) occurs when a family borrows an amount K at time 0 as a home mortgage. Suppose there is a fixed interest rate r per period (usually a month rather than a year). Suppose, too, that there are equal repayments of amount a each period, until the mortgage is paid off after n periods (for example, 360 months = 30 years). The outstanding balance or *principal* b_t on the loan in period t satisfies the difference equation $b_{t+1} = (1+r)b_t - a$, with $b_0 = K$ and $b_n = 0$. This difference equation can be solved by using (4), which gives

$$b_t = (1+r)^t (K - a/r) + a/r$$

But $b_t = 0$ when $t = n$, so $0 = (1+r)^n (K - a/r) + a/r$. Solving for K yields

$$K = \frac{a}{r}[1 - (1+r)^{-n}] = a \sum_{t=1}^{n} (1+r)^{-t} \tag{$*$}$$

The original loan, therefore, is equal to the present discounted value of n equal repayments of amount a each period, starting in period 1. Solving for a instead yields

$$a = \frac{rK}{1 - (1+r)^{-n}} = \frac{rK(1+r)^n}{(1+r)^n - 1} \qquad (**)$$

Formulas $(*)$ and $(**)$ are the same as those derived by a more direct argument in Section 10.6.

PROBLEMS FOR SECTION 10.8

1. Find the solutions of the following difference equations.

   (a) $x_{t+1} = -2x_t$ (b) $6x_{t+1} = 5x_t$ (c) $x_{t+1} = -0.3x_t$

2. Find the solutions of the following difference equations with the given values of x_0:

   (a) $x_{t+1} = x_t - 4$, $x_0 = 0$ (b) $x_{t+1} = \frac{1}{2}x_t + 2$, $x_0 = 6$

   (c) $2x_{t+1} + 6x_t + 5 = 0$, $x_0 = 1$ (d) $x_{t+1} + x_t = 8$, $x_0 = 2$

3. Suppose supply at price P_t is $S(P_t) = \alpha P_t - \beta$ and demand at price P_{t+1} is $D(P_{t+1}) = \gamma - \delta P_{t+1}$. Solve the difference equation $S(P_t) = D(P_{t+1})$. All constants are positive.

REVIEW PROBLEMS FOR CHAPTER 10

1. (a) An amount $5000 earns interest at 3% per year. What will this amount have grown to after 10 years?

   (b) How long does it take for the $5000 to double?

2. An amount of 8000 euros is invested at 5% per year.

   (a) What is the balance in the account after 3 years?

   (b) What is the balance after 13 years?

   (c) How long does it take (approximately) for the balance to reach 32 000 euros?

3. Which is preferable for a borrower: (i) to borrow at the annual interest rate of 11% with interest paid yearly; or (ii) to borrow at annual interest rate 10% with interest paid monthly?

4. Suppose the sum of £15 000 is invested in an account earning interest at an annual rate of 7%. What is the balance after 12 years if interest is compounded continuously?

5. (a) How much has $8000 increased to after 3 years if the annual interest rate is 6%, with continuous compounding?

   (b) How long does it take before the $8000 has doubled?

6. Find the sums of the following infinite series:

   (a) $44 + 44 \cdot 0.56 + 44 \cdot (0.56)^2 + \cdots$

   (b) $\displaystyle\sum_{n=0}^{\infty} 20 \left(\frac{1}{1.2} \right)^n$

   (c) $3 + \dfrac{3 \cdot 2}{5} + \dfrac{3 \cdot 2^2}{5^2} + \cdots + \dfrac{3 \cdot 2^{n-1}}{5^{n-1}} + \cdots$

   (d) $\displaystyle\sum_{j=-2}^{\infty} \frac{1}{20^j}$

7. (a) Find the present discounted value (PDV) of a constant income stream of a dollars per year over the next T years, assuming an interest rate of r annually, compounded continuously.

   (b) What is the limit of the PDV as $T \to \infty$? Compare this result with (10.5.4).

(SM) 8. (a) At the beginning of a year $5000 is deposited in an account earning 4% annual interest. What is the balance after 4 years?

   (b) At the end of each year for four years, $5000 is deposited in an account earning 4% annual interest. What is the balance immediately after the fourth deposit?

   (c) Suppose you had $10 000 in your account on 1st January 1996. You agreed to deposit a fixed amount K each year for 8 years, the first deposit on 1st January 1999. What choice of the fixed amount K will imply that you have a balance of $70 000 immediately after the last deposit? The annual interest rate is 4%.

9. A business borrows 500 000 euros from a bank at the beginning of one year, and is supposed to pay it off in 10 equal instalments at the end of each year, with interest at 7% compounding annually.

   (a) Find the annual payment. What is the total amount paid to the bank?

   (b) What is the total amount if the business has to pay twice a year?

10. Lucy is offered the choice between the following three options:

   (a) She gets $3200 each year for 10 years. First payment due after 1 year.

   (b) She gets $7000 today, and thereafter $3000 each year for 5 years. First payment after 1 year.

   (c) She gets $4000 each year for 10 years. First payment only due after 5 years.

   The annual interest rate is 8%. Calculate the present values of the three options. What would you advise Lucy to choose?

(SM) 11. (a) With reference to Example 10.3.2, suppose that the market value of the tree is $P(t) = 100e^{\sqrt{t}/2}$, so that its present value is $f(t) = 100e^{\sqrt{t}/2}e^{-rt}$. Find the optimal cutting time t^*. (Note that t^* decreases as r increases.) By studying the sign variation of $f'(t)$, show that you have indeed found the maximum. What is t^* if $r = 0.05$?

   (b) Solve the same problem when $P(t) = 200e^{-1/t}$ and $r = 0.04$.

12. The revenue produced by a new oil well is $1 million per year initially ($t = 0$), which is expected to rise uniformly to $5 million per year after 10 years. If we measure time in years and let $f(t)$ denote the revenue (in millions of dollars) per unit of time at time t, it follows that $f(t) = 1 + 0.4t$. If $F(t)$ denotes the total revenue that accumulates over the time interval $[0, t]$, then $F'(t) = f(t)$.

   (a) Calculate the total revenue earned during the 10 year period (i.e. $F(10)$).

   (b) Find the present value of the revenue stream over the time interval $[0, 10]$, if we assume continuously compounded interest at the rate $r = 0.05$ per year.

13. Solve the following difference equations with the given values of x_0:

(a) $x_{t+1} = -0.1x_t, \quad x_0 = 1$ (b) $x_{t+1} = x_t - 2, \quad x_0 = 4$ (c) $2x_{t+1} - 3x_t = 2, \quad x_0 = 2$

FUNCTIONS OF MANY VARIABLES

Mathematics is not a careful march down a well-cleared highway,
but a journey into a strange wilderness, where the explorers often
get lost.
—W.S. Anglin (1992)

So far, this book has been concerned with functions of one variable almost exclusively. Yet a realistic description of many economic phenomena requires considering a large number of variables. For example, one consumer's demand for a good like orange juice depends on its price, on the consumer's income, and on the prices of substitutes like other soft drinks, or complements like some kinds of food.

Previous chapters have presented important properties of functions of one variable. For functions of several variables, most of what economists need to know consists of relatively simple extensions of properties presented in the previous chapters for functions of one variable. Moreover, most of the difficulties already arise in the transition from one variable to two variables. To help students see how to overcome these difficulties, Sections 11.1 to 11.3 deal exclusively with functions of two variables. These have graphs in three dimensions, which it is possible to represent even in two-dimensional figures—though with some difficulty. However, as the previous example of the demand for orange juice suggests, there are many interesting economic problems that can only be represented mathematically by functions of many variables. These are discussed in Sections 11.4 to 11.7. The final Section 11.8 is devoted to the economically important topic of elasticity.

11.1 Functions of Two Variables

We begin with the following definition, where D is a subset of the xy-plane.

FUNCTIONS OF TWO VARIABLES

A function f of two real variables x and y with domain D is a rule that assigns a specified number $f(x, y)$ to each point (x, y) in D.

(1)

If f is a function of two variables, we often let a letter like z denote the value of f at (x, y), so $z = f(x, y)$. Then we call x and y the **independent variables**, or the **arguments** of f, whereas z is called the **dependent variable**, because the value z (in general) depends on the values of x and y. The domain of the function f is then the set of all possible pairs of the independent variables, whereas the **range** is the set of corresponding values of the dependent variable. In economics, x and y are often called the *exogenous* variables, whereas z is the *endogenous* variable.

EXAMPLE 1   Consider the function f that, to every pair of numbers (x, y), assigns the number $2x + x^2y^3$. The function f is thus defined by

$$f(x, y) = 2x + x^2y^3$$

What are $f(1, 0)$, $f(0, 1)$, $f(-2, 3)$, and $f(a + 1, b)$?

Solution: First, $f(1, 0)$ is the value when $x = 1$ and $y = 0$. So $f(1, 0) = 2 \cdot 1 + 1^2 \cdot 0^3 = 2$. Similarly, $f(0, 1) = 2 \cdot 0 + 0^2 \cdot 1^3 = 0$, and $f(-2, 3) = 2(-2) + (-2)^2 \cdot 3^3 = -4 + 4 \cdot 27 = 104$. Finally, we find $f(a + 1, b)$ by replacing x with $a + 1$ and y with b in the formula for $f(x, y)$, giving $f(a + 1, b) = 2(a + 1) + (a + 1)^2 b^3$.

EXAMPLE 2   A study of the demand for milk by R. Frisch and T. Haavelmo found the relationship

$$x = A \frac{m^{2.08}}{p^{1.5}} \qquad (A \text{ is a positive constant})$$

where x is milk consumption, p is the relative price of milk, and m is income per family. This equation defines x as a function of p and m. Note that milk consumption goes up when income m increases, and goes down when the price of milk increases, which seems reasonable.

EXAMPLE 3   A function of two variables appearing in many economic models is

$$F(x, y) = Ax^a y^b \qquad (A, a, \text{ and } b \text{ are constants}) \tag{2}$$

Usually, one assumes that F is defined only for $x > 0$ and $y > 0$. Then F is generally called a **Cobb–Douglas function**.[1] Note that the function defined in the previous example is a Cobb–Douglas function, because we have $x = Ap^{-1.5}m^{2.08}$.

The Cobb–Douglas function is most often used to describe certain production processes. Then x and y are called *input factors*, while $F(x, y)$ is the number of units produced, or the *output*. Also, F is called a *production function*.

---

[1] The function in (2) is named after two American researchers, C. W. Cobb and P. H. Douglas, who applied it (with $a + b = 1$) in a paper that appeared in 1927 on the estimation of production functions. The function should properly be called a "Wicksell function", because the Swedish economist Knut Wicksell (1851–1926) introduced such production functions before 1900.

It is important to become thoroughly familiar with standard functional notation.

EXAMPLE 4   For the function F given in (2), find an expression for $F(2x, 2y)$ and for $F(tx, ty)$, where t is an arbitrary positive number. Find also an expression for $F(x + h, y) - F(x, y)$. Give economic interpretations.

Solution: We find that

$$F(2x, 2y) = A(2x)^a(2y)^b = A2^a x^a 2^b y^b = 2^a 2^b A x^a y^b = 2^{a+b} F(x, y)$$

When F is a production function, this shows that if each of the input factors is doubled, then the output is 2^{a+b} times as large. For example, if $a + b = 1$, then doubling each factor of production implies doubling the output. In the general case,

$$F(tx, ty) = A(tx)^a(ty)^b = At^a x^a t^b y^b = t^a t^b A x^a y^b = t^{a+b} F(x, y) \qquad (*)$$

Formulate this result in your own words. Because of property $(*)$, we call the function F *homogeneous of degree* $a + b$. Homogeneous functions are discussed in Sections 12.6 and 12.7.

Finally, we see that

$$F(x + h, y) - F(x, y) = A(x + h)^a y^b - Ax^a y^b = Ay^b[(x + h)^a - x^a] \qquad (**)$$

This shows the change in output when the first input factor is changed by h units while the other input factor is unchanged. For example, suppose $A = 100$, $a = 1/2$, and $b = 1/4$, in which case $F(x, y) = 100x^{1/2}y^{1/4}$. Now, if we choose $x = 16$, $y = 16$, and $h = 1$, then $(**)$ implies that

$$F(16 + 1, 16) - F(16, 16) = 100 \cdot 16^{1/4}[17^{1/2} - 16^{1/2}] = 100 \cdot 2[\sqrt{17} - 4] \approx 24.6$$

Hence, if we increase the input of the first factor from 16 to 17, while keeping the input of the second factor constant at 16 units, then we increase production by about 24.6 units.

Domains

For functions studied in economics, there are usually explicit or implicit restrictions on the domain D in the xy-plane where the function is defined, as in (1). For instance, if $f(x, y)$ is a production function, we usually assume that the input quantities are nonnegative, so $x \geq 0$ and $y \geq 0$. In economics, it is often crucially important to be clear what are the domains of the functions being used.

In the same way as for functions of one variable, we assume, unless otherwise stated, that the domain of a function defined by a formula is the largest domain in which the formula gives a meaningful and unique value.

Sometimes it is helpful to draw a graph of the domain D in the xy-plane.

EXAMPLE 5   Determine the domains of the functions given by the following formulas, then draw the sets in the xy-plane.

(a) $f(x, y) = \sqrt{x - 1} + \sqrt{y}$ (b) $g(x, y) = \dfrac{2}{(x^2 + y^2 - 4)^{1/2}} + \sqrt{9 - (x^2 + y^2)}$

Solution:

(a) We must require that $x \geq 1$ and $y \geq 0$, for only then do $\sqrt{x-1}$ and $\sqrt{y}$ have any meaning. The (unbounded) domain is indicated in Fig. 1.

(b) $(x^2 + y^2 - 4)^{1/2} = \sqrt{x^2 + y^2 - 4}$ is only defined if $x^2 + y^2 \geq 4$. Moreover, we must have $x^2 + y^2 \neq 4$; otherwise, the denominator is equal to 0. Furthermore, we must require that $9 - (x^2 + y^2) \geq 0$, or $x^2 + y^2 \leq 9$. All in all, therefore, we must have $4 < x^2 + y^2 \leq 9$. Because the graph of $x^2 + y^2 = r^2$ consists of all the points on the circle with centre at the origin and radius r, the domain is the set of points (x, y) that lie outside (but not on) the circle $x^2 + y^2 = 4$, and inside or on the circle $x^2 + y^2 = 9$. This set is shown in Fig. 2, where the solid circle is in the domain, but the dashed circle is outside it.

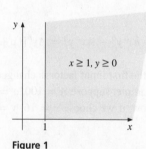

$x \geq 1, y \geq 0$

Figure 1

$4 < x^2 + y^2 \leq 9$

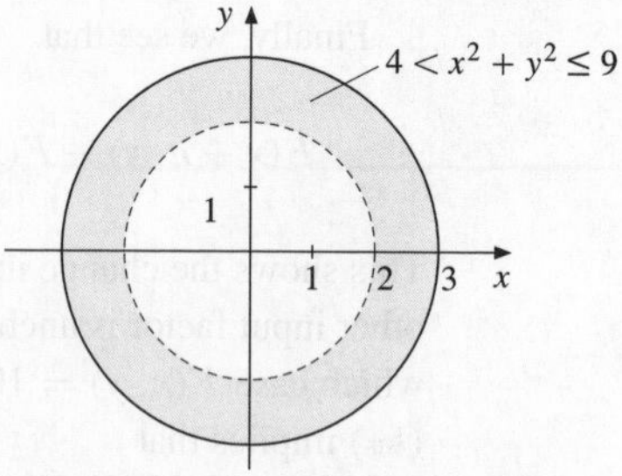

Figure 2

PROBLEMS FOR SECTION 11.1

1. Let $f(x, y) = x + 2y$. Find $f(0, 1)$, $f(2, -1)$, $f(a, a)$, and $f(a + h, b) - f(a, b)$.

2. Let $f(x, y) = xy^2$. Find $f(0, 1)$, $f(-1, 2)$, $f(10^4, 10^{-2})$, $f(a, a)$, $f(a + h, b)$, and $f(a, b + k) - f(a, b)$.

3. Let $f(x, y) = 3x^2 - 2xy + y^3$. Find $f(1, 1)$, $f(-2, 3)$, $f(1/x, 1/y)$, $p = \left[f(x + h, y) - f(x, y)\right]/h$, and $q = \left[f(x, y + k) - f(x, y)\right]/k$.

4. (a) Let $f(x, y) = x^2 + 2xy + y^2$. Find $f(-1, 2)$, $f(a, a)$, and $f(a + h, b) - f(a, b)$.

   (b) Prove that $f(2x, 2y) = 2^2 f(x, y)$ and that $f(tx, ty) = t^2 f(x, y)$ for all t.

5. Let $F(K, L) = 10K^{1/2}L^{1/3}$, for $K \geq 0$ and $L \geq 0$. Find $F(1, 1)$, $F(4, 27)$, $F(9, 1/27)$, $F(3, \sqrt{2})$, $F(100, 1000)$, and $F(2K, 2L)$.

6. Examine for which (x, y) the functions given by the following formulas are defined, then draw the domains of (b) and (c) in the xy-plane.

(a) $\dfrac{x^2 + y^3}{y - x + 2}$ (b) $\sqrt{2 - (x^2 + y^2)}$ (c) $\sqrt{(4 - x^2 - y^2)(x^2 + y^2 - 1)}$

7. Find the domains of the functions defined by the following formulas:

(a) $\dfrac{1}{e^{x+y} - 3}$ (b) $\ln(x - a)^2 + \ln(y - b)^2$ (c) $2\ln(x - a) + 2\ln(y - b)$

11.2 Partial Derivatives with Two Variables

For a function $y = f(x)$ of one variable, the derivative $f'(x)$ is a number which measures the function's rate of change as x changes. For functions of two variables, such as $z = f(x, y)$, we also want to examine how quickly the value of the function changes w.r.t. changes in the values of the independent variables. For example, if $f(x, y)$ is a firm's profit when it uses quantities x and y of two different inputs, we want to know whether and by how much profit can increase as either x or y is varied.

Consider the function

$$z = x^3 + 2y^2 \qquad (*)$$

Suppose first that y is held constant. Then $2y^2$ is constant. Really there is only one variable now. Of course, the rate of change of z w.r.t. x is given by

$$\frac{dz}{dx} = 3x^2$$

On the other hand, we can keep x fixed in $(*)$ and examine how z varies as y varies. This involves taking the derivative of z w.r.t. y while keeping x constant. The result is

$$\frac{dz}{dy} = 4y$$

Obviously, there are many other variations we could study. For example, x and y could vary simultaneously. But in this section, we restrict our attention to variations in *either x or y*.

When we consider functions of two variables, mathematicians (and economists) usually write $\partial z / \partial x$ instead of dz/dx for the derivative of z w.r.t. x when y is held fixed. This slight change of notation, replacing d by ∂, is intended to remind the reader that only one independent variable is changing, with the other(s) held fixed. In the same way, we write $\partial z / \partial y$ instead of dz/dy when y varies and x is held fixed. Hence, we have

$$z = x^3 + 2y^2 \implies \frac{\partial z}{\partial x} = 3x^2 \quad \text{and} \quad \frac{\partial z}{\partial y} = 4y$$

In general, we introduce the following definitions:

$$\frac{d}{dx}(a^x) = \ln a \cdot a^x$$

PARTIAL DERIVATIVES

If $z = f(x, y)$, then

(i) $\partial z/\partial x$ denotes the derivative of $f(x, y)$ w.r.t. x when y is held constant;   (1)

(ii) $\partial z/\partial y$ denotes the derivative of $f(x, y)$ w.r.t. y when x is held constant.

When $z = f(x, y)$, we also denote the derivative $\partial z/\partial x$ by $\partial f/\partial x$, and this is called the **partial derivative** of z (or f) w.r.t. x. Often $\partial z/\partial x$ is pronounced "partial dz by dx". In the same way, $\partial z/\partial y = \partial f/\partial y$ is the **partial derivative** of z (or f) w.r.t. y. Note that $\partial f/\partial x$ is the rate of change of $f(x, y)$ w.r.t. x when y is constant, and correspondingly for $\partial f/\partial y$. Of course, because there are two variables, there are two partial derivatives.

It is usually easy to find the partial derivatives of a function $z = f(x, y)$. To find $\partial f/\partial x$, just think of y as a constant and differentiate $f(x, y)$ w.r.t. x as if f were a function only of x. The rules for finding derivatives of functions of one variable can all be used when we want to compute $\partial f/\partial x$. The same is true for $\partial f/\partial y$. Let us look at some further examples.

EXAMPLE 1   Find the partial derivatives of the following functions:

(a) $f(x, y) = x^3 y + x^2 y^2 + x + y^2$ (b) $f(x, y) = \dfrac{xy}{x^2 + y^2}$

Solution:

(a) We find

$$\frac{\partial f}{\partial x} = 3x^2 y + 2xy^2 + 1 \qquad \text{(holding } y \text{ constant)}$$

$$\frac{\partial f}{\partial y} = x^3 + 2x^2 y + 2y \qquad \text{(holding } x \text{ constant)}$$

(b) For this function the quotient rule gives

$$\frac{\partial f}{\partial x} = \frac{y(x^2 + y^2) - 2xxy}{(x^2 + y^2)^2} = \frac{y^3 - x^2 y}{(x^2 + y^2)^2}, \qquad \frac{\partial f}{\partial y} = \frac{x^3 - y^2 x}{(x^2 + y^2)^2}$$

Observe that the function in (b) is symmetric in x and y, in the sense that the function value is unchanged if we interchange x and y. By interchanging x and y in the formula for $\partial f/\partial x$, therefore, we will find the correct formula for $\partial f/\partial y$. (Find $\partial f/\partial y$ in the usual way and check that the foregoing answer is correct.)

Several other forms of notation are often used to indicate the partial derivatives of $z = f(x, y)$. Some of the most common are

$$\frac{\partial f}{\partial x} = \frac{\partial z}{\partial x} = z'_x = f'_x(x, y) = f'_1(x, y) = \frac{\partial f(x, y)}{\partial x}$$

$$\frac{\partial f}{\partial y} = \frac{\partial z}{\partial y} = z'_y = f'_y(x, y) = f'_2(x, y) = \frac{\partial f(x, y)}{\partial y}$$

Among these, $f_1'(x, y)$ and $f_2'(x, y)$ are the most satisfactory. Here the numerical subscript refers to the position of the argument in the function. Thus, f_1' indicates the partial derivative w.r.t. the first variable, and f_2' w.r.t. the second variable. This notation also reminds us that the partial derivatives themselves are functions of x and y. Finally, $f_1'(a, b)$ and $f_2'(a, b)$ are suitable designations of the values of the partial derivatives at point (a, b) instead of at (x, y). For example, given the function $f(x, y) = x^3y + x^2y^2 + x + y^2$ in Example 1(a), one has

$$f_1'(x, y) = 3x^2y + 2xy^2 + 1 \, , \quad f_1'(a, b) = 3a^2b + 2ab^2 + 1$$

In particular, $f_1'(0, 0) = 1$ and $f_1'(-1, 2) = 3(-1)^2 2 + 2(-1)2^2 + 1 = -1$.

The alternative notation $f_x'(x, y)$ and $f_y'(x, y)$ is often used, but especially in connection with composite functions it is sometimes too ambiguous. For instance, what is the meaning of $f_x'(x^2y, x - y)$?

Remember that the numbers $f_1'(x, y)$ and $f_2'(x, y)$ measure the rate of change of f w.r.t. x and y, respectively. For example, if $f_1'(x, y) > 0$, then a small increase in x will lead to an increase in $f(x, y)$.

EXAMPLE 2   In Example 11.1.2 we studied the function $x = Ap^{-1.5}m^{2.08}$. Find the partial derivatives of x w.r.t. p and m, and discuss their signs.

Solution: We find that $\partial x/\partial p = -1.5Ap^{-2.5}m^{2.08}$ and $\partial x/\partial m = 2.08Ap^{-1.5}m^{1.08}$. Because A, p, and m are positive, $\partial x/\partial p < 0$ and $\partial x/\partial m > 0$. These signs are in accordance with the final remarks in the example.

Formal Definitions of Partial Derivatives

So far the functions have been given by explicit formulas and we have found the partial derivatives by using the ordinary rules for differentiation. If these rules cannot be used, however, we must resort to the formal definition of partial derivative. This is derived from the definition of derivative for functions of one variable in the following rather obvious way.

If $z = f(x, y)$, then with $g(x) = f(x, y)$ (y fixed), the partial derivative of $f(x, y)$ w.r.t. x is simply $g'(x)$. Now, by definition, $g'(x) = \lim_{h \to 0}[g(x + h) - g(x)]/h$. Because $f_1'(x, y) = g'(x)$, it follows that

$$f_1'(x, y) = \lim_{h \to 0} \frac{f(x + h, y) - f(x, y)}{h} \qquad (2)$$

In the same way,

$$f_2'(x, y) = \lim_{k \to 0} \frac{f(x, y + k) - f(x, y)}{k} \qquad (3)$$

If the limit in (2) (or (3)) does not exist, then we say that $f_1'(x, y)$ (or $f_2'(x, y)$) *does not exist*, or that z is *not differentiable* w.r.t. x or y at the point. For instance, the function $f(x, y) = |x| + |y|$ is not differentiable at the point $(x, y) = (0, 0)$.

If h is small in absolute value, then from (2) we obtain the approximation

$$f_1'(x, y) \approx \frac{f(x + h, y) - f(x, y)}{h} \qquad (4)$$

Similarly, if k is small in absolute value,

$$f_2'(x, y) \approx \frac{f(x, y + k) - f(x, y)}{k} \tag{5}$$

These approximations can be interpreted as follows:

(A) The partial derivative $f_1'(x, y)$ is approximately equal to the change in $f(x, y)$ per unit increase in x, holding y constant.

(B) The partial derivative $f_2'(x, y)$ is approximately equal to the change in $f(x, y)$ per unit increase in y, holding x constant. (6)

NOTE 1   The approximations in (6) must be used with caution. Roughly speaking, they will not be too inaccurate provided that the partial derivatives do not vary too much over the actual intervals.

EXAMPLE 3   Let $Y = F(K, L)$ be the number of units produced when K units of capital and L units of labour are used as inputs in a production process. What is the economic interpretation of $F_K'(100, 50) = 5$?

Solution: From (6), $F_K'(100, 50) = 5$ means that, starting from $K = 100$ and holding labour input fixed at 50, output increases by 5 units per unit increase in K.

Higher-Order Partial Derivatives

If $z = f(x, y)$, then $\partial f/\partial x$ and $\partial f/\partial y$ are called **first-order partial derivatives**. These partial derivatives are, in general, again functions of two variables. From $\partial f/\partial x$, provided this derivative is itself differentiable, we can generate two new functions by taking the partial derivatives w.r.t. x and y. In the same way, we can take the partial derivatives of $\partial f/\partial y$ w.r.t. x and y. The four functions we obtain by differentiating twice in this way are called **second-order partial derivatives** of $f(x, y)$. They are expressed as

$$\frac{\partial}{\partial x}\left(\frac{\partial f}{\partial x}\right) = \frac{\partial^2 f}{\partial x^2}, \quad \frac{\partial}{\partial x}\left(\frac{\partial f}{\partial y}\right) = \frac{\partial^2 f}{\partial x \partial y}, \quad \frac{\partial}{\partial y}\left(\frac{\partial f}{\partial x}\right) = \frac{\partial^2 f}{\partial y \partial x}, \quad \frac{\partial}{\partial y}\left(\frac{\partial f}{\partial y}\right) = \frac{\partial^2 f}{\partial y^2}$$

For brevity, we sometimes refer to the first- and second-order "partials", suppressing the word "derivatives".

EXAMPLE 4   For the function in Example 1(a), we obtain

$$\frac{\partial^2 f}{\partial x^2} = 6xy + 2y^2, \quad \frac{\partial^2 f}{\partial y \partial x} = 3x^2 + 4xy = \frac{\partial^2 f}{\partial x \partial y}, \quad \frac{\partial^2 f}{\partial y^2} = 2x^2 + 2$$

As with first-order partial derivatives, several other kinds of notation are also frequently used for second-order partial derivatives. For example, $\partial^2 f/\partial x^2$ is also denoted by $f_{11}''(x, y)$ or $f_{xx}''(x, y)$. In the same way, $\partial^2 f/\partial y \partial x$ can also be written as $f_{12}''(x, y)$ or $f_{xy}''(x, y)$. Note that $f_{12}''(x, y)$ means that we differentiate $f(x, y)$ first w.r.t. the first argument x and then w.r.t. the second argument y. To find $f_{21}''(x, y)$, we must differentiate in the reverse order. In Example 4, these two "mixed" second-order partial derivatives (or "cross-partials") are equal. For most functions $z = f(x, y)$, it will actually be the case that

$$\frac{\partial^2 f}{\partial x \partial y} = \frac{\partial^2 f}{\partial y \partial x} \tag{7}$$

Sufficient conditions for the equality in (7) are given in Theorem 11.6.1.

It is very important to note the exact meaning of the different symbols that have been introduced. If we consider (7), for example, it would be a serious mistake to believe that the two expressions are equal because $\partial x \partial y$ is the same as $\partial y \partial x$. Here the expression on the left-hand side is in fact the derivative of $\partial f/\partial y$ w.r.t. x, and the right-hand side is the derivative of $\partial f/\partial x$ w.r.t. y. It is a remarkable fact, and not a triviality, that the two are usually equal. As another example, we observe that $\partial^2 z/\partial x^2$ is quite different from $(\partial z/\partial x)^2$. For example, if $z = x^2 + y^2$, then $\partial z/\partial x = 2x$. Therefore, $\partial^2 z/\partial x^2 = 2$, whereas $(\partial z/\partial x)^2 = 4x^2$.

Analogously, we define partial derivatives of the third, fourth, and higher orders. For example, we write $\partial^4 z/\partial x \partial y^3 = z_{yyyx}^{(4)}$ when we first differentiate z three times w.r.t. y and then differentiate the result once more w.r.t. x.

Here is an additional example.

EXAMPLE 5   If $f(x, y) = x^3 e^{y^2}$, find the first- and second-order partial derivatives at $(x, y) = (1, 0)$.

Solution: To find $f_1'(x, y)$, we differentiate $x^3 e^{y^2}$ w.r.t. x while treating y as a constant. When y is a constant, so is e^{y^2}. Hence,

$$f_1'(x, y) = 3x^2 e^{y^2} \qquad \text{and so} \qquad f_1'(1, 0) = 3 \cdot 1^2 e^{0^2} = 3$$

To find $f_2'(x, y)$, we differentiate $f(x, y)$ w.r.t. y while treating x as a constant:

$$f_2'(x, y) = x^3 2y e^{y^2} = 2x^3 y e^{y^2} \qquad \text{and so} \qquad f_2'(1, 0) = 0$$

To find the second-order partial $f_{11}''(x, y)$, we must differentiate $f_1'(x, y)$ w.r.t. x once more, while treating y as a constant. Hence,

$$f_{11}''(x, y) = 6x e^{y^2} \qquad \text{and so} \qquad f_{11}''(1, 0) = 6 \cdot 1 e^{0^2} = 6$$

To find $f_{22}''(x, y)$, we must differentiate $f_2'(x, y) = 2x^3 y e^{y^2}$ w.r.t. y once more, while treating x as a constant. Because $y e^{y^2}$ is a product of two functions, each involving y, we use the product rule to obtain

$$f_{22}''(x, y) = (2x^3)(1 \cdot e^{y^2} + y 2y e^{y^2}) = 2x^3 e^{y^2} + 4x^3 y^2 e^{y^2}$$

Evaluating this at $(1, 0)$ gives $f_{22}''(1, 0) = 2$. Moreover,

$$f_{12}''(x, y) = \frac{\partial}{\partial y}[f_1'(x, y)] = \frac{\partial}{\partial y}(3x^2 e^{y^2}) = 3x^2 2y e^{y^2} = 6x^2 y e^{y^2}$$

and

$$f_{21}''(x, y) = \frac{\partial}{\partial x}[f_2'(x, y)] = \frac{\partial}{\partial x}(2x^3 y e^{y^2}) = 6x^2 y e^{y^2}$$

Hence, $f_{12}''(1, 0) = f_{21}''(1, 0) = 0$.

PROBLEMS FOR SECTION 11.2

1. Find $\partial z/\partial x$ and $\partial z/\partial y$ for the following:

(a) $z = 2x + 3y$ (b) $z = x^2 + y^3$ (c) $z = x^3 y^4$ (d) $z = (x + y)^2$

2. Find $\partial z/\partial x$ and $\partial z/\partial y$ for the following:

(a) $z = x^2 + 3y^2$ (b) $z = xy$ (c) $z = 5x^4 y^2 - 2xy^5$ (d) $z = e^{x+y}$

(e) $z = e^{xy}$ (f) $z = e^x/y$ (g) $z = \ln(x + y)$ (h) $z = \ln(xy)$

3. Find $f_1'(x, y)$, $f_2'(x, y)$, and $f_{12}''(x, y)$ for the following:

(a) $f(x, y) = x^7 - y^7$ (b) $f(x, y) = x^5 \ln y$ (c) $f(x, y) = (x^2 - 2y^2)^5$

4. Find all first- and second-order partial derivatives for the following:

(a) $z = 3x + 4y$ (b) $z = x^3 y^2$ (c) $z = x^5 - 3x^2 y + y^6$

(d) $z = x/y$ (e) $z = (x - y)/(x + y)$ (f) $z = \sqrt{x^2 + y^2}$

(SM) 5. Find all the first- and second-order partial derivatives of:

(a) $z = x^2 + e^{2y}$ (b) $z = y \ln x$ (c) $z = xy^2 - e^{xy}$ (d) $z = x^y$

6. Let $F(S, E) = 2.26 \, S^{0.44} E^{0.48}$. (This is an estimated production function for a certain lobster fishery where S denotes the stock of lobsters, E the harvesting effort, and $F(S, E)$ the catch.)

(a) Find $F_S'(S, E)$ and $F_E'(S, E)$.

(b) Show that $SF_S' + EF_E' = kF$ for a suitable constant k.

7. Prove that if $z = (ax + by)^2$, then $xz_x' + yz_y' = 2z$.

8. Let $z = \frac{1}{2} \ln(x^2 + y^2)$. Show that $\partial^2 z/\partial x^2 + \partial^2 z/\partial y^2 = 0$.

9. If a household consumes x units of one good and y units of a second good, its satisfaction is measured by the function $s(x, y) = 2 \ln x + 4 \ln y$. Suppose that the household presently consumes 20 units of the first good and 30 units of the second.

(a) What is the approximate increase in satisfaction from consuming one extra unit of the first good?

(b) What is the approximate increase in satisfaction from consuming one extra unit of the second good?

11.3 Geometric Representation

When studying functions of one variable, we saw how useful it was to represent the function by its graph in a coordinate system in the plane. This section considers how to visualize functions of two variables as having graphs which form surfaces in (three-dimensional) space. We begin by introducing a coordinate system in space.

Recall how any point in a plane can be represented by a pair of real numbers by using two mutually orthogonal coordinate lines: a rectangular coordinate system in the plane. In a similar way, points in space can be represented by triples of real numbers using three mutually orthogonal coordinate lines. In Fig. 1 we have drawn such a coordinate system. The three lines that are orthogonal to each other and intersect at the point O in Fig. 1 are called *coordinate axes*. They are usually called the x-axis, y-axis, and z-axis. We choose units to measure the length along each axis, and select a positive direction on each of them as indicated by the arrows.

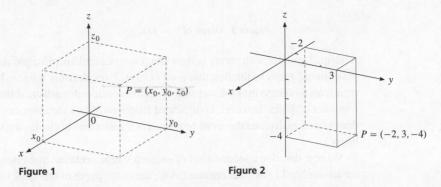

Figure 1   **Figure 2**

The equation $x = 0$ is satisfied by all points in a *coordinate plane* spanned by the y-axis and the z-axis. This is called the yz-plane. There are two other coordinate planes: the xy-plane on which $z = 0$; and the xz-plane on which $y = 0$. We often think of the xy-plane as horizontal, with the z-axis passing vertically through it.

Each coordinate plane divides the space into two *half-spaces*. For example, the xy-plane separates the space into the regions where $z > 0$, above the xy-plane, and $z < 0$, below the xy-plane. The three coordinate planes together divide up the space into 8 *octants*. The octant which has $x \geq 0$, $y \geq 0$, and $z \geq 0$ is called the *nonnegative octant*.

Every point P in space now has an associated triple of numbers (x_0, y_0, z_0) that describes its location, as suggested in Fig. 1. Conversely, it is clear that every triple of numbers also represents a unique point in space in this way. Note in particular that when z_0 is negative, the point (x_0, y_0, z_0) lies below the xy-plane in which $z = 0$. In Fig. 2, we have constructed the point P with coordinates $(-2, 3, -4)$. The point P in Fig. 1 lies in the positive octant.

The Graph of a Function of Two Variables

Suppose $z = f(x, y)$ is a function of two variables defined over a domain D in the xy-plane. The **graph** of the function f is the set of all points $(x, y, f(x, y))$ in the space obtained by letting (x, y) "run through" the whole of D. If f is a sufficiently "nice" function, the graph of f will be a connected surface in the space, like the graph in Fig. 3. In particular, if (x_0, y_0) is a point in the domain D, we see how the point $P = (x_0, y_0, f(x_0, y_0))$ on the surface is obtained by letting $f(x_0, y_0)$ be the "height" of f at (x_0, y_0).

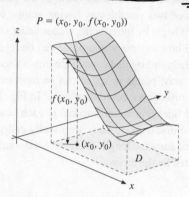

Figure 3 Graph of $y = f(x, y)$

A talented sculptor with plenty of time and resources could in principle construct this three-dimensional graph of the function $z = f(x, y)$. Even drawing a figure like Fig. 3, which represents this graph in two dimensions, requires considerable artistic ability. (Using modern computer graphics, however, complicated functions of two variables can have their graphs drawn fairly easily, and these can be rotated or transformed to display the shape of the graph better.)

We now describe a second kind of geometric representation that often does better when we are confined to two dimensions (as we are in the pages of this book).

Level Curves

Map makers can describe some topographical features of the earth's surface such as hills and valleys even in a plane map. The usual way of doing so is to draw a set of *level curves* or contours connecting points on the map that represent places on the earth's surface with the same elevation above sea level. For instance, there may be such contours corresponding to 100 metres above sea level, others for 200, 300, and 400 metres above sea level, and so on. Off the coast, or in places like the valley of the River Jordan, which drains into the Dead Sea, there may be contours for 100 metres below sea level, etc. Where the contours are closer together, that indicates a hill with a steeper slope. Thus, studying a contour map carefully can give a good idea how the altitude varies on the ground.

The same idea can be used to give a geometric representation of an arbitrary function $z = f(x, y)$. The graph of the function in three-dimensional space is visualized as being cut by horizontal planes parallel to the xy-plane. The resulting intersection between each plane and the graph is then projected onto the xy-plane. If the intersecting plane is $z = c$, then the projection of the intersection onto the xy-plane is called the **level curve** at height c for f. This level curve will consist of points satisfying the equation

$$f(x, y) = c$$

Figure 4 illustrates the construction of such a level curve.

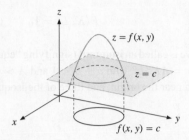

Figure 4 The graph of $z = f(x, y)$ and one of its level curves

EXAMPLE 1   Consider the function of two variables defined by the equation

$$z = x^2 + y^2 \qquad (*)$$

What are the level curves? Draw both a set of level curves and the graph of the function.

Solution: The variable z can only assume values ≥ 0. Each level curve has the equation

$$x^2 + y^2 = c \qquad (**)$$

for some $c \geq 0$. We see that these are circles in the xy-plane centred at the origin and with radius $\sqrt{c}$. See Fig. 5.

As for the graph of $(*)$, all the level curves are circles. For $y = 0$, we have $z = x^2$. This shows that the graph of $(*)$ cuts the xz-plane (where $y = 0$) in a parabola. Similarly, for $x = 0$, we have $z = y^2$, which is the graph of a parabola in the yz-plane. In fact, the graph of $(*)$ is obtained by rotating the parabola $z = x^2$ around the z-axis. The surface (of revolution) is called a **paraboloid**, with its lowest part shown in Fig. 6. Five of the level curves in the xy-plane are also indicated.

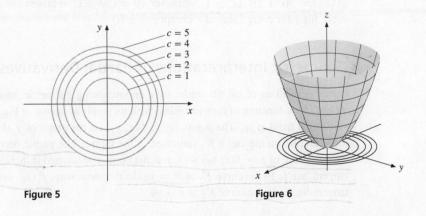

Figure 5

Figure 6

EXAMPLE 2   Suppose $F(K, L)$ denotes a firm's output when its input of capital is K and that of labour is L. A level curve for the function is a curve in the KL-plane given by

$$F(K, L) = Y_0 \qquad (Y_0 \text{ is a constant})$$

This curve is called an **isoquant** (signifying "equal quantity"). For a Cobb–Douglas function $F(K, L) = AK^aL^b$ with $a + b < 1$ and $A > 0$, Figs. 7 and 8 respectively show a part of the graph near the origin, and three of the isoquants.

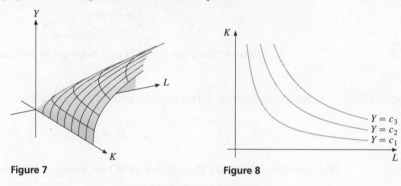

Figure 7   **Figure 8**

EXAMPLE 3   Show that all points (x, y) satisfying $xy = 3$ lie on a level curve for the function

$$g(x, y) = \frac{3(xy + 1)^2}{x^4y^4 - 1}$$

Solution: By substituting $xy = 3$ in the expression for g, we find

$$g(x, y) = \frac{3(xy + 1)^2}{(xy)^4 - 1} = \frac{3(3 + 1)^2}{3^4 - 1} = \frac{48}{80} = \frac{3}{5}$$

This shows that, for all (x, y) where $xy = 3$, the value of $g(x, y)$ is a constant $3/5$. Hence, any point (x, y) satisfying $xy = 3$ is on a level curve (at height $3/5$) for g. (In fact, $g(x, y) = 3(c + 1)^2/(c^4 - 1)$ whenever $xy = c \neq \pm1$, so this equation represents a level curve for g for every value of c except $c \neq \pm1$.)

Geometric Interpretations of Partial Derivatives

Partial derivatives of the first order have an interesting geometric interpretation. Let $z = f(x, y)$ be a function of two variables, with its graph as shown in Fig. 9. Let us keep the value of y fixed at y_0. The points $(x, y, f(x, y))$ on the graph of f that have $y = y_0$ are those that lie on the curve K_y indicated in the figure. The partial derivative $f_x'(x_0, y_0)$ is the derivative of $z = f(x, y_0)$ w.r.t. x at the point $x = x_0$, and is therefore the slope of the tangent line l_y to the curve K_y at $x = x_0$. In the same way, $f_y'(x_0, y_0)$ is the slope of the tangent line l_x to the curve K_x at $y = y_0$.

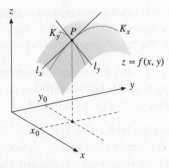

Figure 9

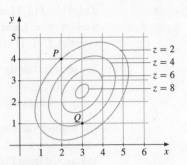

Figure 10

This geometric interpretation of the two partial derivatives can be explained another way. Imagine that the graph of f describes the surface of a mountain, and suppose that we are standing at point P with coordinates $(x_0, y_0, f(x_0, y_0))$ in three dimensions, where the height is $f(x_0, y_0)$ units above the xy-plane. The slope of the terrain at P varies as we look in different directions. In particular, suppose we look in the direction parallel to the positive x-axis. Then $f'_x(x_0, y_0)$ is a measure of the "steepness" in this direction. In the figure, $f'_x(x_0, y_0)$ is negative, because moving from P in the direction given by the positive x-axis will take us downwards. In the same way, we see that $f'_y(x_0, y_0)$ is a measure of the "steepness" in the direction parallel to the positive y-axis. We see that $f'_y(x_0, y_0)$ is positive, meaning that the slope is upward in this direction.

Let us now briefly consider the geometric interpretation of the "direct" second-order derivatives f''_{xx} and f''_{yy}. Consider the curve K_y on the graph of f in the figure. It seems that along this curve, $f''_{xx}(x, y_0)$ is negative, because $f'_x(x, y_0)$ decreases as x increases. In particular, $f''_{xx}(x_0, y_0) < 0$. In the same way, we see that moving along K_x makes $f'_y(x_0, y)$ decrease as y increases, so $f''_{yy}(x_0, y) < 0$ along K_x. In particular, $f''_{yy}(x_0, y_0) < 0$. (The mixed partials, f''_{xy} and f''_{yx}, do not have such easy geometric interpretations.)

EXAMPLE 4   Consider Fig. 10, which shows some level curves of a function $z = f(x, y)$. On the basis of this figure, answer the following questions:

(a) What are the signs of $f'_x(x, y)$ and $f'_y(x, y)$ at the points P and Q? Estimate also the *value* of $f'_x(3, 1)$.

(b) What are the solutions of the equations: (i) $f(3, y) = 4$ and (ii) $f(x, 4) = 6$?

(c) What is the largest value that $f(x, y)$ can attain when $x = 2$, and for which y value does this maximum occur?

Solution:

(a) If you stand at P, you are on the level curve $f(x, y) = 2$. If you look in the direction of the positive x-axis (along the line $y = 4$), then you will see the terrain sloping upwards, because the (nearest) level curves will correspond to larger z values. Hence, $f'_x > 0$. If you stand at P and look in the direction of the positive y-axis (along $x = 2$), the terrain will slope downwards. Thus, at P, we must have $f'_y < 0$. At Q, we find similarly that $f'_x < 0$ and $f'_y > 0$. To estimate $f'_x(3, 1)$, we use $f'_x(3, 1) \approx$

$f(4, 1) - f(3, 1) = 2 - 4 = -2$. (This approximation is actually far from exact. If we keep $y = 1$ and *decrease* x by one unit, then $f(2, 1) \approx 4$, which should give the estimate $f_x'(3, 1) \approx 4 - 4 = 0$. The "map" is not sufficiently finely graded around Q.)

(b) Equation (i) has the solutions $y = 1$ and $y = 4$, because the line $x = 3$ cuts the level curve $f(x, y) = 4$ at $(3, 1)$ and at $(3, 4)$. Equation (ii) has no solutions, because the line $y = 4$ does not meet the level curve $f(x, y) = 6$ at all.

(c) The highest value of c for which the level curve $f(x, y) = c$ has a point in common with the line $x = 2$ is $c = 6$. The largest value of $f(x, y)$ when $x = 2$ is therefore 6, and we see from Fig. 10 that this maximum value is attained when $y \approx 2.2$.

PROBLEMS FOR SECTION 11.3

1. Draw a three-dimensional coordinate system and mark the points

$$P = (3, 0, 0), \qquad Q = (0, 2, 0), \qquad R = (0, 0, -1), \qquad S = (3, -2, 4)$$

(For S, you should draw a box like those in Figs. 1 and 2.)

2. Describe geometrically the set of points (x, y, z) in three dimensions where

   (a) $y = 2$, $\quad z = 3$ (x varies freely)   (b) $y = x$ (z varies freely)

3. Show that $x^2 + y^2 = 6$ is a level curve of $f(x, y) = \sqrt{x^2 + y^2} - x^2 - y^2 + 2$.

4. Show that $x^2 - y^2 = c$ is a level curve of $f(x, y) = e^{x^2}e^{-y^2} + x^4 - 2x^2y^2 + y^4$ for all values of the constant c.

5. Explain why two level curves of the function $z = f(x, y)$ corresponding to different values of z cannot intersect.

6. Let $f(x)$ represent a function of one variable. If we let $g(x, y) = f(x)$, then we have defined a function of two variables, but y is not present in its formula. Explain how the graph of g is obtained from the graph of f. Illustrate with $f(x) = x$ and also with $f(x) = -x^3$.

7. Draw the graphs of the following functions in three-dimensional space, and draw a set of level curves for each of them:

   (a) $z = 3 - x - y$ (b) $z = \sqrt{3 - x^2 - y^2}$

8. Figure 11 shows some level curves for the function $z = f(x, y)$.

   (a) What is $f(2, 3)$? Solve the equation $f(x, 3) = 8$ for x.

   (b) Find the smallest value of $z = f(x, y)$ if $x = 2$. What is the corresponding value of y?

   (c) What are the signs of $f_1'(x, y)$ and $f_2'(x, y)$ at the points A, B, and C? Estimate the values of these two partial derivatives at A.

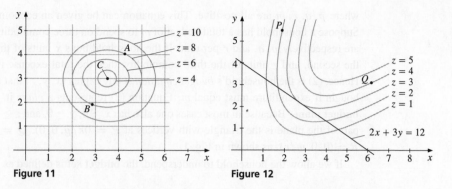

Figure 11   **Figure 12**

SM **9.** Figure 12 shows some level curves for $z = f(x, y)$, together with the line $2x + 3y = 12$.

(a) What are the signs of f'_x and f'_y at the points P and Q?

(b) Find possible solutions of the equations (i) $f(1, y) = 2$ and (ii) $f(x, 2) = 2$.

(c) What is the largest value of $f(x, y)$ among those (x, y) that satisfy $2x + 3y = 12$?

HARDER PROBLEM

SM **10.** Suppose $F(x, y)$ is a function about which nothing is known except that $F(0, 0) = 0$, as well as that $F'_1(x, y) \geq 2$ for all (x, y), and $F'_2(x, y) \leq 1$ for all (x, y). What can be said about the relative sizes of $F(0, 0)$, $F(1, 0)$, $F(2, 0)$, $F(0, 1)$, and $F(1, 1)$? Write down the inequalities that have to hold between these numbers.

11.4 Surfaces and Distance

An equation such as $f(x, y) = c$ in *two* variables x and y can be represented by a point set in the plane, called the graph of the equation. (See Section 5.4.) In a similar way, an equation $g(x, y, z) = c$ in *three* variables x, y, and z can be represented by a point set in space, also called the **graph** of the equation. This graph consists of all triples (x, y, z) satisfying the equation, and will usually form what can be called a **surface** in space.

One of the simplest types of equation in three variables is

$$ax + by + cz = d \qquad \text{(the general equation for a plane in space)} \qquad (1)$$

(with a, b, and c not all 0). Assuming that a and b are not both 0, the graph of this equation intersects the xy-plane when $z = 0$. Then $ax + by = d$, which is a straight line in the xy-plane. In the same way we see that, provided at most one of a, b, and c is equal to zero, the graph intersects the two other coordinate planes in straight lines.

Let us rename the coefficients and consider the equation

$$px + qy + rz = m \qquad (2)$$

where p, q, r, m are all positive. This equation can be given an economic interpretation. Suppose a household has a total budget of m to spend on three commodities, whose prices are respectively p, q, and r per unit. If the household buys x units of the first, y units of the second, and z units of the third commodity, then the total expense is $px + qy + rz$. Hence, (2) is the household's *budget equation*: Only triples (x, y, z) that satisfy (2) can be bought if expenditure must equal m. Equation (2) represents a *plane* in space, called the **budget plane**. Because in most cases one also has $x \geq 0$, $y \geq 0$, and $z \geq 0$, the interesting part of the plane is the triangle with vertices at $P = (m/p, 0, 0)$, $Q = (0, m/q, 0)$, and $R = (0, 0, m/r)$, as shown in Fig. 1.

If we allow the household to underspend, the **budget set** is defined as

$$B = \{ (x, y, z) : px + qy + rz \leq m, \ x \geq 0, \ y \geq 0, \ z \geq 0 \}$$

This represents the three-dimensional body bounded by the three coordinate planes and the budget plane. It generalizes the two-commodity budget set discussed in Example 4.4.7.

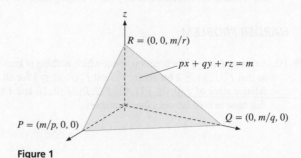

Figure 1

Two rather interesting surfaces that have been drawn by a computer program appear in Figs. 2 and 3. Figure 2 exhibits a surface which is called an **ellipsoid**. (Some readers may recognize its shape as that of a rugby ball.)

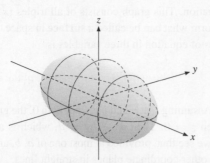

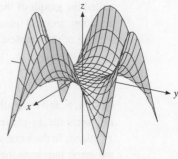

Figure 2 $x^2/a^2 + y^2/b^2 + z^2/c^2 = 1$
where $a > b = c$

Figure 3 $z = x^4 - 3x^2y^2 + y^4$

The Distance Formula

In Section 5.5 we gave the formula for the distance between two points in the plane. Now we derive the corresponding formula for the distance between two points in three-dimensional space.

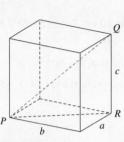

Figure 4   **Figure 5**

Consider a rectangular box with edges of length a, b, and c, as shown in Fig. 4. By Pythagoras's theorem, $(PR)^2 = a^2 + b^2$, and $(PQ)^2 = (PR)^2 + (RQ)^2 = a^2 + b^2 + c^2$, so that the box has diagonal of length $PQ = \sqrt{a^2 + b^2 + c^2}$.

Next we find the distance between two typical points $P = (x_1, y_1, z_1)$ and $Q = (x_2, y_2, z_2)$ in space, as illustrated in Fig. 5. These two points lie precisely at the corners of a rectangular box with edges of lengths $a = |x_2 - x_1|$, $b = |y_2 - y_1|$, and $c = |z_2 - z_1|$. Hence $(PQ)^2 = a^2 + b^2 + c^2 = |x_2 - x_1|^2 + |y_2 - y_1|^2 + |z_2 - z_1|^2 = (x_2 - x_1)^2 + (y_2 - y_1)^2 + (z_2 - z_1)^2$. This motivates the following definition:

DEFINITION OF DISTANCE

The **distance** between (x_1, y_1, z_1) and (x_2, y_2, z_2) is

$$d = \sqrt{(x_2 - x_1)^2 + (y_2 - y_1)^2 + (z_2 - z_1)^2}$$

(3)

EXAMPLE 1   Calculate the distance d between the points $(1, 2, -3)$ and $(-2, 4, 5)$.

Solution: According to formula (3),

$$d = \sqrt{(-2 - 1)^2 + (4 - 2)^2 + (5 - (-3))^2} = \sqrt{(-3)^2 + 2^2 + 8^2} = \sqrt{77} \approx 8.77$$

Let (a, b, c) be a point in space. The sphere with radius r and centre at (a, b, c) is the set of all points (x, y, z) whose distance from (a, b, c) is equal to r. Using the distance formula, we obtain

$$\sqrt{(x - a)^2 + (y - b)^2 + (z - c)^2} = r$$

Squaring each side yields:

EQUATION FOR A SPHERE

The equation for a **sphere** with centre at (a, b, c) and radius r is

$$(x - a)^2 + (y - b)^2 + (z - c)^2 = r^2$$

(4)

EXAMPLE 2   Find the equation for the sphere with centre at $(-2, -2, -2)$ and radius 4.

Solution: According to formula (4), the equation is

$$(x - (-2))^2 + (y - (-2))^2 + (z - (-2))^2 = 4^2 \quad \text{or} \quad (x + 2)^2 + (y + 2)^2 + (z + 2)^2 = 16$$

EXAMPLE 3   How do you interpret the expression $(x + 4)^2 + (y - 3)^2 + (z + 5)^2$? As:

(i) The sphere with centre at the point $(-4, 3, -5)$.

(ii) The distance between the points (x, y, z) and $(-4, 3, -5)$.

(iii) The square of the distance between the points (x, y, z) and $(-4, 3, -5)$.

Solution: Only (iii) is correct.

PROBLEMS FOR SECTION 11.4

1. Sketch graphs of the surfaces in space described by each of the following equations:

   (a) $x = a$ (b) $y = b$ (c) $z = c$

2. Find the distance d between the points

      (a) $(-1, 2, 3)$ and $(4, -2, 0)$ (b) (a, b, c) and $(a + 1, b + 1, c + 1)$

3. Find the equation for the sphere with centre at $(2, 1, 1)$ and radius 5.

4. What is the geometric interpretation of the equation $(x + 3)^2 + (y - 3)^2 + (z - 4)^2 = 25$?

5. The graph of $z = x^2 + y^2$ is a paraboloid (see Fig. 11.3.6). If the point (x, y, z) lies on this paraboloid, interpret the expression $(x - 4)^2 + (y - 4)^2 + \left(z - \frac{1}{2}\right)^2$.

11.5 Functions of More Variables

Many of the most important functions we study in economics, such as the gross domestic product (GDP) of a country, depend on a very large number of variables. Mathematicians and modern economists express this dependence by saying that GDP is a *function* of the different variables.

Any ordered collection of n numbers $(x_1, x_2, \ldots, x_n)$ is called an ***n*-vector**. To save space, n-vectors are often denoted by bold letters. For example, we write $\mathbf{x} = (x_1, x_2, \ldots, x_n)$.

FUNCTIONS OF N VARIABLES

Given any set D of n-vectors, **a function f of n variables $x_1, \ldots, x_n$ with domain D** is a rule that assigns a specified number $f(\mathbf{x}) = f(x_1, \ldots, x_n)$ to each n-vector $\mathbf{x} = (x_1, \ldots, x_n)$ in D.   (1)

EXAMPLE 1   (a) The demand for sugar in the United States in the period 1929–1935 was estimated by T. W. Schultz, who found that it could be described approximately by the formula

$$x = 108.83 - 6.0294p + 0.164w - 0.4217t$$

Here x, the demand for sugar, is a function of three variables: p (the price of sugar), w (a production index), and t (the date, where $t = 0$ corresponds to 1929).

(b) R. Stone estimated the following formula for the demand for beer in the UK:

$$x = 1.058\, x_1^{0.136} x_2^{-0.727} x_3^{0.914} x_4^{0.816}$$

Here the quantity demanded x is a function of four variables: x_1 (the income of the individual), x_2 (the price of beer), x_3 (a general price index for all other commodities), and x_4 (the strength of the beer).

The simpler of the functions in Example 1 is (a). The variables p, w, and t occur here only to the first power, and they are only multiplied by constants, not by each other. Such functions are called *linear*. In general,

$$f(x_1, x_2, \ldots, x_n) = a_1 x_1 + a_2 x_2 + \cdots + a_n x_n + b \tag{2}$$

(where $a_1, a_2, \ldots, a_n$, and b are constants) is a **linear function** in n variables.[2]

Example 1(b) is a special case of the general Cobb–Douglas function

$$F(x_1, x_2, \ldots, x_n) = A x_1^{a_1} x_2^{a_2} \cdots x_n^{a_n} \quad (A, a_1, \ldots, a_n \text{ are constants}; A > 0) \tag{3}$$

defined for $x_1 > 0, x_2 > 0, \ldots, x_n > 0$. We use this function very often in this book.

NOTE 1   Taking the natural logarithm of each side of (3) gives

$$\ln F = \ln A + a_1 \ln x_1 + a_2 \ln x_2 + \cdots + a_n \ln x_n \tag{4}$$

This shows that the Cobb–Douglas function is **log-linear** (or ln-linear), because $\ln F$ is a linear function of $\ln x_1, \ln x_2, \ldots, \ln x_n$.

EXAMPLE 2   Suppose an economist interested in the price of apples records n observations in different stores. Suppose the results are the n positive numbers $x_1, x_2, \ldots, x_n$. In statistics, several different measures for their average value are used. Some of the most common are:

(a)   the **arithmetic** mean: $\bar{x}_A = \dfrac{1}{n}(x_1 + x_2 + \cdots + x_n)$

(b)   the **geometric** mean: $\bar{x}_G = \sqrt[n]{x_1 x_2 \ldots x_n}$

(c)   the **harmonic** mean: $\bar{x}_H = \dfrac{1}{\dfrac{1}{n}\left(\dfrac{1}{x_1} + \dfrac{1}{x_2} + \cdots + \dfrac{1}{x_n}\right)}$

---

[2] This is rather common terminology, although many mathematicians would insist that f should really be called *affine* if $b \neq 0$, and *linear* only if $b = 0$.

Note that $\bar{x}_A$ is a linear function of $x_1, \ldots, x_n$, whereas $\bar{x}_G$ and $\bar{x}_H$ are nonlinear functions. ($\bar{x}_G$ is log-linear.)

For example, if the results of 4 observations are $x_1 = 1$, $x_2 = 2$, $x_3 = 3$, and $x_4 = 4$, then $\bar{x}_A = (1 + 2 + 3 + 4)/4 = 2.5$, $\bar{x}_G = \sqrt[4]{1 \cdot 2 \cdot 3 \cdot 4} = \sqrt[4]{24} \approx 2.21$, and $\bar{x}_H = \left[(1/1 + 1/2 + 1/3 + 1/4)/4\right]^{-1} = 48/25 = 1.92$. In this case $\bar{x}_H < \bar{x}_G < \bar{x}_A$. It turns out that the corresponding weak inequalities

$$\bar{x}_H \leq \bar{x}_G \leq \bar{x}_A \tag{5}$$

are valid in general. Problem 1.6.9 asks you to show (5) for the case $n = 2$. The harmonic mean $\bar{x}_H$ appears in the solutions to Problems 3, 4, and 5.

EXAMPLE 3   An individual must decide what quantities of n different commodities to buy during a given time period. Consumer demand theory often assumes that the individual has a utility function $U(x_1, x_2, \ldots, x_n)$ representing preferences, and that this measures the satisfaction the individual obtains by acquiring x_1 units of good no. 1, x_2 units of good no. 2, and so on. This is an important economic example of a function of n variables, to which we return several times.

One model of consumer demand is the **linear expenditure system**, which is based on the particular utility function

$$U(x_1, x_2, \ldots, x_n) = a_1 \ln(x_1 - c_1) + a_2 \ln(x_2 - c_2) + \cdots + a_n \ln(x_n - c_n)$$

that depends on the $2n$ nonnegative parameters $a_1, a_2, \ldots, a_n$ and $c_1, c_2, \ldots, c_n$. Here, each c_i represents the quantity of the commodity numbered i that the consumer needs to survive. (Some, or even all, of the constants c_i could be equal to 0.) Because $\ln z$ is only defined when $z > 0$, we see that all n inequalities $x_1 > c_1, x_2 > c_2, \ldots, x_n > c_n$ must be satisfied if $U(x_1, x_2, \ldots, x_n)$ is to be defined. Of course, the condition $a_i > 0$ implies that the consumer prefers more of the particular good i.

Continuity

The concept of continuity for functions of one variable may be generalized to functions of several variables. Roughly speaking, a function of n variables is **continuous** if small changes in any or all of the independent variables induce small changes in the function value. Just as in the one-variable case, we have the following useful rule:

CONTINUITY

> Any function of n variables that can be constructed from continuous functions by combining the operations of addition, subtraction, multiplication, division, and functional composition is continuous wherever it is defined.

If a function of one variable is continuous, it will also be continuous when considered as a function of several variables. For example, $f(x, y, z) = x^2$ is a continuous function of x, y, and z. (Small changes in x, y, and z give at most small changes in x^2.)

EXAMPLE 4   Where are the functions given by the following formulas continuous?

$$\text{(a)} \ \ f(x, y, z) = x^2 y + 8x^2 y^5 z - xy + 8z \qquad \text{(b)} \ \ g(x, y) = \frac{xy - 3}{x^2 + y^2 - 4}$$

Solution:

(a) As the sum of products of positive powers, f is defined and continuous for all x, y, and z.

(b) The function g is defined and continuous for all (x, y) except those that lie on the circle $x^2 + y^2 = 4$. There the denominator is zero, and so $g(x, y)$ is not defined.

Euclidean n-Dimensional Space

No concrete geometric interpretation is possible for functions of n variables in the general case when $n \geq 3$. Yet economists still use *geometric language* when dealing with functions of n variables. It is usual to call the set of all possible n-vectors $\mathbf{x} = (x_1, x_2, \ldots, x_n)$ of real numbers the **Euclidean n-dimensional space**, or **n-space**, and to denote it by $\mathbb{R}^n$. For $n = 1$, 2, and 3, we have geometric interpretations of $\mathbb{R}^n$ as a line, a plane, and a three-dimensional space, respectively. But for $n \geq 4$, there is no geometric interpretation.

If $z = f(x_1, x_2, \ldots, x_n) = f(\mathbf{x})$ represents a function of n variables, we define the **graph** of f as the set of all points $(\mathbf{x}, f(\mathbf{x}))$ in $\mathbb{R}^{n+1}$ for which $\mathbf{x}$ belongs to the domain of f. We also call the graph a **surface** (or sometimes a **hypersurface**) in $\mathbb{R}^{n+1}$. For $z = z_0$ (constant), the set of points in $\mathbb{R}^n$ satisfying $f(\mathbf{x}) = z_0$ is called a **level surface** of f. When $f(\mathbf{x})$ is a linear function such as $a_1 x_1 + a_2 x_2 + \cdots + a_n x_n + b$, this surface, which would be a plane if $n = 3$, is called a **hyperplane** when $n > 3$.

In both producer and consumer theory, it is usual to give level surfaces a different name. If $x = f(\mathbf{v}) = f(v_1, v_2, \ldots, v_n)$ is the amount produced when the input quantities of n different factors of production are respectively $v_1, v_2, \ldots, v_n$, the level surfaces where $f(v_1, v_2, \ldots, v_n) = x_0$ (constant) are called *isoquants*, as in Example 11.3.2. On the other hand, if $u = U(\mathbf{x})$ is a utility function that represents the consumer's preferences, the level surface where $U(x_1, x_2, \ldots, x_n) = u_0$ is called an *indifference surface*.

PROBLEMS FOR SECTION 11.5

1. (a) Let $f(x, y, z) = xy + xz + yz$. Find $f(-1, 2, 3)$ and $f(a + 1, b + 1, c + 1) - f(a, b, c)$.

(b) Show that $f(tx, ty, tz) = t^2 f(x, y, z)$ for all t.

2. (a) In a study of milk production, Hjelm and Sandquist found that

$$y = 2.90 \, x_1^{0.015} x_2^{0.250} x_3^{0.350} x_4^{0.408} x_5^{0.030}$$

where y is the output of milk, and $x_1, \ldots, x_5$ are the quantities of five different input factors. (For instance, x_1 is work effort and x_3 is grass consumption.) If all the factors of production were doubled, what would happen to y?

(b) Write the relation in log-linear form.

(SM) **3.** A pension fund decides to invest \$720 million in the shares of XYZ Inc., a company with a volatile share price. Rather than invest all the funds at once and so risk paying an unduly high price, it practises "dollar cost averaging" by investing \$120 million per week in 6 successive weeks. The prices it pays are \$50 per share in the first week, then \$60, \$45, \$40, \$75, and finally \$80 in the sixth week.

   (a) How many shares in total does it buy?

   (b) Which is the most accurate statement of the average price: the arithmetic, the geometric, or the harmonic mean?

4. An American bank A and a European bank E agree a currency swap. In n successive weeks $w = 1, 2, \ldots, n$, bank A will buy \$100 million worth of euros from bank E, at a price p_w per euro determined by the spot exchange rate at the end of week w. After n weeks:

   (a) How many euros will bank A have bought?

   (b) What is the dollar price per euro it will have paid, on average?

HARDER PROBLEM

5. (a) It is observed that three machines A, B, and C produce, respectively, 60, 80, and 40 units of a product during one workday lasting 8 hours (or 480 minutes). The average output is then 60 units per day. We see that A, B, and C use, respectively, 8, 6, and 12 minutes to make one unit. If all machines were equally efficient and jointly produced $60 + 80 + 40 = 180$ units during a day, then how much time would be required to produce each unit? (Note that the answer is not $(8 + 6 + 12)/3$.)

   (b) Suppose that n machines $A_1, A_2, \ldots, A_n$ produce the same product simultaneously during a time interval of length T. Given that the production times per unit are respectively $t_1, t_2, \ldots, t_n$, find the total output Q. Show that if all the machines were equally efficient and together had produced exactly the same total amount Q in the time span T, then the time needed for each machine to produce one unit would be precisely the harmonic mean $\bar{t}_H$ of $t_1, t_2, \ldots, t_n$.

11.6 Partial Derivatives with More Variables

The last section gave several economic examples of functions involving many variables. Accordingly, we need to extend the concept of partial derivative to functions with more than two variables.

PARTIAL DERIVATIVES IN N VARIABLES

> If $z = f(\mathbf{x}) = f(x_1, x_2, \ldots, x_n)$, then $\partial f/\partial x_i$, for $i = 1, 2, \ldots, n$, means the partial derivative of $f(x_1, x_2, \ldots, x_n)$ w.r.t. x_i when all the other variables x_j $(j \neq i)$ are held constant. $\qquad$ (1)

So provided they all exist, there are n partial derivatives of first order, one for each variable x_i, $i = 1, \ldots, n$. Other notation used for the first-order partials of $z = f(x_1, x_2, \ldots, x_n)$ includes

$$\frac{\partial f}{\partial x_i} = \frac{\partial z}{\partial x_i} = \partial z / \partial x_i = z_i' = f_i'(x_1, x_2, \ldots, x_n)$$

EXAMPLE 1   Find the three first-order partials of $f(x_1, x_2, x_3) = 5x_1^2 + x_1 x_2^3 - x_2^2 x_3^2 + x_3^3$.

Solution: We find that

$$f_1' = 10x_1 + x_2^3, \qquad f_2' = 3x_1 x_2^2 - 2x_2 x_3^2, \qquad f_3' = -2x_2^2 x_3 + 3x_3^2$$

As in (11.2.6) we have the following rough approximation:

The partial derivative $\partial z / \partial x_i$ is approximately equal to the per unit change in

$$z = f(x_1, x_2, \ldots, x_n)$$

caused by an increase in x_i, while holding constant all the other x_j ($j \neq i$).

In symbols, for h small one has   (2)

$$f_i'(x_1, \ldots, x_n) \approx$$
$$\frac{f(x_1, \ldots, x_{i-1}, x_i + h, x_{i+1}, \ldots, x_n) - f(x_1, \ldots, x_{i-1}, x_i, x_{i+1}, \ldots, x_n)}{h}$$

For each of the n first-order partials of f, we have n second-order partials:

$$\frac{\partial}{\partial x_j}\left(\frac{\partial f}{\partial x_i}\right) = \frac{\partial^2 f}{\partial x_j \partial x_i} = z_{ij}''$$

Here both i and j may take any value $1, 2, \ldots, n$, so altogether there are n^2 second-order partials.

It is usual to display these second-order partials in an $n \times n$ square array as follows

$$f''(\mathbf{x}) = \begin{pmatrix} f_{11}''(\mathbf{x}) & f_{12}''(\mathbf{x}) & \cdots & f_{1n}''(\mathbf{x}) \\ f_{21}''(\mathbf{x}) & f_{22}''(\mathbf{x}) & \cdots & f_{2n}''(\mathbf{x}) \\ \vdots & \vdots & \ddots & \vdots \\ f_{n1}''(\mathbf{x}) & f_{n2}''(\mathbf{x}) & \cdots & f_{nn}''(\mathbf{x}) \end{pmatrix} \quad \text{(The Hessian)} \quad (3)$$

Such rectangular arrays of numbers (or symbols) are called **matrices**, and (3) is called the **Hessian matrix** of f at $\mathbf{x} = (x_1, x_2, \ldots, x_n)$. See Chapter 15 for more discussion of matrices in general.

The n second-order partial derivatives f_{ii}'' found by differentiating twice w.r.t. the same variable are called *direct second-order partials*; the others, f_{ij}'' where $i \neq j$, are *mixed* or *cross* partials.

EXAMPLE 2   Find the Hessian matrix of $f(x_1, x_2, x_3) = 5x_1^2 + x_1x_2^3 - x_2^2x_3^2 + x_3^3$. (See Example 1.)

Solution: We differentiate the first-order partials found in Example 1. The resulting Hessian is

$$
\begin{pmatrix} f_{11}'' & f_{12}'' & f_{13}'' \\ f_{21}'' & f_{22}'' & f_{23}'' \\ f_{31}'' & f_{32}'' & f_{33}'' \end{pmatrix} = \begin{pmatrix} 10 & 3x_2^2 & 0 \\ 3x_2^2 & 6x_1x_2 - 2x_3^2 & -4x_2x_3 \\ 0 & -4x_2x_3 & -2x_2^2 + 6x_3 \end{pmatrix}
$$

Young's Theorem

If $z = f(x_1, x_2, \ldots, x_n)$, then the two second-order cross-partial derivatives z_{ij}'' and z_{ji}'' are usually equal. That is,

$$
\frac{\partial}{\partial x_j}\left(\frac{\partial f}{\partial x_i}\right) = \frac{\partial}{\partial x_i}\left(\frac{\partial f}{\partial x_j}\right)
$$

This implies that the order of differentiation does not matter. The next theorem makes precise a more general result.

THEOREM 11.6.1 (YOUNG'S THEOREM)

Suppose that all the mth-order partial derivatives of the function $f(x_1, x_2, \ldots, x_n)$ are continuous. If any two of them involve differentiating w.r.t. each of the variables the same number of times, then they are necessarily equal.

The content of this result can be explained as follows: Let $m = m_1 + \cdots + m_n$, and suppose that $f(x_1, x_2, \ldots, x_n)$ is differentiated m_1 times w.r.t. x_1, m_2 times w.r.t. x_2, $\ldots$, and m_n times w.r.t. x_n. (Some of the integers $m_1, \ldots, m_n$ can be zero, of course.) Suppose that the continuity condition is satisfied for these mth-order partial derivatives. Then we end up with the same result no matter what is the order of differentiation, because each of the final partial derivatives is equal to

$$
\frac{\partial^m f}{\partial x_1^{m_1}\partial x_2^{m_2}\ldots\partial x_n^{m_n}}
$$

In particular, for the case when $m = 2$,

$$
\frac{\partial^2 f}{\partial x_j\partial x_i} = \frac{\partial^2 f}{\partial x_i\partial x_j} \qquad (i = 1, 2, \ldots, n; \quad j = 1, 2, \ldots, n)
$$

if both these partials are continuous. A proof of Young's theorem is given in most advanced calculus books. Problem 11 shows that the mixed partial derivatives are not always equal.

Formal Definitions of Partial Derivatives

In Section 11.2, we gave a formal definition of partial derivatives for functions of two variables. This was done by modifying the definition of the (ordinary) derivative for a function of one variable. The same modification works for a function of n variables.

Indeed, if $z = f(x_1, \ldots, x_n)$, then with $g(x_i) = f(x_1, \ldots, x_{i-1}, x_i, x_{i+1}, \ldots, x_n)$, we have $\partial z / \partial x_i = g'(x_i)$. (Here we think of all the variables x_j other than x_i as constants.) If we use the definition of $g'(x_i)$ (see (6.2.1)), we obtain

$$\frac{\partial z}{\partial x_i} = \lim_{h \to 0} \frac{f(x_1, \ldots, x_i + h, \ldots, x_n) - f(x_1, \ldots, x_i, \ldots, x_n)}{h} \tag{4}$$

(The approximation in (2) holds because the fraction on the right in (4) is close to the limit if $h \neq 0$ is small enough.) If the limit in (4) does not exist, then we say that $\partial z / \partial x_i$ *does not exist*, or that z is not differentiable w.r.t. x_i at the point.

Virtually all the functions we consider have continuous partial derivatives everywhere in their domains. If $z = f(x_1, x_2, \ldots, x_n)$ has continuous partial derivatives of first order in a domain D, we call f **continuously differentiable** in D. In this case, f is also called a C^1 **function** on D. If all partial derivatives up to order k exist and are continuous, f is called a C^k **function**.

PROBLEMS FOR SECTION 11.6

1. Calculate $F_1'(1, 1, 1)$, $F_2'(1, 1, 1)$, and $F_3'(1, 1, 1)$ for $F(x, y, z) = x^2 e^{xz} + y^3 e^{xy}$.

SM 2. Calculate all first-order partials of the following functions:

   (a) $f(x, y, z) = x^2 + y^3 + z^4$ (b) $f(x, y, z) = 5x^2 - 3y^3 + 3z^4$

   (c) $f(x, y, z) = xyz$ (d) $f(x, y, z) = x^4 / yz$

   (e) $f(x, y, z) = (x^2 + y^3 + z^4)^6$ (f) $f(x, y, z) = e^{xyz}$

3. Let x and y be the populations of two cities and d the distance between them. Suppose that the number of travellers T between the cities is given by

$$T = kxy/d^n \quad (k \text{ and } n \text{ are positive constants})$$

Find $\partial T / \partial x$, $\partial T / \partial y$, and $\partial T / \partial d$, and discuss their signs.

4. Let g be defined for all (x, y, z) by

$$g(x, y, z) = 2x^2 - 4xy + 10y^2 + z^2 - 4x - 28y - z + 24$$

   (a) Calculate $g(2, 1, 1)$, $g(3, -4, 2)$, and $g(1, 1, a + h) - g(1, 1, a)$.

   (b) Find all partial derivatives of the first and second order.

5. Let $\pi(p, r, w) = \frac{1}{4} p^2 (1/r + 1/w)$. Find the partial derivatives of π w.r.t. p, r, and w.

6. Find all first- and second-order partials of $w(x, y, z) = 3xyz + x^2 y - xz^3$.

7. If $f(x, y, z) = p(x) + q(y) + r(z)$, what are f_1', f_2', and f_3'?

8. Find the Hessian matrices of: (a) $f(x, y, z) = ax^2 + by^2 + cz^2$ (b) $g(x, y, z) = Ax^a y^b z^c$

9. Prove that if $w = \left(\dfrac{x - y + z}{x + y - z}\right)^h$, then

$$x\frac{\partial w}{\partial x} + y\frac{\partial w}{\partial y} + z\frac{\partial w}{\partial z} = 0$$

(SM) **10.** Calculate the first-order partial derivatives of the following function

$$f(x, y, z) = x^{y^z} \qquad x > 0, y > 0, z > 0$$

(You might find it easier first to take the natural logarithm of both sides.)

HARDER PROBLEM

(SM) **11.** Define the function $f(x, y) = xy(x^2 - y^2)/(x^2 + y^2)$ when $(x, y) \neq (0, 0)$, and $f(0, 0) = 0$. Find expressions for $f_1'(0, y)$ and $f_2'(x, 0)$, then show that $f_{12}''(0, 0) = 1$ and $f_{21}''(0, 0) = -1$. Check that Young's theorem is not contradicted. (f_{12}'' and f_{21}'' are discontinuous at $(0, 0)$.)

11.7 Economic Applications

This section considers several economic applications of partial derivatives.

EXAMPLE 1   Consider an agricultural production function $Y = F(K, L, T)$, where Y is the number of units produced, K is capital invested, L is labour input, and T is the area of agricultural land that is used. Then $\partial Y/\partial K = F_K'$ is called the **marginal product of capital**. It is the rate of change of output Y w.r.t. K when L and T are held fixed. Similarly, $\partial Y/\partial L = F_L'$ and $\partial Y/\partial T = F_T'$ are the **marginal products of labour and of land**, respectively. For example, if K is the value of capital equipment measured in dollars, and $\partial Y/\partial K = 5$, then increasing capital input by h units would increase output by approximately $5h$ units.

Suppose, in particular, that F is the Cobb–Douglas function

$$F(K, L, T) = AK^a L^b T^c \qquad (A, a, b, \text{ and } c \text{ are positive constants})$$

Find the marginal products, and the second-order partials. Discuss their signs.

Solution: The marginal products are

$$F_K' = AaK^{a-1}L^bT^c, \qquad F_L' = AbK^aL^{b-1}T^c, \qquad F_T' = AcK^aL^bT^{c-1}$$

Assuming K, L, and T are all positive, the marginal products are positive. Thus, an increase in capital, labour, or land will increase the number of units produced.

The mixed second-order partials (or cross-partials) are

$$F_{KL}'' = AabK^{a-1}L^{b-1}T^c, \qquad F_{KT}'' = AacK^{a-1}L^bT^{c-1}, \qquad F_{LT}'' = AbcK^aL^{b-1}T^{c-1}$$

Check for yourself that F''_{LK}, F''_{TK}, and F''_{TL} give, respectively, the same results. Note that these partials are positive. We call each pair of factors *complementary*, because more of one increases the marginal product of the other.

The direct second-order partials are

$$F''_{KK} = Aa(a-1)K^{a-2}L^bT^c, \quad F''_{LL} = Ab(b-1)K^aL^{b-2}T^c, \quad F''_{TT} = Ac(c-1)K^aL^bT^{c-2}$$

For instance, F''_{KK} is the partial derivative of the marginal product of capital (F'_K) w.r.t. K. If $a < 1$, then $F''_{KK} < 0$, and there is a diminishing marginal product of capital—that is, a small increase in the capital invested will lead to a decrease in the marginal product of capital. We can interpret this to mean that, although small increases in capital cause output to rise $(F'_K > 0)$, this rise occurs at a decreasing rate $(F''_{KK} < 0)$. Similarly for labour (if $b < 1$), and for land (if $c < 1$).

EXAMPLE 2   Let x be an index of the total amount of goods produced and consumed in a society, and let z be a measure of the level of pollution. If $u(x, z)$ measures the total well-being of the society (not a very easy function to estimate!), what signs do you expect $u'_x(x, z)$ and $u'_z(x, z)$ to have? Can you guess what economists usually assume about the sign of $u''_{xz}(x, z)$?

Solution: It is reasonable to expect that well-being increases as the amount of goods increases, but decreases as the level of pollution increases. Hence, we will usually have $u'_x(x, z) > 0$ and $u'_z(x, z) < 0$. According to (11.6.2), $u''_{xz} = (\partial/\partial z)(u'_x)$ is approximately equal to the change in u'_x per unit increase in x, the level of pollution. Moreover, $u'_x \approx$ the increase in welfare per unit increase in x. It is often assumed that $u''_{xz} < 0$. This implies that the increase in welfare obtained by an extra unit of x will decrease when the level of pollution increases. (An analogy: When a confirmed nonsmoker sits in a smoke-filled room, the extra satisfaction from one more piece of cake will decrease if the concentration of smoke increases too much.) Because of Young's theorem 11.6.1, the inequality $u''_{xz} < 0$ also implies that $u''_{zx} < 0$. Thus the increase in welfare obtained from being exposed to one unit less pollution (which is approximately $-u'_z$) increases with consumption x. This accords with the (controversial) view that, as people can afford to consume more, they also become less tolerant of pollution.

PROBLEMS FOR SECTION 11.7

1. The demand for money M in the United States for the period 1929–1952 has been estimated as

$$M = 0.14Y + 76.03(r - 2)^{-0.84} \quad (r > 2)$$

where Y is the annual national income, and the interest rate is $r\%$ per year. Find $\partial M/\partial Y$ and $\partial M/\partial r$ and discuss their signs.

(SM) **2.** If a and b are constants, compute the expression $KY'_K + LY'_L$ for the following:

(a) $Y = AK^a + BL^a$ 　　　(b) $Y = AK^aL^b$ 　　　(c) $Y = \dfrac{K^2L^2}{aL^3 + bK^3}$

3. The demand for a product depends on the price p of the product and on the price q charged by a competing producer. It is

$$D(p, q) = a - bpq^{-\alpha}$$

where a, b, and α are positive constants with $\alpha < 1$. Find $D_p'(p, q)$ and $D_q'(p, q)$, and comment on the signs of the partial derivatives.

4. Let $F(K, L, M) = AK^a L^b M^c$. Show that

$$KF_K' + LF_L' + MF_M' = (a + b + c)F$$

5. Let $D(p, q)$ and $E(p, q)$ be the demands for two commodities when the prices per unit are p and q, respectively. Suppose the commodities are *substitutes* in consumption, such as butter and margarine. What are the normal signs of the partial derivatives of D and E w.r.t. p and q?

6. Find $\partial U / \partial x_i$ when $U(x_1, x_2, \ldots, x_n) = 100 - e^{-x_1} - e^{-x_2} - \cdots - e^{-x_n}$.

HARDER PROBLEM

(SM) **7.** Calculate the expression $KY_K' + LY_L'$ for the CES function $Y = Ae^{\lambda t}\left[aK^{-\varrho} + bL^{-\varrho}\right]^{-\mu/\varrho}$.

11.8 Partial Elasticities

Section 7.7 introduced the concept of elasticity for functions of one variable. Here we study the corresponding concept for functions of several variables. This enables us to distinguish between, for instance, the price and income elasticities of demand, as well as between different price elasticities.

Two Variables

If $z = f(x, y)$, we define the partial elasticity of z w.r.t. x and y by

$$\text{El}_x z = \frac{x}{z}\frac{\partial z}{\partial x}, \qquad \text{El}_y z = \frac{y}{z}\frac{\partial z}{\partial y} \tag{1}$$

Often economists just refer to the elasticity rather than the partial elasticity. Thus, $\text{El}_x z$ is the elasticity of z w.r.t. x when y is held constant, and $\text{El}_y z$ is the elasticity of z w.r.t. y when x is held constant. The number $\text{El}_x z$ is (approximately) the percentage change in z caused by a 1% increase in x when y is held constant, and $\text{El}_y z$ has a corresponding interpretation.

As in Section 7.7, when all the variables are positive, elasticities can be expressed as logarithmic derivatives. Accordingly,

$$\text{El}_x z = \frac{\partial \ln z}{\partial \ln x}, \qquad \text{El}_y z = \frac{\partial \ln z}{\partial \ln y} \tag{2}$$

EXAMPLE 1   Find the (partial) elasticity of z w.r.t. x when   (a) $z = Ax^a y^b$ (b) $z = xye^{x+y}$.

Solution: (a) When finding the elasticity of $Ax^a y^b$ w.r.t. x, the variable y, and thus Ay^b, is held constant. From Example 7.7.1 we obtain $\text{El}_x z = a$. In the same way, $\text{El}_y z = b$.

(b) It is convenient here to use formula (2). Assuming all variables are positive, taking appropriate natural logarithms gives $\ln z = \ln x + \ln y + x + y = \ln x + \ln y + e^{\ln x} + y$. Hence $\text{El}_x z = \partial \ln z / \partial \ln x = 1 + e^{\ln x} = 1 + x$.

EXAMPLE 2   The demand D_1 for potatoes in the United States for the period 1927 to 1941 was estimated to be $D_1 = Ap^{-0.28} m^{0.34}$, where p is the price of potatoes and m is mean income. The demand for apples was estimated to be $D_2 = Bq^{-1.27} m^{1.32}$, where q is the price of apples.

Find the price elasticities of demand, $\text{El}_p D_1$ and $\text{El}_q D_2$, as well as the income elasticities of demand $\text{El}_m D_1$ and $\text{El}_m D_2$, and comment on their signs.

Solution: According to Example 1(a), $\text{El}_p D_1 = -0.28$. If the price of potatoes increases by 1%, demand decreases by approximately 0.28%. Furthermore, $\text{El}_q D_2 = -1.27$, $\text{El}_m D_1 = 0.34$, and $\text{El}_m D_2 = 1.32$.

Both price elasticities $\text{El}_p D_1$ and $\text{El}_q D_2$ are negative, so demand decreases when the price increases in both cases—as seems reasonable. Both income elasticities $\text{El}_m D_1$ and $\text{El}_m D_2$ are positive, so demand increases when mean income increases—as seems reasonable. Note that the demand for apples is more sensitive to both price and income increases than is the demand for potatoes. This also seems reasonable, since at that time potatoes were a more essential commodity than apples for most consumers.

n Variables

If $z = f(x_1, x_2, \ldots, x_n) = f(\mathbf{x})$, we define the **(partial) elasticity** of z (or of f) w.r.t. x_i as the elasticity of z w.r.t. x_i when all the other variables are held constant. Thus,

$$\text{El}_i z = \frac{x_i}{f(\mathbf{x})} \frac{\partial f(\mathbf{x})}{\partial x_i} = \frac{x_i}{z} \frac{\partial z}{\partial x_i} = \frac{\partial \ln z}{\partial \ln x_i} \tag{3}$$

(Of course, the last characterization is only valid when all variables are positive.) The number $\text{El}_i z$ is approximately equal to the percentage change in z caused by a 1% increase in x_i, keeping all the other x_j ($j \neq i$) constant. Among other forms of notation commonly used instead of $\text{El}_i z$, we mention

$$\text{El}_i f(\mathbf{x}), \qquad \text{El}_{x_i} z, \qquad \hat{z}_i \text{ (pronounced "z hat i"),} \qquad \varepsilon_i, \qquad \text{and} \qquad e_i$$

EXAMPLE 3   Suppose $D = Ax_1^{a_1} x_2^{a_2} \cdots x_n^{a_n}$ is defined for all $x_1 > 0$, $x_2 > 0$, $\ldots$, $x_n > 0$, where $A > 0$ and $a_1, a_2, \ldots, a_n$ are constants. Find the elasticity of D w.r.t. x_i, for $i = 1, \ldots, n$.

Solution: Because all the factors except $x_i^{a_i}$ are constant, we can apply (7.7.2) to obtain $\text{El}_i D = a_i$.

As a special case of this example, suppose that $D_i = Am^\alpha p_i^{-\beta} p_j^\gamma$, where m is income, p_i is the own price, and p_j is the price of a substitute good. Then α is the income elasticity of demand defined as in Example 2. On the other hand, $-\beta$ is the elasticity of demand w.r.t. changes in its own price p_i, so it is called the **own-price elasticity** of demand. However, because own-price elasticities of demand are usually negative, one often describes β rather than $-\beta$ as being the own-price elasticity of demand. Finally, γ is the elasticity of demand w.r.t. the price of the specified substitute. By analogy with the cross-partial derivatives defined in Section 11.6, it is called a **cross-price elasticity** of demand.

Note that the proportion of income spent on good i is

$$\frac{p_i D_i}{m} = Am^{\alpha-1} p_i^{1-\beta} p_j^\gamma$$

When the income elasticity $\alpha < 1$, this proportion is a decreasing function of income. Economists describe a good with this property as a *necessity*. On the other hand, when $\alpha > 1$, the proportion of income spent on good i rises with income, in which case economists describe good i as a *luxury*. Referring back to Example 2, these definitions imply that during the period 1927–1941, which includes the years of the Great Depression, potatoes were a necessity, but apples a (relative) luxury.

Problem 4 below considers this distinction between necessities and luxuries for more general demand functions.

PROBLEMS FOR SECTION 11.8

1. Find the partial elasticities of z w.r.t. x and y in the following cases:

   (a) $z = xy$ (b) $z = x^2 y^5$ (c) $z = x^n e^x y^n e^y$ (d) $z = x + y$

2. Let $z = (ax_1^d + bx_2^d + cx_3^d)^g$, where a, b, c, d, and g are constants. Find $\sum_{i=1}^{3} \text{El}_i\, z$.

3. Let $z = x_1^p \cdots x_n^p \exp(a_1 x_1 + \cdots + a_n x_n)$, where $a_1, \ldots, a_n$, and p are constants. Find the partial elasticities of z w.r.t. $x_1, \ldots, x_n$.

(SM) 4. Let $D(p, m)$ indicate a typical consumer's demand for a particular commodity, as a function of its price p and the consumer's own income m. Show that the proportion pD/m of income spent on the commodity increases with income if $\text{El}_m D > 1$ (in which case the good is a "luxury", whereas it is a "necessity" if $\text{El}_m D < 1$).

REVIEW PROBLEMS FOR CHAPTER 11

1. Let $f(x, y) = 3x - 5y$. Calculate $f(0, 1)$, $f(2, -1)$, $f(a, a)$, and $f(a + h, b) - f(a, b)$.

2. Let $f(x, y) = 2x^2 - 3y^2$. Calculate $f(-1, 2)$, $f(2a, 2a)$, $f(a, b+k) - f(a, b)$, and $f(tx, ty) - t^2 f(x, y)$.

3. Let $f(x, y, z) = \sqrt{x^2 + y^2 + z^2}$. Calculate $f(3, 4, 0)$, $f(-2, 1, 3)$, and $f(tx, ty, tz)$ for $t \geq 0$.

4. Let $Y = F(K, L) = 15K^{1/5}L^{2/5}$ denote the number of units produced when K units of capital and L units of labour are used as inputs.

   (a) Compute $F(0, 0)$, $F(1, 1)$, and $F(32, 243)$.

   (b) Find an expression for $F(K + 1, L) - F(K, L)$, and give an economic interpretation.

   (c) Compute $F(32 + 1, 243) - F(32, 243)$, and compare the result with what you get by calculating $F'_K(32, 243)$.

   (d) Show that $F(tK, tL) = t^k F(K, L)$ for a constant k.

5. In a paper by Henderson and Tugwell the annual herring catch is given by the function $Y(K, S) = 0.06157K^{1.356}S^{0.562}$ of the catching effort K and the herring stock S.

   (a) Find $\partial Y/\partial K$ and $\partial Y/\partial S$.

   (b) If K and S are both doubled, what happens to the catch?

6. For which pairs of numbers (x, y) are the functions given by the following formulas defined?

   (a) $3xy^3 - 45x^4 - 3y$ (b) $\sqrt{1 - xy}$ (c) $\ln(2 - (x^2 + y^2))$

7. For which pairs of numbers (x, y) are the functions given by the following formulas defined?

   (a) $\dfrac{1}{\sqrt{x + y - 1}}$ (b) $\sqrt{x^2 - y^2} + \sqrt{x^2 + y^2 - 1}$ (c) $\sqrt{y - x^2} - \sqrt{\sqrt{x} - y}$

8. Complete the following implications:

   (a) $z = (x^2y^4 + 2)^5 \implies \dfrac{\partial z}{\partial x} =$

   (b) $F(K, L) = (\sqrt{K} + \sqrt{L})^2 \implies \sqrt{K}\dfrac{\partial F}{\partial K} =$

   (c) $F(K, L) = (K^a + L^a)^{1/a} \implies KF'_K(K, L) + LF'_L(K, L) =$

   (d) $g(t, w) = \dfrac{3t}{w} + wt^2 \implies \dfrac{\partial^2 g}{\partial w \partial t} =$

   (e) $g(t_1, t_2, t_3) = (t_1^2 + t_2^2 + t_3^2)^{1/2} \implies g'_3(t_1, t_2, t_3) =$

   (f) $f(x, y, z) = 2x^2yz - y^3 + x^2z^2 \implies f'_1(x, y, z) = \quad, f''_{13}(x, y, z) =$

9. Let f be defined for all (x, y) by $f(x, y) = (x - 2)^2(y + 3)^2$.

   (a) Calculate $f(0, 0)$, $f(-2, -3)$, and $f(a + 2, b - 3)$.

   (b) Find f'_x and f'_y.

10. Verify that the points $(-1, 5)$ and $(1, 1)$ lie on the same level curve for the function

$$g(x, y) = (2x + y)^3 - 2x + 5/y$$

11. For each $c \neq 0$, verify that $x - y = c$ is a level curve for $F(x, y) = \ln(x^2 - 2xy + y^2) + e^{2x - 2y}$.

(SM) **12.** (a) If $f(x, y) = x^4 + 2y^2 - 4x^2y + 4y$, find $f_1'(x, y)$ and $f_2'(x, y)$.

    (b) Find all pairs (x, y) which solve both equations $f_1'(x, y) = 0$ and $f_2'(x, y) = 0$.

13. Find the partial elasticities of z w.r.t. x and y in the following cases:

    (a) $z = x^3 y^{-4}$ (b) $z = \ln(x^2 + y^2)$ (c) $z = e^{x+y}$ (d) $z = (x^2 + y^2)^{1/2}$

14. (a) If $F(x, y) = e^{2x}(1 - y)^2$, find $\partial F / \partial y$.

    (b) If $F(K, L, M) = (\ln K)(\ln L)(\ln M)$, find F_L' and F_{LM}''.

    (c) If $w = x^x y^x z^x$, with x, y, and z positive, find w_x' using logarithmic differentiation.

HARDER PROBLEMS

15. Compute $\partial^{p+q} z / \partial y^q \partial x^p$ at $(0, 0)$ for the following:

    (a) $z = e^x \ln(1 + y)$ (b) $z = e^{x+y}(xy + y - 1)$

16. Show that, if $u = Ax^a y^b$, then $u_{xy}''/u_x'u_y'$ can be expressed as a function of u alone. Use this to prove that

$$\frac{1}{u_x'} \frac{\partial}{\partial x} \left(\frac{u_{xy}''}{u_x'u_y'} \right) = \frac{1}{u_y'} \frac{\partial}{\partial y} \left(\frac{u_{xy}''}{u_x'u_y'} \right)$$

12 TOOLS FOR COMPARATIVE STATICS

CHAPTER 12 / TOOLS FOR COMPARATIVE STATICS

*Logic merely sanctions the
conquests of the intuition.*
—J. Hadamard (1945)

Comparative statics is a particular technique that features very prominently in economic analysis. The question it addresses is how economic quantities such as demand and supply, which are determined as endogenous variables that satisfy an equation system, respond to changes in exogenous parameters like price. More generally, what happens to the solution of an optimization problem when the parameters of the problem change? Or to the solution of equations that describe an equilibrium of demand and supply? Simple examples will be studied in this chapter and the next two; more demanding problems are treated in FMEA.

Section 12.5 discusses the concept of elasticity of substitution, which is often used by economists to characterize the "curvature" of level curves.

Homogeneous and homothetic functions are important in economics. They are studied in Sections 12.6 and 12.7. The last sections of the chapter consider linear approximations, then differentials, and finally systems of equations, together with some properties that result from differentiating such systems.

12.1 A Simple Chain Rule

Many economic models involve composite functions. These are functions of one or several variables in which the variables are themselves functions of other basic variables. For example, many models of economic growth regard output as a function of capital and labour, both of which are functions of time. How does output vary with time?

More generally, what happens to the value of a composite function as its basic variables change? This is the general problem we discuss in this and the next section.

Suppose z is a function of x and y, with

$$z = F(x, y)$$

where x and y both are functions of a variable t, with

$$x = f(t), \qquad y = g(t)$$

Substituting for x and y in $z = F(x, y)$ gives the composite function

$$z = F(f(t), g(t))$$

This reduces z to a function of t alone. A change in t will in general lead to changes in both $f(t)$ and $g(t)$, and as a result, z changes. How does z change when t changes? For example, will a small increase in t lead to an increase or a decrease in z? Such questions would become much easier to answer if we could find an expression for dz/dt, the rate of change of z w.r.t. t. This is given by the following rule:

THE CHAIN RULE

When $z = F(x, y)$ with $x = f(t)$ and $y = g(t)$, then

$$\frac{dz}{dt} = F_1'(x, y)\frac{dx}{dt} + F_2'(x, y)\frac{dy}{dt} \tag{1}$$

It is important to understand the precise content of (1). It gives the derivative of $z = F(x, y)$ w.r.t. t when x and y are both differentiable functions of t. This derivative is called the **total derivative** of z w.r.t. t. According to (1), one contribution to the total derivative occurs because the first variable in $F(x, y)$, namely x, depends on t. This contribution is $F_1'(x, y)\, dx/dt$. A second contribution arises because the second variable in $F(x, y)$, namely y, also depends on t. This contribution is $F_2'(x, y)\, dy/dt$. The total derivative dz/dt is the *sum* of the two contributions.

EXAMPLE 1   Find dz/dt when $z = F(x, y) = x^2 + y^3$ with $x = t^2$ and $y = 2t$.

Solution: In this case $F_1'(x, y) = 2x$, $F_2'(x, y) = 3y^2$, $dx/dt = 2t$, and $dy/dt = 2$. So formula (1) gives

$$\frac{dz}{dt} = 2x \cdot 2t + 3y^2 \cdot 2 = 4tx + 6y^2 = 4t^3 + 24t^2$$

where the last equality comes from substituting the appropriate functions of t for x and y respectively. In a simple case like this, we can verify the chain rule by substituting $x = t^2$ and $y = 2t$ in the formula for $F(x, y)$ and then differentiating w.r.t. t. The result is

$$z = x^2 + y^3 = (t^2)^2 + (2t)^3 = t^4 + 8t^3 \implies \frac{dz}{dt} = 4t^3 + 24t^2$$

as before.

EXAMPLE 2   Find dz/dt when $z = F(x, y) = xe^{2y}$ with $x = \sqrt{t}$ and $y = \ln t$.

Solution: Here $F_1'(x, y) = e^{2y}$, $F_2'(x, y) = 2xe^{2y}$, $dx/dt = 1/2\sqrt{t}$, and $dy/dt = 1/t$. Now $y = \ln t$ implies that $e^{2y} = e^{2\ln t} = (e^{\ln t})^2 = t^2$, so formula (1) gives

$$\frac{dz}{dt} = e^{2y}\frac{1}{2\sqrt{t}} + 2xe^{2y}\frac{1}{t} = t^2\frac{1}{2\sqrt{t}} + 2\sqrt{t}\,t^2\frac{1}{t} = \frac{5}{2}t^{3/2}$$

As in Example 1, we can verify the chain rule directly by substituting $x = \sqrt{t}$ and $y = \ln t$ in the formula for $F(x, y)$, implying that $z = xe^{2y} = \sqrt{t} \cdot t^2 = t^{5/2}$, whose derivative is $dz/dt = \frac{5}{2}t^{3/2}$.

Here are some rather typical examples of ways in which economists use (1).

EXAMPLE 3   Let $D = D(p, m)$ denote the demand for a commodity as a function of price p and income m. Suppose that price p and income m vary continuously with time t, so that $p = p(t)$ and $m = m(t)$. Then demand can be determined as a function $D = D(p(t), m(t))$ of t alone. Find an expression for $\dot{D}/D$, the relative rate of growth of D.

Solution: Using (1) we obtain

$$\dot{D} = \frac{\partial D(p, m)}{\partial p}\dot{p} + \frac{\partial D(p, m)}{\partial m}\dot{m}$$

where we have denoted time derivatives by "dots". The first term on the right-hand side gives the effect on demand that arises because the price p is changing, and the second term gives the effect of the change in m. Denoting the price elasticity of demand by $\varepsilon_{Dp} = \text{El}_p\, D$ and the income elasticity of demand by $\varepsilon_{Dm} = \text{El}_m\, D$, we can write the relative rate of growth of D as

$$\frac{\dot{D}}{D} = \frac{p}{D}\frac{\partial D(p, m)}{\partial p}\frac{\dot{p}}{p} + \frac{m}{D}\frac{\partial D(p, m)}{\partial m}\frac{\dot{m}}{m} = \varepsilon_{Dp}\frac{\dot{p}}{p} + \varepsilon_{Dm}\frac{\dot{m}}{m}$$

So the relative rate of growth is found by multiplying the relative rates of change of price and income by their respective elasticities, then adding.

EXAMPLE 4   Let $u(x, z)$ denote the "total well-being" of a society, where x is an index of the total amount of goods produced and consumed, and z is a measure of the level of pollution. Assume that $u_x'(x, z) > 0$ and $u_z'(x, z) < 0$. (See Example 11.7.2.) Suppose the level of pollution z is some increasing function $z = h(x)$ of x, with $h'(x) > 0$. Then total well-being becomes a function

$$U(x) = u(x, h(x))$$

of x alone. Find a necessary condition for $U(x)$ to have a maximum at $x = x^* > 0$, and give this condition an economic interpretation.

Solution: A necessary condition for $U(x)$ to have a maximum at $x^* > 0$ is that $U'(x^*) = 0$. In order to find $U'(x)$, we use the chain rule (1):

$$U'(x) = u'_x(x, h(x)) \cdot 1 + u'_z(x, h(x))h'(x)$$

So $U'(x^*) = 0$ requires that

$$u'_x(x^*, h(x^*)) = -u'_z(x^*, h(x^*))h'(x^*) \tag{$*$}$$

To illustrate this condition, consider increasing x^* by a small amount ξ, which can be positive or negative. By (11.2.6), our gain is approximately $u'_x(x^*, h(x^*))\xi$. On the other hand, the level of pollution increases by about $h'(x^*)\xi$ units. But we lose $u'_z(x^*, h(x^*))$ in well-being per unit increase in pollution. So in all we lose about $u'_z(x^*, h(x^*))h'(x^*)\xi$ from this increase in x^*. Equation $(*)$ just states that what we gain directly from increasing x^* by any small amount ξ can be neither greater nor less than what we lose indirectly through increased pollution: otherwise a small change ξ in the right direction would increase well-being slightly.

We note finally that all the general rules for differentiating functions of one variable turn out to be just special cases of the chain rule (1) (see Problem 5).

Higher-Order Derivatives

Sometimes we use the second derivative of a composite function. A general formula for d^2z/dt^2, based on formula (1), is suggested in Problem 7. Here we derive a special case of interest in optimization theory.

EXAMPLE 5   Suppose

$$z = F(x, y) \quad \text{where} \quad x = x_0 + th, \quad y = y_0 + tk$$

Keeping (x_0, y_0) and (h, k) fixed, z becomes a function only of t. So we can write $z = g(t)$. Find expressions for $g'(t)$ and $g''(t)$. (The function g records what happens to F as one moves away from (x_0, y_0) in the direction (h, k) or, when $t < 0$, in the reverse direction $(-h, -k)$. See Fig. 13.3.2.)

Solution: With $x = x_0 + th$ and $y = y_0 + tk$, we have $g(t) = F(x, y)$. Using (1) we get

$$g'(t) = F'_1(x, y)\frac{dx}{dt} + F'_2(x, y)\frac{dy}{dt} = F'_1(x_0 + th, y_0 + tk)h + F'_2(x_0 + th, y_0 + tk)k$$

To find the second derivative $g''(t)$, we have to differentiate a second time w.r.t. t. This yields

$$g''(t) = \frac{d}{dt}F'_1(x, y)h + \frac{d}{dt}F'_2(x, y)k \tag{$*$}$$

To evaluate the derivatives on the right-hand side, we must use the chain rule (1) again. This gives

$$\frac{d}{dt}F'_1(x, y) = F''_{11}(x, y)\frac{dx}{dt} + F''_{12}(x, y)\frac{dy}{dt} = F''_{11}(x, y)h + F''_{12}(x, y)k$$

$$\frac{d}{dt}F'_2(x, y) = F''_{21}(x, y)\frac{dx}{dt} + F''_{22}(x, y)\frac{dy}{dt} = F''_{21}(x, y)h + F''_{22}(x, y)k$$

Assuming that $F''_{12} = F''_{21}$, inserting these expressions into $(*)$ gives

$$g''(t) = F''_{11}(x, y)h^2 + 2F''_{12}(x, y)hk + F''_{22}(x, y)k^2$$

where $x = x_0 + th$, $y = y_0 + tk$.

A Rough Argument for the Chain Rule

In order to show that the chain rule is valid, none of the earlier rules for derivatives can be applied. Instead, we must go all the way back to the definition of derivative. Letting $\varphi(t)$ denote $F(f(t), g(t))$, we must examine the limit as $\Delta t \to 0$ of the Newton quotient

$$\frac{\varphi(t + \Delta t) - \varphi(t)}{\Delta t} = \frac{F(f(t + \Delta t), g(t + \Delta t)) - F(f(t), g(t))}{\Delta t} \qquad (*)$$

Because $x = f(t)$ and $y = g(t)$, we define $\Delta x = f(t + \Delta t) - f(t)$ and $\Delta y = g(t + \Delta t) - g(t)$, so that $f(t + \Delta t) = x + \Delta x$, $g(t + \Delta t) = y + \Delta y$. Substituting the last two expressions into $(*)$, then subtracting and adding $F(x, y + \Delta y)$, we obtain

$$\frac{\varphi(t + \Delta t) - \varphi(t)}{\Delta t} = \frac{F(x + \Delta x, y + \Delta y) - F(x, y + \Delta y) + F(x, y + \Delta y) - F(x, y)}{\Delta t}$$

whose right-hand side, provided that neither Δx nor Δy is 0, can be expressed as

$$\frac{F(x + \Delta x, y + \Delta y) - F(x, y + \Delta y)}{\Delta x} \frac{\Delta x}{\Delta t} + \frac{F(x, y + \Delta y) - F(x, y)}{\Delta y} \frac{\Delta y}{\Delta t} \qquad (**)$$

We focus on the special case when Δx and Δy are indeed nonzero for all Δt close to 0.[1] Now, as $\Delta t \to 0$, so $\Delta x / \Delta t \to dx/dt = f'(t)$, and $\Delta y / \Delta t \to dy/dt = g'(t)$. In particular, $\Delta x \to 0$ and $\Delta y \to 0$. From the formal definition of partial derivatives (see (2) and (3) of Section 11.2), we see that $[F(x + \Delta x, y + \Delta y) - F(x, y + \Delta y)]/\Delta x$ tends to $F_1'(x, y + \Delta y)$ as $\Delta x \to 0$, and that $[F(x, y + \Delta y) - F(x, y)]/\Delta y$ tends to $F_2'(x, y)$ as $\Delta y \to 0$. Also, as $\Delta t \to 0$, both Δx and Δy tend to 0, and so, because F_1' is a continuous function, $F_1'(x, y + \Delta y) \to F_1'(x, y)$. Finally, combining $(*)$ and $(**)$, then taking limits throughout as $\Delta t \to 0$, we obtain

$$\varphi'(t) = \lim_{\Delta t \to 0} \frac{\varphi(t + \Delta t) - \varphi(t)}{\Delta t} = F_1'(x, y)\frac{dx}{dt} + F_2'(x, y)\frac{dy}{dt}$$

as required.

PROBLEMS FOR SECTION 12.1

1. In the following cases, find dz/dt by using the chain rule (1):

(a) $F(x, y) = x + y^2$, $\quad x = t^2$, $\quad y = t^3$.

(b) $F(x, y) = x^p y^q$, $\quad x = at$, $\quad y = bt$.

(c) Check the answers by first substituting the expressions for x and y and then differentiating.

2. Find dz/dt when:

(a) $F(x, y) = x \ln y + y \ln x$, $\quad x = t + 1$, $\quad y = \ln t$

(b) $F(x, y) = \ln x + \ln y$, $\quad x = Ae^{at}$, $\quad y = Be^{bt}$

3. (a) If $z = F(t, y)$ and $y = g(t)$, find a formula for dz/dt. Consider in particular the case where $z = t^2 + ye^y$ and $y = t^2$.

(b) If $Y = F(K, L)$ and $K = g(L)$, find a formula for dY/dL.

---

[1] This is a "rough" argument because this assumption is not always valid, even when F, f, and g are all C^1 functions.

4. Let $Y = 10KL - \sqrt{K} - \sqrt{L}$. Suppose too that $K = 0.2t + 5$ and $L = 5e^{0.1t}$. Find $(dY/dt)_{t=0}$.

(SM) **5.** What do you get if you apply the chain rule (1) when $F(x, y)$ is as follows?

(a) $x + y$ (b) $x - y$ (c) $x \cdot y$ (d) x/y (e) $G(x)$

Here $x = f(t)$, $y = g(t)$, and $G(x)$ are all differentiable functions.

HARDER PROBLEMS

(SM) **6.** Consider Example 4 and let $u(x, z) = \ln(x^\alpha + z^\alpha) - \alpha \ln z$. Let $z = h(x) = \sqrt[3]{ax^4 + b}$, with the constants α, a, and b all positive. Find the optimal x^* in this case.

(SM) **7.** Suppose that $z = F(x, y)$, $x = g(t)$, and $y = h(t)$. Modify the solution to Example 5 in order to prove that

$$\frac{d^2z}{dt^2} = \frac{\partial z}{\partial x}\frac{d^2x}{dt^2} + \frac{\partial z}{\partial y}\frac{d^2y}{dt^2} + \frac{\partial^2 z}{\partial x^2}\left(\frac{dx}{dt}\right)^2 + 2\frac{\partial^2 z}{\partial x \partial y}\left(\frac{dx}{dt}\right)\left(\frac{dy}{dt}\right) + \frac{\partial^2 z}{\partial y^2}\left(\frac{dy}{dt}\right)^2$$

under appropriate assumptions on F, g, and h.

12.2 Chain Rules for Many Variables

Economists often need even more general chain rules than the simple one for two variables presented in the previous section. Problem 7, for example, considers the example of a railway company whose fares for peak and off-peak fares are set by a regulatory authority. The costs it faces for running enough trains to carry all the passengers depend on demand for both kinds of journey. These demands are obviously affected by both peak and off-peak fares because some passengers will choose when to travel based on the fare difference. The general chain rule we are about to present allows us to work out how these costs change when either fare is increased.

Consider the general problem of this kind where

$$z = F(x, y), \qquad x = f(t, s), \qquad y = g(t, s)$$

In this case, z is a function of both t and s, with

$$z = F(f(t, s), g(t, s))$$

Here it makes sense to look for both partial derivatives $\partial z/\partial t$ and $\partial z/\partial s$. If we keep s fixed, then z is a function of t alone, and we can therefore use the chain rule (1) from the previous section. In the same way, by keeping t fixed, we can differentiate z w.r.t. s. The result is the following:

THE CHAIN RULE

If $z = F(x, y)$ with $x = f(t, s)$ and $y = g(t, s)$, then

(a) $\dfrac{\partial z}{\partial t} = F_1'(x, y)\dfrac{\partial x}{\partial t} + F_2'(x, y)\dfrac{\partial y}{\partial t}$

(b) $\dfrac{\partial z}{\partial s} = F_1'(x, y)\dfrac{\partial x}{\partial s} + F_2'(x, y)\dfrac{\partial y}{\partial s}$

(1)

EXAMPLE 1   Find $\partial z/\partial t$ and $\partial z/\partial s$ when $z = F(x, y) = x^2 + 2y^2$, with $x = t - s^2$ and $y = ts$.

Solution: We obtain

$$F_1'(x, y) = 2x, \quad F_2'(x, y) = 4y, \quad \frac{\partial x}{\partial t} = 1, \quad \frac{\partial x}{\partial s} = -2s, \quad \frac{\partial y}{\partial t} = s, \quad \frac{\partial y}{\partial s} = t$$

Formula (1) therefore gives:

$$\frac{\partial z}{\partial t} = 2x \cdot 1 + 4y \cdot s = 2(t - s^2) + 4tss = 2t - 2s^2 + 4ts^2$$

$$\frac{\partial z}{\partial s} = 2x \cdot (-2s) + 4y \cdot t = 2(t - s^2)(-2s) + 4tst = -4ts + 4s^3 + 4t^2s$$

Check these answers by first expressing z as a function of t and s, then differentiating.

EXAMPLE 2   Find $z_t'(1, 0)$ if $z = e^{x^2} + y^2 e^{xy}$, with $x = 2t + 3s$ and $y = t^2 s^3$.

Solution: We obtain

$$\frac{\partial z}{\partial x} = 2xe^{x^2} + y^3 e^{xy}, \quad \frac{\partial z}{\partial y} = 2ye^{xy} + xy^2 e^{xy}, \quad \frac{\partial x}{\partial t} = 2, \quad \frac{\partial y}{\partial t} = 2ts^3$$

Using somewhat more concise notation, formula (1) gives

$$z_t'(t, s) = \frac{\partial z}{\partial x}\frac{\partial x}{\partial t} + \frac{\partial z}{\partial y}\frac{\partial y}{\partial t} = (2xe^{x^2} + y^3 e^{xy}) \cdot 2 + (2ye^{xy} + xy^2 e^{xy}) \cdot 2ts^3$$

When $t = 1$ and $s = 0$, then $x = 2$ and $y = 0$, so $z_t'(1, 0) = 4e^4 \cdot 2 = 8e^4$.

The General Case

In consumer demand theory economists typically assume that a household's utility depends on the number of units of each good it is able to consume. The number of units consumed will depend in turn on the prices of these goods and on the household's income. Thus the household's utility is related, indirectly, to all the prices and to income. How does utility respond to an increase in one of the prices, or to an increase in income? The following general chain rule extends to this kind of problem.

Suppose that

$$z = F(x_1, \ldots, x_n) \quad \text{with} \quad x_1 = f_1(t_1, \ldots, t_m), \ldots, x_n = f_n(t_1, \ldots, t_m) \quad (2)$$

Substituting for all the variables x_i as functions of the variables t_j into the function F expresses z as a **composite function**

$$z = F(f_1(t_1, \ldots, t_m), \ldots, f_n(t_1, \ldots, t_m))$$

of $t_1, \ldots, t_m$. In vector notation, $z = F(\mathbf{x}(\mathbf{t}))$. An obvious generalization of (1) is as follows:

THE GENERAL CHAIN RULE

When (2) is true, then

$$\frac{\partial z}{\partial t_j} = \frac{\partial z}{\partial x_1}\frac{\partial x_1}{\partial t_j} + \frac{\partial z}{\partial x_2}\frac{\partial x_2}{\partial t_j} + \cdots + \frac{\partial z}{\partial x_n}\frac{\partial x_n}{\partial t_j}, \qquad j = 1, 2, \ldots, m \tag{3}$$

This is an important formula that every economist should understand. A small change in a basic variable t_j sets off a chain reaction. First, every x_i depends on t_j in general, so it changes when t_j is changed. This affects z in turn. The contribution to the total derivative of z w.r.t. t_j that results from the change in x_i is $(\partial z/\partial x_i)(\partial x_i/\partial t_j)$. Formula (3) shows that $\partial z/\partial t_j$ is the sum of all these contributions.

EXAMPLE 3   Example 11.7.1 considered an agricultural production function $Y = F(K, L, T)$, where Y is the size of the harvest, K is capital invested, L is labour, and T is the area of agricultural land used to grow the crop. Suppose that K, L, and T are all functions of time. Then, according to (3), one has

$$\frac{dY}{dt} = \frac{\partial F}{\partial K}\frac{dK}{dt} + \frac{\partial F}{\partial L}\frac{dL}{dt} + \frac{\partial F}{\partial T}\frac{dT}{dt}$$

In the special case when F is the Cobb–Douglas function $F(K, L, T) = AK^a L^b T^c$, then

$$\frac{dY}{dt} = aAK^{a-1}L^b T^c \frac{dK}{dt} + bAK^a L^{b-1} T^c \frac{dL}{dt} + cAK^a L^b T^{c-1}\frac{dT}{dt} \tag{$*$}$$

Denoting time derivatives by "dots", and dividing each term in ($*$) by $Y = AK^a L^b T^c$, we get

$$\frac{\dot{Y}}{Y} = a\frac{\dot{K}}{K} + b\frac{\dot{L}}{L} + c\frac{\dot{T}}{T}$$

The relative rate of change of output is, therefore, a weighted sum of the relative rates of change of capital, labour, and land. The weights are the respective powers a, b, and c.

PROBLEMS FOR SECTION 12.2

1. Use (1) to find $\partial z/\partial t$ and $\partial z/\partial s$ for the following cases:

(a) $z = F(x, y) = x + y^2$, $\quad x = t - s$, $\quad y = ts$

(b) $z = F(x, y) = 2x^2 + 3y^3$, $\quad x = t^2 - s$, $\quad y = t + 2s^3$

(SM) **2.** Using (1), find $\partial z/\partial t$ and $\partial z/\partial s$ for the following cases:

(a) $z = xy^2$, $\quad x = t + s^2$, $\quad y = t^2 s$ $\qquad$ (b) $z = \dfrac{x - y}{x + y}$, $\quad x = e^{t+s}$, $\quad y = e^{ts}$

3. (a) If $z = F(u, v, w)$ where $u = r^2$, $v = -2s^2$, and $w = \ln r + \ln s$, find $\partial z/\partial r$ and $\partial z/\partial s$.

(b) If $z = F(x)$ and $x = f(t_1, t_2)$, find $\partial z/\partial t_1$ and $\partial z/\partial t_2$.

(c) If $x = F(s, f(s), g(s, t))$, find $\partial x/\partial s$ and $\partial x/\partial t$.

(d) If $z = F(u, v, w)$ where $u = f(x, y)$, $v = x^2 h(y)$ and $w = 1/y$, find $\partial z/\partial x$ and $\partial z/\partial y$.

4. Use the general chain rule (3) to find $\partial w/\partial t$ for the following cases:

(a) $w = xy^2 z^3$, $\quad$ with $\quad x = t^2$, $\quad y = s$, $\quad z = t$

(b) $w = x^2 + y^2 + z^2$, $\quad$ with $\quad x = \sqrt{t + s}$, $\quad y = e^{ts}$, $\quad z = s^3$

5. Find expressions for dz/dt when

(a) $z = F(t, t^2, t^3)$ $\qquad\qquad\qquad\qquad$ (b) $z = F(t, f(t), g(t^2))$

6. (a) Suppose $Z = G + Y^2 + r^2$, where Y and r are both functions of G. Find $\partial Z/\partial G$.

(b) Suppose $Z = G + I(Y, r)$, where I is a differentiable function of two variables, and Y, r are both functions of G. Find $\partial Z/\partial G$.

7. Each week a suburban railway company has a long-run cost $C = aQ_1 + bQ_2 + cQ_1^2$ of providing Q_1 passenger kilometres of service during rush hours and Q_2 passenger kilometres during off-peak hours. As functions of the regulated fares p_1 and p_2 per kilometre for the rush hours and off-peak hours respectively, the demands for the two kinds of service are $Q_1 = Ap_1^{-\alpha_1} p_2^{\beta_1}$ and $Q_2 = Bp_1^{\alpha_2} p_2^{-\beta_2}$, where the constants $A, B, \alpha_1, \alpha_2, \beta_1, \beta_2$ are all positive. Assuming that the company runs enough trains to meet the demand, find expressions for the partial derivatives of C w.r.t. p_1 and p_2.

(SM) **8.** (a) If $u = \ln(x^3 + y^3 + z^3 - 3xyz)$, show that

$$(\text{i}) \ x\frac{\partial u}{\partial x} + y\frac{\partial u}{\partial y} + z\frac{\partial u}{\partial z} = 3 \qquad (\text{ii}) \ (x + y + z)\left(\frac{\partial u}{\partial x} + \frac{\partial u}{\partial y} + \frac{\partial u}{\partial z}\right) = 3$$

(b) If $z = f(x^2 y)$, show that $x\dfrac{\partial z}{\partial x} = 2y\dfrac{\partial z}{\partial y}$.

9. (a) Find a formula for $\partial u/\partial r$ when $u = f(x, y, z, w)$ and x, y, z, and w all are functions of two variables r and s.

(b) Suppose $u = xyzw$, where $x = r + s$, $y = r - s$, $z = rs$, $w = r/s$. Find $\partial u/\partial r$ when $(r, s) = (2, 1)$.

12.3   Implicit Differentiation along a Level Curve

Economists often need to differentiate functions that are defined implicitly by an equation. Section 7.2 considered some simple cases; it is a good idea to review those examples now. Here we study the problem from a more general point of view.

Let F be a function of two variables, and consider the equation

$$F(x, y) = c \qquad (c \text{ is a constant})$$

The equation represents a level curve for F. (See Section 11.3.) Suppose this equation defines y implicitly as a function $y = f(x)$ of x in some interval I, as illustrated in Fig. 1. This means that

$$F(x, f(x)) = c \qquad \text{for all } x \text{ in } I \tag{$*$}$$

If f is differentiable, what is the derivative of $y = f(x)$? If the graph of f looks like the one given in Fig. 1, the geometric problem is to find the slope of the graph at each point like P.

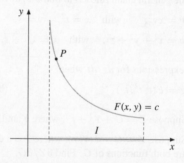

Figure 1 What is the slope at P?

To find an expression for the slope, introduce the auxiliary function u defined for all x in I by $u(x) = F(x, f(x))$. Then $u'(x) = F_1'(x, f(x)) \cdot 1 + F_2'(x, f(x)) \cdot f'(x)$ according to the chain rule. Now, $(*)$ states that $u(x) = c$ for all x in I. The derivative of a constant is 0, so we have $u'(x) = F_1'(x, f(x)) + F_2'(x, f(x)) \cdot f'(x) = 0$. If we replace $f(x)$ by y and solve for $f'(x) = y'$, we reach the conclusion:

SLOPE OF A LEVEL CURVE

$$F(x, y) = c \implies y' = -\frac{F_1'(x, y)}{F_2'(x, y)} \qquad (F_2'(x, y) \neq 0) \tag{1}$$

This is an important result. Before applying this formula for y', however, recall that the pair (x, y) must satisfy the equation $F(x, y) = c$. On the other hand, note that there is no need to solve the equation $F(x, y) = c$ explicitly for y before applying (1) in order to find y'. (See Example 3.)

The same argument with x and y interchanged gives an analogous result to (1). Thus, if x is a continuously differentiable function of y which satisfies $F(x, y) = c$, then

$$F(x, y) = c \implies \frac{dx}{dy} = -\frac{\partial F / \partial y}{\partial F / \partial x} \qquad \left(\frac{\partial F}{\partial x} \neq 0 \right) \tag{2}$$

EXAMPLE 1   Use (1) to find y' when $xy = 5$.

Solution: We put $F(x, y) = xy$. Then $F_1'(x, y) = y$ and $F_2'(x, y) = x$. Hence (1) gives

$$y' = -\frac{F_1'(x, y)}{F_2'(x, y)} = -\frac{y}{x}$$

This confirms the result in Example 7.1.1.

EXAMPLE 2   For the curve given by

$$x^3 + x^2 y - 2y^2 - 10y = 0$$

find the slope and the equation for the tangent at the point $(x, y) = (2, 1)$.

Solution: Let $F(x, y) = x^3 + x^2 y - 2y^2 - 10y$. Then the given equation is equivalent to $F(x, y) = 0$, which is a level curve for F. First, we check that $F(2, 1) = 0$, so $(x, y) = (2, 1)$ is a point on the curve. Also, $F_1'(x, y) = 3x^2 + 2xy$ and $F_2'(x, y) = x^2 - 4y - 10$. So (1) implies that

$$y' = -\frac{3x^2 + 2xy}{x^2 - 4y - 10}$$

For $x = 2$ and $y = 1$ in particular, one has $y' = 8/5$. Then the point–slope formula for a line implies that the tangent at $(2, 1)$ must have the equation $y - 1 = (8/5)(x - 2)$, or $5y = 8x - 11$. See Fig. 2, in which the curve has been drawn by a computer program. Note that, for many values of x, there is more than one corresponding value of y such that (x, y) lies on the curve. For instance, $(2, 1)$ and $(2, -4)$ both lie on the curve. Find y' at $(2, -4)$. (Answer: $y' = 0.4$.)

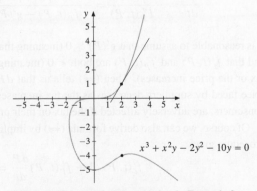

Figure 2 The graph of the equation in Example 2.

EXAMPLE 3   Assume that the equation

$$e^{xy^2} - 2x - 4y = c$$

implicitly defines y as a differentiable function $y = f(x)$ of x. Find a value of the constant c such that $f(0) = 1$, and find y' at $(x, y) = (0, 1)$.

Solution: When $x = 0$ and $y = 1$, the equation becomes $1 - 4 = c$, so $c = -3$. Let $F(x, y) = e^{xy^2} - 2x - 4y$. Then $F_1'(x, y) = y^2 e^{xy^2} - 2$, and $F_2'(x, y) = 2xy e^{xy^2} - 4$. Thus, from (1) we have

$$y' = -\frac{F_1'(x, y)}{F_2'(x, y)} = -\frac{y^2 e^{xy^2} - 2}{2xy e^{xy^2} - 4}$$

When $x = 0$ and $y = 1$, we find $y' = -1/4$. (Note that in this example it is impossible to solve $e^{xy^2} - 2x - 4y = -3$ explicitly for y. Even so, we have managed to find an explicit expression for the derivative of y w.r.t. x.)

Here is an important economic example using a function defined implicitly by an equation.

EXAMPLE 4   We generalize Example 7.2.2, and assume that $D = f(t, P)$ is the demand for a commodity that depends on the price P before tax, as well as on the sales tax per unit, denoted by t. Suppose that $S = g(P)$ is the supply function. At equilibrium, when supply is equal to demand, the equilibrium price $P = P(t)$ depends on t. Indeed, $P = P(t)$ must satisfy the equation

$$f(t, P) = g(P) \qquad (*)$$

for all t in some relevant interval. Suppose that $(*)$ defines P implicitly as a differentiable function of t. Find an expression for dP/dt, then discuss its sign.

Solution: Let $F(t, P) = f(t, P) - g(P)$. Then equation $(*)$ becomes $F(t, P) = 0$, so formula (1) yields

$$\frac{dP}{dt} = -\frac{F_t'(t, P)}{F_P'(t, P)} = -\frac{f_t'(t, P)}{f_P'(t, P) - g'(P)} = \frac{f_t'(t, P)}{g'(P) - f_P'(t, P)} \qquad (**)$$

It is reasonable to assume that $g'(P) > 0$ (meaning that supply increases if price increases) and that $f_t'(t, P)$ and $f_P'(t, P)$ are both < 0 (meaning that demand decreases if either the tax or the price increases). Then $(**)$ tells us that $dP/dt < 0$, implying that the pre-tax price faced by suppliers decreases as the tax increases. Thus the suppliers, as well as the consumers, are adversely affected if the tax on their product rises.

Of course, we can also derive formula $(**)$ by implicit differentiation of $(*)$ w.r.t. t. This procedure gives

$$f_t'(t, P) \cdot 1 + f_P'(t, P)\frac{dP}{dt} = g'(P)\frac{dP}{dt}$$

Solving this equation for dP/dt yields $(**)$ again.

A Formula for the Second Derivative

Sometimes we need to know whether a level curve $F(x, y) = c$ is the graph of a function $y = f(x)$ that is convex or concave. One way to find out is to calculate y'', which is the derivative of $y' = -F_1'(x, y)/F_2'(x, y)$. Write $G(x) = F_1'(x, y)$ and $H(x) = F_2'(x, y)$, where y is a function of x. Our aim now is to differentiate the quotient $y' = -G(x)/H(x)$ w.r.t. x. According to the rule for differentiating quotients,

$$y'' = -\frac{G'(x)H(x) - G(x)H'(x)}{[H(x)]^2} \tag{*}$$

Keeping in mind that y is a function of x, both $G(x)$ and $H(x)$ are composite functions. So we differentiate them both by using the chain rule, thereby obtaining

$$G'(x) = F_{11}''(x, y) \cdot 1 + F_{12}''(x, y) \cdot y'$$

$$H'(x) = F_{21}''(x, y) \cdot 1 + F_{22}''(x, y) \cdot y'$$

Assuming that F is a C^2 function, Young's Theorem (Theorem 11.6.1) implies that $F_{12}'' = F_{21}''$. Replace y' in both the preceding equations by the quotient $-F_1'/F_2'$, and then insert the results into (*). After some algebraic simplification, this yields the formula

$$F(x, y) = c \implies y'' = -\frac{1}{(F_2')^3}[F_{11}''(F_2')^2 - 2F_{12}''F_1'F_2' + F_{22}''(F_1')^2] \tag{3}$$

Occasionally (3) is used in theoretical arguments, but generally it is easier to find y'' by direct differentiation, as in the examples in Section 7.1.

EXAMPLE 5   Use (3) to find y'' when

$$xy = 5$$

Solution: With $F(x, y) = xy$ we have $F_1' = y$, $F_2' = x$, $F_{11}'' = 0$, $F_{12}'' = 1$, and $F_{22}'' = 0$. According to (3), we obtain

$$y'' = -\frac{1}{x^3}(-2 \cdot 1 \cdot y \cdot x) = \frac{2y}{x^2}$$

which is the same result we found in Example 7.1.4.

For those who are already familiar with 3×3 determinants, which this book discusses in Section 16.2, the result in (3) can be expressed in the following more memorable form:

$$F(x, y) = c \implies y'' = \frac{d^2y}{dx^2} = \frac{1}{(F_2')^3} \begin{vmatrix} 0 & F_1' & F_2' \\ F_1' & F_{11}'' & F_{12}'' \\ F_2' & F_{21}'' & F_{22}'' \end{vmatrix} \tag{4}$$

This is valid only if $F_2' \neq 0$, obviously.

1. Use formula (1) with $F(x, y) = 2x^2 + 6xy + y^2$ and $c = 18$ to find y' when y is defined implicitly by $2x^2 + 6xy + y^2 = 18$. Compare with the result in Problem 7.1.5.

(SM) 2. Use formula (1) to find y' for the following level curves. Also find y'' using (3).

 ( ) $x^2 y = 1$ (b) $x - y + 3xy = 2$ (c) $y^5 - x^6 = 0$

(SM) 3. A curve in the xy-plane is given by the equation $2x^2 + xy + y^2 - 8 = 0$.

 (a) Find y', y'', and the equation for the tangent at the point $(2, 0)$.

 (b) Which points on the curve have a horizontal tangent?

4. The equation $3x^2 - 3xy^2 + y^3 + 3y^2 = 4$ defines y implicitly as a function $h(x)$ of x in a neighbourhood of the point $(1, 1)$. Find $h'(1)$.

5. Suppose the demand $D(P, r)$ for a certain commodity (like a luxury car) depends on its price P and the interest rate r. What signs should one expect the partial derivatives of D w.r.t. P and r to have? Suppose the supply S is constant, so that in equilibrium, $D(P, r) = S$. Differentiate implicitly to find dP/dr, and comment on its sign. (Problem 7.2.3 considers a special case.)

6. Let $D = f(R, P)$ denote the demand for a commodity when the price is P and R is advertising expenditure. What signs should one expect the partial derivatives f_R' and f_P' to have? If the supply is $S = g(P)$, equilibrium in the market requires that $f(R, P) = g(P)$. What is dP/dR? Discuss its sign.

7. Let f be a differentiable function of one variable, and let a and b be two constants. Suppose that the equation $x - az = f(y - bz)$ defines z as a differentiable function of x and y. Prove that z satisfies $az_x' + bz_y' = 1$.

12.4 More General Cases

Consider the equation $F(x, y, z) = c$, where c is a constant. In general, this equation determines a surface in three-dimensional space consisting of all the triples (x, y, z) that satisfy the equation. This we called the graph of the equation. Suppose that $z = f(x, y)$ defines implicitly a function that, for all (x, y) in some domain A, satisfies the equation $F(x, y, z) = c$. Then

$$F(x, y, f(x, y)) = c \qquad \text{for all } (x, y) \text{ in } A$$

Suppose F and f are differentiable. Because the function $g(x, y) = F(x, y, f(x, y))$ is equal to the constant c for all $(x, y) \in A$, the partial derivatives g_x' and g_y' must both be 0. However, $g(x, y)$ is a composite function of x and y whose partial derivatives can be found by using the general chain rule (12.2.3.) Therefore,

$$g_x' = F_x' \cdot 1 + F_z' \cdot z_x' = 0, \qquad g_y' = F_y' \cdot 1 + F_z' \cdot z_y' = 0$$

This implies the following expressions for the partial derivatives of $z = f(x, y)$:

$$F(x, y, z) = c \implies z'_x = -\frac{F'_x}{F'_z}, \quad z'_y = -\frac{F'_y}{F'_z} \qquad (F'_z \neq 0) \qquad (1)$$

Using (1) allows formulas for z'_x and z'_y to be found even if it is impossible to solve the equation $F(x, y, z) = c$ explicitly for z as a function of x and y.

EXAMPLE 1   The equation $x - 2y - 3z + z^2 = -2$ defines z as a twice differentiable function of x and y about the point $(x, y, z) = (0, 0, 2)$. Find z'_x and z'_y, and then z''_{xx}, z''_{xy}, and z''_{yy}. Find also the numerical values of all these partial derivatives at $(0, 0)$.

Solution: Let $F(x, y, z) = x - 2y - 3z + z^2$ and $c = -2$. Then $F'_x = 1$, $F'_y = -2$, and $F'_z = 2z - 3$. Whenever $z \neq 3/2$, we have $F'_z \neq 0$, so formula (1) gives

$$z'_x = -\frac{1}{2z - 3}, \qquad z'_y = -\frac{-2}{2z - 3} = \frac{2}{2z - 3}$$

For $x = 0$, $y = 0$, and $z = 2$ in particular, we obtain $z'_x = -1$ and $z'_y = 2$.

We find z''_{xx} by differentiating the expression for z'_x partially w.r.t. x. Keeping in mind that z is a function of x and y, we get $z''_{xx} = (\partial/\partial x)(-(2z - 3)^{-1}) = (2z - 3)^{-2} 2z'_x$. Using the expression for z'_x found above, we have

$$z''_{xx} = \frac{-2}{(2z - 3)^3}$$

Correspondingly,

$$z''_{xy} = \frac{\partial}{\partial y} z'_x = \frac{\partial}{\partial y}[-(2z - 3)^{-1}] = (2z - 3)^{-2} 2z'_y = \frac{4}{(2z - 3)^3}$$

and

$$z''_{yy} = \frac{\partial}{\partial y} z'_y = \frac{\partial}{\partial y}[2(2z - 3)^{-1}] = -2(2z - 3)^{-2} 2z'_y = \frac{-8}{(2z - 3)^3}$$

For $x = y = 0$ and $z = 2$, we get $z''_{xx} = -2$, $z''_{xy} = 4$, and $z''_{yy} = -8$.

EXAMPLE 2   A firm produces $Q = f(L)$ units of a commodity using L units of labour. We assume that $f'(L) > 0$ and $f''(L) < 0$, so f is strictly increasing and strictly concave. (It might be a good idea to look at Problem 3(a) where a special case is considered.)

(a) If the firm gets P euros per unit produced and pays w euros for a unit of labour, write down the profit function, and find the first-order condition for profit maximization at $L^* > 0$.

(b) By implicit differentiation of the first-order condition, examine how changes in P and w influence the optimal choice of L^*.

Solution: (a) The profit function is $\pi(L) = Pf(L) - wL$, so $\pi'(L) = Pf'(L) - w$. Thus an optimal L^* must satisfy

$$Pf'(L^*) - w = 0 \qquad (*)$$

(b) If we define $F(P, w, L^*) = Pf'(L^*) - w$, then $(*)$ is equivalent to $F(P, w, L^*) = 0$. According to formula (1),

$$\frac{\partial L^*}{\partial P} = -\frac{F_P'}{F_{L^*}'} = -\frac{f'(L^*)}{Pf''(L^*)}, \quad \frac{\partial L^*}{\partial w} = -\frac{F_w'}{F_{L^*}'} = -\frac{-1}{Pf''(L^*)} = \frac{1}{Pf''(L^*)}$$

The sign assumptions on f' and f'' imply that $\partial L^*/\partial P > 0$ and $\partial L^*/\partial w < 0$. Thus, the optimal labour input goes up if the price P increases, while it goes down if labour costs increase. This makes economic sense. (Actually, economists would usually prefer to use implicit differentiation rather than relying on formula (1).)

EXAMPLE 3   (**Gains from Search**)   Suppose you intend to buy x^0 units of a particular commodity like flour. Right now, there is the opportunity to buy it at a price of p^0 per unit. But you expect that searching among other sellers will yield a lower price. Let $p(t)$ denote the lowest price per unit you expect to find after searching the market for t hours. It is reasonable to assume that $\dot{p}(t) < 0$. Moreover, since it is usually harder to find lower prices as the search progresses, we assume that $\ddot{p}(t) > 0$. Suppose your hourly wage is w. By searching for t hours, you save $p^0 - p(t)$ dollars for each unit you buy. Since you are buying x^0 units, total savings are $[p^0 - p(t)]x^0$. On the other hand, searching for t hours costs you wt in forgone wages. So the expected profit from searching for t hours is

$$\pi(t) = [p^0 - p(t)]x^0 - wt$$

A necessary first-order condition for $t = t^* > 0$ to maximize profit is that

$$\dot{\pi}(t^*) = -\dot{p}(t^*)x^0 - w = 0 \qquad (*)$$

This condition is also sufficient, because $\ddot{\pi}(t) = -\ddot{p}(t)x^0 < 0$ for all t.

Here is an economic interpretation of the condition $-\dot{p}(t^*)x_0 = w$: Suppose you search for an extra hour. The gain expected from finding a lower price is $[p(t^*) - p(t^* + 1)]x_0$, which is approximately $-\dot{p}(t^*)x_0$. On the other hand you lose an hour's wage. So the first-order condition says that you should search until the marginal gain from searching for an extra hour is just offset by the hourly wage.

The optimal search time t^* depends on x^0 and w. Economists typically want to know how t^* changes as x^0 or w changes. We see that equation $(*)$ is similar to equation $(*)$ in Example 2 (with $x^0 = -P$, $p = f$, and $t^* = L^*$). It follows immediately that

$$\frac{\partial t^*}{\partial x^0} = -\frac{\dot{p}(t^*)}{\ddot{p}(t^*)x^0} > 0, \quad \frac{\partial t^*}{\partial w} = -\frac{1}{\ddot{p}(t^*)x^0} < 0$$

where the signs are as indicated because $\dot{p}(t^*) < 0$, $\ddot{p}(t^*) > 0$, and $x^0 > 0$. Thus, the optimal search time rises as the quantity to be bought increases, and falls as the wage rate rises.

These qualitative results can easily be obtained by a geometric argument. Figure 1 illustrates the optimal search time t^*. It is the value of t at which the tangent to the curve $R = [p^0 - p(t)]x^0$ has slope w, and so is parallel to the line $C = wt$. If x^0 increases, the R curve is magnified vertically but not horizontally, so t^* moves to the right. On the other hand, if w increases, the straight line $C = wt$ will rotate anti-clockwise about the origin, so the optimal t^* will decrease.

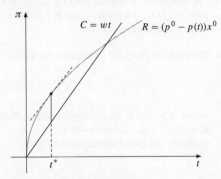

Figure 1 Optimal search

The General Case

The foregoing can be extended to any number of variables. The proof of the following result is a direct extension of the argument we gave for (1), so is left to the reader. Assuming that $\partial F / \partial z \neq 0$, we have

$$F(x_1, \ldots, x_n, z) = c \quad \Longrightarrow \quad \frac{\partial z}{\partial x_i} = -\frac{\partial F / \partial x_i}{\partial F / \partial z}, \qquad i = 1, 2, \ldots, n \qquad (2)$$

PROBLEMS FOR SECTION 12.4

1. Use formula (1) to find $\partial z / \partial x$ for the following:

   (a) $3x + y - z = 0$ (b) $xyz + xz^3 - xy^2z^5 = 1$ (c) $e^{xyz} = 3xyz$

2. Find z'_x, z'_y, and z''_{xy} when $x^3 + y^3 + z^3 - 3z = 0$.

SM 3. (a) Assume in Example 2 that $f(L) = \sqrt{L}$. Write down equation (∗) in this case and find an explicit expression for L^* as a function of P and w. Find the partial derivatives of L^* w.r.t. P and w. Then verify the signs obtained in Example 2.

   (b) Suppose the profit function is replaced by $\pi(L) = Pf(L) - C(L, w)$, where $C(L, w)$ is the cost function. What is the first-order condition for L^* to be optimal in this case? Find the partial derivatives of L^* w.r.t. P and w.

4. The equation $x^y + y^z + z^x = k$, where k is a positive constant, defines z as a positive-valued function of x and y, for $x > 0$ and $y > 0$. Find the partial derivatives of z w.r.t. x and y.

5. Replace $S = g(P)$ in the model of Problem 12.3.6 by $S = g(w, P)$, where w is an index for how favourable the weather has been. Assume $g'_w(w, P) > 0$. (We are studying the market for an agricultural crop.) Equilibrium now requires $f(R, P) = g(w, P)$. Assume that this equation defines P implicitly as a differentiable function of R and w. Find an expression for P'_w, and comment on its sign.

(SM) 6. (a) The function F is defined for all x and y by $F(x, y) = xe^{y-3} + xy^2 - 2y$. Show that the point $(1, 3)$ lies on the level curve $F(x, y) = 4$, and find the equation for the tangent line to the curve at the point $(1, 3)$.

(b) The Nerlove–Ringstad production function $y = y(K, L)$ is defined implicitly by

$$y^{1+c \ln y} = A K^{\alpha} L^{\beta}$$

where A, α, and β are positive constants. Find the marginal productivities of y w.r.t. both K (capital) and L (labour)—that is, find $\partial y/\partial K$ and $\partial y/\partial L$. (*Hint:* Take the logarithm of each side and then differentiate implicitly.)

12.5 Elasticity of Substitution

Economists are often interested in the slope of the tangent to a level curve at a particular point. Often, the level curve is downwards sloping, but economists prefer a positive answer. So we change the sign of the slope defined by (12.3.1), and use a special name:

$$R_{yx} = \frac{F'_1(x, y)}{F'_2(x, y)} \qquad \text{(the \textbf{marginal rate of substitution} of } y \text{ for } x) \tag{1}$$

The marginal rate of substitution has the standard abbreviation MRS. Note that $R_{yx} = -y' \approx -\Delta y/\Delta x$ when we move along the level curve $F(x, y) = c$. If $\Delta x = -1$ in particular, then $R_{yx} \approx \Delta y$. Thus, R_{yx} is approximately the quantity of y we must substitute (add) per unit of x removed, if we are to stay on the same level curve.

EXAMPLE 1   Let $F(K, L) = 100$ be an isoquant for a production function, where K is capital input, L is labour input, and 100 is the output. Look at Fig. 1. At all the points P, Q, and R, 100 units are used. At P a little capital input and a lot of labour input are used. The slope of the isoquant at P is approximately -4, so the MRS at P is approximately 4. This means that for each 4 units of labour that are taken away, adding only one unit of capital will ensure that output remains at (approximately) 100 units. Provided that units are chosen so that capital and labour have the same price, at P capital is more "valuable" than labour. At Q the MRS is approximately 1, so capital and labour are equally "valuable". Finally, at R, the MRS is approximately $1/5$, so at this point approximately 5 units of capital are required to compensate for the loss of one unit of labour.

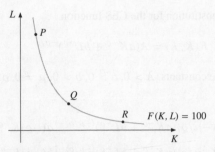

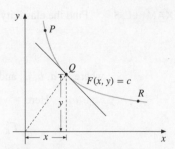

Figure 1 What is the MRS at P, Q, and R? (See Example 1.)

Figure 2 R_{yx} decreases as we move from P to R along the curve

Consider a level curve $F(x, y) = c$ for a function F of two variables, as shown in Fig. 2. The marginal rate of substitution R_{yx} varies along the curve. At point P, the MRS R_{yx} is a large positive number. At Q, the number R_{yx} is about 1, and at R it is about 0.2. As we move along the level curve from left to right, R_{yx} will be strictly decreasing with values in some positive interval I. For each value of R_{yx} in I, there is a corresponding point (x, y) on the level curve $F(x, y) = c$, and thus a corresponding value of y/x. The fraction y/x is therefore a function of R_{yx}, and we define the following:

ELASTICITY OF SUBSTITUTION

When $F(x, y) = c$, the elasticity of substitution between y and x is

$$\sigma_{yx} = \mathrm{El}_{R_{yx}}\left(\frac{y}{x}\right)$$

(2)

Thus, σ_{yx} is the elasticity of the fraction y/x w.r.t. the marginal rate of substitution. Roughly speaking, σ_{yx} is the percentage change in the fraction y/x when we move along the level curve $F(x, y) = c$ far enough so that R_{yx} increases by 1%. Note that σ_{yx} is symmetric in x and y. In fact, $R_{xy} = 1/R_{yx}$, and so the logarithmic formula for elasticities implies that $\sigma_{xy} = \sigma_{yx}$. Also, Problem 3 asks you to work with a (symmetric) expression for the elasticity of substitution in terms of the first- and second-order partial derivatives of F.

EXAMPLE 2   Calculate σ_{KL} for the Cobb–Douglas function $F(K, L) = AK^a L^b$.

Solution: The marginal rate of substitution of K for L is

$$R_{KL} = \frac{F'_L}{F'_K} = \frac{bAK^a L^{b-1}}{aAK^{a-1}L^b} = \frac{b}{a}\frac{K}{L}$$

Thus, $K/L = (a/b)R_{KL}$. The elasticity of the last expression w.r.t. R_{KL} is 1. Hence, $\sigma_{KL} = 1$ for the Cobb–Douglas function.

EXAMPLE 3   Find the elasticity of substitution for the CES function

$$F(K, L) = A(aK^{-\varrho} + bL^{-\varrho})^{-\mu/\varrho}$$

where A, a, b, μ, and ϱ are constants, $A > 0, a > 0, b > 0, \mu \neq 0, \varrho > -1$, and $\varrho \neq 0$.

Solution: Here

$$F_K' = A(-\mu/\varrho)(aK^{-\varrho} + bL^{-\varrho})^{(-\mu/\varrho)-1}a(-\varrho)K^{-\varrho-1}$$

$$F_L' = A(-\mu/\varrho)(aK^{-\varrho} + bL^{-\varrho})^{(-\mu/\varrho)-1}b(-\varrho)L^{-\varrho-1}$$

Hence,

$$R_{KL} = \frac{F_L'}{F_K'} = \frac{b}{a}\frac{L^{-\varrho-1}}{K^{-\varrho-1}} = \frac{b}{a}\left(\frac{K}{L}\right)^{\varrho+1}$$

and therefore

$$\frac{K}{L} = \left(\frac{a}{b}\right)^{1/(\varrho+1)} (R_{KL})^{1/(\varrho+1)}$$

Recalling that the elasticity of Ax^b w.r.t. x is b, definition (2) implies that

$$\sigma_{KL} = \text{El}_{R_{KL}}\left(\frac{K}{L}\right) = \frac{1}{\varrho+1}$$

We have thus shown that the function F has constant elasticity of substitution $1/(\varrho + 1)$. This, of course, is the reason why F is called the **CES function** (where CES stands for "constant elasticity of substitution").

Note that the elasticity of substitution for the CES function tends to 1 as $\varrho \to 0$, which is precisely the elasticity of substitution for the Cobb–Douglas function in the previous example. This accords with the result in Example 7.12.5.

PROBLEMS FOR SECTION 12.5

1. Calculate the elasticity of substitution between y and x for $F(x, y) = 10x^2 + 15y^2$.

2. (a) Find the marginal rate of substitution of y for x in

$$F(x, y) = x^a + y^a \qquad (a \text{ is a constant}, a \neq 0 \text{ and } a \neq 1)$$

   (b) Calculate the elasticity of substitution between y and x.

SM 3. The elasticity of substitution defined in (2) can be expressed in terms of the partial derivatives of the function F:

$$\sigma_{yx} = \frac{-F_1'F_2'(xF_1' + yF_2')}{xy[(F_2')^2F_{11}'' - 2F_1'F_2'F_{12}'' + (F_1')^2F_{22}'']}, \qquad F(x, y) = c$$

   Use this formula to derive the result in Example 2.

12.6 Homogeneous Functions of Two Variables

If $F(K, L)$ denotes the number of units produced when K units of capital and L units of labour are used as inputs, economists often ask: What happens to production if we double the inputs of both capital and labour? Will production rise by more or less than a factor of 2? To answer such and related questions, we introduce the following new concept of **homogeneity** for functions of two variables.

A function f of two variables x and y defined in a domain D is said to be **homogeneous of degree k** if, for all (x, y) in D,

$$f(tx, ty) = t^k f(x, y) \qquad \text{for all } t > 0 \tag{1}$$

Multiplying both variables by a positive factor t will thus multiply the value of the function by the factor t^k.

The degree of homogeneity of a function can be an arbitrary number—positive, zero, or negative. Earlier we determined the degree of homogeneity for several particular functions. For instance, we found in Example 11.1.4 that the Cobb–Douglas function F defined by $F(x, y) = Ax^a y^b$ is homogeneous of degree $a + b$. Here is an even simpler example:

EXAMPLE 1   Show that $f(x, y) = 3x^2 y - y^3$ is homogeneous of degree 3.

Solution: If we replace x by tx and y by ty in the formula for $f(x, y)$, we obtain

$$f(tx, ty) = 3(tx)^2(ty) - (ty)^3 = 3t^2 x^2 ty - t^3 y^3 = t^3(3x^2 y - y^3) = t^3 f(x, y)$$

Thus f is homogeneous of degree 3. If we let $t = 2$, then

$$f(2x, 2y) = 2^3 f(x, y) = 8f(x, y)$$

After doubling both x and y, the value of this function increases by a factor of 8.

Note that the sum of the exponents in each term of the polynomial in Example 1 is equal to 3. In general, a polynomial is homogeneous of degree k if and only if the sum of the exponents in each term is k. Other types of polynomial with different sums of exponents in different terms, such as $f(x, y) = 1 + xy$ or $g(x, y) = x^3 + xy$, are not homogeneous of any degree. (See Problem 6.)

Homogeneous functions of two variables have some important properties of interest to economists. The first is **Euler's theorem**, which says that

$$f(x, y) \text{ is homogeneous of degree } k \iff x f_1'(x, y) + y f_2'(x, y) = k f(x, y) \tag{2}$$

It is easy to demonstrate that when f is homogeneous of degree k, then the right-hand side of (2) is true. Indeed, differentiating each side of (1) w.r.t. t, using the chain rule to differentiate the left-hand side, gives

$$x f_1'(tx, ty) + y f_2'(tx, ty) = kt^{k-1} f(x, y)$$

Putting $t = 1$ gives $x f_1'(x, y) + y f_2'(x, y) = k f(x, y)$ immediately. Theorem 12.7.1 in the next section also proves the converse, and considers the case of n variables.

We note three other interesting general properties of functions $f(x, y)$ that are homogeneous of degree k:

$$f_1'(x, y) \text{ and } f_2'(x, y) \text{ are both homogeneous of degree } k - 1 \tag{3}$$

$$f(x, y) = x^k f(1, y/x) = y^k f(x/y, 1) \qquad \text{(for } x > 0, y > 0) \tag{4}$$

$$x^2 f_{11}''(x, y) + 2xy f_{12}''(x, y) + y^2 f_{22}''(x, y) = k(k - 1) f(x, y) \tag{5}$$

To prove (3), keep t and y constant and differentiate equation (1) partially w.r.t. x. Then $t f_1'(tx, ty) = t^k f_1'(x, y)$, so $f_1'(tx, ty) = t^{k-1} f_1'(x, y)$, thus showing that $f_1'(x, y)$ is homogeneous of degree $k - 1$. The same argument shows that $f_2'(x, y)$ is homogeneous of degree $k - 1$.

We can prove the two equalities in (4) by replacing t in (1) first by $1/x$ and then by $1/y$, respectively.

Finally, to show (5) (assuming that $f(x, y)$ is twice continuously differentiable), we note first that because $f_1'(x, y)$ and $f_2'(x, y)$ are both homogeneous of degree $k - 1$, Euler's theorem in (2) can be applied to f_1' and f_2'. It implies that

$$\begin{aligned} x f_{11}''(x, y) + y f_{12}''(x, y) &= (k - 1) f_1'(x, y) \\ x f_{21}''(x, y) + y f_{22}''(x, y) &= (k - 1) f_2'(x, y) \end{aligned} \tag{6}$$

Let us now multiply the first of these equations by x, the second by y, and then add. Because f is C^2, Young's theorem implies that $f_{12}'' = f_{21}''$, so the result is

$$x^2 f_{11}''(x, y) + 2xy f_{12}''(x, y) + y^2 f_{22}''(x, y) = (k - 1)[x f_1'(x, y) + y f_2'(x, y)]$$

By Euler's theorem, however, $x f_1'(x, y) + y f_2'(x, y) = k f(x, y)$. So (5) is verified.

EXAMPLE 2   Check properties (2) to (5) for the function $f(x, y) = 3x^2 y - y^3$.

Solution: We find that $f_1'(x, y) = 6xy$ and $f_2'(x, y) = 3x^2 - 3y^2$. Hence,

$$x f_1'(x, y) + y f_2'(x, y) = 6x^2 y + 3x^2 y - 3y^3 = 3(3x^2 y - y^3) = 3 f(x, y)$$

Example 1 showed that f is homogeneous of degree 3, so this confirms (2).

Obviously f_1' and f_2' are polynomials that are homogeneous of degree 2, which confirms (3). As for (4), in this case it takes the form

$$3x^2 y - y^3 = x^3[3(y/x) - (y/x)^3] = y^3[3(x/y)^2 - 1]$$

Finally, to show (5), first calculate the second-order partial derivatives, $f_{11}''(x, y) = 6y$, $f_{12}''(x, y) = 6x$, and $f_{22}''(x, y) = -6y$. Hence,

$$\begin{aligned} x^2 f_{11}''(x, y) + 2xy f_{12}''(x, y) + y^2 f_{22}''(x, y) &= 6x^2 y + 12x^2 y - 6y^3 = 6(3x^2 y - y^3) \\ &= 3 \cdot 2 f(x, y) \end{aligned}$$

which confirms (5) as well.

EXAMPLE 3   Suppose that the production function $Y = F(K, L)$ is homogeneous of degree 1. Show that

$$Y/L = f(K/L), \quad \text{where} \quad f(K/L) = F(K/L, 1)$$

(Thus, when a production function involving capital K and labour L is homogeneous of degree 1, one can express the output–labour ratio Y/L as a function of the capital–labour ratio K/L.) Find the form of f when F is the Cobb–Douglas function $AK^a L^b$ with $a + b = 1$.

Solution: Because F is homogeneous of degree 1,

$$Y = F(K, L) = F(L(K/L), L \cdot 1) = LF(K/L, 1) = Lf(K/L)$$

(Really, this is just a special case of (4).) When $F(K, L) = AK^a L^{1-a}$, then $f(K/L) = F(K/L, 1) = A(K/L)^a$. With $k = K/L$, we have $f(k) = Ak^a$.

Geometric Aspects of Homogeneous Functions

Homogeneous functions in two variables have some interesting geometric properties. Let $f(x, y)$ be homogeneous of degree k. Consider a ray in the xy-plane from the origin $(0, 0)$ through the point $(x_0, y_0) \neq (0, 0)$. An arbitrary point on this ray is of the form (tx_0, ty_0) for some positive number t. If we let $f(x_0, y_0) = c$, then $f(tx_0, ty_0) = t^k f(x_0, y_0) = t^k c$. Above any ray in the xy-plane through a point (x_0, y_0), the relevant portion of the graph of f therefore consists of the curve $z = t^k c$, where t measures the distance along the ray from the origin, and $c = f(x_0, y_0)$. A function that is homogeneous of degree k is therefore completely determined if its value is known at one point on each ray through the origin. (See Fig 1.)

In particular, let $k = 1$ so that $f(x, y)$ is homogeneous of degree 1. The curve $z = t^k c$ lying vertically above each relevant ray through the origin is then the straight line $z = tc$. Because of this, it is often said that *the graph of a homogeneous function of degree 1 is generated by straight lines through the origin.* Fig. 2 illustrates this.

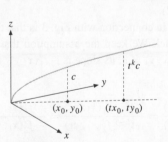

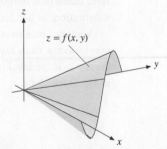

Figure 1   **Figure 2** f is homogeneous of degree 1

We have seen how, for a function $f(x, y)$ of two variables, it is often convenient to consider its level curves in the xy-plane instead of its 3-dimensional graph. What can we say about the level curves of a homogeneous function? It turns out that *for a homogeneous function, even if only one of its level curves is known, then so are all its other level curves.* To see this, consider a function $f(x, y)$ that is homogeneous of degree k, and let $f(x, y) = c$ be one of its level curves, as illustrated in Fig. 3. We now explain how to construct the level curve through an arbitrary point A not lying on $f(x, y) = c$: First, draw the ray through the origin and the point A. This ray intersects the level curve $f(x, y) = c$ at a point D with coordinates (x_1, y_1). The coordinates of A will then be of the form (tx_1, ty_1) for some value of t. (In the figure, $t \approx 1.7$.) In order to construct a new point on the same level curve as A, draw a new ray through the origin. This ray intersects the original level curve $f(x, y) = c$ at (x_2, y_2). Now use the value of t found earlier to determine the new point B with coordinates (tx_2, ty_2). This new point B is on the same level curve as A because $f(tx_2, ty_2) = t^k f(x_2, y_2) = t^k c = t^k f(x_1, y_1) = f(tx_1, ty_1)$. By repeating this construction for different rays through the origin that intersect the level curve $f(x, y) = c$, we can find as many points as we wish on the new level curve $f(x, y) = f(tx_1, ty_1)$.

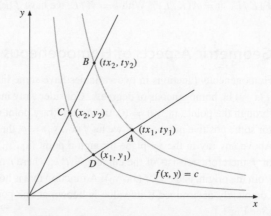

Figure 3   Level curves for a homogeneous function

The foregoing argument shows that a homogeneous function $f(x, y)$ is entirely determined by any one of its level curves and by its degree of homogeneity. The shape of each level curve of a homogeneous function is often determined by specifying its elasticity of substitution, as defined in (12.5.2).

Another point worth noticing in connection with Fig. 3 is that the tangents to the level curves along each ray are parallel. We keep the assumption that f is homogeneous of degree k. If the level curve is $f(x, y) = c$, its slope is $-f_1'(x, y)/f_2'(x, y)$. At the point A in Fig. 3 the slope is

$$-\frac{f_1'(tx_1, ty_1)}{f_2'(tx_1, ty_1)} = -\frac{t^{k-1} f_1'(x_1, y_1)}{t^{k-1} f_2'(x_1, y_1)} = -\frac{f_1'(x_1, y_1)}{f_2'(x_1, y_1)} \qquad (*)$$

where we have used equation (3), expressing the fact that the partial derivatives of f are homogeneous of degree $k - 1$. The equalities in $(*)$ state that the two level curves through A and D have the same slopes at those points. It follows that, at every point along a ray from the origin the slope of the corresponding level curve will be the same. Stated differently, after removing the minus signs, $(*)$ shows that the marginal rate of substitution of y for x is a homogeneous function of degree 0.

1. Show that $f(x, y) = x^4 + x^2 y^2$ is homogeneous of degree 4 by using (1).

2. Find the degree of homogeneity of $x(p, r) = Ap^{-1.5}r^{2.08}$.

(SM) 3. Show that $f(x, y) = xy^2 + x^3$ is homogeneous of degree 3. Verify that the four properties (2) to (5) all hold.

4. See whether the function $f(x, y) = xy/(x^2 + y^2)$ is homogeneous, and check Euler's theorem.

5. Prove the CES function $F(K, L) = A(aK^{-\varrho} + bL^{-\varrho})^{-1/\varrho}$ is homogeneous of degree one. Express $F(K, L)/L$ as a function of $k = K/L$. (See Example 3.)

6. Show that $f(x, y) = x^3 + xy$ is not homogeneous of any degree. (*Hint:* Let $x = y = 1$. Apply (1) with $t = 2$ and $t = 4$ to get a contradiction.)

7. Use the equations (6) with $k = 1$ to show that if $f(x, y)$ is homogeneous of degree 1 for $x > 0$ and $y > 0$, then $f''_{11}(x, y) f''_{22}(x, y) - [f''_{12}(x, y)]^2 \equiv 0$.

8. If $f(x, y)$ is homogeneous of degree 2 with $f'_1(2, 3) = 4$ and $f'_2(4, 6) = 12$, find $f(6, 9)$.

HARDER PROBLEM

(SM) 9. Prove that if $F(x, y)$ is homogeneous of degree 1, then the elasticity of substitution can be expressed as $\sigma_{yx} = F'_1 F'_2/FF''_{12}$. (*Hint:* Use Euler's theorem (2), together with (6) and the result in Problem 12.5.3.)

12.7 Homogeneous and Homothetic Functions

Suppose that f is a function of n variables defined in a domain D. Suppose also that whenever $(x_1, x_2, \ldots, x_n) \in D$ and $t > 0$, the point $(tx_1, tx_2, \ldots, tx_n)$ also lies in D. (A set D with this property is called a **cone**.) We say that f is **homogeneous of degree** k on D if

$$f(tx_1, tx_2, \ldots, tx_n) = t^k f(x_1, x_2, \ldots, x_n) \qquad \text{for all} \quad t > 0 \tag{1}$$

The constant k can be any number—positive, zero, or negative.

EXAMPLE 1   Test the homogeneity of $f(x_1, x_2, x_3) = \dfrac{x_1 + 2x_2 + 3x_3}{x_1^2 + x_2^2 + x_3^2}$.

Solution: Here f is defined on the set D of all points in three-dimensional space excluding the origin. This set is a cone. Also,

$$f(tx_1, tx_2, tx_3) = \frac{tx_1 + 2tx_2 + 3tx_3}{(tx_1)^2 + (tx_2)^2 + (tx_3)^2} = \frac{t(x_1 + 2x_2 + 3x_3)}{t^2(x_1^2 + x_2^2 + x_3^2)} = t^{-1} f(x_1, x_2, x_3)$$

Hence, f is homogeneous of degree -1.

Euler's theorem can be generalized to functions of n variables:

THEOREM 12.7.1   (EULER'S THEOREM)

Suppose f is a differentiable function of n variables in an open domain D, where $\mathbf{x} = (x_1, x_2, \ldots, x_n) \in D$ and $t > 0$ imply $t\mathbf{x} \in D$. Then f is homogeneous of degree k in D if and only if the following equation holds for all $\mathbf{x}$ in D:

$$\sum_{i=1}^{n} x_i f_i'(\mathbf{x}) = kf(\mathbf{x}) \tag{2}$$

Proof: Suppose f is homogeneous of degree k, so (1) holds. Differentiating this equation w.r.t. t (with $\mathbf{x}$ fixed) yields $\sum_{i=1}^{n} x_i f_i'(t\mathbf{x}) = kt^{k-1} f(\mathbf{x})$. Setting $t = 1$ gives (2) immediately.

To prove the converse, assume that (2) is valid for all $\mathbf{x}$ in D. Keep $\mathbf{x}$ fixed and define the function g for all $t > 0$ by $g(t) = t^{-k} f(t\mathbf{x}) - f(\mathbf{x})$. Then differentiating w.r.t. t gives

$$g'(t) = -kt^{-k-1} f(t\mathbf{x}) + t^{-k} \sum_{i=1}^{n} x_i f_i'(t\mathbf{x}) \tag{$*$}$$

Because $t\mathbf{x}$ lies in D, equation (2) must also be valid when each x_i is replaced by tx_i. Therefore, we get $\sum_{i=1}^{n}(tx_i) f_i'(t\mathbf{x}) = kf(t\mathbf{x})$. Applying this to the last term of $(*)$ implies that, for all $t > 0$, one has $g'(t) = -kt^{-k-1} f(t\mathbf{x}) + t^{-k-1} kf(t\mathbf{x}) = 0$. It follows that $g(t)$ must be a constant C. Obviously, $g(1) = 0$, so $C = 0$, implying that $g(t) \equiv 0$. According to the definition of g, this proves that $f(t\mathbf{x}) = t^k f(\mathbf{x})$. Thus, f is indeed homogeneous of degree k. ∎

An interesting version of the Euler equation (2) is obtained by dividing each term of the equation by $f(\mathbf{x})$, provided this number is not 0. Recalling the definition of the partial elasticity ($\mathrm{El}_i \, f(\mathbf{x}) = (x_i/f(\mathbf{x})) f_i'(\mathbf{x})$), we have

$$\mathrm{El}_1 \, f(\mathbf{x}) + \mathrm{El}_2 \, f(\mathbf{x}) + \cdots + \mathrm{El}_n \, f(\mathbf{x}) = k \tag{3}$$

Thus, the sum of the partial elasticities of a function of n variables that is homogeneous of degree k must be equal to k.

The results in (3) to (5) in the previous section can also be generalized to functions of n variables. The proofs are similar, so they can be left to the interested reader. We simply state the general versions of (3) and (5):

If $f(\mathbf{x})$ is homogeneous of degree k, then:

$$f_i'(\mathbf{x}) \text{ is homogeneous of degree } k - 1, \qquad i = 1, 2, \ldots, n \tag{4}$$

$$\sum_{i=1}^{n} \sum_{j=1}^{n} x_i x_j f_{ij}''(\mathbf{x}) = k(k-1) f(\mathbf{x}) \tag{5}$$

Economic Applications

Let us consider some typical examples of homogeneous functions in economics.

EXAMPLE 2   Let $f(\mathbf{v}) = f(v_1, \ldots, v_n)$ denote the output of a production process when the input quantities are $v_1, \ldots, v_n$. It is often assumed that if all the input quantities are scaled by a factor t, then t times as much output as before is produced, so that

$$f(t\mathbf{v}) = tf(\mathbf{v}) \qquad \text{for all} \quad t > 0 \tag{$*$}$$

This implies that f is homogeneous of degree 1. Production functions with this property are said to exhibit *constant returns to scale*.

For any fixed input vector $\mathbf{v}$, consider the function $\varphi(t) = f(t\mathbf{v})/t$. This indicates the average returns to scale—i.e. the average output per unit input when all inputs are rescaled together. For example when $t = 2$, all inputs are doubled. When $t = \frac{3}{4}$, all inputs are reduced proportionally by $\frac{1}{4}$.

Now, when ($*$) holds, then $\varphi(t) = f(\mathbf{v})$, independent of t. Also, a production function that is homogeneous of degree $k < 1$ has *decreasing returns to scale* because $\varphi(t) = t^{k-1} f(\mathbf{v})$ and so $\varphi'(t) < 0$. On the other hand, a production function has *increasing returns to scale* if $k > 1$ because then $\varphi'(t) > 0$.

EXAMPLE 3   The general Cobb–Douglas function $F(v_1, \ldots, v_n) = Av_1^{a_1} \cdots v_n^{a_n}$ is often used as an example of a production function. Prove that it is homogeneous, and examine when it has constant/decreasing/increasing returns to scale. Also show that formula (3) is confirmed.

Solution: Here

$$F(t\mathbf{v}) = A(tv_1)^{a_1} \ldots (tv_n)^{a_n} = At^{a_1}v_1^{a_1} \ldots t^{a_n}v_n^{a_n} = t^{a_1+\cdots+a_n} F(\mathbf{v})$$

So F is homogeneous of degree $a_1 + \cdots + a_n$. Thus it has constant, decreasing, or increasing returns to scale according as $a_1 + \cdots + a_n$ is $= 1$, < 1, or > 1. Because $\mathrm{El}_i F = a_i$, $i = 1, \ldots, n$, we get $\sum_{i=1}^{n} \mathrm{El}_i F = \sum_{i=1}^{n} a_i$, which confirms (3) in this case.

EXAMPLE 4   Consider a market with three commodities with quantities denoted by x, y, and z, whose prices per unit are respectively p, q, and r. Suppose that the demand for one of the commodities by a consumer with income m is given by $D(p, q, r, m)$. Suppose that the three prices and income m are all multiplied by some $t > 0$. (Imagine, for example, that the prices of all commodities rise by 10%. Or that all prices and incomes have been converted into euros from, say, German marks.) Then the consumer's budget constraint $px + qy + rz \leq m$ becomes $tpx + tqy + trz \leq tm$, which is exactly the same constraint. The multiplicative constant t is irrelevant to the consumer. It is therefore natural to assume that the consumer's demand remains unchanged, with

$$D(tp, tq, tr, tm) = D(p, q, r, m)$$

Requiring this equation to be valid for all $t > 0$ means that the demand function D is homogeneous of degree 0. In this case, it is often said that demand is not influenced by "money illusion"; a consumer with 10% more money to spend should realize that nothing has really changed if all prices have also risen by 10%.

As a specific example of a function that is common in demand analysis, consider

$$D(p, q, r, m) = \frac{mp^b}{p^{b+1} + q^{b+1} + r^{b+1}} \qquad (b \text{ is a constant})$$

Here

$$D(tp, tq, tr, tm) = \frac{(tm)(tp)^b}{(tp)^{b+1} + (tq)^{b+1} + (tr)^{b+1}} = D(p, q, r, m)$$

since t cancels out. So the function *is* homogeneous of degree 0.

Sometimes we encounter nonhomogeneous functions of several variables that are, however, homogeneous when regarded as functions of some of the variables only, with the other variables fixed. For instance, the (minimum) cost of producing y units of a single output is often expressed as a function $C(\mathbf{w}, y)$ of y and the vector $\mathbf{w} = (w_1, \ldots, w_n)$ of prices of n different input factors. Then, if all input prices double, one expects cost to double. So economists usually assume that $C(t\mathbf{w}, y) = tC(\mathbf{w}, y)$ for all $t > 0$—i.e. that the cost function is homogeneous of degree 1 in $\mathbf{w}$ (for each fixed y). See Problem 6 for a prominent example.

Homothetic Functions

Let f be a function of n variables $\mathbf{x} = (x_1, \ldots, x_n)$ defined in a cone K. Then f is called **homothetic** provided that

$$\mathbf{x}, \mathbf{y} \in K, \ f(\mathbf{x}) = f(\mathbf{y}), \ t > 0 \ \implies \ f(t\mathbf{x}) = f(t\mathbf{y}) \tag{6}$$

For instance, if f is some consumer's utility function, (6) requires that whenever there is indifference between the two commodity bundles $\mathbf{x}$ and $\mathbf{y}$, then there is also indifference after they have both been magnified or shrunk by the same proportion. (If this consumer is indifferent between 2 litres of soda and 3 litres of juice, she is also indifferent between 4 litres of soda and 6 litres of juice.)

A homogeneous function f of any degree k is homothetic. In fact, it is easy to prove a more general result.

$$\left. \begin{array}{l} H \text{ strictly increasing and} \\ f \text{ is homogeneous of degree } k \end{array} \right\} \implies F(\mathbf{x}) = H(f(\mathbf{x})) \text{ is homothetic} \tag{7}$$

Indeed, suppose that $F(\mathbf{x}) = F(\mathbf{y})$, or equivalently, that $H(f(\mathbf{x})) = H(f(\mathbf{y}))$. Because H is strictly increasing, this implies that $f(\mathbf{x}) = f(\mathbf{y})$. Because f is homogeneous of degree k, it follows that if $t > 0$, then

$$F(t\mathbf{x}) = H(f(t\mathbf{x})) = H(t^k f(\mathbf{x})) = H(t^k f(\mathbf{y})) = H(f(t\mathbf{y})) = F(t\mathbf{y})$$

This proves that $F(\mathbf{x})$ is homothetic. Hence, any strictly increasing function of a homogeneous function is homothetic. It is actually quite common to take this property as the definition of a homothetic function, usually with $k = 1$.[2]

---

[2] Suppose that $F(\mathbf{x})$ is any continuous homothetic function defined on the cone K of vectors $\mathbf{x}$ satisfying $x_i \geq 0, i = 1, \ldots, n$. Suppose too that $F(t\mathbf{x}_0)$ is a strictly increasing function of t for each fixed $\mathbf{x}_0 \neq \mathbf{0}$ in K. Then one can prove that there exists a strictly increasing function H such that $F(\mathbf{x}) = H(f(\mathbf{x}))$, where the function $f(\mathbf{x})$ is homogeneous of degree 1.

The next example shows that not all homothetic functions are homogeneous.

EXAMPLE 5   Show that the function $F(x, y) = xy + 1$, which is obviously not homogeneous, is nevertheless homothetic.

Solution: Define $H(u) = u + 1$. Then H is strictly increasing. The function $f(x, y) = xy$ is homogeneous of degree 2, and $F(x, y) = xy + 1 = H(f(x, y))$. According to (7), F is homothetic. (You can also use definition (6) to show directly that F is homothetic.)

Suppose that $F(\mathbf{x}) = F(x_1, x_2, \ldots, x_n)$ is a differentiable production function, defined for all $(x_1, \ldots, x_n)$ satisfying $x_i \geq 0, i = 1, \ldots, n$. The **marginal rate of substitution** of factor j for factor i is defined by

$$h_{ji}(\mathbf{x}) = \frac{\partial F(\mathbf{x})}{\partial x_i} \bigg/ \frac{\partial F(\mathbf{x})}{\partial x_j}, \qquad i, j = 1, 2, \ldots, n \qquad (8)$$

We claim that if F is a strictly increasing transformation of a homogeneous function (as in (7)), these marginal rates of substitution are homogeneous of degree 0.[3] To prove this, suppose that $F(\mathbf{x}) = H(f(\mathbf{x}))$, where H is strictly increasing and $f(\mathbf{x})$ is homogeneous of degree k. Then $\partial F(\mathbf{x})/\partial x_i = H'(f(\mathbf{x}))(\partial f(\mathbf{x})/\partial x_i)$, implying that

$$\frac{\partial F(\mathbf{x})}{\partial x_i} \bigg/ \frac{\partial F(\mathbf{x})}{\partial x_j} = \frac{\partial f(\mathbf{x})}{\partial x_i} \bigg/ \frac{\partial f(\mathbf{x})}{\partial x_j}, \qquad i, j = 1, 2, \ldots, n$$

because the factor H' can be cancelled. But f is homogeneous of degree k, so we can use (4) to show that, for all $t > 0$,

$$h_{ji}(t\mathbf{x}) = \frac{\partial f(t\mathbf{x})}{\partial x_i} \bigg/ \frac{\partial f(t\mathbf{x})}{\partial x_j} = t^{k-1}\frac{\partial f(\mathbf{x})}{\partial x_i} \bigg/ t^{k-1}\frac{\partial f(\mathbf{x})}{\partial x_j} = h_{ji}(\mathbf{x}), \ i, j = 1, 2, \ldots, n \quad (9)$$

Formula (9) shows precisely that the marginal rates of substitution are homogeneous of degree 0. This generalizes the result for two variables mentioned at the end of Section 12.6.

PROBLEMS FOR SECTION 12.7

(SM) 1. Examine which of the following functions are homogeneous, and find the degree of homogeneity for those that are:

(a) $f(x, y, z) = 3x + 4y - 3z$

(b) $g(x, y, z) = 3x + 4y - 2z - 2$

(c) $h(x, y, z) = \dfrac{\sqrt{x} + \sqrt{y} + \sqrt{z}}{x + y + z}$

(d) $G(x, y) = \sqrt{xy} \ln \dfrac{x^2 + y^2}{xy}$

(e) $H(x, y) = \ln x + \ln y$

(f) $p(x_1, \ldots, x_n) = \sum_{i=1}^{n} x_i^n$

(SM) 2. Examine the homogeneity of the following functions:

(a) $f(x_1, x_2, x_3) = \dfrac{(x_1 x_2 x_3)^2}{x_1^4 + x_2^4 + x_3^4}\left(\dfrac{1}{x_1} + \dfrac{1}{x_2} + \dfrac{1}{x_3}\right)$

(b) $x(v_1, v_2, \ldots, v_n) = A\big(\delta_1 v_1^{-\varrho} + \delta_2 v_2^{-\varrho} + \cdots + \delta_n v_n^{-\varrho}\big)^{-\mu/\varrho}$ (The CES function.)

---

[3] Because of footnote 2, the same must be true if F is any homothetic function with the property that $F(t\mathbf{x})$ is an increasing function of the scalar t for each fixed vector $\mathbf{x}$.

3. Examine the homogeneity of the three means $\bar{x}_A$, $\bar{x}_G$, and $\bar{x}_H$, as defined in Example 11.5.2.

4. D. W. Katzner has considered a utility function $u(\mathbf{x}) = u(x_1, \ldots, x_n)$ with continuous partial derivatives that for some constant a satisfy

$$\sum_{i=1}^{n} x_i \frac{\partial u}{\partial x_i} = a \qquad \text{(for all } x_1 > 0, \ldots, x_n > 0)$$

Show that the function $v(\mathbf{x}) = u(\mathbf{x}) - a \ln(x_1 + \cdots + x_n)$ is homogeneous of degree 0. (*Hint*: Use Euler's theorem.)

(SM) **5.** Which of the following functions $f(x, y)$ are homothetic?

(a) $(xy)^2 + 1$
(b) $\dfrac{2(xy)^2}{(xy)^2 + 1}$
(c) $x^2 + y^3$
(d) $e^{x^2 y}$

HARDER PROBLEMS

6. Suppose that $f(\mathbf{x})$ and $g(\mathbf{x})$ are homogeneous of degree r and s, respectively. Examine whether the following functions h are homogeneous. Determine the degree of homogeneity in each case.

(a) $h(\mathbf{x}) = f(x_1^m, x_2^m, \ldots, x_n^m)$
(b) $h(\mathbf{x}) = (g(\mathbf{x}))^p$
(c) $h = f + g$

(d) $h = fg$
(e) $h = f/g$

(SM) **7.** The **translog cost function** $C(\mathbf{w}, y)$, where $\mathbf{w}$ is the vector of factor prices and y is the level of output, is defined implicitly by

$$\ln C(\mathbf{w}, y) = a_0 + c_1 \ln y + \sum_{i=1}^{n} a_i \ln w_i + \frac{1}{2} \sum_{i,j=1}^{n} a_{ij} \ln w_i \ln w_j + \ln y \sum_{i=1}^{n} b_i \ln w_i$$

Prove that this translog (short for "transcendental logarithmic") function is homogeneous of degree 1 in $\mathbf{w}$, for each fixed y, provided that all the following conditions are met: $\sum_{i=1}^{n} a_i = 1$; $\sum_{i=1}^{n} b_i = 0$; $\sum_{j=1}^{n} a_{ij} = 0$ for all i; and $\sum_{i=1}^{n} a_{ij} = 0$ for all j.

12.8 Linear Approximations

Section 7.4 discussed the linear approximation $f(x) \approx f(a) + f'(a)(x - a)$ for a function of one variable. We will find a similar approximation for functions f of two variables.

For fixed values of x_0, y_0, x, and y, define the function $g(t)$ by

$$g(t) = f(x_0 + t(x - x_0), y_0 + t(y - y_0))$$

We see that $g(0) = f(x_0, y_0)$ and $g(1) = f(x, y)$. Generally, $g(t)$ is the value of f at the point $(x_0 + t(x - x_0), y_0 + t(y - y_0)) = ((1 - t)x_0 + tx, (1 - t)y_0 + ty)$, which lies on the line joining (x_0, y_0) to (x, y). According to the chain rule,

$$g'(t) = f_1'(x_0 + t(x - x_0), y_0 + t(y - y_0))(x - x_0) + f_2'(x_0 + t(x - x_0), y_0 + t(y - y_0))(y - y_0)$$

Putting $t = 0$ and using the approximation $g(1) \approx g(0) + g'(0)$, we obtain the result:

LINEAR APPROXIMATION

The linear approximation to $f(x, y)$ about (x_0, y_0) is

$$f(x, y) \approx f(x_0, y_0) + f'_1(x_0, y_0)(x - x_0) + f'_2(x_0, y_0)(y - y_0)$$

(1)

NOTE 1 The usefulness of approximation (1) depends on the size of the error. Taylor's formula with remainder, presented for the case of one variable in Section 7.6, is extended to n variables in FMEA. One implication of the extended formula is that, as $x \to x_0$ and $y \to y_0$, so approximation (1) will get better, in the sense that the error will tend to 0.

EXAMPLE 1   Find the linear approximation to $f(x, y) = e^{x+y}(xy - 1)$ about $(0, 0)$.

Solution: Here $f(0, 0) = -1$, $f'_1(x, y) = e^{x+y}(xy-1) + e^{x+y}y$ and $f'_2(x, y) = e^{x+y}(xy - 1) + e^{x+y}x$. So $f'_1(0, 0) = -1$ and $f'_2(0, 0) = -1$. Hence, (1) gives

$$e^{x+y}(xy - 1) \approx -1 - x - y$$

For x and y close to 0, the complicated function $z = e^{x+y}(xy - 1)$ is approximated by the simple linear function $z = -1 - x - y$.

Formula (1) can be used to find approximate numerical values of a function near any point where the function and its derivatives are easily evaluated. Consider the following example.

EXAMPLE 2   Let $f(x, y) = xy^3 - 2x^3$. Then $f(2, 3) = 38$. Using (1), find an approximate numerical value for $f(2.01, 2.98)$.

Solution: Here $f'_1(x, y) = y^3 - 6x^2$ and $f'_2(x, y) = 3xy^2$, so $f'_1(2, 3) = 3$ and $f'_2(2, 3) = 54$. Putting $x_0 = 2$, $y_0 = 3$, $x = 2 + 0.01$, and $y = 3 - 0.02$, we obtain

$$f(2.01, 2.98) \approx f(2, 3) + f'_1(2, 3) \cdot 0.01 + f'_2(2, 3) \cdot (-0.02) = 38 + 3(0.01) + 54(-0.02)$$

which equals 36.95. The exact value is $f(2.01, 2.98) = 36.95061792$. The error in the approximation is therefore a bit greater than -0.0006.

The linear approximation in (1) can be generalized to functions of several variables. (See Problem 8.)

LINEAR APPROXIMATION

The linear approximation to $z = f(\mathbf{x}) = f(x_1, \ldots, x_n)$ about $\mathbf{x}^0 = (x_1^0, \ldots, x_n^0)$ is given by

$$f(\mathbf{x}) \approx f(\mathbf{x}^0) + f'_1(\mathbf{x}^0)(x_1 - x_1^0) + \cdots + f'_n(\mathbf{x}^0)(x_n - x_n^0)$$

(2)

Tangent Planes

In (1) the function $f(x, y)$ is approximated by the *linear function*

$$z = f(x_0, y_0) + f_1'(x_0, y_0)(x - x_0) + f_2'(x_0, y_0)(y - y_0)$$

The graph of this linear function is a plane which passes through the point $P = (x_0, y_0, z_0)$, with $z_0 = f(x_0, y_0)$, on the graph of $z = f(x, y)$. This plane is called the **tangent plane** to $z = f(x, y)$ at P:

TANGENT PLANE

At the point (x_0, y_0, z_0) with $z_0 = f(x_0, y_0)$, the tangent plane to the graph of $z = f(x, y)$ has the equation

$$z - z_0 = f_1'(x_0, y_0)(x - x_0) + f_2'(x_0, y_0)(y - y_0)$$

(3)

The tangent plane is illustrated in Fig. 1.

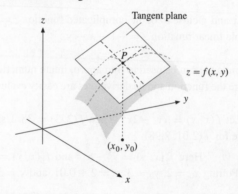

Figure 1 The graph of $z = f(x, y)$ and the tangent plane at P

Does it deserve its name? Look back at Fig. 11.3.9, where l_x and l_y are the tangents at P to the two curves K_x and K_y that lie on the surface. Since the slope of the line l_x is $f_2'(x_0, y_0)$, the points (x, y, z) which lie on l_x are characterized by $x = x_0$ and $z - z_0 = f_2'(x_0, y_0)(y - y_0)$. But we see from (3) that these points also lie in the tangent plane. In the same way we see that the line l_y also lies in the tangent plane. Because the plane which is the graph of (3) is the only one that contains both tangent lines l_x and l_y, it makes good sense to use the term "tangent plane".

EXAMPLE 3   Find the tangent plane at $P = (x_0, y_0, z_0) = (1, 1, 5)$ to the graph of

$$f(x, y) = x^2 + 2xy + 2y^2$$

Solution: Because $f(1, 1) = 5$, P lies on the graph of f. We find that $f_1'(x, y) = 2x + 2y$ and $f_2'(x, y) = 2x + 4y$. Hence, $f_1'(1, 1) = 4$ and $f_2'(1, 1) = 6$. Thus, (3) yields

$$z - 5 = 4(x - 1) + 6(y - 1) \quad \text{or} \quad z = 4x + 6y - 5$$

PROBLEMS FOR SECTION 12.8

1. Find the linear approximation about $(0, 0)$ for the following:

   (a) $f(x, y) = (x + 1)^5(y + 1)^6$ (b) $f(x, y) = \sqrt{1 + x + y}$ (c) $f(x, y) = e^x \ln(1 + y)$

2. Find the linear approximation about (x_0, y_0) for $f(x, y) = Ax^a y^b$.

3. Suppose that $g^*(\mu, \varepsilon) = [(1 + \mu)(1 + \varepsilon)^\alpha]^{1/(1-\beta)} - 1$, with α and β as constants. Show that if μ and ε are close to 0, then

$$g^*(\mu, \varepsilon) \approx \frac{1}{1 - \beta}\mu + \frac{\alpha}{1 - \beta}\varepsilon$$

4. Let $f(x, y) = 3x^2 y + 2y^3$. Then $f(1, -1) = -5$. Use the approximation (1) to estimate the value of $f(0.98, -1.01)$. How large is the error caused by this approximation?

5. (a) With $f(x, y) = 3x^2 + xy - y^2$, compute $f(1.02, 1.99)$ exactly.

   (b) Let $f(1.02, 1.99) = f(1 + 0.02, 2 - 0.01)$ and use (1) to find an approximate numerical value for $f(1.02, 1.99)$. How large is the error?

6. Suppose you have been told that a differentiable function v of two variables satisfies $v(1, 0) = -1$, $v_1'(1, 0) = -4/3$, and $v_2'(1, 0) = 1/3$. Find an approximate value for $v(1.01, 0.02)$.

(SM) 7. Find the tangent planes to the following surfaces at the indicated points:

   (a) $z = x^2 + y^2$ at $(1, 2, 5)$ (b) $z = (y - x^2)(y - 2x^2)$ at $(1, 3, 2)$

HARDER PROBLEMS

(SM) 8. Define

$$g(t) = f(x_1^0 + t(x_1 - x_1^0), \ldots, x_n^0 + t(x_n - x_n^0))$$

Use the approximation $g(1) \approx g(0) + g'(0)$ to derive (2).

9. Let $f(x, y)$ be any differentiable function. Prove that f is homogeneous of degree 1 if and only if the tangent plane at any point on its graph passes through the origin.

12.9 Differentials

Suppose that $z = f(x, y)$ is a differentiable function of two variables. Let dx and dy denote arbitrary real numbers (not necessarily small). Then we define the **differential** of $z = f(x, y)$ at (x, y), denoted by dz or df, so that

$$z = f(x, y) \implies dz = f_1'(x, y)\, dx + f_2'(x, y)\, dy \tag{1}$$

When x is changed to $x + dx$ and y is changed to $y + dy$, then the actual change in the value of the function is the **increment**

$$\Delta z = f(x + dx, y + dy) - f(x, y)$$

If dx and dy are small in absolute value, then Δz can be approximated by dz:

$$\Delta z \approx dz = f_1'(x, y)\, dx + f_2'(x, y)\, dy \qquad \text{(when } |dx| \text{ and } |dy| \text{ are small)} \tag{2}$$

The approximation in (2) follows from (1) in the previous section. We first replace $x - x_0$ by dx and $y - y_0$ by dy, and thus x by $x_0 + dx$ and y by $y_0 + dy$. Finally, in the formula which emerges, replace x_0 by x and y_0 by y. The approximation (2) can be given a geometric interpretation, as illustrated in Fig. 1. The error that arises from replacing Δz by dz results from "following the tangent plane" from P to the point S, rather than "following the graph" to the point R.

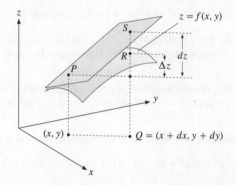

Figure 1   The geometric interpretation of Δz and the differential dz.

Here is an analytical argument. By definition, the tangent plane at $P = (x, y, f(x, y))$ is the set of points (X, Y, Z) satisfying the linear equation

$$Z - f(x, y) = f_1'(x, y)(X - x) + f_2'(x, y)(Y - y)$$

Letting $X = x + dx$ and $Y = y + dy$, we obtain

$$Z = f(x, y) + f_1'(x, y)\, dx + f_2'(x, y)\, dy = f(x, y) + dz$$

The length of the line segment QS in the figure is therefore $f(x, y) + dz$.

NOTE 1 In the literature on mathematics for economists, a common definition of the differential $dz = f_1'(x, y) \, dx + f_2'(x, y) \, dy$ requires that dx and dy be "infinitesimals", or "infinitely small". In this case, it is often claimed, Δz becomes equal to dz. Imprecise ideas of this sort have caused confusion over the centuries since Leibniz first introduced them, and they have largely been abandoned in mathematics. However, in nonstandard analysis, a respectable branch of modern mathematics, a modified version of Leibniz's ideas about infinitesimals can be made precise. There have even been some interesting applications of nonstandard analysis to theoretical economics.

EXAMPLE 1   Let $z = f(x, y) = xy$. Then

$$\Delta z = f(x + dx, y + dy) - f(x, y) = (x + dx)(y + dy) - xy = y \, dx + x \, dy + dx \, dy$$

In this case $dz = f_1'(x, y) \, dx + f_2'(x, y) \, dy = y \, dx + x \, dy$, so $\Delta z - dz = dx \, dy$. The error term is $dx \, dy$, and the approximation is illustrated in Fig. 2. If dx and dy are very small—for example, about 10^{-3}—then the error term $dx \, dy$ is "very, very small"—about 10^{-6} in this example.

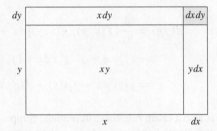

Figure 2   The difference $\Delta z - dz = dx \, dy$

EXAMPLE 2   Let $Y = F(K, L)$ be a production function with K and L as capital and labour inputs, respectively. Then F_K' and F_L' are the marginal products of capital and labour. If dK and dL are arbitrary increments in K and L, respectively, the *differential* of $Y = F(K, L)$ is

$$dY = F_K' \, dK + F_L' \, dL$$

The increment $\Delta Y = F(K + dK, L + dL) - F(K, L)$ in Y can be approximated by dY provided dK and dL are small in absolute value, and so

$$\Delta Y = F(K + dK, L + dL) - F(K, L) \approx F_K' \, dK + F_L' \, dL$$

NOTE 2 If $z = f(x, y)$, we can always find the differential $dz = df$ by first finding the partial derivatives $f_1'(x, y)$ and $f_2'(x, y)$, and then using the definition of dz. Conversely, once we know the differential of a function f of two variables, then we have the partial derivatives: Suppose that $dz = A \, dx + B \, dy$ for all dx and dy. By definition, $dz = f_1'(x, y) \, dx + f_2'(x, y) \, dy$ for all dx and dy. Putting $dx = 1$ and $dy = 0$ yields $A = f_1'(x, y)$. In the same way, putting $dx = 0$ and $dy = 1$ yields $B = f_2'(x, y)$. So

$$dz = A \, dx + B \, dy \quad \Longrightarrow \quad \frac{\partial z}{\partial x} = A \quad \text{and} \quad \frac{\partial z}{\partial y} = B \tag{3}$$

Rules for Differentials

Section 7.4 developed several rules for working with differentials of functions of one variable. The same rules apply to functions of several variables. Indeed, suppose that $f(x, y)$ and $g(x, y)$ are differentiable, with differentials $df = f_1' \, dx + f_2' \, dy$ and $dg = g_1' \, dx + g_2' \, dy$, respectively. If $d(\ \ )$ denotes the differential of whatever is inside the parentheses, then the following rules are exactly the same as (7.4.4):

$$d(af + bg) = a \, df + b \, dg$$

$$d(fg) = g \, df + f \, dg \tag{4}$$

$$d\left(\frac{f}{g}\right) = \frac{g \, df - f \, dg}{g^2}, \quad g \neq 0$$

These rules are also quite easy to prove. For example, the formula for $d(fg)$ is proved as follows (keeping in mind that $(fg)(x, y) = f(x, y) \cdot g(x, y)$):

$$d(fg) = \frac{\partial}{\partial x}[f(x, y) \cdot g(x, y)] \, dx + \frac{\partial}{\partial y}[f(x, y) \cdot g(x, y)] \, dy$$

$$= (f_x' \cdot g + f \cdot g_x') \, dx + (f_y' \cdot g + f \cdot g_y') \, dy$$

$$= g(f_x' \, dx + f_y' \, dy) + f(g_x' \, dx + g_y' \, dy) = g \, df + f \, dg$$

There is also a chain rule for differentials. Suppose that $z = F(x, y) = g(f(x, y))$, where g is a differentiable function of one variable. Then

$$dz = F_x' \, dx + F_y' \, dy = g'(f(x, y)) f_x' \, dx + g'(f(x, y)) f_y' \, dy$$

$$= g'(f(x, y))(f_x' \, dx + f_y' \, dy) = g'(f(x, y)) \, df$$

because $F_x' = g' f_x'$, $F_y' = g' f_y'$, and $df = f_x' \, dx + f_y' \, dy$. Briefly formulated:

$$z = g(f(x, y)) \implies dz = g'(f(x, y)) \, df \tag{5}$$

EXAMPLE 3   Find an expression for dz in terms of dx and dy for the following:

(a) $z = Ax^a + By^b$ (b) $z = e^{xu}$ with $u = u(x, y)$ (c) $z = \ln(x^2 + y)$

Solution:

(a) $dz = A \, d(x^a) + B \, d(y^b) = Aax^{a-1} \, dx + Bby^{b-1} \, dy$

(b) $dz = e^{xu} \, d(xu) = e^{xu}(x \, du + u \, dx) = e^{xu}\{x[u_1'(x, y) \, dx + u_2'(x, y) \, dy] + u \, dx\}$

$$= e^{xu}\{[xu_1'(x, y) + u] \, dx + xu_2'(x, y) \, dy\}$$

(c) $dz = d \ln(x^2 + y) = \dfrac{d(x^2 + y)}{x^2 + y} = \dfrac{2x \, dx + dy}{x^2 + y}$

Invariance of the Differential

Suppose that

$$z = F(x, y), \qquad x = f(t, s), \qquad y = g(t, s)$$

where F, f, and g are all differentiable functions. Thus, z is a composite function of t and s together. Suppose that t and s are changed by dt and ds, respectively. The differential of z is then

$$dz = z'_t \, dt + z'_s \, ds$$

Using the expressions for z'_t and z'_s obtained from the chain rule (12.2.1), we find that

$$\begin{aligned} dz &= [F'_1(x, y)x'_t + F'_2(x, y)y'_t] \, dt + [F'_1(x, y)x'_s + F'_2(x, y)y'_s] \, ds \\ &= F'_1(x, y)(x'_t \, dt + x'_s \, ds) + F'_2(x, y)(y'_t \, dt + y'_s \, ds) \\ &= F'_1(x, y) \, dx + F'_2(x, y) \, dy \end{aligned}$$

where dx and dy denote the differentials of $x = f(t, s)$ and $y = g(t, s)$, respectively, as functions of t and s.

Note especially that the final expression for dz is precisely the definition of the differential of $z = F(x, y)$ when x and y are changed by dx and dy, respectively. *Thus, the differential of z has the same form whether x and y are free variables, or depend on other variables t and s.* This property is referred to as the **invariance** of the differential.

The Differential of a Function of n Variables

The differential of a function $z = f(x_1, x_2, \dots, x_n)$ of n variables is defined in the obvious way as

$$dz = df = f'_1 \, dx_1 + f'_2 \, dx_2 + \cdots + f'_n \, dx_n \tag{6}$$

If the absolute values of $dx_1, \dots, dx_n$ are all small, then again $\Delta z \approx dz$, where Δz is the actual increment of z when $(x_1, \dots, x_n)$ is changed to $(x_1 + dx_1, \dots, x_n + dx_n)$.

The rules for differentials in (4) are valid for functions of n variables, and there is also a general rule for invariance of the differential: *The differential of $z = F(x_1, \dots, x_n)$ has the same form whether $x_1, \dots, x_n$ are free variables, or depend on other basic variables.* The proofs are easy extensions of those for two variables.

PROBLEMS FOR SECTION 12.9

1. Determine the differential of $z = xy^2 + x^3$ by:

(a) computing $\partial z/\partial x$ and $\partial z/\partial y$ and then using the definition of dz.

(b) using the rules in (4).

2. Calculate the differentials of the following:

(a) $z = x^3 + y^3$ (b) $z = xe^{y^2}$ (c) $z = \ln(x^2 - y^2)$

3. Find dz expressed in terms of dx and dy when $u = u(x, y)$ and

(a) $z = x^2 u$ (b) $z = u^2$ (c) $z = \ln(xy + yu)$

SM 4. Find an approximate value for $T = [(2.01)^2 + (2.99)^2 + (6.02)^2]^{1/2}$ by using the approximation $\Delta T \approx dT$.

5. Find dU expressed in terms of dx and dy when $U = U(x, y)$ satisfies the equation

$$Ue^U = x\sqrt{y}$$

6. (a) Differentiate the equation $X = AN^\beta e^{\varrho t}$, where A, β, and ϱ are constants.

(b) Differentiate the equation $X_1 = BX^E N^{1-E}$, where B and E are constants.

7. Calculate the differentials of the following:

(a) $U = a_1 u_1^2 + \cdots + a_n u_n^2$ (b) $U = A(\delta_1 u_1^{-\varrho} + \cdots + \delta_n u_n^{-\varrho})^{-1/\varrho}$

where $a_1, \ldots, a_n$, A, $\delta_1, \ldots, \delta_n$, and ϱ are positive constants.

8. Find dz when

$$z = Ax_1^{a_1} x_2^{a_2} \ldots x_n^{a_n}$$

where $x_1 > 0, x_2 > 0, \ldots, x_n > 0$, and $A, a_1, a_2, \ldots, a_n$ are all constants with A positive. (*Hint:* First, take the natural logarithm of each side.)

HARDER PROBLEM

9. The differential dz defined in (1) is called the *differential of first order*. If f has continuous partial derivatives of second order, we define the *differential of second order* d^2z as the differential $d(dz)$ of $dz = f_1'(x, y) dx + f_2'(x, y) dy$. This implies that

$$d^2z = d(dz) = f_{11}''(x, y)(dx)^2 + 2f_{12}''(x, y) dx\, dy + f_{22}''(x, y)(dy)^2$$

(a) Calculate d^2z for $z = xy + y^2$.

(b) Suppose that $x = t$ and $y = t^2$. Express dz and d^2z in terms of dt, for the function in part (a). Also find d^2z/dt^2, then show that $d^2z \neq (d^2z/dt^2)(dt)^2$. (This example shows that there is no invariance property for the second-order differential.)

12.10 Systems of Equations

Many economic models relate a large number of variables to each other through a system of simultaneous equations. To keep track of the structure of the model, the concept of *degrees of freedom* is very useful.

Let $x_1, x_2, \ldots, x_n$ be n variables. If no restrictions are placed on them then, by definition, there are n *degrees of freedom*, because all n variables can be freely chosen. If the variables are required to satisfy *one* equation of the form $f_1(x_1, x_2, \ldots, x_n) = 0$, then the number of degrees of freedom is usually reduced by 1. Whenever one further "independent" restriction is introduced, the number of degrees of freedom is again reduced by 1. In general, introducing $m < n$ independent restrictions on the variables $x_1, x_2, \ldots, x_n$ means that they satisfy a system of m independent equations having the form

$$
\begin{aligned}
f_1(x_1, x_2, \ldots, x_n) &= 0 \\
f_2(x_1, x_2, \ldots, x_n) &= 0 \\
&\cdots\cdots\cdots\cdots\cdots \\
f_m(x_1, x_2, \ldots, x_n) &= 0
\end{aligned}
\tag{1}
$$

Then, provided that $m < n$, the remaining number of degrees of freedom is $n - m$. The rule that emerges from these considerations is rather vague, especially as it is hard to explain precisely what it means for equations to be "independent". Nevertheless, the following rule is much used in economics and statistics:

THE COUNTING RULE

To find the number of degrees of freedom for a system of equations, count the number of variables, n, and the number of "independent" equations, m. In general, if $n > m$, there are $n - m$ degrees of freedom in the system. If $n < m$, there is no solution to the system.

(2)

This rule of counting variables and equations is used to justify the following economic proposition: "The number of independent targets the government can pursue cannot possibly exceed the number of available policy instruments". For example, if a national government seeks simultaneous low inflation, low unemployment, and stability of its currency's exchange rate against, say, the US dollar, then it needs at least three independent policy instruments.

It should be noted that the counting rule is not generally valid. For example, if 100 variables $x_1, \ldots, x_{100}$ are restricted to satisfy one equation, the rule says that the number of degrees of freedom should be 99. However, if the equation happens to be

$$
x_1^2 + x_2^2 + \cdots + x_{100}^2 = 0
$$

then there is only one solution, $x_1 = x_2 = \ldots = x_{100} = 0$, so there are no degrees of freedom. For the equation $x_1^2 + x_2^2 + \cdots + x_{100}^2 = -1$, even this one solution is lost.

It is obvious that the word "independent" cannot be dropped from the statement of the counting rule. For instance, if we just repeat an equation that has appeared before, the number of degrees of freedom will certainly not be reduced.

The concept of degrees of freedom introduced earlier needs to be generalized.

DEGREES OF FREEDOM FOR A SYSTEM OF EQUATIONS

A system of equations in n variables is said to have k **degrees of freedom** if there is a set of k variables that can be freely chosen, while the remaining $n - k$ variables are uniquely determined once the k free variables have been assigned specific values.

(3)

In order for a system to have k degrees of freedom, it suffices that *there exist k* of the variables that can be freely chosen. We do not require that *any* set of k variables can be chosen freely. If the n variables are restricted to vary within a subset A of $\mathbb{R}^n$, we say that the system has k *degrees of freedom in A.*

The counting rule claims that if the number of equations is larger than the number of variables, then the system is, in general, **inconsistent**—that is, it has no solutions. For example, the system

$$f(x, y) = 0, \qquad g(x, y) = 0, \qquad h(x, y) = 0$$

with two variables and three equations, is usually inconsistent. Each of the equations represents a curve in the plane, and any pair of curves will usually have at least one point in common. But if we add a third equation, the corresponding curve will seldom pass through any points where the first two curves intersect, so the system is usually inconsistent.

So far, we have discussed the two cases $m < n$ and $m > n$. What about the case $m = n$, in which the number of equations is equal to the number of unknowns? Even in the simplest case of one equation in one variable, $f(x) = 0$, such an equation might have any number of solutions. Consider, for instance, the following three different single equations in one variable:

$$x^2 + 1 = 0, \qquad x - 1 = 0, \qquad (x - 1)(x - 2)(x - 3)(x - 4)(x - 5) = 0$$

These have 0, 1, and 5 solutions, respectively. Those of you who know something about trigonometric functions will realize that the simple equation $\sin x = 0$ has infinitely many solutions, namely $x = n\pi$ for any integer n.

In general, a system with as many equations as unknowns is usually **consistent** (that is, has solutions), but it may have several solutions. Economists, however, ideally like their models to have a system of equations that produces a unique, economically meaningful solution, because then the model purports to predict the values of particular economic variables. Based on the earlier discussion, we can at least formulate the following rough rule: *A system of equations does not, in general, have a unique solution unless there are exactly as many equations as unknowns.*

EXAMPLE 1   Consider the macroeconomic model described by the system of equations

(i) $Y = C + I + G$ (ii) $C = f(Y - T)$ (iii) $I = h(r)$ (iv) $r = m(M)$

where f, h, and m are given functions, Y is national income, C is consumption, I is investment, G is public expenditure, T is tax revenue, r is the interest rate, and M is the money supply (or more exactly, the quantity of money in circulation). How many degrees of freedom are there?

Solution: The number of variables is 7 and the number of equations is 4, so according to the counting rule there should be $7 - 4 = 3$ degrees of freedom. Usually macroeconomists regard M, T, and G as the exogenous (free) variables. Then the system will in general determine the endogenous variables Y, C, I, and r as functions of M, T, and G. (For a further analysis of this model, see Example 12.11.3. For a discussion of exogenous and endogenous variables, see Section 12.11.)

EXAMPLE 2   Consider the alternative macroeconomic model

(i) $Y = C + I + G$ (ii) $C = f(Y - T)$ (iii) $G = \overline{G}$

whose variables have the same interpretations as in the previous example. Here the level of public expenditure is a constant, $\overline{G}$. Determine the number of degrees of freedom in the model.

Solution: There are now 5 variables (Y, C, I, G, and T) and 3 equations. Hence, there are 2 degrees of freedom. For suitable functions f, two of the variables can be freely chosen, while allowing the remaining variables to be determined once the values of these 2 are fixed. It is natural to consider I and T as the two free variables. Note that G cannot be chosen as a free variable in this case because G is completely fixed by equation (iii).

PROBLEMS FOR SECTION 12.10

1. Use the counting rule to find the number of degrees of freedom for the following systems of equations:

(a)
$$xu^3 + v = y^2$$
$$3uv - x = 4$$

(b)
$$x_2^2 - x_3^3 + 2y_1 - y_2^3 = 1$$
$$x_1^3 - x_2 + y_1^5 - y_2 = 0$$

(c)
$$f(y + z + w) = x^3$$
$$x^2 + y^2 + z^2 = w^2$$
$$g(x, y) - z^3 = w^3$$

(In (c) assume that f and g are specified functions.)

2. Use the counting rule to find the number of degrees of freedom in the following macroeconomic model (which is studied further in Problem 12.11.6):

(i) $Y = C + I + G$ (ii) $C = F(Y, T, r)$ (iii) $I = f(Y, r)$

(The symbols have the same interpretation as in Example 1. We assume that F and f are specified functions of their respective arguments.)

3. For each of the following equation systems, determine the number of degrees of freedom (if any), and discuss whether the counting rule applies:

(a) $\begin{aligned} 3x - y &= 2 \\ 6x - 2y &= 4 \\ 9x - 3y &= 6 \end{aligned}$
    (b) $\begin{aligned} x - 2y &= 3 \\ x - 2y &= 4 \end{aligned}$
    (c) $\begin{aligned} x - 2y &= 3 \\ 2x - 4y &= 6 \end{aligned}$

(d) $x_1^2 + x_2^2 + \cdots + x_{100}^2 = 1$
    (e) $x_1^2 + x_2^2 + \cdots + x_{100}^2 = -1$

12.11 Differentiating Systems of Equations

This section shows how using differentials can be an efficient way to find the partial derivatives of functions defined implicitly by a system of equations. We begin with three examples.

EXAMPLE 1   Consider the following system of two linear equations in four variables

$$5u + 5v = 2x - 3y$$

$$2u + 4v = 3x - 2y$$

It has 2 degrees of freedom. In fact, it defines u and v as functions of x and y. Differentiate the system and then find the differentials du and dv expressed in terms of dx and dy. Derive the partial derivatives of u and v w.r.t. x and y. Check the results by solving the system explicitly for u and v.

Solution: For both equations, take the differential of each side and use the rules in Section 12.9. The result is

$$5\,du + 5\,dv = 2\,dx - 3\,dy$$

$$2\,du + 4\,dv = 3\,dx - 2\,dy$$

(Note that in a linear system like this, the differentials satisfy the same equations as the variables.) Solving simultaneously for du and dv in terms of dx and dy yields

$$du = -\frac{7}{10}\,dx - \frac{1}{5}\,dy, \qquad dv = \frac{11}{10}\,dx - \frac{2}{5}\,dy$$

We read off the following partial derivatives: $u'_x = -\frac{7}{10}$, $u'_y = -\frac{1}{5}$, $v'_x = \frac{11}{10}$, and $v'_y = -\frac{2}{5}$.

Suppose that instead of finding the differential, we solve the given equation system directly for u and v as functions of x and y. The result is $u = -\frac{7}{10}x - \frac{1}{5}y$ and $v = \frac{11}{10}x - \frac{2}{5}y$. From these expressions we easily confirm the values found for the partial derivatives.

EXAMPLE 2   Consider the system of nonlinear equations

$$u^2 + v = xy$$
$$uv = -x^2 + y^2 \qquad (*)$$

(a) What has the counting rule to say about this system?

(b) Find the differentials of u and v expressed in terms of dx and dy. What are the partial derivatives of u and v w.r.t. x and y?

(c) The point $P = (x, y, u, v) = (1, 0, 1, -1)$ satisfies system $(*)$. If $x = 1$ is increased by 0.01 and $y = 0$ is increased by 0.02, what is the new value of u, approximately?

(d) Calculate u''_{12} at the point P.

Solution: (a) There are 4 variables and 2 equations, so there should be 2 degrees of freedom. Suppose we choose fixed values for x and y. Then there are two equations for determining the two remaining variables, u and v. For example, if $x = 1$ and $y = 0$, then $(*)$ reduces to $u^2 = -v$ and $uv = -1$, from which we find that $u^3 = 1$, so $u = 1$ and $v = -1$. For other values of x and y, it is more difficult to find solutions for u and v. However, it seems reasonable to assume that system $(*)$ defines $u = u(x, y)$ and $v = v(x, y)$ as differentiable functions of x and y, at least if the domain of the pair (x, y) is suitably restricted.

(b) The left- and right-hand sides of each equation in $(*)$ must be equal functions of x and y. So we can equate the differentials of each side to obtain $d(u^2 + v) = d(xy)$ and $d(uv) = d(-x^2 + y^2)$. Using the rules for differentials, we obtain

$$2u\,du + \quad dv = \quad y\,dx + \ x\,dy$$
$$v\,du + u\,dv = -2x\,dx + 2y\,dy$$

Note that by the invariance property of the differential in Section 12.9, this system is valid no matter which pair of variables are independent.

We want to solve the system for du and dv. There are two equations in the two unknowns du and dv of the form

$$A\,du + B\,dv = C$$
$$D\,du + E\,dv = F$$

where, for instance, $A = 2u$, $C = y\,dx + x\,dy$, and so on. Using (2) in Section 2.4, or standard elimination, provided that $v \neq 2u^2$, we find that

$$du = \frac{2x + yu}{2u^2 - v}\,dx + \frac{xu - 2y}{2u^2 - v}\,dy, \qquad dv = \frac{-4xu - yv}{2u^2 - v}\,dx + \frac{4uy - xv}{2u^2 - v}\,dy$$

From the first of these two equations, we obtain immediately that

$$u'_1 = \frac{2x + yu}{2u^2 - v}, \qquad u'_2 = \frac{xu - 2y}{2u^2 - v}$$

Similarly, the partial derivatives of v w.r.t. x and y are the coefficients of dx and dy in the expression for dv. So we have found all the first-order partial derivatives.

(c) We use the approximation $u(x + dx, y + dy) \approx u(x, y) + du$. Letting $x = 1$, $y = 0$, $dx = 0.01$, and $dy = 0.02$, we obtain

$$u(1 + 0.01, 0 + 0.02) \approx u(1, 0) + u'_1(1, 0) \cdot 0.01 + u'_2(1, 0) \cdot 0.02$$
$$= 1 + \tfrac{2}{3} \cdot 0.01 + \tfrac{1}{3} \cdot 0.02 \approx 1 + 0.0133 = 1.0133$$

Note that in this case, it is not easy to find the exact value of $u(1.01, 0.02)$.

(d) We find u''_{12} by using the chain rule as follows:

$$u''_{12} = \frac{\partial}{\partial y}(u'_1) = \frac{\partial}{\partial y}\left(\frac{2x + yu}{2u^2 - v}\right) = \frac{(yu'_2 + u)(2u^2 - v) - (2x + yu)(4uu'_2 - v'_2)}{(2u^2 - v)^2}$$

At the point P where $(x, y, u, v) = (1, 0, 1, -1)$, we obtain $u''_{12} = 1/9$.

EXAMPLE 3 Consider the following macroeconomic model:

(i) $Y = C + I + G$ (ii) $C = f(Y - T)$ (iii) $I = h(r)$ (iv) $r = m(M)$

Here Y is national income, C consumption, I investment, G public expenditure, T tax revenue, r interest rate, and M money supply. (See Example 12.10.1.) If we assume that f, h, and m are differentiable functions with $0 < f' < 1$, $h' < 0$, and $m' < 0$, then these equations will determine Y, C, I, and r as differentiable functions of M, T, and G. Differentiate the system and express the differentials of Y, C, I, and r in terms of the differentials of M, T, and G. Find $\partial Y / \partial T$ and $\partial C / \partial T$, and comment on their signs.

Suppose $P_0 = (M_0, T_0, G_0, Y_0, C_0, I_0, r_0)$ is an initial equilibrium point for the system. If the money supply M, tax revenue T, and public expenditure G are all slightly changed as a result of government policy or central bank intervention, find the approximate changes in national income Y and in consumption C.

Solution: Taking differentials of the system of four equations yields

$$\begin{aligned} dY &= dC + dI + dG \\ dC &= f'(Y - T)(dY - dT) \\ dI &= h'(r) \, dr \\ dr &= m'(M) \, dM \end{aligned} \tag{v}$$

We wish to solve this linear system for the differential changes dY, dC, dI, and dr in the (endogenous) variables Y, C, I, and r, expressing these differentials in terms of the differentials of the (exogenous) policy variables dM, dT, and dG.

From the last two equations in (v), we can find dI and dr immediately. In fact

$$dr = m'(M) \, dM, \qquad dI = h'(r)m'(M) \, dM \tag{vi}$$

Inserting the expression for dI from (vi) into the first equation in (v), while also rearranging the second equation in (v), we obtain the system

$$\begin{aligned} dY - dC &= h'(r)m'(M) \, dM + dG \\ f'(Y - T) \, dY - dC &= f'(Y - T) \, dT \end{aligned}$$

These are two equations to determine the two unknowns dY and dC. Solving for dY and dC, using a simplified notation, we get

$$dY = \frac{h'm'}{1 - f'}\, dM - \frac{f'}{1 - f'}\, dT + \frac{1}{1 - f'}\, dG$$

$$dC = \frac{f'h'm'}{1 - f'}\, dM - \frac{f'}{1 - f'}\, dT + \frac{f'}{1 - f'}\, dG$$

(vii)

which expresses the differentials dY, dC, dI, and dr as linear functions of the differentials dM, dT, and dG. Moreover, the solution is valid because $f' < 1$ by assumption.

From (vii) and (vi), we can at once find the partial derivatives of Y, C, I, and r w.r.t. M, T, and G. For example, $\partial Y/\partial T = \partial C/\partial T = -f'/(1 - f')$ and $\partial r/\partial T = 0$. Note that because $0 < f' < 1$, we have $\partial Y/\partial T = \partial C/\partial T < 0$. Thus, a small increase in the tax level (keeping M and G constant) decreases national income in this model, but not if the extra tax revenue is all spent by the government. For if $dT = dG = dx$ (and $dM = 0$), then $dY = dx$ and $dC = dI = dr = 0$.

If dM, dT, and dG are small in absolute value, then

$$\Delta Y = Y(M_0 + dM, T_0 + dT, G_0 + dG) - Y(M_0, T_0, G_0) \approx dY$$

When computing dY, the partial derivatives are evaluated at the equilibrium point P_0.

WARNING: Some textbooks recommend that students should express macro models like the one in the previous example as a matrix equation and then either use Cramer's rule or matrix inversion to find the solution. Elimination is vastly simpler and drastically reduces the risk of making errors.

EXAMPLE 4

Suppose that the two equations

$$(z + 2w)^5 + xy^2 = 2z - yw$$

$$(1 + z^2)^3 - z^2 w = 8x + y^5 w^2$$

(∗)

define z and w as differentiable functions $z = \varphi(x, y)$ and $w = \psi(x, y)$ of x and y in a neigbourhood around $(x, y, z, w) = (1, 1, 1, 0)$.

(a) Compute $\partial z/\partial x, \partial z/\partial y, \partial w/\partial x$, and $\partial w/\partial y$ at $(1, 1, 1, 0)$ by finding the differentials of (∗).

(b) Use the results in (a) to find an approximate values of $\varphi(1 + 0.1, 1 + 0.2)$.

Solution:

(a) Equating the differentials of each side of the two equations (∗), treated as functions of (x, y), we obtain

$$5(z + 2w)^4(dz + 2\, dw) + y^2\, dx + 2xy\, dy = 2\, dz - w\, dy - y\, dw$$

$$3(1 + z^2)^2 2z\, dz - 2zw\, dz - z^2\, dw = 8\, dx + 5y^4 w^2\, dy + 2y^5 w\, dw$$

At the particular point $(x, y, z, w) = (1, 1, 1, 0)$ this system reduces to

$$\text{(i)} \quad 3\,dz + 11\,dw = -dx - 2\,dy \qquad \text{(ii)} \quad 24\,dz - dw = 8\,dx$$

Solving these two equations simultaneously for dz and dw in terms of dx and dy yields

$$dz = \tfrac{29}{89}\,dx - \tfrac{2}{267}\,dy, \qquad dw = -\tfrac{16}{89}\,dx - \tfrac{16}{89}\,dy$$

Hence, $\partial z/\partial x = 29/89$, $\partial z/\partial y = -2/267$, $\partial w/\partial x = -16/89$, $\partial w/\partial y = -16/89$.

(b) If $x = 1$ is increased by $dx = 0.1$ and $y = 1$ is increased by $dy = 0.2$, the associated change in $z = \varphi(x, y)$ is approximately $dz = (29/89) \cdot 0.1 - (2/267) \cdot 0.2 \approx 0.03$. Hence $\varphi(1 + 0.1, 1 + 0.2) \approx \varphi(1, 1) + dz \approx 1 + 0.03 = 1.03$.

The General Case

When economists deal with systems of equations, notably in comparative static analysis, the variables are usually divided a priori into two types: **endogenous** variables, which the model is intended to determine; **exogenous** variables, which are supposed to be determined by "forces" outside the economic model such as government policy, consumers' tastes, or technical progress. This classification depends on the model in question. Public expenditure, for example, is often treated as exogenous in public finance theory, which seeks to understand how tax changes affect the economy. But it is often endogenous in a "political economy" model which tries to explain how political variables like public expenditure emerge from the political system.

Economic models often give rise to a general system of **structural equations** having the form

$$
\begin{aligned}
f_1(x_1, x_2, \ldots, x_n, y_1, y_2, \ldots, y_m) &= 0 \\
f_2(x_1, x_2, \ldots, x_n, y_1, y_2, \ldots, y_m) &= 0 \\
&\cdots\cdots\cdots\cdots\cdots\cdots\cdots\cdots\cdots\cdots\cdots \\
f_m(x_1, x_2, \ldots, x_n, y_1, y_2, \ldots, y_m) &= 0
\end{aligned}
\tag{1}
$$

Here it is assumed that $x_1, \ldots, x_n$ are the exogenous variables, whereas $y_1, \ldots, y_m$ are the endogenous variables. An "initial equilibrium" or "status quo" solution $(\mathbf{x}^0, \mathbf{y}^0) = (x_1^0, \ldots, x_n^0, y_1^0, \ldots, y_m^0)$ is frequently known, or else assumed to exist. This **equilibrium** might, for instance, represent a state in which there is equality between current supply and demand for each good.

Note that if the counting rule applies, then system (1) with m equations in $n+m$ unknowns has $n + m - m = n$ degrees of freedom. Suppose it defines all the endogenous variables $y_1, \ldots, y_m$ as C^1 functions of $x_1, \ldots, x_n$ in a neighbourhood of $(\mathbf{x}^0, \mathbf{y}^0)$. Then the system can be solved "in principle" for $y_1, \ldots, y_m$ in terms of $x_1, \ldots, x_n$ to give

$$y_1 = \varphi_1(x_1, \ldots, x_n), \ldots, y_m = \varphi_m(x_1, \ldots, x_n) \tag{2}$$

In this case, (2) is said to be the **reduced form** of the structural equation system (1). The endogenous variables have all been expressed as functions of the exogenous variables. The form of the functions $\varphi_1, \varphi_2, \ldots, \varphi_m$ is not necessarily known.

The previous examples showed how we can often find an explicit expression for the partial derivative of any endogenous variable w.r.t. any exogenous variable. The same type of argument can be used in the general case, but a detailed discussion is left for FMEA.

PROBLEMS FOR SECTION 12.11

1. Differentiate the system

$$au + bv = cx + dy$$
$$eu + fv = gx + hy$$

with a, b, c, d, e, f, g, and h as constants, $af \neq be$, and find the partial derivatives of u and v w.r.t. x and y.

2. (a) Differentiate the following system, and solve for du and dv in terms of dx and dy:

$$xu^3 + v = y^2 \qquad (*)$$
$$3uv - x = 4$$

(b) Find u'_x and v'_x by using the results in part (a).

(c) The point $(x, y, u, v) = (0, 1, 4/3, 1)$ satisfies $(*)$. Find u'_x and v'_x at this point.

SM 3. Suppose y_1 and y_2 are implicitly defined as differentiable functions of x_1 and x_2 by

$$f_1(x_1, x_2, y_1, y_2) = 3x_1 + x_2^2 - y_1 - 3y_2^3 = 0$$
$$f_2(x_1, x_2, y_1, y_2) = x_1^3 - 2x_2 + 2y_1^3 - y_2 = 0$$

Find $\partial y_1 / \partial x_1$ and $\partial y_2 / \partial x_1$.

SM 4. A version of the "IS–LM" macroeconomic model originally devised by J. R. Hicks leads to the system of equations

(i) $I(r) = S(Y)$ (ii) $aY + L(r) = M$

Here a is a positive parameter, while I, S, and L are given, continuously differentiable functions.[4] Suppose that the system defines Y and r implicitly as differentiable functions of a and M. Find expressions for $\partial Y / \partial M$ and $\partial r / \partial M$.

5. Find u''_{xx} when u and v are defined as functions of x and y by the equations $xy + uv = 1$ and $xu + yv = 0$.

6. (a) Consider the macroeconomic model

(i) $Y = C + I + G$ (ii) $C = F(Y, T, r)$ (iii) $I = f(Y, r)$

where F and f are continuously differentiable functions, with $F'_Y > 0$, $F'_T < 0$, $F'_r < 0$, $f'_Y > 0$, $f'_r < 0$, and $F'_Y + f'_Y < 1$. Differentiate the system, and express dY in terms of dT, dG, and dr.

(b) What happens to Y if T increases? Or if T and G undergo equal increases?

7. (a) Determine the number of degrees of freedom in the macroeconomic model

(i) $Y = C(Y, r) + I + \alpha$ (ii) $I = F(Y, r) + \beta$ (iii) $M = L(Y, r)$

where Y is national income, r is the interest rate, I is total investments, α is public consumption, β is public investment, and M is the money supply. Here C, F, and L are given differentiable functions.

---

[4] The first "IS equation" involves the investment function I and savings function S. The second "LM equation" involves the liquidity preference function L (the demand for money) and the money supply M. The variable Y denotes national income and r denotes the interest rate.

(b) Differentiate the system. Put $d\beta = dM = 0$ and find dY, dr, and dI expressed in terms of $d\alpha$.

8. A standard macroeconomic model consists of the system of equations

$$\text{(i)} \quad M = \alpha Py + L(r) \qquad \text{(ii)} \quad S(y, r, g) = I(y, r)$$

Here M, α, and P are positive constants, whereas L, S, and I are differentiable functions.

(a) By using the counting rule, explain why it is reasonable to assume that the system, in general, defines y and r as differentiable functions of g.

(b) Differentiate the system and find expressions for dy/dg and dr/dg.

9. (a) The system

$$u^2 v - u = x^3 + 2y^3$$
$$e^{ux} = vy$$

defines u and v as differentiable functions of x and y around the point $P = (x, y, u, v) = (0, 1, 2, 1)$. Find the differentials of u and v expressed in terms of the differentials of x and y. Find $\partial u / \partial y$ and $\partial v / \partial x$ at P.

(b) If x increases by 0.1 and y decreases by 0.2 from their values at P, what are the approximate changes in u and v?

HARDER PROBLEM

10. When there are two goods, consumer demand theory involves the equation system

$$\text{(i)} \quad U_1'(x_1, x_2) = \lambda p_1 \qquad \text{(ii)} \quad U_2'(x_1, x_2) = \lambda p_2 \qquad \text{(iii)} \quad p_1 x_1 + p_2 x_2 = m$$

where $U(x_1, x_2)$ is a given utility function. Suppose that the system defines x_1, x_2, and λ as differentiable functions of p_1, p_2, and m. Find an expression for $\partial x_1 / \partial p_1$.

REVIEW PROBLEMS FOR CHAPTER 12

1. In the following cases, find dz/dt by using the chain rule:

(a) $z = F(x, y) = 6x + y^3$, $x = 2t^2$, $y = 3t^3$.

(b) $z = F(x, y) = x^p + y^p$, $x = at$, $y = bt$

(c) Check the answers by first substituting the expressions for x and y and then differentiating.

2. Let $z = G(u, v)$, $u = \varphi(t, s)$, and $v = \psi(s)$. Find expressions for $\partial z / \partial t$ and $\partial z / \partial s$.

3. Find expressions for $\partial w / \partial t$ and $\partial w / \partial s$ when

$$w = x^2 + y^3 + z^4, \quad x = t + s, \ y = t - s, \ z = st$$

(SM) 4. Suppose production X depends on the number of workers N according to the formula $X = Ng(\varphi(N)/N)$, where g and φ are given differentiable functions. Find expressions for dX/dN and d^2X/dN^2.

5. Suppose that a representative household's demand for a commodity is a function $E(p, m) = Ap^{-a}m^b$ of the price p and income m (where A, a, and b are positive constants).

   (a) Suppose that p and m are both differentiable functions of time t. Then demand E is a function only of t. Find an expression for $\dot{E}/E$ in terms of $\dot{p}/p$ and $\dot{m}/m$.

   (b) Put $p = p_0(1.06)^t$, $m = m_0(1.08)^t$, where p_0 is the price and m_0 is the income at time $t = 0$. Show that in this case $\dot{E}/E = \ln Q$, where $Q = (1.08)^b/(1.06)^a$.

6. The equation
$$x^3 \ln x + y^3 \ln y = 2z^3 \ln z$$
defines z as a differentiable function of x and y in a neighbourhood of the point $(x, y, z) = (e, e, e)$. Calculate $z_1'(e, e)$ and $z_{11}''(e, e)$.

7. What is the elasticity of substitution between y and x when $F(x, y) = x^2 - 10y^2$?

8. Find the marginal rate of substitution (MRS) between y and x when:

   (a) $U(x, y) = 2x^{0.4}y^{0.6}$ (b) $U(x, y) = xy + y$ (c) $U(x, y) = 10(x^{-2} + y^{-2})^{-4}$

9. Find the degree of homogeneity, if any, of the functions:

   (a) $f(x, y) = 3x^3y^{-4} + 2xy^{-2}$ (b) $Y(K, L) = (K^a + L^a)^{2c}e^{K^2/L^2}$

   (c) $f(x_1, x_2) = 5x_1^4 + 6x_1x_2^3$ (d) $F(x_1, x_2, x_3) = e^{x_1+x_2+x_3}$

10. What is the elasticity of substitution between y and x for the function in Problem 8(c)?

(SM) 11. Find the elasticity of y w.r.t. x when $y^2e^{x+1/y} = 3$.

12. Find the degree of homogeneity of the functions:

   (a) $f(x, y) = xg(y/x)$, where g is an arbitrary function of one variable.

   (b) $F(x, y, z) = z^k f(x/z, y/z)$, where f is an arbitrary function of two variables.

   (c) $G(K, L, M, N) = K^{a-b} \cdot L^{b-c} \cdot M^{c-d} \cdot N^{d-a}$ (a, b, c, and d are constants)

13. Suppose the production function $F(K, L)$ defined for $K > 0$, $L > 0$ is homogeneous of degree 1. If $F_{KK}'' < 0$, so that the marginal productivity of capital is a strictly decreasing function of K, prove that $F_{KL}'' > 0$, so that the marginal productivity of capital is strictly increasing as labour input increases. This is called *Wicksell's law*. (*Hint:* Use (6) in Section 12.6.)

14. Show that no generalization of the concept of a homogeneous function emerges if one replaces t^k in definition (12.7.1) by an arbitrary function $g(t)$. (*Hint:* Differentiate the new (1) w.r.t. t, and let $t = 1$. Then use Euler's theorem.)

15. The following system of equations defines $u = u(x, y)$ and $v = v(x, y)$ as differentiable functions of x and y around the point $P = (x, y, u, v) = (1, 1, -1, 0)$:

$$u + xe^y + v = e - 1$$
$$x + e^{u+v^2} - y = e^{-1}$$

Differentiate the system and find the values of u_x', u_y', v_x', and v_y' at that point.

(SM) **16.** (a) An equilibrium model of labour demand and output pricing leads to the following system of equations:

$$pF'(L) - w = 0$$
$$pF(L) - wL - B = 0 \qquad (*)$$

Here F is twice differentiable with $F'(L) > 0$ and $F''(L) < 0$. All the variables are positive. Regard w and B as exogenous, so that p and L are endogenous variables which are functions of w and B. Find expressions for $\partial p/\partial w$, $\partial p/\partial B$, $\partial L/\partial w$, and $\partial L/\partial B$ by implicit differentiation.

(b) What can be said about the signs of these partial derivatives? Show, in particular, that $\partial L/\partial w < 0$.

17. (a) The following system of equations defines $u = u(x, y)$ and $v = v(x, y)$ as differentiable functions of x and y around the point $P = (x, y, u, v) = (1, 1, 1, 2)$:

$$u^\alpha + v^\beta = 2^\beta x + y^3$$
$$u^\alpha v^\beta - v^\beta = x - y$$

where α and β are positive constants. Differentiate the system. Then find $\partial u/\partial x$, $\partial u/\partial y$, $\partial v/\partial x$, and $\partial v/\partial y$ at the point P.

(b) For the function $u(x, y)$ in (a), find an approximation to $u(0.99, 1.01)$.

18. A study of the demand for semiconductors involves the integral

$$S = \int_0^T e^{-rx}(e^{g(T-x)} - 1)\, dx,$$

where T, r and g are positive constants.

(a) Show that

$$r(r + g)S = re^{gT} + ge^{-rT} - (r + g) \qquad (*)$$

(b) The equation $(*)$ defines T as a differentiable function of g, r, and S. Use it to find an expression for $\partial T/\partial g$.

(SM) **19.** (a) Suppose that a vintage car has an appreciating market value given by the function $V(t)$ of time t. Suppose the maintenance cost of the car per unit of time is constant, at m per year. Allowing for continuous time discounting at a rate r per year, the present discounted value from selling the car at time t is $P(t) = V(t)e^{-rt} - \int_0^t me^{-r\tau}\, d\tau$. Show that the optimal choice t^* of t must satisfy

$$V'(t^*) = rV(t^*) + m \qquad (*)$$

and give $(*)$ an economic interpretation.

(b) Show that the standard second-order condition for $P(t)$ to have a strict local maximum at $t^*(r, m)$ reduces to the condition $D = V''(t^*) - rV'(t^*) < 0$.

(c) Find the partial derivatives $\partial t^*/\partial r$ and $\partial t^*/\partial m$, and use the condition derived in the answer to (b) in order to discuss how an economist would interpret their signs.

13

MULTIVARIABLE OPTIMIZATION

At first sight it is curious that a subject as pure and
passionless as mathematics can have anything useful to say
about that messy, ill-structured, chancy world in which we live.
*   Fortunately we find that whenever we comprehend*
what was previously mysterious, there is at the centre
of everything order, pattern and common sense.
—B. H. P. Rivett (1978)

Chapter 8 was concerned with optimization problems involving functions of one variable. Most interesting economic optimization problems, however, require the simultaneous choice of several variables. For example, a profit-maximizing producer of a single commodity chooses not only its output level, but also the quantities of many different inputs. A consumer chooses what quantities of the many different goods to buy.

Most of the mathematical difficulties arise already in the transition from one to two variables. On the other hand, textbooks in economics often illustrate economic problems by using functions of only two variables, for which one can at least draw level curves in the plane. We therefore begin this chapter by studying the two-variable case. The first section presents the basic results, illustrated by relatively simple examples and problems. Then we give a more systematic presentation of the theory with two variables. Subsequently we consider how the theory can be generalized to functions of several variables.

Much of economic analysis involves seeing how the solution to an optimization problem responds when the situation changes—for example, if some relevant parameters change. Thus, the theory of the firm considers how a change in the price of a good that is either an input or an output can affect the optimal quantities of all the inputs and outputs, as well as the maximum profit. Some simple results of this kind are briefly introduced at the end of the chapter.

13.1 Two Variables: Necessary Conditions

Consider a differentiable function $z = f(x, y)$ defined on a set S in the xy-plane. Suppose that f attains its largest value (its maximum) at an interior point (x_0, y_0) of S, as indicated in Fig. 1. If we keep y fixed at y_0, then the function $g(x) = f(x, y_0)$ depends only on x and has its maximum at $x = x_0$. (Geometrically, if P is the highest point on the surface in Fig. 1, then P is certainly also the highest point on the curve through P that has $y = y_0$—i.e. on the curve which is the intersection of the surface with the plane $y = y_0$.) From Theorem 8.1.1 we know that $g'(x_0) = 0$. But for all x, the derivative $g'(x)$ is exactly the same as the partial derivative $f_1'(x, y_0)$. At $x = x_0$, therefore, one has $f_1'(x_0, y_0) = 0$. In the same way, we see that (x_0, y_0) must satisfy $f_2'(x_0, y_0) = 0$, because the function $h(y) = f(x_0, y)$ has its maximum at $y = y_0$. A point (x_0, y_0) where both the partial derivatives are 0 is called a **stationary** (or **critical**) **point** of f.

If f attains its smallest value (its minimum) at an interior point (x_0, y_0) of S, a similar argument shows that the point again must be a stationary point. So we have the following important result:[1]

THEOREM 13.1.1 (NECESSARY CONDITIONS FOR INTERIOR EXTREMA)

A differentiable function $z = f(x, y)$ can have a maximum or minimum at an interior point (x_0, y_0) of S only if it is a **stationary point**—that is, if the point $(x, y) = (x_0, y_0)$ satisfies the two equations

$$f_1'(x, y) = 0, \qquad f_2'(x, y) = 0 \qquad \textbf{(first-order conditions, or FOCs)}$$

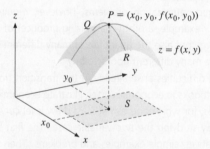

Figure 1 $f(x, y)$ has maximum at P, the highest point on the surface $z = f(x, y)$, where $f_1'(x_0, y_0) = f_2'(x_0, y_0) = 0$.

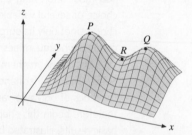

Figure 2 P is a maximum, Q is a local maximum, and R is a saddle point.

In Fig. 2, the three points P, Q, and R are all stationary points, but only P is a maximum. (Later, we shall call Q a *local maximum*, whereas R is a *saddle point*.)

In the following examples and problems only the first-order conditions are considered. The next section explains how to verify that we have found the optimum.

EXAMPLE 1   The function f is defined for all (x, y) by

$$f(x, y) = -2x^2 - 2xy - 2y^2 + 36x + 42y - 158$$

Assume that f has a maximum point. Find it.

---
[1] Interior point is defined precisely in Section 13.5.

Solution: Theorem 13.1.1 applies. So a maximum point (x, y) must be a stationary point satisfying the first-order conditions

$$f_1'(x, y) = -4x - 2y + 36 = 0$$
$$f_2'(x, y) = -2x - 4y + 42 = 0$$

These are two linear equations which determine x and y. We find that $(x, y) = (5, 8)$ is the only pair of numbers which satisfies both equations. Assuming there is a maximum point, these must be its coordinates. The maximum value is $f(5, 8) = 100$. (In Example 13.2.2 we prove that $(5, 8)$ *is* a maximum point.)

EXAMPLE 2   A firm produces two different kinds A and B of a commodity. The daily cost of producing x units of A and y units of B is

$$C(x, y) = 0.04x^2 + 0.01xy + 0.01y^2 + 4x + 2y + 500$$

Suppose that the firm sells all its output at a price per unit of 15 for A and 9 for B. Find the daily production levels x and y that maximize profit per day.

Solution: Profit per day is $\pi(x, y) = 15x + 9y - C(x, y)$, so

$$\pi(x, y) = 15x + 9y - 0.04x^2 - 0.01xy - 0.01y^2 - 4x - 2y - 500$$
$$= -0.04x^2 - 0.01xy - 0.01y^2 + 11x + 7y - 500$$

If $x > 0$ and $y > 0$ maximize profit, then (x, y) must satisfy

$$\frac{\partial \pi}{\partial x} = -0.08x - 0.01y + 11 = 0, \qquad \frac{\partial \pi}{\partial y} = -0.01x - 0.02y + 7 = 0$$

These two linear equations in x and y have the unique solution $x = 100$, $y = 300$, with $\pi(100, 300) = 1100$. (We have not proved that this actually is a maximum. See Problem 13.2.1(a).)

EXAMPLE 3   (**Profit maximization**)   Suppose that $Q = F(K, L)$ is a production function with K as the capital input and L as the labour input. The price per unit of output is p, the cost (or rental) per unit of capital is r, and the wage rate is w. The constants p, r, and w are all positive. The profit π from producing and selling $F(K, L)$ units is then given by the function

$$\pi(K, L) = pF(K, L) - rK - wL \tag{1}$$

If F is differentiable and π has a maximum with $K > 0$, $L > 0$, then the first-order conditions (FOCs) are

$$\pi_K'(K, L) = pF_K'(K, L) - r = 0$$
$$\pi_L'(K, L) = pF_L'(K, L) - w = 0 \tag{$*$}$$

Thus, a necessary condition for profit to be a maximum when $K = K^*$ and $L = L^*$ is that

$$pF_K'(K^*, L^*) = r, \qquad pF_L'(K^*, L^*) = w \qquad (**)$$

The first equation says that r, the price of capital, must equal the sales value at the price p per unit of the marginal product of capital. The second equation has a similar interpretation.

Suppose we think of increasing capital input from the level K^* by 1 unit. How much would be gained? Production would increase by approximately $F_K'(K^*, L^*)$ units. Because each extra unit is priced at p, the revenue gain is approximately $pF_K'(K^*, L^*)$. How much is lost? The answer is r, because this is the price of one unit of capital. These two must be equal.

The second equation in $(**)$ has a similar interpretation: Increasing labour input by one unit from level L^* will lead to the approximate gain $pF_L'(K^*, L^*)$ in revenue, whereas the extra labour cost is w. The profit-maximizing pair (K^*, L^*) thus has the property that the extra revenue from increasing either input by one unit is just offset by the extra cost.

Economists often divide the first-order conditions $(**)$ by the positive price p to reach the alternative form $F_K'(K, L) = r/p$ and $F_L'(K, L) = w/p$. So, to obtain maximum profit, the firm must choose K and L to equate the marginal productivity of capital to its relative price r/p, and also to equate the marginal productivity of labour to its relative price w/p.

Note that the conditions in $(**)$ are necessary, but generally not sufficient for an interior maximum. Sufficient conditions for an optimum are given in Example 13.3.3.

EXAMPLE 4   Find the only possible solution to the following special case of Example 3:

$$\max \pi(K, L) = 12K^{1/2}L^{1/4} - 1.2K - 0.6L$$

Solution: The first-order conditions are

$$\pi_K'(K, L) = 6K^{-1/2}L^{1/4} - 1.2 = 0, \qquad \pi_L'(K, L) = 3K^{1/2}L^{-3/4} - 0.6 = 0$$

These equations imply that $K^{-1/2}L^{1/4} = K^{1/2}L^{-3/4} = 0.2 = 1/5$. Multiplying each side of the first equation here by $K^{1/2}L^{3/4}$ reduces it to $L = K$. Hence $K^{-1/4} = L^{-1/4} = 1/5$. It follows that $K = L = 5^4 = 625$ is the only possible solution. (See Example 13.2.3 for a proof that this is indeed a maximum point.)

EXAMPLE 5   A firm is a monopolist in the domestic market but takes as given the fixed price p_w of its product in the world market. The quantities sold in the two markets are denoted by x_d and x_w, respectively. The price obtained in the domestic market, as a function of its sales, is given by the inverse demand function $p_d = f(x_d)$. The cost function is $c(x_d + x_w)$. (Note that c is here a function of one variable, not a constant.)

(a) Find the profit function $\pi(x_d, x_w)$ and write down the first-order conditions for profit to be maximized at $x_d > 0$, $x_w > 0$. Give economic interpretations of these conditions.

(b) Suppose that the firm in the domestic market is faced with a demand curve whose price elasticity is a constant equal to -2. What is the relationship between the prices in the domestic and world markets?

Solution: (a) The revenue from selling x_d units in the domestic market at the price $p_d = f(x_d)$ is $p_d x_d = f(x_d)x_d$. In the world market the revenue is $p_w x_w$. The profit function is $\pi = \pi(x_d, x_w) = p_d x_d + p_w x_w - c(x_d + x_w)$. Thus the first-order conditions are

(i) $\pi_1' = p_d + (dp_d/dx_d)x_d - c'(x_d + x_w) = 0$,   (ii) $\pi_2' = p_w - c'(x_d + x_w) = 0$

According to (ii), the marginal cost in the world market must equal the price, which is the marginal revenue in this case. In the domestic market the marginal cost must also equal the marginal revenue. Here is an interpretation of (i): Suppose the firm contemplates producing and selling a little extra in its domestic market. The extra revenue per unit increase in output equals p_d minus the loss that arises because of the induced price reduction for all domestic sales. The latter loss is approximately $f'(x_d)x_d = (dp_d/dx_d)x_d$. Since the cost of an extra unit of output is approximately the marginal cost $c'(x_d + x_w)$, condition (i) expresses the requirement that, per unit of extra output, the domestic revenue gain is just offset by the cost increase.

(b) The price elasticity of demand is -2, meaning that $\mathrm{El}_{p_d} x_d = (p_d/x_d)(dx_d/dp_d) = -2$. By the rule for differentiating inverse functions one has $dp_d/dx_d = 1/(dx_d/dp_d)$. It follows that $(dp_d/dx_d)x_d = -\frac{1}{2}p_d$. Then (i) and (ii) imply that $\frac{1}{2}p_d = c'(x_d + x_w) = p_w$, so the world market price is half the domestic market price.

PROBLEMS FOR SECTION 13.1

1. The function f defined for all (x, y) by $f(x, y) = -2x^2 - y^2 + 4x + 4y - 3$ has a maximum. Find the corresponding values of x and y.

2. (a) The function f defined for all (x, y) by $f(x, y) = x^2 + y^2 - 6x + 8y + 35$ has a minimum point. Find it.

   (b) Show that $f(x, y)$ can be written in the form $f(x, y) = (x - 3)^2 + (y + 4)^2 + 10$. Explain why this shows that you have really found the minimum in part (a).

3. In the profit-maximizing problem of Example 3, let $p = 1$, $r = 0.65$, $w = 1.2$, and

   $$F(K, L) = 80 - (K - 3)^2 - 2(L - 6)^2 - (K - 3)(L - 6)$$

   Find the only possible values of K and L that maximize profits.

4. Yearly profits (in millions of dollars) for a firm are given by

   $$P(x, y) = -x^2 - y^2 + 22x + 18y - 102$$

   where x is the amount spent on research (in millions of dollars), and y is the amount spent on advertising (in millions of dollars).

   (a) Find the profits when $x = 10$, $y = 8$ and when $x = 12$, $y = 10$.

   (b) Find the only possible values of x and y that can maximize profits, and the corresponding profit.

13.2   Two Variables: Sufficient Conditions

Suppose f is a function of one variable which is twice differentiable in an interval I. In this case a very simple sufficient condition for a stationary point in I to be a maximum point is that $f''(x) \leq 0$ for all x in I. (See Theorem 8.2.2.) The function f is then called "concave".

For functions of two variables there is a corresponding test for concavity based on the second-order *partial* derivatives. Provided the function has an interior stationary point, this test implies that its graph is a surface shaped like the one in Fig. 13.1.1.

Consider any curve parallel to the xz-plane which lies in the surface, like QPR in that figure. Any such curve is the graph of a concave function of one variable, implying that $f''_{11}(x, y) \leq 0$. A similar argument holds for any curve parallel to the yz-plane which lies in the surface, implying that $f''_{22}(x, y) \leq 0$. In general, however, having these two second-order partial derivatives be nonpositive is *not* sufficient on its own to ensure that the surface is shaped like the one in Fig. 13.1.1. This is clear from the next example.

EXAMPLE 1   The function

$$f(x, y) = 3xy - x^2 - y^2$$

has $f''_{11}(x, y) = f''_{22}(x, y) = -2$. Each curve parallel to the xz-plane that lies in the surface defined by the graph has the equation $z = 3xy_0 - x^2 - y_0^2$ for some fixed y_0. It is therefore a concave parabola. So is each curve parallel to the yz-plane that lies in the surface. But along the line $y = x$ the function reduces to $f(x, x) = x^2$, which is a convex rather than a concave parabola. It follows that f has no maximum (or minimum) at $(0, 0)$, which is the only stationary point.

What Example 1 shows is that conditions ensuring that the graph of f looks like the one in Fig. 13.1.1 cannot ignore the second-order mixed partial derivative $f''_{12}(x, y)$. The following result will be discussed in FMEA. (See the end of Section 13.3 for a proof of the local version.) To formulate the theorem we need a new concept. A set S in the xy-plane is **convex** if, for each pair of points P and Q in S, all the line segment between P and Q lies in S.

THEOREM 13.2.1   (SUFFICIENT CONDITIONS FOR A MAXIMUM OR MINIMUM)

Suppose that (x_0, y_0) is an interior stationary point for a C^2 function $f(x, y)$ defined in a convex set S in $\mathbb{R}^2$.

(a) If for all (x, y) in S,

$$f''_{11}(x, y) \leq 0, \quad f''_{22}(x, y) \leq 0, \quad \text{and} \quad f''_{11}(x, y)f''_{22}(x, y) - \left(f''_{12}(x, y)\right)^2 \geq 0$$

then (x_0, y_0) is a maximum point for $f(x, y)$ in S.

(b) If for all (x, y) in S,

$$f''_{11}(x, y) \geq 0, \quad f''_{22}(x, y) \geq 0, \quad \text{and} \quad f''_{11}(x, y)f''_{22}(x, y) - \left(f''_{12}(x, y)\right)^2 \geq 0$$

then (x_0, y_0) is a minimum point for $f(x, y)$ in S.

NOTE 1   The conditions in part (a) of Theorem 13.2.1 are sufficient for a stationary point to be a maximum point. They are far from being necessary. This is clear from the function whose graph is shown in Fig. 13.1.2, which *has* a maximum at P, but where the conditions in (a) are certainly not satisfied in the whole of its domain.

NOTE 2   If a twice differentiable function $z = f(x, y)$ satisfies the inequalities in (a) throughout a convex set S, it is called **concave**, whereas it is called **convex** if it satisfies the inequalities in (b) throughout S. It follows from these definitions that f is concave if and only if $-f$ is convex, just as in the one-variable case.

There are more general definitions of concave and convex functions which apply to functions that are not necessarily differentiable. These are presented in FMEA. (The one-variable case was briefly discussed in Section 8.7.)

EXAMPLE 2   Show that
$$f(x, y) = -2x^2 - 2xy - 2y^2 + 36x + 42y - 158$$

has a maximum at the stationary point $(x_0, y_0) = (5, 8)$. (See Example 13.1.1.)

Solution: We found that $f_1'(x, y) = -4x - 2y + 36$ and $f_2'(x, y) = -2x - 4y + 42$. Furthermore, $f_{11}'' = -4$, $f_{12}'' = -2$, and $f_{22}'' = -4$. Thus

$$f_{11}''(x, y) \leq 0, \quad f_{22}''(x, y) \leq 0, \quad f_{11}''(x, y)f_{22}''(x, y) - \left(f_{12}''(x, y)\right)^2 = 16 - 4 = 12 \geq 0$$

According to (a) in Theorem 13.2.1, these inequalities guarantee that the stationary point $(5, 8)$ is a maximum point.

EXAMPLE 3   Show that we have found the maximum in Example 13.1.4.

Solution: If $K > 0$ and $L > 0$, we find that

$$\pi_{KK}'' = -3K^{-3/2}L^{1/4}, \qquad \pi_{KL}'' = \tfrac{3}{2}K^{-1/2}L^{-3/4}, \quad \text{and} \quad \pi_{LL}'' = -\tfrac{9}{4}K^{1/2}L^{-7/4}$$

Clearly, $\pi_{KK}'' < 0$, $\pi_{LL}'' < 0$, and moreover,

$$\pi_{KK}''\pi_{LL}'' - (\pi_{KL}'')^2 = \tfrac{27}{4}K^{-1}L^{-3/2} - \tfrac{9}{4}K^{-1}L^{-3/2} = \tfrac{9}{2}K^{-1}L^{-3/2} > 0$$

It follows that the stationary point $(K, L) = (625, 625)$ maximizes profit.

This section concludes with two examples that each involve a constraint. Nevertheless, a simple transformation can be used to convert the problem into the form we have been discussing, without any constraint.

EXAMPLE 4   Suppose that any production by the firm in Example 13.1.2 creates pollution, so it is legally restricted to produce a total of 320 units of the two kinds of output. The firm's problem is then:

$$\max \; -0.04x^2 - 0.01xy - 0.01y^2 + 11x + 7y - 500 \quad \text{subject to} \quad x + y = 320$$

What now are the optimal quantities of the two kinds of output?

Solution: The firm still wants to maximize its profits. But because of the restriction $y = 320 - x$, the new profit function is

$$\hat{\pi}(x) = -0.04x^2 - 0.01x(320 - x) - 0.01(320 - x)^2 + 11x + 7(320 - x) - 500$$

We easily find $\hat{\pi}'(x) = -0.08x + 7.2$, so $\hat{\pi}'(x) = 0$ for $x = 7.2/0.08 = 90$. Since $\hat{\pi}''(x) = -0.08 < 0$ for all x, the point $x = 90$ does maximize $\hat{\pi}$. The corresponding value of y is $y = 320 - 90 = 230$. The maximum profit is 1040.

EXAMPLE 5   A firm has three factories each producing the same item. Let x, y, and z denote the respective output quantities that the three factories produce in order to fulfil an order for 2000 units in total. Hence, $x + y + z = 2000$. The cost functions for the three factories are

$$C_1(x) = 200 + \frac{1}{100}x^2, \qquad C_2(y) = 200 + y + \frac{1}{300}y^3, \qquad C_3(z) = 200 + 10z$$

The total cost of fulfilling the order is thus

$$C(x, y, z) = C_1(x) + C_2(y) + C_3(z)$$

Find the values of x, y, and z that minimize C. (*Hint:* Reduce the problem to one with only two variables by solving $x + y + z = 2000$ for z.)

Solution: Solving the equation $x + y + z = 2000$ for z yields $z = 2000 - x - y$. Substituting this expression for z in the expression for C yields, after simplifying,

$$\hat{C}(x, y) = C(x, y, 2000 - x - y) = \frac{1}{100}x^2 - 10x + \frac{1}{300}y^3 - 9y + 20\,600$$

Any stationary points of $\hat{C}$ must satisfy the two equations

$$\hat{C}_1'(x, y) = \frac{1}{50}x - 10 = 0, \qquad \hat{C}_2'(x, y) = \frac{1}{100}y^2 - 9 = 0$$

The only solution is $x = 500$ and $y = 30$, implying that $z = 1470$. The corresponding value of C is $17\,920$.

The second-order partial derivatives are $\hat{C}_{11}''(x, y) = \frac{1}{50}$, $\hat{C}_{12}''(x, y) = 0$, and $\hat{C}_{22}''(x, y) = \frac{1}{50}y$. It follows that for all $x \geq 0$, $y \geq 0$, one has

$$\hat{C}_{11}''(x, y) \geq 0, \quad \hat{C}_{22}''(x, y) \geq 0, \quad \text{and} \quad \hat{C}_{11}''(x, y)\hat{C}_{22}''(x, y) - \left(\hat{C}_{12}''(x, y)\right)^2 = \frac{y}{2500} \geq 0$$

Part (b) of Theorem 13.2.1 implies that $(500, 30)$ is a minimum point of $\hat{C}$ within the convex domain of points (x, y) satisfying $x \geq 0$, $y \geq 0$. It follows that $(500, 30, 1470)$ is a minimum point of C within the domain of (x, y, z) satisfying $x \geq 0$, $y \geq 0$, $z \geq 0$, and $x + y + z = 2000$.

PROBLEMS FOR SECTION 13.2

1. Prove that the optimum has been found in: (a) Example 13.1.2;   (b) Problem 13.1.1;
   (c) Problem 13.1.3.

2. (a) A firm produces two different kinds A and B of a commodity. The daily cost of producing
   x units of A and y units of B is

   $$C(x, y) = 2x^2 - 4xy + 4y^2 - 40x - 20y + 514$$

   Suppose that the firm sells all its output at a price per unit of \$24 for A and \$12 for B. Find
   the daily production levels x and y that maximize profit.

   (b) The firm is required to produce exactly 54 units per day of the two kinds combined. What
   now is the optimal production plan?

SM 3. Solve the utility-maximizing problem max $U = xyz$ subject to $x + 3y + 4z = 108$, by making
   U a function of y and z by eliminating the variable x.

4. The demands for a monopolist's two products are determined by the equations

   $$p = 25 - x, \qquad q = 24 - 2y$$

   where p and q are prices per unit of the two goods, and x and y are the corresponding quantities.
   The costs of producing and selling x units of the first good and y units of the other are

   $$C(x, y) = 3x^2 + 3xy + y^2$$

   (a) Find the monopolist's profit $\pi(x, y)$ from producing and selling x units of the first good
   and y units of the other.

   (b) Find the values of x and y that maximize $\pi(x, y)$. Verify that you have found the maximum
   profit.

5. A firm produces two goods. The cost of producing x units of good 1 and y units of good 2 is

   $$C(x, y) = x^2 + xy + y^2 + x + y + 14$$

   Suppose that the firm sells all its output of each good at prices per unit of p and q respectively.
   Find the values of x and y that maximize profits. (Assume $\frac{1}{2}p + \frac{1}{2} < q < 2p - 1$ and $p > 1$.)

6. The profit function of a firm is $\pi(x, y) = px + qy - \alpha x^2 - \beta y^2$, where p and q are the prices
   per unit and $\alpha x^2 + \beta y^2$ are the costs of producing and selling x units of the first good and y
   units of the other. The constants are all positive.

   (a) Find the values of x and y that maximize profits. Denote them by x^* and y^*. Verify that
   the second-order conditions are satisfied.

   (b) Define $\pi^*(p, q) = \pi(x^*, y^*)$. Verify that $\partial \pi^*(p, q)/\partial p = x^*$ and $\partial \pi^*(p, q)/\partial q = y^*$.
   Give these results economic interpretations.

7. Find the smallest value of $x^2 + y^2 + z^2$ when we require that $4x + 2y - z = 5$. (Geometrically,
   the problem is to find the point in the plane $4x + 2y - z = 5$ which is closest to the origin.)

8. Show that $f(x, y) = Ax^a y^b - px - qy - r$ (where A, a, b are positive constants, and p, q, and
   r are arbitrary constants) is concave for $x > 0$, $y > 0$ provided that $a + b \leq 1$. (See Note 2.)

13.3 Local Extreme Points

Sometimes one needs to consider *local* extreme points of a function. The point (x_0, y_0) is said to be a **local maximum point** of f in S if $f(x, y) \leq f(x_0, y_0)$ for all pairs (x, y) in S that lie sufficiently close to (x_0, y_0). More precisely, the definition is that there exists a positive number r such that $f(x, y) \leq f(x_0, y_0)$ for all (x, y) in S that lie inside the circle with centre (x_0, y_0) and radius r. If the inequality is strict for $(x, y) \neq (x_0, y_0)$, then (x_0, y_0) is a **strict** local maximum point.

A **(strict) local minimum** point is defined in the obvious way, and it should also be clear what we mean by *local maximum and minimum values*, *local extreme points*, and *local extreme values*. Note how these definitions imply that a global extreme point is also a local extreme point; the converse is not true, of course.

In searching for maximum and minimum points, the first-order conditions were very useful. The same result also applies to the local extreme points:

At any local extreme point in the interior of the domain of a differentiable function, the function must be stationary—i.e. all its first-order partial derivatives are 0.

This observation follows because in the argument for Theorem 13.1.1 it was sufficient to consider the behaviour of the function in a small neighbourhood of the optimal point.

These first-order conditions are necessary for a differentiable function to have a local extreme point. However, a stationary point does not have to be a local extreme point. A stationary point (x_0, y_0) of f which, like point R in Fig. 13.1.2, is neither a local maximum nor a local minimum point, is called a **saddle point** of f. Hence:

A saddle point (x_0, y_0) is a stationary point with the property that there exist points (x, y) arbitrarily close to (x_0, y_0) with $f(x, y) < f(x_0, y_0)$, and there also exist such points with $f(x, y) > f(x_0, y_0)$.

EXAMPLE 1   Show that $(0, 0)$ is a saddle point of $f(x, y) = x^2 - y^2$.

Solution: It is easy to check that $(0, 0)$ is a stationary point at which $f(0, 0) = 0$. Moreover, $f(x, 0) = x^2$ and $f(0, y) = -y^2$, so $f(x, y)$ takes positive and negative values arbitrarily close to the origin. Hence, $(0, 0)$ is a saddle point. See the graph in Fig. 1.

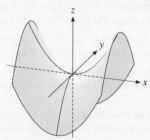

Figure 1 $f(x, y) = x^2 - y^2$. The point $(0, 0)$ is a saddle point

Local extreme points and saddle points can be illustrated by thinking of the mountains in the Himalayas. Every summit is a local maximum, but only the highest (Mount Everest)

is the (global) maximum. The deepest points of the lakes or glaciers are local minima. In every mountain pass there will be a saddle point that is the highest point in one compass direction and the lowest in another.

The stationary points of a function thus fall into three categories:

(a) Local maximum points   (b) Local minimum points   (c) Saddle points

How do we distinguish between these three cases?

Consider first the case when $z = f(x, y)$ has a local maximum at (x_0, y_0). The functions $g(x) = f(x, y_0)$ and $h(y) = f(x_0, y)$ describe the behaviour of f along the straight lines $y = y_0$ and $x = x_0$, respectively (see Fig. 13.1.1). These functions must achieve local maxima at x_0 and y_0, respectively. Therefore, $g''(x_0) = f''_{11}(x_0, y_0) \leq 0$ and $h''(y_0) = f''_{22}(x_0, y_0) \leq 0$.

On the other hand, if $g''(x_0) < 0$ and $h''(y_0) < 0$, then we know that g and h really do achieve local maxima at x_0 and y_0, respectively. Stated differently, the conditions $f''_{11}(x_0, y_0) < 0$ and $f''_{22}(x_0, y_0) < 0$ will ensure that $f(x, y)$ has a local maximum in the directions through (x_0, y_0) that are parallel to the x-axis and the y-axis.

However, note that the signs of $f''_{11}(x_0, y_0)$ and $f''_{22}(x_0, y_0)$ on their own do not reveal much about the behaviour of the graph of $z = f(x, y)$ when we move away from (x_0, y_0) in directions other than the two mentioned. Example 1 illustrated the problem.

It turns out that in order to have a correct second-derivative test for functions f of two variables, the mixed second-order partial $f''_{12}(x_0, y_0)$ must also be considered, just as it had to be in Section 13.2. The following theorem can be used to determine the nature of the stationary points in most cases. (A proof is given at the end of this section.)

THEOREM 13.3.1 (SECOND-DERIVATIVE TEST FOR LOCAL EXTREMA)

Suppose $f(x, y)$ is a C^2 function in a domain S, and let (x_0, y_0) be an interior stationary point of S. Write

$$A = f''_{11}(x_0, y_0), \qquad B = f''_{12}(x_0, y_0), \quad \text{and} \quad C = f''_{22}(x_0, y_0)$$

(a) If $A < 0$ and $AC - B^2 > 0$, then (x_0, y_0) is a (strict) local maximum point.

(b) If $A > 0$ and $AC - B^2 > 0$, then (x_0, y_0) is a (strict) local minimum point.

(c) If $AC - B^2 < 0$, then (x_0, y_0) is a saddle point.

(d) If $AC - B^2 = 0$, then (x_0, y_0) could be a local maximum, a local minimum, or a saddle point.

Note that $AC - B^2 > 0$ in (a) implies that $AC > B^2 \geq 0$, and so $AC > 0$. Thus, if $A < 0$, then also $C < 0$. The condition $C = f''_{22}(x_0, y_0) < 0$ is thus (indirectly) included in the assumptions in (a). The corresponding observation for (b) is also valid.

The conditions in (a), (b), and (c) are usually called (local) **second-order conditions**. Note that these are sufficient conditions for a stationary point to be, respectively, a *strict local* maximum point, a *strict local* minimum point, or a saddle point. None of these conditions is necessary. The result in Problem 5 will confirm (d), because it shows that a stationary point where $AC - B^2 = 0$ can fall into any of the three categories. The second-derivative test is inconclusive in this case.

EXAMPLE 2   Find the stationary points and classify them when $f(x, y) = x^3 - x^2 - y^2 + 8$.

Solution: The stationary points must satisfy the two equations

$$f_1'(x, y) = 3x^2 - 2x = 0 \quad \text{and} \quad f_2'(x, y) = -2y = 0$$

Because $3x^2 - 2x = x(3x - 2)$, we see that the first equation has the solutions $x = 0$ and $x = 2/3$. The second equation has the solution $y = 0$. We conclude that $(0, 0)$ and $(2/3, 0)$ are the only stationary points.

Furthermore, $f_{11}''(x, y) = 6x - 2$, $f_{12}''(x, y) = 0$, and $f_{22}''(x, y) = -2$. A convenient way of classifying the stationary points is to make a table like the following (with A, B, and C defined in the theorem):

(x, y)	A	B	C	$AC - B^2$	Type of point
$(0, 0)$	-2	0	-2	4	Local maximum point
$(2/3, 0)$	2	0	-2	-4	Saddle point

EXAMPLE 3   Consider Example 13.1.3 and suppose that the production function F is twice differentiable. Let (K^*, L^*) be an input pair satisfying the first-order conditions $(**)$ in the example. Define $\Delta(K, L) = F_{KK}''(K, L)F_{LL}''(K, L) - (F_{KL}''(K, L))^2$.

(a) Prove that if

$$F_{KK}''(K, L) \leq 0, \ F_{LL}''(K, L) \leq 0, \ \text{and} \ \Delta(K, L) \geq 0 \quad \text{for all } K \geq 0 \text{ and } L \geq 0 \ (*)$$

then (K^*, L^*) maximizes profit. (According to Note 13.2.2, the product function F is concave.)

(b) Prove also that if

$$F_{KK}''(K^*, L^*) < 0 \text{ and } \Delta(K^*, L^*) > 0 \tag{$**$}$$

then (K^*, L^*) is a local maximum for the profit function.

Solution:

(a) The second-order partials of the profit function are $\pi_{KK}''(K, L) = pF_{KK}''(K, L)$, $\pi_{KL}''(K, L) = pF_{KL}''(K, L)$, and $\pi_{LL}''(K, L) = pF_{LL}''(K, L)$. Since $p > 0$, the conclusion follows from Theorem 13.2.1(a).

(b) In this case the conclusion follows from Theorem 13.3.1(a).

Proof of the Second-Derivative Test

Let $z = f(x, y)$ be the function graphed in Fig. 2, with (x_0, y_0) as a local maximum point. For fixed values of h and k, define the function g of one variable by

$$g(t) = f(x_0 + th, y_0 + tk)$$

This function tells us what happens to f as one moves away from (x_0, y_0) in the direction (h, k), or in the reverse direction $(-h, -k)$.

If f has a local maximum at (x_0, y_0), then $g(t)$ must certainly have a local maximum at $t = 0$. Necessary conditions for this are that $g'(0) = 0$ and $g''(0) \leq 0$. The first- and second-order derivatives of $g(t)$ were calculated in Example 12.1.5. At $t = 0$ the second derivative of g is

$$g''(0) = f_{11}''(x_0, y_0)h^2 + 2f_{12}''(x_0, y_0)hk + f_{22}''(x_0, y_0)k^2 \tag{1}$$

So if f has a local maximum at (x_0, y_0), the expression in (1) must be ≤ 0 for all choices of (h, k).

In this way we have obtained a *necessary* condition for f to have a local maximum at (x_0, y_0). We are often more interested in *sufficient* conditions for a local maximum. For the one-variable function g we know that the conditions $g'(0) = 0$ and $g''(0) < 0$ are sufficient for g to have a local maximum at $t = 0$. It is therefore reasonable to conjecture that we have the following result:

If $f_1'(x_0, y_0) = f_2'(x_0, y_0) = 0$ and the expression in (1) for the second derivative $g''(0)$ is < 0 for all directions $(h, k) \neq (0, 0)$, then (x_0, y_0) is a (strict) local maximum point for f. $\tag{2}$

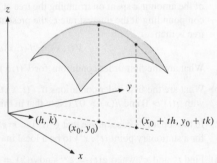

Figure 2

This turns out to be correct, as will be proved in FMEA. Problem 7, however, shows that the expression in (1) really must be negative for all directions (h, k) without exception.

Relying on (2), we can prove part (a) of Theorem 13.3.1. It suffices to verify that

$$A < 0 \quad \text{and} \quad AC - B^2 > 0 \implies Ah^2 + 2Bhk + Ck^2 < 0 \quad \text{for all} \quad (h, k) \neq (0, 0) \tag{3}$$

To this end we "complete the square":

$$Ah^2 + 2Bhk + Ck^2 = A\left[\left(h + \frac{B}{A}k\right)^2 + \frac{AC - B^2}{A^2}k^2\right] \tag{4}$$

The expression in square brackets is obviously ≥ 0, and $= 0$ only if both $h + Bk/A = 0$ and $k = 0$, implying that $h = k = 0$. Because $A < 0$, the right-hand side of (4) is negative for all $(h, k) \neq (0, 0)$, so we have proved (2). $\blacksquare$

1. (a) Find the partial derivatives of first and second order for the function f defined for all (x, y) by $f(x, y) = 5 - x^2 + 6x - 2y^2 + 8y$.

 (b) Find the only stationary point and classify it by using the second-derivative test. What does Theorem 13.2.1 tell us?

2. (a) Find the first- and second-order partial derivatives of $f(x, y) = x^2 + 2xy^2 + 2y^2$.

 (b) Show that the stationary points are $(0, 0)$, $(-1, 1)$, $(-1, -1)$, and classify them.

(SM) 3. (a) Let f be a function of two variables, given by

$$f(x, y) = (x^2 - axy)e^y$$

 where $a \neq 0$ is a constant. Find the stationary points of f and decide for each of them if it is a local maximum point, a local minimum point or a saddle point.

 (b) Let (x^*, y^*) be the stationary point where $x^* \neq 0$, and let $f^*(a) = f(x^*, y^*)$. Find $df^*(a)/da$. Show that if we let $\hat{f}(x, y, a) = (x^2 - axy)e^y$, then

$$\hat{f}_3'(x^*, y^*, a) = \frac{df^*(a)}{da}$$

(SM) 4. (a) Suppose in Example 10.3.2 that the market value of the tree at time t is a function $f(t, x)$ of the amount x spent on trimming the tree at time 0, as well as of t. Assuming continuous compounding at the interest rate r, the present discounted value of the profit earned on the tree is then

$$V(t, x) = f(t, x)e^{-rt} - x$$

 What are the first-order conditions for $V(t, x)$ to have a maximum at $t^* > 0$, $x^* > 0$?

 (b) What are the first-order conditions if $f(t, x)$ takes the separable form $f(t, x) = g(t)h(x)$, with $g(t) > 0$ and $h(x) > 0$? (Note that in this case t^* does not depend on the function h.)

 (c) In the separable case, prove that $g''(t^*) < r^2 g(t^*)$ and $h''(x^*) < 0$ are sufficient conditions for a stationary point (t^*, x^*) to be a local maximum point for V.

 (d) Find t^* and x^* when $g(t) = e^{\sqrt{t}}$ and $h(x) = \ln(x + 1)$, and check the local second-order conditions.

5. Consider the three functions: (a) $z = -x^4 - y^4$ (b) $z = x^4 + y^4$ (c) $z = x^3 + y^3$. Prove that the origin is a stationary point for each one of these functions, and that $AC - B^2 = 0$ at the origin in each case. By studying the functions directly, prove that the origin is respectively a maximum point for (a), a minimum point for (b), and a saddle point for (c).

HARDER PROBLEMS

(SM) 6. (a) Find the domain of the function $f(x, y) = \ln(1 + x^2 y)$.

 (b) Prove that the stationary points are all the points on the y-axis.

 (c) Show that the second-derivative test fails.

 (d) Classify the stationary points by looking directly at the sign of the value of $f(x, y)$. Then look at the figure in the answer section.

7. (a) The graph of $f(x, y) = (y - x^2)(y - 2x^2)$ intersects the xy-plane $z = 0$ in two parabolas. In the xy-plane, draw the domains where f is negative, and where f is positive. Show that $(0, 0)$ is the only stationary point, and that it is a saddle point.

(b) Suppose $(h, k) \neq (0, 0)$ is any direction vector. Let $g(t) = f(th, tk)$ and show that g has a local minimum at $t = 0$, whatever the direction (h, k) may be. (Thus, although $(0, 0)$ is a saddle point, the function has a local minimum at the origin in each direction through the origin.)

13.4 Linear Models with Quadratic Objectives

In this section we consider some other interesting economic applications of optimization theory when there are two variables. Versions of the first example have already appeared in Example 13.1.5 and Problem 13.2.4.

EXAMPLE 1   (**Discriminating Monopolist**) Consider a firm that sells a product in two isolated geographical areas. If it wants to, it can then charge different prices in the two different areas because what is sold in one area cannot easily be resold in the other. As an example, it seems that express mail or courier services find it possible to charge much higher prices in Europe than they can in North America. Another example—pharmaceutical firms often charge much more for the same medication in the USA than they do in Europe or Canada.

Suppose that such a firm also has some monopoly power to influence the different prices it faces in the two separate markets by adjusting the quantity it sells in each. Economists generally use the term "discriminating monopolist" to describe a firm having this power.

Faced with two such isolated markets, the discriminating monopolist has two independent demand curves. Suppose that, in inverse form, these are

$$P_1 = a_1 - b_1 Q_1, \qquad P_2 = a_2 - b_2 Q_2 \qquad (*)$$

for market areas 1 and 2, respectively. Suppose, too, that the total cost is proportional to total production:[2]

$$C(Q) = \alpha(Q_1 + Q_2)$$

As a function of Q_1 and Q_2, total profits are

$$\begin{aligned} \pi(Q_1, Q_2) &= P_1 Q_1 + P_2 Q_2 - \alpha(Q_1 + Q_2) \\ &= (a_1 - b_1 Q_1)Q_1 + (a_2 - b_2 Q_2)Q_2 - \alpha(Q_1 + Q_2) \\ &= (a_1 - \alpha)Q_1 + (a_2 - \alpha)Q_2 - b_1 Q_1^2 - b_2 Q_2^2 \end{aligned}$$

---

[2] It is true that this cost function neglects transport costs. But the point to be made is that, even though supplies to the two areas are perfect substitutes in production, the monopolist will generally be able to earn higher profits by charging different prices, if this is allowed.

We want to find the values of $Q_1 \geq 0$ and $Q_2 \geq 0$ that maximize profits. The first-order conditions are

$$\pi_1'(Q_1, Q_2) = (a_1 - \alpha) - 2b_1Q_1 = 0, \qquad \pi_2'(Q_1, Q_2) = (a_2 - \alpha) - 2b_2Q_2 = 0$$

with the solutions

$$Q_1^* = (a_1 - \alpha)/2b_1, \qquad Q_2^* = (a_2 - \alpha)/2b_2$$

Furthermore, $\pi_{11}''(Q_1, Q_2) = -2b_1$, $\pi_{12}''(Q_1, Q_2) = 0$, and $\pi_{22}''(Q_1, Q_2) = -2b_2$. Hence, for all (Q_1, Q_2)

$$\pi_{11}'' \leq 0, \qquad \pi_{22}'' \leq 0, \qquad \text{and} \qquad \pi_{11}''\pi_{22}'' - (\pi_{12}'')^2 = 4b_1b_2 \geq 0$$

We conclude from Theorem 13.2.1 that if Q_1^* and Q_2^* are both positive, implying that (Q_1^*, Q_2^*) is an interior point in the domain of π, then the pair (Q_1^*, Q_2^*) really does maximize profits.

The corresponding prices can be found by inserting these values in (∗) to get

$$P_1^* = a_1 - b_1Q_1^* = \tfrac{1}{2}(a_1 + \alpha), \qquad P_2^* = a_2 - b_2Q_2^* = \tfrac{1}{2}(a_2 + \alpha)$$

The maximum profit is

$$\pi^* = \frac{(a_1 - \alpha)^2}{4b_1} + \frac{(a_2 - \alpha)^2}{4b_2}$$

Both demands Q_1^* and Q_2^* are positive provided $a_1 > \alpha$ and $a_2 > \alpha$. In this case, P_1^* and P_2^* are both greater than α. This implies that there is no "dumping", with the price in one market less than the cost α. Nor is there any "cross-subsidy", with the losses due to dumping in one market being subsidized out of profits in the other market. It is notable that the optimal prices are independent of b_1 and b_2. More important, note that the prices are *not* the same in the two markets, except in the special case when $a_1 = a_2$. Indeed, $P_1^* > P_2^*$ if and only if $a_1 > a_2$. This says that the price is higher in the market where consumers are willing to pay a higher price for each unit when the quantity is close to zero.

EXAMPLE 2   Suppose that the monopolist in Example 1 has the demand functions

$$P_1 = 100 - Q_1, \qquad P_2 = 80 - Q_2$$

and that the cost function is $C = 6(Q_1 + Q_2)$.

(a) How much should be sold in the two markets to maximize profits? What are the corresponding prices?

(b) How much profit is lost if it becomes illegal to discriminate?

(c) The authorities in market 1 impose a tax of t per unit sold in market 1. Discuss the consequences.

Solution:

(a) Here $a_1 = 100$, $a_2 = 80$, $b_1 = b_2 = 1$, and $\alpha = 6$. Example 1 gives the answers

$$Q_1^* = (100 - 6)/2 = 47, \quad Q_2^* = 37, \quad P_1^* = \tfrac{1}{2}(100 + 6) = 53, \quad P_2^* = 43$$

The corresponding profit is $P_1^* Q_1^* + P_2^* Q_2^* - 6(Q_1^* + Q_2^*) = 3578$.

(b) If price discrimination is not permitted, then $P_1 = P_2 = P$, and $Q_1 = 100 - P$, $Q_2 = 80 - P$, with total demand $Q = Q_1 + Q_2 = 180 - 2P$. Then $P = 90 - \tfrac{1}{2}Q$, so profits are

$$\pi = \left(90 - \tfrac{1}{2}Q\right)Q - 6Q = 84Q - \tfrac{1}{2}Q^2$$

This has a maximum at $Q = 84$ when $P = 48$. The corresponding profit is now 3528, so the loss in profit is $3578 - 3528 = 50$.

(c) With the introduction of the tax, the new profit function is

$$\hat{\pi} = (100 - Q_1)Q_1 + (80 - Q_2)Q_2 - 6(Q_1 + Q_2) - t Q_1$$

We easily see that this has a maximum at $\hat{Q}_1 = 47 - \tfrac{1}{2}t$, $\hat{Q}_2 = 37$, with corresponding prices $\hat{P}_1 = 53 + \tfrac{1}{2}t$, $\hat{P}_2 = 43$. The tax therefore has no influence on the sales in market 2, while the amount sold in market 1 is lowered and the price in market 1 goes up. The optimal profit is easily worked out:

$$\pi^* = (53 + \tfrac{1}{2}t)(47 - \tfrac{1}{2}t) + 43 \cdot 37 - 6(84 - \tfrac{1}{2}t) - t(47 - \tfrac{1}{2}t) = 3578 - 47t + \tfrac{1}{4}t^2$$

So introducing the tax makes the profit fall by $47t - \tfrac{1}{4}t^2$. The authorities in market 1 obtain a tax revenue which is

$$T = t\hat{Q}_1 = t(47 - \tfrac{1}{2}t) = 47t - \tfrac{1}{2}t^2$$

Thus we see that profits fall by $\tfrac{1}{4}t^2$ more than the tax revenue. This amount $\tfrac{1}{4}t^2$ represents the so-called deadweight loss from the tax.

A monopolistic firm faces a downward-sloping demand curve. A *discriminating monopolist* such as in Example 1 faces separate downward-sloping demand curves in two or more isolated markets. A *monopsonistic firm*, on the other hand, faces an upward-sloping supply curve for one or more of its factors of production. Then, by definition, a *discriminating monopsonist* faces two or more upward-sloping supply curves for different kinds of the same input—for example, workers of different race or gender. Of course, discrimination by race or gender is illegal in many countries. The following example, however, suggests one possible reason why firms might want to discriminate if they were allowed to.

EXAMPLE 3   (**Discriminating Monopsonist**)   Consider a firm using quantities L_1 and L_2 of two kinds of labour as its only inputs in order to produce output Q according to the simple production function

$$Q = L_1 + L_2$$

Thus, both output and labour supply are measured so that each unit of labour produces one unit of output. Note especially how the two kinds of labour are essentially indistinguishable, because each unit of each type makes an equal contribution to the firm's output. Suppose, however, that there are two segmented labour markets, with different inverse supply functions specifying the wage that must be paid to attract a given labour supply. Specifically, suppose that

$$w_1 = \alpha_1 + \beta_1 L_1, \qquad w_2 = \alpha_2 + \beta_2 L_2$$

Assume moreover that the firm is competitive in its output market, taking price P as fixed. Then the firm's profits are

$$\pi(L_1, L_2) = PQ - w_1 L_1 - w_2 L_2 = P(L_1 + L_2) - (\alpha_1 + \beta_1 L_1)L_1 - (\alpha_2 + \beta_2 L_2)L_2$$

$$= (P - \alpha_1)L_1 - \beta_1 L_1^2 + (P - \alpha_2)L_2 - \beta_2 L_2^2$$

The firm wants to maximize profits. The first-order conditions are

$$\pi_1'(L_1, L_2) = (P - \alpha_1) - 2\beta_1 L_1 = 0, \qquad \pi_2'(L_1, L_2) = (P - \alpha_2) - 2\beta_2 L_2 = 0$$

These have the solutions

$$L_1^* = \frac{P - \alpha_1}{2\beta_1}, \qquad L_2^* = \frac{P - \alpha_2}{2\beta_2}$$

It is easy to see that the conditions for maximum in Theorem 13.2.1 are satisfied, so that L_1^*, L_2^* really do maximize profits if $P > \alpha_1$ and $P > \alpha_2$. The maximum profit is

$$\pi^* = \frac{(P - \alpha_1)^2}{4\beta_1} + \frac{(P - \alpha_2)^2}{4\beta_2}$$

The corresponding wages are

$$w_1^* = \alpha_1 + \beta_1 L_1^* = \tfrac{1}{2}(P + \alpha_1), \qquad w_2^* = \alpha_2 + \beta_2 L_2^* = \tfrac{1}{2}(P + \alpha_2)$$

Hence, $w_1^* = w_2^*$ only if $\alpha_1 = \alpha_2$. Generally, the wage is higher for the type of labour that demands a higher wage for very low levels of labour supply—perhaps this is the type of labour with better job prospects elsewhere.

EXAMPLE 4   (**Econometrics: Linear Regression**)   Empirical economics is concerned with analysing data in order to try to discern some pattern that helps in understanding the past, and possibly in predicting the future. For example, price and quantity data for a particular commodity such as natural gas may be used in order to try to estimate a demand curve. This might then be used to predict how demand will respond to future price changes. The most commonly used technique for estimating such a curve is *linear regression*.

Suppose it is thought that variable y—say, the quantity demanded—depends upon variable x—say, price or income. Suppose that we have observations (x_t, y_t) of both variables at times $t = 1, 2, \ldots, T$. Then the technique of linear regression seeks to fit a linear function

$$y = \alpha + \beta x$$

to the data, as indicated in Fig. 1.

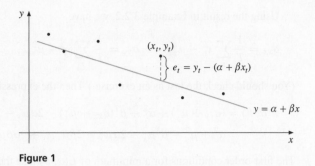

Figure 1

Of course, an exact fit is possible only if there exist numbers α and β for which $y_t = \alpha + \beta x_t$ for $t = 1, 2, \ldots, T$. This is rarely possible. Generally, however α and β may be chosen, one has instead

$$y_t = \alpha + \beta x_t + e_t, \qquad t = 1, 2, \ldots, T$$

where e_t is an *error* or *disturbance* term. Obviously, one hopes that the errors will be small, on average. So the parameters α and β are chosen to make the errors as "small as possible", somehow. One idea would be to make the sum $\sum_{t=1}^{T}(y_t - \alpha - \beta x_t)$ equal to zero. However, in this case, large positive discrepancies would cancel large negative discrepancies. Indeed, the sum of errors could be zero even though the line is very far from giving a perfect or even a good fit. We must somehow prevent large positive errors from cancelling large negative errors. Usually, this is done by minimizing the quadratic "loss" function

$$L(\alpha, \beta) = \frac{1}{T} \sum_{t=1}^{T} e_t^2 = \frac{1}{T} \sum_{t=1}^{T}(y_t - \alpha - \beta x_t)^2 \quad \textbf{(loss function)} \qquad (*)$$

which equals the mean (or average) square error. Expanding the square gives[3]

$$L(\alpha, \beta) = \frac{1}{T} \sum_t (y_t^2 + \alpha^2 + \beta^2 x_t^2 - 2\alpha y_t - 2\beta x_t y_t + 2\alpha\beta x_t)$$

This is a quadratic function of α and β. We shall show how to derive the *ordinary least-squares* estimates of α and β. To do so it helps to introduce some standard notation. Write

$$\mu_x = \frac{x_1 + \cdots + x_T}{T} = \frac{1}{T} \sum_t x_t, \qquad \mu_y = \frac{y_1 + \cdots + y_T}{T} = \frac{1}{T} \sum_t y_t$$

for the *statistical means* of x_t and y_t, and

$$\sigma_{xx} = \frac{1}{T} \sum_t (x_t - \mu_x)^2, \ \sigma_{yy} = \frac{1}{T} \sum_t (y_t - \mu_y)^2, \ \sigma_{xy} = \frac{1}{T} \sum_t (x_t - \mu_x)(y_t - \mu_y)$$

for their *statistical variances*, as well as their *covariance*, respectively. In what follows, we shall assume that the x_t *are not all equal*. Then, in particular, $\sigma_{xx} > 0$.

---

[3] From now on, we often use $\sum_t$ to denote $\sum_{t=1}^{T}$.

Using the result in Example 3.2.2, we have

$$\sigma_{xx} = \frac{1}{T} \sum_t x_t^2 - \mu_x^2, \qquad \sigma_{yy} = \frac{1}{T} \sum_t y_t^2 - \mu_y^2, \qquad \sigma_{xy} = \frac{1}{T} \sum_t x_t y_t - \mu_x \mu_y$$

(You should check the last as an exercise.) Then the expression for $L(\alpha, \beta)$ becomes

$$
\begin{aligned}
L(\alpha, \beta) &= (\sigma_{yy} + \mu_y^2) + \alpha^2 + \beta^2(\sigma_{xx} + \mu_x^2) - 2\alpha\mu_y - 2\beta(\sigma_{xy} + \mu_x\mu_y) + 2\alpha\beta\mu_x \\
&= \alpha^2 + \mu_y^2 + \beta^2\mu_x^2 - 2\alpha\mu_y - 2\beta\mu_x\mu_y + 2\alpha\beta\mu_x + \beta^2\sigma_{xx} - 2\beta\sigma_{xy} + \sigma_{yy}
\end{aligned}
$$

The first-order conditions for a minimum of $L(\alpha, \beta)$ take the form

$$L_1'(\alpha, \beta) = 2\alpha - 2\mu_y + 2\beta\mu_x = 0$$

$$L_2'(\alpha, \beta) = 2\beta\mu_x^2 - 2\mu_x\mu_y + 2\alpha\mu_x + 2\beta\sigma_{xx} - 2\sigma_{xy} = 0$$

Note that $L_2'(\alpha, \beta) = \mu_x L_1'(\alpha, \beta) + 2\beta\sigma_{xx} - 2\sigma_{xy}$. So the values of α and β that make L stationary are given by

$$\hat{\beta} = \sigma_{xy}/\sigma_{xx}, \qquad \hat{\alpha} = \mu_y - \hat{\beta}\mu_x = \mu_y - (\sigma_{xy}/\sigma_{xx})\mu_x \qquad (**)$$

Furthermore, $L_{11}'' = 2$, $L_{12}'' = 2\mu_x$, $L_{22}'' = 2\mu_x^2 + 2\sigma_{xx}$. Thus $L_{11}'' \geq 0$, $L_{22}'' \geq 0$, and

$$L_{11}'' L_{22}'' - (L_{12}'')^2 = 2(2\mu_x^2 + 2\sigma_{xx}) - (2\mu_x)^2 = 4\sigma_{xx} = 4T^{-1} \sum_t (x_t - \mu_x)^2 \geq 0$$

We conclude that the conditions in Theorem 13.2.1(b) are satisfied, and therefore the pair $(\hat{\alpha}, \hat{\beta})$ given by $(**)$ minimizes $L(\alpha, \beta)$. The problem is then completely solved:

The straight line $y = \hat{\alpha} + \hat{\beta}x$, with $\hat{\alpha}$ and $\hat{\beta}$ given by $(**)$, is the one that best fits the observations $(x_1, y_1), (x_2, y_2), \ldots, (x_T, y_T)$, in the sense of minimizing the mean square error in $(*)$.

Note in particular that this estimated straight line passes through the mean (μ_x, μ_y) of the observed pairs (x_t, y_t), $t = 1, \ldots, T$. Also, with a little bit of tedious algebra we obtain

$$L(\alpha, \beta) = (\alpha + \beta\mu_x - \mu_y)^2 + \sigma_{xx}(\beta - \sigma_{xy}/\sigma_{xx})^2 + (\sigma_{xx}\sigma_{yy} - \sigma_{xy}^2)/\sigma_{xx}$$

The first two terms on the right are always nonnegative, and with $\alpha = \hat{\alpha}$ and $\beta = \hat{\beta}$, they are zero, confirming that $\hat{\alpha}$ and $\hat{\beta}$ do give the minimum value of $L(\alpha, \beta)$.

PROBLEMS FOR SECTION 13.4

1. (a) Suppose that the monopolist in Example 1 faces the demand functions

    $$P_1 = 200 - 2Q_1, \qquad P_2 = 180 - 4Q_2$$

    and that the cost function is $C = 20(Q_1 + Q_2)$. How much should be sold in the two markets to maximize total profit? What are the corresponding prices?

    (b) How much profit is lost if it becomes illegal to discriminate?

    (c) Discuss the consequences of imposing a tax of 5 per unit on the product sold in market 1.

(SM) **2.** A firm produces and sells a product in two separate markets. When the price in market A is p per ton, and the price in market B is q per ton, the demand in tons per week in the two markets are, respectively,

$$Q_A = a - bp, \qquad Q_B = c - dq$$

The cost function is $C(Q_A, Q_B) = \alpha + \beta(Q_A + Q_B)$, and all constants are positive.

(a) Find the firm's profit π as a function of the prices p and q, and then find the pair (p^*, q^*) that maximizes profits.

(b) Suppose it becomes unlawful to discriminate by price, so that the firm must charge the same price in the two markets. What price $\hat{p}$ will now maximize profits?

(c) In the case $\beta = 0$, find the firm's loss of profit if it has to charge the same price in both markets. Comment.

3. In Example 1, discuss the effects of a tax imposed in market 1 of t per unit of Q_1.

(SM) **4.** The following table shows the Norwegian gross national product (GNP) and spending on foreign aid (FA) for the period 1970–1973 (in millions of crowns).

Year	1970	1971	1972	1973
GNP	79 835	89 112	97 339	110 156
FA	274	307	436	524

Growth of both GNP and FA was almost exponential during the period. So, approximately:

$$\text{GNP} = Ae^{a(t-t_0)}, \qquad t_0 = 1970$$

Define $x = t - t_0$ and $b = \ln A$. Then $\ln(\text{GNP}) = ax + b$. On the basis of the table above, one gets the following

Year	1970	1971	1972	1973
$y = \ln(\text{GNP})$	11.29	11.40	11.49	11.61

(a) Using the method of least squares, determine the straight line $y = ax + b$ which best fits the data in the last table.

(b) Repeat the method above to estimate c and d, where $\ln(\text{FA}) = cx + d$.

(c) The Norwegian government had a stated goal of eventually giving 1% of its GNP as foreign aid. If the time trends of the two variables had continued as they did during the years 1970–1973, when would this goal have been reached?

(SM) **5. (Duopoly)** Each of two firms A and B produces its own brand of a commodity such as mineral water in amounts denoted by x and y, which are sold at prices p and q per unit, respectively. Each firm determines its own price and produces exactly as much as is demanded. The demands for the two brands are given by

$$x = 29 - 5p + 4q, \qquad y = 16 + 4p - 6q$$

Firm A has total costs $5 + x$, whereas firm B has total costs $3 + 2y$. (Assume that the functions to be maximized have maxima, and at positive prices.)

(a) Initially, the two firms collude in order to maximize their combined profit, as one monopolist would. Find the prices (p, q), the production levels (x, y), and the profits of firms A and B.

(b) Then an anti-trust authority prohibits collusion, so each producer maximizes its own profit, taking the other's price as given.

If q is fixed, how will A choose p? (Find p as a function $p = p_A(q)$ of q.)

If p is fixed, how will B choose q? (Find q as a function $q = q_B(p)$ of p.)

(c) Under the assumptions in part (b), what constant equilibrium prices are possible? What are the production levels and profits in this case?

(d) Draw a diagram with p along the horizontal axis and q along the vertical axis, and draw the "reaction" curves $p_A(q)$ and $q_B(p)$. Show on the diagram how the two firms' prices change over time if A breaks the cooperation first by maximizing its profit, taking B's initial price as fixed, then B answers by maximizing its profit with A's price fixed, then A responds, and so on.

13.5   The Extreme Value Theorem

As with functions of one variable, it is easy to find examples of functions of several variables that do not have any maximum or minimum points. For providing sufficient conditions to ensure that extreme points do exist, however, the extreme value theorem (Theorem 8.4.1) was very useful for functions of one variable. It can be directly generalized to functions of several variables. In order to formulate the theorem, however, we need a few new concepts.

For many of the results concerning functions of one variable, it was important to distinguish between different kinds of domain for the functions. For functions of several variables, the distinction between different kinds of domain is no less important. In the one-variable case, most functions were defined over intervals, and there are not many different kinds of interval. For functions of several variables, however, there are many different kinds of domain. Fortunately, the distinctions that are relevant to the extreme value theorem can be made using only the concepts of open, closed, and bounded sets.

A point (a, b) is called an **interior point** of a set S in the plane if *there exists* a circle centred at (a, b) such that all points strictly inside the circle lie in S. (See Fig. 1.) A set is called **open** if it consists only of interior points. (See the second set illustrated in Fig. 1, where we indicate boundary points that belong to the set by a solid curve, and those that do not by a dashed curve.) The point (a, b) is called a **boundary point** of a set S if *every* circle centred at (a, b) contains points of S as well as points in its complement, as illustrated in the first figure. A boundary point of S does not necessarily lie in S. If S contains all its boundary points, then S is called **closed**. (See the third set in Fig. 1.) Note that a set that contains some but not all of its boundary points, like the last of those illustrated in Fig. 1, is neither open nor closed. In fact, a set is closed if and only if its complement is open.[4]

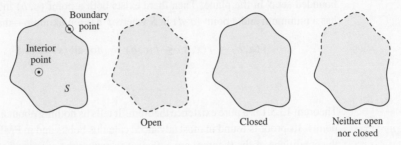

Figure 1

These illustrations give only very loose indications of what it means for a set to be either open or closed. Of course, if a set is not even precisely defined, it is impossible to decide conclusively whether it is open or closed.

In many of the optimization problems considered in economics, sets are defined by one or more inequalities, and boundary points occur where one or more of these inequalities are satisfied with equality. For instance, provided that p, q, and m are positive parameters, the (budget) set of points (x, y) that satisfy the inequalities

$$px + qy \leq m, \quad x \geq 0, \quad y \geq 0 \qquad (*)$$

is closed. This set is a triangle, as shown in Fig. 4.4.12. Its boundary consists of the three sides of the triangle. Each of the three sides corresponds to having one of the inequalities in (*) be satisfied with equality. On the other hand, the set that results from replacing $\leq$ by $<$ and $\geq$ by $>$ in (*) is open.

In general, if $g(x, y)$ is a continuous function and c is a real number, then the sets

$$\{(x, y) : g(x, y) \geq c\}, \qquad \{(x, y) : g(x, y) \leq c\}, \qquad \{(x, y) : g(x, y) = c\}$$

are all closed. If $\geq$ is replaced by $>$, or $\leq$ is replaced by $<$, or $=$ by $\neq$, then the corresponding set becomes open.

A set in the plane is **bounded** if the whole set is contained within a sufficiently large circle. The sets in Fig. 1 and the budget triangle in Fig. 4.4.12 are all bounded. On the other hand, the set of all (x, y) satisfying

$$x \geq 1 \quad \text{and} \quad y \geq 0$$

is a closed, but unbounded set. (See Fig. 11.1.1.) The set is closed because it contains all its boundary points. How would you characterize the set in Fig. 11.1.2? (In fact, it is neither open nor closed, but it is bounded.) A set in the plane that is both closed and bounded is often called **compact**.

We are now ready to formulate the main result in this section.

---

[4] In every day usage the words "open" and "closed" are antonyms: a shop is either open or closed. In topology, however, a set that contains some but not all its boundary points is neither open nor closed. See the last set in Fig. 1.

THEOREM 13.5.1 (EXTREME VALUE THEOREM)

Suppose the function $f(x, y)$ is continuous throughout a nonempty, closed and bounded set S in the plane. Then there exists both a point (a, b) in S where f has a minimum and a point (c, d) in S where f has a maximum—that is,

$$f(a, b) \leq f(x, y) \leq f(c, d) \qquad \text{for all } (x, y) \text{ in } S$$

Theorem 13.5.1 is a pure existence theorem. It tells us nothing about *how to find* the extreme points. Its proof is found in most advanced calculus books and in FMEA. Also, even though the conditions of the theorem are *sufficient* to ensure the existence of extreme points, they are far from necessary. (See Note 8.4.1.)

Finding Maxima and Minima

Sections 13.1 and 13.2 presented some simple cases where we could find the maximum and minimum points of a function of two variables by finding its stationary points. The procedure set out in the following frame covers many additional optimization problems.

FINDING MAXIMA AND MINIMA

Find the maximum and minimum values of a differentiable function $f(x, y)$ defined on a closed, bounded set S in the plane.

Solution:

(I) Find all stationary points of f in the interior of S.

(II) Find the largest value and the smallest value of f on the boundary of S, along with the associated points. (If it is convenient to subdivide the boundary into several pieces, find the largest and smallest value on each piece of the boundary.)   (1)

(III) Compute the values of the function at all the points found in (I) and (II). The largest function value is the maximum value of f in S. The smallest function value is the minimum value of f in S.

We try out this procedure on the function whose graph is depicted in Fig. 2 below. (Because the function is not specified analytically, we can only give a rough geometric argument.) The function has a rectangular domain S of points (x, y) in the xy-plane. The only stationary point of f it includes is (x_0, y_0), which corresponds to the point P of the graph. The boundary of S consists of four straight-line segments. The point R vertically above one corner point of S represents the maximum value of f along the boundary; similarly, Q represents the minimum value of f along the boundary. The only candidates for a maximum/minimum are, therefore, the three points P, Q, and R. By comparing the values of f at these points, we see that P represents the minimum value, whereas R represents the maximum value of f in S.

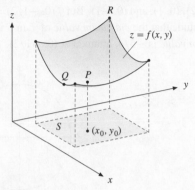

Figure 2

As an aspiring economist you will be glad to hear that most optimization problems in economics, especially those appearing in textbooks, rarely create enough difficulties to call for the full recipe. Usually there is an interior optimum that can be found by equating all the first-order partial derivatives to zero. Conditions that are sufficient for this easier approach to work were already discussed in Section 13.2. Nevertheless, we consider an example of a harder problem which illustrates how the whole recipe is sometimes needed. This recipe is also needed in several of the problems for this section. In particular, Problem 3 gives an economic example.

EXAMPLE 1   Find the extreme values for $f(x, y)$ defined over S when

$$f(x, y) = x^2 + y^2 + y - 1, \qquad S = \{(x, y) : x^2 + y^2 \le 1\}$$

Solution: The set S consists of all the points on or inside the circle of radius 1 centred at the origin, as shown in Fig. 3. The continuous function f will attain both a maximum and a minimum over S, by the extreme value theorem.

According to the preceding recipe, we start by finding all the stationary points in the interior of S. These stationary points satisfy the two equations

$$f_1'(x, y) = 2x = 0, \qquad f_2'(x, y) = 2y + 1 = 0$$

So $(x, y) = (0, -1/2)$ is the only stationary point, and it is in the interior of S, with $f(0, -1/2) = -5/4$.

The boundary of S consists of the circle $x^2 + y^2 = 1$. Note that if (x, y) lies on this circle, then in particular both x and y lie in the interval $[-1, 1]$. Inserting $x^2 + y^2 = 1$ into the expression for $f(x, y)$ shows that, *along the boundary of S*, the value of f is determined by the following function of one variable:

$$g(y) = 1 + y - 1 = y, \qquad y \in [-1, 1]$$

The maximum value of g is 1 for $y = 1$, and then $x = 0$. The minimum value is -1 when $y = -1$, and then again $x = 0$.

We have now found the only three possible candidates for extreme points, namely, $(0, -1/2)$, $(0, 1)$, and $(0, -1)$. But $f(0, -1/2) = -5/4$, $f(0, 1) = 1$, and $f(0, -1) = -1$. We conclude that the *maximum value* of f in S is 1, which is attained at $(0, 1)$, whereas the *minimum value* is $-5/4$, attained at $(0, -1/2)$.

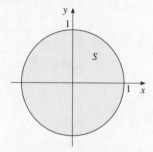

Figure 3 The domain in Example 1

PROBLEMS FOR SECTION 13.5

1. Let $f(x, y) = 4x - 2x^2 - 2y^2$, $S = \{(x, y) : x^2 + y^2 \leq 25\}$.

   (a) Compute $f_1'(x, y)$ and $f_2'(x, y)$, then find the only stationary point for f.

   (b) Find the extreme points for f over S.

SM 2. Find the maximum and minimum points for the following:

   (a) $f(x, y) = x^3 + y^3 - 9xy + 27$ subject to $0 \leq x \leq 4$ and $0 \leq y \leq 4$.

   (b) $f(x, y) = x^2 + 2y^2 - x$ subject to $x^2 + y^2 \leq 1$.

SM 3. In one study of the quantities x and y of natural gas that Western Europe should import from Norway and Siberia, respectively, it was assumed that the benefits were given by the function $f(x, y) = 9x + 8y - 6(x + y)^2$. (The term $-6(x + y)^2$ occurs because the world price of natural gas rises as total imports increase.) Because of capacity constraints, x and y must satisfy $0 \leq x \leq 5$ and $0 \leq y \leq 3$. Finally, for political reasons, it was felt that imports from Norway should not provide too small a fraction of total imports at the margin, so that $x \geq 2(y - 1)$, or equivalently $-x + 2y \leq 2$. Thus, the optimization problem was cast as

$$\max \ f(x, y) = 9x + 8y - 6(x + y)^2 \quad \text{subject to } 0 \leq x \leq 5, \ 0 \leq y \leq 3, \ -x + 2y \leq 2$$

   In the xy-plane, draw the set S of all points satisfying the three constraints, and then solve the problem.

4. (a) Determine values of the constants a, b, and c such that $f(x, y) = ax^2y + bxy + 2xy^2 + c$ has a local minimum at the point $(2/3, 1/3)$ with local minimum value $-1/9$.

   (b) With the values of a, b, and c found in part (a), find the maximum and minimum values of f over $S = \{(x, y) : x \geq 0, y \geq 0, 2x + y \leq 4\}$.

⑤ⓜ **5.** (a) Find all stationary points of $f(x, y) = xe^{-x}(y^2 - 4y)$ and classify them by using the second-derivative test.

(b) Show that f has neither a global maximum nor a global minimum.

(c) Let $S = \{(x, y) : 0 \leq x \leq 5, \ 0 \leq y \leq 4\}$. Prove that f has global maximum and minimum points in S and find them.

(d) Find the slope of the tangent to the level curve $xe^{-x}(y^2 - 4y) = e - 4$ at the point where $x = 1$ and $y = 4 - e$.

6. Which of the following sets are open, closed, bounded, or compact?

(a) $\{(x, y) : 5x^2 + 5y^2 \leq 9\}$ (b) $\{(x, y) : x^2 + y^2 > 9\}$ (c) $\{(x, y) : x^2 + y^2 \leq 9\}$

(d) $\{(x, y) : 2x + 5y \geq 6\}$ (e) $\{(x, y) : 5x + 8y = 8\}$ (f) $\{(x, y) : 5x + 8y > 8\}$

HARDER PROBLEM

7. Give an example of a discontinuous function g of one variable such that the set $\{x : g(x) \leq 1\}$ is not closed.

13.6 Three or More Variables

So far this chapter has considered optimization problems for functions of two variables. In order to understand modern economic theory we definitely have to extend the analysis to an arbitrary number of variables.

The extensions of the definitions of maximum and minimum points, extreme points, etc. are almost obvious. If $f(\mathbf{x}) = f(x_1, \ldots, x_n)$ is a function of n variables defined over a set S in $\mathbb{R}^n$, then $\mathbf{c} = (c_1, \ldots, c_n)$ is a (global) **maximum point** for f in S if

$$f(\mathbf{x}) \leq f(\mathbf{c}) \qquad \text{for all } \mathbf{x} \text{ in } S \tag{1}$$

Suppose that f is a function of n variables defined over a set S in $\mathbb{R}^n$ and that $f(\mathbf{x}) \leq f(\mathbf{c})$ for all $\mathbf{x}$ in S, so $\mathbf{c}$ maximizes f over S. Then $-f(\mathbf{x}) \geq -f(\mathbf{c})$ for all $\mathbf{x}$ in S. Thus, $\mathbf{c}$ maximizes f over S if and only if $\mathbf{c}$ minimizes $-f$ over S. We can use this simple observation to convert maximization problems into minimization problems and vice versa. (Recall the one-variable illustration in Fig. 8.1.1.)

The concepts of interior and boundary points, and of open, closed, and bounded sets, are also easy to generalize. First, define the **distance** between the points $\mathbf{x} = (x_1, \ldots, x_n)$ and $\mathbf{y} = (y_1, \ldots, y_n)$ in $\mathbb{R}^n$ by

$$\|\mathbf{x} - \mathbf{y}\| = \sqrt{(x_1 - y_1)^2 + (x_2 - y_2)^2 + \cdots + (x_n - y_n)^2} \tag{2}$$

For $n = 1, 2$ and 3 this reduces to the distance concept discussed earlier. In particular, if $\mathbf{y} = \mathbf{0}$, then

$$\|\mathbf{x}\| = \sqrt{x_1^2 + x_2^2 + \cdots + x_n^2}$$

is the distance between $\mathbf{x}$ and the origin. The number $\|\mathbf{x}\|$ is also called the **norm** or **length** of the vector $\mathbf{x}$.

An **open (n-dimensional) ball** with centre at $\mathbf{a} = (a_1, \ldots, a_n)$ and radius r is the set of all points $\mathbf{x} = (x_1, \ldots, x_n)$ such that $\|\mathbf{x} - \mathbf{a}\| < r$. The definitions in Section 13.5 of interior point, open set, boundary point, closed set, bounded set, and compact set all become valid for set · in $\mathbb{R}^n$ provided we replace the word "circle" by "ball".

If $g(\mathbf{x}) = g(x_1, \ldots, x_n)$ is a continuous function, and c is a real number, then each of the three sets

$$\{\mathbf{x} : g(\mathbf{x}) \geq c\}, \qquad \{\mathbf{x} : g(\mathbf{x}) \leq c\}, \qquad \{\mathbf{x} : g(\mathbf{x}) = c\}$$

is closed. If $\geq$ is replaced by $>$, $\leq$ by $<$, or $=$ by $\neq$, the corresponding set is open.

If A is an arbitrary set in $\mathbb{R}^n$, we define the **interior** of A as the set of interior points in A. If A is open, the interior of A is equal to the set itself.[5]

A **stationary** (or **critical**) **point** for a function of n variables is a point where all the first-order derivatives are 0. We have the following important generalization of Theorem 13.1.1:

THEOREM 13.6.1 (NECESSARY FIRST-ORDER CONDITIONS)

Suppose f is defined in a set S in $\mathbb{R}^n$ and let $\mathbf{c} = (c_1, \ldots, c_n)$ be an interior point in S where f is differentiable. A necessary condition for $\mathbf{c}$ to be a maximum or minimum point for f is that $\mathbf{c}$ is a stationary point for f—that is, $\mathbf{x} = \mathbf{c}$ satisfies the n equations

$$f_i'(\mathbf{x}) = 0, \qquad i = 1, \ldots, n \qquad \textbf{(first-order conditions}, \text{ or FOCs)}$$

Proof: Keep i ($1 \leq i \leq n$) fixed and define $g(x_i) = f(c_1, \ldots, c_{i-1}, x_i, c_{i+1}, \ldots, c_n)$, whose domain consists of those x_i such that $(c_1, \ldots, c_{i-1}, x_i, c_{i+1}, \ldots, c_n)$ belongs to S. If $\mathbf{c} = (c_1, \ldots, c_n)$ is a maximum (or minimum) point for f, then the function g of one variable must attain a maximum (or minimum) at $x_i = c_i$. Because $\mathbf{c}$ is an interior point of S, it follows that c_i is also an interior point in the domain of g. Hence, according to Theorem 8.1.1, we must have $g'(c_i) = 0$. But $g'(c_i) = f_i'(c_1, \ldots, c_n)$, so the conclusion follows.   ∎

The extreme value theorem is valid also for functions of n variables:

THEOREM 13.6.2 (EXTREME VALUE THEOREM)

Suppose the function f is continuous throughout a nonempty, closed and bounded set S in $\mathbb{R}^n$. Then there exist both a point $\mathbf{d}$ in S where f has a minimum and a point $\mathbf{c}$ in S where f has a maximum—that is,

$$f(\mathbf{d}) \leq f(\mathbf{x}) \leq f(\mathbf{c}) \qquad \text{for all } \mathbf{x} \text{ in } S$$

---

[5] These topological definitions and results are dealt with in some detail in FMEA.

If $f(\mathbf{x})$ is defined over a set S in $\mathbb{R}^n$, then the maximum and minimum points (if there are any) must lie either in the interior of S or on the boundary of S. According to Theorem 13.6.1, if f is differentiable, then any maximum or minimum point in the interior must satisfy the first-order conditions. Consequently, the recipe in (13.5.1) is also valid for any function of n variables defined on a closed and bounded set in $\mathbb{R}^n$.

Both the local and the global second-order conditions for the two-variable case can be generalized to functions of n variables, though they become considerably more complicated. This will be discussed in FMEA.

A Useful Result

A simple result, which is nevertheless of considerable interest in theoretical economics, is often expressed as follows: *Maximizing a function is equivalent to maximizing a strictly increasing transformation of that function.* For instance, suppose we want to find all pairs (x, y) that maximize $f(x, y)$ over a set S in the xy-plane. Then we can just as well try to find those (x, y) that maximize over S any one of the following objective functions:

$$\text{(i) } af(x, y) + b \quad (a > 0) \qquad \text{(ii) } e^{f(x,y)} \qquad \text{(iii) } \ln f(x, y)$$

(In case (iii), we must assume that $f(x, y) > 0$ over S.) The maximum *points* are exactly the same. But the maximum *values* are, of course, quite different. As a concrete example, because the transformation $u \mapsto \ln u$ is strictly increasing when $u > 0$, the problem

$$\text{maximize } e^{x^2 + 2xy^2 - y^3} \text{ subject to } (x, y) \in S$$

has the same solutions for x and y as the problem

$$\text{maximize } x^2 + 2xy^2 - y^3 \text{ subject to } (x, y) \in S$$

In general, it is easy to prove the following result:

THEOREM 13.6.3

Suppose $f(\mathbf{x}) = f(x_1, \ldots, x_n)$ is defined over a set S in $\mathbb{R}^n$, let F be a function of one variable defined over the range of f, and let $\mathbf{c}$ be a point in S. Define g over S by

$$g(\mathbf{x}) = F(f(\mathbf{x}))$$

Then:

(a) If F is increasing and $\mathbf{c}$ maximizes (minimizes) f over S, then $\mathbf{c}$ also maximizes (minimizes) g over S.

(b) If F is strictly increasing, then $\mathbf{c}$ maximizes (minimizes) f over S if and only if $\mathbf{c}$ maximizes (minimizes) g over S.

Proof: (For the maximization case—the argument in the minimization case is entirely similar.)

(a) Because **c** maximizes f over S, we have $f(\mathbf{x}) \le f(\mathbf{c})$ for all **x** in S. But then $g(\mathbf{x}) = F(f(\mathbf{x})) \le F(f(\mathbf{c})) = g(\mathbf{c})$ for all **x** in S, because F is increasing. It follows that **c** maximizes g over S.

(b) If F is also strictly increasing and $f(\mathbf{x}) > f(\mathbf{c})$, then it must be true that $g(\mathbf{x}) = F(f(\mathbf{x})) > F(f(\mathbf{c})) = g(\mathbf{c})$. So $g(\mathbf{x}) \le g(\mathbf{c})$ for all **x** in S implies that $f(\mathbf{x}) \le f(\mathbf{c})$ for all **x** in S. ∎

NOTE 1   The proof of Theorem 13.6.3 is extremely simple. No continuity or differentiability assumptions are required. Instead, the proof is based only on the concepts of maximum/minimum, and of increasing/strictly increasing functions. Some people appear to distrust such simple, direct arguments and replace them by inefficient or even insufficient arguments based on "differentiating everything in sight" in order to use first- or second-order conditions. Such distrust merely makes matters unnecessarily complicated and risks introducing errors.

PROBLEMS FOR SECTION 13.6

1. Each of the following functions has a maximum point. Find it.

(a) $f(x, y, z) = 2x - x^2 + 10y - y^2 + 3 - z^2$

(b) $f(x, y, z) = 3 - x^2 - 2y^2 - 3z^2 - 2xy - 2xz$

2. (a) Suppose $f(x) = e^{-x^2}$ and $F(u) = \ln u$. Verify that $f(x)$ has a maximum at $x = 0$ if and only if $g(x) = F(f(x))$ has a maximum at $x = 0$.

(b) Suppose $f(x) = e^{-x^2}$ and $F(u) = 5$. Then $g(x) = F(f(x)) = 5$. Explain why this example shows that implication (a) in Theorem 13.6.3 cannot be reversed. (Recall that we call a constant function increasing.)

3. Suppose $g(\mathbf{x}) = F(f(\mathbf{x}))$ where $f : \mathbb{R}^n \to \mathbb{R}$ and $F : \mathbb{R} \to \mathbb{R}$ are differentiable functions, with $F' \ne 0$ everywhere. Prove that **x** is a stationary point for f if and only if it is a stationary point for g.

(SM) **4.** Find the first-order partial derivatives of the function of three variables given by

$$f(x, y, z) = -2x^3 + 15x^2 - 36x + 2y - 3z + \int_y^z e^{t^2}\, dt$$

Then determine its eight stationary points.

5. Suggest how to simplify the following problems:

(a) max $\frac{1}{2}\left(e^{x^2+y^2-2x} - e^{-(x^2+y^2-2x)}\right)$ subject to $(x, y) \in S$

(b) max $A x_1^{a_1} \cdots x_n^{a_n}$ subject to $x_1 + x_2 + \cdots + x_n = 1$

Assume in (b) that $A > 0$ and $x_1 > 0, \ldots, x_n > 0$.

13.7 Comparative Statics and the Envelope Theorem

Optimization problems in economics usually involve maximizing or minimizing functions which depend not only on endogenous variables one can choose, but also on one or more exogenous parameters like prices, tax rates, income levels, etc. Although these parameters are held constant during the optimization, they vary according to the economic situation. For example, we may calculate a firm's profit-maximizing input and output quantities while treating the prices it faces as parameters. But then we may want to know how the optimal quantities respond to changes in those prices, or in whatever other exogenous parameters affect the problem we are considering.

Consider first the following simple problem. A function f depends on a single variable x as well as on a single parameter r. We wish to maximize or minimize $f(x, r)$ w.r.t. x while keeping r constant:

$$\max(\min)_x \ f(x, r)$$

The value of x that maximizes (minimizes) f will usually depend on r, so we denote it by $x^*(r)$. Inserting $x^*(r)$ into $f(x, r)$, we obtain

$$f^*(r) = f(x^*(r), r) \quad \text{(the \textbf{value function})}$$

What happens to the value function as r changes? Assuming that $f^*(r)$ is differentiable, the chain rule yields

$$\frac{df^*(r)}{dr} = f_1'(x^*(r), r)\frac{dx^*(r)}{dr} + f_2'(x^*(r), r)$$

If $f(x, r)$ has an extreme point at an interior point $x^*(r)$ in the domain of variation for x, then $f_1'(x^*(r), r) = 0$. It follows that

$$\frac{df^*(r)}{dr} = f_2'(x^*(r), r) \tag{1}$$

Note that when r is changed, then $f^*(r)$ changes for two reasons. First, a change in r changes the value of f^* directly because r is the second variable in $f(x, r)$. Second, a change in r changes the value of the function $x^*(r)$, and hence $f(x^*(r), r)$ is changed indirectly. Formula (1) shows that the total effect is simply found by computing the partial derivative of $f(x^*(r), r)$ w.r.t. r, ignoring entirely the indirect effect of the dependence of x^* on r. At first sight, this seems very surprising. On further reflection, however, you may realize that the first-order condition for $x^*(r)$ to maximize $f(x, r)$ w.r.t. x implies that any small change in x, whether or not it is induced by a small change in r, must have a negligible effect on the value of $f(x^*, r)$.

EXAMPLE 1   Suppose that when a firm produces and sells x units of a commodity, it has revenue $R(x) = rx$, while the cost is $C(x) = x^2$, where r is a positive parameter. The profit is then

$$\pi(x, r) = R(x) - C(x) = rx - x^2$$

Find the optimal choice x^* of x, and verify (1) in this case.

Solution: The quadratic profit function has a maximum when $\pi'_1 = r - 2x = 0$, that is for $x^* = r/2$. So the maximum profit as a function of r is given by $\pi^*(r) = rx^* - (x^*)^2 = r(r/2) - (r/2)^2 = r^2/4$, and then $d\pi^*/dr = r/2$. Using formula (1) is much more direct: because $\pi'_2(x, r) = x$, it implies that $d\pi^*/dr = \pi'_2(x^*(r), r) = x^*(r) = \frac{1}{2}r$.

EXAMPLE 2   In Example 8.6.5 we studied a firm with the profit function $\hat{\pi}(Q, t) = R(Q) - C(Q) - tQ$, where t denoted a tax per unit produced. Let $Q^* = Q^*(t)$ denote the optimal choice of Q as a function of the tax rate t, and let $\pi^*(t)$ be the corresponding value function. Because $\hat{\pi}'_2 = -Q$, formula (1) yields

$$\frac{d\pi^*(t)}{dt} = \hat{\pi}'_2(Q^*(t), t) = -Q^*(t)$$

which is the same result found earlier.

It is easy to generalize (1) to the case with many choice variables and many parameters. We let $\mathbf{x} = (x_1, \ldots, x_n)$, and $\mathbf{r} = (r_1, \ldots, r_k)$. Then we can formulate the following result:

ENVELOPE THEOREM

If $f^*(\mathbf{r}) = \max_{\mathbf{x}} f(\mathbf{x}, \mathbf{r})$ and if $\mathbf{x}^*(\mathbf{r})$ is the value of $\mathbf{x}$ that maximizes $f(\mathbf{x}, \mathbf{r})$, then

$$\frac{\partial f^*(\mathbf{r})}{\partial r_j} = \left[\frac{\partial f(\mathbf{x}, \mathbf{r})}{\partial r_j} \right]_{\mathbf{x}=\mathbf{x}^*(\mathbf{r})} , \quad j = 1, \ldots, k \qquad (2)$$

provided that the partial derivative exists.

Again, $f^*(\mathbf{r})$ is the **value function**. It is easy to prove (2) by using the first-order conditions to eliminate other terms, as in the argument for (1). The same equality holds if we minimize $f(\mathbf{x}, \mathbf{r})$ w.r.t. $\mathbf{x}$ instead of maximize (or even if $\mathbf{x}^*(\mathbf{r})$ is any stationary point).

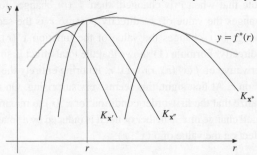

Figure 1   The curve $y = f^*(r)$ is the envelope of all the curves $y = f(\mathbf{x}, r)$

Figure 1 illustrates (2) in the case where there is only one parameter r. For each fixed value of $\mathbf{x}$ there is a curve $K_{\mathbf{x}}$ in the ry-plane, given by the equation $y = f(\mathbf{x}, r)$. Figure 1 shows some of these curves together with the graph of $y = f^*(r)$. For all $\mathbf{x}$ and all r we have $f(\mathbf{x}, r) \leq \max_{\mathbf{x}} f(\mathbf{x}, r) = f^*(r)$. It follows that none of the $K_{\mathbf{x}}$-curves can ever lie above the curve $y = f^*(r)$. On the other hand, for each value of r there is at least one value $\mathbf{x}^*$ of $\mathbf{x}$ such that $f(\mathbf{x}^*, r) = f^*(r)$, namely the choice of $\mathbf{x}^*$ which solves the maximization problem for the given value of r. The curve $K_{\mathbf{x}^*}$ will then just touch the curve $y = f^*(r)$ at the point $(r, f^*(r)) = (r, f(\mathbf{x}^*, r))$, and so must have exactly the same tangent as the graph of $y = f^*(r)$ at this point. Moreover, because $K_{\mathbf{x}^*}$ can never go above this graph, it must have exactly the same tangent as the graph of f^* at the point where the curves touch. The slope of this common tangent, therefore, must be not only df^*/dr, the slope of the tangent to the graph of f^* at $(r, f^*(r))$, but also $\partial f(\mathbf{x}^*, r)/\partial r$, the slope of the tangent to the curve $K_{\mathbf{x}^*}$ at the point $(r, f(\mathbf{x}^*, r))$. Equation (2) follows because $K_{\mathbf{x}^*}$ is the graph of $f(\mathbf{x}^*, r)$ when $\mathbf{x}^*$ is fixed.

As Fig. 1 suggests, the graph of $y = f^*(r)$ is the lowest curve with the property that it lies on or above all the curves $K_{\mathbf{x}}$. So its graph is like an envelope or some "cling film" that is used to enclose or wrap up all these curves. Indeed, a point is on or below the graph if and only if it lies on or below one of the curves $K_{\mathbf{x}}$. For this reason we call the graph of f^* the **envelope** of the family of $K_{\mathbf{x}}$-curves. Also, result (2) is often called the **envelope theorem**.

EXAMPLE 3   In Example 13.1.3, $Q = F(K, L)$ denoted a production function with K as capital input and L as labour input. The price per unit of the product was p, the price per unit of capital was r, and the price per unit of labour was w. The profit obtained by using K and L units of the inputs, then producing and selling $F(K, L)$ units of the product, is given by

$$\hat{\pi}(K, L, p, r, w) = pF(K, L) - rK - wL$$

Here profit has been expressed as a new function $\hat{\pi}$ of the parameters p, r, and w, as well as of the choice variables K and L. We keep p, r, and w fixed and maximize $\hat{\pi}$ w.r.t. K and L. The optimal values of K and L are functions of p, r, and w, which we denote by $K^* = K^*(p, r, w)$ and $L^* = L^*(p, r, w)$. The value function for the problem is $\hat{\pi}^*(p, r, w) = \hat{\pi}(K^*, L^*, p, r, w)$. Usually, $\hat{\pi}^*$ is called the firm's **profit function**, though it would be more accurately described as the "maximum profit function". It is found by taking prices as given and choosing the optimal quantities of all inputs and outputs.

According to (2), one has

$$\frac{\partial \hat{\pi}^*}{\partial p} = F(K^*, L^*) = Q^*, \qquad \frac{\partial \hat{\pi}^*}{\partial r} = -K^*, \qquad \frac{\partial \hat{\pi}^*}{\partial w} = -L^* \qquad (*)$$

These three equalities are instances of what is known in producer theory as **Hotelling's lemma**. An economic interpretation of the middle equality is this: How much profit is lost if the price of capital increases by a small amount? At the optimum the firm uses K^* units of capital, so the answer is K^* per unit increase in the price. See Problem 4 for further interesting relationships.

PROBLEMS FOR SECTION 13.7

1. (a) A firm produces a single commodity and gets p for each unit sold. The cost of producing x units is $ax + bx^2$ and the tax per unit is t. Assume that the parameters are positive with $p > a + t$. The firm wants to maximize its profit. Find the optimal production x^* and the optimal profit π^*.

(b) Prove that $\partial \pi^*/\partial p = x^*$, and give an economic interpretation.

(SM) 2. (a) A firm uses capital K, labour L, and land T to produce Q units of a commodity, where

$$Q = K^{2/3} + L^{1/2} + T^{1/3}$$

Suppose that the firm is paid a positive price p for each unit it produces, and that the positive prices it pays per unit of capital, labour, and land are r, w, and q, respectively. Express the firm's profits as a function π of (K, L, T), then find the values of K, L, and T (as functions of the four prices) that maximize the firm's profits (assuming a maximum exists).

(b) Let Q^* denote the optimal number of units produced and K^* the optimal capital stock. Show that $\partial Q^*/\partial r = -\partial K^*/\partial p$.

3. (a) A firm produces $Q = a \ln(L + 1)$ units of a commodity when labour input is L units. The price obtained per unit is P and price per unit of labour is w, both positive, and with $w < aP$. Write down the profit function π. What choice of labour input $L = L^*$ maximizes profits?

(b) Consider L^* as a function of all the three parameters, $L^*(P, w, a)$, and define $\pi^*(P, w, a) = \pi(L^*, P, w, a)$. Verify that $\partial \pi^*/\partial P = \pi'_P(L^*, P, w, a)$, $\partial \pi^*/\partial w = \pi'_w(L^*, P, w, a)$, and $\partial \pi^*/\partial a = \pi'_a(L^*, P, w, a)$, thus confirming the envelope theorem.

4. With reference to Example 3, assuming that F is a C^2 function, prove the symmetry relations:

$$\frac{\partial Q^*}{\partial r} = -\frac{\partial K^*}{\partial p}, \qquad \frac{\partial Q^*}{\partial w} = -\frac{\partial L^*}{\partial p}, \qquad \frac{\partial L^*}{\partial r} = \frac{\partial K^*}{\partial w}$$

(*Hint:* Using the first result in Example 3 and Young's theorem, we have the equalities $\partial Q^*/\partial r = (\partial/\partial r)(\partial \hat\pi^*/\partial p) = (\partial/\partial p)(\partial \hat\pi^*/\partial r)$. Now use the other results in Example 3.)

(SM) 5. (a) With reference to Example 3 we want to study the factor demand functions—in particular how the optimal choices of capital and labour respond to price changes. By differentiating the first-order conditions (∗∗) in Example 13.1.3, verify that we get

$$F'_K(K^*, L^*)\, dp + pF''_{KK}(K^*, L^*)\, dK + pF''_{KL}(K^*, L^*)\, dL = dr$$
$$F'_L(K^*, L^*)\, dp + pF''_{LK}(K^*, L^*)\, dK + pF''_{LL}(K^*, L^*)\, dL = dw$$

(b) Use this system to find the partials of K^* and L^* w.r.t. p, r, and w. (You might find it easier first to find $\partial K^*/\partial p$ and $\partial L^*/\partial p$ by putting $dr = dw = 0$, etc.)

(c) Assume that the local second-order conditions (∗∗) in Example 13.3.3 are satisfied. What can you say about the signs of the partial derivatives? In particular, show that the factor demand curves are downward sloping as functions of their own factor prices. Verify that $\partial K^*/\partial w = \partial L^*/\partial r$.

(SM) 6. A profit-maximizing monopolist produces two commodities whose quantities are denoted by x_1 and x_2. Good 1 is subsidized at the rate of s per unit and good 2 is taxed at t per unit. The monopolist's profit function is therefore given by

$$\pi(x_1, x_2) = R(x_1, x_2) - C(x_1, x_2) + sx_1 - tx_2$$

where R and C are the firm's revenue and cost functions, respectively. Assume that the partial derivatives of these functions have the following signs:

$$R'_1 > 0, \quad R'_2 > 0, \quad R''_{11} < 0, \quad R''_{12} = R''_{21} < 0, \quad R''_{22} < 0$$
$$C'_1 > 0, \quad C'_2 > 0, \quad C''_{11} > 0, \quad C''_{12} = C''_{21} > 0, \quad C''_{22} > 0$$

(a) Find the first-order conditions for maximum profits.

(b) Write down the local second-order conditions for maximum profits.

(c) Suppose that $x_1^* = x_1^*(s, t)$, $x_2^* = x_2^*(s, t)$ solve the problem. Find the signs of $\partial x_1^*/\partial s$, $\partial x_1^*/\partial t$, $\partial x_2^*/\partial s$, and $\partial x_2^*/\partial t$, assuming that the local second-order conditions are satisfied.

(d) Show that $\partial x_1^*/\partial t = -\partial x_2^*/\partial s$.

REVIEW PROBLEMS FOR CHAPTER 13

1. The function f defined for all (x, y) by $f(x, y) = -2x^2 + 2xy - y^2 + 18x - 14y + 4$ has a maximum. Find the corresponding values of x and y. Use Theorem 13.2.1 to prove that it is a maximum point.

(SM) 2. (a) A firm produces two different kinds A and B of a commodity. The daily cost of producing Q_1 units of A and Q_2 units of B is $C(Q_1, Q_2) = 0.1(Q_1^2 + Q_1 Q_2 + Q_2^2)$. Suppose that the firm sells all its output at a price per unit of $P_1 = 120$ for A and $P_2 = 90$ for B. Find the daily production levels that maximize profits.

(b) If P_2 remains unchanged at 90, what new price (P_1) per unit of A would imply that the optimal daily production level for A is 400 units?

3. (a) The profit obtained by a firm from producing and selling x and y units of two brands of a commodity is given by

$$P(x, y) = -0.1x^2 - 0.2xy - 0.2y^2 + 47x + 48y - 600$$

Find the production levels that maximize profits.

(b) A key raw material is rationed so that total production must be restricted to 200 units. Find the production levels that now maximize profits.

(SM) 4. Find the stationary points of the following functions:

(a) $f(x, y) = x^3 - x^2 y + y^2$ (b) $g(x, y) = xye^{4x^2 - 5xy + y^2}$

(c) $f(x, y) = 4y^3 + 12x^2 y - 24x^2 - 24y^2$

5. Define $f(x, y, a) = ax^2 - 2x + y^2 - 4ay$, where a is a parameter. For each fixed $a \neq 0$, find the point $(x^*(a), y^*(a))$ that makes the function f stationary w.r.t. (x, y). Find also the value function $f^*(a) = f(x^*(a), y^*(a), a)$, and verify the envelope theorem in this case.

(SM) 6. (a) Suppose the production function in Problem 13.7.2 is replaced by $Q = K^a + L^b + T^c$, for parameters $a, b, c \in (0, 1)$. Assuming that a maximum exists, find the values of K, L, and T that maximize the firm's profits.

(b) Let π^* denote the optimal profit as a function of the four prices. Compute the partial derivative $\partial \pi^*/\partial r$.

(c) Verify the envelope theorem in this case.

7. Define $f(x, y)$ for all (x, y) by

$$f(x, y) = e^{x+y} + e^{x-y} - \tfrac{3}{2}x - \tfrac{1}{2}y$$

(a) Find the first- and second-order partial derivatives of f, then show that $f(x, y)$ is convex.

(b) Find the minimum point of $f(x, y)$.

(SM) 8. (a) Find and classify the stationary points of

$$f(x, y) = x^2 - y^2 - xy - x^3$$

(b) Find the domain S where f is concave, and find the largest value f in S.

(SM) 9. Consider the function f defined for all (x, y) by $f(x, y) = \tfrac{1}{2}x^2 - x + ay(x - 1) - \tfrac{1}{3}y^3 + a^2 y^2$, where a is a constant.

(a) Prove that $(x^*, y^*) = (1 - a^3, a^2)$ is a stationary point of f.

(b) Verify the envelope theorem in this case.

(c) Where in the xy-plane is f convex?

(SM) 10. In this problem we will generalize several of the economic examples and problems considered so far. Consider a firm that produces two different goods A and B. If the total cost function is $C(x, y)$ and the prices obtained per unit of A and B are p and q respectively, then the profit is

$$\pi(x, y) = px + qy - C(x, y) \tag{i}$$

(a) Suppose first that the firm has a small share in the markets for both these goods, and so takes p and q as given. Write down and interpret the first-order conditions for $x^* > 0$ and $y^* > 0$ to maximize profits.

(b) Suppose next that the firm has a monopoly in the sale of both goods. The prices are no longer fixed, but chosen by the monopolist, bearing in mind the demand functions

$$x = f(p, q) \quad \text{and} \quad y = g(p, q) \tag{ii}$$

Suppose we solve equations (ii) for p and q to obtain the inverse demand functions

$$p = F(x, y) \quad \text{and} \quad q = G(x, y) \tag{iii}$$

Then profit as a function of x and y is

$$\pi(x, y) = xF(x, y) + yG(x, y) - C(x, y) \tag{iv}$$

Write down and interpret the first-order conditions for $x^* > 0$ and $y^* > 0$ to maximize profits.

(c) Suppose $p = a - bx - cy$ and $q = \alpha - \beta x - \gamma y$, where b and γ are positive. (An increase in the price of either good decreases the demand for that good, but may increase or decrease the demand for the other good.) If the cost function is $C(x, y) = Px + Qy + R$, write down the first-order conditions for maximum profit.

(d) Prove that the (global) second-order conditions are satisfied provided $4\gamma b \geq (\beta + c)^2$.

14

CONSTRAINED OPTIMIZATION

Mathematics is removed from this turmoil of human life, but its
methods and the relations are a mirror, an incredibly pure mirror,
of the relations that link facts of our existence.
—Konrad Knopp (1928)

The previous chapter 13 introduced unconstrained optimization problems with several variables. In economics, however, the variables to be chosen must often satisfy one or more constraints. Accordingly, this chapter considers constrained optimization problems, and studies the method of Lagrange multipliers in some detail. Sections 14.1–14.7 treat equality constraints, with Section 14.7 presenting some comparative static results and the envelope theorem. More general constrained optimization problems allowing inequality constraints are introduced in Sections 14.8–14.10. A much fuller treatment of constrained optimization can be found in FMEA.

14.1 The Lagrange Multiplier Method

A typical economic example of a constrained optimization problem concerns a consumer who chooses how much of the available income m to spend on a good x whose price is p, and how much income to leave over for expenditure y on other goods. Note that the consumer then faces the budget constraint $px + y = m$. Suppose that preferences are represented by the utility function $u(x, y)$. In mathematical terms the consumer's problem can be expressed as

$$\max u(x, y) \quad \text{subject to} \quad px + y = m$$

This is a typical *constrained maximization problem*. In this case, because $y = m - px$, the same problem can be expressed as the *unconstrained maximization* of the function $h(x) = u(x, m - px)$ w.r.t. the single variable x. Indeed, this method of converting a constrained optimization problem involving two variables to a one-variable problem was used in Section 13.2.

When, however, the constraint involves a complicated function, or there are several equality constraints to consider, this substitution method might be difficult or even impossible to carry out in practice. In such cases, economists make much use of the *Lagrange multiplier method.*[1] Actually, this method is often used even for problems that are quite easy to express as unconstrained problems. One reason is that Lagrange multipliers have an important economic interpretation. In addition, a similar method works for many more complicated optimization problems, such as those where the constraints are expressed in terms of inequalities.

We start with the problem of maximizing (or minimizing) a function $f(x, y)$ of two variables, when x and y are restricted to satisfy an equality constraint $g(x, y) = c$. This can be written as

$$\text{max(min)} \quad f(x, y) \quad \text{subject to} \quad g(x, y) = c \tag{1}$$

The first step of the method is to introduce a **Lagrange multiplier**, often denoted by λ, which is associated with the constraint $g(x, y) = c$. Then we define the **Lagrangian** $\mathcal{L}$ by

$$\mathcal{L}(x, y) = f(x, y) - \lambda(g(x, y) - c) \tag{2}$$

in which the expression $g(x, y) - c$, which must be 0 when the constraint is satisfied, has been multiplied by λ. Note that $\mathcal{L}(x, y) = f(x, y)$ for all (x, y) that satisfy the constraint $g(x, y) = c$.

The Lagrange multiplier λ is a constant, so the partial derivatives of $\mathcal{L}(x, y)$ w.r.t. x and y are $\mathcal{L}'_1(x, y) = f'_1(x, y) - \lambda g'_1(x, y)$ and $\mathcal{L}'_2(x, y) = f'_2(x, y) - \lambda g'_2(x, y)$, respectively. As will be explained algebraically and geometrically in Section 14.4, except in rare cases a solution of problem (1) can only be a point (x, y) where, for a suitable value of λ, the first-order partial derivatives of $\mathcal{L}$ vanish, and also the constraint $g(x, y) = c$ is satisfied.

Here is a simple economic application.

EXAMPLE 1   A consumer has the utility function $U(x, y) = xy$ and faces the budget constraint $2x + y = 100$. Find the only solution candidate to the consumer demand problem

$$\text{maximize } xy \quad \text{subject to} \quad 2x + y = 100$$

Solution: The Lagrangian is $\mathcal{L}(x, y) = xy - \lambda(2x + y - 100)$. Including the constraint, the first-order conditions for the solution of the problem are

$$\mathcal{L}'_1(x, y) = y - 2\lambda = 0, \qquad \mathcal{L}'_2(x, y) = x - \lambda = 0, \qquad 2x + y = 100$$

The first two equations imply that $y = 2\lambda$ and $x = \lambda$. So $y = 2x$. Inserting this into the constraint yields $2x + 2x = 100$. So $x = 25$ and $y = 50$, implying that $\lambda = x = 25$.

This solution can be confirmed by the substitution method. From $2x + y = 100$ we get $y = 100 - 2x$, so the problem is reduced to maximizing the unconstrained function $h(x) = x(100 - 2x) = -2x^2 + 100x$. Since $h'(x) = -4x + 100 = 0$ gives $x = 25$, and $h''(x) = -4 < 0$ for all x, this shows that $x = 25$ *is* a maximum point.

---

[1] Named after its discoverer, the Italian-born French mathematician J. L. Lagrange (1736–1813). The Danish economist Harald Westergaard seems to be the first who used it in economics, in 1876.

Example 1 illustrates the following general method:[2]

THE LAGRANGE MULTIPLIER METHOD

To find the only possible solutions of the problem

$$\text{maximize (minimize)} \quad f(x, y) \quad \text{subject to} \quad g(x, y) = c$$

proceed as follows:

(I) Write down the Lagrangian

$$\mathcal{L}(x, y) = f(x, y) - \lambda(g(x, y) - c)$$

where λ is a constant.

(II) Differentiate $\mathcal{L}$ w.r.t. x and y, and equate the partial derivatives to 0.

(III) The two equations in (II), together with the constraint, yield the following three equations:

$$\mathcal{L}'_1(x, y) = f'_1(x, y) - \lambda g'_1(x, y) = 0$$
$$\mathcal{L}'_2(x, y) = f'_2(x, y) - \lambda g'_2(x, y) = 0$$
$$g(x, y) = c$$

(IV) Solve these three equations simultaneously for the three unknowns x, y, and λ. These triples (x, y, λ) are the solution candidates, at least one of which solves the problem (if it has a solution).

The conditions in (III) are called the *first-order conditions* for problem (1).

NOTE 1   Some economists prefer to consider the Lagrangian as a function $\mathcal{L}(x, y, \lambda)$ of three variables. Then the first-order condition $\partial \mathcal{L}/\partial \lambda = -(g(x, y) - c) = 0$ yields the constraint. In this way all the three necessary conditions are obtained by equating the partial derivatives of the (extended) Lagrangian to 0. However, it does seem somewhat unnatural to perform a differentiation to get an obvious necessary condition, namely the constraint equation. Also, this procedure can easily lead to trouble when treating problems with inequality constraints, so we prefer to avoid it.

EXAMPLE 2   A single-product firm intends to produce 30 units of output as cheaply as possible. By using K units of capital and L units of labour, it can produce $\sqrt{K} + L$ units. Suppose the prices of capital and labour are, respectively, 1 and 20. The firm's problem is then:

$$\text{minimize} \quad K + 20L \quad \text{subject to} \quad \sqrt{K} + L = 30$$

Find the optimal choices of K and L.

---

[2] If $g'_1(x, y)$ and $g'_2(x, y)$ both vanish, the method might fail to give the right answer.

Solution: The Lagrangian is $\mathcal{L} = K + 20L - \lambda(\sqrt{K} + L - 30)$, so the first-order conditions are:

$$\mathcal{L}'_K = 1 - \lambda/2\sqrt{K} = 0, \qquad \mathcal{L}'_L = 20 - \lambda = 0, \qquad \sqrt{K} + L = 30$$

The second equation gives $\lambda = 20$, which inserted into the first equation yields $1 = 20/2\sqrt{K}$. It follows that $\sqrt{K} = 10$, and hence $K = 100$. Inserted into the constraint this gives $\sqrt{100} + L = 30$, and hence $L = 20$. The 30 units are therefore produced in the cheapest way when the firm uses 100 units of capital and 20 units of labour. The associated cost is $K + 20L = 500$. (Theorem 14.5.1 will tell us that this is the solution because $\mathcal{L}$ is convex in (K, L).)

An economist would be inclined to ask: What is the additional cost of producing 31 rather than 30 units? Solving the problem with the constraint $\sqrt{K} + L = 31$, we see that still $\lambda = 20$ and $K = 100$, while $L = 31 - 10 = 21$. The associated minimum cost is $100 + 20 \cdot 21 = 520$, so the additional cost is $520 - 500 = 20$. This is precisely equal to the Lagrange multiplier! Thus, in this case the Lagrange multiplier tells us by how much costs increase if the production requirement is increased by one unit from 30 to 31.

EXAMPLE 3   A consumer who has Cobb–Douglas utility function $U(x, y) = Ax^a y^b$ faces the budget constraint $px + qy = m$, where A, a, b, p, q, and m are all positive constants. Find the only solution candidate to the consumer demand problem

$$\max Ax^a y^b \quad \text{subject to} \quad px + qy = m \qquad (*)$$

Solution: The Lagrangian is $\mathcal{L}(x, y) = Ax^a y^b - \lambda(px + qy - m)$, so the first-order conditions are

$$\mathcal{L}'_1(x, y) = aAx^{a-1}y^b - \lambda p = 0, \quad \mathcal{L}'_2(x, y) = bAx^a y^{b-1} - \lambda q = 0, \quad px + qy = m$$

Solving the first two equations for λ yields

$$\lambda = aAx^{a-1}y^b/p = bAx^a y^{b-1}/q$$

Cancelling the common factor $Ax^{a-1}y^{b-1}$ from the last two fractions gives

$$ay/p = bx/q$$

Solving this equation for qy yields $qy = (b/a)px$, which inserted into the budget constraint gives $px + (b/a)px = m$. From this equation we find x and then y. The results are the following **demand functions**:

$$x = x(p, q, m) = \frac{a}{a+b}\frac{m}{p}, \qquad y = y(p, q, m) = \frac{b}{a+b}\frac{m}{q} \qquad (**)$$

(It follows from $(**)$ that for all t one has $x(tp, tq, tm) = x(p, q, m)$ and $y(tp, tq, tm) = y(p, q, m)$, so the demand functions are homogeneous of degree 0. This is as one should expect because, if (p, q, m) is changed to (tp, tq, tm), then the constraint in $(*)$ is unchanged, and so the optimal choices of x and y are unchanged. See also Example 12.7.4.)

The solution we have found makes good sense. In the utility function $Ax^a y^b$, the relative sizes of the coefficients a and b indicate the relative importance of x and y in the individual's preferences. For instance, if a is larger than b, then the consumer values a 1% increase in x more than a 1% increase in y. The product px is the amount spent on the first good, and (∗∗) says that the consumer should spend the fraction $a/(a+b)$ of income on this good and the fraction $b/(a+b)$ on the second good.

Formula (∗∗) can be applied immediately to find the correct answer to thousands of exam problems in mathematical economics courses given each year all over the world! But note that the utility function has to be of the Cobb–Douglas type $Ax^a y^b$. For the problem $\max x^a + y^b$ subject to $px + qy = m$, the solution is not given by (∗∗). (Assuming that $0 < a < 1$, see Problem 9 for the case when $b = 1$, and Problem 14.5.4 for the case when $a = b$.)

WARNING: There is an underlying assumption in problem (∗) that $x \geq 0$ and $y \geq 0$. Thus, we maximize a continuous function $Ax^a y^b$ over a closed bounded set $S = \{(x, y) : px + qy = m, x \geq 0, y \geq 0\}$. According to the extreme value theorem, a maximum must exist. Since utility is 0 when $x = 0$ or when $y = 0$, and positive at the point given by (∗∗), this point indeed solves the problem. Without nonnegativity conditions on x and y, however, the problem might fail to have a maximum. Indeed, consider the problem $\max x^2 y$ subject to $x + y = 1$. For any t, the pair $(x, y) = (-t, 1 + t)$ satisfies the constraint, yet $x^2 y = t^2(1 + t) \to \infty$ as $t \to \infty$, so there is no maximum.

EXAMPLE 4   Examine the general utility maximizing problem with two goods:

$$\text{maximize } u(x, y) \quad \text{subject to} \quad px + qy = m \tag{3}$$

Solution: The Lagrangian is $\mathcal{L}(x, y) = u(x, y) - \lambda(px + qy - m)$, so the first-order conditions are

$$\mathcal{L}'_x(x, y) = u'_x(x, y) - \lambda p = 0 \tag{i}$$

$$\mathcal{L}'_y(x, y) = u'_y(x, y) - \lambda q = 0 \tag{ii}$$

$$px + qy = m \tag{iiii}$$

From equation (i) we get $\lambda = u'_x(x, y)/p$, and from (ii), $\lambda = u'_y(x, y)/q$. Hence,

$$\frac{u'_x(x, y)}{p} = \frac{u'_y(x, y)}{q}, \quad \text{which can be rewritten as} \quad \frac{u'_x(x, y)}{u'_y(x, y)} = \frac{p}{q} \tag{4}$$

The left-hand side of the last equation is the *marginal rate of substitution* (MRS) (see Section 12.5). Utility maximization thus requires equating the MRS to the price ratio p/q.

A geometric interpretation of (4) is that the consumer should choose the point on the budget line at which the slope of the level curve of the utility function, $-u'_x(x, y)/u'_y(x, y)$, is equal to the slope of the budget line, $-p/q$. (See Section 12.3.) Thus at the optimal point the budget line is tangent to a level curve of the utility function, illustrated by point P in

Figure 1. The level curves of the utility function are the *indifference curves*, along which the utility level is constant by definition. Thus, utility is maximized at a point where the budget line is tangent to an indifference curve. The fact that $\lambda = u'_x(x, y)/p = u'_y(x, y)/q$ at point P means that the marginal utility per dollar is the same for both goods. At any other point (x, y) where, for example, $u'_x(x, y)/p > u'_y(x, y)/q$, the consumer can increase utility by shifting expenditure away from y toward x. Indeed, then the increase in utility per extra dollar spent on x would equal $u'_x(x, y)/p$; this exceeds the decrease in utility per dollar reduction in the amount spent on y, which equals $u'_y(x, y)/q$.

As in Example 3, the optimal choices of x and y can be expressed as **demand functions** of (p, q, m), which must be homogeneous of degree zero in the three variables together.

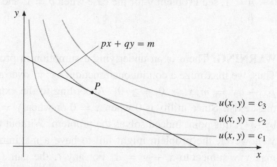

Figure 1 Assuming that $c_1 < c_2 < c_3 < \cdots$, the solution to problem (3) is at P.

PROBLEMS FOR SECTION 14.1

All the following problems have only one solution candidate, which is the optimal solution.

1. (a) Use Lagrange's method to find the only possible solution to the problem:
$$\max xy \quad \text{subject to} \quad x + 3y = 24$$
   (b) Check the solution by using the results in Example 3.

2. Use the Lagrange's method to solve the problem
$$\min -40Q_1 + Q_1^2 - 2Q_1Q_2 - 20Q_2 + Q_2^2 \quad \text{subject to} \quad Q_1 + Q_2 = 15$$

3. Use the results in Example 3 to solve the following problems.
   (a) $\max 10x^{1/2}y^{1/3}$ subject to $2x + 4y = m$.
   (b) $\max x^{1/2}y^{1/2}$ subject to $50\,000x + 0.08y = 1\,000\,000$
   (c) $\max 12x\sqrt{y}$ subject to $3x + 4y = 12$

(SM) 4. Solve the following problems:
   (a) $\min f(x, y) = x^2 + y^2$ subject to $g(x, y) = x + 2y = 4$
   (b) $\min f(x, y) = x^2 + 2y^2$ subject to $g(x, y) = x + y = 12$
   (c) $\max f(x, y) = x^2 + 3xy + y^2$ subject to $g(x, y) = x + y = 100$

5. A person has utility function

$$u(x, y) = 100xy + x + 2y$$

Suppose that the price per unit of x is \$2, and that the price per unit of y is \$4. The person receives \$1000 that all has to be spent on the two commodities x and y. Solve the utility maximization problem.

6. An individual has a Cobb–Douglas utility function $U(m, l) = Am^a l^b$, where m is income and l is leisure. Here A, a, and b are positive constants, with $a + b \leq 1$. A total of T_0 hours are allocated between work W and leisure l, so that $W + l = T_0$. If the hourly wage is w, then $m = wW$, and the individual's problem is

$$\max Am^a l^b \quad \text{subject to} \quad (m/w) + l = T_0$$

Solve the problem by using (∗∗) in Example 3.

7. Solve Problem 13.R.3(b) by using the Lagrange method.

8. A firm produces and sells two commodities. By selling x tons of the first commodity the firm gets a price per ton given by $p = 96 - 4x$. By selling y tons of the other commodity the price per ton is given by $q = 84 - 2y$. The total cost of producing and selling x tons of the first commodity and y tons of the second is given by $C(x, y) = 2x^2 + 2xy + y^2$.

   (a) Show that the firm's profit function is $P(x, y) = -6x^2 - 3y^2 - 2xy + 96x + 84y$.

   (b) Compute the first-order partial derivatives of P, and find its only stationary point.

   (c) Suppose that the firm's production activity causes so much pollution that the authorities limit its output to 11 tons in total. Solve the firm's maximization problem in this case. Verify that the production restrictions do reduce the maximum possible value of $P(x, y)$.

(SM) 9. Consider the utility maximization problem

$$\max x^a + y \quad \text{subject to} \quad px + y = m$$

where all constants are positive, $a \in (0, 1)$.

   (a) Find the demand functions, $x^*(p, m)$ and $y^*(p, m)$.

   (b) Find the partial derivatives of the demand functions w.r.t. p and m, and check their signs.

   (c) How does the optimal expenditure on the x good vary with p? (Check the elasticity of $px^*(p, m)$ w.r.t. p.)

   (d) Put $a = 1/2$. What are the demand functions in this case? Denote the maximal utility as a function of p and m by $U^*(p, m)$, the value function, also called the indirect utility function. Verify that $\partial U^*/\partial p = -x^*(p, m)$.

HARDER PROBLEM

(SM) 10. Consider the problem

$$\max U(x, y) = 100 - e^{-x} - e^{-y} \quad \text{subject to} \quad px + qy = m$$

   (a) Write down the first-order conditions for the problem and solve them for x, y, and λ as functions of p, q, and m. What assumptions are needed for x and y to be nonnegative?

   (b) Verify that x and y are homogeneous of degree 0 as functions of p, q, and m.

14.2   Interpreting the Lagrange Multiplier

Consider again the problem

$$\max(\min) \ f(x, y) \quad \text{subject to} \quad g(x, y) = c$$

Suppose x^* and y^* are the values of x and y that solve this problem. In general, x^* and y^* depend on c. We *assume* that $x^* = x^*(c)$ and $y^* = y^*(c)$ are differentiable functions of c. The associated value of $f(x, y)$ is then also a function of c, with

$$f^*(c) = f(x^*(c), y^*(c)) \tag{1}$$

Here $f^*(c)$ is called the **(optimal) value function** for the problem. Of course, the associated value of the Lagrange multiplier also depends on c, in general. Provided that certain regularity conditions are satisfied, we have the remarkable result that

$$\frac{df^*(c)}{dc} = \lambda(c) \tag{2}$$

Thus, *the Lagrange multiplier $\lambda = \lambda(c)$ is the rate at which the optimal value of the objective function changes with respect to changes in the constraint constant c.*

In particular, if dc is a small change in c, then

$$f^*(c + dc) - f^*(c) \approx \lambda(c) \, dc \tag{3}$$

In economic applications, c often denotes the available stock of some resource, and $f(x, y)$ denotes utility or profit. Then $\lambda(c) \, dc$ measures the approximate change in utility or profit that can be obtained from dc units more (or $-dc$ less, when $dc < 0$). Economists call λ a **shadow price** of the resource. If $f^*(c)$ is the maximum profit when the resource input is c, then (3) says that λ indicates the approximate increase in profit per unit increase in the resource.

Proof of (2) **(assuming that $f^*(c)$ is differentiable):**   Taking the differential of (1) gives

$$df^*(c) = df(x^*, y^*) = f_1'(x^*, y^*) \, dx^* + f_2'(x^*, y^*) \, dy^* \tag{*}$$

But from the first-order conditions we have $f_1'(x^*, y^*) = \lambda g_1'(x^*, y^*)$ and $f_2'(x^*, y^*) = \lambda g_2'(x^*, y^*)$, so (*) can be written as

$$df^*(c) = \lambda g_1'(x^*, y^*) \, dx^* + \lambda g_2'(x^*, y^*) \, dy^* = \lambda [g_1'(x^*, y^*) \, dx^* + g_2'(x^*, y^*) \, dy^*] \tag{**}$$

Moreover, taking the differential of the identity $g(x^*(c), y^*(c)) = c$ yields

$$dg(x^*, y^*) = g_1'(x^*, y^*) \, dx^* + g_2'(x^*, y^*) \, dy^* = dc$$

Substituting the last equality in (**) implies that $df^*(c) = \lambda \, dc$ ∎

EXAMPLE 1   Consider the following generalization of Example 14.1.1:

$$\max xy \quad \text{subject to} \quad 2x + y = m$$

The first-order conditions again give $y = 2x$ with $\lambda = x$. The constraint now becomes $2x + 2x = m$, so $x = m/4$. In the notation introduced above, the solution is

$$x^*(m) = m/4, \qquad y^*(m) = m/2, \qquad \lambda(m) = m/4$$

The value function is therefore $f^*(m) = (m/4)(m/2) = m^2/8$. It follows that $df^*(m)/dm = m/4 = \lambda(m)$. Hence (2) is confirmed. Suppose in particular that $m = 100$. Then $f^*(100) = 100^2/8$. What happens to the value function if $m = 100$ increases by 1? The new value is $f^*(101) = 101^2/8$, so $f^*(101) - f^*(100) = 101^2/8 - 100^2/8 = 25.125$. Note that formula (3) with $dc = 1$ gives $f^*(101) - f^*(100) \approx \lambda(100) \cdot 1 = 25 \cdot 1 = 25$, which is quite close to the exact value 25.125.

EXAMPLE 2   Suppose $Q = F(K, L)$ denotes the output of a state-owned firm when the input of capital is K and that of labour is L. Suppose the prices of capital and labour are r and w, respectively, and that the firm is given a total budget of m to spend on the two input factors. The firm wishes to find the choice of inputs it can afford that maximizes output. So it faces the problem

$$\max F(K, L) \quad \text{subject to} \quad rK + wL = m$$

Solving this problem by using Lagrange's method, the value of the Lagrange multiplier will tells us approximately the increase in output if m is increased by 1 dollar.

Consider, for example, the specific problem

$$\max 120KL \quad \text{subject to} \quad 2K + 5L = m$$

Note that this is mathematically a special case of the problem in Example 14.1.3. Only the notation is different, along with the fact that the consumer has been replaced with a firm. From (∗∗) in Example 14.1.3 we find the solution

$$K^* = \tfrac{1}{4}m, \quad L^* = \tfrac{1}{10}m, \quad \text{with} \quad \lambda = 6m$$

The optimal output is $Q^*(m) = 120K^*L^* = 120\tfrac{1}{4}m\tfrac{1}{10}m = 3m^2$, so $dQ^*/dm = 6m = \lambda$, and (2) is confirmed.

PROBLEMS FOR SECTION 14.2

1. Verify that equation (2) holds for the problem: max x^3y subject to $2x + 3y = m$.

2. (a) With reference to Example 14.1.2, solve the problem

$$\text{minimize } rK + wL \quad \text{subject to} \quad \sqrt{K} + L = Q$$

assuming that $Q > w/2r$, where r, w, and Q are positive constants.

(b) Verify (2) in this case.

3. (a) Consider the problem of minimizing $x^2 + y^2$ subject to $x + 2y = a$ (where a is a constant). Solve the problem by transforming it into an unconstrained optimization problem with one variable.

(b) Show that the Lagrange method leads to the same solution. Verify (2) in this case.

(c) Explain the solution by studying the level curves of $f(x, y) = x^2 + y^2$ and the graph of the straight line $x + 2y = a$. Can you give a geometric interpretation of the problem? Does the corresponding maximization problem have a solution?

(SM) **4.** (a) Solve the utility maximization problem

$$\max U(x, y) = \sqrt{x} + y \quad \text{subject to} \quad x + 4y = 100$$

using the Lagrange method, i.e. find the quantities demanded of the two goods.

(b) Suppose income increases from 100 to 101. What is the exact increase in the optimal value of $U(x, y)$? Compare with the value found in (a) for the Lagrange multiplier.

(c) Suppose we change the budget constraint to $px + qy = m$, but keep the same utility function. Derive the quantities demanded of the two goods if $m > q^2/4p$.

(SM) **5.** (a) Consider the consumer demand problem

$$\max_{x, y} \left[U(x, y) = \alpha \ln(x - a) + \beta \ln(y - b) \right] \quad \text{subject to} \quad px + qy = m \qquad (*)$$

where α, β, a, b, p, q, and m are positive constants with $\alpha + \beta = 1$, and moreover, with $m > ap + bq$. Show that if x^*, y^* solve problem $(*)$, then expenditure on the two goods is given by the two linear functions

$$px^* = \alpha m + pa - \alpha(pa + qb), \qquad qy^* = \beta m + qb - \beta(pa + qb) \qquad (**)$$

of the variables (m, p, q). (This is a special case of the **linear expenditure system** that the British economist R. Stone fitted to UK consumption data in the *Economic Journal*, 1954.)

(b) Let $U^*(p, q, m) = U(x^*, y^*)$ denote the indirect utility function. Show that $\partial U^*/\partial m > 0$ and verify the so-called Roy's identities, $\dfrac{\partial U^*}{\partial p} = -\dfrac{\partial U^*}{\partial m} x^*$ and $\dfrac{\partial U^*}{\partial q} = -\dfrac{\partial U^*}{\partial m} y^*$.

HARDER PROBLEM

(SM) **6.** An oil producer starts extracting oil from a well at time $t = 0$, and ends at a time $t = T$ that the producer chooses. Suppose that the output flow at any time t in the interval $[0, T]$ is $xt(T - t)$ barrels per unit of time, where the intensity x can also be chosen. The total amount of oil extracted in the given time span is thus given by the function $g(x, T) = \int_0^T xt(T - t)\, dt$ of x and T. Assume further that the sales price per barrel at time t is $p = 1 + t$, and that the cost per barrel extracted is equal to αT^2, where α is a positive constant. The profit per unit of time is then $(1 + t - \alpha T^2)xt(T - t)$, so that the total profit earned during the time interval $[0, T]$ is a function of x and T given by $f(x, T) = \int_0^T (1 + t - \alpha T^2)\, xt\, (T - t)\, dt$. If the total amount of extractable oil in the field is M barrels, the producer can choose values of x and T such that $g(x, T) = M$. The producer's problem is thus

$$\max f(x, T) \quad \text{subject to} \quad g(x, T) = M \qquad (*)$$

Find explicit expressions for $f(x, T)$ and $g(x, T)$ by calculating the given integrals, and then solve problem $(*)$. Verify Equation (2) in this case.

14.3 Several Solution Candidates

In all our examples and problems so far, the recipe for solving constrained optimization problems has produced only one solution candidate. In this section we consider a problem where there are several solution candidates. In such cases we have to decide which of the candidates actually solves the problem, assuming it has any solution at all.

EXAMPLE 1   Solve the problem

$$\max \, (\min) \; f(x, y) = x^2 + y^2 \quad \text{subject to} \quad g(x, y) = x^2 + xy + y^2 = 3$$

Solution: The Lagrangian in this case is $\mathcal{L}(x, y) = x^2 + y^2 - \lambda(x^2 + xy + y^2 - 3)$, and the three equations to consider are

$$\mathcal{L}_1'(x, y) = 2x - \lambda(2x + y) = 0 \tag{i}$$
$$\mathcal{L}_2'(x, y) = 2y - \lambda(x + 2y) = 0 \tag{ii}$$
$$x^2 + xy + y^2 - 3 = 0 \tag{iii}$$

Let us eliminate λ from (i) and (ii). From (i) we get $\lambda = 2x/(2x + y)$ provided $y \neq -2x$. Inserting this value of λ into (ii) gives

$$2y = \frac{2x}{2x + y}(x + 2y), \quad \text{or} \quad y^2 = x^2, \quad \text{and so} \quad y = \pm x$$

Suppose $y = x$. Then (iii) yields $x^2 = 1$, so $x = 1$ or $x = -1$. This gives the two solution candidates $(x, y) = (1, 1)$ and $(-1, -1)$, with $\lambda = 2/3$.

Suppose $y = -x$. Then (iii) yields $x^2 = 3$, so $x = \sqrt{3}$ or $x = -\sqrt{3}$. This gives the two solution candidates $(x, y) = (\sqrt{3}, -\sqrt{3})$ and $(-\sqrt{3}, \sqrt{3})$, with $\lambda = 2$.

It remains to consider the case $y = -2x$. Then from (i), $x = 0$ and so $y = 0$. But this contradicts (iii), so this case cannot occur.

We have found the only four points (x, y) that can solve the problem. Furthermore,

$$f(1, 1) = f(-1, -1) = 2, \qquad f(\sqrt{3}, -\sqrt{3}) = f(-\sqrt{3}, \sqrt{3}) = 6$$

We conclude that if the problem has solutions, then $(1, 1)$ and $(-1, -1)$ solve the minimization problem, whereas $(\sqrt{3}, -\sqrt{3})$ and $(-\sqrt{3}, \sqrt{3})$ solve the maximization problem.

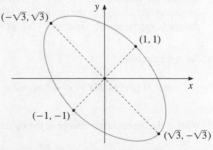

Figure 1 The constraint curve in Example 1

Geometrically, the equality constraint determines an ellipse. The problem is therefore to find what points on the ellipse are nearest to or furthest from the origin. See Fig. 1. It is "geometrically obvious" that such points exist.

Here is an alternative way of proving that $(x, y) = (1, 1)$ minimizes $f(x, y) = x^2 + y^2$ subject to the constraint $x^2 + xy + y^2 = 3$. (The other points can be treated in the same way.) Note, however, that this method works only in special cases.

Let $x = 1 + h$ and $y = 1 + k$. Thus h and k measure the deviation of x and y, respectively, from 1. Then $f(x, y)$ takes the form

$$f(x, y) = (1 + h)^2 + (1 + k)^2 = 2 + 2(h + k) + h^2 + k^2 \qquad (*)$$

If $(x, y) = (1 + h, 1 + k)$ satisfies the constraint, then $(1 + h)^2 + (1 + h)(1 + k) + (1 + k)^2 = 3$, so $h + k = -hk/3 - (h^2 + k^2)/3$. Inserting this expression for $h + k$ into $(*)$ yields

$$f(x, y) = 2 + 2\left[-\tfrac{1}{3}hk - \tfrac{1}{3}(h^2 + k^2)\right] + h^2 + k^2 = 2 + \tfrac{1}{3}(h - k)^2$$

Because $\tfrac{1}{3}(h - k)^2 \geq 0$ for all (h, k), it follows that $f(x, y) \geq 2$ for all values of (x, y). But because $f(1, 1) = 2$, this means that $(1, 1)$ really does minimize $f(x, y)$ subject to the constraint.

PROBLEMS FOR SECTION 14.3

SM **1.** (a) max(min) $3xy$ subject to $x^2 + y^2 = 8$

(b) max(min) $x + y$ subject to $x^2 + 3xy + 3y^2 = 3$

SM **2.** In (b) you can take it for granted that the minimum value exists.

(a) max $x^2 + y^2 - 2x + 1$ subject to $x^2 + 4y^2 = 16$

(b) min $\ln(2 + x^2) + y^2$ subject to $x^2 + 2y = 2$

3. (a) Find the solutions to the necessary conditions for the problem max(min) $f(x, y) = x + y$ subject to $g(x, y) = x^2 + y = 1$.

(b) Explain the solution geometrically by drawing appropriate level curves for $f(x, y)$ together with the graph of the parabola $x^2 + y = 1$. Does the associated minimization problem have a solution?

(c) Replace the constraint by $x^2 + y = 1.1$, and solve the problem in this case. Find the corresponding change in the optimal value of $f(x, y) = x + y$, and check to see if this change is approximately equal to $\lambda \cdot 0.1$, as suggested by (14.2.3).

SM **4.** (a) Solve the problem

$$\text{max } f(x, y) = 24x - x^2 + 16y - 2y^2 \quad \text{subject to} \quad g(x, y) = x^2 + 2y^2 = 44$$

(b) What is the approximate change in the optimal value of $f(x, y)$ if 44 is changed to 45?

14.4 Why the Lagrange Method Works

We have explained the Lagrange multiplier method for solving the problem

$$\max(\min) \; f(x, y) \quad \text{subject to} \quad g(x, y) = c \tag{1}$$

In this section we give a geometric as well as an analytic argument for the method.

A Geometric Argument

The maximization problem in (1) can be given a geometric interpretation, as shown in Fig. 1. The graph of f is like the surface of an inverted bowl, whereas the equation $g(x, y) = c$ represents a curve in the xy-plane. The curve K on the bowl is the one that lies directly above the curve $g(x, y) = c$. (The latter curve is the projection of K onto the xy-plane.) Maximizing $f(x, y)$ without taking the constraint into account gets us to the peak A in Fig. 1. The solution to problem (1), however, is at B, which is the highest point on the curve K. If we think of the graph of f as representing a mountain, and K as a mountain path, then we seek the highest point on the path, which is B. Analytically, the problem is to find the coordinates of B.

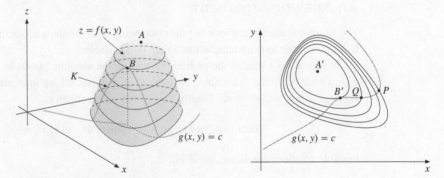

Figure 1 Illustrating a Lagrange problem

The right half of Fig. 1 shows some of the level curves for f, and also indicates the constraint curve $g(x, y) = c$. Now A' represents the point at which $f(x, y)$ has its unconstrained (free) maximum. The closer a level curve of f is to point A', the higher is the value of f along that level curve. We are seeking that point on the constraint curve $g(x, y) = c$ where f has its highest value. If we start at point P on the constraint curve and move along that curve toward A', we encounter level curves with higher and higher values of f.

Obviously, the point Q indicated in Fig. 1 is not the point on $g(x, y) = c$ at which f has its highest value, because the constraint curve passes *through* the level curve of f at that point. Therefore, we can cross a level curve to higher values of f by proceeding further along the constraint curve. However, when we reach point B', we cannot go any higher. It is intuitively clear that B' is the point where the constraint curve touches (without intersecting) a level curve for f.

This observation implies that the slope of the tangent to the curve $g(x, y) = c$ at (x, y) is equal to the slope of the tangent to the level curve of f at that point.

Recall from Section 12.3 that the slope of the level curve $F(x, y) = c$ is given by $dy/dx = -F_1'(x, y)/F_2'(x, y)$. Thus, the condition that the slope of the tangent to $g(x, y) = c$ is equal to the slope of a level curve for $f(x, y)$ can be expressed analytically as:[3]

$$-\frac{g_1'(x, y)}{g_2'(x, y)} = -\frac{f_1'(x, y)}{f_2'(x, y)} \qquad \text{or} \qquad \frac{f_1'(x, y)}{g_1'(x, y)} = \frac{f_2'(x, y)}{g_2'(x, y)} \tag{2}$$

It follows that a necessary condition for (x, y) to solve problem (1) is that the left- and right-hand sides of the last equation in (2) are equal at (x, y). Let λ denote the common value of these fractions. This is the Lagrange multiplier introduced in Section 14.1. With this definition,

$$f_1'(x, y) - \lambda g_1'(x, y) = 0, \qquad f_2'(x, y) - \lambda g_2'(x, y) = 0 \tag{3}$$

Using the Lagrangian from Section 14.1, we see that (3) just tells us that the Lagrangian has a stationary point. An analogous argument for the problem of minimizing $f(x, y)$ subject to $g(x, y) = c$ gives the same condition.

An Analytic Argument

The geometric argument above is quite convincing. But the analytic argument we are about to offer is easier to generalize to more than two variables.

So far we have studied the problem of finding the absolute largest or smallest value of $f(x, y)$ subject to the constraint $g(x, y) = c$. Sometimes we are interested in studying the corresponding local extrema. Briefly formulated, the problem is

$$\text{local max(min)} \ f(x, y) \quad \text{subject to} \quad g(x, y) = c \tag{4}$$

Possible solutions are illustrated in Fig. 2.

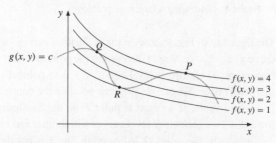

Figure 2 Q, R, and P all satisfy the first-order conditions

The point R is a local minimum point for $f(x, y)$ subject to $g(x, y) = c$, whereas Q and P are local maximum points. The global maximum of $f(x, y)$ subject to $g(x, y) = c$ is

---

[3] Disregard for the moment cases where any denominator is 0.

attained only at P. Each of the points P, Q, and R in Fig. 2 satisfies condition (2), so the first-order conditions are exactly as before. Let us derive them in a way that does not rely on geometric intuition. Except in some special cases, the equation $g(x, y) = c$ defines y implicitly as a differentiable function of x near any local extreme point. Denote this function by $y = h(x)$. According to formula (12.3.1), provided that $g'_2(x, y) \neq 0$, one has

$$y' = h'(x) = -g'_1(x, y)/g'_2(x, y)$$

Now, the objective function $z = f(x, y) = f(x, h(x))$ is, in effect, a function of x alone. By calculating dz/dx while taking into account how y depends on x, we obtain a necessary condition for local extreme points by equating dz/dx to 0. But

$$\frac{dz}{dx} = f'_1(x, y) + f'_2(x, y)y' \qquad \text{(with } y' = h'(x))$$

So substituting the previous expression for $h'(x)$ gives the following necessary condition for (x, y) to solve problem (1):

$$\frac{dz}{dx} = f'_1(x, y) - f'_2(x, y)\frac{g'_1(x, y)}{g'_2(x, y)} = 0 \tag{5}$$

Assuming that $g'_2(x, y) \neq 0$, and defining $\lambda = f'_2(x, y)/g'_2(x, y)$, we deduce that the two equations $f'_1(x, y) - \lambda g'_1(x, y) = 0$ and $f'_2(x, y) - \lambda g'_2(x, y) = 0$ must both be satisfied. Hence, the Lagrangian must be stationary at (x, y). The same result holds (by an analogous argument) provided $g'_1(x, y) \neq 0$. To summarize, one can prove the following precise result:

THEOREM 14.4.1   (LAGRANGE'S THEOREM)

Suppose that $f(x, y)$ and $g(x, y)$ have continuous partial derivatives in a domain A of the xy-plane, and that (x_0, y_0) is both an interior point of A and a local extreme point for $f(x, y)$ subject to the constraint $g(x, y) = c$. Suppose further that $g'_1(x_0, y_0)$ and $g'_2(x_0, y_0)$ are not both 0. Then there exists a unique number λ such that the Lagrangian

$$\mathcal{L}(x, y) = f(x, y) - \lambda\left(g(x, y) - c\right)$$

has a stationary point at (x_0, y_0).

Problem 3 asks you to show how trouble can result from uncritical use of the Lagrange multiplier method, disregarding the assumptions in Theorem 14.4.1. Problem 4 asks you to show what can go wrong if $g'_1(x_0, y_0)$ and $g'_2(x_0, y_0)$ are both 0.

In constrained optimization problems in economics, it is often implicitly assumed that the variables are nonnegative. This was certainly the case for the specific utility maximization problem in Example 14.1.3. Because the optimal solutions were positive, nothing was lost by disregarding the nonnegativity constraints. Here is an example showing that sometimes we must take greater care.

EXAMPLE 1   Consider the utility maximization problem

$$\max xy + x + 2y \quad \text{subject to} \quad 2x + y = m, \quad x \geq 0, \; y \geq 0$$

where we have required that the amount of each good is nonnegative. The Lagrangian is $\mathcal{L} = xy + x + 2y - \lambda(2x + y - m)$. So the first-order conditions (disregarding the nonnegativity constraints for the moment) are $\mathcal{L}'_1 = y + 1 - 2\lambda = 0$, $\mathcal{L}'_2(x, y) = x + 2 - \lambda = 0$. By eliminating λ, we find that $y = 2x + 3$. Inserting this into the budget constraint gives $2x + 2x + 3 = m$, so $x = \frac{1}{4}(m - 3)$. We easily find the corresponding value of y, and the suggested solution that emerges is $x^* = \frac{1}{4}(m - 3)$, $y^* = \frac{1}{2}(m + 3)$. Note that in the case when $m < 3$, then $x^* < 0$, so that the expressions we have found for x^* and y^* do not solve the given problem. The solution in this case is, as shown below, $x^* = 0$, $y^* = m$. (So when income is low, the consumer should spend everything on just one commodity.)

Let us analyse the problem by converting it to one that is unconstrained. To do this, note how the constraint implies that $y = m - 2x$. In order for both x and y to be nonnegative, one must require $0 \leq x \leq m/2$ and $0 \leq y \leq m$. Substituting $y = m - 2x$ into the utility function, we obtain utility as function $U(x)$ of x alone, where

$$U(x) = x(m - 2x) + x + 2(m - 2x) = -2x^2 + (m - 3)x + 2m, \quad x \in [0, m/2]$$

This is a quadratic function with $x = \frac{1}{4}(m - 3)$ as the stationary point. If $m > 3$, it is an interior stationary point for the concave function U, so it is a maximum point. If $m \leq 3$, then $U'(x) = -4x + (m - 3) \leq 0$ for all $x \geq 0$. Because of the constraint $x \geq 0$, it follows that $U(x)$ must have its largest value for $x = 0$.

Optimization problems with inequality constraints are generally known as *nonlinear programming problems*. Some relatively simple cases are discussed in Sections 14.8 and 14.9. A much more systematic treatment of nonlinear programming is included in FMEA.

WARNING: One of the most frequently occurring errors in the economics literature (even in some leading textbooks) concerning the Lagrange multiplier method is the claim that it transforms a constrained optimization problem into one of finding an unconstrained optimum of the Lagrangian. Problem 1 shows that this is wrong. What the method does instead is to transform a constrained optimization problem into one of finding the appropriate stationary points of the Lagrangian. Sometimes these are maximum points, but often they are not.

PROBLEMS FOR SECTION 14.4

1. Consider the problem max xy subject to $x + y = 2$. Show that $(x, y) = (1, 1)$, with $\lambda = 1$, is the only solution of the first-order conditions. (That this is indeed the solution of the problem is easily seen by reducing it to the one-variable problem of maximizing $xy = x(2 - x)$.) But $(1, 1)$ does not maximize the Lagrangian $\mathcal{L}(x, y) = xy - 1 \cdot (x + y - 2)$. Why not?

2. The following text taken from a book on mathematics for management contains *grave* errors. Sort them out. "Consider the general problem of finding the extreme points of $z = f(x, y)$ subject to the constraint $g(x, y) = 0$. Clearly the extreme points must satisfy the pair of equations $f'_x(x, y) = 0$, $f'_y(x, y) = 0$ in addition to the constraint $g(x, y) = 0$. Thus, there are three equations that must be satisfied by the pair of unknowns x, y. Because there are more equations than unknowns, the system is said to be overdetermined and, in general, is difficult to solve. In order to facilitate computation ..." (A description of the Lagrange method follows.)

HARDER PROBLEMS

3. Consider the problem max $f(x, y) = 2x + 3y$ subject to $g(x, y) = \sqrt{x} + \sqrt{y} = 5$.

   (a) Show that the Lagrange multiplier method suggests the wrong solution $(x, y) = (9, 4)$. (Note that $f(9, 4) = 30$, and yet $f(25, 0) = 50$.)

   (b) Solve the problem by studying the level curves of $f(x, y) = 2x + 3y$ together with the graph of the constraint equation. (See Problem 5.4.2.)

   (c) Which assumption of Theorem 14.4.1 is violated?

SM 4. The functions f and g are defined by

$$f(x, y) = (x + 2)^2 + y^2 \quad \text{and} \quad g(x, y) = y^2 - x(x + 1)^2$$

   Find the minimum value of $f(x, y)$ subject to $g(x, y) = 0$. Show that the Lagrange multiplier method cannot locate this minimum. (*Hint:* Draw a graph of $g(x, y) = 0$. Note in particular that $g(-1, 0) = 0$.)

14.5 Sufficient Conditions

Under the hypotheses of Theorem 14.4.1, the Lagrange multiplier method for the problem

$$\max(\min) f(x, y) \quad \text{subject to} \quad g(x, y) = c \tag{1}$$

gives *necessary* conditions for the solution. In order to confirm that we have really found the solution, however, a more careful check is needed. The examples and problems of Section 14.3 have geometric interpretations which strongly suggest we have found the solution. Indeed, if the constraint set is closed and bounded, then the extreme value theorem 13.6.2 guarantees that a continuous function *will* attain both maximum and minimum values over this set. A case in point is Example 14.3.1, where the constraint set *is* closed and bounded (see Fig. 14.3.1), so the continuous function $f(x, y) = x^2 + y^2$ will attain both a maximum value and a minimum value over the constraint set. Since there are 4 points satisfying the first-order conditions, it remains only to check which of them gives f its highest and lowest value. (To test your understanding of when this procedure can be used, explain why it certainly works in Problems 14.3.1(a) and 14.3.2(a), but not in Problem 14.3.2(b), to mention just a few.) Finally, in some cases, ad hoc methods of the kind illustrated at the end of Example 14.3.1 can be used.

Concave/Convex Lagrangian

If (x_0, y_0) does solve problem (1), then the Lagrangian $\mathcal{L}(x, y) = f(x, y) - \lambda(g(x, y) - c)$ is stationary at (x_0, y_0), but $\mathcal{L}$ does not necessarily have a maximum (minimum) at (x_0, y_0) (see Problem 14.4.1). Suppose, however, that $\mathcal{L}(x, y)$ happens to reach a global maximum at (x_0, y_0) — that is, (x_0, y_0) maximizes $\mathcal{L}(x, y)$ among *all* (x, y). Then

$$\mathcal{L}(x_0, y_0) = f(x_0, y_0) - \lambda(g(x_0, y_0) - c) \geq \mathcal{L}(x, y) = f(x, y) - \lambda(g(x, y) - c) \quad (*)$$

for all (x, y). If (x_0, y_0) also satisfies the constraint $g(x_0, y_0) = c$, then from $(*)$ we conclude that $f(x_0, y_0) \geq f(x, y)$ for all (x, y) such that $g(x, y) = c$. Hence, (x_0, y_0) really does solve the maximization problem (1).

A corresponding result is obtained for the minimization problem in (1), provided that $\mathcal{L}(x, y)$ reaches a global minimum at (x_0, y_0).

Next, we recall from Theorem 13.2.1 and Note 13.2.2 that a stationary point (x_0, y_0) for a concave (convex) function really does maximize (minimize) the function. Thus we have the following result:

THEOREM 14.5.1 (CONCAVE/CONVEX LAGRANGIAN)

Consider problem (1) and suppose (x_0, y_0) is a stationary point for the Lagrangian $\mathcal{L}(x, y) = f(x, y) - \lambda(g(x, y) - c)$.

(A) If the Lagrangian is concave, then (x_0, y_0) solves the maximization problem.

(B) If the Lagrangian is convex, then (x_0, y_0) solves the minimization problem.

EXAMPLE 1   Consider a firm that uses positive inputs K and L of capital and labour, respectively, to produce a single output Q according to the Cobb–Douglas production function $Q = F(K, L) = AK^a L^b$, where A, a, and b are positive parameters satisfying $a + b \leq 1$. Suppose that the prices of capital and labour are $r > 0$ and $w > 0$, respectively. The cost-minimizing inputs of K and L must solve the problem

$$\min rK + wL \quad \text{subject to} \quad AK^a L^b = Q$$

Explain why the Lagrangian is convex, so that a stationary point of the Lagrangian must minimize costs. (*Hint:* See Problem 13.2.8.)

Solution: The Lagrangian is $\mathcal{L} = rK + wL - \lambda(AK^a L^b - Q)$, and the first-order conditions are $r = \lambda Aa K^{a-1} L^b$ and $w = \lambda Ab K^a L^{b-1}$, implying that $\lambda > 0$. From Problem 13.2.8 we see that $-\mathcal{L}$ is concave, so $\mathcal{L}$ is convex.

Local Second-Order Conditions

Sometimes we are interested in conditions that are sufficient for (x_0, y_0) to be a local extreme point of $f(x, y)$ subject to $g(x, y) = c$. We start by looking at the expression for dz/dx given by (14.4.5). The condition $dz/dx = 0$ is necessary for local optimality. If also $d^2z/dx^2 < 0$, then a stationary point of the Lagrangian must solve the local maximization problem. The derivative d^2z/dx^2 is just the total derivative of dz/dx w.r.t. x. Assuming that both f and g are C^2 functions, and recalling that y is a function of x, it follows from (14.4.5) that

$$\frac{d^2z}{dx^2} = f_{11}'' + f_{12}''y' - (f_{21}'' + f_{22}''y')\frac{g_1'}{g_2'} - f_2'\frac{(g_{11}'' + g_{12}''y')g_2' - (g_{21}'' + g_{22}''y')g_1'}{(g_2')^2}$$

But f and g are C^2 functions, so $f_{12}'' = f_{21}''$ and $g_{12}'' = g_{21}''$. Moreover, $y' = -g_1'/g_2'$. Also $f_1' = \lambda g_1'$ and $f_2' = \lambda g_2'$, because these are the first-order conditions. Using these relationships to eliminate y' and f_2', as well as some elementary algebra, we obtain

$$\frac{d^2z}{dx^2} = \frac{1}{(g_2')^2}\left[(f_{11}'' - \lambda g_{11}'')(g_2')^2 - 2(f_{12}'' - \lambda g_{12}'')g_1'g_2' + (f_{22}'' - \lambda g_{22}'')(g_1')^2\right]$$

We see that $d^2z/dx^2 < 0$ provided the expression in the square brackets is < 0. Thus we have the following result:

THEOREM 14.5.2 (LOCAL SECOND-ORDER CONDITIONS)

Consider the problem

$$\text{local max(min) } f(x, y) \quad \text{subject to} \quad g(x, y) = c$$

and suppose that (x_0, y_0) satisfies the first-order conditions $f_1'(x, y) = \lambda g_1'(x, y)$, $f_2'(x, y) = \lambda g_2'(x, y)$. Define

$$D(x, y, \lambda) = (f_{11}'' - \lambda g_{11}'')(g_2')^2 - 2(f_{12}'' - \lambda g_{12}'')g_1'g_2' + (f_{22}'' - \lambda g_{22}'')(g_1')^2$$

(A) If $D(x_0, y_0, \lambda) < 0$, then (x_0, y_0) solves the local maximization problem.

(B) If $D(x_0, y_0, \lambda) > 0$, then (x_0, y_0) solves the local minimization problem.

The conditions on the sign of $D(x_0, y_0, \lambda)$ are called the (local) *second-order conditions*.

EXAMPLE 2   Consider the problem

$$\text{local max (min) } f(x, y) = x^2 + y^2 \quad \text{subject to} \quad g(x, y) = x^2 + xy + y^2 = 3$$

In Example 14.3.1 we saw that the first-order conditions give the points $(1, 1)$ and $(-1, -1)$ with $\lambda = 2/3$, as well as $(\sqrt{3}, -\sqrt{3})$ and $(-\sqrt{3}, \sqrt{3})$ with $\lambda = 2$. Use Theorem 14.5.2 to check the local second-order conditions in this case.

Solution: We find that $f_{11}'' = 2$, $f_{12}'' = 0$, $f_{22}'' = 2$, $g_{11}'' = 2$, $g_{12}'' = 1$, and $g_{22}'' = 2$. So

$$D(x, y, \lambda) = (2 - 2\lambda)(x + 2y)^2 + 2\lambda(2x + y)(x + 2y) + (2 - 2\lambda)(2x + y)^2$$

Hence $D(1, 1, \frac{2}{3}) = D(-1, -1, \frac{2}{3}) = 24$ and $D(\sqrt{3}, -\sqrt{3}, 2) = D(-\sqrt{3}, \sqrt{3}, 2) = -24$. From the signs of D, we conclude that $(1, 1)$ and $(-1, -1)$ are local minimum points, whereas $(\sqrt{3}, -\sqrt{3})$ and $(-\sqrt{3}, \sqrt{3})$ are local maximum points. (In Example 14.3.1 we actually proved that these points were *global* extreme points.)

For those who are familiar with 3×3 determinants (see Section 16.2), the rather lengthy expression $D(x, y, \lambda)$ can be written in a symmetric form that is easier to remember. In fact,

$$D(x, y, \lambda) = - \begin{vmatrix} 0 & g_1'(x, y) & g_2'(x, y) \\ g_1'(x, y) & \mathcal{L}_{11}''(x, y) & \mathcal{L}_{12}''(x, y) \\ g_2'(x, y) & \mathcal{L}_{21}''(x, y) & \mathcal{L}_{22}''(x, y) \end{vmatrix} \tag{2}$$

Note that the 2×2 matrix at the bottom right of (2) is the Hessian of the Lagrangian (see Section 11.6). So the determinant is naturally called a **bordered Hessian**; its borders in the first row and first column, apart from the 0 element in the top left position, are the first-order partial derivatives of g.

PROBLEMS FOR SECTION 14.5

1. Use Theorem 14.5.1 to check that the optimal solution is found in Problem 14.1.3(a).

2. Consider the utility maximizing problem max $\ln x + \ln y$ subject to $px + qy = m$. Compute $D(x, y, \lambda)$ in Theorem 14.5.2 in this case, and verify that the second-order condition in that theorem is satisfied. (Note that the Lagrangian is actually concave, as is easily checked, so the unique solution $(x, y) = (m/p, m/2q)$ to the first-order conditions is actually a global constrained maximum for this problem.)

3. Compute $D(x, y, \lambda)$ in Theorem 14.5.2 for Problem 14.2.3(a). Conclusion?

(SM) 4. Prove that $U(x, y) = x^a + y^a$, $a \in (0, 1)$, is concave when $x > 0$, $y > 0$. Solve the consumer demand problem

$$\max x^a + y^a \quad \text{subject to} \quad px + qy = m$$

14.6 Additional Variables and Constraints

Constrained optimization problems in economics usually involve more than just two variables. The typical problem with n variables can be written in the form

$$\max(\min) \ f(x_1, \ldots, x_n) \quad \text{subject to} \quad g(x_1, \ldots, x_n) = c \tag{1}$$

The Lagrange multiplier method presented in the previous sections can be easily generalized. As before, associate a Lagrange multiplier λ with the constraint and form the Lagrangian

$$\mathcal{L}(x_1, \ldots, x_n) = f(x_1, \ldots, x_n) - \lambda\big(g(x_1, \ldots, x_n) - c\big) \tag{2}$$

Next, find all the first-order partial derivatives of $\mathcal{L}$ and equate them to zero, so that

$$\mathcal{L}_1' = f_1'(x_1, \ldots, x_n) - \lambda g_1'(x_1, \ldots, x_n) = 0$$
$$\cdots\cdots\cdots\cdots\cdots\cdots\cdots\cdots\cdots\cdots\cdots\cdots\cdots\cdots\cdots\cdots \tag{3}$$
$$\mathcal{L}_n' = f_n'(x_1, \ldots, x_n) - \lambda g_n'(x_1, \ldots, x_n) = 0$$

These n equations, together with the constraint, form $n + 1$ equations that should be solved simultaneously to determine the $n + 1$ unknowns $x_1, \ldots, x_n$, and λ.

NOTE 1 This method will (in general) fail to give correct necessary conditions if all the first-order partial derivatives of $g(x_1, \ldots, x_n)$ vanish at the stationary point of the Lagrangian. Otherwise, the proof is an easy generalization of the analytic argument in Section 14.4 for the first-order conditions. If, say, $\partial g/\partial x_n \neq 0$, we "solve" $g(x_1, \ldots, x_n) = c$ for x_n near the stationary point, and thus reduce the problem to an unconstrained extremum problem in the remaining $n - 1$ variables $x_1, \ldots, x_{n-1}$.

EXAMPLE 1   Solve the consumer's demand problem

$$\max \ U(x, y, z) = x^2 y^3 z \quad \text{subject to} \quad x + y + z = 12$$

Solution: With $\mathcal{L}(x, y, z) = x^2 y^3 z - \lambda(x + y + z - 12)$, the first-order conditions are

$$\mathcal{L}'_1 = 2xy^3 z - \lambda = 0, \qquad \mathcal{L}'_2 = 3x^2 y^2 z - \lambda = 0, \qquad \mathcal{L}'_3 = x^2 y^3 - \lambda = 0 \qquad (*)$$

If *any* of the variables x, y, and z is 0, then $x^2 y^3 z = 0$, which is *not* the maximum value. So suppose that x, y, and z are all positive. From the two first equations in $(*)$, we have $2xy^3 z = 3x^2 y^2 z$, so $y = 3x/2$. The first and third equations in $(*)$ likewise imply that $z = x/2$. Inserting $y = 3x/2$ and $z = x/2$ into the constraint yields $x + 3x/2 + x/2 = 12$, so $x = 4$. Then $y = 6$ and $z = 2$. Thus, the only possible solution is $(x, y, z) = (4, 6, 2)$.

EXAMPLE 2   Solve the problem

$$\text{minimize} \quad f(x, y, z) = (x - 4)^2 + (y - 4)^2 + \left(z - \tfrac{1}{2}\right)^2 \quad \text{subject to} \quad x^2 + y^2 = z$$

Can you supply a geometric interpretation of the problem?

Solution: The Lagrangian is $\mathcal{L}(x, y, z) = (x-4)^2 + (y-4)^2 + \left(z-\tfrac{1}{2}\right)^2 - \lambda(x^2 + y^2 - z)$, and the first-order conditions are:

$$\mathcal{L}'_1(x, y, z) = 2(x - 4) - 2\lambda x = 0 \tag{i}$$

$$\mathcal{L}'_2(x, y, z) = 2(y - 4) - 2\lambda y = 0 \tag{ii}$$

$$\mathcal{L}'_3(x, y, z) = 2\left(z - \tfrac{1}{2}\right) + \lambda = 0 \tag{iii}$$

$$x^2 + y^2 = z \tag{iv}$$

From (i) we see that $x = 0$ is impossible. Equation (i) thus gives $\lambda = 1 - 4/x$. Inserting this into (ii) and (iii) gives $y = x$ and $z = 2/x$. Using these results, equation (iv) reduces to $2x^2 = 2/x$, that is, $x^3 = 1$, so $x = 1$. It follows that $(x, y, z) = (1, 1, 2)$ is the only solution candidate to the problem.

The expression $(x-4)^2 + (y-4)^2 + (z-1/2)^2$ measures the square of the distance from the point $(4, 4, 1/2)$ to the point (x, y, z). The set of points (x, y, z) that satisfy $z = x^2 + y^2$ is a surface known as a paraboloid, part of which is shown in Fig. 1. The minimization problem is therefore to find that point on the paraboloid which has the smallest (square) distance from $(4, 4, 1/2)$. It is "geometrically obvious" that this problem has a solution. On the other hand, the problem of finding the largest distance from $(4, 4, 1/2)$ to a point on the paraboloid does not have a solution, because the distance can be made as large as we like.

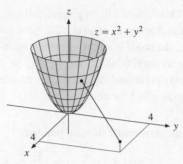

Figure 1

EXAMPLE 3   The general consumer optimization problem with n goods is

$$\max_{x_1,\dots,x_n} U(x_1,\dots,x_n) \quad \text{subject to} \quad p_1 x_1 + \cdots + p_n x_n = m \tag{4}$$

where U is defined for $x_1 \geq 0, \dots, x_n \geq 0$. The Lagrangian is

$$\mathcal{L}(x_1,\dots,x_n) = U(x_1,\dots,x_n) - \lambda(p_1 x_1 + \cdots + p_n x_n - m)$$

The first-order conditions are

$$\mathcal{L}_i'(x_1,\dots,x_n) = U_i'(x_1,\dots,x_n) - \lambda p_i = 0, \qquad i = 1,\dots,n$$

Writing $\mathbf{x} = (x_1,\dots,x_n)$, we have

$$\frac{U_1'(\mathbf{x})}{p_1} = \frac{U_2'(\mathbf{x})}{p_2} = \cdots = \frac{U_n'(\mathbf{x})}{p_n} = \lambda \tag{5}$$

Apart from the last equation, which serves only to determine the Lagrange multiplier λ, we have $n - 1$ equations. (For $n = 2$, there is one equation; for $n = 3$, there are two equations; and so on.) In addition, the constraint must hold. Thus, we have n equations to determine the values of $x_1,\dots,x_n$. From (5) it also follows that

$$\frac{U_j'(\mathbf{x})}{U_k'(\mathbf{x})} = \frac{p_j}{p_k} \qquad \text{for every pair of goods } j \text{ and } k \tag{6}$$

The left-hand side is the marginal rate of substitution (MRS) of good k for good j, whereas the right-hand side is their price ratio, or rate of exchange of good k for good j. So condition (6) equates the MRS for each pair of goods to the corresponding price ratio.

Consider the equations in (5), together with the budget constraint. Assume that this system is solved for $x_1,\dots,x_n$ and λ as functions of $p_1,\dots,p_n$ and m, giving $x_i = D_i(p_1,\dots,p_n,m)$, for $i = 1,\dots,n$. Then $D_i(p_1,\dots,p_n,m)$ gives the amount of the ith commodity demanded by the individual when facing prices $p_1,\dots,p_n$ and income m. For this reason $D_1,\dots,D_n$ are called the **(individual) demand functions**. By the same argument as in Example 14.1.3, the demand functions are homogeneous of degree 0. As one check that you have correctly derived the demand functions, it is a good idea to verify that the functions you find are indeed homogeneous of degree 0, and satisfy the budget constraint.

In the case when the consumer has a Cobb–Douglas utility function, the constrained maximization problem is

$$\max \ A x_1^{a_1} \cdots x_n^{a_n} \quad \text{subject to} \quad p_1 x_1 + \cdots + p_n x_n = m \tag{$*$}$$

where we assume that each "taste" parameter $a_i > 0$. Then the demand functions are

$$D_i(p_1, \ldots, p_n, m) = \frac{a_i}{a_1 + \cdots + a_n} \frac{m}{p_i}, \qquad i = 1, \ldots, n \tag{$**$}$$

(see Problem 8(a)). We see how the pattern of the two-variable case in Example 14.1.3 is repeated, with a constant fraction of income m spent on each good, independent of all prices. Note also that the demand for any good i is completely unaffected by changes in the price of any other good. This is an argument against using Cobb–Douglas utility functions, because we expect realistic demand functions to depend on prices of other goods that are either complements or substitutes.

More Constraints

Occasionally economists need to consider optimization problems with more than one equality constraint (although it is much more common to have many inequality constraints). The corresponding general Lagrange problem is

$$\max(\min) f(x_1, \ldots, x_n) \quad \text{subject to} \quad \begin{cases} g_1(x_1, \ldots, x_n) = c_1 \\ \cdots\cdots\cdots\cdots\cdots \\ g_m(x_1, \ldots, x_n) = c_m \end{cases} \tag{7}$$

The Lagrange multiplier method can be extended to treat problem (7). To do so, associate a Lagrange multiplier with each constraint, then form the Lagrangian sum

$$\mathcal{L}(x_1, \ldots, x_n) = f(x_1, \ldots, x_n) - \sum_{j=1}^{m} \lambda_j \big(g_j(x_1, \ldots, x_n) - c_j\big) \tag{8}$$

Except in special cases, this Lagrangian must be stationary at any optimal point. That is, its partial derivative w.r.t. each variable x_i must vanish. Hence,

$$\frac{\partial \mathcal{L}}{\partial x_i} = \frac{\partial f(x_1, \ldots, x_n)}{\partial x_i} - \sum_{j=1}^{m} \lambda_j \frac{\partial g_j(x_1, \ldots, x_n)}{\partial x_i} = 0, \qquad i = 1, 2, \ldots, n \tag{9}$$

Together with the m equality constraints, these n equations form a total of $n + m$ equations in the $n + m$ unknowns $x_1, \ldots, x_n, \lambda_1, \ldots, \lambda_m$.

EXAMPLE 4   Solve the problem

$$\min \ x^2 + y^2 + z^2 \quad \text{subject to} \quad \begin{cases} x + 2y + z = 30 & \text{(i)} \\ 2x - y - 3z = 10 & \text{(ii)} \end{cases}$$

Solution: The Lagrangian is

$$\mathcal{L}(x, y, z) = x^2 + y^2 + z^2 - \lambda_1(x + 2y + z - 30) - \lambda_2(2x - y - 3z - 10)$$

The first-order conditions (9) require that

$$\frac{\partial \mathcal{L}}{\partial x} = 2x - \lambda_1 - 2\lambda_2 = 0 \tag{iii}$$

$$\frac{\partial \mathcal{L}}{\partial y} = 2y - 2\lambda_1 + \lambda_2 = 0 \tag{iv}$$

$$\frac{\partial \mathcal{L}}{\partial z} = 2z - \lambda_1 + 3\lambda_2 = 0 \tag{v}$$

So there are five equations, (i) to (v), to determine the five unknowns x, y, z, λ_1, and λ_2.
Solving (iii) and (iv) simultaneously for λ_1 and λ_2 gives

$$\lambda_1 = \tfrac{2}{5}x + \tfrac{4}{5}y, \qquad \lambda_2 = \tfrac{4}{5}x - \tfrac{2}{5}y$$

Inserting these expressions for λ_1 and λ_2 into (v) and rearranging yields

$$x - y + z = 0 \tag{vi}$$

This equation together with (i) and (ii) constitutes a system of three linear equations in the
unknowns x, y, and z. Solving this system by elimination gives $(x, y, z) = (10, 10, 0)$. The
corresponding values of the multipliers are $\lambda_1 = 12$ and $\lambda_2 = 4$.

Here is a geometric argument to confirm that we have solved the minimization problem.
Each of the two constraints represents a plane in $\mathbb{R}^3$, and the points satisfying both constraints
consequently lie on the straight line where the two planes intersect. Now $x^2 + y^2 + z^2$
measures (the square of) the distance from the origin to a point on this straight line, which
we want to make as small as possible by choosing the point on the line that is nearest to the
origin. No maximum distance can possibly exist, but it is geometrically obvious that there
is a minimum distance, and it must be attained at this nearest point.

An easier alternative method to solve this particular problem is to reduce it to a one-
variable optimization problem by using (i) and (ii) to get $y = 20 - x$ and $z = x - 10$, the
equations of the straight line where the planes intersect. Then the square of the distance
from the origin is $x^2 + y^2 + z^2 = x^2 + (20 - x)^2 + (x - 10)^2 = 3(x - 10)^2 + 200$, and
this function is easily seen to have a minimum when $x = 10$. See also Problem 5.

PROBLEMS FOR SECTION 14.6

1. Consider the problem min $x^2 + y^2 + z^2$ subject to $x + y + z = 1$.

   (a) Write down the Lagrangian for this problem, and find the only point (x, y, z) that satisfies
   the necessary conditions.

   (b) Give a geometric argument for the existence of a solution. Does the corresponding maximization problem have any solution?

2. Use the result in (∗∗) in Example 3 to solve the utility maximizing problem

   $$\max \ 10x^{1/2}y^{1/3}z^{1/4} \quad \text{subject to} \quad 4x + 3y + 6z = 390$$

3. A consumer's demands x, y, z for three goods are chosen to maximize the utility function

$$U(x, y, z) = x + \sqrt{y} - 1/z \quad (x \geq 0, \ y > 0, \ z > 0)$$

subject to the budget constraint $px + qy + rz = m$, where $p, q, r > 0$ and $m \geq \sqrt{pr} + p^2/4q$.

(a) Write out the first-order conditions for a constrained maximum.

(b) Find the utility-maximizing demands for all three goods as functions of the four variables (p, q, r, m).

(c) Show that the maximized utility is given by the indirect utility function

$$U^*(p, q, r, m) = \frac{m}{p} + \frac{p}{4q} - 2\sqrt{\frac{r}{p}}$$

(d) Find $\partial U^*/\partial m$ and comment on your answer.

4. Each week an individual consumes quantities x and y of two goods, and works for l hours. These three quantities are chosen to maximize the utility function

$$U(x, y, l) = \alpha \ln x + \beta \ln y + (1 - \alpha - \beta) \ln(L - l)$$

which is defined for $0 \leq l < L$ and for $x, y > 0$. Here α and β are positive parameters satisfying $\alpha + \beta < 1$. The individual faces the budget constraint $px + qy = wl$, where w is the wage per hour. Define $\gamma = (\alpha + \beta)/(1 - \alpha - \beta)$. Find the individual's demands x^*, y^*, and labour supply l^* as functions of p, q, and w.

5. Consider the problem in Example 4, and let $(x, y, z) = (10+h, 10+k, l)$. Show that if (x, y, z) satisfies both constraints, then $k = -h$ and $l = h$. Then show that $x^2 + y^2 + z^2 = 200 + 3h^2$. Conclusion?

6. A statistical problem requires solving

$$\min \ a_1^2 x_1^2 + a_2^2 x_2^2 + \cdots + a_n^2 x_n^2 \quad \text{subject to} \quad x_1 + x_2 + \cdots + x_n = 1$$

Here all the constants a_i are nonzero. Solve the problem, taking it for granted that the minimum value exists. What is the solution if one of the a_i's is zero?

(SM) 7. Solve the problem:

$$\max(\min) \ x + y \quad \text{subject to} \quad \begin{cases} x^2 + 2y^2 + z^2 = 1 \\ x + y + z = 1 \end{cases}$$

HARDER PROBLEM

(SM) 8. Consider the consumer optimization problem in Example 3. Find the demand functions when:

(a) $U(x_1, \ldots, x_n) = A x_1^{a_1} \cdots x_n^{a_n} \quad (A > 0, a_1 > 0, \ldots, a_n > 0)$

(b) $U(x_1, \ldots, x_n) = x_1^a + \cdots + x_n^a \quad (0 < a < 1)$

14.7 Comparative Statics

Equation (14.2.2) offers an economic interpretation of the Lagrange multiplier for the case of two variables and one constraint. This can be extended to the Lagrange problem with n variables and m constraints introduced in Section 14.6. That general problem can be written in the form

$$\max(\min)\ f(\mathbf{x}) \quad \text{subject to} \quad g_j(\mathbf{x}) = c_j, \ j = 1, \ldots, m \tag{1}$$

Let $x_1^*, \ldots, x_n^*$ be the values of $x_1, \ldots, x_n$ that satisfy the necessary conditions for the solution to (1). In general, $x_1^*, \ldots, x_n^*$ depend on the values of $c_1, \ldots, c_m$. We assume that each $x_i^* = x_i^*(c_1, \ldots, c_m)$, $i = 1, \ldots, n$ is a differentiable function of $c_1, \ldots, c_m$. The associated value $f^* = f(x_1^*, \ldots, x_n^*)$ of f is then a function of $c_1, \ldots, c_m$ as well.

Indeed, if we put $\mathbf{x}^* = (x_1^*, \ldots, x_n^*)$ and $\mathbf{c} = (c_1, \ldots, c_m)$, the resulting value is

$$f^*(\mathbf{c}) = f(\mathbf{x}^*(\mathbf{c})) = f(x_1^*(\mathbf{c}), \ldots, x_n^*(\mathbf{c})) \tag{2}$$

This function f^* of the right-hand sides of the equality constraints in (1) is called the **(optimal) value function** for problem (1). The m Lagrange multipliers $\lambda_1, \ldots, \lambda_m$ associated with $\mathbf{x}^*$ also depend on $\mathbf{c}$. Provided that certain regularity conditions are satisfied, we have

$$\frac{\partial f^*(\mathbf{c})}{\partial c_i} = \lambda_i(\mathbf{c}), \qquad i = 1, \ldots, m \tag{3}$$

The Lagrange multiplier $\lambda_i = \lambda_i(\mathbf{c})$ for the ith constraint is the rate at which the optimal value of the objective function changes w.r.t. changes in the constant c_i. The number λ_i is referred to as the imputed **shadow price** (or **marginal value**) per unit of resource i.

Suppose we change the components of the vector $\mathbf{c} = (c_1, \ldots, c_m)$ by the respective amounts $\mathbf{dc} = (dc_1, \ldots, dc_m)$. According to (12.8.2), if $dc_1, \ldots, dc_m$ are all small in absolute value, using (3) yields

$$f^*(\mathbf{c} + \mathbf{dc}) - f^*(\mathbf{c}) \approx \lambda_1(\mathbf{c})\,dc_1 + \cdots + \lambda_m(\mathbf{c})\,dc_m \tag{4}$$

EXAMPLE 1   Consider Example 4 in the previous section, and suppose we change the first constraint to $x + 2y + z = 31$ and the second constraint to $2x - y - 3z = 9$. Estimate the corresponding change in the value function by using (4). Find also the new exact value of the value function.

Solution: Using the notation introduced above and the results in Example 14.6.4, we have $c_1 = 30$, $c_2 = 10$, $dc_1 = 1$, $dc_2 = -1$, $\lambda_1(30, 10) = 12$, $\lambda_2(30, 10) = 4$, and $f^*(c_1, c_2) = f^*(30, 10) = 10^2 + 10^2 + 0^2 = 200$. Then (4) yields

$$f^*(30 + 1, 10 - 1) - f^*(30, 10) \approx \lambda_1(30, 10)\,dc_1 + \lambda_2(30, 10)\,dc_2$$
$$= 12 \cdot 1 + 4 \cdot (-1) = 8$$

Thus, $f^*(31, 9) = f^*(30 + 1, 10 - 1) \approx 200 + 8 = 208$.

To find the exact value of $f^*(31, 9)$, observe that (vi) in Example 14.6.4 is still valid. Thus, we have the three equations $x + 2y + z = 31$, $2x - y - 3z = 9$, $x - y + z = 0$, whose solutions for x, y, and z are $151/15$, $31/3$, and $4/15$, respectively. We find that $f^*(31, 9) = 15614/75 \approx 208.19$.

The Envelope Theorem

Using vector notation with $\mathbf{x} = (x_1, \ldots, x_n)$ and $\mathbf{r} = (r_1, \ldots, r_k)$, consider the version

$$\max(\min)_{\mathbf{x}} f(\mathbf{x}, \mathbf{r}) \quad \text{subject to} \quad g_j(\mathbf{x}, \mathbf{r}) = 0, \qquad j = 1, \ldots, m \qquad (5)$$

of the Lagrange problem (1) in which both the objective function f and each of the m different constraint functions g_j depend not only on the vector $\mathbf{x}$ of variables x_i which are to be chosen, but also on the parameter vector $\mathbf{r}$. Suppose that $\lambda_j = \lambda_j(\mathbf{r})$, $j = 1, \ldots, m$ are the Lagrange multipliers obtained from the first-order conditions for problem (5), and let $\mathcal{L}(\mathbf{x}, \mathbf{r}) = f(\mathbf{x}, \mathbf{r}) - \sum_{j=1}^{m} \lambda_j g_j(\mathbf{x}, \mathbf{r})$ be the corresponding Lagrangian. By analogy with (2), let $\mathbf{x}^*(\mathbf{r})$ denote the optimal choice of $\mathbf{x}$ when the parameter vector is $\mathbf{r}$, and define

$$f^*(\mathbf{r}) = f(\mathbf{x}^*(\mathbf{r}), \mathbf{r}) \qquad (6)$$

At the end of this section we prove that *if* $f^*(\mathbf{r})$ *and* $\mathbf{x}^*(\mathbf{r})$ *are differentiable*, the following result holds:

ENVELOPE THEOREM

$$\frac{\partial f^*(\mathbf{r})}{\partial r_i} = \left[\frac{\partial \mathcal{L}(\mathbf{x}, \mathbf{r})}{\partial r_i} \right]_{\mathbf{x}=\mathbf{x}^*(\mathbf{r})}, \quad i = 1, \ldots, k \qquad (7)$$

Economists refer to this as the **envelope theorem**. It is a very useful general result that should be studied carefully. When any parameter r_i is changed, then $f^*(\mathbf{r})$ changes for two reasons: First, a change in r_i changes the vector $\mathbf{r}$ and thus changes $f(\mathbf{x}^*(\mathbf{r}), \mathbf{r})$ directly. Second, a change in r_i changes, in general, all the functions $x_1^*(\mathbf{r}), \ldots, x_n^*(\mathbf{r})$, which changes $f(\mathbf{x}^*(\mathbf{r}), \mathbf{r})$ indirectly. The result in (7) shows that the total effect on the value function of a small change in r_i is found by computing the partial derivative of $\mathcal{L}(\mathbf{x}, \mathbf{r})$ w.r.t. r_i, and evaluating it at $\mathbf{x}^*(\mathbf{r})$, ignoring the indirect effect of the dependence of $\mathbf{x}^*$ on $\mathbf{r}$ altogether. The reason is that any small change in $\mathbf{x}$ that preserves the equality constraints of problem (5) will have a negligible effect on the value of $f(\mathbf{x}^*, \mathbf{r})$.

EXAMPLE 2   For Example 14.6.3, let $U^*(p_1, \ldots, p_n, m)$ denote the maximum utility obtainable when prices are $p_1, \ldots, p_n$ and the income is m. This U^* is called the **indirect utility function.** Using (3) for the Lagrange multiplier λ associated with the budget constraint, we see that

$$\lambda = \frac{\partial U^*}{\partial m} \qquad (8)$$

Thus, λ is the rate of increase in maximum utility as income increases. For this reason, λ is generally called the **marginal utility of income**.

Including the vector $\mathbf{r} = (p_1, \ldots, p_n, m)$ of all parameters, the Lagrangian $\mathcal{L}(\mathbf{x}, \mathbf{r})$ takes the form

$$\mathcal{L}(x_1, \ldots, x_n, p_1, \ldots, p_n, m) = U(x_1, \ldots, x_n) - \lambda(p_1 x_1 + \cdots + p_n x_n - m)$$

Obviously, $\partial \mathcal{L}/\partial m = \lambda$ and $\partial \mathcal{L}/\partial p_i = -\lambda x_i$. Hence, from (7) we get

$$\frac{\partial U^*(p_1, \ldots, p_n, m)}{\partial m} = \frac{\partial \mathcal{L}(x_1^*, \ldots, x_n^*, p_1, \ldots, p_n, m)}{\partial m} = \lambda$$

which repeats (8). Moreover,

$$\frac{\partial U^*(p_1, \ldots, p_n, m)}{\partial p_i} = \frac{\partial \mathcal{L}(x_1^*, \ldots, x_n^*, p_1, \ldots, p_n, m)}{\partial p_i} = -\lambda x_i^*$$

which is the so-called **Roy's identity**.[4] This formula has a nice interpretation: the marginal disutility of a price increase is the marginal utility of income (λ) multiplied by the quantity demanded (x_i^*). Intuitively, this is because, for a small price change, the loss of real income is approximately equal to the change in price multiplied by the quantity demanded.

EXAMPLE 3   As an illustration of Roy's identity, consider the consumer optimization problem with a Cobb–Douglas utility function, as given by ($*$) in Section 14.6 and Problem 14.6.8(a). Substituting the demands, which are given by ($**$) in Section 14.6, into the utility function, we obtain the indirect utility function, where we have defined $a = a_1 + a_2 + \cdots + a_n$,

$$U^*(p_1, \ldots, p_n, m) = A \left(\frac{a_1 m}{a p_1} \right)^{a_1} \cdots \left(\frac{a_n m}{a p_n} \right)^{a_n} = \frac{B m^a}{P(p_1, \ldots, p_n)}$$

where B denotes the constant $A a_1^{a_1} \cdots a_n^{a_n}/a^a$, and $P = P(p_1, \ldots, p_n)$ denotes the function $p_1^{a_1} \cdots p_n^{a_n}$. In fact, P is a homogeneous of degree a **price index**, which is also a Cobb–Douglas function whose powers match those of the original utility function.

This formula for the indirect utility function implies that $\partial U^*/\partial m = B a m^{a-1}/P$, and also that

$$\frac{\partial U^*}{\partial p_i} = -\frac{B m^a}{P^2} \frac{\partial P}{\partial p_i} = -\frac{B m^a}{P^2} \frac{a_i P}{p_i} = -\frac{B a m^{a-1}}{P} \frac{a_i m}{a p_i} = -\frac{\partial U^*}{\partial m} D_i(p_1, \ldots, p_n, m)$$

This confirms Roy's identity for the case of a Cobb–Douglas utility function.

EXAMPLE 4   A firm uses K units of capital and L units of labour to produce $F(K, L)$ units of a commodity. The prices of capital and labour are r and w, respectively. Consider the cost minimization problem

$$\text{minimize} \quad C = rK + wL \quad \text{subject to} \quad F(K, L) = Q$$

where we want to find the values of K and L that minimize the cost of producing Q units. Let $C^* = C(r, w, Q)$ be the value function for the problem. Find $\partial C^*/\partial r$, $\partial C^*/\partial w$, $\partial C^*/\partial Q$.

---

[4] Named after the French economist René Roy. Thus his name should be pronounced like the French word "roi" (meaning king); a very rough English equivalent is "rwa".

Solution: Including the production output requirement Q and the price parameters r and w, the Lagrangian is $\mathcal{L}(K, L, r, w, Q) = rK + wL - \lambda(F(K, L) - Q)$, whose partial derivatives are $\partial \mathcal{L}/\partial r = K$, $\partial \mathcal{L}/\partial w = L$, and $\partial \mathcal{L}/\partial Q = \lambda$. According to the envelope theorem (7),

$$\frac{\partial C^*}{\partial r} = K^*, \qquad \frac{\partial C^*}{\partial w} = L^*, \qquad \frac{\partial C^*}{\partial Q} = \lambda \qquad (*)$$

The first two equalities are instances of **Shephard's lemma.** The last equation shows that λ must equal *marginal cost*, the rate at which minimum cost increases w.r.t. changes in output.

Proof of (7): Using the chain rule to differentiate (6) w.r.t. r_h yields

$$\frac{\partial f^*(\mathbf{r})}{\partial r_h} = \sum_{i=1}^{n} \frac{\partial f(\mathbf{x}^*(\mathbf{r}), \mathbf{r})}{\partial x_i} \frac{\partial x_i^*(\mathbf{r})}{\partial r_h} + \frac{\partial f(\mathbf{x}^*(\mathbf{r}), \mathbf{r})}{\partial r_h} \qquad (i)$$

But the corresponding partial derivative of the Lagrangian evaluated at $(\mathbf{x}^*(\mathbf{r}), \mathbf{r})$ is

$$\frac{\partial \mathcal{L}(\mathbf{x}^*(\mathbf{r}), \mathbf{r})}{\partial r_h} = \frac{\partial f(\mathbf{x}^*(\mathbf{r}), \mathbf{r})}{\partial r_h} - \sum_{j=1}^{m} \lambda_j \frac{\partial g_j(\mathbf{x}^*(\mathbf{r}), \mathbf{r})}{\partial r_h} \qquad (ii)$$

Subtracting each side of (ii) from the corresponding side of (i), we obtain

$$\frac{\partial f^*(\mathbf{r})}{\partial r_h} - \frac{\partial \mathcal{L}(\mathbf{x}^*(\mathbf{r}), \mathbf{r})}{\partial r_h} = \sum_{i=1}^{n} \frac{\partial f(\mathbf{x}^*(\mathbf{r}), \mathbf{r})}{\partial x_i} \frac{\partial x_i^*(\mathbf{r})}{\partial r_h} + \sum_{j=1}^{m} \lambda_j \frac{\partial g_j(\mathbf{x}^*(\mathbf{r}), \mathbf{r})}{\partial r_h} \qquad (iii)$$

Differentiating the left-hand side of each constraint $g_j(\mathbf{x}^*(\mathbf{r}), \mathbf{r}) = 0$ w.r.t. r_h, however, yields

$$\sum_{i=1}^{n} \frac{\partial g_j(\mathbf{x}^*(\mathbf{r}), \mathbf{r})}{\partial x_i} \frac{\partial x_i^*(\mathbf{r})}{\partial r_h} + \frac{\partial g_j(\mathbf{x}^*(\mathbf{r}), \mathbf{r})}{\partial r_h} = 0 \qquad (iv)$$

Using (iv) to substitute for each term $\partial g_j(\mathbf{x}^*(\mathbf{r}), \mathbf{r})/\partial r_h$ in (iii) gives

$$\frac{\partial f^*(\mathbf{r})}{\partial r_h} - \frac{\partial \mathcal{L}(\mathbf{x}^*(\mathbf{r}), \mathbf{r})}{\partial r_h} = \sum_{i=1}^{n} \left[\sum_{i=1}^{n} \frac{\partial f(\mathbf{x}^*(\mathbf{r}), \mathbf{r})}{\partial x_i} - \frac{\partial g_j(\mathbf{x}^*(\mathbf{r}), \mathbf{r})}{\partial x_i} \right] \frac{\partial x_i^*(\mathbf{r})}{\partial r_h} \qquad (v)$$

The terms in square brackets, however, are equal to the partial derivatives $\partial \mathcal{L}(\mathbf{x}^*(\mathbf{r}), \mathbf{r})/\partial x_i$ which the first-order conditions require to be 0 for each $\mathbf{r}$ at the optimum $(\mathbf{x}^*(\mathbf{r}), \mathbf{r})$. ∎

NOTE 1 This proof used only the first-order conditions for problem (5). Therefore, the results in (7) are equally valid if we minimize rather than maximize $f(\mathbf{x}, \mathbf{r})$ w.r.t. $\mathbf{x}$. (Conditions sufficient for f^* to be differentiable are discussed in FMEA.)

PROBLEMS FOR SECTION 14.7

1. (a) Assuming $0 \le a < m/p$, find the solution (x^*, y^*) to the utility maximization problem

$$\max x + a \ln y \quad \text{subject to} \quad px + qy = m$$

(b) Find the indirect utility function $U^*(p, q, m, a) = x^* + \ln y^*$, and compute its partial derivatives w.r.t. p, q, m, and a. Verify the envelope theorem (7).

(SM) **2.** Solve the problem min $x + 4y + 3z$ subject to $x^2 + 2y^2 + \frac{1}{3}z^2 = b$. (Suppose that $b > 0$ and take it for granted that the problem has a solution.) Verify that (3) is valid.

3. (a) A firm has L units of labour at its disposal. Its outputs are three different commodities. Producing x, y, and z units of these commodities requires αx^2, βy^2, and γz^2 units of labour, respectively. Solve the problem

$$\max\ (ax + by + cz) \quad \text{subject to} \quad \alpha x^2 + \beta y^2 + \gamma z^2 = L$$

where a, b, c, α, β, and γ are positive constants.

(b) Put $a = 4$, $b = c = 1$, $\alpha = 1$, $\beta = \frac{1}{4}$, and $\gamma = \frac{1}{5}$, and show that in this case the problem in (a) has the solution $x = \frac{4}{5}\sqrt{L}$, $y = \frac{4}{5}\sqrt{L}$, and $z = \sqrt{L}$. What happens to the maximum value of $4x + y + z$ when L increases from 100 to 101? Find both the exact change and the appropriate linear approximation based on the interpretation of the Lagrange multiplier.

(SM) **4.** (a) Solve the problem

$$\max(\min)\ f(x, y, z) = x^2 + y^2 + z \quad \text{subject to}\ g(x, y, z) = x^2 + 2y^2 + 4z^2 = 1$$

(The graph of the constraint is the surface of an ellipsoid in $\mathbb{R}^3$, a closed and bounded set.)

(b) Suppose the constraint is changed to $x^2 + 2y^2 + 4z^2 = 1.02$. What is the approximate change in the maximum value of $f(x, y, z)$?

(SM) **5.** With reference to Example 4, let $F(K, L) = K^{1/2}L^{1/4}$ and solve the problem, finding explicit expressions for K^*, L^*, C^*, and λ. Verify the equalities $(*)$ in Example 3.

6. With reference to Example 4, assuming that the cost function C^* is a C^2 function, prove the symmetry relation $\partial K^*/\partial w = \partial L^*/\partial r$.

7. (a) Assuming that $m > q^2/4a^2p$, find the utility-maximizing demand functions $x^*(p, q, m, a)$ and $y^*(p, q, m, a)$, as well as the indirect utility function $U^*(p, q, m, a) = x^* + ay^*$, for the problem

$$\max\ \sqrt{x} + ay \quad \text{subject to} \quad px + qy = m$$

(b) Find all four partials of $U^*(p, q, m, a) = x^* + ay^*$ and verify the envelope theorem.

14.8 Nonlinear Programming: A Simple Case

So far this chapter has considered how to maximize or minimize a function subject to equality constraints. The final two sections concern nonlinear programming problems, which involve *inequality* constraints. Some particularly simple inequality constraints are those requiring certain variables to be nonnegative. These often have to be imposed for the solution to make economic sense. In addition, bounds on resource availability are often expressed as inequalities rather than equalities.

In this section we consider the simple **nonlinear programming problem**

$$\max f(x, y) \quad \text{subject to} \quad g(x, y) \leq c \tag{1}$$

with just one inequality constraint. Thus, we seek the largest value attained by $f(x, y)$ in the **admissible** or **feasible** set S of all pairs (x, y) satisfying $g(x, y) \leq c$.

Problems where one wants to minimize $f(x, y)$ subject to $(x, y) \in S$ can be handled by instead studying the problem of maximizing $-f(x, y)$ subject to $(x, y) \in S$.

Using the methods explained in Chapter 13, problem (1) can be solved by classical methods. It involves examining not only the stationary points of f in the interior of the admissible set S, but also the behaviour of f on the boundary of S. However, since the 1950s, economists have generally tackled such problems by using an extension of the Lagrangian multiplier method due originally to H. W. Kuhn and A. W. Tucker.

To apply their method, we begin by writing down a recipe giving all the points (x, y) that can possibly solve problem (1), except in some bizarre cases. The recipe closely resembles the one we used to solve the Lagrange problem max $f(x, y)$ subject to $g(x, y) = c$.

RECIPE FOR SOLVING PROBLEM (1)

A. Associate a constant Lagrange multiplier λ with the constraint $g(x, y) \leq c$, and define the Lagrangian

$$\mathcal{L}(x, y) = f(x, y) - \lambda\big(g(x, y) - c\big)$$

B. Find where $\mathcal{L}(x, y)$ is stationary by equating its partial derivatives to zero:

$$\mathcal{L}_1'(x, y) = f_1'(x, y) - \lambda g_1'(x, y) = 0$$
$$\mathcal{L}_2'(x, y) = f_2'(x, y) - \lambda g_2'(x, y) = 0 \tag{2}$$

C. Introduce the **complementary slackness condition**

$$\lambda \geq 0, \text{ and } \lambda = 0 \text{ if } g(x, y) < c \tag{3}$$

D. Require (x, y) to satisfy the constraint

$$g(x, y) \leq c \tag{4}$$

Find all the points (x, y) that, together with associated values of λ, satisfy all the conditions B, C, and D. These are the solution candidates, at least one of which solves the problem (if it has a solution).

Note that the conditions (2) are exactly the same as those used in the Lagrange multiplier method of Section 14.1. Condition (4) obviously has to be satisfied, so the only new feature is condition (3). In fact, condition (3) is rather tricky. It requires that λ is nonnegative, and moreover that $\lambda = 0$ if $g(x, y) < c$. Thus, if $\lambda > 0$, we must have $g(x, y) = c$. An alternative formulation of this condition is that

$$\lambda \geq 0, \qquad \lambda \cdot [g(x, y) - c] = 0 \tag{5}$$

Later we shall see that even in nonlinear programming, the Lagrange multiplier λ can be interpreted as a "price" per unit associated with increasing the right-hand side c of the "resource constraint" $g(x, y) \leq c$. With this interpretation, prices are nonnegative, and if the resource constraint is not binding because $g(x, y) < c$ at the optimum, this means that the price associated with increasing c by one unit is 0.

The two inequalities $\lambda \geq 0$ and $g(x, y) \leq c$ are **complementary** in the sense that at most one can be "slack"—that is, at most one can hold with inequality. Equivalently, at least one must be an equality.

WARNING: Failure to observe that it *is* possible to have *both* $\lambda = 0$ *and* $g(x, y) = c$ in (3), is probably the most common error that students make when answering questions in exam papers involving nonlinear programming problems.

Parts B and C of the above rule are together called the **Kuhn–Tucker conditions**. Note that these are (essentially) *necessary* conditions for the solution of problem (1). In general, they are far from sufficient. Indeed, suppose one can find a point (x_0, y_0) at which f is stationary and $g(x_0, y_0) < c$. Then the Kuhn–Tucker conditions will automatically be satisfied by (x_0, y_0) together with the Lagrange multiplier $\lambda = 0$. Yet then (x_0, y_0) could be a local or global minimum or maximum, or a saddle point.

NOTE 1 We say that conditions B and C are essentially necessary because the Kuhn–Tucker conditions may not hold for some rather rare constrained optimization problems that fail to satisfy a special technical condition called the "constraint qualification". For details, see FMEA.

NOTE 2 With equality constraints, setting the partial derivative $\partial \mathcal{L}/\partial \lambda$ equal to zero just recovers the constraint $g(x, y) = c$. (See Note 14.1.1.) With an inequality constraint, however, one can have $\partial \mathcal{L}/\partial \lambda = -g(x, y) + c > 0$ if the constraint is slack or inactive at an optimum. For this reason, we advise against differentiating the Lagrangian w.r.t. the multiplier λ, even though several other books advocate this procedure.

In Theorem 14.5.1 we proved that if the Lagrangian is concave, then the first-order conditions in the problem max $f(x, y)$ subject to $g(x, y) = c$ are sufficient for optimality. The corresponding result is also valid for problem (1):

THEOREM 14.8.1 (SUFFICIENT CONDITIONS)

Consider problem (1) and suppose that (x_0, y_0) satisfies conditions (2)–(4).

If the Lagrangian $\mathcal{L}(x, y)$ is concave, then (x_0, y_0) solves the problem.

Proof: Any pair (x_0, y_0) that satisfies conditions (2) must be a stationary point of the Lagrangian. By Theorem 13.2.1, if the Lagrangian is concave, this (x_0, y_0) will give a maximum. So

$$\mathcal{L}(x_0, y_0) = f(x_0, y_0) - \lambda(g(x_0, y_0) - c) \geq \mathcal{L}(x, y) = f(x, y) - \lambda(g(x, y) - c)$$

Rearranging the terms, we obtain

$$f(x_0, y_0) - f(x, y) \geq \lambda[g(x_0, y_0) - g(x, y)] \qquad (*)$$

If $g(x_0, y_0) < c$, then by (3), we have $\lambda = 0$, so $(*)$ implies that $f(x_0, y_0) \geq f(x, y)$ for all (x, y). On the other hand, if $g(x_0, y_0) = c$, then $\lambda[g(x_0, y_0) - g(x, y)] = \lambda[c - g(x, y)]$. Here $\lambda \geq 0$, and $c - g(x, y) \geq 0$ for all (x, y) satisfying the inequality constraint. Hence, (x_0, y_0) solves problem (1).[5] ∎

EXAMPLE 1   A firm has a total of L units of labour to allocate to the production of two goods. These can be sold at fixed positive prices a and b respectively. Producing x units of the first good requires αx^2 units of labour, whereas producing y units of the second good requires βy^2 units of labour, where α and β are positive constants. Find what output levels of the two goods maximize the revenue that the firm can earn by using this fixed amount of labour.

Solution: The firm's revenue maximization problem is

$$\max ax + by \quad \text{subject to} \quad \alpha x^2 + \beta y^2 \leq L$$

The Lagrangian is $\mathcal{L}(x, y) = ax + by - \lambda(\alpha x^2 + \beta y^2 - L)$, and the necessary conditions for (x^*, y^*) to solve the problem are

(i) $\mathcal{L}'_x = a - 2\lambda\alpha x^* = 0,$ (ii) $\mathcal{L}'_y = b - 2\lambda\beta y^* = 0$

(iii) $\lambda \geq 0$, and $\lambda = 0$ if $\alpha(x^*)^2 + \beta(y^*)^2 < L$

We see that λ, x^*, and y^* are all positive, and $\lambda = a/2\alpha x^* = b/2\beta y^*$. So

$$x^* = a/2\alpha\lambda, \quad y^* = b/2\beta\lambda \qquad (*)$$

Because $\lambda > 0$, condition (iii) implies that $\alpha(x^*)^2 + \beta(y^*)^2 = L$. Inserting the expressions for x^* and y^* into the resource constraint yields $a^2/4\alpha\lambda^2 + b^2/4\beta\lambda^2 = L$. It follows that

$$\lambda = \tfrac{1}{2}L^{-1/2}\sqrt{a^2/\alpha + b^2/\beta} \qquad (**)$$

Our recipe has produced the solution candidate with x^* and y^* given by $(*)$, and λ as in $(**)$. The Lagrangian $\mathcal{L}$ is obviously concave, so we have found the solution.

EXAMPLE 2   Solve the problem

$$\max f(x, y) = x^2 + y^2 + y - 1 \quad \text{subject to} \quad g(x, y) = x^2 + y^2 \leq 1$$

---

[5] In fact, as in the argument preceding Theorem 14.5.1, this proof shows that if the Lagrangian achieves a (global) maximum at a point (x_0, y_0) that satisfies conditions (3) and (4) (whether or not the Lagrangian is concave), then (x_0, y_0) solves the problem.

Solution: The Lagrangian is $\mathcal{L}(x, y) = x^2 + y^2 + y - 1 - \lambda(x^2 + y^2 - 1)$. Here the first-order conditions are:

(i) $\mathcal{L}'_1(x, y) = 2x - 2\lambda x = 0$ (ii) $\mathcal{L}'_2(x, y) = 2y + 1 - 2\lambda y = 0$

The complementary slackness condition is

$$\lambda \geq 0, \text{ and } \lambda = 0 \text{ if } x^2 + y^2 < 1 \tag{iii}$$

We want to find all pairs (x, y) that satisfy these conditions for some suitable value of λ.

Conditions (i) and (ii) can be written as $2x(1 - \lambda) = 0$ and $2y(1 - \lambda) = -1$, respectively. The second of these implies that $\lambda \neq 1$, so the first implies that $x = 0$.

Suppose $x^2 + y^2 = 1$ and so $y = \pm 1$ because $x = 0$. Try $y = 1$ first. Then (ii) implies $\lambda = 3/2$ and so (iii) is satisfied. Thus, $(0, 1)$ *with* $\lambda = 3/2$ *is a first candidate for optimality* (because all the conditions (i)–(iii) are satisfied). Next, try $y = -1$. Then condition (ii) yields $\lambda = 1/2$ and (iii) is again satisfied. Thus, $(0, -1)$ *with* $\lambda = 1/2$ *is a second candidate for optimality.*

Consider, finally, the case when $x = 0$ and also $x^2 + y^2 = y^2 < 1$—that is, $-1 < y < 1$. Then (iii) implies that $\lambda = 0$, and so (ii) yields $y = -1/2$. Hence, $(0, -1/2)$ *with* $\lambda = 0$ *is a third candidate for optimality.*

We conclude that there are three candidates for optimality. Now

$$f(0, 1) = 1, \qquad f(0, -1) = -1, \qquad f(0, -1/2) = -5/4$$

Because we want to maximize a continuous function over a closed, bounded set, by the extreme value theorem there is a solution to the problem. Because the only possible solutions are the three points already found, we conclude that $(x, y) = (0, 1)$ solves the maximization problem. (The point $(0, -1/2)$ solves the corresponding minimization problem. We solved both these problems in Example 13.5.1.)

Why Does the Recipe Work?

Suppose (x^*, y^*) solves problem (1). Then either $g(x^*, y^*) < c$, in which case the constraint $g(x^*, y^*) \leq c$ is said to be **inactive** or **slack** at (x^*, y^*), or else $g(x^*, y^*) = c$, in which case the same inequality constraint is said to be **active** or **binding** at (x^*, y^*). The two different cases are illustrated for two different values of c in Figs. 1 and 2, which both display the same four level curves of the objective function f as well. This function is assumed to increase as the level curves shrink. In Fig. 1, the solution (x^*, y^*) to problem (1) is an interior point of the admissible set. On the other hand, in Fig. 2, the solution (x^*, y^*) is at the boundary of the admissible set.

In case the solution (x^*, y^*) satisfies $g(x^*, y^*) < c$, as in Fig. 1, the point (x^*, y^*) is usually an interior maximum of the function f. Then it is a stationary point at which $f'_1(x^*, y^*) = f'_2(x^*, y^*) = 0$. In this case, if we set $\lambda = 0$, then conditions (2) to (4) of the recipe are all satisfied.

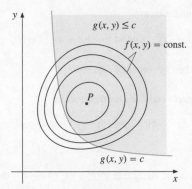

Figure 1 The point $P = (x^*, y^*)$ is an interior point of the admissible set.

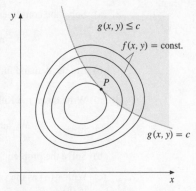

Figure 2 The constraint $g(x, y) \leq c$ is binding at $P = (x^*, y^*)$.

On the other hand, in the case when the constraint is binding at (x^*, y^*), as in Fig. 2, the point (x^*, y^*) solves the Lagrange problem max $f(x, y)$ subject to $g(x, y) = c$ with an equality constraint. Provided that the conditions of Theorem 14.4.1 are all satisfied, there will exist a unique Lagrange multiplier λ such that the Lagrangian satisfies the first-order conditions (2) at (x^*, y^*). It remains to be shown that this Lagrange multiplier λ satisfies $\lambda \geq 0$, thus ensuring that (3) is also satisfied at (x^*, y^*).

To prove that $\lambda \geq 0$, consider the two value functions

$$v(b) = \max\{f(x, y) : g(x, y) \leq b\} \quad \text{and} \quad f^*(b) = \max\{f(x, y) : g(x, y) = b\} \qquad (6)$$

for the versions of problem (1) in which the constant c has been replaced by the variable parameter b, and where $f^*(b)$ arises from the problem where the inequality constraint has been replaced by the corresponding equality constraint. Recall from (14.2.2) that $\lambda = df^*(c)/dc$ if f^* is differentiable at c. We shall now show that $f^*(b) \leq f^*(c)$ when $b \leq c$, thus implying that

$$\lambda = \lim_{c \to b} \frac{f(c) - f(b)}{c - b} = \lim_{c \to b^-} \frac{f(c) - f(b)}{c - b} \geq 0$$

—at least when f^* is differentiable.

Indeed, (6) implies that $f^*(b) \leq v(b)$ for all b, because the equality constraint $g(x, y) = b$ is more stringent than $g(x, y) \leq b$, and imposing a more stringent constraint never allows a higher maximum value. But also, in case $b < c$, the constraint $g(x, y) \leq b$ is more stringent than $g(x, y) \leq c$, from which it follows that $v(b) \leq v(c)$. Finally, because we are discussing the case when the constraint $g(x^*, y^*) = c$ binds at the solution to problem (1), we must have $v(c) = f^*(c)$. Thus, the chain $f^*(b) \leq v(b) \leq v(c) = f^*(c)$ is satisfied whenever $b < c$ (and also when $b = c$). It follows that $f^*(b) \leq f^*(c)$ whenever $b \leq c$, as required.

PROBLEMS FOR SECTION 14.8

1. (a) Solve the problem max $-x^2 - y^2$ subject to $x - 3y \leq -10$.

(b) The pair (x^*, y^*) that solves the problem in (a) also solves the minimization problem min $(x^2 + y^2)$ subject to $x - 3y \leq -10$. Sketch the admissible set S and explain the solution geometrically.

2. (a) Solve the consumer demand problem

$$\max \sqrt{x} + \sqrt{y} \quad \text{subject to} \quad px + qy \leq m$$

(b) Are the demand functions homogeneous of degree 0?

3. (a) Write down the Kuhn–Tucker conditions for the problem

$$\max 4 - \tfrac{1}{2}x^2 - 4y \quad \text{subject to} \quad 6x - 4y \leq a$$

(b) Solve the problem.

(c) With $V(a)$ as the value function, verify that $V'(a) = \lambda$, where λ is the Lagrange multiplier in (b).

4. (a) Write down the Lagrangian and conditions (2)–(3) for the problem

$$\max x^2 + 2y^2 - x \quad \text{subject to} \quad x^2 + y^2 \leq 1$$

(b) Find all pairs (x, y) that satisfy all the necessary conditions. (There are five candidates.) Find the solution to the problem.

(SM) **5.** Consider the problem

$$\max f(x, y) = 2 - (x - 1)^2 - e^{y^2} \quad \text{subject to} \quad x^2 + y^2 \leq a$$

where a is a positive constant.

(a) Write down the Kuhn–Tucker conditions for the solution of the problem. Find the only solution candidate. (You will need to distinguish between the cases $a \in (0, 1)$ and $a \geq 1$.) Prove optimality by using Theorem 14.8.1.

(b) The optimal value of $f(x, y)$ will depend on a. The resulting function $f^*(a)$ is called the *value function* for the problem. Verify that $df^*(a)/da = \lambda$ in both cases.

6. Suppose a firm earns revenue $R(Q) = aQ - bQ^2$ and incurs cost $C(Q) = \alpha Q + \beta Q^2$ as functions of output $Q \geq 0$, where a, b, α, and β are positive parameters. The firm maximizes profit $\pi(Q) = R(Q) - C(Q)$ subject to the constraint $Q \geq 0$. Solve this one-variable problem by the Kuhn–Tucker method, and find conditions for the constraint to bind at the optimum.

14.9 Multiple Inequality Constraints

A fairly general nonlinear programming problem is the following:

$$\max f(x_1, \ldots, x_n) \quad \text{subject to} \quad \begin{cases} g_1(x_1, \ldots, x_n) \leq c_1 \\ \ldots\ldots\ldots\ldots\ldots \\ g_m(x_1, \ldots, x_n) \leq c_m \end{cases} \tag{1}$$

The set of vectors $\mathbf{x} = (x_1, \ldots, x_n)$ that satisfy all the constraints is called the **admissible set** or the **feasible set**. Here is a recipe for solving problem (1):

RECIPE FOR SOLVING THE GENERAL NONLINEAR PROGRAMMING PROBLEM:

Consider the problem

$$\max \ f(\mathbf{x}) \text{ subject to } g_j(\mathbf{x}) \le c_j, \qquad j = 1, \dots, m$$

where $\mathbf{x}$ denotes $(x_1, \dots, x_n)$.

A. Write down the Lagrangian

$$\mathcal{L}(\mathbf{x}) = f(\mathbf{x}) - \sum_{j=1}^{m} \lambda_j (g_j(\mathbf{x}) - c_j)$$

with $\lambda_1, \dots, \lambda_m$ as the Lagrange multipliers associated with the m constraints.

B. Equate all the first-order partial derivatives of $\mathcal{L}(\mathbf{x})$ to 0:

$$\frac{\partial \mathcal{L}(\mathbf{x})}{\partial x_i} = \frac{\partial f(\mathbf{x})}{\partial x_i} - \sum_{j=1}^{m} \lambda_j \frac{\partial g_j(\mathbf{x})}{\partial x_i} = 0, \qquad i = 1, \dots, n$$

C. Impose the complementary slackness conditions:

$$\lambda_j \ge 0, \text{ and } \lambda_j = 0 \text{ if } g_j(\mathbf{x}) < c_j, \qquad j = 1, \dots, m$$

D. Require $\mathbf{x}$ to satisfy the constraints

$$g_j(\mathbf{x}) \le c_j, \qquad j = 1, \dots, m$$

Find all the vectors $\mathbf{x}$ that, together with associated values of $\lambda_1, \dots, \lambda_m$, satisfy conditions B, C, and D. These are the solution candidates, at least one of which solves the problem (if it has a solution). If the Lagrangian is concave in $\mathbf{x}$, then the conditions are sufficient for optimality. Even if $\mathcal{L}(\mathbf{x})$ is not concave, still any vector $\mathbf{x}$ which happens to maximize the Lagrangian while also satisfying C and D must be an optimum.

NOTE 1 Concavity and convexity for functions of several variables are discussed extensively in FMEA. In order for the conditions to be truly necessary, a constraint qualification is needed. See FMEA. The conditions in B and C are called the *Kuhn–Tucker conditions*. Note that minimizing $f(\mathbf{x})$ is equivalent to maximizing $-f(\mathbf{x})$. Also an inequality constraint of the form $g_j(\mathbf{x}) \ge c_j$ can be rewritten as $-g_j(\mathbf{x}) \le -c_j$, whereas an equality constraint $g_j(\mathbf{x}) = c_j$ is equivalent to the double inequality constraint $g_j(\mathbf{x}) \le c_j$ and $-g_j(\mathbf{x}) \le -c_j$. In this way, most constrained optimization problems can be expressed in the form (1).

EXAMPLE 1   Consider the nonlinear programming problem

$$\text{maximize} \quad x + 3y - 4e^{-x-y} \quad \text{subject to} \quad \begin{cases} 2 - x \ge 2y \\ x - 1 \le -y \end{cases}$$

(a) Write down the necessary Kuhn–Tucker conditions for a point (x^*, y^*) to be a solution of the problem. Are the conditions sufficient for optimality?

(b) Solve the problem.

Solution: (a) The first (important) step is to write the problem in the same form as (1):

$$\text{maximize} \quad x + 3y - 4e^{-x-y} \quad \text{subject to} \quad \begin{cases} x + 2y \leq 2 \\ x + \ y \leq 1 \end{cases}$$

The Lagrangian is $\mathcal{L}(x, y) = x + 3y - 4e^{-x-y} - \lambda_1(x + 2y - 2) - \lambda_2(x + y - 1)$. Hence, the Kuhn–Tucker conditions for (x^*, y^*) to solve the problem are:

$$\mathcal{L}_1' = 1 + 4e^{-x^*-y^*} - \lambda_1 - \lambda_2 = 0 \tag{i}$$

$$\mathcal{L}_2' = 3 + 4e^{-x^*-y^*} - 2\lambda_1 - \lambda_2 = 0 \tag{ii}$$

$$\lambda_1 \geq 0, \quad \text{and} \quad \lambda_1 = 0 \text{ if } x^* + 2y^* < 2 \tag{iii}$$

$$\lambda_2 \geq 0, \quad \text{and} \quad \lambda_2 = 0 \text{ if } x^* + y^* < 1 \tag{iv}$$

These conditions are sufficient for optimality because the Lagrangian is easily seen to be concave. (Look at the Hessian matrix of $\mathcal{L}$.)

(b) Subtracting (ii) from (i) we get $-2 + \lambda_1 = 0$ and so $\lambda_1 = 2$. But then (iii) together with $x^* + 2y^* \leq 2$ yields

$$x^* + 2y^* = 2 \tag{v}$$

Suppose $\lambda_2 = 0$. Then from (i), $4e^{-x^*-y^*} = 1$, so $-x^* - y^* = \ln(1/4)$, and then $x^* + y^* = \ln 4 > 1$, a contradiction. Thus λ_2 has to be positive. Then from (iv) and $x^* + y^* \leq 1$ we deduce $x^* + y^* = 1$. Using (v) we see that $x^* = 0$ and $y^* = 1$. Inserting these values for x^* and y^* into (i) and (ii) we find that $\lambda_2 = e^{-1}(4 - e)$, which is positive. We conclude that the solution is: $x^* = 0$ and $y^* = 1$, with $\lambda_1 = 2$, $\lambda_2 = e^{-1}(4 - e)$.

EXAMPLE 2   A worker chooses both consumption c and labour supply l in order to maximize the utility function $\alpha \ln c + (1 - \alpha) \ln(1 - l)$ of consumption c and leisure $1 - l$, where $0 < \alpha < 1$. The worker's budget constraint is $c \leq wl + m$, where m is unearned income. In addition, the worker must choose $l \geq 0$ (otherwise there would be no work!). Solve the worker's problem.

Solution: The worker's constrained maximization problem is

$$\max \alpha \ln c + (1 - \alpha) \ln(1 - l) \quad \text{subject to} \quad c \leq wl + m, \ l \geq 0$$

The Lagrangian is $\mathcal{L}(c, l) = \alpha \ln c + (1 - \alpha) \ln(1 - l) - \lambda(c - wl - m) - \mu l$, and the Kuhn–Tucker conditions for (c^*, l^*) to solve the problem are

$$\mathcal{L}_c' = \frac{\alpha}{c^*} - \lambda = 0 \tag{i}$$

$$\mathcal{L}_l' = \frac{-(1 - \alpha)}{1 - l^*} + \lambda w + \mu = 0 \tag{ii}$$

$$\lambda \geq 0, \quad \text{and} \quad \lambda = 0 \text{ if } c^* < wl^* + m \tag{iii}$$

$$\mu \geq 0, \quad \text{and} \quad \mu = 0 \text{ if } l^* > 0 \tag{iv}$$

From (i) we have $\lambda = \alpha/c^* > 0$. Then (iii) together with the first constraint yield

$$c^* = wl^* + m \tag{v}$$

Case I: $\mu = 0$. Then from (ii) we get $l^* = \alpha - (1-\alpha)m/w$. Using (v) next, $c^* = \alpha(w+m)$, with $\lambda = \alpha/c^* = 1/(w + m)$. The Kuhn–Tucker conditions are all satisfied provided $l^* = \alpha - (1 - \alpha)m/w \geq 0$, that is $m \leq \alpha w/(1 - \alpha)$.

Case II: $\mu > 0$. Then $l^* = 0$, $c^* = m$, and $\lambda = \alpha/c^* = \alpha/m$. From (ii) it follows that $\mu = 1 - \alpha - \alpha w/m$, and $\mu > 0 \iff m > \alpha w/(1 - \alpha)$.

In the last two examples it was not too hard to find which constraints bind (i.e. hold with equality) at the optimum. But with more complicated nonlinear programming problems, this can be harder. A general method for finding all candidates for optimality in a nonlinear programming problem with two constraints can be formulated as follows: First, examine the case where both constraints bind. Next, examine the two cases where only one constraint binds. Finally, examine the case where neither constraint binds. In each case, find all vectors **x**, with associated values of the Lagrange multipliers, that satisfy all the relevant conditions— if any do. Then calculate the value of the objective function for these values of **x**, and retain those **x** with the highest values. Except for perverse problems, this procedure will find the optimum. The next example illustrates how it works in practice.

EXAMPLE 3   Suppose your utility of consuming x_1 units of good A and x_2 units of good B is $U(x_1, x_2) = \ln x_1 + \ln x_2$, and that the prices per unit of A and B are 10 and 5, respectively. You have at most 350 to spend on the two goods. Suppose it takes 0.1 hours to consume one unit of A and 0.2 hours to consume one unit of B. You have at most 8 hours to spend on consuming the two goods. How much of each good should you buy in order to maximize your utility?

Solution: The problem is

$$\max U(x_1, x_2) = \ln x_1 + \ln x_2 \quad \text{subject to} \quad \begin{cases} 10x_1 + 5x_2 \leq 350 \\ 0.1x_1 + 0.2x_2 \leq 8 \end{cases}$$

The Lagrangian is $\mathcal{L} = \ln x_1 + \ln x_2 - \lambda_1(10x_1 + 5x_2 - 350) - \lambda_2(0.1x_1 + 0.2x_2 - 8)$. Necessary conditions for (x_1^*, x_2^*) to solve the problem are that there exist numbers λ_1 and λ_2 such that

$$\mathcal{L}_1' = 1/x_1^* - 10\lambda_1 - 0.1\lambda_2 = 0 \tag{i}$$

$$\mathcal{L}_2' = 1/x_2^* - 5\lambda_1 - 0.2\lambda_2 = 0 \tag{ii}$$

$$\lambda_1 \geq 0, \quad \text{and} \quad \lambda_1 = 0 \text{ if } 10x_1^* + 5x_2^* < 350 \tag{iii}$$

$$\lambda_2 \geq 0, \quad \text{and} \quad \lambda_2 = 0 \text{ if } 0.1x_1^* + 0.2x_2^* < 8 \tag{iv}$$

We start the systematic procedure:

(I) *Both constraints bind.* Then

$$10x_1^* + 5x_2^* = 350 \tag{v}$$

and $0.1x_1^* + 0.2x_2^* = 8$. The solution is $(x_1^*, x_2^*) = (20, 30)$. Inserting these values into (i) and (ii) yields the system $10\lambda_1 + 0.1\lambda_2 = 1/20$ and $5\lambda_1 + 0.2\lambda_2 = 1/30$, with solution $(\lambda_1, \lambda_2) = (1/225, 1/18)$. So we have found a candidate for optimality because all the Kuhn–Tucker conditions are satisfied. (Note that it is important to check that λ_1 and λ_2 are nonnegative.)

(II) *Constraint 1 binds, 2 does not.* Then (v) holds and $0.1x_1^* + 0.2x_2^* < 8$. From (iv) we obtain $\lambda_2 = 0$. Now (i) and (ii) give $x_2^* = 2x_1^*$. Inserting this into (v), we get $x_1^* = 17.5$ and then $x_2^* = 2x_1^* = 35$. But then $0.1x_1^* + 0.2x_2^* = 8.75$, which violates the second constraint. So no candidate arises in this case.

(III) *Constraint 2 binds, 1 does not.* Then $10x_1^* + 5x_2^* < 350$ and $0.1x_1^* + 0.2x_2^* = 8$. From (iii), $\lambda_1 = 0$, and (i) and (ii) yield $0.1x_1^* = 0.2x_2^*$. Inserted into $0.1x_1^* + 0.2x_2^* = 8$ this yields $x_2^* = 20$ and so $x_1^* = 40$. But then $10x_1^* + 5x_2^* = 500$, violating the first constraint. So no candidate arises in this case either.

(IV) *None of the constraints bind.* Then $\lambda_1 = \lambda_2 = 0$ and (i) and (ii) make no sense.

Conclusion: There is only one candidate for optimality, $(20, 30)$. Since the Lagrangian is easily seen to be concave, we have found the solution.

Properties of the Value Function

The optimal value of the objective $f(\mathbf{x})$ in (1) obviously depends on $c_1, \ldots, c_m$. The function defined by

$$f^*(\mathbf{c}) = \max\{ f(\mathbf{x}) : g_j(\mathbf{x}) \le c_j, \ j = 1, \ldots, m \} \tag{2}$$

assigns to each $\mathbf{c} = (c_1, \ldots, c_m)$ the optimal value $f^*(\mathbf{c})$ of f. It is called the **value function** for the problem. The following properties of f^* are very useful:

$$f^*(\mathbf{c}) \text{ is nondecreasing in each variable } c_1, \ldots, c_m \tag{3}$$

$$\text{If } \partial f^*(\mathbf{c})/\partial c_j \text{ exists, then it is equal to } \lambda_j(\mathbf{c}), \quad j = 1, \ldots, m \tag{4}$$

Here property (3) follows immediately because if c_j increases, and all the other c_k are fixed, then the admissible set becomes larger; hence, $f^*(\mathbf{c})$ cannot decrease.

Concerning property (4), each $\lambda_j(\mathbf{c})$ is a Lagrange multiplier coming from the Kuhn–Tucker conditions. However, there is a catch: The value function f^* need not be differentiable. Even if f and $g_1, \ldots, g_m$ are all differentiable, the value function can have sudden changes of slope. Such cases are studied in FMEA.

1. (a) Write down the Lagrangian and the necessary Kuhn–Tucker conditions for the problem

$$\max \tfrac{1}{2}x - y \quad \text{subject to} \quad x + e^{-x} \le y, \ x \ge 0$$

(b) Find the solution to the problem.

(SM) 2. Solve the following consumer demand problem where, in addition to the budget constraint, there is an upper limit $\bar{x}$ which rations how much of the first good can be bought:

$$\max \quad \alpha \ln x + (1 - \alpha) \ln y \quad \text{subject to} \quad px + qy \leq m, \qquad x \leq \bar{x}$$

(SM) 3. (a) Sketch the admissible set S for the problem

$$\max \quad x + y - e^x - e^{x+y} \quad \text{subject to} \quad x + y \geq 4, \ x \geq -1, \ y \geq 1$$

(b) Find all pairs (x, y) that satisfy all the necessary conditions. Find the solution to the problem.

(SM) 4. Consider the problem

$$\max \quad x + ay \quad \text{subject to} \quad x^2 + y^2 \leq 1, \ x + y \geq 0 \qquad (a \text{ is a constant})$$

(a) Sketch the admissible set and write down the necessary conditions.

(b) Find the solution for all values of the constant a.

(SM) 5. Solve the following problem, assuming it has a solution:

$$\max \quad y - x^2 \quad \text{subject to} \quad y \geq 0, \ y - x \geq -2, \ y^2 \leq x$$

(SM) 6. (a) Sketch the admissible set for the problem

$$\max \quad -\left(x + \tfrac{1}{2}\right)^2 - \tfrac{1}{2}y^2 \quad \text{subject to} \quad e^{-x} - y \leq 0 \text{ and } y \leq \tfrac{2}{3}$$

(b) Write down the Kuhn–Tucker conditions, and find the solution of the problem.

7. Consider the problem

$$\max \quad xz + yz \quad \text{subject to} \quad x^2 + y^2 + z^2 \leq 1$$

(a) Write down the Kuhn–Tucker conditions.

(b) Solve the problem.

14.10 Nonnegativity Constraints

Consider the general nonlinear programming problem (14.9.1) once again. Often, variables involved in economic optimization problems must be nonnegative by their very nature. It is not difficult to incorporate such constraints in the formulation of (14.9.1). If $x_1 \geq 0$, for example, this can be represented by the new constraint $h_1(x_1, \ldots, x_n) = -x_1 \leq 0$, and we introduce an additional Lagrange multiplier to go with it. But in order not to have too many Lagrange multipliers, the necessary conditions for the solution of nonlinear programming problems with nonnegativity constraints are sometimes formulated in a slightly different way.

Consider first the problem

$$\max f(x, y) \quad \text{subject to} \quad g(x, y) \leq c, \ x \geq 0, \ y \geq 0 \tag{1}$$

Here we introduce the functions $h_1(x, y) = -x$ and $h_2(x, y) = -y$, so that the constraints in problem (1) become $g(x, y) \leq c$, $h_1(x, y) \leq 0$, and $h_2(x, y) \leq 0$. Applying the recipe for solving (14.9.1), we introduce the Lagrangian

$$\mathcal{L}(x, y) = f(x, y) - \lambda(g(x, y) - c) - \mu_1(-x) - \mu_2(-y)$$

The Kuhn–Tucker conditions are

$$\mathcal{L}_1' = f_1'(x, y) - \lambda g_1'(x, y) + \mu_1 = 0 \tag{i}$$

$$\mathcal{L}_2' = f_2'(x, y) - \lambda g_2'(x, y) + \mu_2 = 0 \tag{ii}$$

$$\lambda \geq 0, \quad \text{and } \lambda = 0 \text{ if } g(x, y) < c \tag{iii}$$

$$\mu_1 \geq 0, \quad \text{and } \mu_1 = 0 \text{ if } x > 0 \tag{iv}$$

$$\mu_2 \geq 0, \quad \text{and } \mu_2 = 0 \text{ if } y > 0 \tag{v}$$

From (i), we have $f_1'(x, y) - \lambda g_1'(x, y) = -\mu_1$. From (iv), we have $-\mu_1 \leq 0$ and $-\mu_1 = 0$ if $x > 0$. Thus, (i) and (iv) are together equivalent to

$$f_1'(x, y) - \lambda g_1'(x, y) \leq 0 \quad (= 0 \text{ if } x > 0) \tag{vi}$$

In the same way, (ii) and (v) are together equivalent to

$$f_2'(x, y) - \lambda g_2'(x, y) \leq 0 \quad (= 0 \text{ if } y > 0) \tag{vii}$$

So the new Kuhn–Tucker conditions are (vi), (vii), and (iii). Note that after replacing (i) and (iv) by (vi), as well as (ii) and (v) by (vii), only the multiplier λ associated with $g(x, y) \leq c$ remains.

The same idea can obviously be extended to the n-variable problem

$$\max f(\mathbf{x}) \quad \text{subject to} \quad \begin{cases} g_1(\mathbf{x}) \leq c_1 \\ \ldots\ldots\ldots \\ g_m(\mathbf{x}) \leq c_m \end{cases}, \quad x_1 \geq 0, \ldots, x_n \geq 0 \tag{2}$$

Briefly formulated, the necessary conditions for the solution of (2) are that, for each $i = 1, \ldots, n$,

$$\frac{\partial f(\mathbf{x})}{\partial x_i} - \sum_{j=1}^{m} \lambda_j \frac{\partial g_j(\mathbf{x})}{\partial x_i} \leq 0 \quad (= 0 \text{ if } x_i > 0) \tag{3}$$

$$\lambda_j \geq 0, \quad \text{with } \lambda_j = 0 \text{ if } g_j(\mathbf{x}) < c_j, \quad j = 1, \ldots, m \tag{4}$$

EXAMPLE 1   Consider the utility maximizing problem

$$\text{maximize } x + \ln(1 + y) \quad \text{subject to} \quad px + y \leq m, \ x \geq 0, \ y \geq 0$$

(a) Write down the necessary Kuhn–Tucker conditions for a point (x^*, y^*) to be a solution.

(b) Find the solution to the problem, for all positive values of p and m.

Solution:

(a) The Lagrangian is $\mathcal{L}(x, y) = x + \ln(1 + y) - \lambda(px + y - m)$, and the Kuhn–Tucker conditions for (x^*, y^*) to be a solution are that there exists a λ such that

$$\mathcal{L}'_1(x^*, y^*) = \qquad 1 - p\lambda \leq 0, \quad \text{and} \quad 1 - p\lambda = 0 \text{ if } x^* > 0 \qquad \text{(i)}$$

$$\mathcal{L}'_2(x^*, y^*) = \frac{1}{1 + y^*} - \lambda \leq 0, \quad \text{and} \quad \frac{1}{1 + y^*} - \lambda = 0 \text{ if } y^* > 0 \qquad \text{(ii)}$$

$$\lambda \geq 0, \quad \text{and} \quad \lambda = 0 \text{ if } px^* + y^* < m \qquad \text{(iii)}$$

In addition $x^* \geq 0$, $y^* \geq 0$, and the budget constraint has to be satisfied, so $px^* + y^* \leq m$.

(b) Note that the Lagrangian is concave, so a point that satisfies the Kuhn–Tucker conditions will be a maximum point. It is clear from (i) that λ cannot be 0. Therefore $\lambda > 0$, so (iii) and $px^* + y^* \leq m$ imply that

$$px^* + y^* = m \qquad \text{(iv)}$$

There are four cases to consider:

I. *Suppose* $x^* = 0$, $y^* = 0$. Since $m > 0$, this is impossible because of (iv).

II. *Suppose* $x^* > 0$, $y^* = 0$. From (ii) and $y^* = 0$ we get $\lambda \geq 1$. Then (i) implies that $p = 1/\lambda \leq 1$. Equation (iv) gives $x^* = m/p$, so we get one candidate for a maximum point:

$$(x^*, y^*) = (m/p, 0), \quad \lambda = 1/p, \quad \text{if } 0 < p \leq 1 \qquad .$$

III. *Suppose* $x^* = 0$, $y^* > 0$. By (iv) we have $y^* = m$. Then (ii) yields $\lambda = 1/(1 + y^*) = 1/(1 + m)$. From (i) we get $p \geq 1/\lambda = m + 1$. This gives one more candidate:

$$(x^*, y^*) = (0, m), \quad \lambda = 1/(1 + m), \quad \text{if } p \geq m + 1$$

IV. *Suppose* $x^* > 0$, $y^* > 0$. With equality in both (i) and (ii), $\lambda = 1/p = 1/(1 + y^*)$. It follows that $y^* = p - 1$, and then $p > 1$ because $y^* > 0$. Equation (iv) implies that $px^* = m - y^* = m - p + 1$, so $x^* = (m + 1 - p)/p$. Since $x^* > 0$, we must have $p < m + 1$. Thus we get one last candidate

$$(x^*, y^*) = ((m + 1 - p)/p, p - 1), \quad \lambda = 1/p, \quad \text{if } 1 < p < m + 1$$

Conclusion: Putting all this together, we see that the solution of the problem is

A. If $0 < p \leq 1$, then $(x^*, y^*) = (m/p, 0)$, with $\lambda = 1/p$. (Case II.)

B. If $1 < p < m + 1$, then $(x^*, y^*) = ((m + 1 - p)/p, p - 1)$, with $\lambda = 1/p$. (Case IV.)

C. If $p \geq m + 1$, then $(x^*, y^*) = (0, m)$, with $\lambda = 1/(m + 1)$. (Case III.)

Note that except in the intermediate case (B) when $1 < p < m + 1$, it is optimal to spend everything on only the cheaper of the two goods — either x in case A, or y in case C. This makes economic sense.

EXAMPLE 2   **(Peak Load Pricing)**   Consider a producer who generates electricity by burning a fuel such as coal or natural gas. The demand for electricity varies between peak periods, during which all the generating capacity is used, and off-peak periods when there is spare capacity. We consider a certain time interval (say, a year) divided into n periods of equal length. Suppose the amounts of electric power sold in these n periods are $x_1, x_2, \ldots, x_n$. Assume that a regulatory authority fixes the corresponding prices at levels equal to $p_1, p_2, \ldots, p_n$. The total operating cost over all n periods is given by the function $C(x_1, \ldots, x_n)$, and k is the output capacity in each period. Let $D(k)$ denote the cost of maintaining output capacity at level k. The producer's total profit is then

$$\pi(x_1, \ldots, x_n, k) = \sum_{i=1}^{n} p_i x_i - C(\mathbf{x}) - D(k)$$

Because the producer cannot exceed capacity k in any period, it faces the constraints

$$x_1 \leq k, \quad \ldots, \quad x_n \leq k \tag{I}$$

We consider the problem of finding $x_1 \geq 0, \ldots, x_n \geq 0$ and $k \geq 0$ such that profit is maximized subject to the capacity constraints (I).

This is a nonlinear programming problem with $n + 1$ variables and n constraints. The Lagrangian $\mathcal{L}$ is

$$\mathcal{L}(x_1, \ldots, x_n, k) = \sum_{i=1}^{n} p_i x_i - C(x_1, \ldots, x_n) - D(k) - \sum_{i=1}^{n} \lambda_i (x_i - k)$$

Following (4) and (5), the choice $(x_1^0, \ldots, x_n^0, k^0) \geq 0$ can solve the problem only if there exist Lagrange multipliers $\lambda_1 \geq 0, \ldots, \lambda_n \geq 0$ such that

$$\frac{\partial \mathcal{L}}{\partial x_i} = p_i - C_i'(x_1^0, \ldots, x_n^0) - \lambda_i \leq 0 \quad (= 0 \text{ if } x_i^0 > 0), \qquad i = 1, \ldots, n \tag{i}$$

$$\frac{\partial \mathcal{L}}{\partial k} = -D'(k^0) + \sum_{i=1}^{n} \lambda_i \leq 0 \quad (= 0 \text{ if } k^0 > 0) \tag{ii}$$

$$\lambda_i \geq 0, \quad \text{and} \quad \lambda_i = 0 \text{ if } x_i^0 < k^0, \qquad i = 1, \ldots, n \tag{iii}$$

Suppose that i is such that $x_i^0 > 0$. Then (i) implies that

$$p_i = C_i'(x_1^0, \ldots, x_n^0) + \lambda_i \tag{iv}$$

If period i is an off-peak period, then $x_i^0 < k^0$ and so $\lambda_i = 0$ by (iii). From (iv) it follows that $p_i = C_i'(x_1^0, \ldots, x_n^0)$. Thus, we see that *the profit-maximizing pattern of output* $(x_1^0, \ldots, x_n^0)$ *will bring about equality between the regulator's price in any off-peak period and the corresponding marginal operating cost.*

On the other hand, λ_j might be positive in a peak period when $x_j^0 = k^0$. If $k^0 > 0$, it follows from (ii) that $\sum_{i=1}^{n} \lambda_i = D'(k^0)$. We conclude that the output pattern will be such that *in peak periods the price set by the regulator will exceed the marginal operating cost by an additional amount* λ_j, *which is really the "shadow price" of the capacity constraint* $x_j^0 \leq k^0$. *The sum of these shadow prices over all peak periods is equal to the marginal capacity cost.*

PROBLEMS FOR SECTION 14.10

1. (a) Consider the utility maximization problem

$$\text{maximize } x + \ln(1 + y) \quad \text{subject to } 16x + y \le 495, \quad x \ge 0, \quad y \ge 0$$

Write down the necessary K–T conditions (with nonnegativity constraints) for a point (x^*, y^*) to be a solution.

(b) Find the solution to the problem.

(c) Estimate by how much utility will increase if income is increased from 495 to 500.

ⓢⓜ 2. Solve the following problem, assuming it has a solution:

$$\max \ xe^{y-x} - 2ey \quad \text{subject to } y \le 1 + x/2, \quad x \ge 0, \quad y \ge 0$$

ⓢⓜ 3. Suppose that optimal capacity utilization by a firm requires that its output quantities x_1 and x_2, along with its capacity level k, should be chosen to solve the problem

$$\max \ (x_1 + 3x_2 - x_1^2 - x_2^2 - k^2) \quad \text{subject to } \ x_1 \le k, \ x_2 \le k, \ x_1 \ge 0, \ x_2 \ge 0, \ k \ge 0$$

Show that $k = 0$ cannot be optimal, and then find the solution.

REVIEW PROBLEMS FOR CHAPTER 14

1. (a) Solve the following problem using the Lagrange multiplier method:

$$\max f(x, y) = 3x + 4y \quad \text{subject to } \ g(x, y) = x^2 + y^2 = 225$$

(b) Suppose 225 is changed to 224. What is the approximate change in the optimal value of f?

2. Using the result (∗∗) in Example 14.1.3, write down the solution to the problem

$$\max \ f(x, y) \quad \text{subject to } \ px + qy = m$$

in each of the cases:

(a) $f(x, y) = 25x^2 y^3$ (b) $f(x, y) = x^{1/5} y^{2/5}$ (c) $f(x, y) = 10\sqrt{x} \sqrt[3]{y}$

ⓢⓜ 3. (a) By selling x tons of one commodity the firm gets a price per ton given by $p(x)$. By selling y tons of another commodity the price per ton is $q(y)$. The cost of producing and selling x tons of the first commodity and y tons of the second is given by $C(x, y)$. Write down the firm's profit function and find necessary conditions for $x^* > 0$ and $y^* > 0$ to solve the problem. Give economic interpretations of the necessary conditions.

(b) Suppose that the firm's production activity causes so much pollution that the authorities limit its output to no more than m tons of total output. Write down the necessary conditions for $\hat{x} > 0$ and $\hat{y} > 0$ to solve the problem.

4. (a) Suppose $U(x, y)$ denotes the utility enjoyed by a person when having x hours of leisure per day (24 hours) and y units per day of other goods. The person gets an hourly wage of w and pays an average price of p per unit of the other goods, so that

$$py = w(24 - x) \tag{$*$}$$

assuming that the person spends all that is earned. Show that maximizing $U(x, y)$ subject to the constraint ($*$) leads to the equation

$$pU_1'(x, y) = wU_2'(x, y) \tag{$**$}$$

(b) Suppose that the equations ($*$) and ($**$) define x and y as differentiable functions $x(p, w)$, $y(p, w)$ of p and w. Show that, with appropriate conditions on $U(x, y)$,

$$\frac{\partial x}{\partial w} = \frac{(24 - x)(wU_{22}'' - pU_{12}'') + pU_2'}{p^2 U_{11}'' - 2pwU_{12}'' + w^2 U_{22}''}$$

(SM) **5.** (a) Solve the problem

$$\max(\min) \; x^2 + y^2 - 2x + 1 \quad \text{subject to} \quad \tfrac{1}{4}x^2 + y^2 = b$$

where b is a constant $> \frac{4}{9}$. (The constraint has a graph that is an ellipse in the xy-plane. So it defines a closed and bounded set.)

(b) If $f^*(b)$ denotes the value function for the maximization problem, verify that $df^*(b)/db = \lambda$, where λ is the corresponding Lagrange multiplier.

6. Consider the utility maximization problem (14.1.3) with a separable utility function $u(x, y) = v(x) + w(y)$, where $v'(x) > 0$, $w'(y) > 0$, $v''(x) \leq 0$, and $w''(y) \leq 0$.

(a) State the first-order conditions for utility maximization.

(b) Why are these conditions sufficient for optimality?

(SM) **7.** (a) Consider the problem

$$\min \; f(x, y) = x^2 - 2x + 1 + y^2 - 2y \quad \text{subject to} \quad g(x, y) = (x + y)\sqrt{x + y + b} = 2\sqrt{a}$$

where a and b are positive constants and x and y are positive. Suppose that (x, y) solves the problem. Show that x and y must then satisfy the equations

$$x = y \quad \text{and} \quad 2x^3 + bx^2 = a \tag{$*$}$$

(b) The equations in ($*$) define x and y as differentiable functions of a and b. Find expressions for $\partial x/\partial a$, $\partial^2 x/\partial a^2$, and $\partial x/\partial b$.

(SM) **8.** Solve the problem

$$\max \; f(x, y) = 10 - (x - 2)^2 - (y - 1)^2 \quad \text{subject to} \quad g(x, y) = x^2 + y^2 \leq a$$

for all $a > 0$.

(SM) **9.** (a) Consider the nonlinear programming problem

$$\text{maximize} \quad xy \quad \text{subject to} \quad \begin{cases} x^2 + ry^2 \leq m \\ \qquad x \geq 1 \end{cases}$$

Here r and m are positive constants, $m > 1$. Write down the necessary Kuhn–Tucker conditions for a point (x^*, y^*) to be a solution of the problem.

(b) Solve the problem.

(c) Let $V(r, m)$ denote the value function. Compute $\partial V(r, m)/\partial m$. Comment? Verify that $\partial V(r, m)/\partial r = \partial \mathcal{L}/\partial r$, where $\mathcal{L}$ is the Lagrangian.

10. Suppose the firm of Example 8.5.1 earns revenue $R(Q)$ and incurs cost $C(Q)$ as functions of output $Q \geq 0$, where $R'(Q) > 0$, $C'(Q) > 0$, $R''(Q) < 0$, and $C''(Q) > 0$ for all $Q \geq 0$. The firm maximizes profit $\pi(Q) = R(Q) - C(Q)$ subject to $Q \geq 0$. Write down the first-order conditions for the solution to this problem, and find sufficient conditions for the constraint to bind at the optimum.

11. (a) A firm uses K and L units of two inputs to produce $\sqrt{KL}$ units of a product, where $K > 0$, $L > 0$. The input factor costs are r and w per unit, respectively. The firm wants to minimize the costs of producing at least Q units. Formulate the nonlinear programming problem that emerges. Reformulate it as a maximization problem, then write down the Kuhn–Tucker conditions for the optimum. Solve these conditions to determine K^* and L^* as functions of (r, w, Q).

(b) Define the minimum cost function as $c^*(r, w, Q) = rK^* + wL^*$. Verify that $\partial c^*/\partial r = K^*$ and $\partial c^*/\partial w = L^*$, and give these results economic interpretations.

MATRIX AND VECTOR ALGEBRA

Indeed, models basically play the same role in economics as in fashion.
They provide an articulated frame on which to show off your material to advantage,
. . . a useful role, but fraught with the dangers that the designer
may get carried away by his personal inclination for the model,
while the customer may forget that the model is more streamlined than reality.
—J. H. Drèze (1984)

Most mathematical models used by economists ultimately involve a system of several equations, which usually express how one or more endogenous variables depend on several exogenous parameters. If these equations are all linear, the study of such systems belongs to an area of mathematics called **linear algebra**. Even if the equations are nonlinear, much may be learned from linear approximations around the solution we are interested in—for example, how the solution changes in response to small shocks to the exogenous parameters. Indeed, such models lie right at the heart of the econometric techniques that form the basis of most modern empirical economic analysis.

The analysis and even the comprehension of systems of linear equations becomes much easier if we use some key mathematical concepts such as matrices, vectors, and determinants. These, as well as their application to economic models, will be introduced in this chapter and in the next.

Actually, the usefulness of linear algebra extends far beyond its ability to solve systems of linear equations. For instance, in the theory of differential and difference equations, in linear and nonlinear optimization theory, in statistics and econometrics, the methods of linear algebra are used extensively.

15.1 Systems of Linear Equations

Section 2.4 has already introduced systems of two simultaneous linear equations in two variables. Subsequently in later chapters, notably Chapter 14, we have encountered up to five linear equations in five unknowns. These systems were solved in an ad hoc manner. It is now time to study systems of linear equations more systematically.

The first key step is to introduce suitable notation for what may be a large linear system of equations. Specifically, we consider m equations in n unknowns, where m may be greater than, equal to, or less than n. If the unknowns are denoted by $x_1, \ldots, x_n$, we usually write such a system in the form

$$
\begin{aligned}
a_{11}x_1 + a_{12}x_2 + \cdots + a_{1n}x_n &= b_1 \\
a_{21}x_1 + a_{22}x_2 + \cdots + a_{2n}x_n &= b_2 \\
&\cdots\cdots\cdots\cdots\cdots\cdots\cdots\cdots \\
a_{m1}x_1 + a_{m2}x_2 + \cdots + a_{mn}x_n &= b_m
\end{aligned}
\tag{1}
$$

Here $a_{11}, a_{12}, \ldots, a_{mn}$ are called the *coefficients* of the system, and $b_1, \ldots, b_m$ are called the *right-hand sides*. All are real numbers.

Note carefully the order of the subscripts. In general, a_{ij} is the coefficient in the ith equation of the jth variable (x_j). One or more of these coefficients may be 0—indeed, the system usually becomes easier to analyse and solve if a high proportion of the coefficients are 0.

A **solution** of system (1) is an ordered set or list of numbers $s_1, s_2, \ldots, s_n$ that satisfies all the equations simultaneously when we put $x_1 = s_1, x_2 = s_2, \ldots, x_n = s_n$. Usually, a solution is written as $(s_1, s_2, \ldots, s_n)$. Note that the order in which we write the components is essential in the sense that if $(s_1, s_2, \ldots, s_n)$ satisfies (1), then $(s_n, s_{n-1}, \ldots, s_1)$, say, will usually *not* be a solution.

If system (1) has at least one solution, it is said to be **consistent**. When the system has no solution, it is said to be **inconsistent**.

EXAMPLE 1   To check your understanding of the notation used, write down the system of equations (1) when $n = m = 3$ and $a_{ij} = i + j$ for $i, j = 1, 2, 3$, while $b_j = j$ for $j = 1, 2, 3$. Verify that $(x_1, x_2, x_3) = (2, -1, 0)$ is a solution, but that $(x_1, x_2, x_3) = (2, 0, -1)$ is not.

Solution: The coefficients are $a_{11} = 1 + 1 = 2$, $a_{12} = 1 + 2 = 3$, etc. Set out in full, the system of equations is

$$
\begin{aligned}
2x_1 + 3x_2 + 4x_3 &= 1 \\
3x_1 + 4x_2 + 5x_3 &= 2 \\
4x_1 + 5x_2 + 6x_3 &= 3
\end{aligned}
$$

Inserting $(x_1, x_2, x_3) = (2, -1, 0)$ we see that all the equations are satisfied, so this is a solution. On the other hand, if we change the order of the numbers 2, -1 and 0 to form the triple $(x_1, x_2, x_3) = (2, 0, -1)$, then $2x_1 + 3x_2 + 4x_3 = 0$, so the first equation is not satisfied, and $(2, 0, -1)$ is not a solution to the system. (In fact, the general solution is $(x_1, x_2, x_3) = (2 + t, -1 - 2t, t)$, with t an arbitrary real number. In the terminology of Section 12.5 the system has one degree of freedom.)

There are computer programs that make it easy to check whether a system like (1) is consistent, and if it is, to find possible solutions, even if there are thousands of equations and unknowns. Still, economists need to understand the general theory of such equation systems so that they can follow theoretical arguments and conclusions related to linear models.

1. Decide which of the following single equations in the variables x, y, z, and w are linear and which are not. (In (f), a and b are nonnegative constants.)

(a) $3x - y - z - w = 50$

(b) $\sqrt{3}x + 8xy - z + w = 0$

(c) $3(x + y - z) = 4(x - 2y + 3z)$

(d) $3.33x - 4y + \dfrac{800}{3}z = 3$

(e) $(x - y)^2 + 3z - w = -3$

(f) $2a^2x - \sqrt{b}y + (2 + \sqrt{a})z = b^2$

2. Let x_1, y_1, x_2, and y_2 be given numbers and consider the following equations in the variables a, b, c, and d. (In *almost* all other cases in this book, a, b, c, and d denote constants!)

$$ax_1^2 + bx_1y_1 + cy_1^2 + d = 0$$
$$ax_2^2 + bx_2y_2 + cy_2^2 + d = 0$$

Is this a linear system of equations in a, b, c, and d?

3. Write down the system of equations (1) when $n = 4$, $m = 3$, and $a_{ij} = i + 2j + (-1)^i$ for $i = 1, 2, 4$, $j = 1, 2, 3$, while $b_j = 2^j$ for $j = 1, 2, 3$.

4. Write system (1) out in full when $n = m = 4$ and $a_{ij} = 1$ for all $i \neq j$, while $a_{ii} = 0$ for $i = 1$, 2, 3, 4. Sum the four equations to derive a simple equation for $\sum_{i=1}^{4} x_i$, then solve the whole system.

5. Consider a collection of n individuals, each of whom owns a definite quantity of m different commodities. Let a_{ij} be the number of units of commodity i owned by individual j, where $i = 1, 2, \ldots, m$, while $j = 1, 2, \ldots, n$.

(a) What does the list $(a_{1j}, a_{2j}, \ldots, a_{mj})$ represent?

(b) Explain in words what $a_{11} + a_{12} + \cdots + a_{1n}$ and $a_{i1} + a_{i2} + \cdots + a_{in}$ express.

(c) Let p_i denote the price per unit of commodity i ($i = 1, 2, \ldots, m$). What is the total value of the commodities owned by individual j?

SM 6. T. Haavelmo devised a model of the US economy for the years 1929–1941 based on the following equations:

(i) $c = 0.712y + 95.05$

(ii) $s = 0.158(c + x) - 34.30$

(iii) $y = c + x - s$

(iv) $x = 93.53$

Here x denotes total investment, y is disposable income, s is the total saving by firms, and c is total consumption. Write the system of equations in the form (1) when the variables appear in the order x, y, s, and c. Then find the solution of the system.

15.2   Matrices and Matrix Operations

A **matrix** is simply a rectangular array of numbers considered as one mathematical object. When there are m **rows** and n **columns** in the array, we have an m-by-n matrix (written as $m \times n$). We usually denote a matrix with bold capital letters such as $\mathbf{A}$, $\mathbf{B}$, and so on. In general, an $m \times n$ matrix is of the form

$$\mathbf{A} = \begin{pmatrix} a_{11} & a_{12} & \dots & a_{1n} \\ a_{21} & a_{22} & \dots & a_{2n} \\ \vdots & \vdots & & \vdots \\ a_{m1} & a_{m2} & \dots & a_{mn} \end{pmatrix} \tag{1}$$

In this book any array like (1) will be enclosed with large parentheses surrounding the numbers. Note, however, that some writers replace the parentheses in (1) with large square brackets.

The matrix $\mathbf{A}$ in (1) is said to have **order** $m \times n$. The mn numbers that constitute $\mathbf{A}$ are called its **elements** or **entries**. In particular, a_{ij} denotes the element in the ith row and the jth column. For brevity, the $m \times n$ matrix in (1) is often expressed as $(a_{ij})_{m \times n}$, or more simply as (a_{ij}), if the order $m \times n$ is either obvious or unimportant.

A matrix with either only one row or only one column is called a **vector**. It is usual to distinguish between a **row vector**, which has only one row, and a **column vector**, which has only one column. It is usual to denote row or column vectors by small bold letters like $\mathbf{x}$ or $\mathbf{y}$ rather than capital letters.

EXAMPLE 1 $\mathbf{A} = \begin{pmatrix} 3 & -2 \\ 5 & 8 \end{pmatrix}$, $\mathbf{B} = (-1, \quad 2, \quad \sqrt{3}, \quad 16)$, $\mathbf{C} = \begin{pmatrix} -1 & 2 \\ 8 & 5 \\ 7 & 6 \\ 1 & 1 \end{pmatrix}$

are matrices. Of these, $\mathbf{A}$ is 2×2, $\mathbf{B}$ is 1×4 (and so a row vector), and $\mathbf{C}$ is 4×2. Also $a_{21} = 5$ and $c_{32} = 6$. Note that c_{23} is undefined because $\mathbf{C}$ only has two columns.

EXAMPLE 2   Construct the 4×3 matrix $\mathbf{A} = (a_{ij})_{4 \times 3}$ with $a_{ij} = 2i - j$.

Solution: The matrix $\mathbf{A}$ has $4 \cdot 3 = 12$ entries. Because $a_{ij} = 2i - j$, it follows that $a_{11} = 2 \cdot 1 - 1 = 1$, $a_{12} = 2 \cdot 1 - 2 = 0$, $a_{13} = 2 \cdot 1 - 3 = -1$, and so on. The complete matrix is

$$\mathbf{A} = \begin{pmatrix} 2 \cdot 1 - 1 & 2 \cdot 1 - 2 & 2 \cdot 1 - 3 \\ 2 \cdot 2 - 1 & 2 \cdot 2 - 2 & 2 \cdot 2 - 3 \\ 2 \cdot 3 - 1 & 2 \cdot 3 - 2 & 2 \cdot 3 - 3 \\ 2 \cdot 4 - 1 & 2 \cdot 4 - 2 & 2 \cdot 4 - 3 \end{pmatrix} = \begin{pmatrix} 1 & 0 & -1 \\ 3 & 2 & 1 \\ 5 & 4 & 3 \\ 7 & 6 & 5 \end{pmatrix}$$

If $m = n$, so that the matrix has the same number of columns as rows, it is called a **square matrix** of order n. If $\mathbf{A} = (a_{ij})_{n \times n}$, then the elements $a_{11}, a_{22}, \dots, a_{nn}$ constitute the **main diagonal** that runs from the top left (a_{11}) to the bottom right (a_{nn}). For instance, the matrix $\mathbf{A}$ in Example 1 is a square matrix of order 2, whose main diagonal consists of the numbers 3 and 8. Note that only a square matrix can have such a main diagonal.

EXAMPLE 3   Consider the general linear system

$$
\begin{aligned}
a_{11}x_1 + a_{12}x_2 + \cdots + a_{1n}x_n &= b_1 \\
a_{21}x_1 + a_{22}x_2 + \cdots + a_{2n}x_n &= b_2 \\
&\cdots\cdots\cdots\cdots\cdots\cdots\cdots\cdots\cdots\cdots\cdots\cdots\cdots\cdots \\
a_{m1}x_1 + a_{m2}x_2 + \cdots + a_{mn}x_n &= b_m
\end{aligned}
\tag{2}
$$

of m equations in the unknown variables x_j ($j = 1, 2, \ldots, n$). It is natural to represent the coefficients of the n unknowns in (2) by the $m \times n$ matrix $\mathbf{A}$ that is arranged as in (1). Then $\mathbf{A}$ is called the **coefficient matrix** of (2). For instance, the coefficient matrix of

$$
\begin{aligned}
3x_1 - 2x_2 + 6x_3 &= 5 \\
5x_1 + x_2 + 2x_3 &= -2
\end{aligned}
\quad \text{is} \quad
\begin{pmatrix} 3 & -2 & 6 \\ 5 & 1 & 2 \end{pmatrix}
$$

One can also represent the numbers b_i ($i = 1, 2, \ldots, m$) on the right-hand side of (2) by an $m \times 1$ matrix, or column vector, often denoted by $\mathbf{b}$.

EXAMPLE 4   Consider a chain of stores with four outlets labelled B_1, B_2, B_3, and B_4, each selling eight different commodities, $V_1, V_2, \ldots, V_8$. Let a_{ij} denote the dollar value of the sales of commodity V_i at outlet B_j during a certain month. A suitable way of recording this data is in the 8×4 matrix or "spreadsheet"

$$
\mathbf{A} = \begin{pmatrix}
a_{11} & a_{12} & a_{13} & a_{14} \\
a_{21} & a_{22} & a_{23} & a_{24} \\
\vdots & \vdots & \vdots & \vdots \\
a_{81} & a_{82} & a_{83} & a_{84}
\end{pmatrix}
$$

The 8 rows refer to the 8 commodities, whereas the 4 columns refer to the 4 outlets. For instance, if $a_{73} = 225$, this means that the sales of commodity 7 at outlet 3 were worth \$225 for the month in question.

Matrix Operations

So far matrices have been regarded as just rectangular arrays of numbers that can be useful for storing information. The real motivation for introducing matrices, however, is that there are useful rules for manipulating them that correspond (to some extent) with the familiar rules of ordinary algebra.

First, let us agree how to define equality between matrices of the same order. If $\mathbf{A} = (a_{ij})_{m \times n}$ and $\mathbf{B} = (b_{ij})_{m \times n}$ are both $m \times n$ matrices, then $\mathbf{A}$ and $\mathbf{B}$ are said to be **equal**, and we write $\mathbf{A} = \mathbf{B}$, provided that $a_{ij} = b_{ij}$ for all $i = 1, 2, \ldots, m$, and $j = 1, 2, \ldots, n$. Thus, two matrices $\mathbf{A}$ and $\mathbf{B}$ are equal if they have the same order *and* if all their corresponding entries are equal. If $\mathbf{A}$ and $\mathbf{B}$ are *not* equal, then we write $\mathbf{A} \neq \mathbf{B}$.

EXAMPLE 5   When is $\begin{pmatrix} 3 & t-1 \\ 2t & u \end{pmatrix} = \begin{pmatrix} t & 2v \\ u+1 & t+w \end{pmatrix}$?

Solution: Both are 2×2 matrices. Since both have four elements, equality requires the four equations $3 = t$, $t - 1 = 2v$, $2t = u + 1$, and $u = t + w$ to be satisfied. By solving these simultaneous equations, it follows that the two matrices are equal if and only if $t = 3$, $v = 1$, $u = 5$, and $w = 2$. Then both matrices are equal to $\begin{pmatrix} 3 & 2 \\ 6 & 5 \end{pmatrix}$.

Let us return to Example 4, where the 8×4 matrix $\mathbf{A}$ represents the dollar values of total sales of the 8 commodities at the 4 outlets in a certain month. Suppose that the dollar values of sales for the next month are given by a corresponding 8×4 matrix $\mathbf{B} = (b_{ij})_{8 \times 4}$. The total sales revenues from each commodity in each of the outlets in the course of these 2 months combined would then be given by a new 8×4 matrix $\mathbf{C} = (c_{ij})_{8 \times 4}$, where $c_{ij} = a_{ij} + b_{ij}$ for $i = 1, \ldots, 8$ and for $j = 1, \ldots, 4$. Matrix $\mathbf{C}$ is called the "sum" of $\mathbf{A}$ and $\mathbf{B}$, and we write $\mathbf{C} = \mathbf{A} + \mathbf{B}$.

In general, if $\mathbf{A} = (a_{ij})_{m \times n}$ and $\mathbf{B} = (b_{ij})_{m \times n}$ are two matrices of the same order, we define the **sum** of $\mathbf{A}$ and $\mathbf{B}$ as the $m \times n$ matrix $(a_{ij} + b_{ij})_{m \times n}$. Thus,

$$\mathbf{A} + \mathbf{B} = (a_{ij})_{m \times n} + (b_{ij})_{m \times n} = (a_{ij} + b_{ij})_{m \times n} \tag{3}$$

So we add two matrices of the same order by adding their corresponding entries.

If α is a real number, we define $\alpha \mathbf{A}$ by

$$\alpha \mathbf{A} = \alpha(a_{ij})_{m \times n} = (\alpha a_{ij})_{m \times n} \tag{4}$$

Thus, to multiply a matrix by a scalar, multiply *each* entry in the matrix by that scalar. Returning to the chain of stores, the matrix equation $\mathbf{B} = 2\mathbf{A}$ would mean that all the entries in $\mathbf{B}$ are twice the corresponding elements in $\mathbf{A}$—that is, the sales revenue for each commodity in each of the outlets has exactly doubled from one month to the next. (Of course, this is a rather unlikely event.) Equivalently, $2\mathbf{A} = \mathbf{A} + \mathbf{A}$.

EXAMPLE 6   Compute $\mathbf{A} + \mathbf{B}$, $3\mathbf{A}$, and $(-\frac{1}{2})\mathbf{B}$, if $\mathbf{A} = \begin{pmatrix} 1 & 2 & 0 \\ 4 & -3 & -1 \end{pmatrix}$ and $\mathbf{B} = \begin{pmatrix} 0 & 1 & 2 \\ 1 & 0 & 2 \end{pmatrix}$.

Solution:

$$\mathbf{A} + \mathbf{B} = \begin{pmatrix} 1 & 3 & 2 \\ 5 & -3 & 1 \end{pmatrix}, \quad 3\mathbf{A} = \begin{pmatrix} 3 & 6 & 0 \\ 12 & -9 & -3 \end{pmatrix}, \quad (-\tfrac{1}{2})\mathbf{B} = \begin{pmatrix} 0 & -\tfrac{1}{2} & -1 \\ -\tfrac{1}{2} & 0 & -1 \end{pmatrix}$$

The matrix $(-1)\mathbf{A}$ is usually denoted by $-\mathbf{A}$, and the difference between the two matrices $\mathbf{A}$ and $\mathbf{B}$ of the same dimension, $\mathbf{A} - \mathbf{B}$, means the same as $\mathbf{A} + (-1)\mathbf{B}$. In our chain store example, $\mathbf{B} - \mathbf{A}$ denotes the (net) change in sales revenue for each commodity from each outlet between one month and the next. Positive components represent increases and negative components represent decreases.

With the definitions given earlier, it is easy to derive some useful rules. Let $\mathbf{A}$, $\mathbf{B}$, and $\mathbf{C}$ be arbitrary $m \times n$ matrices, and let α and β be real numbers. Also, let $\mathbf{0}$ denote the $m \times n$ matrix consisting only of zeros, called the **zero matrix**. Then:

RULES FOR MATRIX ADDITION AND MULTIPLICATION BY SCALARS

(a) $(\mathbf{A} + \mathbf{B}) + \mathbf{C} = \mathbf{A} + (\mathbf{B} + \mathbf{C})$

(b) $\mathbf{A} + \mathbf{B} = \mathbf{B} + \mathbf{A}$

(c) $\mathbf{A} + \mathbf{0} = \mathbf{A}$

(d) $\mathbf{A} + (-\mathbf{A}) = \mathbf{0}$ (5)

(e) $(\alpha + \beta)\mathbf{A} = \alpha\mathbf{A} + \beta\mathbf{A}$

(f) $\alpha(\mathbf{A} + \mathbf{B}) = \alpha\mathbf{A} + \alpha\mathbf{B}$

Each of these rules follows directly from the definitions and the corresponding rules for ordinary numbers.

Because of rule (5)(a), there is no need to put parentheses in expressions like $\mathbf{A} + \mathbf{B} + \mathbf{C}$. Note also that definitions (3) and (4) imply that $\mathbf{A} + \mathbf{A} + \mathbf{A}$ is equal to $3\mathbf{A}$.

PROBLEMS FOR SECTION 15.2

1. Construct the matrix $\mathbf{A} = (a_{ij})_{3 \times 3}$, where $a_{ii} = 1$ for $i = 1, 2, 3$, and $a_{ij} = 0$ for $i \neq j$.

2. Evaluate $\mathbf{A} + \mathbf{B}$ and $3\mathbf{A}$ when $\quad \mathbf{A} = \begin{pmatrix} 0 & 1 \\ 2 & 3 \end{pmatrix} \quad$ and $\quad \mathbf{B} = \begin{pmatrix} 1 & -1 \\ 5 & 2 \end{pmatrix}$.

3. For what values of u and v does $\begin{pmatrix} (1-u)^2 & v^2 & 3 \\ v & 2u & 5 \\ 6 & u & -1 \end{pmatrix} = \begin{pmatrix} 4 & 4 & u \\ v & -3v & u-v \\ 6 & v+5 & -1 \end{pmatrix}$?

4. Evaluate $\mathbf{A} + \mathbf{B}$, $\mathbf{A} - \mathbf{B}$, and $5\mathbf{A} - 3\mathbf{B}$ when

$$\mathbf{A} = \begin{pmatrix} 0 & 1 & -1 \\ 2 & 3 & 7 \end{pmatrix} \quad \text{and} \quad \mathbf{B} = \begin{pmatrix} 1 & -1 & 5 \\ 0 & 1 & 9 \end{pmatrix}$$

15.3 Matrix Multiplication

The rules we just gave for adding or subtracting matrices, and for multiplying a matrix by a scalar, should seem quite natural. The rule for matrix multiplication, however, is more subtle.[1] We motivate it by considering how to manipulate an equation system.

---

[1] It is tempting to define the product of two matrices $\mathbf{A} = (a_{ij})_{m \times n}$ and $\mathbf{B} = (b_{ij})_{m \times n}$ of the same dimensions this way: The product of $\mathbf{A}$ and $\mathbf{B}$ is simply the matrix $\mathbf{C} = (c_{ij})_{m \times n}$ where $c_{ij} = a_{ij}b_{ij}$ is obtained by multiplying the entries of the two matrices term by term. This is a respectable matrix operation and, in fact, matrix $\mathbf{C}$ is called the *Hadamard product* of $\mathbf{A}$ and $\mathbf{B}$. However, the definition of matrix multiplication that we give is by far the one most used in linear algebra.

Consider, for example, the following two linear equation systems:

(i) $\begin{aligned} z_1 &= a_{11}y_1 + a_{12}y_2 + a_{13}y_3 \\ z_2 &= a_{21}y_1 + a_{22}y_2 + a_{23}y_3 \end{aligned}$

(ii) $\begin{aligned} y_1 &= b_{11}x_1 + b_{12}x_2 \\ y_2 &= b_{21}x_1 + b_{22}x_2 \\ y_3 &= b_{31}x_1 + b_{32}x_2 \end{aligned}$

The matrices of coefficients appearing on the right-hand sides of these two systems of equations are, respectively,

$$\mathbf{A} = \begin{pmatrix} a_{11} & a_{12} & a_{13} \\ a_{21} & a_{22} & a_{23} \end{pmatrix} \quad \text{and} \quad \mathbf{B} = \begin{pmatrix} b_{11} & b_{12} \\ b_{21} & b_{22} \\ b_{31} & b_{32} \end{pmatrix}$$

System (i) expresses the z variables in terms of the y's, whereas in (ii), the y's are expressed in terms of the x's. So the z variables must be related to the x variables. Indeed, take the expressions for y_1, y_2, and y_3 in (ii) and insert them into (i). The result is

$$z_1 = a_{11}(b_{11}x_1 + b_{12}x_2) + a_{12}(b_{21}x_1 + b_{22}x_2) + a_{13}(b_{31}x_1 + b_{32}x_2)$$
$$z_2 = a_{21}(b_{11}x_1 + b_{12}x_2) + a_{22}(b_{21}x_1 + b_{22}x_2) + a_{23}(b_{31}x_1 + b_{32}x_2)$$

Rearranging the terms yields

$$z_1 = (a_{11}b_{11} + a_{12}b_{21} + a_{13}b_{31})x_1 + (a_{11}b_{12} + a_{12}b_{22} + a_{13}b_{32})x_2$$
$$z_2 = (a_{21}b_{11} + a_{22}b_{21} + a_{23}b_{31})x_1 + (a_{21}b_{12} + a_{22}b_{22} + a_{23}b_{32})x_2$$

The coefficient matrix of this system is, therefore,

$$\mathbf{C} = \begin{pmatrix} a_{11}b_{11} + a_{12}b_{21} + a_{13}b_{31} & a_{11}b_{12} + a_{12}b_{22} + a_{13}b_{32} \\ a_{21}b_{11} + a_{22}b_{21} + a_{23}b_{31} & a_{21}b_{12} + a_{22}b_{22} + a_{23}b_{32} \end{pmatrix}$$

The matrix $\mathbf{A}$ is 2×3 and $\mathbf{B}$ is 3×2. Thus, $\mathbf{B}$ *has as many rows as* $\mathbf{A}$ *has columns*. The matrix $\mathbf{C}$ is 2×2. Note that if we let $\mathbf{C} = (c_{ij})_{2 \times 2}$, then the number

$$c_{11} = a_{11}b_{11} + a_{12}b_{21} + a_{13}b_{31}$$

in the first row and first column is obtained by multiplying each of the three elements in the first row of $\mathbf{A}$ by the corresponding element in the first column of $\mathbf{B}$, and then adding these three products. We call the resulting expression $a_{11}b_{11} + a_{12}b_{21} + a_{13}b_{31}$ the "inner product" of the first row in $\mathbf{A}$ with the first column in $\mathbf{B}$. Likewise, c_{12} is the inner product of the first row in $\mathbf{A}$ and the second column in $\mathbf{B}$, and so on. Generally, each element c_{ij} is the inner product of the ith row in $\mathbf{A}$ and the jth column in $\mathbf{B}$.

The matrix $\mathbf{C}$ is called the **(matrix) product** of $\mathbf{A}$ and $\mathbf{B}$, and we write $\mathbf{C} = \mathbf{AB}$. Here is a numerical example.

EXAMPLE 1

$$\begin{pmatrix} 1 & 0 & 3 \\ 2 & 1 & 5 \end{pmatrix} \begin{pmatrix} 1 & 3 \\ 2 & 5 \\ 6 & 2 \end{pmatrix} = \begin{pmatrix} 1 \cdot 1 + 0 \cdot 2 + 3 \cdot 6 & 1 \cdot 3 + 0 \cdot 5 + 3 \cdot 2 \\ 2 \cdot 1 + 1 \cdot 2 + 5 \cdot 6 & 2 \cdot 3 + 1 \cdot 5 + 5 \cdot 2 \end{pmatrix} = \begin{pmatrix} 19 & 9 \\ 34 & 21 \end{pmatrix}$$

In order to extend the argument to general matrices, assume that as in (i) the variables $z_1, \ldots, z_m$ are expressed linearly in terms of $y_1, \ldots, y_n$, and that as in (ii), the variables $y_1, \ldots, y_n$ are expressed linearly in terms of $x_1, \ldots, x_p$. Then $z_1, \ldots, z_m$ can be expressed linearly in terms of $x_1, \ldots, x_p$. Provided that the matrix **B** does indeed have as many rows as **A** has columns, the result we get leads directly to the following definition:

MATRIX MULTIPLICATION

Suppose that $\mathbf{A} = (a_{ij})_{m \times n}$ and that $\mathbf{B} = (b_{ij})_{n \times p}$. Then the product $\mathbf{C} = \mathbf{AB}$ is the $m \times p$ matrix $\mathbf{C} = (c_{ij})_{m \times p}$, whose element in the ith row and the jth column is the inner product

$$c_{ij} = \sum_{r=1}^{n} a_{ir} b_{rj} = a_{i1}b_{1j} + a_{i2}b_{2j} + \cdots + a_{ik}b_{kj} + \cdots + a_{in}b_{nj} \tag{1}$$

of the ith row of **A** and the jth column of **B**.

Note that to get c_{ij} we multiply each component a_{ir} in the ith row of **A** by the corresponding component b_{rj} in the jth column of **B**, then add all the products. One way of visualizing matrix multiplication is this:

$$\begin{pmatrix} a_{11} & \cdots & a_{1k} & \cdots & a_{1n} \\ \vdots & & \vdots & & \vdots \\ a_{i1} & \cdots & a_{ik} & \cdots & a_{in} \\ \vdots & & \vdots & & \vdots \\ a_{m1} & \cdots & a_{mk} & \cdots & a_{mn} \end{pmatrix} \cdot \begin{pmatrix} b_{11} & \cdots & b_{1j} & \cdots & b_{1p} \\ \vdots & & \vdots & & \vdots \\ b_{k1} & \cdots & b_{kj} & \cdots & b_{kp} \\ \vdots & & \vdots & & \vdots \\ b_{n1} & \cdots & b_{nj} & \cdots & b_{np} \end{pmatrix} = \begin{pmatrix} c_{11} & \cdots & c_{1j} & \cdots & c_{1p} \\ \vdots & & \vdots & & \vdots \\ c_{i1} & \cdots & c_{ij} & \cdots & c_{ip} \\ \vdots & & \vdots & & \vdots \\ c_{m1} & \cdots & c_{mj} & \cdots & c_{mp} \end{pmatrix}$$

It bears repeating that the matrix product **AB** is defined only if the number of columns in **A** is equal to the number of rows in **B**. Also, if **A** and **B** are two matrices, then **AB** might be defined, even if **BA** is not. For instance, if **A** is 6×3 and **B** is 3×5, then **AB** is defined (and is 6×5), whereas **BA** is not defined.

EXAMPLE 2   Let $\mathbf{A} = \begin{pmatrix} 0 & 1 & 2 \\ 2 & 3 & 1 \\ 4 & -1 & 6 \end{pmatrix}$ and $\mathbf{B} = \begin{pmatrix} 3 & 2 \\ 1 & 0 \\ -1 & 1 \end{pmatrix}$. Compute the matrix product **AB**. Is the product **BA** defined?

Solution: **A** is 3×3 and **B** is 3×2, so **AB** is a 3×2 matrix:

$$\mathbf{AB} = \begin{pmatrix} 0 & 1 & 2 \\ 2 & 3 & 1 \\ 4 & -1 & 6 \end{pmatrix} \begin{pmatrix} 3 & 2 \\ 1 & 0 \\ -1 & 1 \end{pmatrix} = \begin{pmatrix} -1 & 2 \\ 8 & 5 \\ 5 & 14 \end{pmatrix}$$

(We have indicated how the element in the second row and first column of **AB** is found. It is the inner product of the second row in **A** and the first column in **B**; this is $2 \cdot 3 + 3 \cdot 1 + 1 \cdot (-1) = 8$.) The matrix product **BA** is not defined because the number of columns in **B** ($= 2$) is not equal to the number of rows in **A** ($= 3$).

NOTE 1 In the previous example, **AB** was defined but **BA** was not. Even in cases in which **AB** and **BA** are both defined, they are usually not equal. See Problem 1 and the subsection "Errors to Avoid" in Section 15.4. When we write **AB**, we say that we **premultiply B** by **A**, whereas in **BA** we **postmultiply B** by **A**.

EXAMPLE 3   Initially, three firms A, B, and C (numbered 1, 2, and 3) share the market for a certain commodity. Firm A has 20% of the market, B has 60%, and C has 20%. In the course of the next year, the following changes occur:

$$\begin{cases} A \text{ keeps 85\% of its customers, while losing 5\% to } B \text{ and 10\% to } C \\ B \text{ keeps 55\% of its customers, while losing 10\% to } A \text{ and 35\% to } C \\ C \text{ keeps 85\% of its customers, while losing 10\% to } A \text{ and 5\% to } B \end{cases}$$

We can represent market shares of the three firms by means of a *market share vector*, defined as a column vector **s** whose components are all nonnegative and sum to 1. Define the matrix **T** and the initial market share vector **s** by

$$\mathbf{T} = \begin{pmatrix} 0.85 & 0.10 & 0.10 \\ 0.05 & 0.55 & 0.05 \\ 0.10 & 0.35 & 0.85 \end{pmatrix} \quad \text{and} \quad \mathbf{s} = \begin{pmatrix} 0.2 \\ 0.6 \\ 0.2 \end{pmatrix}$$

Notice that t_{ij} is the percentage of j's customers who become i's customers in the next period. So **T** is called the *transition matrix*.

Compute the vector **Ts**, show that it is also a market share vector, and give an interpretation. What is the interpretation of **T(Ts)**, **T(T(Ts))**, ...?

Solution:

$$\mathbf{Ts} = \begin{pmatrix} 0.85 & 0.10 & 0.10 \\ 0.05 & 0.55 & 0.05 \\ 0.10 & 0.35 & 0.85 \end{pmatrix} \begin{pmatrix} 0.2 \\ 0.6 \\ 0.2 \end{pmatrix} = \begin{pmatrix} 0.25 \\ 0.35 \\ 0.40 \end{pmatrix}$$

Because $0.25 + 0.35 + 0.40 = 1$, the product **Ts** is also a market share vector. The first entry in **Ts** is obtained from the calculation

$$0.85 \cdot 0.2 + 0.10 \cdot 0.6 + 0.10 \cdot 0.2 = 0.25$$

Here $0.85 \cdot 0.2$ is A's share of the market that it retains after 1 year, $0.10 \cdot 0.6$ is the share A gains from B, and $0.10 \cdot 0.2$ is the share A gains from C. The sum is therefore A's total share of the market after 1 year. The other entries in **Ts** can be interpreted similarly, so **Ts** must be the new market share vector after 1 year. Then **T(Ts)** is the market share vector after one more year—that is, after 2 years, and so on. (In Problem 7, you are asked to compute **T(Ts)**.)

Systems of Equations in Matrix Form

The definition of matrix multiplication was introduced in order to allow systems of equations to be manipulated. Indeed, it turns out that we can write linear systems of equations very compactly by means of matrix multiplication. For instance, consider the system

$$3x_1 + 4x_2 = 5$$
$$7x_1 - 2x_2 = 2$$

Now define $\mathbf{A} = \begin{pmatrix} 3 & 4 \\ 7 & -2 \end{pmatrix}$, $\mathbf{x} = \begin{pmatrix} x_1 \\ x_2 \end{pmatrix}$, and $\mathbf{b} = \begin{pmatrix} 5 \\ 2 \end{pmatrix}$. Then we see that

$$\mathbf{Ax} = \begin{pmatrix} 3 & 4 \\ 7 & -2 \end{pmatrix} \begin{pmatrix} x_1 \\ x_2 \end{pmatrix} = \begin{pmatrix} 3x_1 + 4x_2 \\ 7x_1 - 2x_2 \end{pmatrix}$$

So the original system is equivalent to the matrix equation

$$\mathbf{Ax} = \mathbf{b}$$

Consider the general linear system (15.1.1) with m equations and n unknowns. Suppose we define

$$\mathbf{A} = \begin{pmatrix} a_{11} & a_{12} & \cdots & a_{1n} \\ a_{21} & a_{22} & \cdots & a_{2n} \\ \vdots & \vdots & & \vdots \\ a_{m1} & a_{m2} & \cdots & a_{mn} \end{pmatrix}, \quad \mathbf{x} = \begin{pmatrix} x_1 \\ x_2 \\ \vdots \\ x_n \end{pmatrix}, \quad \mathbf{b} = \begin{pmatrix} b_1 \\ b_2 \\ \vdots \\ b_m \end{pmatrix}$$

So $\mathbf{A}$ is $m \times n$ and $\mathbf{x}$ is $n \times 1$. The matrix product $\mathbf{Ax}$ is then defined and is $m \times 1$. It follows that

$$a_{11}x_1 + a_{12}x_2 + \cdots + a_{1n}x_n = b_1$$
$$a_{21}x_1 + a_{22}x_2 + \cdots + a_{2n}x_n = b_2$$
$$\dots\dots\dots\dots\dots\dots\dots\dots\dots\dots\dots \qquad \text{can be written as} \qquad \mathbf{Ax} = \mathbf{b}$$
$$a_{m1}x_1 + a_{m2}x_2 + \cdots + a_{mn}x_n = b_m$$

This very concise notation turns out to be extremely useful.

PROBLEMS FOR SECTION 15.3

1. Compute the products $\mathbf{AB}$ and $\mathbf{BA}$, if possible, for the following:

(a) $\mathbf{A} = \begin{pmatrix} 0 & -2 \\ 3 & 1 \end{pmatrix}$, $\mathbf{B} = \begin{pmatrix} -1 & 4 \\ 1 & 5 \end{pmatrix}$

(b) $\mathbf{A} = \begin{pmatrix} 8 & 3 & -2 \\ 1 & 0 & 4 \end{pmatrix}$, $\mathbf{B} = \begin{pmatrix} 2 & -2 \\ 4 & 3 \\ 1 & -5 \end{pmatrix}$

(c) $\mathbf{A} = \begin{pmatrix} 0 \\ -2 \\ 4 \end{pmatrix}$, $\mathbf{B} = (0, \ -2, \ 3)$

(d) $\mathbf{A} = \begin{pmatrix} -1 & 0 \\ 2 & 4 \end{pmatrix}$, $\mathbf{B} = \begin{pmatrix} 3 & 1 \\ -1 & 1 \\ 0 & 2 \end{pmatrix}$

2. Given the matrices $\mathbf{A} = \begin{pmatrix} 2 & 4 \\ 1 & 2 \end{pmatrix}$, $\mathbf{B} = \begin{pmatrix} -2 & 4 \\ 1 & -2 \end{pmatrix}$, $\mathbf{C} = \begin{pmatrix} 2 & 3 \\ 6 & 9 \end{pmatrix}$, $\mathbf{D} = \begin{pmatrix} 1 & 1 \\ 1 & 3 \end{pmatrix}$,

   calculate   (i) $3\mathbf{A} + 2\mathbf{B} - 2\mathbf{C} + \mathbf{D}$ (ii) $\mathbf{AB}$ (iii) $\mathbf{C}(\mathbf{AB})$.

3. Let $\mathbf{A} = \begin{pmatrix} 1 & 2 & -3 \\ 5 & 0 & 2 \\ 1 & -1 & 1 \end{pmatrix}$, $\mathbf{B} = \begin{pmatrix} 3 & -1 & 2 \\ 4 & 2 & 5 \\ 2 & 0 & 3 \end{pmatrix}$, $\mathbf{C} = \begin{pmatrix} 4 & 1 & 2 \\ 0 & 3 & 2 \\ 1 & -2 & 3 \end{pmatrix}$.

   Find the matrices $\mathbf{A} + \mathbf{B}$, $\mathbf{A} - \mathbf{B}$, $\mathbf{AB}$, $\mathbf{BA}$, $\mathbf{A}(\mathbf{BC})$, and $(\mathbf{AB})\mathbf{C}$.

4. Write out three matrix equations corresponding to the following systems:

   (a) $\begin{aligned} x_1 + x_2 &= 3 \\ 3x_1 + 5x_2 &= 5 \end{aligned}$
   (b) $\begin{aligned} x_1 + 2x_2 + x_3 &= 4 \\ x_1 - x_2 + x_3 &= 5 \\ 2x_1 + 3x_2 - x_3 &= 1 \end{aligned}$
   (c) $\begin{aligned} 2x_1 - 3x_2 + x_3 &= 0 \\ x_1 + x_2 - x_3 &= 0 \end{aligned}$

5. Consider the three matrices $\mathbf{A} = \begin{pmatrix} 2 & 2 \\ 1 & 5 \end{pmatrix}$, $\mathbf{B} = \begin{pmatrix} 2 & 0 \\ 3 & 2 \end{pmatrix}$, and $\mathbf{I} = \begin{pmatrix} 1 & 0 \\ 0 & 1 \end{pmatrix}$.

   (a) Find a matrix $\mathbf{C}$ satisfying $(\mathbf{A} - 2\mathbf{I})\mathbf{C} = \mathbf{I}$.

   (b) Is there a matrix $\mathbf{D}$ satisfying $(\mathbf{B} - 2\mathbf{I})\mathbf{D} = \mathbf{I}$?

(SM) 6. (a) If $\mathbf{A}$ is an $m \times n$ matrix and $\mathbf{B}$ is another matrix such that both products $\mathbf{AB}$ and $\mathbf{BA}$ are defined, what must be the dimensions of $\mathbf{B}$?

   (b) Find all matrices $\mathbf{B}$ that "commute" with $\mathbf{A} = \begin{pmatrix} 1 & 2 \\ 2 & 3 \end{pmatrix}$ in the sense that $\mathbf{BA} = \mathbf{AB}$.

7. In Example 3, compute $\mathbf{T}(\mathbf{Ts})$.

15.4 Rules for Matrix Multiplication

In Section 15.2 we set out some rather obvious algebraic rules for matrix addition and multiplication by a scalar. Matrix multiplication is a more complicated operation, so we must carefully examine what rules apply. We have already noticed that the commutative law $\mathbf{AB} = \mathbf{BA}$ does NOT hold in general. The following three important rules *are* generally valid, however.

If $\mathbf{A}$, $\mathbf{B}$, and $\mathbf{C}$ are matrices whose dimensions are such that the given operations are defined, and α is an arbitrary scalar, then:

RULES FOR MATRIX MULTIPLICATION

$(\mathbf{AB})\mathbf{C} = \mathbf{A}(\mathbf{BC})$	**(associative law)**	(1)
$\mathbf{A}(\mathbf{B} + \mathbf{C}) = \mathbf{AB} + \mathbf{AC}$	**(left distributive law)**	(2)
$(\mathbf{A} + \mathbf{B})\mathbf{C} = \mathbf{AC} + \mathbf{BC}$	**(right distributive law)**	(3)
$(\alpha\mathbf{A})\mathbf{B} = \mathbf{A}(\alpha\mathbf{B}) = \alpha(\mathbf{AB})$		(4)

Note that both the left and right distributive laws are stated here because, unlike for numbers, matrix multiplication is not *commutative*, and so $\mathbf{A}(\mathbf{B} + \mathbf{C}) \neq (\mathbf{B} + \mathbf{C})\mathbf{A}$ in general.

EXAMPLE 1   Verify rules (1)–(4), where α is an arbitrary scalar, for the following matrices:

$$\mathbf{A} = \begin{pmatrix} 1 & 2 \\ 0 & 1 \end{pmatrix}, \qquad \mathbf{B} = \begin{pmatrix} 0 & -1 \\ 3 & 2 \end{pmatrix}, \qquad \mathbf{C} = \begin{pmatrix} 1 & 1 \\ 2 & 1 \end{pmatrix}$$

Solution: All operations of multiplication and addition are defined, with

$$\mathbf{AB} = \begin{pmatrix} 6 & 3 \\ 3 & 2 \end{pmatrix}, \qquad (\mathbf{AB})\mathbf{C} = \begin{pmatrix} 6 & 3 \\ 3 & 2 \end{pmatrix}\begin{pmatrix} 1 & 1 \\ 2 & 1 \end{pmatrix} = \begin{pmatrix} 12 & 9 \\ 7 & 5 \end{pmatrix}$$

$$\mathbf{BC} = \begin{pmatrix} -2 & -1 \\ 7 & 5 \end{pmatrix}, \qquad \mathbf{A}(\mathbf{BC}) = \begin{pmatrix} 1 & 2 \\ 0 & 1 \end{pmatrix}\begin{pmatrix} -2 & -1 \\ 7 & 5 \end{pmatrix} = \begin{pmatrix} 12 & 9 \\ 7 & 5 \end{pmatrix}$$

Thus, $(\mathbf{AB})\mathbf{C} = \mathbf{A}(\mathbf{BC})$ in this case. Moreover,

$$\mathbf{B} + \mathbf{C} = \begin{pmatrix} 1 & 0 \\ 5 & 3 \end{pmatrix}, \qquad \mathbf{A}(\mathbf{B} + \mathbf{C}) = \begin{pmatrix} 1 & 2 \\ 0 & 1 \end{pmatrix}\begin{pmatrix} 1 & 0 \\ 5 & 3 \end{pmatrix} = \begin{pmatrix} 11 & 6 \\ 5 & 3 \end{pmatrix}$$

and

$$\mathbf{AC} = \begin{pmatrix} 5 & 3 \\ 2 & 1 \end{pmatrix}, \qquad \mathbf{AB} + \mathbf{AC} = \begin{pmatrix} 6 & 3 \\ 3 & 2 \end{pmatrix} + \begin{pmatrix} 5 & 3 \\ 2 & 1 \end{pmatrix} = \begin{pmatrix} 11 & 6 \\ 5 & 3 \end{pmatrix}$$

So $\mathbf{A}(\mathbf{B} + \mathbf{C}) = \mathbf{AB} + \mathbf{AC}$. You should verify the right distributive law (3), as well as rule (4), for yourself.

Proof of (1): Suppose $\mathbf{A} = (a_{ij})_{m \times n}$, $\mathbf{B} = (b_{ij})_{n \times p}$, and $\mathbf{C} = (c_{ij})_{p \times q}$. It is easy to verify that these dimensions imply that $(\mathbf{AB})\mathbf{C}$ and $\mathbf{A}(\mathbf{BC})$ are both defined as $m \times q$ matrices. We have to prove that their corresponding elements are all equal.

The element in row i and column l of $(\mathbf{AB})\mathbf{C}$ is denoted by $[(\mathbf{AB})\mathbf{C}]_{il}$, and it is the inner product of the ith row in $\mathbf{AB}$ and the lth column in $\mathbf{C}$. Using the notation for sums, we see that

$$[(\mathbf{AB})\mathbf{C}]_{il} = \sum_{k=1}^{p}\left(\sum_{j=1}^{n} a_{ij}b_{jk}\right)c_{kl} = \sum_{j=1}^{n} a_{ij}\left(\sum_{k=1}^{p} b_{jk}c_{kl}\right) = [\mathbf{A}(\mathbf{BC})]_{il}$$

where the two double sums are equal because they both give the sum of all the pn terms $a_{ij}b_{jk}c_{kl}$, where j runs from 1 to n and k runs from 1 to p. This proves (1). ∎

Proving rule (1) involves checking in detail that each element of $(\mathbf{AB})\mathbf{C}$ equals the corresponding element of $\mathbf{A}(\mathbf{BC})$. The same sort of check is required to prove the other three rules. We leave these proofs to the reader.

Because of (1), parentheses are not required in a matrix product such as $\mathbf{ABC}$. Of course, a corresponding result is valid for products of more factors.

A useful technique in matrix algebra is to prove new results by using (1)–(4), rather than examining individual elements. For instance, suppose we are asked to prove that if $\mathbf{A} = (a_{ij})$ and $\mathbf{B} = (b_{ij})$ are both $n \times n$ matrices, then

$$(\mathbf{A} + \mathbf{B})(\mathbf{A} + \mathbf{B}) = \mathbf{AA} + \mathbf{AB} + \mathbf{BA} + \mathbf{BB} \tag{5}$$

According to (2),

$$(A + B)(A + B) = (A + B)A + (A + B)B$$

By (3), one has $(A + B)A = AA + BA$ and $(A + B)B = AB + BB$, from which we see that $(*)$ follows.

Powers of Matrices

If A is a square matrix, the associative law (1) allows us to write AA as A^2, and AAA as A^3, and so on. In general,

$$A^n = AA \cdots A \qquad (A \text{ is repeated } n \text{ times})$$

EXAMPLE 2   Let $A = \begin{pmatrix} 1 & -1 \\ 0 & 1 \end{pmatrix}$. Compute A^2, A^3, and A^4. Then guess the general form of A^n, and confirm your guess by induction on n. (For induction, see Section 3.7.)

Solution: We find that

$$A^2 = AA = \begin{pmatrix} 1 & -2 \\ 0 & 1 \end{pmatrix}, \quad A^3 = A^2A = \begin{pmatrix} 1 & -3 \\ 0 & 1 \end{pmatrix}, \quad A^4 = A^3A = \begin{pmatrix} 1 & -4 \\ 0 & 1 \end{pmatrix}$$

A reasonable guess, therefore, is that for all natural numbers n,

$$A^n = \begin{pmatrix} 1 & -n \\ 0 & 1 \end{pmatrix} \qquad\qquad (*)$$

We confirm this by induction on n. Formula $(*)$ *is* correct for $n = 1$. As the induction hypothesis, we suppose that $(*)$ holds for $n = k$—that is,

$$A^k = \begin{pmatrix} 1 & -k \\ 0 & 1 \end{pmatrix}$$

Then

$$A^{k+1} = A^k A = \begin{pmatrix} 1 & -k \\ 0 & 1 \end{pmatrix}\begin{pmatrix} 1 & -1 \\ 0 & 1 \end{pmatrix} = \begin{pmatrix} 1 & -k-1 \\ 0 & 1 \end{pmatrix}$$

This completes the induction step showing that, if $(*)$ holds for $n = k$, then it holds for $n = k + 1$. It follows that $(*)$ holds for all natural numbers n.

EXAMPLE 3   Suppose P and Q are $n \times n$ matrices such that $PQ = Q^2P$. Prove that $(PQ)^2 = Q^6P^2$.

Solution: The proof is simple if we use (1) and $PQ = Q^2P$ repeatedly:

$$(PQ)^2 = (PQ)(PQ) = (Q^2P)(Q^2P) = (Q^2P)Q(QP) = Q^2(PQ)(QP)$$

$$= Q^2(Q^2P)(QP) = Q^2Q^2(PQ)P = Q^2Q^2(Q^2P)P = Q^2Q^2Q^2P^2 = Q^6P^2$$

It would be essentially impossible to prove this equality by looking at individual elements. Note carefully that $(PQ)^2$ is *not* equal to P^2Q^2.

The Identity Matrix

The **identity matrix** of order n, denoted by $\mathbf{I}_n$ (or often just by $\mathbf{I}$), is the $n \times n$ matrix having ones along the main diagonal and zeros elsewhere:

$$\mathbf{I}_n = \begin{pmatrix} 1 & 0 & \cdots & 0 \\ 0 & 1 & \cdots & 0 \\ \vdots & \vdots & \ddots & \vdots \\ 0 & 0 & \cdots & 1 \end{pmatrix}_{n \times n} \qquad \text{(identity matrix)}$$

If $\mathbf{A}$ is any $m \times n$ matrix, it is easy to verify that $\mathbf{AI}_n = \mathbf{A}$. Likewise, if $\mathbf{B}$ is any $n \times m$ matrix, then $\mathbf{I}_n\mathbf{B} = \mathbf{B}$. In particular,

$$\mathbf{AI}_n = \mathbf{I}_n\mathbf{A} = \mathbf{A} \qquad \text{(for every } n \times n \text{ matrix } \mathbf{A}) \tag{6}$$

Thus, $\mathbf{I}_n$ is the matrix equivalent of 1 in the real number system. In fact, it is the only matrix with this property. To prove this, suppose $\mathbf{E}$ is an arbitrary $n \times n$ matrix such that $\mathbf{AE} = \mathbf{A}$ for all $n \times n$ matrices $\mathbf{A}$. Putting $\mathbf{A} = \mathbf{I}_n$ in particular yields $\mathbf{I}_n\mathbf{E} = \mathbf{I}_n$. But $\mathbf{I}_n\mathbf{E} = \mathbf{E}$ according to (6). So $\mathbf{E} = \mathbf{I}_n$.

Errors to Avoid

The rules of matrix algebra make many arguments very easy. But it is essential to avoid using rules that do not work when multiplying general matrices, even if they do work for numbers (or for 1×1 matrices). For example, consider equation (5). It is tempting to simplify the expression $\mathbf{AA} + \mathbf{AB} + \mathbf{BA} + \mathbf{BB}$ on the right-hand side to $\mathbf{AA} + 2\mathbf{AB} + \mathbf{BB}$. This is wrong! Even when $\mathbf{AB}$ and $\mathbf{BA}$ are both defined, $\mathbf{AB}$ is not necessarily equal to $\mathbf{BA}$. As the next example shows, matrix multiplication is *not* commutative.

EXAMPLE 4   Let $\mathbf{A}$ and $\mathbf{B}$ be the matrices $\mathbf{A} = \begin{pmatrix} 2 & 0 \\ 0 & 3 \end{pmatrix}$, $\mathbf{B} = \begin{pmatrix} 0 & 1 \\ 1 & 0 \end{pmatrix}$.
Show that $\mathbf{AB} \neq \mathbf{BA}$.

Solution: $\mathbf{AB} = \begin{pmatrix} 0 & 2 \\ 3 & 0 \end{pmatrix}$ and $\mathbf{BA} = \begin{pmatrix} 0 & 3 \\ 2 & 0 \end{pmatrix}$. Hence, $\mathbf{AB} \neq \mathbf{BA}$.

If a and b are real numbers, then $ab = 0$ implies that either a or b is 0. The corresponding result is not true for matrices. In fact, $\mathbf{AB}$ can be the zero matrix even if neither $\mathbf{A}$ nor $\mathbf{B}$ is the zero matrix.

EXAMPLE 5   Let $\mathbf{A} = \begin{pmatrix} 3 & 1 \\ 6 & 2 \end{pmatrix}$, $\mathbf{B} = \begin{pmatrix} 1 & 2 \\ -3 & -6 \end{pmatrix}$. Compute $\mathbf{AB}$.

Solution: $\mathbf{AB} = \begin{pmatrix} 3 & 1 \\ 6 & 2 \end{pmatrix}\begin{pmatrix} 1 & 2 \\ -3 & -6 \end{pmatrix} = \begin{pmatrix} 0 & 0 \\ 0 & 0 \end{pmatrix}$.

For real numbers, if $ab = ac$ and $a \neq 0$, then $b = c$, because we can cancel by multiplying each side of the equation by $1/a$. The corresponding cancellation "rule" is not valid for matrices. Example 5 illustrates this point also: There $\mathbf{AB} = \mathbf{A0}$ and $\mathbf{A} \neq \mathbf{0}$, yet $\mathbf{B} \neq \mathbf{0}$.

So we have found examples showing that in general:

$$\mathbf{AB} \neq \mathbf{BA} \tag{7}$$

$$\mathbf{AB} = \mathbf{0} \text{ does not imply that either } \mathbf{A} \text{ or } \mathbf{B} \text{ is } \mathbf{0} \tag{8}$$

$$\mathbf{AB} = \mathbf{AC} \text{ and } \mathbf{A} \neq \mathbf{0} \text{ do not imply that } \mathbf{B} = \mathbf{C} \tag{9}$$

Here (7) says that matrix multiplication is not **commutative** in general, whereas (9) shows us that the cancellation law is generally invalid for matrix multiplication. (The cancellation law *is valid* if $\mathbf{A}$ has a so-called inverse. See Section 16.6.)

The following two examples illustrate natural applications of matrix multiplication.

EXAMPLE 6   A firm uses raw materials $R_1, R_2, \ldots, R_m$ to produce the commodities $V_1, V_2, \ldots, V_n$. For $i = 1, \ldots, m$ and $j = 1, \ldots, n$, we let a_{ij} be the quantity of raw material R_i which is needed to produce each unit of commodity V_j. These quantities form the matrix

$$\mathbf{A} = (a_{ij})_{m \times n} = \begin{pmatrix} a_{11} & a_{12} & \cdots & a_{1n} \\ a_{21} & a_{22} & \cdots & a_{2n} \\ \vdots & \vdots & & \vdots \\ a_{m1} & a_{m2} & \cdots & a_{mn} \end{pmatrix}$$

Suppose that the firm plans a monthly production of u_j units of each commodity V_j, $j = 1, 2, \ldots, n$. This plan can be represented by an $n \times 1$ matrix (column vector) $\mathbf{u}$, called the firm's monthly production vector:

$$\mathbf{u} = \begin{pmatrix} u_1 \\ u_2 \\ \vdots \\ u_n \end{pmatrix}$$

Since a_{i1}, in particular, is the amount of raw material R_i which is needed to produce one unit of commodity V_1, it follows that $a_{i1}u_1$ is the amount of raw material R_i which is needed to produce u_1 units of commodity V_1. Similarly $a_{ij}u_j$ is the amount needed for u_j units of V_j $(j = 2, \ldots, n)$. The total monthly requirement of raw material R_i is therefore

$$a_{i1}u_1 + a_{i2}u_2 + \cdots + a_{in}u_n = \sum_{j=1}^{n} a_{ij}u_j$$

This is the inner product of the ith row vector in $\mathbf{A}$ and the column vector $\mathbf{u}$. The firm's monthly requirement vector $\mathbf{r}$ for all raw materials is therefore given by the matrix product $\mathbf{r} = \mathbf{Au}$. Thus $\mathbf{r}$ is an $m \times 1$ matrix, or a column vector.

Suppose that the prices of the m raw materials are respectively $p_1, p_2, \ldots, p_m$ per unit. If we define the price vector $\mathbf{p} = (p_1, p_2, \ldots, p_m)$, then the total monthly cost K of acquiring the required raw materials to produce the vector $\mathbf{u}$ is $\sum_{i=1}^{m} p_i r_i$. This sum can also be written as the matrix product $\mathbf{pr}$. Hence, $K = \mathbf{pr} = \mathbf{p}(\mathbf{Au}) = \mathbf{pAu}$. (Since matrix multiplication is associative, it is unnecessary to use parentheses.)

EXAMPLE 7   Figure 1 indicates the number of daily international flights between major airports in three different countries A, B, and C. The number attached to each connecting line shows how many flights there are between the two airports. For instance, from airport b_3 in country B there are 4 flights to airport c_3 in country C each day, but none to airport c_2 in country C.

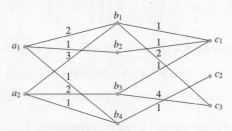

Figure 1

The relevant data can also be represented by the two matrices

$$\mathbf{P}: \quad \begin{matrix} & b_1 & b_2 & b_3 & b_4 \\ a_1 \\ a_2 \end{matrix}\begin{pmatrix} 2 & 1 & 0 & 1 \\ 3 & 0 & 2 & 1 \end{pmatrix} \qquad \mathbf{Q}: \quad \begin{matrix} & c_1 & c_2 & c_3 \\ b_1 \\ b_2 \\ b_3 \\ b_4 \end{matrix}\begin{pmatrix} 1 & 0 & 2 \\ 1 & 0 & 0 \\ 1 & 0 & 4 \\ 0 & 1 & 0 \end{pmatrix}$$

Each element p_{ij} of the matrix $\mathbf{P}$ represents the number of daily flights between a_i and b_j, while each element q_{jk} of $\mathbf{Q}$ represents the number of daily flights between b_j and c_k. How many ways are there of getting from a_i to c_k using two flights, with one connection in country B? Between a_2 and c_3, for example, there are $3 \cdot 2 + 0 \cdot 0 + 2 \cdot 4 + 1 \cdot 0 = 14$ possibilities. This is the inner product of the second row vector in $\mathbf{P}$ and the third column vector in $\mathbf{Q}$. The same reasoning applies for each a_i and c_k. So the total number of flight connections between the different airports in countries A and C is given by the matrix product

$$\mathbf{R} = \mathbf{PQ} = \begin{pmatrix} 2 & 1 & 0 & 1 \\ 3 & 0 & 2 & 1 \end{pmatrix}\begin{pmatrix} 1 & 0 & 2 \\ 1 & 0 & 0 \\ 1 & 0 & 4 \\ 0 & 1 & 0 \end{pmatrix} = \begin{pmatrix} 3 & 1 & 4 \\ 5 & 1 & 14 \end{pmatrix}$$

PROBLEMS FOR SECTION 15.4

1. Verify the distributive law $\mathbf{A}(\mathbf{B} + \mathbf{C}) = \mathbf{AB} + \mathbf{AC}$ when

$$\mathbf{A} = \begin{pmatrix} 1 & 2 \\ 3 & 4 \end{pmatrix}, \qquad \mathbf{B} = \begin{pmatrix} 2 & -1 & 1 & 0 \\ 3 & -1 & 2 & 1 \end{pmatrix}, \qquad \mathbf{C} = \begin{pmatrix} -1 & 1 & 1 & 2 \\ -2 & 2 & 0 & -1 \end{pmatrix}$$

(SM) 2. Compute the matrix product $(x, y, z)\begin{pmatrix} a & d & e \\ d & b & f \\ e & f & c \end{pmatrix}\begin{pmatrix} x \\ y \\ z \end{pmatrix}$.

3. Verify by actual multiplication that $(\mathbf{AB})\mathbf{C} = \mathbf{A}(\mathbf{BC})$ if

$$\mathbf{A} = \begin{pmatrix} a_{11} & a_{12} \\ a_{21} & a_{22} \end{pmatrix}, \qquad \mathbf{B} = \begin{pmatrix} b_{11} & b_{12} \\ b_{21} & b_{22} \end{pmatrix}, \qquad \mathbf{C} = \begin{pmatrix} c_{11} & c_{12} \\ c_{21} & c_{22} \end{pmatrix}$$

4. Compute: (a) $\begin{pmatrix} 1 & 0 & 0 \\ 0 & 1 & 0 \\ 0 & 0 & 1 \end{pmatrix} \begin{pmatrix} 5 & 3 & 1 \\ 2 & 0 & 9 \\ 1 & 3 & 3 \end{pmatrix}$ (b) $(1, \quad 2, \quad -3) \begin{pmatrix} 1 & 0 & 0 \\ 0 & 1 & 0 \\ 0 & 0 & 1 \end{pmatrix}$

5. If $\mathbf{A}$ and $\mathbf{B}$ are square matrices of order n, prove that, in general

$$\text{(a) } (\mathbf{A} + \mathbf{B})(\mathbf{A} - \mathbf{B}) \neq \mathbf{A}^2 - \mathbf{B}^2 \quad \text{(b) } (\mathbf{A} - \mathbf{B})(\mathbf{A} - \mathbf{B}) \neq \mathbf{A}^2 - 2\mathbf{AB} + \mathbf{B}^2$$

Find a necessary and sufficient condition for equality to hold in each case.

6. A square matrix $\mathbf{A}$ is said to be **idempotent** if $\mathbf{A}^2 = \mathbf{A}$.

(a) Show that $\begin{pmatrix} 2 & -2 & -4 \\ -1 & 3 & 4 \\ 1 & -2 & -3 \end{pmatrix}$ is idempotent.

(b) Show that if $\mathbf{AB} = \mathbf{A}$ and $\mathbf{BA} = \mathbf{B}$, then $\mathbf{A}$ and $\mathbf{B}$ are both idempotent.

(c) Show that if $\mathbf{A}$ is idempotent, then $\mathbf{A}^n = \mathbf{A}$ for all positive integers n.

7. Suppose that $\mathbf{P}$ and $\mathbf{Q}$ are $n \times n$ matrices and that $\mathbf{P}^3\mathbf{Q} = \mathbf{PQ}$. Prove that $\mathbf{P}^5\mathbf{Q} = \mathbf{PQ}$.

HARDER PROBLEM

(SM) 8. (a) For the general 2×2 matrix $\mathbf{A} = \begin{pmatrix} a & b \\ c & d \end{pmatrix}$, prove that $\mathbf{A}^2 = (a + d)\mathbf{A} - (ad - bc)\mathbf{I}_2$.

(b) Use (a) to find an example of a 2×2 matrix $\mathbf{A}$ such that $\mathbf{A}^2 = \mathbf{0}$, but $\mathbf{A} \neq \mathbf{0}$.

(c) Use part (a) to show that if any 2×2 matrix $\mathbf{A}$ satisfies $\mathbf{A}^3 = \mathbf{0}$, then $\mathbf{A}^2 = \mathbf{0}$. (*Hint:* Multiply the equality in part (a) by $\mathbf{A}$, and use the equality $\mathbf{A}^3 = \mathbf{0}$ to derive an equation, which you should then multiply by $\mathbf{A}$ once again.)

15.5 The Transpose

Consider any $m \times n$ matrix $\mathbf{A}$. The **transpose** of $\mathbf{A}$, denoted by $\mathbf{A}'$, is defined as the $n \times m$ matrix whose first column is the first row of $\mathbf{A}$, whose second column is the second row of $\mathbf{A}$, and so on. Thus,

$$\mathbf{A} = \begin{pmatrix} a_{11} & a_{12} & \cdots & a_{1n} \\ a_{21} & a_{22} & \cdots & a_{2n} \\ \vdots & \vdots & & \vdots \\ a_{m1} & a_{m2} & \cdots & a_{mn} \end{pmatrix} \implies \mathbf{A}' = \begin{pmatrix} a_{11} & a_{21} & \cdots & a_{m1} \\ a_{12} & a_{22} & \cdots & a_{m2} \\ \vdots & \vdots & & \vdots \\ a_{1n} & a_{2n} & \cdots & a_{mn} \end{pmatrix} \tag{1}$$

So we can write $\mathbf{A}' = (a'_{ij})$, where $a'_{ij} = a_{ji}$. The subscripts i and j have to be interchanged because the jth row of $\mathbf{A}$ becomes the jth column of $\mathbf{A}'$, whereas the ith column of $\mathbf{A}$ becomes the ith row of $\mathbf{A}'$.

EXAMPLE 1   Let $\mathbf{A} = \begin{pmatrix} -1 & 0 \\ 2 & 3 \\ 5 & -1 \end{pmatrix}$, $\mathbf{B} = \begin{pmatrix} 1 & -1 & 0 & 4 \\ 2 & 1 & 1 & 1 \end{pmatrix}$. Find $\mathbf{A}'$ and $\mathbf{B}'$.

Solution: $\mathbf{A}' = \begin{pmatrix} -1 & 2 & 5 \\ 0 & 3 & -1 \end{pmatrix}$, $\mathbf{B}' = \begin{pmatrix} 1 & 2 \\ -1 & 1 \\ 0 & 1 \\ 4 & 1 \end{pmatrix}$.

The following rules apply to matrix transposition:

RULES FOR TRANSPOSITION

(a) $(\mathbf{A}')' = \mathbf{A}$

(b) $(\mathbf{A} + \mathbf{B})' = \mathbf{A}' + \mathbf{B}'$

(c) $(\alpha \mathbf{A})' = \alpha \mathbf{A}'$

(d) $(\mathbf{AB})' = \mathbf{B}'\mathbf{A}'$

(2)

Proof: Verifying the first three rules is very easy, and you should prove them in detail, using the fact that $a'_{ij} = a_{ji}$ for each i, j. To prove rule (d), suppose that $\mathbf{A}$ is $m \times n$ and $\mathbf{B}$ is $n \times p$. Then $\mathbf{A}'$ is $n \times m$, $\mathbf{B}'$ is $p \times n$, $\mathbf{AB}$ is $m \times p$, $(\mathbf{AB})'$ is $p \times m$, and $\mathbf{B}'\mathbf{A}'$ is $p \times m$. Thus, $(\mathbf{AB})'$ and $\mathbf{B}'\mathbf{A}'$ have the same order. It remains to prove that corresponding elements in the two matrices are equal.

The rs element in $(\mathbf{AB})'$ is the sr element in $\mathbf{AB}$, which is $a_{s1}b_{1r} + a_{s2}b_{2r} + \cdots + a_{sn}b_{nr}$. On the other hand, the rs element in $\mathbf{B}'\mathbf{A}'$ is $b_{1r}a_{s1} + b_{2r}a_{s2} + \cdots + b_{nr}a_{sn}$. The two sums are clearly equal. So we have proved rule (d).   ∎

EXAMPLE 2   Let $\mathbf{x}$ be the column vector $(x_1, x_2, \ldots, x_n)'$. Then $\mathbf{x}'$ is a row vector of n elements. The product $\mathbf{x}'\mathbf{x}$ is $\sum_{i=1}^{n} x_i^2$. This equals $\|\mathbf{x}\|^2$, the square of the norm of $\mathbf{x}$. (See Section 13.6.) The reverse product $\mathbf{xx}'$, however, is an $n \times n$ matrix whose ij element is equal to $x_i x_j$.

Symmetric Matrices

Square matrices with the property that they are symmetric about the main diagonal are called **symmetric**. For example,

$$\begin{pmatrix} -3 & 2 \\ 2 & 0 \end{pmatrix}, \qquad \begin{pmatrix} 2 & -1 & 5 \\ -1 & -3 & 2 \\ 5 & 2 & 8 \end{pmatrix}, \qquad \begin{pmatrix} a & b & c \\ b & d & e \\ c & e & f \end{pmatrix}$$

are all symmetric. Symmetric matrices are characterized by the fact that they are equal to their own transposes:

The matrix $\mathbf{A}$ is **symmetric** $\iff$ $\mathbf{A} = \mathbf{A}'$

Hence, matrix $\mathbf{A} = (a_{ij})_{n \times n}$ is symmetric iff $a_{ij} = a_{ji}$ for all i, j.

EXAMPLE 3   If $\mathbf{X}$ is an arbitrary $m \times n$ matrix, show that $\mathbf{XX}'$ and $\mathbf{X}'\mathbf{X}$ are both symmetric.

Solution: First, note that $\mathbf{XX}'$ is $m \times m$, whereas $\mathbf{X}'\mathbf{X}$ is $n \times n$. Using rules (d) and (a) in (2), we find that

$$(\mathbf{XX}')' = (\mathbf{X}')'\mathbf{X}' = \mathbf{XX}'$$

This proves that $\mathbf{XX}'$ is symmetric. Prove the other equality in a similar way.

PROBLEMS FOR SECTION 15.5

1. Find the transposes of $\mathbf{A} = \begin{pmatrix} 3 & 5 & 8 & 3 \\ -1 & 2 & 6 & 2 \end{pmatrix}$, $\mathbf{B} = \begin{pmatrix} 0 \\ 1 \\ -1 \\ 2 \end{pmatrix}$, $\mathbf{C} = (1, 5, 0, -1)$.

2. Let $\mathbf{A} = \begin{pmatrix} 3 & 2 \\ -1 & 5 \end{pmatrix}$, $\mathbf{B} = \begin{pmatrix} 0 & 2 \\ 2 & 2 \end{pmatrix}$, and $\alpha = -2$. Compute $\mathbf{A}'$, $\mathbf{B}'$, $(\mathbf{A} + \mathbf{B})'$, $(\alpha\mathbf{A})'$, $\mathbf{AB}$, $(\mathbf{AB})'$, $\mathbf{B}'\mathbf{A}'$, and $\mathbf{A}'\mathbf{B}'$. Then verify all the rules in (2) for these particular values of $\mathbf{A}$, $\mathbf{B}$, and α.

3. Show that $\mathbf{A} = \begin{pmatrix} 3 & 2 & 3 \\ 2 & -1 & 1 \\ 3 & 1 & 0 \end{pmatrix}$ and $\mathbf{B} = \begin{pmatrix} 0 & 4 & 8 \\ 4 & 0 & 13 \\ 8 & 13 & 0 \end{pmatrix}$ are symmetric.

4. For what values of a is $\begin{pmatrix} a & a^2 - 1 & -3 \\ a + 1 & 2 & a^2 + 4 \\ -3 & 4a & -1 \end{pmatrix}$ symmetric?

5. Is the product of two symmetric matrices necessarily symmetric?

SM 6. If $\mathbf{A}_1$, $\mathbf{A}_2$, and $\mathbf{A}_3$ are matrices for which the given products are defined, show that

$$(\mathbf{A}_1\mathbf{A}_2\mathbf{A}_3)' = \mathbf{A}_3'\mathbf{A}_2'\mathbf{A}_1'$$

Generalize to products of n matrices.

7. An $n \times n$ matrix $\mathbf{P}$ is said to be **orthogonal** if $\mathbf{P}'\mathbf{P} = \mathbf{I}_n$.

   (a) For $\lambda = \pm 1/\sqrt{2}$, show that $\mathbf{P} = \begin{pmatrix} \lambda & 0 & \lambda \\ \lambda & 0 & -\lambda \\ 0 & 1 & 0 \end{pmatrix}$ is orthogonal.

   (b) Show that the 2×2 matrix $\begin{pmatrix} p & -q \\ q & p \end{pmatrix}$ is orthogonal if and only if $p^2 + q^2 = 1$.

   (c) Show that the product of two orthogonal $n \times n$ matrices is orthogonal.

SM 8. Define the two matrices $\mathbf{T}$ and $\mathbf{S}$ by $\mathbf{T} = \begin{pmatrix} p & q & 0 \\ \frac{1}{2}p & \frac{1}{2} & \frac{1}{2}q \\ 0 & p & q \end{pmatrix}$, $\mathbf{S} = \begin{pmatrix} p^2 & 2pq & q^2 \\ p^2 & 2pq & q^2 \\ p^2 & 2pq & q^2 \end{pmatrix}$, and assume that $p + q = 1$.

   (a) Prove that $\mathbf{T} \cdot \mathbf{S} = \mathbf{S}$, $\mathbf{T}^2 = \frac{1}{2}\mathbf{T} + \frac{1}{2}\mathbf{S}$, and $\mathbf{T}^3 = \frac{1}{4}\mathbf{T} + \frac{3}{4}\mathbf{S}$.

   (b) Conjecture formulas for constants α_n, β_n such that $\mathbf{T}^n = \alpha_n\mathbf{T} + \beta_n\mathbf{S}$ for $n = 2, 3, \ldots$, then prove the formulas by induction.

15.6 Gaussian Elimination

One way of solving simultaneous equations is by eliminating unknowns, introduced as Method 2 in Section 2.4 for the case of two equations in two unknowns. This procedure can be extended to larger equation systems. Because it is very efficient, it is the starting point for computer programs. Consider first the following example.

EXAMPLE 1   Find all possible solutions of the system

$$
\begin{aligned}
2x_2 - x_3 &= -7 \\
x_1 + x_2 + 3x_3 &= 2 \\
-3x_1 + 2x_2 + 2x_3 &= -10
\end{aligned}
\tag{i}
$$

Solution: The idea will be to eliminate one unknown x_1 from both the second and third equations, and then to eliminate x_2 from the third equation, which remains with only the unknown x_3. We begin, however, by interchanging the first two equations, which certainly will not alter the set of solutions. We obtain

$$
\begin{aligned}
x_1 + x_2 + 3x_3 &= 2 \\
2x_2 - x_3 &= -7 \\
-3x_1 + 2x_2 + 2x_3 &= -10
\end{aligned}
\tag{ii}
$$

This has removed x_1 from the second equation. The next step is to use the first equation in (ii) to eliminate x_1 from the third equation. This is done by adding three times the first equation to the last equation. (The same result is obtained if we solve the first equation for x_1 to obtain $x_1 = -x_2 - 3x_3 + 2$, and then substitute this into the last equation.) This gives

$$
\begin{aligned}
x_1 + x_2 + 3x_3 &= 2 \\
2x_2 - x_3 &= -7 \\
5x_2 + 11x_3 &= -4
\end{aligned}
\tag{iii}
$$

Having eliminated x_1, the next step in the systematic procedure is to multiply the second equation in (iii) by 1/2, so that the coefficient of x_2 becomes 1. Thus,

$$
\begin{aligned}
x_1 + x_2 + 3x_3 &= 2 \\
x_2 - \tfrac{1}{2}x_3 &= -\tfrac{7}{2} \\
5x_2 + 11x_3 &= -4
\end{aligned}
\tag{iv}
$$

Next, eliminate x_2 from the last equation by multiplying the second equation by -5 and adding the result to the last equation. This gives:

$$
\begin{aligned}
x_1 + x_2 + 3x_2 &= 2 \\
x_2 - \tfrac{1}{2}x_3 &= -\tfrac{7}{2} \\
\tfrac{27}{2}x_3 &= \tfrac{27}{2}
\end{aligned}
\tag{v}
$$

Finally, multiply the last equation by $\tfrac{2}{27}$ to obtain $x_3 = 1$. Now the other two unknowns can easily be found by "back substitution": Inserting $x_3 = 1$ into the second equation in (v) gives $x_2 = -3$, and the first equation in (v) subsequently yields $x_1 = 2$. Therefore the only solution of the given system is $(x_1, x_2, x_3) = (2, -3, 1)$.

Our elimination procedure led to a "staircase" in system (v), with x_1, x_2, and x_3 as *leading entries*. In matrix notation, we have

$$\begin{pmatrix} 1 & 1 & 3 \\ 0 & 1 & -\frac{1}{2} \\ 0 & 0 & 1 \end{pmatrix} \begin{pmatrix} x_1 \\ x_2 \\ x_3 \end{pmatrix} = \begin{pmatrix} 2 \\ -\frac{7}{2} \\ 1 \end{pmatrix}$$

The matrix of coefficients on the left-hand side is *upper triangular* because all entries below the main diagonal are 0. Moreover, the diagonal elements are all 1.

The solution method illustrated in this example is called **Gaussian elimination**. The operations performed on the given system of equations in order to arrive at system (v) are called **elementary row operations**. These come in three different kinds:

1. Interchange any pair of rows, as in the step from (i) to (ii) in the above solution.
2. Multiply any row by a scalar, as in the steps from (iii) to (iv) and from (iv) to (v) in the above solution.
3. Add any multiple of one row to a different row, as in the steps from (ii) to (iii) and from (iv) to (v) in the above solution.

Sometimes the elementary row operations are continued until we also obtain zeros above the leading entries. In the example above, this takes three more operations of type 3. The first is as indicated in

$$\begin{aligned} x_1 + x_2 + 3x_3 &= 2 \\ x_2 - \tfrac{1}{2}x_3 &= -\tfrac{7}{2} \quad -1 \\ x_3 &= 1 \end{aligned} \tag{vi}$$

which results in

$$\begin{aligned} x_1 \quad\;\; + \tfrac{7}{2}x_3 &= \tfrac{11}{2} \\ x_2 - \tfrac{1}{2}x_3 &= -\tfrac{7}{2} \\ x_3 &= 1 \qquad \tfrac{1}{2} \quad -\tfrac{7}{2} \end{aligned} \tag{vii}$$

The above display indicates the next *two* operations, affecting rows 1 and 2 respectively. The result is the simple equation system $x_1 = 2$, $x_2 = -3$, and $x_3 = 1$.

Let us apply this method to another example.

EXAMPLE 2   Find all possible solutions of the following system of equations:

$$\begin{aligned} x_1 + 3x_2 - \;\; x_3 &= 4 \\ 2x_1 + \;\; x_2 + \;\; x_3 &= 7 \\ 2x_1 - 4x_2 + 4x_3 &= 6 \\ 3x_1 + 4x_2 \qquad\quad &= 11 \end{aligned}$$

Solution: We begin with three operations to remove x_1 from equations 2, 3, and 4:

$$
\begin{aligned}
x_1 + 3x_2 - x_3 &= 4 \quad\; -2 \;\; -2 \;\; -3 \\
2x_1 + x_2 + x_3 &= 7 \;\longleftarrow\!\rfloor \\
2x_1 - 4x_2 + 4x_3 &= 6 \;\longleftarrow \\
3x_1 + 4x_2 \phantom{{}+4x_3} &= 11 \;\longleftarrow
\end{aligned}
$$

The result is

$$
\begin{aligned}
x_1 + 3x_2 - x_3 &= 4 \\
-5x_2 + 3x_3 &= -1 \quad -\tfrac{1}{5} \\
-10x_2 + 6x_3 &= -2 \\
-5x_2 + 3x_3 &= -1
\end{aligned}
$$

where we have also indicated the next operation of multiplying row 2 by $-\tfrac{1}{5}$. Further operations on the result lead to

$$
\begin{aligned}
x_1 + 3x_2 - x_3 &= 4 \\
x_2 - \tfrac{3}{5}x_3 &= \tfrac{1}{5} \quad 10 \;\; 5 \\
-10x_2 + 6x_3 &= -2 \;\longleftarrow\!\rfloor \\
-5x_2 + 3x_3 &= -1 \;\longleftarrow
\end{aligned}
\qquad \text{then} \qquad
\begin{aligned}
x_1 + 3x_2 - x_3 &= 4 \;\longleftarrow \\
x_2 - \tfrac{3}{5}x_3 &= \tfrac{1}{5} \quad -3 \\
0 &= 0 \\
0 &= 0
\end{aligned}
$$

We have now constructed the staircase. The last two equations are superfluous, and we continue by creating zeros above the leading entry x_2:

$$
\begin{aligned}
x_1 \phantom{{}+3x_2} + \tfrac{4}{5}x_3 &= \tfrac{17}{5} \\
x_2 - \tfrac{3}{5}x_3 &= \tfrac{1}{5}
\end{aligned}
\qquad \text{or} \qquad
\begin{aligned}
x_1 &= -\tfrac{4}{5}x_3 + \tfrac{17}{5} \\
x_2 &= \tfrac{3}{5}x_3 + \tfrac{1}{5}
\end{aligned}
\qquad (*)
$$

Clearly, x_3 can be chosen freely, after which x_1 and x_2 are uniquely determined by $(*)$. Putting $x_3 = t$, we can represent the solution set as:

$$
(x_1, x_2, x_3) = \left(-\tfrac{4}{5}t + \tfrac{17}{5},\; \tfrac{3}{5}t + \tfrac{1}{5},\; t\right) \qquad (t \text{ is any real number})
$$

We say that the solution set of the system has *one degree of freedom*, since one of the variables can be freely chosen. (See Section 12.10.) If this variable is given a fixed value, then the other two variables are uniquely determined.

GAUSSIAN ELIMINATION METHOD

(1) Make a staircase with 1 as the coefficient for each nonzero leading entry.

(2) Produce 0's above each leading entry.

(3) The general solution is found by expressing the unknowns that occur as leading entries in terms of those unknowns that do not. The latter unknowns (if there are any) can be chosen freely. The number of unknowns that can be chosen freely (possibly 0) is the number of **degrees of freedom**.

This description of the recipe assumes that the system has solutions. However, the Gaussian elimination method (also called the Gauss–Jordan method) can also be used to show that a linear system of equations is inconsistent—that is, it has no solutions.

Before showing you an example of this, let us introduce a device that considerably reduces the amount of notation needed. Looking back at the last two examples, we realize that we only need to know the coefficients of the system of equations and the right-hand side vector, while the variables only serve to indicate in which column the different coefficients belong. Thus, Example 2 can be represented by **augmented coefficient matrices** (i.e. each has the corresponding vector of right-hand sides as an extra column) as follows:

$$
\begin{pmatrix} 1 & 3 & -1 & 4 \\ 2 & 1 & 1 & 7 \\ 2 & -4 & 4 & 6 \\ 3 & 4 & 0 & 11 \end{pmatrix} \begin{matrix} -2 & -2 & -3 \end{matrix} \sim \begin{pmatrix} 1 & 3 & -1 & 4 \\ 0 & -5 & 3 & -1 \\ 0 & -10 & 6 & -2 \\ 0 & -5 & 3 & -1 \end{pmatrix} \begin{matrix} -1/5 \end{matrix}
$$

$$
\sim \begin{pmatrix} 1 & 3 & -1 & 4 \\ 0 & 1 & -3/5 & 1/5 \\ 0 & -10 & 6 & -2 \\ 0 & -5 & 3 & -1 \end{pmatrix} \begin{matrix} 10 & 5 \end{matrix} \sim \begin{pmatrix} 1 & 3 & -1 & 4 \\ 0 & 1 & -3/5 & 1/5 \\ 0 & 0 & 0 & 0 \\ 0 & 0 & 0 & 0 \end{pmatrix} \begin{matrix} -3 \end{matrix}
$$

$$
\sim \begin{pmatrix} 1 & 0 & 4/5 & 17/5 \\ 0 & 1 & -3/5 & 1/5 \\ 0 & 0 & 0 & 0 \\ 0 & 0 & 0 & 0 \end{pmatrix}
$$

We have performed *elementary row operations* on the different 4×4 augmented matrices, and we have used the equivalence symbol $\sim$ between two matrices when the latter has been obtained by using elementary operations on the former. This is justified because such operations do always produce an equivalent system of equations. Note carefully how the system of equations in Example 2 is represented by the first matrix, and how the last matrix represents the system $x_1 + \frac{4}{5}x_3 = \frac{17}{5}$, $x_2 - \frac{3}{5}x_3 = \frac{1}{5}$.

EXAMPLE 3   For what values of the numbers a, b, and c does the following system have solutions? Find the solutions when they exist.

$$
\begin{aligned}
x_1 - 2x_2 + x_3 + 2x_4 &= a \\
x_1 + x_2 - x_3 + x_4 &= b \\
x_1 + 7x_2 - 5x_3 - x_4 &= c
\end{aligned}
$$

Solution: We represent the system by its augmented matrix, then perform elementary row operations as required by the Gaussian method:

$$
\begin{pmatrix} 1 & -2 & 1 & 2 & a \\ 1 & 1 & -1 & 1 & b \\ 1 & 7 & -5 & -1 & c \end{pmatrix} \begin{matrix} -1 & -1 \end{matrix} \sim \begin{pmatrix} 1 & -2 & 1 & 2 & a \\ 0 & 3 & -2 & -1 & b-a \\ 0 & 9 & -6 & -3 & c-a \end{pmatrix} \begin{matrix} -3 \end{matrix}
$$

$$
\sim \begin{pmatrix} 1 & -2 & 1 & 2 & a \\ 0 & 3 & -2 & -1 & b-a \\ 0 & 0 & 0 & 0 & 2a-3b+c \end{pmatrix}
$$

The last row represents the equation $0 \cdot x_1 + 0 \cdot x_2 + 0 \cdot x_3 + 0 \cdot x_4 = 2a - 3b + c$. The system therefore has solutions only if $2a - 3b + c = 0$. In this case the last row has only zeros, and we continue using elementary operations till we end up with the following matrix:

$$\begin{pmatrix} 1 & 0 & -1/3 & 4/3 & \frac{1}{3}(a+2b) \\ 0 & 1 & -2/3 & -1/3 & \frac{1}{3}(b-a) \\ 0 & 0 & 0 & 0 & 0 \end{pmatrix} \quad \text{and thus} \quad \begin{cases} x_1 & -\frac{1}{3}x_3 + \frac{4}{3}x_4 = \frac{1}{3}(a+2b) \\ x_2 - \frac{2}{3}x_3 - \frac{1}{3}x_4 = \frac{1}{3}(b-a) \end{cases}$$

Here x_3 and x_4 can be freely chosen. Once they have been chosen, however, x_1 and x_2 are uniquely determined linear functions of $s = x_3$ and $t = x_4$:

$$x_1 = \tfrac{1}{3}(a+2b) + \tfrac{1}{3}s - \tfrac{4}{3}t$$
$$x_2 = \tfrac{1}{3}(b-a) + \tfrac{2}{3}s + \tfrac{1}{3}t$$

(s and t arbitrary real numbers, $2a - 3b + c = 0$)

For $2a - 3b + c \neq 0$ the given system is inconsistent, so has no solutions.

PROBLEMS FOR SECTION 15.6

1. Solve the following systems by Gaussian elimination.

(a) $\begin{aligned} x_1 + x_2 &= 3 \\ 3x_1 + 5x_2 &= 5 \end{aligned}$

(b) $\begin{aligned} x_1 + 2x_2 + x_3 &= 4 \\ x_1 - x_2 + x_3 &= 5 \\ 2x_1 + 3x_2 - x_3 &= 1 \end{aligned}$

(c) $\begin{aligned} 2x_1 - 3x_2 + x_3 &= 0 \\ x_1 + x_2 - x_3 &= 0 \end{aligned}$

2. Use Gaussian elimination to discuss what are the possible solutions of the following system for different values of a and b:

$$\begin{aligned} x + y - z &= 1 \\ x - y + 2z &= 2 \\ x + 2y + az &= b \end{aligned}$$

(SM) 3. Find the values of c for which the system

$$\begin{aligned} 2w + x + 4y + 3z &= 1 \\ w + 3x + 2y - z &= 3c \\ w + x + 2y + z &= c^2 \end{aligned}$$

has a solution, and find the complete solution for these values of c.

(SM) 4. Consider the two systems of equations:

(a) $\begin{aligned} ax + y + (a+1)z &= b_1 \\ x + 2y + z &= b_2 \\ 3x + 4y + 7z &= b_3 \end{aligned}$

(b) $\begin{aligned} \tfrac{3}{4}x + y + \tfrac{7}{4}z &= b_1 \\ x + 2y + z &= b_2 \\ 3x + 4y + 7z &= b_3 \end{aligned}$

Find the values of a for which (a) has a unique solution, and find all solutions to system (b).

15.7 Vectors

Recall that a matrix with only one row is also called a **row vector**, and a matrix with only one column is called a **column vector**. We refer to both types as **vectors**. As remarked in Section 15.2, vectors are typically denoted by small bold letters. Thus, if $\mathbf{a}$ is a $1 \times n$ row vector, we write

$$\mathbf{a} = (a_1, a_2, \ldots, a_n)$$

Here, the numbers $a_1, a_2, \ldots, a_n$ are called the **components** (or **coordinates**) of the vector, and a_i is its ith component or ith coordinate. (Recall that when we consider $\mathbf{a}$ as a matrix, $a_1, \ldots, a_n$ are called entries or elements.) If we want to emphasize that a vector has n components, we refer to it as an **n-vector**. Alternatively, if $\mathbf{a}$ is an n-vector, then we say that it has **dimension n**.

It is clear that the row vector $(7, 13, 4)$ and the column vector $\begin{pmatrix} 7 \\ 13 \\ 4 \end{pmatrix}$ contain exactly the same information—the numbers and their order are the same, only the arrangement of the numbers is different. In fact, following the ideas presented in Chapter 11, both the row and the column vector are represented by the same point in 3-dimensional space $\mathbb{R}^3$. And any n-vector is represented by a point in n-dimensional space $\mathbb{R}^n$.

Operations on Vectors

Since a vector is just a special types of matrix, the algebraic operations introduced for matrices are equally valid for vectors. So:

(A) Two n-vectors $\mathbf{a}$ and $\mathbf{b}$ are **equal** if and only if all their corresponding components are equal; we then write $\mathbf{a} = \mathbf{b}$.

(B) If $\mathbf{a}$ and $\mathbf{b}$ are two n-vectors, their **sum**, denoted by $\mathbf{a} + \mathbf{b}$, is the n-vector obtained by adding each component of $\mathbf{a}$ to the corresponding component of $\mathbf{b}$.[2]

(C) If $\mathbf{a}$ is an n-vector and t is a real number, we define $t\mathbf{a}$ as the n-vector whose components are t times the corresponding components in $\mathbf{a}$.

(D) The **difference** between two n-vectors $\mathbf{a}$ and $\mathbf{b}$ is defined as $\mathbf{a} - \mathbf{b} = \mathbf{a} + (-1)\mathbf{b}$.

If $\mathbf{a}$ and $\mathbf{b}$ are two n-vectors and t and s are real numbers, the n-vector $t\mathbf{a} + s\mathbf{b}$ is said to be a **linear combination** of $\mathbf{a}$ and $\mathbf{b}$. In symbols, using column vectors,

$$t \begin{pmatrix} a_1 \\ a_2 \\ \vdots \\ a_n \end{pmatrix} + s \begin{pmatrix} b_1 \\ b_2 \\ \vdots \\ b_n \end{pmatrix} = \begin{pmatrix} ta_1 + sb_1 \\ ta_2 + sb_2 \\ \vdots \\ ta_n + sb_n \end{pmatrix}$$

Here is an interpretation: Suppose $\mathbf{a}$ and $\mathbf{b}$ are commodity vectors, whose jth components are quantities of commodity number j. Now, if t persons all buy the same commodity vector

---

[2] If two vectors do not have the same dimension, their sum is simply not defined, nor is their difference. Nor should one add a row vector to a column vector, even if they have the same number of elements.

a and s persons all buy commodity vector **b**, then the vector $t\mathbf{a} + s\mathbf{b}$ represents the total commodity vector bought by all $t + s$ persons combined.

Of course, the rules for matrix addition and multiplication by scalars in (15.2.5) apply to vectors also.

The Inner Product

Let us consider four different commodities—say, apples, bananas, cherries and dates. Suppose you buy the commodity vector $\mathbf{x} = (5, 3, 6, 7)$. This means, of course, that you buy 5 units—say, kilos—of the first commodity, 3 kilos of the second commodity, etc. Suppose the prices per kilo of these four different commodities are given by the price vector $\mathbf{p} = (4, 5, 3, 8)$, meaning that the price per kilo of the first good is 4, that of the second is 5, etc. Then the total value of the commodity vector you buy is $4 \cdot 5 + 5 \cdot 3 + 3 \cdot 6 + 8 \cdot 7 = 109$. The result of this operation on the two vectors **p** and **x** is often written as $\mathbf{p} \cdot \mathbf{x}$ and is called the *inner product* or *scalar product* or *dot product* of **p** and **x**. In general, we have the following definition (formulated for row vectors):

INNER PRODUCT

The **inner product** of the n-vectors $\mathbf{a} = (a_1, a_2, \ldots, a_n)$ and $\mathbf{b} = (b_1, b_2, \ldots, b_n)$ is defined as

$$\mathbf{a} \cdot \mathbf{b} = a_1 b_1 + a_2 b_2 + \cdots + a_n b_n = \sum_{i=1}^{n} a_i b_i \tag{1}$$

Note that the inner (scalar) product of two vectors is not a vector but a *number* (or scalar). It is obtained by simply multiplying all pairs (a_j, b_j), $j = 1, 2, \ldots, n$, of the corresponding components in the two vectors **a** and **b**, and then finally adding the results. Note that $\mathbf{a} \cdot \mathbf{b}$ is *defined only if* **a** and **b** are both of the same dimension.

In the case when **p** is a price vector whose components are measured in dollars per kilo, and **x** is a commodity vector whose components are measured in kilos, then each product $p_j x_j$ is an amount of money measured in dollars, as is the inner product $\mathbf{p} \cdot \mathbf{x} = \sum_{j=1}^{n} p_j x_j$.

EXAMPLE 1 If $\mathbf{a} = (1, -2, 3)$ and $\mathbf{b} = (-3, 2, 5)$, compute $\mathbf{a} \cdot \mathbf{b}$.

Solution: We get $\mathbf{a} \cdot \mathbf{b} = 1 \cdot (-3) + (-2) \cdot 2 + 3 \cdot 5 = 8$.

Note that according to the definition of the matrix product **AB**, the ijth element of the product is the inner product of the ith row vector of **A** and the jth column vector of **B**.

The inner product is defined for any two n-vectors. If $\mathbf{a} = (a_1, \ldots, a_n)'$ and $\mathbf{b} = (b_1, \ldots, b_n)'$ both happen to be $n \times 1$ matrices, then the transpose $\mathbf{a}'$ of **a** is a $1 \times n$ matrix, and the matrix product $\mathbf{a}'\mathbf{b}$ is defined as a 1×1 matrix. In fact,

$$\mathbf{a}'\mathbf{b} = a_1 b_1 + a_2 b_2 + \cdots + a_n b_n$$

Because 1×1 matrices behave exactly as ordinary numbers with respect to addition and multiplication, we can regard the inner product of **a** and **b** as the matrix product $\mathbf{a}'\mathbf{b}$.

It is usual in economics to regard a typical vector **x** as a column vector, unless otherwise specified. This is especially true if it is a quantity or commodity vector. Another common convention is to regard a price vector as a row vector, often denoted by $\mathbf{p}'$ to suggest that it is the transpose of a column vector. Then $\mathbf{p}'\mathbf{x}$ is the 1×1 matrix whose single element is equal to the inner product $\mathbf{p} \cdot \mathbf{x}$.

Important properties of the inner product follow:

RULES FOR THE INNER PRODUCT

If **a**, **b**, and **c** are n-vectors and α is a scalar, then

(a) $\mathbf{a} \cdot \mathbf{b} = \mathbf{b} \cdot \mathbf{a}$

(b) $\mathbf{a} \cdot (\mathbf{b} + \mathbf{c}) = \mathbf{a} \cdot \mathbf{b} + \mathbf{a} \cdot \mathbf{c}$ (2)

(c) $(\alpha \mathbf{a}) \cdot \mathbf{b} = \mathbf{a} \cdot (\alpha \mathbf{b}) = \alpha (\mathbf{a} \cdot \mathbf{b})$

(d) $\mathbf{a} \cdot \mathbf{a} > 0 \iff \mathbf{a} \neq \mathbf{0}$

Proof: Rules (a) and (c) are easy consequences of the definition.

To prove rule (b), apply the distributive law for matrix multiplication (15.4.2) when **a** is $1 \times n$ whereas **b** and **c** are $n \times 1$.

To prove rule (d), it suffices to note that $\mathbf{a} \cdot \mathbf{a} = a_1^2 + a_2^2 + \cdots + a_n^2$. This is always nonnegative, and is zero only if all the a_i's are 0.   ∎

PROBLEMS FOR SECTION 15.7

1. Compute $\mathbf{a} + \mathbf{b}$, $\mathbf{a} - \mathbf{b}$, $2\mathbf{a} + 3\mathbf{b}$, and $-5\mathbf{a} + 2\mathbf{b}$ when $\mathbf{a} = \begin{pmatrix} 2 \\ -1 \end{pmatrix}$ and $\mathbf{b} = \begin{pmatrix} 3 \\ 4 \end{pmatrix}$.

2. Let $\mathbf{a} = (1, 2, 2)$, $\mathbf{b} = (0, 0, -3)$, and $\mathbf{c} = (-2, 4, -3)$. Find the following:

$$\mathbf{a} + \mathbf{b} + \mathbf{c}, \qquad \mathbf{a} - 2\mathbf{b} + 2\mathbf{c}, \qquad 3\mathbf{a} + 2\mathbf{b} - 3\mathbf{c}$$

3. If $3(x, y, z) + 5(-1, 2, 3) = (4, 1, 3)$, find x, y, and z.

4. (a) If $\mathbf{x} + \mathbf{0} = \mathbf{0}$, what do you know about the components of **x**?

(b) If $0\mathbf{x} = \mathbf{0}$, what do you know about the components of **x**?

5. Express the vector $(4, -11)$ as a linear combination of $(2, -1)$ and $(1, 4)$.

6. Solve the vector equation $4\mathbf{x} - 7\mathbf{a} = 2\mathbf{x} + 8\mathbf{b} - \mathbf{a}$ for **x** in terms of **a** and **b**.

7. If $\mathbf{a} = \begin{pmatrix} 2 \\ -1 \end{pmatrix}$ and $\mathbf{b} = \begin{pmatrix} 3 \\ 4 \end{pmatrix}$, find $\mathbf{a} \cdot \mathbf{a}$, $\mathbf{a} \cdot \mathbf{b}$, and $\mathbf{a} \cdot (\mathbf{a} + \mathbf{b})$. Verify that $\mathbf{a} \cdot \mathbf{a} + \mathbf{a} \cdot \mathbf{b} = \mathbf{a} \cdot (\mathbf{a} + \mathbf{b})$.

8. For what values of x is the inner product of $(x, x - 1, 3)$ and $(x, x, 3x)$ equal to 0?

9. A residential construction company plans to build several houses of three different types: 5 of type A, 7 of type B, and 12 of type C. Write down a 3-dimensional vector $\mathbf{x}$ whose coordinates give the number of houses of each type. Suppose that each house of type A requires 20 units of timber, type B requires 18 units, and type C requires 25 units. Write down a vector $\mathbf{u}$ that gives the different timber quantities required for one house of each of the three different types A, B, and C. Find the total timber requirement by computing the inner product $\mathbf{u} \cdot \mathbf{x}$.

10. A firm produces nonnegative output quantities $z_1, z_2, \ldots, z_n$ of n different goods, using as inputs the nonnegative quantities $x_1, x_2, \ldots, x_n$ of the same n goods. For each good i ($i = 1, \ldots, n$), define $y_i = z_i - x_i$ as the net output of good i, and let p_i be the price of good i. Let $\mathbf{p} = (p_1, \ldots, p_n)$, $\mathbf{x} = (x_1, \ldots, x_n)$ (the **input vector**), $\mathbf{y} = (y_1, \ldots, y_n)$ (the **net output vector**), and $\mathbf{z} = (z_1, \ldots, z_n)$ (the **output vector**).

    (a) Calculate the firm's revenue and its costs.

    (b) Show that the firm's profit is given by the inner product $\mathbf{p} \cdot \mathbf{y}$. What if $\mathbf{p} \cdot \mathbf{y}$ is negative?

11. A firm produces the first of two different goods as its output, using the second good as its input. Its net output vector (see Problem 10) is $\begin{pmatrix} 2 \\ -1 \end{pmatrix}$. The price vector it faces is $(1, 3)$. Find the firm's (a) input vector, (b) output vector, (c) costs, (d) revenue, (e) value of net output, and (f) profit or loss.

15.8 Geometric Interpretation of Vectors

Vectors, in contrast to general matrices, are easily interpreted geometrically. Actually, the word "vector" is originally Latin and was used to mean both "carrier" and "passenger". In particular, the word is related to the act of moving a person or object from one place to another. Following this idea, a biologist is likely to think of a "vector" as a carrier of disease, such as mosquitoes are for malaria.

In the xy-plane, any shift can be described by the distance a_1 moved in the x-direction and by the distance a_2 moved in the y-direction. A movement in the plane is therefore uniquely determined by an ordered pair or 2-vector (a_1, a_2). Geometrically, such a movement can be illustrated by an arrow from the start point P to the end point Q, as shown in Fig. 1. If we make a parallel displacement of the arrow so that it starts at P' and ends at Q', the resulting arrow will represent exactly the same shift, because the x and y components are still a_1 and a_2, respectively. The vector from P to Q is denoted by $\overrightarrow{PQ}$, and we refer to it as a **geometric vector** or *directed line segment*. Two geometric vectors that have the same direction and the same length are said to be equal (in much the same way as the two fractions 2/6 and 1/3 are equal because they represent the same real number).

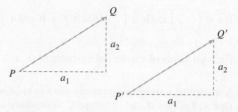

Figure 1

Suppose that the geometric vector **a** involves a movement from $P = (p_1, p_2)$ to $Q = (q_1, q_2)$. Then the pair (a_1, a_2) that describes the movement in both the x and y directions is given by $a_1 = q_1 - p_1$, $a_2 = q_2 - p_2$, or by $(a_1, a_2) = (q_1, q_2) - (p_1, p_2)$. This is illustrated in Fig. 2. On the other hand, if the pair (a_1, a_2) is given, the corresponding shift is obtained by moving a_1 units in the direction of the x-axis, as well as a_2 units in the direction of the y-axis. If we start at the point $P = (p_1, p_2)$, then we arrive at the point Q with coordinates $(q_1, q_2) = (p_1 + a_1, p_2 + a_2)$, also shown in Fig. 2.

This correspondence makes it a matter of convenience whether we think of a vector as an ordered pair of numbers (a_1, a_2), or as a directed line segment such as $\overrightarrow{PQ}$ in Fig. 2.

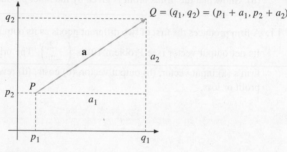

Figure 2

Vector Operations

If we represent vectors by directed line segments, the vector operations $\mathbf{a} + \mathbf{b}$, $\mathbf{a} - \mathbf{b}$, and $t\mathbf{a}$ can be given interesting geometric interpretations. Let $\mathbf{a} = (a_1, a_2)$ and $\mathbf{b} = (b_1, b_2)$ both start at the origin $(0, 0)$ of the coordinate system.

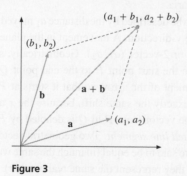

Figure 3   **Figure 4**

The sum $\mathbf{a} + \mathbf{b}$ shown in Fig. 3 is the diagonal in the parallelogram determined by the two sides $\mathbf{a}$ and $\mathbf{b}$. The geometric reason for this can be seen from Fig. 4, in which the two right-angled triangles OSR and PTQ are congruent. Thus, OR is parallel to PQ and has the same length, so $OPQR$ is a parallelogram. (This parallelogram law of adding vectors will be familiar to those who have studied physics. If $\mathbf{a}$ and $\mathbf{b}$ represent two forces acting on a particle at O, then the single combined force $\mathbf{a} + \mathbf{b}$ acting on the particle will produce the same result.) The parallelogram law of addition is also illustrated in Fig. 5. One way of interpreting this figure is that if $\mathbf{a}$ takes you from O to P and $\mathbf{b}$ takes you on from P to Q, then the combined movement $\mathbf{a} + \mathbf{b}$ takes you from O to Q. Moreover, looking at Fig. 4 again, $\mathbf{b}$ takes you from O to R, whereas $\mathbf{a}$ takes you on from R to Q. So the combined movement $\mathbf{b} + \mathbf{a}$ takes you from O to Q. Of course, this verifies that $\mathbf{a} + \mathbf{b} = \mathbf{b} + \mathbf{a}$.

Figure 6 gives a geometric interpretation to the vector $\mathbf{a} - \mathbf{b}$. Note carefully the direction of the geometric vector $\mathbf{a} - \mathbf{b}$. And note that $\mathbf{b} + (\mathbf{a} - \mathbf{b}) = \mathbf{a} = (\mathbf{a} - \mathbf{b}) + \mathbf{b}$.

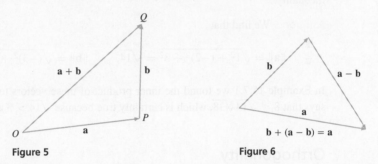

Figure 5   **Figure 6**

The geometric interpretation of $t\mathbf{a}$, where t is any real number, is also straightforward. If $t > 0$, then $t\mathbf{a}$ is the vector with the same direction as $\mathbf{a}$ and whose length is t times the length of $\mathbf{a}$. If $t < 0$, the direction is reversed and the length is multiplied by the absolute value of t. Indeed, multiplication by t is like rescaling the vector $\mathbf{a}$; that is why the number t is often called a **scalar**.

3-Space and n-Space

The plane is often also called 2-space and denoted $\mathbb{R}^2$. We represent a point or a vector in a plane by a pair of real numbers using two mutually orthogonal coordinate lines.

In a similar way, any point or vector in 3-space $\mathbb{R}^3$ can be represented by a triple of real numbers using three mutually orthogonal coordinate lines, as explained in Section 11.3. Any 3-vector (a_1, a_2, a_3) can be considered in an obvious way as a geometric vector or movement in 3-space $\mathbb{R}^3$. As with ordered pairs in the plane, there is a natural correspondence between ordered triples (a_1, a_2, a_3) and geometric vectors regarded as directed line segments. The parallelogram law of addition remains valid in $\mathbb{R}^3$, as does the geometric interpretation of the multiplication of a vector by a scalar.

The set $\mathbb{R}^n$ of all n-vectors was introduced in Section 11.5. When $n \geq 4$, it has no natural spatial interpretation. Nevertheless, geometric language is sometimes still used to discuss properties of $\mathbb{R}^n$, because many properties of $\mathbb{R}^2$ and $\mathbb{R}^3$ carry over to $\mathbb{R}^n$. In particular, the rules for addition, subtraction, and scalar multiplication of vectors remain exactly the same.

Lengths of Vectors and the Cauchy–Schwarz Inequality

If $\mathbf{a} = (a_1, a_2, \ldots, a_n)$, we define the **length** (or **norm**) of the vector $\mathbf{a}$, denoted by $\|\mathbf{a}\|$, as $\|\mathbf{a}\| = \sqrt{\mathbf{a} \cdot \mathbf{a}}$, or

$$\|\mathbf{a}\| = \sqrt{a_1^2 + a_2^2 + \cdots + a_n^2} \qquad (1)$$

According to (13.6.2), $\|\mathbf{a}\|$ is the distance from the origin $(0, 0, \ldots, 0)$ to $(a_1, a_2, \ldots, a_n)$. In Problem 4.6.9 you were asked to prove a famous inequality. Using the notation we have just introduced, this inequality can be expressed as $(\mathbf{a} \cdot \mathbf{b})^2 \leq \|\mathbf{a}\|^2 \|\mathbf{b}\|^2$, or equivalently, as

$$|\mathbf{a} \cdot \mathbf{b}| \leq \|\mathbf{a}\| \cdot \|\mathbf{b}\| \qquad \textbf{(Cauchy–Schwarz inequality)} \qquad (2)$$

EXAMPLE 1   For the two vectors $\mathbf{a} = (1, -2, 3)$ and $\mathbf{b} = (-3, 2, 5)$, check the Cauchy–Schwarz inequality.

Solution: We find that

$$\|\mathbf{a}\| = \sqrt{1^2 + (-2)^2 + 3^2} = \sqrt{14}, \qquad \|\mathbf{b}\| = \sqrt{(-3)^2 + 2^2 + 5^2} = \sqrt{38}$$

In Example 15.7.1 we found the inner product of these vectors to be 8. So inequality (2) says that $8 \leq \sqrt{14}\sqrt{38}$, which is certainly true because $\sqrt{14} > 3$ and $\sqrt{38} > 6$.

Orthogonality

Consider Fig. 7, which exhibits three vectors, $\mathbf{a}$, $\mathbf{b}$, and $\mathbf{a} - \mathbf{b}$ in $\mathbb{R}^2$ or $\mathbb{R}^3$.

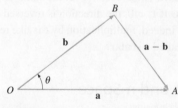

Figure 7

According to Pythagoras's theorem, the angle θ between the two vectors $\mathbf{a}$ and $\mathbf{b}$ is a right angle ($= 90°$) if and only if $(OA)^2 + (OB)^2 = (AB)^2$, or $\|\mathbf{a}\|^2 + \|\mathbf{b}\|^2 = \|\mathbf{a} - \mathbf{b}\|^2$. This implies that $\theta = 90°$ if and only if

$$\mathbf{a} \cdot \mathbf{a} + \mathbf{b} \cdot \mathbf{b} = (\mathbf{a} - \mathbf{b}) \cdot (\mathbf{a} - \mathbf{b}) = \mathbf{a} \cdot \mathbf{a} - \mathbf{a} \cdot \mathbf{b} - \mathbf{b} \cdot \mathbf{a} + \mathbf{b} \cdot \mathbf{b} \qquad (*)$$

Because $\mathbf{a} \cdot \mathbf{b} = \mathbf{b} \cdot \mathbf{a}$, equality $(*)$ requires $2\mathbf{a} \cdot \mathbf{b} = 0$, and so $\mathbf{a} \cdot \mathbf{b} = 0$. When the angle between two vectors $\mathbf{a}$ and $\mathbf{b}$ is $90°$, they are said to be **orthogonal**, and we write $\mathbf{a} \perp \mathbf{b}$. Thus, we have proved that two vectors in $\mathbb{R}^2$ or $\mathbb{R}^3$ are orthogonal if and only if their inner product is 0. In symbols:

$$\mathbf{a} \perp \mathbf{b} \quad \Longleftrightarrow \quad \mathbf{a} \cdot \mathbf{b} = 0 \qquad (3)$$

For pairs of vectors in $\mathbb{R}^n$, we *define* orthogonality between **a** and **b** by (3).

NOTE 1 (This relies on some elementary trigonometry.) Let **a** and **b** be two nonzero vectors in $\mathbb{R}^n$. Define the *angle* θ between them by

$$\cos\theta = \frac{\mathbf{a}\cdot\mathbf{b}}{\|\mathbf{a}\|\cdot\|\mathbf{b}\|} \qquad (\theta \in [0,\pi]) \tag{4}$$

Definition (4) makes sense because the Cauchy–Schwarz inequality implies that the right-hand side has an absolute value ≤ 1. Note also that according to (4), $\cos\theta = 0$ iff $\mathbf{a}\cdot\mathbf{b} = 0$. This agrees with (3) because for $\theta \in [0,\pi]$, we have $\cos\theta = 0$ iff $\theta = \pi/2$.

EXAMPLE 2   Suppose we repeatedly observe a commodity's price and the quantity demanded. After n observations we have n pairs $(p_1, d_1), (p_2, d_2), \ldots, (p_n, d_n)$, where p_i represents the price and d_i is the demand at observation i, $i = 1, 2, \ldots, n$. Define the statistical means

$$\bar{p} = \frac{1}{n}\sum_{i=1}^n p_i, \qquad \bar{d} = \frac{1}{n}\sum_{i=1}^n d_i$$

and

$$\mathbf{a} = (p_1 - \bar{p},\ p_2 - \bar{p},\ \ldots,\ p_n - \bar{p}), \quad \mathbf{b} = (d_1 - \bar{d},\ d_2 - \bar{d},\ \ldots,\ d_n - \bar{d})$$

In statistics, the ratio $\cos\theta$ defined by (4) is called the **correlation coefficient**, often denoted by ρ. It is a measure of the degree of "correlation" between the prices and demand quantities in the data. When $\rho = 1$, there is a positive constant $\alpha > 0$ such that $d_i - \bar{d} = \alpha(p_i - \bar{p})$, implying that demand and price are *perfectly correlated*. It is more plausible, however, that $\rho = -1$ because this relationship holds for some $\alpha < 0$. Generally, if $\rho > 0$ the variables are *positively correlated*, whereas if $\rho < 0$ the variables are *negatively correlated*, and if $\rho = 0$ they are *uncorrelated*.

EXAMPLE 3   (**Orthogonality in econometrics**)   In the earlier example of linear regression (Example 13.4.4), the regression coefficients α and β were chosen to minimize the *mean squared error* loss function

$$L(\alpha, \beta) = \frac{1}{T}\sum_{t=1}^T e_t^2 = \frac{1}{T}\sum_{t=1}^T (y_t - \alpha - \beta x_t)^2$$

This required choosing $\hat{\alpha} = \mu_y - (\sigma_{xy}/\sigma_{xx})\mu_x$ and $\hat{\beta} = \sigma_{xy}/\sigma_{xx}$, where μ_x and μ_y denote the means of x_t and y_t respectively, whereas σ_{xx} is the variance of x_t, and σ_{xy} is the covariance of x_t with y_t. The resulting errors become $\hat{e}_t = y_t - \hat{\alpha} - \hat{\beta}x_t = y_t - \mu_y - (\sigma_{xy}/\sigma_{xx})(x_t - \mu_x)$. By definition of μ_x and μ_y, one has

$$\frac{1}{T}\sum_{t=1}^T \hat{e}_t = 0 \tag{$*$}$$

In addition,

$$\frac{1}{T}\sum_{t=1}^T \hat{e}_t x_t = \frac{1}{T}\sum_{t=1}^T x_t y_t - \mu_x\mu_y - \frac{\sigma_{xy}}{\sigma_{xx}}\left(\frac{1}{T}\sum_{t=1}^T x_t^2 - \mu_x^2\right) = \sigma_{xy} - \frac{\sigma_{xy}}{\sigma_{xx}}\sigma_{xx} = 0 \tag{$**$}$$

Define the vectors $\mathbf{1} = (1, 1\ldots, 1)$, $\mathbf{x} = (x_1, \ldots, x_T)$, and $\hat{\mathbf{e}} = (\hat{e}_1, \ldots, \hat{e}_T)$. Then equation ($*$) shows that the inner product of $\hat{\mathbf{e}}$ and $\mathbf{1}$ is 0. Moreover, equation ($**$) shows that the inner product of $\hat{\mathbf{e}}$ and $\mathbf{x}$ is 0.

Note that $L(\alpha, \beta) = (1/T)\|\mathbf{y} - \alpha\mathbf{1} - \beta\mathbf{x}\|^2$. Geometrically, the scalars $\hat{\alpha}$ and $\hat{\beta}$ are chosen so that the vector $\hat{\mathbf{y}} = \hat{\alpha}\mathbf{1} + \hat{\beta}\mathbf{x}$ in the plane containing the vectors $\mathbf{0}, \mathbf{1}$, and $\mathbf{x}$ is as close as possible to $\mathbf{y}$ in the T-dimensional space $\mathbb{R}^T$.[3] This involves having the vector $\mathbf{y} - \hat{\mathbf{y}} = \hat{\mathbf{e}}$ be orthogonal to $\mathbf{1}$ and $\mathbf{x}$, and to every other vector $\alpha\mathbf{1} + \beta\mathbf{x}$ in this plane. Accordingly, $\hat{\mathbf{y}}$ is called the **orthogonal projection** of $\mathbf{y}$ onto this plane.

PROBLEMS FOR SECTION 15.8

1. Let $\mathbf{a} = (5, -1)$ and $\mathbf{b} = (-2, 4)$. Compute $\mathbf{a} + \mathbf{b}$ and $-\frac{1}{2}\mathbf{a}$, and illustrate with geometric vectors starting at the origin.

(SM) 2. (a) Let $\mathbf{a} = (3, 1)$ and $\mathbf{b} = (-1, 2)$. Define $\mathbf{x} = \lambda\mathbf{a} + (1 - \lambda)\mathbf{b}$. Compute $\mathbf{x}$ when $\lambda = 0, 1/4$, 1/2, 3/4, and 1. Illustrate.

   (b) If $\lambda \in [0, 1]$, what set of points does $\mathbf{x} = \lambda\mathbf{a} + (1 - \lambda)\mathbf{b}$ trace out? Show that if $\lambda \in \mathbb{R}$, then $\mathbf{x}$ traces out the whole straight line through $(3, 1)$ and $(-1, 2)$.

3. Let $\mathbf{a} = (1, 2, 2)$, $\mathbf{b} = (0, 0, -3)$, and $\mathbf{c} = (-2, 4, -3)$. Compute $\|\mathbf{a}\|$, $\|\mathbf{b}\|$, and $\|\mathbf{c}\|$, and verify that (2) holds for $\mathbf{a}$ and $\mathbf{b}$.

4. (a) Let $\mathbf{a} = (1, 2, 1)$, $\mathbf{b} = (-3, 0, -2)$. Find numbers x_1 and x_2 such that $x_1\mathbf{a} + x_2\mathbf{b} = (5, 4, 4)$.

   (b) Prove that there are no real numbers x_1 and x_2 satisfying $x_1\mathbf{a} + x_2\mathbf{b} = (-3, 6, 1)$.

5. Check which of these pairs of vectors are orthogonal:

   (a) $(1, 2)$ and $(-2, 1)$ (b) $(1, -1, 1)$ and $(-1, 1, -1)$ (c) $(a, -b, 1)$ and $(b, a, 0)$

6. For what values of x are $(x, -x - 8, x, x)$ and $(x, 1, -2, 1)$ orthogonal?

HARDER PROBLEMS

7. Show that any two different columns of an orthogonal matrix (see Problem 15.5.7) are orthogonal vectors, as are any two different rows.

8. If $\mathbf{a}$ and $\mathbf{b}$ are n-vectors, prove the *triangle inequality* $\|\mathbf{a} + \mathbf{b}\| \leq \|\mathbf{a}\| + \|\mathbf{b}\|$.
   (*Hint:* $\|\mathbf{a} + \mathbf{b}\|^2 = (\mathbf{a} + \mathbf{b}) \cdot (\mathbf{a} + \mathbf{b})$. Then use (2).)

15.9 Lines and Planes

Let $\mathbf{a} = (a_1, a_2, a_3)$ and $\mathbf{b} = (b_1, b_2, b_3)$ be two distinct vectors in $\mathbb{R}^3$. We can think of them as arrows from the origin to the points with coordinates (a_1, a_2, a_3) and (b_1, b_2, b_3), respectively. The straight line L passing through these two points is shown in Fig. 1.

---

[3] Planes are discussed in the next section.

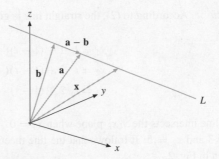

Figure 1

Let t be a real number and put $\mathbf{x} = \mathbf{b} + t(\mathbf{a} - \mathbf{b}) = t\mathbf{a} + (1 - t)\mathbf{b}$. Then $t = 0$ gives $\mathbf{x} = \mathbf{b}$ and $t = 1$ gives $\mathbf{x} = \mathbf{a}$. As t decreases, the point $\mathbf{x}$ moves to the left in Fig. 1; as t increases, $\mathbf{x}$ moves to the right. By the geometric rule for adding vectors extended from $\mathbb{R}^2$ to $\mathbb{R}^3$, the vector marked $\mathbf{x}$ in Fig. 1 is approximately $\mathbf{b} + 2.5(\mathbf{a} - \mathbf{b})$. As t runs through all the real numbers, so $\mathbf{x}$ describes the whole straight line L.

For $\mathbb{R}^n$, we introduce the following definition:

LINE IN N-SPACE

The line L in $\mathbb{R}^n$ through the two distinct points $\mathbf{a} = (a_1, \ldots, a_n)$ and $\mathbf{b} = (b_1, \ldots, b_n)$ is the set of all $\mathbf{x} = (x_1, \ldots, x_n)$ satisfying

$$\mathbf{x} = t\mathbf{a} + (1 - t)\mathbf{b} \qquad \text{for some real number } t$$

(1)

By using the coordinates of $\mathbf{a}$ and $\mathbf{b}$, (1) is equivalent to

$$x_1 = ta_1 + (1 - t)b_1, x_2 = ta_2 + (1 - t)b_2, \ldots, x_n = ta_n + (1 - t)b_n \qquad (2)$$

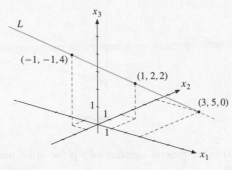

Figure 2

EXAMPLE 1   Describe the straight line in $\mathbb{R}^3$ through the two points $(1, 2, 2)$ and $(-1, -1, 4)$. Where does it meet the x_1x_2-plane?

Solution: According to (2), the straight line is given by the equations:

$$x_1 = t \cdot 1 + (1 - t)(-1) = 2t - 1$$
$$x_2 = t \cdot 2 + (1 - t)(-1) = 3t - 1$$
$$x_3 = t \cdot 2 + (1 - t) \cdot 4 \quad = 4 - 2t$$

This line intersects the x_1x_2-plane when $x_3 = 0$. Then $4 - 2t = 0$, so $t = 2$, implying that $x_1 = 3$ and $x_2 = 5$. It follows that the line meets the x_1x_2-plane at the point $(3, 5, 0)$, as shown in Fig. 2.

Suppose $\mathbf{p} = (p_1, \ldots, p_n) \in \mathbb{R}^n$. The straight line L passing through $(p_1, \ldots, p_n)$ in the same direction as the vector $\mathbf{a} = (a_1, \ldots, a_n)$ is given by

$$\mathbf{x} = \mathbf{p} + t\mathbf{a} \qquad (t \text{ is any real number}) \tag{3}$$

Hyperplanes

As shown in Fig. 3, a plane $\mathcal{P}$ in $\mathbb{R}^3$ is defined by one point $\mathbf{a} = (a_1, a_2, a_3)$ in the plane, as well as one vector $\mathbf{p} = (p_1, p_2, p_3) \neq (0, 0, 0)$ which is orthogonal or perpendicular to any line in the plane. Then the vector $\mathbf{p}$ is said to be a **normal** to the plane. Thus, if $\mathbf{x} = (x_1, x_2, x_3)$ is any point in $\mathcal{P}$ other than $\mathbf{a}$, then the vector $\mathbf{x} - \mathbf{a}$ is in a direction orthogonal to $\mathbf{p}$. Therefore, the inner product of $\mathbf{p}$ and $\mathbf{x} - \mathbf{a}$ must be 0, so that

$$\mathbf{p} \cdot (\mathbf{x} - \mathbf{a}) = 0 \quad \text{or} \quad (p_1, p_2, p_3) \cdot (x_1 - a_1, x_2 - a_2, x_3 - a_3) = 0 \tag{4}$$

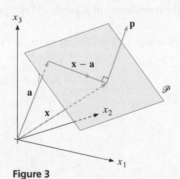

Figure 3

So (4) is the general equation of a plane in $\mathbb{R}^3$ passing through the point $\mathbf{a}$ with normal $\mathbf{p} \neq \mathbf{0}$.

EXAMPLE 2   Find the equation for the plane in $\mathbb{R}^3$ through $\mathbf{a} = (2, 1, -1)$ with $\mathbf{p} = (-1, 1, 3)$ as a normal. Does the line in Example 1 intersect this plane?

Solution: Using (4), the equation is

$$-1 \cdot (x_1 - 2) + 1 \cdot (x_2 - 1) + 3(x_3 - (-1)) = 0 \quad \text{or} \quad -x_1 + x_2 + 3x_3 = -4$$

The line is given by the three equations $x_1 = 2t - 1$, $x_2 = 3t - 1$, and $x_3 = 4 - 2t$. If it meets this plane, then we must have

$$-(2t - 1) + (3t - 1) + 3(4 - 2t) = -4$$

Solving this equation for t yields $t = 16/5$, and so the point of intersection is given by

$$x_1 = 32/5 - 1 = 27/5, \quad x_2 = 43/5, \quad x_3 = -12/5$$

Motivated by this characterization of a plane in $\mathbb{R}^3$, we introduce the following general definition in $\mathbb{R}^n$.

HYPERPLANE IN N-SPACE

The hyperplane H in $\mathbb{R}^n$ through $\mathbf{a} = (a_1, \ldots, a_n)$ which is orthogonal to the nonzero vector $\mathbf{p} = (p_1, \ldots, p_n)$ is the set of all points $\mathbf{x} = (x_1, \ldots, x_n)$ satisfying

$$\mathbf{p} \cdot (\mathbf{x} - \mathbf{a}) = 0$$

(5)

Note that if the normal vector $\mathbf{p}$ is replaced by the scalar multiple $s\mathbf{p}$, where $s \neq 0$, then precisely the same set of vectors $\mathbf{x}$ will satisfy the hyperplane equation.

Using the coordinate representation of the vectors, the hyperplane has the equation

$$p_1(x_1 - a_1) + p_2(x_2 - a_2) + \cdots + p_n(x_n - a_n) = 0 \tag{6}$$

or

$$p_1 x_1 + p_2 x_2 + \cdots + p_n x_n = A, \quad \text{where} \quad A = p_1 a_1 + p_2 a_2 + \cdots + p_n a_n$$

EXAMPLE 3   A person has an amount m to spend on n different commodities, whose prices per unit are $p_1, p_2, \ldots, p_n$, respectively. This person can afford any commodity vector $\mathbf{x} = (x_1, x_2, \ldots, x_n)$ that satisfies the budget inequality

$$p_1 x_1 + p_2 x_2 + \cdots + p_n x_n \leq m \tag{7}$$

When (7) is satisfied with equality, it describes the *budget (hyper)plane* whose normal is the price vector $(p_1, p_2, \ldots, p_n)$.

Usually, it is implicitly assumed that $x_1 \geq 0, x_2 \geq 0, \ldots, x_n \geq 0$. See Fig. 11.4.1 for the case $n = 3$. Note that in this figure the vector (p, q, r) is normal to the plane.

1. Find the equation for the line:

(a) that passes through points $(3, -2, 2)$ and $(10, 2, 1)$.

(b) that passes through point $(1, 3, 2)$ and has the same direction as $(0, -1, 1)$.

2. The line L is given by $x_1 = -t + 2$, $x_2 = 2t - 1$, and $x_3 = t + 3$.

(a) Verify that the point $\mathbf{a} = (2, -1, 3)$ lies on L, but that $(1, 1, 1)$ does not.

(b) Find the equation for the plane $\mathcal{P}$ through $\mathbf{a}$ that is orthogonal to L.

(c) Find the point P where L intersects the plane $3x_1 + 5x_2 - x_3 = 6$.

(SM) **3.** Find the equation for the plane through the points $(1, 0, 2)$, $(5, 2, 1)$, and $(2, -1, 4)$.

4. The price vector is $(2, 3, 5)$ and you can afford the commodity vector $(10, 5, 8)$. What inequality describes your budget constraint? (See Example 3.)

5. (a) Show that $\mathbf{a} = (-2, 1, -1)$ is a point in the plane $-x + 2y + 3z = 1$.

(b) Find the equation for the normal at $\mathbf{a}$ to the plane in part (a).

1. Construct the two matrices $\mathbf{A} = (a_{ij})_{2\times3}$, where (a) $a_{ij} = i + j$ and (b) $a_{ij} = (-1)^{i+j}$.

2. Using the matrices

$$\mathbf{A} = \begin{pmatrix} 2 & 0 \\ -1 & 1 \end{pmatrix}, \quad \mathbf{B} = \begin{pmatrix} -1 & 2 \\ 1 & -1 \end{pmatrix}, \quad \mathbf{C} = \begin{pmatrix} 2 & 3 \\ 1 & 4 \end{pmatrix}, \quad \mathbf{D} = \begin{pmatrix} 1 & 1 & 1 \\ 1 & 3 & 4 \end{pmatrix}$$

calculate (where possible),

(a) $\mathbf{A} - \mathbf{B}$ (b) $\mathbf{A} + \mathbf{B} - 2\mathbf{C}$ (c) $\mathbf{AB}$ (d) $\mathbf{C}(\mathbf{AB})$ (e) $\mathbf{AD}$ (f) $\mathbf{DC}$

3. Using the matrices in Problem 2, compute (where possible),

(a) $2\mathbf{A} - 3\mathbf{B}$ (b) $(\mathbf{A} - \mathbf{B})'$ (c) $(\mathbf{C}'\mathbf{A}')\mathbf{B}'$ (d) $\mathbf{C}'(\mathbf{A}'\mathbf{B}')$ (e) $\mathbf{D}'\mathbf{D}$ (f) $\mathbf{D}\mathbf{D}'$

4. Write the following systems of equations in matrix notation:

(a)
$$\begin{aligned} 2x_1 - 5x_2 &= 3 \\ 5x_1 + 8x_2 &= 5 \end{aligned}$$

(b)
$$\begin{aligned} x + y + z + t &= a \\ x + 3y + 2z + 4t &= b \\ x + 4y + 8z &= c \\ 2x \quad\quad + z - t &= d \end{aligned}$$

(c)
$$\begin{aligned} ax + y + (a+1)z &= b_1 \\ x + 2y + z &= b_2 \\ 3x + 4y + 7z &= b_3 \end{aligned}$$

5. Let $\mathbf{A} = \begin{pmatrix} 0 & 1 & -2 \\ 3 & 4 & 5 \\ -6 & 7 & 15 \end{pmatrix}$, $\mathbf{B} = \begin{pmatrix} 0 & -5 & 3 \\ 5 & 2 & -1 \\ -4 & 2 & 0 \end{pmatrix}$, $\mathbf{C} = \begin{pmatrix} 6 & -2 & -3 \\ 2 & 0 & 1 \\ 0 & 5 & 7 \end{pmatrix}$.

Find the matrices $\mathbf{A} + \mathbf{B}$, $\mathbf{A} - \mathbf{B}$, $\mathbf{AB}$, $\mathbf{BA}$, $\mathbf{A}(\mathbf{BC})$, and $(\mathbf{AB})\mathbf{C}$.

6. Find real numbers a, b, and x such that $\begin{pmatrix} a & b \\ x & 0 \end{pmatrix}\begin{pmatrix} 2 & 1 \\ 1 & 1 \end{pmatrix} - \begin{pmatrix} 1 & 0 \\ 2 & 1 \end{pmatrix}\begin{pmatrix} a & b \\ x & 0 \end{pmatrix} = \begin{pmatrix} 2 & 1 \\ 4 & 4 \end{pmatrix}$.

7. (a) Let $\mathbf{A} = \begin{pmatrix} a & b & 0 \\ -b & a & b \\ 0 & -b & a \end{pmatrix}$, where a and b are arbitrary constants. Find $\mathbf{AA} = \mathbf{A}^2$.

   (b) A square matrix $\mathbf{B}$ is called *skew-symmetric* if $\mathbf{B} = -\mathbf{B}'$, where $\mathbf{B}'$ is the transpose of $\mathbf{B}$. Show that if $\mathbf{C}$ is an arbitrary matrix such that $\mathbf{C}'\mathbf{BC}$ is defined, then $\mathbf{C}'\mathbf{BC}$ is skew-symmetric if $\mathbf{B}$ is. When is the matrix $\mathbf{A}$ defined in (a) skew-symmetric?

   (c) If $\mathbf{A}$ is any square matrix, prove that $\mathbf{A}_1 = \frac{1}{2}(\mathbf{A}+\mathbf{A}')$ is symmetric and that $\mathbf{A}_2 = \frac{1}{2}(\mathbf{A}-\mathbf{A}')$ is skew-symmetric. Verify that $\mathbf{A} = \mathbf{A}_1 + \mathbf{A}_2$, and explain in your own words what you have proved.

(SM) 8. Solve the following equation systems by Gaussian elimination.

   (a) $\begin{aligned} x_1 + 4x_2 &= 1 \\ 2x_1 + 2x_2 &= 8 \end{aligned}$ (b) $\begin{aligned} 2x_1 + 2x_2 - x_3 &= 2 \\ x_1 - 3x_2 + x_3 &= 0 \\ 3x_1 + 4x_2 - x_3 &= 1 \end{aligned}$ (c) $\begin{aligned} x_1 + 3x_2 + 4x_3 &= 0 \\ 5x_1 + x_2 + x_3 &= 0 \end{aligned}$

9. Use Gaussian elimination to find for what values of a the following system has solutions. Then find all the possible solutions.

$$\begin{aligned} x + ay + 2z &= 0 \\ -2x - ay + z &= 4 \\ 2ax + 3a^2y + 9z &= 4 \end{aligned}$$

10. Let $\mathbf{a} = (-1, 5, 3)$, $\mathbf{b} = (1, 1, -3)$, and $\mathbf{c} = (-1, 2, 8)$. Compute $\|\mathbf{a}\|$, $\|\mathbf{b}\|$, and $\|\mathbf{c}\|$. Then verify that the Cauchy–Schwarz inequality holds for $\mathbf{a}$ and $\mathbf{b}$.

(SM) 11. A firm has two plants that produce outputs of three different goods. Its total labour force is fixed. When a fraction λ of its labour force is allocated to its first plant and a fraction $1 - \lambda$ to its second plant (with $0 \leq \lambda \leq 1$), the total output of the three different goods are given by the vector $\lambda(8, 4, 4) + (1 - \lambda)(2, 6, 10) = (6\lambda + 2, -2\lambda + 6, -6\lambda + 10)$.

   (a) Is it possible for the firm to produce either of the two output vectors $\mathbf{a} = (5, 5, 7)$ and $\mathbf{b} = (7, 5, 5)$ if output cannot be thrown away?

   (b) How do your answers to part (a) change if output can be thrown away?

   (c) How will the revenue-maximizing choice of the fraction λ depend upon the selling prices (p_1, p_2, p_3) of the three goods? What condition must be satisfied by these prices if both plants are to remain in use?

(SM) 12. If $\mathbf{P}$ and $\mathbf{Q}$ are $n \times n$ matrices with $\mathbf{PQ} - \mathbf{QP} = \mathbf{P}$, prove that $\mathbf{P}^2\mathbf{Q} - \mathbf{QP}^2 = 2\mathbf{P}^2$ and $\mathbf{P}^3\mathbf{Q} - \mathbf{QP}^3 = 3\mathbf{P}^3$. Then use induction to prove that $\mathbf{P}^k\mathbf{Q} - \mathbf{QP}^k = k\mathbf{P}^k$ for $k = 1, 2, \ldots$.

16

DETERMINANTS AND INVERSE MATRICES

You know we all became mathematicians
for the same reason: We were lazy.
—Max Rosenlicht (1949)

This chapter continues the study of linear algebra. The first topic discussed is the *determinant* of a square matrix. It is one number that does indeed determine some key properties of the n^2 elements of an $n \times n$ matrix. Some economists regard determinants as almost obsolete because calculations that rely on them are very inefficient when the matrix is large. Nevertheless, they are important in several areas of mathematics that interest economists.

After introducing determinants, we consider the fundamentally important concept of the *inverse* of a square matrix and its main properties. Inverse matrices play a major role in the study of systems of linear equations, and in econometrics, for deriving a linear relationship that fits a data set as well as possible. Cramer's rule for the solution of a system of n linear equations and n unknowns is discussed next. Although it is not efficient for solving systems of equations with more than 3 unknowns, Cramer's rule is often used in theoretical studies. An important theorem on homogeneous systems of equations is also discussed. The chapter concludes with a brief introduction to the Leontief model.

16.1 Determinants of Order 2

Consider the pair of linear equations with its associated coefficient matrix:

$$
\begin{array}{cc}
\begin{aligned}
a_{11}x_1 + a_{12}x_2 &= b_1 \\
a_{21}x_1 + a_{22}x_2 &= b_2
\end{aligned}, &
\mathbf{A} = \begin{pmatrix} a_{11} & a_{12} \\ a_{21} & a_{22} \end{pmatrix}
\end{array}
\tag{1}
$$

Solving the equation system (1) in the usual way (see Section 2.4) yields

$$
x_1 = \frac{b_1 a_{22} - b_2 a_{12}}{a_{11}a_{22} - a_{21}a_{12}}, \qquad
x_2 = \frac{b_2 a_{11} - b_1 a_{21}}{a_{11}a_{22} - a_{21}a_{12}}
\tag{2}
$$

The two fractions have a common denominator D, equal to $a_{11}a_{22} - a_{21}a_{12}$. The number D must be nonzero for (2) to be valid, in which case system (1) has a unique solution specified by (2). In this sense, the value of the denominator determines whether system (1) has a unique solution. In fact, $D = a_{11}a_{22} - a_{21}a_{12}$ is called the **determinant** of the matrix $\mathbf{A}$. The determinant of $\mathbf{A}$ is denoted by either $\det(\mathbf{A})$ or, more usually as in this book, by $|\mathbf{A}|$. Thus,

$$|\mathbf{A}| = \begin{vmatrix} a_{11} & a_{12} \\ a_{21} & a_{22} \end{vmatrix} = a_{11}a_{22} - a_{21}a_{12} \tag{3}$$

for any 2×2 matrix $\mathbf{A}$. Such a determinant is said to have **order** 2. For the special case of order 2 determinants, the rule for calculating $|\mathbf{A}|$ is: (a) multiply the elements on the main diagonal; (b) multiply the off-diagonal elements; (c) subtract the product of the off-diagonal elements from the product of the diagonal elements.

EXAMPLE 1
$$\begin{vmatrix} 4 & 1 \\ 3 & 2 \end{vmatrix} = 4 \cdot 2 - 3 \cdot 1 = 5, \quad \begin{vmatrix} b_1 & a_{12} \\ b_2 & a_{22} \end{vmatrix} = b_1 a_{22} - b_2 a_{12}, \quad \begin{vmatrix} a_{11} & b_1 \\ a_{21} & b_2 \end{vmatrix} = b_2 a_{11} - b_1 a_{21}$$

NOTE 1 Geometrically, each of the two equations in (1) represents the graph of a straight line. If $|\mathbf{A}| \neq 0$, then the two lines intersect at a unique point (x_1, x_2) given by (2). If $|\mathbf{A}| = 0$, the expressions for x_1 and x_2 become meaningless—indeed, in this case, equation system (1) either has no solution (because the two lines are parallel), or else has infinitely many solutions (because the two lines coincide).

From Example 1, we see that the *numerators* of the expressions for x_1 and x_2 in (2) can also be written as determinants. Indeed, provided that $|\mathbf{A}| \neq 0$, one has

$$x_1 = \frac{\begin{vmatrix} b_1 & a_{12} \\ b_2 & a_{22} \end{vmatrix}}{|\mathbf{A}|}, \quad x_2 = \frac{\begin{vmatrix} a_{11} & b_1 \\ a_{21} & b_2 \end{vmatrix}}{|\mathbf{A}|} \tag{4}$$

This is a special case of a result referred to as **Cramer's rule**.[1] It is quite convenient when there are only two equations in two unknowns. But it is easier to solve many macroeconomic equation systems in particular by simple substitution. (See Problem 8.)

EXAMPLE 2   Use (4) to find the solutions of

$$2x_1 + 4x_2 = 7$$
$$2x_1 - 2x_2 = -2$$

Solution:

$$x_1 = \frac{\begin{vmatrix} 7 & 4 \\ -2 & -2 \end{vmatrix}}{\begin{vmatrix} 2 & 4 \\ 2 & -2 \end{vmatrix}} = \frac{-6}{-12} = \frac{1}{2}, \quad x_2 = \frac{\begin{vmatrix} 2 & 7 \\ 2 & -2 \end{vmatrix}}{\begin{vmatrix} 2 & 4 \\ 2 & -2 \end{vmatrix}} = \frac{-18}{-12} = \frac{3}{2}$$

Check by substitution that $x_1 = 1/2$, $x_2 = 3/2$ really is a solution.

---

[1] Named after the Swiss mathematician Gabriel Cramer, 1704–1752.

EXAMPLE 3   Use (4) to find Q_1^D and Q_2^D in terms of the parameters when

$$2(b + \beta_1)Q_1^D + bQ_2^D = a - \alpha_1$$

$$bQ_1^D + 2(b + \beta_2)Q_2^D = a - \alpha_2$$

Solution: The determinant of the coefficient matrix is

$$\Delta = \begin{vmatrix} 2(b + \beta_1) & b \\ b & 2(b + \beta_2) \end{vmatrix} = 4(b + \beta_1)(b + \beta_2) - b^2$$

Provided $\Delta \neq 0$, by (4) the solution for Q_1^D is

$$Q_1^D = \frac{\begin{vmatrix} a - \alpha_1 & b \\ a - \alpha_2 & 2(b + \beta_2) \end{vmatrix}}{\Delta} = \frac{2(b + \beta_2)(a - \alpha_1) - b(a - \alpha_2)}{\Delta}$$

with a similar expression for Q_2^D.

In the next section Cramer's rule is extended to 3 equations in 3 unknowns, and then in Section 16.8 to n equations in n unknowns.

A Geometric Interpretation

Determinants of order 2 have a nice geometric interpretation. If the two rows of the matrix are represented as the vectors shown in Fig. 1, then its determinant equals the shaded area of the parallelogram. If we interchange the two rows, however, the determinant becomes a negative number equal to minus this shaded area.

Figure 2 illustrates why the result claimed in Fig. 1 is true. We want to find area T. Note that $2T_1 + 2T_2 + 2T_3 + T = (a_{11} + a_{21})(a_{12} + a_{22})$, where $T_1 = a_{12}a_{21}$, $T_2 = \frac{1}{2}a_{21}a_{22}$, and $T_3 = \frac{1}{2}a_{11}a_{12}$. Hence $T = a_{11}a_{22} - a_{21}a_{12}$, by elementary algebra.

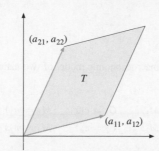

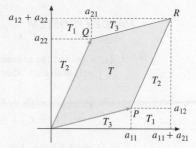

Figure 1 The area T is the absolute value of the determinant $\begin{vmatrix} a_{11} & a_{12} \\ a_{21} & a_{22} \end{vmatrix}$

Figure 2 $2T_1 + 2T_2 + 2T_3 + T = (a_{11} + a_{21})(a_{12} + a_{22})$

PROBLEMS FOR SECTION 16.1

1. Calculate the following determinants:

(a) $\begin{vmatrix} 3 & 0 \\ 2 & 6 \end{vmatrix}$ (b) $\begin{vmatrix} a & a \\ b & b \end{vmatrix}$ (c) $\begin{vmatrix} a + b & a - b \\ a - b & a + b \end{vmatrix}$ (d) $\begin{vmatrix} 3^t & 2^t \\ 3^{t-1} & 2^{t-1} \end{vmatrix}$

2. Illustrate the geometric interpretation in Fig. 1 for the determinant in Problem 1(a).

3. Use Cramer's rule (4) to solve the following systems of equations for x and y. Test the answers by substitution.

(a) $\begin{aligned} 3x - y &= 8 \\ x - 2y &= 5 \end{aligned}$
(b) $\begin{aligned} x + 3y &= 1 \\ 3x - 2y &= 14 \end{aligned}$
(c) $\begin{aligned} ax - by &= 1 \\ bx + ay &= 2 \end{aligned}$

4. Given the matrix $\mathbf{A} = \begin{pmatrix} a & 3 \\ b & 1 \end{pmatrix}$. Find numbers a and b such that $\operatorname{tr}(\mathbf{A}) = 0$ and $|\mathbf{A}| = -10$.

(The **trace** of a square matrix $\mathbf{A}$ is the sum of its diagonal elements, denoted by $\operatorname{tr}(\mathbf{A})$.)

5. Find the solutions to the equation $\begin{vmatrix} 2 - x & 1 \\ 8 & -x \end{vmatrix} = 0$

6. Let $\mathbf{A} = \begin{pmatrix} a_{11} & a_{12} \\ a_{21} & a_{22} \end{pmatrix}$ and $\mathbf{B} = \begin{pmatrix} b_{11} & b_{12} \\ b_{21} & b_{22} \end{pmatrix}$. Show that $|\mathbf{AB}| = |\mathbf{A}| \cdot |\mathbf{B}|$.

7. Find two 2×2 matrices $\mathbf{A}$ and $\mathbf{B}$ such that $|\mathbf{A} + \mathbf{B}| \neq |\mathbf{A}| + |\mathbf{B}|$.

8. Use Cramer's rule to find Y and C when

$$Y = C + I_0 + G_0, \qquad C = a + bY$$

where Y is the national product and C is private consumption. The symbols I_0 (private investment), G_0 (public consumption and investment), a, and b all represent constants, with $b < 1$. (Actually, this is a typical case in which one should *not* use Cramer's rule, because Y and C can be found much more simply. How?)

HARDER PROBLEM

(SM) **9.** (a) Consider the following linked macroeconomic model of two nations, $i = 1, 2$, that trade only with each other:

$$\begin{aligned} Y_1 &= C_1 + A_1 + X_1 - M_1; & C_1 &= c_1 Y_1; & M_1 &= m_1 Y_1 = X_2 \\ Y_2 &= C_2 + A_2 + X_2 - M_2; & C_2 &= c_2 Y_2; & M_2 &= m_2 Y_2 = X_1 \end{aligned}$$

Here, for $i = 1, 2$, Y_i is income, C_i is consumption, A_i is (exogenous) autonomous expenditure, X_i denotes exports, and M_i denotes imports of country i. Interpret the two equations $M_1 = X_2$ and $M_2 = X_1$.

(b) Given the system of 8 equations in 8 unknowns in part (a), use substitution to reduce it to a pair of simultaneous equations in the endogenous variables Y_1 and Y_2. Then solve for the equilibrium values of Y_1, Y_2 as functions of the exogenous variables A_1, A_2.

(c) How does an increase in A_1 affect Y_2? Interpret your answer.

16.2   Determinants of Order 3

Consider the system of three linear equations in three unknowns

$$a_{11}x_1 + a_{12}x_2 + a_{13}x_3 = b_1$$
$$a_{21}x_1 + a_{22}x_2 + a_{23}x_3 = b_2 \qquad (1)$$
$$a_{31}x_1 + a_{32}x_2 + a_{33}x_3 = b_3$$

Here the coefficient matrix $\mathbf{A}$ is 3×3. By applying the method of elimination along with some rather heavy algebraic computation, this system can be solved eventually for x_1, x_2, and x_3 except in a degenerate case. The resulting expression for x_1 is

$$x_1 = \frac{b_1a_{22}a_{33} - b_1a_{23}a_{32} - b_2a_{12}a_{33} + b_2a_{13}a_{32} + b_3a_{12}a_{23} - b_3a_{22}a_{13}}{a_{11}a_{22}a_{33} - a_{11}a_{23}a_{32} + a_{12}a_{23}a_{31} - a_{12}a_{21}a_{33} + a_{13}a_{21}a_{32} - a_{13}a_{22}a_{31}}$$

We shall not triple the demands on the reader's patience and eyesight by giving the corresponding expressions for x_2 and x_3. However, we do claim that these expressions share the same denominator as that given for x_1. This common denominator is called the **determinant** of $\mathbf{A}$, denoted by $\det(\mathbf{A})$ or $|\mathbf{A}|$, which is zero in the degenerate case. Thus, the determinant is defined as

$$|\mathbf{A}| = \begin{vmatrix} a_{11} & a_{12} & a_{13} \\ a_{21} & a_{22} & a_{23} \\ a_{31} & a_{32} & a_{33} \end{vmatrix} = \begin{cases} a_{11}a_{22}a_{33} - a_{11}a_{23}a_{32} + a_{12}a_{23}a_{31} \\ \quad - a_{12}a_{21}a_{33} + a_{13}a_{21}a_{32} - a_{13}a_{22}a_{31} \end{cases} \qquad (2)$$

Expansion by Cofactors

Consider the sum of the six terms in (2). It looks quite messy, but the method of expansion by cofactors makes it easy to write down all the terms. First, note that each of the three elements a_{11}, a_{12}, and a_{13} in the first row of $\mathbf{A}$ appears in exactly two terms of (2). In fact, $|\mathbf{A}|$ can be written as

$$|\mathbf{A}| = a_{11}(a_{22}a_{33} - a_{23}a_{32}) - a_{12}(a_{21}a_{33} - a_{23}a_{31}) + a_{13}(a_{21}a_{32} - a_{22}a_{31})$$

Applying the rule for evaluating determinants of order 2, we see that this is the same as

$$|\mathbf{A}| = a_{11} \begin{vmatrix} a_{22} & a_{23} \\ a_{32} & a_{33} \end{vmatrix} - a_{12} \begin{vmatrix} a_{21} & a_{23} \\ a_{31} & a_{33} \end{vmatrix} + a_{13} \begin{vmatrix} a_{21} & a_{22} \\ a_{31} & a_{32} \end{vmatrix} \qquad (3)$$

In this way, the computation of a determinant of order 3 can be reduced to calculating three determinants of order 2. Note that a_{11} is multiplied by the second-order determinant obtained by deleting the *first* row and the *first* column of $|\mathbf{A}|$. Likewise, a_{12}, with a minus sign attached to it, is multiplied by the determinant obtained by deleting the *first* row and the *second* column of $|\mathbf{A}|$. Finally, a_{13} is multiplied by the determinant obtained by deleting the *first* row and the *third* column of $|\mathbf{A}|$.

EXAMPLE 1   Use (3) to calculate $|\mathbf{A}| = \begin{vmatrix} 3 & 0 & 2 \\ -1 & 1 & 0 \\ 5 & 2 & 3 \end{vmatrix}$.

Solution:

$$|\mathbf{A}| = 3 \cdot \begin{vmatrix} 1 & 0 \\ 2 & 3 \end{vmatrix} - 0 \cdot \begin{vmatrix} -1 & 0 \\ 5 & 3 \end{vmatrix} + 2 \cdot \begin{vmatrix} -1 & 1 \\ 5 & 2 \end{vmatrix} = 3 \cdot 3 - 0 + 2 \cdot (-2 - 5) = -5.$$

EXAMPLE 2   Use (3) to prove that $|\mathbf{A}| = \begin{vmatrix} 1 & a & a^2 \\ 1 & b & b^2 \\ 1 & c & c^2 \end{vmatrix} = (b-a)(c-a)(c-b)$.

Solution:

$$|\mathbf{A}| = 1 \cdot \begin{vmatrix} b & b^2 \\ c & c^2 \end{vmatrix} - a \cdot \begin{vmatrix} 1 & b^2 \\ 1 & c^2 \end{vmatrix} + a^2 \cdot \begin{vmatrix} 1 & b \\ 1 & c \end{vmatrix} = bc^2 - b^2c - ac^2 + ab^2 + a^2c - a^2b$$

You are not supposed to "see" that these six terms can be written as $(b-a)(c-a)(c-b)$. Rather, you should expand $(b-a)[(c-a)(c-b)]$ and verify the equality that way.

A careful study of the numerator in the expression for x_1 in the beginning of this section reveals that it can also be written as a determinant. The same is true of the corresponding formulas for x_2 and x_3. In fact, if $|\mathbf{A}| \neq 0$, then one has

$$x_1 = \frac{\begin{vmatrix} b_1 & a_{12} & a_{13} \\ b_2 & a_{22} & a_{23} \\ b_3 & a_{32} & a_{33} \end{vmatrix}}{|\mathbf{A}|}, \quad x_2 = \frac{\begin{vmatrix} a_{11} & b_1 & a_{13} \\ a_{21} & b_2 & a_{23} \\ a_{31} & b_3 & a_{33} \end{vmatrix}}{|\mathbf{A}|}, \quad x_3 = \frac{\begin{vmatrix} a_{11} & a_{12} & b_1 \\ a_{21} & a_{22} & b_2 \\ a_{31} & a_{32} & b_3 \end{vmatrix}}{|\mathbf{A}|} \quad (4)$$

This is Cramer's rule for the solution of (1). (See Section 16.8 for a full proof of (4) for the general case of n equations in n unknowns.)

NOTE 1   In the determinants appearing in the numerators of x_1, x_2, and x_3 of (4), observe how the right-hand column in (1),

$$\begin{pmatrix} b_1 \\ b_2 \\ b_3 \end{pmatrix}$$

shifts from the first column when solving for x_1, to the second column when solving for x_2, and then to the third column when solving for x_3. This makes it very easy to remember Cramer's rule.

NOTE 2   The method in (3) for calculating the value of a 3×3 determinant is called *cofactor expansion along row* 1. If we focus on the elements in row i instead of row 1, we again find that $|\mathbf{A}| = a_{i1}C_{i1} + a_{i2}C_{i2} + a_{i3}C_{i3}$, where for $j = 1, 2, 3$, the factor C_{ij} equals $(-1)^{i+j}$ times the determinant of the 2×2 matrix we get by deleting row i and column j from $\mathbf{A}$. Thus, we can also find the value of the determinant by cofactor expansion along row i for any $i = 1, 2, 3$. Moreover, it turns out that for $j = 1, 2,$ or 3, we also have $|\mathbf{A}| = a_{1j}C_{1j} + a_{2j}C_{2j} + a_{3j}C_{3j}$. In other words, we can calculate the determinant by cofactor expansion along column j. See Section 16.5 for more about cofactor expansion.

EXAMPLE 3   Solve the following system of equations by using Cramer's rule:

$$2x_1 + 2x_2 - x_3 = -3$$
$$4x_1 \qquad + 2x_3 = 8$$
$$6x_2 - 3x_3 = -12$$

Solution: In this case, the determinant $|\mathbf{A}|$ in (4) is seen to be

$$|\mathbf{A}| = \begin{vmatrix} 2 & 2 & -1 \\ 4 & 0 & 2 \\ 0 & 6 & -3 \end{vmatrix} = -24$$

The numerators in (4) are (verify!)

$$\begin{vmatrix} -3 & 2 & -1 \\ 8 & 0 & 2 \\ -12 & 6 & -3 \end{vmatrix} = -12, \quad \begin{vmatrix} 2 & -3 & -1 \\ 4 & 8 & 2 \\ 0 & -12 & -3 \end{vmatrix} = 12, \quad \begin{vmatrix} 2 & 2 & -3 \\ 4 & 0 & 8 \\ 0 & 6 & -12 \end{vmatrix} = -72$$

Hence, (4) yields the solution $x_1 = (-12)/(-24) = 1/2$, $x_2 = 12/(-24) = -1/2$, and $x_3 = (-72)/(-24) = 3$. Inserting this into the original system of equations verifies that this is a correct answer.

A Geometric Interpretation

Like determinants of order 2, those of order 3 also have a geometric interpretation which is shown and explained in Fig. 1.

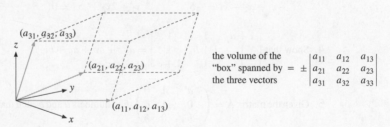

$$\text{the volume of the "box" spanned by the three vectors} = \pm \begin{vmatrix} a_{11} & a_{12} & a_{13} \\ a_{21} & a_{22} & a_{23} \\ a_{31} & a_{32} & a_{33} \end{vmatrix}$$

Figure 1

The rows of the determinant correspond to three different 3-vectors represented in the diagram. These vectors determine a box which is not rectangular with right-angles at each of its six corners, but a distorted "parallelepiped" which has six faces that are all parallelograms whose opposite edges are parallel.

Sarrus's Rule

Here is an alternative way of evaluating determinants of order 3 that many people find convenient. Write down the determinant twice, except that the last column in the second determinant should be omitted:

$$\begin{matrix} a_{11} & a_{12} & a_{13} & a_{11} & a_{12} \\ a_{21} & a_{22} & a_{23} & a_{21} & a_{22} \\ a_{31} & a_{32} & a_{33} & a_{31} & a_{32} \end{matrix} \tag{5}$$

First, multiply along the three lines falling to the right, giving all these products a plus sign:

$$a_{11}a_{22}a_{33} + a_{12}a_{23}a_{31} + a_{13}a_{21}a_{32}$$

Then multiply along the three lines rising to the right, giving all these products a minus sign:

$$-a_{11}a_{23}a_{32} - a_{12}a_{21}a_{33} - a_{13}a_{22}a_{31}$$

The sum of all the six terms is exactly equal to formula (2) for $|\mathbf{A}|$. It is important to note that this rule, known as **Sarrus's rule**, *does not generalize* to determinants of order higher than 3.

PROBLEMS FOR SECTION 16.2

(SM) **1.** Use (3) or Sarrus's rule to calculate the following determinants:

(a) $\begin{vmatrix} 1 & -1 & 0 \\ 1 & 3 & 2 \\ 1 & 0 & 0 \end{vmatrix}$
(b) $\begin{vmatrix} 1 & -1 & 0 \\ 1 & 3 & 2 \\ 1 & 2 & 1 \end{vmatrix}$
(c) $\begin{vmatrix} a & b & c \\ 0 & d & e \\ 0 & 0 & f \end{vmatrix}$
(d) $\begin{vmatrix} a & 0 & b \\ 0 & e & 0 \\ c & 0 & d \end{vmatrix}$

2. Let $\mathbf{A} = \begin{pmatrix} 1 & -1 & 0 \\ 1 & 3 & 2 \\ 1 & 2 & 1 \end{pmatrix}$ and $\mathbf{B} = \begin{pmatrix} 1 & 2 & 3 \\ 2 & 3 & 4 \\ 0 & 1 & -1 \end{pmatrix}$.

Calculate $\mathbf{AB}$, $|\mathbf{A}|$, $|\mathbf{B}|$, $|\mathbf{A}| \cdot |\mathbf{B}|$, and $|\mathbf{AB}|$. (Note that $|\mathbf{AB}| = |\mathbf{A}| \cdot |\mathbf{B}|$.)

(SM) **3.** Use Cramer's rule to solve the following systems of equations. Check your answers.

(a) $\begin{aligned} x_1 - x_2 + x_3 &= 2 \\ x_1 + x_2 - x_3 &= 0 \\ -x_1 - x_2 - x_3 &= -6 \end{aligned}$
(b) $\begin{aligned} x_1 - x_2 &= 0 \\ x_1 + 3x_2 + 2x_3 &= 0 \\ x_1 + 2x_2 + x_3 &= 0 \end{aligned}$
(c) $\begin{aligned} x + 3y - 2z &= 1 \\ 3x - 2y + 5z &= 14 \\ 2x - 5y + 3z &= 1 \end{aligned}$

4. Show that $\begin{vmatrix} 1+a & 1 & 1 \\ 1 & 1+b & 1 \\ 1 & 1 & 1+c \end{vmatrix} = abc + ab + ac + bc.$

5. Given the matrix $\mathbf{A} = \begin{pmatrix} a & 1 & 0 \\ 0 & -1 & a \\ -b & 0 & b \end{pmatrix}$, find numbers a and b such that $\mathrm{tr}(\mathbf{A}) = 0$ and $|\mathbf{A}| = 12$.

($\mathrm{tr}(\mathbf{A})$ is the sum of the diagonal elements.)

6. Solve the equation:

$$\begin{vmatrix} 1-x & 2 & 2 \\ 2 & 1-x & 2 \\ 2 & 2 & 1-x \end{vmatrix} = 0$$

7. (a) Calculate the determinant of $\mathbf{A}_t = \begin{pmatrix} 1 & t & 0 \\ -2 & -2 & -1 \\ 0 & 1 & t \end{pmatrix}$, and show that it is never 0.

(b) Show that for a certain value of t, one has $\mathbf{A}_t^3 = \mathbf{I}_3$.

(SM) **8.** Consider the simple macro model described by the three equations

(i) $Y = C + A_0$ (ii) $C = a + b(Y - T)$ (iii) $T = d + tY$

where Y is income, C is consumption, T is tax revenue, A_0 is the constant (exogenous) autonomous expenditure, and a, b, d, and t are all positive parameters. Find the equilibrium values of the endogenous variables Y, C, and T by: (A) successive elimination or substitution; (B) writing the equations in matrix form and applying Cramer's rule.

16.3 Determinants of Order n

This section gives a definition of determinant that is particularly useful when proving general results. If you are not so interested in these proofs, you might skip this section and rely instead on expansion by cofactors (explained in Section 16.5) in all your work on determinants.

For a 3×3 matrix $\mathbf{A} = (a_{ij})_{3\times3}$, the determinant can be written as the sum

$$a_{11}a_{22}a_{33} - a_{11}a_{23}a_{32} + a_{12}a_{23}a_{31} - a_{12}a_{21}a_{33} + a_{13}a_{21}a_{32} - a_{13}a_{22}a_{31} \qquad (1)$$

A closer examination of this sum reveals a definite pattern. Each term is the product of three different elements of the matrix. Each product contains one element from each row of $\mathbf{A}$. Moreover, these elements all lie in different columns of the matrix. In fact, the elements in the six terms are chosen from the matrix $\mathbf{A}$ according to the pattern shown by the circles in Fig. 1 (disregard the lines for a moment).

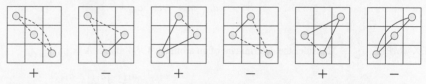

Figure 1

In a 3×3 matrix, there are precisely 6 different ways of picking three elements with one element from each row and one element from each column. All the 6 corresponding products appear in (1). How do we determine the sign of each term in (1)? In Fig. 1, we have joined each pair of circles in every box by a line, which is solid if the line rises to the right, but dashed if the line falls to the right. Using the solid lines drawn in each of the 6 boxes, the following rule emerges:

THE SIGN RULE

To determine the sign of any term in the sum, mark in the array all the elements appearing in that term. Join all possible pairs of these elements with lines. These lines will then either fall or rise to the right. If the number of the rising lines is even, then the corresponding term is assigned a plus sign; if it is odd, it is assigned a minus sign. $\qquad (2)$

Let us apply this rule to the six boxes in Fig. 1. In the first box, for example, no lines rise, so $a_{11}a_{22}a_{33}$ has a plus sign. In box 4, exactly one line rises, so $a_{12}a_{21}a_{33}$ has a minus sign. And so on.

Suppose $\mathbf{A} = (a_{ij})_{n\times n}$ is an arbitrary $n \times n$ matrix. Suppose we pick n elements from $\mathbf{A}$, including exactly one element from each row and exactly one element from each column. Take the product of these n elements, giving an expression of the form

$$a_{1r_1} \cdot a_{2r_2} \cdot \ldots \cdot a_{nr_n}$$

where the second subscripts $r_1, r_2, \ldots, r_n$ represent a shuffling (or permutation) of the numbers $1, 2, \ldots, n$. The numbers $1, 2, \ldots, n$ can be permuted in $n! = 1 \cdot 2 \ldots (n-1)n$ different ways: For the first element, there are n choices; for each of these first choices, there are $n-1$ choices for the second element; and so on. So there are $n!$ different products of n factors to consider.

Now we define the determinant of $\mathbf{A}$, $\det(\mathbf{A})$ or $|\mathbf{A}|$, as follows:

DEFINITION OF DETERMINANT

Let $\mathbf{A}$ be an $n \times n$ matrix. Then $|\mathbf{A}|$ is a sum of $n!$ terms where:

1. Each term is the product of n elements of the matrix, with one element from each row and one element from each column. Moreover, every product of n factors, in which each row and each column is represented exactly once, must appear in this sum.

2. The sign of each term is found by applying the sign rule (2).

Using $(\pm)$ to denote the appropriate choice of either a plus or minus sign, one can write

$$|\mathbf{A}| = \begin{vmatrix} a_{11} & a_{12} & \cdots & a_{1n} \\ a_{21} & a_{22} & \cdots & a_{2n} \\ \vdots & \vdots & \ddots & \vdots \\ a_{n1} & a_{n2} & \cdots & a_{nn} \end{vmatrix} = \sum (\pm) a_{1r_1} a_{2r_2} \ldots a_{nr_n} \tag{3}$$

EXAMPLE 1   Consider the determinant of an arbitrary 4×4 matrix $\mathbf{A} = \left(a_{ij} \right)_{4 \times 4}$:

$$|\mathbf{A}| = \begin{vmatrix} a_{11} & a_{12} & a_{13} & a_{14} \\ a_{21} & a_{22} & a_{23} & a_{24} \\ a_{31} & a_{32} & a_{33} & a_{34} \\ a_{41} & a_{42} & a_{43} & a_{44} \end{vmatrix}$$

It consists of $4! = 4 \cdot 3 \cdot 2 \cdot 1 = 24$ terms. One of these terms is $a_{13}a_{21}a_{32}a_{44}$, and the corresponding factors are the boxed elements in the array. What sign should this term have? According to the sign rule, the term should have the plus sign because there are two rising lines. (We have omitted the dashed lines, because these do not count.)

Check that the four indicated terms in the following sum have been given the correct sign:

$$|\mathbf{A}| = a_{11}a_{22}a_{33}a_{44} - a_{12}a_{21}a_{33}a_{44} + \cdots + a_{13}a_{21}a_{32}a_{44} - \cdots + a_{14}a_{23}a_{32}a_{41}$$

Note that there are 20 other terms which we have left out.

The determinant of an $n \times n$ matrix is called a **determinant of order n**. In general, it is difficult to evaluate determinants by using the definition directly, even if n is only 4 or 5. If $n > 5$, the work is usually enormous. For example, if $n = 6$, then $n! = 720$, and so there are 720 terms in the sum defining the determinant. Fortunately there are other methods based on the elementary row operations discussed in Section 15.6 that reduce the work considerably. There are several standard computer programs for evaluating determinants.

In a few special cases, it is easy to evaluate a determinant even if the order is high. For instance,

$$\begin{vmatrix} a_{11} & a_{12} & \cdots & a_{1n} \\ 0 & a_{22} & \cdots & a_{2n} \\ \vdots & \vdots & \ddots & \vdots \\ 0 & 0 & \cdots & a_{nn} \end{vmatrix} = a_{11}a_{22} \ldots a_{nn} \tag{4}$$

Here all the elements *below* the main diagonal are 0. The matrix whose determinant is given in (4) is called **upper triangular** because all the nonzero terms lie in the triangle on or above the main diagonal. Such a determinant can be evaluated by taking the product of all the elements on the main diagonal. To see why, note that in order to have a term that is not 0, we have to choose a_{11} from column 1. From column 2, we cannot choose a_{12}, because we have already picked the element a_{11} from the first row. Hence, from column 2, we have to pick a_{22} in order to have a term different from 0. From the third column, we have to pick a_{33}, and so on. Thus, only the term $a_{11}a_{22}\ldots a_{nn}$ can be $\neq 0$. The sign of this term is plus because no line joining any pair of elements appearing in the product rises to the right.

If a matrix is a transpose of an upper triangular matrix, so that all elements above the main diagonal are 0, then the matrix is **lower triangular**. By using essentially the same argument as for (4), we see that the determinant of a lower triangular matrix is also equal to the product of the elements on its main diagonal:

$$\begin{vmatrix} a_{11} & 0 & \cdots & 0 \\ a_{21} & a_{22} & \cdots & 0 \\ \vdots & \vdots & \ddots & \vdots \\ a_{n1} & a_{n2} & \cdots & a_{nn} \end{vmatrix} = a_{11}a_{22}\ldots a_{nn} \tag{5}$$

PROBLEMS FOR SECTION 16.3

(SM) 1. Use the definition of determinant to calculate the following:

(a) $\begin{vmatrix} 1 & 0 & 0 & 0 \\ 0 & 2 & 0 & 0 \\ 0 & 0 & 3 & 0 \\ 0 & 0 & 0 & 4 \end{vmatrix}$ (b) $\begin{vmatrix} 1 & 0 & 0 & 1 \\ 0 & 1 & 0 & 0 \\ 0 & 0 & 1 & 0 \\ a & b & c & d \end{vmatrix}$ (c) $\begin{vmatrix} 1 & 0 & 0 & 2 \\ 0 & 1 & 0 & -3 \\ 0 & 0 & 1 & 4 \\ 2 & 3 & 4 & 11 \end{vmatrix}$

2. Suppose that the two $n \times n$ matrices **A** and **B** are both upper triangular. Show that $|\mathbf{AB}| = |\mathbf{A}||\mathbf{B}|$.

3. The determinant of the following 5×5 matrix consists of $5! = 120$ terms. One of them is the product of the boxed elements. Write this term with its correct sign.

$$\begin{matrix} a_{11} & \boxed{a_{12}} & a_{13} & a_{14} & a_{15} \\ a_{21} & a_{22} & \boxed{a_{23}} & a_{24} & a_{25} \\ a_{31} & a_{32} & a_{33} & a_{34} & \boxed{a_{35}} \\ \boxed{a_{41}} & a_{42} & a_{43} & a_{44} & a_{45} \\ a_{51} & a_{52} & a_{53} & \boxed{a_{54}} & a_{55} \end{matrix}$$

4. Write the term indicated by the marked boxes with its correct sign. (See the previous problem.)

$$\begin{matrix} a_{11} & a_{12} & a_{13} & a_{14} & \boxed{a_{15}} \\ a_{21} & a_{22} & a_{23} & \boxed{a_{24}} & a_{25} \\ a_{31} & \boxed{a_{32}} & a_{33} & a_{34} & a_{35} \\ a_{41} & a_{42} & \boxed{a_{43}} & a_{44} & a_{45} \\ \boxed{a_{51}} & a_{52} & a_{53} & a_{54} & a_{55} \end{matrix}$$

5. Solve the following equation for x:

$$\begin{vmatrix} 2-x & 0 & 3 & 0 \\ 1 & 2-x & 0 & 3 \\ 0 & 0 & 2-x & 0 \\ 0 & 0 & 1 & 2-x \end{vmatrix} = 0$$

16.4   Basic Rules for Determinants

The definition of the determinant of an $n \times n$ matrix $\mathbf{A}$ implies a number of important properties. All are of theoretical interest, but they also make it simpler to evaluate determinants.

THEOREM 16.4.1   (RULES FOR DETERMINANTS)

Let $\mathbf{A}$ be an $n \times n$ matrix. Then:

A. If all the elements in a row (or column) of $\mathbf{A}$ are 0, then $|\mathbf{A}| = 0$.

B. $|\mathbf{A}'| = |\mathbf{A}|$, where $\mathbf{A}'$ is the transpose of $\mathbf{A}$.

C. If all the elements in a single row (or column) of $\mathbf{A}$ are multiplied by a number α, the determinant is multiplied by α.

D. If two rows (or two columns) of $\mathbf{A}$ are interchanged, the determinant changes sign, but the absolute value remains unchanged.

E. If two of the rows (or columns) of $\mathbf{A}$ are proportional, then $|\mathbf{A}| = 0$.

F. The value of the determinant of $\mathbf{A}$ is unchanged if a multiple of one row (or one column) is added to a different row (or column) of $\mathbf{A}$.

G. The determinant of the product of two $n \times n$ matrices $\mathbf{A}$ and $\mathbf{B}$ is the product of the determinants of each of the factors:

$$|\mathbf{AB}| = |\mathbf{A}| \cdot |\mathbf{B}| \tag{1}$$

H. If α is a real number,

$$|\alpha\mathbf{A}| = \alpha^n |\mathbf{A}| \tag{2}$$

NOTE 1   It should be recalled that (usually) the determinant of a sum is *not* the sum of the determinants:

$$|\mathbf{A} + \mathbf{B}| \neq |\mathbf{A}| + |\mathbf{B}| \qquad \text{(in general)} \tag{3}$$

An example of this general inequality was asked for in Problem 16.1.7.

NOTE 2   Our geometric interpretations of determinants of order 2 and 3 support several of these rules. For example, rule C with (say) $\alpha = 2$, reflects the fact that if one of the vectors in Figure 16.1.1 (16.2.1) is doubled in length, then the area (volume) is twice as big. Try to give geometric interpretations of rules A, B, D, E, and H.

Proofs for most of these properties are given at the end of this section. First, however, let us illustrate them in some special cases of 2×2 matrices.

Rule A: $\begin{vmatrix} a_{11} & a_{12} \\ 0 & 0 \end{vmatrix} = a_{11} \cdot 0 - a_{12} \cdot 0 = 0$

Rule B: $|\mathbf{A}| = \begin{vmatrix} a_{11} & a_{12} \\ a_{21} & a_{22} \end{vmatrix} = a_{11}a_{22} - a_{12}a_{21}, \quad |\mathbf{A}'| = \begin{vmatrix} a_{11} & a_{21} \\ a_{12} & a_{22} \end{vmatrix} = a_{11}a_{22} - a_{12}a_{21}$

We see that $|\mathbf{A}'|$ has exactly the same terms as $|\mathbf{A}|$. In particular, $|\mathbf{A}'| = |\mathbf{A}|$.

Rule C: $\begin{vmatrix} a_{11} & a_{12} \\ \alpha a_{21} & \alpha a_{22} \end{vmatrix} = a_{11}(\alpha a_{22}) - a_{12}(\alpha a_{21}) = \alpha(a_{11}a_{22} - a_{12}a_{21}) = \alpha \begin{vmatrix} a_{11} & a_{12} \\ a_{21} & a_{22} \end{vmatrix}$

Rule D: $\begin{vmatrix} a_{21} & a_{22} \\ a_{11} & a_{12} \end{vmatrix} = a_{21}a_{12} - a_{11}a_{22} = -(a_{11}a_{22} - a_{12}a_{21}) = - \begin{vmatrix} a_{11} & a_{12} \\ a_{21} & a_{22} \end{vmatrix}$

Rule E: $\begin{vmatrix} a_{11} & a_{12} \\ \beta a_{11} & \beta a_{12} \end{vmatrix} = a_{11}(\beta a_{12}) - a_{12}(\beta a_{11}) = \beta(a_{11}a_{12} - a_{11}a_{12}) = 0$

Let us also see how rule E helps to confirm (partly) the result in Example 16.2.2. Note that the product $(b - a)(c - a)(c - b)$ is 0 if $b = a$, $c = a$, or $c = b$, and in each of these three cases, two rows of the matrix are proportional, in fact equal.

Rule F: Multiply each entry in the first row of a determinant of order 2 by α and add it to the corresponding entry in the second row. Then the determinant does not change its value. (Note carefully the way in which we indicate this operation—see also Section 15.6.)

$$\begin{vmatrix} a_{11} & a_{12} \\ a_{21} & a_{22} \end{vmatrix} \begin{matrix} \alpha \\ \hookleftarrow \end{matrix} = \begin{vmatrix} a_{11} & a_{12} \\ a_{21} + \alpha a_{11} & a_{22} + \alpha a_{12} \end{vmatrix} = a_{11}(a_{22} + \alpha a_{12}) - a_{12}(a_{21} + \alpha a_{11})$$

$$= a_{11}a_{22} + \alpha a_{11}a_{12} - a_{12}a_{21} - \alpha a_{12}a_{11} = a_{11}a_{22} - a_{12}a_{21}$$

$$= \begin{vmatrix} a_{11} & a_{12} \\ a_{21} & a_{22} \end{vmatrix}$$

Rule G: Problem 16.1.6 has already asked for a proof of this rule for 2×2 matrices.

Rule H: $\begin{vmatrix} \alpha a_{11} & \alpha a_{12} \\ \alpha a_{21} & \alpha a_{22} \end{vmatrix} = \alpha a_{11}\alpha a_{22} - \alpha a_{12}\alpha a_{21} = \alpha^2(a_{11}a_{22} - a_{12}a_{21}) = \alpha^2 \begin{vmatrix} a_{11} & a_{12} \\ a_{21} & a_{22} \end{vmatrix}$

Theorem 16.4.1 exhibits some of the most important rules for determinants. Confidence in dealing with them comes only from doing many problems.

Rule F is particularly useful for evaluating large or complicated determinants.[2] The idea is to convert the matrix into one that is (upper or lower) triangular. This is just the same procedure as that used in the Gaussian elimination method described in Section 15.6. We give two examples involving 3×3 matrices.

EXAMPLE 1

$$\begin{vmatrix} 1 & 5 & -1 \\ -1 & 1 & 3 \\ 3 & 2 & 1 \end{vmatrix} \begin{matrix} 1 \\ \hookleftarrow \end{matrix} = \begin{vmatrix} 1 & 5 & -1 \\ -1+1 & 1+5 & 3+(-1) \\ 3 & 2 & 1 \end{vmatrix} = \begin{vmatrix} 1 & 5 & -1 \\ 0 & 6 & 2 \\ 3 & 2 & 1 \end{vmatrix} \begin{matrix} -3 \\ \hookleftarrow \end{matrix}$$

$$= \begin{vmatrix} 1 & 5 & -1 \\ 0 & 6 & 2 \\ 0 & -13 & 4 \end{vmatrix} \begin{matrix} \frac{13}{6} \\ \hookleftarrow \end{matrix} = \begin{vmatrix} 1 & 5 & -1 \\ 0 & 6 & 2 \\ 0 & 0 & 25/3 \end{vmatrix} = 1 \cdot 6 \cdot \frac{25}{3} = 50$$

---

[2] To calculate a general 10×10 determinant using the definition directly requires no fewer than $10! - 1 = 3\,628\,799$ operations of addition or multiplication! Systematic use of rule F can reduce the required number of operations to about 380.

Here, 1 times the first row has been added to the second row in order to obtain a zero in the first column. Then (-3) times the first row has been added to the third, which gives a second zero in the first column. Thereafter, 13/6 times the second row has been added to the third, which creates an extra zero in the second column. Note the way in which we have indicated these operations. In the end, they produce an upper triangular matrix whose determinant is easy to evaluate by means of formula (16.3.4).

In the next example, the first two steps involve more than one operation simultaneously.

EXAMPLE 2
$$\begin{vmatrix} a+b & a & a \\ a & a+b & a \\ a & a & a+b \end{vmatrix} = \begin{vmatrix} 3a+b & 3a+b & 3a+b \\ a & a+b & a \\ a & a & a+b \end{vmatrix}$$

$$= (3a+b)\begin{vmatrix} 1 & 1 & 1 \\ a & a+b & a \\ a & a & a+b \end{vmatrix} = (3a+b)\begin{vmatrix} 1 & 1 & 1 \\ 0 & b & 0 \\ 0 & 0 & b \end{vmatrix}$$

$$= (3a+b)\cdot 1 \cdot b \cdot b = b^2(3a+b)$$

EXAMPLE 3   Check that $|\mathbf{AB}| = |\mathbf{A}| \cdot |\mathbf{B}|$ when $\mathbf{A} = \begin{pmatrix} 1 & 5 & -1 \\ -1 & 1 & 3 \\ 3 & 2 & 1 \end{pmatrix}$, $\mathbf{B} = \begin{pmatrix} 3 & 0 & 2 \\ -1 & 1 & 0 \\ 5 & 2 & 3 \end{pmatrix}$.

Solution: Here $|\mathbf{A}| = 50$ (as in Example 1) and you should verify that $|\mathbf{B}| = -5$. Moreover, multiplying the two matrices yields

$$\mathbf{AB} = \begin{pmatrix} -7 & 3 & -1 \\ 11 & 7 & 7 \\ 12 & 4 & 9 \end{pmatrix}$$

Using Sarrus's rule, or otherwise, we find that $|\mathbf{AB}| = -250$. Thus $|\mathbf{AB}| = |\mathbf{A}| \cdot |\mathbf{B}|$.

On the proof of Theorem 16.4.1:

Rule A: Each of the $n!$ terms in the determinant must take one element from the row (or column) consisting of only zeros, so the whole determinant is 0.

Rule B: Each term in $|\mathbf{A}|$ is the product of entries chosen from $\mathbf{A}$ to include exactly one element from each row and one element from each column. Exactly the same terms, therefore, must appear in $|\mathbf{A}'|$ also. One can prove that the signs are also the same, but we skip the proof. (The proof of this property and the others we leave unproved are found in most books on linear algebra.)

Rule C: Let $\mathbf{B}$ be the matrix obtained from $\mathbf{A}$ by multiplying every element in a certain row (or column) of $\mathbf{A}$ by α. Then each term in the sum defining $|\mathbf{B}|$ is the corresponding term in the sum defining $|\mathbf{A}|$ multiplied by α. Hence, $|\mathbf{B}| = \alpha|\mathbf{A}|$.

Rule D: If two rows are interchanged, or two columns, the terms involved in the definition of determinant in Section 16.3 remain the same, except that the sign of each term is reversed. Showing this, however, involves a somewhat intricate argument, so we offer only this brief explanation.

Rule E: By using rule C, the factor of proportionality can be put outside the determinant. The determinant then has two equal rows (columns). If we interchange the two rows that are equal, the determinant will be exactly the same. But according to rule D, the determinant has changed its sign. Hence, $|\mathbf{A}| = -|\mathbf{A}|$, which means that $2|\mathbf{A}| = 0$, and so $|\mathbf{A}| = 0$.

Rule F: Symbolically, the proof of this rule is as follows, for the case when the scalar multiple α of row i is added to row j:

$$\sum(\pm)a_{1r_1}\ldots a_{ir_i}\ldots(a_{jr_j}+\alpha a_{ir_j})\ldots a_{nr_n}$$
$$=\sum(\pm)a_{1r_1}\ldots a_{ir_i}\ldots a_{jr_j}\ldots a_{nr_n}+\alpha\sum(\pm)a_{1r_1}\ldots a_{ir_i}\ldots a_{ir_j}\ldots a_{nr_n}$$
$$=|\mathbf{A}|+\alpha\cdot 0=|\mathbf{A}|$$

(The last sum is zero because it is equal to a determinant with rows i and j equal.)

Rule G: The proof of this rule for the case $n=2$ is the object of Problem 16.1.6. The case when $\mathbf{A}$ and $\mathbf{B}$ are both upper triangular is covered in Problem 16.3.2. One can prove the general case by using elementary row and column operations to convert $\mathbf{A}$ and $\mathbf{B}$ as well as $\mathbf{AB}$ to upper triangular form, but we omit the proof.

Rule H: The matrix $\alpha\mathbf{A}$ is obtained by multiplying *each* entry in $\mathbf{A}$ by α. By rule C, $|\alpha\mathbf{A}|$ is then equal to $\alpha^n|\mathbf{A}|$, because each of the n rows has α as a factor in each entry.

PROBLEMS FOR SECTION 16.4

1. Let $\mathbf{A}=\begin{pmatrix}1&2\\3&4\end{pmatrix}$, $\mathbf{B}=\begin{pmatrix}3&4\\5&6\end{pmatrix}$.

    (a) Calculate $\mathbf{AB}$, $\mathbf{BA}$, $\mathbf{A'B'}$, and $\mathbf{B'A'}$.

    (b) Show that $|\mathbf{A}|=|\mathbf{A'}|$ and $|\mathbf{AB}|=|\mathbf{A}|\cdot|\mathbf{B}|$. Is $|\mathbf{A'B'}|=|\mathbf{A'}|\cdot|\mathbf{B'}|$?

2. Let $\mathbf{A}=\begin{pmatrix}2&1&3\\1&0&1\\1&2&5\end{pmatrix}$. Write down $\mathbf{A'}$, then show that $|\mathbf{A}|=|\mathbf{A'}|$.

3. Evaluate the following determinants as simply as possible:

    (a) $\begin{vmatrix}3&0&1\\1&0&-1\\2&0&5\end{vmatrix}$ (b) $\begin{vmatrix}1&2&3&4\\0&-1&2&4\\0&0&3&-1\\-3&-6&-9&-12\end{vmatrix}$ (c) $\begin{vmatrix}a_1-x&a_2&a_3&a_4\\0&-x&0&0\\0&1&-x&0\\0&0&1&-x\end{vmatrix}$

4. Let $\mathbf{A}$ and $\mathbf{B}$ be 3×3 matrices with $|\mathbf{A}|=3$ and $|\mathbf{B}|=-4$. Where it is possible, determine the unique numerical value of $|\mathbf{AB}|$, $3|\mathbf{A}|$, $|-2\mathbf{B}|$, $|4\mathbf{A}|$, $|\mathbf{A}|+|\mathbf{B}|$, and $|\mathbf{A}+\mathbf{B}|$. Which, if any, have an undetermined numerical value?

5. If $\mathbf{A}=\begin{pmatrix}a&1&4\\2&1&a^2\\1&0&-3\end{pmatrix}$, calculate $\mathbf{A}^2$ and $|\mathbf{A}|$.

6. Prove that each of the following determinants is zero:

(a) $\begin{vmatrix} 1 & 2 & 3 \\ 2 & 4 & 5 \\ 3 & 6 & 8 \end{vmatrix}$ (b) $\begin{vmatrix} 1 & a & b+c \\ 1 & b & c+a \\ 1 & c & a+b \end{vmatrix}$ (c) $\begin{vmatrix} x-y & x-y & x^2-y^2 \\ 1 & 1 & x+y \\ y & 1 & x \end{vmatrix}$

7. Let $\mathbf{X} = \begin{pmatrix} 1 & 0 & 0 \\ 1 & 1 & 1 \\ 1 & 2 & 0 \\ 1 & 0 & 1 \end{pmatrix}$. Calculate $\mathbf{X}'\mathbf{X}$ and $|\mathbf{X}'\mathbf{X}|$.

8. If $\mathbf{A}_a = \begin{pmatrix} a & 2 & 2 \\ 2 & a^2+1 & 1 \\ 2 & 1 & 1 \end{pmatrix}$, calculate $|\mathbf{A}_a|$ and $|\mathbf{A}_1^6|$.

9. Show that an orthogonal matrix $\mathbf{P}$ (see Problem 15.5.7) must have determinant 1 or -1.

10. A square matrix $\mathbf{A}$ of order n is called **involutive** if $\mathbf{A}^2 = \mathbf{I}_n$.

(a) Show that the determinant of an involutive matrix is 1 or -1.

(b) Show that $\begin{pmatrix} -1 & 0 \\ 0 & -1 \end{pmatrix}$ and $\begin{pmatrix} a & 1-a^2 \\ 1 & -a \end{pmatrix}$ are involutive (for all a).

(c) Show that $\mathbf{A}$ is involutive $\iff (\mathbf{I}_n - \mathbf{A})(\mathbf{I}_n + \mathbf{A}) = \mathbf{0}$.

11. Determine which of the following equalities are (generally) true/false:

(a) $\begin{vmatrix} a & b \\ c & d \end{vmatrix} = -\begin{vmatrix} a & -b \\ c & -d \end{vmatrix} = 2\begin{vmatrix} \frac{1}{2}a & \frac{1}{2}b \\ \frac{1}{2}c & \frac{1}{2}d \end{vmatrix}$ (b) $\begin{vmatrix} a & b \\ c & d \end{vmatrix} = \begin{vmatrix} a & b \\ 0 & 0 \end{vmatrix} + \begin{vmatrix} 0 & 0 \\ c & d \end{vmatrix}$

(c) $\begin{vmatrix} a & b \\ c & d \end{vmatrix} = \begin{vmatrix} 0 & b \\ 0 & d \end{vmatrix} + \begin{vmatrix} a & b \\ c & d \end{vmatrix} = \begin{vmatrix} a & 0 & b \\ -1 & 1 & 0 \\ c & 0 & d \end{vmatrix}$ (d) $\begin{vmatrix} a & b \\ c & d \end{vmatrix} = \begin{vmatrix} a & b \\ c-2a & d-2b \end{vmatrix}$

12. Let $\mathbf{B}$ be a given $n \times n$ matrix. An $n \times n$ matrix $\mathbf{P}$ is said to *commute* with $\mathbf{B}$ if $\mathbf{BP} = \mathbf{PB}$. Show that if $\mathbf{P}$ and $\mathbf{Q}$ both commute with $\mathbf{B}$, then $\mathbf{PQ}$ will also commute with $\mathbf{B}$.

HARDER PROBLEMS

13. Without computing the determinants, show that

$$\begin{vmatrix} b^2+c^2 & ab & ac \\ ab & a^2+c^2 & bc \\ ac & bc & a^2+b^2 \end{vmatrix} = \begin{vmatrix} 0 & c & b \\ c & 0 & a \\ b & a & 0 \end{vmatrix}^2$$

(SM) **14.** Prove the following useful result: $D_n = \begin{vmatrix} a+b & a & \dots & a \\ a & a+b & \dots & a \\ \vdots & \vdots & \ddots & \vdots \\ a & a & \dots & a+b \end{vmatrix} = b^{n-1}(na+b)$.

(*Hint:* Study Example 2.)

16.5 Expansion by Cofactors

According to the definition in Section 16.3, the determinant of an $n \times n$ matrix $\mathbf{A} = (a_{ij})$ is a sum of $n!$ terms. Each term contains one element from each row and one element from each column. Consider in particular row i: pick out all the terms that have a_{i1} as a factor, then all the terms that have a_{i2} as a factor, and so on. Because all these terms have precisely one factor from row i, in this way we get all the terms of $|\mathbf{A}|$. So we can write

$$|\mathbf{A}| = a_{i1}C_{i1} + a_{i2}C_{i2} + \cdots + a_{ij}C_{ij} + \cdots + a_{in}C_{in} \tag{1}$$

This is called the *expansion of* $|\mathbf{A}|$ *in terms of the elements of the ith row.* The coefficients $C_{i1}, \ldots, C_{in}$ are the **cofactors** of the elements $a_{i1}, \ldots, a_{in}$, and equation (1) is called the *cofactor expansion of* $|\mathbf{A}|$ *along row i.*

Similarly, one has the *cofactor expansion of* $|\mathbf{A}|$ *down column j,* which is

$$|\mathbf{A}| = a_{1j}C_{1j} + a_{2j}C_{2j} + \cdots + a_{ij}C_{ij} + \cdots + a_{nj}C_{nj} \tag{2}$$

What makes expansions (1) and (2) extremely useful is that in general each cofactor C_{ij} can be found by applying the following procedure to the determinant $|\mathbf{A}|$: First, delete row i and column j to arrive at a determinant of order $n - 1$, which is called a **minor**. Second, multiply the minor by the factor $(-1)^{i+j}$. This gives the cofactor.

In symbols, the cofactor C_{ij} is given by

$$C_{ij} = (-1)^{i+j} \begin{vmatrix} a_{11} & \cdots & a_{1,j-1} & a_{1j} & a_{1,j+1} & \cdots & a_{1n} \\ a_{21} & \cdots & a_{2,j-1} & a_{2j} & a_{2,j+1} & \cdots & a_{2n} \\ \vdots & & \vdots & \vdots & \vdots & & \vdots \\ a_{i1} & \cdots & a_{i,j-1} & \boxed{a_{ij}} & a_{i,j+1} & \cdots & a_{in} \\ \vdots & & \vdots & \vdots & \vdots & & \vdots \\ a_{n1} & \cdots & a_{n,j-1} & a_{nj} & a_{n,j+1} & \cdots & a_{nn} \end{vmatrix} \tag{3}$$

where lines have been drawn through row i and column j, which are to be deleted from the matrix. We skip the proof. If we look back at (16.2.3), however, it confirms (3) in a special case. Indeed, put $|\mathbf{A}| = a_{11}C_{11} + a_{12}C_{12} + a_{13}C_{13}$. Then

$$C_{11} = (-1)^{1+1} \begin{vmatrix} a_{22} & a_{23} \\ a_{32} & a_{33} \end{vmatrix}, \quad C_{12} = (-1)^{1+2} \begin{vmatrix} a_{21} & a_{23} \\ a_{31} & a_{33} \end{vmatrix}, \quad C_{13} = (-1)^{1+3} \begin{vmatrix} a_{21} & a_{22} \\ a_{31} & a_{32} \end{vmatrix}$$

precisely in accordance with (16.2.3).

Generally, formula (3) is rather complicated. Test your understanding of it by studying the following example.

EXAMPLE 1   Check that the cofactor of the element c in the determinant

$$|\mathbf{A}| = \begin{vmatrix} 3 & 0 & 0 & 2 \\ 6 & 1 & \boxed{c} & 2 \\ -1 & 1 & 0 & 0 \\ 5 & 2 & 0 & 3 \end{vmatrix} \quad \text{is} \quad C_{23} = (-1)^{2+3} \begin{vmatrix} 3 & 0 & 2 \\ -1 & 1 & 0 \\ 5 & 2 & 3 \end{vmatrix}$$

Find the value of $|\mathbf{A}|$ by using (2) and Example 16.2.1.

Solution: Because the element c is in row 2 and column 3, its cofactor has been written correctly. To find the numerical value of $|\mathbf{A}|$ we use the cofactor expansion down its *third column* (because it has so many zeros). This yields

$$|\mathbf{A}| = a_{23}C_{23} = c\,(-1)^{2+3}\begin{vmatrix} 3 & 0 & 2 \\ -1 & 1 & 0 \\ 5 & 2 & 3 \end{vmatrix} = c\,(-1)(-5) = 5c$$

Example 1 shows a case in which expansion by cofactors is particularly simple because there are many zeros in the third column. If the zeros are not there initially, we can often create them by appealing to rule F in Theorem 16.4.1. Two examples illustrate the method.

EXAMPLE 2
$$\begin{vmatrix} 3 & -1 & 2 \\ 0 & -1 & -1 \\ 6 & 1 & 2 \end{vmatrix} \overset{-2}{\underset{\longleftarrow}{}} = \begin{vmatrix} 3 & -1 & 2 \\ 0 & -1 & -1 \\ 0 & 3 & -2 \end{vmatrix} \overset{(*)}{=} 3\begin{vmatrix} -1 & -1 \\ 3 & -2 \end{vmatrix} = 3(2+3) = 15$$

To derive the equality labelled $(*)$, expand by column 1.

EXAMPLE 3
$$\begin{vmatrix} 2 & 0 & 3 & -1 \\ 0 & 4 & 0 & 0 \\ 0 & 1 & -1 & 2 \\ 3 & 2 & 5 & -3 \end{vmatrix} \overset{(*)}{=} (-1)^{2+2} \cdot 4 \begin{vmatrix} 2 & 3 & -1 \\ 0 & -1 & 2 \\ 3 & 5 & -3 \end{vmatrix} \overset{-3/2}{\underset{\longleftarrow}{}}$$

$$= 4\begin{vmatrix} 2 & 3 & -1 \\ 0 & -1 & 2 \\ 0 & 1/2 & -3/2 \end{vmatrix} \overset{(**)}{=} 4 \cdot 2 \begin{vmatrix} -1 & 2 \\ 1/2 & -3/2 \end{vmatrix} = 8\left(\tfrac{3}{2} - \tfrac{2}{2}\right) = 4$$

For equality $(*)$, expand by row 2. For equality $(**)$, expand by column 1.

Expansion by Alien Cofactors

According to the cofactor expansions (1) and (2), if each element a_{ij} in any row (or column) of a determinant is multiplied by the corresponding cofactor C_{ij} and then all the products are added, the result is the value of the determinant. What happens if we multiply the elements of a row by the cofactors of a different (alien) row? Or the elements of a column by the cofactors of an alien column? Consider the following example.

EXAMPLE 4   If $\mathbf{A} = (a_{ij})_{3\times3}$, then the cofactor expansion of $|\mathbf{A}|$ along the second row is

$$|\mathbf{A}| = a_{21}C_{21} + a_{22}C_{22} + a_{23}C_{23}$$

Suppose we replace the elements a_{21}, a_{22}, and a_{23} by a, b, and c. Then C_{21}, C_{22}, and C_{23} remain unchanged, so the cofactor expansion of the new determinant along its second row is

$$\begin{vmatrix} a_{11} & a_{12} & a_{13} \\ a & b & c \\ a_{31} & a_{32} & a_{33} \end{vmatrix} = aC_{21} + bC_{22} + cC_{23} \tag{$*$}$$

In particular, if we replace a, b, and c by a_{11}, a_{12}, and a_{13}, or by a_{31}, a_{32}, and a_{33}, then the determinant in $(*)$ is 0 because two rows are equal. Hence,

$$a_{11}C_{21} + a_{12}C_{22} + a_{13}C_{23} = 0$$

$$a_{31}C_{21} + a_{32}C_{22} + a_{33}C_{23} = 0$$

That is, the sum of the products of the elements in either row 1 or row 3 multiplied by the cofactors of the elements in row 2 is zero.

Obviously, the argument used in this example can be generalized: If we multiply the elements of any row by the cofactors of an alien row, and then add the products, the result is 0. Similarly if we multiply the elements of a column by the cofactors of an alien column, then add.

We summarize all the results in this section in the following theorem:

THEOREM 16.5.1 (COFACTOR EXPANSION OF A DETERMINANT)

Let $\mathbf{A} = (a_{ij})_{n \times n}$. Suppose that the cofactors C_{ij} are defined as in (3). Then:

$$a_{i1}C_{i1} + a_{i2}C_{i2} + \cdots + a_{in}C_{in} = |\mathbf{A}|$$

$$a_{i1}C_{k1} + a_{i2}C_{k2} + \cdots + a_{in}C_{kn} = 0 \qquad (k \neq i)$$

$$a_{1j}C_{1j} + a_{2j}C_{2j} + \cdots + a_{nj}C_{nj} = |\mathbf{A}|$$

$$a_{1j}C_{1k} + a_{2j}C_{2k} + \cdots + a_{nj}C_{nk} = 0 \qquad (k \neq j)$$

Theorem 16.5.1 says that an expansion of a determinant by row i in terms of the cofactors of row k vanishes when $k \neq i$, and is equal to $|\mathbf{A}|$ if $k = i$. Likewise, an expansion by column j in terms of the cofactors of column k vanishes when $k \neq j$, and is equal to $|\mathbf{A}|$ if $k = j$.

PROBLEMS FOR SECTION 16.5

(SM) **1.** Calculate the following determinants:

(a) $\begin{vmatrix} 1 & 2 & 4 \\ 1 & 3 & 9 \\ 1 & 4 & 16 \end{vmatrix}$

(b) $\begin{vmatrix} 1 & 2 & 3 & 4 \\ 0 & -1 & 0 & 11 \\ 2 & -1 & 0 & 3 \\ -2 & 0 & -1 & 3 \end{vmatrix}$

(c) $\begin{vmatrix} 2 & 1 & 3 & 3 \\ 3 & 2 & 1 & 6 \\ 1 & 3 & 0 & 9 \\ 2 & 4 & 1 & 12 \end{vmatrix}$

2. Calculate the following determinants:

(a) $\begin{vmatrix} 0 & 0 & a \\ 0 & b & 0 \\ c & 0 & 0 \end{vmatrix}$

(b) $\begin{vmatrix} 0 & 0 & 0 & a \\ 0 & 0 & b & 0 \\ 0 & c & 0 & 0 \\ d & 0 & 0 & 0 \end{vmatrix}$

(c) $\begin{vmatrix} 0 & 0 & 0 & 0 & 1 \\ 0 & 0 & 0 & 5 & 1 \\ 0 & 0 & 3 & 1 & 2 \\ 0 & 4 & 0 & 3 & 4 \\ 6 & 2 & 3 & 1 & 2 \end{vmatrix}$

16.6   The Inverse of a Matrix

Suppose that α is a real number different from 0. Then there is a unique number α^{-1} with the property that $\alpha\alpha^{-1} = \alpha^{-1}\alpha = 1$. We call α^{-1} the (multiplicative) inverse of α. We saw in Section 15.4 that the identity matrix $\mathbf{I}$ (with 1's along the main diagonal and 0's elsewhere) is the matrix equivalent of 1 in the real number system.[3] This makes the following terminology seem natural.

Given a matrix $\mathbf{A}$, we say that $\mathbf{X}$ is an **inverse** of $\mathbf{A}$ if there exists a matrix $\mathbf{X}$ such that

$$\mathbf{AX} = \mathbf{XA} = \mathbf{I} \tag{1}$$

Then $\mathbf{A}$ is said to be **invertible**. Because $\mathbf{XA} = \mathbf{AX} = \mathbf{I}$, the matrix $\mathbf{A}$ is also an inverse of $\mathbf{X}$—that is, $\mathbf{A}$ and $\mathbf{X}$ are inverses of each other. Note that the two matrix products $\mathbf{AX}$ and $\mathbf{XA}$ are defined and equal only if $\mathbf{A}$ and $\mathbf{X}$ are square matrices of the same order. *Thus, only square matrices can have inverses.* But not even all square matrices have inverses, as (b) in the following example shows.

EXAMPLE 1   (a) Show that $\mathbf{A} = \begin{pmatrix} 5 & 6 \\ 5 & 10 \end{pmatrix}$ and $\mathbf{X} = \begin{pmatrix} 1/2 & -3/10 \\ -1/4 & 1/4 \end{pmatrix}$ are inverses of each other.

(b) Show that $\mathbf{A} = \begin{pmatrix} 1 & 0 \\ 0 & 0 \end{pmatrix}$ has no inverse.

Solution:

(a) $\begin{pmatrix} 5 & 6 \\ 5 & 10 \end{pmatrix}\begin{pmatrix} 1/2 & -3/10 \\ -1/4 & 1/4 \end{pmatrix} = \begin{pmatrix} 5/2 - 6/4 & -15/10 + 6/4 \\ 5/2 - 10/4 & -15/10 + 10/4 \end{pmatrix} = \begin{pmatrix} 1 & 0 \\ 0 & 1 \end{pmatrix}$

and likewise we verify that $\mathbf{XA} = \mathbf{I}$.

(b) Observe that for all real numbers x, y, z, and w,

$$\begin{pmatrix} 1 & 0 \\ 0 & 0 \end{pmatrix}\begin{pmatrix} x & y \\ z & w \end{pmatrix} = \begin{pmatrix} x & y \\ 0 & 0 \end{pmatrix}$$

So there is no way of choosing x, y, z, and w to make the product of these two matrices equal to $\mathbf{I}$. Thus, $\begin{pmatrix} 1 & 0 \\ 0 & 0 \end{pmatrix}$ has no inverse.

The following questions arise:

A. *Which matrices have inverses?*

B. *Can a given matrix have more than one inverse?*

C. *How do we find the inverse if it exists?*

As for question A, it is easy to find a *necessary* condition for a matrix $\mathbf{A}$ to have an inverse. In fact, from (1) and rule G in Theorem 16.4.1, it follows that $|\mathbf{AX}| = |\mathbf{A}| \cdot |\mathbf{X}| = |\mathbf{I}|$. Using

---

[3] From now on, we write $\mathbf{I}$ instead of $\mathbf{I}_n$ whenever the order n of the identity matrix seems obvious.

(16.3.4), we see that the identity matrix of any order has determinant 1. Thus, if $\mathbf{X}$ is an inverse of $\mathbf{A}$, then $|\mathbf{A}| \cdot |\mathbf{X}| = 1$. We conclude from this equation that $|\mathbf{A}| \neq 0$ is a necessary condition for $\mathbf{A}$ to have an inverse, because $|\mathbf{A}| = 0$ would lead to a contradiction.

As we shall see in the next section, the condition $|\mathbf{A}| \neq 0$ is also *sufficient* for $\mathbf{A}$ to have an inverse. Hence, for any square matrix $\mathbf{A}$,

$$\mathbf{A} \text{ has an inverse} \iff |\mathbf{A}| \neq 0 \tag{2}$$

A square matrix $\mathbf{A}$ is said to be **singular** if $|\mathbf{A}| = 0$ and **nonsingular** if $|\mathbf{A}| \neq 0$. According to (2), a matrix has an inverse if and only if it is nonsingular.

Concerning question B, the answer is no—a matrix cannot have more than one inverse. Indeed, suppose that $\mathbf{X}$ satisfies (1) and that $\mathbf{AY} = \mathbf{I}$ for some other square matrix $\mathbf{Y}$. Then

$$\mathbf{Y} = \mathbf{IY} = (\mathbf{XA})\mathbf{Y} = \mathbf{X}(\mathbf{AY}) = \mathbf{XI} = \mathbf{X}$$

A similar argument shows that if $\mathbf{YA} = \mathbf{I}$, then $\mathbf{Y} = \mathbf{X}$. *Thus, the inverse of $\mathbf{A}$ is unique if it exists.*

If the inverse of $\mathbf{A}$ exists, it is usually written $\mathbf{A}^{-1}$. Whereas for numbers we can write $a^{-1} = 1/a$, the symbol $\mathbf{I}/\mathbf{A}$ has *no* meaning. *There are no rules for dividing matrices.* Note also that even if the product $\mathbf{A}^{-1}\mathbf{B}$ is defined, it is usually quite different from $\mathbf{BA}^{-1}$ because matrix multiplication is not commutative, in general.

The full answer to question C is given in the next section. Here we only consider the case of 2×2 matrices.

EXAMPLE 2   Find the inverse of $\mathbf{A} = \begin{pmatrix} a & b \\ c & d \end{pmatrix}$ (when it exists).

Solution: We find a 2×2 matrix $\mathbf{X}$ such that $\mathbf{AX} = \mathbf{I}$, after which it is easy to check that $\mathbf{XA} = \mathbf{I}$. Solving $\mathbf{AX} = \mathbf{I}$ requires finding numbers x, y, z, and w such that

$$\begin{pmatrix} a & b \\ c & d \end{pmatrix} \begin{pmatrix} x & y \\ z & w \end{pmatrix} = \begin{pmatrix} 1 & 0 \\ 0 & 1 \end{pmatrix}$$

Matrix multiplication implies that

$$ax + bz = 1, \qquad ay + bw = 0$$
$$cx + dz = 0, \qquad cy + dw = 1$$

Note that we have two different systems of equations here. One is given by the two equations on the left, and the other by the two equations on the right. Both these systems have $\mathbf{A}$ as a common coefficient matrix. If $|\mathbf{A}| = ad - bc \neq 0$, solving the two pairs of simultaneous equations separately using Cramer's rule from Section 16.1 yields

$$x = \frac{d}{ad - bc}, \qquad z = \frac{-c}{ad - bc}, \qquad y = \frac{-b}{ad - bc}, \qquad w = \frac{a}{ad - bc}$$

Hence, we have proved the following result, assuming that $|\mathbf{A}| = ad - bc \neq 0$:

$$\mathbf{A} = \begin{pmatrix} a & b \\ c & d \end{pmatrix} \quad \Longrightarrow \quad \mathbf{A}^{-1} = \frac{1}{ad - bc} \begin{pmatrix} d & -b \\ -c & a \end{pmatrix} \tag{3}$$

Note that in the inverse matrix, the diagonal elements of the original 2×2 matrix are switched, whereas the off-diagonal elements just change sign.

For square matrices of order 3, one can use Cramer's rule (16.2.4) to derive a formula for the inverse. Again, the requirement for the inverse to exist is that the determinant of the coefficient matrix is not 0. Full details will be given in Section 16.7.

Some Useful Implications

If $\mathbf{A}^{-1}$ is the inverse of $\mathbf{A}$, then $\mathbf{A}^{-1}\mathbf{A} = \mathbf{I}$ and $\mathbf{A}\mathbf{A}^{-1} = \mathbf{I}$. Actually, each of these equations implies the other, in the sense that

$$\mathbf{A}\mathbf{X} = \mathbf{I} \quad \Longrightarrow \quad \mathbf{X} = \mathbf{A}^{-1} \tag{4}$$

$$\mathbf{Y}\mathbf{A} = \mathbf{I} \quad \Longrightarrow \quad \mathbf{Y} = \mathbf{A}^{-1} \tag{5}$$

To prove (4), suppose $\mathbf{A}\mathbf{X} = \mathbf{I}$. Then $|\mathbf{A}| \cdot |\mathbf{X}| = 1$, and so $|\mathbf{A}| \neq 0$. Hence, by (2), $\mathbf{A}^{-1}$ exists. Multiplying $\mathbf{A}\mathbf{X} = \mathbf{I}$ from the left by $\mathbf{A}^{-1}$ yields $\mathbf{X} = \mathbf{A}^{-1}$. The proof of (5) is almost the same.

Implications (4) and (5) are used repeatedly in proving properties of the inverse. Here are two examples.

EXAMPLE 3   Find the inverse of the $n \times n$ matrix $\mathbf{A}$ if $\mathbf{A} - \mathbf{A}^2 = \mathbf{I}$.

Solution: The matrix equation $\mathbf{A} - \mathbf{A}^2 = \mathbf{I}$ yields $\mathbf{A}(\mathbf{I} - \mathbf{A}) = \mathbf{I}$. But then it follows from (4) that $\mathbf{A}$ has the inverse $\mathbf{A}^{-1} = \mathbf{I} - \mathbf{A}$.

EXAMPLE 4   Let $\mathbf{B}$ be a $n \times n$ matrix such that $\mathbf{B}^2 = 3\mathbf{B}$. Prove that there exists a number s such that $\mathbf{I} + s\mathbf{B}$ is the inverse of $\mathbf{I} + \mathbf{B}$.

Solution: Because of (5), it suffices to find a number s such that $(\mathbf{I} + s\mathbf{B})(\mathbf{I} + \mathbf{B}) = \mathbf{I}$. Now,

$$(\mathbf{I} + s\mathbf{B})(\mathbf{I} + \mathbf{B}) = \mathbf{I}\mathbf{I} + \mathbf{I}\mathbf{B} + s\mathbf{B}\mathbf{I} + s\mathbf{B}^2 = \mathbf{I} + \mathbf{B} + s\mathbf{B} + 3s\mathbf{B} = \mathbf{I} + (1 + 4s)\mathbf{B}$$

which is equal to $\mathbf{I}$ provided $1 + 4s = 0$. The right choice of s is thus $s = -1/4$.

Properties of the Inverse

We shall now prove some useful rules for the inverse.

THEOREM 16.6.1 (PROPERTIES OF THE INVERSE)

Let $\mathbf{A}$ and $\mathbf{B}$ be invertible $n \times n$ matrices. Then:

(a) $\mathbf{A}^{-1}$ is invertible, and $(\mathbf{A}^{-1})^{-1} = \mathbf{A}$.

(b) $\mathbf{AB}$ is invertible, and $(\mathbf{AB})^{-1} = \mathbf{B}^{-1}\mathbf{A}^{-1}$.

(c) The transpose $\mathbf{A}'$ is invertible, and $(\mathbf{A}')^{-1} = (\mathbf{A}^{-1})'$.

(d) $(c\mathbf{A})^{-1} = c^{-1}\mathbf{A}^{-1}$ whenever c is a number $\neq 0$.

Proof: In each case, we use (4):

(a) We have $\mathbf{A}^{-1}\mathbf{A} = \mathbf{I}$, so $\mathbf{A} = (\mathbf{A}^{-1})^{-1}$.

(b) To prove that $\mathbf{X} = \mathbf{B}^{-1}\mathbf{A}^{-1}$ is the inverse of $\mathbf{AB}$, we just verify that $(\mathbf{AB})\mathbf{X}$ is equal to $\mathbf{I}$. In fact, $(\mathbf{AB})\mathbf{X} = (\mathbf{AB})(\mathbf{B}^{-1}\mathbf{A}^{-1}) = \mathbf{A}(\mathbf{BB}^{-1})\mathbf{A}^{-1} = \mathbf{AIA}^{-1} = \mathbf{AA}^{-1} = \mathbf{I}$.

(c) Applying rule (15.5.2)(d) with $\mathbf{B} = \mathbf{A}^{-1}$ gives $(\mathbf{A}^{-1})'\mathbf{A}' = (\mathbf{AA}^{-1})' = \mathbf{I}' = \mathbf{I}$. By (5), it follows that $(\mathbf{A}')^{-1} = (\mathbf{A}^{-1})'$.

(d) Here rule (15.4.4) implies that $(c\mathbf{A})(c^{-1}\mathbf{A}^{-1}) = cc^{-1}\mathbf{AA}^{-1} = 1 \cdot \mathbf{I} = \mathbf{I}$, so $c^{-1}\mathbf{A}^{-1} = (c\mathbf{A})^{-1}$. ∎

NOTE 1 It is important to think carefully through the implications of the four rules in Theorem 16.6.1 and to understand their uses. A somewhat dramatic but possibly mythical story might help you to appreciate rule (c). Some decades ago a team of (human) calculators was working in a central bureau of statistics. After 3 weeks of hard work, they finally found the inverse $\mathbf{A}^{-1}$ of a 20×20 matrix $\mathbf{A}$. Then the boss came along and said: "Sorry, I was really interested in the inverse of the transpose of $\mathbf{A}$". Panic—until they realized that property (c) would save them from having to redo all the calculations. They simply transposed the inverse matrix that it had taken 3 weeks to find, because according to (c), the inverse of the transpose is the transpose of the inverse.

NOTE 2 Suppose that $\mathbf{A}$ is invertible and also symmetric—that is, $\mathbf{A}' = \mathbf{A}$. Then rule (c) implies that $(\mathbf{A}^{-1})' = (\mathbf{A}')^{-1} = \mathbf{A}^{-1}$, so $\mathbf{A}^{-1}$ is symmetric. *The inverse of a symmetric matrix is symmetric.*

NOTE 3 Rule (b) can be extended to products of several matrices. For instance, if $\mathbf{A}$, $\mathbf{B}$, and $\mathbf{C}$ are all invertible $n \times n$ matrices, then

$$(\mathbf{ABC})^{-1} = [(\mathbf{AB})\mathbf{C}]^{-1} = \mathbf{C}^{-1}(\mathbf{AB})^{-1} = \mathbf{C}^{-1}(\mathbf{B}^{-1}\mathbf{A}^{-1}) = \mathbf{C}^{-1}\mathbf{B}^{-1}\mathbf{A}^{-1}$$

where rule (b) has been used twice. Note the assumption in (b) that $\mathbf{A}$ and $\mathbf{B}$ are both $n \times n$ matrices. In statistics and econometrics, we often consider products of the form $\mathbf{XX}'$, where $\mathbf{X}$ is $n \times m$, with $n \neq m$. Then $\mathbf{XX}'$ is $n \times n$. If the determinant $|\mathbf{XX}'|$ is not 0, then $(\mathbf{XX}')^{-1}$ exists, but (b) does not apply because $\mathbf{X}^{-1}$ and $\mathbf{X}'^{-1}$ are only defined if $n = m$.

NOTE 4 It is a common fallacy to misinterpret (d). For instance, a correct application of (d) yields $\left(\frac{1}{2}\mathbf{A}\right)^{-1} = 2\mathbf{A}^{-1}$.

Solving Equations by Matrix Inversion

Let $\mathbf{A}$ be any $n \times n$ matrix. If $\mathbf{B}$ is an arbitrary matrix, we consider whether there are matrices $\mathbf{X}$ and $\mathbf{Y}$ of suitable order such that

$$(*) \quad \mathbf{AX} = \mathbf{B} \qquad\qquad (**) \quad \mathbf{YA} = \mathbf{B}$$

In case $(*)$, the matrix $\mathbf{B}$ must have n rows, while in case $(**)$, $\mathbf{B}$ must have n columns. Provided these conditions are satisfied, we have the following result:

THEOREM 16.6.2

Provided that $|\mathbf{A}| \neq 0$, one has:

$$\mathbf{AX} = \mathbf{B} \iff \mathbf{X} = \mathbf{A}^{-1}\mathbf{B} \tag{6}$$

$$\mathbf{YA} = \mathbf{B} \iff \mathbf{Y} = \mathbf{BA}^{-1} \tag{7}$$

Proof: Provided that $|\mathbf{A}| \neq 0$, we can multiply each side of the equation $\mathbf{AX} = \mathbf{B}$ in (6) on the left by $\mathbf{A}^{-1}$. This yields $\mathbf{A}^{-1}(\mathbf{AX}) = \mathbf{A}^{-1}\mathbf{B}$. Because $(\mathbf{A}^{-1}\mathbf{A})\mathbf{X} = \mathbf{IX} = \mathbf{X}$, we conclude that $\mathbf{X} = \mathbf{A}^{-1}\mathbf{B}$ is the only possible solution of the equation. On the other hand, by substituting $\mathbf{X} = \mathbf{A}^{-1}\mathbf{B}$ into $\mathbf{AX} = \mathbf{B}$, we see that it really satisfies the equation.

The proof of (7) is similar—postmultiply each side of $\mathbf{YA} = \mathbf{B}$ by $\mathbf{A}^{-1}$. ∎

EXAMPLE 5 Solve the following system of equations by using Theorem 16.6.2:

$$2x + y = 3$$
$$2x + 2y = 4$$

Solution: Suppose we define the matrices

$$\mathbf{A} = \begin{pmatrix} 2 & 1 \\ 2 & 2 \end{pmatrix}, \qquad \mathbf{x} = \begin{pmatrix} x \\ y \end{pmatrix}, \qquad \mathbf{b} = \begin{pmatrix} 3 \\ 4 \end{pmatrix}$$

Then the system is equivalent to the matrix equation $\mathbf{Ax} = \mathbf{b}$. Because $|\mathbf{A}| = 2 \neq 0$, matrix $\mathbf{A}$ has an inverse, and according to Theorem 16.6.2, $\mathbf{x} = \mathbf{A}^{-1}\mathbf{b}$. Hence

$$\begin{pmatrix} x \\ y \end{pmatrix} = \mathbf{A}^{-1}\begin{pmatrix} 3 \\ 4 \end{pmatrix} = \begin{pmatrix} 1 & -1/2 \\ -1 & 1 \end{pmatrix}\begin{pmatrix} 3 \\ 4 \end{pmatrix} = \begin{pmatrix} 1 \\ 1 \end{pmatrix}$$

where we have used (3) to find $\mathbf{A}^{-1}$. The solution is therefore $x = 1$, $y = 1$. (Check by substitution that this really is the correct solution. Clearly, solving by systematic elimination is easier.)

PROBLEMS FOR SECTION 16.6

1. Prove that: (a) $\begin{pmatrix} 3 & 0 \\ 2 & -1 \end{pmatrix}^{-1} = \begin{pmatrix} 1/3 & 0 \\ 2/3 & -1 \end{pmatrix}$ (b) $\begin{pmatrix} 1 & 1 & -3 \\ 2 & 1 & -3 \\ 2 & 2 & 1 \end{pmatrix}^{-1} = \begin{pmatrix} -1 & 1 & 0 \\ 8/7 & -1 & 3/7 \\ -2/7 & 0 & 1/7 \end{pmatrix}$

2. Find numbers a and b that make $\mathbf{A}$ the inverse of $\mathbf{B}$ when

$$\mathbf{A} = \begin{pmatrix} 2 & -1 & -1 \\ a & 1/4 & b \\ 1/8 & 1/8 & -1/8 \end{pmatrix} \quad \text{and} \quad \mathbf{B} = \begin{pmatrix} 1 & 2 & 4 \\ 0 & 1 & 6 \\ 1 & 3 & 2 \end{pmatrix}$$

3. Solve the following systems of equations by using Theorem 16.6.2. (See Example 5.)

(a) $\begin{aligned} 2x - 3y &= 3 \\ 3x - 4y &= 5 \end{aligned}$ (b) $\begin{aligned} 2x - 3y &= 8 \\ 3x - 4y &= 11 \end{aligned}$ (c) $\begin{aligned} 2x - 3y &= 0 \\ 3x - 4y &= 0 \end{aligned}$

4. Let $\mathbf{A} = \dfrac{1}{2}\begin{pmatrix} -1 & -\sqrt{3} \\ \sqrt{3} & -1 \end{pmatrix}$. Show that $\mathbf{A}^3 = \mathbf{I}_2$. Use this to find $\mathbf{A}^{-1}$.

5. (a) Given $\mathbf{A} = \begin{pmatrix} 0 & 1 & 0 \\ 0 & 1 & 1 \\ 1 & 0 & 1 \end{pmatrix}$, calculate $|\mathbf{A}|$, $\mathbf{A}^2$, $\mathbf{A}^3$, and $\mathbf{A}^3 - 2\mathbf{A}^2 + \mathbf{A} - \mathbf{I}_3$. Use the last calculation to show that $\mathbf{A}$ has an inverse and $\mathbf{A}^{-1} = (\mathbf{A} - \mathbf{I}_3)^2$.

   (b) Find a matrix $\mathbf{P}$ such that $\mathbf{P}^2 = \mathbf{A}$. Are there other matrices with this property?

6. (a) Let $\mathbf{A} = \begin{pmatrix} 2 & 1 & 4 \\ 0 & -1 & 3 \end{pmatrix}$. Calculate $\mathbf{AA}'$, $|\mathbf{AA}'|$, and $(\mathbf{AA}')^{-1}$.

   (b) The matrices $\mathbf{AA}'$ and $(\mathbf{AA}')^{-1}$ in part (a) are both symmetric. Is this a coincidence?

7. (a) If $\mathbf{A}$, $\mathbf{P}$, and $\mathbf{D}$ are square matrices such that $\mathbf{A} = \mathbf{PDP}^{-1}$, show that $\mathbf{A}^2 = \mathbf{PD}^2\mathbf{P}^{-1}$.

   (b) Show by induction that $\mathbf{A}^m = \mathbf{PD}^m\mathbf{P}^{-1}$ for any positive integer m.

(SM) 8. Given $\mathbf{B} = \begin{pmatrix} -1/2 & 5 \\ 1/4 & -1/2 \end{pmatrix}$, calculate $\mathbf{B}^2 + \mathbf{B}$, $\mathbf{B}^3 - 2\mathbf{B} + \mathbf{I}$, and then find $\mathbf{B}^{-1}$.

9. Suppose that $\mathbf{X}$ is an $m \times n$ matrix and that $|\mathbf{X}'\mathbf{X}| \neq 0$. Show that the matrix

$$\mathbf{A} = \mathbf{I}_m - \mathbf{X}(\mathbf{X}'\mathbf{X})^{-1}\mathbf{X}'$$

is idempotent—that is, $\mathbf{A}^2 = \mathbf{A}$. (See Problem 15.4.6.)

10. Given $\mathbf{A} = \begin{pmatrix} -2 & 0 & 1 \\ 1 & -1 & 5 \end{pmatrix}$, $\mathbf{B} = \begin{pmatrix} 3 & 1 \\ 0 & 1 \\ -1 & 2 \end{pmatrix}$, $\mathbf{C} = \begin{pmatrix} 1 & 2 \\ 3 & 4 \end{pmatrix}$, $\mathbf{D} = \begin{pmatrix} -9 & 3 \\ -8 & 17 \end{pmatrix}$.
    Find a matrix $\mathbf{X}$ that satisfies $\mathbf{AB} + \mathbf{CX} = \mathbf{D}$.

11. (a) Let $\mathbf{C}$ be an $n \times n$ matrix that satisfies $\mathbf{C}^2 + \mathbf{C} = \mathbf{I}$. Show that $\mathbf{C}^{-1} = \mathbf{I} + \mathbf{C}$.

    (b) Show that $\mathbf{C}^3 = -\mathbf{I} + 2\mathbf{C}$ and $\mathbf{C}^4 = 2\mathbf{I} - 3\mathbf{C}$.

16.7 A General Formula for the Inverse

The previous section presents the most important facts about the inverse and its properties. As such, it contains "what every economist should know". It is less important for most economists to know much about how to calculate the inverses of large matrices, because powerful computer programs are available.

Nevertheless, this section presents an explicit formula for the inverse of any nonsingular $n \times n$ matrix $\mathbf{A}$. Though this formula is extremely inefficient for computing inverses of large matrices, it does have theoretical interest. The key to this formula are the rules for the cofactor expansion of determinants.

Let $C_{11}, \ldots, C_{nn}$ denote the cofactors of the elements in $\mathbf{A}$. By Theorem 16.5.1, cofactor expansion yields n^2 equations of the form

$$a_{i1}C_{k1} + a_{i2}C_{k2} + \cdots + a_{in}C_{kn} = \begin{cases} |\mathbf{A}| & \text{if } i = k \\ 0 & \text{if } i \neq k \end{cases} \tag{*}$$

for $i, k = 1, \ldots, n$. The sums on the left-hand side look very much like those appearing in matrix products. In fact, the n^2 different equations in $(*)$ reduce to the single matrix equation

$$\begin{pmatrix} a_{11} & a_{12} & \cdots & a_{1n} \\ \vdots & \vdots & & \vdots \\ a_{i1} & a_{i2} & \cdots & a_{in} \\ \vdots & \vdots & & \vdots \\ a_{n1} & a_{n2} & \cdots & a_{nn} \end{pmatrix} \begin{pmatrix} C_{11} & \cdots & C_{k1} & \cdots & C_{n1} \\ C_{12} & \cdots & C_{k2} & \cdots & C_{n2} \\ \vdots & & \vdots & & \vdots \\ C_{1n} & \cdots & C_{kn} & \cdots & C_{nn} \end{pmatrix} = \begin{pmatrix} |\mathbf{A}| & 0 & \cdots & 0 \\ 0 & |\mathbf{A}| & \cdots & 0 \\ \vdots & \vdots & \ddots & \vdots \\ 0 & 0 & \cdots & |\mathbf{A}| \end{pmatrix}$$

Here the matrix on the right-hand equals $|\mathbf{A}| \cdot \mathbf{I}_n$. Let $\mathbf{C}^+ = (C_{ij})$ denote the matrix of cofactors. Then the second matrix in the product on the left-hand side has its row and column indices interchanged. Thus, it is the *transpose* $(\mathbf{C}^+)'$ of that matrix, which is called the **adjoint** of $\mathbf{A}$, and denoted by adj($\mathbf{A}$). Thus,

$$\text{adj}(\mathbf{A}) = (\mathbf{C}^+)' = \begin{pmatrix} C_{11} & \cdots & C_{k1} & \cdots & C_{n1} \\ C_{12} & \cdots & C_{k2} & \cdots & C_{n2} \\ \vdots & & \vdots & & \vdots \\ C_{1n} & \cdots & C_{kn} & \cdots & C_{nn} \end{pmatrix} \tag{1}$$

The previous equation, therefore, can be written as $\mathbf{A} \, \text{adj}(\mathbf{A}) = |\mathbf{A}| \cdot \mathbf{I}$. In case $|\mathbf{A}| \neq 0$, this evidently implies that $\mathbf{A}^{-1} = (1/|\mathbf{A}|) \cdot \text{adj}(\mathbf{A})$. We have proved the general formula for the inverse:

THEOREM 16.7.1 (GENERAL FORMULA FOR THE INVERSE)

Any square matrix $\mathbf{A} = (a_{ij})_{n \times n}$ with determinant $|\mathbf{A}| \neq 0$ has a unique inverse $\mathbf{A}^{-1}$ satisfying $\mathbf{A}\mathbf{A}^{-1} = \mathbf{A}^{-1}\mathbf{A} = \mathbf{I}$. This is given by

$$\mathbf{A}^{-1} = \frac{1}{|\mathbf{A}|} \cdot \text{adj}(\mathbf{A})$$

If $|\mathbf{A}| = 0$, then there is no matrix $\mathbf{X}$ such that $\mathbf{A}\mathbf{X} = \mathbf{X}\mathbf{A} = \mathbf{I}$.

EXAMPLE 1   Let $\mathbf{A} = \begin{pmatrix} 2 & 3 & 4 \\ 4 & 3 & 1 \\ 1 & 2 & 4 \end{pmatrix}$. Show that $\mathbf{A}$ has an inverse and find the inverse.

Solution: According to Theorem 16.7.1, $\mathbf{A}$ has an inverse if and only if $|\mathbf{A}| \neq 0$. Here we find that $|\mathbf{A}| = -5$, so the inverse exists. The cofactors are

$$C_{11} = \begin{vmatrix} 3 & 1 \\ 2 & 4 \end{vmatrix} = 10, \quad C_{12} = -\begin{vmatrix} 4 & 1 \\ 1 & 4 \end{vmatrix} = -15, \quad C_{13} = \begin{vmatrix} 4 & 3 \\ 1 & 2 \end{vmatrix} = 5$$

$$C_{21} = -\begin{vmatrix} 3 & 4 \\ 2 & 4 \end{vmatrix} = -4, \quad C_{22} = \begin{vmatrix} 2 & 4 \\ 1 & 4 \end{vmatrix} = 4, \quad C_{23} = -\begin{vmatrix} 2 & 3 \\ 1 & 2 \end{vmatrix} = -1$$

$$C_{31} = \begin{vmatrix} 3 & 4 \\ 3 & 1 \end{vmatrix} = -9, \quad C_{32} = -\begin{vmatrix} 2 & 4 \\ 4 & 1 \end{vmatrix} = 14, \quad C_{33} = \begin{vmatrix} 2 & 3 \\ 4 & 3 \end{vmatrix} = -6$$

Hence, the inverse of **A** is

$$\mathbf{A}^{-1} = \frac{1}{|\mathbf{A}|} \begin{pmatrix} C_{11} & C_{21} & C_{31} \\ C_{12} & C_{22} & C_{32} \\ C_{13} & C_{23} & C_{33} \end{pmatrix} = -\frac{1}{5} \begin{pmatrix} 10 & -4 & -9 \\ -15 & 4 & 14 \\ 5 & -1 & -6 \end{pmatrix}$$

(Check the result by showing that $\mathbf{A}\mathbf{A}^{-1} = \mathbf{I}$.)

Finding Inverses by Elementary Row Operations

Theorem 16.7.1 presented a general formula for the inverse of a nonsingular matrix. Although this formula is important theoretically, it is computationally useless for matrices much larger than 2×2. An efficient way of finding the inverse of an invertible $n \times n$ matrix **A** is based on using elementary operations in a systematic way: First form the $n \times 2n$ matrix $(\mathbf{A} : \mathbf{I})$ by writing down the n columns of **A** followed by the n columns of **I**. Then apply elementary row operations to this matrix in order to transform it to an $n \times 2n$ matrix $(\mathbf{I} : \mathbf{B})$ whose first n columns are all the columns of **I**. It will follow that $\mathbf{B} = \mathbf{A}^{-1}$. If it is impossible to perform such row operations, then **A** has no inverse. The method is illustrated by the following example.

EXAMPLE 2   Find the inverse of $\mathbf{A} = \begin{pmatrix} 1 & 3 & 3 \\ 1 & 3 & 4 \\ 1 & 4 & 3 \end{pmatrix}$.

Solution: First, write down the 3×6 matrix whose first three columns are the columns of **A** and whose next three columns are the columns of the 3×3 identity matrix:

$$\begin{pmatrix} 1 & 3 & 3 & \vdots & 1 & 0 & 0 \\ 1 & 3 & 4 & \vdots & 0 & 1 & 0 \\ 1 & 4 & 3 & \vdots & 0 & 0 & 1 \end{pmatrix}$$

The idea is now to use elementary operations on this matrix so that, in the end, the three first columns constitute an identity matrix. Then the last three columns constitute the inverse of **A**.

To start, we multiply the first row by -1 and add the result to the second row. This gives a zero in the second row and the first column. You should be able then to understand the other operations used and why they are chosen.

$$\begin{pmatrix} 1 & 3 & 3 & \vdots & 1 & 0 & 0 \\ 1 & 3 & 4 & \vdots & 0 & 1 & 0 \\ 1 & 4 & 3 & \vdots & 0 & 0 & 1 \end{pmatrix} \begin{matrix} -1 \\ \hookleftarrow \end{matrix} \sim \begin{pmatrix} 1 & 3 & 3 & \vdots & 1 & 0 & 0 \\ 0 & 0 & 1 & \vdots & -1 & 1 & 0 \\ 1 & 4 & 3 & \vdots & 0 & 0 & 1 \end{pmatrix} \begin{matrix} -1 \\ \hookleftarrow \end{matrix}$$

$$\sim \begin{pmatrix} 1 & 3 & 3 & \vdots & 1 & 0 & 0 \\ 0 & 0 & 1 & \vdots & -1 & 1 & 0 \\ 0 & 1 & 0 & \vdots & -1 & 0 & 1 \end{pmatrix} \begin{matrix} \\ -3 \end{matrix} \sim \begin{pmatrix} 1 & 0 & 3 & \vdots & 4 & 0 & -3 \\ 0 & 0 & 1 & \vdots & -1 & 1 & 0 \\ 0 & 1 & 0 & \vdots & -1 & 0 & 1 \end{pmatrix} \begin{matrix} \hookleftarrow \\ -3 \end{matrix}$$

$$\sim \begin{pmatrix} 1 & 0 & 0 & \vdots & 7 & -3 & -3 \\ 0 & 0 & 1 & \vdots & -1 & 1 & 0 \\ 0 & 1 & 0 & \vdots & -1 & 0 & 1 \end{pmatrix} \hookleftarrow \sim \begin{pmatrix} 1 & 0 & 0 & \vdots & 7 & -3 & -3 \\ 0 & 1 & 0 & \vdots & -1 & 0 & 1 \\ 0 & 0 & 1 & \vdots & -1 & 1 & 0 \end{pmatrix}$$

We conclude that

$$\mathbf{A}^{-1} = \begin{pmatrix} 7 & -3 & -3 \\ -1 & 0 & 1 \\ -1 & 1 & 0 \end{pmatrix}$$

(Check that $\mathbf{AA}^{-1} = \mathbf{I}$.)

PROBLEMS FOR SECTION 16.7

(SM) 1. Use Theorem 16.7.1 to calculate the inverses of the following matrices, if they exist:

(a) $\mathbf{A} = \begin{pmatrix} 2 & 3 \\ 4 & 5 \end{pmatrix}$ (b) $\mathbf{B} = \begin{pmatrix} 1 & 0 & 2 \\ 2 & -1 & 0 \\ 0 & 2 & -1 \end{pmatrix}$ (c) $\mathbf{C} = \begin{pmatrix} 1 & 0 & 0 \\ -3 & -2 & 1 \\ 4 & -16 & 8 \end{pmatrix}$

2. Find the inverse of $\mathbf{A} = \begin{pmatrix} -2 & 3 & 2 \\ 6 & 0 & 3 \\ 4 & 1 & -1 \end{pmatrix}$.

(SM) 3. Let $\mathbf{A} = \begin{pmatrix} 0.2 & 0.6 & 0.2 \\ 0 & 0.2 & 0.4 \\ 0.2 & 0.2 & 0 \end{pmatrix}$. Find $(\mathbf{I} - \mathbf{A})^{-1}$.

(SM) 4. Repeated observations of an empirical phenomenon lead to p different systems of equations

$$
\begin{aligned}
a_{11}x_1 + \cdots + a_{1n}x_n &= b_{1k} \\
&\cdots\cdots\cdots\cdots\cdots\cdots \qquad (k = 1, \ldots, p) \qquad (*) \\
a_{n1}x_1 + \cdots + a_{nn}x_n &= b_{nk}
\end{aligned}
$$

which all share the same $n \times n$ coefficient matrix (a_{ij}). Explain how to find the solutions $(x_{k1}, \ldots, x_{kn})$ $(k = 1, \ldots, p)$ of all the systems simultaneously by using row operations to get

$$\begin{pmatrix} a_{11} & \cdots & a_{1n} & b_{11} & \cdots & b_{1p} \\ \vdots & \ddots & \vdots & \vdots & & \vdots \\ a_{n1} & \cdots & a_{nn} & b_{n1} & \cdots & b_{np} \end{pmatrix} \sim \begin{pmatrix} 1 & \cdots & 0 & b_{11}^* & \cdots & b_{1p}^* \\ \vdots & \ddots & \vdots & \vdots & & \vdots \\ 0 & \cdots & 1 & b_{1n}^* & \cdots & b_{np}^* \end{pmatrix}$$

What then is the solution of the system of equations $(*)$ for $k = r$?

(SM) 5. Use the method in Example 2 to calculate the inverses (provided they exist) of the following matrices (check each result by verifying that $\mathbf{AA}^{-1} = \mathbf{I}$).

(a) $\mathbf{A} = \begin{pmatrix} 1 & 2 \\ 3 & 4 \end{pmatrix}$ (b) $\mathbf{A} = \begin{pmatrix} 1 & 2 & 3 \\ 2 & 4 & 5 \\ 3 & 5 & 6 \end{pmatrix}$ (c) $\mathbf{A} = \begin{pmatrix} 3 & 2 & -1 \\ -1 & 5 & 8 \\ -9 & -6 & 3 \end{pmatrix}$

16.8 Cramer's Rule

Cramer's rule for solving n linear equations in n unknowns is a direct generalization of the same rule for systems of equations with 2 or 3 unknowns. Consider the system

$$
\begin{aligned}
a_{11}x_1 + a_{12}x_2 + \cdots + a_{1n}x_n &= b_1 \\
a_{21}x_1 + a_{22}x_2 + \cdots + a_{2n}x_n &= b_2 \\
&\cdots\cdots\cdots\cdots\cdots\cdots\cdots \\
a_{n1}x_1 + a_{n2}x_2 + \cdots + a_{nn}x_n &= b_n
\end{aligned}
\tag{1}
$$

Let D_j denote the determinant obtained from $|\mathbf{A}|$ by replacing the jth column vector with the column vector whose components are $b_1, b_2, \ldots, b_n$. Thus,

$$
D_j =
\begin{vmatrix}
a_{11} & \cdots & a_{1j-1} & b_1 & a_{1j+1} & \cdots & a_{1n} \\
a_{21} & \cdots & a_{2j-1} & b_2 & a_{2j+1} & \cdots & a_{2n} \\
\vdots & & \vdots & \vdots & \vdots & & \vdots \\
a_{n1} & \cdots & a_{nj-1} & b_n & a_{nj+1} & \cdots & a_{nn}
\end{vmatrix},
\qquad j = 1, \ldots, n
\tag{2}
$$

The cofactor expansion of D_j down its jth column gives

$$
D_j = C_{1j}b_1 + C_{2j}b_2 + \cdots + C_{nj}b_n
\tag{3}
$$

where the cofactors C_{ij} are given by (16.5.3). Now we have the following result:

THEOREM 16.8.1 (CRAMER'S RULE)

The general linear system of equations (1) with n equations and n unknowns has a unique solution if and only if $\mathbf{A}$ is nonsingular ($|\mathbf{A}| \neq 0$). The solution is

$$
x_1 = \frac{D_1}{|\mathbf{A}|}, \quad x_2 = \frac{D_2}{|\mathbf{A}|}, \quad \ldots, \quad x_n = \frac{D_n}{|\mathbf{A}|}
\tag{4}
$$

where $D_1, D_2, \ldots, D_n$ are defined by (2).

Proof of the "if" part: Suppose $|\mathbf{A}| \neq 0$. System (1) can be written in the form

$$
\begin{pmatrix}
a_{11} & a_{12} & \cdots & a_{1n} \\
a_{21} & a_{22} & \cdots & a_{2n} \\
\vdots & \vdots & \ddots & \vdots \\
a_{n1} & a_{n2} & \cdots & a_{nn}
\end{pmatrix}
\begin{pmatrix}
x_1 \\ x_2 \\ \vdots \\ x_n
\end{pmatrix}
=
\begin{pmatrix}
b_1 \\ b_2 \\ \vdots \\ b_n
\end{pmatrix}
$$

Using the formula for the inverse of the coefficient matrix yields

$$
\begin{pmatrix}
x_1 \\ x_2 \\ \vdots \\ x_n
\end{pmatrix}
= \frac{1}{|\mathbf{A}|}
\begin{pmatrix}
C_{11} & C_{21} & \cdots & C_{n1} \\
C_{12} & C_{22} & \cdots & C_{n2} \\
\vdots & \vdots & \ddots & \vdots \\
C_{1n} & C_{2n} & \cdots & C_{nn}
\end{pmatrix}
\begin{pmatrix}
b_1 \\ b_2 \\ \vdots \\ b_n
\end{pmatrix}
\tag{$*$}
$$

where the cofactors C_{ij} are given by (16.5.3). From (∗), we have

$$x_j = \frac{1}{|\mathbf{A}|}[C_{1j}b_1 + C_{2j}b_2 + \cdots + C_{nj}b_n] = \frac{D_j}{|\mathbf{A}|}, \qquad j = 1, 2, \ldots, n$$

where the last equality follows from the previous equation (3). This proves (4).
The "only if" part will be discussed in Note 2 below, and proved in FMEA.   ∎

EXAMPLE 1   Find the solutions of the following system for all values of p.

$$\begin{aligned}
px + y &= 1 \\
x - y + z &= 0 \\
2y - z &= 3
\end{aligned}$$

Solution: The coefficient matrix has determinant

$$|\mathbf{A}| = \begin{vmatrix} p & 1 & 0 \\ 1 & -1 & 1 \\ 0 & 2 & -1 \end{vmatrix} = 1 - p$$

According to Theorem 16.8.1, the system has a unique solution if $1 - p \neq 0$—that is, if $p \neq 1$. In this case, the determinants in (2) are

$$D_1 = \begin{vmatrix} 1 & 1 & 0 \\ 0 & -1 & 1 \\ 3 & 2 & -1 \end{vmatrix}, \qquad D_2 = \begin{vmatrix} p & 1 & 0 \\ 1 & 0 & 1 \\ 0 & 3 & -1 \end{vmatrix}, \qquad D_3 = \begin{vmatrix} p & 1 & 1 \\ 1 & -1 & 0 \\ 0 & 2 & 3 \end{vmatrix}$$

whose numerical values are $D_1 = 2$, $D_2 = 1 - 3p$, and $D_3 = -1 - 3p$. Then (4) yields for $p \neq 1$

$$x = \frac{D_1}{|\mathbf{A}|} = \frac{2}{1 - p}, \qquad y = \frac{D_2}{|\mathbf{A}|} = \frac{1 - 3p}{1 - p}, \qquad z = \frac{D_3}{|\mathbf{A}|} = \frac{-1 - 3p}{1 - p}$$

On the other hand, in case $p = 1$, the first equation becomes $x + y = 1$. Yet adding the last two of the original equations implies that $x + y = 3$. There is no solution to these two contradictory equations in case $p = 1$.   ▌

NOTE 1 It might be instructive to solve this problem by using Gaussian elimination, starting by interchanging the first two equations.

Homogeneous Systems of Equations

Consider the special case in which the right-hand side of the system of equations (1) consists only of zeros. The system is then called **homogeneous**. A homogeneous system will always have the so-called **trivial solution** $x_1 = x_2 = \cdots = x_n = 0$. In many problems, one is interested in knowing when a homogeneous system has **nontrivial** solutions.

THEOREM 16.8.2 (NONTRIVIAL SOLUTIONS OF HOMOGENEOUS SYSTEMS)

The homogeneous linear system of equations with n equations and n unknowns

$$a_{11}x_1 + a_{12}x_2 + \cdots + a_{1n}x_n = 0$$
$$a_{21}x_1 + a_{22}x_2 + \cdots + a_{2n}x_n = 0$$
$$\cdots\cdots\cdots\cdots\cdots\cdots\cdots\cdots\cdots\cdots\cdots\cdots\cdots \tag{5}$$
$$a_{n1}x_1 + a_{n2}x_2 + \cdots + a_{nn}x_n = 0$$

has nontrivial solutions if and only if the coefficient matrix $\mathbf{A} = \left(a_{ij}\right)_{n \times n}$ is singular (that is, if and only if $|\mathbf{A}| = 0$).

Proof of the "only if" part: Suppose that $|\mathbf{A}| \neq 0$. Then, by Cramer's rule, $x_1, \ldots, x_n$ are given by (4). But the numerator in each of these fractions is 0, because each of the determinants $D_1, \ldots, D_n$ contains a column consisting entirely of zeros. Then the system only has the trivial solution. In other words: *System (5) has nontrivial solutions only if the determinant $|\mathbf{A}|$ vanishes.*

As for the "if" part, concepts from FMEA can be used to show that, if $|\mathbf{A}| = 0$, then the rank of $\mathbf{A}$ is less than n, so system (5) has at least one degree of freedom. That is, apart from the trivial solution, there are infinitely many nontrivial solutions which take the form $\alpha\mathbf{x}$ where $\mathbf{x} \neq \mathbf{0}$, and α is an arbitrary nonzero scalar. ∎

NOTE 2 We now consider the "only if" part of Theorem 16.8.1. In case $|\mathbf{A}| = 0$, there are two possibilities. First, the equation system (1), which we write in matrix form $\mathbf{Ax} = \mathbf{b}$, may have no solutions. Second, it may have at least one particular solution $\mathbf{x}^P$. But the homogeneous system has solutions $\alpha\mathbf{x}$ satisfying $\mathbf{A}\alpha\mathbf{x} = \mathbf{0}$. So all vectors of the form $\mathbf{x}^P + \alpha\mathbf{x}$ are also solutions of the equation system. In particular, (1) has a unique solution only if $|\mathbf{A}| \neq 0$.

EXAMPLE 2   Examine for what values of λ the following system of equations has nontrivial solutions.

$$5x + 2y + z = \lambda x$$
$$2x + y = \lambda y$$
$$x + z = \lambda z$$

Solution: The variables x, y, and z appear on both sides of the equations, so we start by putting the system into standard form:

$$(5 - \lambda)x + 2y + z = 0$$
$$2x + (1 - \lambda)y = 0$$
$$x + (1 - \lambda)z = 0$$

According to Theorem 16.8.2, this system has a nontrivial solution if and only if the coefficient matrix is singular:

$$\begin{vmatrix} 5 - \lambda & 2 & 1 \\ 2 & 1 - \lambda & 0 \\ 1 & 0 & 1 - \lambda \end{vmatrix} = 0$$

The value of the determinant is found to be $\lambda(1-\lambda)(\lambda-6)$. Hence, system (1) has nontrivial solutions if and only if $\lambda = 0, 1$, or 6.

NOTE 3 Actually, using terminology explained in FMEA, this example asks us to find the eigenvalues of the matrix $\begin{pmatrix} 5 & 2 & 1 \\ 2 & 1 & 0 \\ 1 & 0 & 1 \end{pmatrix}$.

PROBLEMS FOR SECTION 16.8

(SM) **1.** Use Cramer's rule to solve the following two systems of equations:

(a) $\begin{array}{rcl} x + 2y - z &=& -5 \\ 2x - y + z &=& 6 \\ x - y - 3z &=& -3 \end{array}$

(b) $\begin{array}{rcl} x + y & = 3 \\ x \quad\ + z & = 2 \\ y + z + u & = 6 \\ y \quad\ + u & = 1 \end{array}$

2. Use Theorem 16.8.1 to prove that the following system of equations has a unique solution for all values of b_1, b_2, b_3, and find the solution.

$$\begin{array}{rcl} 3x_1 + x_2 & = b_1 \\ x_1 - x_2 + 2x_3 & = b_2 \\ 2x_1 + 3x_2 - x_3 & = b_3 \end{array}$$

(SM) **3.** Prove that the homogeneous system of equations

$$\begin{array}{rcl} ax + by + cz &=& 0 \\ bx + cy + az &=& 0 \\ cx + ay + bz &=& 0 \end{array}$$

has a nontrivial solution if and only if $a^3 + b^3 + c^3 - 3abc = 0$.

16.9 The Leontief Model

In order to illustrate why linear systems of equations are important in economics, we briefly discuss a simple example of the Leontief model.

EXAMPLE 1   Once upon a time, in an ancient land perhaps not too far from Norway, an economy consisted of three industries—fishing, forestry, and boat building.

To produce 1 ton of fish requires the services of α fishing boats.

To produce 1 ton of timber requires β tons of fish, as extra food for the energetic foresters.

To produce 1 fishing boat requires γ tons of timber.

These are the only inputs needed for each of these three industries. Suppose there is no final (external) demand for fishing boats. Find what gross outputs each of the three industries must produce in order to meet the final demands of d_1 tons of fish to feed the general population, plus d_2 tons of timber to build houses.

Solution: Let x_1 denote the total number of tons of fish to be produced, x_2 the total number of tons of timber, and x_3 the total number of fishing boats.

Consider first the demand for fish. Because βx_2 tons of fish are needed to produce x_2 units of timber, and because the final demand for fish is d_1, we must have $x_1 = \beta x_2 + d_1$. (Producing fishing boats does not require fish as an input, so there is no term with x_3.) In the case of timber, a similar argument shows that the equation $x_2 = \gamma x_3 + d_2$ must be satisfied. Finally, for boat building, only the fishing industry needs boats; there is no final demand in this case, and so $x_3 = \alpha x_1$. Thus, the following three equations must be satisfied:

$$\text{(i)} \ \ x_1 = \beta x_2 + d_1 \qquad \text{(ii)} \ \ x_2 = \gamma x_3 + d_2 \qquad \text{(iii)} \ \ x_3 = \alpha x_1 \qquad\qquad (*)$$

One way to solve these equations begins by using (iii) to insert $x_3 = \alpha x_1$ into (ii). This gives $x_2 = \gamma \alpha x_1 + d_2$, which inserted into (i) yields $x_1 = \alpha \beta \gamma x_1 + \beta d_2 + d_1$. Solving this last equation for x_1 gives $x_1 = (d_1 + \beta d_2)/(1 - \alpha \beta \gamma)$. The corresponding expressions for the two other variables are easily found, and the results are:

$$x_1 = \frac{d_1 + \beta d_2}{1 - \alpha \beta \gamma}, \qquad x_2 = \frac{\alpha \gamma d_1 + d_2}{1 - \alpha \beta \gamma}, \qquad x_3 = \frac{\alpha d_1 + \alpha \beta d_2}{1 - \alpha \beta \gamma} \qquad\qquad (**)$$

Clearly, this solution for (x_1, x_2, x_3) only makes sense when $\alpha \beta \gamma < 1$. In fact, if $\alpha \beta \gamma \geq 1$, it is impossible for this economy to meet any positive final demands for fish and timber—production in the economy is too inefficient.

The General Leontief Model

In Example 1 we considered a simple example of the Leontief model. More generally, the Leontief model describes an economy with n interlinked industries, each of which produces a single good using only one process of production. To produce its good, each industry must use inputs from at least some other industries. For example, the steel industry needs goods from the iron mining and coal industries, as well as from many other industries. In addition to supplying its own good to other industries that need it, each industry also faces an external demand for its product from consumers, governments, foreigners, and so on. The amount needed to meet this external demand is called the *final demand*.

Let x_i denote the total number of units of good i that industry i is going to produce in a certain year. Furthermore, let

$$a_{ij} = \text{the number of units of good } i \text{ needed to produce one unit of good } j \qquad (1)$$

We assume that input requirements are directly proportional to the amount of the output produced. Then

$$a_{ij} x_j = \text{the number of units of good } i \text{ needed to produce } x_j \text{ units of good } j \qquad (2)$$

In order that x_1 units of good 1, x_2 units of good 2, ..., x_n units of good n can all be produced, industry i needs to supply a total of

$$a_{i1}x_1 + a_{i2}x_2 + \cdots + a_{in}x_n$$

units of good i. If we require industry i also to supply b_i units to meet final demand, then equilibrium between supply and demand requires that

$$x_i = a_{i1}x_1 + a_{i2}x_2 + \cdots + a_{in}x_n + b_i$$

This goes for all $i = 1, 2, \ldots, n$. So we arrive at the following system of equations:

$$
\begin{aligned}
x_1 &= a_{11}x_1 + a_{12}x_2 + \cdots + a_{1n}x_n + b_1 \\
x_2 &= a_{21}x_1 + a_{22}x_2 + \cdots + a_{2n}x_n + b_2 \\
&\cdots\cdots\cdots\cdots\cdots\cdots\cdots\cdots\cdots\cdots\cdots\cdots \\
x_n &= a_{n1}x_1 + a_{n2}x_2 + \cdots + a_{nn}x_n + b_n
\end{aligned}
\tag{3}
$$

Note that in the first equation, x_1 appears on the left-hand side as well as in the first term on the right-hand side. In the second equation, x_2 appears on the left-hand side as well as in the second term on the right-hand side, and so on. Moving all terms involving $x_1, \ldots, x_n$ to the left-hand side and rearranging gives the system of equations

$$
\begin{aligned}
(1-a_{11})x_1 - \quad & a_{12}x_2 - \cdots - \quad & a_{1n}x_n = b_1 \\
- a_{21}x_1 + (1-a_{22})x_2 - \cdots - \quad & a_{2n}x_n = b_2 \\
\cdots\cdots\cdots\cdots\cdots\cdots\cdots\cdots\cdots\cdots\cdots\cdots & \\
- a_{n1}x_1 - \quad & a_{n2}x_2 - \cdots + (1-a_{nn})x_n = b_n
\end{aligned}
\tag{4}
$$

This system of equations is called the **Leontief system**. The numbers a_{11}, a_{12}, ..., a_{nn} are called **input** (or **technical**) **coefficients**. Given any collection of final demand quantities $(b_1, b_2, \ldots, b_n)$, a solution $(x_1, x_2, \ldots, x_n)$ of (4) will give outputs for each industry such that the combined interindustry and final demands can just be met. Of course, only nonnegative values for x_i make sense.

It is natural to use matrix algebra to study the Leontief model. Define the following matrices:

$$
\mathbf{A} = \begin{pmatrix} a_{11} & a_{12} & \cdots & a_{1n} \\ a_{21} & a_{22} & \cdots & a_{2n} \\ \vdots & \vdots & \ddots & \vdots \\ a_{n1} & a_{n2} & \cdots & a_{nn} \end{pmatrix}, \qquad \mathbf{x} = \begin{pmatrix} x_1 \\ x_2 \\ \vdots \\ x_n \end{pmatrix}, \qquad \mathbf{b} = \begin{pmatrix} b_1 \\ b_2 \\ \vdots \\ b_n \end{pmatrix}
\tag{5}
$$

The elements of the matrix $\mathbf{A}$ are the input coefficients, so it is called the **input** or **Leontief matrix**. Recall that the element a_{ij} denotes the number of units of commodity i which is needed to produce one unit of commodity j.

With these definitions, system (3) can expressed as

$$\mathbf{x} = \mathbf{A}\mathbf{x} + \mathbf{b} \tag{6}$$

This equation is evidently equivalent to the equation $\mathbf{x} - \mathbf{Ax} = \mathbf{b}$. If $\mathbf{I}_n$ denotes the identity matrix of order n, then $(\mathbf{I}_n - \mathbf{A})\mathbf{x} = \mathbf{I}_n\mathbf{x} - \mathbf{Ax} = \mathbf{x} - \mathbf{Ax}$, so that (3) is equivalent to

$$(\mathbf{I}_n - \mathbf{A})\mathbf{x} = \mathbf{b} \tag{7}$$

which is the matrix equivalent of system (4). (Note in particular that "$\mathbf{x} - \mathbf{Ax} = (1 - \mathbf{A})\mathbf{x}$" is meaningless, since $1 - \mathbf{A}$ (where 1 is the number 1) is meaningless.)

Suppose now that we introduce prices into the Leontief model, and that

$$p_i \text{ is the price of a unit of commodity } i$$

Because a_{ij} denotes the number of units of commodity i needed to produce one unit of commodity j, the sum

$$a_{1j}p_1 + a_{2j}p_2 + \cdots + a_{nj}p_n$$

is the total cost of the n commodities needed to produce one unit of commodity j. The expression

$$p_j - a_{1j}p_1 - a_{2j}p_2 - \cdots - a_{nj}p_n$$

is the difference between the price of one unit of commodity j and the cost of producing that unit. This is called **unit value added** in sector j. If we denote this unit value added by v_j, then for all sectors:

$$\begin{aligned} p_1 - a_{11}p_1 - a_{21}p_2 - \cdots - a_{n1}p_n &= v_1 \\ p_2 - a_{12}p_1 - a_{22}p_2 - \cdots - a_{n2}p_n &= v_2 \\ &\cdots\cdots\cdots\cdots\cdots\cdots\cdots\cdots \\ p_n - a_{1n}p_1 - a_{2n}p_2 - \cdots - a_{nn}p_n &= v_n \end{aligned} \tag{8}$$

Note that the input–output coefficients a_{ij} appear in transposed order. If we define

$$\mathbf{p} = \begin{pmatrix} p_1 \\ p_2 \\ \vdots \\ p_n \end{pmatrix} \quad \text{and} \quad \mathbf{v} = \begin{pmatrix} v_1 \\ v_2 \\ \vdots \\ v_n \end{pmatrix} \tag{9}$$

we see that (8) can be written in the matrix form $\mathbf{p} - \mathbf{A}'\mathbf{p} = \mathbf{v}$, or

$$(\mathbf{I}_n - \mathbf{A}')\mathbf{p} = \mathbf{v} \tag{10}$$

By using the rules for transposition in (15.5.2), we can express (10) in an alternative way. Transposing each side of (10) gives

$$\mathbf{p}'(\mathbf{I}_n - \mathbf{A}) = \mathbf{v}' \tag{11}$$

since $\mathbf{I}'_n = \mathbf{I}_n$ and $(\mathbf{A}')' = \mathbf{A}$. We see that the two systems (7) and (11) are closely related.

1. In Example 1 let $\alpha = 1/2$, $\beta = 1/4$, $\gamma = 2$, $d_1 = 100$, and $d_2 = 80$. Write down system (∗) in this case and find the solution of the system. Confirm the results by using the general formulas in (∗∗).

2. Consider an economy divided into an agricultural sector (A) and an industrial sector (I). To produce one unit in sector A requires $1/6$ unit from A and $1/4$ unit from I. To produce one unit in sector I requires $1/4$ unit from A and $1/4$ unit from I. Suppose final demands in each of the two sectors are 60 units.

   (a) Write down the Leontief system for this economy.

   (b) Find the number of units that have to be produced in each sector in order to meet the final demands.

3. Consider the Leontief model (4).

   (a) What is the interpretation of the condition that $a_{ii} = 0$ for all i?

   (b) What is the interpretation of the sum $a_{i1} + a_{i2} + \cdots + a_{in}$?

   (c) What is the interpretation of the vector of input coefficients $(a_{1j}, a_{2j}, \ldots, a_{nj})$?

   (d) Can you give any interpretation to the sum $a_{1j} + a_{2j} + \cdots + a_{nj}$?

4. Write down system (4) when $n = 2$, $a_{11} = 0.2$, $a_{12} = 0.3$, $a_{21} = 0.4$, $a_{22} = 0.1$, $b_1 = 120$, and $b_2 = 90$. What is the solution to this system?

5. Consider an input–output model with three sectors. Sector 1 is heavy industry, sector 2 is light industry, and sector 3 is agriculture. Suppose that the input requirements are given by the following table:

	Heavy industry	Light industry	Agriculture
Units of heavy industry goods	$a_{11} = 0.1$	$a_{12} = 0.2$	$a_{13} = 0.1$
Units of light industry goods	$a_{21} = 0.3$	$a_{22} = 0.2$	$a_{23} = 0.2$
Units of agri-cultural goods	$a_{31} = 0.2$	$a_{32} = 0.2$	$a_{33} = 0.1$

Suppose the final demands for the three goods are 85, 95, and 20 units, respectively. If x_1, x_2, and x_3 denote the number of units that have to be produced in the three sectors, write down the Leontief system for the problem. Verify that $x_1 = 150$, $x_2 = 200$, and $x_3 = 100$ is a solution.

6. Write down the input matrix for the simple Leontief model of Example 1. Compare the condition for efficient production discussed in that example with the requirement that the sum of the elements of each column in the input matrix be less than 1.

7. Suppose that $\mathbf{x} = \mathbf{x}_0$ is a solution of (7) and that $\mathbf{p}' = \mathbf{p}'_0$ is a solution of (11). Prove that $\mathbf{p}'_0 \mathbf{b} = \mathbf{v}' \mathbf{x}_0$.

1. Calculate the following determinants:

(a) $\begin{vmatrix} 5 & -2 \\ 3 & -2 \end{vmatrix}$ (b) $\begin{vmatrix} 1 & a \\ a & 1 \end{vmatrix}$ (c) $\begin{vmatrix} (a+b)^2 & a-b \\ (a-b)^2 & a+b \end{vmatrix}$ (d) $\begin{vmatrix} 1-\lambda & 2 \\ 2 & 4-\lambda \end{vmatrix}$

2. Calculate the determinants:

(a) $\begin{vmatrix} 2 & 2 & 3 \\ 0 & 3 & 5 \\ 0 & 4 & 6 \end{vmatrix}$ (b) $\begin{vmatrix} 4 & 5 & 6 \\ 5 & 6 & 8 \\ 6 & 7 & 9 \end{vmatrix}$ (c) $\begin{vmatrix} 31 & 32 & 33 \\ 32 & 33 & 35 \\ 33 & 34 & 36 \end{vmatrix}$

(*Hint:* In (b) and (c) you should perform suitable elementary operations.)

3. Find **A** when $(\mathbf{A}^{-1} - 2\mathbf{I}_2)' = -2 \begin{pmatrix} 1 & 1 \\ 1 & 0 \end{pmatrix}$.

4. Let $\mathbf{A}_t = \begin{pmatrix} 1 & 0 & t \\ 2 & 1 & t \\ 0 & 1 & 1 \end{pmatrix}$ and $\mathbf{B} = \begin{pmatrix} 1 & 0 & 0 \\ 0 & 0 & 1 \\ 0 & 1 & 0 \end{pmatrix}$.

(a) For what values of t does $\mathbf{A}_t$ have an inverse?

(b) Find a matrix **X** such that $\mathbf{B} + \mathbf{X}\mathbf{A}_1^{-1} = \mathbf{A}_1^{-1}$.

SM 5. Define the two 3×3 matrices $\mathbf{A} = \begin{pmatrix} q & -1 & q-2 \\ 1 & -p & 2-p \\ 2 & -1 & 0 \end{pmatrix}$, $\mathbf{E} = \begin{pmatrix} 1 & 1 & 1 \\ 1 & 1 & 1 \\ 1 & 1 & 1 \end{pmatrix}$.

Calculate $|\mathbf{A}|$ and $|\mathbf{A} + \mathbf{E}|$. For what values of p and q does $\mathbf{A} + \mathbf{E}$ have an inverse? Why does **BE** not have an inverse for any 3×3 matrix **B**?

6. For what values of t does the system of equations

$$-2x + 4y - tz = t - 4$$
$$-3x + y + tz = 3 - 4t$$
$$(t-2)x - 7y + 4z = 23$$

have a unique solution for the three variables x, y, and z? (Use Cramer's rule.)

7. Prove that if **A** is an $n \times n$ matrix such that $\mathbf{A}^4 = \mathbf{0}$, then $(\mathbf{I} - \mathbf{A})^{-1} = \mathbf{I} + \mathbf{A} + \mathbf{A}^2 + \mathbf{A}^3$.

SM 8. (a) Let **U** be the $n \times n$ matrix where all the elements are 1. Show that

$$(\mathbf{I}_n + a\mathbf{U})(\mathbf{I}_n + b\mathbf{U}) = \mathbf{I}_n + (a + b + nab)\mathbf{U}$$

for all real numbers a and b.

(b) Use the result in (a) to find the inverse of $\mathbf{A} = \begin{pmatrix} 4 & 3 & 3 \\ 3 & 4 & 3 \\ 3 & 3 & 4 \end{pmatrix}$.

9. Let **A**, **B**, **C**, **X**, and **Y** be $n \times n$ matrices, with $|\mathbf{A}| \neq 0$, which satisfy the two equations

(i) $\mathbf{AX} + \mathbf{Y} = \mathbf{B}$ (ii) $\mathbf{X} + 2\mathbf{A}^{-1}\mathbf{Y} = \mathbf{C}$

Find **X** and **Y** expressed in terms of **A**, **B**, and **C**.

(SM) **10.** (a) For what values of a does the system of equations

$$
\begin{aligned}
ax + y + \;\;4z &= 2 \\
2x + y + a^2 z &= 2 \\
x \qquad - \;\;3z &= a
\end{aligned}
\qquad (*)
$$

have one, none, or infinitely many solutions?

(b) Replace the right-hand sides 2, 2, and a in $(*)$ by b_1, b_2, and b_3, respectively. Find a necessary and sufficient condition for the new system of equations to have infinitely many solutions.

11. (a) Let $\mathbf{A} = \begin{pmatrix} 11 & -6 \\ 18 & -10 \end{pmatrix}$. Compute $|\mathbf{A}|$. Show that there exists a real number c such that $\mathbf{A}^2 + c\mathbf{A} = 2\mathbf{I}_2$, and then find the inverse of $\mathbf{A}$.

(b) Show that there is no 2×2 matrix $\mathbf{B}$ such that $\mathbf{B}^2 = \mathbf{A}$.

12. Suppose that $\mathbf{A}$ and $\mathbf{B}$ are invertible $n \times n$ matrices. Show that if $\mathbf{A}'\mathbf{A} = \mathbf{I}_n$, then $(\mathbf{A}'\mathbf{B}\mathbf{A})^{-1} = \mathbf{A}'\mathbf{B}^{-1}\mathbf{A}$.

13. Examine for what values of the constants a and b the system of equations

$$
\begin{aligned}
ax + y &= 3 \\
x + z &= 2 \\
y + az + bu &= 6 \\
y + u &= 1
\end{aligned}
$$

has a unique solution in the unknowns x, y, z, and u. When it exists, find this unique solution (expressed in terms of a and b).

HARDER PROBLEMS

14. The 3×3 matrix $\mathbf{B}$ satisfies the equation $\mathbf{B}^3 = -\mathbf{B}$. Show that $\mathbf{B}$ cannot have an inverse. (*Hint:* Use (16.4.1).)

(SM) **15.** (a) Prove that $\begin{vmatrix} a + x & b + y \\ c & d \end{vmatrix} = \begin{vmatrix} a & b \\ c & d \end{vmatrix} + \begin{vmatrix} x & y \\ c & d \end{vmatrix}$.

(b) Suppose $\mathbf{A}$, $\mathbf{B}$, and $\mathbf{C}$ are $n \times n$ matrices that differ only in the rth row, and suppose the rth row in $\mathbf{C}$ is obtained by adding the entries in the rth row of $\mathbf{A}$ to the corresponding entries in the rth row of $\mathbf{B}$. Prove that then $|\mathbf{A}| + |\mathbf{B}| = |\mathbf{C}|$. (*Hint:* Expand according to the rth row of $\mathbf{C}$.)

(SM) **16.** Solve the following equation for x: $\begin{vmatrix} x & a & x & b \\ b & x & a & x \\ x & b & x & a \\ a & x & b & x \end{vmatrix} = 0$.

17

LINEAR PROGRAMMING

If one would take statistics about which mathematical problem is using up most of the computer time in the world, then (not counting database handling problems like sorting and searching) the answer would probably be linear programming.
—L. Lovász (1980)

L inear programming is the name used to describe constrained optimization problems in which the objective is to maximize or minimize a linear function subject to linear inequality constraints. Because of its extensive use in economic decision problems, all economists should know something about the basic theory of linear programming.

In principle, *any* linear programming problem (often called an LP problem) can be solved numerically, provided that a solution exists. This is because the *simplex method* introduced by G. B. Dantzig in 1947 provides a very efficient numerical algorithm that finds the solution in a finite number of steps. As the above quotation from Lovász indicates, the simplex method has made linear programming a mathematical technique of immense practical importance. It is reported that when Mobil Oil Company's multimillion-dollar computer system was installed in 1958, it paid off this huge investment in two weeks by doing linear programming.[1] That said, the simplex method will not be discussed in this book. After all, faced with a nontrivial LP problem, it is natural to use one of the great number of available LP computer programs to find the solution. In any case, it is probably more important for economists to understand the basic theory of LP than the details of the simplex method.

Indeed, the importance of LP extends even beyond its practical applications. In particular, the duality theory of linear programming is a basis for understanding key theoretical properties of more complicated optimization problems with an even larger range of interesting economic applications.

17.1 A Graphical Approach

A general linear programming problem with only two decision variables involves maximizing or minimizing a linear function

$$z = c_1 x_1 + c_2 x_2 \qquad \text{(objective function)}$$

---

[1] Joel Franklin, "Mathematical methods of economics", *The American Mathematical Monthly*, 1983, Vol. 90, no. 4.

subject to m linear constraints

$$a_{11}x_1 + a_{12}x_2 \le b_1$$
$$a_{21}x_1 + a_{22}x_2 \le b_2 \quad \text{(inequality constraints)}$$
$$\ldots\ldots\ldots\ldots\ldots\ldots$$
$$a_{m1}x_1 + a_{m2}x_2 \le b_m$$

Usually, we also impose explicit nonnegativity constraints on x_1 and x_2:

$$x_1 \ge 0, \quad x_2 \ge 0 \quad \text{(nonnegativity constraints)}$$

Note that having a $\le$ sign rather than $\ge$ in each inequality constraint is merely a convention because any inequality of the alternative form $ax_1 + bx_2 \ge c$ is equivalent to the inequality $-ax_1 - bx_2 \le -c$.

LP problems with only two decision variables can be solved by a simple graphical method.

EXAMPLE 1   A baker has 150 kilograms of flour, 22 kilos of sugar, and 27.5 kilos of butter with which to make two types of cake. Suppose that making one dozen A cakes requires 3 kilos of flour, 1 kilo of sugar, and 1 kilo of butter, whereas making one dozen B cakes requires 6 kilos of flour, 0.5 kilo of sugar, and 1 kilo of butter. Suppose that the profit from one dozen A cakes is 20 and from one dozen B cakes is 30. How many dozen A cakes (x_1) and how many dozen B cakes (x_2) will maximize the baker's profit?

Solution: An output of x_1 dozen A cakes plus x_2 dozen B cakes needs a total of $3x_1 + 6x_2$ kilos of flour. Because there are only 150 kilos of flour, the inequality

$$3x_1 + 6x_2 \le 150 \quad \text{(flour constraint)}$$

must hold. Similarly, for sugar,

$$x_1 + 0.5x_2 \le 22 \quad \text{(sugar constraint)}$$

and for butter,

$$x_1 + x_2 \le 27.5 \quad \text{(butter constraint)}$$

Of course, $x_1 \ge 0$ and $x_2 \ge 0$. The profit obtained from producing x_1 dozen A cakes and x_2 dozen B cakes is

$$z = 20x_1 + 30x_2$$

In short, the problem is to

$$\max \; z = 20x_1 + 30x_2 \;\text{ subject to }\; \begin{cases} 3x_1 + 6x_2 \le 150 \\ x_1 + 0.5x_2 \le 22 \\ x_1 + x_2 \le 27.5 \end{cases} \quad x_1 \ge 0, \; x_2 \ge 0 \quad \text{(i)}$$

This problem will now be solved graphically.

The output pair (x_1, x_2) is called *feasible* (or *admissible*) for problem (i) if all the five constraints are satisfied. Look at the flour constraint, $3x_1 + 6x_2 \leq 150$. If we use all the flour, then $3x_1 + 6x_2 = 150$, and we call the corresponding straight line the *flour border*. We can find similar "borders" for the other two inputs. Figure 1 shows the three straight lines that represent the flour border, the sugar border, and the butter border. In order for (x_1, x_2) to be feasible, it has to be on or below (to the "south-west" of) *each* of the three borders simultaneously. Because constraints $x_1 \geq 0$ and $x_2 \geq 0$ restrict (x_1, x_2) to the nonnegative quadrant, the set of admissible pairs for problem (i) is the shaded set S shown in Fig. 2. (This set S is a so-called *convex polyhedron*, and the five corner points O, A, B, C, and D are called *extreme points* of the set S.)

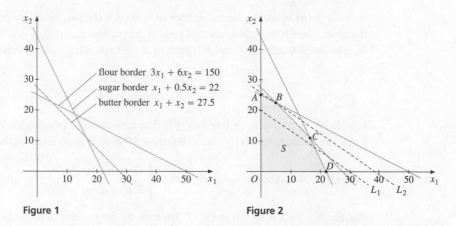

Figure 1   **Figure 2**

A baker might think of finding the point in the feasible region that maximizes profit by calculating $20x_1 + 30x_2$ at each point of S and picking the highest value. In practice, this is impossible because there are infinitely many feasible points. Let us argue this way instead. Can the baker obtain a profit of 600? If so, the straight line $20x_1 + 30x_2 = 600$ must have points in common with S. This line is represented in Fig. 2 by dashed line L_1. It does have points in common with S. (One of them is $(x_1, x_2) = (0, 20)$, where no A cakes are produced, but 20 dozen B cakes are, and the profit *is* $20 \cdot 0 + 30 \cdot 20 = 600$.) Can the baker do better? Yes. For instance, the straight line $20x_1 + 30x_2 = 601$ also has points in common with S and the profit is 601. In fact, the straight lines

$$20x_1 + 30x_2 = c \qquad (c \text{ is a constant})$$

are all parallel to $20x_1 + 30x_2 = 600$. As c increases, the line moves out farther and farther to the north-east. It is clear that the straight line that has the highest value of c and still has a point in common with S is dashed line L_2 in the figure. It touches set S at point B. Note that B is at the intersection of the flour border and the butter border. Its coordinates, therefore, satisfy the two equations: $3x_1 + 6x_2 = 150$ and $x_1 + x_2 = 27.5$. Solving these two simultaneous equations yields $x_1 = 5$ and $x_2 = 22.5$. So the baker maximizes profit by baking 5 dozen A cakes and 22.5 dozen B cakes. This uses all the available flour and butter, but $22 - 5 - 0.5 \cdot 22.5 = 5.75$ kilos of sugar are left over. The profit earned is $20x_1 + 30x_2 = 775$.

EXAMPLE 2   A firm is producing two goods, A and B. It has two factories that jointly produce the two goods in the following quantities (per hour):

	Factory 1	Factory 2
Good A	10	20
Good B	25	25

The firm receives an order for 300 units of A and 500 units of B. The costs of operating the two factories are 10 000 and 8 000 per hour. Formulate the linear programming problem of minimizing the total cost of meeting this order.

Solution: Let u_1 and u_2 be the number of hours that the two factories operate to produce the order. Then $10u_1 + 20u_2$ units of good A are produced, and $25u_1 + 25u_2$ units of good B. Because 300 units of A and 500 units of B are required, u_1 and u_2 must satisfy

$$10u_1 + 20u_2 \geq 300$$
$$25u_1 + 25u_2 \geq 500$$

(i)

In addition, of course, $u_1 \geq 0$ and $u_2 \geq 0$. The total costs of operating the two factories for u_1 and u_2 hours, respectively, are $10\,000\,u_1 + 8\,000\,u_2$. The problem is, therefore,

$$\text{min } 10\,000\,u_1 + 8\,000\,u_2 \quad \text{subject to} \quad \begin{cases} 10u_1 + 20u_2 \geq 300 \\ 25u_1 + 25u_2 \geq 500 \end{cases} \quad u_1 \geq 0,\ u_2 \geq 0$$

The feasible set S is shown in Fig. 3. Because the inequalities in (i) are of the $\geq$ type and all the coefficients of u_1 and u_2 are positive, the feasible set lies to the north-east. Figure 3 includes three of the level curves $10\,000u_1 + 8\,000u_2 = c$, marked L_1, L_2, and L_3. These three correspond to the values $100\,000$, $160\,000$, and $240\,000$ of the cost level c. As c increases, the level curve moves farther and farther to the north-east.

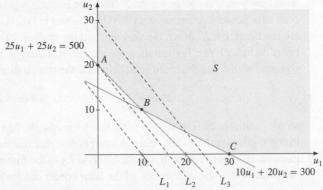

Figure 3

The solution to the minimization problem is clearly the level curve that touches the feasible set S at point A with coordinates $(0, 20)$. Hence, the optimal solution is to operate factory 2 for 20 hours and not to use factory 1 at all, with minimum cost $160\,000$.

The graphical method of solving linear programming problems works well when there are only two decision variables. One can extend the method to the case with three decision variables. Then the feasible set is a convex polyhedron in 3-space, and the level surfaces of the objective function are planes in 3-space. However, it is not easy to visualize the solution in such cases. For more than three decision variables, no graphical method is available. (By using duality theory, however, one can solve LP problems graphically when *either* the number of unknowns *or* the number of constraints is less than or equal to 3. See Section 17.5.)

Both the previous examples had optimal solutions. If the feasible region is unbounded, however, a (finite) optimal solution might not exist, as is the case in Problem 4.

The General LP Problem

The general LP problem is that of maximizing or minimizing

$$z = c_1 x_1 + \cdots + c_n x_n \qquad \textbf{(objective function)} \tag{1}$$

with $c_1, \ldots, c_n$ as given constants, subject to m constraints

$$
\begin{aligned}
a_{11} x_1 + \cdots + a_{1n} x_n &\leq b_1 \\
a_{21} x_1 + \cdots + a_{2n} x_n &\leq b_2 \qquad \textbf{(inequality constraints)} \\
&\cdots\cdots\cdots\cdots\cdots\cdots\cdots \\
a_{m1} x_1 + \cdots + a_{mn} x_n &\leq b_m
\end{aligned}
\tag{2}
$$

where the elements a_{ij} and b_k are given constants. Usually, we assume explicitly that

$$x_1 \geq 0, \ \ldots, \ x_n \geq 0 \qquad \textbf{(nonnegativity constraints)} \tag{3}$$

There is no essential difference between a minimization problem and a maximization problem, because the optimal solution $(x_1^*, \ldots, x_n^*)$ that minimizes (1) subject to (2) and (3) also maximizes $-z$. An n-vector $(x_1, \ldots, x_n)$ that satisfies (2) and (3) is called **feasible** or **admissible**.

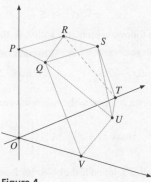

Figure 4

The set of feasible points is a so-called *convex polyhedron* in the *nonnegative orthant* of n-space. A typical example in 3-space is shown in Fig. 4. The points O, P, Q, R, S, T, U, and V are called *extreme points*. The 15 line segments OP, OT, OV, etc. joining two extreme points that are marked in Fig. 4 (including RT which is indicated with a dashed line because it is hidden behind the solid polyhedron) are called *edges*. The flat portions of the boundary which are triangles or quadrilaterals lying within three or four of these edges are called *faces*. In n-space, any convex polyhedron also has extreme points, edges, and faces. If n and m are large, the number of extreme points can be astronomical.[2] Nevertheless, the simplex method can solve such problems. It relies on the fact that if an LP problem has a solution, there must be a solution at an extreme point. Accordingly the method provides a procedure for moving repeatedly between adjacent extreme points of the polyhedron, along its edges, in such a way that the value of the objective function never decreases. The procedure terminates when it reaches an extreme point where no move to an adjacent extreme point will increase the value of the objective function. We have then reached the optimal solution.

PROBLEMS FOR SECTION 17.1

1. Use the graphical method to solve the following LP problems:

   (a) max $3x_1 + 4x_2$ s.t. $\begin{cases} 3x_1 + 2x_2 \le 6 \\ x_1 + 4x_2 \le 4 \end{cases}$ $\quad x_1 \ge 0,\ x_2 \ge 0$

   (b) min $10u_1 + 27u_2$ s.t. $\begin{cases} u_1 + 3u_2 \ge 11 \\ 2u_1 + 5u_2 \ge 20 \end{cases}$ $\quad u_1 \ge 0,\ u_2 \ge 0$

2. Use the graphical method to solve the following LP problems:

   (a) max $2x_1 + 5x_2$ s.t. $\begin{cases} -2x_1 + 3x_2 \le 6 \\ 7x_1 - 2x_2 \le 14 \\ x_1 + x_2 \le 5 \end{cases}$ $\quad x_1 \ge 0,\ x_2 \ge 0$

   (b) max $8x_1 + 9x_2$ s.t. $\begin{cases} x_1 + 2x_2 \le 8 \\ 2x_1 + 3x_2 \le 13 \\ x_1 + x_2 \le 6 \end{cases}$ $\quad x_1 \ge 0,\ x_2 \ge 0$

   (c) max $-2x_1 + x_2$ s.t. $\quad 0 \le x_1 - 3x_2 \le 3,\ \ x_1 \ge 2,\ \ x_1 \ge 0,\ \ x_2 \ge 0$

(SM) 3. Set A consists of all (x_1, x_2) satisfying

$$-2x_1 + x_2 \le 2, \quad x_1 + 2x_2 \le 8, \quad x_1 \ge 0, \quad x_2 \ge 0$$

   Solve the following problems with A as the feasible set:

   (a) max x_2 (b) max x_1 (c) max $3x_1 + 2x_2$

   (d) min $2x_1 - 2x_2$ (e) max $2x_1 + 4x_2$ (f) min $-3x_1 - 2x_2$

4. (a) Is there a solution to the following problem?

$$\text{max } x_1 + x_2 \quad \text{s.t.} \quad \begin{cases} -x_1 + x_2 \le -1 \\ -x_1 + 3x_2 \le 3 \end{cases} \quad x_1 \ge 0,\ x_2 \ge 0$$

   (b) Is there a solution if the objective function is $z = -x_1 - x_2$?

---

[2] The typical extreme point has n of the $n + m$ inequality constraints holding with equality. Thus, there can be as many as $(n + m)!/n!m!$ extreme points. For example, if $n = 50$ and $m = 60$ (which is quite small by the standards of the problems that can be solved numerically), then there can be as many as $110!/50!60!$ or more than $6 \cdot 10^{31}$ extreme points.

5. Replace the objective function in Example 1 by $20x_1 + tx_2$. For what values of t will the maximum profit still be at $x_1 = 5$ and $x_2 = 22.5$?

6. A firm produces two types of television set, an inexpensive type (A) and an expensive type (B). The firm earns a profit of 700 from each TV of type A, and 1000 for each TV of type B. There are three stages of the production process, each requiring its own specialized kind of labour. Stage I requires 3 units of labour on each set of type A and 5 units of labour on each set of type B. The total available quantity of labour for this stage is 3900. Stage II requires 1 unit of labour on each set of type A and 3 units on each set of type B. The total labour available for this stage is 2100 units. At stage III, 2 units of labour are needed for each type, and 2200 units of labour are available. How many TV sets of each type should the firm produce to maximize its profit?

17.2 Introduction to Duality Theory

Confronted with an optimization problem involving scarce resources, an economist will often ask: What happens to the optimal solution if the availability of the resources changes? For linear programming problems, answers to questions like this are intimately related to the so-called duality theory of LP. As a point of departure, let us again consider the baker's problem in Example 17.1.1.

EXAMPLE 1   Suppose the baker were to stumble across an extra kilo of flour that had been hidden away in storage. How much would this extra kilo add to his maximum profit? How much would an extra kilo of sugar contribute to profit? Or an extra kilo of butter?

Solution: If the baker finds an extra kilo of flour, the flour border would become $3x_1 + 6x_2 = 151$. It is clear from Fig. 17.1.2 that the feasible set S will expand slightly and point B will move slightly up along the butter border. The new optimal point B' will be at the intersection of the lines $3x_1 + 6x_2 = 151$ and $x_1 + x_2 = 27.5$. Solving these equations gives $x_1 = 14/3$ and $x_2 = 137/6$. The objective function attains the value $20(14/3) + 30(137/6) = 2335/3 = 775 + 10/3$. So profit rises by $10/3$.

If the baker finds an extra kilo of sugar, the feasible set will expand, but the optimal point is still at B. Recall that at the optimum in the original problem, the baker had 5.75 kilos of unused sugar. There is no extra profit.

An extra kilo of butter would give a new optimal point at the intersection of the lines $3x_1 + 6x_2 = 150$ and $x_1 + x_2 = 28.5$. Solving these equations gives $x_1 = 7$ and $x_2 = 21.5$ with $20x_1 + 30x_2 = 775 + 10$. Profit rises by 10.

These results can be summarized as follows:

(a) An extra kilo of flour would increase the optimal z by $10/3$.

(b) An extra kilo of sugar would increase the optimal z by 0.

(c) An extra kilo of butter would increase the optimal z by 10.

The three numbers $u_1^* = 10/3$, $u_2^* = 0$, and $u_3^* = 10$ are related to the flour, sugar, and butter constraints, respectively. They are the *marginal* profits from an extra kilo of each ingredient. These numbers have many interesting properties we shall now explore.

Suppose (x_1, x_2) is a feasible pair in the problem, so that the three constraints in Example 17.1.1 are satisfied. Multiply the first constraint by 10/3, the second by 0, and the third by 10. Because the multipliers are all ≥ 0, the inequalities are preserved. That is,

$$(10/3)(3x_1 + 6x_2) \leq (10/3) \cdot 150$$
$$0(x_1 + 0.5x_2) \leq 0 \cdot 22$$
$$10(x_1 + x_2) \leq 10 \cdot 27.5$$

Now add all these inequalities, using the obvious fact that if $A \leq B$, $C \leq D$, and $E \leq F$, then $A + C + E \leq B + D + F$. The result is $10x_1 + 20x_2 + 10x_1 + 10x_2 \leq \frac{10}{3} \cdot 150 + 10 \cdot 27.5$, which reduces to

$$20x_1 + 30x_2 \leq 775$$

Thus, using the "magic" numbers u_1^*, u_2^*, and u_3^* defined above, we have proved that if (x_1, x_2) is any feasible pair, then the objective function has to be less than or equal to 775. Because $x_1 = 5$ and $x_2 = 22.5$ give z the value 775, we have in this way *proved algebraically* that $(5, 22.5)$ *is* a solution!

The Dual Problem

The pattern revealed in the last example turns up in all linear programming problems. In fact, the numbers u_1^*, u_2^*, and u_3^* are solutions to a new LP problem called the *dual*.

Recall the baker's problem, now called the *primal* and denoted by (P). It was

$$\max\ 20x_1 + 30x_2 \text{ subject to } \begin{cases} 3x_1 + 6x_2 \leq 150 \\ x_1 + 0.5x_2 \leq 22 \\ x_1 + x_2 \leq 27.5 \end{cases} \quad x_1 \geq 0,\ x_2 \geq 0 \qquad \text{(P)}$$

Suppose the baker gets tired of running the business. (After all, baking cakes this plain is hardly exciting.) An entrant wants to take over and buy all the ingredients. The baker intends to charge a price u_1 for each kilo of flour, u_2 for each kilo of sugar, and u_3 for each kilo of butter. Because one dozen A cakes requires 3 kilos of flour and 1 kilo each of sugar and butter, the baker will charge $3u_1 + u_2 + u_3$ for the ingredients needed to produce a dozen A cakes. The baker originally had a profit of 20 for each dozen A cakes, and he wants to earn at least as much from these ingredients if he quits. Hence, the baker insists that the prices (u_1, u_2, u_3) must satisfy

$$3u_1 + u_2 + u_3 \geq 20$$

Otherwise, it would be more profitable to use the ingredients himself to produce A cakes.

If the baker also wants to earn at least as much as before for the ingredients needed to produce a dozen B cakes, the requirement is

$$6u_1 + 0.5u_2 + u_3 \geq 30$$

Presumably, the entrant wants to buy the baker's resources as inexpensively as possible. The total cost of 150 kilos of flour, 22 kilos of sugar, and 27.5 kilos of butter is $150u_1 +$

$22u_2 + 27.5u_3$. In order to pay as little as possible while having the baker accept the offer, the entrant should suggest prices $u_1 \geq 0$, $u_2 \geq 0$, and $u_3 \geq 0$, that solve the LP problem

$$\min\ 150u_1 + 22u_2 + 27.5u_3 \quad \text{subject to} \quad \begin{cases} 3u_1 + \quad u_2 + u_3 \geq 20 \\ 6u_1 + 0.5u_2 + u_3 \geq 30 \end{cases} \tag{D}$$

which is called the *dual* of the primal problem (P), and so labelled (D).

Suppose the baker lets the entrant take over the business and charges prices that solve problem (D). Will the baker earn as much as before? It turns out that the answer is yes. The solution to (D) is $u_1^* = 10/3$, and $u_2^* = 0$, and $u_3^* = 10$, so the amount the baker gets for selling the resources is $150u_1^* + 22u_2^* + 27.5u_3^* = 775$, which is precisely the maximum value of the objective function in problem (P). The entrant pays for each ingredient exactly the marginal profit for that ingredient which was calculated previously. In particular, the price of sugar is zero, because the baker has more than he can use optimally.

The primal problem (P) and dual problem (D) turn out to be closely related. Let us explain in general how to construct the dual of an LP problem.

The General Case

Consider the general LP problem

$$\max\ c_1 x_1 + \cdots + c_n x_n \quad \text{subject to} \quad \begin{cases} a_{11}x_1 + \cdots + a_{1n}x_n \leq b_1 \\ \dots\dots\dots\dots\dots\dots \\ a_{m1}x_1 + \cdots + a_{mn}x_n \leq b_m \end{cases} \tag{1}$$

with nonnegativity constraints $x_1 \geq 0, \ldots, x_n \geq 0$. Its **dual** is the LP problem

$$\min\ b_1 u_1 + \cdots + b_m u_m \quad \text{subject to} \quad \begin{cases} a_{11}u_1 + \cdots + a_{m1}u_m \geq c_1 \\ \dots\dots\dots\dots\dots\dots \\ a_{1n}u_1 + \cdots + a_{mn}u_m \geq c_n \end{cases} \tag{2}$$

with nonnegativity constraints $u_1 \geq 0, \ldots, u_m \geq 0$. Note that problem (2) is constructed using exactly the same coefficients $c_1, \ldots, c_n, a_{11}, \ldots, a_{mn}$, and $b_1, \ldots, b_m$ as in (1).

In the **primal** problem (1), there are n variables $x_1, \ldots, x_n$ and m constraints (disregarding the nonnegativity constraints). In the dual (2), there are m variables $u_1, \ldots, u_m$ and n constraints. Whereas the primal is a maximization problem, the dual is a minimization problem. In both problems, all variables are nonnegative. There are m "less than or equal to" constraints in the primal problem (1), but n "greater than or equal to" constraints in the dual problem (2). The coefficients of the objective function in either problem are the right-hand side elements of the constraints in the other problem. Finally, the two matrices formed by the coefficients of the variables in the constraints in the primal and dual problems are transposes of each other, because they take the form

$$\mathbf{A} = \begin{pmatrix} a_{11} & a_{12} & \cdots & a_{1n} \\ a_{21} & a_{22} & \cdots & a_{2n} \\ \vdots & \vdots & & \vdots \\ a_{m1} & a_{m2} & \cdots & a_{mn} \end{pmatrix} \quad \text{and} \quad \mathbf{A}' = \begin{pmatrix} a_{11} & a_{21} & \cdots & a_{m1} \\ a_{12} & a_{22} & \cdots & a_{m2} \\ \vdots & \vdots & & \vdots \\ a_{1n} & a_{2n} & \cdots & a_{mn} \end{pmatrix} \tag{3}$$

Check carefully that problem (D) really is the dual of problem (P) in the sense just explained. Due to the symmetry between the two problems, we call each the dual of the other.

Matrix Formulation

Let us introduce the following column vectors (i.e. matrices with one column):

$$\mathbf{x} = \begin{pmatrix} x_1 \\ \vdots \\ x_n \end{pmatrix}, \qquad \mathbf{c} = \begin{pmatrix} c_1 \\ \vdots \\ c_n \end{pmatrix}, \qquad \mathbf{b} = \begin{pmatrix} b_1 \\ \vdots \\ b_m \end{pmatrix}, \qquad \mathbf{u} = \begin{pmatrix} u_1 \\ \vdots \\ u_m \end{pmatrix} \tag{4}$$

When $\mathbf{y}$ and $\mathbf{z}$ are vectors, $\mathbf{y} \leq \mathbf{z}$ means that each component of $\mathbf{y}$ is less than or equal to the corresponding component of $\mathbf{z}$, with $\mathbf{y} \geq \mathbf{z}$ as the reverse inequality.

Then the primal can be written as follows (with $\mathbf{A}$ and $\mathbf{A}'$ given by (3)):

$$\max \mathbf{c}'\mathbf{x} \text{ subject to } \mathbf{A}\mathbf{x} \leq \mathbf{b}, \ \mathbf{x} \geq \mathbf{0} \tag{5}$$

And the dual can be written as min $\mathbf{b}'\mathbf{u}$ subject to $\mathbf{A}'\mathbf{u} \geq \mathbf{c}$, $\mathbf{u} \geq \mathbf{0}$. It is more convenient, however, to write the dual in a slightly different way. Transposing $\mathbf{A}'\mathbf{u} \geq \mathbf{c}$ using the rules in (15.5.2) yields $\mathbf{u}'\mathbf{A} \geq \mathbf{c}'$, and moreover $\mathbf{b}'\mathbf{u} = \mathbf{u}'\mathbf{b}$. So the dual can be written as

$$\min \mathbf{u}'\mathbf{b} \text{ subject to } \mathbf{u}'\mathbf{A} \geq \mathbf{c}', \ \mathbf{u}' \geq \mathbf{0} \tag{6}$$

PROBLEMS FOR SECTION 17.2

⅏ **1.** Consider Problem 17.1.1(a).

(a) Replace the constraint $3x_1 + 2x_2 \leq 6$ by $3x_1 + 2x_2 \leq 7$. Find the new optimal solution and compute the increase u_1^* in the objective function.

(b) Replace the constraint $x_1 + 4x_2 \leq 4$ by $x_1 + 4x_2 \leq 5$. Find the new optimal solution and compute the increase u_2^* in the objective function.

(c) By the same argument as in Example 1, prove that if (x_1, x_2) is feasible in the original problem, then the objective function can never be larger than 36/5.

2. Write down the dual to Problem 17.1.2 (b).

3. Write down the duals to Problems 17.1.1 (a) and (b).

4. (a) Use the graphical method to find the solution to the following LP problem:

$$\max x_1 + x_2 \quad \text{s.t.} \quad \begin{cases} x_1 + 2x_2 \leq 14 \\ 2x_1 + \ x_2 \leq 13 \end{cases} \qquad x_1 \geq 0, \ x_2 \geq 0$$

(b) Write down the dual and find its solution.

17.3 The Duality Theorem

This section presents the main results relating the solution of an LP problem to that of its dual. We begin by considering the baker's problem yet again.

EXAMPLE 1 Consider problems (P) and (D) in Section 17.2. Suppose that (x_1, x_2) is an arbitrary feasible pair in (P), which means that $x_1 \geq 0$, $x_2 \geq 0$, and the three $\leq$ inequalities in (P) are all satisfied. Let (u_1, u_2, u_3) be an arbitrary feasible triple in (D). Multiply the $\leq$ inequalities in (P) by the nonnegative numbers u_1, u_2, and u_3, respectively, and then add the inequalities. The result is the new inequality

$$(3x_1 + 6x_2)u_1 + (x_1 + 0.5x_2)u_2 + (x_1 + x_2)u_3 \leq 150u_1 + 22u_2 + 27.5u_3$$

Rearranging the terms on the left-hand side yields

$$(3u_1 + u_2 + u_3)x_1 + (6u_1 + 0.5u_2 + u_3)x_2 \leq 150u_1 + 22u_2 + 27.5u_3 \qquad \text{(i)}$$

Similarly, we multiply the $\geq$ inequalities in (D) by the nonnegative numbers x_1 and x_2, respectively, and add the results. This gives

$$(3u_1 + u_2 + u_3)x_1 + (6u_1 + 0.5u_2 + u_3)x_2 \geq 20x_1 + 30x_2 \qquad \text{(ii)}$$

From (i) and (ii) together, it follows that

$$150u_1 + 22u_2 + 27.5u_3 \geq 20x_1 + 30x_2 \qquad \text{(iii)}$$

for all feasible (x_1, x_2) in problem (P) and for all feasible (u_1, u_2, u_3) in problem (D). Thus, the objective function in the dual problem is always greater than or equal to the objective function of the primal problem, whatever feasible (x_1, x_2) and (u_1, u_2, u_3) are chosen.

The inequality (iii) is valid for the feasible pair $(x_1, x_2) = (5, 22.5)$ in particular. For each feasible triple (u_1, u_2, u_3), we therefore obtain $150u_1 + 22u_2 + 27.5u_3 \geq 20 \cdot 5 + 30 \cdot 22.5 = 775$. It follows that if we can find a feasible triple (u_1^*, u_2^*, u_3^*) for problem (D) such that $150u_1^* + 22u_2^* + 27.5u_3^* = 775$, then (u_1^*, u_2^*, u_3^*) must solve problem (D), because no lower value of the objective function is obtainable. In Section 17.2, we saw that for $(u_1^*, u_2^*, u_3^*) = (10/3, 0, 10)$, the objective function in the dual did have the value 775. Hence, $(10/3, 0, 10)$ solves the dual problem.

Our analysis of this example illustrates two significant general results in LP theory. Here is the first:

THEOREM 17.3.1

If $(x_1, \ldots, x_n)$ is feasible in the primal problem (17.2.1) and $(u_1, \ldots, u_m)$ is feasible in the dual problem (17.2.2), then

$$b_1u_1 + \cdots + b_mu_m \geq c_1x_1 + \cdots + c_nx_n \qquad (1)$$

So the dual objective function has a value that is always at least as large as that of the primal.

Proof: Multiply the m inequalities in (17.2.1) by the nonnegative numbers $u_1, \ldots, u_m$, then add. Also, multiply the n inequalities in (17.2.2) by the nonnegative numbers $x_1, \ldots, x_n$, then add. These two operations yield the two inequalities

$$(a_{11}x_1 + \cdots + a_{1n}x_n)u_1 + \cdots + (a_{m1}x_1 + \cdots + a_{mn}x_n)u_m \leq b_1u_1 + \cdots + b_mu_m$$

$$(a_{11}u_1 + \cdots + a_{m1}u_m)x_1 + \cdots + (a_{1n}u_1 + \cdots + a_{mn}u_m)x_n \geq c_1x_1 + \cdots + c_nx_n$$

By rearranging the terms on the left-hand side of each inequality, we see that each is equal to the double sum $\sum_{i=1}^{m} \sum_{j=1}^{n} a_{ij}u_ix_j$. So (1) follows immediately.   ∎

From Theorem 17.3.1 we can derive a second significant result:

THEOREM 17.3.2

Suppose that $(x_1^*, \ldots, x_n^*)$ and $(u_1^*, \ldots, u_m^*)$ are feasible in problems (17.2.1) and (17.2.2), respectively, and that

$$c_1x_1^* + \cdots + c_nx_n^* = b_1u_1^* + \cdots + b_mu_m^* \qquad (2)$$

Then $(x_1^*, \ldots, x_n^*)$ solves the primal problem (17.2.1) and $(u_1^*, \ldots, u_m^*)$ solves dual problem (17.2.2).

Proof: Let $(x_1, \ldots, x_n)$ be an arbitrary feasible n-vector for problem (17.2.1). Using (1) with $u_1 = u_1^*, \ldots, u_m = u_m^*$, as well as (2), yields

$$c_1x_1 + \cdots + c_nx_n \leq b_1u_1^* + \cdots + b_mu_m^* = c_1x_1^* + \cdots + c_nx_n^*$$

This proves that $(x_1^*, \ldots, x_n^*)$ solves (17.2.1).

Suppose that $(u_1, \ldots, u_m)$ is feasible for problem (17.2.2). Then (1) and (2) together imply that

$$b_1u_1 + \cdots + b_mu_m \geq c_1x_1^* + \cdots + c_nx_n^* = b_1u_1^* + \cdots + b_mu_m^*$$

This proves that $(u_1^*, \ldots, u_m^*)$ solves (17.2.2).   ∎

Theorem 17.3.2 shows that if we are able to find *feasible* solutions for problems (17.2.1) and (17.2.2) that give the same value to the relevant objective function in each of the two problems, then these feasible solutions are, in fact, *optimal* solutions.

The most important result in duality theory is the following:

THEOREM 17.3.3   (THE DUALITY THEOREM)

Suppose the primal problem (17.2.1) has a (finite) optimal solution. Then the dual problem (17.2.2) also has a (finite) optimal solution, and the corresponding values of the objective functions are equal. If the primal has no bounded optimum, then the dual has no feasible solution. Symmetrically, if the primal has no feasible solution, then the dual has no bounded optimum.

The proofs of Theorems 17.3.1 and 17.3.2 were very simple. It is much more difficult to prove the first statement in Theorem 17.3.3 concerning the existence of a solution to the dual, and we shall not attempt to provide a proof here. The last statement in Theorem 17.3.3, however, follows readily from inequality (1). For if $(u_1, \ldots, u_m)$ is any feasible solution to the dual problem, then $b_1 u_1 + \cdots + b_m u_m$ is a finite number greater than or equal to *any* number $c_1 x_1 + \cdots + c_n x_n$ when $(x_1, \ldots, x_n)$ is feasible in the primal. This puts an upper bound on the possible values of $c_1 x_1 + \cdots + c_n x_n$.

NOTE 1　An instructive exercise is to formulate and prove Theorems 17.3.1 and 17.3.2 using matrix algebra. Let us do so for Theorem 17.3.1. Suppose $\mathbf{x}$ is feasible in (17.2.5) and $\mathbf{u}$ is feasible in (17.2.6). Then $\mathbf{u}'\mathbf{b} \geq \mathbf{u}'(\mathbf{A}\mathbf{x}) = (\mathbf{u}'\mathbf{A})\mathbf{x} \geq \mathbf{c}'\mathbf{x}$. Note carefully how these inequalities correspond to those we established in the earlier proof of Theorem 17.3.1.

PROBLEMS FOR SECTION 17.3

(SM) **1.** (a) Solve the following problem by a graphical argument:

$$\max \quad 2x + 7y \quad \text{subject to} \quad \begin{cases} 4x + 5y \leq 20 \\ 3x + 7y \leq 21 \end{cases} \quad x \geq 0, \quad y \geq 0$$

(b) Write down the dual and solve it by a graphical argument.

(c) Are the values of the objective functions equal? (If not, then according to Theorem 17.3.3, you have made a mistake.)

2. Write down the dual to the problem in Example 17.1.2 and solve it. Check that the optimal values of the objective functions are equal.

(SM) **3.** (a) A firm produces small and medium television sets. The profit is 400 for each small and 500 for each medium television set. Each television has to be processed on three different assembly lines. Each small television requires respectively 2, 1, and 1 hour on lines 1, 2, and 3. The corresponding numbers for the medium television sets are 1, 4, and 2. Suppose lines 1 and 2 both have a capacity of at most 16 hours per day, and line 3 has a capacity of at most 11 hours per day. Let x_1 and x_2 denote the number of small and medium television sets that are produced per day. Show that in order to maximize profits per day, one must solve the following problem:

$$\max \quad 400x_1 + 500x_2 \quad \text{subject to} \quad \begin{cases} 2x_1 + x_2 \leq 16 \\ x_1 + 4x_2 \leq 16 \\ x_1 + 2x_2 \leq 11 \end{cases} \quad x_1 \geq 0, \quad x_2 \geq 0$$

(b) Solve this problem graphically.

(c) Suppose the firm could increase its capacity by 1 hour a day on just one of its assembly lines. Which line should have its capacity increased?

17.4 A General Economic Interpretation

This section gives an economic interpretation of the general LP problem (17.2.1) and its dual (17.2.2). Think of a firm that produces one or more different kinds of output using m different **resources** as inputs. There are n different **activities** (or processes) involved in the production process. A typical activity is characterized by the fact that running it at unit level requires a certain amount of each resource. If a_{ij} is the number of units of resource i that are needed to run activity j at unit level, the vector with components $a_{1j}, a_{2j}, \ldots, a_{mj}$ expresses the m different total resource requirements for running activity j at unit level. If we run the activities at levels $x_1, \ldots, x_n$, the total resource requirement can be expressed as the column vector

$$x_1 \begin{pmatrix} a_{11} \\ \vdots \\ a_{m1} \end{pmatrix} + \cdots + x_n \begin{pmatrix} a_{1n} \\ \vdots \\ a_{mn} \end{pmatrix}$$

If the available resources are $b_1, \ldots, b_m$, then the feasible activity levels are those that satisfy the m constraints in (17.2.1). The nonnegativity constraints reflect the fact that we cannot run the activities at negative levels.

Each activity brings a certain "reward". Let c_j denote the reward (or value) earned by running activity j at unit level. The total reward from running the n activities at levels $x_1, \ldots, x_n$ is then $c_1 x_1 + \cdots + c_n x_n$. So the firm faces the problem of solving the following LP problem: *Find those levels for the n activities that maximize the total reward, subject to the given resource constraints.*

The baker's problem in Example 17.1.1 provides an illustration. The two activities are baking the two different types of cake, and there are three resources—flour, sugar, and butter.

Let us turn to the dual problem (17.2.2). In order to remain in business, the firm has to use some resources. Each resource, therefore, has a value or price. Let u_j be the price associated with one unit of resource j. Rather than think of u_j as a market price for resource j, we should think of it as measuring the relative contribution that one unit of resource j makes to the total economic reward. Because these are not real market prices, they are often called **shadow prices**.

Because $a_{1j}, a_{2j}, \ldots, a_{mj}$ are the quantities of each of the m resources needed to run activity j at unit level, $a_{1j}u_1 + a_{2j}u_2 + \cdots + a_{mj}u_m$ is the total (shadow) cost of running activity j at unit level. Because c_j is the reward earned by running activity j at unit level, the difference

$$c_j - (a_{1j}u_1 + a_{2j}u_2 + \cdots + a_{mj}u_m)$$

can be regarded as the (shadow) *profit* from running activity j at unit level. Note that the jth constraint in the dual problem (17.2.2) says that the (shadow) profit from running activity j at unit level is ≤ 0.

The objective function $Z = b_1 u_1 + \cdots + b_m u_m$ in the dual LP problem measures the (shadow) value of the initial stock of all the resources. The dual problem is, therefore: *Among all choices of nonnegative shadow prices $u_1, \ldots, u_m$ such that the profit from running each activity at unit level is ≤ 0, find those prices which together minimize the (shadow) value of the initial resources.*

The Optimal Dual Variables as Shadow Prices

Consider again the primal problem (17.2.1). What happens to the optimal value of the objective function if the numbers $b_1, \ldots, b_m$ change? If the changes $\Delta b_1, \ldots, \Delta b_m$ are positive, then the feasible set increases and the new optimal value of the objective function cannot be smaller. (Usually it increases.) The following analysis also applies when some or all the changes $\Delta b_1, \ldots, \Delta b_m$ are negative.

Suppose $(x_1^*, \ldots, x_n^*)$ and $(x_1^* + \Delta x_1, \ldots, x_n^* + \Delta x_n)$ are optimal solutions to the primal problem when the right-hand sides of the constraints are respectively $(b_1, \ldots, b_m)$ and $(b_1 + \Delta b_1, \ldots, b_m + \Delta b_m)$. Typically, if $\Delta b_1, \ldots, \Delta b_m$ are all sufficiently small, the duals of the two problems have the same optimal solution $u_1^*, \ldots, u_m^*$. Then, according to Theorem 17.3.3, one has

$$c_1 x_1^* + \cdots + c_n x_n^* = b_1 u_1^* + \cdots + b_m u_m^*$$
$$c_1(x_1^* + \Delta x_1) + \cdots + c_n(x_n^* + \Delta x_n) = (b_1 + \Delta b_1)u_1^* + \cdots + (b_m + \Delta b_m)u_m^*$$

Hence, by subtraction,

$$c_1 \Delta x_1 + \cdots + c_n \Delta x_n = u_1^* \Delta b_1 + \cdots + u_m^* \Delta b_m$$

Here the left-hand side is the change we obtain in the objective function in (1) when b_1, $\ldots, b_m$ are changed by $\Delta b_1, \ldots, \Delta b_m$, respectively. Denoting this change in z by Δz^*, we obtain

$$\Delta z^* = u_1^* \Delta b_1 + \cdots + u_m^* \Delta b_m \tag{1}$$

NOTE 1   The assumption underlying (1) is that the numbers b_j do not change enough to cause the optimal dual variables to change. If $\Delta b_j = 1$, while all $\Delta b_i = 0$ for $i \neq j$, then $\Delta z^* = u_j^*$. This accords with the results in Example 17.2.1.

PROBLEMS FOR SECTION 17.4

1. Consider Problem 17.3.1. We found that the optimal solution of this problem was $x^* = 0$ and $y^* = 3$, with $z^* = 2x^* + 7y^* = 21$. The optimal solution of the dual was $u_1^* = 0$ and $u_2^* = 1$. Suppose we change 20 to 20.1 and 21 to 20.8. What is the corresponding change in the objective function?

(SM) **2.** (a) A firm produces two goods A and B. The firm earns a profit of 300 from each unit of good A, and 200 from each unit of B. There are three stages of the production process. Good A requires 6 hours in production, then 4 hours in assembly, and finally 5 hours of packing. The corresponding numbers for B are 3, 6, and 5, respectively. The total number of hours available for the three stages are 54, 48, and 50, respectively. Formulate and solve the LP problem of maximizing profits subject to the given constraints.

(b) Write down and solve the dual problem.

(c) By how much would the optimal profit increase if the firm gets 2 hours more preparation time and 1 hour more packing time?

17.5   Complementary Slackness

Consider again the baker's problem (P) in Section 17.2 and its dual (D). The solution to (P) was $x_1^* = 5$ and $x_2^* = 22.5$, with the first and the third inequalities both satisfied with equality. The solution to the dual was $u_1^* = 10/3$, $u_2^* = 0$, and $u_3^* = 10$, with both inequalities in the dual satisfied with equality. Thus, in this example

$$x_1^* > 0, \ x_2^* > 0 \implies \begin{cases} \text{the first and second inequalities} \\ \text{in the dual are satisfied with equality} \end{cases}$$

$$u_1^* > 0, \ u_3^* > 0 \implies \begin{cases} \text{the first and third inequalities} \\ \text{in the primal are satisfied with equality} \end{cases}$$

We interpret the second implication this way: Because the shadow prices of flour and butter are positive, the optimal solution requires all the available flour and butter to be used, but not all the available sugar, so its shadow price is zero—it is not a scarce resource.

Implications like this hold more generally. Indeed, consider the problem

$$\max \ c_1 x_1 + c_2 x_2 \quad \text{subject to} \quad \begin{cases} a_{11}x_1 + a_{12}x_2 \le b_1 \\ a_{21}x_1 + a_{22}x_2 \le b_2 \\ a_{31}x_1 + a_{32}x_2 \le b_3 \end{cases} \quad x_1 \ge 0, \ x_2 \ge 0 \qquad \text{(i)}$$

and its dual

$$\min \ b_1 u_1 + b_2 u_2 + b_3 u_3 \quad \text{subject to} \quad \begin{cases} a_{11}u_1 + a_{21}u_2 + a_{31}u_3 \ge c_1 \\ a_{12}u_1 + a_{22}u_2 + a_{32}u_3 \ge c_2 \end{cases} \qquad \text{(ii)}$$

with u_1, u_2, and $u_3 \ge 0$. Suppose (x_1^*, x_2^*) solves (i) and (u_1^*, u_2^*, u_3^*) solves (ii). Then

$$\text{(iii)} \quad \begin{matrix} a_{11}x_1^* + a_{12}x_2^* \le b_1 \\ a_{21}x_1^* + a_{22}x_2^* \le b_2 \\ a_{31}x_1^* + a_{32}x_2^* \le b_3 \end{matrix} \quad \text{and} \quad \text{(iv)} \quad \begin{matrix} a_{11}u_1^* + a_{21}u_2^* + a_{31}u_3^* \ge c_1 \\ a_{12}u_1^* + a_{22}u_2^* + a_{32}u_3^* \ge c_2 \end{matrix}$$

Multiply the three inequalities in (iii) by the three nonnegative numbers u_1^*, u_2^*, and u_3^*, respectively. Then add the results. This yields the inequality

$$(a_{11}x_1^* + a_{12}x_2^*)u_1^* + (a_{21}x_1^* + a_{22}x_2^*)u_2^* + (a_{31}x_1^* + a_{32}x_2^*)u_3^* \le b_1 u_1^* + b_2 u_2^* + b_3 u_3^* \qquad \text{(v)}$$

Multiply the two inequalities in (iv) by x_1^* and x_2^*, respectively, and then add. This gives

$$(a_{11}u_1^* + a_{21}u_2^* + a_{31}u_3^*)x_1^* + (a_{12}u_1^* + a_{22}u_2^* + a_{32}u_3^*)x_2^* \ge c_1 x_1^* + c_2 x_2^* \qquad \text{(vi)}$$

But the left-hand sides of the inequalities (v) and (vi) are rearrangements of each other. Moreover, by the duality theorem of LP (Theorem 17.3.3), their right-hand sides are the equal values of the primal and dual. Hence, both inequalities in (v) and (vi) can be replaced by *equalities*. In particular, we can rearrange the equality version of (v) to obtain

$$(a_{11}x_1^* + a_{12}x_2^* - b_1)u_1^* + (a_{21}x_1^* + a_{22}x_2^* - b_2)u_2^* + (a_{31}x_1^* + a_{32}x_2^* - b_3)u_3^* = 0$$

Because (x_1^*, x_2^*) is feasible, (iii) implies that each term in parentheses is ≤ 0. But each $u_i \geq 0$, so the left-hand side is the sum of three ≤ 0 terms. If any is < 0, so is their sum. But the sum is 0, so each term is 0. Thus,

$$(a_{j1}x_1^* + a_{j2}x_2^* - b_j)u_j^* = 0, \quad j = 1, 2, 3$$

We conclude that

$$a_{j1}x_1^* + a_{j2}x_2^* \leq b_j, \quad \text{with } a_{j1}x_1^* + a_{j2}x_2^* = b_j \text{ if } u_j^* > 0, \quad j = 1, 2, 3$$

Using the fact that $\geq$ in (vi) can be replaced by =, and reasoning in exactly the same way as above, we also get

$$a_{1i}u_1^* + a_{2i}u_2^* + a_{3i}u_3^* \geq c_i, \quad \text{with } a_{1i}u_1^* + a_{2i}u_2^* + a_{3i}u_3^* = c_i \text{ if } x_i^* > 0, \quad i = 1, 2$$

These last two sets of inequalities (or equalities) are called **complementary slackness conditions**. The arguments used to show their necessity extend in a straightforward way to the general case. Furthermore, the same complementary slackness conditions are also sufficient for optimality. Here is a general statement and proof:

THEOREM 17.5.1 (COMPLEMENTARY SLACKNESS)

Suppose that the primal problem (17.2.1) has an optimal solution $\mathbf{x}^* = (x_1^*, \ldots, x_n^*)$, whereas the dual (17.2.2) has an optimal solution $\mathbf{u}^* = (u_1^*, \ldots, u_m^*)$. Then for $i = 1, \ldots, n$, and $j = 1, \ldots, m$,

$$a_{1i}u_1^* + \cdots + a_{mi}u_m^* \geq c_i, \quad \text{with} \quad a_{1i}u_1^* + \cdots + a_{mi}u_m^* = c_i \text{ if } x_i^* > 0 \qquad (1)$$

$$a_{j1}x_1^* + \cdots + a_{jn}x_n^* \leq b_j, \quad \text{with} \quad a_{j1}x_1^* + \cdots + a_{jn}x_n^* = b_j \text{ if } u_j^* > 0 \qquad (2)$$

Conversely, if $\mathbf{x}^*$ and $\mathbf{u}^*$ have all their components nonnegative and satisfy (1) and (2), then $\mathbf{x}^*$ and $\mathbf{u}^*$ solve the primal problem (17.2.1) and the dual (17.2.2), respectively.

Proof: Suppose $\mathbf{x}^*$ solves (17.2.1) and $\mathbf{u}^*$ solves (17.2.2). Using the matrix notation of (17.2.5) and (17.2.6), it follows that

$$\mathbf{A}\mathbf{x}^* \leqq \mathbf{b} \quad \text{and} \quad (\mathbf{u}^*)'\mathbf{A} \geqq \mathbf{c}' \qquad (i)$$

Multiplying the first inequality in (i) on the left by $(\mathbf{u}^*)' \geqq \mathbf{0}$ and the second inequality on the right by $\mathbf{x}^* \geqq \mathbf{0}$ yields

$$(\mathbf{u}^*)'\mathbf{A}\mathbf{x}^* \leqq (\mathbf{u}^*)'\mathbf{b} \quad \text{and} \quad (\mathbf{u}^*)'\mathbf{A}\mathbf{x}^* \geqq \mathbf{c}'\mathbf{x}^* \qquad (ii)$$

According to Theorem 17.3.3, $(\mathbf{u}^*)'\mathbf{b} = \mathbf{c}'\mathbf{x}^*$. So both inequalities in (ii) must be equalities. They can be written as

$$(\mathbf{u}^*)'(\mathbf{A}\mathbf{x}^* - \mathbf{b}) = 0 \quad \text{and} \quad ((\mathbf{u}^*)'\mathbf{A} - \mathbf{c}')\mathbf{x}^* = 0 \qquad (iii)$$

But these two equations are equivalent to the two equalities

$$\sum_{j=1}^{m} u_j^*(a_{j1}x_1^* + \cdots + a_{jn}x_n^* - b_j) = 0 \qquad (iv)$$

$$\sum_{i=1}^{n} (a_{1i}u_1^* + \cdots + a_{mi}u_m^* - c_i)x_i^* = 0 \qquad (v)$$

For $j = 1, \ldots, m$ one has both $u_j^* \geq 0$ and $a_{j1}x_1^* + \cdots + a_{jn}x_n^* - b_j \leq 0$. So each term in the sum (iv) is ≤ 0. If any term is negative, so is their sum; but the sum of all m terms is 0, so each term in (iv) must be 0 as well. Therefore,

$$u_j^*(a_{j1}x_1^* + \cdots + a_{jn}x_n^* - b_j) = 0, \qquad j = 1, \ldots, m \tag{vi}$$

Now (2) follows immediately. Property (1) is proved in the same way by noting how (v) implies that

$$x_i^*(a_{1i}u_1^* + \cdots + a_{mi}u_m^* - c_i) = 0, \qquad i = 1, \ldots, n \tag{vii}$$

Suppose on the other hand that $\mathbf{x}^*$ and $\mathbf{u}^*$ have all their components nonnegative and satisfy (1) and (2) respectively. It follows immediately that (vi) and (vii) are satisfied. So summing over j and i, respectively, we obtain (iv) and (v). These equations imply that $\sum_{j=1}^m b_j u_j^* = \sum_{j=1}^m \sum_{i=1}^n a_{ji} x_i^* u_j^*$ and also $\sum_{i=1}^n c_i x_i^* = \sum_{i=1}^n \sum_{j=1}^m a_{ji} u_j^* x_i^*$. Because the two double sums are equal, $\sum_{j=1}^m b_j u_j^* = \sum_{i=1}^n c_i x_i^*$. So according to Theorem 17.3.2, $\mathbf{x}^*$ solves problem (1) and $\mathbf{u}^*$ solves the dual. ∎

NOTE 1   Using the economic interpretations we gave in Section 17.4, conditions (1) and (2) can be interpreted as follows:

If the optimal solution of the primal problem implies that activity i is in operation ($x_i^* > 0$), then the (shadow) profit from running that activity at unit level is 0.

If the shadow price of resource j is positive ($u_j^* > 0$), then all the available stock of resource j must be used in any optimum.

How Complementary Slackness Can Help Solve LP Problems

If the solution to either the primal or the dual problem is known, then the complementary slackness conditions can help find the solution to the other problem by determining which constraints are slack, and so which hold with equality. Let us look at an example.

EXAMPLE 1   Write down the dual of the following LP problem and solve it by a graphical argument.

$$\max 3x_1 + 4x_2 + 6x_3 \text{ subject to } \begin{cases} 3x_1 + x_2 + x_3 \leq 2 \\ x_1 + 2x_2 + 6x_3 \leq 1 \end{cases}, \quad x_1 \geq 0, \, x_2 \geq 0, \, x_3 \geq 0 \tag{i}$$

Then use complementary slackness to solve (i).

Solution: The dual problem is

$$\min 2u_1 + u_2 \text{ subject to } \begin{cases} 3u_1 + u_2 \geq 3 \\ u_1 + 2u_2 \geq 4 \\ u_1 + 6u_2 \geq 6 \end{cases}, \quad u_1 \geq 0, \, u_2 \geq 0 \tag{ii}$$

Using the graphical solution technique shown in Example 17.1.2, we find the solution $u_1^* = 2/5$, and $u_2^* = 9/5$. Then $3u_1^* + u_2^* = 3$, and $u_1^* + 2u_2^* = 4$, and $u_1^* + 6u_2^* > 6$.

What do we know about the solution (x_1^*, x_2^*, x_3^*) to (i)? According to (2), because $u_1^* > 0$ and $u_2^* > 0$, both inequalities in (i) are satisfied with equality. So

$$3x_1^* + x_2^* + x_3^* = 2 \qquad \text{and} \qquad x_1^* + 2x_2^* + 6x_3^* = 1 \tag{iii}$$

Next, since $u_1^* + 6u_2^* > 6$, the complementary slackness condition (1) implies that $x_3^* = 0$. Letting $x_3^* = 0$ in (iii) and solving for x_1^* and x_2^* gives

$$x_1^* = 3/5, \qquad x_2^* = 1/5, \qquad x_3^* = 0$$

This is the solution to problem (i). Note that the optimal values of the objective functions in the two problems are indeed equal: $2u_1^* + u_2^* = 13/5$ and $3x_1^* + 4x_2^* + 6x_3^* = 13/5$, just as they should be according to the duality theorem.

The Kuhn–Tucker Theorem Applied to Linear Programmes

The general linear programming problem

$$\max c_1 x_1 + \cdots + c_n x_n \text{ s.t. } \begin{cases} a_{11}x_1 + \cdots + a_{1n}x_n \le b_1 \\ \dots\dots\dots\dots\dots\dots\dots \\ a_{m1}x_1 + \cdots + a_{mn}x_n \le b_m \end{cases}, \quad x_1 \ge 0, \dots, x_n \ge 0 \quad (3)$$

is obviously a special case of the general nonlinear programming problem

$$\max f(x_1, \dots, x_n) \text{ s.t. } \begin{cases} g_1(x_1, \dots, x_n) \le c_1 \\ \dots\dots\dots\dots\dots \\ g_m(x_1, \dots, x_n) \le c_m \end{cases}, \quad x_1 \ge 0, \dots, x_n \ge 0 \quad (4)$$

that was studied in Section 14.9.

Let us see what form the conditions (14.10.3) and (14.10.4) take in the linear case. If we let $\lambda_j = u_j^*$ for $j = 1, \dots, m$, the conditions become

$$c_i - (a_{1i}u_1^* + \cdots + a_{mi}u_m^*) \le 0 \quad (= 0 \text{ if } x_i^* > 0), \qquad i = 1, \dots, n \quad (5)$$

$$u_j^* \ge 0 \quad (= 0 \text{ if } a_{j1}x_1^* + \cdots + a_{jn}x_n^* < b_j), \qquad j = 1, \dots, m \quad (6)$$

When combined with the requirement that $\mathbf{x}^*$ satisfy the constraints in problem (3), these conditions are precisely the complementary slackness conditions in Theorem 17.5.1.

Duality when Some Constraints Are Equalities

Suppose that one of the m constraints in the primal problem is the equality

$$a_{i1}x_1 + \cdots + a_{in}x_n = b_i \tag{$*$}$$

rather than the corresponding inequality in (17.2.1). In order to put the problem into the standard form, we can replace $(*)$ by the two inequalities

$$a_{i1}x_1 + \cdots + a_{in}x_n \le b_i \qquad \text{and} \qquad -a_{i1}x_1 - \cdots - a_{in}x_n \le -b_i \tag{$**$}$$

Constraint (∗) thus gives rise to two dual variables u_i' and u_i''. For each $j = 1, \ldots, n$ the term $a_{ij}u_i$ in the sum on the left-hand side of the constraint $\sum_{k=1}^{m} a_{kj}u_k \geq c_j$ in (17.2.2) gets replaced by $a_{ij}u_i' - a_{ij}u_i''$. Therefore, we can replace the two variables u_i' and u_i'' with the single variable $u_i = u_i' - u_i''$, but then there is no restriction on the sign of u_i. We see that *if the ith constraint in the primal is an equality, then the ith dual variable has an unrestricted sign*. This is consistent with the economic interpretation we have given. If we are forced to use all of resource i, then it is not surprising that the resource may have a negative shadow price—it may be something that is harmful in excess. For instance, if the baker of Example 17.1.1 was forced to include all the stock of sugar in the cakes, the best point in Fig. 17.1.2 would be C, not B. Some profit would be lost.

From the symmetry between the primal and the dual, we realize now that *if one of the variables in the primal has an unrestricted sign, then the corresponding constraint in the dual is an equality*.

PROBLEMS FOR SECTION 17.5

1. Consider Problem 17.3.1. The solution of the primal was $x^* = 0$, and $y^* = 3$, with $u_1^* = 0$, $u_2^* = 1$ as the solution of the dual. Verify that (1) and (2) are satisfied in this case.

2. (a) Solve the following problem graphically:

$$\min\ y_1 + 2y_2 \ \text{s.t.} \begin{cases} y_1 + 6y_2 \geq 15 \\ y_1 + y_2 \geq 5 \\ -y_1 + y_2 \geq -5 \\ y_1 - 2y_2 \geq -20 \end{cases} \quad y_1 \geq 0,\ y_2 \geq 0$$

   (b) Write down the dual problem and solve it.

   (c) What happens to the optimal dual variables if the constraint $y_1 + 6y_2 \geq 15$ is changed to $y_1 + 6y_2 \geq 15.1$?

(SM) 3. A firm produces two commodities A and B. The firm has three factories that jointly produce both commodities in the amounts per hour given in the following table:

	Factory 1	Factory 2	Factory 3
Commodity A	10	20	20
Commodity B	20	10	20

The firm receives an order for 300 units of A and 500 units of B. The costs per hour of running factories 1, 2, and 3 are respectively 10 000, 8000, and 11 000.

   (a) Let y_1, y_2, and y_3, respectively, denote the number of hours for which the three factories are used. Write down the linear programming problem of minimizing the costs of fulfilling the order.

   (b) Write down the dual and solve it. Then find the solution of the problem in part (a).

   (c) By how much will the minimum cost of production increase if the cost per hour in factory 1 increases by 100?

HARDER PROBLEM

4. Consider the LP problem

$$\max\ 3x_1 + 2x_2 \quad \text{s.t.} \quad \begin{cases} x_1 + x_2 & \le 3 \\ 2x_1 + x_2 - x_3 \le 1 \\ x_1 + 2x_2 - 2x_3 \le 1 \end{cases} \quad x_1 \ge 0,\ x_2 \ge 0,\ x_3 \ge 0$$

(a) Suppose x_3 is a fixed number. Solve the problem if $x_3 = 0$ and if $x_3 = 3$.

(b) Formulate and solve the problem for any fixed value of x_3 in $[0, \infty)$. The maximal value of $3x_1 + 2x_2$ becomes a function of x_3. Find this function and maximize it.

(c) Do the results in part (b) say anything about the solution to the original problem, in which x_3 can also be chosen?

REVIEW PROBLEMS FOR CHAPTER 17

1. (a) Solve the LP problem

$$\max\ x + 2y \text{ subject to } \begin{cases} x + y \le 4 \\ -x + y \le 1 \\ 2x - y \le 3 \end{cases} \quad x \ge 0,\ y \ge 0$$

(b) Formulate and solve the dual problem.

(SM) 2. Consider the LP problem

$$\min\ 16y_1 + 6y_2 - 8y_3 - 15y_4 \quad \text{s.t.} \quad \begin{cases} -y_1 + y_2 - 2y_3 - 4y_4 \ge -1 \\ 2y_1 - 2y_2 - y_3 - 5y_4 \ge 1 \end{cases}$$

where $y_i \ge 0, i = 1, 2, 3, 4$.

(a) Write down the dual problem and solve it.

(b) Find the solution to the primal problem.

(c) If the first constraint in the primal is changed to $-y_1 + y_2 - 2y_3 - 4y_4 \ge k$, for what values of k will the solution of the dual occur at the same point as for $k = -1$?

3. (a) Solve the LP problem: $\min\ 5x + y$ subject to $\begin{cases} 4x + y \ge 4 \\ 2x + y \ge 3 \\ 3x + 2y \ge 2 \\ -x + 2y \ge -2 \end{cases}$, $x \ge 0,\ y \ge 0$

(b) Formulate the dual problem and solve it.

(SM) **4.** A firm produces x_1 cars and x_2 trucks per month. Suppose each car requires 0.04% of the capacity per month in the body division, 0.025% of the capacity per month in the motor division, and 0.05% of the capacity per month on the specialized car assembly line. The corresponding numbers for trucks are 0.03% in the body division, 0.05% in the motor division, and 0.08% on the specialized truck assembly line. The firm can therefore deliver x_1 cars and x_2 trucks per month provided the following inequalities are satisfied:

$$0.04x_1 + 0.03x_2 \le 100$$
$$0.025x_1 + 0.05x_2 \le 100$$
$$0.05x_1 \le 100 \qquad (*)$$
$$0.08x_2 \le 100$$

with $x_1 \ge 0$, $x_2 \ge 0$. Suppose the profit per car is $500 - ax_1$, where a is a nonnegative constant, while the profit per truck is 250. The firm thus seeks to solve the problem

$$\max \ (500 - ax_1)x_1 + 250x_2 \quad \text{subject to } (*)$$

(a) Solve the problem graphically if $a = 0$.

(b) Write down conditions (14.10.3) and (14.10.4) for the problem when $a \ge 0$.

(c) Use the conditions obtained in (b) to examine for which values of $a \ge 0$ the solution is the same as for $a = 0$.

(SM) **5.** The production of three goods requires using two machines. Machine 1 can be utilized for b_1 hours, while machine 2 can be utilized for b_2 hours. The time spent for the production of one unit of each good is given by the following table:

	Machine 1	Machine 2
Good 1	3	2
Good 2	1	2
Good 3	4	1

The profits per unit produced of the three goods are 6, 3, and 4, respectively.

(a) Write down the linear programming problem this leads to.

(b) Show that the dual is

$$\min \ b_1 y_1 + b_2 y_2 \quad \text{s.t.} \quad \begin{cases} 3y_1 + 2y_2 \ge 6 \\ y_1 + 2y_2 \ge 3 \\ 4y_1 + \ y_2 \ge 4 \end{cases} \quad y_1 \ge 0, \ y_2 \ge 0$$

Solve this problem geometrically for $b_1 = b_2 = 100$.

(c) Solve the problem in (a) when $b_1 = b_2 = 100$.

(d) If machine 1 increases its capacity to 101, while $b_2 = 100$, what is the new maximal profit?

(e) The maximum value of the profit in problem (a) is a function F of b_1 and b_2. What is the degree of homogeneity of the function F?

GEOMETRY

Let no one ignorant of geometry enter this door.
—Entrance to Plato's Academy

This appendix is to remind the reader about some simple formulas and results from geometry that are occasionally useful for economists, and sometimes used in this book.

Triangles

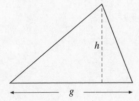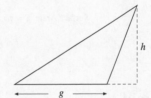

Area: $A = \frac{1}{2}gh$

Circles

Area: $A = \pi r^2$

Circumference: $C = 2\pi r$

Area: $A = \frac{1}{2}xr$

Rectangular Box

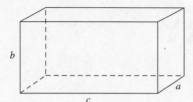

Volume: $V = abc$

Surface Area: $S = 2ab + 2ac + 2bc$

Sphere (Ball)

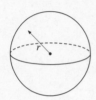

Volume: $V = \frac{4}{3}\pi r^3$

Surface Area: $S = 4\pi r^2$

Cone

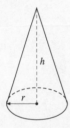

Volume: $V = \frac{1}{3}\pi r^2 h$

Surface Area: $S = \pi r^2 + \pi r\sqrt{h^2 + r^2}$

Pyramid

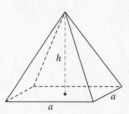

Volume: $V = \frac{1}{3}a^2 h$

Surface Area: $S = a^2 + a\sqrt{a^2 + 4h^2}$

Angles

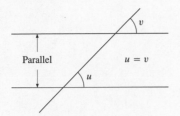 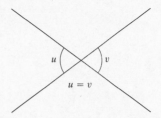

Proportions

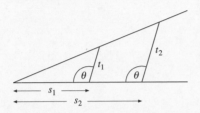

$t_1/s_1 = t_2/s_2$

Sum of Angles in a Triangle

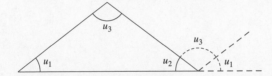

$u_1 + u_2 + u_3 = 180°$

Pythagoras's Theorem

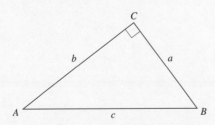

$\angle C = 90° \iff a^2 + b^2 = c^2$

The Greek Alphabet

A α	alpha	H η	eta	N ν	nu	T τ	tau
B β	beta	$\Theta\ \theta\ \vartheta$	theta	$\Xi\ \xi$	xi	$\Upsilon\ \upsilon$	upsilon
$\Gamma\ \gamma$	gamma	I ι	iota	O o	omicron	$\Phi\ \phi\ \varphi$	phi
$\Delta\ \delta$	delta	K κ	kappa	$\Pi\ \pi$	pi	X χ	chi
E $\epsilon\ \varepsilon$	epsilon	$\Lambda\ \lambda$	lambda	P $\rho\ \varrho$	rho	$\Psi\ \psi$	psi
Z ζ	zeta	M μ	mu	$\Sigma\ \sigma$	sigma	$\Omega\ \omega$	omega

ANSWERS TO THE PROBLEMS

Chapter 1

1.1

1. (a) True.   (b) False. -5 is smaller than -3, so on the number line it is to the left of -3.   (c) False. -13 is an integer, but not a natural number.   (d) True. Every natural number is rational. For example $5 = 5/1$.   (e) False, since $3.1415 = 31415/10000$, the quotient of two integers. (Note that 3.1415 is only an approximation to the irrational number π).   (f) False. Counterexample: $\sqrt{2} + (-\sqrt{2}) = 0$.   (g) True.   (h) True.

2. There is obviously no finite sequence of digits that repeats itself indefinitely, because one extra zero is added between each successive pair of ones: $1.01001000100001000001\ldots$

1.2

1. (a) $10^3 = 10 \cdot 10 \cdot 10 = 1000$ (b) $(-0.3)^2 = 0.09$ (c) $4^{-2} = 1/16$ (d) $(0.1)^{-1} = 1/0.1 = 10$

2. (a) $4 = 2^2$ (b) $1 = 2^0$ (c) $64 = 2^6$ (d) $1/16 = 2^{-4}$

3. (a) 15^3 (b) $\left(-\frac{1}{3}\right)^3$ (c) 10^{-1} (d) 10^{-7} (e) t^6 (f) $(a-b)^3$ (g) $a^2 b^4$ (h) $(-a)^3$

4. (a) $2^5 \cdot 2^5 = 2^{5+5} = 2^{10}$ (b) $3^8 \cdot 3^{-2} \cdot 3^{-3} = 3^{8-2-3} = 3^3$ (c) $(2x)^3 = 2^3 x^3 = 8x^3$
   (d) $(-3xy^2)^3 = (-3)^3 x^3 (y^2)^3 = -27x^3 y^6$

5. (a) $\dfrac{p^{24} p^3}{p^4 p} = p^{24+3-4-1} = p^{22}$ (b) $\dfrac{a^4 b^{-3}}{(a^2 b^{-3})^2} = \dfrac{a^4 b^{-3}}{a^4 b^{-6}} = a^{4-4} b^{-3-(-6)} = b^3$
   (c) $\dfrac{3^4 (3^2)^6}{(-3)^{15} 3^7} = \dfrac{3^4 3^{12}}{-3^{15} 3^7} = -3^{-6}$ (d) $\dfrac{p^\gamma (pq)^\sigma}{p^{2\gamma+\sigma} q^{\sigma-2}} = p^{-\gamma} q^2$

6. (a) $2^6 = 64$ (b) $64/27$ (c) $8/3$ (d) x^9 (e) y^{12} (f) $8x^3 y^3$ (g) $10^{-2} = 1/100$ (h) k^4 (i) $(x+1)^2$

7. (a) Because $4\pi(3r)^2 = 4\pi 3^2 r^2 = 9(4\pi r^2)$, the surface area increases by the factor 9.
   (b) When r increases by 16%, it increases by a factor of 1.16, and r^2 increases by the factor $(1.16)^2 = 1.3456$, and thus the surface area increases by 34.56%.

8. (a) False. $a^0 = 1$.   (b) True. $c^{-n} = 1/c^n$ for all $c \neq 0$.   (c) True. $a^m \cdot a^m = a^{m+m} = a^{2m}$.
   (d) False (unless $m = 0$ or $ab = 1$). $a^m b^m = (ab)^m$.   (e) False (unless $m = 1$). For example, $(a+b)^2$ is equal to $a^2 + 2ab + b^2$.   (f) False (unless $a^m b^n = 1$). For example, $a^2 b^3$ is not equal to $(ab)^{2+3} = (ab)^5 = a^5 b^5$.

9. (a) $x^3 y^3 = (xy)^3 = 3^3 = 27$ (b) $(ab)^4 = (-2)^4 = 16$ (c) $(a^8)^0 = 1$ for all $a \neq 0$.
   (d) $(-1)^{2n} = [(-1)^2]^n = 1^n = 1$

10. (a) $150 \cdot 0.13 = 19.5$ (b) $2400 \cdot 0.06 = 144$ (c) $200 \cdot 0.055 = 11$ 11. $\$1.50$ cheaper, which is 15% of $\$10$.

12. (a) With an interest rate of 11% per year, then in 8 years, an initial investment of 50 dollars will be worth $50 \cdot (1.11)^8 \approx 115.23$ dollars.   (b) Given a constant interest rate of 12% per year, then in 20 years, an initial investment of 10 000 pounds will be worth $10\,000 \cdot (1.12)^{20} \approx 96\,462.93$ pounds.   (c) $5000 \cdot (1.07)^{-10} \approx 2541.75$ euros is what you should have invested 10 years ago in order to have 5000 euros today, given the constant interest rate of 7%.

13. (a) $12\,000 \cdot (1.04)^{15} \approx 21611.32$ (b) $50\,000 \cdot (1.06)^{-5} \approx 37362.91$ **14.** $p \approx 95.3\%$, since $(1.25)^3 = 1.9531$.

15. (a) The profit was higher in 1990. $((1 + 0.2)(1 - 0.17) = 1.2 \cdot 0.83 = 0.996.)$
(b) If the decrease in profits from 1991 to 1992 were $p\%$, then profits in 1990 and 1992 would be equal provided
$1.2 \cdot (1 - p/100) = 1$, or $p = 100(1 - 1/1.2) = 100/6 \approx 16.67$.

1.3

1. (a) 1 (b) 6 (c) -18 (d) -18 (e) $3x + 12$ (f) $45x - 27y$ (g) 3 (h) 0 (i) -1

2. (a) $3a^2 - 5b$ (b) $-2x^2 + 3x + 4y$ (c) t (d) $2r^3 - 6r^2s + 2s^3$

3. (a) $-3n^2 + 6n - 9$ (b) $x^5 + x^2$ (c) $4n^2 - 11n + 6$ (d) $-18a^3b^3 + 30a^3b^2$ (e) $a^3b - ab^3$
(f) $x^3 - 6x^2y + 11xy^2 - 6y^3$

4. (a) $acx^2 + (ad + bc)x + bd$ (b) $4 - t^4$ (c) $[(u - v)(u + v)]^2 = (u^2 - v^2)^2 = u^4 - 2u^2v^2 + v^4$

5. (a) $2t^3 - 5t^2 + 4t - 1$ (b) 4 (c) $x^2 + y^2 + z^2 + 2xy + 2xz + 2yz$ (d) $4xy + 4xz$

6. (a) $x^2 + 4xy + 4y^2$ (b) $1/x^2 - 2 + x^2$ (c) $9u^2 - 30uv + 25v^2$ (d) $4z^2 - 25w^2$

7. (a) $201^2 - 199^2 = (201 + 199)(201 - 199) = 400 \cdot 2 = 800$ (b) $u^2 - 4u + 4 = (u - 2)^2 = 1$ so $u - 2 = \pm 1$,
and $u = 1$ or $u = 3$. (c) $\dfrac{(a + 1)^2 - (a - 1)^2}{(b + 1)^2 - (b - 1)^2} = \dfrac{a^2 + 2a + 1 - (a^2 - 2a + 1)}{b^2 + 2b + 1 - (b^2 - 2b + 1)} = \dfrac{4a}{4b} = \dfrac{a}{b}$

8. $1000^2/(252^2 - 248^2) = 1000^2/(252 + 248)(252 - 248) = 1000^2/500 \cdot 4 = 500$

9. (a) $(a + b)^3 = (a + b)^2(a + b) = (a^2 + 2ab + b^2)(a + b) = a^3 + 3a^2b + 3ab^2 + b^3$
(b) $(a - b)^3 = (a - b)^2(a - b) = (a^2 - 2ab + b^2)(a - b) = a^3 - 3a^2b + 3ab^2 - b^3$
(c) and (d): Expand the right-hand sides.

10. (a) $3 \cdot 7 \cdot xxyyy$ (b) $3(x - 3y + 9z)$ (c) $aa(a - b)$ (d) $2 \cdot 2 \cdot 2xy(xy - 2)$

11. (a) $2 \cdot 2 \cdot 7aabbb$ (b) $2 \cdot 2(x + 2y - 6z)$ (c) $2x(x - 3y)$ (d) $2aabb(3a + 2b)$ (e) $7x(x - 7y)$
(f) $5xyy(1 - 3x)(1 + 3x)$ (g) $(4 + b)(4 - b)$ (h) $3(x + 2)(x - 2)$

12. (a) $(x - 2)(x - 2)$ (b) $2 \cdot 2ts(t - 2s)$ (c) $2 \cdot 2(2a + b)(2a + b)$ (d) $5x(x + \sqrt{2}y)(x - \sqrt{2}y)$

13. (a) $(a + 2b)(a + 2b)$ (b) $KL(K - L)$ (c) $K^{-5}(K - L)$ (d) $(3z - 4w)(3z + 4w)$ (e) $-\frac{1}{5}(x - 5y)(x - 5y)$
(f) $(a^2 - b^2)(a^2 + b^2) = (a + b)(a - b)(a^2 + b^2)$

14. (a) $(5 + a)(x + y)$ (b) $u^2 - v^2 + 3(u + v) = (u + v)(u - v) + 3(u + v) = (u + v)(u - v + 3)$ (c) $(P + Q)(P^2 + Q^2)$

15. (a) $KK(K - L)$ (b) $KL(L^2 + 1)$ (c) $(L + K)(L - K)$ (d) $(K - L)(K - L)$ (e) $KL(K - 2L)(K - 2L)$
(f) $K^{-6}(K^3 - 1) = K^{-6}(K - 1)(K^2 + K + 1)$, using Problem 9(c).

1.4

1. (a) 2/7 (b) 13/12 (c) 5/24 (d) 2/25 (e) 9/5 (f) 1/2 (g) 1/2 (h) 11/27

2. (a) $3x/2$ (b) $3a/5$ (c) 1/5 (d) $\frac{1}{12}(-5x + 11)$ (e) $-1/(6b)$ (f) $1/b$

3. (a) $\dfrac{5 \cdot 5 \cdot 13}{5 \cdot 5 \cdot 5 \cdot 5} = \dfrac{13}{25}$ (b) $\dfrac{ab^2}{8c^2}$ (c) $\dfrac{2}{3}(a - b)$ (d) $\dfrac{P(P + Q)(P - Q)}{(P + Q)^2} = \dfrac{P(P - Q)}{P + Q}$

4. (a) 1/2 (b) 6 (c) 5/7 (d) 9/2

5. (a) $\dfrac{4}{x^2 - 4}$ (b) $\dfrac{21}{2(2x + 1)}$ (c) $\dfrac{a}{a - 3b}$ (d) $\dfrac{1}{4ab(a + 2)}$ (e) $\dfrac{-3t^2}{t + 2}$ (f) $4(1 - a)$

6. (a) $\dfrac{2 - 3x^2}{x(x + 1)}$ (b) $\dfrac{-2t}{4t^2 - 1}$ (c) $\dfrac{7x^2 + 1}{x^2 - 4}$ (d) $x + y$ (e) $\dfrac{y^2 - x^2}{y^2 + x^2}$ (f) $\dfrac{y - x}{y + x}$

7. $\dfrac{-8x}{x^2 + 2xy - 3y^2}$ **8.** (a) 400 (b) $\dfrac{-n}{n - 1}$ (c) 1 (d) $\dfrac{1}{(x - 1)^2}$ (e) $\dfrac{-2x - h}{x^2(x + h)^2}$ (f) $\dfrac{2x}{x - 1}$

1.5

1. (a) 3   (b) 40   (c) 10   (d) 5   (e) 1/6   (f) 0.7   (g) 0.1   (h) 1/5

2. (a) =. (Both expressions are equal to 20.)   (b) $\neq$. In fact, $\sqrt{25+16} = \sqrt{41} \neq 9 = \sqrt{25} + \sqrt{16}$.
(c) $\neq$. (Put $a = b = 1$.)   (d) =. In fact, $(\sqrt{a+b})^{-1} = [(a+b)^{1/2}]^{-1} = (a+b)^{-1/2}$.

3. (a) 81   (b) 4   (c) 623   (d) 15   (e) -1 (f) $2^x - 2^{x-1} = 2^{x-1}(2-1) = 2^{x-1} = 4$ for $x = 3$.

4. (a) $\frac{6}{7}\sqrt{7}$ (b) 4   (c) $\frac{1}{8}\sqrt{6}$ (d) 1   (e) $\frac{1}{6}\sqrt{6}$ (f) $\dfrac{2\sqrt{2y}}{y}$ (g) $\dfrac{\sqrt{2x}}{2}$ (h) $x + \sqrt{x}$

5. (a) $\frac{1}{2}(\sqrt{7} - \sqrt{5})$ (b) $4 - \sqrt{15}$ (c) $-x(\sqrt{3} + 2)$ (d) $\dfrac{(\sqrt{x} - \sqrt{y})^2}{x - y}$ (e) $\sqrt{x+h} + \sqrt{x}$ (f) $\dfrac{1}{x}(2\sqrt{x+1} - x - 2)$

6. (a) $\sqrt[3]{125} = 5$ because $5^3 = 125$.   (b) $(243)^{1/5} = 3$ because $3^5 = 243$.   (c) -2 (d) $\sqrt[3]{0.008} = 0.2$

7. (a) $\sqrt[3]{55} \approx 3.80295$ (b) $(160)^{1/4} \approx 3.55656$ (c) $(2.71828)^{1/5} \approx 1.22140$ (d) $(1.0001)^{10000} \approx 2.718146$

8. $40(1 + p/100)^{12} = 60$ gives $(1 + p/100)^{12} = 1.5$, and therefore $1 + p/100 = (1.5)^{1/12}$. Solving this for p yields
$p = 100[(1.5)^{1/12} - 1] \approx 3.44$.

9. (a) 9   (b) 1/4   (c) $16^{-2.25} = 16^{-9/4} = \left(\sqrt[4]{16}\right)^{-9} = 2^{-9} = 1/512$ (d) $(1/3^{-2})^{-2} = 1/3^4 = 1/81$

10. (a) $3x^p y^{2q} z^{4r}$ (b) $(x+15)^{4/3-5/6} = (x+15)^{1/2} = \sqrt{x+15}$ (c) $\dfrac{8x^{2/3}y^{1/4}z^{-1/2}}{-2x^{1/3}y^{5/2}z^{1/2}} = -4x^{1/3}y^{-9/4}z^{-1}$

11. (a) $a^{\frac{1}{2}\frac{2}{3}\frac{3}{4}\frac{4}{5}} = a^{1/5}$ (b) $a^{\frac{1}{2}+\frac{2}{3}+\frac{3}{4}+\frac{4}{5}} = a^{163/60}$ (c) $9a^7/2$ (d) $a^{1/4}$ **12.** Only (b) and (c) are generally valid.

13. $x < 4$. (If $x > 0$, then $32x^{3/2} > 4x^3$ if and only if $8x^{3/2} > x^3$, which is equivalent to $8 > x^{3/2}$, and so
$x < 8^{2/3} = 4$.)

1.6

1. (a), (b), (d), (f), and (h) are valid, (c), (e), and (g) are not valid.

2. (a) $x \geq -8$ (b) $x < -9$ (c) All x.   (d) $x \leq 25/2$ (e) $x \leq 19/7$ (f) $t > -17/12$

3. (a) $-2 < x < 1$ (b) $x < -4$ or $x > 3$ (c) $-5 \leq a \leq 5$

4. (a) $-7 < x < -2$ (b) $n \geq 160$ or $n < 0$ (c) $0 \leq g \leq 2$ (d) $p \geq -1$ and $p \neq 2$ (e) $-4 < n < -10/3$
(f) $-1 < x < 0$ or $0 < x < 1$. (Hint: $x^4 - x^2 = x^2(x+1)(x-1)$.)

5. (a) $x > 1$ or $x < -4$ (b) $x > -4$ and $x \neq 1$ (c) $1 \leq x \leq 2$ (d) $x < 1$ and $x \neq 1/5$ (e) $1/5 < x < 1$
(f) $x < 0$ (g) $-3 < x < -2$ or $x > 0$ (h) $x \neq 2$ (i) $x \leq 0$

6. (a) $-41/6 < x \leq 2/3$ (b) $x < -1/5$ (c) $-1 < x < 0$

7. (a) Yes   (b) No, put $x = \frac{1}{2}$, for example.   (c) No, not for $x \leq 0$.   (d) Yes, because the inequality is equivalent to
$x^2 - 2xy + y^2 \geq 0$, or $(x - y)^2 \geq 0$, which *is* satisfied for all x and y.

8. (a) We have $C = \frac{5}{9}(F - 32)$, so we must solve $4 \leq \frac{5}{9}(F - 32) \leq 6$ for F. The result is $39.2° \leq F \leq 42.8°$.
(b) Between 2.2°C and 4.4°C, approximately.

9. $(\sqrt{a} - \sqrt{b})^2 = a - 2\sqrt{ab} + b \geq 0$ yields $a + b \geq 2\sqrt{ab}$; dividing by 2 gives $m_A \geq m_G$. Because $(\sqrt{a} - \sqrt{b})^2 = 0$
is equivalent to $a = b$, one also has $m_A > m_G$ unless $a = b$. The inequality $m_G \geq m_H$ follows easily from the hint.

1.7

1. $|2 \cdot 0 - 3| = 3$, $|2 \cdot \frac{1}{2} - 3| = 2$, $|2 \cdot \frac{7}{2} - 3| = 4$

2. (a) $|5 - 3(-1)| = 8$, $|5 - 3 \cdot 2| = 1$, $|5 - 3 \cdot 4| = 7$ (b) $x = 5/3$ (c) $|5 - 3x| = 5 - 3x$ for $x \leq 5/3$, $= 3x - 5$
for $x > 5/3$

3. (a) $x = -1$ and $x = 4$ (b) $-2 \leq x \leq 2$ (c) $1 \leq x \leq 3$ (d) $-1/4 \leq x \leq 1$ (e) $x > \sqrt{2}$ or $x < -\sqrt{2}$
(f) $1 \leq x^2 \leq 3$, i.e. $1 \leq x \leq \sqrt{3}$ or $-\sqrt{3} \leq x \leq -1$

4. (a) $4.999 < x < 5.001$ (b) $|x - 5| < 0.001$

Review Problems for Chapter 1

1. (a) $3(50 - x)$ (b) $\dfrac{x}{y + 100}$ (c) If the price before VAT is p, then the price after VAT is $p + 20p/100 =$
$p(1+0.2) = 1.2p$. Thus $a = 1.2p$, so $p = \dfrac{a}{1.2}$.   (d) $p_1x_1 + p_2x_2 + p_3x_3$ (e) $F + bx$ (f) $(F + cx)/x = F/x + c$
(g) After the $p\%$ raise, his salary is $L + pL/100 = L(1 + p/100)$. A $q\%$ raise of this new salary gives the final
answer: $L(1 + p/100)(1 + q/100)$.

2. (a) $5^3 = 5 \cdot 5 \cdot 5 = 125$ (b) $10^{-3} = 1/10^3 = 1/1000$ (c) $1/3^{-3} = 3^3 = 27$ (d) -1000 (e) 3
(f) $(3^{-2})^{-3} = 3^6 = 729$ (g) -1 (h) $\left(-\frac{1}{2}\right)^{-3} = \frac{1}{(-\frac{1}{2})^3} = \frac{1}{-\frac{1}{8}} = -8$

3. (a) 1 (b) Undefined.   (c) 1 (d) 1 4. (a) $2^{-6} = 1/64$ (b) $\frac{3}{2} - \frac{3}{4} = \frac{3}{4}$ (c) $-45/4$ (d) 1

5. (a) $16x^4$ (b) 4 (c) $6xyz$ (d) $a^{27}b^9$ (e) a^3 (f) x^{-15}

6. (a) $0.12 \cdot 300 = 36$ (b) $0.05 \cdot 2000 = 100$ (c) $0.065 \cdot 1500 = 97.5$

7. (a) Given a growth rate of 1% per year, then in 8 years, a population which was 100 million has grown to $100 \cdot$
$(1.01)^8 \approx 108$ million.   (b) Given an interest rate of 15% per year, then in 10 years, an initial investment of 50 000
yen will be worth $50\,000 \cdot (1.15)^{10} \approx 202\,277$ yen.   (c) $6000 \cdot (1.03)^{-8} \approx 4736$ euros is what you should have
deposited 8 years ago in order to have 6000 euros today, given the constant interest rate of 3%.

8. (a) $100\,000(1.08)^{10} \approx 215\,892$ (b) $25\,000(1.08)^{-6} \approx 15\,754$

9. (a) $a^2 - a$ (b) $x^2 + 4x - 21$ (c) $-3 + 3\sqrt{2}$ (d) $3 - 2\sqrt{2}$ (e) $x^3 - 3x^2 + 3x - 1$ (f) $1 - b^4$
(g) $1 - x^4$ (h) $x^4 + 4x^3 + 6x^2 + 4x + 1$

10. (a) $x^3y^3 = (x^{-1}y^{-1})^{-3} = 3^{-3} = 1/27$ (b) $(x^{-3})^6(x^2)^2 = x^{-18}x^4 = x^{-14} = (x^7)^{-2} = 2^{-2} = 1/4$
(c) $(z/xy)^6 = (xy/z)^{-6} = [(xy/z)^{-2}]^3 = 3^3 = 27$ (d) $(abc)^4 = (a^{-1}b^{-1}c^{-1})^{-4} = (1/4)^{-4} = 4^4 = 256$

11. (a) $5(5x - 1)$ (b) $xx(3 - xy)$ (c) $(\sqrt{50} - x)(\sqrt{50} + x)$ (d) $a(a - 2b)^2$

12. (a) $(5 + a)(x + 2y)$ (b) $(a + b)(c - d)$ (c) $(a + 2)(x + y)$ (d) $(2x - y)(x + 5z)$ (e) $(p - q)(p + q + 1)$
(f) $(u - v)(u - v)(u + v)$

13. (a) $16^{1/4} = \sqrt[4]{16} = 2$ (b) $243^{-1/5} = 1/\sqrt[5]{243} = 1/3$ (c) $5^{1/7} \cdot 5^{6/7} = 5^{1/7+6/7} = 5^1 = 5$ (d) $4^{-3/2} = 1/8$
(e) $64^{1/3} + \sqrt[3]{125} = 4 + 5 = 9$ (f) $(-8/27)^{2/3} = (\sqrt[3]{-8/27})^2 = (-2/3)^2 = 4/9$ (g) $(-1/8)^{-2/3} + (1/27)^{-2/3} =$
$(\sqrt[3]{-1/8})^{-2} + (\sqrt[3]{1/27})^{-2} = (-1/2)^{-2} + (1/3)^{-2} = 4 + 9 = 13$ (h) $\dfrac{1000^{-2/3}}{\sqrt[3]{5^{-3}}} = \dfrac{(\sqrt[3]{1000})^{-2}}{5^{-1}} = \dfrac{10^{-2}}{5^{-1}} = \dfrac{1}{20}$

14. (a) $8 = 2^3$, so $x = 3/2$ (b) $1/81 = 3^{-4}$, so $3x + 1 = -4$ or $x = -5/3$ (c) $x^2 - 2x + 2 = 2$, so $x = 0$ or $x = 2$.

15. (a) $5 + x = 3$, so $x = -2$.   (b) $3^x - 3^{x-2} = 3^{x-2}(3^2 - 1) = 3^{x-2} \cdot 8$, so $3^{x-2} = 3$, and thus $x = 3$.
(c) $3^x \cdot 3^{x-1} = 3^{2x-1} = 81 = 3^4$ provided $x = 2.5$.   (d) $3^5 + 3^5 + 3^5 = 3 \cdot 3^5 = 3^6$, so $x = 6$.
(e) $4^{-6} + 4^{-6} + 4^{-6} + 4^{-6} = 4 \cdot 4^{-6} = 4^{-5}$, so $x = -5$.   (f) $\dfrac{2^{26} - 2^{23}}{2^{26} + 2^{23}} = \dfrac{2^{23}(2^3 - 1)}{2^{23}(2^3 + 1)} = \dfrac{7}{9}$, so $x = 7$.

16. (a) $\dfrac{2s}{4s^2 - 1}$ (b) $\dfrac{7}{3 - x}$ (c) $\dfrac{1}{x + y}$ 17. (a) $\frac{1}{5}a^2b$ (b) $x - y$ (c) $\dfrac{2a - 3b}{2a + 3b}$ (d) $\dfrac{x(x + 2)}{2 - x}$

18. (a) $x < 13/2$ (b) $y \geq -3$ (c) Valid for all x.   (d) $x < 29/14$ (e) $-1 \leq x \leq 13/3$
(f) $-\sqrt{6} \leq x \leq -\sqrt{2}$ or $\sqrt{2} \leq x \leq \sqrt{6}$

19. (a) $30 + 0.16x$ (b) Smallest number of hours: 7.5. Largest number of hours: 10.

20. $2\pi(r + 1) - 2\pi r = 2\pi$, where r is the radius of the Earth (as an approximate sphere). So the extended rope is only
about 6.28 m longer!

21. (a) Put $p/100 = r$. Then the given expression becomes $a + ar - (a + ar)r = a(1 - r^2)$, as required.
(b) $\$2000 \cdot 1.05 \cdot 0.95 = \$1995$.   (c) The result is precisely the formula in (a).   (d) With the notation used in the
answer to (a), we have: $a - ar + (a - ar)r = a(1 - r^2)$, which is the same expression as in (a).

22. (a) No, for example, $-1 > -2$, but $(-1)^2 < (-2)^2$.   (b) Suppose $a > b$ so that $a - b > 0$. If also $a + b > 0$, then $a^2 - b^2 = (a + b)(a - b) > 0$, so $a^2 > b^2$.

23. (a) $2 > 1$ and $1/2 < 1/1$. Also, $-1 > -2$ and $1/(-1) < -1/2$. On the other hand, $2 > -1$ and $1/2 > 1/(-1)$. (b) If $ab > 0$ and $a > b$, then $1/b - 1/a = (a - b)/ab > 0$, so $1/b > 1/a$. (Also, if $ab < 0$ and $a > b$, then $1/b - 1/a = (a - b)/ab < 0$, so $1/b < 1/a$.)

24. (i) For any number c, $|c| = \sqrt{c^2}$. Then $|ab| = \sqrt{(ab)^2} = \sqrt{a^2 b^2} = \sqrt{a^2}\sqrt{b^2} = |a| \cdot |b|$.
(ii) Either $a = |a|$ or $a = -|a|$, so $-|a| \leq a \leq |a|$. Likewise, $-|b| \leq b \leq |b|$. Adding these inequalities yields $-|a| - |b| \leq a + b \leq |a| + |b|$, and thus $|a + b| \leq |a| + |b|$.

25. See SM.

Chapter 2

2.1

1. (a) $x = 5$ (b) $x = 3$ (c) $x = 6$ (d) Any x is a solution. (e) $x = -12$ (f) $x = 1$
(g) $x = -5$. (*Hint:* $x^2 + 10x + 25 = (x + 5)^2$.) (h) $x = -1$

2. (a) $x = 3$ (b) $x = -7$ (c) $x = -28/11$ (d) $x = 5/11$ (e) $x = 1$ (f) $x = 121$

3. (a) $x = 0$ (b) $x = -6$ (c) $x = 5$

4. (a) $2x + 5 = x - 3$. Solution: $x = -8$.   (b) With x as the smallest number, $x + (x + 1) + (x + 2) = 10 + 2x$, so $x = 7$, and the numbers are 7, 8, and 9.   (c) If x is Jane's regular hourly wage, then $38x + (48 - 38)2x = 812$. Solution: $x = 14$.   (d) $1500 + 12x/100 = 2100$. Solution: $x = 5000$.   (e) $\frac{2}{3}x + \frac{1}{4}x + 100\,000 = x$. Solution: $x = 1\,200\,000$.

5. (a) $y = 17/23$ (b) $x = -4$ (c) $z = 4$ (d) $p = 15/16$

6. She buys $y/9$ kilos of apples, $y/6$ kilos of bananas, and $y/18$ kilos of cherries, for a total of $\left(\frac{1}{9} + \frac{1}{6} + \frac{1}{18}\right) y = \left(\frac{2+3+1}{18}\right) y = \frac{6}{18} y = \frac{1}{3} y$ kilos. She pays 3 euros per kilo of fruit.

2.2

1. (iii) $Y = 3000$. $\left(Y = \dfrac{a}{1 - b} + \dfrac{1}{1 - b}\bar{I} = \dfrac{500}{1 - 0.8} + \dfrac{100}{1 - 0.8} = 2500 + 500 = 3000.\right)$ (iv) $Y = 7500$

2. (a) $x = \frac{1}{2}\left(\dfrac{1}{a} + \dfrac{1}{b}\right)$ (b) $x = \dfrac{dA - b}{a - cA}$ (c) $x = \dfrac{p^2}{4w^2}$ (d) $x = -\dfrac{1}{1 + a}$ (e) $x = \pm\dfrac{b}{a}$ (f) $x = 0$

3. (a) $p = 20q/3 - 14/15$ (b) $P = (S - \alpha)/\beta$ (c) $g = 2A/h$ (d) $r = (3V/4\pi)^{1/3}$ (e) $L = (Y_0 A^{-1} K^{-\alpha})^{1/\beta}$

4. (a) $x = (a - b)/(\alpha - \beta)$ (b) $p = (3q + 5)^2/q$ (c) $Y = 100$ (d) $K = (2wQ^4/r)^{1/3}$ (e) $L = rK/2w$
(f) $K = \frac{1}{32} p^4 r^{-3} w^{-1}$

5. (a) $s = \dfrac{tT}{T - t}$ (b) $M = \dfrac{(B + \alpha L)^2}{KL}$ (c) $z = \dfrac{4xy - x + 2y}{x + 4y}$ (d) $T = N\left(1 - \dfrac{V}{C}\right)$

2.3

1. (a) $x(15 - x) = 0$, so $x = 0$ and $x = 15$ (b) $p = \pm 4$ (c) $q = 3$ and $q = -4$ (d) No solution. (e) $x = 0$ and $x = 3$ (f) $x = 2$. (Note that $x^2 - 4x + 4 = (x - 2)^2$.)

2. (a) $x^2 - 5x + 6 = (x - 2)(x - 3) = 0$ for $x = 2$ and for $x = 3$. (With $x^2 - 5x = -6$, completing the square gives $x^2 - 5x + (5/2)^2 = (5/2)^2 - 6 = 25/4 - 6 = 1/4$, or $(x - 5/2)^2 = 1/4$. Hence, $x - 5/2 = \pm 1/2$.)
(b) $y^2 - y - 12 = (y - 4)(y + 3) = 0$ for $y = 4$ and for $y = -3$ (c) No solutions and no factorization.
(d) $-\frac{1}{4}x^2 + \frac{1}{2}x + \frac{1}{2} = -\frac{1}{4}\left[x - \left(1 + \sqrt{3}\right)\right]\left[x - \left(1 - \sqrt{3}\right)\right] = 0$ for $x = 1 \pm \sqrt{3}$

(e) $m^2 - 5m - 3 = \left[m - \frac{1}{2}(5 + \sqrt{37})\right]\left[m - \frac{1}{2}(5 - \sqrt{37})\right] = 0$ for $m = \frac{1}{2}(5 \pm \sqrt{37})$

(f) $0.1p^2 + p - 2.4 = 0.1(p - 2)(p + 12) = 0$ for $p = 2$ and $p = -12$

3. (a) $r = -13, r = 2$ (b) $p = -16, p = 1$ (c) $K = 100, K = 200$ (d) $r = -\sqrt{3}, r = \sqrt{2}$
(e) $x = -0.5, x = 0.8$ (f) $p = -1/6, p = 1/4$

4. (a) $x = 1, x = 2$ (b) $t = \frac{1}{10}(1 \pm \sqrt{61})$ (c) $x = \frac{1}{4}(3 \pm \sqrt{13})$ (d) $x = \frac{1}{3}(-7 \pm \sqrt{5})$ (e) $x = -300, x = 100$
(f) $x = \frac{1}{6}(5 \pm \sqrt{13})$

5. (a) With sides of length x and y, $2x + 2y = 40$ and $xy = 75$. So x satisfies $x^2 - 20x + 75 = 0$, with the solutions $x = 5$ or $x = 15$. (b) 2 and 3. (c) The shorter side is 16 cm, the longer 30 cm. (d) 50 km/h.

6. (a) $x = -2, \ x = 0, \ x = 2$. ($x(x^2 - 4) = 0$ or $x(x + 2)(x - 2) = 0$) (b) $x = -2, \ x = -1, \ x = 1, \ x = 2$.
(Let $x^2 = u$.) (c) $z = -1/3, \ z = 1/5$. (Let $z^{-1} = u$.)

2.4

1. (a) $x = 8, \ y = 3$ (b) $x = 1/2, \ y = 1/3$ (c) $x = 1.1, \ y = -0.3$

2. (a) $x = 1, \ y = -1$ (b) $x = -4, \ y = 7$ (c) $x = -7/2, \ y = 10/3$

3. (a) $K = 2.8, \ L = 5.75$ (b) $p = 2, \ q = 3$ (c) $r = 2.1, \ s = 0.1$

4. (a) 39 and 13 (b) $120 for a table and $60 for a chair. (c) 30 of quality A and 20 of quality B.
(d) $8000 at 7.2% and $2000 at 5% interest.

2.5

1. (a) $x = 0$ and $x = -3$ (b) $x = 0$ and $x = 1/2$ (c) $x = 1$ and $x = 3$ (d) $x = -5/2$ (e) No solutions.
(f) $x = 0$ and $x = -1$

2. (a) No solutions. (b) $x = -1$ (c) $x = -3/2$ (d) $x = 0$ and $x = 1/2$

3. (a) $z = 0$ or $z = a/(1 - a - b)$ for $a + b \neq 1$. For $a + b = 1$ the only solution is $z = 0$.
(b) $\lambda = -1$ or $\mu = 0$ or $x = y$ (c) $\lambda = 0$ and $\mu \neq \pm 1$, or $\mu = 2$ (d) $a = 2$ or $b = 0$ or $\lambda = -1$

Review Problems for Chapter 2

1. (a) $x = 12$ (b) $x = 3$ (c) $x = -3/2$ (d) $x = -19$ (e) $x = 11/7$ (f) $x = 39$

2. (a) $x = 0$ (b) $x = -6$ (c) $x = 5$ (d) $x = -1$

3. (a) $x = \frac{2}{3}(y - 3) + y = \frac{2}{3}y - 2 + y = \frac{5}{3}y - 2$, or $\frac{5}{3}y = x + 2$, so $y = \frac{3}{5}(x + 2)$.
(b) $ax - cx = b + d$, or $(a - c)x = b + d$, so $x = (b + d)/(a - c)$.
(c) $\sqrt{L} = Y_0/AK$, so squaring each side yields $L = (Y_0/AK)^2$. (d) $qy = m - px$, so $y = (m - px)/q$.
(e) Put $s = 1/(1 + r)$. Then $s = (a + bc)/(1 - c)$, so $r = (1/s) - 1 = [(1 - a) - c(1 + b)]/(a + bc)$
(f) Multiplying by $(Px + Q)^{1/3}$ yields $Px + Px + Q = 0$, and so $x = -Q/2P$.

4. (a) From (ii) and (iii), $C = b(Y - tY) = b(1 - t)Y$, which inserted into (i) and solved for Y yields $Y = \dfrac{\bar{I} + G}{1 - b(1 - t)}$.

Then $C = \dfrac{b(1 - t)(\bar{I} + G)}{1 - b(1 - t)}$. (b) Note that $0 < b(1 - t) < 1$. When t increases, Y and $1 - t$ both decrease, and so therefore must $C = b(1 - t)Y$.

5. (a) $K = 225L^{2/3}$ (b) $r = 100(2^{1/t} - 1)$ (c) $x_0 = (p/ab)^{1/(b-1)}$ (d) $b = \lambda^{1/\rho}\left(c^{-\rho} - (1 - \lambda)a^{-\rho}\right)^{-1/\rho}$

6. (a) $z = 0$ or $z = 8$ (b) $x = -7$ or $x = 5$ (c) $p = -7$ or $p = 2$ (d) $p = 1/4$ or $p = 1/3$ (e) $y = 4 \pm \sqrt{31}$
(f) $x = -7$ or $x = 6$

7. (a) $x = \pm 2$ or $x = 5$ (b) $x = -4$. ($x^4 + 1$ is never 0.)   (c) $\lambda = 1$ or $x = y$

8. If he invested \$$x$ at 15% interest and \$$y$ at 20%, then $0.15x + 0.20y = 275$. Also, $x + y = 1500$. Solving this system yields $x = 500$, $y = 1000$.

9. $5^{3x} = 25^{y+2} = 5^{2(y+2)}$ so that $3x = 2(y + 2)$. With $x - 2y = 8$ this gives $x = -2$ and $y = -5$, so $x - y = 3$.

10. (a) Let $u = 1/x$ and $v = 1/y$. Then the system reduces to $2u + 3v = 4$, $3u - 2v = 19$, with solution $u = 5$, $v = -2$, and so $x = 1/u = 1/5$, $y = 1/v = -1/2$.   (b) Let $u = \sqrt{x}$ and $v = \sqrt{y}$. Then $3u + 2v = 2$, $2u - 3v = 1/4$, with solution $u = 1/2$, $v = 1/4$, so $x = 1/4$, $y = 1/16$.   (c) With $u = x^2$ and $v = y^2$, we get $u + v = 13$, $4u - 3v = 24$, with solution $u = 9$, $v = 4$, and so $x = \pm 3$ and $y = \pm 2$.

Chapter 3

3.1

1. (a) $1 + 2 + 3 + \cdots + 10 = 55$ (b) $(5 \cdot 3^0 - 2) + (5 \cdot 3^1 - 3) + (5 \cdot 3^2 - 4) + (5 \cdot 3^3 - 5) + (5 \cdot 3^4 - 6) = 585$
(c) $1 + 3 + 5 + 7 + 9 + 11 = 36$ (d) $2^{2^0} + 2^{2^1} + 2^{2^2} = 2^1 + 2^2 + 2^4 = 22$ (e) $2 \cdot 10 = 20$
(f) $2/1 + 3/2 + 4/3 + 5/4 = 73/12$

2. (a) $2\sqrt{0} + 2\sqrt{1} + 2\sqrt{2} + 2\sqrt{3} + 2\sqrt{4} = 2(3 + \sqrt{2} + \sqrt{3})$
(b) $(x + 0)^2 + (x + 2)^2 + (x + 4)^2 + (x + 6)^2 = 4(x^2 + 6x + 14)$
(c) $a_{1i}b^2 + a_{2i}b^3 + a_{3i}b^4 + \cdots + a_{ni}b^{n+1}$ (d) $f(x_0)\Delta x_0 + f(x_1)\Delta x_1 + f(x_2)\Delta x_2 + \cdots + f(x_m)\Delta x_m$

3. (a) $\displaystyle\sum_{k=1}^{n} 4k$ (b) $\displaystyle\sum_{k=1}^{n} k^3$ (c) $\displaystyle\sum_{k=0}^{n} (-1)^k \frac{1}{2k+1}$ (d) $\displaystyle\sum_{k=1}^{n} a_{ik}b_{kj}$ (e) $\displaystyle\sum_{n=1}^{5} 3^n x^n$ (f) $\displaystyle\sum_{j=3}^{p} a_i^j b_{i+j}$ (g) $\displaystyle\sum_{k=0}^{p} a_{i+k}^{k+3} b_{i+k+3}$

(h) $\displaystyle\sum_{k=0}^{3} (81\,297 + 198k)$

4. $\dfrac{2 \cdot 3 + 3 \cdot 5 + 4 \cdot 7}{1 \cdot 3 + 2 \cdot 5 + 3 \cdot 7} \cdot 100 = \dfrac{6 + 15 + 28}{3 + 10 + 21} \cdot 100 = \dfrac{49}{34} \cdot 100 \approx 144.12$

5. (a) $\displaystyle\sum_{k=1}^{10} (k-2)t^k = \sum_{m=-1}^{8} mt^{m+2}$ (b) $\displaystyle\sum_{n=0}^{N} 2^{n+5} = \sum_{j=1}^{N+1} 32 \cdot 2^{j-1}$

6. (a) The total number of people moving within the EEA from nation i.
(b) The total number of people moving within the EEA to nation j.

7. (a), (c), (d), and (e) are always true; (b) and (f) are generally not true.

3.2

1. $\sum_{k=1}^{n}(k^2 + 3k + 2) = \sum_{k=1}^{n} k^2 + 3\sum_{k=1}^{n} k + \sum_{k=1}^{n} 2 = \frac{1}{6}n(n+1)(2n+1) + 3\left[\frac{1}{2}n(n+1)\right] + 2n = \frac{1}{3}n(n^2 + 6n + 11)$.

2. $(a + b)^6 = a^6 + 6a^5b + 15a^4b^2 + 20a^3b^3 + 15a^2b^4 + 6ab^5 + b^6$. (The coefficients are those in the seventh row of Pascal's triangle in the text.)

3. (a) In both sums, all terms cancel pairwise, except $-a_1$, the last term within the first parentheses, and a_9 (or, generally, a_n), the first term within the last parentheses.   (b) (i) $1 - (1/51) = 50/51$ (ii) $3^{13} - 3$ (iii) $ar(r^n - 1)$

4. (a) $\dbinom{5}{3} = \dfrac{5 \cdot 4 \cdot 3}{1 \cdot 2 \cdot 3} = \dfrac{5 \cdot 4 \cdot 3 \cdot 2 \cdot 1}{1 \cdot 2 \cdot 3 \cdot 2 \cdot 1} = \dfrac{5!}{3!\,2!} = \dfrac{5!}{2!\,3!}$. In general, $\dbinom{m}{k} = \dfrac{m(m-1)\cdots(m-k+1)}{k!} =$
$\dfrac{m(m-1)\cdots(m-k+1)\cdot(m-k)!}{k!(m-k)!} = \dfrac{m!}{(m-k)!\,k!}$.

(b) $\binom{8}{3} = 56$. Also, $\binom{8}{8-3} = \binom{8}{5} = 56$; $\binom{8}{3} + \binom{8}{3+1} = 56 + 70 = 126$ and $\binom{8+1}{3+1} = \binom{9}{4} = 126$.

(c) $\binom{m}{k} = \dfrac{m!}{(m-k)!k!} = \binom{m}{m-k}$ and $\binom{m}{k} + \binom{m}{k+1} = \dfrac{m!}{(m-k)!k!} + \dfrac{m!}{(m-k-1)!(k+1)!} = $

$\dfrac{m!(k+1+m-k)}{(m-k)!(k+1)!} = \dfrac{(m+1)!}{(m-k)!(k+1)!} = \binom{m+1}{k+1}$.

5. $\sum_{i=0}^{n-1}(a+id) = \sum_{i=0}^{n-1} a + d\sum_{i=0}^{n-1} i = na + d\frac{1}{2}[1+(n-1)](n-1) = na + \frac{1}{2}n(n-1)d$. Using this formula, the sum Gauss (allegedly) computed is: $100 \cdot 81297 + \frac{1}{2}100 \cdot 99 \cdot 198 = 9\,109\,800$. (One does not have to use summation signs. The sum is $a + (a+d) + (a+2d) + \cdots + (a+(n-1)d)$. There are n terms. The sum of all the a's is na. The rest is $d(1+2+\cdots+n-1)$. Then use formula (4).)

3.3

1. (a) $\displaystyle\sum_{i=1}^{3}\sum_{j=1}^{4} i \cdot 3^j = \sum_{i=1}^{3}(i \cdot 3 + i \cdot 9 + i \cdot 27 + i \cdot 81) = \sum_{i=1}^{3} 120i = 720$ (b) $5 + \frac{3113}{3600}$

(c) $\frac{1}{6}mn(2n^2 + 3n + 3m + 4)$ (d) $\frac{1}{3}m(m+1)(m+2)$

2. (a) The total number of units of good i.   (b) The total number of units of all goods owned by person j.
(c) The total number of units of goods owned by the group as a whole.

3. $\sum_{j=1}^{i} a_{ij}$ is the sum of all the i numbers in the ith row, so in the first double sum we sum all these m row sums. $\sum_{i=j}^{m} a_{ij}$ is the sum of all the $m-j+1$ numbers in the jth column, so in the second double sum we sum all these m column sums.

4. See SM.

3.4

1. (a) $2x - 4 = 2 \implies x = 3$ (b) $x = 3 \implies 2x - 4 = 2$ (c) $x = 1 \implies x^2 - 2x + 1 = 0$ (d) $x^2 > 4 \iff |x| > 2$

2. $x = 2$. ($x = -1, 0$, and 1 make the equation meaningless. Multiplying each term by the common denominator $x(x-1)(x+1)$ yields $2x(x^2 - 3x + 2) = 0$, or $2x(x-1)(x-2) = 0$. Hence, $x = 2$ is the only solution.)

3. (a) $\implies$ true, $\impliedby$ false   (b) $\implies$ false, $\impliedby$ true   (c) $\implies$ true, $\impliedby$ false   (d) $\implies$ and $\impliedby$ both true
(e) $\implies$ false ($0 \cdot 5 = 0 \cdot 4$, but $5 \neq 4$), $\impliedby$ true   (f) $\implies$ true, $\impliedby$ false

4. (a) $x \geq 0$ is necessary, but not sufficient.   (b) $x \geq 50$ is sufficient, but not necessary.
(c) $x \geq 4$ is necessary and sufficient.

5. (a) Squaring both sides and rearranging yields $x^2 = 9$, so $x = \pm 3$. Only $x = 3$ is a solution.
(b) Squaring both sides and rearranging yields $x(x+5) = 0$. Both $x = 0$ and $x = -5$ are solutions.
(c) The equivalent equation $|x|^2 - 2|x| - 3 = 0$ gives $|x| = 3$ or $|x| = -1$. Only $x = \pm 3$ are solutions.

6. (a) No solutions.   (b) $x = 20$

7. (a) Iff. (Note: $\sqrt{4}$ means 2, not ± 2.)   (b) Only if   (c) Only if   (d) Iff   (e) If   (f) Only if

8. (a) $x + \sqrt{x+4} = 2 \implies \sqrt{x+4} = 2 - x \implies x + 4 = 4 - 4x + x^2 \implies x^2 - 5x = 0 \overset{(i)}{\implies} x - 5 = 0 \overset{(ii)}{\impliedby} x = 5$.
Here implication (i) is incorrect ($x^2 - 5x = 0 \implies x - 5 = 0$ or $x = 0$.) Implication (ii) is correct, but it breaks the chain of implications.   (b) $x = 0$. (After correcting implication (i), we see that the given equation implies $x = 5$ or $x = 0$. But only $x = 0$ is a solution; $x = 5$ solves $x - \sqrt{x+4} = 2$.)

9. (a) $x < 0$ or $y < 0$ (b) $x < a$ for at least one x.   (c) $x < 5$ or $y < 5$, or both.   (d) There exists an $\varepsilon > 0$ such that B is not satisfied for any $\delta > 0$.   (e) Someone may not like cats.   (f) Someone never loves anyone.

3.5

1. (b), (d), and (e) all express the same condition. (a) and (c) are different.

2. (a) Logically the two statements are equivalent.   (b) Appending the second statement is still an expressive poetic reinforcement.

3. If x and y are *not* both odd, at least one of them must be even. If, for example, $x = 2n$, where n is an integer, then $xy = 2ny$ is also even.

3.6

1. (a) $5 \in C$, $D \subseteq C$, and $B = C$ are true. The three others are false.   (b) $A \cap B = \{2\}$, $A \cup B = \{2, 3, 4, 5, 6\}$, $A \setminus B = \{3, 4\}$, $B \setminus A = \{5, 6\}$, $(A \cup B) \setminus (A \cap B) = \{3, 4, 5, 6\}$, $A \cup B \cup C \cup D = \{2, 3, 4, 5, 6\}$, $A \cap B \cap C = \{2\}$, and $A \cap B \cap C \cap D = \emptyset$.

2. $F \cap B \cap C$ is the set of all female biology students in the university choir; $M \cap F$ the female mathematics students; $((M \cap B) \setminus C) \setminus T$ the students who study both mathematics and biology but neither play tennis nor belong to the university choir.

3. $50 - 35 = 15$ liked only coffee, $40 - 35 = 5$ liked only tea, 35 liked both, and 10 did not like either. In all there were $15 + 5 + 35 + 10 = 65$ who responded.

4. (a) $B \subset M$ (b) $F \cap B \cap C \neq \emptyset$ (c) $T \cap B = \emptyset$ (d) $F \setminus (T \cup C) \subset B$

5. The $2^3 = 8$ subsets of $\{a, b, c\}$ are the set itself, the empty set, $\{a\}$, $\{b\}$, $\{c\}$, $\{a, b\}$, $\{a, c\}$, and $\{b, c\}$. The $2^4 = 16$ subsets of $\{a, b, c, d\}$ are the 8 preceding sets together with $\{d\}$, $\{a, d\}$, $\{b, d\}$, $\{c, d\}$, $\{a, b, d\}$, $\{a, c, d\}$, $\{b, c, d\}$, and $\{a, b, c, d\}$.

6. (b) and (c) are true, the others are wrong. (Counterexample for (a), (d), and (f): $A = \{1, 2\}$, $B = \{1\}$, $C = \{1, 3\}$. As for (e), note in particular that $A \cup B = A \cup C = A$ whenever B and C are subsets of A, even if $B \neq C$.)

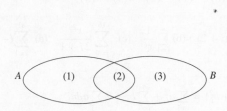

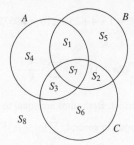

Figure A3.6.7   Figure A3.6.8

7. (a) Look at Fig. A3.6.7. $n(A \cup B)$ is the sum of the numbers of elements in (1), (2), and (3) respectively—that is, $n(A \setminus B) + n(A \cap B) + n(B \setminus A)$. But $n(A) + n(B)$ is the number of elements in (1) and (2) together, plus the number of elements in (2) and (3) together. Thus, the elements in (2) are counted twice. Hence, you must subtract $n(A \cap B)$, the number of elements in (2), to have equality.   (b) Look again at Fig. A3.6.7. $n(A \setminus B)$ is the number of elements in (1). $n(A) - n(A \cap B)$ is the number of elements in (1) and (2) together, minus the number of elements in (2). Hence, it is the number of elements in (1).

8. (a) Consider Fig. A3.6.8, and let n_k denote the number of people in the set marked S_k, for $k = 1, 2, \ldots, 8$. Obviously $n_1 + n_2 + \cdots + n_8 = 1000$. The responses imply that: $n_1 + n_3 + n_4 + n_7 = 420$; $n_1 + n_2 + n_5 + n_7 = 316$; $n_2 + n_3 + n_6 + n_7 = 160$; $n_1 + n_7 = 116$; $n_3 + n_7 = 100$; $n_2 + n_7 = 30$; $n_7 = 16$, and $n_8 = 334$. From these equations we easily find $n_1 = 100$, $n_2 = 14$, $n_3 = 84$, $n_4 = 220$, $n_5 = 186$, $n_6 = 46$, $n_7 = 16$. (i) $n_3 + n_4 = 304$ had read A but not B; (ii) $n_6 = 46$; (iii) $n_8 = 334$.

(b) We find $n(A \setminus B) = n_3 + n_4 = 304$, $n(C \setminus (A \cup B)) = n_6 = 46$, and $n(\Omega \setminus (A \cup B \cup C)) = n_8 = 334$. The last equality is a special case of $n(\Omega \setminus D) = n(\Omega) - n(D)$. (The number of persons who are in Ω, but not in D, is the number of persons in all of Ω minus the number of those who are in D.)

3.7

1. For $n = 1$, both sides are 1. Suppose (∗) is true for $n = k$. Then $1 + 2 + 3 + \cdots + k + (k+1) = \frac{1}{2}k(k+1) + (k+1) = \frac{1}{2}(k+1)(k+2)$, which is (∗) for $n = k+1$. Thus, by induction, (∗) is true for all n.

2. We prove only (3.2.6); the proof of (3.2.5) is very similar, but slightly easier. For $n = 1$ the LHS and the RHS of (3.2.6) are both equal to 1. As the induction hypothesis, suppose (3.2.6) is true for $n = k$, so that $\sum_{i=1}^{k} i^3 = 1^3 + 2^3 + \cdots + k^3 = [\frac{1}{2}k(k+1)]^2$. Then $\sum_{i=1}^{k+1} i^3 = \sum_{i=1}^{k} i^3 + (k+1)^3 = [\frac{1}{2}k(k+1)]^2 + (k+1)^3 = (k+1)^2(\frac{1}{4}k^2 + k + 1)$. But this last expression is equal to $\frac{1}{4}(k+1)^2(k^2 + 4k + 4) = [\frac{1}{2}(k+1)(k+2)]^2$, which proves that (3.2.6) is true for $n = k+1$. By induction, we have proved (3.2.6).

3. Easy induction proof.   **4.** See SM.

5. The induction argument is wrong for $k = 1$: Take two professors A and B. Send A outside. B has the same income as himself. Bring A back, and send B outside. A has the same income as himself. But this does *not* imply that the two professors have the same income! (The induction argument is correct for all $k > 1$, because then the two professors sent out have the same income as the others.)

Review Problems for Chapter 3

1. (a) $\dfrac{1}{1 \cdot 3} + \dfrac{1}{2 \cdot 4} + \dfrac{1}{3 \cdot 5} + \dfrac{1}{4 \cdot 6} = \dfrac{17}{30}$ (b) $2^2 + 4^2 + 6^2 + 8^2 + 10^2 = 220$ (c) $\dfrac{0}{2} + \dfrac{1}{3} + \dfrac{2}{4} + \dfrac{3}{5} + \dfrac{4}{6} = \dfrac{21}{10} = 2.1$

2. (a) $1^2 \cdot 4 + 2^2 \cdot 5 + 3^2 \cdot 6 + 4^2 \cdot 7 = 4 + 20 + 54 + 112 = 190$ (b) $1 - \frac{1}{6} = \frac{5}{6}$ (c) $1^{-2} + 2^{-1} + 3^0 + 4^1 + 5^2 + 6^3 = 1 + 1/2 + 1 + 4 + 25 + 216 = 495/2$ (d) $\displaystyle\sum_{i=0}^{4} \binom{4}{i} = \binom{4}{0} + \binom{4}{1} + \binom{4}{2} + \binom{4}{3} + \binom{4}{4} = 1 + 4 + 6 + 4 + 1 = 16$

3. (a) $\displaystyle\sum_{n=1}^{100}(2n+1)$ (b) $\displaystyle\sum_{k=1}^{96}\dfrac{k+1}{k}$ **4.** (a) $\displaystyle\sum_{i=4}^{38} i(i+2)$ (b) $\displaystyle\sum_{i=1}^{n}\dfrac{1}{x^i}$ (c) $\displaystyle\sum_{j=0}^{16}\dfrac{x^{2j}}{2j+1}$ (d) $\displaystyle\sum_{k=1}^{81}(-1)^{k-1}\dfrac{1}{k}$

5. (a) Correct. Both sums are equal to $a_1 + a_2 + \cdots + a_n$.

(b) Wrong in general. $\displaystyle\sum_{i=1}^{n}(a_i + b_i)^2 = \sum_{i=1}^{n}(a_i^2 + 2a_i b_i + b_i^2) = \sum_{i=1}^{n} a_i^2 + \sum_{i=1}^{n} b_i^2 + 2\sum_{i=1}^{5} a_i b_i$.

(c) Correct. Both sums are equal to $5a_{1,j} + 5a_{2,j} + \cdots + 5a_{n+1,j}$.

(d) Wrong in general. $\displaystyle\sum_{i=1}^{3}\dfrac{a_i}{b_i} = \dfrac{a_1}{b_1} + \dfrac{a_2}{b_2} + \dfrac{a_3}{b_3}$, while $\dfrac{\sum_{i=1}^{3} a_i}{\sum_{i=1}^{3} b_i} = \dfrac{a_1 + a_2 + a_3}{b_1 + b_2 + b_3}$, and the two expressions are obviously not equal. (For example, put all a_i and b_i equal to 1.)

6. (a) $\Rightarrow$ true, $\Leftarrow$ false.   (b) $\Rightarrow$ false, $\Leftarrow$ true.   (c) $\Rightarrow$ true, $\Leftarrow$ false.   (d) $\Rightarrow$ and $\Leftarrow$ both true.

7. $A \cap B = \{1, 4\}$; $A \cup B = \{1, 3, 4, 6\}$; $A \setminus B = \{3\}$; $B \setminus A = \{6\}$; $(A \cup B) \setminus (A \cap B) = \{3, 6\}$; $A \cup B \cup C \cup D = \{1, 2, 3, 4, 5, 6\}$; $A \cap B \cap C = \{4\}$; and $A \cap B \cap C \cap D = \emptyset$.

8. $A \cap B = \emptyset$; $A \cup B = \{1, 2, 4, 6, 11\}$; $\Omega \setminus B = \{1, 3, 4, 5, 6, 7, 8, 9, 10\}$; $\complement A = \Omega \setminus A = \{2, 3, 5, 7, 8, 9, 10, 11\}$

9. (a) 100   (b) 670   (c) 95   **10.** (a) $R = 10\,200$ (b) $S = 55\,055$

11. (a) $(1+x)^2 = 1 + 2x + x^2 \geq 1 + 2x$ for all x since $x^2 \geq 0$.   (b) $(1+x)^3 = 1 + 3x + 3x^2 + x^3 = 1 + 3x + x^2(3+x) \geq 1 + 3x$ for all $x \geq -3$, since $x^2(3+x) \geq 0$ for all $x \geq -3$.   (c) See SM.

Chapter 4

4.2

1. (a) $f(0) = 1$, $f(-1) = 2$, $f(1/2) = 5/4$, and $f(\sqrt{2}) = 3$
(b) (i) For all x.   (ii) When $x = 1/2$.   (iii) When $x = \pm\sqrt{1/2} = \pm\frac{1}{2}\sqrt{2}$.

2. $F(0) = F(-3) = 10$, $F(a + h) - F(a) = 10 - 10 = 0$

3. (a) $f(0) = 0$, $f(a) = a^2$, $f(-a) = a^2 - (-a - a)^2 = -3a^2$, and $f(2a) = 0$
b) $3f(a) + f(-2a) = 3a^2 + [a^2 - (-2a - a)^2] = 3a^2 + a^2 - 9a^2 = -5a^2$

4. (a) $f(-1/10) = -10/101$, $f(0) = 0$, $f(1/\sqrt{2}) = \sqrt{2}/3$, $f(\sqrt{\pi}) = \sqrt{\pi}/(1 + \pi)$, $f(2) = 2/5$
(b) $f(-x) = -x/(1 + (-x)^2) = -x/(1 + x^2) = -f(x)$ and $f(1/x) = (1/x)/[1 + (1/x)^2] = (1/x) \cdot x^2/[1 + (1/x)^2] \cdot x^2 = x/(1 + x^2) = f(x)$.

5. $F(0) = 2$, $F(-3) = \sqrt{19}$, $F(t + 1) = \sqrt{t^2 + 3}$

6. (a) $C(0) = 1000$, $C(100) = 41\,000$, and $C(101) - C(100) = 501$.
(b) $C(x + 1) - C(x) = 2x + 301 =$ incremental cost of increasing production from x to $x + 1$.

7. (a) $D(8) = 4$, $D(10) = 3.4$, and $D(10.22) = 3.334$.   (b) $P = 10.9$

8. (a) $f(tx) = 100(tx)^2 = 100t^2x^2 = t^2f(x)$ (b) $P(tx) = (tx)^{1/2} = t^{1/2}x^{1/2} = t^{1/2}P(x)$

9. (a) $b(0) = 0$, $b(50) = 100/11$, $b(100) = 200$ (b) $b(50 + h) - b(50)$ is the additional cost of removing $h\%$ more than 50% of the impurities.

10. (a) No: $f(2 + 1) = f(3) = 18$, whereas $f(2) + f(1) = 8 + 2 = 10$.   (b) Yes: $f(2 + 1) = f(2) + f(1) = -9$.
(c) No: $f(2 + 1) = f(3) = \sqrt{3} \approx 1.73$, whereas $f(2) + f(1) = \sqrt{2} + 1 \approx 2.41$.

11. (a) $f(a + b) = A(a + b) = Aa + Ab = f(a) + f(b)$ (b) $f(a + b) = 10^{a+b} = 10^a \cdot 10^b = f(a) \cdot f(b)$

12. See Figs. A4.2.12a and A4.2.12b.

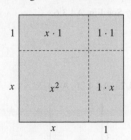

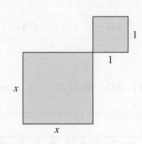

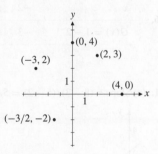

Figure A4.2.12a The area
is $(x + 1)^2 = x^2 + 2x + 1$

Figure A4.2.12b The area
is $x^2 + 1$

Figure A4.3.1

13. (a) $x \leq 5$ (b) $x \neq 0$ and $x \neq 1$ (c) $-3 < x \leq 1$ or $x > 2$

14. (a) Defined for $x \neq 2$, i.e. $D_f = (-\infty, 2) \cup (2, \infty)$ (b) $f(8) = 5$
(c) $f(x) = \dfrac{3x + 6}{x - 2} = 3 \iff 3x + 6 = 3(x - 2) \iff 6 = -6$, which is impossible.

15. Since g obviously is defined for $x \geq -2$, $D_g = [-2, \infty)$. Note that $g(-2) = 1$, and $g(x) \leq 1$ for all $x \in D_f$. As x increases from -2 to ∞, $g(x)$ decreases from 1 to $-\infty$, so $R_g = (-\infty, 1]$.

4.3

1. See Fig. A4.3.1.

2. (a) $f(-5) = 0$, $f(-3) = -3$, $f(-2) = 0$, $f(0) = 2$, $f(3) = 4$, $f(4) = 0$ (b) $D_f = [-5, 4]$, $R_f = [-3, 4]$

3.

x	0	1	2	3	4
$g(x) = -2x + 5$	5	3	1	-1	-3

See Fig. A4.3.3.

4.

x	-2	-1	0	1	2	3	4
$h(x) = x^2 - 2x - 3$	5	0	-3	-4	-3	0	5

See Fig. A4.3.4.

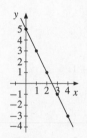

Figure A4.3.3ny

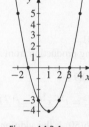

Figure A4.3.4ny

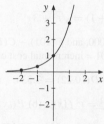

Figure A4.3.5

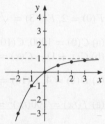

Figure A4.3.6

5.

x	-2	-1	0	1	2
$F(x) = 3^x$	1/9	1/3	1	3	9

See Fig. A4.3.5.

6.

x	-2	-1	0	1	2	3
$G(x) = 1 - 2^{-x}$	-3	-1	0	1/2	3/4	7/8

See Fig. A4.3.6.

4.4

1. (a) Slope $= (8 - 3)/(5 - 2) = 5/3$ (b) $-2/3$ (c) $51/5$ **2.** See Figs. A4.4.2a, A4.4.2b, A4.4.2c

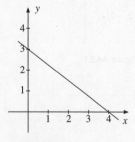

Figure A4.4.2a

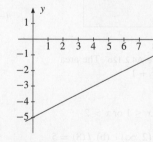

Figure A4.4.2b

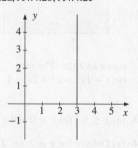

Figure A4.4.2c

3. If $D = a + bP$, then $a + 10b = 200$, and $a + 15b = 150$. Solving for a and b yields $a = 300$ and $b = -10$, so
$D = 300 - 10P$.

4. L_1: The slope is 1, and the point–slope formula with $(x_1, y_1) = (0, 2)$ and $a = 1$ gives $y = x + 2$.

L_2: Using the point–point formula with $(x_1, y_1) = (0, 3)$ and $(x_2, y_2) = (5, 0)$ yields $y - 3 = \frac{0-3}{5-0}x$, or $y = -\frac{3}{5}x + 3$. L_3 is $y = 1$, with slope 0.

L_4 is $y = 3x - 14$, with slope 3. L_5 is $y = \frac{1}{9}x + 2$, with slope 1/9.

5. (a), (b), and (d) are all linear; (c) is not, it is quadratic.

6. If P is the price of Q copies, then applying the point–point formula gives $P - 1400 = \frac{3000-1400}{500-100}(Q - 100)$ or $P = 1000 + 4Q$. The price of printing 300 copies is therefore $P = 1000 + 4 \cdot 300 = 2200$.

7. (a) L_1: $y - 3 = 2(x - 1)$ or $y = 2x + 1$ (b) L_2: $y - 2 = \frac{3-2}{3-(-2)}[x - (-2)]$ or $y = x/5 + 12/5$
(c) L_3: $y = -x/2$ (d) L_4: $x/a + y/b = 1$, or $y = -bx/a + b$.

8. (a) See Figs. A4.4.8a, A4.4.8b, and A4.4.8c.

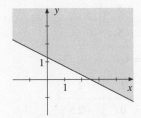

Figure A4.4.8a

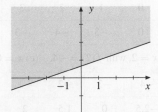

Figure A4.4.8b

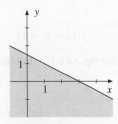

Figure A4.4.8c

9. For (a), shown in Fig. A4.4.9a, the solution is $x = 3$, $y = -2$. For (b), shown in Fig. A4.4.9b, the solution is $x = 2$, $y = 0$. For (c), shown in Fig. A4.4.9c, there are no solutions, because the two lines are parallel.

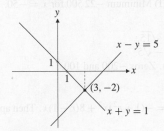

Figure A4.4.9a

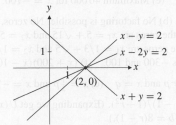

Figure A4.4.9b

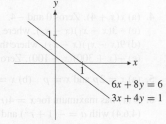

Figure A4.4.9c

10. See Fig. A4.4.10. Each arrow points to the side of the line where the relevant inequality is satisfied. The shaded triangle is the required set.

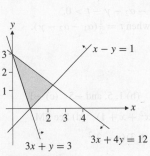

Figure A4.4.10

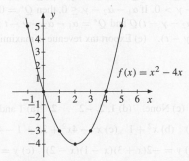

Figure A4.6.1

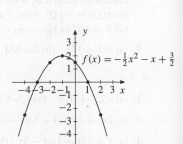

Figure A4.6.2

4.5

1. 0.78   **2.** (a) $75 - 3P^e = 20 + 2P^e$, and hence $P^e = 11$.   (b) $P^e = 90$

3. The point–point formula gives $C - 200 = \dfrac{275 - 200}{150 - 100}(x - 100)$, or $C = \dfrac{3}{2}x + 50$.

4. $C = 0.8y + 100$. (With $C = ay + b$, we are told that $900 = 1000a + b$ and $a = 80/100 = 0.8$, so $b = 100$.)

5. (a) $P(t) = 20\,000 - 2000t$ (b) $W(t) = 500 - 50t$

6. (a) April 1960 corresponds to $t = 9/4$, when $N(9/4) = -17\,400 \cdot (9/4) + 151\,000 = 111\,850$.
(b) $-17\,400\,t + 151\,000 = 0$ implies $t = 8.68$, which corresponds roughly to September 1966.

4.6

1. (a)

x	-1	0	1	2	3	4	5
$f(x) = x^2 - 4x$	5	0	-3	-4	-3	0	5

See Fig. A4.6.1.   (b) Minimum at $x = 2$, with $f(2) = -4$.   (c) $x = 0$ and $x = 4$.

2. (a)

x	-4	-3	-2	-1	0	1	2
$f(x) = -\frac{1}{2}x^2 - x + \frac{3}{2}$	-2.5	0	1.5	2	1.5	0	-2.5

See Fig. A4.6.2.   (b) Maximum at $x = -1$ with $f(-1) = 2$.   (c) $x = -3$ and $x = 1$.   (d) $f(x) > 0$ in $(-3, 1)$, $f(x) < 0$ for $x < -3$ and for $x > 1$.

3. (a) Minimum -4 for $x = -2$.   (b) Minimum 9 for $x = -3$.   (c) Maximum 45 for $x = 5$.
(d) Minimum -45 for $x = 1/3$.   (e) Maximum 40 000 for $x = -100$.   (f) Minimum $-22\,500$ for $x = -50$.

4. (a) $x(x + 4)$. Zeros 0 and -4.   (b) No factoring is possible. No zeros.
(c) $-3(x - x_1)(x - x_2)$, where the zeros are $x_1 = 5 + \sqrt{15}$ and $x_2 = 5 - \sqrt{15}$.
(d) $9(x - x_1)(x - x_2)$, where the zeros are $x_1 = 1/3 + \sqrt{5}$ and $x_2 = 1/3 - \sqrt{5}$.
(e) $-(x + 300)(x - 100)$. Zeros -300 and 100.   (f) $(x + 200)(x - 100)$. Zeros -200 and 100.

5. (a) $x = 2p$ and $x = p$ (b) $x = p$ and $x = q$ (c) $x = \frac{1}{2}p$ and $x = -2q$

6. $U(x)$ has maximum for $x = 4(r - 1)/(1 + r^2)$. (Expanding we get $U(x) = -(1 + r^2)x^2 + 8(r - 1)x$. Then apply (4.6.4) with $a = -(1 + r^2)$ and $b = 8(r - 1)$.)

7. (a) The areas when $x = 100, 250$, and 350 are $100 \cdot 400 = 40\,000$, $250 \cdot 250 = 62\,500$, and $350 \cdot 150 = 52\,500$, respectively.   (b) The area is $A = (250 + x)(250 - x) = 62\,500 - x^2$, which obviously has its maximum for $x = 0$. Then the rectangle is a square.

8. (a) $\pi(Q) = (P_{UK} - P_G - \gamma)Q = -\frac{1}{2}Q^2 + (\alpha_1 - \alpha_2 - \gamma)Q$.   (b) Using (4), we see that $Q^* = \alpha_1 - \alpha_2 - \gamma$ maximizes profit if $\alpha_1 - \alpha_2 - \gamma > 0$. If $\alpha_1 - \alpha_2 - \gamma \le 0$, then $Q^* = 0$.
(c) $\pi(Q) = -\frac{1}{2}Q^2 + (\alpha_1 - \alpha_2 - \gamma - t)Q$ and $Q^* = \alpha_1 - \alpha_2 - \gamma - t$ if $\alpha_1 - \alpha_2 - \gamma - t > 0$.
(d) $T = tQ^* = t(\alpha_1 - \alpha_2 - \gamma - t)$.   (e) Export tax revenue is maximized when $t = \frac{1}{2}(\alpha_1 - \alpha_2 - \gamma)$.

9. (a) $361 \le 377$ (b) See SM.

4.7

1. (a) $-2, -1, 1, 3$ (b) $1, -6$ (c) None.   (d) $1, 2, -2$ **2.** (a) 1 and -2 (b) 1, 5, and -5 (c) -1

3. (a) $2x^2 + 2x + 4 + 3/(x - 1)$ (b) $x^2 + 1$ (c) $x^3 - 4x^2 + 3x + 1 - 4x/(x^2 + x + 1)$ (d) See SM.

4. (a) $y = \frac{1}{2}(x + 1)(x - 3)$ (b) $y = -2(x + 3)(x - 1)(x - 2)$ (c) $y = \frac{1}{2}(x + 3)(x - 2)^2$

5. (a) $x + 4$ (b) $x^2 + x + 1$ (c) $-3x^2 - 12x$

6. $c^4 + 3c^2 + 5 \geq 5 \neq 0$ for every choice of c, so the division has to leave a remainder.

7. Expand the right-hand side. (Note that $R(x) \to c/a$ as $x \to \infty$.)   **8.** $E = \alpha\left(x - (\beta + \gamma)\right) + \dfrac{\alpha\beta(\beta + \gamma)}{x + \beta}$

4.8

1. See Fig. A4.8.1.   **2.** (a) 1.6325269   (b) 36.4621596

3. (a) $2^3 = 8$, so $x = 3/2$ (b) $1/81 = 3^{-4}$, so $3x + 1 = -4$, and therefore $x = -5/3$ (c) $x^2 - 2x + 2 = 2$, so $x^2 - 2x = 0$, implying that $x = 0$ or $x = 2$.

4. (a): C   (b): D   (c): E   (d): B   (e): A   (f): F: $y = 2 - (1/2)^x$

5. (a) $3^{5t}9^t = 3^{5t}(3^2)^t = 3^{5t+2t} = 3^{7t}$ and $27 = 3^3$, so $7t = 3$, and then $t = 3/7$.   (b) $9^t = (3^2)^t = 3^{2t}$ and $(27)^{1/5}/3 = (3^3)^{1/5}/3 = 3^{3/5}/3 = 3^{-2/5}$, and then $2t = -2/5$, so $t = -1/5$.

6. $V = (4/3)\pi r^3$ implies $r^3 = 3V/4\pi$ and so $r = (3V/4\pi)^{1/3}$. Hence, $S = 4\pi r^2 = 4\pi(3V/4\pi)^{2/3} = \sqrt[3]{36\pi}\, V^{2/3}$.

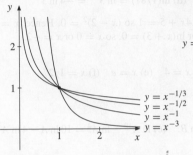

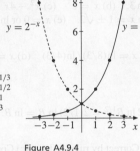

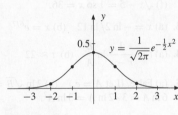

Figure A4.8.1   Figure A4.9.4   Figure A4.9.5

4.9

1. The doubling time t^* is determined by $(1.0072)^{t^*} = 2$. Using a calculator, we find $t^* \approx 96.6$.

2. $P(t) = 1.22 \cdot 1.034^t$. The doubling time t^* is given by the equation $(1.034)^{t^*} = 2$, and we find $t^* \approx 20.7$ (years).

3. The amount of savings after t years: $100\,(1 + 12/100)^t = 100 \cdot (1.12)^t$.

t	1	2	5	10	20	30	50
$100 \cdot (1.12)^t$	112	125.44	176.23	310.58	964.63	2995.99	28 900.21

4. The graphs are drawn in Fig. A4.9.4.

x	-3	-2	-1	0	1	2	3
2^x	1/8	1/4	1/2	1	2	4	8
2^{-x}	8	4	2	1	1/2	1/4	1/8

5. The graph is drawn in Fig. A4.9.5. We have the following table:

x	-2	-1	0	1	2
$y = \frac{1}{\sqrt{2\pi}}e^{-\frac{1}{2}x^2}$	0.05	0.24	0.40	0.24	0.05

6. We find $(1.035)^t = 3.91 \cdot 10^5/5.1 \approx 76666.67$, and using a calculator we find $t \approx 327$. So the year is $1969 + 327 = 2296$. This is when every Zimbabwean would have only 1 m² of land on average.

7. If the initial time is t, the doubling time t^* is given by the equation $Aa^{t+t^*} = 2Aa^t$, which implies $Aa^t a^{t^*} = 2Aa^t$, so $a^{t^*} = 2$, independent of t.

8. (b) and (d) do not define exponential functions. (In (f): $y = (1/2)^x$.)

9. (a) $16(1.19)^5 \approx 38.18$ (b) $4.40(1.19)^{10} \approx 25.06$ (c) $250\,000(1.19)^4 \approx 501\,335$

10. Suppose $y = Ab^x$, with $b > 0$. Then in (a), since the graph passes through the points $(x, y) = (0, 2)$ and $(x, y) = (2, 8)$, we get $2 = Ab^0$, or $A = 2$, and $8 = 2b^2$, so $b = 2$. Hence, $y = 2 \cdot 2^x$.
   In (b), $\frac{2}{3} = Ab^{-1}$ and $6 = Ab$. It follows that $A = 2$ and $b = 3$, and so $y = 2 \cdot 3^x$.
   In (c), $4 = Ab^0$ and $1/4 = Ab^4$. It follows that $A = 4$ and $b^4 = 1/16$, and so $b = 1/2$. Thus, $y = 4(1/2)^x$.

4.10

1. (a) $\ln 9 = \ln 3^2 = 2 \ln 3$ (b) $\frac{1}{2} \ln 3$ (c) $\ln \sqrt[5]{3^2} = \ln 3^{2/5} = \frac{2}{5} \ln 3$ (d) $\ln(1/81) = \ln 3^{-4} = -4 \ln 3$

2. (a) $\ln 3^x = x \ln 3 = \ln 8$, so $x = \ln 8/\ln 3$. (b) $x = e^3$ (c) $x^2 - 4x + 5 = 1$ so $(x-2)^2 = 0$. Hence, $x = 2$.
   (d) $x(x-2) = 1$ or $x^2 - 2x - 1 = 0$, so $x = 1 \pm \sqrt{2}$. (e) $x = 0$ or $\ln(x+3) = 0$, so $x = 0$ or $x = -2$.
   (f) $\sqrt{x} - 5 = 1$ so $x = 36$.

3. (a) $x = -\ln 2/\ln 12$ (b) $x = e^{6/7}$ (c) $x = \ln(8/3)/\ln(4/3)$ (d) $x = 4$ (e) $x = e$ (f) $x = 1/27$

4. (a) $t = \dfrac{1}{r-s} \ln \dfrac{B}{A}$ (b) $t \approx 22$

5. (a) False. (Let $A = e$.) (b) $2 \ln \sqrt{B} = 2 \ln B^{1/2} = 2(1/2) \ln B = \ln B$. (c) $\ln A^{10} - \ln A^4 = 10 \ln A - 4 \ln A = 6 \ln A = 3 \cdot 2 \ln A = 3 \ln A^2$.

6. (a) Wrong. (Put $A = B = C = 1$.) (b) Correct by rule (2)(b). (c) Correct. (Use (2)(b) twice.)
   (d) Wrong. (If $A = e$ and $p = 2$, then the equality becomes $0 = \ln 2$.) (e) Correct by (2)(c).
   (f) Wrong. (Put $A = 2$, $B = C = 1$.)

7. (a) $\exp\big[\ln(x)\big] - \ln\big[\exp(x)\big] = e^{\ln x} - \ln e^x = x - x = 0$ (b) $\ln\big[x^4 \exp(-x)\big] = 4 \ln x - x$ (c) x^2/y^2

Review Problems for Chapter 4

1. (a) $f(0) = 3$, $f(-1) = 30$, $f(1/3) = 2$, $f(\sqrt[3]{2}) = 3 - 27(2^{1/3})^3 = 3 - 27 \cdot 2 = -51$
   (b) $f(x) + f(-x) = 3 - 27x^3 + 3 - 27(-x)^3 = 3 - 27x^3 + 3 + 27x^3 = 6$

2. (a) $F(0) = 1$, $F(-2) = 0$, $F(2) = 2$, and $F(3) = 25/13$ (b) $F(x) = 1 + \dfrac{4}{x + 4/x}$ tends to 1 as x becomes large
   positive or negative. (c) See Fig. A4.R.2.

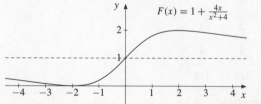

Figure A4.R.2   Figure A4.R.9

3. (i) $f(x) \leq g(x)$ when $-2 \leq x \leq 3$. (ii) $f(x) \leq 0$ when $-1 \leq x \leq 3$. (iii) $g(x) \geq 0$ when $x \leq 3$.

4. (a) $x^2 \geq 1$, i.e. $x \geq 1$ or $x \leq -1$.   (b) The square root is defined if $x \geq 4$, but $x = 4$ makes the denominator 0, so we must require $x > 4$.   (c) We must have $(x-3)(5-x) \geq 0$, i.e. $3 \leq x \leq 5$ (use a sign diagram).

5. (a) $C(0) = 100$, $C(100) = 24\,100$, and $C(101) - C(100) = 24\,542 - 24\,100 = 442$.
(b) $C(x+1) - C(x) = 4x + 42$ is the additional cost of producing one more than x units.

6. (a) Slope -4 (b) Slope $-3/4$ (c) Solving for y gives $y = b - (b/a)x$, so the slope is $-b/a$.

7. (a) The point–slope formula gives $y - 3 = -3(x+2)$, or $y = -3x - 3$.
(b) The point–point formula gives $y - 5 = \dfrac{7-5}{2-(-3)}(x-(-3))$, or $y = 2x/5 + 31/5$.
(c) $y - b = \dfrac{3b-b}{2a-a}(x-a)$, or $y = (2b/a)x - b$.

8. $f(2) = 3$ and $f(-1) = -3$ give $2a + b = 3$ and $-a + b = -3$, so $a = 2$, $b = -1$. Hence $f(x) = 2x - 1$ and $f(-3) = -7$. (Or use the point–point formula.)

9. The graph is drawn in Fig. A4.R.9.

x	-5	-4	-3	-2	-1	0	1
$y = x^2 e^x$	0.17	0.29	0.45	0.54	0.37	0	2.7

10. $(1, -3)$ belongs to the graph if $a + b + c = -3$, $(0, -6)$ belongs to the graph if $c = -6$, and $(3, 15)$ belongs to the graph if $9a + 3b + c = 15$. It follows that $a = 2$, $b = 1$, and $c = -6$.

11. (a) $\pi = \left(1000 - \frac{1}{3}Q\right)Q - \left(800 + \frac{1}{5}Q\right)Q - 100Q = 100Q - \frac{8}{15}Q^2$. Here $Q = 1500/16 = 93.75$ maximizes π.
(b) $\hat{\pi} = 100Q - \frac{8}{15}Q^2 - 10Q = 90Q - \frac{8}{15}Q^2$. So $\hat{Q} = 1350/16 = 84.375$ maximizes $\hat{\pi}$.

12. The new profit is $\pi_t = 100Q - \frac{5}{2}Q^2 - tQ$, which is maximized at $Q_t = \frac{1}{5}(100 - t)$.

13. (a) The profit function is $\pi(x) = 100x - 20x - 0.25x^2 = 80x - 0.25x^2$, which has a maximum at $x^* = 160$.
(b) The profit function is $\pi_t(x) = 80x - 0.25x^2 - 10x$, which has a maximum at $x^* = 140$.
(c) The profit function is $\pi_t(x) = (p - t - \alpha)x - \beta x^2$, which has a maximum at $x^* = (p - \alpha - t)/2\beta$.

14. (a) $p(x) = x(x-3)(x+4)$ (b) $q(x) = 2(x-2)(x+4)(x - 1/2)$

15. (a) $x^3 - x - 1$ is not 0 for $x = 1$, so the division leaves a remainder.   (b) $2x^3 - x - 1$ is 0 for $x = 1$, so the division leaves no remainder.   (c) $x^3 - ax^2 + bx - ab$ is 0 for $x = a$, so the division leaves no remainder.
(d) $x^{2n} - 1$ is 0 for $x = -1$, so the division leaves no remainder.

16. We use (4.7.5). (a) $p(2) = 8 - 2k = 0$ for $k = 4$.   (b) $p(-2) = 4k^2 + 2k - 6 = 0$ for $k = -3/2$ and $k = 1$.
(c) $p(-2) = -26 + k = 0$ for $k = 26$.   (d) $p(1) = k^2 - 3k - 4 = 0$ for $k = -1$ and $k = 4$.

17. The other roots are $x = -3$ and $x = 5$.

18. $(1 + p/100)^{15} = 2$ gives $p = 100(2^{1/15} - 1) \approx 4.7$ as the percentage rate.

19. $a > 0$, $b < 0$, $c < 0$, $p > 0$, $q < 0$, and $r < 0$.

20. (a) Assume $F = aC + b$. Then $32 = a \cdot 0 + b$ and $212 = a \cdot 100 + b$. Therefore $a = 180/100 = 9/5$ and $b = 32$, so $F = 9C/5 + 32$.   (b) If $X = 9X/5 + 32$, then $X = -40$.

21. (a) $\ln x = \ln e^{at+b} = at + b$, so $t = (\ln x - b)/a$.   (b) $-at = \ln(1/2) = \ln 1 - \ln 2 = -\ln 2$, so $t = (\ln 2)/a$.
(c) $e^{-\frac{1}{2}t^2} = 2^{1/2}\pi^{1/2}2^{-3}$, so $-\frac{1}{2}t^2 = \frac{1}{2}\ln 2 + \frac{1}{2}\ln \pi - 3\ln 2 = -\frac{5}{2}\ln 2 + \frac{1}{2}\ln \pi$, so $t^2 = 5\ln 2 - \ln \pi = \ln(32/\pi)$,
and finally, $t = \pm\sqrt{\ln(32/\pi)}$.

22. See SM.

Chapter 5

5.1

1. (a) $y = x^2 + 1$ has the graph of $y = x^2$ shifted up by 1. See Fig. A5.1.1a. (b) $y = (x + 3)^2$ has the graph of $y = x^2$ moved 3 units to the left. See Fig. A5.1.1b. (c) $y = 3 - (x + 1)^2$ has the graph of $y = x^2$ turned upside down, then with $(0, 0)$ shifted to $(-1, 3)$. See Fig. A5.1.1c.

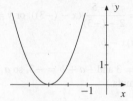
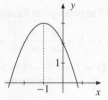

Figure A5.1.1a   Figure A5.1.1b   Figure A5.1.1c

2. (a) The graph of $y = f(x)$ is moved 2 units to the right. See Fig. A5.1.2a. (b) The graph of $y = f(x)$ is moved downwards by 2 units. See Fig. A5.1.2b. (c) The graph of $y = f(x)$ is reflected about the y-axis. See Fig. A5.1.2c.

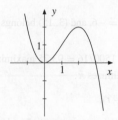
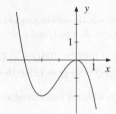
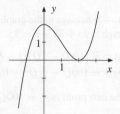

Figure A5.1.2a   Figure A5.1.2b   Figure A5.1.2c

3. The equilibrium condition is $106 - P = 10 + 2P$, and thus $P = 32$. The corresponding quantity is $Q = 106 - 32 = 74$. See Fig. A5.1.3.

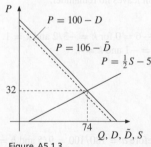
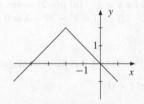
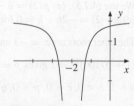

Figure A5.1.3   Figure A5.1.4   Figure A5.1.5

4. Move $y = |x|$ two units to the left. Then reflect the graph about the x-axis, and then move the graph up 2 units. See Fig. A5.1.4.

5. Draw the graph of $y = 1/x^2$. Move it two units to the left. Then reflect the graph about the x-axis, and then move the graph up 2 units to get Fig. A5.1.5.

6. $f(y^*-d) = f(y^*) - c$ gives $A(y^*-d) + B(y^*-d)^2 = Ay^* + B(y^*)^2 - c$, or $Ay^* - Ad + B(y^*)^2 - 2Bdy^* + Bd^2 = Ay^* + B(y^*)^2 - c$. It follows that $y^* = [Bd^2 - Ad + c]/2Bd$.

5.2

1. See Fig. A5.2.1. **2.** See Figs. A5.2.2a to A5.2.2c.

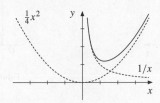

Figure A5.2.1

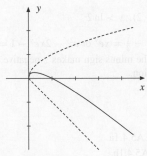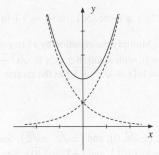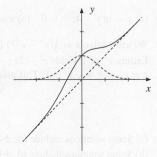

| Figure A5.2.2a | Figure A5.2.2b | Figure A5.2.2c |

3. $(f+g)(x) = 3x$, $(f-g)(x) = 3x - 2x^3$, $(fg)(x) = 3x^4 - x^6$, $(f/g)(x) = 3/x^2 - 1$, $f(g(1)) = f(1) = 2$, and $g(f(1)) = g(2) = 8$

4. If $f(x) = 3x + 7$, then $f(f(x)) = f(3x+7) = 3(3x+7)+7 = 9x+28$. $f(f(x^*)) = 100$ requires $9x^*+28 = 100$, and so $x^* = 8$.

5. $\ln(\ln e) = \ln 1 = 0$, while $(\ln e)^2 = 1^2 = 1$.

5.3

1. $P = \frac{1}{3}(64 - 10D)$ **2.** $P = (157.8/D)^{10/3}$

3. (a) Domain and range: $\mathbb{R}$; $x = -y/3$. (b) Domain and range: $\mathbb{R} \setminus 0$; $x = 1/y$.
(c) Domain and range: $\mathbb{R}$; $x = y^{1/3}$. (d) Domain $[4, \infty)$, range $[0, \infty)$; $x = (y^2 + 2)^2$.

4. (a) The domain of f^{-1} is $\{-4, -2, 0, 2, 4, 6, 8\}$. $f^{-1}(2) = -1$ (b) $f(x) = 2x + 4$, $f^{-1}(x) = \frac{1}{2}x - 2$

5. $f(x) = x^2$ is not one-to-one over $(-\infty, \infty)$, and therefore has no inverse. Over $[0, \infty)$, f is strictly increasing and has therefore the inverse $f^{-1}(x) = \sqrt{x}$.

6. (a) $f(x) = x/2$ and $g(x) = 2x$ are inverse functions. (b) $f(x) = 3x - 2$ and $g(x) = \frac{1}{3}(x + 2)$ are inverse functions. (c) $C = \frac{5}{9}(F - 32)$ and $F = \frac{9}{5}C + 32$ are inverse functions.

7. $f^{-1}(C)$ determines the cost of C kilograms of carrots.

8. (a) See Fig. A5.3.8a. (b) See Fig. A5.3.8b. Triangles OBA and OBC are congruent. The point half-way between the two points A and C is $B = (\frac{1}{2}(a + b), \frac{1}{2}(a + b))$.

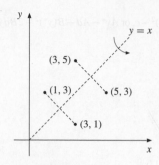

Figure A5.3.8a

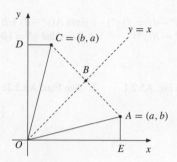

Figure A5.3.8b

9. (a) $f^{-1}(x) = (x^3 + 1)^{1/3}$ (b) $f^{-1}(x) = \dfrac{2x + 1}{x - 1}$ (c) $f^{-1}(x) = \left(1 - (x - 2)^5\right)^{1/3}$

10. (a) $x = \ln y - 4$, $y > 0$ (b) $x = e^{y+4}$, $y \in (-\infty, \infty)$ (c) $x = 3 + \ln(e^y - 2)$, $y > \ln 2$

11. We must solve $x = \frac{1}{2}(e^y - e^{-y})$ for y. Multiply the equation by e^y to get $\frac{1}{2}e^{2y} - \frac{1}{2} = xe^y$ or $e^{2y} - 2xe^y - 1 = 0$. Letting $e^y = z$ yields $z^2 - 2xz - 1 = 0$, with solution $z = x \pm \sqrt{x^2 + 1}$. The minus sign makes z negative, so $z = e^y = x + \sqrt{x^2 + 1}$. This gives $y = \ln\left(x + \sqrt{x^2 + 1}\right)$ as the inverse function.

5.4

1. (a) Some solutions include $\left(0, \pm\sqrt{3}\right)$, $\left(\pm\sqrt{6}, 0\right)$, and $\left(\pm\sqrt{2}, \pm\sqrt{2}\right)$. See Fig. A5.4.1a.
(b) Some solutions include $(0, \pm 1)$, $\left(\pm 1, \pm\sqrt{2}\right)$, and $\left(\pm 3, \pm\sqrt{10}\right)$. See Fig. A5.4.1b.

2. We see that we must have $x \geq 0$ and $y \geq 0$. If (a, b) lies on the graph, so does (b, a), so the graph is symmetric about the line $y = x$ and includes the points $(25, 0)$, $(0, 25)$, and $(25/4, 25/4)$. See Fig. A5.4.2.

3. $F(100\,000) = 4070$. The graph is the thick line sketched in Fig. A5.4.3.

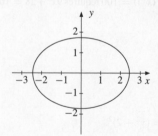

Figure A5.4.1a

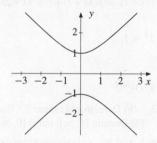

Figure A5.4.1b

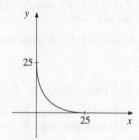

Figure A5.4.2

5.5

1. (a) $\sqrt{(2 - 1)^2 + (4 - 3)^2} = \sqrt{2}$ (b) $\sqrt{5}$ (c) $\frac{1}{2}\sqrt{205}$ (d) $\sqrt{x^2 + 9}$ (e) $2|a|$ (f) $2\sqrt{2}$

2. $(5 - 2)^2 + (y - 4)^2 = 13$, or $y^2 - 8y + 12 = 0$, with solutions $y = 2$ and $y = 6$. Geometric explanation: The circle with centre at $(2, 4)$ and radius $\sqrt{13}$ intersects the line $x = 5$ at two points. See Fig. A5.5.2.

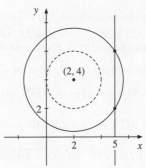

Figure A5.4.3   Figure A5.5.2

3. (a) 5.362   (b) $\sqrt{(2\pi)^2 + (2\pi - 1)^2} = \sqrt{8\pi^2 - 4\pi + 1} \approx 8.209$

4. (a) $(x - 2)^2 + (y - 3)^2 = 16$ (b) Since the circle has centre at $(2, 5)$, its equation is $(x - 2)^2 + (y - 5)^2 = r^2$. Since $(-1, 3)$ lies on the circle, $(-1 - 2)^2 + (3 - 5)^2 = r^2$, so $r^2 = 13$.

5. (a) Completing the squares yields $(x + 5)^2 + (y - 3)^2 = 4$, so the circle has centre at $(-5, 3)$ and radius 2.
(b) $(x + 3)^2 + (y - 4)^2 = 12$, which has centre at $(-3, 4)$ and radius $\sqrt{12} = 2\sqrt{3}$.

6. The condition is that $\sqrt{(x + 2)^2 + y^2} = 2\sqrt{(x - 4)^2 + y^2}$, which reduces to $(x - 6)^2 + y^2 = 4^2$.

7. We can write the formula as $cxy - ax + dy - b = 0$. Comparing with (5), $A = C = 0$ and $B = c$, so $4AC < B^2$ reduces to $0 < c^2$, that is $c \neq 0$, precisely the condition assumed in Example 4.7.7.

8. See SM.

5.6

1. Only (c) does not define a function. (Rectangles with equal areas can have different perimeters.)

2. The function in (b) is one-to-one and has an inverse: the rule mapping each youngest child alive today to his/her mother. (Though the youngest child of a mother with several children will have been different at different dates.) The function in (d) is one-to-one and has an inverse: the rule mapping the surface area to the volume. The function in (e) is one-to-one and has an inverse: the rule that maps (u, v) to $(u - 3, v)$. The function in (a) is many-to-one, in general, and so has no inverse.

Review Problems for Chapter 5

1. The shifts of $y = |x|$ are the same as those of $y = x^2$ in Problem 5.1.1. See Figs. A5.R.1(a)–(c).

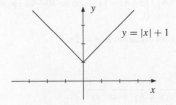

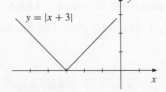

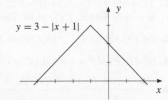

Figure A5.R.1a   Figure A5.R.1b   Figure A5.R.1c

2. $(f + g)(x) = x^2 - 2$, $(f - g)(x) = 2x^3 - x^2 - 2$, $(fg)(x) = x^2(1 - x)(x^3 - 2)$, $(f/g)(x) = (x^3 - 2)/x^2(1 - x)$, $f(g(1)) = f(0) = -2$, and $g(f(1)) = g(-1) = 2$.

3. (a) Equilibrium condition: $150 - \frac{1}{2}P^* = 20 + 2P^*$, which gives $P^* = 52$ and $Q^* = 20 + 2P^* = 124$.
(b) $S = 20 + 2(\hat{P} - 2) = 16 + 2\hat{P}$, so $S = D$ when $5\hat{P}/2 = 134$. Hence $\hat{P} = 53.6$, $\hat{Q} = 123.2$.
(c) Before the tax, $R^* = P^*Q* = 6448$. After the tax, $\hat{R} = (\hat{P} - 2)\hat{Q} = 51.6 \cdot 123.2 = 6357.12$.

4. $P = (64 - 10D)/3$ **5.** $P = 24 - \frac{1}{5}D$

6. (a) $x = 50 - \frac{1}{2}y$ (b) $x = \sqrt[5]{y/2}$ (c) $x = \frac{1}{3}[2 + \ln(y/5)]$, $y > 0$

7. (a) $y = \ln(2 + e^{x-3})$, $x \in \mathbb{R}$ (b) $y = -\dfrac{1}{\lambda}\ln a - \dfrac{1}{\lambda}\ln\left(\dfrac{1}{x} - 1\right)$, $x \in (0, 1)$

8. (a) $\sqrt{13}$ (b) $\sqrt{17}$ (c) $\sqrt{(2 - 3a)^2} = |2 - 3a|$. (Note that $2 - 3a$ is the correct answer only if $2 - 3a \geq 0$, i.e. $a \leq 2/3$. Test by putting $a = 3$.)

9. $(x - 2)^2 + (y + 3)^2 = 25$ (b) $(x + 2)^2 + (y - 2)^2 = 65$

10. $(x - 3)^2 + (y - 2)^2 = (x - 5)^2 + (y + 4)^2$, which reduces to $x - 3y = 7$. See Fig. A5.R.10.

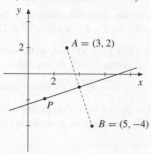

Figure A5.R.10

11. The function cannot be one-to-one, because at least two persons out of any five must have the same blood group.

Chapter 6

6.1

1. $f(3) = 2$. The tangent passes through $(0, 3)$, so has slope $-1/3$. Thus, $f'(3) = -1/3$.   **2.** $g(5) = 1, g'(5) = 1$

6.2

1. $f(5+h) - f(5) = 4(5+h)^2 - 4 \cdot 5^2 = 4(25 + 10h + h^2) - 100 = 40h + 4h^2$. So $[f(5+h) - f(5)]/h = 40 + 4h \to 40$ as $h \to 0$. Hence, $f'(5) = 40$. This accords with (6) when $a = 4$ and $b = c = 0$.

2. (a) $f'(x) = 6x + 2$ (b) $f'(0) = 2$, $f'(-2) = -10$, $f'(3) = 20$. The tangent equation is $y = 2x - 1$.

3. (a) $dD(P)/dP = -b$ (b) $C'(x) = 2qx$

4. $\dfrac{f(x + h) - f(x)}{h} = \dfrac{1/(x+h) - 1/x}{h} = \dfrac{x - (x+h)}{hx(x+h)} = \dfrac{-h}{hx(x+h)} = \dfrac{-1}{x(x+h)} \xrightarrow[h\to 0]{} -\dfrac{1}{x^2}$

5. (a) $f'(0) = 3$ (b) $f'(1) = 2$ (c) $f'(3) = -1/3$ (d) $f'(0) = -2$ (e) $f'(-1) = 0$ (f) $f'(1) = 4$

6. (a) $f(x+h) - f(x) = a(x+h)^2 + b(x+h) + c - (ax^2 + bx + c) = 2ahx + bh + ah^2$, so $[f(x+h) - f(x)]/h = 2ax + b + ah \to 2ax + b$ as $h \to 0$. Thus $f'(x) = 2ax + b$.
(b) $f'(x) = 0$ for $x = -b/2a$. The tangent is parallel to the x-axis at the minimum/maximum point.

7. $f'(a) < 0$, $f'(b) = 0$, $f'(c) > 0$, $f'(d) < 0$

8. (a) Expand the left-hand side. (b) Use the identity in (a). (c) Letting $h \to 0$, the formula follows. (Recall that $\sqrt{x} = x^{1/2}$ and $1/\sqrt{x} = x^{-1/2}$.)

9. (a) $f'(x) = 3ax^2 + 2bx + c$. (b) Put $a = 1$ and $b = c = d = 0$ to get the result in Example 2. Then put $a = 0$ to get a quadratic expression as in Problem 6(a).

10. $\dfrac{(x+h)^{1/3} - x^{1/3}}{h} = \dfrac{1}{(x+h)^{2/3} + (x+h)^{1/3}x^{1/3} + x^{2/3}} \to \dfrac{1}{3x^{2/3}}$ as $h \to 0$, and $\dfrac{1}{3x^{2/3}} = \dfrac{1}{3}x^{-2/3}$.

6.3

1. $f'(x) = 2x - 4$, so $f(x)$ is decreasing in $(-\infty, 2]$, increasing in $[2, \infty)$.

2. $f'(x) = -3x^2 + 8x - 1 = -3(x - x_0)(x - x_1)$, where $x_0 = \frac{1}{3}(4 - \sqrt{13}) \approx 0.13$ and $x_1 = \frac{1}{3}(4 + \sqrt{13}) \approx 2.54$. Then $f(x)$ is decreasing in $(-\infty, x_0]$, increasing in $[x_0, x_1]$, and decreasing in $[x_1, \infty)$.

3. If $x_2 > x_1$, then $x_2^3 - x_1^3 = (x_2 - x_1)\left[\left(x_1 + \frac{1}{2}x_2\right)^2 + \frac{3}{4}x_2^2\right] > 0$, since the bracket is positive. This shows that $f(x) = x^3$ is strictly increasing.

6.4

1. $C'(100) = 203$ and $C'(x) = 2x + 3$.

2. I is the fixed cost, whereas k is the marginal cost, and also the (constant) incremental cost of producing each additional unit.

3. (a) $S'(Y) = b$ (b) $S'(Y) = 0.1 + 0.0004Y$ 4. $T'(y) = t$, so the marginal tax rate is constant.

5. $\dot{x}(0) = -3$: During the first minute approximately 3 barrels are extracted.

6. (a) $C'(x) = 3x^2 - 180x + 7500$ (b) $x = 30$. ($C'(x)$ has a minimum at $x = 180/6 = 30$, using (4.6.3).)

7. (a) $\pi'(Q) = 24 - 2Q$. $Q^* = 12$. (b) $R'(Q) = 500 - Q^2$ (c) $C'(Q) = -3Q^2 + 428.4Q - 7900$

8. (a) $C'(x) = 2a_1x + b_1$. (b) $C'(x) = 3a_1x^2$.

6.5

1. (a) 3 (b) $-1/2$ (c) $13^3 = 2197$ (d) 40 (e) 1 (f) $-3/4$

2. (a) 0.6931 (b) 1.0986 (c) 0.4055 (Actually, using the result in Example 7.12.2, the precise values of these limits are $\ln 2$, $\ln 3$, and $\ln(3/2)$, respectively.)

3. (a)

x	0.9	0.99	0.999	1	1.001	1.01	1.1
$\dfrac{x^2 + 7x - 8}{x - 1}$	8.9	8.99	8.999	*	9.001	9.01	9.1

*not defined

(b) $x^2 + 7x - 8 = (x - 1)(x + 8)$, so $(x^2 + 7x - 8)/(x - 1) = x + 8 \to 9$ as $x \to 1$.

4. (a) 5 (b) 1/5 (c) 1 (d) -2 (e) $3x^2$ (f) h^2

5. (a) 1/6 (b) $-\infty$ (does not exist). (c) 2 (d) $\sqrt{3}/6$ (e) $-2/3$ (f) 1/4

6. (a) 4 (b) 5 (c) 6 (d) $2a + 2$ (e) $2a + 2$ (f) $4a + 4$

7. (a) $x^3 - 8 = (x-2)(x^2+2x+4)$, so the limit is $1/6$.   (b) $\lim_{h\to 0}[\sqrt[3]{27+h}-3]/h = \lim_{u\to 3}(u-3)/(u^3-27)$, and $u^3 - 27 = (u-3)(u^2+3u+9)$, so the limit is $1/27$.   (c) $x^n - 1 = (x-1)(x^{n-1}+x^{n-2}+\cdots+x+1)$, so the limit is n.

6.6

1. (a) 0 (b) $4x^3$ (c) $90x^9$ (d) 0. (Remember that π is a constant!)   **2.** (a) $2g'(x)$ (b) $-\frac{1}{6}g'(x)$ (c) $\frac{1}{3}g'(x)$

3. (a) $6x^5$ (b) $33x^{10}$ (c) $50x^{49}$ (d) $28x^{-8}$ (e) x^{11} (f) $4x^{-3}$ (g) $-x^{-4/3}$ (h) $3x^{-5/2}$

4. (a) $8\pi r$ (b) $A(b+1)y^b$ (c) $(-5/2)A^{-7/2}$

5. In (6.2.1) (the definition of the derivative), choose $h = x - a$ so that $a + h$ is replaced by x, and $h \to 0$ implies $x \to a$. For $f(x) = x^2$ we get $f'(a) = 2a$.

6. (a) $F(x) = \frac{1}{3}x^3 + C$ (b) $F(x) = x^2 + 3x + C$ (c) $F(x) = x^{a+1}/(a+1) + C$. (In all cases C is an arbitrary constant.)

7. (a) With $f(x) = x^2$ and $a = 5$, $\displaystyle\lim_{h\to 0}\frac{(5+h)^2 - 5^2}{h} = \lim_{h\to 0}\frac{f(a+h) - f(a)}{h} = f'(a) = f'(5)$. On the other hand, $f'(x) = 2x$, so $f'(5) = 10$, so the limit is 10.   (b) Let $f(x) = x^5$. Then $f'(x) = 5x^4$, and the limit is equal to $f'(1) = 5\cdot 1^4 = 5$.   (c) Let $f(x) = 5x^2 + 10$. Then $f'(x) = 10x$, and this is the value of the limit.

6.7

1. (a) 1 (b) $1 + 2x$ (c) $15x^4 + 8x^3$ (d) $32x^3 + x^{-1/2}$ (e) $\frac{1}{2} - 3x + 15x^2$ (f) $-21x^6$

2. (a) $\frac{6}{5}x - 14x^6 - \frac{1}{2}x^{-1/2}$ (b) $4x(3x^4 - x^2 - 1)$ (c) $10x^9 + 5x^4 + 4x^3 - x^{-2}$. (Expand and differentiate.)

3. (a) $-6x^{-7}$ (b) $\frac{3}{2}x^{1/2} - \frac{1}{2}x^{-3/2}$ (c) $-(3/2)x^{-5/2}$ (d) $-2/(x-1)^2$ (e) $-4x^{-5} - 5x^{-6}$ (f) $34/(2x+8)^2$ (g) $-33x^{-12}$ (h) $(-3x^2 + 2x + 4)/(x^2 + x + 1)^2$

4. (a) $\dfrac{3}{2\sqrt{x}(\sqrt{x}+1)^2}$ (b) $\dfrac{4x}{(x^2+1)^2}$ (c) $\dfrac{-2x^2+2}{(x^2-x+1)^2}$

5. (a) $f'(L^*) < f(L^*)/L^*$. See Figure A6.7.5. The tangent at P has the slope $f'(L^*)$. We "see" that the tangent at P is less steep than the straight line from the origin to P, which has the slope $f(L^*)/L^* = g(L^*)$. (The inequality follows directly from the characterization of differentiable concave functions in FMEA, Theorem 2.4.1.)
(b) $\frac{d}{dL}(f(L)/L) = \frac{1}{L}(f'(L) - f(L)/L)$, as in Example 6.

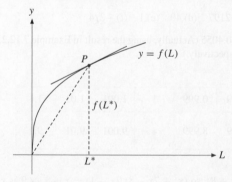

Figure A6.7.5

6. (a) $[2, \infty)$ (b) $\left[-\sqrt{3}, 0\right]$ and $\left[\sqrt{3}, \infty\right)$ (c) $\left[-\sqrt{2}, \sqrt{2}\right]$ (d) $(-\infty, \frac{1}{2}(-1-\sqrt{5})]$ and $[0, \frac{1}{2}(-1+\sqrt{5})]$.

7. (a) $y = -3x + 4$ (b) $y = x - 1$ (c) $y = (17x - 19)/4$ (d) $y = -(x-3)/9$

8. $\dot{R}(t) = \dot{p}(t)x(t) + p(t)\dot{x}(t)$. $R(t)$ increases for two reasons. First, $R(t)$ increases because of the price increase. This increase is proportional to the amount of extraction $x(t)$ and is equal to $\dot{p}(t)x(t)$. But $R(t)$ also rises because extraction increases. Its contribution to the rate of change of $R(t)$ must be proportional to the price, and is equal to $p(t)\dot{x}(t)$. $\dot{R}(t)$, the total rate of change of $R(t)$, is the sum of these two parts.

9. (a) $(ad - bc)/(ct + d)^2$ (b) $a\left(n + \frac{1}{2}\right)t^{n-1/2} + nbt^{n-1}$ (c) $-(2at + b)/(at^2 + bt + c)^2$

10. The product rule yields $f'(x) \cdot f(x) + f(x) \cdot f'(x) = 1$, so $2f'(x) \cdot f(x) = 1$. Hence, $f'(x) = 1/2f(x) = 1/2\sqrt{x}$.

11. If $f(x) = 1/x^n$, the quotient rule yields $f'(x) = (0 \cdot x^n - 1 \cdot nx^{n-1})/(x^n)^2 = -nx^{-n-1}$, which is the power rule.

6.8

1. (a) $dy/dx = (dy/du)(du/dx) = 20u^{4-1}\,du/dx = 20(1 + x^2)^3 2x = 40x(1 + x^2)^3$
(b) $dy/dx = (1 - 6u^5)\,(du/dx) = (-1/x^2)\left(1 - 6(1 + 1/x)^5\right)$

2. (a) $dY/dt = (dY/dV)(dV/dt) = (-3)5(V + 1)^4 t^2 = -15t^2(t^3/3 + 1)^4$
(b) $dK/dt = (dK/dL)(dL/dt) = AaL^{a-1}b = Aab(bt + c)^{a-1}$

3. (a) $y' = -5(x^2 + x + 1)^{-6}(2x + 1)$ (b) $y' = \frac{1}{2}\left[x + (x + x^{1/2})^{1/2}\right]^{-1/2}\left(1 + \frac{1}{2}(x + x^{1/2})^{-1/2}\left(1 + \frac{1}{2}x^{-1/2}\right)\right)$
(c) $y' = ax^{a-1}(px + q)^b + x^a bp(px + q)^{b-1} = x^{a-1}(px + q)^{b-1}[(a + b)px + aq]$

4. $(dY/dt)_{t=t_0} = (dY/dK)_{t=t_0} \cdot (dK/dt)_{t=t_0} = Y'(K(t_0))K'(t_0)$ **5.** $dY/dt = F'\big(h(t)\big) \cdot h'(t)$

6. $x = b - \sqrt{ap - c} = b - \sqrt{u}$, with $u = ap - c$. Then $\dfrac{dx}{dp} = -\dfrac{1}{2\sqrt{u}}u' = -\dfrac{a}{2\sqrt{ap - c}}$.

7. (i) $h'(x) = f'(x^2)2x$ (ii) $h'(x) = f'\big(x^n g(x)\big)\big(nx^{n-1}g(x) + x^n g'(x)\big)$

8. $b(t)$ is the total fuel consumption after t hours. $b'(t) = B'\big(s(t)\big)s'(t)$, so the rate of fuel consumption per hour is equal to the rate per kilometre multiplied by the speed in kph.

9. $dC/dx = q\left(25 - \frac{1}{2}x\right)^{-1/2}$ **10.** (a) $y' = 5(x^4)^4 \cdot 4x^3 = 20x^{19}$ (b) $y' = 3(1 - x)^2(-1) = -3 + 6x - 3x^2$

11. (a) (i) $g(5)$ is the amount accumulated if the interest rate is 5 % per year. (ii) $g'(5)$ is (very roughly) the increase in the accumulated value if the interest rate increases by 1%. ($g'(5) \approx [g(5.1) - g(5)]/0.1 \approx 154.8$ gives a better approximation.) (b) $g(p) = 1000(1 + p/100)^{10}$ is the final amount after 10 years if the interest rate was $p\%$ per year. $g(5) = 1000(1 + 5/100)^{10} \approx 1629$. Moreover, $g'(p) = 1000 \cdot 10(1 + p/100)^9 \cdot 1/100 = 100 \cdot (1 + p/100)^9$, so $g'(5) = 100 \cdot (1 + 5/100)^9 \approx 155$.

12. (a) $1 + f'(x)$ (b) $2f(x)f'(x) - 1$ (c) $4\big[f(x)\big]^3 f'(x)$ (d) $2xf(x) + x^2 f'(x) + 3\big[f(x)\big]^2 f'(x)$
(e) $f(x) + xf'(x)$ (f) $f'(x)/2\sqrt{f(x)}$ (g) $[2xf(x) - x^2 f'(x)]/(f(x))^2$ (h) $[2xf(x)f'(x) - 3(f(x))^2]/x^4$

6.9

1. (a) $y'' = 20x^3 - 36x^2$ (b) $y'' = (-1/4)x^{-3/2}$ (c) $y' = 20x(1 + x^2)^9$, $y'' = 20(1 + x^2)^9 + 20x \cdot 9 \cdot 2x(1 + x^2)^8 = 20(1 + x^2)^8(1 + 19x^2)$

2. $d^2y/dx^2 = (1 + x^2)^{-1/2} - x^2(1 + x^2)^{-3/2} = (1 + x^2)^{-3/2}$

3. (a) $y'' = 18x$ (b) $Y''' = 36$ (c) $d^3z/dt^3 = -2$ (d) $f^{(4)}(1) = 84\,000$

4. $g'(t) = \dfrac{2t(t - 1) - t^2}{(t - 1)^2} = \dfrac{t^2 - 2t}{(t - 1)^2}$, $g''(t) = \dfrac{2}{(t - 1)^3}$, so $g''(2) = 2$.

5. With simplified notation: $y' = f'g + fg'$, $y'' = f''g + f'g' + f'g' + fg'' = f''g + 2f'g' + fg''$, $y''' = f'''g + f''g' + 2f''g' + 2f'g'' + f'g'' + fg''' = f'''g + 3f''g' + 3f'g'' + fg'''$.

6. $L = (2t - 1)^{-1/2}$, so $dL/dt = -\frac{1}{2} \cdot 2(2t - 1)^{-3/2} = -(2t - 1)^{-3/2}$, so $d^2L/dt^2 = 3(2t - 1)^{-5/2}$.

7. (a) $R = 1/2$ (b) $R = 3$ (c) $R = \rho$ **8.** Because $g(u)$ is not concave.

9. The defence secretary: $P' < 0$. Gray: $P' \geq 0$ and $P'' < 0$. **10.** $d^3L/dt^3 > 0$

6.10

1. (a) $y' = e^x + 2x$ (b) $y' = 5e^x - 9x^2$ (c) $y' = (1 \cdot e^x - xe^x)/e^{2x} = (1-x)e^{-x}$
 (d) $y' = [(1+2x)(e^x+1) - (x+x^2)e^x]/(e^x+1)^2 = [1 + 2x + e^x(1 + x - x^2)]/(e^x+1)^2$
 (e) $y' = -1 - e^x$ (f) $y' = x^2 e^x(3+x)$ (g) $y' = e^x(x-2)/x^3$ (h) $y' = 2(x + e^x)(1 + e^x)$

2. (a) $dx/dt = (b + 2ct)e^t + (a + bt + ct^2)e^t = (a + b + (b + 2c)t + ct^2)e^t$
 (b) $\dfrac{dx}{dt} = \dfrac{3qt^2te^t - (p + qt^3)(1 + t)e^t}{t^2 e^{2t}} = \dfrac{-qt^4 + 2qt^3 - pt - p}{t^2 e^t}$
 (c) $x' = [2(at + bt^2)(a + 2bt)e^t - (at + bt^2)^2 e^t]/(e^t)^2 = [t(a + bt)(-bt^2 + (4b - a)t + 2a)]e^{-t}$

3. (a) $y' = -3e^{-3x}$, $y'' = 9e^{-3x}$ (b) $y' = 6x^2 e^{x^3}$, $y'' = 6xe^{x^3}(3x^3 + 2)$ (c) $y' = -x^{-2}e^{1/x}$, $y'' = x^{-4}e^{1/x}(2x + 1)$
 (d) $y' = 5(4x - 3)e^{2x^2 - 3x + 1}$, $y'' = 5e^{2x^2 - 3x + 1}(16x^2 - 24x + 13)$

4. (a) $(-\infty, \infty)$ (b) $[0, 1/2]$ (c) $(-\infty, -1]$ and $[0, 1]$

5. (a) $y' = 2xe^{-2x}(1 - x)$. y is increasing in $[0, 1]$. (b) $y' = e^x(1 - 3e^{2x})$. y is increasing in $(-\infty, -\frac{1}{2}\ln 3]$.
 (c) $y' = (2x + 3)e^{2x}/(x + 2)^2$. y is increasing in $[-3/2, \infty)$.

6. (a) $e^{e^x}e^x = e^{e^x + x}$ (b) $\frac{1}{2}(e^{t/2} - e^{-t/2})$ (c) $-\dfrac{e^t - e^{-t}}{(e^t + e^{-t})^2}$ (d) $z^2 e^{z^3}(e^{z^3} - 1)^{-2/3}$

7. (a) $y' = 5^x \ln 5$ (b) $y' = 2^x + x2^x \ln 2 = 2^x(1 + x \ln 2)$ (c) $y' = 2x2^{x^2}(1 + x^2 \ln 2)$
 (d) $y' = e^x 10^x + e^x 10^x \ln 10 = e^x 10^x(1 + \ln 10)$

6.11

1. (a) $y' = 1/x + 3$, $y'' = -1/x^2$ (b) $y' = 2x - 2/x$, $y'' = 2 + 2/x^2$ (c) $y' = 3x^2 \ln x + x^2$, $y'' = x(6\ln x + 5)$
 (d) $y' = (1 - \ln x)/x^2$, $y'' = (2\ln x - 3)/x^3$

2. (a) $x^2 \ln x(3 \ln x + 2)$ (b) $x(2\ln x - 1)/(\ln x)^2$ (c) $10(\ln x)^9/x$ (d) $2\ln x/x + 6\ln x + 18x + 6$

3. (a) $1/(x \ln x)$ (b) $-x/(1 - x^2)$ (c) $e^x(\ln x + 1/x)$ (d) $e^{x^3}(3x^2 \ln x^2 + 2/x)$ (e) $e^x/(e^x + 1)$
 (f) $(2x + 3)/(x^2 + 3x - 1)$ (g) $-2e^x(e^x - 1)^{-2}$ (h) $(4x - 1)e^{2x^2 - x}$

4. (a) $x > -1$ (b) $1/3 < x < 1$ (c) $x \neq 0$ **5.** (a) $|x| > 1$ (b) $x > 1$ (c) $x \neq e^e$ and $x > 1$

6. (a) $(-2, 0]$. (y is defined only in $(-2, 2)$.) (b) $[e^{-1/3}, \infty)$. ($y' = x^2(3\ln x + 1)$, $x > 0$.)
 (c) $[e, e^3]$. ($y' = (1 - \ln x)(\ln x - 3)/2x^2$, $x > 0$.)

7. (a) (i) $y = x - 1$ (ii) $y = 2x - 1 - \ln 2$ (iii) $y = x/e$ (b) (i) $y = x$ (ii) $y = 2ex - e$ (iii) $y = -e^{-2}x - 4e^{-2}$

8. (a) $f'(x)/f(x) = -2/3(x^2 - 1)$ (b) $f'(x)/f(x) = 2\ln x + 2$
 (c) $f'(x)/f(x) = 1/(2x - 4) + 2x/(x^2 + 1) + 4x^3/(x^4 + 6)$

9. (a) $(2x)^x(1 + \ln 2 + \ln x)$ (b) $x^{\sqrt{x} - \frac{1}{2}}\left(\frac{1}{2}\ln x + 1\right)$ (c) $\frac{1}{2}(\sqrt{x})^x(\ln x + 1)$

10. $\ln y = v \ln u$, so $y'/y = v' \ln u + vu'/u$ and therefore $y' = u^v(v' \ln u + vu'/u)$. (Alternative: $y = (e^{\ln u})^v = e^{v \ln u}$, and then use the chain rule.)

11. (a) Let $f(x) = e^x - (1 + x + \frac{1}{2}x^2)$. Then $f(0) = 0$ and $f'(x) = e^x - (1 + x) > 0$ for all $x > 0$, as shown in the problem. Hence $f(x) > 0$ for all $x > 0$, and the inequality follows. For (b) and (c) see SM.

Review Problems for Chapter 6

1. $[f(x + h) - f(x)]/h = [(x + h)^2 - (x + h) + 2 - x^2 + x - 2]/h = [2xh + h^2 - h]/h = 2x + h - 1 \to 2x - 1$ as $h \to 0$, so $f'(x) = 2x - 1$.

2. $[f(x + h) - f(x)]/h = -6x^2 + 2x - 6xh - 2h^2 + h \to -6x^2 + 2x$ as $h \to 0$, so $f'(x) = -6x^2 + 2x$.

3. (a) $y' = 2$, $y'' = 0$ (b) $y' = 3x^8$, $y'' = 24x^7$ (c) $y' = -x^9$, $y'' = -9x^8$ (d) $y' = 21x^6$, $y'' = 126x^5$
(e) $y' = 1/10$, $y'' = 0$ (f) $y' = 5x^4 + 5x^{-6}$, $y'' = 20x^3 - 30x^{-7}$ (g) $y' = x^3 + x^2$, $y'' = 3x^2 + 2x$
(h) $y' = -x^{-2} - 3x^{-4}$, $y'' = 2x^{-3} + 12x^{-5}$

4. Because $C'(1000) \approx C(1001) - C(1000)$, if $C'(1000) = 25$, the additional cost of producing 1 more than 1000 units is approximately 25. It is profitable to increase production if each unit is sold for 30.

5. (a) $y = -3$ and $y' = -6x = -6$ at $x = 1$, so $y - (-3) = (-6)(x - 1)$, or $y = -6x + 3$.
(b) $y = -14$ and $y' = 1/2\sqrt{x} - 2x = -31/4$ at $x = 4$, so $y = -(31/4)x + 17$.
(c) $y = 0$ and $y' = (-2x^3 - 8x^2 + 6x)/(x + 3)^2 = -1/4$ at $x = 1$, so $y = (-1/4)(x - 1)$.

6. $A'(100) \approx A(101) - A(100)$, so the additional cost of increasing the area from 100 to 101 m^2 is approximately \$250.

7. (a) $f(x) = x^3 + x$, so $f'(x) = 3x^2 + 1$.   (b) $g'(w) = -5w^{-6}$ (c) $h(y) = y(y^2 - 1) = y^3 - y$, so $h'(y) = 3y^2 - 1$.
(d) $G'(t) = (-2t^2 - 2t + 6)/(t^2 + 3)^2$ (e) $\varphi'(\xi) = (4 - 2\xi^2)/(\xi^2 + 2)^2$ (f) $F'(s) = -(s^2 + 2)/(s^2 + s - 2)^2$

8. (a) $2at$ (b) $a^2 - 2t$ (c) $2x\varphi - 1/2\sqrt{\varphi}$

9. (a) $y' = 20uu' = 20(5 - x^2)(-2x) = 40x^3 - 200x$ (b) $y' = \dfrac{1}{2\sqrt{u}} \cdot u' = \dfrac{-1}{2x^2\sqrt{1/x - 1}}$

10. (a) $dZ/dt = (dZ/du)(du/dt) = 3(u^2 - 1)^2 2u3t^2 = 18t^5(t^6 - 1)^2$
(b) $dK/dt = (dK/dL)(dL/dt) = (1/2\sqrt{L})(-1/t^2) = -1/2t^2\sqrt{1 + 1/t}$

11. (a) $\dot{x}/x = 2\dot{a}/a + \dot{b}/b$ (b) $\dot{x}/x = \alpha\dot{a}/a + \beta\dot{b}/b$ (c) $\dot{x}/x = (\alpha + \beta)(\alpha a^{\alpha-1}\dot{a} + \beta b^{\beta-1}\dot{b})/(a^\alpha + b^\beta)$

12. $dR/dt = (dR/dS)(dS/dK)(dK/dt) = \alpha S^{\alpha-1}\beta\gamma K^{\gamma-1}Apt^{p-1} = A\alpha\beta\gamma pt^{p-1}S^{\alpha-1}K^{\gamma-1}$

13. (a) $h'(L) = apL^{a-1}(L^a + b)^{p-1}$ (b) $C'(Q) = a + 2bQ$ (c) $P'(x) = ax^{1/q-1}(ax^{1/q} + b)^{q-1}$

14. (a) $y' = -7e^x$ (b) $y' = -6xe^{-3x^2}$ (c) $y' = xe^{-x}(2 - x)$ (d) $y' = e^x[\ln(x^2 + 2) + 2x/(x^2 + 2)]$
(e) $y' = 15x^2e^{5x^3}$ (f) $y' = x^3e^{-x}(x - 4)$ (g) $y' = 10(e^x + 2x)(e^x + x^2)^9$ (h) $y' = 1/2\sqrt{x}(\sqrt{x} + 1)$

15. (a) Increases in $[1, \infty)$.   (b) Increases when $x \geq 0$.   (c) Increases in $(-\infty, 1]$ and in $[2, \infty)$.

16. (a) $d\pi/dQ = P(Q) + QP'(Q) - c$ (b) $d\pi/dL = PF'(L) - w$

Chapter 7

7.1

1. Differentiating w.r.t. x yields (∗) $6x + 2y' = 0$, so $y' = -3x$. Solving the given equation for y yields $y = 5/2 - 3x^2/2$, and then $y' = -3x$.

2. Implicit differentiation yields (∗) $2xy + x^2(dy/dx) = 0$, and so $dy/dx = -2y/x$. Differentiating (∗) implicitly w.r.t. x gives $2y + 2x(dy/dx) + 2x(dy/dx) + x^2(d^2y/dx^2) = 0$. Inserting the result for dy/dx, and simplifying yields $d^2y/dx^2 = 6y/x^2$. These results follows more easily by differentiating $y = x^{-2}$ twice.

3. (a) $y' = (1 + 3y)/(1 - 3x) = -5/(1 - 3x)^2$, $y'' = 6y'/(1 - 3x) = -30/(1 - 3x)^3$
(b) $y' = 6x^5/5y^4 = (6/5)x^{1/5}$, $y'' = 6x^4y^{-4} - (144/25)x^{10}y^{-9} = (6/25)x^{-4/5}$

4. $2u + v + u(dv/du) - 3v^2(dv/du) = 0$, so $dv/du = (2u + v)/(3v^2 - u)$. Hence $dv/du = 0$ when $v = -2u$ (provided $3v^2 - u \neq 0$). Substituting for v in the original equation yields $8u^3 - u^2 = 0$. So the only point on the curve where $dv/du = 0$ and $u \neq 0$ is $(u, v) = (1/8, -1/4)$.

5. Differentiating w.r.t. x yields ($*$) $4x + 6y + 6xy' + 2yy' = 0$, so $y' = -(2x + 3y)/(3x + y) = -8/5$ at $(1, 2)$. Differentiating ($*$) w.r.t. x yields $4 + 6y' + 6y' + 6xy'' + 2(y')^2 + 2yy'' = 0$. Substituting $x = 1$, $y = 2$, and $y' = -8/5$ yields $y'' = 126/125$.

6. (a) $2x + 2yy' = 0$, and solve for y' to get $y' = -x/y$. (b) $1/2\sqrt{x} + y'/2\sqrt{y} = 0$, and solve for y' to get $y' = -\sqrt{y/x}$. (c) $4x^3 - 4y^3 y' = 2xy^3 + x^2 3y^2 y'$, and solve for y' to get $y' = 2x(2x^2 - y^3)/y^2(3x^2 + 4y)$. (d) $e^{xy}(y + xy') - 2xy - x^2 y' = 0$, and solve for y' to get $y' = y(2x - e^{xy})/x(e^{xy} - x)$.

7. ($*$) $2y + 2xy' - 6yy' = 0$. Inserting $x = 6$, $y = 1$ yields $2 + 12y' - 6y' = 0$, so $y' = -1/3$. Differentiating ($*$) w.r.t. x yields $2y' + 2y' + 2xy'' - 6y'y' - 6yy'' = 0$. Inserting $x = 6$, $y = 1$, and $y' = -1/3$ gives $y'' = 1/3$.

8. (a) $y' = \dfrac{g'(x) - y}{x - 3y^2}$ (b) $y' = \dfrac{2x - g'(x + y)}{g'(x + y) - 2y}$ (c) $y' = \dfrac{2y(xg'(x^2 y) - xy - 1)}{x(2xy + 2 - xg'(x^2 y))}$

9. Differentiation w.r.t. x yields $3x^2 F(xy) + x^3 F'(xy)(y + xy') + e^{xy}(y + xy') = 1$. Then put $x = 1$, $y = 0$ to obtain $y' = 1/(F'(0) + 1)$. (Note that F is a function of only one variable, with argument xy.)

10. (a) $y' = \dfrac{x[a^2 - 2(x^2 + y^2)]}{y[2(x^2 + y^2) + a^2]}$ (b) $(\pm\frac{1}{4}a\sqrt{6}, \pm\frac{1}{4}a\sqrt{2})$, where all four sign combinations are allowed.

7.2

1. Implicit differentiation w.r.t. P, with Q as a function of P, yields $(dQ/dP) \cdot P^{1/2} + Q\frac{1}{2}P^{-1/2} = 0$. Thus $dQ/dP = -\frac{1}{2}QP^{-1} = -19/P^{3/2}$.

2. (a) $1 = C''(Q^*)(dQ^*/dP)$, so $dQ^*/dP = 1/C''(Q^*)$ (b) $dQ^*/dP > 0$, which is reasonable because if the price received by the producer increases, the optimal production should increase.

3. Taking first the natural logarithm on both sides yields $\ln A - \alpha \ln P - \beta \ln r = \ln S$. Differentiating with respect to r we have $-(\alpha/P)(dP/dr) - \beta/r = 0$. It follows that $dP/dr = -(\beta/\alpha)(P/r) < 0$. So a rise in the interest rate depresses demand, and the price falls to compensate.

4. (a) $Y = f(Y) + I + \bar{X} - g(Y)$, $dY/dI = 1/[1 - f'(Y) + g'(Y)]$. If $g'(Y) > 0$, then $dY/dI > 0$. (b) $d^2 Y/dI^2 = (f'' - g'')/(1 - f' + g')^3$

5. Differentiating ($*$) w.r.t. P yields $f''(P+t)(dP/dt+1)^2 + f'(P+t)d^2P/dt^2 = g''(P)(dP/dt)^2 + g'(P)d^2P/dt^2$. With simplified notation $f''(P' + 1)^2 + f'P'' = g''(P')^2 + g'P''$. Substituting $P' = f'/(g' - f')$ and solving for P'', we get $P'' = [f''(g')^2 - g''(f')^2]/(g' - f')^3$.

6. (a) Differentiating ($*$) w.r.t. t yields $f'(P)(dP/dt) = g'((1 - t)P)[-P + (1 - t)(dP/dt)]$, and so

$$\frac{dP}{dt} = \frac{-Pg'((1-t)P)}{f'(P) - (1-t)g'((1-t)P)}$$

(b) The numerator as well as the denominator is negative, so dP/dt is positive. Increasing the tax on the producers increases the price.

7.3

1. $f(1) = 1$ and $f'(x) = 2e^{2x-2} = 2$ for $x = 1$. So according to (3), $g'(1) = 1/f'(1) = 1/2$. The inverse function is $g(x) = 1 + \frac{1}{2}\ln x$, so $g'(x) = 1/2x = 1/2$ for $x = 1$.

2. (a) $f'(x) = x^2\sqrt{4 - x^2} + \frac{1}{3}x^3 \dfrac{-2x}{2\sqrt{4 - x^2}} = \dfrac{4x^2(3 - x^2)}{3\sqrt{4 - x^2}}$. f increases in $[-\sqrt{3}, \sqrt{3}]$, and decreases in $[-2, -\sqrt{3}]$ and in $[\sqrt{3}, 2]$. See Fig. A7.3.2. (b) f has an inverse in the interval $[0, \sqrt{3}]$ because f is strictly increasing there. $g'(\frac{1}{3}\sqrt{3}) = 1/f'(1) = 3\sqrt{3}/8$.

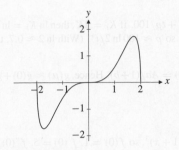

Figure A7.3.2

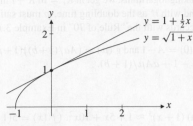

$y = 1 + \frac{1}{2}x$

$y = \sqrt{1+x}$

Figure A7.4.1

3. (a) $f'(x) = e^{x-3}/(e^{x-3} + 2) > 0$ for all x, so f is strictly increasing. $f(x) \to \ln 2$ as $x \to -\infty$ and $f(x) \to \infty$ as $x \to \infty$, so the range of f is $(\ln 2, \infty)$.   (b) $g(x) = 3 + \ln(e^x - 2)$, defined on the range of f.
(c) $f'(3) = 1/g'(f(3)) = 1/3$

4. $dD/dP = -0.3 \cdot 157.8 P^{-1.3} = -47.34 P^{-1.3}$, so $dP/dD = 1/(dD/dP) \approx -0.021 P^{1.3}$.

5. (a) $dx/dy = -e^{x+5} = -1/y$ (b) $dx/dy = -1 - 3e^x$ (c) $dx/dy = x(3y^2 - x^2)/(2 + 3x^2y - y^3)$

7.4

1. If $f(x) = \sqrt{1+x}$, then $f'(x) = 1/(2\sqrt{1+x})$, so $f(0) = 1$ and $f'(0) = 1/2$. Hence, (1) gives $\sqrt{1+x} \approx 1 + \frac{1}{2}(x - 0) = 1 + \frac{1}{2}x$. See Fig. A7.4.1.

2. $(5x + 3)^{-2} \approx 1/9 - 10x/27$. ($f(0) = 1/9$, $f'(x) = -10(5x + 3)^{-3}$, so $f'(0) = -10/27$.)

3. (a) $(1 + x)^{-1} \approx 1 - x$ (b) $(1 + x)^5 \approx 1 + 5x$ (c) $(1 - x)^{1/4} \approx 1 - \frac{1}{4}x$

4. $F(1) = A$ and $F'(K) = \alpha A K^{\alpha-1}$, so $F'(1) = \alpha A$. Then $F(K) \approx F(1) + F'(1)(K - 1) = A + \alpha A(K - 1) = A(1 + \alpha(K - 1))$.

5. (a) $30x^2\, dx$ (b) $15x^2\, dx - 10x\, dx + 5\, dx$ (c) $-3x^{-4}\, dx$ (d) $(1/x)\, dx$ (e) $(px^{p-1} + qx^{q-1})\, dx$
(f) $(p + q)x^{p+q-1}\, dx$ (g) $rp(px + q)^{r-1}\, dx$ (h) $(pe^{px} + qe^{qx})\, dx$

6. (a) If $f(x) = (1 + x)^m$, then $f(0) = 1$ and $f'(0) = m$, so $1 + mx$ is the linear approximation to $f(x)$ about $x = 0$.
(b) (i) $\sqrt[3]{1.1} = (1 + 1/10)^{1/3} \approx 1 + (1/3)(1/10) \approx 1.033$ (ii) $\sqrt[5]{33} = 2(1 + 1/32)^{1/5} \approx 2(1 + 1/160) = 2.0125$
(iii) $\sqrt[3]{9} = 2(1 + 1/8)^{1/3} \approx 2(1 + 1/24) \approx 2.083$ (iv) $(0.98)^{25} = (1 - 0.02)^{25} = (1 - 1/50)^{25} \approx 1 - 1/2 = 1/2$

7. (a) (i) $\Delta y = 0.61$, $dy = 0.6$ (ii) $\Delta y = 0.0601$, $dy = 0.06$
(b) (i) $\Delta y = 0.011494$, $dy = 0.011111$ (ii) $\Delta y = 0.001115$, $dy = 0.001111$
(c) (i) $\Delta y = 0.012461$, $dy = 0.0125$ (ii) $\Delta y = 0.002498$, $dy = 0.0025$

8. (a) $y' = -3/2$ (b) $y(x) \approx -\frac{3}{2}x + \frac{3}{2}$

9. (a) $A(r + dr) - A(r)$ is the shaded area in Fig. A7.4.9. It is approximately equal to the length of the inner circle, $2\pi r$, times dr.   (b) $V(r + dr) - V(r)$ is the volume of the shell between the sphere with radius $r + dr$ and the sphere with radius r. It is approximately equal to the surface area $4\pi r^2$ of the inner sphere times the thickness dr of the shell.

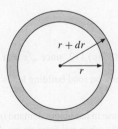

$r + dr$

r

Figure A7.4.9

10. Taking logarithms, we get $\ln K_t = \ln K + t \ln(1 + p/100) \approx \ln K + tp/100$. If $K_t = 2K$, then $\ln K_t = \ln 2 + \ln K$, and with t^* as the doubling time, p must satisfy $\ln 2 \approx t^* p/100$, so $p \approx 100 \ln 2/t^*$. (With $\ln 2 \approx 0.7$, this result accords with the "Rule of 70" in Example 3.)

11. $g(0) = A - 1$ and $g'(\mu) = \big(Aa/(1+b)\big)(1+\mu)^{[a/(1+b)]-1}$, so $g'(0) = Aa/(1+b)$. Hence, $g(\mu) \approx g(0) + g'(0)\mu = A - 1 + aA\mu/(1+b)$.

7.5

1. (a) $(1+x)^5 \approx 1 + 5x + 10x^2$. ($f'(x) = 5(1+x)^4$, $f''(x) = 20(1+x)^3$, so $f(0) = 1$, $f'(0) = 5$, $f''(0) = 20$, so $f(x) \approx 1 + x + \frac{1}{2}20x^2 = 1 + x + 10x^2$.) (b) $AK^\alpha \approx A + \alpha A(K-1) + \frac{1}{2}\alpha(\alpha-1)A(K-1)^2$
(c) $(1 + \frac{3}{2}\varepsilon + \frac{1}{2}\varepsilon^2)^{1/2} \approx 1 + \frac{3}{4}\varepsilon - \frac{3}{32}\varepsilon^2$ (d) $(1-x)^{-1} \approx 1 + x + x^2$. ($f'(x) = (-1)(1-x)^{-2}(-1) = (1-x)^{-2}$, $f''(x) = 2(1-x)^{-3}$, etc.)

2. $x - \frac{1}{2}x^2 + \frac{1}{3}x^3 - \frac{1}{4}x^4 + \frac{1}{5}x^5$ **3.** $-5 + \frac{5}{2}x - \frac{15}{8}x^2$

4. Follows from formula (1) with $f = U$, $a = y$, $x = y + M - s$.

5. Implicit differentiation yields: $(*)$ $3x^2y + x^3y' + 1 = \frac{1}{2}y^{-1/2}y'$. Inserting $x = 0$ and $y = 1$ gives $1 = \big(\frac{1}{2}\big)1^{-1/2}y'$, so $y' = 2$. Differentiating $(*)$ once more w.r.t. x yields $6xy + 3x^2y' + 3x^2y' + x^3y'' = -\frac{1}{4}y^{-3/2}(y')^2 + \frac{1}{2}y^{-1/2}y''$. Inserting $x = 0$, $y = 1$, and $y' = 2$ gives $y'' = 2$. Hence, $y(x) \approx 1 + 2x + x^2$.

6. We find $\dot{x}(0) = 2[x(0)]^2 = 2$. Differentiating the expression for $\dot{x}(t)$ yields $\ddot{x}(t) = x(t) + t\dot{x}(t) + 4[x(t)]\dot{x}(t)$, and so $\ddot{x}(0) = x(0) + 4[x(0)]\dot{x}(0) = 1 + 4 \cdot 1 \cdot 2 = 9$. Hence, $x(t) \approx x(0) + \dot{x}(0)t + \frac{1}{2}\ddot{x}(0)t^2 = 1 + 2t + \frac{9}{2}t^2$.

7. Use (5) with $x = \sigma\sqrt{t/n}$, keeping only three terms on the right-hand side.

8. Use (2) with $f(x) = (1+x)^n$ and $x = p/100$. Then $f'(x) = n(1+x)^{n-1}$ and $f''(x) = n(n-1)(1+x)^{n-2}$. The approximation follows.

9. $h'(x) = \dfrac{(px^{p-1} - qx^{q-1})(x^p + x^q) - (x^p - x^q)(px^{p-1} + qx^{q-1})}{(x^p + x^q)^2} = \dfrac{2(p-q)x^{p+q-1}}{(x^p + x^q)^2}$, so $h'(1) = \frac{1}{2}(p-q)$.
Since $h(1) = 0$, we get $h(x) \approx h(1) + h'(1)(x-1) = \frac{1}{2}(p-q)(x-1)$.

7.6

1. From Problem 7.5.2, $f(0) = 0$, $f'(0) = 1$, $f''(0) = -1$, and $f'''(c) = 2(1+c)^{-3}$. Then (3) gives $f(x) = f(0) + \frac{1}{1!}f'(0)x + \frac{1}{2!}f''(0)x + \frac{1}{3!}f'''(c)x^3 = x - \frac{1}{2}x^2 + \frac{1}{3}(1+c)^{-3}x^3$.

2. (a) $\sqrt[3]{25} = 3(1 - 2/27)^{1/3} \approx 3(1 - \frac{1}{3}\frac{2}{27} - \frac{1}{9}\frac{4}{27^2}) \approx 2.924$
(b) $\sqrt[5]{33} = 2(1 + 1/32)^{1/5} \approx 2(1 + \frac{1}{5 \cdot 32} - \frac{2}{25}\frac{1}{32^2}) \approx 2.0125$

3. $(1 + 1/8)^{1/3} = 1 + 1/24 - 1/576 + R_3(1/8)$, where $0 < R_3(1/8) < 5/(81 \cdot 8^3)$. Thus, $\sqrt[3]{9} = 2(1+1/8)^{1/3} \approx 2.080$, with three correct decimals.

4. (a) $1 + \frac{1}{3}x - \frac{1}{9}x^2$ (b) and (c) see SM.

7.7

1. In each case we use (2): (a) -3 (b) 100 (c) $1/2$, since $\sqrt{x} = x^{1/2}$.   (d) $-3/2$, since $A/x\sqrt{x} = Ax^{-3/2}$.

2. $\mathrm{El}_K T = 1.06$. A 1% increase in expenditure on road building leads to an increase in the traffic volume of approximately 1.06 %.

3. (a) A 10% increase in fares leads to a decrease in passenger demand of approximately 4%.   (b) One reason could be that for long-distance travel, more people fly when rail fares go up. Another reason could be that many people may commute 60 km, whereas almost nobody commutes 300 km, and commuters' demand is likely to be less elastic.

4. (a) $\text{El}_x\, e^{ax} = (x/e^{ax})ae^{ax} = ax$ (b) $\text{El}_x \ln x = (x/\ln x)(1/x) = 1/\ln x$ (c) $\text{El}_x(x^p e^{ax}) =$

$\dfrac{x}{x^p e^{ax}}(px^{p-1}e^{ax} + x^p ae^{ax}) = p + ax$ (d) $\text{El}_x(x^p \ln x) = \dfrac{x}{x^p \ln x}(px^{p-1}\ln x + x^p(1/x)) = p + 1/\ln x$

5. $\text{El}_x(f(x))^p = \dfrac{x}{(f(x))^p}\, p(f(x))^{p-1} f'(x) = p\dfrac{x}{f(x)} f'(x) = p\, \text{El}_x\, f(x)$

6. Using (2), $\text{El}_r\, D = 1.23$. A 1% increase in income leads to an increase in the demand of approximately 1.23%.

7. $\ln m = -0.02 + 0.19 \ln N$. When $N = 480\,000$, then $m \approx 11.77$.

8. $\text{El}_x\, Af(x) = \dfrac{x}{Af(x)}\, Af'(x) = \dfrac{x}{f(x)} f'(x) = \text{El}_x\, f(x)$

$\text{El}_x\,(A + f(x)) = \dfrac{x}{A + f(x)} f'(x) = \dfrac{f(x)xf'(x)/f(x)}{A + f(x)} = \dfrac{f(x)\,\text{El}_x\, f(x)}{A + f(x)}$

9. We prove only (d) (for the rest see SM): $\text{El}_x(f + g) = \dfrac{x(f' + g')}{f + g} = \dfrac{f(xf'/f) + g(xg'/g)}{f + g} = \dfrac{f\,\text{El}_x\, f + g\,\text{El}_x\, g}{f + g}$

10. (a) -5 (b) $\dfrac{1 + 2x}{1 + x}$ (c) $\dfrac{30x^3}{x^3 + 1}$ (d) $\text{El}_x\, 5x^2 = 2$, so $\text{El}_x(\text{El}_x\, 5x^2) = 0$ (e) $\dfrac{2x^2}{1 + x^2}$

(f) $\text{El}_x\left(\dfrac{x - 1}{x^5 + 1}\right) = \text{El}_x(x - 1) - \text{El}_x(x^5 + 1) = \dfrac{x\,\text{El}_x\, x}{x - 1} - \dfrac{x^5\,\text{El}_x\, x^5}{x^5 + 1} = \dfrac{x}{x - 1} - \dfrac{5x^5}{x^5 + 1}$

7.8

1. Only the function in (a) is not continuous.

2. f is discontinuous at $x = 0$. g is continuous at $x = 2$. The graphs of f and g are shown in Figs. A7.8.2a and A7.8.2b.

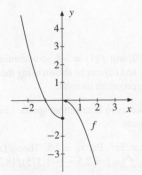

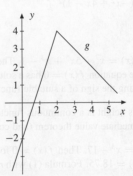

Figure A7.8.2a   Figure A7.8.2b

3. (a) Continuous for all x.   (b) Continuous for all $x \neq 1$.   (c) Continuous for all $x < 2$.   (d) Continuous for all x.
(e) Continuous for all x where $x \neq \sqrt{3} - 1$ and $x \neq -\sqrt{3} - 1$.   (f) Continuous for all $x > 0$.

4. See Fig. A7.8.4; y is discontinuous at $x = a$.

5. $a = 5$. (The straight line $y = ax - 1$ and the parabola $y = 3x^2 + 1$ must meet when $x = 1$, which is true if and only if $a = 5$.)

6. See Fig. A7.8.6. (This example shows that the commonly seen statement: "if the inverse function exists, the original and the inverse function must both be monotonic" is wrong. This claim is correct for a continuous function on an interval, however.)

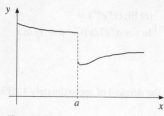

Figure A7.8.4

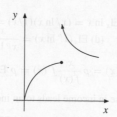

Figure A7.8.6

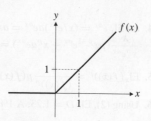

Figure A7.9.6

7.9

1. (a) -4 (b) 0 (c) 2 (d) $-\infty$ (e) ∞ (f) $-\infty$

2. (a) $\dfrac{x-3}{x^2+1} = \dfrac{1/x - 3/x^2}{1+1/x^2} \to 0$ as $x \to \infty$.   (b) $\sqrt{\dfrac{2+3x}{x-1}} = \sqrt{\dfrac{3+2/x}{1-1/x}} \to \sqrt{3}$ as $x \to \infty$.   (c) a^2

3. $\lim\limits_{x\to\infty} f_i(x) = \infty$ for $i = 1, 2, 3$; $\lim\limits_{x\to\infty} f_4(x) = 0$. Then: (a) ∞ (b) 0 (c) $-\infty$ (d) 1 (e) 0 (f) ∞ (g) 1 (h) ∞

4. (a) $y = x - 1$ ($x = -1$ is a vertical asymptote).   (b) $y = 2x - 3$ (c) $y = 3x + 5$ ($x = 1$ is a vertical asymptote). (d) $y = 5x$ ($x = 1$ is a vertical asymptote).

5. $y = Ax + A(b-c) + d$ is an asymptote as $x \to \infty$. ($x = -c$ is not an asymptote because $x \geq 0$.)

6. $f'(0^+) = 1$ and $f'(0^-) = 0$. See Fig. A7.9.6.

7. $f'(x) = \dfrac{3(x-1)(x+1)}{(-x^2+4x-1)^2}$. $f(x)$ is increasing in $(-\infty, -1]$, in $\left[1, 2+\sqrt{3}\,\right]$, and in $\left(2+\sqrt{3}, \infty\right)$. See Fig. SM7.9.7.

7.10

1. (a) Let $f(x) = x^7 - 5x^5 + x^3 - 1$. Then f is continuous, $f(-1) = 2$, and $f(1) = -4$, so according to Theorem 7.10.1, the equation $f(x) = 0$ has a solution in $(-1, 1)$. Parts (b), (c), and (d) can be shown using the same method of evaluating the sign of a suitable function at the end points of the appropriate interval.

2. A person's height is a continuous function of time (even if growth occurs in intermittent spurts, often overnight). The intermediate value theorem (and common sense) give the conclusion.

3. Let $f(x) = x^3 - 17$. Then $f(x) = 0$ for $x = \sqrt[3]{17}$. Moreover, $f'(x) = 3x^2$. Put $x_0 = 2.5$. Then $f(x_0) = -1.375$ and $f'(x_0) = 18.75$. Formula (1) with $n = 0$ yields $x_1 = x_0 - f(x_0)/f'(x_0) = 2.5 - (-1.375)/18.75 \approx 2.573$.

4. Integer root: $x = -3$. Newton's method gives $-1.879, 0.347$, and 1.534 for the three other roots.

5. Approximate solution: $x = 2$. Put $f(x) = (2x)^x - 15$. Then $f'(x) = (2x)^x[\ln(2x) + 1]$. Formula (1) with $n = 0$ yields $x_1 = x_0 - f(x_0)/f'(x_0) = 2 - f(2)/f'(2) = 2 - 1/[16(\ln 4 + 1)] \approx 1.9738$.

6. If $f(x_0)$ and $f'(x_0)$ have the same sign (as in Fig. 2), then (1) implies that $x_1 < x_0$. But if they have opposite signs, then $x_1 > x_0$.

7.11

1. (a) $\alpha_n = \dfrac{(3/n)-1}{2-(1/n)} \to -\dfrac{1}{2}$ as $n \to \infty$ (b) $\beta_n = \dfrac{1+(2/n)-(1/n^2)}{3-(2/n^2)} \to \dfrac{1}{3}$ as $n \to \infty$ (c) $-1/6$ (d) $-1/6$
(e) $= -3/2$ (f) $\sqrt{(1/3)-(-1/2)} = \sqrt{5/6} = \sqrt{30}/6$

2. (a) When $n \to \infty$, $2/n \to 0$ and so $5 - 2/n \to 5$.   (b) When $n \to \infty$, $\dfrac{n^2 - 1}{n} = n - 1/n \to \infty$.

(c) When $n \to \infty$, $\dfrac{3n}{\sqrt{2n^2 - 1}} = \dfrac{3n}{n\sqrt{2 - 1/n^2}} = \dfrac{3}{\sqrt{2 - 1/n^2}} \to \dfrac{3}{\sqrt{2}} = \dfrac{3\sqrt{2}}{2}$.

3. For a fixed number x, put $x/n = 1/m$. Then $n = mx$, and as $n \to \infty$, so $m \to \infty$. Hence $(1 + x/n)^n = (1 + 1/m)^{mx} = [(1 + 1/m)^m]^x \to e^x$ as $m \to \infty$.

7.12

1. (a) $\lim\limits_{x \to 3} \dfrac{3x^2 - 27}{x - 3} = \dfrac{\text{``0''}}{0} = \lim\limits_{x \to 3} \dfrac{6x}{1} = 18$, (or using $3x^2 - 27 = 3(x - 3)(x + 3)$).

(b) $\lim\limits_{x \to 0} \dfrac{e^x - 1 - x - \frac{1}{2}x^2}{3x^3} = \dfrac{\text{``0''}}{0} = \lim\limits_{x \to 0} \dfrac{e^x - 1 - x}{9x^2} = \dfrac{\text{``0''}}{0} = \lim\limits_{x \to 0} \dfrac{e^x - 1}{18x} = \dfrac{\text{``0''}}{0} = \lim\limits_{x \to 0} \dfrac{e^x}{18} = \dfrac{1}{18}$

(c) $\lim\limits_{x \to 0} \dfrac{e^{-3x} - e^{-2x} + x}{x^2} = \dfrac{\text{``0''}}{0} = \lim\limits_{x \to 0} \dfrac{-3e^{-3x} + 2e^{-2x} + 1}{2x} = \dfrac{\text{``0''}}{0} = \lim\limits_{x \to 0} \dfrac{9e^{-3x} - 4e^{-2x}}{2} = \dfrac{5}{2}$

2. (a) $\lim\limits_{x \to a} \dfrac{x^2 - a^2}{x - a} = \dfrac{\text{``0''}}{0} = \lim\limits_{x \to a} \dfrac{2x}{1} = 2a$, (or using $x^2 - a^2 = (x + a)(x - a)$).

(b) $\lim\limits_{x \to 0} \dfrac{2(1 + x)^{1/2} - 2 - x}{2(1 + x + x^2)^{1/2} - 2 - x} = \dfrac{\text{``0''}}{0} = \lim\limits_{x \to 0} \dfrac{(1 + x)^{-1/2} - 1}{(1 + 2x)(1 + x + x^2)^{-1/2} - 1} = \dfrac{\text{``0''}}{0} =$

$\lim\limits_{x \to 0} \dfrac{-\frac{1}{2}(1 + x)^{-3/2}}{2(1 + x + x^2)^{-1/2} + (1 + 2x)^2(-\frac{1}{2})(1 + x + x^2)^{-3/2}} = -\dfrac{1}{3}$

3. (a) $\frac{1}{2}$ (b) 3 (c) 2 (d) $-\frac{1}{2}$ (e) $\frac{3}{8}$ (f) -2

4. (a) $\lim\limits_{x \to \infty} \dfrac{\ln x}{x^{1/2}} = \dfrac{\text{``}\infty\text{''}}{\infty} = \lim\limits_{x \to \infty} \dfrac{1/x}{(1/2)x^{-1/2}} = \lim\limits_{x \to \infty} \dfrac{2}{x^{1/2}} = 0$ (b) 0. (Write $x \ln x = \dfrac{\ln x}{1/x}$, and then use l'Hôpital's rule.)   (c) $+\infty$. (Write $xe^{1/x} - x = x(e^{1/x} - 1) = (e^{1/x} - 1)/(1/x)$, and then use l'Hôpital's rule.)

5. The second fraction is not "0/0". The correct limit is $5/2$.

6. $L = \lim\limits_{v \to 0^+} \dfrac{1 - (1 + v^\beta)^{-\gamma}}{v} = \dfrac{\text{``0''}}{0} = \lim\limits_{v \to 0^+} \dfrac{\gamma(1 + v^\beta)^{-\gamma - 1}\beta v^{\beta - 1}}{1}$. If $\beta = 1$, then $L = \gamma$.
If $\beta > 1$, then $L = 0$, and if $\beta < 1$, then $L = \infty$.

7. $\lim\limits_{x \to \infty} \dfrac{f(x)}{g(x)} = \lim\limits_{t \to 0^+} \dfrac{f(1/t)}{g(1/t)} = \dfrac{\text{``0''}}{0} = \lim\limits_{t \to 0^+} \dfrac{f'(1/t)(-1/t^2)}{g'(1/t)(-1/t^2)} = \lim\limits_{t \to 0^+} \dfrac{f'(1/t)}{g'(1/t)} = \lim\limits_{x \to \infty} \dfrac{f'(x)}{g'(x)}$

8. See SM.

Review Problems for Chapter 7

1. (a) $y' = -5$, $y'' = 0$ (b) Differentiating w.r.t. x yields $y^3 + 3xy^2y' = 0$, so $y' = -y/3x$. Differentiating $y' = -y/3x$ w.r.t. x yields $y'' = -[y'3x - 3y]/9x^2 = -[(-y/3x)3x - 3y]/9x^2 = 4y/9x^2$. Because $y = 5x^{-1/3}$, we get $y' = -(5/3)x^{-4/3}$ and $y'' = (20/9)x^{-7/3}$. The answers from differentiating $y = 5x^{-1/3}$ are the same.
(c) $2y'e^{2y} = 3x^2$, so $y' = (3x^2/2)e^{-2y}$. Then $y'' = 3xe^{-2y} + \frac{1}{2}3x^2e^{-2y}(-2y') = 3xe^{-2y} - \frac{1}{2}9x^4e^{-4y}$. From the given equation we get $2y = \ln x^3 = 3\ln x$, so $y = \frac{3}{2}\ln x$, and then $y' = \frac{3}{2}x^{-1}$, $y'' = -\frac{3}{2}x^{-2}$. By noting that $e^{-2y} = e^{-3\ln x} = (e^{\ln x})^{-3} = x^{-3}$ and $e^{-4y} = (e^{-2y})^2 = x^{-6}$, verify that the answers are the same.

2. $5y^4y' - y^2 - 2xyy' = 0$, so $y' = \dfrac{y^2}{5y^4 - 2xy} = \dfrac{y}{5y^3 - 2x}$.   Because $y = 0$ makes the given equation meaningless, y' is never 0.

3. Differentiating w.r.t. x yields $3x^2 + 3y^2y' = 3y + 3xy'$. When $x = y = 3/2$, then $y' = -1$. See Fig. A7.R.3.

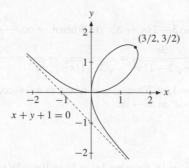

Figure A7.R.3

4. (a) $y' = -4/13$. (Implicit differentiation yields (∗) $2xy + x^2y' + 9y^2y' = 0$.)
   (b) Differentiating (∗) w.r.t. x yields: $2y + 2xy' + 2xy' + x^2y'' + 18yy'y' + 9y^2y'' = 0$. Inserting $x = 2$, $y = 1$, and $y' = -4/13$ gives the answer.

5. $\frac{1}{3}K^{-2/3}L^{1/3} + \frac{1}{3}K^{1/3}L^{-2/3}(dL/dK) = 0$, so $dL/dK = -L/K$.

6. Differentiation w.r.t. x gives $y'/y + y' = -2/x - 0.4(\ln x)/x$. Solving for y' gives $y' = \dfrac{-(2/x)(1 + \frac{1}{5}\ln x)}{1 + 1/y}$ which is 0 for $1 + \frac{1}{5}\ln x = 0$, i.e. $\ln x = -5$, and then $x = e^{-5}$.

7. (a) Straightforward. (b) $dY/dI = f'((1 - \beta)Y - \alpha)(1 - \beta)(dY/dI) + 1$. Solving for dY/dI yields
$$\frac{dY}{dI} = \frac{1}{1 - (1 - \beta)f'((1 - \beta)Y - \alpha)}.$$
   (c) Since $f' \in (0, 1)$ and $\beta \in (0, 1)$, we get $(1 - \beta)f'((1 - \beta)Y - \alpha) \in (0, 1)$, so $dY/dI > 0$.

8. (a) Differentiating w.r.t. x yields $2x - y - xy' + 4yy' = 0$, so $y' = (y - 2x)/(4y - x)$. (b) Horizontal tangent at $(1, 2)$ and $(-1, -2)$. ($y' = 0$ when $y = 2x$. Insert this into the given equation.) Vertical tangents at $(2\sqrt{2}, \sqrt{2}/2) \approx (2.8, 0.7)$ and at $(-2\sqrt{2}, -\sqrt{2}/2) \approx (-2.8, -0.7)$. (Vertical tangent when the denominator in the expression for y' is 0, i.e. when $x = 4y$.) See Fig. A in the book.

9. (a) $y' = \dfrac{2 - 2xy}{x^2 - 9y^2} = -\dfrac{1}{2}$ at $(-1, 1)$. (b) Vertical tangent at $(0, 0)$, $(-3, -1)$, and $(3, 1)$. (Vertical tangent requires the denominator of y' to be 0, i.e. $x = \pm 3y$. $y = 3y$ inserted into the given equation yields $y^3 = y$, so $y = 0$, $y = 1$, or $y = -1$. The corresponding values for x are 0, 3, and -3. Inserting $y = -3x$ gives no new points.) Horizontal tangent requires $y' = 0$, i.e. $xy = 1$. But inserting $y = 1/x$ into the given equation yields $x^4 = -3$, which has no solution. All these findings accord with Fig. B in the book.

10. (a) $D_f = (-1, 1)$, $R_f = (-\infty, \infty)$. (b) The inverse is $g(y) = (e^{2y} - 1)/(e^{2y} + 1)$. $g'(\frac{1}{2}\ln 3) = 3/4$.

11. (a) $f(e^2) = 2$ and $f(x) = \ln x(\ln x - 1)^2 = 0$ for $\ln x = 0$ and for $\ln x = 1$, so $x = 1$ or $x = e$.
   (b) $f'(x) = (3/x)(\ln x - 1)(\ln x - 1/3) > 0$ for $x > e$, and so f is strictly increasing in $[e, \infty)$. It therefore has an inverse h. According to (7.3.3), because $f(e^2) = 2$, we have $h'(2) = 1/f'(e^2) = e^2/5$.

12. (a) $f(x) \approx \ln 4 + \frac{1}{2}x - \frac{1}{8}x^2$ (b) $g(x) \approx 1 - \frac{1}{2}x + \frac{3}{8}x^2$ (c) $h(x) \approx x + 2x^2$

13. (a) $x\, dx/\sqrt{1 + x^2}$ (b) $8\pi r\, dr$ (c) $400K^3\, dK$ (d) $-3x^2\, dx/(1 - x^3)$

14. $df(x) = f'(x)\, dx = 3x^2\, dx/2\sqrt{1 + x^3}$. Moreover, $\Delta f(2) \approx df(2) = 3 \cdot 2^2(0.2)/2\sqrt{1 + 2^3} = 0.4$.

15. Let $x = \frac{1}{2}$ and $n = 5$ and use formula (7.6.6). $\sqrt{e} \approx 1.649$, correct to 3 decimals.

16. $y' + (1/y)y' = 1$, or (∗) $yy' + y' = y$. When $y = 1$, $y' = 1/2$. Differentiating (∗) w.r.t. x yields $(y')^2 + yy'' + y'' = y'$. With $y = 1$ and $y' = 1/2$, we find $y'' = 1/8$, so $y(x) \approx 1 + \frac{1}{2}x + \frac{1}{16}x^2$.

17. (a) For all $x \neq 0$. (b) Continuous for all $x > 0$. ($x^2 + 2x + 2$ is never 0.) (c) Continuous for all x in $(-2, 2)$.

18. (a) $1 = f'(y^2)2yy'$, so $y' = \dfrac{1}{2yf'(y^2)}$ (b) $y^2 + x2yy' = f'(x) - 3y^2y'$, and so $y' = \dfrac{f'(x) - y^2}{y(2x + 3y)}$

(c) $f'(2x + y)(2 + y') = 1 + 2yy'$, so $y' = \dfrac{1 - 2f'(2x + y)}{f'(2x + y) - 2y}$

19. $\text{El}_r(D_{\text{marg}}) = -0.165$ and $\text{El}_r(D_{\text{mah}}) = 2.39$. When income increased by 1%, the demand for margarine decreased by approximately 0.165%, while the demand for meals away from home increased by approximately 2.39%.

20. (a) 5 (using (7.7.2)). (b) 1/3 (using $\sqrt[3]{x} = x^{1/3}$ and (7.7.2)). (c) $\text{El}_x(x^3 + x^5) = \dfrac{x}{x^3 + x^5}(3x^2 + 5x^4) =$
$(5x^2 + 3)/(x^2 + 1)$, using (7.7.1). (Alternative: Use Problem 7.7.9.) (d) $2x/(x^2 - 1)$

21. Put $f(x) = x^3 - x - 5$. Then $f'(x) = 3x^2 - 1$. Taking $x_0 = 2$, formula (7.10.1) with $n = 1$ gives $x_1 = 2 - f(2)/f'(2) = 2 - 1/11 \approx 1.909$.

22. f is continuous, $f(1) = e - 3 < 0$ and $f(4) = e^2 - 3 > 0$. From Theorem 7.10.1(i), there is a zero for f in $(1, 4)$. Because $f'(x) > 0$, the solution is unique. Formula (7.10.1) yields $x_1 = 1 - f(1)/f'(1) = -1 + 6/e \approx 1.21$.

23. (a) 2 (b) Tends to $+\infty$. (c) No limit exists. (d) $-1/6$. (e) 1/5 (f) 1/16 (g) 1 (h) $-1/16$ (i) 0

24. Does not exist if $b \neq d$. If $b = d$, the limit is $(a - c)/2\sqrt{b}$.

25. $\lim_{x \to 0} \dfrac{a^x - b^x}{e^{ax} - e^{bx}} = \dfrac{\text{"0"}}{0} = \lim_{x \to 0} \dfrac{a^x \ln a - b^x \ln b}{ae^{ax} - be^{bx}} = \dfrac{\ln a - \ln b}{a - b}$

26. $x_1 = 0.9 - f(0.9)/f'(0.9) \approx 0.9247924$, $x_2 = x_1 - f(x_1)/f'(x_1) \approx 0.9279565$, $x_3 = x_2 - f(x_2)/f'(x_2) \approx 0.9280338$, and $x_4 = x_3 - f(x_3)/f'(x_3) \approx 0.9280339$. It seems that the answer correct to 3 decimals is 0.928.

Chapter 8

8.1

1. (a) $f(0) = 2$ and $f(x) \leq 2$ for all x (we divide 8 by a number greater than or equal to 4), so $x = 0$ maximizes $f(x)$. (b) $g(-2) = -3$ and $g(x) \geq -3$ for all x, so $x = -2$ minimizes $g(x)$. $g(x) \to \infty$ as $x \to \infty$, so there is no maximum. (c) $h(x)$ has its largest value 1 when $1 + x^4$ is the smallest, namely for $x = 0$, and $h(x)$ has its smallest value 1/2 when $1 + x^4$ is the largest, namely for $x = \pm 1$.

2. (a) Minimum -1 at $x = 0$. ($F(0) = -1$ and $-2/(2 + x^2) \geq -1$ for all x because $2 + x^2 \geq 2$ and so $2/(2 + x^2) \leq 1$.) No maximum. (b) Maximum 2 at $x = 1$. No minimum.

(c) Minimum 99 at $x = 0$. No maximum. (When $x \to \pm \infty$, $H(x) \to 100$.)

8.2

1. $y' = 1.06 - 0.08x$. $y' \geq 0$ for $x \leq 13.25$ and $y' \leq 0$ for $x \geq 13.25$, so y has a maximum at $x = 13.25$.

2. $h'(x) = \dfrac{8(2 - \sqrt{3}x)(2 + \sqrt{3}x)}{(3x^2 + 4)^2}$. The function has a maximum at $x = 2\sqrt{3}/3$ and a minimum at $x = -2\sqrt{3}/3$.

3. $h'(t) = 1/2\sqrt{t} - \frac{1}{2} = (1 - \sqrt{t})/2\sqrt{t}$. We see that $h'(t) \geq 0$ in $[0, 1]$ and $h'(t) \leq 0$ in $[1, \infty)$. According to Theorem 8.2.1(a), $t = 1$ maximizes $h(t)$.

4. $f'(x) = [4x(x^4 + 1) - 2x^2 4x^3]/(x^4 + 1)^2$, then simplify and factor. f on $[0, \infty)$ has maximum 1 at $x = 1$, because $f(x)$ increases in $[0, 1]$ and decreases in $[1, \infty)$.

5. $g'(x) = 3x^2 \ln x + x^3/x = 3x^2(\ln x + \frac{1}{3})$. $g'(x) = 0$ when $\ln x = -\frac{1}{3}$, i.e. $x = e^{-1/3}$. We see that $g'(x) \leq 0$ in $(0, e^{-1/3}]$ and $g'(x) \geq 0$ in $[e^{-1/3}, \infty)$, so $x = e^{-1/3}$ minimizes $g(x)$. Since $g(x) \to \infty$ as $x \to \infty$, there is no maximum.

6. $f'(x) = 3e^x(e^{2x} - 2)$. $f'(x) = 0$ when $e^{2x} = 2$, so $x = \frac{1}{2} \ln 2$. If $x < \frac{1}{2} \ln 2$ then $f'(x) < 0$, and if $x > \frac{1}{2} \ln 2$ then $f'(x) > 0$, so $x = \frac{1}{2} \ln 2$ is a minimum point. $f(x) = e^x(e^{2x} - 6)$ tends to $+\infty$ as $x \to \infty$, so f has no maximum.

7. $y' = xe^{-x}(2 - x)$ is positive in $(0, 2)$ and negative in $(2, 4)$, so y has a maximum $4e^{-2} \approx 0.54$ at $x = 2$.

8. (a) $x = \frac{1}{3} \ln 2$ is a minimum point. (b) $x = \frac{1}{3}(a + 2b)$ is a maximum point. (c) $x = \frac{1}{3}$ is a maximum point.

9. $d'(x) = 2(x - a_1) + 2(x - a_2) + \cdots + 2(x - a_n) = 2[nx - (a_1 + a_2 + \cdots + a_n)]$. So $d'(x) = 0$ for $x = \bar{x}$, where $\bar{x} = \frac{1}{n}(a_1 + a_2 + \cdots + a_n)$, the *arithmetic mean* of $a_1, a_2, \ldots, a_n$. Since $d''(x) = 2n > 0$, $\bar{x}$ minimizes $d(x)$.

10. (a) $x_0 = (1/\alpha) \ln(A\alpha/k)$. (b) See SM.

8.3

1. (a) $\pi(L) = 320\sqrt{L} - 40L$, so $\pi'(L) = \dfrac{160}{\sqrt{L}} - 40 = \dfrac{40(4 - \sqrt{L})}{\sqrt{L}}$. We see that $\pi'(L) \geq 0$ for $0 \leq L \leq 16$, $\pi'(16) = 0$, and $\pi'(L) \leq 0$ for $L \geq 16$, so $L = 16$ maximizes profits.
(b) The profit function is $\pi(L) = f(L) - wL$, so the first-order condition is $\pi'(L^*) = f'(L^*) - w = 0$.
(c) The first-order condition in (b) defines L^* as a function of w. Differentiating w.r.t. w: $f''(L^*)(\partial L^*/\partial w) - 1 = 0$, or $(\partial L^*/\partial w) = 1/f''(L^*) < 0$. (If the price of labour increases, the optimal labour input decreases.)

2. (a) $Q^* = \frac{1}{2}(a - k)$, $\pi(Q^*) = \frac{1}{4}(a - k)^2$ (b) $d\pi(Q^*)/dk = -\frac{1}{2}(a - k) = -Q^*$ (c) $s = a - k$

3. See Figs. A8.3.3a and A8.3.3b. The volume in cm^3 is as given. $V'(x) = 12(x - 3)(x - 9)$. V has maximum 432 at $x = 3$. The box has maximum volume when the square cut out from each corner has sides of length 3 cm.

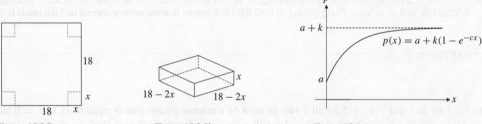

Figure A8.3.3a   Figure A8.3.3b   Figure A8.3.4

4. $p'(x) = kce^{-cx}$, $p''(x) = -kc^2e^{-cx}$. No maximum exists, and $p(x) \to a + k$ as $x \to \infty$. See Fig. A8.3.4.

5. $\overline{T}'(W) = a\dfrac{pb(bW + c)^{p-1}W - (bW + c)^p}{W^2} = a(bW + c)^{p-1}\dfrac{bW(p - 1) - c}{W^2}$, which is 0 for $W^* = c/b(p - 1)$. This must be the minimum point because $\overline{T}'(W)$ is negative for $W < W^*$ and positive for $W > W^*$.

8.4

1. $f'(x) = 8x - 40 = 0$ for $x = 5$. $f(0) = 80$, $f(5) = -20$, and $f(8) = 16$. Maximum 80 for $x = 0$. Minimum -20 for $x = 5$. See Fig. A8.4.1.

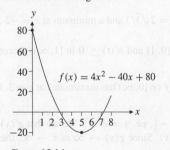

Figure A8.4.1

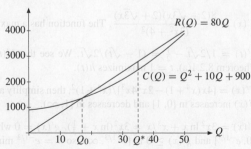

Figure A8.5.2

2. (a) Max. -1 at $x = 0$. Min. -7 at $x = 3$.   (b) Max. 10 at $x = -1$ and $x = 2$. Min. 6 at $x = 1$.
(c) Max. $5/2$ at $x = 1/2$ and $x = 2$. Min. 2 at $x = 1$.   (d) Max. 4 at $x = -1$. Min. $-6\sqrt{3}$ at $x = \sqrt{3}$.
(e) Max. $4.5 \cdot 10^9$ at $x = 3000$. Min. 0 at $x = 0$.

3. $g'(x) = \frac{2}{5}xe^{x^2}(1 - e^{2-2x^2})$. Stationary points: $x = 0$ and $x = \pm 1$. Here $x = 2$ is a maximum point, $x = 1$ and $x = -1$ are minimum points. (Note that $g(2) = \frac{1}{5}(e^4 + e^{-2}) > g(0) = \frac{1}{5}(1 + e^2)$.)

4. (a) Total commission is, respectively, \$4819, \$4900, \$4800, and $C = \frac{1}{10}(60 + x)(800 - 10x) = 4800 + 20x - x^2$, $x \in [0, 20]$. (When there are $60 + x$ passengers, the charter company earns $800 - 10x$ from each, so they earn $\$(60+x)(800 - 10x)$. The sports club earns $1/10$ of that amount.)   (b) The quadratic function C has its maximum for $x = 10$, so the maximum commission is with 70 travellers.

5. (a) $f(x) = \ln x(\ln x - 1)^2$. $f(e^{1/3}) = 4/27$, $f(e^2) = 2$, $f(e^3) = 12$. Zeros: $x = 1$ and $x = e$.
(b) $f'(x) = (3/x)(\ln x - 1)(\ln x - 1/3)$. Minimum 0 at $x = 1$ and at $x = e$. Maximum 12 at $x = e^3$.
(c) $f'(x) > 0$ in $[e, e^3]$, so $f(x)$ has an inverse. $g'(2) = 1/f'(e^2) = e^2/5$.

6. (a) $x^* = 3/2$ (b) $x^* = \sqrt{2}/2$ (c) $x^* = \sqrt{12}$ (d) $x^* = \sqrt{3}$

7. There is at least one point where you must be heading in the direction of the straight line joining A to B (even if that straight line hits the shore).

8. f is not continuous at $x = -1$ and $x = 1$. It has no maximum because $f(x)$ is arbitrarily close to 1 for x sufficiently close to 1. But there is no value of x for which $f(x) = 1$. Similarly, there is no minimum.

9. f has a maximum at $x = 1$ and a minimum at all $x > 1$. (Draw your own graph.) Yet the function is discontinuous at $x = 1$, and its domain of definition is neither closed nor bounded.

8.5

1. $\pi(Q) = 10Q - \frac{1}{1000}Q^2 - (5000 + 2Q) = 8Q - \frac{1}{1000}Q^2 - 5000$. Since $\pi'(Q) = 8 - \frac{1}{500}Q = 0$ for $Q = 4000$, and $\pi''(Q) = -\frac{1}{500} < 0$, $Q = 4000$ maximizes profits.

2. (a) See Fig. A8.5.2.   (b) (i) The requirement is $\pi(Q) \geq 0$ and $Q \in [0, 50]$, that is $-Q^2 + 70Q - 900 \geq 0$ and $Q \in [0, 50]$. The firm must produce at least $Q_0 = 35 - 5\sqrt{13} \approx 17$ units. (ii) Profits are maximized at $Q^* = 35$.

3. Profits: $\pi(x) = -0.003x^2 + 120x - 500\,000$, which is maximized at $x = 20\,000$.

4. (i) $Q^* = 450$ (ii) $Q^* = 550$ (iii) $Q^* = 0$

5. (a) $\pi(Q) = QP(Q) - C(Q) = -0.01Q^2 + 14Q - 4500$, which is maximized at $Q = 700$.
(b) $\text{El}_Q P(Q) = (Q/P(Q))P'(Q) = Q/(Q - 3000) = -1$ for $Q^* = 1500$.
(c) $R(Q) = QP(Q) = 18Q - 0.006Q^2$, so $R'(Q) = 18 - 0.012Q = 0$ for $Q^* = 1500$.

6. $\pi'(Q) = P - abQ^{b-1} = 0$ when $Q^{b-1} = P/ab$, i.e. $Q = (P/ab)^{1/(b-1)}$. Moreover, $\pi''(Q) = -ab(b-1)Q^{b-2} < 0$ for all $Q > 0$, so this is a maximum point.

8.6

1. $f'(x) = 3x^2 - 12 = 0$ at $x = \pm 2$. A sign diagram shows that $x = 2$ is a local minimum point and $x = -2$ is a local maximum point. Since $f''(x) = 6x$, this is confirmed by Theorem 8.6.2.

2. (a) No local extreme points.   (b) Local maximum 10 at $x = -1$. Local minimum 6 at $x = 1$.
(c) Local maximum -2 at $x = -1$. Local minimum 2 at $x = 1$.
(d) Local maximum $6\sqrt{3}$ at $x = -\sqrt{3}$. Local minimum $-6\sqrt{3}$ at $x = \sqrt{3}$.
(e) No local maximum point. Local minimum $1/2$ at $x = 3$.
(f) Local maximum 2 at $x = -2$. Local minimum -2 at $x = 0$.

3. (a) $D_f = [-6, 0) \cup (0, \infty)$; $f(x) > 0$ in $(-6, -2) \cup (0, \infty)$.   (b) Local maximum $\frac{1}{2}\sqrt{2}$ at $x = -4$. Local minima $(8/3)\sqrt{3}$ at $x = 6$, and 0 at $x = -6$ (where $f'(x)$ is undefined).   (c) $f(x) \to -\infty$ as $x \to 0^-$, $f(x) \to \infty$ as $x \to 0^+$, $f(x) \to \infty$ as $x \to \infty$, and $f'(x) \to 0$ as $x \to \infty$. f attains neither a maximum nor a minimum.

4. Look at the point a. Since the graph shows $f'(x)$, $f'(x) < 0$ to the left of a, $f'(a) = 0$, and $f'(x) > 0$ to the right of a, so a is a local minimum point. At the points b and e, $f'(x) > 0$ on both sides of the points, so they cannot be extreme points. At c, f has a local maximum, and d is a local minimum point.

5. (a) $f'(x) = 3x^2 + 2ax + b$, $f''(x) = 6x + 2a$. $f'(0) = 0$ requires $b = 0$. $f''(0) \geq 0$ requires $a \geq 0$. If $a = 0$ and $b = 0$, then $f(x) = x^3 + c$, which does not have a local minimum at $x = 0$. Hence, f has a local minimum at 0 if and only if $a > 0$ and $b = 0$.
   (b) $f'(1) = 0$ and $f'(3) = 0$ require $3 + 2a + b = 0$ and $27 + 6a + b = 0$, which means that $a = -6$ and $b = 9$.

6. (a) $f'(x) = x^2 e^x (3 + x)$. Use a sign diagram to show that $x = -3$ is a local (and global) minimum point. No local maximum points. ($x = 0$ is an inflection point (see next section).   (b) $g'(x) = x2^x (2 + x \ln 2)$. $x = 0$ is a local minimum point and $x = -2/\ln 2$ is a local maximum point.

7. $f'(x) = 3x^2 + a$. See SM.

8.7

1. (a) $f'(x) = 3x^2 + 3x - 6 = 3(x-1)(x+2)$, so $x = -2$ and $x = 1$ are stationary points. A sign diagram reveals that f increases in $(-\infty, -2]$ and in $[1, \infty)$.   (b) $f''(x) = 6x + 3 = 0$ for $x = -1/2$ and $f''(x)$ changes sign around $x = -1/2$, so this is an inflection point.

2. (a) $f''(x) = 2x(x^2 - 3)/(1 + x^2)^3$. f is convex in $[-\sqrt{3}, 0]$ and in $[\sqrt{3}, \infty)$. Inflection points: $x = -\sqrt{3}, 0, \sqrt{3}$.
   (b) $g''(x) = 4(1+x)^{-3} > 0$ when $x > -1$, so g is (strictly) convex in $(-1, \infty)$. No inflection points.
   (c) $h''(x) = (2+x)e^x$, so h is convex in $[-2, \infty)$ and $x = -2$ is an inflection point.

3. (a) $x = -1$ is a local (and global) maximum point, $x = 0$ is an inflection point.
   (b) $x = 1$ is a local (and global) minimum point, $x = 2$ is an inflection point.
   (c) $x = 3$ is a local maximum point, $x = 0, 3 - \sqrt{3}$, and $3 + \sqrt{3}$ are inflection points.
   (d) $x = \sqrt{e}$ is a local (and global) maximum point, $x = e^{5/6}$ is an inflection point.
   (e) $x = 0$ is a local (and global) minimum point, $x = -\ln 2$ is an inflection point.
   (f) $x = -\sqrt{2}$ is a local minimum point, $x = \sqrt{2}$ is a local maximum point, $x = 1 - \sqrt{3}$ and $x = 1 + \sqrt{3}$ are inflection points.

4. (a) For $x > 0$ one has $R = p\sqrt{x}$, $C = wx + F$, and $\pi(x) = p\sqrt{x} - wx - F$.   (b) $\pi'(x) = 0$ when $w = p/2\sqrt{x}$. (Marginal cost = price times marginal product.) Then $x = p^2/4w^2$. Moreover, $\pi''(x) = -\frac{1}{4}px^{-3/2} < 0$ for all $x > 0$, so profit is maximized over $(0, \infty)$. When $x = p^2/4w^2$, then $\pi = p^2/2w - p^2/4w - F = p^2/4w - F$. So this is a profit maximum if $F \leq p^2/4w$; otherwise, the firm does better not to start up and to choose $x = 0$.

5. $x = -2$ and $x = 4$ are minimum points, whereas $x = 2$ is a (possibly local) maximum point. Moreover, $x = 0$, $x = 1$, $x = 3$, and $x = 5$ are inflection points.

6. $a = -2/5$, $b = 3/5$ ($f(-1) = 1$ gives $-a + b = 1$. Moreover, $f'(x) = 3ax^2 + 2bx$ and $f''(x) = 6ax + 2b$, so $f''(1/2) = 0$ yields $3a + 2b = 0$.)

7. $C''(x) = 6ax + 2b$, so $C(x)$ is concave in $[0, -b/3a]$, convex in $[-b/3a, \infty)$. $x = -b/3a$ is the inflection point.

8. See Fig. A8.7.8. Use definition (2).

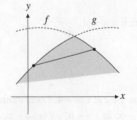

Figure A8.7.8

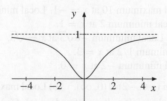

Figure A8.R.1

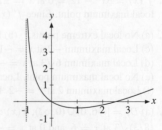

Figure A8.R.6

Review Problems for Chapter 8

1. (a) $f'(x) = \dfrac{4x}{(x^2+2)^2}$. Thus $f(x)$ decreases for $x \le 0$, increases for $x \ge 0$. (b) $f''(x) = 4(2-3x^2)/(x^2+2)^3$.

Inflection points at $x = \pm\frac{1}{3}\sqrt{6}$. (c) $f(x) \to 1$ as $x \to \pm\infty$. See Fig. A8.R.1.

2. (a) $Q'(L) = 3L(8 - \frac{1}{20}L) = 0$ for $L^* = 160$, and $Q(L)$ is increasing in $[0, 160]$, decreasing in $[160, 200]$, so $Q^* = 160$ maximizes $Q(L)$. Output per worker is $Q(L)/L = 12L - \frac{1}{20}L^2$, and this quadratic function has maximum at $L^{**} = 120$. (b) $Q'(120) = Q(120)/120 = 720$. In general (see Example 6.7.6), $(d/dL)(Q(L)/L) = (1/L)(Q'(L) - Q(L)/L)$. If $L > 0$ maximizes output per worker, one must have $Q'(L) = Q(L)/L$.

3. If the side parallel to the river is y and the other side is x, $2x + y = 1000$, so $y = 1000 - 2x$. The area of the enclosure is $xy = 1000x - 2x^2$, and this quadratic function has maximum when for $x = 250$, and then $y = 500$.

4. (a) $\pi = -0.0016Q^2 + 44Q - 0.0004Q^2 - 8Q - 64\,000 = -0.002Q^2 + 36Q - 64\,000$, and $Q = 9000$ maximizes π.

(b) $\text{El}_Q\, C(Q) = \dfrac{Q}{C(Q)}C'(Q) = \dfrac{0.0008Q^2 + 8Q}{0.0004Q^2 + 8Q + 64\,000} \approx 0.12$ when $Q = 1000$. This means that if Q increases from 1000 by 1%, then costs will increase by about 0.12%.

5. The profit as a function of Q is $\pi(Q) = PQ - C = (a - bQ^2)Q - \alpha + \beta Q = -bQ^3 + (a+\beta)Q - \alpha$. Then $\pi'(Q) = -3bQ^2 + a + \beta$, which is 0 for $Q^2 = (a+\beta)/3b$, and so $Q = \sqrt{(a+\beta)/3b}$. This value of Q maximizes the profit because $\pi''(Q) = -6bQ \le 0$ for all $Q \ge 0$.

6. (a) g is defined for $x > -1$. (b) $g'(x) = 1 - 2/(x+1) = (x-1)/(x+1)$, $g''(x) = 2/(x+1)^2$. (c) Since $g'(x) < 0$ in $(-1, 1)$, $g'(1) = 0$ and $g'(x) > 0$ in $(1, \infty)$, $x = 1$ is a (global) minimum point. Since $g''(x) > 0$ for all $x > -1$, the function g is convex and there are no inflection points. When $x \to (-1)^-$, $g(x) \to \infty$ and when $x \to \infty$, $g(x) \to \infty$. See figure A8.R.6.

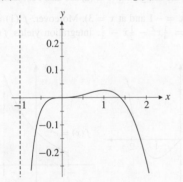

Figure A8.R.7

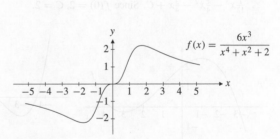

Figure A8.R.11

7. (a) $D_f = (-1, \infty)$. (b) A sign diagram shows that $f'(x) \ge 0$ in $(-1, 1]$ and $f'(x) \le 0$ in $[1, \infty)$. Hence $x = 1$ is a maximum point. f has no minimum. $f''(x) = \dfrac{-x(x^2 + x - 1)}{(x+1)^2} = 0$ for $x = 0$ and $x = \frac{1}{2}(\sqrt{5} - 1)$. ($x = \frac{1}{2}(-\sqrt{5} - 1)$ is outside the domain.) Since $f''(x)$ changes sign around these points, they are both inflection points. (c) $f(x) \to -\infty$ as $x \to (-1)^+$. See Figure A8.R.7.

8. (a) h is increasing in $(-\infty, \frac{1}{2}\ln 2\,]$ and decreasing in $[\,\frac{1}{2}\ln 2, \infty)$, so h has a maximum at $x = \frac{1}{2}\ln 2$. It has no minimum. (b) h is strictly increasing in $(-\infty, 0]$ (with range $(0, 1/3]$), and therefore has an inverse. The inverse is $h^{-1}(y) = \ln(1 - \sqrt{1 - 8y^2}) - \ln(2y)$. See Figure SM8.R.8 in SM.

9. (a) $f'(x) = 4e^{4x} + 8e^x - 32e^{-2x}$, $f''(x) = 16e^{4x} + 8e^x + 64e^{-2x}$ (b) $f'(x) = 4e^{-2x}(e^{3x} + 4)(e^{3x} - 2)$, so $f(x)$ is increasing in $[\frac{1}{3}\ln 2, \infty)$, decreasing in $(-\infty, \frac{1}{3}\ln 2]$. $f''(x) > 0$ for all x so f is strictly convex. (c) $\frac{1}{3}\ln 2$ is a (global) minimum. No maximum exists because $f(x) \to \infty$ as $x \to \infty$.

10. (a) D_f is the set of all $x \neq \pm\sqrt{a}$. $f(x)$ is positive in $(-\sqrt{a}, 0)$ and in $(\sqrt{a}, \infty)$. (b) $f(x)$ is increasing in $(-\infty, -\sqrt{3a})$ and in $(\sqrt{3a}, \infty)$, decreasing in $(-\sqrt{3a}, -\sqrt{a})$, in $(-\sqrt{a}, \sqrt{a})$, and in $(\sqrt{a}, \sqrt{3a})$. It follows that $x = -\sqrt{3a}$ is a local maximum point and $x = \sqrt{3a}$ is a local minimum point. (c) Inflection points at $-3\sqrt{a}, 0,$ and $3\sqrt{a}$.

11. $x = \sqrt{3}$ is a maximum point, $x = -\sqrt{3}$ is a minimum point, and $x = 0$ is an inflection point. See Fig. A8.R.11.

Chapter 9

9.1

1. (a) $\frac{1}{14}x^{14} + C$ (b) $\frac{2}{5}x^2\sqrt{x} + C$. $(x\sqrt{x} = x \cdot x^{1/2} = x^{3/2}.)$ (c) $2\sqrt{x} + C$. $(1/\sqrt{x} = x^{-1/2}.)$ (d) $\frac{8}{15}x^{\frac{15}{8}} + C$. $\left(\sqrt{x\sqrt{x\sqrt{x}}} = \sqrt{x\sqrt{x^{3/2}}} = \sqrt{x \cdot x^{3/4}} = \sqrt{x^{7/4}} = x^{7/8}.\right)$

2. (a) $-e^{-x} + C$ (b) $4e^{\frac{1}{4}x} + C$ (c) $-\frac{3}{2}e^{-2x} + C$ (d) $(1/\ln 2)2^x + C$

3. (a) $C(x) = \frac{3}{2}x^2 + 4x + 40$. $\left(C(x) = \int (3x + 4)\, dx = \frac{3}{2}x^2 + 4x + C. \ C(0) = 40 \text{ gives } C = 40.\right)$
   (b) $C(x) = \frac{1}{2}ax^2 + bx + C_0$

4. (a) $\frac{1}{4}t^4 + t^2 - 3t + C$ (b) $\frac{1}{3}(x-1)^3 + C$ (c) $\frac{1}{3}x^3 + \frac{1}{2}x^2 - 2x + C$ (d) $\frac{1}{4}(x+2)^4 + C$
   (e) $\frac{1}{3}e^{3x} - \frac{1}{2}e^{2x} + e^x + C$ (f) $\frac{1}{3}x^3 - 3x + 4\ln|x| + C$

5. (a) $\frac{2}{5}y^2\sqrt{y} - \frac{8}{3}y\sqrt{y} + 8\sqrt{y} + C$ (b) $\frac{1}{3}x^3 - \frac{1}{2}x^2 + x - \ln|x+1| + C$ (c) $\frac{1}{32}(1+x^2)^{16} + C$

6. (a) and (b): Differentiate the right-hand side and check that you get the integrand. (For (a) see also Problem 9.5.5.)

7. See Fig. A9.1.7. $f'(x) = A(x+1)(x-3)$ (because $f'(x)$ is 0 at $x = -1$ and at $x = 3$). Moreover, $f'(1) = -1$. This implies that $A = 1/4$, so that $f'(x) = \frac{1}{4}(x+1)(x-3) = \frac{1}{4}x^2 - \frac{1}{2}x - \frac{3}{4}$. Integration yields $f(x) = \frac{1}{12}x^3 - \frac{1}{4}x^2 - \frac{3}{4}x + C$. Since $f(0) = 2$, $C = 2$.

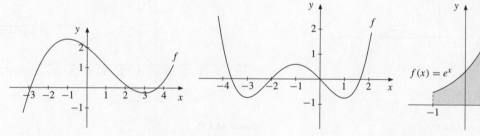

Figure A9.1.7   Figure A9.1.8   Figure A9.2.2

8. The graph of $f'(x)$ in Fig. 2 can be that of a cubic function, with roots at $-3, -1,$ and $1,$ and with $f'(0) = -1$. So $f'(x) = \frac{1}{3}(x+3)(x+1)(x-1) = \frac{1}{3}x^3 + x^2 - \frac{1}{3}x - 1$. If $f(0) = 0$, integrating gives $f(x) = \frac{1}{12}x^4 + \frac{1}{3}x^3 - \frac{1}{6}x^2 - x$. Fig. A9.1.8 is the graph of this f.

9. Differentiate the right-hand side and check that you get the integrand.

10. (a) Differentiate the right-hand side. (Once we have learned integration by substitution in Section 9.6, this will be an easy problem.) (b) (i) $\frac{1}{10}(2x+1)^5 + C$ (ii) $\frac{2}{3}(x+2)^{3/2} + C$ (iii) $-2\sqrt{4-x} + C$

11. (a) $F(x) = \int (\frac{1}{2}e^x - 2x)\, dx = \frac{1}{2}e^x - x^2 + C$. $F(0) = \frac{1}{2}$ implies $C = 0$.
    (b) $F(x) = \int (x - x^3)\, dx = \frac{1}{2}x^2 - \frac{1}{4}x^4 + C$. $F(1) = \frac{5}{12}$ implies $C = \frac{1}{6}$.

12. The general form for f' is $f'(x) = \frac{1}{3}x^3 + A$, so that for f is $f(x) = \frac{1}{12}x^4 + Ax + B$. If we require that $f(0) = 1$ and $f'(0) = -1$, then $B = 1$ and $A = -1$, so $f(x) = \frac{1}{12}x^4 - x + 1$.

13. $f(x) = -\ln x + \frac{1}{20}x^5 + x^2 - x - \frac{1}{20}$

9.2

1. (a) $A = \int_0^1 x^3\,dx = \Big|_0^1 \frac{1}{4}x^4 = \frac{1}{4}1^4 - \frac{1}{4}0^4 = \frac{1}{4}$.   (b) $A = \int_0^1 x^{10}\,dx = \Big|_0^1 \frac{1}{11}x^{11} = \frac{1}{11}$

2. (a) $\int_0^2 3x^2\,dx = \Big|_0^2 x^3 = 8$ (b) $1/7$ (c) $e - 1/e$. (See the shaded area in Fig. A9.2.2.)   (d) $9/10$

3. See Fig. A9.2.3. $A = -\int_{-2}^{-1} x^{-3}\,dx = -\Big|_{-2}^{-1}(-\frac{1}{2})x^{-2} = -[-\frac{1}{2} - (-\frac{1}{8})] = \frac{3}{8}$

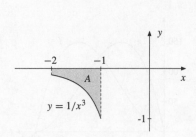

Figure A9.2.3

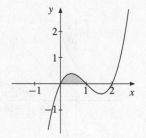

Figure A9.2.6

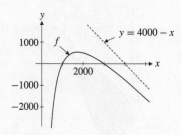

Figure A9.2.7

4. $A = \frac{1}{2}\int_{-1}^1 (e^x + e^{-x})\,dx = \frac{1}{2}\Big|_{-1}^1 (e^x - e^{-x}) = e - e^{-1}$

5. (a) $\int_0^1 x\,dx = \Big|_0^1 \frac{1}{2}x^2 = \frac{1}{2}$ (b) $16/3$ (c) $5/12$ (d) $-12/5$ (e) $41/2$ (f) $\ln 2 + 5/2$

6. (a) $f'(x) = 3x^2 - 6x + 2 = 0$ when $x_0 = 1 - \frac{1}{3}\sqrt{3}$ and $x_1 = 1 + \frac{1}{3}\sqrt{3}$. $f(x)$ increases in $(-\infty, x_0)$ and in (x_1, ∞).
(b) See Fig. A9.2.6. The shaded area is $\frac{1}{4}$.

7. (a) $f'(x) = -1 + 3000\,000/x^2 = 0$ for $x = \sqrt{3000\,000} = 1000\sqrt{3}$. (Recall $x > 0$.) $x = 1000\sqrt{3}$ maximizes profits. See Fig. A9.2.7.   (b) $I = \frac{1}{2000}\Big|_{1000}^{3000} (4000x - \frac{1}{2}x^2 - 3\,000\,000 \ln x) = 2000 - 1500 \ln 3 \approx 352$

8. (a) $6/5$ (b) $26/3$ (c) $\alpha(e^\beta - 1)/\beta$ (d) $-\ln 2$

9.3

1. (a) $\Big|_0^5 (\frac{1}{2}x^2 + \frac{1}{3}x^3) = 325/6$ (b) 0 (c) $\ln 9$ (d) $e - 1$ (e) -136 (f) $687/64$
(g) $\int_0^4 \frac{1}{2}x^{1/2}\,dx = \Big|_0^4 \frac{1}{2}\cdot\frac{2}{3}x^{3/2} = \frac{8}{3}$ (h) $\int_1^2 \frac{1+x^3}{x^2}\,dx = \int_1^2 \left(\frac{1}{x^2} + x\right) dx = \Big|_1^2 \left(-\frac{1}{x} + \frac{1}{2}x^2\right) = 2$

2. $\int_c^b f(x)\,dx = \int_a^b f(x)\,dx - \int_a^c f(x)\,dx = 8 - 4 = 4$

3. Let $A = \int_0^1 f(x)\,dx$ and $B = \int_0^1 g(x)\,dx$. Then from (i) and (ii), $A - 2B = 6$ and $2A + 2B = 9$, from which we find $A = 5$ and $B = -1/2$, and then $I = A - B = 11/2$.

4. (a) $1/(p + q + 1) + 1/(p + r + 1)$ (b) $f(x) = 4x^3 - 3x^2 + 5$

5. (a) $\Big|_0^3 [\frac{1}{9} e^{3t-2} + \ln(t + 2)] = \frac{1}{9}(e^7 - e^{-2}) + \ln(5/2)$ (b) $83/15$ (c) $2\sqrt{2} - 3/2$
   (d) $A[b - 1 + (b - c) \ln[(b + c)/(1 + c)]] + d \ln b$

6. (a) From formula (6), $F'(x) = x^2 + 2$. To find $G'(x)$ use formula (8). We get $G'(x) = [(x^2)^2 + 2]2x = 2x^5 + 4x$.
   (b) $H'(t) = 2t K (t^2) e^{-\rho t^2}$ (use formula (8)).

7. We use formulas (6), (7), and (8). (a) t^2 (b) $-e^{-t^2}$ (c) $2/\sqrt{t^4 + 1}$
   (d) $(f(2) - g(2)) \cdot 0 - (f(-\lambda) - g(-\lambda)) \cdot (-1) = f(-\lambda) - g(-\lambda)$

8. From $y^2 = 3x$ we get $x = \frac{1}{3} y^2$, which inserted into the other equation gives $y+1 = (\frac{1}{3} y^2 - 1)^2$, or $y(y^3 - 6y - 9) = 0$. Here $y^3 - 6y - 9 = (y - 3)(y^2 + 3y + 3)$, with $y^2 + 3y + 3$ never 0. So $(0, 0)$ and $(3, 3)$ are the only points of intersection. $A = \int_0^3 (\sqrt{3x} - x^2 + 2x) \, dx = 6$. See Fig. A9.3.8.

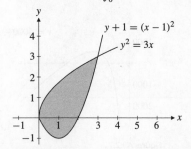

Figure A9.3.8

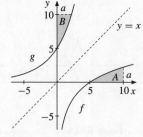

Figure A9.3.10

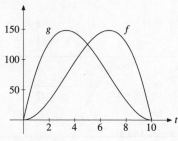

Figure A9.4.5

9. $W(T) = (K/T) \Big|_0^T (-1/\varrho) e^{-\varrho t} = K(1 - e^{-\varrho T})/\varrho T$

10. (a) $g(x) = e^{x/2} + 4e^{x/4}$ defined on $(-\infty, \infty)$.   (b) See Fig. A9.3.10.   (c) $A = 10a + 14 - 8\sqrt{14} \approx 6.26$.

9.4

1. $x(t) = K - \int_0^t \bar{u} e^{-as} \, ds = K - \bar{u}(1 - e^{-at})/a$. Note that $x(t) \to K - \bar{u}/a$ as $t \to \infty$. If $K \geq \bar{u}/a$, the well will never be exhausted.

2. (a) $m = 2b \ln 2$ (b) $x(p) = nABp^\gamma b^{\delta-1}(2^{\delta-1} - 1)/(\delta - 1)$

3. $T = \frac{1}{r} \ln(1 + rS)$. $(S = \Big|_0^T (1/r)e^{rt} = (e^{rT} - 1)/r$, so $e^{rT} - 1 = rS$, and solve for T.)

4. (a) $K(5) - K(0) = \int_0^5 (3t^2 + 2t + 5) \, dt = 175$ (b) $K(T) - K_0 = (T^3 - t_0^3) + (T^2 - t_0^2) + 5(T - t_0)$

5. (a) See Fig. A9.4.5.   (b) $\int_0^t \big(g(\tau) - f(\tau)\big) \, d\tau = \int_0^t \big(2\tau^3 - 30\tau^2 + 100\tau\big) \, d\tau = \frac{1}{2} t^2 (t - 10)^2 \geq 0$ for all t.

   (c) $\int_0^{10} p(t)f(t) \, dt = \int_0^{10} \big(-t^3 + 9t^2 + 11t - 11 + 11/(t + 1)\big) \, dt = 940 + 11 \ln 11 \approx 966.38,$

   $\int_0^{10} p(t)g(t) \, dt = \int_0^{10} \big(t^3 - 19t^2 + 79t + 121 - 121/(t + 1)\big) \, dt = 3980/3 - 121 \ln 11 \approx 1036.52.$
   Profile g should be chosen.

6. The equilibrium quantity is $Q^* = 600$, where $P^* = 80$. Then, $\text{CS} = \displaystyle\int_0^{600} (120 - 0.2Q)\,dQ = 36\,000$, and

$\text{PS} = \displaystyle\int_0^{600} (60 - 0.1Q)\,dQ = 18\,000$.

7. Equilibrium when $6000/(Q^* + 50) = Q^* + 10$. The only positive solution is $Q^* = 50$, and then $P^* = 60$.

$\text{CS} = \displaystyle\int_0^{50} \left[\frac{6000}{Q + 50} - 60 \right] dQ = \Big|_0^{50} [6000 \ln(Q+50) - 60Q] = 6000 \ln 2 - 3000$, $\text{PS} = \displaystyle\int_0^{50} (50 - Q)\,dQ = 1250$

9.5

1. (a) Use (1) with $f(x) = x$ and $g'(x) = e^{-x}$: $\displaystyle\int xe^{-x}\,dx = x(-e^{-x}) - \int 1 \cdot (-e^{-x})\,dx = -xe^{-x} - e^{-x} + C$.

(b) $\frac{3}{4}xe^{4x} - \frac{3}{16}e^{4x} + C$ (c) $-x^2 e^{-x} - 2xe^{-x} - 3e^{-x} + C$ (d) $\frac{1}{2}x^2 \ln x - \frac{1}{4}x^2 + C$

2. (a) $\displaystyle\int_{-1}^{1} x\ln(x+2)\,dx = \Big|_{-1}^{1} \frac{1}{2}x^2 \ln(x+2) - \int_{-1}^{1} \frac{1}{2}x^2 \frac{1}{x+2}\,dx = \frac{1}{2}\ln 3 - \frac{1}{2}\int_{-1}^{1}\left(x - 2 + \frac{4}{x+2}\right) dx = 2 - \frac{3}{2}\ln 3$

(b) $8/(\ln 2) - 3/(\ln 2)^2$ (c) $e - 2$ (d) $7\frac{11}{15}$

3. (a) $\displaystyle\int_1^4 \sqrt{t}\,\ln t\,dt = \int_1^4 t^{1/2} \ln t\,dt = \Big|_1^4 \frac{2}{3}t^{3/2} \ln t - \frac{2}{3}\int_1^4 t^{3/2}(1/t)\,dt = \frac{16}{3}\ln 4 - \frac{2}{3}\Big|_1^4 \frac{2}{3}t^{3/2} = \frac{16}{3}\ln 4 - \frac{28}{9}$

(b) $\displaystyle\int_0^2 (x - 2)e^{-x/2}\,dx = \Big|_0^2 (x - 2)(-2)e^{-x/2} - \int_0^2 (-2)e^{-x/2}\,dt = -4 - 4\Big|_0^2 e^{-x/2} = -4 - 4(e^{-1} - 1) = -4e^{-1}$

(c) $\displaystyle\int_0^3 (3 - x)3^x\,dx = \Big|_0^3 (3 - x)(3^x/\ln 3) - \int_0^3 (-1)(3^x/\ln 3)\,dx = 26/(\ln 3)^2 - 3/\ln 3$

4. The general formula follows from (1), and yields $\displaystyle\int \ln x\,dx = x\ln x - x + C$.

5. Use (1) with $f(x) = \ln x$ and $g'(x) = x^\rho$. (Alternatively, simply differentiate the right-hand side.)

6. (a) $br^{-2}[1 - (1 + rT)e^{-rT}]$ (b) $ar^{-1}(1 - e^{-rT}) + br^{-2}[1 - (1 + rT)e^{-rT}]$

(c) $ar^{-1}(1 - e^{-rT}) - br^{-2}[1 - (1 + rT)e^{-rT}] + cr^{-3}[2(1 - e^{-rT}) - 2rTe^{-rT} - r^2T^2e^{-rT}]$

9.6

1. (a) $\frac{1}{9}(x^2 + 1)^9 + C$. (Substitute $u = x^2 + 1$, $du = 2x\,dx$.)   (b) $\frac{1}{11}(x + 2)^{11} + C$. (Substitute $u = x + 2$.)

(c) $\ln |x^2 - x + 8| + C$. (Substitute $u = x^2 - x + 8$.)

2. (a) $\frac{1}{24}(2x^2 + 3)^6 + C$. (Substitute $u = 2x^2 + 3$, so $du = 4x\,dx$.)   (b) $\frac{1}{3}e^{x^3+2} + C$. (Substitute $u = e^{x^3+2}$.)

(c) $\frac{1}{4}\big(\ln(x + 2)\big)^2 + C$. (Substitute $u = \ln(x + 2)$.)   (d) $\frac{2}{5}(1 + x)^{5/2} - \frac{2}{3}(1 + x)^{3/2} + C$. (Substitute $u = \sqrt{1 + x}$.)

(e) $\dfrac{-1}{2(1 + x^2)} + \dfrac{1}{4(1 + x^2)^2} + C$ (f) $\frac{2}{15}(4 - x^3)^{5/2} - \frac{8}{9}(4 - x^3)^{3/2} + C$

3. (a) With $u = \sqrt{1 + x^2}$, $u^2 = 1 + x^2$, so $u\,du = x\,dx$. If $x = 0$, then $u = 1$; if $x = 1$, then $u = \sqrt{2}$.

Hence, $\displaystyle\int_0^1 x\sqrt{1 + x^2}\,dx = \int_1^{\sqrt{2}} u^2\,du = \Big|_1^{\sqrt{2}} \frac{1}{3}u^3 = \frac{1}{3}(2\sqrt{2} - 1)$.   (b) $1/2$. (Let $u = \ln y$.)

(c) $\frac{1}{2}(e^2 - e^{2/3})$. (Let $u = 2/x$.)

(d) Method 1: $\displaystyle\int_5^8 \frac{x}{x - 4}\,dx = \int_5^8 \frac{x - 4 + 4}{x - 4}\,dx = \int_5^8 \left(1 + \frac{4}{x - 4}\right) dx = \Big|_5^8 [(x + 4\ln(x - 4)] = 3 + 4\ln 4$

Method 2: Performing the division $x \div (x - 4)$ leads to the same result as in Method 1.

Method 3: Introduce the new variable $u = x - 4$, Then $du = dx$ and $x = u + 4$. When $x = 5$, $u = 1$, and when

$x = 8$, $u = 4$, so $L = \displaystyle\int_1^4 \frac{u + 4}{u}\,du = \int_1^4 \left(1 + \frac{4}{u}\right) du = \Big|_1^4 (u + 4\ln u) = 3 + 4\ln 4$.

4. $\int_3^x \frac{2t-2}{t^2-2t}\,dt = \left|_3^x \ln(t^2-2t) = \ln(x^2-2x) - \ln 3 = \ln\frac{1}{3}(x^2-2x) = \frac{2}{3}x - 1$. Hence, $x^2 - 4x + 3 = 0$, with solutions $x = 1$ and $x = 3$. But only $x = 3$ is in the specified domain. So the solution is $x = 3$.

5. Substitute $z = x(t)$. Then $dz = \dot{x}(t)dt$, and the result follows using (2).

6. (a) $1/70$. $((x^4 - x^9)(x^5 - 1)^{12} = -x^4(x^5 - 1)^{13}$.) (b) $2\sqrt{x}\ln x - 4\sqrt{x} + C$. (Let $u = \sqrt{x}$.) (c) $8/3$

7. (a) $2\ln(1 + e^2) - 2\ln(1 + e)$ (b) $\ln 2 - \ln(e^{-1/3} + 1)$ (c) $7 + 2\ln 2$

8. Substitute $u = x^{1/6}$. Then $I = 6\int \frac{u^8}{1 - u^2}\,du$. Here $u^8 \div (-u^2 + 1) = -u^6 - u^4 - u^2 - 1 + 1/(-u^2 + 1)$. It follows that $I = -\frac{6}{7}x^{7/6} - \frac{6}{5}x^{5/6} - 2x^{1/2} - 6x^{1/6} - 3\ln|1 - x^{1/6}| + 3\ln|1 + x^{1/6}| + C$.

9. We find $f(x) = \frac{1}{a-b}\left[\frac{ac+d}{x-a} - \frac{bc+d}{x-b}\right]$.

(a) $\int \frac{x\,dx}{(x+1)(x+2)} = \int \frac{-1\,dx}{x+1} + \int \frac{2\,dx}{x+2} = -\ln|x+1| + 2\ln|x+2| + C$

(b) $\int \frac{(1-2x)\,dx}{(x+3)(x-5)} = \int \left[-\frac{7}{8}\frac{1}{x+3} - \frac{9}{8}\frac{1}{x-5}\right]dx = -\frac{7}{8}\ln|x+3| - \frac{9}{8}\ln|x-5| + C$

9.7

1. (a) $\int_1^b x^{-3}\,dx = \left|_1^b (-\frac{1}{2}x^{-2}) = \frac{1}{2} - \frac{1}{2}b^{-2} \to \frac{1}{2}$ as $b \to \infty$. So $\int_1^\infty \frac{1}{x^3}\,dx = \frac{1}{2}$.

(b) $\int_1^b x^{-1/2}\,dx = \left|_1^b 2x^{1/2} = 2b^{1/2} - 2 \to \infty$ as $b \to \infty$, so the integral diverges.

(c) 1 (d) $\int_0^a (x/\sqrt{a^2 - x^2})\,dx = -\left|_0^a \sqrt{a^2 - x^2} = a$

2. (a) $\int_{-\infty}^{+\infty} f(x)\,dx = \int_a^b \frac{1}{b-a}\,dx = \frac{1}{b-a}\left|_a^b x = \frac{1}{b-a}(b-a) = 1$

(b) $\int_{-\infty}^{+\infty} xf(x)\,dx = \frac{1}{b-a}\int_a^b x\,dx = \frac{1}{2(b-a)}\left|_a^b x^2 = \frac{1}{2(b-a)}(b^2 - a^2) = \frac{1}{2}(a+b)$

(c) $\frac{1}{3(b-a)}\left|_a^b x^3 = \frac{1}{3}\frac{b^3 - a^3}{b-a} = \frac{1}{3}(a^2 + ab + b^2)$

3. Using a simplified notation and the result in Example 1, we have:

(a) $\int_0^\infty x\lambda e^{-\lambda x}\,dx = -\left|_0^\infty xe^{-\lambda x} + \int_0^\infty e^{-\lambda x}\,dx = 1/\lambda$ (b) $1/\lambda^2$ (c) $2/\lambda^3$

4. The first integral diverges because $\int_0^b [x/(1+x^2)]\,dx = \left|_0^b \frac{1}{2}\ln(1+x^2) = \frac{1}{2}\ln(1+b^2) \to \infty$ as $b \to \infty$. On the other hand, $\int_{-b}^b [x/(1+x^2)]\,dx = \left|_{-b}^b \frac{1}{2}\ln(1+x^2) = 0$ for all b, so the limit as $b \to \infty$ is 0.

5. (a) f has a maximum at $(e^{1/3}, 1/3e)$, but no minimum. (b) $\int_0^1 x^{-3}\ln x\,dx$ diverges. $\int_1^\infty x^{-3}\ln x\,dx = 1/4$.

6. $\frac{1}{1+x^2} \leq \frac{1}{x^2}$ for $x \geq 1$, and $\int_1^b \frac{dx}{x^2} = \left|_1^b -\frac{1}{x} = 1 - \frac{1}{b} \xrightarrow[b\to\infty]{} 1$, so by Theorem 9.7.1 the integral converges.

7. See SM.

8. (a) $z = \int_0^\tau (1/\tau)e^{-rs}\,ds = (1 - e^{-r\tau})/r\tau$ (b) $z = \int_0^\tau 2(\tau - s)\tau^{-2}e^{-rs}\,ds = (2/r\tau)\left[1 - (1/r\tau)(1 - e^{-r\tau})\right]$.

9. $\int x^{-2}dx = -x^{-1} + C$. So evaluating $\int_{-1}^{1} x^{-2}dx$ as $\Big|_{-1}^{1} -x^{-1}$ gives the nonsensical answer -2. The error arises because x^{-2} diverges to $+\infty$ as $x \to 0$. (In fact, $\int_{-1}^{1} x^{-2}dx$ diverges to $+\infty$.)

10. Using the answer to Problem 9.6.6(b), $\int_{h}^{1} (\ln x/\sqrt{x})\,dx = \Big|_{h}^{1} (2\sqrt{x}\ln x - 4\sqrt{x}) = -4 - (2\sqrt{h}\ln h - 4\sqrt{h}) \to -4$ as $h \to 0^{+}$, so the given integral converges to -4. ($\sqrt{h}\ln h = \ln h/h^{-1/2} \to 0$, by l'Hôpital's rule.)

11. $\int_{1}^{A} [k/x - k^{2}/(1 + kx)]\,dx = k\ln[1/(1/A + k)] - k\ln[1/(1 + k)] \to k\ln(1/k) - k\ln[1/(1 + k)] = \ln(1 + 1/k)^{k}$ as $A \to \infty$. So $I_{k} = \ln(1 + 1/k)^{k}$, which tends to $\ln e = 1$ as $k \to \infty$.

12. See SM.

9.8

1. The functions in (c) and (d) are the only ones that have a constant relative rate of increase. This accords with (3). (Note that $2^{t} = e^{(\ln 2)t}$.)

2. (a) $K(t) = (K_{0} - I/\delta)e^{-\delta t} + I/\delta$ (b) (i) $K(t) = 200 - 50e^{-0.05t}$ and $K(t)$ tends to 200 from below as $t \to \infty$. (ii) $K(t) = 200 + 50e^{-0.05t}$, and $K(t)$ tends to 200 from above as $t \to \infty$.

3. $N(t) = P(1 - e^{-kt})$. Then $N(t) \to P$ as $t \to \infty$.

4. $\dot{N}(t) = 0.02N(t) + 4 \cdot 10^{4}$. The solution with $N(0) = 2 \cdot 10^{6}$ is $N(t) = 2 \cdot 10^{6}(2e^{0.02t} - 1)$.

5. $P(10) = 705$ gives $641e^{10k} = 705$, or $e^{10k} = 705/641$. Taking the natural logarithm of both sides yields $10k = \ln(705/641)$, so $k = 0.1\ln(705/641) \approx 0.0095$. $P(15) \approx 739$ and $P(40) \approx 938$.

6. The percentage surviving after t seconds satisfies $p(t) = 100e^{-\delta t}$, where $p(7) = 70.5$ and so $\delta = -\ln 0.705/7 \approx 0.05$. Thus $p(30) = 100e^{-30\delta} \approx 22.3\%$ are still alive after 30 seconds. Because $100e^{-\delta t} = 5$ when $t \approx \ln 20/0.05 \approx 60$, it takes about 60 seconds to kill 95%.

7. (a) $x = Ae^{-0.5t}$ (b) $K = Ae^{0.02t}$ (c) $x = Ae^{-0.5t} + 10$ (d) $K = Ae^{0.2t} - 500$ (e) $x = 0.1/(3 - Ae^{0.1t})$ and $x \equiv 0$.   (f) $K = 1/(2 - Ae^{t})$ and $K \equiv 0$.

8. (a) $y(t) = 250 + \dfrac{230}{1 + 8.2e^{-0.34t}}$.   (b) $y(t) \to 480$ as $t \to \infty$. See Fig. A9.8.8.

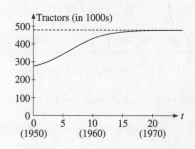

Figure A9.8.8

9. (a) Using (7) we find $N(t) = 1000/(1 + 999e^{-0.39t})$. After 20 days, $N(20) \approx 710$ have developed influenza. (b) $800 = \dfrac{1000}{1 + 999e^{-0.39t^{*}}} \iff 999e^{-0.39t^{*}} = \dfrac{1}{4}$, so $e^{-0.39t^{*}} = 1/3996$, and so $0.39t^{*} = \ln 3996$. $t^{*} \approx 21$ days. (c) After about 35 days, 999 will have or have had influenza. $N(t) \to 1000$ as $t \to \infty$.

10. See SM.

11. At about 11.26. (Measuring time in hours, with $t = 0$ being 12 noon, one has $\dot{T} = k(20 - T)$ with $T(0) = 35$ and $T(1) = 32$. So the body temperature at time t is $T(t) = 20 + 15e^{-kt}$ with $k = \ln(5/4)$. Assuming that the temperature was the normal 37 degrees at the time of death t^*, then $t^* = -\ln(17/15)/\ln(5/4) \approx -0.56$ hours, or about 34 minutes before 12.00.)

9.9

1. The equation is separable: $\int x^4\, dx = \int (1 - t)\, dt$, $\frac{1}{5}x^5 = t - \frac{1}{2}t^2 + C_1$, $x^5 = 5t - \frac{5}{2}t^2 + 5C_1$, $x = \sqrt[5]{5t - \frac{5}{2}t^2 + 5C_1} = \sqrt[5]{5t - \frac{5}{2}t^2 + C}$, with $C = 5C_1$. $x(1) = 1$ yields $C = -3/2$.

2. (a) $x = \sqrt[3]{\frac{3}{2}e^{2t} + C}$ (b) $x = -\ln(e^{-t} + C)$ (c) $x = Ce^{3t} - 6$ (d) $x = \sqrt[7]{(1 + t)^7 + C}$ (e) $x = Ce^{2t} + \frac{1}{2}t + \frac{1}{4}$
(f) $x = Ce^{-3t} + \frac{1}{2}e^{t^2 - 3t}$

3. The equation is separable: $dk/k = s\alpha e^{\beta t}\, dt$, so $\ln k = \frac{s\alpha}{\beta}e^{\beta t} + C_1$, or $k = e^{\frac{s\alpha}{\beta}e^{\beta t}}e^{C_1} = Ce^{\frac{s\alpha}{\beta}e^{\beta t}}$. With $k(0) = k_0$, we have $k_0 = Ce^{\frac{s\alpha}{\beta}}$, and thus $k = k_0 e^{\frac{s\alpha}{\beta}(e^{\beta t} - 1)}$.

4. (a) $\dot{Y} = \alpha(a - 1)Y + \alpha(b + \bar{I})$ (b) $Y = \left(Y_0 - \dfrac{b + \bar{I}}{1 - a}\right)e^{-\alpha(1 - a)t} + \dfrac{b + \bar{I}}{1 - a} \to \dfrac{b + \bar{I}}{1 - a}$ as $t \to \infty$.

5. (a) From (iii), $L = L_0 e^{\beta t}$, so $\dot{K} = \gamma K^\alpha L_0 e^{\beta t}$, a separable equation. (b) $K = \left[\dfrac{(1 - \alpha)\gamma}{\beta}L_0(e^{\beta t} - 1) + K_0^{1 - \alpha}\right]^{1/(1 - \alpha)}$

6. $\dfrac{t}{x}\dfrac{dx}{dt} = a$ is separable: $\dfrac{dx}{x} = a\dfrac{dt}{t}$, so $\int \dfrac{dx}{x} = a\int \dfrac{dt}{t}$. Integrating yields $\ln x = a \ln t + C_1$, so $x = e^{a \ln t + C_1} = (e^{\ln t})^a e^{C_1} = Ct^a$, with $C = e^{C_1}$. This shows that the only type of function which has constant elasticity is $x = Ct^a$.

Review Problems for Chapter 9

1. (a) $-16x + C$ (b) $5^5 x + C$ (c) $3y - \frac{1}{2}y^2 + C$ (d) $\frac{1}{2}r^2 - \frac{16}{5}r^{5/4} + C$ (e) $\frac{1}{9}x^9 + C$
(f) $\frac{2}{7}x^{7/2} + C$. ($x^2\sqrt{x} = x^2 \cdot x^{1/2} = x^{5/2}$.) (g) $-\frac{1}{4}p^{-4} + C$ (h) $\frac{1}{4}x^4 + \frac{1}{2}x^2 + C$

2. (a) $e^{2x} + C$ (b) $\frac{1}{2}x^2 - \frac{25}{2}e^{2x/5} + C$ (c) $-\frac{1}{3}e^{-3x} + \frac{1}{3}e^{3x} + C$ (d) $2\ln|x + 5| + C$

3. (a) $\displaystyle\int_0^{12} 50\, dx = \Big|_0^{12} 50x = 600$ (b) $\displaystyle\int_0^2 (x - \frac{1}{2}x^2)\, dx = \Big|_0^2 (\frac{1}{2}x^2 - \frac{1}{6}x^3) = \frac{2}{3}$
(c) $\displaystyle\int_{-3}^3 (u + 1)^2\, du = \Big|_{-3}^3 \frac{1}{3}(u + 1)^3\, du = 24$ (d) $\displaystyle\int_1^5 \frac{2}{z}\, dz = \Big|_1^5 2\ln z = 2\ln 5$ (e) $3\ln(8/3)$
(f) $I = \displaystyle\int_0^4 v\sqrt{v^2 + 9}\, dv = \Big|_0^4 \frac{1}{3}(v^2 + 9)^{3/2} = 98/3$. (Or introduce $z = \sqrt{v^2 + 9}$. Then $z^2 = v^2 + 9$ and $2z\, dz = 2v\, dv$, or $v\, dv = z\, dz$. When $v = 0$, $z = 3$, when $v = 4$, $z = 5$, so $I = \displaystyle\int_3^5 z^2\, dz = \Big|_3^5 \frac{1}{3}z^3 = 98/3$.)

4. (a) $5/4$ (b) $31/20$ (c) -5 (d) $e - 2$ (e) $52/9$ (f) $\frac{1}{3}\ln(6/5)$ (g) $(1/256)(3e^4 + 1)$ (h) $2e^{-1}$.

5. (a) $10 - 18\ln(14/9)$. (Substitute $z = 9 + \sqrt{x}$.) (b) $886/15$. (Substitute $z = \sqrt{t + 2}$.)
(c) $195/4$. (Substitute $z = \sqrt[3]{19x^3 + 8}$.)

6. (a) $F'(x) = 4(\sqrt{x} - 1)$. ($\displaystyle\int_4^x (u^{1/2} + xu^{-1/2})\, du = \Big|_4^x \frac{2}{3}u^{3/2} + 2xu^{1/2} = \frac{8}{3}x^{3/2} - \frac{16}{3} - 4x$.)
(b) We use (9.3.8). $F'(x) = \ln x - (\ln\sqrt{x})(1/2\sqrt{x}) = \ln x - \ln x/4\sqrt{x}$.

7. $C(Y) = 0.69Y + 1000$ **8.** $C(x) = \frac{\alpha}{\beta}(e^{\beta x} - 1) + \gamma x + C_0$

9. Let $\int_{-1}^{3} (f(x)\,dx = A$ and $\int_{-1}^{3} g(x))\,dx = B$. Then $A + B = 6$ and $3A + 4B = 9$, from which we find $A = 15$ and $B = -9$. Then $I = A + B = 6$.

10. (a) $P^* = 70$, $Q^* = 600$. CS 9000, PS = 18000. See Fig. A9.R.10(a).
(b) $P^* = Q^* = 5$, CS $= 50\ln 2 - 25$, PS $= 1.25$. See Fig. A9.R.10(b).

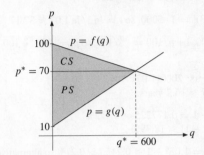

Figure A9.R.10(a)

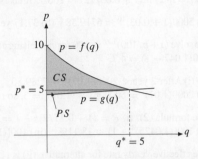

Figure A9.R.10(b)

11. (a) $f'(t) = 4\ln t(2 - \ln t)/t^2$, $f''(t) = 8[(\ln t)^2 - 3\ln t + 1]/t^3$. (b) $(e^2, 16/e^2)$ is a local maximum point, $(1, 0)$ is a local (and global) minimum point. See Fig. A9.R.11. (c) Area $= 32/3$. (*Hint:* $\int f(t)\,dt = \dfrac{4}{3}(\ln t)^3 + C$.)

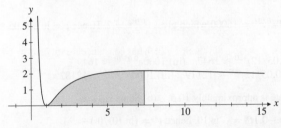

Figure A9.R.11

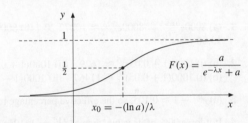

Figure A9.R.16

12. (a) $x = Ae^{-3t}$ (b) $x = Ae^{-4t} + 3$ (c) $x = 1/(Ae^{-3t} - 4)$ and $x \equiv 0$. (d) $x = Ae^{-\frac{1}{3}t}$ (e) $x = Ae^{-2t} + 5/3$
(f) $x = 1/(Ae^{-\frac{1}{2}t} - 2)$ and $x \equiv 0$.

13. (a) $x = 1/(C - \frac{1}{2}t^2)$ and $x(t) \equiv 0$. (b) $x = Ce^{-3t/2} - 5$ (c) $x = Ce^{3t} - 10$ (d) $x = Ce^{-5t} + 2t - \frac{2}{5}$
(e) $x = Ce^{-t/2} + \frac{2}{3}e^t$ (f) $x = Ce^{-3t} + \frac{1}{3}t^2 - \frac{2}{9}t + \frac{2}{27}$

14. (a) $V(x) = (V_0 + b/a)e^{-ax} - b/a$ (b) $V(x^*) = 0$ yields $x^* = (1/a)\ln(1 + aV_0/b)$.
(c) $0 = V(\hat{x}) = (V_m + b/a)e^{-a\hat{x}} - b/a$ yields $V_m = (b/a)(e^{a\hat{x}} - 1)$.
(d) $x^* = (1/0.001)\ln(1 + 0.001 \cdot 12\,000/8) \approx 916$, and $V_m = (8/0.001)(e^{0.001 \cdot 1200} - 1) = 8000(e^{1.2} - 1) \approx 18561$.

15. (a) $\int_0^{\infty} f(r)\,dr = \int_0^{\infty} (1/m)e^{-r/m}\,dr = 1$ (as in Example 9.7.1) and $\int_0^{\infty} rf(r)\,dr = \int_0^{\infty} r(1/m)e^{-r/m}\,dr = m$
(as in Problem 9.7.3(a)), so the mean income is m.
(b) $x(p) = n\int_0^{\infty} (ar - bp)f(r)\,dr = n\left(a\int_0^{\infty} rf(r)\,dr - bp\int_0^{\infty} f(r)\,dr\right) = n(am - bp)$

16. (a) Verify that $F'(x) = f(x)$. $\lim_{x\to\infty} F(x) = 1$ and $\lim_{x\to-\infty} F(x) = 0$.
(b) $\int_{-\infty}^{x} f(t)\,dt = \lim_{a\to-\infty} \int_a^{x} f(t)\,dt = \lim_{a\to-\infty} [F(x) - F(a)] = F(x)$, by (a). Since $F'(x) = f(x) > 0$ for all x,
$F(x)$ is strictly increasing. For (c) and (d) see Fig. A9.R.16 and SM.

Chapter 10

10.1

1. (a) (i) $8000(1 + 0.05/12)^{5 \cdot 12} \approx 10266.87$ (ii) $8000(1 + 0.05/365)^{5 \cdot 365} \approx 10272.03$
   (b) $t = \ln 2/\ln(1 + 0.05/12) \approx 166.7$. It takes approximately $166.7/12 \approx 13.9$ years.

2. (a) $5000(1 + 0.03)^{10} \approx 6719.58$ (b) 37.17 years. ($5000(1.03)^t = 3 \cdot 5000$, so $t = \ln 3/\ln 1.03 \approx 37.17$.)

3. We solve $(1 + p/100)^{100} = 100$ for p. Raising each side to $1/100$, $1 + p/100 = \sqrt[100]{100}$, so $p = 100(\sqrt[100]{100} - 1) \approx 100(1.047 - 1) = 4.7$.

4. (a) (i) After 2 years: $2000(1.07)^2 = 2289.80$ (ii) After 10 years: $2000(1.07)^{10} \approx 3934.30$
   (b) $2000(1.07)^t = 6000$ gives $(1.07)^t = 3$, so $t = \ln 3/\ln 1.07 \approx 16.2$ years.

5. Use formula (2). (i) $R = (1 + 0.17/2)^2 - 1 = (1 + 0.085)^2 - 1 = 0.177225$ or 17.72%
   (ii) $100[(1.0425)^4 - 1] \approx 18.11\%$ (iii) $100[(1 + 0.17/12)^{12} - 1] \approx 18.39\%$

6. The effective yearly rate for alternative (ii) is $(1 + 0.2/4)^4 - 1 = 1.05^4 - 1 \approx 0.2155 > 0.215$, so alternative (i) is (slightly) cheaper.

7. (a) $12\,000 \cdot (1.04)^{15} \approx 21\,611.32$ (b) $50\,000 \cdot (1.05)^{-5} \approx 39\,176.31$ (c) $100[(1.02)^{12} - 1] \approx 26.82\%$

8. Let the nominal yearly rate be r. By (2), $0.28 = (1 + r/4)^4 - 1$, so $r = 4(\sqrt[4]{1.28} - 1) \approx 0.25$, or 25%.

10.2

1. (a) $8000e^{0.05 \cdot 5} = 8000e^{0.25} \approx 10272.20$ (b) $8000e^{0.05t} = 16000$ which gives $e^{0.05t} = 2$. Hence $t = \ln 2/0.05 \approx 13.86$ years.

2. (a) (i) $1000(1 + 0.05)^{10} \approx 1629$ (ii) $1000(1 + 0.05/12)^{120} \approx 1647$ (iii) $1000e^{0.05 \cdot 10} \approx 1649$
   (b) (i) $1000(1 + 0.05)^{50} \approx 11467$ (ii) $1000(1 + 0.05/12)^{600} \approx 12119$ (iii) $1000e^{0.05 \cdot 50} \approx 12182$

3. (a) $e^{0.1} - 1 \approx 0.105$, so the effective percentage rate is approximately 10.5.   (b) Same answer.

4. If it loses 90% of its value, then $e^{-0.1t^*} = 1/10$, so $-0.1t^* = -\ln 10$, hence $t^* = (\ln 10)/0.1 \approx 23$.

5. $e^{-0.06t^*} = 1/2$, so $t^* = \ln 2/0.06 \approx 11.55$ years.   **6.** See SM.

10.3

1. (i) The present value is $350\,000 \cdot 1.08^{-10} \approx 162\,117.72$.   (ii) $350\,000 \cdot e^{-0.08 \cdot 10} \approx 157\,265.14$

2. (i) The present value is $50\,000 \cdot 1.0575^{-5} \approx 37\,806.64$.   (ii) $50\,000 \cdot e^{-0.0575 \cdot 5} \approx 37\,506.83$

3. (a) We find $f'(t) = 0.05(t + 5)(35 - t)e^{-t}$. Obviously, $f'(t) > 0$ for $t < 35$ and $f'(t) < 0$ for $t > 35$, so $t = 35$ maximizes f (with $f(35) \approx 278$). (b) $f(t) \to 0$ as $t \to \infty$. See the graph in Fig. A10.3.3.

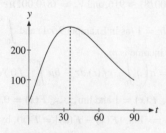

Figure A10.3.3

10.4

1. $s_n = \frac{3}{2}\left(1 - \left(\frac{1}{3}\right)^n\right) \to \frac{3}{2}$ as $n \to \infty$, so $\displaystyle\sum_{n=1}^{\infty} \frac{1}{3^{n-1}} = \frac{3}{2}$.

2. We use formula (5): (a) $\dfrac{1/5}{1 - 1/5} = 1/4$ (b) $\dfrac{0.1}{1 - 0.1} = \dfrac{0.1}{0.9} = \dfrac{1}{9}$ (c) $\dfrac{517}{1 - 1/1.1} = 5687$

(d) $\dfrac{a}{1 - 1/(1+a)} = 1 + a$ (e) $\dfrac{5}{1 - 3/7} = \dfrac{35}{4}$

3. (a) Geometric series with quotient $1/8$. Its sum is $8/(1 - 1/8) = 64/7$.   (b) Geometric with quotient -3. It diverges.   (c) Geometric, with sum $2^{1/3}/(1 - 2^{-1/3})$.   (d) Not geometric. (In fact, one can show that the series converges with sum $\ln 2$.)

4. (a) Quotient $k = 1/p$. Converges to $1/(p - 1)$ for $|p| > 1$.
(b) Quotient $k = 1/\sqrt{x}$. Converges to $x\sqrt{x}/(\sqrt{x} - 1)$ for $\sqrt{x} > 1$, that is, for $x > 1$.
(c) Quotient $k = x^2$. Converges to $x^2/(1 - x^2)$ for $|x| < 1$.

5. Geometric series with quotient $(1 + p/100)^{-1}$. Its sum is $b/[1 - (1 + p/100)^{-1}] = b(1 + 100/p)$.

6. The resources will be exhausted partway through the year 2028.

7. $1824 \cdot 1.02 + 1824 \cdot 1.02^2 + \cdots + 1824 \cdot 1.02^n = (1824/0.02)(1.02^{n+1} - 1.02)$ must equal $128\,300$. So $n \approx 43.77$. The resources will last until year 2037.

8. (a) $f(t) = \dfrac{P(t)}{e^{rt} - 1}$ (b) Use $f'(t^*) = 0$.   (c) $P'(t^*)/P(t^*) \to 1/t^*$ as $r \to 0$.

9. The general term does not approach 0 as $n \to \infty$ in any of these three cases, so each of the series is divergent.

10. (a) A geometric series with quotient $100/101$ that converges to 100.   (b) Diverges according to (11).
(c) Converges according to (11).   (d) Diverges because the nth term $s_n = (1 + n)/(4n - 3) \to 1/4$ as $n \to \infty$.
(e) Geometric series with quotient $-1/2$ that converges to $-1/3$.
(f) Geometric series with quotient $1/\sqrt{3}$ converging to $\sqrt{3}/(\sqrt{3} - 1)$.

11. See SM.

10.5

1. Use (2) with $n = 15$, $r = 0.12$, and $a = 3500$. This gives $P_{15} = \dfrac{3500}{0.12}\left(1 - \dfrac{1}{(1.12)^{15}}\right) \approx 23\,838$.

2. (a) 10 years ago the amount was: $100\,000(1.04)^{-10} \approx 67556.42$
(b) $10\,000(1.06^3 + 1.06^2 + 1.06 + 1) = 10\,000(1.06^4 - 1)/(1.06 - 1)) \approx 43\,746.16$

3. The future value after 10 years of (i) is obviously \$13\,000, whereas according to (3), the corresponding value of (ii) is $F_{10} = (1000/0.06)(1.06^{10} - 1) \approx 13\,180.80$. So (ii) is worth more.

4. Offer (a) is better, because the present value of (b) is $4600\dfrac{1 - (1.06)^{-5}}{1 - (1.06)^{-1}} \approx 20\,539$.

5. $\dfrac{1500}{0.08} = 18\,750$ (using (4)).

6. If the largest amount is a, then according to formula (4), $a/r = K$, so that $a = rK$.

7. This is a geometric series with first term $a = D/(1 + r)$ and quotient $k = (1 + g)/(1 + r)$. It converges if and only if $k < 1$, i.e. if and only if $g < r$. The sum is $\dfrac{a}{1 - k} = \dfrac{D/(1+r)}{1 - (1+g)/(1+r)} = \dfrac{D}{r - g}$.

8. PDV $= \displaystyle\int_0^{15} 500 e^{-0.06t}\, dt = 500 \left. (-1/0.06)e^{-0.06t} \right|_0^{15} = (500/0.06)\left[1 - e^{-0.9}\right] \approx 4945.25$.

$$\text{FDV} = e^{0.06 \cdot 15}\text{PDV} = e^{0.9}\text{PDV} \approx 2.4596 \cdot 4945.25 \approx 12163.3.$$

10.6

1. Using formula (2) we find that the annual payments are: $a = 0.07 \cdot 80\,000/(1 - (1.07)^{-10}) \approx 11\,390.20$.

2. Using (2) we get $a = (0.07/12) \cdot 80\,000/[1 - (1 + 0.07/12)^{-120}] \approx 928.87$.

3. (a) $(8000/0.07)[1.07^6 - 1] \approx 57\,226.33$. (Formula (10.5.3).) Four years after the last deposit you have $57\,226.33 \cdot 1.07^4 \approx 75\,012.05$.   (b) With annual compounding: $r = 3^{1/20} - 1 \approx 0.0565$, so the rate of interest is about 5.65 %. With continuous compounding, $e^{20r} = 3$, so that $r = \ln 3/20 \approx 0.0549$, so the rate of interest is about 5.49 %.

4. Schedule (b) has present value $\dfrac{12\,000 \cdot 1.115}{0.115}[1 - (1.115)^{-8}] \approx 67\,644.42$. Schedule (c) has present value $22\,000 + \dfrac{7000}{0.115}[1 - (1.115)^{-12}] \approx 66\,384.08$. Thus schedule (c) is cheapest. When the interest rate becomes 12.5 %, schedules (b) and (c) have present values equal to 65\,907.61 and 64\,374.33, respectively, so (c) is cheapest in this case too.

10.7

1. r must satisfy $-50\,000 + 30\,000/(1+r) + 30\,000/(1+r)^2 = 0$. With $s = 1/(1+r)$, this yields $s^2 + s - 5/3 = 0$, with positive solution $s = -1/2 + \sqrt{23/12} \approx 0.884$, so that $r \approx 0.13$.

2. Equation (1) is here $a/(1+r) + a/(1+r)^2 + \cdots = -a_0$, which yields $a/r = -a_0$, so $r = -a/a_0$.

3. By hypothesis, $f(0) = a_0 + a_1 + \cdots + a_n > 0$. Also, $f(r) \to a_0 < 0$ as $r \to \infty$. Moreover, $f'(r) = -a_1(1+r)^{-2} - 2a_2(1+r)^{-3} - \cdots - na_n(1+r)^{-n-1} < 0$, so $f(r)$ is strictly decreasing. This guarantees that there is a unique internal rate of return, with $r > 0$.

4. \$ 1.55 million. $(400\,000(1/1.175 + (1/1.175)^2 + \cdots + (1/1.175)^7) \approx 1\,546\,522.94.)$

5. See SM.

6. Applying (10.5.2) with $a = 1000$ and $n = 5$ gives the equation $P_5 = (1000/r)[1 - 1/(1+r)^5] = 4340$ to be solved for r. For $r = 0.05$, the present value is \$4329.48; for $r = 0.045$, the present value is \$4389.98. Because $dP_5/dr < 0$, it follows that p is a little less than 5%.

10.8

1. (a) $x_t = x_0(-2)^t$ (b) $x_t = x_0(5/6)^t$ (c) $x_t = x_0(-0.3)^t$

2. (a) $x_t = -4t$. (See line 1 below (4).)   (b) $x_t = 2(1/2)^t + 4$ (c) $x_t = (13/8)(-3)^t - 5/8$ (d) $x_t = -2(-1)^t + 4$

3. Equilibrium requires $\alpha P_t - \beta = \gamma - \delta P_{t+1}$, or $P_{t+1} = -(\alpha/\delta)P_t + (\beta + \gamma)/\delta$. Using (4) we obtain $P_t = \left(-\dfrac{\alpha}{\delta}\right)^t \left(P_0 - \dfrac{\beta + \gamma}{\alpha + \delta}\right) + \dfrac{\beta + \gamma}{\alpha + \delta}$.

Review Problems for Chapter 10

1. (a) $5000 \cdot 1.03^{10} \approx 6719.58$ (b) $5000(1.03)^{t^*} = 10\,000$, so $(1.03)^{t^*} = 2$, or $t^* = \ln 2/\ln 1.03 \approx 23.45$.

2. (a) $8000 \cdot 1.05^3 = 9261$ (b) $8000 \cdot 1.05^{13} \approx 15\,085.19$ (c) $(1.05)^{t^*} = 4$, so $t^* = \ln 4/1.05 \approx 28.5$

3. If you borrow \$$a$ at the annual interest rate of 11% with interest paid yearly, then the debt after 1 year is equal to $a(1 + 11/100) = a(1.11)$; if you borrow at annual interest rate 10% with interest paid monthly, your debt after 1 year will be $a(1 + 10/(12 \cdot 100))^{12} \approx 1.1047a$, so schedule (ii) is preferable.

4. $15\,000e^{0.07 \cdot 12} \approx 34\,745.50$ 5. (a) $8000e^{0.06 \cdot 3} \approx 9577.74$ (b) $t^* = \ln 2/0.06 \approx 11.6$

6. We use formula (10.4.5): (a) $\dfrac{44}{1-0.56} = 100$ (b) The first term is 20 and the quotient is $1/1.2$, so the sum is

$\dfrac{20}{1-1/1.2} = 120$.   (c) $\dfrac{3}{1-2/5} = 5$

(d) The first term is $(1/20)^{-2} = 400$ and the quotient is $1/20$, so the sum is $\dfrac{400}{1-1/20} = 8000/19$.

7. (a) $\displaystyle\int_0^T ae^{-rt}\,dt = (a/r)(1-e^{-rT})$ (b) a/r, the same as (10.5.4).

8. (a) $5000(1.04)^4 = 5849.29$ (b) $21\,232.32$ (c) $K \approx 5990.49$

9. (a) According to formula (10.6.2), the annual payment is: $500\,000 \cdot 0.07(1.07)^{10}/(1.07^{10}-1) \approx 71\,188.80$. The total amount is $10 \cdot 71\,188.80 = 711\,888$.   (b) If the person has to pay twice a year, the biannual payment is $500\,000 \cdot 0.035(1.035)^{20}/(1.035^{20}-1) \approx 35\,180.50$. The total amount is then $20 \cdot 35\,180.50 = 703\,610.80$.

10. (a) Present value: $(3200/0.08)[1-(1.08)^{-10}] = 21\,472.26$.   (b) Present value: $7000+(3000/0.08)[1-1.08^{-5}] = 18\,978.13$.   (c) Four years ahead the present value is $(4000/0.08)[1-(1.08)^{-10}] = 26\,840.33$. The present value when Lucy makes her choice is $26\,840.33 \cdot 1.08^{-4} = 19\,728.44$. She should choose option (a).

11. (a) $t^* = 1/16r^2 = 25$ for $r = 0.05$.   (b) $t^* = 1/\sqrt{r} = 5$ for $r = 0.04$.

12. (a) $F(10) - F(0) = \displaystyle\int_0^{10}(1+0.4t)\,dt = \Big|_0^{10}(t+0.2t^2) = 30$. (Note: the total revenue is $F(10) - F(0) = F(10)$.)
(b) See Example 9.5.3.

13. (a) $x_t = (-0.1)^t$ (b) $x_t = -2t + 4$ (c) $x_t = 4\left(\tfrac{3}{2}\right)^t - 2$

Chapter 11

11.1

1. $f(0,1) = 1 \cdot 0 + 2 \cdot 1 = 2$, $f(2,-1) = 0$, $f(a,a) = 3a$, and $f(a+h,b) - f(a,b) = h$

2. $f(0,1) = 0$, $f(-1,2) = -4$, $f(10^4, 10^{-2}) = 1$, $f(a,a) = a^3$, $f(a+h,b) = (a+h)b^2 = ab^2 + hb^2$, and $f(a, b+k) - f(a,b) = 2abk + ak^2$.

3. $f(1,1) = 2$, $f(-2,3) = 51$, $f(1/x, 1/y) = 3/x^2 - 2/xy + 1/y^3$, $p = 6x + 3h - 2y$, $q = -2x + 3y^2 + 3yk + k^2$

4. (a) $f(-1,2) = 1$, $f(a,a) = 4a^2$, $f(a+h,b) - f(a,b) = 2(a+b)h + h^2$
(b) $f(tx, ty) = (tx)^2 + 2(tx)(ty) + (ty)^2 = t^2(x^2 + 2xy + y^2) = t^2 f(x,y)$ for all t, including $t = 2$.

5. $F(1,1) = 10$, $F(4,27) = 60$, $F(9, 1/27) = 10$, $F(3, \sqrt{2}) = 10\sqrt{3} \cdot \sqrt[6]{2}$, $F(100, 1000) = 1000$, $F(2K, 2L) = 10 \cdot 2^{5/6} K^{1/2} L^{1/3} = 2^{5/6} F(K, L)$

6. (a) The denominator must be different from 0, so the function is defined for those (x, y) where $y \neq x - 2$.
(b) We can only take the square root of nonnegative numbers, so we must require $2 - (x^2 + y^2) \geq 0$, i.e. $x^2 + y^2 \leq 2$.
(c) Put $a = x^2 + y^2$. We must have $(4 - a)(a - 1) \geq 0$, i.e. $1 \leq a \leq 4$. (Use a sign diagram.)
The domains in (b) and (c) are the shaded sets shown in Figs. A11.1.6b and A11.1.6c.

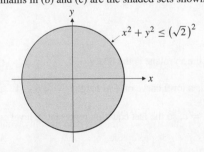

Figure A11.1.6b

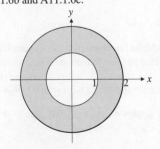

Figure A11.1.6c

7. (a) $e^{x+y} \neq 3$, that is $x + y \neq \ln 3$ (b) Since $(x-a)^2 \geq 0$ and $(y-b)^2 \geq 0$, it suffices to have $x \neq a$ and $y \neq b$, because then we take ln of positive numbers. (c) $x > a$ and $y > b$. (Note that $\ln(x-a)^2 = 2\ln|x-a|$, which is equal to $2\ln(x-a)$ only if $x > a$.)

11.2

1. (a) $\partial z/\partial x = 2$, $\partial z/\partial y = 3$ (b) $\partial z/\partial x = 2x$, $\partial z/\partial y = 3y^2$ (c) $\partial z/\partial x = 3x^2 y^4$, $\partial z/\partial y = 4x^3 y^3$
   (d) $\partial z/\partial x = \partial z/\partial y = 2(x+y)$

2. (a) $\partial z/\partial x = 2x$, $\partial z/\partial y = 6y$ (b) $\partial z/\partial x = y$, $\partial z/\partial y = x$ (c) $\partial z/\partial x = 20x^3 y^2 - 2y^5$, $\partial z/\partial y = 10x^4 y - 10xy^4$
   (d) $\partial z/\partial x = \partial z/\partial y = e^{x+y}$ (e) $\partial z/\partial x = ye^{xy}$, $\partial z/\partial y = xe^{xy}$ (f) $\partial z/\partial x = e^x/y$, $\partial z/\partial y = -e^x/y^2$
   (g) $\partial z/\partial x = \partial z/\partial y = 1/(x+y)$ (h) $\partial z/\partial x = 1/x$, $\partial z/\partial y = 1/y$

3. (a) $f_1'(x, y) = 7x^6$, $f_2'(x, y) = -7y^6$, $f_{12}''(x, y) = 0$ (b) $f_1'(x, y) = 5x^4 \ln y$, $f_2'(x, y) = x^5/y$, $f_{12}''(x, y) = 5x^4/y$ (c) $f(x, y) = (x^2 - 2y^2)^5 = u^5$, where $u = x^2 - 2y^2$. Then $f_1'(x, y) = 5u^4 u_1' = 5(x^2 - 2y^2)^4 2x = 10x(x^2 - 2y^2)^4$. In the same way, $f_2'(x, y) = 5u^4 u_2' = 5(x^2 - 2y^2)^4(-4y) = -20y(x^2 - 2y^2)^4$. Finally, $f_{12}''(x, y) = (\partial/\partial y)(10x(x^2 - 2y^2)^4) = 10x4(x^2 - 2y^2)^3(-4y) = -160xy(x^2 - 2y^2)^3$.

4. (a) $z_x' = 3$, $z_y' = 4$, and $z_{xx}'' = z_{xy}'' = z_{yx}'' = z_{yy}'' = 0$ (b) $z_x' = 3x^2 y^2$, $z_y' = 2x^3 y$, $z_{xx}'' = 6xy^2$, $z_{yy}'' = 2x^3$, and $z_{xy}'' = 6x^2 y$ (c) $z_x' = 5x^4 - 6xy$, $z_y' = -3x^2 + 6y^5$, $z_{xx}'' = 20x^3 - 6y$, $z_{yy}'' = 30y^4$, and $z_{xy}'' = -6x$
   (d) $z_x' = 1/y$, $z_y' = -x/y^2$, $z_{xx}'' = 0$, $z_{yy}'' = 2x/y^3$, and $z_{xy}'' = -1/y^2$ (e) $z_x' = 2y(x+y)^{-2}$, $z_y' = -2x(x+y)^{-2}$, $z_{xx}'' = -4y(x+y)^{-3}$, $z_{yy}'' = 4x(x+y)^{-3}$, and $z_{xy}'' = 2(x-y)(x+y)^{-3}$ (f) $z_x' = x(x^2 + y^2)^{-1/2}$, $z_y' = y(x^2 + y^2)^{-1/2}$, $z_{xx}'' = y^2(x^2 + y^2)^{-3/2}$, $z_{yy}'' = x^2(x^2 + y^2)^{-3/2}$, and $z_{xy}'' = -xy(x^2 + y^2)^{-3/2}$

5. (a) $z_x' = 2x$, $z_y' = 2e^{2y}$, $z_{xx}'' = 2$, $z_{yy}'' = 4e^{2y}$, $z_{xy}'' = 0$ (b) $z_x' = y/x$, $z_y' = \ln x$, $z_{xx}'' = -y/x^2$, $z_{yy}'' = 0$, $z_{xy}'' = 1/x$
   (c) $z_x' = y^2 - ye^{xy}$, $z_y' = 2xy - xe^{xy}$, $z_{xx}'' = -y^2 e^{xy}$, $z_{yy}'' = 2x - x^2 e^{xy}$, $z_{xy}'' = 2y - e^{xy} - xye^{xy}$
   (d) $z_x' = yx^{y-1}$, $z_y' = x^y \ln x$, $z_{xx}'' = y(y-1)x^{y-2}$, $z_{yy}'' = x^y(\ln x)^2$, $z_{xy}'' = x^{y-1} + yx^{y-1} \ln x$

6. (a) $F_S' = 2.26 \cdot 0.44 S^{-0.56} E^{0.48} = 0.9944 S^{-0.56} E^{0.48}$, $F_E' = 2.26 \cdot 0.48 S^{0.44} E^{-0.52} = 1.0848 S^{0.44} E^{-0.52}$
   (b) $SF_S' + EF_E' = S \cdot 2.26 \cdot 0.44 S^{-0.56} E^{0.48} + E \cdot 2.26 \cdot 0.48 S^{0.44} E^{-0.52} = 0.44 F + 0.48 F = 0.92 F$, so $k = 0.92$.

7. $xz_x' + yz_y' = x[2a(ax + by)] + y[2b(ax + by)] = (ax + by)2(ax + by) = 2(ax + by)^2 = 2z$

8. $\partial z/\partial x = x/(x^2+y^2)$, $\partial z/\partial y = y/(x^2+y^2)$, $\partial^2 z/\partial x^2 = (y^2 - x^2)/(x^2+y^2)^2$, and $\partial^2 z/\partial y^2 = (x^2 - y^2)/(x^2+y^2)^2$. Thus, $\partial^2 z/\partial x^2 + \partial^2 z/\partial y^2 = 0$.

9. (a) $s_x'(x, y) = 2/x$, so $s_x'(20, 30) = 2/20 = 1/10$. (b) $s_y'(x, y) = 4/y$, so $s_y'(20, 30) = 4/30 = 2/15$.

11.3

1. See Fig. A11.3.1.

2. (a) A straight line through $(0, 2, 3)$ parallel to the x-axis.
   (b) A plane parallel to the z-axis whose intersection with the xy-plane is the line $y = x$.

3. If $x^2 + y^2 = 6$, then $f(x, y) = \sqrt{6} - 4$, so $x^2 + y^2 = 6$ is a level curve of f at height $c = \sqrt{6} - 4$.

4. $f(x, y) = e^{x^2 - y^2} + (x^2 - y^2)^2 = e^c + c^2$ when $x^2 - y^2 = c$, so the last equation represents a level curve of f at height $e^c + c^2$.

5. At the point of intersection f would have two different values, which is impossible when f is a function.

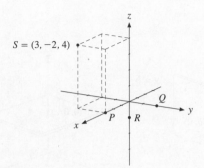

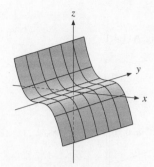

Figure A11.3.1   Figure A11.3.6

6. Generally, the graph of $g(x, y) = f(x)$ in 3-space consists of a surface traced out by moving the graph of $z = f(x)$ parallel to the y-axis in both directions. The graph of $g(x, y) = x$ is the plane through the y-axis at a 45° angle with the xy-plane. The graph of $g(x, y) = -x^3$ is shown in Fig. A11.3.6. (Only a portion of the unbounded graph is indicated, of course.)

7. See Figs. A11.3.7a and b. (Note that only a portion of the graph is indicated in part (a).)

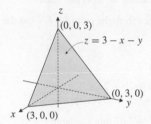

Figure A11.3.7a

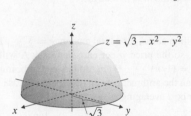

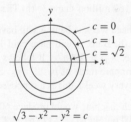

Figure A11.3.7b

8. (a) The point $(2, 3)$ lies on the level curve $z = 8$, so $f(2, 3) = 8$. The points $(x, 3)$ are those on the line $y = 3$ parallel to the x-axis. This line intersects the level curve $z = 8$ when $x = 2$ and $x = 5$.
(b) As y varies with $x = 2$ fixed, the minimum of $f(2, y)$ is 8 when $y = 3$.   (c) At A, any move in the direction of increasing x with y held fixed reaches higher level curves, so $f_1'(x, y) > 0$. Similarly, any move in the direction of increasing y with x held fixed reaches higher level curves, so $f_2'(x, y) > 0$.   At B: $f_1'(x, y) < 0$, $f_2'(x, y) < 0$.   At C: $f_1'(x, y) = 0$, $f_2'(x, y) = 0$. Finally, to increase z by 2 units when moving away from A, the required increases in x and y are approximately 1 and 0.6 respectively. Hence, $f_1' \approx 2/1 = 2$ and $f_2' \approx 2/0.6 = 10/3$.

9. (a) $f_x' > 0$ and $f_y' < 0$ at P, whereas $f_x' < 0$ and $f_y' > 0$ at Q.   (b) (i) No solutions among points shown in the figure. (ii) $x \approx 2$ and $x \approx 6$ (c) The highest level curve that meets the line is $z = 3$, so 3 is the largest value.

10. See SM.

11.4

1. See Fig. A11.4.1.

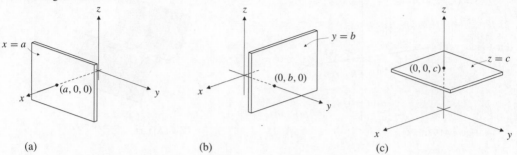

(a) (b) (c)

Figure A11.4.1

2. (a) $d = \sqrt{(4-(-1))^2 + (-2-2)^2 + (0-3)^2} = \sqrt{25+16+9} = \sqrt{50} = 5\sqrt{2}$
(b) $d = \sqrt{(a+1-a)^2 + (b+1-b)^2 + (c+1-c)^2} = \sqrt{3}$

3. $(x-2)^2 + (y-1)^2 + (z-1)^2 = 25$ **4.** The sphere with centre at $(-3, 3, 4)$ and radius 5.

5. $(x-4)^2 + (y-4)^2 + (z-\frac{1}{2})^2$ measures the square of the distance from the point $(4, 4, \frac{1}{2})$ to the point (x, y, z) on the paraboloid.

11.5

1. (a) $f(-1, 2, 3) = 1$ and $f(a+1, b+1, c+1) - f(a, b, c) = 2a + 2b + 2c + 3$.
(b) $f(tx, ty, tz) = (tx)(ty) + (tx)(tz) + (ty)(tz) = t^2(xy + xz + yz) = t^2 f(x, y, z)$

2. (a) Because 1.053 is the sum of exponents, y would become $2^{1.053} \approx 2.07$ times as large.
(b) $\ln y = \ln 2.9 + 0.015 \ln x_1 + 0.25 \ln x_2 + 0.35 \ln x_3 + 0.408 \ln x_4 + 0.03 \ln x_5$

3. (a) 13.167 million shares.   (b) The harmonic mean.

4. (a) In each week w bank A will have bought $100/p_w$ million euros, for a total amount $e = \sum_{w=1}^{n} 100/p_w$ million euros. (b) Bank A will have paid $100n$ million dollars, so the price p per euro that bank A will have paid, on average, is $p = 100n/e$. It follows that $1/p = e/100n = (1/n)\sum_{w=1}^{n} 1/p_w$ dollars per euro, implying that p is the harmonic mean of $p_1, \ldots, p_n$. Since this is lower than the arithmetic mean (except in the case when p_w is the same every week), this is a supposed advantage of dollar cost averaging.

5. (a) Each machine would produce 60 units per day, so each unit produced would require $480/60 = 8$ minutes.
(b) Total output is $\sum_{i=1}^{n}(T/t_i) = T\sum_{i=1}^{n}(1/t_i)$. If all n machines were equally efficient, the time needed for each unit would be $nT/T\sum_{i=1}^{n}(1/t_i) = n/\sum_{i=1}^{n}(1/t_i)$, the harmonic mean of $t_1, \ldots, t_n$.

11.6

1. $F_1'(x, y, z) = 2xe^{xz} + x^2ze^{xz} + y^4e^{xy}$, so $F_1'(1, 1, 1) = 4e$; $F_2'(x, y, z) = 3y^2e^{xy} + xy^3e^{xy}$, so $F_2'(1, 1, 1) = 4e$; $F_3'(x, y, z) = x^3e^{xz}$, so $F_3'(1, 1, 1) = e$.

2. (a) $f_1' = 2x$, $f_2' = 3y^2$, and $f_3' = 4z^3$ (b) $f_1' = 10x$, $f_2' = -9y^2$, and $f_3' = 12z^3$ (c) $f_1' = yz$, $f_2' = xz$, and $f_3' = xy$ (d) $f_1' = 4x^3/yz$, $f_2' = -x^4/y^2z$, and $f_3' = -x^4/yz^2$ (e) $f_1' = 12x(x^2 + y^3 + z^4)^5$, $f_2' = 18y^2(x^2 + y^3 + z^4)^5$, and $f_3' = 24z^3(x^2 + y^3 + z^4)^5$ (f) $f_1' = yze^{xyz}$, $f_2' = xze^{xyz}$, and $f_3' = xye^{xyz}$

3. $\partial T/\partial x = ky/d^n$ and $\partial T/\partial y = kx/d^n$ are both positive, so that the number of travellers increases if the size of either city increases, which is reasonable. $\partial T/\partial d = -nkxy/d^{n+1}$ is negative, so that the number of travellers decreases if the distance between the cities increases, which is also reasonable.

4. (a) $g(2, 1, 1) = -2$, $g(3, -4, 2) = 352$, and $g(1, 1, a + h) - g(1, 1, a) = 2ah + h^2 - h$.
(b) $g_1' = 4x - 4y - 4$, $g_2' = -4x + 20y - 28$, $g_3' = 2z - 1$. The second-order partials are: $g_{11}'' = 4$, $g_{12}'' = -4$,
$g_{13}'' = 0$, $g_{21}'' = -4$, $g_{22}'' = 20$, $g_{23}'' = 0$, $g_{31}'' = 0$, $g_{32}'' = 0$, and $g_{33}'' = 2$.

5. $\partial\pi/\partial p = \frac{1}{2}p(1/r + 1/w)$, $\partial\pi/\partial r = -\frac{1}{4}p^2/r^2$, $\partial\pi/\partial w = -\frac{1}{4}p^2/w^2$

6. First-order partials: $w_1' = 3yz + 2xy - z^3$, $w_2' = 3xz + x^2$, $w_3' = 3xy - 3xz^2$. Second-order partials: $w_{11}'' = 2y$,
$w_{12}'' = w_{21}'' = 3z + 2x$, $w_{13}'' = w_{31}'' = 3y - 3z^2$, $w_{22}'' = 0$, $w_{23}'' = w_{32}'' = 3x$, $w_{33}'' = -6xz$.

7. $f_1' = p'(x)$, $f_2' = q'(y)$, $f_3' = r'(z)$

8. (a) $\begin{pmatrix} 2a & 0 & 0 \\ 0 & 2b & 0 \\ 0 & 0 & 2c \end{pmatrix}$ (b) $\begin{pmatrix} a(a-1)g/x^2 & abg/xy & acg/xz \\ abg/xy & b(b-1)g/y^2 & bcg/yz \\ acg/xz & bcg/yz & c(c-1)g/z^2 \end{pmatrix}$, in concise form.

9. Put $w = u^h$, where $u = (x - y + z)/(x + y - z)$. Then $\partial w/\partial x = hu^{h-1}\partial u/\partial x$, $\partial w/\partial y = hu^{h-1}\partial u/\partial y$,
and $\partial w/\partial z = hu^{h-1}\partial u/\partial z$. With $v = x + y - z$, we get $\partial u/\partial x = (2y - 2z)/v^2$, $\partial u/\partial y = -2x/v^2$, and
$\partial u/\partial z = 2x/v^2$. Hence $x\partial w/\partial x + y\partial w/\partial y + z\partial w/\partial z = hu^{h-1}v^{-2}[x(2y - 2z) + y(-2x) + z2x] = 0$. (In the
terminology of Section 12.7, the function w is homogeneous of degree 0. Euler's theorem 12.7.1 yields the result
immediately.)

10. $f_x' = y^z x^{y^z-1}$, $f_y' = zy^{z-1}(\ln x)x^{y^z}$, $f_z' = y^z(\ln x)(\ln y)x^{y^z}$

11. See SM.

11.7

1. $\partial M/\partial Y = 0.14$ and $\partial M/\partial r = -0.84 \cdot 76.03(r - 2)^{-1.84} = -63.8652(r - 2)^{-1.84}$. So $\partial M/\partial Y$ is positive and
$\partial M/\partial r$ is negative, which accords with standard economic intuition.

2. (a) $KY_K' + LY_L' = aY$ (b) $KY_K' + LY_L' = (a + b)Y$ (c) $KY_K' + LY_L' = Y$

3. $D_p'(p, q) = -bq^{-\alpha}$, $D_q'(p, q) = bp\alpha q^{-\alpha-1}$. So $D_p'(p, q) < 0$, showing that demand decreases as price increases.
And $D_q'(p, q) > 0$, showing that demand increases as the price of a competing product increases.

4. $F_K' = aF/K$, $F_L' = bF/L$, and $F_M' = cF/M$, so $KF_K' + LF_L' + MF_M' = (a + b + c)F$.

5. $\partial D/\partial p$ and $\partial E/\partial q$ are normally negative, because the demand for a commodity goes down when its price increases.
If the commodities are substitutes, this means that demand increases when the price of the other good increases.
So the usual signs are $\partial D/\partial q > 0$ and $\partial E/\partial p > 0$.

6. $\partial U/\partial x_i = e^{-x_i}$, for $i = 1, \ldots, n$ **7.** $KY_K' + LY_L' = \mu Y$

11.8

1. (a) $\text{El}_x z = 1$ and $\text{El}_y z = 1$ (b) $\text{El}_x z = 2$ and $\text{El}_y z = 5$ (c) $\text{El}_x z = n + x$ and $\text{El}_y z = n + y$
(d) $\text{El}_x z = x/(x + y)$ and $\text{El}_y z = y/(x + y)$

2. Let $z = u^g$ with $u = ax_1^d + bx_2^d + cx_3^d$. Then $\text{El}_1 z = \text{El}_u u^g \text{El}_1 u = g(x_1/u)adx_1^{d-1} = adgx_1^d/u$. Similarly,
$\text{El}_2 z = bdgx_2^d/u$ and $\text{El}_3 z = cdgx_3^d/u$, so $\text{El}_1 z + \text{El}_2 z + \text{El}_3 z = dg(ax_1^d + bx_2^d + cx_3^d)/u = dg$. (This result
follows easily from the fact that z is homogeneous of degree dg and from the elasticity form (12.7.3) of the Euler
equation.)

3. $\text{El}_i z = p + a_i x_i$ for $i = 1, \ldots, n$.   **4.** See SM.

Review Problems for Chapter 11

1. $f(0, 1) = -5$, $f(2, -1) = 11$, $f(a, a) = -2a$, and $f(a + h, b) - f(a, b) = 3h$

2. $f(-1, 2) = -10$, $f(2a, 2a) = -4a^2$, $f(a, b + k) - f(a, b) = -6bk - 3k^2$, $f(tx, ty) - t^2 f(x, y) = 0$

3. $f(3, 4, 0) = 5$, $f(-2, 1, 3) = \sqrt{14}$, and $f(tx, ty, tz) = \sqrt{t^2 x^2 + t^2 y^2 + t^2 z^2} = t f(x, y, z)$

4. (a) $F(0, 0) = 0$, $F(1, 1) = 15$, and $F(32, 243) = 15 \cdot 2 \cdot 9 = 270$.
(b) $F(K + 1, L) - F(K, L) = 15(K + 1)^{1/5} L^{2/5} - 15 K^{1/5} L^{2/5} = 15 L^{2/5}[(K + 1)^{1/5} - K^{1/5}]$ is the extra output from 1 more unit of capital, approximately equal to the marginal productivity of capital.
(c) $F(32 + 1, 243) - F(32, 243) \approx 1.667$. Moreover, $F'_K(K, L) = 3 K^{-4/5} L^{2/5}$, so $F'_K(32, 243)$
$= 3 \cdot 32^{-4/5} 243^{2/5} = 3 \cdot 2^{-4} \cdot 3^2 = 27/16 \approx 1.6875$. As expected, $F(32 + 1, 243) - F(32, 243)$ is close to $F'_K(32, 243)$.   (d) F is homogeneous of degree 3/5.

5. (a) $\partial Y / \partial K \approx 0.083 K^{0.356} S^{0.562}$ and $\partial Y / \partial S \approx 0.035 K^{1.356} S^{-0.438}$.
(b) The catch becomes $2^{1.356 + 0.562} = 2^{1.918} \approx 3.779$ times higher.

6. (a) All (x, y) (b) For $xy \le 1$ (c) For $x^2 + y^2 < 2$

7. (a) $x + y > 1$ (b) $x^2 \ge y^2$ and $x^2 + y^2 \ge 1$. So $x^2 + y^2 \ge 1$ and $|x| \ge |y|$.   (c) $y \ge x^2$, $x \ge 0$, and $\sqrt{x} \ge y$.
So $0 \le x \le 1$ and $\sqrt{x} \ge y \ge x^2$.

8. (a) $\partial z / \partial x = 10 x y^4 (x^2 y^4 + 2)^4$ (b) $\sqrt{K} (\partial F / \partial K) = 2\sqrt{K} (\sqrt{K} + \sqrt{L})(1/2\sqrt{K}) = \sqrt{K} + \sqrt{L}$
(c) $K F'_K + L F'_L = K(1/a) a K^{a-1} (K^a + L^a)^{1/a-1} + L(1/a) a L^{a-1} (K^a + L^a)^{1/a-1} =$
$(K^a + L^a)(K^a + L^a)^{1/a-1} = F$ (d) $\partial g / \partial t = 3/w + 2wt$, so $\partial^2 g / \partial w \partial t = -3/w^2 + 2t$
(e) $g'_3 = t_3 (t_1^2 + t_2^2 + t_3^2)^{-1/2}$ (f) $f'_1 = 4xyz + 2xz^2$, $f''_{13} = 4xy + 4xz$

9. (a) $f(0, 0) = 36$, $f(-2, -3) = 0$, $f(a + 2, b - 3) = a^2 b^2$ (b) $f'_x = 2(x - 2)(y + 3)^2$, $f'_y = 2(x - 2)^2 (y + 3)$

10. Because $g(-1, 5) = g(1, 1) = 30$, the two points are on the same level curve.

11. If $x - y = c \ne 0$, then $F(x, y) = \ln(x - y)^2 + e^{2(x-y)} = \ln c^2 + e^{2c}$, a constant.

12. (a) $f'_1(x, y) = 4x^3 - 8xy$, $f'_2(x, y) = 4y - 4x^2 + 4$ (b) Stationary points: $(0, -1)$, $(\sqrt{2}, 1)$, and $(-\sqrt{2}, 1)$.

13. (a) $\text{El}_x z = 3$, $\text{El}_y z = -4$ (b) $\text{El}_x z = 2x^2/(x^2 + y^2) \ln(x^2 + y^2)$, $\text{El}_y z = 2y^2/(x^2 + y^2) \ln(x^2 + y^2)$
(c) $\text{El}_x z = \text{El}_x (e^x e^y) = \text{El}_x e^x = x$, $\text{El}_y z = y$ (d) $\text{El}_x z = x^2/(x^2 + y^2)$, $\text{El}_y z = y^2/(x^2 + y^2)$

14. (a) $\partial F / \partial y = e^{2x} 2(1 - y)(-1) = -2e^{2x}(1 - y)$.   (b) $F'_L = (\ln K)(\ln M)/L$, $F'_{LK} = (\ln M)/KL$
(c) $w = x^x y^x z^x$ gives $\ln w = x \ln x + x \ln y + x \ln z$, and so by implicit differentiation, $w'_x/w = 1 \cdot \ln x + x(1/x) +$
$\ln y + \ln z$, implying that $w'_x = w(\ln x + 1 + \ln y + \ln z) = x^x y^x z^x (\ln(xyz) + 1)$.

15. (a) Begin by differentiating w.r.t. x to obtain $\partial^p z / \partial x^p = e^x \ln(1 + y)$ for any natural number p. Differentiating this repeatedly w.r.t. y yields first $\partial^{p+1} / \partial y \partial x^p = e^x (1 + y)^{-1}$, then $\partial^{p+2} / \partial y^2 \partial x^p = e^x (-1)(1 + y)^{-2}$, and so on. By induction on q, one has $\partial^{p+q} / \partial y^q \partial x^p = e^x (-1)^{q-1} (q - 1)! (1 + y)^{-q}$, which becomes $(-1)^{q-1}(q - 1)!$ at $(x, y) = (0, 0)$.

16. $u'_x = au/x$ and $u'_y = bu/y$, so $u''_{xy} = au'_y/x = abu/xy$. Hence, $u''_{xy}/u'_x u'_y = 1/u$ ($u \ne 0$). Then,

$$\frac{1}{u'_x} \frac{\partial}{\partial x} \left(\frac{u''_{xy}}{u'_x u'_y} \right) = \frac{1}{u'_x} \cdot \frac{-u'_x}{u^2} = -\frac{1}{u^2} = \frac{1}{u'_y} \frac{\partial}{\partial y} \left(\frac{u''_{xy}}{u'_x u'_y} \right)$$

Chapter 12

12.1

1. (a) $dz/dt = F'_1(x, y) dx/dt + F'_2(x, y) dy/dt = 1 \cdot 2t + 2y \cdot 3t^2 = 2t + 6t^5$
(b) $dz/dt = px^{p-1} y^q a + qx^p y^{q-1} b = x^{p-1} y^{q-1}(apy + bqx) = a^p b^q (p + q) t^{p+q-1}$ (c) In part (a), $z = t^2 + (t^3)^2 = t^2 + t^6$, so $dz/dt = 2t + 6t^5$. In part (b), $z = (at)^p \cdot (bt)^q = a^p b^q t^{p+q}$, so $dz/dt = a^p b^q (p + q) t^{p+q-1}$.

2. (a) $dz/dt = (\ln y + y/x) \cdot 1 + (x/y + \ln x)(1/t) = \ln(\ln t) + \ln t/(t + 1) + (t + 1)/t \ln t + \ln(t + 1)/t$
(b) $dz/dt = Aae^{at}/x + Bbe^{bt}/y = a + b$

3. These problems are important because there are many economic applications like this with incompletely specified functions.
   (a) $dz/dt = F_1'(t, y) + F_2'(t, y)g'(t)$. If $F(t, y) = t^2 + ye^y$ and $g(t) = t^2$, then $F_1'(t, y) = 2t$, $F_2'(t, y) = e^y + ye^y$, and $g'(t) = 2t$. Hence $dz/dt = 2t(1 + e^{t^2} + t^2 e^{t^2})$.   (b) $dY/dL = F_K'(K, L)g'(L) + F_L'(K, L)$

4. $dY/dt = \left(10L - \frac{1}{2}K^{-1/2}\right)0.2 + \left(10K - \frac{1}{2}L^{-1/2}\right)0.5e^{0.1t} = 35 - 7\sqrt{5}/100$ when $t = 0$ and so $K = L = 5$.

5. The usual rules in Sections 6.7 and 6.8 for differentiating (a) a sum; (b) a difference; (c) a product; (d) a quotient; (e) a composite function of one variable.

6. $x^* = \sqrt[4]{3b/a}$ 7. See SM.

12.2

1. (a) $\partial z/\partial t = F_1'(x, y)\partial x/\partial t + F_2'(x, y)\partial y/\partial t = 1 \cdot 1 + 2ys = 1 + 2ts^2$,
   $\partial z/\partial s = (\partial z/\partial x)(\partial x/\partial s) + (\partial z/\partial y)(\partial y/\partial s) = 1 \cdot (-1) + 2yt = -1 + 2t^2s$
   (b) $\partial z/\partial t = 4x2t + 9y^2 = 8tx + 9y^2 = 8t^3 - 8ts + 9t^2 + 36ts^3 + 36s^6$
   $\partial z/\partial s = 4x(-1) + 9y^2 6s^2 = -4x + 54s^2 y^2 = -4t^2 + 4s + 54t^2 s^2 + 216ts^5 + 216s^8$

2. (a) $\partial z/\partial t = y^2 + 2xy2ts = 5t^4 s^2 + 4t^3 s^4$, $\partial z/\partial s = y^2 2s + 2xyt^2 = 2t^5 s + 4t^4 s^3$
   (b) $\dfrac{\partial z}{\partial t} = \dfrac{2(1 - s)e^{ts+t+s}}{(e^{t+s} + e^{ts})^2}$ and $\dfrac{\partial z}{\partial s} = \dfrac{2(1 - t)e^{ts+t+s}}{(e^{t+s} + e^{ts})^2}$

3. It is important to do these problems, because in economic applications, functions are often not completely specified.
   (a) $\partial z/\partial r = 2r\partial F/\partial u + (1/r)\partial F/\partial w$, $\partial z/\partial s = -4s\partial F/\partial v + (1/s)\partial F/\partial w$
   (b) $\partial z/\partial t_1 = F'(x)f_1'(t_1, t_2)$, $\partial z/\partial t_2 = F'(x)f_2'(t_1, t_2)$
   (c) $\partial x/\partial s = F_1' + F_2' f'(s) + F_3' g_1'(s, t)$, $\partial x/\partial t = F_3' g_2'(s, t)$
   (d) $\partial z/\partial x = F_1' f_1'(x, y) + F_2' 2xh(y)$ and $\partial z/\partial y = F_1' f_2'(x, y) + F_2' x^2 h'(y) + F_3'(-1/y^2)$.

4. (a) $\dfrac{\partial w}{\partial t} = \dfrac{\partial w}{\partial x}\dfrac{\partial x}{\partial t} + \dfrac{\partial w}{\partial y}\dfrac{\partial y}{\partial t} + \dfrac{\partial w}{\partial z}\dfrac{\partial z}{\partial t} = y^2 z^3 \cdot 2t + 2xyz^3 \cdot 0 + 3xy^2 z^2 \cdot 1 = 5s^2 t^4$
   (b) $\dfrac{\partial w}{\partial t} = 2x\dfrac{\partial x}{\partial t} + 2y\dfrac{\partial y}{\partial t} + 2z\dfrac{\partial z}{\partial t} = \dfrac{x}{\sqrt{t+s}} + 2sye^{ts} = 1 + 2se^{2ts}$

5. (a) We can write $z = F(u_1, u_2, u_3)$, with $u_1 = t$, $u_2 = t^2$ and $u_3 = t^3$. Then
   $\dfrac{dz}{dt} = F_1'\dfrac{du_1}{dt} + F_2'\dfrac{du_2}{dt} + F_3'\dfrac{du_3}{dt} = F_1'(t, t^2, t^3) + F_2'(t, t^2, t^3)2t + F_3'(t, t^2, t^3)3t^2$.
   (b) $z = F(t, f(t), g(t^2)) \Rightarrow \dfrac{dz}{dt} = F_1'(t, f(t), g(t^2)) + F_2'(t, f(t), g(t^2))f'(t) + F_3'(t, t^2, t^3)g'(t^2)2t$

6. (a) $\partial Z/\partial G = 1 + 2Y\partial Y/\partial G + 2r\partial r/\partial G$ (b) $\partial Z/\partial G = 1 + I_1'(Y, r)\partial Y/\partial G + I_2'(Y, r)\partial r/\partial G$

7. $\partial C/\partial p_1 = a\partial Q_1/\partial p_1 + b\partial Q_2/\partial p_1 + 2cQ_1\partial Q_1/\partial p_1 = -\alpha_1 A(a + 2cAp_1^{-\alpha_1} p_2^{\beta_1})p_1^{-\alpha_1-1} p_2^{\beta_1} + \alpha_2 bBp_1^{\alpha_2-1} p_2^{-\beta_2}$
   $\partial C/\partial p_2 = \beta_1 A(a + 2cAp_1^{-\alpha_1} p_2^{\beta_1})p_1^{-\alpha_1} p_2^{\beta_1-1} - \beta_2 bBp_1^{\alpha_2} p_2^{-\beta_2-1}$

8. See SM.   9. (a) $\dfrac{\partial u}{\partial r} = \dfrac{\partial f}{\partial x}\dfrac{\partial x}{\partial r} + \dfrac{\partial f}{\partial y}\dfrac{\partial y}{\partial r} + \dfrac{\partial f}{\partial z}\dfrac{\partial z}{\partial r} + \dfrac{\partial f}{\partial w}\dfrac{\partial w}{\partial r}$ (b) $\dfrac{\partial u}{\partial r} = yzw + xzw + xyws + xyz(1/s) = 28$

12.3

1. Formula (1) gives $y' = -F_1'/F_2' = -(4x + 6y)/(6x + 2y) = -(2x + 3y)/(3x + y)$.

2. (a) Put $F(x, y) = x^2 y$. Then $F_1' = 2xy$, $F_2' = x^2$, $F_{11}'' = 2y$, $F_{12}'' = 2x$, $F_{22}'' = 0$, so $y' = -F_1'/F_2' = -2xy/x^2 = -2y/x$. Moreover, using equation (3), $y'' = -(1/(F_2')^3)\left[F_{11}''(F_2')^2 - 2F_{12}''F_1'F_2' + F_{22}''(F_1')^2\right] = -(1/x^6)[2yx^4 - 2(2x)(2xy)x^2] = 6y/x^2$. (See also Problem 7.1.2.)   For (b) and (c), see the answers to Problem 7.1.3.

3. (a) $y' = -4$ and $y'' = -14$ at $(2, 0)$. The tangent has the equation $y = -4x + 8$.
(b) Two points: $(a, -4a)$ and $(-a, 4a)$, where $a = 2\sqrt{7}/7$.

4. With $F(x, y) = 3x^2 - 3xy^2 + y^3 + 3y^2$, we have $F_1'(x, y) = 6x - 3y^2$ and $F_2'(x, y) = -6xy + 3y^2 + 6y$, so according to (12.3.1), $h'(x) = y' = -(6x - 3y^2)/(-6xy + 3y^2 + 6y)$. For x near 1 and so (x, y) near $(1, 1)$, we have $h'(1) = -(6 - 3)/(-6 + 3 + 6) = -1$.

5. $D_P' < 0$ and $D_r' < 0$. Differentiating the equation w.r.t. r yields $D_P'(dP/dr) + D_r' = 0$, and so $dP/dr = -D_r'/D_P' < 0$. So a rise in the interest rate depresses demand, and the price falls to compensate.

6. $dP/dR = f_R'(R, P)/(g'(P) - f_P'(R, P))$. It is plausible that $f_R'(R, P) > 0$ (demand increases as advertising expenditure increases), and $g'(P) > 0$, $f_P'(R, P) < 0$, so $dP/dR > 0$.

7. Differentiating the equation w.r.t. x gives (i) $1 - az_x' = f'(y - bz)(-bz_x')$. Differentiating w.r.t. y gives (ii) $-az_y' = f'(y - bz)(1 - bz_y')$. If $bz_x' \neq 0$, solving (i) for f' and inserting it into (ii) yields $az_x' + bz_y' = 1$. If $bz_x' = 0$, then (i) implies $az_x' = 1$. But then $z_x' \neq 0$, so $b = 0$ and then again $az_x' + bz_y' = 1$.

12.4

1. (a) With $F(x, y) = 3x + y - z$, the given equation is $F(x, y, z) = 0$, and $\partial z/\partial x = -F_1'/F_3' = -3/(-1) = 3$.
(b) $\partial z/\partial x = -(yz + z^3 - y^2 z^5)/(xy + 3xz^2 - 5xy^2 z^4)$ (c) With $F(x, y, z) = e^{xyz} - 3xyz$, the given equation is $F(x, y, z) = 0$. Now, $F_x'(x, y, z) = yze^{xyz} - 3yz$, $F_z'(x, y, z) = xye^{xyz} - 3xy$, so (12.4.1) gives $z_x' = -F_x'/F_z' = -(yze^{xyz} - 3yz)/(xye^{xyz} - 3xy) = -yz(e^{xyz} - 3)/xy(e^{xyz} - 3) = -z/x$. (Actually, the equation $e^c = 3c$ has two solutions. From $xyz = c$ (c a constant) we find z_x' much more easily.)

2. Differentiating partially w.r.t. x yields $(*)$ $3x^2 + 3z^2 z_x' - 3z_x' = 0$, so $z_x' = x^2/(1 - z^2)$. By symmetry, $z_y' = y^2/(1 - z^2)$. To find z_{xy}'', differentiate $(*)$ w.r.t. y to obtain $6zz_y'z_x' + 3z^2 z_{xy}'' - 3z_{xy}'' = 0$, so $z_{xy}'' = 2zx^2 y^2/(1 - z^2)^3$. (Alternatively, differentiate $z_x' = x^2/(1 - z^2)$ w.r.t. y, treating z as a function of y and using the expression for z_y'.)

3. (a) $L^* = P^2/4w^2$, $\partial L^*/\partial P = P/2w^2 > 0$ and $\partial L^*/\partial w = -P^2/2w^3 < 0$.
(b) First-order condition: $Pf'(L^*) - C_L'(L^*, w) = 0$. $\partial L^*/\partial P = -f'(L^*)/(Pf''(L^*) - C_{LL}''(L^*, w))$, $\partial L^*/\partial w = C_{Lw}''(L^*, w)/(Pf''(L^*) - C_{LL}''(L^*, w))$.

4. Use formula (12.4.1). $z_x' = -\dfrac{yx^{y-1} + z^x \ln z}{y^z \ln y + xz^{x-1}}$ and $z_y' = -\dfrac{x^y \ln x + zy^{z-1}}{y^z \ln y + xz^{x-1}}$

5. Implicit differentiation gives $f_P'(R, P)P_w' = g_w'(w, P) + g_P'(w, P)P_w'$. Hence $P_w' = -g_w'(w, P)/(g_P'(w, P) - f_P'(R, P)) < 0$ because $g_w' > 0$, $g_P' > 0$, and $f_P' < 0$.

6. (a) $F(1, 3) = 4$. The equation for the tangent is $y - 3 = -(F_x'(1, 3)/F_y'(1, 3))(x - 1)$ with $F_x'(1, 3) = 10$ and $F_y'(1, 3) = 5$, so $y = -2x + 5$. (b) $\partial y/\partial K = \alpha y/K(1 + 2c \ln y)$, $\partial y/\partial L = \beta y/L(1 + 2c \ln y)$

12.5

1. The marginal rate of substitution is $R_{yx} = 20x/30y$, so $y/x = (2/3)(R_{yx})^{-1}$, whose elasticity is $\sigma_{yx} = -1$.

2. (a) $R_{yx} = (x/y)^{a-1} = (y/x)^{1-a}$ (b) $\sigma_{yx} = \text{El}_{R_{yx}}(y/x) = \text{El}_{R_{yx}}(R_{yx})^{1/(1-a)} = 1/(1 - a)$

3. See SM.

12.6

1. $f(tx, ty) = (tx)^4 + (tx)^2(ty)^2 = t^4 x^4 + t^2 x^2 t^2 y^2 = t^4(x^4 + x^2 y^2) = t^4 f(x, y)$, so f is homogeneous of degree 4.

2. $x(tp, tr) = A(tp)^{-1.5}(tr)^{2.08} = At^{-1.5}p^{-1.5}t^{2.08}r^{2.08} = t^{-1.5}t^{2.08}Ap^{-1.5}r^{2.08} = t^{0.58}x(p, r)$, so the function is homogeneous of degree 0.58. (Alternatively, use the result in Example 11.1.4.)

3. $f(tx, ty) = (tx)(ty)^2 + (tx)^3 = t^3(xy^2 + x^3) = t^3 f(x, y)$. f is homogeneous of degree 3. For the rest, see SM.

4. $f(tx, ty) = (tx)(ty)/[(tx)^2 + (ty)^2] = t^2xy/t^2[x^2 + y^2] = f(x, y) = t^0 f(x, y)$, so f is homogeneous of degree 0. Using the formulas for the partial derivatives of this function in Example 11.2.1(b), we get $x\dfrac{\partial f}{\partial x} + y\dfrac{\partial f}{\partial y} = \dfrac{xy^3 - x^3y + x^3y - xy^3}{(x^2 + y^2)^2} = 0 = 0 \cdot f$, as claimed by Euler's theorem.

5. $F(tK, tL) = A(a(tK)^{-\varrho} + b(tL)^{-\varrho})^{-1/\varrho} = A(t^{-\varrho}aK^{-\varrho} + t^{-\varrho}bL^{-\varrho})^{-1/\varrho} = (t^{-\varrho})^{-1/\varrho}A(aK^{-\varrho} + bL^{-\varrho})^{-1/\varrho} = tF(K, L)$. Using Example 12.6.3, we get $F(K, L)/L = F(K/L, 1) = A[a(K/L)^{-\rho} + b]^{-1/\rho}$.

6. Definition (1) requires that for some number k one has $t^3x^3 + t^2xy = t^k(x^3 + xy)$ for all $t > 0$ and all (x, y). In particular, for $x = y = 1$, we must have $t^3 + t^2 = 2t^k$. For $t = 2$, we get $12 = 2 \cdot 2^k$, or $2^k = 6$. For $t = 4$, we get $80 = 2 \cdot 4^k$, or $4^k = 40$. But $2^k = 6$ implies $4^k = 36$. So the two values of k must actually be different, implying that f is not homogeneous of any degree.

7. From (6), with $k = 1$, we get $f''_{11} = (-y/x)f''_{12}$ and $f''_{22} = (-x/y)f''_{21}$. With $f''_{12} = f''_{21}$ we get $f''_{11}f''_{22} - (f''_{12})^2 = (-y/x)f''_{12}(-x/y)f''_{12} - (f''_{12})^2 = 0$.

8. $f'_2(4, 6) = f'_2(2 \cdot 2, 2 \cdot 3) = 2f'_2(2, 3)$ because $f'_2(x, y)$ is homogeneous of degree 1. (See (12.6.3).) But then $f'_2(2, 3) = 12/2 = 6$. By Euler's theorem (12.6.2), $2f(2, 3) = 2f'_1(2, 3) + 3f'_2(2, 3) = 2 \cdot 4 + 3 \cdot 6 = 26$. Hence $f(2, 3) = 13$, and then $f(6, 9) = f(3 \cdot 2, 3 \cdot 3) = 3^2 f(2, 3) = 9 \cdot 13 = 117$, where we used definition (12.6.1).

9. See SM.

12.7

1. (a) Homogeneous of degree 1. (b) Not homogeneous. (c) Homogeneous of degree $-1/2$.
(d) Homogeneous of degree 1. (e) Not homogeneous. (f) Homogeneous of degree n.

2. (a) Homogeneous of degree 1. (b) Homogeneous of degree μ.

3. All are homogeneous of degree 1, as is easily checked by using (1).

4. $v'_i = u'_i - a/(x_1 + \cdots + x_n)$, so $\sum_{i=1}^n x_i v'_i = \sum_{i=1}^n x_i u'_i - \sum_{i=1}^n ax_i/(x_1 + \cdots + x_n) = a - [a/(x_1 + \cdots + x_n)]\sum_{i=1}^n x_i = a - a = 0$. By Euler's theorem, v is homogeneous of degree 0.

5. (a) Homothetic. (b) Homothetic. (c) Not homothetic. (d) Homothetic.

6. (a) $h(t\mathbf{x}) = f((tx_1)^m, \ldots, (tx_n)^m) = f(t^mx_1^m, \ldots, t^mx_n^m) = (t^m)^r f(x_1^m, \ldots, x_n^m) = t^{mr}h(\mathbf{x})$, so h is homogeneous of degree mr. (b) Homogeneous of degree sp. (c) Homogeneous of degree r for $r = s$, not homogeneous for $r \neq s$. (d) Homogeneous of degree $r + s$. (e) Homogeneous of degree $r - s$.

7. See SM.

12.8

1. We use the approximation $f(x, y) \approx f(0, 0) + f'_1(0, 0)x + f'_2(0, 0)y$. (a) $f'_1(x, y) = 5(x + 1)^4(y + 1)^6$ and $f'_2(x, y) = 6(x + 1)^5(y + 1)^5$, so $f_1(0, 0) = 5$ and $f'_2(0, 0) = 6$. Since $f(0, 0) = 1$, $f(x, y) \approx 1 + 5x + 6y$.
(b) $f'_1(x, y) = f'_2(x, y) = \frac{1}{2}(1 + x + y)^{-1/2}$, so $f'_1(0, 0) = f'_2(0, 0) = 1/2$. Since $f(0, 0) = 1$, $f(x, y) \approx 1 + \frac{1}{2}x + \frac{1}{2}$.
(c) $f'_1(x, y) = e^x \ln(1 + y)$, $f'_2(x, y) = e^x/(1 + y)$, so $f'_1(0, 0) = 0$ and $f'_2(0, 0) = 1$. Since $f(0, 0) = 0$, $f(x, y) \approx y$.

2. $f(x, y) \approx Ax_0^a y_0^b + aAx_0^{a-1}y_0^b(x - x_0) + bAx_0^a y_0^{b-1}(y - y_0) = Ax_0^a y_0^b[1 + a(x - x_0)/x_0 + b(y - y_0)/y_0]$

3. Write the function in the form $g^*(\mu, \varepsilon) = (1 + \mu)^a(1 + \varepsilon)^{\alpha a} - 1$, where $a = 1/(1 - \beta)$. Then $\partial g^*(\mu, \varepsilon)/\partial \mu = a(1 + \mu)^{a-1}(1 + \varepsilon)^{\alpha a}$ and $\partial g^*(\mu, \varepsilon)/\partial \varepsilon = (1 + \mu)^a \alpha a(1 + \varepsilon)^{\alpha a-1}$. Hence, $g^*(0, 0) = 0$, $\partial g^*(0, 0)/\partial \mu = a$, $\partial g^*(0, 0)/\partial \varepsilon = \alpha a$, and $g^*(\mu, \varepsilon) \approx a\mu + \alpha a\varepsilon = (\mu + \alpha\varepsilon)/(1 - \beta)$.

4. $f(0.98, -1.01) \approx -5 - 6(-0.02) + 9(-0.01) = -4.97$. The exact value is -4.970614, so the error is 0.000614.

5. (a) $f(1.02, 1.99) = 1.1909$ (b) $f(1.02, 1.99) \approx f(1, 2) + 0.02 \cdot 8 - 0.01 \cdot (-3) = 1.19$. The error is 0.0009.

6. $v(1.01, 0.02) \approx v(1,0) + v_1'(1,0) \cdot 0.01 + v_2'(1,0) \cdot 0.02 = -1 - 1/150$

7. (a) $z = 2x + 4y - 5$ (b) $z = -10x + 3y + 3$

8. See SM.

9. The tangent plane (3) passes through $(x, y, z) = (0, 0, 0)$ if and only if $-f(x_0, y_0) = f_1'(x_0, y_0)(-x_0) + f_2'(x_0, y_0)(-y_0)$. According to Euler's theorem this equation holds for all (x_0, y_0) if and only if f is homogeneous of degree 1.

12.9

1. Both (a) and (b) give: $dz = (y^2 + 3x^2)dx + 2xy\, dy$.

2. We can either use the definition of the differential, (12.9.1), or the rules for differentials, as we do here.
(a) $dz = d(x^3) + d(y^3) = 3x^2\, dx + 3y^2\, dy$ (b) $dz = (dx)e^{y^2} + x(de^{y^2})$. Here $d(e^{y^2}) = e^{y^2}dy^2 = e^{y^2}2y\, dy$, so $dz = e^{y^2}dx + 2xye^{y^2}dy = e^{y^2}(dx + 2xy\, dy)$.
(c) $dz = d\ln u$, where $u = x^2 - y^2$. Then $dz = \dfrac{1}{u}du = \dfrac{2x\, dx - 2y\, dy}{x^2 - y^2}$.

3. (a) $dz = 2xu\, dx + x^2(u_x'\, dx + u_y'\, dy)$ (b) $dz = 2u(u_x'\, dx + u_y'\, dy)$
(c) $dz = \dfrac{1}{xy + yu}\left[(y + yu_x')\, dx + (x + u + yu_y')\, dy\right]$

4. $T \approx 7.015714$.

5. Taking the differential of each side of the equation gives $d(Ue^U) = d(x\sqrt{y})$, and so $e^U\, dU + Ue^U\, dU = \sqrt{y}\, dx + (x/2\sqrt{y})\, dy$. Solving for dU yields $dU = \sqrt{y}\, dx/(e^U + Ue^U) + x\, dy/2\sqrt{y}(e^U + Ue^U)$.

6. (a) $dX = A\beta N^{\beta-1}e^{\varrho t}dN + AN^\beta \varrho e^{\varrho t}dt$ (b) $dX_1 = BEX^{E-1}N^{1-E}dX + B(1-E)X^E N^{-E}dN$

7. (a) $dU = 2a_1 u_1\, du_1 + \cdots + 2a_n u_n\, du_n$ (b) $dU = A(\delta_1 u_1^{-\varrho} + \cdots + \delta_n u_n^{-\varrho})^{-1-1/\varrho}(\delta_1 u_1^{-\varrho-1}du_1 + \cdots + \delta_n u_n^{-\varrho-1}du_n)$

8. $d(\ln z) = a_1 d(\ln x_1) + \cdots + a_n d(\ln x_n)$, so $dz/z = a_1 dx_1/x_1 + a_2 dx_2/x_2 + \cdots + a_n dx_n/x_n$.

9. (a) $d^2 z = 2\, dx\, dy + 2(dy)^2$ (b) $dz/dt = 3t^2 + 4t^3$ and then $(d^2 z/dt^2)(dt)^2 = (6t + 12t^2)(dt)^2$. On the other hand, the expression for $d^2 z$ derived from (a) is equal to $(4t + 8t^2)(dt)^2$.

12.10

1. (a) $4 - 2 = 2$ (b) $5 - 2 = 3$ (c) $4 - 3 = 1$

2. There are 6 variables Y, C, I, G, T, and r, and 3 equations. So there are $6 - 3 = 3$ degrees of freedom.

3. Let m denote the number of equations and n the number of unknowns. (a) $m = 3, n = 2$; infinitely many solutions. (b) $m = n = 2$; no solutions. (c) $m = n = 2$; infinitely many solutions. (d) $m = 1, n = 100$; infinitely many solutions. (e) $m = 1, n = 100$; no solutions. We see that the counting rule fails dramatically.

12.11

1. Differentiating yields the two equations $a\, du + b\, dv = c\, dx + d\, dy$ and $e\, du + f\, dv = g\, dx + h\, dy$. Solving these for du and dv yields $du = [(cf - bg)\, dx + (df - bh)\, dy]/D$ and $dv = [(ag - ce)\, dx + (ah - de)\, dy]/D$, where $D = af - be$. The required partial derivatives are then easily read off.

2. (a) Differentiating yields $u^3\, dx + x3u^2\, du + dv = 2y\, dy$ and $3v\, du + 3u\, dv - dx = 0$. Solving for du and dv with $D = 9xu^3 - 3v$ yields $du = (-3u^4 - 1)\, dx/D + 6yu\, dy/D$ and $dv = (3xu^2 + 3u^3v)\, dx/D - 6yv\, dy/D$.
(b) $u_x' = (-3u^4 - 1)/D$, $v_x' = (3xu^2 + 3u^3v)/D$ (c) $u_x' = 283/81$ and $v_x' = -64/27$.

3. $\partial y_1/\partial x_1 = (3 - 27x_1^2 y_2^2)/J$ and $\partial y_2/\partial x_1 = (3x_1^2 + 18y_1^2)/J$ with $J = 1 + 54y_1^2 y_2^2$.

4. $\partial Y/\partial M = I'(r)/(aI'(r) + L'(r)S'(Y))$ and $\partial r/\partial M = S'(Y)/(aI'(r) + L'(r)S'(Y))$.

5. Differentiation w.r.t. x yields $y + u'_x v + uv'_x = 0$ and $u + xu'_x + yv'_x = 0$. Solving for u'_x and v'_x, we get

$$u'_x = \frac{u^2 - y^2}{yv - xu} = \frac{u^2 - y^2}{2yv}, \quad v'_x = \frac{xy - uv}{yv - xu} = \frac{2xy - 1}{2yv}$$

where we substituted $xu = -yv$ and $uv = 1 - xy$. Differentiating u'_x w.r.t. x finally yields

$$u''_{xx} = \frac{\partial^2 u}{\partial x^2} = \frac{\partial}{\partial x} u'_x = \frac{2uu'_x 2yv - (u^2 - y^2)2yv'_x}{4y^2 v^2} = \frac{(u^2 - y^2)(4uv - 1)}{4y^2 v^3}$$

(The answer to this problem can be expressed in many different ways.)

6. (a) Differentiation yields the equations: $dY = dC + dI + dG$, $dC = F'_Y dY + F'_T dT + F'_r dr$, and $dI = f'_Y dY + f'_r dr$. Hence, $dY = (F'_T dT + dG + (F'_r + f'_r) dr)/(1 - F'_Y - f'_Y)$.
(b) $\partial Y/\partial T = F'_T/(1 - F'_Y - f'_Y) < 0$, so Y decreases as T increases. But if $dT = dG$ with $dr = 0$, then $dY = (1 + F'_T)dT/(1 - F'_Y - f'_Y)$, which is positive provided that $F'_T > -1$.

7. (a) $6 - 3 = 3$ (b) Differentiating, then gathering all terms in dY, dr, and dI on the left-hand side, we obtain
(i) $(C'_Y - 1) dY + C'_r dr + dI = -d\alpha$ (ii) $F'_Y dY + F'_r dr - dI = -d\beta$ (iii) $L'_Y dY + L'_r dr = dM$.
With $d\beta = dM = 0$ we get $dY = -(L'_r/D) d\alpha$, $dr = (L'_Y/D) d\alpha$, and $dI = [(F'_r L'_Y - F'_Y L'_r)/D] d\alpha$, where $D = L'_r(C'_Y + F'_Y - 1) - L'_Y(C'_r + F'_r)$.

8. (a) There are 3 variables and 2 equations, so there is (in general) one degree of freedom.
(b) Differentiation gives $0 = \alpha P dy + L'(r) dr$ and $S'_y dy + S'_r dr + S'_g dg = I'_y dy + I'_r dr$. We find $dy/dg = -L'(r)S'_g/D$ and $dr/dg = \alpha P S'_g/D$, where $D = L'(r)(S'_y - I'_y) - \alpha P(S'_r - I'_r)$.

9. (a) Differentiation yields $2uv\, du + u^2\, dv - du = 3x^2\, dx + 6y^2\, dy$, and $e^{ux}(u\, dx + x\, du) = v\, dy + y\, dv$. At P these equations become $3\, du + 4\, dv = 6\, dy$ and $dv = 2\, dx - dy$. Hence $du = 2dy - (4/3)\, dv = -(8/3)\, dx + (10/3)\, dy$. So $\partial u/\partial y = 10/3$ and $\partial v/\partial x = 2$.
(b) $\Delta u \approx du = -(8/3)0.1 + (10/3)(-0.2) = -14/15 \approx -0.93$, $\quad \Delta v \approx dv = 2(0.1) + (-1)(-0.2) = 0.4$

10. Taking differentials and putting $dp_2 = dm = 0$ gives: (i) $U''_{11}\, dx_1 + U''_{12}\, dx_2 = p_1\, d\lambda + \lambda\, dp_1$;
(ii) $U''_{21}\, dx_1 + U''_{22}\, dx_2 = p_2\, d\lambda$; (iii) $p_1\, dx_1 + dp_1\, x_1 + p_2\, dx_2 = 0$. Solving for dx_1 we obtain, in particular, $\partial x_1/\partial p_1 = [\lambda p_2^2 + x_1(p_2 U''_{12} - p_1 U''_{22})]/(p_1^2 U''_{22} - 2p_1 p_2 U''_{12} + p_2^2 U''_{11})$.

Review Problems for Chapter 12

1. (a) $dz/dt = 6 \cdot 4t + 3y^2 9t^2 = 24t + 27t^2 y^2 = 24t + 243t^8$ (b) $dz/dt = px^{p-1}a + py^{p-1}b = pt^{p-1}(a^p + b^p)$
(c) In part (a), $z = 6(2t^2) + (3t^3)^3 = 12t^2 + 27t^9$, so $dz/dt = 24t + 243t^8$. In part (b), $z = (at)^p + (bt)^p = a^p t^p + b^p t^p$, so $dz/dt = (a^p + b^p)pt^{p-1}$.

2. $\partial z/\partial t = G'_1(u, v)\phi'_1(t, s)$ and $\partial z/\partial s = G'_1(u, v)\phi'_2(t, s) + G'_2(u, v)\psi'(s)$

3. $\partial w/\partial t = 2x \cdot 1 + 3y^2 \cdot 1 + 4z^3 s = 2x + 3y^2 + 4sz^3 = 4s^4 t^3 + 3s^2 + 3t^2 - 6ts + 2s + 2t$,
$\partial w/\partial s = 2x - 3y^2 + 4tz^3 = 4s^3 t^4 - 3s^2 - 3t^2 + 6ts + 2s + 2t$

4. $dX/dN = g(u) + g'(u)(\varphi'(N) - u)$, where $u = \varphi(N)/N$, and $d^2 X/dN^2 = (1/N)g''(u)(\varphi'(N) - u)^2 + g'(u)\varphi''(N)$.

5. (a) Take the natural logarithm, $\ln E = \ln A - a \ln p + b \ln m$, and then differentiate to get $\dot{E}/E = -a(\dot{p}/p) + b(\dot{m}/m)$. (b) $\ln p = \ln p_0 + t \ln(1.06)$, so $\dot{p}/p = \ln 1.06$. Likewise, $\dot{m}/m = \ln 1.08$. Then $\dot{E}/E = -a \ln 1.06 + b \ln 1.08 = \ln(1.08^b/1.06^a) = \ln Q$.

6. Differentiating each side w.r.t. x while holding y constant gives $3x^2 \ln x + x^2 = (6z^2 \ln z + 2z^2)z'_1$. When $x = y = z = e$, this gives $z'_1 = 1/2$. Differentiating a second time, $6x \ln x + 5x = (12z \ln z + 10z)(z'_1)^2 + (6z^2 \ln z + 2z^2)z''_{11}$. When $x = y = z = e$ and $z'_1 = 1/2$, this gives $z''_{11} = 11/16e$.

7. $R_{yx} = F'_x/F'_y = -x/10y$. Hence $y/x = -(1/10)R_{yx}^{-1}$, and so $\sigma_{yx} = \mathrm{El}_{R_{yx}}(y/x) = -1$.

8. (a) MRS $= R_{yx} = U'_x/U'_y = 2y/3x$ (b) MRS $= R_{yx} = y/(x+1)$ (c) MRS $= R_{yx} = (y/x)^3$

9. (a) -1 (b) $2ac$ (c) 4. (d) Not homogeneous. (If F were homogeneous, then by Euler's theorem, for some constant k, we would have $x_1 e^{x_1+x_2+x_3} + x_2 e^{x_1+x_2+x_3} + x_3 e^{x_1+x_2+x_3} = k e^{x_1+x_2+x_3}$ for all positive x_1, x_2, x_3, and so $x_1 + x_2 + x_3 = k$. This is evidently impossible.)

10. Since $y/x = (R_{yx})^{1/3}$, $\sigma_{yx} = \mathrm{El}_{R_{yx}}(y/x) = 1/3$.

11. $\mathrm{El}_x\, y = xy/(1-2y)$. (*Hint:* Take the elasticity w.r.t x of $y^2 e^x e^{1/y} = 3$.)   **12.** (a) 1 (b) k (c) 0

13. Since F is homogeneous of degree 1, according to (12.6.6), we have $K F''_{KK} + L F''_{KL} = 0$, so that $F''_{KL} = -(K/L)F''_{KK} > 0$ since $F''_{KK} < 0$ and $K > 0, L > 0$.

14. Differentiate $f(tx_1, \ldots, tx_n) = g(t) f(x_1, \ldots, x_n)$ w.r.t. t and put $t = 1$, as in the proof of Euler's theorem (Theorem 12.7.1). This yields $\sum_{i=1}^{n} x_i f'_i(x_1, \ldots, x_n) = g'(1) f(x_1, \ldots, x_n)$. Thus, by Euler's theorem, f must be homogeneous of degree $g'(1)$. In fact, $g(t) = t^k$ where $k = g'(1)$.

15. $du + e^y\, dx + xe^y\, dy + dv = 0$ and $dx + e^{u+v^2}\, du + e^{u+v^2} 2v\, dv - dy = 0$. At the given point, these equations reduce to $du + dv = -e\, dx - e\, dy$ and $du = -e\, dx + e\, dy$, implying that $u'_x = -e$, $u'_y = e$, $v'_x = 0$, and $v'_y = -2e$.

16. (a) $\partial p/\partial w = L/F(L)$, $\partial p/\partial B = 1/F(L)$, $\partial L/\partial w = (F(L) - L F'(L))/pF(L)F''(L)$, $\partial L/\partial B = -F'(L)/pF(L)F''(L)$ (b) See SM.

17. (a) $\alpha u^{\alpha-1}\, du + \beta v^{\beta-1}\, dv = 2^\beta\, dx + 3y^2\, dy$ and $\alpha u^{\alpha-1} v^\beta\, du + u^\alpha \beta v^{\beta-1}\, dv - \beta v^{\beta-1}\, dv = dx - dy$. At P we find $\partial u/\partial x = 2^{-\beta}/\alpha$, $\partial u/\partial y = -2^{-\beta}/\alpha$, $\partial v/\partial x = (2^\beta - 2^{-\beta})/\beta 2^{\beta-1}$, $\partial v/\partial y = (2^{-\beta} + 3)/\beta 2^{\beta-1}$.
(b) $u(0.99, 1.01) \approx u(1,1) + \partial u(1,1)/\partial x \cdot (-0.01) + \partial u(1,1)/\partial y \cdot 0.01 = 1 - 2^{-\beta}/100\alpha - 2^{-\beta}/100\alpha = 1 - 2^{-\beta}/50\alpha$.

18. (a) $S = \displaystyle\int_0^T e^{-rx}(e^{gT-gx} - 1)\, dx = e^{gT} \int_0^T e^{-(r+g)x}\, dx - \int_0^T e^{-rx}\, dx = \dfrac{e^{gT} - e^{-rT}}{r+g} + \dfrac{e^{-rT} - 1}{r}$, and therefore $r(r+g)S = re^{gT} + ge^{-rT} - (r+g)$. (b) Implicit differentiation w.r.t. g yields $rS = re^{gT}(T + g\partial T/\partial g) + e^{-rT} + ge^{-rT}(-r\partial T/\partial g) - 1$, so $\partial T/\partial g = [rS + 1 - rTe^{gT} - e^{-rT}]/rg(e^{gT} - e^{-rT})$.

19. (a) Economic interpretation of $(*)$: How much do we gain by waiting one year? Approximately $V'(t^*)$. How much do we lose? Forgone interest $rV(t^*)$ plus the yearly cost m. (b) and (c) see SM.

Chapter 13

13.1

1. The first-order conditions $f'_1(x, y) = -4x + 4 = 0$ and $f'_2(x, y) = -2y + 4 = 0$ are both satisfied when $x = 1$ and $y = 2$.

2. (a) $f'_1(x, y) = 2x - 6$ and $f'_2(x, y) = 2y + 8$, which are both zero at the only stationary point $(x, y) = (3, -4)$.
(b) $f(x, y) = x^2 - 6x + 3^2 + y^2 + 8y + 4^2 + 35 - 3^2 - 4^2 = (x-3)^2 + (y+4)^2 + 10 \geq 10$ for all (x, y), whereas $f(3, -4) = 10$, so $(3, -4)$ minimizes f.

3. $F'_K = -2(K-3) - (L-6)$ and $F'_L = -4(L-6) - (K-3)$, so the first-order conditions yield $-2(K-3) - (L-6) = 0.65$, $-4(L-6) - (K-3) = 1.2$. The only solution of these two simultaneous equations is $(K, L) = (2.8, 5.75)$.

4. (a) $P(10, 8) = P(12, 10) = 98$ (b) First-order conditions: $P'_x = -2x + 22 = 0$, $P'_y = -2y + 18 = 0$. It follows that $x = 11$ and $y = 9$, where profits are $P(11, 9) = 100$.

13.2

1. We check that the conditions in part (a) of Theorem 13.2.1 are satisfied in all three cases:
(a) $\partial^2 \pi/\partial x^2 = -0.08 \leq 0$, $\partial^2 \pi/\partial y^2 = -0.02 \leq 0$, and $(\partial^2 \pi/\partial x^2)(\partial^2 \pi/\partial y^2) - (\partial^2 \pi/\partial x \partial y)^2 = 0.0015 \geq 0$.

(b) $f_{11}'' = -4$, $f_{12}'' = 0$, and $f_{22}'' = -2$ for all (x, y).
(c) With $\pi = F(K, L) - 0.65K - 1.2L$, $\pi_{KK}'' = -2$, $\pi_{KL}'' = -1$, and $\pi_{LL}'' = -4$.

2. (a) Profit: $\pi(x, y) = 24x + 12y - C(x, y) = -2x^2 - 4y^2 + 4xy + 64x + 32y - 514$. Maximum at $x = 40$, $y = 24$, with $\pi(40, 24) = 1150$. Since $\pi_{11}'' = -4 \le 0$, $\pi_{22}'' = -8 \le 0$, and $\pi_{11}''\pi_{22}'' - (\pi_{12}'')^2 = 16 \ge 0$, this is the maximum.
(b) $x = 34$, $y = 20$. (With $y = 54 - x$, profits are $\hat{\pi} = -2x^2 - 4(54 - x)^2 + 4x(54 - x) + 64x + 32(54 - x) - 514 = -10x^2 + 680x - 10450$, which has a maximum at $x = 34$. Then $y = 54 - 34 = 20$. The maximum value is 1110.)

3. Maximum 3888 at $x = 36$, $y = 12$, $z = 9$.

4. (a) $\pi(x, y) = px + qy - C(x, y) = (25 - x)x + (24 - 2y)y - (3x^2 + 3xy + y^2) = -4x^2 - 3xy - 3y^2 + 25x + 24y$.
(b) $\pi_1' = -8x - 3y + 25 = 0$ and $\pi_2' = -3x - 6y + 24 = 0$ when $(x, y) = (2, 3)$. Moreover, then $\pi_{11}'' = -8 \le 0$, $\pi_{22}'' = -6 \le 0$, and $\pi_{11}''\pi_{22}'' - (\pi_{12}'')^2 = (-8)(-6) - (-3)^2 = 39 \ge 0$. So $(x, y) = (2, 3)$ maximizes profits.

5. The profit is $\pi(x, y) = px + qy - x^2 - xy - y^2 - x - y - 14$. Profit is stationary at $x^* = \frac{1}{3}(2p - q - 1)$ and $y^* = \frac{1}{3}(-p + 2q - 1)$. Provided that $q < 2p - 1$ and $q > \frac{1}{2}(p + 1)$, the sufficient conditions in Theorem 13.2.1 for an interior point (x^*, y^*) to maximize profits are easily seen to be satisfied.

6. (a) $x^* = p/2\alpha$, $y^* = q/2\beta$, and the second-order conditions are satisfied.
(b) $\pi^*(p, q) = px^* + qy^* - \alpha(x^*)^2 - \beta(y^*)^2 = p^2/4\alpha + q^2/2\beta$. Hence $\partial\pi^*(p, q)/\partial p = p/2\alpha = x^*$. So increasing the price p by one unit increases the optimal profit by approximately x^*, the output of the first good. $\partial\pi^*(p, q)/\partial q = y^*$ has a similar interpretation.

7. The constraint implies that $z = 4x + 2y - 5$. Using this to substitute for z, we choose (x, y) to minimize $P(x, y) = x^2 + y^2 + (4x + 2y - 5)^2$ w.r.t. x and y. The first-order conditions are: $P_1' = 34x + 16y - 40 = 0$, $P_2' = 16x + 10y - 20 = 0$, with solution $x = 20/21$, $y = 10/21$. Since $P_{11}'' = 34$, $P_{12}'' = 16$, and $P_{22}'' = 10$, the second-order conditions for minimum are satisfied. The minimum value is $525/441$.

8. $f_{11}'' = a(a - 1)Ax^{a-2}y^b$, $f_{12}'' = f_{21}'' = abAx^{a-1}y^{b-1}$, and $f_{22}'' = b(b - 1)Ax^a y^{b-2}$. Thus, $f_{11}''f_{22}'' - (f_{12}'')^2 = abA^2x^{2a-2}y^{2b-2}[1 - (a + b)]$. Suppose that $a + b \le 1$. Then $a \le 1$ and $b \le 1$ as well. If $x > 0$ and $y > 0$, then $f_{11}'' \le 0$ and $f_{22}'' \le 0$, and $f_{11}''f_{22}'' - (f_{12}'')^2 \ge 0$. We conclude from Note 2 that f is concave for $x > 0$, $y > 0$.

13.3

1. (a) $f_1' = -2x + 6$, $f_2' = -4y + 8$, $f_{11}'' = -2$, $f_{12}'' = 0$, and $f_{22}'' = -4$.   (b) $(3, 2)$ is a local maximum point, because $A = -2 < 0$ and $AC - B^2 = 8 > 0$. Theorem 13.2.1 implies that $(3, 2)$ is a (global) maximum point.

2. (a) $f_1' = 2x + 2y^2$, $f_2' = 4xy + 4y$, $f_{11}'' = 2$, $f_{12}'' = 4y$, $f_{22}'' = 4x + 4$
(b) $f_2' = 0 \iff 4y(x + 1) = 0 \iff x = -1$ or $y = 0$. If $x = -1$, then $f_1' = 0$ for $y = \pm 1$. If $y = 0$, then $f_1' = 0$ for $x = 0$. Thus we get the three stationary points classified in the table:

(x, y)	A	B	C	$AC - B^2$	Type of stationary point:
$(0, 0)$	2	0	4	8	Local minimum point
$(-1, 1)$	2	4	0	-16	Saddle point
$(-1, -1)$	2	-4	0	-16	Saddle point

3. (a) $(0, 0)$ is a saddle point and $(-a, -2)$ is a local minimum point.   (b) $df^*(a)/da = -2ae^{-2}$

4. (a) $f_t'(t^*, x^*) = rf(t^*, x^*)$ and $f_x'(t^*, x^*) = e^{rt^*}$ (b) $g'(t^*) = rg(t^*)$ and $h'(x^*) = e^{rt^*}/g(t^*)$ (c) See SM.
(d) $t^* = 1/4r^2$, $x^* = e^{1/4r} - 1$

5. In all three cases $(0, 0)$ is a stationary point where $z = 0$ and $A = B = C = 0$, so $AC - B^2 = 0$. In case (a), $z \le 0$ for all (x, y), so the origin is a maximum point. In case (b), $z \ge 0$ for all (x, y), so the origin is a minimum point. In (c), z takes positive and negative values at points arbitrarily close to the origin, so it is a saddle point.

6. (a) f is defined for $x = 0$ and for $y > -1/x^2$. (b) $f_1'(x, y) = 2xy/(1 + x^2y)$ and $f_2'(x, y) = x^2/(1 + x^2y)$. Here $f_1' = f_2' = 0$ at all points $(0, b)$ with $b \in \mathbb{R}$. (c) Because $AC - B^2 = 0$ when $(x, y) = (0, b)$, the second-derivative test fails. (d) Note that $f(0, b) = 0$ at any stationary point $(0, b)$. By considering the sign of $f(x, y) = \ln(1 + x^2y)$ in the neighbourhood of any stationary point, one sees that f has: a local maximum point if $b < 0$; a saddle point if $b = 0$; and a local minimum point if $b > 0$. See Fig. A13.3.6.

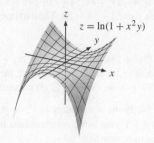

Figure A13.3.6

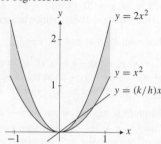

Figure A13.3.7

7. (a) See Fig. A13.3.7. The domain where $f(x, y)$ is negative is shaded. The origin is easily seen to be the only stationary point, and $f(0, 0) = 0$. As the figure shows, $f(x, y)$ takes positive and negative values for points arbitrary close to $(0, 0)$, so the origin is a saddle point. (b) $g(t) = f(th, tk) = (tk - t^2h^2)(tk - 2t^2h^2) = 2h^4t^4 - 3h^2kt^3 + k^2t^2$, so $g'(t) = 8h^4t^3 - 9h^2kt^2 + 2k^2t$ and $g''(t) = 24h^4t^2 - 18h^2kt + 2k^2$. So $g'(0) = 0$ and $g''(0) = 2k^2$. Thus $t = 0$ is a minimum point for $k \neq 0$. For $k = 0$, $g(t) = 2t^4h^4$, which has a minimum at $t = 0$.

13.4

1. (a) $\pi = P_1Q_1 + P_2Q_2 - C(Q_1, Q_2) = -2Q_1^2 - 4Q_2^2 + 180Q_1 + 160Q_2$, which has a maximum at $Q_1^* = 45$, $Q_2^* = 20$, with $P_1^* = 110$, $P_2^* = 100$, and $\pi^* = 5650$ (b) Let $P = P_1 = P_2$. Then $Q_1 = 100 - \frac{1}{2}P$, $Q_2 = 45 - \frac{1}{4}P$, so profit as a function of P is $\widehat{\pi} = (P - 20)(Q_1 + Q_2) = (P - 20)(145 - \frac{3}{4}P) = -\frac{3}{4}P^2 + 160P - 2900$, which is maximized when $P = 320/3$. Corresponding profit: $16900/3$. Lost profit: $5650 - 16900/3 = 50/3$.
(c) New profit: $\widetilde{\pi} = -2Q_1^2 - 4Q_2^2 + 175Q_1 + 160Q_2$, with maximum at $Q_1 = 43.75$, $Q_2 = 20$, with prices $P_1 = 112.50$ and $P_2 = 100$. Profit is 5428.125. The number of units sold in market 1 goes down, the price goes up and profits are lower. In market 2 the number of units sold and the price are unchanged.

2. (a) $\pi = -bp^2 - dq^2 + (a + \beta b)p + (c + \beta d)q - \alpha - \beta(a + c)$, $p^* = (a + \beta b)/2b$, $q^* = (c + \beta d)/2d$. The second-order conditions are obviously satisfied because $\pi_{11}'' = -2b$, $\pi_{12}'' = 0$, and $\pi_{22}'' = -2d$.
(b) $\hat{p} = (a + c + \beta(b + d))/2(b + d)$. (c) See SM.

3. Imposing a tax of t per unit sold in market area 1 means that the new profit function is $\widehat{\pi}(Q_1, Q_2) = \pi(Q_1, Q_2) - tQ_1$. The optimal choice of production in market area 1 is then $\widehat{Q}_1 = (a_1 - \alpha - t)/2b_1$ (see the text), and the tax revenue is $T(t) = t(a_1 - \alpha - t)/2b_1 = [t(a_1 - \alpha) - t^2]/2b_1$. This quadratic function has a maximum when $T'(t) = 0$, so $t = \frac{1}{2}(a_1 - \alpha)$.

4. (a) $\hat{a} = 0.105$ and $\hat{b} = 11.29$. (b) $\hat{c} = 0.23$, $\hat{d} = 5.575$. (c) The goal would have been reached in 1979.

5. (a) $p = 9$, $q = 8$, $x = 16$, $y = 4$. A's profit is 123, whereas B's is 21. (b) Firm A's profit is maximized at $p = p_A(q) = \frac{1}{5}(2q + 17)$. Firm B's profit is maximized at $q = q_B(p) = \frac{1}{3}(p + 7)$. (c) Equilibrium occurs where $p = 5$, $q = 4$, $x = 20$, $y = 12$. A gets 75, B gets 21. (d) See SM.

13.5

1. (a) $f_1'(x, y) = 4 - 4x$ and $f_2'(x, y) = -4y$. The only stationary point is $(1, 0)$, with $f(1, 0) = 2$.
(b) $f(x, y)$ has maximum 2 at $(1, 0)$ and minimum -70 at $(-5, 0)$. (A maximum and a minimum exist, by the extreme value theorem. Along the boundary, the function value is $4x - 50$, with $x \in [-5, 5]$. So its maximum along the boundary is -30 at $x = 5$ and its minimum is -70 at $x = -5$.)

2. (a) Maximum 91 at $(0, 4)$ and at $(4, 0)$. Minimum 0 at $(3, 3)$.

(b) Maximum 9/4 at $(-1/2, \sqrt{3}/2)$ and at $(-1/2, -\sqrt{3}/2)$. Minimum $-1/4$ at $(1/2, 0)$.

3. See Fig. A13.5.3. No stationary points in the interior. The maximum value of f is 27/8 at $(3/4, 0)$.

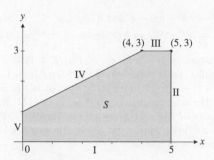

Figure A13.5.3

4. (a) The first-order conditions $2axy + by + 2y^2 = 0$ and $ax^2 + bx + 4xy = 0$ must have $(x, y) = (2/3, 1/3)$ as a solution. So $a = 1$ and $b = -2$. Also $c = 1/27$, so that $f(2/3, 1/3) = -1/9$. Because $A = f_{11}''(2/3, 1/3) = 2/3$, $B = f_{12}''(2/3, 1/3) = 2/3$, and $C = f_{22}''(2/3, 1/3) = 8/3$, Theorem 13.3.1 shows that this is a local minimum.

(b) Maximum 193/27 at $(2/3, 8/3)$. Minimum $-1/9$ at $(2/3, 1/3)$.

5. (a) $(1, 2)$ is a local minimum; $(0, 0)$ and $(0, 4)$ are saddle points.   (b) Note that $f(x, 1) = -3xe^{-x} \to \infty$ as $x \to -\infty$, and $f(-1, y) = -e(y^2 - 4y) \to -\infty$ as $y \to \infty$.   (c) f has a minimum $-4/e$ at $(1, 2)$, and maximum 0 at all $(x, 0)$ and $(x, 4)$ satisfying $x \in [0, 5]$, as well as at all $(0, y)$ satisfying $y \in [0, 4]$.

(d) $y' = 0$ when $x = 1$ and $y = 4 - e$.

6. (a) Closed and bounded, so compact.   (b) Open and unbounded.   (c) Closed and bounded, so compact.

(d) Closed and unbounded.   (e) Closed and unbounded.   (f) Open and unbounded.

7. Let $g(x) = 1$ in $[0, 1)$, $g(x) = 2$ in $[1, 2]$. Then g is discontinuous at $x = 1$, and the set $\{x : g(x) \le 1\} = [0, 1)$ is not closed. (Draw your own graph of g.)

13.6

1. (a) The first-order conditions $f_x'(x, y, z) = 2 - 2x = 0$, $f_y'(x, y, z) = 10 - 2y = 0$, and $f_z'(x, y, z) = -2z = 0$ have a unique solution $(x, y, z) = (1, 5, 0)$, which must then be the maximum point.   (b) The first-order conditions are $f_x'(x, y, z) = -2x - 2y - 2z = 0$, $f_y'(x, y, z) = -4y - 2x = 0$, $f_z'(x, y, z) = -6z - 2x = 0$. From the last two equations we get $y = -\frac{1}{2}x$ and $z = -\frac{1}{3}x$. Inserting this into the first equation we get $-2x + x + \frac{2}{3}x = 0$, and thus $x = 0$, implying that $y = z = 0$. So $(x, y, z) = (0, 0, 0)$ is the maximum point.

2. (a) $f(x) = e^{-x^2}$ and $g(x) = F(f(x)) = \ln(e^{-x^2}) = -x^2$ both have a unique maximum at $x = 0$.

(b) Only $x = 0$ maximizes $f(x)$. But $g(x) = 5$ is maximized at every point x because it is a constant.

3. By the chain rule, $g_i'(\mathbf{x}) = F'(f(\mathbf{x}))f_i'(\mathbf{x})$ for $i = 1, 2, \ldots, n$. Because $F' \ne 0$ everywhere, the assertion follows.

4. $f_x' = -6x^2 + 30x - 36$, $f_y' = 2 - e^{y^2}$, $f_z' = -3 + e^{z^2}$. The 8 stationary points are $(x, y, z) = (3, \pm\sqrt{\ln 2}, \pm\sqrt{\ln 3})$, and $(x, y, z) = (2, \pm\sqrt{\ln 2}, \pm\sqrt{\ln 3})$, where all combinations of signs are allowed.

5. (a) Because $F(u) = \frac{1}{2}(e^u - e^{-u})$ is strictly increasing, the problem is equivalent to: max $x^2 + y^2 - 2x$ subject to $(x, y) \in S$.   (b) The problem is equivalent to: max $\ln A + a_1 \ln x_1 + \cdots + a_n \ln x_n$ subject to $x_1 + \cdots + x_n = 1$.

13.7

1. (a) The profit is $\pi = px - ax - bx^2 - tx$, which has a maximum at $x^* = (p-a-t)/2b$, with $\pi^* = (p-a-t)^2/4b$.
(b) $\partial \pi^*/\partial p = 2(p-a-t)/4b = x^*$. If we increase p by 1 dollar, then the optimal profit increases by x^* dollars.
(For each of the x^* units sold the revenue increases by 1 dollar.)

2. (a) $\pi = p(K^{2/3} + L^{1/2} + T^{1/3}) - rK - wL - q$, and $K^* = \frac{8}{27}p^3 r^{-3}$, $L^* = \frac{1}{4}p^2 w^{-2}$, $T^* = \frac{1}{3\sqrt{3}}p^{3/2}q^{-3/2}$
(b) $Q^* = \frac{4}{9}p^2 r^{-2} + \frac{1}{2}pw^{-1} + \frac{1}{\sqrt{3}}p^{1/2}q^{-1/2}$, so $\partial Q^*/\partial r = -\frac{8}{9}p^2 r^{-3} = -\partial K^*/\partial p$

3. (a) $\pi = \pi(L, P, w, a) = Pa\ln(L+1) - wL$, $\pi'_L = Pa/(L+1) - w = 0$ for $L = aP/w - 1$. Since
$\pi''_{LL} = -aP/(L+1)^2 < 0$ for all L, profit is maximized at $L^* = aP/w - 1$.
(b) $\pi'_P(L^*, P, w, a) = a\ln(L^*+1) = a\ln(aP/w)$, $\pi'_w(L^*, P, w, a) = -L^* = 1 - aP/w$, and $\pi'_a(L^*, P, w, a) = P\ln(L^*+1) = P\ln(aP/w)$. The value function is $\pi^*(P, w, a) = \pi(L^*, P, w, a) = aP\ln(L^*+1) - wL^* = aP\ln(aP/w) - aP + w = aP\ln a + aP\ln P - aP\ln w - aP + w$. Then $\partial \pi^*/\partial P = a\ln a + a\ln P + aP/P - a\ln w - a = a\ln(aP/w)$. $\partial \pi^*/\partial w = -aP/w + 1$. Finally, $\partial \pi^*/\partial a = P\ln a + aP/a + P\ln P - P\ln w - P = P\ln(aP/w)$.
The envelope theorem is confirmed in all cases.

4. $\partial Q^*/\partial r = (\partial/\partial r)(\partial \hat{\pi}^*/\partial p) = (\partial/\partial p)(\partial \hat{\pi}^*/\partial r) = (\partial/\partial p)(-K^*) = -\partial K^*/\partial p$. The other equalities are proved in a similar way.

5. (a) See SM.   (b) Suppressing the fact that the partials are evaluated at (K^*, L^*), we get

$$\frac{\partial K^*}{\partial p} = \frac{-F'_K F''_{LL} + F'_L F''_{KL}}{p(F''_{KK} F''_{LL} - (F''_{KL})^2)}, \quad \frac{\partial L^*}{\partial p} = \frac{-F'_L F''_{KK} + F'_K F''_{LK}}{p(F''_{KK} F''_{LL} - (F''_{KL})^2)}, \quad \frac{\partial K^*}{\partial r} = \frac{F''_{LL}}{p(F''_{KK} F''_{LL} - (F''_{KL})^2)},$$

$$\frac{\partial L^*}{\partial r} = \frac{-F''_{LK}}{p(F''_{KK} F''_{LL} - (F''_{KL})^2)}, \quad \frac{\partial K^*}{\partial w} = \frac{-F''_{KL}}{p(F''_{KK} F''_{LL} - (F''_{KL})^2)}, \quad \frac{\partial L^*}{\partial w} = \frac{F''_{KK}}{p(F''_{KK} F''_{LL} - (F''_{KL})^2)}.$$

(c) We see that $\partial K^*/\partial r$ and $\partial L^*/\partial w$ are both negative. Since we have no information about the sign of F''_{KL}, the signs of the other partials are not determined by the sufficient conditions for profit maximization. We observe that $\partial K^*/\partial w = \partial L^*/\partial r$, since $F''_{KL} = F''_{LK}$.

6. (a) First-order conditions: (i) $R'_1 - C'_1 + s = 0$, (ii) $R'_2 - C'_2 - t = 0$.   (b) $\pi''_{11} = R''_{11} - C''_{11} < 0$ and $D = \pi''_{11}\pi''_{22} - (\pi''_{12})^2 = (R''_{11} - C''_{11})(R''_{22} - C''_{22}) - (R''_{12} - C''_{12})^2 > 0$.   For (c) and (d) see SM.

Review Problems for Chapter 13

1. The first-order conditions $f'_1(x, y) = -4x + 2y + 18 = 0$ and $f'_2(x, y) = 2x - 2y - 14 = 0$ are satisfied at $(x, y) = (2, -5)$. Moreover, $f''_{11} = -4$, $f''_{12} = 2$, and $f''_{22} = -2$, so $f''_{11}f''_{22} - (f''_{12})^2 = 4$. The conditions in (a) in Theorem 13.2.1 are satisfied.)

2. (a) $(Q_1, Q_2) = (500, 200)$ (b) $P_1 = 105$

3. (a) Stationary points where $P'_1(x, y) = -0.2x - 0.2y + 47 = 0$ and $P'_2(x, y) = -0.2x - 0.4y + 48 = 0$. It follows that $x = 230$ and $y = 5$. Moreover, $P''_{11} = -0.2 \leq 0$, $P''_{12} = -0.2$, and $P''_{22} = -0.4 \leq 0$. Since also $P''_{11}P''_{22} - (P''_{12})^2 = 0.04 \geq 0$, $(230, 5)$ maximizes profit.   (b) With $x + y = 200$, and so $y = 200 - x$, the new profit function is $\hat{\pi}(x) = f(x, 200 - x) = -0.1x^2 + 39x + 1000$. This function is easily seen to have maximum at $x = 195$. Then $y = 200 - 195 = 5$.

4. (a) Stationary points at $(0, 0$ and $(3, 9/2)$.   (b) $(0, 0)$, $(\frac{1}{2}\sqrt{2}, \sqrt{2})$, $(-\frac{1}{2}\sqrt{2}, -\sqrt{2})$ (c) $(0, 0)$, $(0, 4)$, $(2, 2)$, and $(-2, 2)$.

5. Stationary points are where $f'_x(x, y, a) = 2ax - 2 = 0$ and $f'_y(x, y, a) = 2y - 4a = 0$, or $x = x^*(a) = 1/a$ and $y = y^*(a) = 2a$. The value function is $f^*(a) = a(1/a)^2 - 2(1/a) + (2a)^2 - 4a(2a) = -(1/a) - 4a^2$. Thus $(d/da)f^*(a) = (1/a^2) - 8a$. On the other hand $(\partial/\partial a)f(x, y, a) = x^2 - 4y = (1/a^2) - 8a$ at $(x^*(a), y^*(a))$. This verifies the envelope theorem.

6. (a) $K^* = (ap/r)^{1/(1-a)}$, $L^* = (bp/w)^{1/(1-b)}$, $T^* = (cp/q)^{1/(1-c)}$. For (b) and (c) see SM.

7. (a) $f_1' = e^{x+y} + e^{x-y} - \frac{3}{2}$, $f_2' = e^{x+y} - e^{x-y} - \frac{1}{2}$, $f_{11}'' = e^{x+y} + e^{x-y}$, $f_{12}'' = e^{x+y} - e^{x-y}$, $f_{22}'' = e^{x+y} + e^{x-y}$. It follows that $f_{11}'' \geq 0$, $f_{22}'' \geq 0$, and $f_{11}'' f_{22}'' - (f_{12}'')^2 = (e^{x+y} + e^{x-y})^2 - (e^{x+y} - e^{x-y})^2 = 4e^{x+y}e^{x-y} = 4e^{2x} \geq 0$, so f is convex.

(b) At the stationary point, $e^{x+y} = 1$ and $e^{x-y} = \frac{1}{2}$, so $x + y = 0$ and $x - y = -\ln 2$. The stationary point is therefore $(x, y) = (-\frac{1}{2}\ln 2, \frac{1}{2}\ln 2)$, where $f(x, y) = \frac{1}{2}(3 + \ln 2)$. Because f is convex, this is the minimum.

8. (a) $(0, 0)$ saddle point, $(5/6, -5/12)$ local maximum point.   (b) $f_{11}'' = 2 - 6x \leq 0 \iff x \geq 1/3$, while $f_{22}'' = -2 \leq 0$, and $f_{11}'' f_{22}'' - (f_{12}'')^2 = 12x - 5 \geq 0 \iff x \geq 5/12$. We conclude that f is concave if and only if $x \geq 5/12$. The largest value of f in S is $125/432$, obtained at $(5/6, -5/12)$.

9. (a) $f_1'(x, y) = x - 1 + ay$, $f_2'(x, y) = a(x - 1) - y^2 + 2a^2 y$, which are both 0 at $(x, y) = (1 - a^3, a^2)$. For (b) and (c), see SM.

10. (a) $p = C_x'(x^*, y^*)$ and $q = C_y'(x^*, y^*)$ are the familiar conditions that at the optimum the price of each good should equal marginal cost.   (b) With a simplified notation, at the optimum (x^*, y^*), $\hat{\pi}_x' = F + xF_x' + yG_x' - C_x' = 0$ and $\hat{\pi}_y' = xF_y' + G + yG_y' - C_y' = 0$. The interpretation is that marginal revenue = marginal cost, as usual, with the twist that a change in output of either good affects revenue in the other market as well.   (c) The profit function is $\pi = x(a - bx - cy) + y(\alpha - \beta x - \gamma y) - Px - Qy - R$, and the first-order conditions are $\partial \pi / \partial x = a - 2bx - cy - \beta y - P = 0$, $\partial \pi / \partial y = -cx + \alpha - \beta x - 2\gamma y - Q = 0$.
(d) $\partial^2 \pi / \partial x^2 = -2b$, $\partial^2 \pi / \partial y^2 = -2\gamma$, $\partial^2 \pi / \partial x \partial y = -(\beta + c)$. The direct partials of order 2 are negative and $\Delta = (\partial^2 \pi / \partial x^2)(\partial^2 \pi / \partial y^2) - (\partial^2 \pi / \partial x \partial y)^2 = 4\gamma b - (\beta + c)^2$, so the conclusion follows.

Chapter 14

14.1

1. (a) $\mathcal{L}(x, y) = xy - \lambda(x + 3y - 24)$. The first-order conditions $\mathcal{L}_1' = y - \lambda = 0$, $\mathcal{L}_2' = x - 3\lambda = 0$ imply that $x = 3y$. Inserted this into the constraint yields $3y + 3y = 24$, so $y = 4$, and then $x = 12$.   (b) Using (**) in Example 3 with $a = b = p = 1$, $q = 3$, and $m = 24$, we have $x = \frac{1}{2}(24/1) = 12$, $y = \frac{1}{2}(24/3) = 4$.

2. With $\mathcal{L} = -40Q_1 + Q_1^2 - 2Q_1 Q_2 - 20Q_2 + Q_2^2 - \lambda(Q_1 + Q_2 - 15)$, the first-order conditions are: $\mathcal{L}_1' = -40 + 2Q_1 - 2Q_2 - \lambda = 0$, $\mathcal{L}_2' = -2Q_1 - 20 + 2Q_2 - \lambda = 0$. It follows that $-40 + 2Q_1 - 2Q_2 = -2Q_1 - 20 + 2Q_2$, and so $Q_1 - Q_2 = 5$. This equation and the constraint together give the solution $Q_1 = 10$, $Q_2 = 5$, with $\lambda = -30$.

3. (a) According to (**) in Example 3, $x = \frac{3}{10}m$ and $y = \frac{1}{10}m$.   (b) $x = 10$, $y = 6\,250\,000$ (c) $x = 8/3$, $y = 1$

4. (a) $(x, y) = (4/5, 8/5)$ with $\lambda = 8/5$.   (b) $(x, y) = (8, 4)$ with $\lambda = 16$.   (c) $(x, y) = (50, 50)$ with $\lambda = 250$.

5. The budget constraint is $2x + 4y = 1000$, so with $\mathcal{L}(x, y) = 100xy + x + 2y - \lambda(2x + 4y - 1000)$, the first-order conditions are $\mathcal{L}_1' = 100y + 1 - 2\lambda = 0$ and $\mathcal{L}_2' = 100x + 2 - 4\lambda = 0$. From these equations, by eliminating λ, we get $x = 2y$, which inserted into the constraint gives $2x + 2x = 1000$. So $x = 250$ and $y = 125$.

6. $m = awT_0/(a + b)$, $l = bT_0/(a + b)$

7. The problem is: max $-0.1x^2 - 0.2xy - 0.2y^2 + 47x + 48y - 600$ subject to $x + y = 200$. With $\mathcal{L}(x, y) = -0.1x^2 - 0.2xy - 0.2y^2 + 47x + 48y - 600 - \lambda(x + y - 200)$, the first-order conditions are $\mathcal{L}_1' = -0.2x - 0.2y + 47 - \lambda = 0$ and $\mathcal{L}_2' = -0.2x - 0.4y + 48 - \lambda = 0$. Eliminating x and λ yields $y = 5$, and then the budget constraint gives $x = 195$, with $\lambda = 7$.

8. (a) $P(x, y) = (96 - 4x)x + (84 - 2y)y - 2x^2 - 2xy - y^2 = -6x^2 - 3y^2 - 2xy + 96x + 84y$
(b) $P_x'(x, y) = -12x - 2y + 96$, $P_y'(x, y) = -6y - 2x + 84$. The only stationary point is $(x, y) = (6, 12)$.
(c) With $\mathcal{L}(x, y) = -6x^2 - 3y^2 - 2xy + 96x + 84y - \lambda(x + y - 11)$, $\mathcal{L}_1' = -12x - 2y + 96 - \lambda = 0$, $\mathcal{L}_2' = -6y - 2x + 84 - \lambda = 0$. Eliminating λ yields $10x - 4y = 12$. The constraint is $x + y = 11$. Solving these two equations simultaneously gives $x = 4$, $y = 7$. Since $P(4, 7) = 673 < P(6, 12) = 792$, the production restriction reduces profit by 119.

9. (a) $x^*(p, m) = a^\gamma p^{-\gamma}$ where $\gamma = 1/(1 - a)$, and $y^*(p, m) = m - a^\gamma p^{1-\gamma}$. (b)–(d) see SM.

10. (a) $x(p, q, m) = [m + q \ln(q/p)]/(p + q)$, $y(p, q, m) = [m + p \ln(p/q)]/(p + q)$ (b) Direct verification.

14.2

1. According to $(**)$ in Example 14.1.3, the solution is $x^* = 3m/8$, $y^* = m/12$, with $\lambda = 9m^3/512$. The value function is $f^*(m) = (x^*)^3 y^* = 9m^4/2048$, so we see that $df^*(m)/dm = 9m^3/512 = \lambda$.

2. (a) With $\mathcal{L} = rK + wL - \lambda(\sqrt{K} + L - Q)$, the first-order conditions are $\mathcal{L}'_K = r - \lambda/2\sqrt{K^*} = 0$, $\mathcal{L}'_L = w - \lambda = 0$. Inserting λ from the last equation into the first yields $\sqrt{K^*} = w/2r$. Then $K^* = w^2/4r^2$ and from the constraint $L^* = Q - w/2r$. (b) The value function is $C^*(Q) = rK^* + wL^* = wQ - w^2/4r$, and so $dC^*(Q)/dQ = w = \lambda$.

3. (a) $x + 2y = a$ yields $y = \frac{1}{2}a - \frac{1}{2}x$, and then $x^2 + y^2 = x^2 + (\frac{1}{2}a - \frac{1}{2}x)^2 = \frac{5}{4}x^2 - \frac{1}{2}ax + \frac{1}{4}a^2$. This quadratic function has a minimum at $x = a/5$, and then $y = 2a/5$. (b) $\mathcal{L}(x, y) = x^2 + y^2 - \lambda(x + 2y - a)$. The necessary conditions are $\mathcal{L}'_1 = 2x - \lambda = 0$, $\mathcal{L}'_2 = 2y - 2\lambda = 0$, implying that $2x = y$. From the constraint, $x = a/5$ and then $y = 2a/5$, $\lambda = 2a/5$. (c) See Fig. A14.2.3. Find the point on the straight line $x + 2y = a$ which has the smallest distance from the origin. The corresponding maximization problem has no solution.

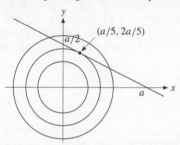

Figure A14.2.3

4. (a) $x^* = 4$, $y^* = 24$, $\lambda = 1/4$. (b) $\hat{y} = 97/4$, $\hat{x} = 4$. $\Delta U = 105/4 - 104/4 = 1/4$, the value of the Lagrange multiplier from (a). (There is exact equality here because U is linear in one of the variables.) (c) $x^* = q^2/4p^2$, $y^* = m/q - q/4p$. (Note that $y^* > 0$ if and only if $m > q^2/4p$.)

5. (a) First-order conditions: (i) $\alpha/(x^* - a) = \lambda p$; (ii) $\beta/(y^* - b) = \lambda q$. Hence $px^* = pa + \alpha/\lambda$ and $qy^* = qb + \beta/\lambda$. Use the budget constraint to eliminate λ. The expressions for px^* and qy^* follow. (b) $U^* = \alpha[\ln \alpha + \ln(m - (ap + bq)) - \ln p] + \beta[\ln \beta + \ln(m - (ap + bq)) - \ln q]$. The results follow.

6. $f(x, T) = -\frac{1}{6}\alpha x T^5 + \frac{1}{12}x T^4 + \frac{1}{6}x T^3$, $g(x, T) = \frac{1}{6}x T^3$. The solution of $(*)$ is $x = 384\alpha^3 M$, $T = 1/4\alpha$, $f^*(M) = M + M/16\alpha$, with $\lambda = 1 + 1/16\alpha$. Clearly, $\partial f^*(M)/\partial M = \lambda$, which confirms (2).

14.3

1. (a) $(2, 2)$ and $(-2, -2)$ are the only possible solutions of the maximization problem, and $(-2, 2)$ and $(2, -2)$ are the only possible solutions of the minimization problem. (b) $(3, -1)$ solves the maximization problem and $(-3, 1)$ solves the minimization problem.

2. (a) Maximum at $(x, y, \lambda) = (-4, 0, 5/4)$, minimum at $(x, y, \lambda) = (4/3, \pm 4\sqrt{2}/3, 1/4)$. (b) Minimum points: $(\sqrt[4]{2}, 1 - \frac{1}{2}\sqrt{2})$ and $(-\sqrt[4]{2}, 1 - \frac{1}{2}\sqrt{2})$

3. (a) $\mathcal{L} = x + y - \lambda(x^2 + y - 1)$. The equations $\mathcal{L}'_1 = 1 - 2\lambda x = 0$, $\mathcal{L}'_2 = 1 - \lambda = 0$, and $x^2 + y = 1$ have the solution $x = 1/2$, $y = 3/4$, and $\lambda = 1$. (b) See Fig. A14.3.3. The minimization problem has no solution because $f(x, 1 - x^2) = x + 1 - x^2 \to -\infty$ as $x \to \infty$. (c) New solution: $x = 0.5$ and $y = 0.85$. The change in the value function is $f^*(1.1) - f^*(1) = (0.5 + 0.85) - (0.5 + 0.75) = 0.1$. Because $\lambda = 1$, one has $\lambda \cdot dc = 1 \cdot 0.1 = 0.1$. So, in this case, (14.2.3) is satisfied with equality. (This is because of the special form of the functions f and g.)

4. (a) $x = 6$, $y = 2$ (b) The approximate change is 1.

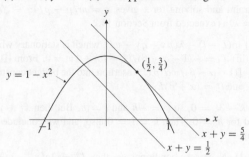

Figure A14.3.3

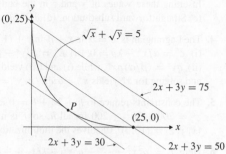

Figure A14.4.3

14.4

1. $\mathcal{L}(x, y) = xy - \lambda(x + y - 2)$, so the first-order conditions are $y - \lambda = 0$, $x - \lambda = 0$, with the unique solution $x = y = \lambda = 1$ satisfying the constraint $x + y = 2$. Then, when $\lambda = 1$, one has $\mathcal{L}(2, 2) = 2 > \mathcal{L}(1, 1) = 1$, so $(1, 1)$ is not a maximum point for $\mathcal{L}$. (In fact, $\mathcal{L}(x, y)$ has a saddle point at $(1, 1)$.)

2. The problem with systems of three equations and two unknowns is not that they are merely difficult to solve but that they are usually inconsistent—i.e., it is *impossible* to solve them. The equations $f_x'(x, y) = f_y'(x, y) = 0$ are NOT valid at the optimal point.

3. (a) With $\mathcal{L} = 2x + 3y - \lambda(\sqrt{x} + \sqrt{y} - 5)$, $\mathcal{L}_1'(x, y) = 2 - \lambda/2\sqrt{x} = 0$, $\mathcal{L}_2'(x, y) = 3 - \lambda/2\sqrt{y} = 0$. Thus $y = 4x/9$, so $x = 9$ and $y = 4$.   (b) See Fig. A14.4.3. Move the line $2x + 3y = c$ as far as possible in the north-east direction. So the solution is at $(x, y) = (0, 25)$.   (c) $g(x, y)$ is continuously differentiable only on the set A of (x, y) such that $x > 0$ and $y > 0$, so the theorem does not apply at the point $(x, y) = (0, 25)$.

4. The minimum is 1 at $(x, y) = (-1, 0)$.

14.5

1. $\mathcal{L} = 10x^{1/2}y^{1/3} - \lambda(2x + 4y - m)$ is concave in (x, y) (Problem 13.2.8), so Theorem 14.5.1 applies.

2. With $\mathcal{L} = \ln x + \ln y - \lambda(px + qy - m)$, $\mathcal{L}_x' = 1/x - p\lambda$, $\mathcal{L}_y' = 1/y - q\lambda$, $\mathcal{L}_{xx}'' = -1/x^2$, $\mathcal{L}_{xy}'' = 0$, and $\mathcal{L}_{yy}'' = -1/y^2$. Moreover, $g_x' = p$ and $g_y' = q$. Hence $D(x, y, \lambda) = -q^2/x^2 - p^2/y^2 < 0$. Condition (A) in Theorem 14.5.2 is satisfied.

3. $D(x, y, \lambda) = 10$, so Theorem 14.5.2 tells us that $(a/5, 2a/5)$ is a local minimum.

4. $U_{11}''(x, y) = a(a - 1)x^{a-2} \leq 0$, $U_{22}''(x, y) = a(a - 1)y^{a-2} \leq 0$, and $U_{12}''(x, y) = 0$, so U is concave. The solution is $x = mp^{1/(a-1)}/R$, $y = mq^{1/(a-1)}/R$, where $R = p^{a/(a-1)} + q^{a/(a-1)}$.

14.6

1. (a) $\mathcal{L}(x, y, z) = x^2 + y^2 + z^2 - \lambda(x + y + z - 1)$, so $\mathcal{L}_x' = 2x - \lambda = 0$, $\mathcal{L}_y' = 2y - \lambda = 0$, $\mathcal{L}_z' = 2z - \lambda = 0$. It follows that $x = y = z$. The only solution of the necessary conditions is $(1/3, 1/3, 1/3)$ with $\lambda = 2/3$.
(b) The problem is to find the shortest distance from the origin to a point in the plane $x + y + z = 1$. The corresponding maximization problem has no solution.

2. $x = \dfrac{1/2}{1/2 + 1/3 + 1/4} \dfrac{390}{4} = 45$, $y = \dfrac{1/3}{1/2 + 1/3 + 1/4} \dfrac{390}{3} = 40$, $z = \dfrac{1/4}{1/2 + 1/3 + 1/4} \dfrac{390}{6} = 15$

3. (a) With the Lagrangian $\mathcal{L} = x + \sqrt{y} - 1/z - \lambda(px + qy + rz - m)$, the first-order conditions are:
(i) $\partial\mathcal{L}/\partial x = 1 - \lambda p = 0$;   (ii) $\partial\mathcal{L}/\partial y = \frac{1}{2}y^{-1/2} - \lambda q = 0$;   (iii) $\partial\mathcal{L}/\partial z = z^{-2} - \lambda r = 0$.

(b) From the equations in (a) we get $\lambda = 1/p$, and then $\frac{1}{2} y^{-1/2} = q/p$, and so $y = p^2/4q^2$, and finally, $z = \sqrt{p/r}$. Inserting these values of y and z in the budget constraint and solving for x gives $x = m/p - p/4q - \sqrt{r/p}$.
(c) Straightforward substitution. (d) $\partial U^*/\partial m = 1/p = \lambda$, as expected from Section 14.2.

4. The Lagrangian is $\mathcal{L} = \alpha \ln x + \beta \ln y + (1 - \alpha - \beta) \ln(L - l) - \lambda(px + qy - wl)$, which is stationary when: (i) $\mathcal{L}'_x = \alpha/x - \lambda p = 0$; (ii) $\mathcal{L}'_y = \beta/y^* - \lambda q = 0$; (iii) $\mathcal{L}'_l = -(1 - \alpha - \beta)/(L - l^*) + \lambda w = 0$. From (i) and (ii), $qy^* = (\beta/\alpha)px^*$, while (i) and (iii) yield $l^* = L - [(1 - \alpha - \beta)/w\alpha]px^*$. Insertion into the budget constraint and solving for x^* yields $x^* = \alpha wL/p$, $y^* = \beta wL/q$, and $l^* = (\alpha + \beta)L$.

5. The constraints reduce to $h + 2k + l = 0$ and $2h - k - 3l = 0$, so $k = -h$ and $l = h$. But then $x^2 + y^2 + z^2 = 200 + 3h^2 \geq 200$ for all h, so f is maximized for $h = 0$. Then $k = l = 0$ also, and we conclude that $(x, y, z) = (10, 10, 0)$ solves the minimization problem.

6. Here $\mathcal{L} = a_1^2 x_1^2 + \cdots + a_n^2 x_n^2 - \lambda(x_1 + \cdots + x_n - 1)$. Necessary conditions are that $\mathcal{L}'_j = 2a_j^2 x_j - \lambda = 0$, $j = 1, \ldots, n$, and so $x_j = \lambda/2a_j^2$. Inserted into the constraint, this implies that $1 = \frac{1}{2}\lambda(1/a_1^2 + \cdots + 1/a_n^2)$. Thus, for $j = 1, \ldots, n$, we have $x_j = 1/a_j^2(1/a_1^2 + \cdots + 1/a_n^2) = 1/a_j^2 \sum_{i=1}^{n}(1/a_i^2)$. If at least one a_i is 0, the minimum value is 0, which is attained by letting a corresponding x_i be 1, with the other x_j all equal to 0.

7. $(x, y, z) = (0, 0, 1)$ with $\lambda = -1/2$ and $\mu = 1$ yields the minimum, $(x, y, z) = (4/5, 2/5, -1/5)$ with $\lambda = 1/2$ and $\mu = 1/5$ yields the maximum.

8. (a) $x_j = a_j m/p_j(a_1 + \cdots + a_n)$ for $k = 1, \ldots, n$.

(b) $x_j = mp_j^{-1/(1-a)} \Big/ \sum_{i=1}^{n} p_i^{-a/(1-a)}$ for $j = 1, \ldots, n$.

14.7

1. (a) With $\mathcal{L} = x + a \ln y - \lambda(px + qy - m)$, $\mathcal{L}'_1 = 1 - \lambda p = 0$, $\mathcal{L}'_2 = a/y^* - \lambda q = 0$. Thus $\lambda = 1/p$, which inserted into the second equality yields $y^* = ap/q$. From the budget constraint we get $x^* = m/p - a$. The Lagrangian is concave, so this is the solution. (b) $U^* = x^* + a \ln y^* = m/p - a + a \ln a + a \ln p - a \ln q$. Then $\partial U^*/\partial p = -m/p^2 + a/p$, $\partial U^*/\partial q = -a/q$, $\partial U^*/\partial m = 1/p$, and $\partial U^*/\partial a = \ln a + \ln p - \ln q$. On the other hand, $\partial \mathcal{L}/\partial p = -\lambda x$, $\partial \mathcal{L}/\partial q = -\lambda y$, $\partial \mathcal{L}/\partial m = \lambda$, and $\partial \mathcal{L}/\partial a = \ln y$. When we evaluate these four partials at (x^*, y^*), we see that the envelope theorem is confirmed.

2. The minimum point is $(x^*, y^*, z^*) = (a, 2a, 9a)$, where $a = -\sqrt{b}/6$, with $\lambda = -3/\sqrt{b}$. The value of the objective function is $f^*(b) = x^* + 4y^* + 3z^* = -6\sqrt{b}$, and $df^*(b)/db = -3/\sqrt{b} = \lambda$.

3. (a) $x = aM/\alpha$, $y = bM/\beta$, $z = cM/\gamma$, $\lambda = 1/2M$, where $M = \sqrt{L}/\sqrt{a^2/\alpha + b^2/\beta + c^2/\gamma}$. (The first-order conditions give $x = a/2\lambda\alpha$, $y = b/2\lambda\beta$, $z = c/2\lambda\gamma$. Substituting in the constraint and solving for λ gives the solution.) (b) We find that $M = \sqrt{L}/5$, and the given values of x, y, and z follow. For $L = 100$ one has $M = 2$ and $\lambda = 1/4$. The increase in the maximal value as L increases from 100 to 101, is approximately $\lambda \cdot 1 = 0.25$. The actual increase is $5(\sqrt{101} - \sqrt{100}) \approx 0.249378$.

4. (a) $\left(\frac{1}{4}\sqrt{15}, 0, \frac{1}{8}\right)$ and $\left(-\frac{1}{4}\sqrt{15}, 0, \frac{1}{8}\right)$ (with $\lambda = 1$) both solve the maximization problem, while $\left(0, 0, -\frac{1}{2}\right)$ solves the minimization problem. (b) $\Delta f^* \approx \lambda \Delta c = 1 \cdot 0.02 = 0.02$

5. $K^* = 2^{1/3} r^{-1/3} w^{1/3} Q^{4/3}$, $L^* = 2^{-2/3} r^{2/3} w^{-2/3} Q^{4/3}$, $C^* = 3 \cdot 2^{-2/3} r^{2/3} w^{1/3} Q^{4/3}$, $\lambda = 2^{4/3} r^{2/3} w^{1/3} Q^{1/3}$. The equalities $(*)$ are easily verified.

6. $\dfrac{\partial K^*}{\partial w} = \dfrac{\partial}{\partial w}\left(\dfrac{\partial C^*}{\partial r}\right) = \dfrac{\partial}{\partial r}\left(\dfrac{\partial C^*}{\partial w}\right) = \dfrac{\partial L^*}{\partial r}$, using the first and second equalities in $(*)$ in Example 3.

7. (a) With $\mathcal{L} = \sqrt{x} + ay - \lambda(px + qy - m)$, the first-order conditions for (x^*, y^*) to solve the problem are (i) $\mathcal{L}'_x = 1/2\sqrt{x^*} - \lambda p = 0$, (ii) $\mathcal{L}'_y = a - \lambda q = 0$. Thus $\lambda = a/q$, and $x^*(p, q, a, m) = q^2/4a^2 p^2$, $y^*(p, q, a, m) = m/q - q/4a^2 p$. The Lagrangian is concave in (x, y), so this is the solution. The indirect utility function is $U^*(p, q, a, m) = \sqrt{x^*} + ay^* = q/4ap + am/q$.
(b) The partial derivatives of U^* w.r.t. the parameters are $\partial U^*/\partial p = -q/4ap^2$, $\partial U^*/\partial q = 1/4ap - am/q^2$,

$\partial U^*/\partial m = a/q$, and $\partial U^*/\partial a = -q/4a^2p+m/q$. On the other hand, with $\mathcal{L}(x, y, p, q, a, m) = \sqrt{x}+ay-\lambda(px+qy-m)$, the partial derivatives of $\mathcal{L}$ evaluated at (x^*, y^*) are $\partial \mathcal{L}^*/\partial p = -\lambda x^* = -(a/q)(q^2/4a^2p^2) = -q/4ap^2$, $\partial \mathcal{L}^*/\partial q = -\lambda y^* = -(a/q)(m/q - q/4a^2p) = 1/4ap - am/q^2$, $\partial \mathcal{L}^*/\partial m = \lambda$, and $\partial \mathcal{L}^*/\partial a = y^* = m/q - q/4a^2p$. The envelope theorem is confirmed in all cases.

14.8

1. (a) With $\mathcal{L} = -x^2 - y^2 - \lambda(x - 3y + 10)$, (2) and (3) yield (i) $\mathcal{L}'_x = -2x - \lambda = 0$; (ii) $\mathcal{L}'_y = -2y + 3\lambda = 0$; (iii) $\lambda \geq 0$ with $\lambda = 0$ if $x - 3y < -10$. Suppose $\lambda = 0$. Then (i) and (ii) imply $x = y = 0$, contradicting $x - 3y \leq -10$. Thus $\lambda > 0$ and from (iii), $x - 3y = -10$. Furthermore, (i) and (ii) imply $\lambda = -2x = \frac{2}{3}y$, so $y = -3x$. Inserting this into $x - 3y = -10$ yields $x = -1$, and then $y = 3$. Since the Lagrangian is easily seen to be concave, the solution is $(x, y) = (-1, 3)$.   (b) See Fig. A14.8.1. The solution is the point on the line $x - 3y = -10$ that is closest to the origin.

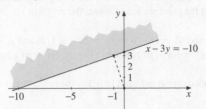

Figure A14.8.1

2. (a) The Kuhn–Tucker conditions yield (i) $\frac{1}{2\sqrt{x}} - \lambda p = 0$, (ii) $\frac{1}{2\sqrt{y}} - \lambda q = 0$, (iii) $\lambda \geq 0$, and $\lambda = 0$ if $px + qy < m$. Clearing fractions in (i) and (ii) gives $1 = 2\lambda p\sqrt{x} = 2\lambda q\sqrt{y}$, from which we infer that x, y, λ are all positive, and also that $y = p^2x/q^2$. Because $\lambda > 0$, the budget constraint $px + qy = m$ holds, implying that $x = mq/(pq + p^2)$. The corresponding value for y is easily found, and the demand functions are

$$x = x(p, q, m) = \frac{mq}{p(p+q)}, \qquad y = y(p, q, m) = \frac{mp}{q(p+q)}$$

These demand functions solve the problem because $\mathcal{L}(x, y)$ is easily seen to be concave.
(b) It is easy to see that the demand functions are homogeneous of degree 0, as expected.

3. (a) With $\mathcal{L} = 4 - \frac{1}{2}x^2 - 4y - \lambda(6x - 4y - a)$, the Kuhn–Tucker conditions are: (i) $\partial \mathcal{L}/\partial x = -x - 6\lambda = 0$; (ii) $\partial \mathcal{L}/\partial y = -4 + 4\lambda = 0$; (iii) $\lambda \geq 0$ ($\lambda = 0$ if $6x - 4y < a$).
(b) From (ii), $\lambda = 1$, so (i) gives $x = -6$. From (iii) and the given constraint, $y = -9 - \frac{1}{4}a$. The Lagrangian is concave, so we have found the solution.   (c) $V(a) = a + 22$, so $V'(a) = 1 = \lambda$.

4. (a) $\mathcal{L}(x, y) = x^2+2y^2-x-\lambda(x^2+y^2-1)$. The Kuhn–Tucker conditions: (i) $2x-1-2\lambda x = 0$; (ii) $4y-2\lambda y = 0$; (iii) $\lambda \geq 0$ with $\lambda = 0$ if $x^2 + y^2 < 1$.   (b) From (ii), $y(2 - \lambda) = 0$, so either (I) $y = 0$ or (II) $\lambda = 2$.
(I) $y = 0$. If $\lambda = 0$, then from (i), $x = 1/2$ and $(x, y) = (1/2, 0)$ is a candidate for optimum (since it satisfies all the Kuhn–Tucker conditions). If $y = 0$ and $\lambda > 0$, then from (iii) and $x^2 + y^2 \leq 1$, $x^2 + y^2 = 1$. But then $x = \pm 1$, so $(x, y) = (\pm 1, 0)$ are candidates, with $\lambda = 1/2$ and $3/2$, respectively.
(II) $\lambda = 2$. Then from (i), $x = -1/2$ and (iii) gives $y^2 = 3/4$, so $y = \pm\sqrt{3}/2$. So $(-1/2, \pm\sqrt{3}/2)$ are the two remaining candidates with $\lambda = 2$. The maximum value is 9/4 at $(-1/2, \sqrt{3}/2)$ and at $(-1/2, -\sqrt{3}/2)$. The extreme value theorem confirms that this is the solution.

5. (a) For $0 < a < 1$, the solution is $x = \sqrt{a}$, $y = 0$, and $\lambda = a^{-1/2} - 1$; for $a \geq 1$, it is $x = 1$, $y = 0$, and $\lambda = 0$. Because the Lagrangian is concave, these give the respective maxima.   (b) For $a \in (0, 1)$, $f^*(a) = 2\sqrt{a} - a$, and $df^*(a)/da = \lambda$. If $a \geq 1$, then $f^*(a) = 1$, so $df^*(a)/da = 0 = \lambda$.

6. With $\mathcal{L} = aQ - bQ^2 - \alpha Q - \beta Q^2 + \lambda Q$, the Kuhn–Tucker conditions for Q^* to solve the problem are: (i) $d\mathcal{L}/dQ = a - \alpha - 2(b + \beta)Q^* + \lambda = 0$; (ii) $\lambda \geq 0$, with $\lambda = 0$ if $Q^* > 0$. By Theorem 14.8.1, these

conditions are also sufficient because the Lagrangian is concave. We find that $Q^* = (a - \alpha)/2(b + \beta)$ and $\lambda = 0$ if $a > \alpha$, whereas $Q^* = 0$ and $\lambda = \alpha - a$ if $a \le \alpha$. (See also Example 4.6.2.)

14.9

1. (a) Writing the constraints as $g_1(x, y) = x + e^{-x} - y \le 0$ and $g_2(x, y) = -x \le 0$, the Lagrangian is $\mathcal{L} = \frac{1}{2}x - y - \lambda_1(x + e^{-x} - y) - \lambda_2(-x)$. The Kuhn–Tucker conditions are then: (i) $\frac{1}{2} - \lambda_1(1 - e^{-x}) + \lambda_2 = 0$; (ii) $-1 + \lambda_1 = 0$; (iii) $\lambda_1 \ge 0$, with $\lambda = 0$ if $x + e^{-x} < y$; (iv) $\lambda_2 \ge 0$, with $\lambda = 0$ if $x > 0$.   (b) From (ii), $\lambda_1 = 1$, so from (iii), $x + e^{-x} = y$. Either $x = 0$ or $x > 0$. In the latter case, (iv) implies that $\lambda_2 = 0$. Then (i) implies $\frac{1}{2} - (1 - e^{-x}) = 0$, or $e^{-x} = \frac{1}{2}$. Hence $x = \ln 2$, and so $y = x + e^{-x} = \ln 2 + \frac{1}{2}$. If $x = 0$, then (i) implies $\lambda_2 = -\frac{1}{2}$, which contradicts $\lambda_2 \ge 0$. We conclude that $(x, y) = (\ln 2, \ln 2 + \frac{1}{2})$ is the only point satisfying the Kuhn–Tucker conditions, with $(\lambda_1, \lambda_2) = (1, 0)$. (By sketching the constraint set and studying the level curves $\frac{1}{2}x - y = c$, it is easy to see that the point we found solves the problem.)

2. If $m \le p\bar{x}/\alpha$, then $x^* = m\alpha/p$ and $y^* = (1 - \alpha)m/q$, with $\lambda = 1/m$ and $\mu = 0$.
If $m > p\bar{x}/\alpha$, then $x^* = \bar{x}$ and $y^* = (m - p\bar{x})/q$, $\lambda = (1 - \alpha)/(m - p\bar{x})$, and $\mu = (\alpha m - p\bar{x})/\bar{x}(m - p\bar{x})$.

3. (a) The admissible set is the shaded region in Fig. A14.9.3.   (b) $(x^*, y^*) = (-1, 5)$

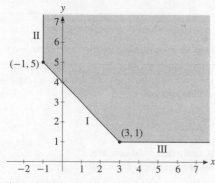

Figure A14.9.3

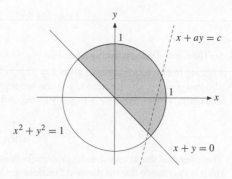

Figure A14.9.4

4. (a) The admissible set and one of the level curves for $x + ay$ are shown in Fig. A14.9.4.

(b) $(x^*, y^*) = \begin{cases} \left(\frac{1}{2}\sqrt{2}, -\frac{1}{2}\sqrt{2}\right) & \text{if } a \le -1 \\ \left(1/\sqrt{1 + a^2}, a/\sqrt{1 + a^2}\right) & \text{if } a > -1 \end{cases}$

5. $(x, y) = (4^{-2/3}, 4^{-1/3})$

6. (a) See Fig. A14.9.6.   (b) Solution: $(x^*, y^*) = (\ln(3/2), 2/3)$, with $\lambda = 3[\ln(3/2) + 1/2]$, $\mu = 3\ln(3/2) + 5/6$.

7. (a) With $\mathcal{L} = xz + yz - \lambda(x^2 + y^2 + z^2 - 1)$, the conditions are (i) $z - 2\lambda x = 0$; (ii) $z - 2\lambda y = 0$; (iii) $x + y - 2\lambda z = 0$;   (iv) $\lambda \ge 0$, with $\lambda = 0$ if $x^2 + y^2 + z^2 < 1$.   (b) If $\lambda = 0$, there is a stationary point at $x = y = z = 0$, but this is not a maximum. If $\lambda > 0$ then (i) and (ii) imply that $x = y = z/2\lambda$. Next, (iii) implies that $z/\lambda = 2\lambda z$, so $\lambda^2 = 1/2$, so $\lambda = \frac{1}{2}\sqrt{2}$ because $\lambda > 0$. Finally, (iv) implies that $x^2 + y^2 + z^2 = z^2/2\lambda^2 + z^2 = 1$, so $z^2 = 1/2$. The maximum points are at $(\frac{1}{2}, \frac{1}{2}, \frac{1}{2}\sqrt{2})$ and $(-\frac{1}{2}, -\frac{1}{2}, -\frac{1}{2}\sqrt{2})$, with $\lambda = \frac{1}{2}\sqrt{2}$. The extreme value theorem guarantees the existence of a maximum.

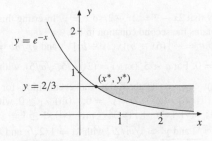

Figure A14.9.6

14.10

1. (a) With $\mathcal{L}(x, y) = x + \ln(1 + y) - \lambda(16x + y - 495)$, the K–T conditions for (x^*, y^*) to be a solution are:
(i) $\mathcal{L}_1'(x^*, y^*) = 1 - 16\lambda \leq 0 \, (= 0 \text{ if } x^* > 0)$ (ii) $\mathcal{L}_2'(x^*, y^*) = \dfrac{1}{1 + y^*} - \lambda \leq 0 \, (= 0 \text{ if } y^* > 0)$
(iii) $\lambda \geq 0$, with $\lambda = 0$ if $16x^* + y^* < 495$ (iv) $x^* \geq 0, \, y^* \geq 0$ (v) $16x^* + y^* \leq 495$.
(b) Note that the Lagrangian is concave, so a point that satisfies the K–T conditions will be a maximum point. From (i), $\lambda \geq 1/16 > 0$, so (iii) and (v) imply (vi) $16x^* + y^* = 495$. Suppose $x^* = 0$. Then (v) gives $y^* = 495$, and from (ii), $\lambda = 1/496$, contradicting $\lambda \geq 1/16$. Hence, $x^* > 0$, and so by (i), $\lambda = 1/16$. Suppose $y^* = 0$. Then (ii) implies $\lambda \geq 1$, contradicting $\lambda = 1/16$. Thus $y^* > 0$, and so from (ii), $y^* = 15$ and then (v) yields $x^* = 30$. So the only solution to the K–T conditions is $(x^*, y^*) = (30, 15)$, with $\lambda = 1/16$.
(c) Utility will increase by approximately $\lambda \cdot 5 = 5/16$. (Actually, the new solution is $(30\tfrac{5}{16}, 15)$, and the increase in utility is exactly 5/16. This is because the utility function has a special "quasi-linear" form.)

2. $(x, y) = (1, 0)$ is the only point satisfying all the conditions.

3. The only possible solution is $(x_1^*, x_2^*, k^*) = (1/2, \, 3/4, \, 3/4)$, with $\lambda = 0$ and $\mu = 3/2$.

Review Problems for Chapter 14

1. (a) With λ as the Lagrange multiplier, the first-order conditions imply $3 - 2\lambda x = 0$ and $4 - 2\lambda y = 0$, so $3y = 4x$. Inserting these into the constraint yields $x^2 = 81$, so $x = \pm 9$. Since the Lagrangian is concave, the solution is at $x = 9, \, y = 12$, with $\lambda = 1/6$.   (b) Using (14.2.3), $f^*(225 - 1) - f^*(225) \approx \lambda(-1) = -1/6$.

2. (a) $x = 2m/5p, \, y = 3m/5q$ (b) $x = m/3p, \, y = 2m/3q$ (c) $x = 3m/5p, \, y = 2m/5q$

3. (a) $\pi = xp(x) + yq(y) - C(x, y)$. The first-order conditions (i) $p(x^*) = C_1'(x^*, y^*) - x^* p'(x^*)$ and (ii) $q(y^*) = C_2'(x^*, y^*) - y^* q'(y^*)$. See SM for the economic interpretations.   (b) With $\mathcal{L} = xp(x) + yq(y) - C(x, y) - \lambda(x + y - m)$, the first-order conditions for $(\hat{x}, \hat{y})$ to solve the problem are $\mathcal{L}_1' = p(\hat{x}) + \hat{x} p'(\hat{x}) - C_1'(\hat{x}, \hat{y}) - \lambda = 0$, $\mathcal{L}_2' = q(\hat{y}) + \hat{y} q'(\hat{y}) - C_2'(\hat{x}, \hat{y}) - \lambda = 0$.

4. (a) The Lagrangian is $\mathcal{L}(x, y) = U(x, y) - \lambda[py - w(24 - x)]$. The first-order conditions imply $pU_1' = wU_2' = \lambda wp$, which immediately yields (**). (b) Differentiating (*) and (**) w.r.t. w gives $py_w' = 24 - x - wx_w'$ and $p(U_{11}'' x_w' + U_{12}'' y_w') = U_2' + w(U_{21}'' x_w' + U_{22}'' y_w')$. Solving these equations yields the given formula for $x_w' = \partial x / \partial w$.

5. (a) $x = -2\sqrt{b}, \, y = 0$ solves the maximization problem. $x = 4/3, \, y = \pm\sqrt{b - 4/9}$ solves the minimization problem.   (b) For $x = -2\sqrt{b}, \, y = 0$, $f^*(b) = 4b + 4\sqrt{b} + 1$. Since $\lambda = 4 + 2/\sqrt{b}$, the suggested equality is easily verified.

6. (a) With $\mathcal{L}(x, y) = v(x) + w(y) - \lambda(px + qy - m)$, the first-order conditions yield $v'(x) = \lambda p$ and $w'(y) = \lambda q$. Thus $v'(x)/w'(y) = p/q$.   (b) Since $\mathcal{L}_{xx}'' = v''(x)$, $\mathcal{L}_{yy}'' = w''(y)$, and $\mathcal{L}_{xy}'' = 0$, we see that the Lagrangian is concave.

7. (a) The first-order conditions imply that $2x - 2 = 2y - 2$, so $x = y$. Inserting this into the constraint equation and squaring, then simplifying, one obtains the second equation in (∗).
   (b) $\partial x/\partial a = 1/2x(3x + b)$, $\partial^2 x/\partial a^2 = -\frac{1}{4}(6x + b)[x(3x + b)]^{-3}$, and $\partial x/\partial b = -x/2(3x + b)$.

8. For $a \geq 5$, $(x, y) = (2, 1)$ with $\lambda = 0$. For $a < 5$, $(x, y) = (2\sqrt{a/5}, \sqrt{a/5})$, with $\lambda = \sqrt{5/a} - 1$.

9. (a) With $\mathcal{L} = xy - \lambda_1(x^2 + ry^2 - m) - \lambda_2(-x + 1)$, the Kuhn–Tucker conditions for (x^*, y^*) to solve the problem are:
   (i) $\mathcal{L}'_1 = y^* - 2\lambda_1 x^* + \lambda_2 = 0$; (ii) $\mathcal{L}'_2 = x^* - 2r\lambda_1 y^* = 0$; (iii) $\lambda_1 \geq 0$, with $\lambda_1 = 0$ if $(x^*)^2 + r(y^*)^2 < m$;
   (iv) $\lambda_2 \geq 0$, with $\lambda_2 = 0$ if $x^* > 1$; (v) $(x^*)^2 + r(y^*)^2 \leq m$; (vi) $x^* \geq 1$
   (b) Solution: For $m \geq 2$, $x^* = \sqrt{m/2}$ and $y^* = \sqrt{m/2r}$, with $\lambda_1 = 1/2\sqrt{r}$ and $\lambda_2 = 0$. For $1 < m < 2$, $x^* = 1$, $y^* = \sqrt{(m - 1)/r}$, with $\lambda_1 = 1/2\sqrt{r(m - 1)}$ and $\lambda_2 = (2 - m)/\sqrt{r(m - 1)}$. (c) See SM.

10. With the Lagrangian $\mathcal{L} = R(Q) - C(Q) - \lambda(-Q)$, the first-order conditions for Q^* to solve the problem are:
    (i) $R'(Q^*) - C'(Q^*) + \lambda = 0$; (ii) $\lambda \geq 0$, with $\lambda = 0$ if $Q^* > 0$. These conditions are also sufficient for optimality because the Lagrangian is concave in Q. A sufficient (and necessary) condition for $Q^* = 0$ to be optimal is that $\pi'(0) \leq 0$, or equivalently, $R'(0) \leq C'(0)$. (Draw a figure.)

11. (a) The maximization problem is: $\max(-rK - wL)$ subject to $-\sqrt{KL} \leq -Q$. With the Lagrangian $\mathcal{L} = -rK - wL - \lambda(-\sqrt{KL} + Q)$, the Kuhn–Tucker conditions for (K^*, L^*) to solve the problem are:
    (i) $\mathcal{L}'_K = -r + \lambda(\sqrt{L^*}/2\sqrt{K^*}) = 0$; (ii) $\mathcal{L}'_L = -w + \lambda(\sqrt{K^*}/2\sqrt{L^*}) = 0$; (iii) $\lambda \geq 0$ ($\lambda = 0$ if $\sqrt{K^*L^*} > Q$).
    Obviously $\lambda = 0$ would contradict (i) and (ii), so $\lambda > 0$ and (iv) $\sqrt{K^*L^*} = Q$. Eliminating λ from (i) and (ii), we find $L^* = rK^*/w$. Then (iv) yields $K^* = Q\sqrt{w/r}$ and $L^* = Q\sqrt{r/w}$.
    (b) $c^*(r, w, Q) = rK^* + wL^* = 2Q\sqrt{rw}$, so $\partial c^*/\partial r = Q\sqrt{w/r} = K^*$. If the price of capital r increases by 1, then the minimum cost will increase by about K^*, the optimal choice of capital input. The equation $\partial c^*/\partial w = Q\sqrt{r/w} = L^*$ has a similar interpretation.

Chapter 15

15.1

1. (a), (c), (d), and (f) are linear, (b) and (e) are nonlinear.

2. Yes, it is linear in a, b, c, and d.

3. $2x_1 + 4x_2 + 6x_3 + 8x_4 = 2$
   $5x_1 + 7x_2 + 9x_3 + 11x_4 = 4$
   $4x_1 + 6x_2 + 8x_3 + 10x_4 = 8$

4. The system is
$$\begin{cases} x_2 + x_3 + x_4 = b_1 \\ x_1 \quad\quad + x_3 + x_4 = b_2 \\ x_1 + x_2 \quad\quad + x_4 = b_3 \\ x_1 + x_2 + x_3 \quad\quad = b_4 \end{cases}, \text{ with solution } \begin{cases} x_1 = -\frac{2}{3}b_1 + \frac{1}{3}(b_2 + b_3 + b_4) \\ x_2 = -\frac{2}{3}b_2 + \frac{1}{3}(b_1 + b_3 + b_4) \\ x_3 = -\frac{2}{3}b_3 + \frac{1}{3}(b_1 + b_2 + b_4) \\ x_4 = -\frac{2}{3}b_4 + \frac{1}{3}(b_1 + b_2 + b_3) \end{cases}$$

(Adding the 4 equations, then dividing by 3, gives $x_1 + x_2 + x_3 + x_4 = \frac{1}{3}(b_1 + b_2 + b_3 + b_4)$. Subtracting each of the original equations in turn from this new equation gives the expressions for $x_1, \ldots, x_4$. Systematic elimination of the variables starting by eliminating (say) x_4 is an alternative solution method.)

5. (a) The commodity bundle owned by individual j. (b) $a_{i1} + a_{i2} + \cdots + a_{in}$ is the total stock of commodity i. The first case is when $i = 1$. (c) $p_1 a_{1j} + p_2 a_{2j} + \cdots + p_m a_{mj}$

6. The solution is $x = 93.53$, $y \approx 482.11$, $s \approx 49.73$, and $c \approx 438.31$.

15.2

1. $A = \begin{pmatrix} 1 & 0 & 0 \\ 0 & 1 & 0 \\ 0 & 0 & 1 \end{pmatrix}$ 2. $A + B = \begin{pmatrix} 1 & 0 \\ 7 & 5 \end{pmatrix}$, $3A = \begin{pmatrix} 0 & 3 \\ 6 & 9 \end{pmatrix}$

3. $u = 3$ and $v = -2$. (Equating the elements in row 1 and column 3 gives $u = 3$. Then, equating those in row 2 and column 3 gives $u - v = 5$ and so $v = -2$. The other elements then need to be checked, but this is obvious.)

4. $A + B = \begin{pmatrix} 1 & 0 & 4 \\ 2 & 4 & 16 \end{pmatrix}$, $A - B = \begin{pmatrix} -1 & 2 & -6 \\ 2 & 2 & -2 \end{pmatrix}$, and $5A - 3B = \begin{pmatrix} -3 & 8 & -20 \\ 10 & 12 & 8 \end{pmatrix}$

15.3

1. (a) $AB = \begin{pmatrix} 0 & -2 \\ 3 & 1 \end{pmatrix}\begin{pmatrix} -1 & 4 \\ 1 & 5 \end{pmatrix} = \begin{pmatrix} 0 \cdot (-1) + (-2) \cdot 1 & 0 \cdot 4 + (-2) \cdot 5 \\ 3 \cdot (-1) + 1 \cdot 1 & 3 \cdot 4 + 1 \cdot 5 \end{pmatrix} = \begin{pmatrix} -2 & -10 \\ -2 & 17 \end{pmatrix}$

and $BA = \begin{pmatrix} 12 & 6 \\ 15 & 3 \end{pmatrix}$. (b) $AB = \begin{pmatrix} 26 & 3 \\ 6 & -22 \end{pmatrix}$ and $BA = \begin{pmatrix} 14 & 6 & -12 \\ 35 & 12 & 4 \\ 3 & 3 & -22 \end{pmatrix}$

(c) $AB = \begin{pmatrix} 0 & 0 & 0 \\ 0 & 4 & -6 \\ 0 & -8 & 12 \end{pmatrix}$ and $BA = (16)$, a 1×1 matrix. (d) AB is not defined. $BA = \begin{pmatrix} -1 & 4 \\ 3 & 4 \\ 4 & 8 \end{pmatrix}$

2. (i) $\begin{pmatrix} -1 & 15 \\ -6 & -13 \end{pmatrix}$ (ii) $AB = \begin{pmatrix} 0 & 0 \\ 0 & 0 \end{pmatrix}$ (iii) From (ii) it follows that $C(AB) = \begin{pmatrix} 0 & 0 \\ 0 & 0 \end{pmatrix}$.

3. $A + B = \begin{pmatrix} 4 & 1 & -1 \\ 9 & 2 & 7 \\ 3 & -1 & 4 \end{pmatrix}$, $A - B = \begin{pmatrix} -2 & 3 & -5 \\ 1 & -2 & -3 \\ -1 & -1 & -2 \end{pmatrix}$, $AB = \begin{pmatrix} 5 & 3 & 3 \\ 19 & -5 & 16 \\ 1 & -3 & 0 \end{pmatrix}$, $BA = \begin{pmatrix} 0 & 4 & -9 \\ 19 & 3 & -3 \\ 5 & 1 & -3 \end{pmatrix}$,

$(AB)C = A(BC) = \begin{pmatrix} 23 & 8 & 25 \\ 92 & -28 & 76 \\ 4 & -8 & -4 \end{pmatrix}$

4. (a) $\begin{pmatrix} 1 & 1 \\ 3 & 5 \end{pmatrix}\begin{pmatrix} x_1 \\ x_2 \end{pmatrix} = \begin{pmatrix} 3 \\ 5 \end{pmatrix}$ (b) $\begin{pmatrix} 1 & 2 & 1 \\ 1 & -1 & 1 \\ 2 & 3 & -1 \end{pmatrix}\begin{pmatrix} x_1 \\ x_2 \\ x_3 \end{pmatrix} = \begin{pmatrix} 4 \\ 5 \\ 1 \end{pmatrix}$ (c) $\begin{pmatrix} 2 & -3 & 1 \\ 1 & 1 & -1 \end{pmatrix}\begin{pmatrix} x_1 \\ x_2 \\ x_3 \end{pmatrix} = \begin{pmatrix} 0 \\ 0 \end{pmatrix}$

5. (a) $A - 2I = \begin{pmatrix} 0 & 2 \\ 1 & 3 \end{pmatrix}$. The matrix C must be 2×2. With $C = \begin{pmatrix} c_{11} & c_{12} \\ c_{21} & c_{22} \end{pmatrix}$, we need $\begin{pmatrix} 0 & 2 \\ 1 & 3 \end{pmatrix}\begin{pmatrix} c_{11} & c_{12} \\ c_{21} & c_{22} \end{pmatrix} =$

$\begin{pmatrix} 1 & 0 \\ 0 & 1 \end{pmatrix}$, or $\begin{pmatrix} 2c_{21} & 2c_{22} \\ c_{11} + 3c_{21} & c_{12} + 3c_{22} \end{pmatrix} = \begin{pmatrix} 1 & 0 \\ 0 & 1 \end{pmatrix}$. It follows that $c_{11} = -3/2$, $c_{12} = 1$, $c_{21} = 1/2$, and $c_{22} = 0$.

(b) $B - 2I = \begin{pmatrix} 0 & 0 \\ 3 & 0 \end{pmatrix}$, so the first row of any product matrix $(B - 2I)D$ must be $(0, 0)$. Hence, no such matrix D can possibly exist.

6. (a) The product AB is defined only if B has n rows. And BA is defined only if B has m columns. So B must be an $n \times m$ matrix. (b) $B = \begin{pmatrix} w - y & y \\ y & w \end{pmatrix}$, for arbitrary y, w.

7. $T(Ts) = \begin{pmatrix} 0.85 & 0.10 & 0.10 \\ 0.05 & 0.55 & 0.05 \\ 0.10 & 0.35 & 0.85 \end{pmatrix}\begin{pmatrix} 0.25 \\ 0.35 \\ 0.40 \end{pmatrix} = \begin{pmatrix} 0.2875 \\ 0.2250 \\ 0.4875 \end{pmatrix}$

15.4

1. $A(B + C) = AB + AC = \begin{pmatrix} 3 & 2 & 6 & 2 \\ 7 & 4 & 14 & 6 \end{pmatrix}$ **2.** $(ax^2 + by^2 + cz^2 + 2dxy + 2exz + 2fyz)$ (a 1×1 matrix)

3. It is straightforward to show that $(AB)C$ and $A(BC)$ are both equal to the 2×2 matrix $D = (d_{ij})_{2 \times 2}$ whose four elements are $d_{ij} = a_{i1}b_{11}c_{1j} + a_{i1}b_{12}c_{2j} + a_{i2}b_{21}c_{1j} + a_{i2}b_{22}c_{2j}$ for $i = 1, 2$ and $j = 1, 2$.

4. (a) $\begin{pmatrix} 5 & 3 & 1 \\ 2 & 0 & 9 \\ 1 & 3 & 3 \end{pmatrix}$ (b) $(1, 2, -3)$

5. Equality in (a) as well as in (b) if and only if $\mathbf{AB} = \mathbf{BA}$. $((\mathbf{A} + \mathbf{B})(\mathbf{A} - \mathbf{B}) = \mathbf{A}^2 - \mathbf{AB} + \mathbf{BA} - \mathbf{B}^2 \neq \mathbf{A}^2 - \mathbf{B}^2$ unless $\mathbf{AB} = \mathbf{BA}$. The other case is similar.)

6. (a) Direct verification by matrix multiplication. (b) $\mathbf{AA} = (\mathbf{AB})\mathbf{A} = \mathbf{A}(\mathbf{BA}) = \mathbf{AB} = \mathbf{A}$, so $\mathbf{A}$ is idempotent. Then just interchange $\mathbf{A}$ and $\mathbf{B}$ to show that $\mathbf{B}$ is idempotent. (c) As the induction hypothesis, suppose that $\mathbf{A}^k = \mathbf{A}$, which is true for $k = 1$. Then $\mathbf{A}^{k+1} = \mathbf{A}^k\mathbf{A} = \mathbf{AA} = \mathbf{A}$, which completes the proof by induction.

7. If $\mathbf{P}^3\mathbf{Q} = \mathbf{PQ}$, then $\mathbf{P}^5\mathbf{Q} = \mathbf{P}^2(\mathbf{P}^3\mathbf{Q}) = \mathbf{P}^2(\mathbf{PQ}) = \mathbf{P}^3\mathbf{Q} = \mathbf{PQ}$.

8. (a) Direct verification. (b) $\mathbf{A} = \begin{pmatrix} 1 & 1 \\ -1 & -1 \end{pmatrix}$ (c) See SM.

15.5

1. $\mathbf{A}' = \begin{pmatrix} 3 & -1 \\ 5 & 2 \\ 8 & 6 \\ 3 & 2 \end{pmatrix}$, $\mathbf{B}' = (0, 1, -1, 2)$, $\mathbf{C}' = \begin{pmatrix} 1 \\ 5 \\ 0 \\ -1 \end{pmatrix}$

2. $\mathbf{A}' = \begin{pmatrix} 3 & -1 \\ 2 & 5 \end{pmatrix}$, $\mathbf{B}' = \begin{pmatrix} 0 & 2 \\ 2 & 2 \end{pmatrix}$, $(\mathbf{A} + \mathbf{B})' = \begin{pmatrix} 3 & 1 \\ 4 & 7 \end{pmatrix}$, $(\alpha\mathbf{A})' = \begin{pmatrix} -6 & 2 \\ -4 & -10 \end{pmatrix}$, $\mathbf{AB} = \begin{pmatrix} 4 & 10 \\ 10 & 8 \end{pmatrix}$,

$(\mathbf{AB})' = \begin{pmatrix} 4 & 10 \\ 10 & 8 \end{pmatrix} = \mathbf{B}'\mathbf{A}'$, and $\mathbf{A}'\mathbf{B}' = \begin{pmatrix} -2 & 4 \\ 10 & 14 \end{pmatrix}$. Verifying the rules in (2) is now very easy.

3. Equation (1) implies that $\mathbf{A} = \mathbf{A}'$ and $\mathbf{B} = \mathbf{B}'$.

4. Symmetry requires $a^2 - 1 = a + 1$ and $a^2 + 4 = 4a$. The second equation has the unique root $a = 2$, which also satisfies the first equation.

5. No! For example: $\begin{pmatrix} 0 & 0 \\ 0 & 1 \end{pmatrix}\begin{pmatrix} 1 & 1 \\ 1 & 1 \end{pmatrix} = \begin{pmatrix} 0 & 0 \\ 1 & 1 \end{pmatrix}$.

6. $(\mathbf{A}_1\mathbf{A}_2\mathbf{A}_3)' = (\mathbf{A}_1(\mathbf{A}_2\mathbf{A}_3))' = (\mathbf{A}_2\mathbf{A}_3)'\mathbf{A}_1' = (\mathbf{A}_3'\mathbf{A}_2')\mathbf{A}_1' = \mathbf{A}_3'\mathbf{A}_2'\mathbf{A}_1'$. For the general case use induction.

7. (a) Direct verification. (b) $\begin{pmatrix} p & q \\ -q & p \end{pmatrix}\begin{pmatrix} p & -q \\ q & p \end{pmatrix} = \begin{pmatrix} p^2 + q^2 & 0 \\ 0 & p^2 + q^2 \end{pmatrix} = \begin{pmatrix} 1 & 0 \\ 0 & 1 \end{pmatrix} \iff p^2 + q^2 = 1$.

(c) If $\mathbf{P}'\mathbf{P} = \mathbf{Q}'\mathbf{Q} = \mathbf{I}_n$, then $(\mathbf{PQ})'(\mathbf{PQ}) = (\mathbf{Q}'\mathbf{P}')(\mathbf{PQ}) = \mathbf{Q}'(\mathbf{P}'\mathbf{P})\mathbf{Q} = \mathbf{Q}'\mathbf{I}_n\mathbf{Q} = \mathbf{Q}'\mathbf{Q} = \mathbf{I}_n$.

8. (a) $\mathbf{TS} = \begin{pmatrix} p^3 + p^2q & 2p^2q + 2pq^2 & pq^2 + q^3 \\ \frac{1}{2}p^3 + \frac{1}{2}p^2 + \frac{1}{2}p^2q & p^2q + pq + pq^2 & \frac{1}{2}pq^2 + \frac{1}{2}q^2 + \frac{1}{2}q^3 \\ p^3 + p^2q & 2p^2q + 2pq^2 & pq^2 + q^3 \end{pmatrix} = \mathbf{S}$ because $p + q = 1$.

A similar argument shows that $\mathbf{T}^2 = \frac{1}{2}\mathbf{T} + \frac{1}{2}\mathbf{S}$. To derive the formula for $\mathbf{T}^3$, multiply each side of the last equation on the left by $\mathbf{T}$.

(b) The appropriate formula is $\mathbf{T}^n = 2^{1-n}\mathbf{T} + (1 - 2^{1-n})\mathbf{S}$.

15.6

1. (a) Gaussian elimination yields

$$\begin{pmatrix} 1 & 1 & 3 \\ 3 & 5 & 5 \end{pmatrix} \overset{-3}{\underleftarrow{\quad}} \sim \begin{pmatrix} 1 & 1 & 3 \\ 0 & 2 & -4 \end{pmatrix} {}_{1/2} \sim \begin{pmatrix} 1 & 1 & 3 \\ 0 & 1 & -2 \end{pmatrix} \overset{}{\underleftarrow{-1}} \sim \begin{pmatrix} 1 & 0 & 5 \\ 0 & 1 & -2 \end{pmatrix}$$

The solution is therefore $x_1 = 5$, $x_2 = -2$. (b) Gaussian elimination yields

$$\begin{pmatrix} 1 & 2 & 1 & 4 \\ 1 & -1 & 1 & 5 \\ 2 & 3 & -1 & 1 \end{pmatrix} \begin{matrix} \underleftarrow{-1} \\ \underleftarrow{\quad} \end{matrix} {}_{-2} \sim \begin{pmatrix} 1 & 2 & 1 & 4 \\ 0 & -3 & 0 & 1 \\ 0 & -1 & -3 & -7 \end{pmatrix} {}_{-1/3} \sim \begin{pmatrix} 1 & 2 & 1 & 4 \\ 0 & 1 & 0 & -1/3 \\ 0 & -1 & -3 & -7 \end{pmatrix} \begin{matrix} \underleftarrow{\quad} \\ {}_{1} {}_{-2} \end{matrix}$$

$$\sim \begin{pmatrix} 1 & 0 & 1 & 14/3 \\ 0 & 1 & 0 & -1/3 \\ 0 & 0 & -3 & -22/3 \end{pmatrix} {}_{-1/3} \sim \begin{pmatrix} 1 & 0 & 1 & 14/3 \\ 0 & 1 & 0 & -1/3 \\ 0 & 0 & 1 & 22/9 \end{pmatrix} \overset{}{\underleftarrow{-1}} \sim \begin{pmatrix} 1 & 0 & 0 & 20/9 \\ 0 & 1 & 0 & -1/3 \\ 0 & 0 & 1 & 22/9 \end{pmatrix}$$

The solution is therefore: $x_1 = 20/9$, $x_2 = -1/3$, $x_3 = 22/9$
(c) Solution: $x_1 = (2/5)s$, $x_2 = (3/5)s$, $x_3 = s$, with s an arbitrary real number.

2. Using Gaussian elimination to eliminate x from the second and third equations, and then y from the third equation,

we arrive at the following augmented matrix: $\begin{pmatrix} 1 & 1 & -1 & 1 \\ 0 & 1 & -3/2 & -1/2 \\ 0 & 0 & a+5/2 & b-1/2 \end{pmatrix}$.

For any z, the first two equations imply that $y = -\frac{1}{2} + \frac{3}{2}z$ and $x = 1 - y + z = \frac{3}{2} - \frac{1}{2}z$. From the last equation we see that for $a \neq -\frac{5}{2}$, there is a unique solution with $z = (b - \frac{1}{2})/(a + \frac{5}{2})$. For $a = -\frac{5}{2}$, there are no solutions if $b \neq \frac{1}{2}$, but there is one degree of freedom if $b = \frac{1}{2}$ (with z arbitrary).

3. For $c = 1$ and for $c = -2/5$ the solution is $x = 2c^2 - 1 + t$, $y = s$, $z = t$, $w = 1 - c^2 - 2s - 2t$, for arbitrary s and t. For other values of c there are no solutions.

4. (a) Move the first row down to row number three and use Gaussian elimination. There is a unique solution if and only if $a \neq 3/4$. (b) If $b_1 \neq \frac{1}{4}b_3$ there is no solution. If $b_1 = \frac{1}{4}b_3$, there is an infinite set of solutions that take the form $x = -2b_2 + b_3 - 5t$, $y = \frac{3}{2}b_2 - \frac{1}{2}b_3 + 2t$, $z = t$, with $t \in \mathbb{R}$.

15.7

1. $\mathbf{a} + \mathbf{b} = \begin{pmatrix} 5 \\ 3 \end{pmatrix}$, $\mathbf{a} - \mathbf{b} = \begin{pmatrix} -1 \\ -5 \end{pmatrix}$, $2\mathbf{a} + 3\mathbf{b} = \begin{pmatrix} 13 \\ 10 \end{pmatrix}$, and $-5\mathbf{a} + 2\mathbf{b} = \begin{pmatrix} -4 \\ 13 \end{pmatrix}$

2. $\mathbf{a} + \mathbf{b} + \mathbf{c} = (-1, 6, -4)$, $\mathbf{a} - 2\mathbf{b} + 2\mathbf{c} = (-3, 10, 2)$, $3\mathbf{a} + 2\mathbf{b} - 3\mathbf{c} = (9, -6, 9)$

3. By the definitions of vector addition and multiplication of a vector by a real number, the left-hand side of the equation is the vector $(3x - 5, 3y + 10, 3z + 15)$. Since two vectors are equal if and only if they are component-wise equal, this vector equation is equivalent to the equation system $3x - 5 = 4$, $3y + 10 = 1$, and $3z + 15 = 3$, with the obvious solution $x = 3$, $y = -3$, $z = -4$.

4. (a) $x_i = 0$ for all i. (b) Nothing, because $0 \cdot \mathbf{x} = \mathbf{0}$ for all $\mathbf{x}$.

5. We need to find numbers t and s such that $t(2, -1) + s(1, 4) = (4, -11)$. This vector equation is equivalent to $(2t + s, -t + 4s) = (4, -11)$. Equating the two components gives the system (i) $2t + s = 4$ (ii) $-t + 4s = -11$. This system has the solution $t = 3$, $s = -2$, so $(4, -11) = 3(2, -1) - 2(1, 4)$.

6. $4\mathbf{x} - 2\mathbf{x} = 7\mathbf{a} + 8\mathbf{b} - \mathbf{a}$, so $2\mathbf{x} = 6\mathbf{a} + 8\mathbf{b}$, and $\mathbf{x} = 3\mathbf{a} + 4\mathbf{b}$.

7. $\mathbf{a} \cdot \mathbf{a} = 5$, $\mathbf{a} \cdot \mathbf{b} = 2$, and $\mathbf{a} \cdot (\mathbf{a} + \mathbf{b}) = 7$. We see that $\mathbf{a} \cdot \mathbf{a} + \mathbf{a} \cdot \mathbf{b} = \mathbf{a} \cdot (\mathbf{a} + \mathbf{b})$.

8. The inner product of the two vectors is $x^2 + (x - 1)x + 3 \cdot 3x = x^2 + x^2 - x + 9x = 2x^2 + 8x = 2x(x + 4)$, which is 0 for $x = 0$ and $x = -4$.

9. $\mathbf{x} = (5, 7, 12)$, $\mathbf{u} = (20, 18, 25)$, $\mathbf{u} \cdot \mathbf{x} = 526$

10. (a) The firm's revenue is $\mathbf{p} \cdot \mathbf{z}$. Its costs are $\mathbf{p} \cdot \mathbf{x}$. (b) Profit = revenue – costs = $\mathbf{p} \cdot \mathbf{z} - \mathbf{p} \cdot \mathbf{x} = \mathbf{p} \cdot (\mathbf{z} - \mathbf{x}) = \mathbf{p} \cdot \mathbf{y}$. If $\mathbf{p} \cdot \mathbf{y} < 0$, the firm makes a loss equal to $-\mathbf{p} \cdot \mathbf{y}$.

11. (a) Input vector $= \begin{pmatrix} 0 \\ 1 \end{pmatrix}$ (b) Output vector $= \begin{pmatrix} 2 \\ 0 \end{pmatrix}$ (c) Cost $= (1, 3)\begin{pmatrix} 0 \\ 1 \end{pmatrix} = 3$ (d) Revenue $= (1, 3)\begin{pmatrix} 2 \\ 0 \end{pmatrix} = 2$

(e) Value of net output $= (1, 3)\begin{pmatrix} 2 \\ -1 \end{pmatrix} = 2 - 3 = -1$. (f) Loss = cost – revenue = $3 - 2 = 1$, so profit $= -1$.

15.8

1. $\mathbf{a} + \mathbf{b} = (3, 3)$ and $-\frac{1}{2}\mathbf{a} = (-2.5, 0.5)$. See Fig. A15.8.1.

2. (a) $\lambda = 0$ gives $\mathbf{x} = (-1, 2) = \mathbf{b}$, $\lambda = 1/4$ gives $\mathbf{x} = (0, 7/4)$, $\lambda = 1/2$ gives $\mathbf{x} = (1, 3/2)$, $\lambda = 3/4$ gives $\mathbf{x} = (2, 5/4)$, and $\lambda = 1$ gives $\mathbf{x} = (3, 1) = \mathbf{a}$. See Fig. A15.8.2. (b) When λ runs through $[0, 1]$, $\mathbf{x}$ will trace out the line segment joining the end points of $\mathbf{a}$ and $\mathbf{b}$ in Fig. A15.8.2. See SM.

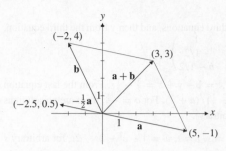

Figure A15.8.1

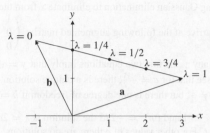

Figure A15.8.2

3. $\|\mathbf{a}\| = 3$, $\|\mathbf{b}\| = 3$, $\|\mathbf{c}\| = \sqrt{29}$. Also, $|\mathbf{a} \cdot \mathbf{b}| = 6 \leq \|\mathbf{a}\| \cdot \|\mathbf{b}\| = 9$

4. (a) $x_1(1, 2, 1) + x_2(-3, 0, -2) = (x_1 - 3x_2, 2x_1, x_1 - 2x_2) = (5, 4, 4)$ when $x_1 = 2$ and $x_2 = -1$.
   (b) x_1 and x_2 would have to satisfy $x_1(1, 2, 1) + x_2(-3, 0, -2) = (-3, 6, 1)$. Then $x_1 - 3x_2 = -3$, $2x_1 = 6$, and $x_1 - 2x_2 = 1$. The first two equations yield $x_1 = 3$ and $x_2 = 2$; then the last equation is not satisfied.

5. The pairs of vectors in (a) and (c) are orthogonal; the pair in (b) is not.

6. The vectors are orthogonal if and only if their inner product is 0—that is, if and only if $x^2 - x - 8 - 2x + x = x^2 - 2x - 8 = 0$, which is the case for $x = -2$ and $x = 4$.

7. If $\mathbf{P}$ is orthogonal and $\mathbf{c}_i$ and $\mathbf{c}_j$ are two different columns of $\mathbf{P}$, then $\mathbf{c}_i'\mathbf{c}_j$ is the element in row i and column j of $\mathbf{P}'\mathbf{P} = \mathbf{I}$, so $\mathbf{c}_i'\mathbf{c}_j = 0$. If $\mathbf{r}_i$ and $\mathbf{r}_j$ are two different rows of $\mathbf{P}$, then $\mathbf{r}_i\mathbf{r}_j'$ is the element in row i and column j of $\mathbf{PP}' = \mathbf{I}' = \mathbf{I}$, so again $\mathbf{r}_i\mathbf{r}_j' = 0$.

8. $(\|\mathbf{a}\| + \|\mathbf{b}\|)^2 = \|\mathbf{a}\|^2 + 2\|\mathbf{a}\| \cdot \|\mathbf{b}\| + \|\mathbf{b}\|^2$, whereas $\|\mathbf{a} + \mathbf{b}\|^2 = (\mathbf{a} + \mathbf{b}) \cdot (\mathbf{a} + \mathbf{b}) = \|\mathbf{a}\|^2 + 2\mathbf{a} \cdot \mathbf{b} + \|\mathbf{b}\|^2$. It follows that $(\|\mathbf{a}\| + \|\mathbf{b}\|)^2 - \|\mathbf{a} + \mathbf{b}\|^2 = 2(\|\mathbf{a}\| \cdot \|\mathbf{b}\| - \mathbf{a} \cdot \mathbf{b}) \geq 0$ by the Cauchy–Schwarz inequality (2).

15.9

1. (a) $x_1 = 3t + 10(1 - t) = 10 - 7t$, $x_2 = (-2)t + 2(1 - t) = 2 - 4t$, and $x_3 = 2t + (1 - t) = 1 + t$
   (b) $x_1 = 1$, $x_2 = 3 - t$, and $x_3 = 2 + t$

2. (a) To show that $\mathbf{a}$ lies on L, put $t = 0$.   (b) The direction of L is given by $(-1, 2, 1)$, and the equation of $\mathcal{P}$ is $(-1)(x_1 - 2) + 2(x_2 - (-1)) + 1 \cdot (x_3 - 3) = 0$, or $-x_1 + 2x_2 + x_3 = -1$.
   (c) We must have $3(-t + 2) + 5(2t - 1) - (t + 3) = 6$, and so $t = 4/3$. Thus $P = (2/3, 5/3, 13/3)$.

3. $x_1 - 3x_2 - 2x_3 = -3$ 4. $2x + 3y + 5z \leq m$, with $m \geq 75$.

5. (a) Direct verification.   (b) $(x_1, x_2, x_3) = (-2, 1, -1) + t(-1, 2, 3) = (-2 - t, 1 + 2t, -1 + 3t)$

Review Problems for Chapter 15

1. (a) $\mathbf{A} = \begin{pmatrix} 2 & 3 & 4 \\ 3 & 4 & 5 \end{pmatrix}$ (b) $\mathbf{A} = \begin{pmatrix} 1 & -1 & 1 \\ -1 & 1 & -1 \end{pmatrix}$

2. (a) $\mathbf{A} - \mathbf{B} = \begin{pmatrix} 3 & -2 \\ -2 & 2 \end{pmatrix}$ (b) $\mathbf{A} + \mathbf{B} - 2\mathbf{C} = \begin{pmatrix} -3 & -4 \\ -2 & -8 \end{pmatrix}$ (c) $\mathbf{AB} = \begin{pmatrix} -2 & 4 \\ 2 & -3 \end{pmatrix}$ (d) $\mathbf{C(AB)} = \begin{pmatrix} 2 & -1 \\ 6 & -8 \end{pmatrix}$
   (e) $\mathbf{AD} = \begin{pmatrix} 2 & 2 & 2 \\ 0 & 2 & 3 \end{pmatrix}$ (f) $\mathbf{DC}$ is not defined.

3. (a) $2\mathbf{A} - 3\mathbf{B} = \begin{pmatrix} 7 & -6 \\ -5 & 5 \end{pmatrix}$ (b) $(\mathbf{A} - \mathbf{B})' = \begin{pmatrix} 3 & -2 \\ -2 & 2 \end{pmatrix}$ (c) and (d): $(\mathbf{C}'\mathbf{A}')\mathbf{B}' = \mathbf{C}'(\mathbf{A}'\mathbf{B}') = \begin{pmatrix} -6 & 5 \\ -4 & 5 \end{pmatrix}$
   (e) Not defined.   (f) $\mathbf{D}'\mathbf{D} = \begin{pmatrix} 2 & 4 & 5 \\ 4 & 10 & 13 \\ 5 & 13 & 17 \end{pmatrix}$

4. (a) $\begin{pmatrix} 2 & -5 \\ 5 & 8 \end{pmatrix} \begin{pmatrix} x_1 \\ x_2 \end{pmatrix} = \begin{pmatrix} 3 \\ 5 \end{pmatrix}$ (b) $\begin{pmatrix} 1 & 1 & 1 & 1 \\ 1 & 3 & 2 & 4 \\ 1 & 4 & 8 & 0 \\ 2 & 0 & 1 & -1 \end{pmatrix} \begin{pmatrix} x \\ y \\ z \\ t \end{pmatrix} = \begin{pmatrix} a \\ b \\ c \\ d \end{pmatrix}$ (c) $\begin{pmatrix} a & 1 & a+1 \\ 1 & 2 & 1 \\ 3 & 4 & 7 \end{pmatrix} \begin{pmatrix} x \\ y \\ z \end{pmatrix} = \begin{pmatrix} b_1 \\ b_2 \\ b_3 \end{pmatrix}$

5. $\mathbf{A} + \mathbf{B} = \begin{pmatrix} 0 & -4 & 1 \\ 8 & 6 & 4 \\ -10 & 9 & 15 \end{pmatrix}$, $\mathbf{A} - \mathbf{B} = \begin{pmatrix} 0 & 6 & -5 \\ -2 & 2 & 6 \\ -2 & 5 & 15 \end{pmatrix}$, $\mathbf{AB} = \begin{pmatrix} 13 & -2 & -1 \\ 0 & 3 & 5 \\ -25 & 74 & -25 \end{pmatrix}$,

$\mathbf{BA} = \begin{pmatrix} -33 & 1 & 20 \\ 12 & 6 & -15 \\ 6 & 4 & 18 \end{pmatrix}$, $(\mathbf{AB})\mathbf{C} = \mathbf{A}(\mathbf{BC}) = \begin{pmatrix} 74 & -31 & -48 \\ 6 & 25 & 38 \\ -2 & -75 & -26 \end{pmatrix}$

6. The matrix products on the left-hand side are $\begin{pmatrix} 2a+b & a+b \\ 2x & x \end{pmatrix}$ and $\begin{pmatrix} a & b \\ 2a+x & 2b \end{pmatrix}$, whose difference is $\begin{pmatrix} a+b & a \\ x-2a & x-2b \end{pmatrix}$. Equating this to the matrix $\begin{pmatrix} 2 & 1 \\ 4 & 4 \end{pmatrix}$ on the right-hand side yields $a+b = 2$, $a = 1$, $x - 2a = 4$, and $x - 2 = 4$. It follows that $a = b = 1$, $x = 6$.

7. (a) $\mathbf{A}^2 = \begin{pmatrix} a^2 - b^2 & 2ab & b^2 \\ -2ab & a^2 - 2b^2 & 2ab \\ b^2 & -2ab & a^2 - b^2 \end{pmatrix}$ (b) $(\mathbf{C}'\mathbf{BC})' = \mathbf{C}'\mathbf{B}'(\mathbf{C}')' = \mathbf{C}'(-\mathbf{B})\mathbf{C} = -\mathbf{C}'\mathbf{BC}$. $\mathbf{A}$ is skew-symmetric if and only if $a = 0$.   (c) $\mathbf{A}_1' = \frac{1}{2}(\mathbf{A}' + \mathbf{A}'') = \frac{1}{2}(\mathbf{A}' + \mathbf{A}) = \mathbf{A}_1$, so $\mathbf{A}_1$ is symmetric. It is equally easy to prove that $\mathbf{A}_2$ is skew-symmetric, as well as that any square matrix $\mathbf{A}$ is therefore the sum $\mathbf{A}_1 + \mathbf{A}_2$ of a symmetric matrix $\mathbf{A}_1$ and a skew-symmetric matrix $\mathbf{A}_2$.

8. (a) $\begin{pmatrix} 1 & 4 & 1 \\ 2 & 2 & 8 \end{pmatrix} \begin{matrix} -2 \\ \hookleftarrow \end{matrix} \sim \begin{pmatrix} 1 & 4 & 1 \\ 0 & -6 & 6 \end{pmatrix} -1/6 \sim \begin{pmatrix} 1 & 4 & 1 \\ 0 & 1 & -1 \end{pmatrix} \begin{matrix} \hookleftarrow \\ -4 \end{matrix} \sim \begin{pmatrix} 1 & 0 & 5 \\ 0 & 1 & -1 \end{pmatrix}$

The solution is $x_1 = 5$, $x_2 = -1$.   (b) Solution: $x_1 = 3/7$, $x_2 = -5/7$, $x_3 = -18/7$.
(c) Solution: $x_1 = (1/14)x_3$, $x_2 = -(19/14)x_3$, where x_3 is arbitrary. (One degree of freedom.)

9. We use the Gaussian method:

$$\begin{pmatrix} 1 & a & 2 & 0 \\ -2 & -a & 1 & 4 \\ 2a & 3a^2 & 9 & 4 \end{pmatrix} \begin{matrix} 2 \\ \hookleftarrow \\ \longleftarrow \end{matrix} \begin{matrix} -2a \\ \\ \end{matrix} \sim \begin{pmatrix} 1 & a & 2 & 0 \\ 0 & a & 5 & 4 \\ 0 & a^2 & 9-4a & 4 \end{pmatrix} \begin{matrix} \\ -a \\ \hookleftarrow \end{matrix} \sim \begin{pmatrix} 1 & a & 2 & 0 \\ 0 & a & 5 & 4 \\ 0 & 0 & 9-9a & 4-4a \end{pmatrix}$$

For $a = 1$, the last equation is superfluous and the solution is $x = 3t - 4$, $y = -5t + 4$, $z = t$, with t arbitrary. If $a \neq 1$, we have $(9 - 9a)z = 4 - 4a$, so $z = 4/9$. The two other equations then become $x + ay = -8/9$ and $ay = 16/9$. If $a = 0$, there is no solution. If $a \neq 0$, the solution is $x = -8/3$, $y = 16/9a$, and $z = 4/9$.

10. $\|\mathbf{a}\| = \sqrt{35}$, $\|\mathbf{b}\| = \sqrt{11}$, and $\|\mathbf{c}\| = \sqrt{69}$. Also, $|\mathbf{a} \cdot \mathbf{b}| = |(-1) \cdot 1 + 5 \cdot 1 + 3 \cdot (-3)| = |-5| = 5$, and $\sqrt{35}\sqrt{11} = \sqrt{385}$ is obviously greater than 5, so the Cauchy–Schwarz inequality is satisfied.

11. (a) To produce $\mathbf{a}$, put $\lambda = 1/2$. To produce $\mathbf{b}$ would require $6\lambda + 2 = 7$, $-2\lambda + 6 = 5$, and $-6\lambda + 10 = 5$, but these equations have no solution.   For (b) and (c) see SM.

12. Because $\mathbf{PQ} = \mathbf{QP} + \mathbf{P}$, multiplying on the left by $\mathbf{P}$ gives $\mathbf{P}^2\mathbf{Q} = (\mathbf{PQ})\mathbf{P} + \mathbf{P}^2 = (\mathbf{QP} + \mathbf{P})\mathbf{P} + \mathbf{P}^2 = \mathbf{QP}^2 + 2\mathbf{P}^2$. See SM for details of how to repeat this argument for higher powers of $\mathbf{P}$.

Chapter 16

16.1

1. (a) $3 \cdot 6 - 2 \cdot 0 = 18$ (b) $ab - ba = 0$ (c) $(a+b)^2 - (a-b)^2 = 4ab$ (d) $3^t 2^{t-1} - 3^{t-1} 2^t = 3^{t-1} 2^{t-1}(3-2) = 6^{t-1}$

2. See Fig. A16.1.2. The shaded parallelogram has area $3 \cdot 6 = 18 = \begin{vmatrix} 3 & 0 \\ 2 & 6 \end{vmatrix}$.

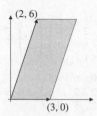

Figure A16.1.2

3. (a) Cramer's rule gives $x = \dfrac{\begin{vmatrix} 8 & -1 \\ 5 & -2 \end{vmatrix}}{\begin{vmatrix} 3 & -1 \\ 1 & -2 \end{vmatrix}} = \dfrac{-16+5}{-6+1} = \dfrac{11}{5}$, $y = \dfrac{\begin{vmatrix} 3 & 8 \\ 1 & 5 \end{vmatrix}}{\begin{vmatrix} 3 & -1 \\ 1 & -2 \end{vmatrix}} = \dfrac{15-8}{-6+1} = \dfrac{7}{-5} = -\dfrac{7}{5}$.

(b) $x = 4$ and $y = -1$ (c) $x = \dfrac{a+2b}{a^2+b^2}$, $y = \dfrac{2a-b}{a^2+b^2}$, $(a^2+b^2 \neq 0)$

4. The numbers a and b must satisfy $a + 1 = 0$ and $a - 3b = -10$, so $a = -1$ and $b = 3$.

5. Expanding the determinant, $(2-x)(-x) - 8 = 0$, that is $x^2 - 2x - 8 = 0$, so $x = -2$ or $x = 4$.

6. The matrix product is $\mathbf{AB} = \begin{pmatrix} a_{11}b_{11} + a_{12}b_{21} & a_{11}b_{12} + a_{12}b_{22} \\ a_{21}b_{11} + a_{22}b_{21} & a_{21}b_{12} + a_{22}b_{22} \end{pmatrix}$, implying that

$|\mathbf{AB}| = (a_{11}b_{11} + a_{12}b_{21})(a_{21}b_{12} + a_{22}b_{22}) - (a_{11}b_{12} + a_{12}b_{22})(a_{21}b_{11} + a_{22}b_{21})$. On the other hand, $|\mathbf{A}||\mathbf{B}| = (a_{11}a_{22} - a_{12}a_{21})(b_{11}b_{22} - b_{12}b_{21})$. A tedious process of expanding each expression, then cancelling four terms in the expression of $|\mathbf{A}||\mathbf{B}|$, reveals that the two expressions are equal.

7. If $\mathbf{A} = \mathbf{B} = \begin{pmatrix} 1 & 0 \\ 0 & 1 \end{pmatrix}$, then $|\mathbf{A} + \mathbf{B}| = 4$, whereas $|\mathbf{A}| + |\mathbf{B}| = 2$. ($\mathbf{A}$ and $\mathbf{B}$ can be chosen almost arbitrarily.)

8. Write the system as $\begin{cases} Y - C = I_0 + G_0 \\ -bY + C = a \end{cases}$. Then Cramer's rule yields

$$Y = \dfrac{\begin{vmatrix} I_0 + G_0 & -1 \\ a & 1 \end{vmatrix}}{\begin{vmatrix} 1 & -1 \\ -b & 1 \end{vmatrix}} = \dfrac{a + I_0 + G_0}{1-b}, \quad C = \dfrac{\begin{vmatrix} 1 & I_0 + G_0 \\ -b & a \end{vmatrix}}{\begin{vmatrix} 1 & -1 \\ -b & 1 \end{vmatrix}} = \dfrac{a + b(I_0 + G_0)}{1-b}$$

The expression for Y is most easily found by substituting the second equation into the first, and then solving for Y. Then use $C = a + bY$ to find C.

9. (a) $X_1 = M_2$ because nation 1's exports are nation 2's imports. Similarly, $X_2 = M_1$.
(b) Substituting for X_1, X_2, M_1, M_2, C_1, and C_2 gives: (i) $Y_1(1 - c_1 + m_1) - m_2 Y_2 = A_1$;
(ii) $Y_2(1 - c_2 + m_2) - m_1 Y_1 = A_2$. Using Cramer's rule with $D = (1 - c_2 + m_2)(1 - c_1 + m_1) - m_1 m_2$ yields

$$Y_1 = [A_2 m_2 + A_1(1 - c_2 + m_2)]/D, \qquad Y_2 = [A_1 m_1 + A_2(1 - c_1 + m_1)]/D$$

(c) Y_2 increases when A_1 increases.

16.2

1. (a) -2 (b) -2 (c) adf (d) $e(ad - bc)$

2. $\mathbf{AB} = \begin{pmatrix} -1 & -1 & -1 \\ 7 & 13 & 13 \\ 5 & 9 & 10 \end{pmatrix}$, $|\mathbf{A}| = -2$, $|\mathbf{B}| = 3$, $|\mathbf{AB}| = |\mathbf{A}| \cdot |\mathbf{B}| = -6$

3. (a) $x_1 = 1$, $x_2 = 2$, and $x_3 = 3$ (b) $x_1 = x_2 = x_3 = 0$ (c) $x = 1$, $y = 2$, and $z = 3$

4. By Sarrus's rule the determinant is $(1 + a)(1 + b)(1 + c) + 1 + 1 - (1 + b) - (1 + a) - (1 + c)$, which reduces to the given expression.

5. $\text{tr}(\mathbf{A}) = a + b - 1 = 0$ and thus $b = 1 - a$. Also, $|\mathbf{A}| = -2ab = 12$, and so $-2a(1 - a) = 12$, or $a^2 - a - 6 = 0$. The roots of this equation are $a = 3$ and $a = -2$. Thus the solutions are $(a, b) = (3, -2)$ or $(a, b) = (-2, 3)$.

6. By Sarrus's rule, the determinant is $(1 - x)^3 + 8 + 8 - 4(1 - x) - 4(1 - x) - 4(1 - x) = -x^3 + 3x^2 + 9x + 5 = (5 - x)(x + 1)^2$, so $x = -1$ or $x = 5$.

7. (a) $|\mathbf{A}_t| = 2t^2 - 2t + 1 = 2(t - \frac{1}{2})^2 + \frac{1}{2} > 0$ for all t. (Alternatively, show that the quadratic polynomial has no real zeros.)   (b) $\mathbf{A}_t^3 = \begin{pmatrix} 1 & 2t - 2t^2 & t - t^2 \\ 4t - 4 & 5t - 4 & -t^2 + 4t - 3 \\ 2 - 2t & t^2 - 4t + 3 & t^3 - 2t + 2 \end{pmatrix}$. We find that $\mathbf{A}_t^3 = \mathbf{I}_3$ for $t = 1$.

8. $Y = (a - bd + A_0)/[1 - b(1 - t)]$, $C = (a - bd + A_0 b(1 - t))/[1 - b(1 - t)]$,
$T = [t(a + A_0) + (1 - b)d]/[1 - b(1 - t)]$

16.3

1. (a) $1 \cdot 2 \cdot 3 \cdot 4 = 24$ (b) $d - a$ (c) $1 \cdot 1 \cdot 1 \cdot 11 - 1 \cdot 1 \cdot 4 \cdot 4 - 1 \cdot (-3) \cdot 1 \cdot 3 - 2 \cdot 1 \cdot 1 \cdot 2 = 0$

2. With $\mathbf{A} = \begin{pmatrix} a_{11} & a_{12} & \cdots & a_{1n} \\ 0 & a_{22} & \cdots & a_{2n} \\ \vdots & \vdots & \ddots & \vdots \\ 0 & 0 & \cdots & a_{nn} \end{pmatrix}$ and $\mathbf{B} = \begin{pmatrix} b_{11} & b_{12} & \cdots & b_{1n} \\ 0 & b_{22} & \cdots & b_{2n} \\ \vdots & \vdots & \ddots & \vdots \\ 0 & 0 & \cdots & b_{nn} \end{pmatrix}$,

the product $\mathbf{AB}$ is easily seen to be upper triangular, with the elements $a_{11}b_{11}, a_{22}b_{22}, \ldots, a_{nn}b_{nn}$ on the main diagonal. The determinant $|\mathbf{AB}|$ is, according to (4), the product of the n numbers $a_{ii}b_{ii}$. On the other hand, $|\mathbf{A}| = a_{11}a_{22} \cdots a_{nn}$, and $|\mathbf{B}| = b_{11}b_{22} \cdots b_{nn}$, so the required equality follows immediately.

3. $+a_{12}a_{23}a_{35}a_{41}a_{54}$. (Four lines between pairs of boxed elements rise as one goes to the right.)

4. $-a_{15}a_{24}a_{32}a_{43}a_{51}$. (There are nine lines that rise to the right.)

5. Carefully examining the determinant reveals that its only nonzero term is the product of its diagonal elements. So the equation is $(2 - x)^4 = 0$, whose only solution is $x = 2$.

16.4

1. (a) $\mathbf{AB} = \begin{pmatrix} 13 & 16 \\ 29 & 36 \end{pmatrix}$, $\mathbf{BA} = \begin{pmatrix} 15 & 22 \\ 23 & 34 \end{pmatrix}$, $\mathbf{A'B'} = \begin{pmatrix} 15 & 23 \\ 22 & 34 \end{pmatrix}$, $\mathbf{B'A'} = \begin{pmatrix} 13 & 29 \\ 16 & 36 \end{pmatrix}$

(b) $|\mathbf{A}| = |\mathbf{A'}| = -2$ and $|\mathbf{B}| = |\mathbf{B'}| = -2$. So $|\mathbf{AB}| = 4 = |\mathbf{A}| \cdot |\mathbf{B}|$ and $|\mathbf{A'B'}| = |\mathbf{A'}| \cdot |\mathbf{B'}| = 4$.

2. $\mathbf{A'} = \begin{pmatrix} 2 & 1 & 1 \\ 1 & 0 & 2 \\ 3 & 1 & 5 \end{pmatrix}$, $|\mathbf{A}| = |\mathbf{A'}| = -2$

3. (a) 0 (one column has only zeros).   (b) 0 (rows 1 and 4 are proportional).   (c) $(a_1 - x)(-x)^3 = x^4 - a_1 x^3$. (Use the definition of a determinant and observe that at most one term is nonzero.)

4. $|\mathbf{AB}| = |\mathbf{A}||\mathbf{B}| = -12$, $3|\mathbf{A}| = 9$, $|-2\mathbf{B}| = (-2)^3(-4) = 32$, $|4\mathbf{A}| = 4^3|\mathbf{A}| = 4^3 \cdot 3 = 192$, $|\mathbf{A}| + |\mathbf{B}| = -1$, whereas $|\mathbf{A} + \mathbf{B}|$ is not determined.

5. $\mathbf{A}^2 = \begin{pmatrix} a^2 + 6 & a + 1 & a^2 + 4a - 12 \\ a^2 + 2a + 2 & 3 & 8 - 2a^2 \\ a - 3 & 1 & 13 \end{pmatrix}$ and $|\mathbf{A}| = a^2 - 3a + 2$.

6. (a) The first and the second columns are proportional, so the determinant is 0 by part E of Theorem 16.4.1.
(b) Add the second column to the third. This makes the first and third columns proportional.

(c) The term $x - y$ is a common factor for each entry in the first row. If $x \neq y$, the first two rows are proportional. If $x = y$, the first row has all elements 0. In either case the determinant is 0.

7. $\mathbf{X}'\mathbf{X} = \begin{pmatrix} 4 & 3 & 2 \\ 3 & 5 & 1 \\ 2 & 1 & 2 \end{pmatrix}$ and $|\mathbf{X}'\mathbf{X}| = 10$

8. By Sarrus's rule, for example, $|\mathbf{A}_a| = a(a^2 + 1) + 4 + 4 - 4(a^2 + 1) - a - 4 = a^2(a - 4)$, so $|\mathbf{A}_1| = -3$ and $|\mathbf{A}_1^6| = |\mathbf{A}_1|^6 = (-3)^6 = 729$. (Note how much easier this is than first finding $\mathbf{A}_1^6$ and then evaluating its determinant.)

9. Because $\mathbf{P}'\mathbf{P} = \mathbf{I}_n$, it follows from (16.4.1) and (16.3.4) that $|\mathbf{P}'||\mathbf{P}| = |\mathbf{I}_n| = 1$. But $|\mathbf{P}'| = |\mathbf{P}|$ by rule B in Theorem 16.4.1, so $|\mathbf{P}|^2 = 1$. Hence, $|\mathbf{P}| = \pm 1$.

10. (a) Because $\mathbf{A}^2 = \mathbf{I}_n$ it follows from (16.4.1) that $|\mathbf{A}|^2 = |\mathbf{I}_n| = 1$, and so $|\mathbf{A}| = \pm 1$. (b) Direct verification by matrix multiplication. (c) We have $(\mathbf{I}_n - \mathbf{A})(\mathbf{I}_n + \mathbf{A}) = \mathbf{I}_n \cdot \mathbf{I}_n - \mathbf{A}\mathbf{I}_n + \mathbf{I}_n\mathbf{A} - \mathbf{A}\mathbf{A} = \mathbf{I}_n - \mathbf{A} + \mathbf{A} - \mathbf{A}^2 = \mathbf{I}_n - \mathbf{A}^2$, and this expression equals $\mathbf{0}$ if and only if $\mathbf{A}^2 = \mathbf{I}_n$.

11. (a) The first equality is true, the second is false. (The second equality becomes true if the factor 2 is replaced by 4.) (b) Generally false. (Both determinants on the right are 0, even if $ad - bc \neq 0$.) (c) Both equalities are true. (d) True. (The second determinant is the result of subtracting 2 times row 1 of the first determinant from its row 2.)

12. We want to show that $\mathbf{B}(\mathbf{PQ}) = (\mathbf{PQ})\mathbf{B}$. Using the associative law for matrix multiplication, we get

$$\mathbf{B}(\mathbf{PQ}) = (\mathbf{BP})\mathbf{Q} \overset{(1)}{=} (\mathbf{PB})\mathbf{Q} = \mathbf{P}(\mathbf{BQ}) \overset{(2)}{=} \mathbf{P}(\mathbf{QB}) = (\mathbf{PQ})\mathbf{B}.$$

This shows that $\mathbf{PQ}$ does indeed commute with $\mathbf{B}$. (At (1) we used the fact that $\mathbf{BP} = \mathbf{PB}$, and at (2) we used $\mathbf{BQ} = \mathbf{QB}$.)

13. Let $\mathbf{A} = \begin{pmatrix} 0 & c & b \\ c & 0 & a \\ b & a & 0 \end{pmatrix}$. Then compute $\mathbf{A}^2$ and recall (16.4.1).

14. Start by adding each of the last $n - 1$ rows to the first row. Each element in the first row then becomes $na + b$. Factor this out of the determinant. Next, add the first row multiplied by $-a$ to all the other $n - 1$ rows. The result is an upper triangular matrix whose diagonal elements are $1, b, b, ..., b$, with product equal to b^{n-1}. The conclusion follows easily.

16.5

1. (a) 2. (Subtract row 1 from both row 2 and row 3 to get a determinant whose first column has elements $1, 0, 0$. Then expand by the first column.) (b) 30 (c) 0. (Columns 2 and 4 are proportional.)

2. In each of these cases we keep expanding by the last (remaining) column. The answers are: (a) $-abc$ (b) $abcd$ (c) $1 \cdot 5 \cdot 3 \cdot 4 \cdot 6 = 360$

16.6

1. (a) Using (16.6.4): $\begin{pmatrix} 3 & 0 \\ 2 & -1 \end{pmatrix} \cdot \begin{pmatrix} 1/3 & 0 \\ 2/3 & -1 \end{pmatrix} = \begin{pmatrix} 1 & 0 \\ 0 & 1 \end{pmatrix}$. (b) Use (16.6.4).

2. $\mathbf{AB} = \begin{pmatrix} 1 & 0 & 0 \\ a+b & 2a+1/4+3b & 4a+3/2+2b \\ 0 & 0 & 1 \end{pmatrix} = \mathbf{I}$ if and only if $a+b = 4a+3/2+2b = 0$ and $2a+1/4+3b = 1$. This is true if and only if $a = -3/4$ and $b = 3/4$.

3. (a) $\begin{pmatrix} x \\ y \end{pmatrix} = \begin{pmatrix} 2 & -3 \\ 3 & -4 \end{pmatrix}^{-1} \begin{pmatrix} 3 \\ 5 \end{pmatrix} = \begin{pmatrix} -4 & 3 \\ -3 & 2 \end{pmatrix} \begin{pmatrix} 3 \\ 5 \end{pmatrix} = \begin{pmatrix} 3 \\ 1 \end{pmatrix}$

(b) $\begin{pmatrix} x \\ y \end{pmatrix} = \begin{pmatrix} -4 & 3 \\ -3 & 2 \end{pmatrix} \begin{pmatrix} 8 \\ 11 \end{pmatrix} = \begin{pmatrix} 1 \\ -2 \end{pmatrix}$ (c) $\begin{pmatrix} x \\ y \end{pmatrix} = \begin{pmatrix} -4 & 3 \\ -3 & 2 \end{pmatrix} \begin{pmatrix} 0 \\ 0 \end{pmatrix} = \begin{pmatrix} 0 \\ 0 \end{pmatrix}$

4. From $\mathbf{A}^3 = \mathbf{I}$, it follows that $\mathbf{A}^2\mathbf{A} = \mathbf{I}$, so $\mathbf{A}^{-1} = \mathbf{A}^2 = \frac{1}{2} \begin{pmatrix} -1 & \sqrt{3} \\ -\sqrt{3} & -1 \end{pmatrix}$.

5. (a) $|\mathbf{A}| = 1$, $\mathbf{A}^2 = \begin{pmatrix} 0 & 1 & 1 \\ 1 & 1 & 2 \\ 1 & 1 & 1 \end{pmatrix}$, $\mathbf{A}^3 = \begin{pmatrix} 1 & 1 & 2 \\ 2 & 2 & 3 \\ 1 & 2 & 2 \end{pmatrix}$. Direct verification yields $\mathbf{A}^3 - 2\mathbf{A}^2 + \mathbf{A} - \mathbf{I}_3 = \mathbf{0}$.

The last equality is equivalent to $\mathbf{A}(\mathbf{A}^2 - 2\mathbf{A} + \mathbf{I}_3) = \mathbf{A}(\mathbf{A} - \mathbf{I}_3)^2 = \mathbf{I}_3$, so $\mathbf{A}^{-1} = (\mathbf{A} - \mathbf{I}_3)^2$.

(b) Choose $\mathbf{P} = (\mathbf{A} - \mathbf{I}_3)^{-1} = \begin{pmatrix} 0 & 0 & 1 \\ 1 & 0 & 1 \\ 0 & 1 & 0 \end{pmatrix}$, so that $\mathbf{A} = [(\mathbf{A} - \mathbf{I}_3)^2]^{-1} = \mathbf{P}^2$. The matrix $-\mathbf{P}$ also works.

6. (a) $\mathbf{A}\mathbf{A}' = \begin{pmatrix} 21 & 11 \\ 11 & 10 \end{pmatrix}$, $|\mathbf{A}\mathbf{A}'| = 89$, and $(\mathbf{A}\mathbf{A}')^{-1} = \frac{1}{89}\begin{pmatrix} 10 & -11 \\ -11 & 21 \end{pmatrix}$.   (b) No, $\mathbf{A}\mathbf{A}'$ is always symmetric by

Example 15.5.3. Then $(\mathbf{A}\mathbf{A}')^{-1}$ is symmetric by Note 2.

7. (a) $\mathbf{A}^2 = (\mathbf{P}\mathbf{D}\mathbf{P}^{-1})(\mathbf{P}\mathbf{D}\mathbf{P}^{-1}) = \mathbf{P}\mathbf{D}(\mathbf{P}^{-1}\mathbf{P})\mathbf{D}\mathbf{P}^{-1} = \mathbf{P}\mathbf{D}\mathbf{I}\mathbf{D}\mathbf{P}^{-1} = \mathbf{P}\mathbf{D}^2\mathbf{P}^{-1}$.

(b) Suppose the formula is valid for $m = k$. Then $\mathbf{A}^{k+1} = \mathbf{A}\mathbf{A}^k = \mathbf{P}\mathbf{D}\mathbf{P}^{-1}(\mathbf{P}\mathbf{D}^k\mathbf{P}^{-1}) = \mathbf{P}\mathbf{D}(\mathbf{P}^{-1}\mathbf{P})\mathbf{D}^k\mathbf{P}^{-1}$
$= \mathbf{P}\mathbf{D}\mathbf{I}\mathbf{D}^k\mathbf{P}^{-1} = \mathbf{P}\mathbf{D}\mathbf{D}^k\mathbf{P}^{-1} = \mathbf{P}\mathbf{D}^{k+1}\mathbf{P}^{-1}$.

8. $\mathbf{B}^2 + \mathbf{B} = \mathbf{I}$, $\mathbf{B}^3 - 2\mathbf{B} + \mathbf{I} = \mathbf{0}$, and $\mathbf{B}^{-1} = \mathbf{B} + \mathbf{I} = \begin{pmatrix} 1/2 & 5 \\ 1/4 & 1/2 \end{pmatrix}$.

9. Let $\mathbf{B} = \mathbf{X}(\mathbf{X}'\mathbf{X})^{-1}\mathbf{X}'$. Then $\mathbf{A}^2 = (\mathbf{I}_m - \mathbf{B})(\mathbf{I}_m - \mathbf{B}) = \mathbf{I}_m - \mathbf{B} - \mathbf{B} + \mathbf{B}^2$. Here $\mathbf{B}^2 = (\mathbf{X}(\mathbf{X}'\mathbf{X})^{-1}\mathbf{X}')(\mathbf{X}(\mathbf{X}'\mathbf{X})^{-1}\mathbf{X}')$
$= \mathbf{X}(\mathbf{X}'\mathbf{X})^{-1}(\mathbf{X}'\mathbf{X})(\mathbf{X}'\mathbf{X})^{-1}\mathbf{X}' = \mathbf{X}(\mathbf{X}'\mathbf{X})^{-1}\mathbf{X}' = \mathbf{B}$. Thus, $\mathbf{A}^2 = \mathbf{I}_m - \mathbf{B} - \mathbf{B} + \mathbf{B} = \mathbf{I}_m - \mathbf{B} = \mathbf{A}$.

10. $\mathbf{A}\mathbf{B} = \begin{pmatrix} -7 & 0 \\ -2 & 10 \end{pmatrix}$, so $\mathbf{C}\mathbf{X} = \mathbf{D} - \mathbf{A}\mathbf{B} = \begin{pmatrix} -2 & 3 \\ -6 & 7 \end{pmatrix}$. But $\mathbf{C}^{-1} = \begin{pmatrix} -2 & 1 \\ 3/2 & -1/2 \end{pmatrix}$, so $\mathbf{X} = \begin{pmatrix} -2 & 1 \\ 0 & 1 \end{pmatrix}$.

11. (a) If $\mathbf{C}^2 + \mathbf{C} = \mathbf{I}$, then $\mathbf{C}(\mathbf{C} + \mathbf{I}) = \mathbf{I}$, and so $\mathbf{C}^{-1} = \mathbf{C} + \mathbf{I} = \mathbf{I} + \mathbf{C}$.

(b) Because $\mathbf{C}^2 = \mathbf{I} - \mathbf{C}$, it follows that $\mathbf{C}^3 = \mathbf{C}^2\mathbf{C} = (\mathbf{I} - \mathbf{C})\mathbf{C} = \mathbf{C} - \mathbf{C}^2 = \mathbf{C} - (\mathbf{I} - \mathbf{C}) = -\mathbf{I} + 2\mathbf{C}$. Moreover,
$\mathbf{C}^4 = \mathbf{C}^3\mathbf{C} = (-\mathbf{I} + 2\mathbf{C})\mathbf{C} = -\mathbf{C} + 2\mathbf{C}^2 = -\mathbf{C} + 2(\mathbf{I} - \mathbf{C}) = 2\mathbf{I} - 3\mathbf{C}$.

16.7

1. (a) $\begin{pmatrix} -5/2 & 3/2 \\ 2 & -1 \end{pmatrix}$ (b) $\frac{1}{9}\begin{pmatrix} 1 & 4 & 2 \\ 2 & -1 & 4 \\ 4 & -2 & -1 \end{pmatrix}$ (c) The matrix has no inverse.

2. The inverse is $\frac{1}{|\mathbf{A}|}\begin{pmatrix} C_{11} & C_{21} & C_{31} \\ C_{12} & C_{22} & C_{32} \\ C_{13} & C_{23} & C_{33} \end{pmatrix} = \frac{1}{72}\begin{pmatrix} -3 & 5 & 9 \\ 18 & -6 & 18 \\ 6 & 14 & -18 \end{pmatrix}$. **3.** $(\mathbf{I} - \mathbf{A})^{-1} = \frac{5}{62}\begin{pmatrix} 18 & 16 & 10 \\ 2 & 19 & 8 \\ 4 & 7 & 16 \end{pmatrix}$

4. When $k = r$, the solution to the system is $x_1 = b_{1r}^*, x_2 = b_{2r}^*, \ldots, x_n = b_{nr}^*$.

5. (a) $\mathbf{A}^{-1} = \begin{pmatrix} -2 & 1 \\ 3/2 & -1/2 \end{pmatrix}$ (b) $\begin{pmatrix} 1 & -3 & 2 \\ -3 & 3 & -1 \\ 2 & -1 & 0 \end{pmatrix}$ (c) There is no inverse.

16.8

1. (a) $x = 1$, $y = -2$, and $z = 2$ (b) $x = -3$, $y = 6$, $z = 5$, and $u = -5$

2. The determinant of the system is equal to -10, so the solution is unique. The determinants in (2) are

$$D_1 = \begin{vmatrix} b_1 & 1 & 0 \\ b_2 & -1 & 2 \\ b_3 & 3 & -1 \end{vmatrix}, \quad D_2 = \begin{vmatrix} 3 & b_1 & 0 \\ 1 & b_2 & 2 \\ 2 & b_3 & -1 \end{vmatrix}, \quad D_3 = \begin{vmatrix} 3 & 1 & b_1 \\ 1 & -1 & b_2 \\ 2 & 3 & b_3 \end{vmatrix}$$

Expanding each of these determinants by the column (b_1, b_2, b_3), we find that $D_1 = -5b_1 + b_2 + 2b_3$, $D_2 = 5b_1 - 3b_2 - 6b_3$, $D_3 = 5b_1 - 7b_2 - 4b_3$. Hence, $x_1 = \frac{1}{2}b_1 - \frac{1}{10}b_2 - \frac{1}{5}b_3$, $x_2 = -\frac{1}{2}b_1 + \frac{3}{10}b_2 + \frac{3}{5}b_3$, $x_3 = -\frac{1}{2}b_1 + \frac{7}{10}b_2 + \frac{2}{5}b_3$.

3. Show that the determinant of the coefficient matrix is equal to $-(a^3 + b^3 + c^3 - 3abc)$, and use Theorem 16.8.2.

16.9

1. $x_1 = \frac{1}{4}x_2 + 100$, $x_2 = 2x_3 + 80$, $x_3 = \frac{1}{2}x_1$. Solution: $x_1 = 160$, $x_2 = 240$, $x_3 = 80$.

2. (a) Let x and y denote total production in industries A and I, respectively. Then $x = \frac{1}{6}x + \frac{1}{4}y + 60$ and $y = \frac{1}{4}x + \frac{1}{4}y + 60$. So $\frac{5}{6}x - \frac{1}{4}y = 60$ and $-\frac{1}{4}x + \frac{3}{4}y = 60$.   (b) The solution is $x = 320/3$ and $y = 1040/9$.

3. (a) No sector delivers to itself. (b) The total amount of good i needed to produce one unit of each good.
(c) This column vector gives the number of units of each good which are needed to produce one unit of good j.
(d) No meaningful economic interpretation. (The goods are usually measured in different units, so it is meaningless to add them together. As the saying goes: "Don't add apples and oranges!")

4. $0.8x_1 - 0.3x_2 = 120$ and $-0.4x_1 + 0.9x_2 = 90$, with solution $x_1 = 225$ and $x_2 = 200$.

5. The Leontief system for this three-sector model is

$$0.9x_1 - 0.2x_2 - 0.1x_3 = 85$$
$$-0.3x_1 + 0.8x_2 - 0.2x_3 = 95 \,,$$
$$-0.2x_1 - 0.2x_2 + 0.9x_3 = 20$$

which does have the claimed solution.

6. The input matrix is $A = \begin{pmatrix} 0 & \beta & 0 \\ 0 & 0 & \gamma \\ \alpha & 0 & 0 \end{pmatrix}$. The sums of the elements in each column are less than 1 provided $\alpha < 1$, $\beta < 1$, and $\gamma < 1$, respectively. Then, in particular, the product $\alpha\beta\gamma < 1$.

7. The quantity vector x_0 must satisfy (∗) $(I_n - A)x_0 = b$ and the price vector p'_0 must satisfy (∗∗) $p'_0(I_n - A) = v'$. Multiplying (∗∗) from the right by x_0 yields $v'x_0 = (p'_0(I_n - A))x_0 = p'_0((I_n - A)x_0) = p'_0 b$.

Review Problems for Chapter 16

1. (a) $5(-2) - (-2)3 = -4$ (b) $1 - a^2$ (c) $6a^2b + 2b^3$ (d) $\lambda^2 - 5\lambda$

2. (a) -4 (b) 1. (Subtract row 1 from rows 2 and 3. Then subtract twice row 2 from row 3. The resulting determinant has only one nonzero term in its third row.)   (c) 1. (Use exactly the same row operations as in (b).)

3. Transposing each side yields $A^{-1} - 2I_2 = -2\begin{pmatrix} 1 & 1 \\ 1 & 0 \end{pmatrix}$, so $A^{-1} = 2I_2 - 2\begin{pmatrix} 1 & 1 \\ 1 & 0 \end{pmatrix} = \begin{pmatrix} 2 & 0 \\ 0 & 2 \end{pmatrix} - \begin{pmatrix} 2 & 2 \\ 2 & 0 \end{pmatrix} = \begin{pmatrix} 0 & -2 \\ -2 & 2 \end{pmatrix}$. Hence, using (16.6.3), $A = \begin{pmatrix} 0 & -2 \\ -2 & 2 \end{pmatrix}^{-1} = -\frac{1}{4}\begin{pmatrix} 2 & 2 \\ 2 & 0 \end{pmatrix} = \begin{pmatrix} -1/2 & -1/2 \\ -1/2 & 0 \end{pmatrix}$.

4. (a) $|A_t| = t + 1$, so A_t has an inverse if and only if $t \neq -1$.   (b) Multiplying the given equation from the right by A_1 yields $BA_1 + X = I_3$. Hence $X = I_3 - BA_1 = \begin{pmatrix} 0 & 0 & -1 \\ 0 & 0 & -1 \\ -2 & -1 & 0 \end{pmatrix}$.

5. $|\mathbf{A}| = (p+1)(q-2)$, $|\mathbf{A}+\mathbf{E}| = 2(p-1)(q-2)$. $\mathbf{A}+\mathbf{E}$ has an inverse for $p \neq 1$ and $q \neq 2$. Obviously, $|\mathbf{E}| = 0$. Hence $|\mathbf{BE}| = |\mathbf{B}||\mathbf{E}| = 0$, so $\mathbf{BE}$ has no inverse.

6. The determinant of the coefficient matrix is $\begin{vmatrix} -2 & 4 & -t \\ -3 & 1 & t \\ t-2 & -7 & 4 \end{vmatrix} = 5t^2 - 45t + 40 = 5(t-1)(t-8)$. So by Cramer's rule, there is a unique solution if and only if $t \neq 1$ and $t \neq 8$.

7. We see that $(\mathbf{I} - \mathbf{A})(\mathbf{I} + \mathbf{A} + \mathbf{A}^2 + \mathbf{A}^3) = \mathbf{I} + \mathbf{A} + \mathbf{A}^2 + \mathbf{A}^3 - \mathbf{A} - \mathbf{A}^2 - \mathbf{A}^3 - \mathbf{A}^4 = \mathbf{I} - \mathbf{A}^4 = \mathbf{I}$. Then use (16.6.4).

8. (a) $(\mathbf{I}_n + a\mathbf{U})(\mathbf{I}_n + b\mathbf{U}) = \mathbf{I}_n^2 + b\mathbf{U} + a\mathbf{U} + ab\mathbf{U}^2 = \mathbf{I}_n + (a + b + nab)\mathbf{U}$, because $\mathbf{U}^2 = n\mathbf{U}$, as is easily verified.
   (b) $\mathbf{A}^{-1} = \dfrac{1}{10}\begin{pmatrix} 7 & -3 & -3 \\ -3 & 7 & -3 \\ -3 & -3 & 7 \end{pmatrix}$.

9. From the first equation, $\mathbf{Y} = \mathbf{B} - \mathbf{AX}$. Inserting this into the second equation and solving for $\mathbf{X}$, yields $\mathbf{X} = 2\mathbf{A}^{-1}\mathbf{B} - \mathbf{C}$. Moreover, $\mathbf{Y} = \mathbf{AC} - \mathbf{B}$.

10. (a) For $a \neq 1$ and $a \neq 2$, there is a unique solution. If $a = 1$, there is no solution. If $a = 2$, there are infinitely many solutions.   (b) When $a = 1$ and $b_1 - b_2 + b_3 = 0$, or when $a = 2$ and $b_1 = b_2$, there are infinitely many solutions.

11. (a) $|\mathbf{A}| = -2$. $\mathbf{A}^2 - 2\mathbf{I}_2 = \begin{pmatrix} 11 & -6 \\ 18 & -10 \end{pmatrix} = \mathbf{A}$, so $\mathbf{A}^2 + c\mathbf{A} = 2\mathbf{I}_2$ if $c = -1$.
   (b) If $\mathbf{B}^2 = \mathbf{A}$, then $|\mathbf{B}|^2 = |\mathbf{A}| = -2$, which is impossible.

12. Note first that if $\mathbf{A}'\mathbf{A} = \mathbf{I}_n$, then rule (16.6.5) implies that $\mathbf{A}' = \mathbf{A}^{-1}$, so $\mathbf{AA}' = \mathbf{I}_n$. But then $(\mathbf{A}'\mathbf{B}^{-1}\mathbf{A})(\mathbf{A}'\mathbf{BA}) = \mathbf{A}'\mathbf{B}^{-1}(\mathbf{AA}')\mathbf{BA} = \mathbf{A}'\mathbf{B}^{-1}\mathbf{I}_n\mathbf{BA} = \mathbf{A}'(\mathbf{B}^{-1}\mathbf{B})\mathbf{A} = \mathbf{A}'\mathbf{I}_n\mathbf{A} = \mathbf{A}'\mathbf{A} = \mathbf{I}_n$. By rule (16.6.5) again, it follows that $(\mathbf{A}'\mathbf{BA})^{-1} = \mathbf{A}'\mathbf{B}^{-1}\mathbf{A}$.

13. For once we use "unsystematic elimination". Solve the first equation to get $y = 3 - ax$, then the second to get $z = 2 - x$, and the fourth to get $u = 1 - y$. Substituting for all these in the third equation gives the result $3 - ax + a(2 - x) + b(1 - 3 + ax) = 6$ or $a(b-2)x = -2a + 2b + 3$. There is a unique solution provided that $a(b-2) \neq 0$. The solution is:

$$x = \frac{2b - 2a + 3}{a(b-2)}, \qquad y = \frac{2a + b - 9}{b - 2}, \qquad z = \frac{2ab - 2a - 2b - 3}{a(b-2)}, \qquad u = \frac{7 - 2a}{b - 2}$$

14. $|\mathbf{B}^3| = |\mathbf{B}|^3$. Because $\mathbf{B}$ is a 3×3-matrix, we have $|-\mathbf{B}| = (-1)^3|\mathbf{B}| = -|\mathbf{B}|$. Since $\mathbf{B}^3 = -\mathbf{B}$, it follows that $|\mathbf{B}|^3 = -|\mathbf{B}|$, and so $|\mathbf{B}|(|\mathbf{B}|^2 + 1) = 0$. The last equation implies $|\mathbf{B}| = 0$, and thus $\mathbf{B}$ can have no inverse.

15. (a) The determinant on the left is equal to $(a + x)d - c(b + y) = (ad - bc) + (dx - cy)$, and this is the sum of the determinants on the right.   (b) For simplicity look at the case $r = 1$.

16. For $a \neq b$ the solutions are $x_1 = \frac{1}{2}(a + b)$ and $x_2 = -\frac{1}{2}(a + b)$. If $a = b$, the determinant is 0 for all values of x.

Chapter 17

17.1

1. (a) From Fig. A17.1.1a we see that the solution is at the intersection of the two lines $3x_1 + 2x_2 = 6$ and $x_1 + 4x_2 = 4$. Solution: $\max = 36/5$ for $(x_1, x_2) = (8/5, 3/5)$.   (b) From Fig. A17.1.1b we see that the solution is at the intersection of the two lines $u_1 + 3u_2 = 11$ and $2u_1 + 5u_2 = 20$. Solution: $\min = 104$ for $(u_1, u_2) = (5, 2)$.

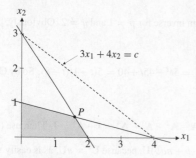

Figure A17.1.1a

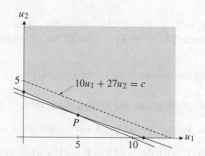

Figure A17.1.1b

2. (a) A graph shows that the solution is at the intersection of the lines $-2x_1 + 3x_2 = 6$ and $x_1 + x_2 = 5$. Hence max = 98/5 for $(x_1, x_2) = (9/5, 16/5)$.   (b) The solution satisfies $2x_1 + 3x_2 = 13$ and $x_1 + x_2 = 6$. Hence max = 49 for $(x_1, x_2) = (5, 1)$ (c) The solution satisfies $x_1 - 3x_2 = 0$ and $x_2 = 2$. Hence max = $-10/3$ for $(x_1, x_2) = (2, 2/3)$.

3. (a) max = 18/5 for $(x_1, x_2) = (4/5, 18/5)$.   (b) max = 8 for $(x_1, x_2) = (8, 0)$.
(c) max = 24 for $(x_1, x_2) = (8, 0)$.   (d) min = $-28/5$ for $(x_1, x_2) = (4/5, 18/5)$.
(e) max = 16 for all (x_1, x_2) of the form $(x_1, 4 - \frac{1}{2}x_1)$ where $x_1 \in [4/5, 8]$.
(f) min= -24 for $(x_1, x_2) = (8, 0)$ (follows from the answer to (c)).

4. (a) No maximum exists. Consider Fig. A17.1.4. By increasing c, the dashed level curve $x_1 + x_2 = c$ moves to the north-east and so this function can take arbitrarily large values and still have points in common with the shaded set.
(b) Maximum at $P = (1, 0)$. The level curves are the same as in (a), but the direction of increase is reversed.

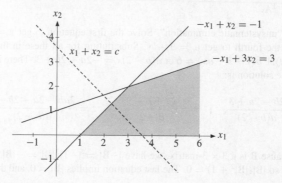

Figure A17.1.4

5. The slope of the line $20x_1 + tx_2 = c$ must lie between $-1/2$ (the slope of the flour border) and -1 (the slope of the butter border). For $t = 0$, the line is vertical and the solution is the point D in Fig. 2 in the text. For $t \neq 0$, the slope of the line is $-20/t$. Thus, $-1 \leq -20/t \leq -1/2$, which implies that $t \in [20, 40]$.

6. The LP problem is: max $700x + 1000y$ subject to $\begin{cases} 3x + 5y \leq 3900 \\ x + 3y \leq 2100 \\ 2x + 2y \leq 2200 \end{cases}$, $x \geq 0$, $y \geq 0$

A figure showing the admissible set and an appropriate level line for the objective function will show that the solution is at the point where the two lines $3x + 5y = 3900$ and $2x + 2y = 2200$ intersect. Solving these equations yields $x = 800$ and $y = 300$. The firm should produce 800 sets of type A and 300 of type B.

17.2

1. (a) $(x_1, x_2) = (2, 1/2)$ and $u_1^* = 4/5$.   (b) $(x_1, x_2) = (7/5, 9/10)$ and $u_2^* = 3/5$.
(c) Multiplying the two $\leq$ constraints by $4/5$ and $3/5$, respectively, then adding, we obtain
$(4/5)(3x_1 + 2x_2) + (3/5)(x_1 + 4x_2) \leq 6 \cdot (4/5) + 4 \cdot (3/5)$, which reduces to $3x_1 + 4x_2 \leq 36/5$.

2. $\min 8u_1 + 13u_2 + 6u_3$ subject to $\begin{cases} u_1 + 2u_2 + u_3 \geq 8 \\ 2u_1 + 3u_2 + u_3 \geq 9 \end{cases}$, $u_1 \geq 0, \; u_2 \geq 0, \; u_3 \geq 0$

3. (a) $\min 6u_1 + 4u_2$ subject to $\begin{cases} 3u_1 + \; u_2 \geq 3 \\ 2u_1 + 4u_2 \geq 4 \end{cases}$, $u_1 \geq 0, \; u_2 \geq 0$

(b) $\max 11x_1 + 20x_2$ subject to $\begin{cases} x_1 + 2x_2 \leq 10 \\ 3x_1 + 5x_2 \leq 27 \end{cases}$, $x_1 \geq 0, \; x_2 \geq 0$

4. (a) A graph shows that the solution is at the intersection of the lines $x_1 + 2x_2 = 14$ and $2x_1 + x_2 = 13$. Hence
$\max = 9$ for $(x_1^*, x_2^*) = (4, 5)$.

(b) The dual is $\min 14u_1 + 13u_2$ subject to $\begin{cases} u_1 + 2u_2 \geq 1 \\ 2u_1 + u_2 \geq 1 \end{cases}$, $u_1 \geq 0, \; u_2 \geq 0$. A graph shows that the solution
is at the intersection of the lines $u_1 + 2u_2 = 1$ and $2u_1 + u_2 = 1$. Hence $\min = 9$ for $(u_1^*, u_2^*) = (1/3, 1/3)$.

17.3

1. (a) $x = 0$ and $y = 3$ gives $\max = 21$. See Fig. A17.3.1a, where the optimum is at P.

(b) The dual problem is $\min 20u_1 + 21u_2$ subject to $\begin{cases} 4u_1 + 3u_2 \geq 2 \\ 5u_1 + 7u_2 \geq 7 \end{cases}$, $u_1 \geq 0, \; u_2 \geq 0$.   It has the solution

$u_1 = 0$ and $u_2 = 1$, which gives $\min = 21$. See Fig. A17.3.1b.   (c) Yes.

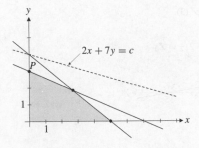

Figure A17.3.1a

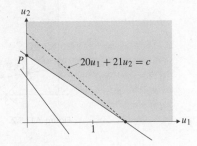

Figure A17.3.1b

2. $\max 300x_1 + 500x_2$ subject to $\begin{cases} 10x_1 + 25x_2 \leq 10\,000 \\ 20x_1 + 25x_2 \leq \; 8\,000 \end{cases}$, $x_1 \geq 0, \; x_2 \geq 0$

The solution can be found graphically. It is $x_1^* = 0$, $x_2^* = 320$, and the value of the objective function is $160\,000$,
the same value found in Example 17.1.2 for the optimal value of the primal objective function.

3. (a) The profit from selling x_1 small and x_2 medium television sets is $400x_1 + 500x_2$. The first constraint, $2x_1 + x_2 \leq 16$,
says that we cannot use more hours in division 1 than the hours available. The other constraints have similar
interpretations.   (b) $\max = 3800$ for $x_1 = 7$ and $x_2 = 2$.   (c) Division 1 should have its capacity increased.

17.4

1. According to formula (1), $\Delta z^* = u_1^* \Delta b_1 + u_2^* \Delta b_2 = 0 \cdot 0.1 + 1 \cdot (-0.2) = -0.2$.

2. (a) max $300x_1 + 200x_2$ subject to $\begin{cases} 6x_1 + 3x_2 \le 54 \\ 4x_1 + 6x_2 \le 48, \\ 5x_1 + 5x_2 \le 50 \end{cases}$ $x_1 \ge 0,\, x_2 \ge 0$

where x_1 and x_2 are the number of units produced of A and B, respectively. Solution: $(x_1, x_2) = (8, 2)$.

(b) Dual solution: $(u_1, u_2, u_3) = (100/3, 0, 20)$.   (c) Increase in optimal profit: $\Delta\pi^* = u_1^* \cdot 2 + u_3^* \cdot 1 = 260/3$.

17.5

1. $4u_1^* + 3u_2^* = 3 > 2$ and $x^* = 0$; $5u_1^* + 7u_2^* = 7$ and $y^* = 3 > 0$. Also $4x^* + 5y^* = 15 < 20$ and $u_1^* = 0$; $3x^* + 7y^* = 21$ and $u_2^* = 1 > 0$. So (1) and (2) are satisfied.

2. (a) See Figure A17.5.2. The minimum is attained at $(y_1^*, y_2^*) = (3, 2)$.

(b) The dual is: max $15x_1 + 5x_2 - 5x_3 - 20x_4$ s.t. $\begin{cases} x_1 + x_2 - x_3 + x_4 \le 1 \\ 6x_1 + x_2 + x_3 - 2x_4 \le 2 \end{cases}$, $x_j \ge 0,\, j = 1, \ldots, 4$.

The maximum is at $(x_1^*, x_2^*, x_3^*, x_4^*) = (1/5, 4/5, 0, 0)$.   (c) If the first constraint is changed to $y_1 + 6y_2 \ge 15.1$, the solution of the primal is still at the intersection of the lines (1) and (2) in Fig. A17.5.2, but with (1) shifted up slightly. The solution of the dual is completely unchanged. In both problems the optimal value increases by $(15.1 - 15) \cdot x_1^* = 0.02$.

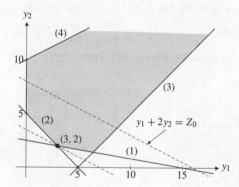

Figure A17.5.2

3. (a) min $10\,000y_1 + 8\,000y_2 + 11\,000y_3$ subject to $\begin{cases} 10y_1 + 20y_2 + 20y_3 \ge 300 \\ 20y_1 + 10y_2 + 20y_3 \ge 500 \end{cases}$, $y_1 \ge 0,\, y_2 \ge 0,\, y_3 \ge 0$

(b) The dual is: max $300x_1 + 500x_2$ subject to $\begin{cases} 10x_1 + 20x_2 \le 10\,000 \\ 20x_1 + 10x_2 \le 8\,000, \\ 20x_1 + 20x_2 \le 11\,000 \end{cases}$ $x_1 \ge 0,\, x_2 \ge 0$

Solution: max $= 255\,000$ for $x_1 = 100$ and $x_2 = 450$. Solution of the primal: min $= 255\,000$ for $(y_1, y_2, y_3) = (20, 0, 5)$.   (c) The minimum cost will increase by 2000.

4. (a) For $x_3 = 0$, the solution is $x_1 = x_2 = 1/3$. For $x_3 = 3$, the solution is $x_1 = 1$ and $x_2 = 2$.
(b) Let z_{max} denote the maximum value of the objective function. If $0 \le x_3 \le 7/3$, then $z_{max}(x_3) = 2x_3 + 5/3$ for $x_1 = 1/3$ and $x_2 = x_3 + 1/3$. If $7/3 < x_3 \le 5$, then $z_{max}(x_3) = x_3 + 4$ for $x_1 = x_3 - 2$ and $x_2 = 5 - x_3$. If $x_3 > 5$, then $z_{max}(x_3) = 9$ for $x_1 = 3$ and $x_2 = 0$. Because $z_{max}(x_3)$ is increasing, the maximum is 9 for $x_3 \ge 5$.
(c) The solution to the original problem is $x_1 = 3$ and $x_2 = 0$, with x_3 as an arbitrary number ≥ 5.

Review Problems for Chapter 17

1. (a) $x^* = 3/2$, $y^* = 5/2$. (A diagram shows that the solution is at the intersection of $x + y = 4$ and $-x + y = 1$.)

(b) The dual is min $4u_1 + u_2 + 3u_3$ subject to $\begin{cases} u_1 - u_2 + 2u_3 \geq 1 \\ u_1 + u_2 - u_3 \geq 2 \end{cases}$, $u_1 \geq 0$, $u_2 \geq 0$, $u_3 \geq 0$.

Using complementary slackness, the solution of the dual is: $u_1^* = 3/2$, $u_2^* = 1/2$, and $u_3^* = 0$.

2. (a) max $-x_1 + x_2$ subject to $\begin{cases} -x_1 + 2x_2 \leq 16 \\ x_1 - 2x_2 \leq 6 \\ -2x_1 - x_2 \leq -8 \\ -4x_1 - 5x_2 \leq -15 \end{cases}$, $x_1 \geq 0$, $x_2 \geq 0$. Maximum 8 at $(x_1, x_2) = (0, 8)$.

(b) $(y_1, y_2, y_3, y_4) = (\frac{1}{2}(b + 1), 0, b, 0)$ for any b satisfying $0 \leq b \leq 1/5$.

(c) The maximand for the dual becomes $kx_1 + x_2$. The solution is unchanged provided that $k \leq -1/2$.

3. (a) $x^* = 0$, $y^* = 4$. (A diagram shows that the solution is at the intersection of $x = 0$ and $4x + y = 4$.)

(b) The dual problem is:

$$\text{max } 4u_1 + 3u_2 + 2u_3 - 2u_4 \quad \text{subject to} \quad \begin{cases} 4u_1 + 2u_2 + 3u_3 - u_4 \leq 5 \\ u_1 + u_2 + 2u_3 + 2u_4 \leq 1 \end{cases} \quad u_1, u_2, u_3, u_4 \geq 0$$

By complementary slackness, its solution is: $u_1^* = 1$, $u_2^* = u_3^* = u_4^* = 0$.

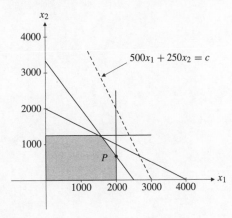

Figure A17.R.4

4. (a) See Fig. A17.R.4. The solution is at P, where $(x_1, x_2) = (2000, 2000/3)$;   (b) See SM.   (c) $a \leq 1/24$

5. (a) If the numbers of units produced of the three goods are x_1, x_2, and x_3, the profit is $6x_1 + 3x_2 + 4x_3$, and the time spent on the two machines is $3x_1 + x_2 + 4x_3$ and $2x_1 + 2x_2 + x_3$, respectively. The LP problem is therefore

$$\text{max } 6x_1 + 3x_2 + 4x_3 \quad \text{subject to} \quad \begin{cases} 3x_1 + x_2 + 4x_3 \leq b_1 \\ 2x_1 + 2x_2 + x_3 \leq b_2 \end{cases}, \quad x_1, x_2, x_3 \geq 0$$

(b) The dual problem is obviously as given. Optimum at $P = (y_1^*, y_2^*) = (3/2, 3/4)$.   (c) $x_1^* = x_2^* = 25$.   For (d) and (e) see SM.

INDEX